天津市统计局 编

Compiled by Tianjin Municipal Bureau of Statistics

天津统计年鉴

TIANJIN STATISTICAL YEARBOOK

2004

(总第20期 No. 20)

中英文对照

Chinese/English

中国统计出版社

China Statistics Press

发展的天津 Development of Tianjin

>> 天津市生产总值（亿元）
Gross Domestic Product of Tianjin (100 million yuan)

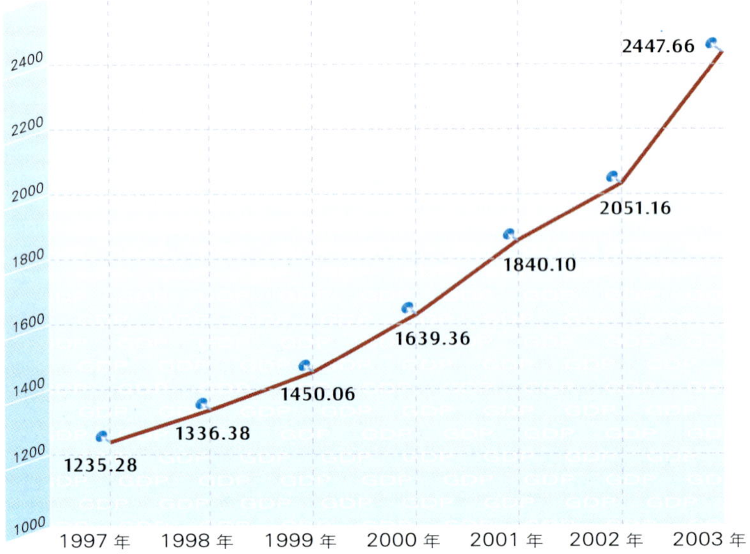

>> 天津市人均生产总值（元）
Per Capita Gross Domestic Product of Tianjin (yuan)

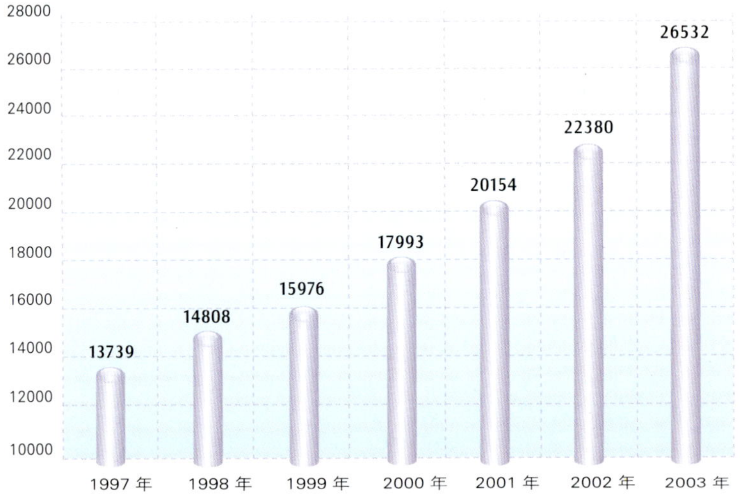

>> 天津市生产总值构成(%)
Composition of Gross Domestic Product (%)

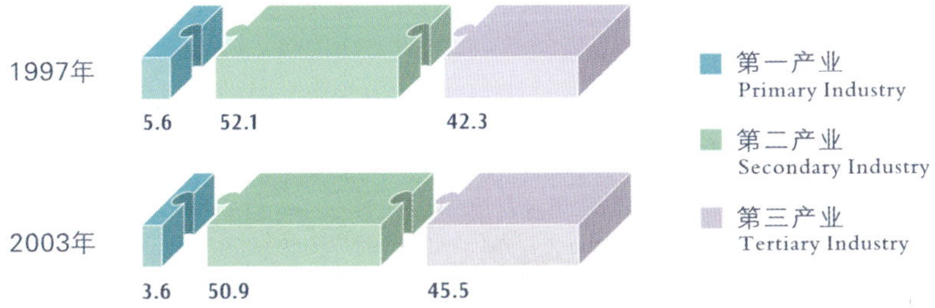

全市财政收入（亿元）
Total Financial Revenue (100 million yuan)

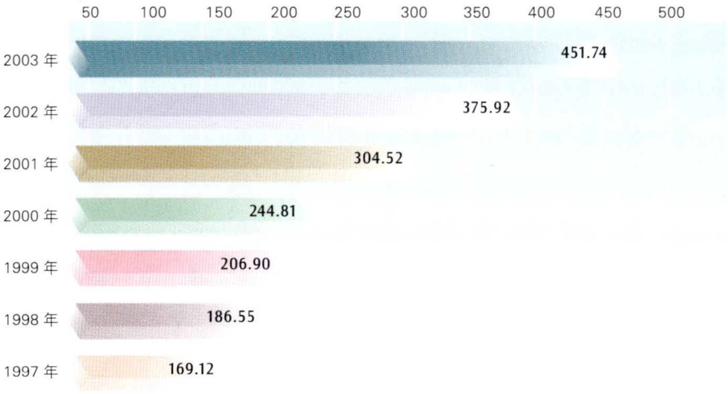

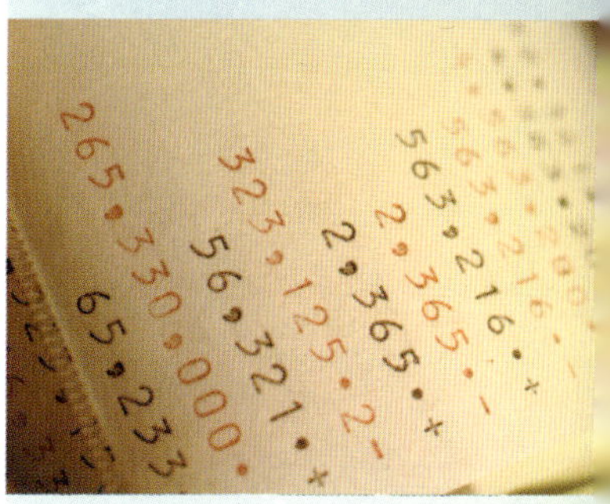

天津的一天
One Day in Tianjin

地区生产总值6.71亿元
Gross Domestic Product 6.71 million yuan

第三产业增加值3.05亿元
Value-added of Tertiary Industry 305 million yuan

工业增加值3.11亿元
Value-added of Industry 3.11 million yuan

社会消费品零售总额2.94亿元
Total Retail Sales of Consumer Goods 294 million yuan

全市财政收入12376万元
Total Financial Revenue 123.76 million yuan

原油产量3.61万吨
Output of Crude Oil 36,100 tons

钢产量1.55万吨
Output of Steel 15,500 tons

港口货物吞吐量44.3万吨
Freight Handled at Port 443,000 tons

社会货物运输量97万吨
Freight Traffic 970,000 tons

接待来津国际旅游者1340人次
Reception of International Tourists 1,340 man-times

外贸出口总值3938万美元
Total Value of Exports in Foreign Trade 39.38 million USD

竣工房屋建筑面积3.44万平方米
Floor Space of Building Completed 34,400 sq.m

邮电业务总量3170万元
Business Value of Post and Telecommunications 31.7 million yuan

生活用电量869万千瓦小时
Living Consumption of Electricity 8.69 million kw

生活用水量81.7万吨
Living Consumption Water 817,000 tons

生活用天然气和煤气82.5万立方米
Living Consumption of Natural Gas and Coal Gas 825,000 cu.m

人口构成(%)
Composition of Population

1997年

- 非农业: 57.3%
  Non-agricultural
- 农　业: 42.7%
  Agricultural

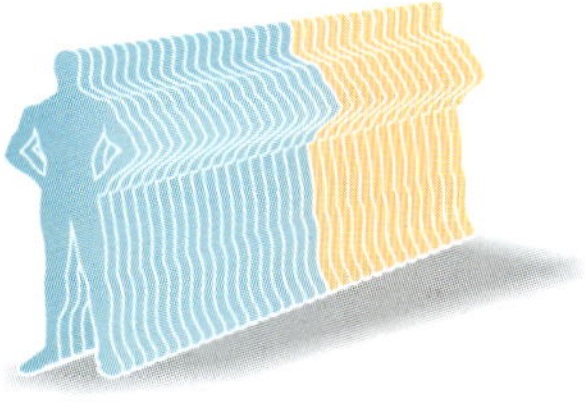

2003年

- 非农业: 59.4%
  Non-agricultural
- 农　业: 40.6%
  Agricultural

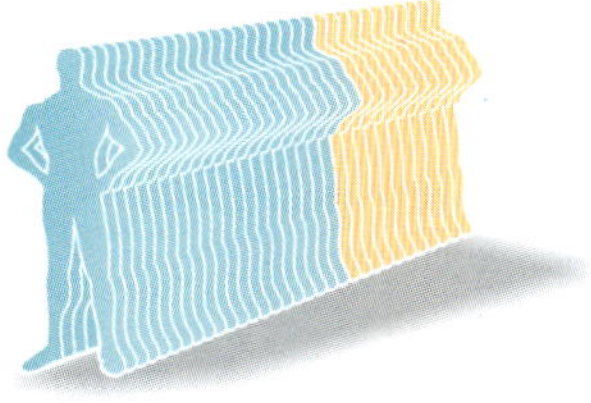

全社会固定资产投资与城市基础设施投资（亿元）
Total Investment in Fixed Assets and Urban Infrastructure Investment (100 million yuan)

- 全社会固定资产投资
  Total Investment in Fixed Assets
- 城市基础设施投资
  Urban Infrastructure Investment

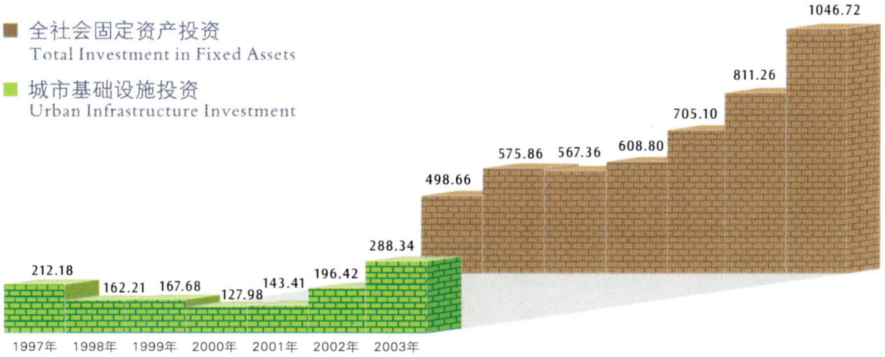

发展的天津 Development of Tianjin

>> 商品房销售面积与商品房住宅销售面积（万平方米）
Floor Space of Commercial Buildings and Residential Buildings Sold (10000 sq. m)

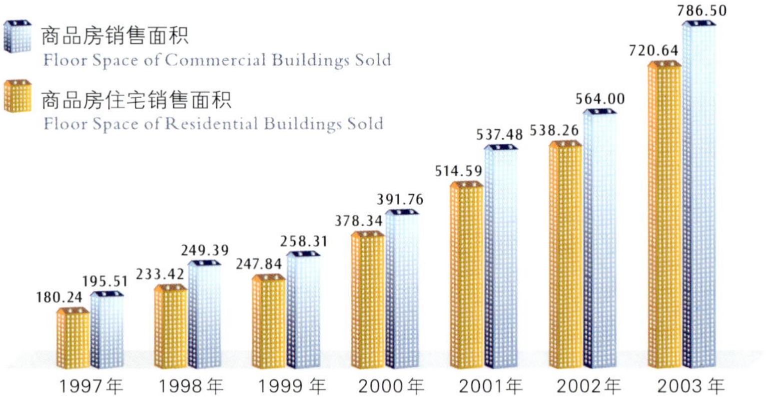

>> 城市绿化覆盖率(%)
Coverage Rate of Afforestation in Urban Areas (%)

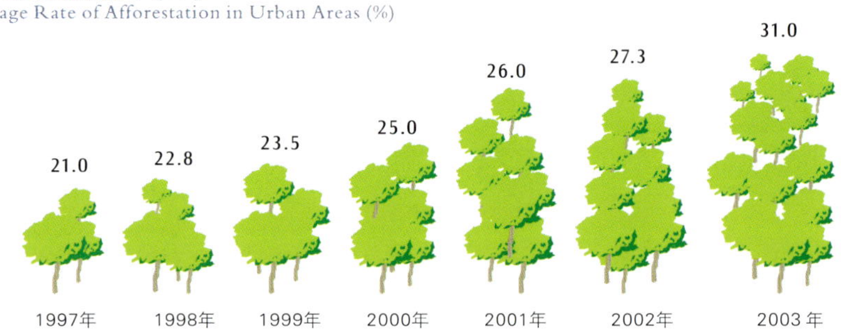

>> 城市居民人均可支配收入（元）
Per Capita Annual Disposable Income of Urban Households (yuan)

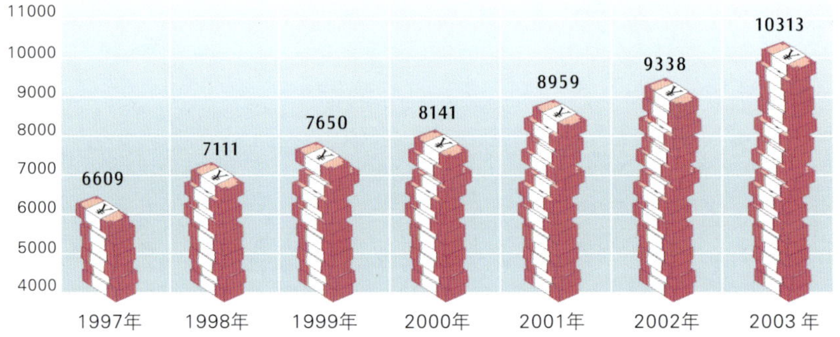

>> 城市居民人均消费性支出构成(%)
Composition of Per Capita Annual Expenditures for Consumption of Urban Households (%)

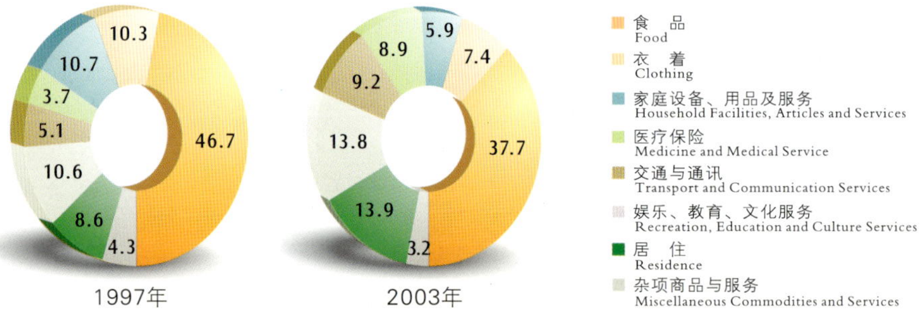

2003年限额以上工业总产值构成(%)
Composition of Industrial Output Value Above Designated Size(%) ,2003

按经济类型分 by Ownership

产值总计 4049.61亿元
Total Output Value
(100 million yuan)

- 国有经济 14.8% State-owned
- 外商投资经济 40.3% Foreign Funded
- 集体经济 11.0% Collective-owenership
- 港澳台商投资经济 6.5% Hongkong, Macao and Taiwan Funded
- 私有经济 5.7% Private and Individual
- 其 它 21.7% Others

港口货物吞吐量（万吨）
Volune of Freight Handled at Ports (10,000 tons)

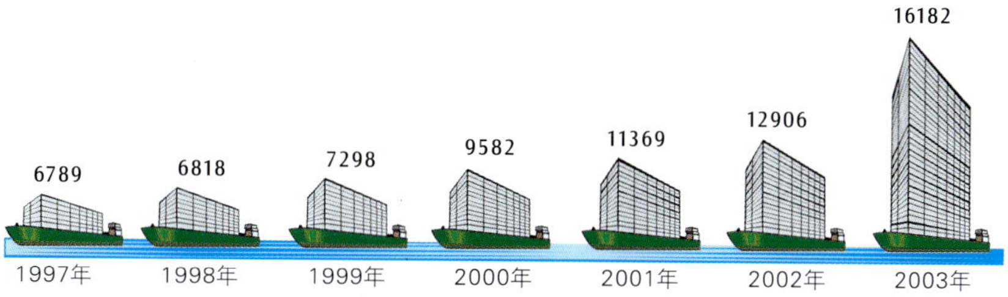

邮电业务总量（亿元）
Business Volume of Post and Telecommunication Services (100 million yuan)

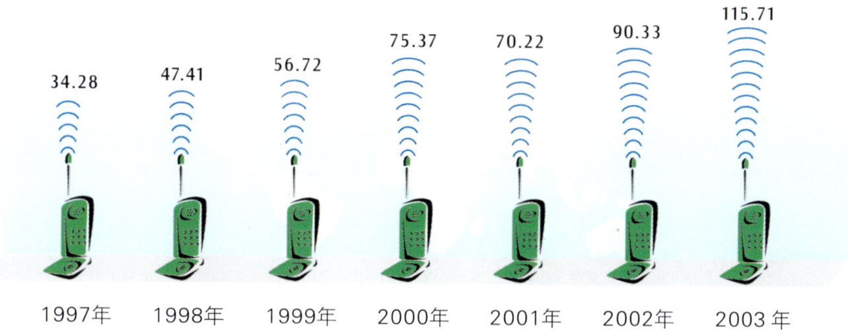

社会消费品零售总额（亿元）
Total Retail Sales of Consumer Goods (100 million yuan)

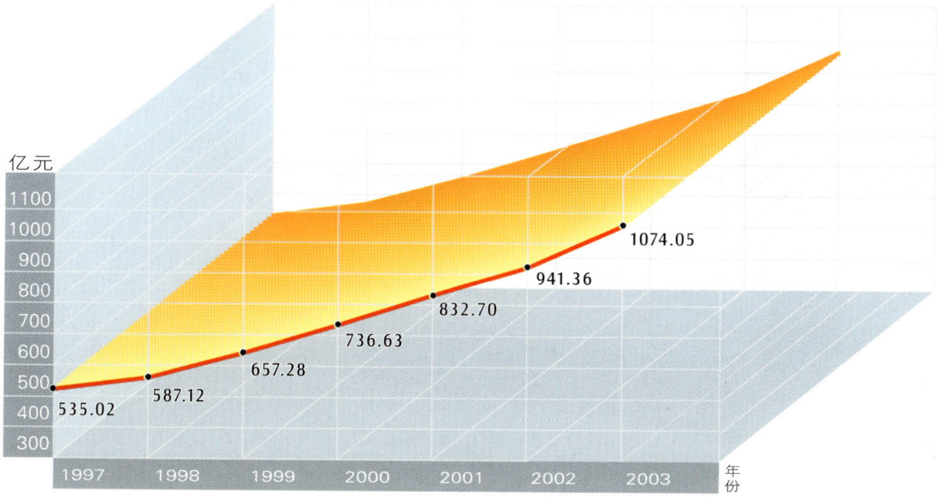

发展的 Development of 天津 Tianjin

>> 外贸进出口总值（亿美元）
Total Value of Imports & Exports in Foreign Trade (100 million USD)

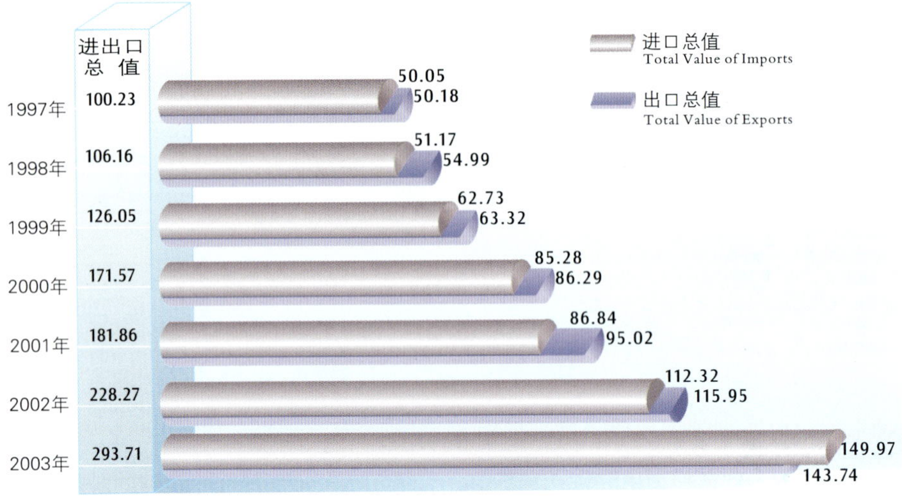

>> 至2003年末按国别（地区）分利用外资构成(%)
Composition of Accumulative Foreign Investmant Used by Country (Region) by the End of 2003 (%)

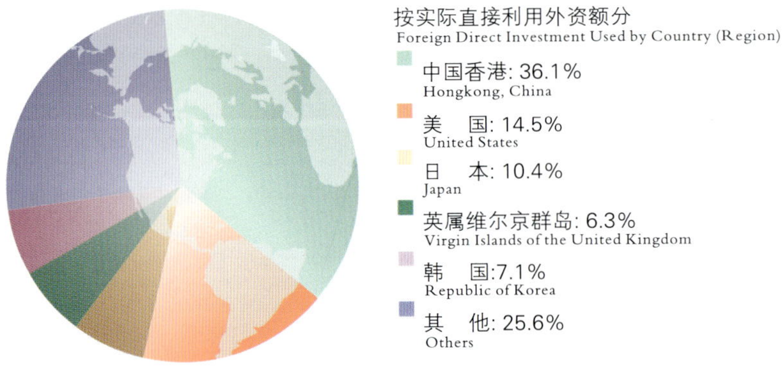

>> 城乡居民储蓄存款余额（亿元）
Savings Deposits of Urban and Rural Households

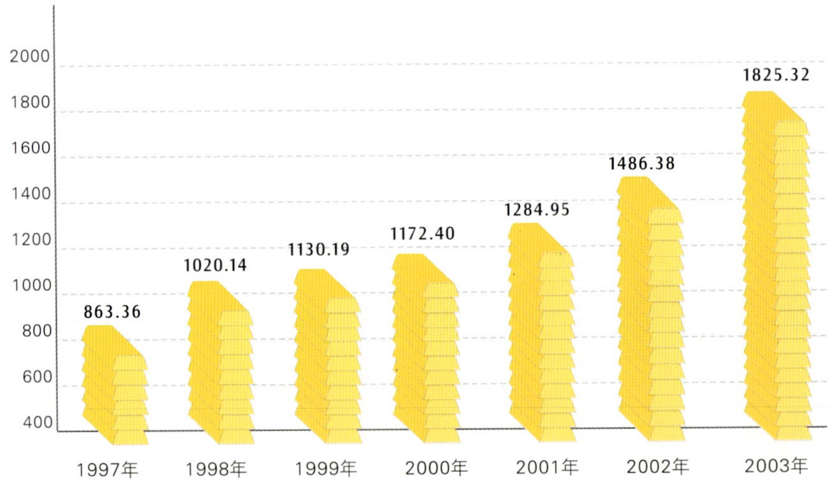

平均每万人口拥有大学生（人）
Number of University or College Students Per 10,000 Population (persons)

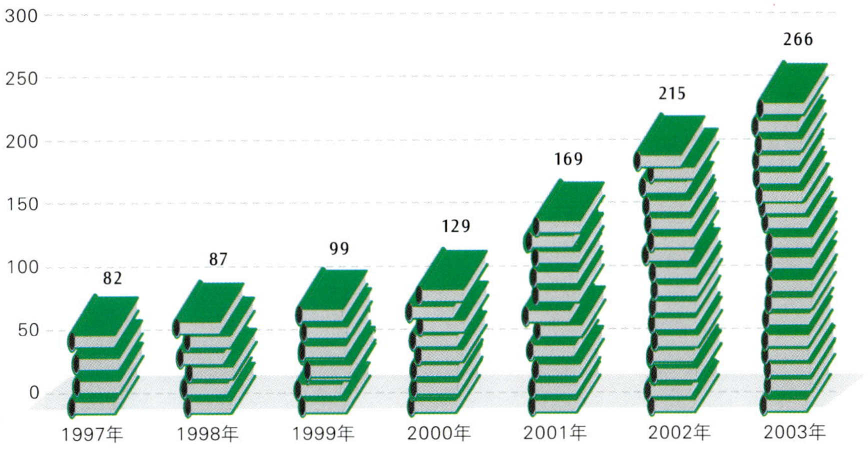

各类学校在校学生数（万人）
Students Enrollment by Type of School (10,000 persons)

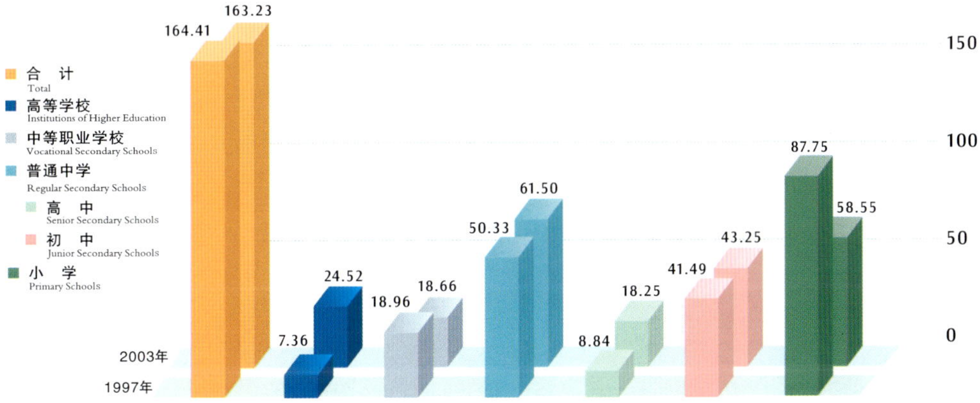

滨海新区生产总值（亿元）
Gross Domestic Product of New Coastal Area (100 million yuan)

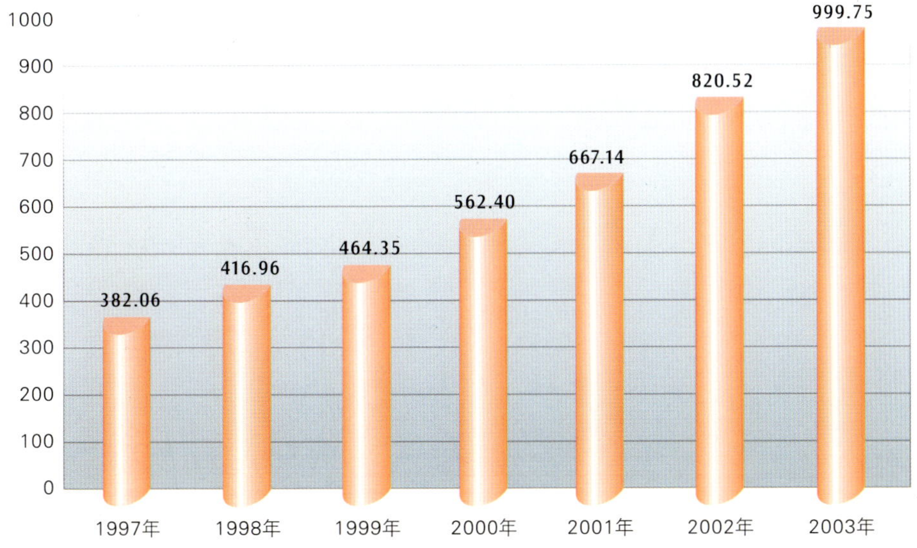

编 者 说 明

一、《天津统计年鉴》是一部全面反映天津市国民经济和社会发展情况的大型资料工具书，创刊于 1984 年，逐年出版，形成系列。本书以其丰富翔实的统计资料而成为社会各界了解天津、认识天津最具权威性的工具资料书。

二、《天津统计年鉴－2004》全书中英文对照，同步配备电子版光盘。

三、书内文字资料载有："天津概况"，"2003 年天津市国民经济和社会发展统计公报"，"2003 年天津市人均生产总值突破 3000 美元"等一系列反映 2003 年天津市各行业发展的分析文章。为方便读者使用，书中在每篇后附有统计指标解释。索引中标明了全书结构。

四、本年鉴的统计数据大部分取自统计年报，少部分来自抽样调查和专业部门统计资料。

五、本年鉴所使用的度量衡单位均采用国际统一标准计量单位。

六、本年鉴中部分数据的合计数和相对数由于四舍五入取舍不同而产生的计算误差，均未做机械调整。

七、本年鉴表中的符号使用说明："空格"表示该项统计指标无数据、数据不足本表最小单位或数据不详；"＃"表示其中的主要项；由于版面原因，部分计量单位如：100 000 000 用 10^8 表示，10 000 用 10^4 表示。

八、由于同普查结果衔接、国家统计制度变化或主管部门提供的数据有调整等原因，年鉴中部分指标的历史年度数据有变动。读者在使用历史资料时，凡以前年度的年鉴与本年鉴数据有出入的，均以本年鉴为准。

九、《天津统计年鉴》公开出版以来，受到了国内外广大读者的关心和支持，对本年鉴的内容和编辑工作提出了许多宝贵意见，对此我们深表谢意。限于我们的水平，书中难免还有不足之处，敬请广大读者继续给予批评指正，帮助我们进一步改进年鉴编辑工作，更好地为广大读者服务。

Preface

Ⅰ. Tianjin Statistical Yearbook is a large – sized statistics publication to reflect various aspects of Tianjin′s economic and social development, which was started in 1984 and published year after year, having become a series of yearbooks. Possessing plentiful and detailed statistical materials, the yearbook has become the most authoritative statistics publication for various circles to understand and know Tianjin.

Ⅱ. Tianjin Statistical Yearbook 2004 is written in Chinese & English, and is equipped with electric CD.

Ⅲ. Written materials in the book include: Survey of Tianjin, Statistical Communique on the 2003 National Economic and Social Development of the City of Tianjin , The Per Capita GDP of the City of Tianjin Exceeding 3,000 US $, a series of reports reflecting the development of Tianjin in 2003 and so on. In order to help readers using these statistical materials better, Explanatory Notes On Main Statistical Indicators are attached after each chapter. Whose structure is marked in the index.

Ⅳ. The major data sources of this book are obtained from annual statistical report, a few from sample surveys and materials of departments statistics.

Ⅴ. The units of measurement used in this book are internationally standard measurement units.

Ⅵ. Statistical discrepancies due to rounding are not adjusted in this book.

Ⅶ. Notations used in this book: "(blank)" indicates the data not available or the figure is not large enough to be measured with the smallest unit in the table. "#" indicates the major items of the total. When the unit is 100,000,000, we shorten some of them as 10^8, 10,000 we shorten some of them as 10^4, so as to save the space for printing.

Ⅷ. As a result of joining with various census, change of statistics institution, data adjustment of special department and so on, some data in this yearbook are different with former yearbook. when using historical data, users should take the data of this book as standard.

Ⅸ. Since Tianjin Statistical Yearbook had been published openly, we have been concerned and supported by the readers at home and abroad. They advance much valuable suggestion on content and edition of the yearbook, we deeply thanks for this all. Based on our limited level, perhaps there are some mistakes in this book, we welcome all of the readers give us your criticism in order to help us further improving our edition level, and providing services for the readers better.

篇目索引

SUBJECT INDEX

目 录

CONTENTS

一、综　　合
GENERAL SURVEY

二、人口和劳动就业

POPULATION，LABOR AND EMPLOYMENT

三、固定资产投资
INVESTMENT IN FIXED ASSETS

四、价格指数
PRICE INDICES

五、人民生活
PEOPLE'S LIFE

六、农村经济

RURAL ECONOMY

七、工　业
INDUSTRY

八、建筑业
CONSTRUCTION

九、交通运输和邮电通信
TRANSPORTATION,POST AND TELECOMMUNICATIONS

十、批发零售贸易餐饮业
WHOLESALE,RETAIL TRADE AND CATERING SERVICES

十一、对外经济贸易和旅游
FOREIGN ECONOMY TRADE AND TOURISM

十二、财政和金融
GOVERNMENT FINANCE AND BANKING

十三、城市建设和环境保护
URBAN CONSTRUCTION AND ENVIRONMENT PROTECTION

十四、教　　育
EDUCATION

十五、科学技术

SCIENCE & TECHNOLOGY

十六、卫生、社会保障和社会福利

PUBLIC HEALTH,SOCIAL SECURITY AND SOCIAL WELFARE

十七、文化、体育
CULTURE,SPORTS

十八、公共管理和社会组织
PUBLIC MANAGEMENT AND SOCIAL ORGANIZATIONS

十九、滨海新区

NEW COASTAL AREA

二十、企业改革与市场发展
REFORM OF ENTERPRISE AND DEVELOPMENT OF MARKET

二十一、排行榜
SENIORITY BY MAIN STATISTICAL INDICATORS

二十二、区县基本情况
BASIC STATISTICS ON DISTRICTS AND COUNTIES

天 津 概 况

一、自然地理 全市总面积 11919.7 平方公里,其中平原面积占全市陆地总面积的 94%。天津地处华北平原东北部,北依燕山,东临渤海,海岸线北起涧河,南至歧口,长 130 多公里。气候属暖温带半湿润大陆季风气候,四季分明,景象多姿。主要河流有海河、南运河、北运河、子牙河、大清河、永定河等。毗邻北京,是华北、西北广大地区的出海口。

二、人口、行政区划 2003年全市常住户籍人口 926.00 万人,其中市辖区人口 758.78 万人。现辖 15 个区、3 个县。市辖区有和平区、河东区、河西区、南开区、河北区、红桥区、塘沽区、汉沽区、大港区、东丽区、西青区、津南区、北辰区、武清区、宝坻区;市辖县有宁河县、静海县、蓟县。

三、名胜古迹 天津历史遗址多,出土文物丰富,有 37 处国家级和市级重点文物保护单位。其中有始建于隋朝的大型木结构庙宇—蓟县独乐寺,已有 1000 多年的历史。有蓟县黄崖关长城,全长 41 公里,多种不同造型的古台 1000 多座,险峻、雄奇,素有“蓟北锁钥”之称。有号称“京东第一山 ”的蓟县盘山,山势雄伟,层峦叠秀,建筑与自然山水浑然一体。此外,还有天后宫、文庙、大悲院、清真大寺、天尊阁、天成寺、大沽口炮台、望海楼教堂、广东会馆以及周恩来青年时代在天津革命活动纪念馆等。天津的建筑具有古建筑、近代建筑和现代建筑并存的特色,有“万国建筑博物馆”之称。由于开埠较早,且有 9 国租界,以风格各异的小洋楼为特色,保留着 19 世纪末到20世纪初东西方各国的各类建筑 1000 多幢。

天津有驰名天下的四大民间艺术。“泥人张”彩塑艺术闻名全国,饮誉世界。“杨柳青年画” 历史悠久,深受国际友人青睐。“魏记风筝”获 1914 年巴拿马国际博览会金奖。以“刻砖刘”为代表的建筑装饰砖雕,使天津刻砖成为中国独一无二的民间建筑工艺。

四、食文化 津菜已具有 300 多年历史和上千个品种,烹饪技艺独具特色,突出了津沽地方特点,以鲜咸为主,软嫩酥烂,主料突出,配料考究、色鲜味醇。传统菜有罾蹦鲤鱼、目鱼烧肉、炸溜软硬飞禽、虎皮肘子等。名菜有:红扒鱼翅、清炒虾仁、烹大虾、蟹黄鱼翅、鸡丝银针、烧干贝、扒鲍鱼、酸沙紫蟹等。另外,全国正宗鲁、苏、川、粤、浙、湘、闽、皖八大菜系,也均在津门落户。天津还有特色小菜 90 多种,花色冷拼 45 种,风味小吃 90 多种,除闻名中外的天津狗不理包子、耳朵眼炸糕、桂发祥麻花老“三绝”食品外,1998 年“猫不闻”饺子又在全国被评为天津第四“绝”。还有张记果仁、曹记驴肉、大福来锅巴菜、石头门坎素包子、芝兰斋糕干以及贴饽饽熬小鱼等特色小吃。传统的大饼、棒槌果子、老豆腐、锅巴菜、豆浆、馄饨、摊煎饼果子等,更是天津人每天早点不可缺少的肴食。

五、产业 天津是中国北方最大的沿海开放城市,是环渤海地区的经济中心。2003 年,全市国内生产总值为 2447.66 亿元,其中第一产业增加值为 89.66 亿元,占 3.6%;第二产业增加值为 1245.29 亿元,占 50.9%;第三产业增加值为1112.71 亿元,占 45.5%。2003年人均国内生产总值达到 26532 元。

天津农业是城郊型农业。粮食生产以小麦、玉米、稻谷为主,经济作物主要有花生、棉花等,水果有苹果、梨、桃、枣、葡萄、柿子等,并盛产板栗、核桃和红果。天津外临渤海,内接九河,有丰富的水产资源。海水产品有带鱼、黄花鱼、小黄鱼、对虾和贝类等,淡水产品有河蟹、鲤鱼、鲫鱼、鲢鳙、蛤蜊等。天津的许多名优农产品驰名中外,“小站稻”以国家优质米的身份出口日本、古巴和东南亚,盘山的盖柿、天津板栗、紫蟹、银鱼等也在国内久负盛名。

天津是中国近代工业的发祥地,工业门类齐全,综合配套能力强。2003 年销售收入在 500万元以上的工业企业有 5341 家,工业总产值达 4049.61 亿元。一大批新型行业和产品如微型汽车、彩色电视机、摩托车、电梯、大型无缝钢管、乙烯、电子通讯设备等产品逐步形成规模。以电子信息、光机电一体化、生物技术和医药、新材料新能源等为主的高新技术产业发展较快，占规模以上工业总产值的比重已达30.5%。

天津是一个历史悠久的商埠，商业、饮食业、服务业都比较发达。近年来又陆续新建、扩建了鼓楼商业街等十余处大型商业设施，全市万米以上大型购物中心达50多个。全市有限额以上零售贸易机构242家，其中百货商场55家，超级市场26家。世界500强中已有22家跨国商贸集团在津设场建店。2003年全市社会消费品零售总额为1074.05亿元。

六、基础设施 经过多年的建设与改造，现已形成以港口为中心的海陆空为一体的高度发达的立体交叉网络。天津港是中国北方最大的综合性贸易港口，拥有全国最大的集装箱码头，有108个港口泊位，其中万吨级以上泊位54个，与世界上160多个国家和地区的300多个港口保持着贸易往来。2003年港口货物吞吐量达16182万吨。天津滨海国际机场有数十条国际国内航线，实施以货为主，客货兼营的经营战略，其目标是建成北方的航空货运中心（物流中心）。天津铁路枢纽是京山、京沪两大铁路干线的交汇处，中国北方铁路运输枢纽。天津公路四通八达，京塘、京哈、津渝、京福、京淄，京同六条国家级公路途经天津，沟通了天津与东北三省、华北大部、浙江、江苏、山东、广东和福建各省区的公路交通往来，市内已建成以3条环线，14条放射线为骨架的城市道路网。邮电通讯已形成了市话、长途、微波及卫星等配套的信息传递系统，2003年全市邮电业务总量完成115.7亿元。电话交换机总容量达402.5万门，长途自动交换机容量达265427路端，电话机（含移动）装机总数761.9万部。

七、对外经济 目前，已有欧、亚、美、澳各大洲的110个国家和地区在津投资。在世界500强企业中，已有98家在津投资，投资项目达228个。截至2003年末，全市累计批准客商投资企业15990个，协议外资额453.01亿美元，全市实际利用外资318.09亿美元。已形成了多领域、多层次、全方位的对外开放格局。2003年，天津口岸进出口贸易总值461.67亿美元，天津外贸出口总值为143.7亿美元。出口商品的国家和地区主要有日本、香港、美国、韩国、德国、英国等。出口商品主要有服装、机电产品、纺织品、化工产品等。

八、教育、科技、文化 天津教育文化事业发达，是我国北方人才密集地区之一，南开大学，天津大学享誉中外。2003年，全市共有各级各类学校2070所，在校学生163.20万人，其中高等学校37所，在校学生24.50万人，普通中学664所，在校学生61.5万人，学龄儿童入学率100%。全市国有单位拥有专业科技人员46.50万人，平均每万人口有科技人员460人，每万名从业人员有科技人员2435人；全市共有公共图书馆、博物馆48个，电视节目16套。

九、居民生活 2003年全市城市居民人均可支配收入10313元，人均消费性支出7868元，人均住房使用面积16.7平方米，每百户拥有彩色电视机134.5台，电冰箱98.5台，家用电脑34.7台，电话95.2部，移动电话机77.8部；2003年农民人均年纯收入5861元，生活消费支出3015元，人均住房面积24.44平方米，每百户拥有彩色电视机110台，电冰箱75台，洗衣机90台，摩托车45辆，家用电脑7台，移动电话机54部。

A SURVEY OF TIANJIN

Ⅰ. Natural Geography

The city covers a total area of 11,919.7 square kilometers, of which, its plain as a part, accounting for 94 percent. It is situated in the Northeast part of the North China's plain, with the Yan Mountains on the north and Bohai Sea on the east. It runs more than 130 kilometers in its coastline from its north end located at Jianhe to the south one at Qikou and lies in the temperate zone with a semi—humid and continental monsoon climate, beautiful in the sight—seeing within the different seasons. Lying near to Beijing, it is a port through which exports from a vast area of North China and Northwest China could be made available oversea. Its main rivers include Haihe river, the South Canal, the North Canal, Ziya river, Daqing river and Yongding river, etc.

Ⅱ. Population & Administrative Division

The permanent registered population of Tianjin was 9.2600 million in 2003, of the total, those living in the districts under city administration were 7.5878 million. It has 15 districts(Heping, Hedong, Hexi, Nankai, Hebei, Hongqiao, Tanggu, Hangu, Dagang, Dongli, Xiqing, Jinnan, Beichen, Wuqing and Baodi)and 3 counties(Ninghe, Jinghai and Jixian).

Ⅲ. Places of Historic Interest and Scenic Beauty

In Tianjin, there are some places of historic interest and scenic beauty had been unearthed, of which, 37 have been in major preservation by the state and the local government. It has over one thousand years history since the Temple of Dule was built in Sui Dynasty with a large scale and the oldest —existing wooden structures in Jixian; more than 1,000 peculiarly—shaped forts with ancientry are in the 41—kilometer—long Great Wall at Jixian county's Huangyaguan, looking ridgy, grand and marvellous, which are known as the key to the lock in northern part of Jixian county. Panshan Mountain is reputed to be grand and be "the First Mountain East of Beijing", with its peaks rising higher and more beautiful than another. Local buildings have been integrated with rivers and mountains. The Tianjin—based historic interest and scenic beauty also comprise Tianhou Temple, the Temple of Confucious, Dabei Buddhistic Monastery, the Grand Mosque, Tianzun pavilion, Dagu forts, Wanghailou Church, Guangdong Guild Hall, Zhou Enlai & Deng Yingchao Memorial Hall where exhibits their revolutionary activities they had gone in for when they were in days of their youth. The buildings in Tianjin keeping the ancient, mordern times and modernized style have been considered as "Multi—country Architectural Museum". Within Tianjin stand over a thousand of Xiaoyanglou (2 to 3—storey buildings foreigners built) in the different styles of the western and eastern countries during the days from the end of 19th century to the earlier 20th century one, when the land in Tianjin was on lease to, but actually seized by foreigners from nine countries and put under their colonial rule, in the earlier opening of the Tianjin—based port abroad.

Tianjin is famous for its 4 folk arts: the painted clay figures by"Clay—Sculptor Zhang" as known well to all parts of China and of the world; "New Year" pictures produced in the town of Yangliuqing with a long history, that find favour in foreign friends' eyes; Wei—made kites popular so much to win a gold medal at the Panama International Fair in 1914; the carved bricks by "Brick—Carver Liu" being uniquely of Tianjin's folk arts put into use of buildings—related decorations in China.

Ⅳ. Food Culture

In Tianjin, there are over 1,000— variety dishes being fresh, smooth and soft, and saltish with a rich taste, in more than 300—year history, which are prepared by local cuisines, from local perfect raw materials for cooking, together with good flavouring. The traditional dishes have included the fried and stewed carps, meat braised together with carps, deep fried and sauteed birds, "tiger skin" pork elbow, etc. And the excellent dishes have shark's fins braised and brown sauce, sauted shrimps, cooked prawns, shark's fins with crab roe, shredded chicken and mushroom, braised scallops, braised abalone, sourish purple crab paste. In addition, 8—style cookeries as accepted generally by all Chinese have been made in Tianjin, in spite of their being originally from respectively Shandong, Suzhou, Sichuan, Guangdong, Zhejiang, Hunan, Fujian and Anhui, and also it has over 90 varieties of specially—flavoured and ordinary dishes, 45 varieties of cold dishes and over 90 snacks with the local flavor. In the case of Tianjin flavour, besides, 3 "second—to—none" foods are well—known to parts of China and foreign countries for: Goubuli Baozi, Erduoyan Zhagao, Guifaxiang Mahua. In 1998, "Maobuwen" Jiaozi, another food in flavors, was awarded in China the title of the 4th "second—to—none" food in Tianjin. Still, other locally—known snacks include: Zhang's Guo ren, Cao—cooked donkey meat, Dafulai Guobacai, ShiTouMenKan Vegetable Baozi, Zhilanzhai Gaogan, Tiebobo Aoxiaoyu. However, Tianjin people are accustomed to breakfasting necessarily on Dabing, Bangchui Guozi, bean curd with flavorings, Guoba Cai, soya—bean milk, Huntun, Jianbing Guozi.

Ⅴ. Production Fields

Tianjin is the largest opening coastal city of North China and the economic center of the Bohai Coastal Region. Its gross domestic product (GDP) was 244.766 billion yuan in 2003, of which, the primary industry reached 8.966 billion yuan of the value—added, its share in GDP was 3.6 percent; the value—added of secondary industry was 124.529 billion yuan, its share in GDP was 50.9 percent; the value—added of the tertiary industry was 111.271 billion yuan, its share in GDP was 45.5 percent. The per capita GDP was 26,532 yuan in 2003.

Involved in its suburban and county—oriented agriculture, Tianjin has been in production not only of both grain including wheat, corn, rice and economic corps related with peanut, cotton, but also of fruits i.e. apple, pear, peach, date, grape, tomato, chestnut, walnut and haw. Located at the west tip of Bohai Bay, however, Tianjin is rich in such sea—resource products as hairtail, yellow croaker, little yellow croaker, prawns and scallops and, also, in the fresh water—resource products as river crab, carp, clam from its 9 rivers there within. And it has a great number of agricultural products renowned at home and abroad, for example, "Xiao Zhan" rice with the up—to—date quality spelt out by the state, that is available for export to Japan, Cuba and to the Southeast Asian countries. Moreover, persimmon from Panshan Mountain, purple crab and white bait, all have come to a long—standing fame within China, too. As the origins in the development of China's modern industry, meanwhile, Tianjin is in a position to have a large variety of industries and supply their own parts and components for their multi—purpose needs; in 2003, its total industrial output value reached 404.961 billion yuan from 5,341 industrial enterprises, which total annual sales exceed 5 million yuan. A large number of new industrial departments and products had gradually grown to a reasonable scale so variously that they appeared with mini—vehicles, color TV sets, motorcycle, elevator, the big—sized seamless steel pipe, ethylene and electric communication equipment. It has further been able to develop its high and new technology industry as involved not only in electronic communications but also in the biology and medicine, and in new—found energies and materials, with their output value accounting for 30.5 percent of total industrial one.

Tianjin as a commercial port with a long history has developed more rapidly in commerce, catering and services. In recent years, more than 10 large business establishment including Gulou Trade Street have been reconstructed. Thus there are more than 50 shopping centers with an area of more than ten thousand square meters. Business mode of retail trade above designated size 242, department store was 55, supermarket was 26. Of the top 500 enterprises in the world, 22 had developed business in Tianjin. The retail of whole social consumer goods reached 107.405 billion yuan in 2003 in the city.

Ⅵ. Infrastructure

By having made every effort on construction and transformation of infrastructure for several years, the people in Tianjin had its harbor linked up all—sidedly with the railway, the air and the highway as well as with the sea, which appeared a well—developed network of the traffic to and from all directions by way of the above said transport. Tianjin Harbor, as the largest comprehensive and commercial one in North China, boasts China's biggest containerized cargo dock consisting of 108 berths including 54 over 10—thousand—ton ones to make it convenient to contact 300 harbors, for the business, in more than 160 countries and regions all over the world, thus handling 161.82 million—ton cargo in 2003. Tianjin Binhai International Airport is dealing in several tens domestic and international air routes. It has carried out the strategy of passenger and cargo transport in coordination and its target is to be Cargo Air Transport Center(Logistics Center) in North China. At the junction of the Beijing—Shanhaiguan and Beijing—Shanghai railways is the Tianjin Railway Transit Hub as the railway transit hub of North China. It has highways accessible to all directions. There is 6 state—run highways (Beijing—Tangshan, Beijing—Haerbin, Tianjin—Chongqing, Beijing—Fujian, Beijing—Zibo and Beijing—Datong) to link up their traffics between Tianjin and regions both of North China and of 9 provinces(Heilongjiang, Jilin, Liaoning, Zhejiang, Jiangsu, Shandong, Guangdong and Fujian). A urban traffic net has been developed of 3 circulating roads built within the city and of 14 the key streets widened and lengthened in Tianjin city. The Information Transit System has been established to consist of urban districts and its counties call, the long—distance call together with microwave and satellite to form a complete sets of post and communication. The turnover of the posts and telecommunication services in 2003 was 11.57 billion yuan at 2000 constant prices, the total capacity of phone call exchange amounts to 4.025 million lines, that of the automatic long—distance exchange to 265,427 circuits and telephone as installed to 7.619 million sets.

Ⅶ. Foreign Economic Relations

By now, the foreign—funds investment has been made in Tianjin by firms from 110 countries situated respectively in Europe, Asia, America and Australian Oceania. In top 500 strong corporations, for example, there are 98 corporations establishing 228 investment projects in Tianjin. There are 15,990 foreign—funded and joint—venture enterprises approved locally by the end of 2003. Total amount of foreign capital to be utilized through the signed agreement and contracts totaled USD 45.301 billion. Total amount of foreign capital actually used totaled USD 31.809 billion. Therefore, a wide opening to the world region in Tianjin has come into being through which a quite number of fields at all levels and different localities are all presented toward their march to the world. In 2003, total value of imports & exports reached USD 46.167 billion including USD 14.37 billion for exports, through Tianjin Harbor, garments, electrical—machinery products, textiles and chemicals are exported to Japan, HongKong, U.S.A., South Korea, Germany and the U.K.

Ⅷ. Education, Science & Technology and Culture

The education and culture affairs develop quite good, Tianjin is one of regions which own a lot of talents in North China, Nankai University and Tianjin University are well—known at home and abroad. In 2003, there were 2,070 schools at all levels, with 1.6320 million students respectively inclusive of 37 institutions of higher education with 245.0 thousand students and of 664 ordinary middle schools with 615.0thousand students. And the proportion of enrollment of primary—school—age was 100 percent. There are more than 465.0 thousand technicians in specialities of natural science in state—owned units of the city; on an average, there were 460 technicians per 10 thousand population and 2,435 technicians per 10 thousand staff and employees. Throughout the city, there were 16 sets TV programs and 48 public libraries and museums open to the public.

Ⅸ. People's Life

In 2003, per capita annual disposable income of urban households was 10,313 yuan and per capita living expenditures for consumption was 7,868 yuan, per capita using house space was 16.7 square meters in urban areas. The number of color TV sets owned by per hundred households was 134.5, refrigerators was 98.5, micro—computer was 34.7 , telephones was 95.2 ,mobile telephone subscribers was 77.8 . The average net annual income and expenditures of peasants was 5,861 yuan and 3,015 yuan respectively, the per capita dwelling space in rural area was 24.44 square meters. The number of color TV sets owned by per hundred rural households was 110, refrigerators was 75, washing machines was 90, motorcycles was 45, micro—computer was 7, mobile telephone subscribers was 54.

2003年天津市国民经济和社会发展统计公报

天津市统计局

2004年2月20日

2003年是我市实施“三步走”战略的第一年。全市人民在市委、市政府领导下，以邓小平理论和“三个代表”重要思想为指导，深入贯彻党的十六大和市委八届三次全会精神，全面启动五大战略举措，扎实苦干，开拓创新，积极应对国内外形势的新变化，在取得抗击非典阶段性重大胜利的同时，经济发展上了一个新台阶，社会事业全面进步。全市主要经济指标增幅创近年最好水平，人均生产总值突破3000美元，“三步走”战略第一步目标胜利实现。

一、经济发展

经济总量

国民经济快速健康发展。全年实现全市生产总值2386.94亿元，按可比价格计算，比上年增长14.5%，增速比上年加快2个百分点，创1996年以来最高增幅，居全国各省市自治区前列。全市人均生产总值由上年的22380元增加到25874元，按当年汇率折算，折合3126美元，比上年增长13.8%。

三次产业全面发展。第一产业完成增加值89.7亿元，增长6.1%。第二产业是推动全市经济快速增长的主要力量，完成增加值1212.34亿元，增长17.8%，比上年加快3.5个百分点，对全市经济增长的贡献率达到62.8%。第三产业积极化解非典负面影响，完成增加值1084.9亿元，增长11.5%。三次产业的比重分别为3.7%、50.8%和45.5%。

财政收入大幅增长。辖区内财政收入718.3亿元，比上年增长22.8%，其中全市财政收入完成451.74亿元，增长20.2%，增幅较上年提高1.8个百分点。增值税、消费税、营业税、企业所得税、个人所得税分别增长16.7%、32.7%、24.5%、13.6%和18.7%。全年财政支出350.01亿元，比上年增长16.6%。其中基本建设支出增长34.7%；科教文卫支出增长17.7%。

劳动就业

就业和再就业工作取得新进展。2003年全市新增就业岗位18.1万个，比上年增加4.1万个，增长29.3%。安置下岗失业人员12.1万人，比上年增加3.1万人，增长34.4%，首次实现新增就业人员数量大于新增下岗失业人员。全市社会从业人员510.9万人，比上年增长3.7%，其中第一产业83.19万人，第二产业219.43万人，第三产业208.28万人；城镇社会从业人员299.95万人，比上年增长1.4%。全年人才和劳务市场共接待292.26万人次进场择业洽谈，61.22万人次达成初步意向。城镇登记失业率为3.8%，比上年下降0.1个百分点。

价　格

消费价格总体保持平稳。全年城市居民消费价格总水平比上年上升1.0%。其中食品类价格受四季度粮油等商品价格上扬的拉动上升3.3%，衣着类价格下降11.9%，家庭设备用品及维修服务价格下降3.5%，交通和通讯类价格下降3.0%。全年城市商品零售价格总水平比上年下降2.6%。

生产和投资领域价格上升明显。全年工业品出厂价格比上年上升2.5%，原材料、燃料及动力购进价格比上年上升8.7%，固定资产投资价格上升2.6%。

土地和房屋价格普遍上升，全年土地交易价格上升3.0%，房屋销售价格上升4.1%，其中商品房销售价格上涨4.0%，私房交易价格上涨5.0%，房屋租赁价格上升0.9%。

固定资产投资

固定资产投资总量上了一个新台阶。全年全社会固定资产投资完成1046.72亿元，比上年增长29.0%，增幅比上年提高13.9个百分点，为1995来以来最高水平。投资呈现多元化。国有投资528.60亿元，比上年增长28.2%；民间投资314.00亿元，增长33.8%；外商及港澳台商投资204.12亿元，增长24.3%；民间投资占全社会投资的比重达到30%，比上年提高1.1个百分点。地方单位投资892.14亿元，增长31.6%；中央单位投资154.58亿元，增长15.5%。从产业投向看，第一产业投资9.38亿元，增长26.8%；第二产业投资402.3亿元，增长24.1%，其中工业投入382.5亿元，增长23.5%；第三产业投资635.04亿元，增长32.3%。第三产业投资占全市的比重为60.7%，交通运输邮电业、房地产业、文教卫生等社会事业和城市建设投资分别增长42.5%、32.2%、76.5%和75.4%。

农　业

农业生产稳步发展。全年农业总产值193.50亿元，比上年增长6.2%。其中种植业产值88.80亿元，增长2.2%；畜牧业产值77.00亿元，增长11.0%；渔业产值26.10亿元，增长5.1%；林业产值1.60亿元，增长2.4%。

农业结构调整进一步深化。养殖业占农业总产值的比重达到53.3%，比上年提高1.7个百分点；经济作物占农作物播种面积的比重达到58.0%，比上年提高6.7个百分点。

农业产业化经营成效显著。至年末，全市已有龙头企业396个，资产1000万元以上的企业120个。其中被列为国家级龙头企业7个，市级龙头企业36个。全市进入农业产业化体系的农户占农户总数的60%。全市无公害蔬菜基地、畜禽基地、牛奶基地和水产基地分别达到552个、98个、112个和68个。

主要农副产品产量增加。全年棉花产量9.47万吨，比上年增长51.8%；蔬菜产量602.78万吨，增长3.2%；肉类总产量52.41万吨，增长16.8%；禽蛋产量24.25万吨，下降0.9%；奶类产量43.23万吨，增长28.7%；水产品产量29.83万吨，增长4.4%。受播种面积减少及气候条件影响，全年粮食总产量119.29万吨，比上年减产18.53万吨；平均亩产308.1公斤，比上年增产12.9公斤。

工　业

工业生产增势强劲。全市工业完成增加值1103.37亿元，比上年增长18.4%；完成总产值4370.76亿元，增长24.1%，其中规模以上工业完成增加值1027.79亿元，增长20.1%；完成总产值4049.61亿元，增长26.1%。

重工业增速和比重继续提高。规模以上工业完成轻工业增加值242.19亿元，比上年增长16.0%，完成总产值1095.39亿元，增长20.8%；完成重工业增加值785.60亿元，增长22.1%，完成总产值2954.22亿元，增长28.7%。轻重工业产值比例为27:73。

优势产业带动作用明显。电子信息、汽车、医药、冶金、化工以及新能源等六大优势行业完成工业总产值2775.04亿元，增长28.9%，占规模以上工业总产值的比重达到68.5%，对工业增长的贡献率达到79.2%。

高新技术产业发展迅速。高新技术企业完成总产值1235.87亿元，比上年增长22.6%，占规模以上工业总产值比重为30.5%。新产品开发和产品出口规模扩大。全年新产品产值971.51亿元，增长22.6%；全市工业完成出口交货值983.91亿元，增长20.6%。

全年主要产品产量如下：

	单位	2003年	比上年增长(%)
原油	万吨	1316.30	8.3
天然气	亿立方米	8.49	-4.4
原盐	万吨	220.48	-8.3
发电量	亿千瓦时	319.95	18.9
生铁	万吨	342.65	20.3
钢	万吨	565.95	17.4
成品钢材	万吨	1031.47	42.6
无缝钢管	万吨	91.67	9.2
水泥	万吨	449.31	17.7

乙烯	万吨	23.00	8.1
纯碱	万吨	82.01	3.2
烧碱	万吨	79.89	25.2
化学纤维	万吨	29.76	30.7
移动电话机	万部	3139.72	10.0
轿车	万辆	17.25	82.7
摩托车	万辆	114.80	37.7
内燃机	万千瓦	973.91	81.7
纱	万吨	7.45	-8.1
布	亿米	2.51	1.2
食用植物油	万吨	17.35	-12.6
方便主食品	万吨	14.47	32.0
葡萄酒	万吨	3.05	10.5
房间空气调节器	万台	241.83	99.0
微波炉	万台	969.87	68.2
彩色显象管	万只	268.41	21.0
电子元件	亿只	840.77	13.2
显示器	万部	677.83	24.8

工业产销衔接较好。规模以上工业完成销售产值4004.37亿元，比上年增长21.6%。工业产品销售率为98.88%，其中重工业为99.43%，轻工业为97.41%；国有企业为100.34%，外商及港澳台商投资企业为99.59%，股份制企业为98.58%。

工业经济效益继续提升。规模以上工业企业经济效益综合指数为147.6，比上年提高14.5点。企业利润大幅增长，全年实现利税总额391.06亿元，增长24.6%。其中实现利润231.88亿元，增长30.2%；实现税金159.18亿元，增长17.3%。

建筑业

投资规模扩张拉动建筑业增长。全年建筑业完成增加值108.97亿元，比上年增长12.1%；完成总产值498.66亿元，增长46.6%。全年房屋建筑施工面积3348.22万平方米，增长35.3%；房屋建筑竣工面积1601.05万平方米，增长54.3%。全市建筑施工企业共承接施工项目22863个。按产值计算的全员劳动生产率人均达15.25万元，增长29.8%。

交通运输邮电仓储业

交通邮电业综合服务能力明显增强。全市交通运输邮电仓储业完成增加值256.03亿元，比上年增长14.7%，增幅比上年提高2.9个百分点。

以港口为中心的海陆空立体交通网络进一步发展。天津港15万吨级航道一期及北大防波堤项目竣工。天津港已与世界上160多个国家和地区的300多个港口建立业务联系，港口货物吞吐量16181.6万吨，比上年增长25.4%，其中进口5270万吨，增长28.4%，出口10911.6万吨，增长24.0%。集装箱吞吐量301.5万国际标准箱，增长25.2%。综合运输能力进一步加强。全年各种运输方式完成货物运输总量39532.66万吨，比上年增长13.6%。其中，铁路运输10082.1万吨，增长11.8%；公路运输20114万吨，增长6.8%；水路运输8762.75万吨，增长36.8%。全年客运量4668.1万人，增长0.7%。机场旅客吞吐量110.1万人次，增长0.8%；机场货邮吞吐量5.66万吨，增长13.9%。

电信和邮政业务大幅上升。全年邮电业务总量完成111.97亿元，比上年增长24.2%。其中电信业务总量103亿元，增长26.1%，实现电信业务收入66.2亿元，增长12.2%。年末长途光缆线路总长度达到2704.08公里，增长42.2%。局用电话交换机总容量403.35万门。全市公网固定电话和移动电话用户达到737.7万户，增长22.3%。公网固定电话用户达到354.3万户，净增58.3万户，增长19.7%。移动电话用户达到383.4万户，净增76.3万户，增长24.8%。全市公网电话本地通话量达到140亿次，增长11.1%，短信业务总量达到14.69亿条。全年邮政业务总量8.97亿元，增长5.7%，发送函件22033.93万件，增长8.5%，特快专递321.5万件，增长11.8%。

国内商业

商业流通规模继续扩大。全市批发零售贸易餐饮业完成增加值211.92亿元，比上年增长10.8%。

市场的积聚作用明显。2003年末，全市共有各类市场760个，其中生产资料市场123个，消费品市场608个，生产要素市场29个。各类市场成交额712.79亿元，比上年增长16.2%。年成交额超亿元商品市场全年成交额498.39亿元，占市场总成交额的69.9%。

零售餐饮市场经历了4、5月份的短期波动后迅速回升。全年社会消费品零售总额1074.05亿元，比上年增长14.1%。其中批发零售贸易业零售额727.1亿元，增长12.5%；餐饮业零售额109.91亿元，增长7.2%。家居用品及装修装饰、通信器材、文体用品、汽车等新的消费热点逐渐升温。限额以上批零贸易业全年通讯器材零售额增长1.1倍，家具类增长18.4%，汽车增长1倍，体育娱乐用品类增长49.9%。

流通业招商引资取得新成果。年内又有易初莲花、欧倍德、沃尔玛、百盛、灿坤等知名集团在津投资建店。截至年末，外资零售业店场达120多家，世界500强中已有22家跨国商贸集团在津设场建店。北京物美、温州麦购等国内知名连锁集团纷纷来津投资建店。商业设施建设增势迅猛。全年开工面积129万平方米，竣工面积108.7万平方米。

金融保险业

金融保险服务力度显著加大。全市金融保险业实现增加值91.81亿元，比上年增长24.7%。年末全市各类金融机构达2837家，其中银行类机构1594家，非银行类机构1243家。渤海银行获国家批准筹建。年末金融机构从业人员达4.7万人。

金融业对外开放步伐加快。花旗银行在津设立分行，截至年末，在津外资银行分行15家，外资银行代表处4家，获准经营人民币业务的外资银行有8家，其中6家已经开展业务。总部设在天津的外资保险公司2家，外资保险驻津代表处3家。

当年新增存贷款创历史最高水平。截止2003年末，全市中外金融机构本外币存款余额达到4362.6亿元，比上年末增长29.9%，净增额为1003.77亿元，比上年净增额多增503.74亿元；本外币贷款余额达到3791.22亿元，比上年末增长32.1%，净增额为920.31亿元，比上年净增额多增537.63亿元.其中，中长期贷款余额1573.93亿元，比上年末增长64.3%。个人消费贷款增长加快，年末余额达到261.42亿元，比上年末增长29.8%，其中住房贷款余额218.84亿元，比上年末增长28.6%。

证券市场平稳。截止2003年末，本市共有境内上市股票23只，其中当年上市1只。各类证券成交额1322亿元，比上年增长12.1%，其中股票交易额1123亿元，增长8.8%。全年调剂外汇总额13亿美元，比上年增长41.9%。

保险业务规模不断扩大。全年保费收入75.31亿元，比上年增长16.0%，其中财产险保费收入15.56亿元，增长8.0%，人身险保费收入59.75亿元，增长18.0%，。支付各项赔款给付17.36亿元，比上年增长51.0%，其中财产险赔款10.11亿元，增长48.0%；人身险给付7.25亿元，增长56.0%。年内太平保险天津分公司和恒安标准人寿保险公司相继开业。至年末，全市有各类保险公司14家，其中财产保险公司7家，人身险保险公司7家。保险中介机构17家，其中保险代理公司12家，保险经纪公司2家，保险公估公司3家。

房地产业

需求扩大拉动了房地产业的大发展。全市房地产业增加值为119.87亿元，增长17.4%，增幅比上年提高13个百分点。受海河开发和路桥建设带动，房地产开发投资大幅增长，全年完成211.39亿元，增长20.2%。商品房销售创历史最高纪录。全年实现商品房现房销售面积786.5万平方米，销售收入202.3亿元，分别比上年增长39.5%和43.4%。存量房交易688.3万平方米，比上年增长94.8%；成交金额86.3亿元，增长1.2倍。其中私房成交面积504.6万平方米，增长1.2倍；成交金额71.4亿元，增长1.3倍。公房置换面积183.7万平方米，增长49%；置换金额14.9亿元，增长55.2%。

二、改革开放

所有制结构

所有制结构调整取得新进展，非公有制经济比重继续提高。全市公有制经济实现增加值1302.33亿元，占全市生产总值的比重为54.6%；非公有制经济增加值1084.61亿元，比重为45.4%，比上年提高3.5个百分点。其中外商及港澳台商经济增加值530.83亿元，占全市生产总值的22.2%，比上年提高1.5个百分点，私营个体经济增加值539.45亿元，占全市生产总值的22.6%，比上年提高2.6个百分点。

各种所有制工业企业共同发展。全年国有及国有控股工业企业完成工业总产值1456.51亿元，比上年增长28.6%。在规模以上工业企业中，股份制工业企业总产值1172.56亿元，比上年增长29.4%；外商及港澳台商投资工业企业总产值1896.06亿元，增长30.3%。股份制和外商及港澳台商投资工业企业总产值合计占规模以上工业总产值的比重达到75.8%。

私营个体经济发展壮大。全市私营个体经济年末注册资金969.45亿元，比年初增加401亿元，增长70.5%；私营和个体经营户达到24.78万户，比年初增加1.44万户；从业人员92.09万人，比年初增加15.14万人；全年实现税收34.97亿元，增长41.4%。《关于进一步加快个体私营经济发展的意见》及相关配套政策的实施，为私营个体经济向公交、供水、燃气、供热、污水处理、垃圾处理等行业发展开辟了新的空间。

国有资产管理与国有企业改革

经济体制改革继续深化，市场化程度进一步提高。新的财政体制和税收体制改革方案出台实施。农村税费改革试点顺利进行。整顿规范土地市场秩序，制定和实施了国有土地有偿使用管理办法。产权交易中心完成交易额151亿元，并与北京、河北、河南、山东、山西等地产权交易机构组建了中国北方产权交易共同市场。

国有企业改革迈出重要步伐。工业加大了大集团重组和中小企业改制力度。完成了钢管公司48.5亿元股权回购，实现了医药、纺织、工程机械行业的重组整合。全年有106户工业中小企业完成了股权改制，已分块搞活58户，累计有364户竞争力差的企业退出市场，提高了中小企业整体素质。天津港股份制改造取得重要突破。商业重组改革力度继续加大。全年有12家大中型商业企业实行股份制改造，7家集团实现内部资源优势整合，组建了津食集团和百货大楼集团，劝华集团整合重组进入实施阶段，采取多种方式退出国有资本的小企业超过500家。

行政审批制度改革

政府行政审批制度改革进一步深化，2003年对原有的审批事项进行了第三轮清理，取消审批事项121项，转变管理方式事项55项，经过三轮清理，累计精简审批事项达到666项。进行了企业工商登记并联审批改革试点。

社会保障

企业养老保险扩面征缴工作取得重大进展。年末参保缴费企业职工人数达到168.5万人，比上年末增加3.85万人。企业基本养老保险基金征缴收入为62.28亿元，增加10.34亿元。由养老保险统筹基金支付的企业离退休人员养老金月人均水平达到707元，比上年增长19%。年末全市参保缴费的职工达到175.8万人，参加基本养老保险的离退休人员为97.61万人。

医疗保险改革进一步深化。制定了完善城镇职工基本医疗保险制度的10项政策措施。年末全市参加基本医疗保险人数为242.92万人，比上年末增加34.42万人。其中：职工165.17万人、退休人员77.75万人，分别比上年末增加25.97万人和8.45万人。按企事业划分来看，企业参加基本医疗保险人数为192.4万人，机关和事业单位为50.52万人，分别比上年增加27.48万人和6.94万人。

失业保险参保人数增加，领取失业保险金人数下降。年末失业保险参保人数193.45万人，比上年末增加3.9万人；领取失业保险金的失业人员9.5万人，比上年末减少2.9万人。

国内合作

内联招商引资实现高增长，区域经济合作取得新进展。全年吸引外地在津投资协议额172.2亿元，增长80.5%，实际利用内资112.2亿元，增长83.7%。外地企业在津投资超过500万元的项目有273个，主要投向房地产开发和商贸物流业。我市与“三北”地区的经贸往来进一步加强，签定合作项目35个，合作金额达25.9亿元。加强了京津冀区域经济合作。京津两市商定增建京津高速公路南北两个通道，加强京津两市经济发展重点区域的联系，加强天津港为北京的服务，实现京津两大机场共同发展。

天津对甘肃省、西藏昌都地区、重庆龙宝移民开发区的对口支援和帮扶工作进一步加强，有力地促进了当地经济的发展。

对外贸易

对外贸易规模进一步扩大。全市外贸进出口总值293.71亿美元，比上年增长28.7%。其中进口149.97亿美元，增长33.5%；出口143.74亿美元，增长24%。加工贸易出口仍占主体，一般贸易出口增长加快。全年加工贸易出口91.47亿美元，增长17.4%，占全市外贸出口的比重为63.6%。一般贸易出口48.36亿美元，增长35.1%，增幅比上年提高28.1个百分点。外商及港澳台商投资企业、个体私营企业出口增长幅度高。外商及港澳台商投资企业出口114.27亿美元，增长25.4%，占全市出口比重为79.5%；个体私营企业出口增长2.1倍。对美国、欧盟、日本、韩国和东盟等五个主要出口市场的出口额分别增长8.9%～43.6%，合计占全市出口的比重达到78.9%。

出口商品结构继续优化，机电产品和高新技术产品出口高速增长。机电产品出口91.8亿美元，增长24%，占全市出口比重为63.9%，机电产品中的高新技术产品出口48.1亿美元，增长48%。

口岸辐射作用不断增强。全年天津口岸进出口总值461.67亿美元，比上年增长26.4%，其中进口202.1亿美元，增长23.2%；出口259.57亿美元，增长28.9%。在天津口岸进出口总值中，外省市的比重达到51.7%，北京、河北、山西进出口货值居前三位，分别占20.3%、10.7%和3.6%。

吸收外资

利用外资步伐加快。全年新批三资企业941家，比上年增长15.3%；直接利用外资合同额35.13亿美元，增长74.3%；实际到位16.33亿美元，增长62.9%。全年新批投资额在500万美元以上的大项目198个，增长60.9%。来自日本、意大利、新加坡、德国、英国、香港等国家和地区的直接利用外资合同额分别增长1～4.5倍。世界500强企业中，已有98家来津投资。企业增资踊跃，全年增资企业达到382家，增资总额10.95亿美元，其中外方增资额9.23亿美元。制造业招商引资占主导地位，直接利用外资合同额21.54亿美元，增长94.7%，占全市的61.3%，电子通信、交通运输设备、化学原料、机械设备、医药制造业等行业引资均超过1.5亿美元。服务业利用外资也保持较快增长，直接利用外资合同额13.28亿美元，增长48.6%。

对外承包工程和劳务合作

对外经济合作发展迅速。全年对外承包工程、劳务合作、设计咨询业务共实现营业额4.05亿美元，比上年增长51.0%。全市具有对外经济合作经营资格的企业59家，对外工程承包和劳务合作业务遍及80多个国家和地区，涉及工业、农业、建筑业、服务业等领域，年末在国外劳务人员1.13万人。全年引进国外先进技术成交合同381项，合同金额9.67亿美元。新批境外机构51个，其中在境外投资生产企业38家，总投资4250.74万美元，在总投资额中中方投资3796.42万美元。

旅　游

受非典影响，国际旅游略有下降，国内旅游小幅增长。全市共有星级宾馆85家，旅行社233家，其中国际旅行社19家，国内旅行社214家。全年共接待国际旅游人数48.9万人次，比上年下降3.4%，其中外国人45.6万人次。国际旅游外汇收入3.29亿美元，下降3.8%。全年接待国内旅游者3751.12万人次，比上年增长1.1%；国内旅游收入395.02亿元，增长1.3%。全市共有5.31万人次出国旅游，旅游花费7.83亿元。旅游资源开发力度加大。当年建成玉龙滑雪场和天津热带植物观光园，天津国际游乐港、“东方公主”号游轮等一批在建旅游项目和设施进展顺利。

滨海新区

滨海新区在全市经济发展中的地位明显提高。滨海新区实现生产总值970亿元，比上年增长20.0%。新区地方财政收入57.73亿元，增长21.0%；实现工业总产值2133.21亿元，增长30.3%；完成固定资产投资464.08亿元，增长65.2%；外贸出口89.87亿美元，增长24.8%，占全市外贸出口的62.5%；直接利用外资合同额24.46亿美元，增长58.2%，占全市的69.6%。

天津经济技术开发区实现生产总值445.23亿元，比上年增长25.1%，主要经济指标在国家级开发区中继续保持领先。第二产业增加值354.90亿元，增长28.3%，占全区生产总值的比重达到79.7%。工业总产值超亿元的企业达到108家，比上年增加20家，产值合计占全区的91.8%。电子通讯、机械制造、医药化工、食品饮料等四大支柱行业完成工业产值占全区工业总产值的91.4%。

天津港保税区实现生产总值83亿元，比上年增长38.2%。国际物流中心建设迈上新台阶。保税及非保税货物进出区总值92.30亿美元，增长42.0%。保税区已成为汽车、汽车零部件、电子产品及电子元器件、钢材、机械设备等商品的物流分拨配送基地，其中自保税区分拨、销售的进口汽车达4.9万辆，继续保持全国领先地位。海港保税区、空港物流加工区、空港国际物流区已开工建设。

三、城市建设和管理

海河两岸综合开发

海河两岸综合开发改造全面启动。海河清淤216万立方米，堤岸改造完成8.9公里。海河东路、海河西路等 4 条道路基本建成，慈海桥、大沽桥开工建设，狮子林桥成功顶升。六大节点规划编制完成，古文化街海河楼商贸区、运河经济文化商贸区、大悲院商贸区开工建设。全年海河两岸综合开发完成投资56亿元。

基础设施建设和城市绿化

城市基础设施建设全面铺开，进展顺利。全年城市基础设施投资263.67亿元，比上年增长34.2%，占全市的比重达到25.2%，主要投向地铁、轻轨、港口、公路等重要基础设施项目。津蓟、唐津高速公路竣工通车。津滨轻轨开始试运行。地铁一号线进入主体施工阶段。新增高速公路里程179公里。完成了海河东路、金钟河大街、卫国道等一批主干道路的扩建，四化河、北塘排水河、月牙河二期 3 条河道改造全面完成。拓宽和打通了西湖道、复康路等一批卡口道路。城市灯光夜景建设初具规模。完成了207幢高层建筑、510幢多层建筑、158幢特色风貌建筑整体灯光装饰，156幢大中型公共建筑实施了里光外透，安装了76处绿地小品灯光。

新建银河公园、海河外滩公园等一批绿地广场和社区公园，全市新增城市绿化面积2500万平方米，建成区绿化覆盖率达到31%，城市人均公共绿地面积6.5平方米，比上年增加0.9平方米。

公用事业

城市交通更加便捷。年内新开公交线路15条，开通10条校车线，延长60条公交线路，至年末，全市公交运营线路达到351条，公交运营车辆6158辆，运营出租车31939辆。全年公交客运达6.22亿人次。进一步改善运营环境，年内更新车辆800余部，新建公交枢纽站 3 处。

公用事业取得新进展。全市自来水综合生产能力368万立方米，全年自来水售水量6.3亿立方米，其中生活用水3.05亿立方米。家庭燃气用户208万户，年末城市居民家庭燃气气化率97%。集中供热普及率达到77.2%，比上年提高3.1个百分点。旧楼区环境改造治理取得突破，65处旧住宅区纳入物业管理。

环境保护和治理

环境综合整治取得新成效。年末全市有环境监测站20个，创建国家环保模范城市六大工程进展顺利。

天津市危险废物处理处置中心建成投入使用。西青区杨柳青镇被国家命名为全国首批环境优美镇。开展了“百万市民环境大清整”活动,有效地促进了环境卫生、城市管理和文明程度的提高。

大气环境质量继续改善,可吸入颗粒物均值较上年下降3.6%。全年空气质量达二级良好水平以上天数为264天,占全年总天数的72.3%。烟尘控制区60个,烟尘控制面积557.3平方公里。

声环境质量处于较好水平。其中城市区域环境噪音平均声级为55分贝,与上年持平;道路交通噪音平均声级为68.2分贝,比上年下降0.2分贝。环境噪声达标区总面积539.1平方公里,覆盖率为78%,比上年提高2个百分点。

水环境治理状况良好。加强了对于桥水库库区和引滦、引黄河道水质巡查和监测,引滦和引黄天津段总体水质较好,饮用水源地各月水质达标率均为100%。

生态环境保护力度加大。全市生态示范区6个,自然保护区8个,自然保护区面积15.33万公顷。建成了以蓟县中上元古界地质自然保护区为核心的蓟县国家地质公园。

信息化建设

信息基础设施建设水平进一步提升。宽带城域网建设完成,光缆总长度达到1.9万千米,宽带无线微波已覆盖市区,核心交换能力达到2000G,城市出口带宽达到21.2G。天津电信通信枢纽工程、互联网数据中心等重大信息基础功能平台相继投入使用,提升了面向社会和公众的信息服务能力。新闻浏览、视频点播、信息查询、远程教育、远程医疗、视频会议、网络游戏等被广泛使用。

信息技术应用继续扩大。2003年全市38个委办局的248项审批项目实现了网上受理,受理范围占市级行政审批总数的40%。口岸信息平台、工商并联审批、企业信用、知识产权、民政管理、网上纳税、网上政府采购等重点工程的实施,有效地提高了政府城市管理、市场监督和为民服务的能力。互联网拨号上网用户达到206万户,比上年增加56万户;互联网专线用户达到1949户,新增631户;互联网宽带用户达到18.9万户,新增16.9万户。医保联网顺利起步,联网医院达到101家。以“校校通”、校园通和远程教育为主的教育信息化发展迅速。今晚报呼叫中心和津工超市合作,开通了电话销售和网上销售服务。自来水远程抄表已在市内一些大型住宅区实现。网上房屋交易市场集中了995个楼盘、879个开发企业的信息。全市13家金融机构共发行银行卡1823万张,清算交易金额66.6亿元,比上年增长2.2倍。发放公务卡1.6万张。城市公共汽车一卡通进一步普及。

四、社会事业

科　技

科技创新能力进一步提高。全年取得市级科技成果1203项,其中属于国际领先水平59项,达到国际先进水平311项。全年获国家科学技术奖14项。全市累计实施重大高新技术产业化项目66项,科技成果应用率80%以上。为神舟五号飞船提供了高效电源和导航设备。全市专利申请量达到6812件,比上年增长27.1%,其中发明专利申请比上年增长60.8%,占全市专利申请量的48.9%,授权专利2505件。科技队伍继续扩大,市属国有企事业单位专业技术人员32.3万人。当年新增中国科学院和中国工程院院士5位,在津两院院士共计28位,其中中国科学院院士13位,中国工程院院士15位。成功举办了“第三届PECC投资博览会暨2003中国(天津)计算机软件网络与通信产品展览会”和“信息化与新型工业化道路论坛”。

科技创新体系建设得到加强。IC设计与数字产品、动力电池等一批科技专项启动实施,生物技术、海水淡化等领域的科技攻关取得新进展。华苑软件产业园被确定为国家级软件出口基地。至年末,全市共有国家级和市级企业技术中心90家。技术市场成交活跃。全年技术交易市场共签订技术合同7278项,合同成交额42亿元,比上年增长15.6%。

新技术产业园区实力不断增强。全年园区实现技工贸总收入668.95亿元,比上年增长35.3%;技工贸总产值561.97亿元,增长35%;利润总额25.73亿元,增长34%;税金总额28.84亿元,增长31.9%;出口销售收入13.63亿美元,增长30.3%。

教　育

高等教育规模继续扩大。全市普通高校和高等职业技术学院37所，当年招生8.6万人，比上年增长24.1%，年末共有在校学生24.5万人，毕业4万人；全年招收研究生0.85万人，比上年增长29.4%，在学研究生2.1万人，毕业研究生0.33万人；中等职业学校当年招生4.4万人，比上年增长9.2%，在校学生13.5万人。高等教育毛入学率达到49%，比上年提高了5个百分点。

中小学教育质量不断提高。全市在校初中学生40.6万人，毕业生14万人；普通高中当年招生7万人，比上年增长18.7%，在校高中学生18.3万人，毕业生4.5万人；高中阶段入学率93.1%。小学当年招生8.5万人，在校学生61万人，毕业生13.2万人。幼儿园在园幼儿20万人，学龄儿童入学率99.97%，小学生升学率98.97%。全市各区县小学全部进入实施新课程的实验。

教育布局进一步得到有效调整。首批31所示范高中学校全部建成并投入使用。医大“211”工程和一批模范小学开工建设。

文　化

文化艺术、新闻出版、广播影视、图书、档案事业成绩斐然。年末全市共有艺术表演团体15个，文化馆、科技馆19个，博物馆16个，公共图书馆31个。天津博物馆、泰达会展中心和图书馆相继建成，进一步提高了城市文化品位。全年共出版各类报纸82386.51万份，杂志4609.72万册，图书6772.39万册。全市现有广播节目7套，综合人口覆盖率为100%；市级电视节目7套，综合人口覆盖率为99%，全市有线电视用户达到180万户。成功地举办了“中国民族戏曲优秀剧目大汇演”、首届老年文化艺术节、第二届家庭文化艺术节、第四届滨海艺术节、毛主席诗词音乐会等大型文化活动。推出了京剧《华子良》、芭蕾舞剧《精卫》、话剧《为你喝彩》等艺术精品。创作演出了《我们必胜》特别文艺节目和“我们携手同行”系列文艺节目。

卫　生

卫生事业稳步发展。年末全市共有卫生机构2671个，其中医院500个，卫生防疫机构25个，妇幼保健所(站)11个。年末卫生机构拥有床位4.27万张，比上年增长0.9%，其中医院、卫生院床位4.16万张，增长0.8%。全市拥有专业卫生技术人员6.1万人，比上年增加0.4万人，其中医生2.59万人。每万人拥有医生27.8人，拥有医院床位44.6张。卫生资源调整进展顺利。改造了海河医院和一中心医院，完成传染病医院一期工程和人民医院主体工程。社区卫生服务和农村卫生服务网络基本形成。

非典型肺炎防治工作取得阶段性重大胜利。出现非典疫情后，全市及时封锁疫点疫区，切断传染源，制定了各项防控措施，建成一批发热门诊和留观所，建立了非典医疗救治体系，仅用28天就控制了疫情。

体　育

竞技体育硕果累累。我市运动员在全国高水平比赛中共获金牌16枚，银牌13枚，铜牌19枚；在亚洲三大赛中获得金牌9枚，银牌1枚，铜牌2枚。在世界三大赛上获得金牌5枚，银牌3枚，铜牌1枚。天津女排获全国联赛和锦标赛冠军。网球、武术、女子佩剑、男子吊环等项目进一步确立了在全国的优势地位。成功举办了第十二届亚洲男排锦标赛、国际室内田径邀请赛、丰田杯国际乒乓球邀请赛等十多项国内外赛事。天津奥林匹克中心体育场开工建设。

群众体育蓬勃开展。全面实施《全民健身计划纲要》二期工程，在全市18个区县配建了23套全民健身工程，在267片居民小区配建了364处健身设施。在全市开展了“阳光健身活动”，举办了首届国际山野运动大会，创编了第一套市民广播体操。

社会福利与救助

社会福利事业不断发展。国家抚恤、补助各类优抚对象24547人，全市低保对象26.74万人，其中城镇低保对象24.13万人，与上年相比减少了近6万人。各种福利院床位16478张，收养10910人。全市有救助站7个，全年救助58857人天。全市社区服务设施1901处，社区服务中心102个。农村社会保障网络覆盖率达到

74.3%。全年销售社会福利彩票1.06亿元，筹集福利资金0.39亿元。

五、人口与人民生活

人　口

人口增长继续得到有效控制。2003年末全市常住人口1011.30万人，比上年末增加4.12万人；年末户籍人口926.00万人，比上年增加6.95万人，其中农业人口376.26万人，比上年减少1.65万人，非农业人口549.74万人，增加8.60万人。全年人口出生率为7.14‰，比上年下降0.35个千分点；人口死亡率为6.04‰，与上年持平；人口自然增长率为1.10‰，比上年下降0.35个千分点。

居民收入与储蓄

城乡居民收入实现较快增长。全年城镇单位从业人员人均劳动报酬18628元，比上年增长14.8%。据抽样调查，全年城市居民人均可支配收入(按新口径计算)10313元，增长10.5%；农民人均纯收入5861元，增长10.3%。居民储蓄增量高于上年。年末城乡居民储蓄存款余额1991.76亿元，比年初增加332.27亿元，比上年净增额多增114.66亿元。

居民消费

城乡居民消费同步增长。城市居民人均消费性支出7868元，增长9.4%。其中居住、交通通讯和医疗保健三项支出分别增长了17.5%、26.5%和11.7%。农村居民人均生活消费支出3015元，增长8.5%，其中居住、交通通讯支出分别增长20.1%和10.8%。居民生活质量进一步提高。绿色健康家电、现代通讯工具成为新的消费热点。年末城市居民每百户家庭拥有影碟机49.6部，空调器90.9台，移动电话77.8部，电脑34.1台，吸尘器24.3台，饮水机31.3台，淋浴热水器82.7台。农村居民每百户拥有彩电110台，洗衣机90台，空调器32台，影碟机31部，电脑 7 台。

居　住

城乡居民居住条件和环境继续改善。全年房屋拆迁总量突破450万平方米，综合整修旧楼区324片，近百万居民受益。城市居民人均住房建筑面积23.10平方米，使用面积17.46平方米，比上年增加0.8平方米。农村居民人均住房面积24.44平方米，比上年增加0.1平方米。

经济和社会发展中存在的主要问题是：第三产业发展还不够快；部分国有中小企业尚未摆脱困境；就业和再就业压力仍比较大；城乡居民整体收入水平还不够高，部分群众的生活还比较困难；部分商品及原材料价格出现上涨过快苗头。

注：1.2003年各项统计数据为快报数。

2.按国家统计局规定，各地区 GDP 中文名称由“国内生产总值”改为“地区生产总值”，本公报中“全市生产总值”即为原“国内生产总值”。

3.全市生产总值、各产业增加值和总产值绝对数按当年价格计算，增长速度按可比价格计算。

4.规模以上工业企业包括全部国有企业和年销售收入在500万元及以上的其他各类型工业企业。

5.利用外资的相关指标口径与上年有所调整，增长速度按可比口径计算。

6.城市居民人均可支配收入指标新口径与原口径相比，扣除了个人缴纳的养老保险基金、失业保险基金、医疗保险基金、住房公积金和出售财物收入。

STATISTICAL COMMUNIQUE ON THE 2003 NATIONAL ECONOMIC AND SOCIAL DEVELOPMENT OF THE CITY OF TIANJIN

Tianjin Municipal Bureau of Statistics

February 20, 2004

The year of 2003 is the first year of implementing "Three－step" development strategy. Under the leadership of Tianjin Municipal Party Committee and Tianjin Municipal Government, the people of Tianjin guided by Deng Xiaoping Theory and the important thought of "Three Represents", went deep into carrying through the spirit of the 16th National Congress of CPC and the Third Plenary Session of the 8thTianjin Municipal Party Committee, Five strategic measures were completely started. Tianjin people actively response to the new changes in the international and domestic situation, devoted every effort to eliminate the negative effect brought by the SARS epidemic with a pioneering spirit and worked diligently. The city's economy exceeded to a new step, social undertakings progressed in a comprehensive way. The main indicators of economy in 2003 presented the fastest increase in recent years. The per capita GDP exceeded 3,000 US＄, the Step 1 aim of "Three－step" development strategy was successfully realized.

Ⅰ. Economic Development

Economic Strength

The national economy of Tianjin developed rapidly and soundly. The gross domestic product of Tianjin was 238.694 billion yuan, up by 14.5percent in comparable prices, 2.0 percentage points higher than that in 2002. The economic growth was the fastest one since 1996 and listed the leading position among all provinces, municipalities and autonomous regions. The per capita GDP grew from 22,380 yuan of the previous year to 25,874 yuan, or 3,126 US＄ equivalent at current exchange rate, up by 13.8 percent.

The three industries developed completely. The primary industry reached 8.97 billion yuan of the value－added, up by 6.1 percent over last year. The secondary industry remained a main motive force for the municipal economic growth, the value－added of secondary industry was 121.234 billion yuan, up by 17.8 percent over last year and 3.5 percentage points higher than that in 2002, it contributed 62.8 percent to Tianjin's economic growth. Eliminating the negative effect brought by the SARS epidemic, the value－added of the tertiary industry was 108.49 billion yuan, up by 11.5 percent. The proportion of the three industries was 3.7 percent, 50.8 percent and 45.5 percent respectively.

Financial revenue grew rapidly The year's total financial revenue of area under Tianjin's jurisdiction was 71.83 billion yuan, up by 22.8 percent, of which,. the total financial revenue of Tianjin amounted to 45.174 billion yuan, up by 20.2 percent and 1.8 percentage points higher than that in 2002. The added value tax, consumption tax, operational tax, enterprises income tax and individual income tax increased by 16.7 percent, 32.7 percent, 24.5 percent, 13.6 percent and 18.7 percent respectively. The annual financial expenditure was 35.001 billion yuan, up by 16.6 percent, of which, the expenditure of capital construction increased by 34.7 percent, the expenditure of science, education, culture and public health increased by 17.7 percent.

Labor Employment

New progress was made in employment and re - employment. New increase of job positions was 0.181 million, 41,000 more than 2002, up by 29.3 percent. In 2003, 0.121 million laid - off workers were re - employed, 31,000 more than 2002, up by 34.4 percent. This is the first time that amount of new increased employed personnel exceeded new increased laid - off workers. Employed personnel totaled 5.109 million, up by 3.7 percent, of which, those in primary industry were 0.8319 million, those in secondary industry were 2.1943 million, those in tertiary industry were 2.0828 million. Urban employed personnel totaled 2.9995 million, up by 1.4 percent. In 2003, the talent and labor market received 2.9226 million people looking for jobs, 0.6122 million of them formed initial intention of their jobs. In 2003, the registered unemployment rate in the city and towns was 3.8 percent, 0.1 percentage point lower than that in 2002.

Price

The consumer price remained steady. Urban consumer price increased by 1.0 percent in 2003. Of which, food increased by 3.3 percent due to the rising of grain and oil at the fourth quarter, clothing decreased by 11.9 percent, household appliances, articles and repair services decreased by 3.5 percent, transport and telecommunications decreased by 3.0 percent. Urban commodity retail price decreased by 2.6 percent than 2002.

The price of production and investment rose obviously. The ex - factory price increased by 2.5 percent, the purchasing price of raw material, fuel and power increased by 8.7 percent, the price of investment in fixed assets increased by 2.6 percent.

The price of land and housing rose slightly. The price of land exchange increased by 3.0 percent, the selling price of housing increased by 4.1 percent, of which, the price of commercial housing increased by 4.0 percent, the price of private housing increased by 5.0 percent, the renting price of housing increased by 0.9 percent.

Investment In Fixed Assets

The growth of investment in fixed assets of the city took a new stride, totaled 104.672 billion yuan in 2003, up by 29.0 percent over the previous year and 13.9 percentage points higher than that in 2002, creating the fastest record since 1995. The city brought variety to invest. Of this total, the investment of state - owned units was 52.86 billion yuan, up 28.2 percent; that of non - state - owned home - funded enterprises was 31.4 billion yuan, up 33.8 percent; that of foreign - funded enterprises was 20.412 billion yuan, up 24.3 percent. The proportion of non - state - owned home - funded enterprises to total investment in fixed assets was 30 percent, 1.1 percentage points higher than that in 2002. The local units completed 89.214 billion yuan, up 31.6 percent; the central units completed 15.458 billion yuan, up by 15.5 percent. Investment in primary industry was 0.938 billion yuan, up 26.8 percent; that in secondary industry was 40.23 billion yuan, up 24.1 percent, of which, the industry investment was 38.25 billion yuan, up 23.5 percent; that in tertiary industry was 63.504 billion yuan, up 32.3 percent, the proportion of tertiary industry was 60.7 percent, the investment of transportation and post, real estate, culture, education and public health, city construction increased by 42.5 percent, 32.2 percent, 76.5 percent and 75.4 percent respectively.

Agriculture

Agriculture developed stably. The gross agriculture product was 19.35 billion yuan, up by 6.2 percent than previous year, of farming 8.88 billion yuan, up by 2.2 percent; of animal husbandry 7.7 billion yuan, up by 11.0 percent; of fishery 2.61 billion yuan, up by 5.1 percent; of forestry 0.16 billion yuan, up by 2.4 percent.

The adjustment of agriculture structure continued to deepen. In the gross agriculture product, the proportion of fish-breeding and poultry-raising was 53.3 percent, 1.7 percentage points higher than that in 2002. The proportion of economic crop in total agricultural crops rose to 58.0 percent, 6.7 percentage points higher than that in 2002.

Great achievement was obtained in industrialized management of agriculture. By the end of 2003, there were 396 leading enterprises; including 120 enterprises with capital of over 10 million yuan. Of which, 7 enterprises were named as state-level leading enterprise, 36 were named as municipal-level leading enterprises. The rural households involved in cooperated peasant organizations accounted for 60 percent of total rural households. There were 552 harmfulness vegetable bases, 98 poultry bases, 112 milk bases and 68 aquatic products bases.

The major farm and sideline products output increased in 2003. That of cotton was 94,700 tons, up by 51.8 percent; vegetable was 6.0278 million tons, up by 3.2 percent; that of meat was 0.5241 million tons, up by 16.8 percent; that of eggs was 0.2425 million tons, down by 0.9 percent; that of milk was 0.4323 million tons, up by 28.7 percent, that of aquatic products was 0.2983 million tons, up by 4.4 percent. Effected by the decrease of sown areas and weather, the output of grain was 1.1929 million tons, decreased 0.1853 million tons than 2002; the output of per mu was 308.1 kilogram, increased 12.9 kilogram.

Industry

The industrial production developed rapidly. The value-added of industry was 110.337 billion yuan, up 18.4 percent; the total gross output value of industry was 437.076 billion yuan, up 24.1 percent; of which, the value-added of industry above designated size(all state-owned enterprises and others with annual sales of exceed 5 million yuan, same to next) was 102.779 billion yuna, up 20.1 percent, the gross output value of industry above designated size was 404.961 billion yuan, up 26.1 percent.

The growth rate and proportion of heavy industry continued to improve. The value-added of light industry above designated size was 24.219 billion yuan, up by 16.0 percent over the previous year, the gross output value of light industry was 109.539 billion yuan, up 20.8 percent; the value-added of heavy industry above designated size was 78.56 billion yuan, up by 22.1 percent, the gross output value of heavy industry was 295.422 billion yuan, up 28.7 percent. The proportion of light industry and heavy industry was 27:73.

The promotion function of advantageous industries was obvious. The total output value of electro-communication, automobile, medical and pharmaceutical industry, smelting of metals, chemical industry and new power was 277.504 billion yuan, up 28.9 percent, accounting for 68.5 percent of the gross output value of industry above designated size, contributing 79.2 percent to the growth of industry.

Development was quick in the high & new technology industry. The gross output value of industry of the high & new technology industry was 123.587 billion yuan, up 22.6 percent over last year and its share in the gross output value of industry above designated size was 30.5 percent. The scale of new products and exports of industrial products was expanded, the value of new products of the year was 97.151 billion yuan, up 22.6 percent; the value of exports of industrial products fulfilled 98.391 billion yuan, up 20.6 percent.

The following lists the output of major products:

	Unit	2003	**Increase over** 2002(%)
Crude oil	10,000 tons	1,316.30	8.3
Natural gas	100 million cubic meters	8.49	-4.4
Crude salt	10,000 tons	220.48	-8.3
Electricity	100 million kwh	319.95	18.9
Pig iron	10,000 tons	342.65	20.3
Steel	ditto	565.95	17.4
Finished steels	ditto	1,031.47	42.6
Seamless steel tube	ditto	91.67	9.2
Cement	ditto	449.31	17.7
Ethylene	ditto	23.00	8.1
Soda ash	ditto	82.01	3.2
Caustic soda	ditto	79.89	25.2
Chemical fiber	ditto	29.76	30.7
Mobile phone	10,000 sets	3,139.72	10.0
Car	10,000	17.25	82.7
Motorcycle	ditto	114.80	37.7
Internal combustion engine	10,000 kw	973.91	81.7
Yarn	10,000 tons	7.45	-8.1
Cloth	100 million meters	2.51	1.2
Vegetable oil	10,000 tons	17.35	-12.6
Staple Food	ditto	14.47	32.0
Wine	ditto	3.05	10.5
Air Conditioner	10,000	241.83	99.0
Microwave Oven	10,000	969.87	68.2
Tricolor Tube	10,000	268.41	21.0
Electronic Element	100 million units	840.77	13.2
Monitor	10,000	677.83	24.8

The production and marketing situation were adapted to each other better. The sales output value was 400.437 billion yuan, up 21.6 percent. The sales ratio of industrial products was 98.88 percent, of which, that of heavy industry was 99.43 percent, that of light industry was 97.41 percent, that of state-owned enterprises was 100.34 percent, of foreign funded enterprises was 99.59 percent, of share-holding enterprises was 98.58 percent.

The economic efficiency continued to improve. The overall coefficient of economic benefit in industrial enterprises reached 147.6, representing an increase of 14.5 points over the previous year. The profit of enterprises grew rapidly, profit and tax totaled 39.106 billion yuan, up 24.6 percent, of which, profit totaled 23.188 billion yuan, up 30.2 percent, tax totaled 15.918 billion yuan, up 17.3 percent.

Construction

Construction industry grew effected by the increasing of investment. The value - added of the city's construction industry was 10.897 billion yuan, up by 12.1 percent. The output value of construction totaled 49.866 billion yuan, up by 46.6 percent. Floor space of building under construction totaled 33.4822 million square meters, up 35.3 percent; floor space of building completed totaled 16.0105 million square meters, up 54.3 percent The construction enterprises contracted a total of 22,863 construction projects. The all - personnel labor productivity was 152,500 yuan per person calculated by output value, up by 29.8 percent.

Transportation, Posts & Telecommunications and Storage

The comprehensive service function was enhanced obviously. The value - added of transportation, posts and store industries in 2003 was 25.603 billion yuan, up by 14.7 percent, 2.9 percentage points higher than that in 2002.

A well - developed network of the traffic appeared which Tianjin port linked all - sided with the railway, the air and the highway as well as the sea. The Phase I of 150,000 - ton class channel and Beida Breakwater put into use. Tianjin port contacted 300 ports for the business in more than 160 countries and regions all over the world. In 2003, the cargoes loaded and unloaded at Tianjin Port weighed 161.816 million tons, up 25.4 percent over 2002, of which, the cargoes that get into the port weighed 52.7 million tons, up 28.4 percent, the cargoes that get out of the port weighed 109.116 million tons, up 24.0 percent. As for the transportation of containers, 3.015 million international standard containers were loaded or unloaded in 2003, up 25.2 percent. The comprehensive transport capacity was enhanced. The total volume of cargo transport was 395.3266 million tons, up by 13.6 percent over the previous year. Of this total, the cargo transportation by railways was 100.821 million tons, up 11.8 percent; by highways, 201.14 million tons, up 6.8 percent; by water transport, 87.6275 million tons, up 36.8 percent. The volume of passenger transportation was 46.681 million person - times, up by 0.7 percent over the previous year. Airport passenger handling capacity was 1.101 million person - times, up by 0.8percent; airport cargo & mail handling capacity was 56,600 tons, up 13.9 percent.

Posts and telecommunications developed rapidly. The business transactions of postal and telecommunication service in 2003 was 11.197 billion yuan, up by 24.2 percent, of which, the business transactions of telecommunication service was 10.3 billion yuan, up 26.1 percent, the business revenue of telecommunication service was 6.62 billion yuan, up 12.2 percent. By the end of 2003, the length of long - distance optical cable reached 2,704.08 kilometers, up 42.2 percent. The total telephone switch capacity was 4.0335 million telephones. The total number of fixed telephone users and mobile phone users was 7.377 million, up 22.3 percent. Fixed telephone users numbered 3.543 million, 0.583 million more than the previous year, up by 19.7 percent. Mobile phone users numbered 3.834 million, 0.763 million than the previous year, up 24.8 percent. The calling transactions of public network reached 14 billion times, up 11.1 percent, the business transaction of mobile SMS reached 1.469 billion messages. The business transactions of postal service was 0.897 billion yuan, up 5.7 percent, letters delivered reached 220.3393 million, up by 8.5 percent, the express mail reached 3.215 million, up by 11.8 percent.

Domestic Commerce

The scale of commerce circulation was enlarged. The value - added of wholesale, retail and catering trade completed in 2003 was 21.192 billion yuan, up by 10.8 percent.

The gather role of markets was obvious. By eh end of 2003, there were 760 markets in Tianjin, including 123 markets of production material, 608 consumer goods markets, 29 markets of production factor. The volume of trade of all markets was 71.279 billion yuan, up 16.2 percent. The volume of trade of the markets with annual volume of trade of over 100 million yuan was 49.839 billion yuan in 2003, and sharing 69.9 percent of total volume of trade.

The retail and catering markets bounced back quickly after the short-term drop took in April and May. In 2003, the total sales volume of retailed consumer goods was 107.405 billion yuan, up by 14.1 percent. Of which, the sales volume of wholesale and retail trade was 72.71 billion yuan, up 12.5 percent; of catering trade, 10.991 billion yuan, up 7.2 percent. Rapid growth was recorded in sales of household articles, housing decoration, communication means, cultural and sports articles and automobiles. Calculated by statistics on retail and wholesale enterprises above designed size, the retail of selling communication means increased by 1.1 times; the retail of selling furniture increased by 18.4 percent; the retail of selling automobiles increased by 1.0 times, the retail of selling cultural and sports articles increased by 49.9 percent.

New achievement was made in absorbing investment in the field of circulation. In 2003, many world famous groups such as Lotus Supercenter, OBI, Wal-Mart, Parkson, Chankun, developed their business in Tianjin. By the end of 2003, there were more than 120 foreign capital retail stores, of the top 500 enterprises in the world, 22 had developed business in Tianjin. Some domestic chain groups such as Meijing Wumei and Wenzhou Maigou also invested and developed in Tianjin. The construction of commercial facilities developed rapidly, Floor space of commercial facilities under construction totaled 1.29 million square meters, floor space of commercial facilities completed totaled 1.087 million square meters.

Finance and Insurance

The service function of finance and insurance sector was enhanced obviously. The value-added of the city's finance and insurance industry was 9.181 billion yuan in 2003, up by 24.7 percent. At the end of the year, there were 2,837 financial institutions of various kinds - 1,594 banking institutions and 1,243 non-banking institutions, which employed a staff of 47,000 people. Bohai Bank was approved to establish by the state.

The pace of opening to the outside world of finance and insurance was quickened. Citibank founded its branch in Tianjin. By the end of 2003, there were 15 branches and 4 representative offices of foreign-funded banks, 8 foreign-funded banks in Tianjin were authorized to deal with RMB business, of which, 6 foreign-funded banks had done business. There were 2 foreign-funded insurance companies that their headquarters located in Tianjin and 3 foreign-funded insurance representative offices.

The new increased deposit and loan created the highest record in history. By end of 2003, the balance of saving deposits in various forms in all home-funded and foreign-funded financial institutions of Tianjin totaled 436.26 billion yuan, 100.377 billion yuan more than the previous year and 50.374 billion yuan more than the net increased saving deposits in 2002, up 29.9 percent over the end of previous year. The year-end value of loans in various forms in all home-funded and foreign-funded financial institutions stood at 379.122 billion yuan, 92.031 billion yuan more than the previous year and 53.763 billion yuan more than the net increased loans in 2002, up 32.1 percent over the end of previous year. Of which, medium and long-term loans totaled 157.393 billion yuan, up 64.3 percent over the end of previous year. Loans to individual consumers increased quickly, the balance stood at 26.142 billion yuan, up 29.8 percent over the end of previous year, of which, the balance of housing loans stood at 21.884 billion yuan, up 28.6 percent over the end of previous year.

Securities market developed steadily. By the end of 2003, there were 23 listed stocks in the city, of which one stock had just got listed within the year. The total securities business volume was 132.2 billion yuan, up 12.1 percent over the previous year, including stock transaction volume of 112.3 billion yuan, up 8.8 percent. The yearly adjustment volume of exchange was US$ 1.3 billion, up 41.9 percent.

The scope of insurance business was expanded continuously. In 2003, the insurance premium of Tianjin totaled 7.531 billion yuan, up by 16.0 percent over the previous year. Of this total, the premium of property insurance was 1.556 billion yuan, up 8.0 percent, that of life insurance was 5.975 billion yuan, up 18.0 percent. The insurance companies paid an indemnity of 1.736 billion yuan as reparation for various insurance programs, up 51.0 percent, of which, the indemnity of property insurance was 1.011 billion yuan, up 48.0 percent, the indemnity on life insurance was 0.725 billion yuan, up 56.0 percent. Taiping Insurance Tianjin Corporation and Hengan Standard Life Insurance Corporation opened business in 2003. By the end of 2003, there were 14 insurance corporations in Tianjin, of which, there were 7 property insurance corporations and 7 life insurance corporations. There were 17 insurance agents in Tianjin, including 12 insurance agent corporations, 2 insurance management corporations and 3 insurance quotation corporations.

Real Estate

Real estate industry developed rapidly along with the arousing of requirement. The added value of real estate was 11.987 billion yuan, up 17.4 percent, 13 percentage points higher than that in 2002. Effected by the developing of Haihe River and construction of roads and bridges, investment in real estate grew rapidly, totaled 21.139 billion yuan, up by 20.2 percent. The sales of commercial housiing created a new record in the history. In the year, the total floor space of sold commercial housing was 7.865 million square meters, sales revenue totaled 20.23 billion yuan, up by 39.5 percent and 43.4 percent respectively. The total floor space of sold and bought existing housing was 6.883 million square meters, up 94.8 percent; which brought value of 8.63 billion yuan, up 1.2 times. Of which, the floor space of sold and bought individual housing was 5.046 million square meters, up 1.2 times and brought value of 7.14 billion yuan, up 1.3 times. The total floor space of sold and bought public housing was 1.837 million square meters, up 49 percent and brought value of 1.49 billion yuan, up 55.2 percent.

II Reform and Opening up to the Outside World

Ownership Structure

New progress was made in adjustment of ownership structure, the proportion of non-public-owned economy continued to increase. The added value of public-owned economy was 130.233 billion yuan, accounting for 54.6 percent of Tianjin's GDP; that of non-public-owned economy was 108.461 billion yuan, accounting for 45.4 percent of Tianjin's GDP, 3.5 percentage points higher than that in 2002. Of which, the added value of foreign funded enterprises was 53.083 billion yuan, accounting for 22.2 percent of GDP, 1.5 percentage points higher than that in 2002, that of private and individual economy was 53.945 billion yuan, accounting for 22.6 percent, 2.6 percentage points higher than that in 2002.

All kinds of industry developed fully. Among the total industrial output value of industrial enterprises above designated size, the industrial output value of state-owned and state-holding enterprises was 145.651 billion yuan, up 28.6 percent; that of share-holding enterprises was 117.256 billion yuan, up 29.4 percent; that of foreign funded enterprises was 189.606 billion yuan, up 30.3 percent. The industrial output value of state-holding enterprises and foreign funded enterprises accounted for 75.8 percent of the total industrial output value above designated size.

The private and individual economy developed continuously. The registered capital of private and individual economy totaled 96.945 billion yuan, 40.1 billion yuan more than the beginning of the year, up by 70.5 percent; by the end of 2003, the number of private and individual economy was 247.8 thousand, 14.4 thousand more than the beginning of the year; there were 920.9 thousand personnel in private and individual economy, 151.4thousand more than the beginning of the year; the taxes totaled 3.497 billion yuan, up 41.4 percent. Along with the implementing of "the suggestion on quickening to develop private and individual economy" and related policies, private and individual economy began to develop in the fields of public traffic, water, gas and heating supply, sewage treatment, garbage treatment and so on.

Management of State - owned Assets and Reform of State - owned Enterprises

The reform of economic system continued to deepen, the market economy developed continuously. The reform scheme of new finance system and tax system began to implement. The experimental units of rural tax reform ran smoothly. The city restructured the order of land market, established and implemented the management system of state - owned land non - free using. The city sealed transactions of property rights involving 15.1 billion yuan, founded North China Property Right Transaction Common Market with Beijing, Hebei province, Henan province, Shandong province, Shanxi province and so on.

New progress was made in reform of state - owned enterprises. Great effort was made in the reestablishment of large - sized industrial groups and the reform of medium and small enterprises system. In 2003, the city completed the re - buy of share ownership of Tianjin Steel Pipe Corporation involving 4.85 billion yuan, realized the reestablishment of medicine, textile and engineering machinery sectors. There were 106 medium and small industrial enterprises complete the reform of share ownership, 58 enterprises re - appear the vitality. A total of 364 enterprises with low competition ability had withdrew the market. The whole strength of medium and small enterprises enhanced. Great achievement was made in the reform of Tianjin Port. The reestablishment of commercial enterprises continued to develop. In 2003, there were 12 large and medium - sized commercial enterprises complete the share - holding reform, 7 groups complete the reorganization of interior structure. The city established Jinshi Group and Department Store Group, reestablished Quanye - Hualian Group. There were over 500 small enterprises withdraw state - owned capital using kinds of pattern.

Reform of Administrative Examination and Approval System

The reform of administrative examination and approval system continued to deepen. In 2003, the city carried out the third management for original approval items, cancelled 121 items and changed 55 items on management way. After three times of management, a total of 666 items were simplified. The city also carried out the experimental units on enterprises registering and the reform of union of administrative examination and approval.

Social Security

Great progress was made in participating pension insurance and paying insurance funds. By the end of 2003, 1.685 million staff and workers participated in pension insurance and paid insurance funds, 38.5 thousand staff and workers more than the end of previous year. Income of pension insurance totaled 6.228 billion yuan, 1.034 billion yuan more than previous year. Per capita old age pension of retired pensioners paid by pension insurance funds was 707 yuan, up by 19 percent over previous year. By the end of the year, a total of 1.758 million staff and workers participated in pension insurance and paid insurance funds, 0.9761 million retired pensioners participated in pension insurance.

The reform of medical insurance further deepened. The city formulated 10 policies on improving basic medical insurance of urban employees. By the end of 2003, 2.4292 million persons participated in basic medical insurance, 0.3442 million persons more than the end of previous year. Of which, 1.6517 million staff and workers and 0.7775 million retired persons participated in basic medical insurance, an increase of 0.2597 million and 0.0845 million over the end of previous year respectively. Grouped by enterprise, institution and agency, for enterprises, 1.924 million persons, institution and agency, 0.5052 million persons, an increase of 0.2748 million and 0.0694 million over previous year respectively.

More people participated in unemployment insurance, less people received unemployment insurance funds. By the end of 2003, 1.9345 million persons participated in unemployment insurance, 0.039 million more than the end of previous year; 0.095 million persons received unemployment insurance funds, 0.029 million less than the end of previous year.

Domestic Cooperation

The utilization of capitals from other domestic regions increased rapidly, new progress was made in cooperation of district economy. In 2003, the contracted utilization of capitals from other domestic regions reached 17.22 billion yuan, up by 80.5 percent, the actual investment was 11.22 billion yuan, up by 83.7 percent. Among all the projects, the number of projects with investment of over 5 million yuan was 273, mainly focused on real estate and trade logistics. The economic trade activities among Tianjin and Northeast China, North China and Northwest China regions was further enhanced, the contracted projects was 35, involving contracted capital of 2.59 billion yuan. Tianjin enhanced the cooperation of Beijing, Tianjin and Hebei province. Bejing and Tianjin decided to newly build two roads for Jing－Jin expressway, strengthened the relation of key areas of the two cities. Tianjin port would improve the service for Beijing, Beijing Airport and Tianjin Airport developed together.

Assistance and support of Tianjin to GanShu, Changdu of Tibet and Longbao Immigration District of ChongQing was further enhanced and promoted the development of local economy.

Foreign Trade

Foreign trade continued to develop. The total of foreign trade import and export was 29.371 billion US$, up by 28.7 percent. In which, import was 14.997 billion US$, up by 33.5 percent, export was 14.374 billion US$, up by 24.0 percent. Exports of processing trade continued to be the major part, exports of general trade quickened to develop. In 2003, exports of processing trade was 9.147 billion US$, increased by 17.4 percent, accounting for 63.6 percent of total exports. Exports of general trade was 4.836 billion US$, up by 35.1 percent, 28.1 percentage points high than that in 2002. The exports of foreign and Hongkong, Macao, Taiwan funded enterprises, private enterprises increased rapidly. The exports of foreign and Hongkong, Macao, Taiwan funded enterprises was 11.427 billion US$, up 25.4 percent, accounting for 79.5 percent of total exports; the exports of private enterprises increased by 2.1 times. Exports to the United States, EU, Japan, Korea and ASEAN increased by from 8.9 percent to 43.6 percent, the five major exports markets accounted for 78.9 percent of total exports.

The structure of exports was further optimized, the exports of electrical－machinery products and high and new technology products grew rapidly. In 2003, the exports of electrical－machinery products completed 9.18 billion US$, up 24 percent, accounting for 63.9 percent of the city's total exports. The exports of high and new technology products totaled 4.81 billion US $, up 48 percent.

The radiate function of Tianjin port was remarkably strengthened. In 2003, the total volume of import and export through Tianjin Port was 46.167 billion US $, up by 26.4 percent. In which, import was 20.21 billion US $, up by 23.2 percent, and export was 25.957 billion US $, up by 28.9 percent. Among the total import and export, the proportion of other provinces and municipalities was 51.7 percent, Beijing, Hebei and Shanxi occupied the first three positions, accounting for 20.3 percent, 10.7 percent and 3.6 percent respectively.

Introduction of Foreign Investment

Foreign investment quickened to grow. In 2003, 941 foreign - funded enterprise projects was approved in Tianjin, a rise of 15.3 percent over 2002 ; the contracted foreign investment increased by 74.3 percent up to 3.513 billion US $, the actual foreign direct investment was 1.633 billion US $, up 62.9 percent. A total of 198 large projects whose total investment is above 5 million US $ was approved, increased by 60.9 percent. The contracted foreign investment from Japan, Italy, Singapore, Germany, United Kingdom and Hongkong increased by 1 time to 4.5 times respectively. Of the top 500 enterprises in the world, 98 had already invested in Tianjin. Enterprises actively increased investment in Tianjin. In this year, a total of 382 enterprises increased investment involving investment of 1.095 billion US $, of which, foreign investment totaled 0.923 billion US $. Foreign investment in manufacturing held the dominant position, the contracted foreign investment totaled 2.154 billion US $, up 94.7 percent, accounting for 61.3 percent of total investment in Tianjin, the investment in electronic and telecommunications, transport equipment, chemical raw materials, machinery equipment, medical and pharmaceutical products all exceeded 0.15 billion US $. The foreign investment in tertiary industry increased rapidly, the contracted investment in 2003 was 1.328 billion US $, up by 48.6 percent.

Foreign Contract Projects and Labor Cooperation

Overseas economic cooperation developed rapidly. In 2003 , Tianjin concluded turnover of 0.405 billion US $ in the field of foreign contract projects, labor cooperation and design consulting, up by 51.0 percent. A total of 59 enterprises were approved to undertake overseas economic cooperation, carried out business with more than 80 countries and regions in the world, covering the fields of industry, agriculture, construction, tertiary industry. At the end of the year, 11,300 workers from Tianjin were working abroad. The city signed 381 contracts of advanced technologies from abroad with the total contracted value of 0.967 billion US $. The construction of 51 overseas agencies had been approved of, including 38 manufacturing enterprises with the total investment of 42.5074 million US $, including Chinese investment of 37.9642 million US $.

Tourism

Under the influence of SARS epidemic, the international tourism of Tianjin saw a slight decrease, domestic tourism saw a slight increase. There were altogether 85 star hotels, 233 travel agencies, including 19 international travel agencies and 214 domestic travel agencies. In 2003, overseas tourists to Tianjin numbered 489 thousand, down by 3.4 percent from the previous year, including 456 thousand foreigners. Foreign exchange incomes from overseas tourists stood at 0.329 billion US $, down by 3.8 percent. Domestic tourists to Tianjin numbered 37.5112 million, up by 1.1 percent; incomes from domestic tourists were 39.502 billion yuan, up 1.3 percent. Meanwhile, 53,100 Tianjin residents also traveled abroad, spending a total of 0.783 billion yuan. Tianjin actively developed tourism resource. In this year, it constructed Yulong Skiing Field and Tianjin Tropical Botanical Touring Garden, some tourism projects and facilities were constructing smoothly, including Tianjin International Pleasure Port and "East Princess" Pleasure-boat.

New Coastal Area

The role of New Coastal Area in promoting Tianjin's economic development was improved obviously. The gross domestic product (GDP)of 2003 was 97 billion yuan, up by 20.0 percent over the previous year. The local financial revenue was 5.773 billion yuan, up 21.0 percent; the total industrial output value was 213.321 billion yuan, up by 30.3 percent; the investment in fixed assets was 46.408 billion yuan, up by 65.2 percent; export was 8.987 billion US $, up 24.8 percent, accounting for 62.5 percent of the city's total export; the total contracted foreign investment was 2.446 billion US $, up by 58.2 percent, accounting for 69.6 percent of the city.

Tianjin Economic-Technological Development Area (TEDA) realized 44.523 billion yuan of added value in 2003, up 25.1 percent over previous year. The major economic indices of TEDA remained on the top of national development areas. The added value of its secondary industry was 35.49 billion yuan, up 28.3 percent, accounting for 79.7 percent of its total GDP. There were 108 enterprises whose total industrial output value is above 0.1 billion yuan, 20 enterprise more than that in 2002, the total output value of these enterprises accounted for 91.8 percent of the total output value of TEDA. In 2003, the total output value of the four pillar industries, namely electrocommunication, machinery manufacturing, medicine and chemical industry, catering industry, accounted for 91.4 percent of the total output value of TEDA.

In 2003, Tianjin Port Free Trade Zone (TPFTZ) realized 8.3 billion yuan of added value, up 38.2 percent. The construction of International Circulation Center forged to a new step. The total value of goods entering or leaving TPFTZ was 9.23 billion US $, up 42.0 percent. TPFTZhad become circulation base of automobile & its parts, electronic products, electronic element, steel, machinery equipment and other goods, the automobiles of entering, leaving and selling from TPFTZ numbered 49,000, remaining the top position in China. TPFTZ were constructing port free trade area, the airport circulating and processing area and international circulating area.

Ⅲ Urban Construction and Management

Comprehensive Development and Rebuilding along Haihe River

Comprehensive development and rebuilding project along Haihe River started completely. In this year, a total of 2.16 million cubic meters silt were cleared, 8.9 kilometer of dike shore completed reconstruction. The construction of Haihe East Road, Haihe West Road and other two roads completed basically, Cihai bridge and Dagu bridge began to construct, Sizilin bridge was successfully promoted. The programming of six projects was finished, the construction of Gulou trade area of ancient culture street, canal culture trade area, Dabeiyuan trade area started in this year. The investment of comprehensive development and rebuilding project along Haihe River in 2003 totaled 5.6 billion yuan.

Construction of Infrastructure and Urban Greening

Construction of city infrastructure developed smoothly. Investment in city infrastructure construction reached 26.367 billion yuan, up 34.2 percent, accounting for 25.2 percent of total investment, mainly used for subway, light rail, port and highways. Jin-Ji expressway and Tang-Jin expressway were opened to traffic. Jin－Bin light rail was put into trail operation. The construction of Subway Line1 started in the year. The length of newly increased expressway was 179 kilometers. The extension of some main roads including Haihe East Road, Jinzhonghe Street, Weiguo Road completed, the reconstruction of Sihua River, Beitang draining River and the first－phase of Yueya River also completed. Some roads including Xihu Road and Fukang Road were joined up. The construction of light night view was initially completed. There were 207 high buildings, 510 multi－layers buildings and 158 special features buildings complete light decoration, 156 large and medium－sized public install outside－seeing light, 76 scenic green areas install lights.

In this year, the city built some green square and gardens, including Yinhe Gargen and Haihe Outside Pool Garden. The newly increased green area totaled 25 million square meters, the green coverage rate grew to 31 percent, the per capita public green area in the city reached 6.5 square meters, 0.9 square meter more than that in 2002.

Public Utilities

City transit became more convenient. There were 15 bus lines and 10 school bus lines open, 60 bus lines extend the length of lines in 2003. By the end of 2003, There were 351 bus lines, bus running in Tianjin numbered 6,158, a total of 31,939 taxicabs were in operation for passengers. 0.622 billion passengers were transported by buses. The city continued to improve running environment, renewed 800 buses and built 3 public transit hub stations in this year.

New progress was made in public utilities. The production capacity of tap water reached 3.68 million cubic meters, there was 0.63 billion cubic meters of tap water sold in the year, of which, 0.305 billion cubic maters were sod for living water. At the end of 2003, there were 2.08 million gas users in Tianjin, the gasification rate of fuel for urban households was 97 percent. The thermal rate was 77.2 percent, 3.1 percentage points higher than that in 2002. New achievement was made in management of old residential zones, a total of 65 old residential zones were brought into property management.

Environmental Protection and Control

New achievement was made in environmental control. By the end of 2003, there were 20 environmental monitoring stations in operation. Six projects of constructing Tianjin into a model city in terms of environment protection ran smoothly. Tianjin Dangerous Waste Products Handling Center put into use. Xiqing Yangliuqing Town was named the first national beautiful towns in this year. A total of 1,000,000 citizens took part in environment cleaning activity, effectively improving the environmental hygiene, urban management and civilization level.

Air quality was improved continuously, Content of PM_{10} in the air was down by 3.6 percent. There were 264 days in which the air quality was at and above Grade II, accounting for 72.3 percent of the total of yearly days. The city had 60 smoke and dust control zones with the total space of 557.3 square kilometers.

Voice quality maintained a good level. The average sound level was 55 decibel, maintaining the same level in 2002; the equivalent sound level of traffic noise was 68.2 decibel, 0.2 decibel lower than that in 2002. There were 539.1 square kilometers where the noise pollution was brought under the specified level, the coverage rate reached 78 percent, 2 percentage points higher than that in previous year.

Water environment control progressed good. The city strengthened the check and supervision of water quality of Yuqiao Reservoir, Luanhe River and Yellow River led to Tianjin, the drinking water was 100 percent in terms of quality.

Ecological environment protection continued to enhance. Tianjin had 6 ecological demonstration areas and 8 nature protection areas with the total area of 153,300 hectares. Tianjin built Jixian National Geological Park, the core part was the Grand Canyon Nature Protection Area.

Information Construction

The information infrastructure had been further developed. The construction of broad - band network completed, There were 19,000 km of optic fiber had been laid, broad - band wireless microwave had covered the whole city, the kernel capacity of the trunk board - band network reached 2,000 Gbps, the brand width at the exit of the city was 21.2 Gbps. Some key information function platform put into use and improved the information service ability for society and public, including Tianjin Telecommunications Engineering and Internet Data Center. Many services were used broadly, such as news review, ordering TV program, searching information, remote education, remote hospital, TV meeting and network game.

The scope of IT application kept expanding. In 2003, 248 items of 38 government departments began to be examined and approved by network, accounting for 40 percent of total approved items. A lot of key projects began to implemented and improved the ability of city management, market supervision and service for public, including Tianjin Port Information Platform, Industry and Business Merged Examination and Approval, Enterprise Credit, Intelligent Property Right, Domestic Affairs Management, Net Paying Tax and Net Government Purchasing. By the end of the year, there were 2.06 million Internet users in Tianjin, 0.56 million more than that in 2002; 1,949 Internet special - line users, 631 more than that in 2002; 0.189 million Internet board - band users and 0.169 million more than that in 2002. Net medical insurance started smoothly, a total of 101 hospitals took part in the network. Education informatization developed rapidly(including school - to - school e - communication, campus networks and remote education). Evening News Public Service Center united Jingong Supermarket opened telephone sales and net sales. Tap water remote recording system began to use in some large - sized residential zones. Net house trade market collected the information of 995 projects of 879 real estate enterprises. 13 financial institutions issued 18.23 million of bank cards, the transaction value totaled 6.66 billion yuan, up 2.2 times than previous year. The city issued 16,000 pieces of official business cards. The "All - in - one" card of public transit became further popular.

Ⅳ Social Undertakings

Science and Technology

Innovation ability in science and technology continued to improve. In 2003, the city reported 1,203 items of municipal - level scientific and technological achievement. Among the major achievement, 59 items leading in the world, 311 items are world advanced level. In 2003, 14 national awards for science and technology were received. A total of 66 projects in high and new technology had been implemented, of which 80 percent had been put into operation. The city provided efficient battery and navigable equipment for Shenzhou No.5 airship. There were 6,812 applications for patent received in 2003, up 27.1 percent over previous year, of which, invention applications increased by 60.8 percent and accounting for 48.9 percent of total applications, 2,505 patents were authorized. Tianjin continued to expand its contingent of scientific and technological workers, work units in the state economic sector employed a total of 323,000 technical workers in various specialized fields. In 2003, 5 Tianjin scientists became academicians of the Chinese Academy of Sciences and the Chinese Engineering Academy. By the end of the year, Tianjin had 28 academicians, including 13 academicians of the Chinese Academy of Sciences and 15 academicians of the Chinese engineering Academy. The city successfully hosted The Third PECC Investment Exposition and China(Tianjin) Computer Software Network & Communications Products Exposition and The Forum on Informatization and New Industrialization.

Innovation system in science and technology was enhanced. A number of projects started to implement, including IC design, digit products and motive battery. New progress was made in scientific research of biology technology and sea water downplays. Huayuan Software Park was named state - level software export base. By the end of 2003, the city had 90 city - level and state - level enterprise technology centers. Technology market was brisk. In 2003, a total of 7,278 contracts on the transfer of technology were signed involving a transaction value of 4.2 billion yuan, up by 15.6 percent.

The strength of Hi - tech Industry Park was enhanced. The total of income from technology, industry and trade was 66.895 billion yuan, up by 35.3 percent. The total value of output was 56.197 billion yuan, up by 35 percent. Profit completed was 2.573 billion yuan, up by 34 percent, tax was 2.884 billion yuan, up 31.9 percent. The sales income earned from export was 1.363 billion US $, up by 30.3 percent.

Education

Enrollment of higher education was enlarged continuously. In 2003, Tianjin had 37 regular institutions of higher learning and advanced vocational and technical colleges. They enrolled 86 thousand students, up 24.1 percent, the total number of their students reached 245 thousand by the end of 2003, the number of students graduated from higher education was 40,000. There were 8,500 enrolled graduated students, up 29.4 percent, the number of graduated students reached 21,000, the number of graduated students graduated from higher education was 3,300. Secondary vocational schools enrolled 44,000, up 9.2 percent, the total number of students reached 135,000. The gross entrance rate of high education in Tianjin was 49 percent, 5 percentage points higher than the previous year.

The teaching quality of middle and primary schools was improved. There were 406 thousand junior school students and graduated 140 thousand; the regular senior schools enrolled 70 thousand students in 2003, up 18.7 percent, the number of students in senior high schools reached 183 thousand, graduated 45 thousand; for senior high school, the entrance rate was 93.1 percent. The primary schools had 610 thousand pupils including 85 thousand new entrants, graduated 132 thousand. There were 200 thousand children in kindergartens, the attendance rate of school - age children was 99.97 percent, the enrollment rate of junior secondary schools was 98.97 percent. The primary schools began to try out new courses.

The distribution of education was adjusted effectively. The first 31 high - quality senior middle schools completed construction and put into use. The construction of "211" project of Tianjin Medical University and a number of high - quality primary schools started.

Culture

Great achievement was made in culture and art, press and publication, radio, film and television, library and film - protection. By end of 2003, the city had 15 art - performing groups, 19 culture and scientific technology centers, 16 museums, 31 public libraries. The city built Tianjin Museum, TEDA Meeting Exhibition Center and Library, the cultural status was further improved. Newspapers issued were 823.8651 million copies, magazines, 46.0972 million copies; books, 67.7239 million copies. The Tianjin People's Radio Station had presented seven programs, the coverage rate of population was 100 percent; Tianjin TV had seven channels and the coverage rate of population was 99 percent, there were 1.8 million households covered by cable television networks.. In 2003, the city successfully hosted a series of cultural activities, including China Race Drama Excellent Programs Performance, the First Old People Culture and Art Festival, the

Second Family Culture and Art Festival, the Fourth Binhai Art Festival and Chairman Mazedong Poem Phrase Concert. The city performed Peking opera "Hua Ziliang", ballet opera "Jingwei" and drama "Applause for you". They also performed special program "We should win" and "We goes forward holding the hands".

Public Health

Public health developed stably. By end of 2003, there were 2,671 medical and health facilities and in which, 500 hospitals, 25 public health and epidemic prevention and cure facilities and 11 women and children health facilities. By end of the year, these facilities had 42.7 thousand beds, up 0.9 percent, of which, hospitals had 41.6 thousand beds, up 0.8 percent. There were 61 thousand professional public health personnel including 25.9 thousand doctors, 4,000 more than that in previous year. There were 27.8 doctors and 44.6 hospital beds per 10,000 persons. The resource of health care was adjusted smoothly. The city rebuilt Haihe Hospital and Tianjin No.1 Hospital, completed the construction of the Phase I of Tianjin Infectious Disease Hospital and Tianjin People Hospital. The medical service network in communities and rural area took shape initially.

Phased achievement was made in prevention and cure of SARS epidemic. Upon the occurrence of SARS epidemic, the city built SARS curing system, blockaded the epidemic areas preliminarily and cut off epidemic source, established a series of prevention measures and a number of fever out-patient service. SARS epidemic was controlled in 28 days.

Sports

Great achievement was made in athletic sports. Tianjin athletes won 16 gold medals, 13 silver medals and 19 bronze medals in the domestic games. In the Asian Games, the city's athletes won 9 gold medals, 1 silver medal and 2 bronze medals. During international games, the athletes from the city won 5 gold medal, 3 silver medals and 1 bronze medal. Tianjin women volleyball team won champion in national championships. A number of sports items occupied a dominant position in domestic games, including tennis, martial arts, women fencing and man ring. Tianjin successfully hosted more than 10 domestic and international games, such as the twelfth Asia Men Volleyball Championships, International Indoors Track and Field Events Invitational Game, "Toyota Cup" International Table Tennis Invitational Game. The construction of Tianjin Olympic Central Stadium started.

The mass sports developed vigorously. The city implemented the phase II of national fit-keeping outline, built 23 national fit-keeping engineering in 18 districts and counties, built 364 projects in 267 residential zones. Tianjin developed "sunshine fit-keeping activity", hosted the first International Countryside Sports Meeting, created the first citizenry broadcast gymnastics.

Social Welfare and Relief

Social relief developed continuously. A total of 24,547 received social relief, 267.4 thousand residents benefited from the city's fund for ensuring a minimum standard of living, of which, the urban residents numbered 241.3 thousand, 60,000 less than that in 2002. There were 16,478 beds in social welfare institutions and received 10,910 inmates. The city had 7 relief stations, receiving 58,857 person/day. There were 1,901 community service facilities, 102 community service centers. The coverage of social security network in Tianjin's rural area reached 74.3 percent. In 2003, 0.106 billion yuan worth of social-welfare lottery tickets were issued, raising 0.039 billion yuan worth of social funds.

Ⅴ Population and People's Life

Population

The increase of population was controlled effectively. By end of 2003, the city's permanent resident population reached 10.113 million and that was 41.2 thousand more than the previous year. The registered population was 9.26 million, increased 69.5 thousand more than the previous year. Among the total population, 3.7626 million were agriculture population and 16.5 thousand less than the previous year, 5.4974 million were non-agriculture population and 86 thousand more than last year. The birth rate of the population was 7.14‰, 0.35 per thousand points lower than the previous year. The mortality rate was 6.04‰, maintaining the same growing level; the natural growth rate of the population was 1.10‰, down 0.35 per thousand points.

Personal Income and Savings

The income of the urban and rural residents increased quickly. The per capita reward of urban employed personnel worked in units was 18,628 yuan, up by 14.8 percent. The per capita annual disposable income of urban residents(calculated on new coverage) was 10,313 yuan, up by 10.5 percent. The average net annual income of the peasants was 5,861 yuan, up by 10.3 percent. The newly increased savings deposit in 2003 was higher than the previous year. By the end of 2003, the balance of urban and rural residents' savings deposit totaled 199.176 billion yuan, 33.227 billion yuan more than the beginning of this year, 11.466 billion yuan more than tthe net increased saving deposits in 2002.

Personal Consumption

Personal consumption increased synchronously. The per capita consuming expenditure was 7,868 yuan, up by 9.4 percent expenditure for housing, transport and telecommunication, medicine and medical service increased by 17.5, 26.5 and 11.7 percent respectively. The per capita annual living expenditures of rural households was 3,015 yuan, up by 8.5 percent, expenditure for housing, transport and telecommunication increased by 20.1 percent and 10.8 percent respectively. The residents' life quality continued to improve. Green household appliances, modern communication products, entered local families. By the end of year, the number of VCD/DVD players owned by per hundred urban households was 49.6, air-conditioners was 90.9, mobile phone was 77.8, computers was 34.1, vacuum was 24.3,drinking machine was 31.3,shower heater was 82.7. The number of color TV sets owned by per hundred rural households was 110, washing machines was 90, air-conditioners was 32, VCD/DVD players was 31, computer was 7.

Housing Conditions

The dwelling condition and the living environment of the urban and rural residents further improved. In 2003, houses demolished were 4.5 million square meters, the city renovated 324 old residential areas and improved the living environment of 1,000,000 residents. By end of 2003, the per capita construction house space in the urban area reached 23.1 square meters, the using space was 17.46 square meters, 0.8 square meter more than that in 2002. The per capita dwelling space in the rural area was 24.44 square meters, 0.1 square meters more than the previous year.

Major problems that remained in economic performance and social development included: the development of the tertiary industry was not quick; some state-owned middle & small-sized enterprises operated facing to difficulties; there were pressure in employment and re- employment; the income level of urban and rural residents was not high, the living of some people were difficult; the price of some goods and raw materials appeared the evidence of growing too quick.

Note:

1. All figures in the communique are preliminary statistics.
2. According to the regulation of National Bureau of Statistics, Gross domestic product of each region is named gross region product in Chinese, the gross domestic product of Tianjin in the communiqué refer to original GDP.
3. The gross domestic product of Tianjin, the value-added and output value are calculated at the current price of the year, where as growth rates are calculated at comparable prices.
4. Industrial enterprises above designated size refer to all state-owned enterprises and other enterprises with annual sales of over 5 million yuan.
5. The coverage of relative indicators of foreign investment is adjusted in this year, the growth rates are calculated at comparable prices.
6. Compared the new coverage to old one, the per capita annual disposable income of urban residents deducts the part paid by individual of pension insurance funds, unemployment insurance funds, medical insurance funds and housing funds and income of selling wealth and properties.

2003年天津市人均生产总值突破3000美元

2003年是天津市实施“三步走”战略的第一年。全市各方面深入贯彻党的十六大和市委八届三次全会精神，全面启动五大战略举措，扎实苦干，开拓创新，积极化解非典负面影响，主要经济指标增幅创近年最好水平。投资拉动和工业推动作用突出，金融支持力度增强，出口、消费、利用外资全面发力，财政收入、城乡居民收入增长加快，经济增长质量和速度同步提高，国民经济继续保持了持续快速协调健康发展的良好局面，人均生产总值突破3000美元，“三步走”战略第一步目标胜利实现。

2003年天津市生产总值完成2447.66亿元，按可比价格计算，比上年增长14.8%，增速比上年加快2.3个百分点，创1996年以来最高增幅。人均生产总值达到26532元，折合3206美元，圆满完成“三步走”战略第一步目标。全年经济运行主要呈现以下八大特点：

特点之一：成功抵御非典冲击，经济发展全面提速

2003年，天津市成功抵御了非典疫情对经济发展的冲击，保持了全市经济发展持续、快速向上的好势头。分季度经济运行情况看，一季度全市经济增长14.9%，实现了高起步。二季度，突发的非典疫情对经济发展造成了一定冲击，但是由于市委、市政府果断采取有效措施，努力把非典的不利影响降低到了最低限度，全市经济运行没有出现大的波动，GDP增长率为12.6%，仍保持了较快增长的态势。三季度，随着非典疫情的解除，全市经济迅速恢复，GDP增长15.2%，四季度经济进一步攀升，GDP增长达到15.4%，创四个季度运行的最高水平。这表明天津市经济抵御风险、稳健运行的能力进一步增强。

分三次产业看，第一产业稳定增长，完成增加值89.66亿元，增长6.1%。农业总产值完成193.44亿元，增长6.6%。农业结构继续优化，养殖业占农业总产值的比重达到53.6%，比上年提高2个百分点；经济作物占农作物播种面积的比重达到58%，比上年提高6.7个百分点。

第二产业是推动全市经济快速增长的主要力量，完成增加值1245.29亿元，增长18.0%，比上年加快3.7个百分点，对全市经济增长的贡献率达到62.4%。其中工业增加值完成1136.24亿元，增长18.6%，比上年加快4个百分点，工业拉动全市经济增长8.7个百分点，贡献率达58.7%。

第三产业是非典影响比较大的产业，在抗击非典中仍保持较快增长，完成增加值1112.71亿元，增长11.8%，其中，交通邮电仓储业增加值增长12.4%，金融保险业增加值增长25.5%，房地产业增加值增长17.6%，这三个行业的快速增长有效弥补了非典疫情对第三产业带来的负面影响。

特点之二：工业增势强劲，规模以上工业总产值突破4000亿元

2003年全市规模以上工业总产值完成4049.61亿元，增长26.1%。工业生产的主要特点：一是重工业成为拉动工业增长的主动力。重工业完成工业总产值2954.22亿元，增长28.7%，产值占全市工业的73%，增长速度快于轻工业7.9个百分点。二是优势产业带动作用明显，形成多点支撑的新格局。电子信息、汽车、医药、冶金、化工以及新能源等六大优势产业完成工业总产值2775.04亿元，增长28.9%，占规模以上工业总产值的比重达到68.5%，对全市工业增长的贡献率达到79.2%。三是外商及港澳台商投资企业和国有及国有控股企业生产增速加快，全年工业总产值分别完成1896.06亿元和1456.51亿元，分别增长30.3%和28.6%，增幅分别比上年加快2.5个和11个百分点。四是重点产品大幅增长。钢和成品钢材产量分别达到565.95万吨和1031.47万吨，分别增长17.4%和42.6%；轿车产量达17.25万辆，增长82.7%；大规模半导体集成电路3.69亿块，增长12.6%；移动电话机3139.72万部，增长10%；微波炉969.87万台，增长68.2%；空调器241.84万台，增长99%；显示器677.83万部，增长24.8%。五是工业企业产销衔接较好，经济效益综合指数较上年明显提高。2003年规模以上工业产品产销率98.88%，工业企业经济效益综合指数为147.6，比上年提高14.5点。工业企业利润大幅增长，实现利税总额401.35亿元，增长23.5%，其中实现利润237.62亿元，增长27.6%。

特点之三：固定资产投资规模明显扩张，全社会投资突破1000亿元

2003年全市全社会固定资产投资实现高起步、高增长，累计完成1046.72亿元，增长29%，增幅比上年提高13.9个百分点，为1995来以来最高水平。固定资产投资的主要特点：一是投资结构进一步优化。工业投资居各行业之首，完成投资382.5亿元，增长23.5%，占全社会固定资产投资的比重达到36.5%。城市基础设施投资力度加大，完成投资263.67亿元，增长34.2%，占全市的比重达到25.2%。二是重点项目进展顺利。64个重点项目完成投资312.29亿元。海河两岸综合开发全面启动，全年完成投资50.4亿元；天钢东移、钢管公司二期、津蓟和丹拉高速公路、15万吨级航道一期及北大防波堤等24个重点项目竣工；津滨轻轨试通车；地铁一号线、丰田轿车二期、大沽化20万吨聚氯乙烯等项目进展加快。三是房地产开发投资受海河开发和路桥建设带动大幅增长。全年完成投资211.39亿元，增长20.2%。四是中央和地方投资同步增长，民间投资增势迅猛。全年地方单位完成投资893.73亿元，增长31.9%；中央单位完成投资152.99亿元，增长14.5%。五大战略举措的全面推进吸引了大量民间投资，全年民间投资额达到314亿元，增长33.8%，占全社会投资的比重达到30%，比上年提高1.1个百分点。五是融资渠道进一步拓宽，建设资金到位情况好于往年。全年资金到位1111.5亿元，增长33%，其中国内贷款311.2亿元，增长79.2%，自筹482.48亿元，增23.3%。

特点之四：消费品市场稳中有升，房地产市场持续活跃

居民消费经历了4、5月份的短期波动后迅速回升，消费支出并没有因为非典的影响而降低。全年社会消费品零售总额突破1000亿元，达到1074.05亿元，增长14.1%，增幅比上年提高1个百分点。家居装修装饰、通信器材、文体用品、汽车等新的消费热点逐渐升温，私人轿车和个人住房消费构成了消费升级的基本动力。据对天津市限额以上批零贸易业统计，2003年通讯器材零售额增长1.1倍；家具类增长18.4%；汽车增长1倍；体育娱乐用品类零售额增长49.9%。消费结构进一步升级，城市居民人均消费性支出7867.53元，同比增长9.4%，服务性消费增长迅速，其中居住、交通通讯和医疗保健三项支出增幅居前，分别增长了17.5%、26.5%和11.7%。

海河综合开发和城市基础设施建设带动了房屋的大规模拆迁。全年拆迁量突破450万平方米。房地产投资占到了今年全市固定资产投资总量的20%以上。房地产市场呈现"价升销畅"的活跃局面，商品房销售创历史最高纪录。全年实现商品房现房销售面积786.5万平方米，销售收入198.04亿元，分别比上年增长39.5%和41.2%。

特点之五：对外开放进一步扩大，滨海新区拉动作用显著

天津口岸辐射作用进一步增强。2003年天津口岸进出口货值461.67亿美元，比上年增长26.4%，其中进口202.1亿美元，增长23.2%；出口259.57亿美元，增长28.9%。在天津口岸进出口货值中，外省市的比重达到51.7%，北京、河北、山西进出口货值居前三位，分别占20.3%、10.7%和3.6%。

外贸出口呈现快速增长。全年外贸出口总值达到143.74亿美元，比上年增长24%，增幅较上年提高2个百分点。2003年天津市外贸出口的主要特点：一是加工贸易出口仍占主体，一般贸易出口增长加快。全年加工贸易出口91.47亿美元，增长17.4%，占全市外贸出口的比重为63.6%。一般贸易出口48.36亿美元，增长35.1%，增幅比上年提高28.1个百分点。二是三资企业、个体私营企业出口高于全市出口平均增幅。三资企业出口114.27亿美元，增长25.4%，占全市出口比重为79.5%；个体私营企业出口1.63亿美元，增长2.1倍。三是出口商品结构明显优化，机电产品和高新技术产品出口高速增长。机电产品出口91.8亿美元，增长24%，占全市出口比重为63.9%，机电产品中的高新技术产品出口48.1亿美元，增长48%。四是对主要贸易伙伴出口平稳增长，目前美国、欧盟、日本、韩国和东盟是天津市五个主要出口市场，分别增长8.9%～43.6%，合计占全市出口的比重达到78.9%。

利用外资保持较高增幅。全年累计新批三资企业941家，增长15.3%；合同外资金额35.13亿美元，增长74.3%；实际到位16.33亿美元，增长62.9%。制造业招商引资占主导地位，合同外资额21.54亿美元，增长94.7%，占全部合同外资额的61.3%。服务业利用外资保持较快增长，合同外资额13.28亿美元，增长48.6%。来自日本、意大利、新加坡、德国、英国、香港等国家和地区的合同外资额分别增长1～4.5倍。外商企业增资踊跃，全市增资企业达到382家，增资总额10.95亿美元，其中外方增资额9.23亿美元。

经过近10年的建设和发展，滨海新区已成为全市最大的经济增长点，积聚了强大的发展后劲。全年滨海新区生产总值完成999.75亿元，增长20.4%。实现工业总产值2133.21亿元，增长30.3%；完成固定资产投资464.08亿元，增长65.2%；外贸出口89.38亿美元，增长24.1%，占全市外贸出口的62.2%；合同外资金额24.52亿美元，增长58.5%，占全市合同外资额的69.8%。天津港的发展尤为迅速，港口吞吐量达到1.62亿吨，增长25.4%，其中集装箱吞吐量301.5万标准箱，增长25.2%。

特点之六：财政收入增幅超过20%，金融对经济增长的支撑力度明显加大

全市财政收入累计完成451.74亿元，增长20.2%，增幅较上年提高1.8个百分点。地方一般预算收入完成204.53亿元，增长24.8%，增幅较上年提高7.9个百分点。增值税、营业税、所得税、消费税均保持较快增长。

全市金融机构存贷款大幅增长，增加额创历史最高水平。金融运行呈现以下四个特点：一是存款大量增加，全市金融机构当年新增存款突破1000亿元。截止2003年末，全市中外金融机构本外币存款余额达到4362.6亿元，比上年末增长29.9%，净增额为1003.77亿元，同比多增503.74亿元。其中，居民储蓄存款余额达到1825.32亿元，比年初增加338.94亿元，同比多增137.55亿元。二是贷款大幅增长，年末全市中外金融机构本外币贷款余额达到3791.22亿元，比上年末增长32.1%，净增额为920.31亿元，同比多增537.63亿元，其中，中长期贷款余额1573.93亿元，同比多增398.1亿元。三是个人消费贷款增长加快，年末余额达到261.42亿元，比上年末增长29.9%。四是金融保险业成为第三产业中发展最快的行业。全年增加值增幅达到25.5%，创近6年来最高水平，金融保险业增加值占第三产业的比重为9.6%，比上年提高2个百分点。

特点之七：私营个体经济发展壮大，中小企业成为新增长点

结合天津市五大战略举措的实施，一批鼓励私营个体经济和中小企业发展的政策措施相继出台，私营经济和中小企业发展日趋活跃，成为天津市经济发展中的新增长点。

截止2003年末，全市私营个体户数达到24.78万户，比年初增加1.44万户；从业人员92.09万人，比年初增加15.14万人；期末注册资金969.45亿元，比年初增加401亿元，增长70.5%；全年完成销售及营业收入680.82亿元，增长41.6%，其中私营企业增长65.2%；实现税收34.97亿元，增长41.4%，其中私营企业增长57.4%。

中小企业成为全市工业增长的重要支撑点。全市规模以上中小型工业企业完成工业总产值1670.16亿元，增长36.3%，高于全市平均增幅10.2个百分点，占全市规模以上工业总产值的比重达到41.2%。

特点之八：就业和再就业工作取得新突破，城乡居民收入继续提高

2003年全市新增就业岗位18.1万个，安置下岗失业人员12.1万人，首次实现新增就业量大于新增下岗失业人员，城镇登记失业率为3.8%。

随着天津市经济的快速发展，特别是就业的进一步扩大，提高职工最低工资标准，增加机关事业单位职工工资和离退休人员离退休费等措施的出台和落实，城乡居民收入保持较快增长。2003年全市城镇单位从业人员劳动报酬总额350.6亿元，增长14.6%，人均劳动报酬18511元，增长14.6%，其中企业单位人均劳动报酬增长16.0%。全年城乡居民收入增长超过了预期目标，城市居民人均可支配收入（按新口径计算）达到10312.91元，增长10.4%；农民人均纯收入5861元，增长10.3%。

2003年，在国际形势复杂多变、非典疫情冲击、市场竞争激烈的情况下，天津市经济取得显著成绩，确实来之不易。2003年天津市经济增长提速的主要因素可以概括为五个方面：一是多年奋斗积聚的能量不断释放。“三五八十”四大奋斗目标提前全面实现，不仅使天津市经济实力显著增强，而且也为今后的发展积蓄了后劲，为新阶段天津市经济继续在快车道上运行提供了动力。二是宏观调控能力进一步增强。二季度受非典疫情的冲击，天津市经济发展受到局部影响，市委、市政府坚持一手抓防治非典，一手抓经济建设，果断采取措施，并对受非典冲击较大的行业给以扶持，确保了全市经济迅速回升。三是随着改革开放的不断深入，企业发展的内在动力逐步增强，微观经济景气度明显改善。据对全市8大行业的企业景气调查显示，2003年天津市企业产品订货、劳动力需求、流动资金等指标景气指数均为近年最好水平。四是国内、国际经济环境明显改善。2003年我国正处在经济周期的上升阶段，经济发展普遍加快，主要经济指标增长达到近年最高水平。同时美、日、欧世界三大经济体均呈现复苏势头，为天津市经济发展提供了较好的外部环境。五是“三步走”战略和五大战略举措全面实施，进一步调动了全市各方面的积极性和创造性，为天津市经济的快速发展提供了新的动力。

（黄瑛）

工业经济发展创历史新高

2003年，天津工业各种所有制经济竞相发展，规模以上工业增加值突破1000亿元，总产值突破4000亿元，重工业比重上升到73%，九家集团进入产值百亿元行列，成品钢材产量超过1000万吨，原油超过1300万吨，手机超过3100万部，汽车产量达17.2万辆，六大优势产业拉动作用明显，企业经济效益继续提高。

一、工业经济运行的主要特点

（一）工业生产在高平台上实现高增长，创历史年度最好水平

2003年，天津工业生产始终处于较高运行平台之上。一季度高开高走，全市规模以上工业增加值同比增长22.2%；二季度受“非典”影响，增势有所减缓，但没有改变快速增长的基本运行趋势，上半年增加值同比增长20.2%；全年工业增加值总量突破1000亿元，达到1027.79亿元，比上年增长20.1%；其中12月份完成100.56亿元，首次突破百亿大关。全年总产值总量突破4000亿元，完成4049.61亿元，同比增长26.1%。工业生产无论是总量，还是增长速度都实现了历史性的突破。

（二）重工业发展提速，重点产品生产迈上新台阶

2003年以来，随着工业结构调整的不断推进，天津工业结构重化工日趋明显，重工业生产总量大，发展速度快。全年全市重工业完成总产值2954.22亿元，生产增速高达28.7%，高于轻工业生产7.9个百分点，也高于上年同期2.7个百分点，重工业比重占73%，比上年提高3.5个百分点，拉动整个工业生产增长达19.4个百分点。重工业的产销衔接情况也比较好，全年产销率达99.43%，高于全市平均水平0.55个百分点。

2003年，全市主要工业产品产量生产形势良好，重点产品生产迈上新台阶。从能源类产品看，生产原油1316.3万吨，发电量320.0亿千瓦小时；从主要原材料产品看，生产乙烯23万吨、聚脂31.9万吨、生铁342.6万吨、钢565.9万吨、成品钢材1031.5万吨，水泥449.3万吨。另外，汽车生产17.2万辆，手机3139.7万部，彩色显像管、显示器、工业锅炉、摩托车、内燃机、微波炉、空调、吸尘器等产品生产规模及增速也上了一个新台阶。

（三）大型集团地位突出，优势产业作用明显

2003年，电子仪表工业公司、摩托罗拉（中国）电子公司、中国石化天津石油化工公司、汽车工业（集团）公司、市大港石油（集团）有限公司、中海石油天津分公司、渤海化工集团公司、冶金集团（控股）有限公司和市钢管公司九家集团公司实现总产值均超百亿元，合计完成总产值1757.02亿元，年平均增速达28.0%，占全市工业比重达43.4%。其中电子仪表公司，摩托罗拉公司分别完成产值总量达400亿元左右，两者产值合计约全市工业的20%左右，影响举足轻重。

被列入五大战略举措之一加快发展的电子信息、汽车、化工、冶金、生物技术及现代医药、新能源及环保产业六大优势产业实现了高增长。全年完成工业总产值2775.04亿元，同比增长28.9%，占全市规模以上工业的比重达到68.5%，比上年提高0.9个百分点，对全市工业增长的贡献率达79.2%，拉动作用更加明显。

（四）多种所有制竞相发展，中小企业增长加快

在各种经济类型中，经济总量最大的外商及港澳台商投资企业生产增势强劲，完成总产值1896.06亿元，同比增长30.3%，增幅比全市平均水平高4.2个百分点，比上年提高2.5个百分点，对全市工业增长的贡献率为67.1%，拉动全市工业增长17.5个百分点；股份制企业完成总产值1172.56亿元，比上年增长29.4%。

2003年，国有及国有控股企业完成总产值1456.51亿元，比上年增长28.6%；私营工业完成总产值232.51亿元，同比增长41.2%，占全市工业经济总量比重由上年的4.0%提高到5.7%，拉动全市工业增长1.8个百分点，保持了良好发展态势。

中小企业成为全市工业增长的主要支撑点。规模以上中小企业完成总产值1670.16亿元，同比增长36.3%，高于全市平均水平10.2个百分点，对全市工

业经济增长的贡献率为51.6%，拉动全市工业增长13.5个百分点。

（五）工业产销衔接状况良好，经济效益继续提高

2003年，天津工业产销衔接状况进一步改善，全年产销率达98.88%，使工业产品库存在生产规模迅速扩大的前提下总体仍保持较低水平。年末产成品资金占用183.84亿元，同比上升2.0%，明显低于同时期生产和销售的增长速度。

2003年，全市规模以上工业企业经济效益综合指数为157.81，比上年提高24.7个百分点。其中：工业企业总资产贡献率为9.89%，同比提高1.23个百分点；全员劳动生产率为9.32万元/人，同比增长33.7%。全年累计实现利税总额401.35亿元，比上年同期增长23.5%，实现利润总额237.62亿元，增长27.6%，实现税金总额163.73亿元，增长17.9%。在全市利润总额中，盈利企业盈利额290.02亿元，增长17.6%，亏损企业亏损额52.40亿元，下降13.2%。

二、工业经济保持快速增长的主要原因

一是"嫁改调"聚集的能量正在释放。8年"嫁改调"，天津走出了一条利用外资嫁接改造老企业的创新之路。1994－2002年，全市工业累计嫁接改造国有老工业项目1220项，利用外资73.87亿美元。通过嫁接改造引进了资金、技术和管理，形成了一批拳头产品，实现了投资主体多元化，现代企业制度的建立进一步到位，使天津老工业基地的地位和作用得到巩固，为天津更大发展提供了有力的支撑。

二是良好的外部环境拉动了冶金等行业的快速增长。今年以来，由于国家继续实行积极的财政政策，固定资产投资增长较快，基础设施建设增势不减。冶金市场，特别是黑色冶金市场出现供不应求局面，产品价格也达到历史少有的高水平，全年全市黑色冶金出厂价格指数达122.6，使钢铁企业生产规模、经济效益大幅提高。2003年，全市黑色金属冶炼压延加工业完成总产值430.14亿元，增长42.9%，冶金集团、天铁集团、钢管公司实现工业总产值分别比上年增长41.5%、38.0%、41.1%，分别比上年提高17.3、20、11.2个百分点，以上三个集团全年实现利润分别比上年同期净增5.53亿元、4.33亿元和0.68亿元。

三是消费结构升级拉动。随着经济的持续发展，居民收入和生活水平的不断提高，消费观念、消费结构和消费层次发生了很大变化，汽车、住房成为新的消费热点。2003年，受汽车市场的强力带动，交通运输设备制造业成为带动全市工业生产增长和效益提高作用最突出的行业之一。全行业全年完成总产值314.60亿元，比上年增长54.7%，对工业增长的贡献率位居全市第2位；全年该行业实现利润21.42亿元，比上年（亏损11.5亿元）减亏增利32.92亿元。此外，在住房消费的带动下，建材、建筑装修装饰产品也呈现较快发展势头，对经济发展起到了较大的推动作用。

四是新项目发挥作用明显。三星手机、威驰轿车、LG家电、天钢扩能、PVC扩能、天安股份大输液等200余个技改和利用外资项目，全年新增产值超过300亿元，占全市净增产值的比重超过40%。电子仪表、汽车等总公司分别拉动全市工业增长9.5和3.5个百分点。这些新增长点的形成改变了过去依靠少数大企业拉动的局面，表明天津工业的结构趋于合理，抗风险能力大大增强。

（寇枫）

农业经济保持稳步发展

2003年，天津农村各级政府和广大干部群众认真贯彻落实十六大和中央、市委农村工作会议精神，紧紧围绕全面建设小康社会的奋斗目标和"三步走"发展战略，进一步强化农业基础地位，不断优化农业经济结构，继续加快推进农业产业化进程，积极拓展农产品流通市场，大力提升农业生产整体效益，努力克服"非典"疫情不利影响，全市农业经济继续在高水平基础上保持稳步发展。

一、农业经济效益增速加快，结构调整拉动作用明显提高

2003年，全市完成农、林、牧、渔业总产值193.44亿元，按可比口径计算，同比增长6.6%；实现农、林、牧、渔业增加值89.66亿元，按可比口径计算，比上年增长6.5%；农林牧渔业总产值和增加值增幅分别比上年提高0.6和0.4个百分点。2003年，全市畜牧水产养殖业产值占农、林、牧、渔业总产值的比重达53.6%，比上年提高2.1个百分点；棉、油、菜、果、花等经济作物产值占种植业产值的比重为83.0%，同比提高2.3个百分点，对推动全市农村经济稳步发展发挥

了重要作用。

（一）粮食继续调减，棉花生产大幅增长，蔬菜保持稳步发展

全市粮食总产量119.29万吨，比上年减产13.4%，其中：夏粮产量35.91万吨，减产18.6%，秋粮产量83.38万吨，减产11.0%。粮食产量继续调减主要是播种面积大幅减少所致。全年粮食播种面积387.17万亩，比上年减播79.71万亩，减少17.1%。其中，夏粮播种面积117.42万亩，减播26.43万亩，减少18.4%；秋粮播种面积269.76万亩，减播53.27万亩，减少16.5%。粮田面积减播主要是由于一方面各区县继续加大对种植业结构调整力度，使粮食作物面积因种植业内部结构调整主动调减了47万多亩，约占退粮面积的60%左右；另一方面是受干旱气候影响，播种期土壤缺墒严重，使粮田被动减播约计32万亩。

2003年，各区县在主动调减粮田面积的同时，进一步扩大了棉花、蔬菜等经济作物的种植面积，特别是棉花作物受市场价格大幅上扬的拉动，呈现出强劲的增长势头。2003年，全市棉花播种面积105.90万亩，比上年增播38.68万亩，增长57.5%；棉花总产量达9.47万吨，比上年增长51.8%，双创历史最高水平。

蔬菜生产作为种植业结构调整的重要组成部分，继续保持了稳步发展的良好态势。广大菜农努力克服干旱气候的不利影响，通过积极采用节水灌溉技术，扩大保护地种植面积，增加反季节蔬菜种植等有效措施，使经济效益不断提高，生产总量快速增长。2003年全市蔬菜种植面积为201.95万亩，比上年增长4.9%，蔬菜总产量达602.78万吨，同比增长3.2%。

（二）林业生产继续向生态公益林方向发展

随着小城镇建设的快速发展和防风制沙工作力度的不断加大，各县区着力推进城镇、村庄和通道绿化建设，扩大封山育林面积。2003年，全市年末实有林地面积由上年的262.88万亩提高到273.21万亩，增长3.9%。其中，用材林和封山育林面积分别达4.7万亩和19.02万亩，同比分别增长15.1%和18.8%；年末实有育苗面积11.85万亩，同比增长29.5%，林业生产加速发展开始起步。

（三）畜牧业生产的快速发展，对全市农业经济稳定增长发挥重要作用

生猪生产形势继续好转，草食牲畜和家禽养殖业快速发展。自2003年年初，天津生猪价格逐步止跌回升，特别是下半年以来，猪肉价格不断攀升。由于养猪效益的逐步回升，加之各级政府加大对畜牧业生产的扶植力度，农民养猪积极性普遍提高。全年生猪出栏412.94万头，同比增长14.0%。同时，牛羊等草食牲畜和家禽养殖业生产随着结构调整步伐的加快得到进一步发展，全年牛、羊和家禽的出栏量分别达到32.82万头、142.45万只和9441.88万只，同比分别增长了17.5%、14.2%和18.0%。

蛋鸡生产基本稳定。2003年天津蛋鸡生产受价格持续低迷影响，饲养量有所下降。但蛋鸡生产者经过近年鸡蛋价格的几次波动后从心理承受能力到经营方式都已基本适应，做为取得和增加收入的重要来源渠道，绝大部分生产者仍能保持冷静、平和的心态，蛋鸡生产基本维持稳定，无明显波动。全市禽蛋产量为24.25万吨，与上年基本持平。全市蛋鸡存栏为1741.08万只，比上年增长了1.6%。

畜禽产品产量全面增长。全年肉类总产量为52.41万吨，比上年同期增长16.8%。其中猪肉产量30.56万吨，增长17.1%；牛、羊肉产量分别为5.41万吨和3.12万吨，同比分别增长18.8%和10.0%；禽肉产量12.81万吨，增长17.7%；牛奶产量43.23万吨，增长28.7%。

畜牧业生产实现快速增长的主要原因：一是广大生产者面对2003年畜禽市场价格逐渐回升的势头，及时调整生产规模。通过引进优新品种，加强生产管理，并采用自繁自育自配饲料等低投入、高产出的方法，使畜牧业生产经济效益得到提高，产出量不断增加。农民出售一头生猪大约盈利150元左右，出售一头肥羊可盈利60元左右。良好的生产效益使农民的生产积极性大大提高，补栏热情较为高涨。据统计，全市年末猪、牛、羊存栏分别比上年同期增长了12.7%、15.1%和13.6%。二是各级政府积极加强结构调整的工作力度，通过狠抓畜禽生产的基地建设，使畜禽生产逐步向专业化、规模经营化、产业化方向发展，极大地增强了生产者抵御市场风险的能力。三是各级畜牧主管部门积极采取措施，制定各项优惠扶持政策，通过投放小额贴息贷款等政策，调动饲养者的积极性，有利地促进了畜牧业经济的快速发展；四是畜牧业投资建设力度不断加大，一批龙头骨干企业不断形成和发展壮大。

2003年，全市畜牧业产值为77.22亿元，比上年增长13.6%。拉动农、林、牧、渔业总产值提高4.3个百分点。

（四）渔业生产保持稳定，内部结构有所调整

2003年以来，天津的渔业生产者和各级管理部门继续以市场为导向，以提高渔业经济效益为中心，针对近海捕捞资源不断匮乏的现状，及时调整内部结构，努力克服干旱气候影响，渔业生产继续保持稳定发展。全年水产品总产量为29.83万吨，比上年增长4.4%。其中，海水产品5.09万吨，减少3.7%；淡水产品24.74万吨，增长6.3%。

二、农产品生产价格继续上升

2003年，天津主要农产品生产价格一路攀升，全年农产品生产价格总指数为104.4（以上年同期为100，下同），同比上升4.4%。

（一）种植业产品生产价格涨势强劲

2003年种植业产品生产价格指数为110.8，比全国平均水平高3.33个百分点，成为近年来增长幅度最大的一年。其中小麦平均生产价格为1.05元/公斤，同比上升1.9%；玉米、稻谷生产价格分别为0.99元/公斤和1.34元/公斤，同比分别上升7.2%和6.2%；豆类作物平均生产价格为2.36元/公斤，同比上升9.1%。棉花价格大幅攀升，价格指数高达128.8；蔬菜价格继续提高，全年蔬菜综合平均生产价格为0.92元/公斤，比上年上涨了13.3%。

（二）畜牧业产品生产价格有升有降，总体呈上升趋势

2003年，畜牧业产品生产价格指数为103.3，呈现稳步上扬态势。分主要品种看，生猪价格每公斤达到6.49元，比上年同期上涨7.7%。鸡蛋价格扭转连年低价徘徊的局面，全年平均价格比上年上升了1.6%。牛羊肉和牛奶的市场需求平稳，价格稳定。家禽价格由于生产量的持续扩大，生产价格同比下降3.6%。

（三）渔业产品价格继续回落，全年水产品生产价格比去年同期下降7.3%，其中淡水鱼类价格下降7.5%。

三、农业产业化经营水平进一步提高

一是龙头企业发展加快，带动能力加强。全市资产在100万元以上、经工商注册的农业产业化龙头企业达到396个，比上年增长11%；共带动农户34万户，占总农户数的35.7%，比上年提高了7.8个百分点。全市进入农业产业化体系的农户达到67.2万户，占农户总数的60%。

二是产业化利益联结机制不断完善。通过引导和规范龙头企业、中介组织与农户签订合同契约，发展订单农业和股份合作制经营，促进了利益联结形式逐步向“公司＋中介组织＋农户”和农民专业合作经济组织办企业的方向发展，利益联结机制由松散型向紧密型发展。全市有合同契约关系的农户达25万户，占进入产业化体系农户数的37.2%，比上年提高了16.2个百分点。

三是设施农业规模进一步扩大。全市农业设施园区达99个，面积41万亩；各类养殖小区达到1500多个，养殖业设施化程度较上年提高10多个百分点。

四是农业标准体系初步建立。生猪、黄瓜、韭菜、鲜奶等50%的重点农产品基本实现了依标生产。全市无公害蔬菜基地、畜禽基地、牛奶基地和水产基地已分别达到366个、62个、68个和34个，无公害饲料生产企业达到了35家。全市有72个品牌、200个产品获得农业名牌产品称号。

四、促进农业经济发展的几点建议

一是认真落实国家对种粮农民的支持政策和措施。进一步完善对种粮农民的直接补贴制度，抓住机遇，加快实施优质粮食产业工程，充分发挥天津粮食生产的特色和优势，从根本上保护种粮农民的利益，保护粮食综合生产能力，把发展粮食生产和增加农民收入结合起来，增加农民收入。

二是切实抓好当前农业生产。要引导农民加强越冬作物特别是小麦的田间管理，加快弱苗的转化，做好春耕备播工作，密切注意小麦病虫害的防治，力争夏粮取得好的收成，为全年粮食丰收打下良好基础。

三是继续加大财政支农力度，鼓励和引导农民增加投入，进一步改善农村基础设施和农业生产条件，增强农业生产能力。同时，要建立完善科学有效的抗灾减灾体系，最大限度地减少灾害损失，确保农业生产和农村经济持续稳定发展。

四是继续大力发展农业产业化经营，进一步增强龙头企业对农户的带动能力；加快发展农副产品加工业，建立健全农业现代化服务体系。围绕信息服务、科技推广、良种繁育体系、农产品质量标准体系、安全

检验检测体系等方面，尽快建立完整的服务体系，以推动农业产业化、市场化的发展进程。

（韩爱兵）

总量突破千亿　增幅再创新高

2003年，天津紧密围绕“三步走”发展战略，不断加大固定资产投资组织工作力度。虽然遭遇非典疫情冲击，但全市投资实现了开局高起步、发展高速度，全年完成投资突破千亿大关，增幅创1995年以来新高。不仅为“三步走”开局之年经济继续保持两位数增长提供了有力支持，同时为第二步目标的实施夯实了基础。

2003年，全市投资总体呈现高开高走，高位运行的基本态势，主要特点为：

一、投资增长速度明显加快，投资进度不断提前

2003年全社会固定资产投资以49.2％的高增长起步，上半年增长44.5％，前三季度增长48.7％，全年投资增幅达到29％，增幅创出自1995年以来新高。特别是国有及其他经济类型投资，连续11个月保持40％以上的高速增长，对全市经济增长目标的实现起到了重要的支撑作用。同时，城乡集、个体投资一季度增长4.7％，二季度增长15.6％，三季度增长19.5％，全年增长14.1％，保持了良好的发展态势。

在投资增长速度明显加快的同时，全市各方面对投资工作高度重视，组织力度不断加大。其中：海河开发基础设施、地铁一号线、津滨轻轨等市重点项目坚持冬季施工，节假日不停工，带动全市投资整体进度不断提前。“非典”出现以后，各单位更是把加大投资力度作为落实中央和市委要求，夺取防治“非典”和经济发展双胜利的重要措施，千方百计加快项目建设，全年四个季度完成投资的比例由2000年的1:2:2:5调整为2003年的1:3:3:3，投资进度大幅度提前。

二、投资结构继续改善，基础设施和工业投入力度进一步加大

2003年，天津投资规模继续扩大，三次产业投资全面增长。第一产业投资完成2.2亿元，同比增长75.7％；第二产业投资完成316.6亿元，同比增长22.9％；第三产业投资完成615.1亿元，同比增长34.9％。三次产业投资比重由上年末的0.1:35.5:64.4调整为本年末的0.2:33.9:65.9，三产投资比重进一步上升。在第三产业投资中，交通运输邮电业、房地产业、文教卫生和城建行业投资增长较快，增幅分别为42.2％、34.7％、83％、75.4％。

在地铁、轻轨、港口、公路等重要基础设施建设项目的带动下，全市基础设施投资在连续几年高增长的基础上继续保持了较快的增长速度。全年基础设施投资完成288.3亿元，增长46.8％，高于全市平均水平16.1个百分点。同时，天津继续加大老企业改造力度，加快工业东移步伐，随着六大支柱产业和十二大产品制造基地建设进展加快，新一轮嫁改调全面启动，全年工业投入达到306.7亿元，增长23.7％，其中：地方工业技改投资138.8亿元，增长25.4％，增幅超过全部工业1.7个百分点。

三、中央和地方投资共同增长，重点项目建设进展顺利

中央在津单位投资摆脱了连续三年下滑的局面，在中海石油勘探开发等项目完成投资大幅度增长的带动下，出现了强劲的反弹态势，增幅达到14.5％。地方投资受到海河综合开发、工业战略东移及区县投资增长较多的拉动，支撑作用进一步增强，全年完成投资780.9亿元，增长34.4％，增幅同比提高14.6个百分点，占全社会投资比重83.6％，同比提高2.3个百分点。

2003年，天津共安排重点建设项目64个，计划投资342.4亿元，占全市总规模的34％。这些项目安排早、启动快，进展好，完成工作量大幅度增加，有效拉动了全市投资的强劲增长。截止年底，64个市重点建设项目完成投资313.2亿元，比上年增加了126.3亿元。其中：天钢东移、钢管公司二套轧机改造、津蓟和丹拉高速公路天津南段、市内道路及卡口改造、示范高中校、滨江金耀广场等24个项目已建成交付使用，其余大部分项目也基本达到进度要求。

四、拆迁带火楼市，房地产市场繁荣活跃

2003年是继大规模危陋平房改造之后旧房拆迁量最多的一年，全年房屋拆迁总量突破450万平方米，强力拉动了对商品房和二手房市场的刚性需求；同时由于消费结构升级和居民消费观念的转变，贷款买房、卖旧买新已成为市场购房的主流，促进了住房梯次结构的形成，为天津房地产业带来了巨大的发展空间。

受海河综合开发和城市建设的强力拉动，天津

2003年房地产投资完成211.4亿元，现房销售786.5万平方米，同比增长20.2%和39.5%，分别高于上年同期11.2个和34.6个百分点。房地产市场呈现出以下特点：(1)开发规模扩大，先导指标增长。全年土地购置面积增长87.4%，土地开发面积增长29.7%，预示房地产开发后劲较强。(2)供求总量基本平衡，空置面积下降。全市商品房竣工面积增长22.1%，现房销售面积增长39.5%，表明目前房地产市场供销两旺，总体保持平衡；同时全年商品房空置面积比上年下降了141.6万平方米，其中空置一年以上的减少了49.5万平方米，降幅分别为29.2%和36.3%。(3)各种用途房屋全面旺销，带动价格上涨。由于金融商贸、旅游文化等第三产业的迅速发展和鼓励大型公建开发的优惠政策继续推行，全年住宅、办公楼、公建项目出现了全面旺销的良好势头，销售面积同比增长33.9%、1.3倍和1.7倍；受需求的强力拉动，现房销售价格平均每平方米比上年同期上涨84元。

五、融资渠道进一步拓宽，企业自主投资机制初步形成

2003年全市各方面多渠道筹划建设资金，靠扩大招商引资、经营城市、资本运作、吸引民间资金等多种手段，使建设资金到位率大幅度提高，有力促进了投资的增长。一方面，政府加强了对土地市场的管理和宏观调控，规范了国有土地有偿使用办法，确保了土地出让收益；另一方面，一些单位按照市场化方式，公开招投标拍卖冠名权、广告发布权等也取得了一定的收益。全年累计到位建设资金1111.5亿元，同比增长33%，资金来源结构也发生了很大变化，国家预算内资金比重明显下降，由2002年的2.4%下降到2003年的1.3%；国内贷款、自筹资金和其他资金所占比重迅速上升，由2002年的80.8%上升到2003年的85.7%。说明影响投资增长的动力机制中，政策性因素在不断减弱，市场机制因素在不断提高，投资自主增长的能力在不断增强。天津的投资增长格局，已经开始由政策推动为主导向市场推动为主的方向转变。

六、民间投资总量进一步攀升，增幅超过全社会投资平均水平

随着全社会固定资产投资规模的整体扩张和一系列积极扶持、鼓励民间投资相关政策的落实，加之民间资本的积累和自身经济实力的提高，天津包括集体投资、私营投资和个体投资在内的民间投资近几年来有了长足的发展，在全社会固定资产投资中的地位逐年提高，已经成为促进天津投资发展的一支不可忽视的生力军。2003年全市民间投资达到314亿元，同比增长33.8%，超过全社会平均增幅4.8个百分点，占全社会投资的比重达到30%，比2002年提高1.1个百分点。若加上外商投资，二者投资总量将占到全社会投资的半壁江山。

（毛涛）

积极创新贸易方式
奋力开拓出口市场

2003年是极不平凡的一年，复杂多变的国际形势和突如其来的"非典"疫情，给天津外经贸工作带来了前所未有的困难与挑战。在市委、市政府的正确领导下，全市人民紧紧围绕"三步走"战略和五大举措，全力克服"非典"等诸多不利因素影响，奋力拼搏，使天津对外贸易保持了快速增长，成为拉动全市国民经济快速增长的重要力量。

一、出口再创新高，有力地带动了全市国民经济快速增长

2003年，全市实现外贸进出口总额293.71亿美元，比上年增长28.7%。其中，出口完成143.74亿美元，增长24%；进口149.97亿美元，增长33.5%。进口和出口均实现快速增长，而且出口规模持续攀升，创历史最高水平，2003年当年新增出口额达到27.93亿美元标志着天津出口规模跃上了一个新台阶。2003年国民经济增长对外贸出口的依存度达到49.98%，比上年提高2.48个百分点。

二、出口商品结构继续优化

2003年天津外贸出口不仅增长速度快，出口规模明显扩大，而且出口商品结构继续得到优化，天津实施的科技兴贸战略进一步收到实效。主要体现在：一是技术含量和附加值相对较高的机电产品出口大增。2003年，全市机电产品出口达91.8亿美元，增长24%，占全市外贸出口总额的63.9%。二是高新技术产品出口显著增长。2003年天津高新技术产品出口57.95亿美元，增长27.5%，占全市出口总额的40.3%。

2003年，天津工业制成品出口127.33亿美元，比上年同期增长22.6%；占全市出总额的比重88.6%；

初级产品出口16.32亿美元，比上年同期增长37.8%，占全市外贸出口的比重为11.4%。

在25种重点出口商品中，2003年全年出口手机及零件24.97亿美元，增长38.4%；计算机与技术产品出口7.17亿美元，增长57.6%；电子元器件出口11.21亿美元，增长17.1%；微波炉出口2.95亿美元，增长33.2%；原油出口9.15亿美元，增长45.1%；服装出口8.56亿美元，增长12.3%；纺织品出口4.69亿美元，增长12.8%；家具出口2.37亿美元，增长24.6%；集装箱出口1.97亿美元，增长53.1%；空调、自行车及零部件和体育用品出口分别比去年同期增长1.2倍、81.2%和58.4%。

三、积极开拓新出口市场成效明显

加速实施市场多元化战略是天津保持外贸进出口持续快速增长的重要举措，为此，天津在努力保持原有出口市场的同时，积极开拓新的国际市场，目前已收到明显效果。2003年，天津外贸出口的国际市场已扩大为190余个国家和地区，除了保持发展亚洲、非洲、南北美洲的国家和地区出口市场规模外，对大洋洲的出口也有了明显增长，多元化市场格局已基本形成。

2003年天津对亚洲出口保持增长的主要国家和地区有：韩国、台湾、新加坡、菲律宾和香港等，出口分别比上年增长32.3%、20.8%、71.4%、26.7%和27.3%。对非洲出口2.32亿美元，增长26.6%。对欧洲出口24.6亿美元，增长40.6%。对北美洲出口43.58亿美元，增长15%，其中对美国出口增长14.5%。

四、贸易方式不断创新，区域对外贸易发展迅速

2003年，全市出口超亿美元的区域达到16个，占全市出口总额的98.5%。保税区被国家授权放开外贸经营权试点，当年出口2.71亿美元，增长97.6%。此外，2003年天津在积极推动民营企业扩大出口方面不断加大力度，建立了外贸创业园，目前有60余家出口型企业落户创业园，全年新增出口额达到1亿美元。

五、经营结构发生明显变化

伴随着天津外贸体制改革的不断深化，全市外贸经营队伍也有了很大发展，使经营单位结构发生了较大变化。2003年，全年新批各类进出口企业859家，增长85.5%，新增有出口实绩企业575家，出口额2.69亿美元。2003年天津各类企业出口均有不同程度的增长。国有企业出口24.75亿美元，增长14.2%，占全市出口总额的17.2%；外商投资企业出口大幅增长，出口额达到114.27亿美元，增长25.4%，占全市出口总额的79.5%；集体企业出口3.09亿美元，增长16.5%；私营企业出口1.63亿美元，增长2.1倍。

六、出口贸易方式发生变化

天津对外贸易呈现“大进大出”的特征，进料加工扮演着重要角色。我国加入WTO对进料加工出口有利，而天津沿海开放城市的区位优势和不断改善提高的工艺、管理水平相结合，以及相对较低的劳动力资源对天津进一步扩大进料加工出口产生了积极的促进作用。2003年天津进料加工贸易出口83.13亿美元，增长18%，占全市出口总额的57.8%。在进料加工出口增长的同时，一般贸易出口开始回升，全年出口48.36亿美元，增长35.1%，占全市出口总额的33.6%。

七、口岸功能进一步增强

通过强化口岸功能，提高服务水平，天津的港口优势得到了进一步的发挥，口岸进出口贸易也有了长足发展。2003年经天津口岸的进出口总额达到461.67亿美元，增长26.4%；其中出口259.57亿美元，比上年增长28.9%；进口202.1亿美元，比上年增长23.2%。海港吞吐量1.62吨，港口集装箱吞吐量301.54万箱，分别增长25.4%和25.2%。空港旅客吞吐量110.16万人次。口岸通关服务中心的建立和口岸通关信息平台的开通，特别是口岸各单位的共同努力，天津口岸的通关效率已经达到国内先进水平。

（程新娣）

抢抓机遇　扩大开放
利用外资再创辉煌

2003年随着天津市“三五八十”四大奋斗目标的全面实现和“三步走”战略第一步任务的全面完成，全市各系统各部门紧紧围绕市委、市政府提出的“整体推进，协调发展，追求高水平，实现新跨越”的要求，积极克服“非典”疫情带来的负面影响，抢抓机遇，进一步扩大开放，利用外资再创辉煌。2003年全年，全市新批外商投资项目941个，同比增长15.3%；合同投资总额59.12亿美元，同比下降7.7%；合同外资额35.13

亿美元,同比增长74.3%,高于全年工作目标34.3个百分点。全年实际直接利用外资16.33亿美元,同比增长62.9%,高于全年工作目标22.9个百分点。

2003年市委、市政府继续把对外开放作为全市工作的战略之举,下大力气积极扩大招商引资渠道,不断创新招商思路、体制和方式。通过采取电话招商、网上招商、委托招商、代理招商等一系列措施,多方式、多渠道加强与外商的联系,千方百计促成利用外资大项目的落实。如充分发挥互联网作用,及时向海内外商务机构和投资商发布天津市经济动态、外资政策、投资项目、专业服务等信息,提供专业化、国际化的信息服务,同时注意发挥使馆商务处和各个办事处等境外商务机构的作用,增加有效沟通渠道。通过采取上述措施,天津市对外商投资大项目的引资成效显著。2003年全市新批合同投资总额在500万美元以上的项目达198个;合同外资额达到21.31亿美元,同比增长76%。截止2003年底,世界500强企业有98家来津投资,投资项目达到251个,合同外资额67亿美元,占全市合同外资额的比重为14.8%。

世界500强企业的大举进入,带动了国内外一批中小配套企业来津投资。截至2003年末天津市已累计批准成立外商投资企业项目15990项,合同外资额达到453.01亿美元。

通过积极落实市委、市政府2003年年初提出的优化发展环境的各项任务,使全市的投资环境进一步改善。特别是通过加强对各类外商投资企业的服务,及时掌握情况,抓紧协调解决企业反映的问题,进一步增强了外商在津投资的信心,外商投资企业增资踊跃。全年,全市外商投资企业中有增资的企业为382家;增资总额达到10.95亿美元,其中,外方增资额为9.23亿美元,比上年增长了66.6% 。

在做好第二产业招商引资工作的基础上,积极顺应我国加入WTO后外商加大对我国服务业投资的新特点,采取有力措施加快第三产业招商引资力度。2003年天津市制造业对外招商引资仍然占主导,第三产业招商引资保持快速增长。2003年全年,制造业的合同外资额为21.54亿美元,同比增长94.7%,占全市合同外资额的比重为61.3%。全年,第三产业共新批企业338家,合同外资额13.28亿美元,同比增长48.6%,占全市直接利用外资合同额的37.8%。

2003年全市新批外商投资项目仍以外商独资为主,并且外商独资企业的合同外资额快速增长。2003年全年,全市外商独资企业合同外资额为27.48亿美元,同比增长96.6%。合资企业合同外资额增速较快,同比增长40.2%;合作企业合同外资额同比下降23.4%。

2003年中国香港、日本、德国、新加坡等国家或地区的合同外资额成倍增长,美国、韩国、中国台湾等国家或地区的合同外资额增长也较快。2003年全年全市直接利用外资合同额中,来自中国香港9.55亿美元,同比增长1.3倍;日本的直接利用外资合同额为5.53亿美元,同比增长2.1倍;德国1.08亿美元,增长1.1倍;新加坡0.62亿美元,增长1.6倍;美国5.34亿美元,同比增长46.4%;韩国2.99亿美元,增长69%;中国台湾1.46亿美元,同比增长19.6%。

天津经济技术开发区、天津港保税区和高科技产业园区成为2003年全市招商引资的亮点。2003年天津经济技术开发区合同外资额12.77亿美元,增长57.1%,占全市合同外资额的比重为36.4%;天津港保税区合同外资额9.67亿美元,增长84%,占全市合同外资额的比重为27.5%;农口十二个区县2003年合同外资额9.48亿美元,增长74.9%;市内六个中心区2003年合同外资额1.59亿美元,增长86.5%。

在建立新型招商机制上,筹备建立了多方出资、共同受益的新型招商企业——天津德元投资顾问公司。狠抓了海外中小企业招商机制的创新,形成海外招商、"中心"孵化、小区落户的三级配套服务系统,为国际中小企业落户天津营造新型服务环境。在商业、保险、旅游等方面积极寻找合作伙伴,提前介入,提前洽谈。

另据统计,2003年全年全市实际直接利用外资16.33亿美元,同比增长62.9%。其中:开发区实际直接利用外资6.33亿美元,同比增长54.3%;保税区实际直接利用外资4.02亿美元,同比增长71%;农口十二个区县实际直接利用外资4.76亿美元,同比增长81%。

外商投资企业生产经营实现快速发展。2003年全市三资企业生产运行良好,主要经济指标保持快速增长。2003年全市三资企业实现总产值1932.7亿元,同比增长19.9%;实现销售收入2233.07亿元,同比增长23.6%;出口快速增长,出口额达114.27亿美元,同比增长25.4%,占全市外贸出口的比重达到79.5%;实现利润总额97.6亿元,同比增长27.8%;实缴税金总额99.78亿元,同比增长9.5%。2003年全市三资企业实现增加值530.83亿元，已占全市生产总值的22.2%。三资经济的快速发展，有力地带动了全市国民经济的快速发展。

（张辉）

开拓奋进的天津旅游业

2003年是天津旅游业经受“非典”严峻考验、奋力实现恢复和振兴的一年。全市旅游业各单位认真贯彻落实市委、市政府加快服务业发展的战略构想，抢抓机遇，迎难而上，与时俱进，在困境中开拓创新。2003年全年国际旅游接待的主要指标接近2002年历史最好水平，国内旅游快速全面地恢复和振兴，为天津市国民经济保持持续快速发展的良好态势，为实现天津市“三步走”战略第一步目标做出了贡献。

一、积极做好国际旅游客源市场的恢复工作，国际旅游人数接近2002年水平

2003年四月下旬。突如其来的“非典”疫情使天津市旅游业蓬勃发展的良好势头受到前所未有的巨大冲击，为了挽回“非典”疫情给天津市旅游业所造成的巨大损失，天津市旅游管理部门在“非典”疫情过后，组织区县旅游部门、旅游企业赴德国、日本、意大利、法国、荷兰等国家和我国香港等地区开展了大规模巡回促销活动。由于天津市对外旅游宣传促销的及时到位，使国际旅游客源市场和接待人数提前两年恢复到2002年水平，全年天津市共接待海外旅游者达48.90万人次，同比下降3.4%，接待人数已接近2002年水平。其中，外国人为45.61万人次，占接待总人数的93.3%；港澳台同胞3.29万人次。

二、国内旅游快速恢复，且发展势头强劲

在“非典”疫情解除后，天津市旅游部门积极组织自救，以中国国际旅行社组织了由医务人员及社会各界人士的家乡游活动迈出第一步开始，由于措施得力，天津市国内旅游用了较短的时间就实现了恢复和振兴。2003年全年，天津市接待国内旅游人数3751.12万人次，同比增长1.1%；旅游收入395.02亿元，同比增长1.3%。其中，天津市接待外埠一日游游客人数为903.15万人次，同比下降1.4%；主要是天津市接待北京市民到天津一日游的游客下降幅度较大，全年接待北京市民到天津一日游的游客人数为312.28万人次，同比下降23.9%，主要是京津两地受“非典”疫情影响的时间较长所致，从“非典”疫情解除后的天津市旅游市场看，天津仍然是北京及周边地区的旅游热点地区之一。

三、旅游接待能力进一步提高，旅游环境大大改善

2003年以来，特别是“非典”时期，天津市各旅游行业各部门苦练内功，不断夯实基础，提高服务质量，抵抗风险能力增强。同时，天津市旅游综合接待能力也明显增强，截止2003年底，已经拥有星级宾馆85座，客房1.16万间，床位2.04万张；国际、国内旅行社达231家，其中，国际旅行社19家；国家A级景区景点14家。

具有天津近代史文化底蕴和天津特色的旅游项目已初步形成，滨海、蓟县、西青和市区四大旅游圈已确立。以轻轨风景线、“基辅”号航母、海河外滩公园、泰达新貌等为主构成的滨海风情游，津蓟绿色通道、盘山新景观、农家乐生态游为主构成的蓟县山野游，杨柳青古镇风情街、热带植物观光园、峰山药王庙等为主构的西青古镇民俗游，绚丽多姿，名街、名河、名馆、名园和灯光夜景等构成的市区都市观光游，这些都成为2003年天津市旅游的突出亮点。

到2003年底天津旅游环境得到明显改善。第一，完善了市内三环十七射道路体系；开通了天津至汉城、大阪、名古屋、明斯克、基辅国际航线，目前已与国内30多个城市（包括香港）通航；天津至神户、仁川海上客运通航；津蓟、津承等旅游专线列车和京津、京塘快速列车运营，使本市初步形成了陆、海、空立体的交通网络。第二，拥有发达的邮电通讯系统。到2003年末全市长途光缆线路长度已达到6477.1公里，局用交换机容量已达402.5万门，移动电话交换机容量已达515万门，可与世界上多个国家和地区直拨电话。第三，城市面貌发生了巨大的变化。社会治安始终保持全国最好的地区之一。旅游环境的明显改善为今后旅游业的跨越式发展提供了有利的条件。

（张辉）

天津运输邮电仓储业蓬勃发展

2003年，随着天津基础设施建设投资力度的加大及国民经济的快速发展，作为国民经济动脉的交通运输和邮政电信业呈现出良好的发展态势，综合运输能力不断增强，城市载体功能进一步提高，为整个国民经济的正常运行提供了坚实的保障。全年主营业务收入在500万元及以上的交通运输、仓储及邮电业企业实现增加值143.42亿元，比上年增长15.2%。其中，交通运输业增加值80.12亿元，增长14.9%；邮政电信业增加值56.20亿元，增长14.4%；仓储业增加值7.10亿元，增长26.0%。

一、交通运输业较快发展

2003年，天津交通运输业努力克服"非典"带来的直接影响，继续保持了增长势头。全年各种运输方式完成客运量3507万人，比上年增长1.4%；完成旅客周转量92.74亿人公里，增长0.2%。完成货运量3.53亿吨，增长13.7%；完成货物周转量8169亿吨公里，增长26.0%。

（一）公路运输功能增强

2003年天津路网质量进一步提高，运输功能不断增强。全市公路通车里程10168公里，比上年增长4.9%，其中等级公路9901公里，增长8.5%，占全部公路的97.4%。在等级公路中高速公路517公里，比上年增加186公里，增长56.2%。随着路网建设的日趋完善，公路运输方便快捷的特点得以充分发挥，民用车辆拥有量及客、货运量也得到快速发展。截至2003年底，天津拥有民用车已达100.55万辆，其中当年新注册9.57万辆，私人汽车拥有量已达30.96万辆。全年公路共发送旅客 2109万人，比上年增加239万人，增长12.8%；完成货运量2.01亿吨，比上年增长2.6%。在各种运输方式中公路客、货运量所占比重分别达到60.1%和56.9%。

（二）铁路客、货运有涨有落

铁路运输仍是当前中远途旅客、货物运输最主要的运输方式。截至 2003年底，天津铁路延展里程4455公里，营业里程1454公里，拥有机车519台，其中内燃机车464台，电力机车54台。全年发送旅客1281万人，比上年下降14.5%；货物运输量5662万吨，比上年增长25.3%。铁路运输在各种运输方式中客、货运比重分别为36.5%和16.1%。

（三）水上运输，特别是海洋货物运输增长明显加快

依仗天津市得天独厚的地理位置，大力发展海洋货物运输业已成为天津开发海洋经济的重点工作之一。2003年底，天津拥有民用运输机动船114艘，总载重量500.32万吨位。全年货运量8944万吨，增长38.6%。水上货运占各种货物运输方式的25.4%，比上年提高了4.6个百分点。

（四）航空运输业明显增强

伴随着人们生活水平的不断提高，人们出行选乘交通工具的方式也在逐渐改变。2003年，天津空港全年飞机累计起降 2 万架次，完成机场旅客吞吐量110.1万人，增长0.8%。完成货邮运量1.28万吨，增长14.2%。

二、港口发展实现新跨越

（一）内、外贸货物吞吐量保持快速增长

2003年，天津及周边地区进出口贸易持续增长，促进了港口货物吞吐量快速增长。天津港口货物吞吐量实现了一年上三个千万吨的新台阶，港口货物吞吐量继续保持着出港大于进港、外贸大于内贸的结构。全年完成货物吞吐量1.62亿吨，比上年净增3276万吨，增长25.4%。完成内贸货物吞吐量0.74亿吨，增长25.8%，增幅比上年提高12.3个百分点，其中进港0.16亿吨，增长33.0%，出港0.58亿吨，增长23.9%；完成外贸货物吞吐量0.88亿吨，增长24.9%，其中进港0.36亿吨，增长26.4%，出港0.52亿吨，增长24.0%。从全港货物内、外贸结构上看，内、外贸货物吞吐量比为45.9:54.1。从进、出港的结构看，进、出港货物吞吐量比为32.6:67.4。

（二）货物流向更加合理

天津港口内贸进港货物主要以大连、绥中、宁波、青岛的石油及制品和福建、山东沿海的矿建材料为主，这两项货物占内贸进港货物吞吐量的69%。内贸出港主要以运往华东、华南的煤炭和钢铁为主，这两项货物约占内贸出港货物吞吐量的80.5%。外贸进港的货物主要以日本、韩国的机械设备和石油、化工原料，印度和澳大利亚的金属矿石为主，这四个国家的进港货物吞吐量占全部外贸进港货物吞吐量的57.9%。外贸出港货物主要以煤炭和其他杂货为主，煤炭占全部外贸出港货物吞吐量的54.9%。从整个外贸进、出港货物吞吐量完成情况看，主要流向亚洲58.6%；欧洲13.1%；大洋洲11.9%；北美洲6.4%；南美洲6%；非洲1.9%。

（三）支柱性货物类稳定增长

煤炭、石油、金属矿石和集装箱是天津港四大支柱性货物类。2003年，煤炭及制品完成吞吐量0.68亿

吨，比上年增长18.8%，占货物吞吐量的41.7%；石油及制品完成0.15亿吨，增长47.4%，占货物吞吐量的9.1%；金属矿石完成0.17亿吨，增长43.7%，占货物吞吐量的10.8%；完成集装箱吞吐量301.5万国际标准箱，增长25.2%，集装箱按重量吨计算吞吐量为0.34亿吨，增长20.9%，占货物吞吐量的20.9%，四大支柱性货物类合计占全部吞吐量的82.6%。

三、邮政、电信业务快速增长

2003年，全市完成邮电业务总量115.71亿元，比上年增长28.1%。其中，邮政业务总量8.97亿元，增长5.7%；电信业务总量106.74亿元，增长30.7%，呈现出了良好的发展态势。

（一）电信业务稳步增长，通信能力不断增强

由于投资力度的加大，2003年，全市新增局用电话交换机容量15.9万门，达到402.5万门；长途光缆线路长度达到2386.6公里，增长38.4%，长途电话交换机容量达到26.5万路端，新增移动交换机容量158万户，达到515万户。

通信业务迅猛发展。近年来，用户对电信业务个性化、多元化需求不断提高，为电信行业的竞争提供了源源不断的动力。电信业务价值的创造已不仅是通过运营规模，更重要的是依靠拓展业务范围和提高服务质量来实现，电信以其便利性和个性化特点使其拥有量迅速上升，2003年底，天津电话（含固定电话、移动电话、小灵通）用户761.91万部，比上年增加160.46万部。全市电话普及率由上年的65.4部/百人增加到82.3部/百人，比上年增加了16.9部/百人。同时，随着宽带网的建设及计算机应用的快速发展，现代化的网络技术对经济建设及人民生活发挥了越来越重要的作用。数据通信业务高速增长，2003年底天津互联网用户达到204.57万户，比上年净增7.96万户，增长63.7%。

（二）邮政业务不断增长

2003年，天津邮政企业积极拓展业务领域，邮政业务总量持续增长。据统计，2003年天津邮政业务总量8.97亿元，比上年增长5.7%。发送函件2.2亿件，比上年增长9.4%；特快专递321.5万件，增长11.8%；邮政储蓄期末余额达到117.47亿元，增长16.7%。

（卢智伟）

现代流通业快速发展
商业经济运行良好

2003年天津商业企业认真贯彻落实市第八次党代会和市委八届三次、四次全会精神，按照"三步走"战略部署，全面启动和推进实施五大战略举措，深化改革，奋力开拓，积极化解非典负面影响，有力地促进了流通和消费市场的进一步活跃。

一、商贸流通规模进一步扩大

2003年，天津商贸流通业蓬勃发展，规模进一步扩大。全年限额以上批发零售贸易业商品购进总额1858.60亿元，比上年增长37.0%；商品销售总额1915.45亿元，比上年增长33.2%。

（一）对外开放成效显著

2003年随着天津对外招商引资力度加大，使天津商业经济呈现出对外开放的良好格局，全年新批批零贸易业、餐饮业191家，比上年增长9.14%，合同外资额4.43亿美元，增长52.4%，实际直接利用外资2.31亿美元，增长46.9%。据对全市限额以上外商及港澳台投资企业统计，2003年实现销售164.16亿元，增长57.9%。

（二）生产资料销售呈现回升势头

随着固定资产投资增长和全国物资市场需求的扩大，拉动天津生产资料市场出现回升势头，增速不断加快。天津限额以上贸易企业全年销售生产资料1086.87亿元，比上年增长36.0%，增幅提高22.4个百分点。

金属材料和石油成为生产资料市场的两大增长点。2003年，天津原材料、燃料、动力购进价格始终在高价位运行，比上年同期上涨8.7%，其中黑色金属材料价格上涨19.6%。今年以来，天津燃油价格升降频繁，全年累计下来，93号汽油价格上涨11.5%、90号柴油价格上涨19.0%。全市限额以上贸易企业金属材料销售425.74亿元，比上年增长42.3%；销售石油571.44亿元，比上年增长35.2%，煤炭、化工材料的需求也呈增长态势。

（三）对外贸易规模进一步扩大，生产资料和机械设备行业拉动进口大幅增长

2003年，天津限额以上批零贸易企业出口总额139.69亿元，比上年增长6.1%；进口总额92.81亿元，比上年增长62.1%，其中生产资料批发业和机械

设备、五金交电及电子产品批发业进口增幅较高，全年进口额达68.06亿元，比上年增长81.1%，拉动全市进口增长53.2个百分点。

二、消费品市场购销活跃，零售总额保持快速增长

2003年，随着天津国民经济快速发展和城乡居民收入水平提高，商业部门努力开拓市场，积极引导消费，大力调整商品结构，使消费品市场继续保持购销活跃的势头。全年消费品零售总额保持快速增长，全市实现社会消费品零售总额1074.05亿元，比上年增长14.1%。

（一）商业经济体制改革继续深入，零售市场所有制格局发生新变化

2003年天津商业经济改革和结构调整向纵深发展，零售市场的所有制格局显著变化。国有经济市场份额减少，个体、私营经济快速发展。全年国有及集体经济零售额实现273.06亿元，比上年增长9.9%，占全市零售额的比重由上年的26.4%下降至25.4%。外商及港澳台投资经济平稳发展，实现零售额36.98亿元，与上年基本持平，占全市比重由3.9%下降至3.4%。个体、私营经济规模进一步扩大，全年共实现零售额363.51亿元，比上年增长23.6%，高出全市平均水平9.5个百分点，占全市的比重已达33.8%，比上年提高2.8个百分点。

（二）餐饮市场保持活跃势头

餐饮业年内不断推出各种形式的美食节和烹饪大赛，充分激发了餐饮市场的活力，形成了正餐、快餐、特色小吃相配套，正宗菜系和特色菜品互为衬托的餐饮市场，迎合了消费需求。同时，餐饮行业通过采取连锁经营和开办餐饮超市等新的经营业态以及基础设施规模扩大和档次的提高，进一步增强了天津餐饮行业的服务功能和发展潜力。尽管4、5两月受到“非典”疫情的严重冲击，全年餐饮业仍实现零售额109.91亿元，比上年增长7.2%。

（三）用品类商品增长加快

2003年天津零售市场吃、穿、用三类商品零售额全面增长，其中用品类零售额增幅最高。全年吃的商品零售额395.70亿元，增长5.9%；穿的商品零售额186.18亿元，增长16.9%；用的商品零售额475.01亿元，增长20.8%；烧的商品零售额17.16亿元，增长12.9%。用的商品零售额增幅分别比吃、穿、烧三类商品高14.9、3.9和7.9个百分点。

（四）受“非典”疫情影响，零售市场呈V型波动

受“非典”疫情影响，2003年天津社会消费品零售总额呈现前高后低再回升并趋于平稳的运行轨迹。一季度零售市场在春节市场的带动下实现了高起步，零售总额同比增长15.2%。二季度突如其来的“非典”疫情对零售市场造成严重冲击，5月份天津零售额同比下降1.3%。影响二季度零售总额增幅比一季度回落5个百分点。进入三季度，“非典”的影响基本消除，市场迅速回升，下半年零售总额同比增长15.4%，超过一季度增速。

三、新的消费热点不断涌现，消费领域进一步拓宽

近年来，随着生活水平的提高和消费观念的转变，天津消费品市场进入了由普通家电向汽车、数码家电等时尚商品的过渡时期。在统计的25大类商品中，销售增长的有18类，其中体育娱乐用品类、电子出版物及音像制品类、通讯器材、汽车等商品比较畅销。随着家庭对汽车消费需求的扩大和经济型轿车价格的下降，汽车销售持续增长。2003年，全市限额以上批零贸易企业零售汽车2.39万辆，比上年增长19.0%，实现零售额22.70亿元，增长1.01倍。由于小灵通业务的开通和优惠的资费，得到更多用户的认可；另外，随着手机彩屏、彩信、摄像、录音等功能的日臻完善，手机的升级换代带动了新一轮的消费高潮。2003年，通讯器材类商品销售增势强劲，全年零售8.11亿元，比上年增长1.13倍。大规模的海河综合开发和市政建设带动了房地产市场购销两旺，受住宅消费升温拉动，家居、建材、家电持续旺销。

四、限额以上贸易企业销售规模扩大，实现利润总体水平提高

2003年天津限额以上贸易企业实现商品销售收入1605.33亿元，比上年增长32.3%；实现利润总额15.20亿元，净增6.03亿元，增长65.8%，其中批发业增长57.7%，零售业1.93倍。分行业看，实现利润主要集中在石油及制品批发业、汽车、摩托车及零配件批发业、金属及金属矿批发业、非金属矿及制品批发业、烟草制品批发业和纺织品、服装和鞋帽零售业，拉动全市限额以上企业利润总额增长66.2个百分点。

（张琦）

商品交易市场
发展迅速　繁荣兴旺

天津商品交易市场经过多年的培育和发展，规模不断扩大，功能不断增强，初步形成了一个门类齐全、吞吐量大，辐射力强的农产品、工业品、生产资料的市场体系。市场发展已从量的扩张转向质的提高。商品交易市场的发展和市场体系的形成，对扩大就业、带动相关产业的发展发挥了重要作用，给天津经济增添了生机与活力。

一、大型市场发展迅速，龙头作用显著

2003年末，全市各类市场总数达701个，其中生产资料市场118个，消费品市场583个。各类商品市场的交易范围进一步扩大，基本形成了以大型批发市场为龙头，区域市场为骨干，初级市场为基础，多层次、多门类的市场体系。2003年全市各类市场实现成交额712.79亿元，比上年增长16.24%。其中52个亿元以上的骨干市场总成交额达到418.48亿元，按可比口径，比上年增长23.59%，占全市商品交易市场成交总额的58.7 %。

2003年全市共有21个消费品批发市场和7个生产资料批发市场年交易额超5亿元。这些大市场吸引了大批国内外有实力的代理商、经销商进场经营，交易商品涉及上百个大类，辐射全国20多个省区，在我国北方乃至全国的影响日益突出。大胡同小百货市场在继续做好原有市场经营的基础上，与万隆集团两强联合进行万隆大胡同商业中心项目的开发和建设，打造天津商业航空母舰，构建新型的商业中心区。目前19个单体建设计划中的18个已完成竣工、入住和开业。中心招商率已超过80%，一个总建筑面积达到40余万平方米，设施一流、规划科学、布局合理、北方最大、国内先进的大胡同商贸城已初具规模。经营商品多达30多个大类，数万个品种，商品远销俄罗斯、美国等十几个国家，日客流量高峰可达30万人次，被誉为“小商品大流通，南货北销旺地”。大胡同小百货批发市场2002年实现成交额51亿元，跻身全国百强市场。天津不锈钢材市场积极采用全新的用人机制和管理机制，经过一年多的培育和发展，现已成为全国最大的不锈钢材市场和北方不锈钢材集散地。为搞活区域经济发挥了重要作用。天津石化交易市场“前店后库”的市场运作模式进一步完善。橡胶、塑料等大品种的交易量及交易价格在本市及周边地区发挥了十分重要的影响，服务于本市经济建设的作用更加明显。到该市场考查，要求入场的企业络绎不绝，市场的知名度和影响在不断扩大。

二、市场建设向现代化方向迈进

网络技术的应用正在深刻改变着传统的商品交易形式和运作方式，网上交易、电子销售、无店铺买卖等现代化交易形式和手段快速发展。近年来，天津一些大型批发交易市场按照国际惯例，以现代化通讯设备，规范化的交易方式，多功能的综合服务，实现了市场建设的现代化。金钟农产品批发交易市场始终把“依法治场，科学管理”放在建设市场、发展市场的首位。目前，市场管理实现了收费、财务、核算、发布信息、经营户管理的电脑化管理，具有完善的微机结算系统，促进了市场管理的现代化水平，并且与农业部连网，实行了网络化管理，已初步成为在国内有影响力的果菜行情发布中心。何庄子蔬菜批发市场已形成购、销、储、运一条龙服务和组织网络，电子结算系统和电子监控、农药检测等7个现代化电子商务管理系统正在建设中。一些现代化程度较高的市场还具备了网上交易、电子交易的能力。如中国天津粮油批发交易市场以计算机网络建设为重点，实现了电子竞价交易系统的技术创新，网上网下交易并驾齐驱，相辅相成。其他一些大型批发市场也相继建立了大容量、高质量的信息网，以指导供销企业的交易行为。环渤海建筑材料中心批发交易市场与北方网合作，将计算机网络定位为商品报价中心、家居文化传播中心，并以信息的形式发布出来，随时把采集到的最新价格信息、产销和供求信息、订单及一些相关情况提供给商户，既满足了商户需求又方便与国内外客户的联系，为经营者和消费者创造了良好的交易环境，进而以快速灵通的信息优势扩大了国内外的影响，交易规模不断扩大。该市场已发展成为年成交额超20亿元的国家级建材批发市场。

三、联合重组步伐加快，大市场建设成效明显

近几年大市场的重组与联合取得了明显成效：王顶堤集团完成了红旗农贸市场的迁扩建一期工程和天津汽车城的建设；大胡同与万隆集团合作组建的万隆大胡同置业有限公司已初步完成建筑面积30多万平方米的大胡同商业中心市场的建设，为建设小商品批发交易集散中心打下了坚实的基础；塘沽滨海陶瓷市场和华北建材陶瓷市场每年成交近百万吨的陶瓷，辐射华北、东北、西北等地区，合作后成为三北地区著名的建材陶瓷集散中心。

四、带动相关产业发展，开辟了就业新渠道

随着近年来市场建设步伐的加快，带动了天津工业、农业、餐饮业、交通通讯业、旅游等行业的发展。利用闲置厂房、仓储设施兴办的环渤海建材、轻纺商城、北方日用工业品中心批发市场、不锈钢材市场等多家市场，使数十万平米房地产和相关设施得到重新利用，创造了新的就业岗位。为繁荣经济、扩大就业，带动产业，美化市容做出了积极贡献。仅不锈钢材市场在一期市场就解决了原厂地五金工具三厂200余人的再就业问题，同时安置区内下岗职工300多人。

五、服务功能不断增强，经营范围不断扩大

伴随着市场的发展，市场的服务功能也在逐步增强，如石化交易中心市场为入场商户提供集办公、商务、居住、生活为一体的用房，银行进驻市场，为客户提供优质快捷的结算、融资等服务，该市场主办的《天津化工信息》网刊为客户发布和提供商情信息，提供仓库和铁路及危险品运输等配套服务；宝钢储菱钢材交易市场的剪切加工和仓储物流为一体的特色服务及客户一票委托的全程服务等，有助于入场商客提高经营的效率和效益。各亿元市场在搞好硬件投入的同时，不断强化服务竞争意识，将市场的统一管理与业主的分散经营结合起来，促进了市场健康、有序发展。

六、品牌化发展趋势明显

为适应市场竞争，一些企业大打品牌战略，实现了产供销一条龙。如：近两年，金钟蔬菜批发交易市场投资6000多万元对市场进行改造扩建，积极适应市场需求，不断实现市场创新，延伸经营领域，向产供销一条龙方向发展，大力培育有影响力的交易商、经纪人队伍，实现市场与生产基地的紧密结合，引导农民根据市场需求开展订单农业，形成了比较稳定的蔬菜交易货源，带动本市及周边地区200万亩蔬菜种植面积，每年为菜农实现纯收入10亿元以上。建立和完善了与基地、农户之间稳定的购销关系和合理的利益联结机制，现已在天津郊区、河北、珠海、山东等地区发展订单农户 9496 户，形成的稳定基地面积达7.7万亩，每年为市场提供2.5亿公斤无公害蔬菜，保证了全市市场的均衡交易。在广东珠海建设的果菜基地及加工车间，作为市场产品出口港澳的中转站和“南菜北调”的重要基地，所经销的“金钟”牌果菜已打入港澳及东南亚市场。现已走向了一条品牌托市场，市场带基地，基地连农户的产供销一体化独具特色的蔬菜产业化之路。与此同时，积极探索连锁经营等新业态，在市内建立绿色果菜销售连锁店，目前已有10家，该市场正在由出租摊位型向市场经营型转变。又如，环渤海建材批发市场牢固树立品牌意识，积极发展代理业务，市场囊括了206户国内外知名品牌，创立了“末位淘汰制”、“市场先行赔付制”，通过了IS09002国际质量体系认证，并成功举办了十届全国建材会，吸引了大批的经营者和消费者来此交易，月均成交额突破1.67亿，已成为天津最大的建材交易市场，其影响力和辐射力不断增强。

（赵忆群）

坚持发展外向型经济
滨海新区功能全面提升

2003 年，滨海新区各单位在市委、市政府的领导下，在新区工委的指导下，全面贯彻党的十六大和市委八届三次全会精神，紧紧围绕全市“三步走”战略和五大战略举措，坚持发展外向型经济，全面提升区域功能。新区经济在2002年提前一年实现“十年基本建成滨海新区”后，2003年继续保持了快速健康的发展态势，为实现滨海新区新一轮发展目标打下了坚实基础。

一、国民经济快速健康运行，各功能区优势突出

2003 年，新区经济发展快速健康运行。一季度生产总值增长22.6%，实现了高起步；上半年和前三季度分别增长21.0%和20.5%，保持快速增长；全年实现生产总值999.75亿元，增长20.4%。新区三次产业全面发展，第三产业增速提高。第一产业结构调整效果明显，实现增加值7.39亿元，增长17.1%；第二产业对经济的贡献不断提高，实现增加值693.18亿元，增长20.8%；第三产业发展加快，实现增加值299.18亿元，增长19.6%，增幅比上年提高3.0个百分点。

开发区以高新技术为主的加工制造功能进一步增强。全年实现生产总值445.23亿元，增长25.1%，主要经济指标在国家级开发区中继续保持领先地位。

全年实现高新技术产品产值719.87亿元，增长25.3%，占全区工业总产值的57.5%，电子信息、生物医药、新能源及新材料等高新技术产业快速健康发展。

保税区充分发挥自由贸易功能，一个集海港和空港于一体的国际物流体系正在形成。全年实现生产总值83.02亿元，增长38.2%，其中，交通运输仓储及贸易业实现增加值70.50亿元，对全区经济增长的贡献率达81.0%。全区全年实现货物进出区总值92.31亿美元，比上年净增27.31亿美元，增长42.0%。

塘沽区不断加快商业布局结构和经营业态调整，综合服务功能增强。购物中心、连锁超市等新型商业业态发展势头强劲，规模效应进一步显现。全年实现生产总值53.19亿元，同比增长25.6%，增幅位居全市十八个区县之首，以商贸、旅游为主的服务业实现增加值39.50亿元，对区属经济增长的贡献率达68.7%。

汉沽区加大基础设施建设，为经济快速发展提供有力保障。全年固定资产投资成倍增长，总量规模和发展速度均创历史最好水平。实现生产总值22.21亿元，增长15.3%。

大港区进一步加快城乡一体化进程，优化农业结构，突出工业特色，加快小城镇建设。全年实现生产总值53.24亿元，增长22.0%，其中，农业实现增加值1.30亿元，增长22.8%；工业实现增加值24.24亿元，增长21.2%，工业对经济的贡献率达45.5%。迎宾广场、古海岸遗迹博物馆等设施相继建成，垃圾处理厂三期工程、污排管网工程、污水处理厂一期工程等先后投入使用。

二、工业经济保持快速增长，现代化工业基地建设加快

2003年是新区新一轮发展战略实施的起始年，工业通过大力发展优势行业，提高科技含量，工业生产实现了高速增长。全年完成工业总产值2133.21亿元，比上年增长30.3%。实现工业增加值641.92亿元，增长20.4%，工业对新区经济增长的贡献率达65.3%。工业快速增长的主要特点：

一是支柱产业支撑作用显著，大中型企业拉动作用明显。电子通讯、石油开采和石油化工、海洋化工、现代冶金、机械制造、生物医药、食品加工7大支柱产业全年实现产值1900亿元，占新区工业总产值的比重达90%。摩托罗拉(中国)电子有限公司、中海石油(中国)有限公司天津分公司、中国石油化工股份有限公司天津分公司、天津三星通信技术有限公司等实现产值前10名企业共实现工业总产值1351.90亿元，占新区工业比重达63.4%。天津三星通信技术有限公司等8家三星骨干企业、天津丰田汽车有限公司、天津乐金大沽化学有限公司全年保持快速发展，成为新区工业增长的新亮点。

二是开发区加大技术创新，工业结构不断优化，拉动作用明显。全区完成工业总产值1251.40亿元，增长30.2%，占新区工业总产值的比重为58.7%。实现高新技术产值719.87亿元，增长25.3%。高技术导向型、出口导向型工业产品产量快速增长，全年彩色电视机产量比上年增长78.0%，半导体器件产量增长57.0%，移动电话机产量增长8.6%，轿车产量增长22.2倍。摩托罗拉、霍尼韦尔、斯坦雷、富士通天、松下汽车电子等跨国公司相继在区内设立了研发机构，一批工程中心、研究中心及科技创新群体为提高工业的科技含量提供了有力的技术支持。

三是外商及港澳台商投资企业快速增长，全年完成工业总产值1307.48亿元，增长28.5%，对新区工业增长的贡献率为57.9%。

四是工业产销衔接良好，经济效益提高。全年实现销售产值2125.07亿元，产销率达99.6%，比全市高0.7个百分点。限额以上独立核算工业企业实现销售收入2029.76亿元，增长22.3%，实现利润总额124.13亿元，增长10.1%。

三、出口和利用外资增势强劲，对外开放步伐加快

2003年，新区抢抓全球经济复苏、美元贬值等刺激我国出口的外部机遇，努力改善投资环境，加大支持出口力度，全年始终保持强劲的增长势头。一季度完成出口19.92亿美元，增长48.1%；上半年出口平稳增长，完成39.20亿美元，增长38.1%；前三季度出口达到61.92亿美元，增长30.0%；四季度外贸出口加快，全年累计完成出口89.38亿美元，增长24.1%，占全市出口比重达62.2%。2003年新区外贸出口依存度为75.9%，比上年提高2.5个百分点。

从各区出口完成情况看：(1)开发区仍是中流砥柱。全年完成出口68.86亿美元，增长20.7%，占新区出口的比重为77.0%。出口保持快速增长的原因：一是全区大企业拉动作用明显。出口额超过1000万美元的企业有43家，出口总额64.25亿美元，占全区比重为93.3%，出口超亿美元的企业有9家，出口总额51.67亿美元，占全区比重为75.0%。二是大宗出口产品作用不断增强。移动电话、集成电路、激光唱机和视盘机、彩色电视机等出口额前10种产品占全区出口总额的比重达73.5%。三是出口商品结构更趋合理，机电产品和高新技术产品出口分别完成39.20亿美元和34.05亿美元，占全区出口总额的56.9%和49.4%。四是主要出口市场增势较好。美国仍为最大出口市场，完成出口25.57亿美元，占全区出口总额的37.1%，增长14.5%；对欧盟、东盟及德国、韩国等主要贸易伙伴的出口共占全区出口的44.6%，分别增长58.2%、34.2%、71.5%和20.2%。(2)各区出口均呈增长态势。保税区全年完成出口5.00亿美元，增长31.5%；塘沽、汉沽及大港三区分别完成出口1.86亿美元、0.38亿美元及2.97亿美元，分别增长80.8%、4.1%及31.9%。

2003年，新区抓住跨国公司对我国加大转移的契机，克服“非典”等不利因素，优化招商政策，扩大招商规模，提高引资质量，取得显著成效。全年直接利用外资合同金额24.52亿美元，增长58.5%，实际直接利用外资12.15亿美元，增长47.6%。主要特点：一是大型跨国公司投资增多。美国丹纳赫集团、荷兰阿克苏诺贝尔涂料、比利时绿源及日本松下汽车电子、京瓷太阳能电池、马来西亚北亚渤迪等知名企业相继落户新区；二是大项目增长快。新区全年新批三资企业458家，增长33.5%，其中500万美元以上的大项目142家，增长43.4%，占全市198个大项目的71.7%，开发区全年新批1000美元以上项目50家，其中全球500强项目9家。开发区和保税区仍是利用外资的主体。开发区直接利用外资合同金额12.78亿美元，增长43.0%，实际直接利用外资6.33亿美元，增长54.3%。保税区直接利用外资合同金额9.67亿美元，增长83.9%，实际直接利用外资4.02亿美元，增长71.0%。两区实现直接利用外资合同金额和实际直接利用外资占新区的比重分别91.8%和85.1%。

四、固定资产投资高位运行，现代化新城区建设加快

2003年是新区固定资产投资规模最大，增速最高的一年。全年固定资产投资呈现高开高走，快速稳定增长态势。年初以54.4%的高速度开工建设；一季度增长75.5%，增速进一步加快；上半年和前三季度分别增长76.6%及74.4%，保持快速增长。全年完成固定资产投资464.08亿元，增长65.2%。其中基本建设投资257.81亿元，增长56.5%，更新改造投资112.01亿元，增长40.7%，房地产开发投资80.49亿元，增长1.5倍。

投资结构继续改善，二、三产业趋于协调。从产业投向看，第一产业完成投资1.51亿元，比上年下降1.2%；第二产业完成投资211.56亿元，增长59.6%；第三产业完成投资251.01亿元，增长71.0%。三次产业的投资结构为:0.3:45.6:54.1。

基础设施和重点项目建设加快，新区面貌焕然一新，城市载体和服务功能增强。全年基础设施投资122.57亿元，完成年计划的102.1%，占新区固定资产投资的26.4%。全长45.79公里的津滨轻轨竣工通车，全年累计投资24.67亿元；海河外滩公园、泰达市民广场、航母旅游等环境工程共完成投资9.38亿元。一批重点项目相继完工，丹拉公路支线天津南段投资9.50亿元、泰达国际心血管病医院投资5.46亿元、泰达图书馆投资3.03亿元。泰达足球场、国际会议中心、滨海金融区等项目建设进展顺利。

工业投资力度加大。随着天津市工业东移步伐加快及新一轮嫁改调全面启动，新区工业投入不断增长。天钢东移全年累计投资28.58亿元，钢管公司二套轧机投资6.03亿元，大港发电厂投资4.59亿元。同时，油田加大勘探力度，中海石油(中国)有限公司天津分公司投资50.84亿元，中国石油大港油田分公司投资17.59亿元。2003年，开发区工业项目固定资产投资额超过千万元以上的项目有79个，超过亿元的项目13个，为区内经济发展提供了后劲。

各区投资增势强劲，对经济增长拉动作用显著。开发区完成投资130.53亿元，增长26.8%，保税区完成投资31.20亿元，增长1.0倍，塘沽区完成投资23.80亿元，增长42.2%，汉沽区完成投资9.61亿元，增长1.6倍，大港区完成投资13.05亿元，增长17.0%。

五、港口、贸易、物流功能增强，服务业发展空间扩大

天津港“航线开发与货源开发相互促进”取得实效，港口货物集散功能进一步增强。2003年，天津港实现新的历史性突破，货物吞吐量和集装箱吞吐量均创历史最好水平，全年完成货物吞吐量16182万吨，同比增长25.4%，完成集装箱吞吐量301.54万TEU，同

比增长25.2%。港口功能进一步增强:一是支柱性货类稳定增长。全年经济的增长带动了电力、石油、金属矿石等能源和原材料需求的增加,煤炭、石油、金属矿及集装箱四大支柱性货类实现全港吞吐量的82.6%;二是大型专业化泊位作用增强。全港年吞吐量超过500万吨的泊位达到10个,完成的吞吐量占全港货物吞吐量的44%;三是港口建设加大,提高了港口吞吐能力。全年完成投资21.43亿元,增长26.5%,其中基本建设完成投资20.21亿元,增长25.9%,更新改造完成投资1.22亿元,增长37.6%,集装箱物流中心、北大防坡堤、十五万吨级航道、东突堤北侧集装箱码头改扩建等工程进展顺利。

保税区充分发挥区位优势,贸易、物流功能不断增强。2003年,保税区通过加快通关速度,便捷外汇结算,进一步完善贸易环境,对内、对外贸易取得双丰收。全年完成进出口总额36.19亿美元,增长70.7%。2003年,保税区加快对物流业的扶持力度,一方面大力引进知名物流企业,全年引进物流企业47家,比上年增长14.5倍。同时积极扩展物流基地发展空间,全面建设海港保税区、空港物流加工区和空港国际物流区,并搭建了三区相互联接的公共信息平台,国际物流中心建设迈上新台阶。进口汽车成为拉动全区物流业快速增长的主导因素,全年共分拨、销售进口汽车4.9万部,增长13.6%,继续保持全国领先地位。

商贸、旅游、会展等现代服务业不断发展。2003年,解放路步行街、友谊名都等一批商贸设施陆续建成开业;基辅号航母、舰船游乐港等旅游项目如期落位;国际大学生龙舟赛、亚洲男排锦标赛及PECC国际贸易投资博览会等一系列活动在新区举办,展示了天津滨海新区的形象,扩大了影响力,带动了新区服务业的发展。

总的看,2003年新区在功能开发、结构调整和扩大开放等方面取得显著成效,在区域经济发展中的战略地位进一步增强。2004年是天津市实施“三步走”战略第二步目标的第一年,也是滨海新区新一轮发展的关键年,按照全市“整体推进,协调发展,追求高水平,实现新跨越”的工作总要求,新区各单位要继续保持开拓创新、奋力拼搏的精神,进一步坚持深化改革,扩大开放,实现新区更大的发展目标。

(王稳)

城镇就业总量继续增加
劳动报酬增势强劲

2003年,天津市各行各业认真贯彻落实市委、市政府部署,积极化解非典带来的负面影响,国民经济保持了持续、快速、健康发展,“三步走”战略第一步目标胜利实现。就业和再就业工作收到明显效果,城镇单位从业人员劳动报酬增势强劲,呈现职工收入与经济增长协调发展的良好态势。

一、城镇从业人员的现状及特点

截止2003年底,天津市拥有城镇从业人数259.12万人。包括:城镇单位从业人员204.21万人;私营经济从业人员42.45万人;个体经济从业人员12.46万人。城镇第一产业从业人员为1.41万人;第二产业为112.52万人;第三产业为145.19万人。三次产业分别比上年增加0.21万人、5.82万人和2.67万人。第三产业从业人员占全部从业人员的比重已达56.03%。

(一)国有、集体经济单位从业人员继续减少

2003年底,天津市城镇国有、集体经济单位从业人员为115.53万人,比上年减少8.77万人,下降7.1%。

1、2003年,国有经济的从业人员为101.57万人,比2002年减少6.22万人,下降5.8%;集体经济从业人员为13.96万人,减少了2.51万人,下降了15.2%。国有经济、集体经济占全部从业人员的比重由上年的49.62%下降为44.59%,下降了5.03个百分点。

2、在国有经济中,企业减员仍是单位减员的主因。2003年国有企业、机关、事业单位从业人员分别为56.58万人、12.36万人和32.64万人,企业比上年减少了6.70万人、机关增加了0.70万人,事业减少了0.21万人。

3、减员主要集中在制造业。2003年,天津市国有、集体城镇单位从业人员中,第二产业为39.79万人,比上年减少5.82万人。其中:制造业减少3.58万人。

(二)非公有制经济从业人数大量增加

2003年,天津市非公有制经济从业人员为143.59万人,比上年增加17.44万人,增长13.8%。非公有制经济从业人员占全部从业人员的比重为55.4%,比上年提高5个百分点。但在非公有制经济

中，不同类型单位的从业人员走势差异较大。

1、城镇私营经济从业人员持续上升，而个体经济从业人员则有所下降。2003年，天津市城镇私营经济从业人员为42.45万人，比上年增加6.76万人，增长18.9%；个体经济从业人员为12.46万人，比上年减少0.61万人，下降了4.67%。

2、三资企业从业人员增加较多。截止2003年底，天津市三资企业的从业人员为45.60万人，比上年增加了4.39万人，增长了10.7%。其中：港、澳、台商投资企业从业人员11.45万人，比上年减少0.07万人，下降了0.6%；外商投资企业从业人员34.15万人，比上年增加4.47万人，增长15.1%。

3、联营企业、股份制企业、有限责任公司等单位从业人员有较大增加。2003年底，天津市达41.54万人，比上年增加了5.35万人，增长了14.8%。

二、城镇单位从业人员劳动报酬总额增长加快

2003年，天津市城镇单位共发放从业人员劳动报酬总额350.6亿元，比上年增加44.8亿元，增长14.6%，增长幅度比上年提高了5个百分点，创五年来增幅最高水平。

(一)各种经济类型单位劳动报酬增长全面提速

2003年，国有经济单位从业人员劳动报酬总额194.8亿元，比上年增加12.4亿元，增长6.8%；集体经济为15.5亿元，比上年减少0.1亿元，同比降低了0.9%；由于企业的改组改制，其他经济(包括三资企业、联营企业、股份制企业、有限责任公司等，下同)从业人员队伍不断壮大，由去年的62.9万人增加到今年的75.5万人，其他经济单位在从业人员和人均劳动报酬分别比上年增长20%和12.6%的双重作用下，劳动报酬总额达到140.3亿元，比上年增加32.5亿元，增长30.2%。三种经济类型单位从业人员劳动报酬总额增速分别比上年提高了3.4、7.3和4.1个百分点，对天津市劳动报酬总额增长的贡献率分别为27.7%、-0.3%和72.6%。其他经济单位是各经济类型中增长最快、对天津市增长拉动作用最大的。

(二)企业单位劳动报酬增长创近年来最好水平

2003年，天津市企业单位发放劳动报酬总额264.6亿元，比上年增加36.3亿元，增长15.9%，增速比上年提高了6.8个百分点，创近年来最好水平。其中地方企业比上年增长达到19.3%，成为拉动天津市劳动报酬总额加快增长的主要因素。事业单位为62.2亿元，比上年增加5.7亿元，增长10.1%，增幅较上年回落了0.6个百分点；机关单位为23.8亿元，比上年增加2.7亿元，增长12.9%，增幅较上年提高了0.2个百分点。

三、各类单位从业人员人均劳动报酬快速增长

(一)经济发展带动从业人员劳动报酬水平同步增长

2003年，天津市经济增长的质量和速度同步提高，综合实力显著增强，天津市GDP增长达到14.5%，比上年提高2个百分点，为从业人员劳动报酬的快速增长奠定了坚实的物质基础。天津市城镇单位从业人员人均劳动报酬达到18511元，比上年增加2358元，增长14.6%，增速较上年提高了0.7个百分点。从业人员劳动报酬水平增长与经济发展相适应。

从经济类型看，国有经济单位人均劳动报酬为18929元，比上年增加2307元，增长13.9%；集体经济为10865元，比上年增加1719元，增长18.8%；股份有限公司达到24033元，是天津市平均水平的1.3倍；外商投资企业为21098元；各种联营公司为18182元；有限责任公司为18417元；股份合作公司为16452元；港澳台投资企业为16875元。

(二)企业单位职工收入增速领先

2003年，天津市企业经济效益稳步提高，从业人员劳动报酬增长加快，人均劳动报酬达到18347元，比上年增加2536元，增长16.0%，增幅较上年提高了2个百分点。企业单位在天津市单位从业人员中的比重占到76.1%，其劳动报酬的加快增长成为拉动天津市城镇单位从业人员劳动报酬增长的主要动力。与此同时，事业机关单位从业人员劳动报酬继续保持增长态势，但增幅回落。2003年，事业单位人均劳动报酬为18717元，比上年增加1789元，增长10.6%；机关单位为19915元，比上年增加1724元，增长9.5%。增幅分别比上年回落了2.6和5.3个百分点。2003年，企业单位人均劳动报酬增加额分别高于事业、机关单位747元和812元，增速分别快于事业、机关单位5.4和6.5个百分点。人均劳动报酬差距进一步缩小，以企业单位为1，2002年三者之间的比例为1:1.07:1.15，2003年缩小到1:1.02:1.09。企业单位人均劳动报酬与事业、机关单位的差额由2002年的1117元、2380元缩小到2003年的370元和1568元。

(三)八个行业收入水平突破2万元，一个行业突

破3万元

从国民经济20个行业看，12大行业从业人员人均劳动报酬高于天津市平均水平。其中8大行业收入水平突破2万元，涉及从业人员44.7万人，占全部城镇单位从业人员的23.4%。与上年相比，人均收入2万元以上的多了23.8万人，占全部从业人员比重上升了12.1个百分点。

信息传输、计算机服务和软件业以高科技含量劳动和高附加值产品，使劳动报酬水平遥遥领先，已突破3万元，位居20行业之首，达到33441元，比位居第二的电力、燃气及水的生产和供应业高出7652元，高于天津市平均水平14930元。其次是电力、燃气及水的生产和供应业25789元；位居第三位的是金融业24060元。

行业间劳动报酬差距呈扩大趋势。水平最高的信息传输、计算机服务和软件业人均劳动报酬是天津市平均水平的1.8倍，而最低的住宿和餐饮业仅相当于天津市平均水平的67.2%，最高与最低的行业收入水平差距达到20995元。

（杨霞）

城市居民家庭收入持续快速增长
消费结构升级 生活质量提高

2003年在全面建设小康社会的热潮中，全市人民齐心合力战胜了突如其来的"非典"疫情，经济保持健康快速增长，顺利实现了"三步走"第一步发展目标，为进一步提高城乡居民生活水平和改善居民生活环境，提高城市居民生活质量创造了条件。

据市城调队抽样调查资料显示，2003年城市居民家庭人均可支配收入为10313元，比上年增长10.5%；居民家庭人均消费性支出为7868元，比上年增长9.4%。

一、居民家庭可支配收入保持了较好增长势头

2003年，在积极发展非公有制经济政策的推动下，私营、个体经济快速发展，拓宽了就业渠道；天津各系统的企业和行政机关事业单位认真落实市委、市政府关于努力增加职工收入的精神，使全市城镇单位从业人员劳动报酬总额加快增长，城市居民的收入水平继续提高。

（一）工薪收入是拉动居民家庭收入增长的主要因素

2003年天津城市居民家庭收入中来自工薪方面的收入家庭人均为6664元，比上年增长10.1%，占居民家庭总收入的60.7%。其中，工资及补贴收入家庭人均6386元，比上年增长10.8%。工薪收入的增长额在家庭总收入的增长额中占54.1%。

工薪收入增长的主要因素，一是2002年年末机关、事业单位增资和企业职工工资增长及年终奖的影响；二是2003年企业职工工资较大幅度的增长和11、12月份机关、事业单位两次提高职工工资的影响。

（二）经营净收入稳步增长

2003年居民家庭收入中来自个体经营净收入家庭人均为469元，比上年增长7.1%。主要是大力发展非公所有制经济，实施一系列优惠扶植政策，特别是在"非典"时期，通过减免税收等优惠政策，保证了个体私营经济效益的稳步增长。

（三）转移性收入明显增长

2003年居民家庭收入中来自转移性收入家庭人均为3743元，比上年增长16.0%。主要是年内提高了机关事业单位离退休人员工资及企业离退休人员生活补贴。据调查，2003年养老金及离退休金收入家庭人均2851元，比上年增长22.2%。

（四）财产性收入下降

2003年居民家庭收入中来自财产性方面的收入家庭人均为96元，比上年下降22.3%。主要是股息与红利收入比上年下降46.9%，但利息及房屋租金收入则分别比上年增长18.3%和88.8%。

二、居民家庭消费性支出稳步增长，消费结构升级，生活质量提高

（一）交通和通讯支出增势强劲

2003年居民家庭用于交通和通讯支出人均为721元，比上年增长26.5%。其中，居民家庭交通支出比上年增长了22.5%；通信支出比上年增长29.4%。

由于各种家用经济型轿车已开始进入居民家庭，交通工具开始了新一轮的升级换代。调查资料显示，到2003年末，天津城市居民家庭百户拥有家用汽车2.2辆，比上年增加了1辆，增长83.3%。居民家庭用于通信服务支出比上年增长了26.9%。到2003年年末，居民家庭百户拥有手机已达77.8部，比上年增长72.1%。

（二）居住消费增幅显著

2003年居民家庭用于居住方面的支出家庭人均为1096元，比上年增长17.5%。其中，居民租赁房屋支出人均141元，比上年增长12.0%；住房装潢支出人均295元，比上年增长20.8%。生活质量的改善使居民家庭用于水电燃料等方面支出增加，人均611元，比上年增长38.1%。

（三）杂项商品和服务支出明显增长，个人用品上档次讲时尚

2003年居民家庭用于杂项商品和服务方面支出人均为258元，比上年增长15.9%。随着生活水平的不断提高，居民购买个人饰品及用品支出增加，档次提高。其中，金银珠宝饰品支出比上年增长30.4%；化妆品支出比上年增长12.3%；理发洗澡费比上年增长7.4%。

（四）食品消费稳步增长，饮食注重营养保健

2003年居民家庭用于食品支出人均为2964元，比上年增长13.7%。其中，粮油类支出比上年增长13.2%，居民家庭全年人均粮食购买量比上年增长8.1%；油脂类购买量比上年增长17.6%。肉禽蛋水产品类支出比上年增长13.3%。蔬菜类支出比上年增长18.8%，居民家庭全年人均鲜菜购买量比上年增长11.2%。糕点、奶及奶制品支出比上年增长20.5%。

居民家庭饮食更加注重营养、保健和时令安全。调查资料显示，2003年居民家庭人均用于鲜奶及酸奶支出分别为89元和17元，比上年分别增长36.9%和60.8%，购买量分别比上年增长36.7%和56.7%。水产品、干鲜瓜果和瓶装饮用水人均支出分别为272元、242元和13元，比上年分别增长17.3%、12.6%和13.8%。其中瓶装饮用水购买量比上年增长36.5%。另外，随着人们饮食观念的转变，居民家庭在外用餐支出明显增加，人均612元，比上年增长13.3%。

（五）医疗保健支出继续增长

2003年居民家庭用于医疗保健支出家庭人均698元，比上年增长11.7%。

2003年的非典疫情使天津市居民健康意识逐步增强。调查资料显示，2003年居民家庭用于药品费比上年增长19.1%；滋补保健品支出比上年增长1.1倍；保健器具支出比上年增长91.1%。

（六）设备用品及服务支出下降，新兴耐用消费品成为消费热点

2003年居民家庭用于设备用品及服务支出人均为467元，比上年下降6.7%。

在家庭日用耐用消费品中，冰箱、洗衣机的霸主地位已风光不再，一些新兴的家庭耐用消费品成为本年度居民家庭消费热点。调查资料显示，到2003年末，城市居民家庭百户拥有微波炉61.4台、空调器90.9台、取暖器21.8台、淋浴热水器82.7台、消毒碗柜1.4台、饮水机31.3台、吸尘器24.3台，分别比上年增长20.1%、12.4%、84.7%、4.7%、1.1倍、61.9%和15.0%。

（七）娱乐文教服务支出有所下降，素质教育费用提高

2003年居民家庭用于娱乐文教服务支出人均1084元，比上年下降5.8%。其中，文化娱乐耐用消费品比上年下降8.6%；文化娱乐服务支出比上年下降10.2%；教育支出比上年下降3.4%。

建立学习型社会，追求人的发展高素质，已经成为当今社会人们的共识。统计资料显示，2003年城市居民家庭人均用于参加各类培训班、成人教育和家教费用支出人均为31元、73元和11元，分别比上年增长63.8%、61.8%和9.0%。

另外，一些文娱耐用消费品拥有量也呈上升趋势。到2003年末，居民家庭百户拥有家用电脑34.1台、摄像机3.4台、影碟机49.6台、健身器材5.4套，分别比上年增长29.8%、27.3%、10.1%和35.0%。

（八）衣着支出略有下降，成衣档次提高

2003年居民家庭用于衣着支出人均为580元，比上年下降0.6%。其中，衣着材料比上年下降18.4%；衣着加工费比上年下降5.7%。

生活水平的提高使广大居民家庭从过去买布做衣转变为越来越多地选择购买成衣。资料显示，居民家庭用于购买每件成衣服装的价格比上年增长了9.6%。

三、非消费性支出显著增长

（一）购建房支出增势强劲

2003年随着天津市新一轮的城市危陋平房改造和城市基础设施建设以及海河开发，拆迁安置货币化拉动了城市居民家庭住房消费。全年城市居民家庭人均用于购建房支出为1640元，比上年增长29.0%。调查资料还显示，城市居民家庭2003年用于购买住房

的贷款人均为561元，比上年增长1.1倍。

（二）居民家庭社会保障意识增强

广大居民家庭保障意识的增强促使居民社会保险支出增加。统计资料显示，2003年城市居民家庭人均用于社会保障支出571元，比上年增长27.4%。其中，家庭人均缴纳养老基金215元，比上年增长26.3%；缴纳住房公积金278元，比上年增长31.4%；缴纳医疗保险基金50元，比上年增长25.0%；缴纳失业保险基金24元，比上年增长32.3%。

（三）居民家庭转移性支出和财产性支出显著增长

2003年天津城市居民家庭人均用于转移性支出为999元，比上年增长29.3%。其中，车辆保险基金支出比上年增长2.9倍；财产性支出比上年增长1.2倍。

（吴向晨）

农村居民收入进一步提高 生活水平又上新台阶

2003年，天津农村居民人均纯收入达到5861元，比去年同期增加546元，增长10.3%，继续保持两位数增长，在收入持续快速增长的同时，人均生活消费支出达到3015元，首次突破3000元大关，比上年增加237元，增长8.5%。

一、农村居民收入快速增长

（一）家庭经营第一产业纯收入加快增长

2003年，随着农业结构调整的力度加大，特别是棉花种植面积首次超过百万亩，加之农产品价格的大幅上扬，家庭经营第一产业纯收入增长明显加快，人均达到1533元，增长10.9%，比去年加快4.8个百分点，占纯收入的比重为26.2%，为纯收入增长贡献了2.8个百分点，贡献率为27.7%。从内部结构看，农业纯收入人均1178元，同比增加118元，增长11.1%，占第一产业纯收入的比重为76.8%，对第一产业纯收入增长的贡献率达到78.1%，是第一产业增收的最重要的支撑点；畜牧业纯收入人均166元，同比增加26元，增长18.6%，对第一产业纯收入增长的贡献率为17.2%；渔业纯收入人均175元，同比增加7元，增长4.2%，对第一产业纯收入增长的贡献率为4.6%；林业纯收入人均14元，与去年持平。

（二）工资性收入继续增加

2003年，天津农村居民在各种单位劳动得到的工资性收入人均达到3248元，比上年增加309元，增长10.5%，占纯收入的比重为55.4%，工资性收入为人均纯收入增长贡献了5.8个百分点，贡献率为56.6%，仍是农民增收的主要支撑点。工资性收入的持续增长主要得益于本地劳务经济的快速发展。2003年，天津农民在本乡地域内劳动得到的各种工资性收入人均达到2371元，同比增加293元，增长14.1%，拉动工资性收入提高10.0个百分点，对工资性收入增长的贡献率达94.8%。本地劳务收入占工资性收入的比重为73.0%，比上年提高了2.3个百分点。其中农民在本地企业劳动得到的收入人均2143元，同比增加214元，增长11.1%。

受"非典"疫情影响，部分外出农民返乡，天津农村居民外出从业收入明显减少，人均为201元，同比减少22元，下降9.9%，减缓工资性收入提高0.7个百分点，占工资性收入的比重为6.2%，比上年下降了1.4个百分点。

农民从乡村集体和国家行政事业单位等非企业组织中劳动得到的工资性收入继续增加，人均达到676元，同比增加38元，增长6.0%，拉动工资性收入提高1.3个百分点，对工资性收入增长的贡献率为12.3%，占工资性收入的比重为20.8%，比上年下降了0.9个百分点。

（三）家庭经营二、三产业纯收入增速放缓

2003年，受"非典"疫情影响，天津农民家庭经营二、三产业纯收入增速明显放缓，人均816元，比上年增加58元，增长7.7%，增幅比上年低9.6个百分点。为人均纯收入增长贡献1.1个百分点，贡献率为10.6%，比上年降低了12.2个百分点。家庭经营二、三产业纯收入占纯收入的比重为13.9%。分行业看，经营工业纯收入增长18.2%，回落19.2个百分点；建筑业增长7.8%，回落3.5个百分点；交通运输、仓储和邮政业增长7.4%，回落19.9个百分点；批发和零售业增长11.6%，回落15.1个百分点；社会服务业增长6.9%，回落5.2个百分点；文教卫生业增长3.8%，回落26.2个百分点。

（四）转移性、财产性收入增长迅速

2003年，天津农村居民来自转移性、财产性等非经营性的纯收入人均达到264元，比上年增加28元，增长11.9%，为人均纯收入增长贡献了0.5个百分点，贡献率为5.1%，比上年提高0.6个百分点，占纯收入的比重为4.5%。其增长特点：一是随着农村固定资产投资规模的不断扩大和城市化进程的不断加快，农民因土地征用而获得的补偿收入显著增加，人均达到57元，占转移性、财产性纯收入的比重已达21.6%；二是受国家调整工资政策的影响，居住在农村的离退休职工的退休金或养老金收入快速增长，人均增至54元，增长20.0%；三是外来打工人员增多，农民出租房屋等获得的租金收入大幅增长，人均达到42元，增长20.0%。

二、生活消费水平明显提高

（一）食品消费支出增长较快，恩格尔系数略有上升

2003年，天津农村居民人均食品消费支出为1156元，同比增加94元，增长8.9%，拉动生活消费支出提高了3.4个百分点，贡献率为39.7%。食品支出占生活消费支出的比重，即恩格尔系数为38.3%，与2002年相比，提高了0.1个百分点。

（二）居住和交通通讯仍为农村居民消费的亮点

2003年农村居民用于居住方面的支出人均达到694元，同比增加116元，增长20.1%，比上年提高了8.7个百分点，拉动生活消费支出提高4.2个百分点，贡献率为48.9% 。用于交通通讯方面的消费支出人均达到216元，同比增加21元，增长10.8%，拉动生活消费支出提高了0.8个百分点，贡献率为8.9%。从拥有量看：电话机和手机每百户拥有量达到84部和54部，分别比上年增长5.0%和50.0%；生活用汽车3辆，与上年持平。

（三）文教娱乐和医疗保健消费支出稳步增长

2003年，天津农村居民人均文教娱乐用品及服务支出246元，同比增加12元，增长5.1%，拉动生活消费支出提高0.4个百分点，贡献率为5.1%；人均医疗保健支出230元，同比增加10元，增长4.5%，拉动生活消费支出提高0.4个百分点，贡献率为4.2%。

（四）衣着消费小幅增长

2003年，农村居民人均衣着消费支出266元，同比增加3元，增长1.1%。

（五）家庭设备及用品消费支出下降，拥有量增加

2003年，天津农村居民用于购买家庭设备、用品及服务的消费支出人均为105元，同比减少8元，下降7.1%。但随着家用电器市场价格的下降，农村居民购买家庭设备的数量继续增长，主要家庭设备拥有量进一步增加。2003年末，洗衣机、空调机和微波炉每百户拥有量分别达到90台、32台和10台，比上年分别增长4.7%、23.1%和42.9%。

（六）服务性消费大幅增长

随着农村居民物质生活水平的不断提高，人们的消费观念悄然变化，农村居民家庭用于服务性消费的支出得到快速增长。2003年，天津农村居民服务性消费支出人均达到800.16元，同比增加89.64元，增长12.6%，占生活消费支出的比重达到26.5%，比上年提高0.9个百分点。

（王福泉）

居民消费价格水平小幅回升

2003年天津市国民经济持续快速发展，特别是投资的快速增长、工业发展以及出口形势良好，在有效推动经济快速增长的同时，也促进了物价运行形势随之有所好转，物价低迷状况有所缓解。居民消费价格同比指数自2002年9月份止跌回升以来持续12个月在100以上，虽然2003年9月份以后的3个月，由于上年上调的学杂费翘尾影响的结束，居民消费价格又出现负增长，但对全年居民消费价格水平的增长幅度影响并不大。与上年相比，2003年全年居民消费价格指数为101.0，比2002年高出1.4个百分点。

2003年商品零售价格同比指数呈现先扬后抑再回升的“V”字型走势。但从总体上看，商品零售价格水平依然呈现明显的下降态势。这也是自2001年5月份商品零售价格同比指数再次下降以来，持续了32个月的下降走势。2003年全年商品零售价格指数为97.4，降幅与2002年持平。

一、服务项目价格水平虽仍呈现刚性上涨态势，但对总指数的拉升作用明显减弱

2003年天津市安排的调价项目采取审慎稳妥的态度，只在上半年安排上调了管道煤气的收费；9月份起托幼保育费收费标准有所上调；公园门票和录像电影票价格在价格上调的同时，实行淡旺季浮动价格收费标准。上述项目对总指数的拉升作用有限，只影响居民消费价格指数上涨0.7个百分点。同时，由于

天津市2002年服务项目价格的走势前低后高，上调的房租、学杂费等翘尾影响在2003年下半年相继结束后，服务项目价格涨幅开始明显回落，拉动居民消费价格总指数上升的力度进一步减弱。特别是2003年9月份，服务项目中影响力度最大的学杂费翘尾影响结束后，当月居民消费价格指数重现负增长的局面。2003年全年天津市服务项目价格水平同比上涨7.8%，共影响居民消费价格指数上涨2个百分点。

二、农副产品等食品涨价直接推动居民消费价格指数的上升

受国际和国内市场供求关系的影响，2003年天津市粮食价格扭转了自2002年下半年以来连续下跌的态势，呈现出“刚性”上扬。2003年以来，特别是10月份以后，粮食、食用油等农产品价格出现的短期内持续大面积地上涨，这在近6年来还是首次。近几年来国家退耕还林、退耕还湖政策的实施，农业结构调整力度的加大，以及前一阶段种粮效益相对较低，长期"低价"徘徊的粮价影响了农民种粮的积极性，使粮食的种植面积逐步减少。而我国北方地区粮食生产受春旱和生长期低温阴雨，南方地区受洪涝灾害以及持续干旱的影响，粮食收成减产，与此同时，农户存在一定的惜卖心理也使得粮食供需缺口进一步加大，市场供需矛盾趋紧，在市场调节下，粮食价格普遍上涨。2003年10月份以后，我国的大豆进口明显减少，同时由于在2003年秋季，我国部分大豆主产区受灾严重，大豆收获量大幅度下降，进一步加剧了大豆供求矛盾。许多食用油生产厂家原料供应不足，生产停滞，豆油上市量减少，供应紧张；另一方面，居民的集中购买及少数居民的抢购现象，也使得豆油的供求矛盾更加突出，豆油价格骤涨。尽管后期天津市油脂类价格有所回落，但仍在高价位运行，从全年情况看，2003年全年天津市粮食价格水平同比上涨2.1%，油脂类价格水平同比上涨11.5%。

粮价的变动具有“一价带百价”的敏感效应。对整个食品市场价格走势起着举足轻重的作用。粮食价格的上涨不仅直接拉动食品和居民消费价格总水平的上涨，而且带动以粮食为主要原料的饲养业价格的上涨。另外，非典时期部分养殖业如蛋鸡接雏减少，仔猪存栏下降，经过一段滞后期后，对市场的影响开始显现，鲜蛋、猪肉上市量的减少，直接引起价格的上扬。与上年相比，鲜蛋和猪肉价格分别上涨2.3%和4.4%。

随着农产品种植结构调整力度的加大和农产品优质化进程的加快，天津市蔬菜的生产向产业化、设施化方向发展，绿色产品、无公害产品的种植面积和比重不断增长，在质量得以提高的同时，农产品的内在比价也不断提升。另外，2002年冬天的严寒、2003年春天的阴雨以及全国大范围干旱旱情对种植业尤其是蔬菜种植业产生了较大的影响。年内全国范围的持续高温干旱，以及部分省市遭遇水灾、暴雨和台风等异常天气的影响下蔬菜产量下降，以及受运输等非市场因素的影响，导致蔬菜上市量明显减少，蔬菜价格陡扬的现象也波及到天津市。从全年的整体情况看，天津市鲜菜价格水平比上年上涨23.8%，影响食品类价格指数上涨1.9个百分点，影响总指数上涨0.6个百分点，成为拉动价格总水平回升的重要因素。

三、供大于求的格局下，大多数工业消费品价格降多涨少的状况依然存在

在上世纪八十年代末九十年代初形成的一轮消费热潮结束之后，经过十几年的培育和引导以及消费能力的不断积聚，天津市消费结构出现升级趋势，加之扩大内需成效的进一步显现，经济自主增长的动力逐步增强，并逐步成为拉动经济保持快速增长的持久动力和消费需求扩张的主要支撑力。住房、汽车、通讯、旅游、教育和文化体育休闲等消费热点日益成熟并持续升温，引导了房地产、汽车、电子、通信、旅游等行业的快速增长。此外，2003年天津市如火如荼进行的海河综合开发和城市基础设施建设，在强力带动破旧房屋的大规模拆迁，改变市容市貌的同时，也有力地拉动了建材、装修、装饰、家具以及家电等行业生产及销售。在消费热点需求的强劲增长下，生产者根据市场需求积极调整生产结构，商品市场质量和供求结构不断改善，市场供求有所好转，商品供求矛盾有所缓解。但由于工业消费品供大于求的格局基本没有改变，一些商品的供求矛盾依然突出，穿用商品的价格降多涨少的状况依然存在；衣着、家庭设备用品、交通和通信类价格持续下滑走势。同时由于下岗失业压力较大，居民消费后移而使被动储蓄增加，加剧了供大于求的矛盾，影响了物价的有效回升。除服务性收费项目以及由于棉花、原油价格上涨导致衣着材料以及部分成品油价格上扬外，2003年天津市的工业消费品市场依然沉浸在一片降价声中，衣着类价格水平同比下降11.9%，影响总指数下降0.9个百分点，并成为拉动价格总水平下行的重要因素。此外，医疗保健和个人用品类价格水平同比下降6.0%，家庭设备用品及维修服务类价格水平同比下降3.5%，交通和通信类价格水平同比下降了3.0%。

（张栩）

工业品价格涨势明显

今年天津工业生产持续保持快速发展，与此同时，反映工业经济运行状况的工业品价格指数也呈现积极变化，扭转了天津工业品出厂价格连续两年下降的局面，出现止跌转升的态势，原材料、燃料及动力购进价格持续在高位运行。2003年，全市工业品出厂价格指数比上年增长2.5%，原材料、燃料及动力购进价格比上年增长8.7%。

一、工业品价格运行的主要特点

（一）工业品出厂和原材料购进价格高于上年水平，但各月价格变化波动较大

2003年工业品出厂价格总水平高于上年，指数为102.5。全年各月价格指数的变动呈现出一条波浪曲线。前8个月出厂价格一直高于上年同期水平，但涨幅不断回落，9、10月份略显下降，11和12月份价格回升。2003年，原材料、燃料及动力购进价格总指数为108.7。各月均高于上年同期水平，各月涨幅波动变化较大。2003年各月工业品出厂和原材料购进同比价格指数具体走势如下：

	1月	2月	3月	4月	5月	6月
工业品出厂价格指数	105.9	107.5	107.3	103.7	101.4	100.2
原材料购进价格指数	108.8	110.4	112.2	108.8	106.9	105.6

	7月	8月	9月	10月	11月	12月
工业品出厂价格指数	101.2	101.6	99.4	99.3	100.5	101.6
原材料购进价格指数	105.9	107.5	107.3	108.4	110.3	112.2

（二）重工业产品价格上涨，轻工业产品价格仍下降

与上年相比，重工业产品价格水平上涨5.1%。在重工业产品中采掘工业产品价格涨幅最大，同比上涨24.7%；其次是原料工业产品价格上涨13.5%；加工工业产品价格下降2.5%。在轻工业产品中，以农产品为原料的产品价格同比上涨3.6%，以非农产品为原料的产品价格同比下降1.9%，拉动轻工业产品价格下降0.4%。重工业产品价格涨幅高于轻工业的格局仍未改变。

（三）行业价格涨跌各半

在天津工业品出厂价格统计涉及的35个工业行业大类中，与上年价格相比，17个行业产品出厂价格上涨，17个行业产品出厂价格下降，各占全部行业大类的48.6%，涨价、降价两种趋势各半。价格涨幅较大的行业有：石油和天然气开采业，黑色金属冶炼及压延加工业，水的生产和供应业，石油加工和化学纤维制造业，与上年相比分别上涨26.1%、22.6%、16.5%、15.6%和14.4%。降幅较大的行业有：通信设备、计算机及其他电子设备制造业，产品价格下降13.9%；交通运输设备制造业，产品价格下降6.9%。

（四）原材料、燃料、动力购进价格持续走高

2003年，原材料、燃料、动力购进价格始终在高价位运行，涨幅比上年上涨8.7%。在原材料九大类分组中，除其它工业原材料及半成品类和木材及纸浆类价格下降外，其余八大类呈不同程度上涨。在价格上涨的八类原材料中，农副产品类价格上涨幅度为最大，同比上涨22.5%；其它依次是黑色金属材料类、燃料动力类和化工原料类，价格分别上涨19.6%、13.1%和11.3%。

二、影响工业品价格上涨的主要原因

（一）原材料价格上涨，成本推动因素增强

2003年，原材料、燃料、动力购进价格总指数108.7。涨幅比上年上涨8.7%，增加了产品的生产成本，进而推动其出厂价格上涨。以纺织行业为例，纺织产品价格的变动主要受棉花、化学纤维等原材料价格影响。2003年，我国产棉区受灾，棉花减产；此外，受国际市场棉花、化纤等纺织原料价格上涨等因素的影响，2003年天津纺织企业购进棉花价格上涨42.9%，纺织原料价格上涨6.2%，拉动纺织产品出厂价格上升7.9%。受原料大豆、玉米等粮食价格上涨影响，农副食品加工产品出厂价格上涨幅度较大。其中，与上年相比，大豆油出厂价格上涨18.3%；蛋白饲料出厂价格上涨9.0%；配合饲料出厂价格上涨7.8%；拉动农副食品加工业涨幅比上年上升10.7个百分点。纺织业和农副食品加工业产品价格上涨成为工业品出厂价格总水平攀升的"新生力军"。

（二）受国际形势及市场价格波动的影响

受"美伊"战争的影响，从2003年年初开始国际市

场原油价格大幅攀升，导致国内石油价格大幅度上涨，天津石油工业产品出厂价格大幅上扬，一季度石油和天然气开采业产品价格同比上涨71.2%。4月份后随着战争结束，价格逐步趋于稳定。2003年原油出厂价格比上年上涨27.4%，拉动工业品出厂价格总水平上涨1.2个百分点。原油价格上涨带动成品油及其下游产品价格不同程度的上涨。石油加工及炼焦业产品价格同比上涨15.6%；化学原料及化学制品制造业产品价格同比上涨8.4%。

（三）受国内需求拉动及市场因素影响

2003年天津经济保持良好的发展态势，固定资产投资增长强劲，城市基础建设、房地产业快速发展，汽车工业产销两旺等都大大增加了对钢材的需求量，加之生产钢材的原料如铁矿石、铁精粉、煤等价格相继上涨，推动钢材价格持续大幅上涨。与上年相比，黑色金属冶炼及压延加工业产品价格上涨22.6%。其中，普碳钢坯上涨27.0%、线材上涨31.3%、螺纹钢上涨32.8%、中厚钢板上涨42.7%。

（四）移动通讯设备、轿车及汽车配件出厂价格下降是影响工业品出厂价格总水平上升幅度低的主要原因。受移动电话市场竞争进一步加剧的影响，价格继续下降，与上年相比移动电话出厂价格下降20.1%，拉动价格总指数下降1.9个百分点。为了保住市场份额，夏利轿车再次降低出厂价格，其中：排气量1.3升夏利轿车与上年相比下降5.7%。微型客车受市场竞争影响，企业也下调微型客车出厂价格，与上年相比下降12.4%。与此同时为配合整车价格下降，汽车配件出厂价格也多次降价，与上年相比汽车配件出厂价格下降11.4%，拉动价格总指数下降0.2个百分点。

（郑萍）

房地产价格持续上涨

2003年天津房地产业在拉动内需、鼓励消费和大规模城市建设的宏观经济背景下，已经进入了一个高速发展时期，在强劲市场需求的依托下，2003年天津房地产业投资、施工、拆迁、销售等各项指标呈全面增长态势，海河综合开发改造、城市基础设施建设为天津房地产的发展注入新的活力，房地产市场急剧升温，商品房销售异常火爆，房地产二级市场交易异常活跃，房屋价格上涨迅猛，有力地推动天津经济和城市建设的全面发展。与上年相比，2003年，房屋销售价格上升4.1%，房屋租赁价格上升0.9%，土地交易价格上升3.0%。

一、2003年天津房地产价格变动特点

（一）房地产销售价格全面上升，价格涨幅逐季增加

2003年天津房屋销售价格指数为104.1，比上年价格上涨4.1%，其价格涨幅比2002年价格涨幅增加1.3个百分点。

从房屋销售环比价格变化情况来看，与上季度相比，除一季度价格下降0.2%外，二、三、四季度的环比价格均呈上升走势，分别上升1.3%、2.8%、4.2%；从同比价格指数变化情况来看，与上年同期相比，各季度同比价格均为上升势头，并呈逐季加大的走势，分别上涨1.5%、2.8%、4.6%、7.5%，在四季度达到近年的最高涨幅。

从2003年各类房屋价格变化看，与上年相比，商品房销售价格上涨4.0%，其中：住宅类中经济适用房上涨6.6%，普通住宅上涨3.2%；非住宅类中的商品用房上涨3.3%；私房交易价格上涨5.0%。

（二）房屋租赁价格总水平变化不大，各季同比价格有升有降

2003年天津房屋租赁价格指数为100.9，仅比上年价格上涨0.9%，其价格涨幅比2002年价格涨幅回落5.1个百分点。

从房屋租赁环比价格变动情况来看，前三季度价格保持平稳，四季度仅上涨0.1%，各季指数变化不大。从同比价格变化来看，各季价格升降各异，与上年同期相比，1、2季度均上涨4.7%，3、4季度分别下降1.3%、3.8%。

（三）土地交易价格继续上涨

2003年天津土地交易价格指数为103.0，比上年上涨3.0%，比上年的上涨幅度高0.2个百分点，继续保持近年来的上涨趋势。

（四）天津房地产价格指数低于全国平均水平，排位居中间位次

与全国房地产价格指数相比，虽然天津房地产价格有一定幅度的上涨，但仍低于全国平均涨幅，排位居中间位次。其中房屋销售价格低0.7个百分点，在全国35大城市排位中居第9位；房屋租赁价格低5.3

个百分点，居第15位；土地交易价格低1.2个百分点，居第18位。

与其它直辖市相比，天津房屋销售价格指数分别比上海、重庆低16个、2.0个百分点，比北京高3.8个百分点；房屋租赁价格指数分别比北京、上海低7.8个、1.5个百分点，比重庆0.4个百分点；土地交易价格指数比上海、重庆低12.5个、12.1个百分点，比北京高2.4个百分点。

二、影响天津房地产价格持续上涨的主要原因

（一）大规模城市建设拉动住房需求

2003年天津全面启动海河两岸综合开发改造和地铁、轻轨等重大基础设施的建设，加大危旧房屋的拆迁力度，全市拆迁面积达500万平方米。由于天津对拆迁居民实行货币化安置，这部分居民只有持币购房，形成对各类房屋的政策性的刚性需求。这是天津今年房地产价格大幅度上升的一个重要原因。

（二）住房供需矛盾拉动房价上升

今年天津继续出台鼓励居民购房的各种政策，加之居民收入水平的逐步提高，大大促进了居民的购房热情，使房地产市场交易空前活跃。尤其是经济适用住房和价格大多在2500元至3500元普通住宅，比较适宜工薪阶层的购买能力，较为热销。但此类房屋开发数量不能满足市场需求，房价张幅较大。随着天津投资环境的不断改善，个体私营企业不断增加，房屋价格的不断攀升，居民投资性购房呈上升趋势。受市场需求影响，2003年，商业用房价格比上年上升3.3%。加之股市低迷等各种因素影响，转向房产投资，二次购房和购多处房产的人已有所增多。

（三）土地拍卖价格大幅上扬

随着天津土地管理制度的不断完善、规范，经营城市理念不断深化，天津土地使用权只能通过拍卖的市场方式进行交易。今年以来，部分土地成交价格皆攀新高，有的拍卖价甚至高出起拍价几倍。其原因有：一是天津城区环境较好的土地经过几年的开发已所剩无几，这使得原来就十分稀少的城市土地资源更趋紧张，从而加剧地价的上升。二是去年下半年以来，受房屋市场销售异常火爆和供求关系的影响，土地价格大幅上升，从而推动房价上升。

（四）住房二级市场发展，进一步活跃了房地产市场

2003年私有住房交易十分活跃，从下半年开始，价格一路呈上涨趋势。3、4季度分别比上年同期上涨7.1%和10.1%。这主要是由于二手房市场刚起步时，由于住房档次低，地理位置较偏，房子旧，价格相对较低。近两年，二手房交易的档次也在不断提高，一些地段较好，房子较新的二手房逐渐增多，交易量的增加，同时也带动了价格的上涨。人们对二手房的概念和认识也有了一些改变。2003年天津出台了降低交易费用、方便房屋交易等措施，鼓励二手房上市交易，这些措施的实施极大的活跃了住房二级市场。住房二级市场的发展，对于天津房地产市场的发展起着较大影响。

（五）房屋建筑成本不断增加

随着房地产开发市场的日臻完善，对房屋建筑质量的要求越来越高。根据建设部的要求，天津自去年提高了房屋建筑材料质量标准，如粘土砖的取缔、楼板要求采用浇铸式等，使房屋建筑成本有所增加。另一方面从天津目前的开发情况看，房屋结构优化程度的不断提高，天津房地产开发企业创品牌，创优质服务，房屋开发由过去的实用、经济型为主，而进入了居住舒适、安康的阶段。房屋从规划、设计，配套设施、绿化面积及周边环境等方面都有较大提高，在一定程度上，使房屋开发费用有所增加，从而影响房屋价格有所提高。

（逄玉涛）

企业经营状况继续向好
企业家信心十足

今年以来，全市各地区、各部门按照市委八届三次全会提出的"三步走"战略，全面启动五大战略举措，积极化解"非典"负面影响，经济增长速度和质量同步提高，全市经济继续在高增长平台上稳步运行，"三步走"战略第一步奋斗目标胜利实现。据对全市八大行业，800家企业景气调查显示，企业家信心指数和企业景气指数都在较高的水平上平稳运行，反映企业生产和运行的主要景气指标明显提高，微观经济的运行质量显著提升。

一、2003年企业景气运行的总体态势

2003年，天津经济发展喜人。全市生产总值完成2386.94亿元，同比增长14.5%。天津宏观经济走势的稳步推进，得益于天津经济的基础细胞—企业的生

机勃勃。调查显示，本年度虽然有“非典”疫情的出现，但天津企业家信心不减，指数走势强劲，各季企业家信心指数都在较高的位置上平稳运行，全年企业家信心指数平均值为127.06，成为自1999年以来的最高年份，表现出企业家们对天津经济发展前景的坚定信心。从企业景气指数全年走势看，一季度全市企业实现高起步，企业景气指数达到126.93，比去年同期提高14.74点，为1999年以来同期最好水平，进入二季度，面对“非典”，天津企业经受住了考验，全市企业景气指数为107.01，依然保持在景气临界点以上，疫情缓解后的三季度天津企业迅速恢复，企业景气指数达到122.62，由二季度的“微景气”区间跳过“相对景气”区间，重新回到一季度的“较为景气区间”。四季度，天津企业再次发力，较三季度再度上扬1.82点，达到124.44点，全年企业景气运行的轨迹呈现"V"字形。

二、2003年企业景气运行中的亮点

（一）“三步走”战略激发企业家信心，企业家信心指数高于去年

本年度，虽然存在"非典"疫情的影响，但随着"三步走"战略的全面实施，企业家对行业看法乐观，信心十足，企业家信心指数全年平均值为127.06，较去年上扬3.44点。其中工业、房地产业、建筑业以及交通运输、仓储及邮电通信业增幅居前，企业家信心指数分别为128.89、160.74、143.36和112.64，增幅分别为6.58点、14.64点、19.59点和7.72点。从不同注册类型企业来看，国有企业、集体企业、私营企业、有限责任公司的企业家信心指数较去年有不同程度的提高，企业家信心指数分别为119.17、96.64、125.55和135.35，增幅分别为0.84点、13.29点10.28点和5.98点。从企业规模看，大型及特大型企业和中小型企业的企业家信心指数全年平均值较去年均有增加，其中大型及特大型企业企业家信心指数全年平均为152.89，位于“较强景气”区间，较去年增7.73点，中小型企业企业家信心指数全年平均为112.14，位于"相对景气"区间，较去年增2.27点。

（二）需求拉动，工业、建筑业、房地产业、批发和零售业以及交通运输、仓储及邮电通信业成为全年最景气的行业

从行业自身发展历程来看，房地产业、批发和零售业以及交通运输、仓储及邮电通信业三个行业本年度全年企业景气指数平均值均为1999年以来的历年最好水平，尤其是在"非典"疫情影响之下，取得这样的成绩就更显可贵。建筑业企业虽然全年景气运行总体情况较2002年略低，但景气指数依然较高，且其在"非典"疫情肆虐的二季度表现突出，当季景气指数为146.8，在全市八大行业中位居首位。今年四季度该行业景气指数为150.93，在全市八大行业中首次超过150的大关，步入"较强景气"区间。从全年各行业景气指数的对比来看，房地产业景气指数以135.7的全年平均值位居首位，其次为工业全年企业景气指数平均值为126.11，建筑业景气指数以123.86，位居第三。

（三）主要景气指标改善明显

从评价企业运行质量的各项综合指标上看，企业流动资金、固定资产投资以及劳动力需求三项指标全年景气指数平均值分别为79.77、111.2和99.04，成为近年来年度景气指数最高均值。如果以2002年为基准，本年度增幅最大的综合指标为劳动力需求指标，较去年上扬5.93点，其次为流动资金指标，景气指数较去年上扬5.18点，同时，固定资产投资上扬幅度也达4.59点。

（四）中小企业和民营经济成为今年亮点

大型及特大型企业以及中小型企业，均为本年一季度企业运行高起步做出了贡献，其中大型及特大型企业一季度企业景气指数达到160.06，位于"较强景气"区间，较去年同期上扬18.43点，中小型企业景气指数为109.56，较去年同期上扬12.3点。二季度“非典”疫情突如其来，两种规模类型企业景气状况均有所回落，其中大型及特大型企业回落至125.25，降幅达34.81点，中小型企业回落至88.64，降幅达20.92点。随着疫情的缓解，两种规模类型的企业均快速回升，体现出天津企业顽强的生命力和快速恢复生产的能力。四季度的数据再次显示出了天津企业的活力，两种规模类型的企业景气指数在三季度急剧回升的基础上，四季度又同时继续回升，其中大型及特大型企业三季度回升至147.07，较二季度回升幅度达21.82，四季度再次发力，达到149.75，上扬幅度达2.68点。中小型企业，三季度企业景气指数大幅上扬23.86点，回升至112.5，四季度再度上扬0.48点，景气指数高达112.98，成为近年来各季度最佳值。

从不同注册类型企业来看，股份有限公司、国有企业以及集体企业景气指数较去年均有不同程度的提高，其中股份有限公司类企业本年度企业景气指数平均值为148.95，较去年上扬7.83点，在“较为景气”

区间高质量运行。集体企业全年企业景气指数平均值为87.75，较去年上扬3.12。国有企业全年企业景气指数平均值为113.31，较去年上扬2.63点。从各注册类型企业纵向比较来看，股份有限公司类企业本年度以企业景气指数148.95高居各行业之首，打破了外商及港澳台企业长期的领先地位，企业景气指数全年平均值之高，在各类型企业中也属罕见。

（五）骨干企业作用明显

从各类重点企业看，各类重点企业在全市经济发展中起到了骨干作用，本年度继续保持了强劲的发展势头。全市上市公司企业景气指数达144.72，在“较为景气”区间中高质量的运行，较去年同期上扬7.45点。国家试点企业集团成员企业景气指数较去年上扬21.09点，达到130.23，同样位于“较为景气”区间。国家重点企业本年度企业景气指数高达167.5，位于“较强景气”区间。各类骨干企业景气指数均远高于全市平均水平，起到了拉动全市企业景气指数总体向好的骨干作用。

三、企业运行中需要关注的重要迹象

（一）原材料价格上扬，企业利润下降

本年度，企业运行中需要关注的重要迹象是主要原材料及能源的供应紧张，价格上扬，利润降低。全市八大行业利润总体指标景气指数全年均值为101.27，较去年下降9.29点，利润降低的主要因素是在产品的销售情况变化不大的情况下，企业主要原材料及能源购进价格的上涨幅度大幅超过产品销售价格的上涨。以工业为例，产品的销售景气指数全年平均为122.62，位于"较为景气"区间，较去年变化不大，而本年度主要原材料及能源购进价格景气指数全年平均为62.69，位于“较为不景气”区间，较去年大幅下降32.92点，同时产品的销售价格景气指数全年为90.33，仍位于景气临界点以下，较去年仅上扬9.15点。从主要原材料及能源价格上扬的覆盖面上看，以今年11月份为例，在原材料九大类分组中，除其它工业原材料及半成品类和木材及纸浆类价格下降外，其余七大类呈不同程度上涨。在价格上涨的七类原材料中，黑色金属材料类价格上涨幅度为最大，上涨26.1%；其它依次是农副产品类、纺织原料类和有色金属材料类，价格分别上涨25.0%、17.6%和16.7%。另外从建筑业层面看，建筑业原材料购进价格也普遍上升，原材料购进价格景气指数只有57.43，位于“较为不景气”区间。同时，在流通领域，商品的进货价格也有不同程度的提高。

（二）外商及港澳台企业增幅略缓，小口径社会服务业乏力

本年度，外商及港澳台企业景气指数全年平均为126.36，虽仍处于“较为景气”区间，但与自身相比，景气状况有所回落，本年度的企业景气指数成为1999年以来各年度的最低水平，较去年同期下降17.93点。致使全年景气指数偏低的原因与“非典”疫情不无关系，一季度，该类企业景气指数为142.72，保持着以往的良好的发展势头，二季度受“非典”疫情影响，景气指数大幅回落30.45点，达到112.27，由“较为景气”区间，回落至少有的“相对景气”区间，三季度，随着疫情的缓解，景气指数回升了12.85点，为125.12，仍为1999年以来的同期景气最低水平，三季度景气指数仅小幅回升0.22点，达到125.34。本年度，小口径调查的社会服务业正如前文行业走势描述中概括的企业景气状况不甚乐观，社会对该行业的需求小幅下降，该行业收费价格下调，营业收入减少，固定资产投资减少，对劳动力的需求减少。

（翟凤建）

注：为更好地分析和理解企业景气指数，我们将景气区间作如下划分：180以上为“非常景气”区间，[180,150）为“较强景气”区间，[150,120）为“较为景气”区间，[120,110）为“相对景气”区间，[110,100）为“微景气”区间，100为景气临界点，（100,90]为“微弱不景气”区间，（90,80]为“相对不景气”区间，（80,50为“较为不景气”区间，（50,20]为“较重不景气”区间，20以下为“严重不景气”区间。另：景气调查所涉及的行业不含第一产业

飞速发展的社会事业

2003年，随着天津经济的快速发展，有力地带动了社会事业的长足进步。科技、教育、文化、卫生、体育、环保等各项事业蓬勃发展，成果丰硕。

科技创新实力再创新高。全年取得市级科技成果1203项，其中达到国际领先水平59项，达到国际先进水平311项。获国家科学技术奖14项。获天津市科学技术奖246项，其中获二等奖以上 77 项，占获奖总

数的31.3%，获国际科技合作奖1项，科技重大成就奖1项。研发投入有所增加。独立自然科研机构开展课题研究1520项，比上年增长3.3%，其中研发项目达到685项，增长9.4%；科技人员投入4746人，经费投入4.39亿元，分别增长10.1%和21.8%，其中研发人员和研发经费分别增长15.3%和24.7%。

国家重点项目投入提高。2003年理工农医类高等院校开展各类课题研究4645项，增加523项，增长12.7%。科技人员投入4730人，增长2.5%。科技经费投入5.20亿元，增长17.1%。其中国家“863”项目达到75项，增长1.3倍；人员投入 84人，增长44.8%；经费投入0.09亿元，增长68.4%。国家自然科学基金项目达到450项，增长13.1%；人员投入448人，增长21.1%；经费投入0.35亿元，增长13.3%。

企业科技投入和产出均有新突破。我国企业技术创新工作受到各级政府和企业的高度重视，企业技术创新的潜在因素逐步得以发挥，企业技术创新的投入力度明显加大，2003年大中型工业企业科技人员2.65万人，比上年增长14.2%。科技经费投入42.68亿元，增加13.51亿元，增长46.3%。其中研发经费17.12亿元，增长13.6 %。企业已逐渐成为天津市研发活动的投资主体。新产品销售收入达到852.53亿元，增加148.68亿元，增长21.1%。新产品利润33.18亿元，增长7.2%。专利申请2516件，增加1244件，增长近一倍。

新技术产业园区实力不断增强。截至2003年年底，园区企业达到4700家，增长4.4%。技工贸总产值561.96亿元，增长34.9%。技工贸总收入668.94亿元，增长34.2%。利润总额25.73亿元，增长8.6%。出口创汇总额13.63亿元，增长5.7%。

技术创新活动更加活跃。三项专利申请和批准量大幅增长。随着我国加入WTO以及知识产权管理体制与国际的逐渐接轨，天津市企事业各界对知识产权的保护意识逐渐增强，三项专利的申请及批准量逐年递增，发明、实用新型和外观设计三种专利申请量在上年大幅度增长的基础上，再度上涨，达到6812件，增长27.2%，其中发明专利达到3328件，增长61.0%。企业专利意识在逐年提高，在职务发明中企业专利申请量达到2791件，占职务发明数的80.8%，创天津历史最高，居全国前列；技术交易市场共签订技术合同7278项，增长5.7%。技术合同成交额42.00亿元，增长15.6%。其中签订技术开发合同2349项，增长43.1%，占技术合同总数的32.3%。成交额27.86亿元，增长69.2%，占技术合同成交总额三分之二之多。

高等教育快速发展。截止2003年末，天津市共有普通高等院校37所；在校本、专科学生24.52万人，比去年同期增长24.5 %，当年毕业生4.02万人，增长47.4 %。硕士以上学历教育步伐加快，博士和硕士研究生数量不断增加，2003年在校博士生、硕士生分别为4304人和16353人，比去年同期增长23.0%和31.6%，当年毕业博士和硕士生分别为585人和2667人。中等职业学校在校学生13.47万人，当年招生4.41万人，比上年增长7.9%。为了不断提升职业教育层次结构，积极探索5年制高职教学改革，确定16所中职学校和10所高职学院进行“三、二分段”改革试验，2000人的招生计划全部完成。2003年高职学生所占比重提高到35%以上。高等教育毛入学率达到49%，比上年提高了5个百分点。

中小学教育质量不断提高。截止2003年末全市共有普通中学 664所，普通初中在校学生和毕业生分别为43.25万人和13.93万人；普通高中当年招生6.99万人，比上年增长18.7%，高中在校生18.25万人，毕业生4.5万人，同比分别增长15.6%和8.4%；高中阶段入学率93.1%。全市共有小学1136所，当年招生8.5万人，在校学生58.54万人，毕业生13.2万人。幼儿园在园幼儿19.96万人，入园率达88.2%，学龄儿童入学率为99.97%，小学生升学率达98.97%。小学课程改革实验工作已在全市铺开，提前两年率先实现了国家确定的改革目标。

中小学布局调整工程成绩显著。首批31所示范高中学校全部建成并投入使用。校均占地面积达80亩，建筑面积由改造前的56万平米，提高到115万平米。招生规模达到1.47万人，全市高中阶段新生接受优质教育的比例已经达到65%以上。此外，一批模范小学也已开工建设。"再建几所南开、耀华式的学校，满足广大人民群众的教育需求"的战略部署，已经如期实现。

文化事业百花齐放，成绩斐然。截止2003年末，全市共有艺术表演团体15个，文化馆、科技馆19个，博物馆16个，公共图书馆31个。天津博物馆、泰达会展中心和图书馆相继建成，进一步提高了城市文化品位。成功地举办了"中国民族戏曲优秀剧目大汇演"、首届老年文化艺术节、第二届家庭文化艺术节、第四届滨海艺术节、毛主席诗词音乐会等大型文化活动。推出了京剧《华子良》、芭蕾舞剧《精卫》、话剧《为你喝彩》等艺术精品。创作演出了《我们必胜》特别文艺节目和"我们携手同行"系列文艺节目。一大批优秀剧目分获中宣部“五个一工程”奖、文化部“文华大奖”、中国京剧艺术节金奖、国家电影华表奖、全国舞剧观摩演出(比赛)优秀剧目奖和第二届全国木偶皮影比赛最高奖“金狮奖”。现代京剧《华子良》继荣获中宣部“五个一工程”奖、文化部“文华大奖”和中国京剧艺术节金奖之后,又在激烈的竞争中脱颖而出,入选国家舞台艺术十大精品。在第十二届全国“群星奖”评选中,天津市取得3金、3银、5铜的好成绩,并有15件美术、书法、摄影作品获优秀奖。

新闻出版业双效俱佳,成果丰硕。近年来,天津市新闻出版工作努力把握正确的舆论导向,始终把社会效益放在首位,贴近实际,贴近生活,贴近群众,唱响主旋律,把好喉舌关,创造出许多人民群众喜闻乐见、丰富多彩的作品,实现思想性、艺术性、观赏性的统一,不断满足人民群众日益增长的精神文化需求。在第六届国家图书奖评选工作中,有两种图书获提名奖,有13种图书分获单项奖;百花出版社的《小说月报》获第二届国家期刊奖。截止2003年底,全市共有图书出版单位13家、音像出版单位5家、电子出版单位2家和2家光盘复制单位;拥有对外公开发行的期刊245种、报纸45种。全市共出版各类报纸82386.51万份,杂志4609.72万册,图书6772.39万册。极大地丰富了广大群众的业余文化生活。

广播电视事业协调发展,迅猛前进。2003年,天津市广播电视事业积极发挥集团优势,努力树立新标准、制定新目标、展现新面貌,解放思想,开拓创新,抢抓机遇,争创一流,使天津广播电视事业取得突飞猛进的发展,形成了广播电视共荣,无线有线同兴,网站网络并举,"声屏报"协调发展的格局。2003年全市现有广播节目7套,平均每日播出时间为148.32小时,较2002年的130.07小时增18.25小时,增长14.0%。广播人口综合覆盖率达100%。市级电视节目7套,较去年增加1套科技频道。平均每周播出时间为863.33小时,同比增加143.51小时,增长20.6%。电视人口综合覆盖率达99%,全市有线电视用户达到180万户。全年发行广播电视报1026万份,生产录音、录像磁带和光盘共计8万盘。广播电视事业已步入了蓬勃发展的快车道。

卫生事业稳步发展。截止2003年末,全市共有卫生机构2671个,其中医院500个,卫生防疫机构25个,妇幼保健所(站)11个。年末卫生机构拥有床位4.27万张,比上年增长0.9%,其中医院、卫生院床位4.16万张,增长0.8%。全市拥有专业卫生技术人员6.1万人,比上年增加0.4万人,其中医生2.59万人。每万人拥有医生27.8人,拥有医院床位44.6张。卫生资源调整进展顺利。改造了海河医院和一中心医院,完成传染病医院一期工程和人民医院主体工程。社区卫生服务和农村卫生服务网络基本形成。

非典型肺炎防治工作取得阶段性重大胜利。出现非典疫情后,全市及时封锁疫点疫区,切断传染源,制定了各项防控措施,建成一批发热门诊和留观所,建立了非典医疗救治体系,使疫情得到了很好控制。

竞技体育实力明显增强,硕果累累。截止2003年底,天津市运动员在全国高水平比赛中共获金牌16枚,银牌13枚,铜牌19枚;在亚洲三大赛中获得金牌9枚,银牌1枚,铜牌2枚。在世界三大赛上获得金牌5枚,银牌3枚,铜牌1枚。天津女排获全国联赛和锦标赛冠军。网球、武术、女子佩剑、男子吊环等项目进一步确立了在全国的优势地位。成功举办了第十二届亚洲男排锦标赛、国际室内田径邀请赛、丰田杯国际乒乓球邀请赛等十多项国内外赛事。天津奥林匹克中心体育场开工建设。

群众体育蓬勃开展,方兴未艾。2003年,天津市群众体育继续坚持以构建群众性多元化服务体系为重点,全面实施《全民健身计划纲要》二期工程,继续加大建设群众体育设施的力度,完成了第六批全民健身工程的配建工作和旧楼区配建体育健身设施工作。在全市18个区县配建了23套全民健身工程,完善了部分健身广场,修建了大批体育彩票健身中心,在267片居民小区配建了364处健身设施。在全市开展了“阳光健身活动”,举办了首届国际山野运动大会。创编了第一套市民广播体操,成为全国创立省市广播体操的第一个省市。

“非典”期间,在全国率先提出“积极锻炼,决战非典”的口号,积极组织市民开展丰富多彩的体育活动,倡导和推广“户外分散、小型多样、因地制宜、科学安全”的健身方式,使抗击“非典”由被动防御进入到主动出击，实现了战略转移，为最后胜利发挥了积极的作用。

环境综合整治取得新成效。截止2003年末，全市共有环境监测站20个，创建国家环保模范城市六大工程进展顺利。天津市危险废物处理处置中心建成投入使用。西青区杨柳青镇被国家命名为全国首批环境优美镇。开展了“百万市民环境大清整”活动，有效地促进了环境卫生、城市管理和文明程度的提高。

环境空气质量基本稳定。2003年全市可吸入颗粒物均值较上年下降3.6%。全年空气质量达二级良好水平以上天数为264天，占全年总天数的72.3%。烟尘控制区60个，烟尘控制面积557.3平方公里。

饮用水源水质基本保持良好。加强了对于桥水库库区和引滦、引黄河道水质巡查和监测，引滦和引黄天津段总体水质较好，饮用水源地各月水质达标率均为100%。

声环境质量持续改善。2003年城市区域环境噪音平均声级为55分贝，与上年持平；道路交通噪音平均声级为68.2分贝，比上年下降0.2分贝。环境噪声达标区总面积539.1平方公里，覆盖率为78%，比上年提高 2 个百分点。

生态环境保护工作成效显著。截止2003年底，全市共有生态示范区 6 个，自然保护区 8 个，自然保护区面积达15.33万公顷。建成了以蓟县中上元古界地质自然保护区为核心的蓟县国家地质公园；西青、汉沽、武清区被国家批准列为第八批全国生态示范区建设试点；宝坻区生态示范区建设试点已通过市级预验收，并具备国家验收条件；宁河、大港生态示范区建设取得阶段性进展。

（郭秀兰　穆菁）

十六大以来天津市经济体制改革进展情况

党的十六大以来，天津市认真贯彻党的十六大、十六届三中全会和市委八届三次全会精神，按照市委提出的“新世纪新阶段，改革要有新突破”的总体要求，紧紧围绕“三步走”战略的实施，积极推进各项改革工作，充分发挥市场配置资源的作用，为全市国民经济保持快速增长创造良好的体制环境。

一、国有经济战略性调整步伐加快，老工业基地的竞争力显著增强

十六大以来，天津市加快实施新一轮嫁接改造调整，用创新的思路，把国有企业的调整重组和盘活存量资产、债务重组、技术改造以及工业东移结合起来，加快布局结构调整，重点发展优势产业，提高国有经济整体质量，增强国有经济带动作用。市医药集团打破地域界限，通过转让45%的股权，引进战略投资伙伴。股权转让收益用于建设抗生素、中药、生物制药基地，增强发展后劲。市纺织集团通过实施债务重组，盘活现有资产，利用土地级差地租，整体东移，并采用世界一流的技术和装备进行改造，把改革、改组、改造结合起来，建设现代化纺织工业园。市钢管公司通过实施债权回购，债权变为股权，形成多元投资主体。进一步完善了公司治理结构，规范公司运作。在新一轮嫁改调中，东移搬迁的企业，采取合资、合作、股权转让等方式，一半以上完成了规范的改制工作。全市工业系统的356个由重点国有企业改制形成的股份制企业中，国有资本的控制力明显增强，支配范围增大了一倍。

二、不断优化体制环境，鼓励个私经济做大做强

今年以来，天津市不断改善个私经济发展的体制环境，有关部门拟定出台《关于进一步加快个体私营经济发展的意见》及相关配套政策，在投资、金融、土地、税收、市场准入等方面创造公平竞争的环境，维护个私企业合法权益，支持个私经济做大做强。选择了一批有实力、有发展前景的私营企业集团，列入天津市重点支持的大企业、大集团范围。进一步放开市场，允许个私经济进入公交、供水、燃气、供热、污水处理、垃圾处理等市政公用行业。拟定了关于鼓励私营企业参与国企改革的暂行规定和规范操作意见，鼓励个私企业通过收购、兼并、控股参股等方式，参与国有中小企业改组改制，实现规模化发展。通过发展中介服务机构和要素市场，完善市场服务体系，使个私经济成为天津市重要的经济增长点。

三、发挥市场机制作用，加快城市建设步伐

今年以来，在落实五大战略举措中，以海河综合开发为突破口，城市建设取得重大进展，海河开发基础设施、房地产开发以及64个市级重点项目相继开工，截止到目前，全市全社会固定资产投资近千亿。一是按照政府推动、市场运作的要求，组建天津市基础设施建设投资公司及四个专项投资公司，积极吸引社会资本，多渠道筹集建设开发资金。二是整顿规范土地市场秩序，制定和公布了土地有偿出让管理办法，统一收购外环以内市区可用开发的土地，经营性土地供应实行公开招标、挂牌、拍卖、转让制度，增加政府收益，全年土地转让政府纯收益可达到12.5亿元。三是完善产权交易市场，产权交易中心建立了产权交易信息网络，进一步扩大业务和服务范围，为推动企业产权流动，促进境内外投资者并购境内企业搭建服务平台。四是加快港口改革和建设。按照国家的要求，拟定港口下放管理体制改革的方案，组建了天津港集团有限公司。进一步明确加快港口建设的目标和措施，从今年起到2010年，总投资预计273亿元，其中近3年140亿元，实现港口吞吐量和集装箱运量比2002年翻一番。今年港口吞吐量可达1.55亿吨，同比增长20％。五是推进金融业改革和发展。围绕建设北方重要的经济中心和现代化港口城市，重点抓了发展金融机构、开放金融市场、创新金融业务三个方面的工作。抓紧筹建中外合资金融和保险机构，吸引各类金融机构在天津开展业务。目前，各银行已向工商企业提供贷款授信额度1400亿元。全市金融机构本外币贷款比今年年初增加了近900亿元，是去年全年新增额的两倍多。六是加强了京津冀区域经济合作。京津两市商定增建京津高速公路南北两个通道，加强京津两市经济发展重点区域的联系，加强天津港为北京的服务，实现京津两大机场共同发展。京津两市高速公路通道一体化建设，有利于加强两市间经济和社会发展的全面合作，实现优势互补，共同繁荣。

四、积极推进就业分配体制改革，完善社会保障制度

今年以来，天津市把再就业工作摆到更加突出的位置，用积极的态度、发展的办法开发就业岗位，完善和落实就业政策，建立健全市场就业机制，就业工作取得明显成效。目前，全市新增就业岗位12万个，比上年同期增长70％，其中安置下岗失业人员9.5万人，比上年同期增长3.4万人。城镇登记失业人员12.3万人，城镇登记失业率3.84％，比去年末下降0.07个百分点。领取城镇最低生活保障金人员24.9万人，比去年末减少5.2万人。天津市自1998年以来首次实现就业人数大于下岗失业人数。

分配制度改革方面。一是建立了企业工资正常增长机制，完善职工收入增长指标考核体系，不断加大考核力度。及时出台了工资指导线，采取有效措施，确保收入增长目标的落实。完善欠薪报告、预警制度，确保低收入群体工资水平的提高，保护劳动者合法权益。二是推行工资集体协商制度，继续扩大自主决定工资水平办法，扩大工资集体协商试点范围，特别是在非公有制企业中推行工资集体协商制度。三是有关部门修订了《天津市最低工资保障规定》，明确各类用工条件下确定和调整职工月最低工资标准的要素依据，对保障职工工资收益做出具体规定。

完善社会保障制度方面。一是下大力量抓好社会保险征缴和扩面工作，强化社会保险基金的保障能力。为进一步完善天津市社会保障体系，市政府提出了扩大城镇职工社会保险覆盖范围的重点目标和要求，并通过建立城镇劳动力资源综合统计制度和建立经营性工作绩效通报及依法参保情况公告制度，形成有效的监督制约机制。二是出台了六项改进和完善城镇职工基本医疗保险制度的政策措施，取得了较好的效果。有关部门根据国家要求，研究了工伤保险实施办法，2004年开始执行。

五、深化行政审批制度改革，加快政府职能转变

今年以来，按照合理、合法、效能、责任、监督五项原则，天津市对原有的审批事项进行了第三轮清理，累计精简审批事项达到666项。各部门对保留的审批事项，逐项规范操作程序，最大限度精简环节，做到便民高效。在9个行业推行企业登记注册照前并联审批方法，企业注册等候时间平均减少一半以上，取得十分良好的效果。通过改革行政审批制度，使政府职能逐步转向制定战略规划、提供政策支持、搞好市场监管、改善公共服务等方面，进一步减少了对市场的干预，政府为市场主体服务和创造良好发展环境的作用得到有效发挥。

积极推进政府法制建设，围绕确立制度、规范权责、保障权益，加强立法工作，维护好投资、交易、价格、信用和各种公共行为的市场秩序，提高政府部门依法行政能力。

（市体改办 李力）

第1篇 CHAPTER 1

综　合

GENERAL SURVEY

1-1 行政建制
ADMINISTRATIVE DIVISIONS
（2003年底）
（END OF 2003）

单位：个 (unit)

项目	Item	街道办事处 Subdistrict Offices	居民委员会 Resident's Committees	镇政府 Town Governments	乡政府 Township Governments	村民委员会 Village Committees
全 市	**Total**	**101**	**1 753**	**120**	**20**	**3 836**
一、市辖区	**Districts Under City Administration**	**100**	**1 698**	**73**	**9**	**2 220**
1.市内六个区	Six Central Districts	63	1 228			
和平区	Heping District	6	91			
河东区	Hedong District	13	232			
河西区	Hexi District	12	251			
南开区	Nankai District	12	254			
河北区	Hebei District	10	215			
红桥区	Hongqiao District	10	185			
2.滨海三个区	Three Coastal Districts	21	250	8		165
塘沽区	Tanggu District	11	131	1		34
汉沽区	Hangu District	5	45	4		58
大港区	Dagang District	5	74	3		73
3.其他六个区	Other Six Districts	16	220	65	9	2 055
东丽区	Dongli District	5	43	3	1	109
西青区	Xiqing District	2	59	7		149
津南区	Jinnan District		25	8		165
北辰区	Beichen District	3	52	9		126
武清区	Wuqing District	6	19	19	5	741
宝坻区	Baodi District		22	19	3	765
二、市辖县	**Counties Under City Administration**	**1**	**55**	**47**	**11**	**1 616**
宁河县	Ninghe County		22	11	3	283
静海县	Jinghai County		18	16	2	384
蓟 县	Jixian County	1	15	20	6	949

资料来源：天津市民政局。
Information Source: Tianjin Municipal Civil Affairs Bureau.

1－2　土地面积(2003 年)
AREA OF LAND,2003

分组	Groups	面积 Area (平方公里) (sq. km)	占全市土地总面积比重(%) Percentage to Total Area(%)
全市土地总面积	**Total Land Area**	**11 919.70**	**100.0**
1.农用地	**Land for Agricultural Production**	**7 201.47**	**60.4**
耕　地	Cultivated Land	4 754.80	39.9
园　地	Garden Plot	368.17	3.1
林　地	Afforested Land	359.43	3.0
牧草地	Grassland	6.07	0.1
其他农用地	Others	1 713.00	14.3
2.建设用地	**Land for Construction**	**3 141.50**	**26.4**
居民点及工矿用地	Land for Residents and Industry	2 353.19	19.8
交通用地	Land for Transportation	146.02	1.2
水利设施用地	Land for Water Conservancy	642.29	5.4
3.未利用地面积	**Unused Area**	**1 576.73**	**13.2**
未利用土地	Unused Soil	554.77	4.7
其他土地	Other Land	1 021.96	8.5

资料来源:天津市规划和国土资源局。
Information Source:Tianjin Municipal Bureau of Programming,Land and Resources.

1－3　城市建设用地
CITY CONSTRUCTION LAND－USED

单位:平方公里　(sq. km)

指标	Item	2001	2002	2003
建成区面积	**Developed Area**	**424.06**	**453.99**	**487.47**
市中心区	Central Districts	248.05	251.25	253.63
塘沽区	Tanggu District	90.33	102.11	108.69
#开发区	TEDA	16.70	18.83	23.00
保税区	TPFTZ	4.64	4.70	5.00
汉沽区	Hangu District	15.62	15.60	15.60
大港区	Dagang District	41.95	41.95	41.95
西青区	Xiqing District			15.40
津南区	Jinnan District			6.92
武清区	Wuqing District	16.44	29.34	31.04
宝坻区	Baodi District	11.67	13.74	14.24
城市建设用地	**City Construction Land－used**	**424.06**	**453.99**	**487.47**
居住用地	Dwelling	108.89	116.86	119.81
公共设施用地	Public Facilities	41.29	44.36	51.02
工业用地	Industry	95.86	106.48	116.87
仓储用地	Warehouse	40.37	39.89	34.67
对外交通用地	Traffic	20.88	23.03	20.36
道路广场用地	Road and Square	40.45	42.21	44.16
市政公用设施用地	Public Ficilities of Municipal Administration	12.49	14.04	14.07
绿　地	Green Land	22.75	27.09	45.19
特殊用地	Special Land	41.08	40.03	41.32

资料来源:天津市建委。
Information Source:Tianjin Municipal Urban & Rural Construction Commission.

1-4 气象资料(2003 年)

METEOROLOGICAL DATA,2003

月 份 Month	平均气温 Average Temperature (℃)	最高气温 The Highest Temperature (℃)	最低气温 The Lowest Temperature (℃)	相对湿度 Average Relative Humidity (%)	日照时数 (小时) Hours of Sunshine (hour)	降水量 (毫米) Precipitation (mm)	一日最大降水量 (毫米) Largest Precipita-tion in a Day (mm)	平均风速 (米/秒) Average Wind Speed (m/sec)
一 月 January	-2.0	11.3	-10.4	59.0	126.9	1.4	0.9	1.5
二 月 February	1.6	12.5	-7.6	60.0	102.6	2.0	1.2	1.3
三 月 March	7.1	23.4	-1.6	61.0	127.9	11.6	7.7	1.5
四 月 April	16.0	30.8	7.2	50.0	178.3	15.1	10.8	1.8
五 月 May	21.8	32.6	11.0	57.0	200.9	49.5	26.5	1.6
六 月 June	24.9	37.7	15.3	57.0	185.7	139.9	77.9	1.4
七 月 July	26.5	35.4	21.0	71.0	122.7	152.3	87.4	1.3
八 月 August	26.2	35.3	17.0	72.0	198.3	129.3	94.3	1.0
九 月 September	21.6	31.8	13.7	72.0	130.9	34.4	12.5	1.2
十 月 October	14.1	22.5	4.4	59.0	176.8	161.9	114.4	1.3
十一月 November	4.9	20.7	-3.3	63.0	80.4	26.8	12.5	1.3
十二月 December	0.9	11.3	-6.9	51.0	143.7	0.0	0.0	1.1

1-5 各区气象资料(2003 年)

METEOROLOGICAL DATA OF DISTRICT,2003

地 区 Region	最高气温 The Highest Temperature (℃)	最低气温 The Lowest Temperature (℃)	全年平均气温 Annual Average Temperature (℃)	平均相对湿度 Average Relative Humidity (%)	日照时数 (小时) Hours of Sunshine (hour)	降水量 (毫米) Precipitation (mm)	无霜期 (天) Non-Frosting Period (day)	雾天数 (天) Foggy Days (day)
市 区 Urban District	37.7	-10.4	13.6	61	1 775.1	724.2	243	13
塘沽区 Tanggu District	35.6	-12.3	13.0	63	2 064.0	586.2	233	21
汉沽区 Hangu District	35.0	-14.3	12.2	67	2 351.0	685.1	214	26
大港区 Dagang District	37.4	-12.9	13.0	64	2 339.0	602.1	242	20
东丽区 Dongli District	37.5	-11.7	13.0	63	2 293.3	629.9	224	23
西青区 Xiqing District	36.9	-13.0	12.8	68	1 993.6	647.5	201	16
津南区 Jinnan District	37.8	-12.0	13.0	62	2 134.0	685.4	230	21
北辰区 Beichen District	36.6	-13.7	12.8	64	1 992.6	526.4	219	27
武清区 Wuqing District	36.4	-12.3	12.9	64	1 980.1	637.7	239	16
宝坻区 Baodi District	35.7	-15.2	12.1	63	2 037.0	412.1	214	29
宁河县 Ninghe County	35.2	-15.0	12.4	69	2 218.9	534.7	233	19
静海县 Jinghai County	37.3	-14.8	13.0	61	2 175.6	758.3	214	28
蓟 县 Jixian County	36.0	-13.9	12.8	61	1 949.0	607.9	212	19

资料来源:天津气候服务中心。
Information Source:Tianjin Meteorological Service Center.

1-6 国民经济各行业法人单位和企业法人单位(2003年)
INSTITUTIONAL UNITS AND ENTERPRISE INSTITUTIONAL UNITS BY SECTOR, 2003

单位:个 (unit)

项目	Item	法人单位 Institutional Units	企业法人单位 Enterprise Institutional Units
总计	**Total**	**105 927**	**86 353**
第一产业	**Primary Industry**	**1 022**	**553**
农、林、牧、渔业	Farming, Forestry, Animal Husbandry and Fishery	1 022	553
农业	Farming	158	137
林业	Forestry	35	25
畜牧业	Animal Husbandry	151	129
渔业	Fishery	111	99
农、林、牧、渔服务业	FFAF Services	567	163
第二产业	**Secondary Industry**	**38 025**	**37 964**
采矿业	Minerals Mining	219	219
煤炭开采和洗选业	Coal Mining and Dressing	9	9
石油和天然气开采业	Petroleum and Natural Gas Extraction	25	25
黑色金属矿采选业	Ferrous Metals Mining and Dressing	4	4
有色金属矿采选业	Nonferrous Metals Mining and Dressing	5	5
非金属矿采选业	Nonmetal Minerals Mining and Dressing	172	172
其他采矿业	Other Minerals Mining	4	4
制造业	Manufacturing	33 123	33 107
农副食品加工业	Agricultural Products and Byproducts Processing	978	971
食品制造业	Food Manufacturing	1 049	1 049
饮料制造业	Beverage Manufacturing	396	396
烟草制品业	Tobacco Processing	5	5
纺织业	Textile Industry	1 390	1 390
纺织服装鞋帽制造业	Textile Garments, Shoes, Caps Manufacturing	1 706	1 704
皮革毛皮羽毛(绒)及其制品业	Leather, Furs, Down and Related Products	410	410
木材加工及木、竹、藤、棕、草制品业	Timber Processing, Bamboo, Cane, Palm Fiber and Straw Products	443	443
家具制造业	Furniture Manufacturing	431	431
造纸及纸制品业	Papermaking and Paper Products	1 057	1 057
印刷业和记录媒介的复制	Printing and Record Medium Reproduction	963	963
文教体育用品制造业	Cultural, Educational and Sports Goods	475	475
石油加工、炼焦及核燃料加工业	Petroleum Processing, Coking and Nuclear Fuel Processing	152	152
化学原料及其制品制造业	Raw Chemical Materials and Chemical Products	2 838	2 838
医药制造业	Medical and Pharmaceutical Products	389	389
化学纤维制造业	Chemical Fiber	83	83
橡胶制品业	Rubber Products	542	542
塑料制品业	Plastic Products	1 526	1 526
非金属矿物制品业	Nonmetal Mineral Products	1 497	1 494
黑色金属冶炼及压延加工业	Smelting and Pressing of Ferrous Metals	575	575
有色金属冶炼及压延加工业	Smelting and Pressing of Nonferrous Metals	334	334
金属制品业	Metal Products	3 529	3 528
通用设备制造业	General Purpose Equipment Manufacturing	3 206	3 205
专用设备制造业	Special Purpose Equipment Manufacturing	1 862	1 860
交通运输设备制造业	Transport Equipment Manufacturing	2 566	2 566

注:本表行业分类为国标GB/T4754—2002标准,1-13表同。
Note: Sector listed in this table is classified by the standard of GB/T4754—2002, same as following table 1-13.

1-6续表1 Continued
单位:个 (unit)

项 目	Item	法人单位 Institutional Units	企业法人单位 Enterprise Institutional Units
电气机械及器材制造业	Electric Equipment and Machinery	1 714	1 714
通信设备、计算机及其他电子设备制造业	Telecommunications Equipment,Computer and Other Electronic Equipment Manufacturing	1 143	1 143
仪器仪表及文化、办公用机械制造业	Instruments,Meters,Cultural and Office Machinery	888	888
工艺品及其他制造业	Handiwork and Other Manufacturing	957	957
废弃资源和废旧材料回收加工业	Waste Resources and Materials Recovering and Processing	19	19
电力、燃气及水的生产和供应业	Production and Supply of Electric Power,Gas and Water	274	236
电力、热力的生产和供应业	Production and Supply of Power and Heating Energy	142	110
燃气生产和供应业	Production and Supply of Gas	68	68
水的生产和供应业	Production and Supply of Water	64	58
建筑业	Construction	4 409	4 402
房屋和土木工程建筑业	Building and Civil Engineering	1 246	1 239
建筑安装业	Building Installation	1 345	1 345
建筑装饰业	Building Decoration	1 403	1 403
其他建筑业	Others	415	415
第三产业	**Tertiary Industry**	**66 880**	**47 836**
交通运输、仓储和邮政业	Transport, Storage, Post Services	3 444	3 156
铁路运输业	Railway Transport	45	43
道路运输业	Highway Transport	635	570
城市公共交通业	City Public Traffic	612	603
水上运输业	Waterway Transport	293	207
航空运输业	Air Transport	61	61
管道运输业	Pipeline Transport	1	1
装卸搬运和其他运输服务业	Load & Unload and Others	1 020	990
仓储业	Storage Services	746	650
邮政业	Post Services	31	31
信息传输、计算机服务和软件业	Information Transmitting, Computer Services and Software	1 138	1 111
电信和其他信息传输服务业	Telecommunication and Others Information Transmitting Services	202	180
计算机服务业	Computer Services	298	294
软件业	Software	638	637
批发和零售业	Wholesale and Retail Trade	28 339	28 316
批发业	Wholesale	15 771	15 750
零售业	Retail Trade	12 568	12 566
住宿和餐饮业	Accommodation and Catering Services	2 332	2 279
住宿业	Accommodation	680	628
餐饮业	Catering Service	1 652	1 651
金融业	Finance	487	485
银行业	Banking	279	279
证券业	Securities	85	85
保险业	Insurance	80	79
其他金融活动	Others	43	42
房地产业	Real Estate	2 610	2 401
房地产业	Real Estate	2 610	2 401
租赁和商务服务业	Leasing and Business Services	4 297	2 973
租赁业	Leasing Serving	257	256
商务服务业	Business Serving	4 040	2 717
科学研究、技术服务和地质勘察业	Scientific Research, Technical Services and Geological Prospecting	5 452	3 659

1－6 续表 2　Continued

单位:个 (unit)

项　目	Item	法人单位 Institutional Units	企业法人单位 Enterprise Institutional Units
研究与试验发展	R&D	404	163
专业技术服务业	Special Technical Services	2 892	2 314
科技交流和推广服务业	Science Exchanges and Technology Expansion	2 103	1 145
地质勘察业	Geological Prospecting	53	37
水利、环境和公共设施管理业	Management for Water Conservancy, Environment and Public Facilities	794	215
水利管理业	Management for Water Conservancy	332	26
环境管理业	Management for Environment	239	84
公共设施管理业	Management for Public Facilities	223	105
居民服务和其他服务业	Resident Services and Other Social Services	2 653	2 171
居民服务业	Resident Services	1 568	1 315
其他服务业	Other Social Services	1 085	856
教　育	Education	3 111	355
卫生、社会保障和社会福利业	Health Care, Social Security and Social Welfare	1 191	61
卫　生	Health Care	820	29
社会保障业	Social Security	100	16
社会福利业	Social Welfare	271	16
文化、体育和娱乐业	Culture, Sports and Recreational Services	1 244	480
新闻出版业	News Publication	80	35
广播、电视、电影和音像业	Broadcast, TV, Movies Record, and video Industry	218	51
文化艺术业	Culture and Art	404	78
体　育	Sports	184	43
娱乐业	Recreational Services	358	273
公共管理和社会组织	Public Management and Social Organizations	9 712	104
中国共产党机关	Chinese Communist Party Organizations	198	1
国家机构	Government Organizations	1 814	67
人民政协和民主党派	The People's Political Consultative Conferance Committees and Democracy Party Groupings	33	
群众团体、社会团体和宗教组织	Mass Organizations, Social Organizations and Religious Groups	1 968	5
基层群众自治组织	Grass－roots Mass Autonomy Organizations	5 699	31
国际组织	International Organizations	76	70

1－7　法人单位和企业法人单位(2003年)

(按登记注册类型划分)

INSTITUTIONAL UNITS AND ENTERPRISE INSTITUTIONAL UNITS,2003

(BY REGISTRATION STATUS)

单位:个　　(unit)

项　目	Item	法人单位 Institutional units	企业法人单位 Enterprise Institutional Units
总　计	**Total**	**105 927**	**86 353**
1.内资企业	**Domestic－funded Enterprises**	**98 907**	**79 451**
国有企业	State－owned Enterprises	17 308	8 223
集体企业	Collective－owned Enterprises	24 136	22 690
股份合作企业	Cooperative Enterprises	1 576	1 572
联营企业	Joint Ownership Enterprises	736	689
国有联营企业	State Joint Ownership Enterprises	162	155
集体联营企业	Collective Joint Ownership Enterprises	144	142
国有与集体联营	State－owned and Collective Joint Ownership Enterprises	184	184
其他联营企业	Other Joint Ownership Enterprises	246	208
有限责任公司	Limited Liability Corporations	14 319	11 975
国有独资公司	Sole State－owned Corporations	294	284
其他有限责任公司	Other Limited Liability Corporations	14 025	11 691
股份有限公司	Share Holding Corporations Ltd.	1 177	1 173
私营企业	Private Enterprises	32 666	32 356
#私营独资企业	Sole Private Enterprises	10 351	10 126
私营有限责任公司	Private Limited Liability Corporations	19 054	19 047
私营股份有限公司	Private Share Holding Corporations Ltd.	806	805
其他内资企业	Other Domestic－funded Enterprises	6 989	773
2.港澳台商投资企业	**Enterprises with Investment from Hongkong,Macao and Taiwan**	**2 493**	**2 465**
与港澳台商合资经营企业	Hongkong,Macao and Taiwan Joint Venture	1 140	1 127
与港澳台商合作经营企业	Hongkong,Macao and Taiwan Cooperative Operation	109	107
港澳台商独资企业	Hongkong,Macao and Taiwan Funded	1 226	1 214
港澳台商投资股份有限公司	Hongkong,Macao and Taiwan Share Holding Corporations Ltd.	18	17
3.外商投资企业	**Foreign Funded Enterprises**	**4 527**	**4 437**
中外合资经营企业	Chinese－foreign Joint Venture	1 498	1 476
中外合作经营企业	Chinese－foreign Cooperative Operation	199	196
外商独资企业	Foreign－funded Sole Enterprise	2 701	2 638
外商投资股份有限公司	Foreign－funded Share Holding Corporations Ltd.	129	127

1－8 主要年份国民经济主要指标和增长速度

MAIN INDICATORS AND INCREASE RATE OF NATIONAL ECONOMY IN MAIN YEARS

年 份 Year	户籍人口数（万人）Registered Population (10 000 persons)	社会从业人员数（万人）Number of Persons Employed (10 000 persons)	#城镇单位从业人员 Persons Employed in Urban Units	地 区 生产总值（亿元）Gross Domestic Product (100 million yuan)	人均地区生产总值（元）Per Capita GDP (yuan)	社会劳动生产率（元/人）Society Labour Productivity (yuan/person)
1952	439.22	159.50	45.18	12.80	299	825
1957	529.65	186.50	86.24	24.11	468	1 311
1962	595.63	203.80	106.48	24.25	414	1 166
1965	637.80	227.50	120.30	35.96	571	1 602
1970	652.70	270.20	135.81	50.99	791	1 960
1975	702.86	328.60	181.46	69.73	1 011	2 232
1978	724.27	366.70	217.40	82.65	1 160	2 300
1980	748.91	394.79	242.69	103.52	1 392	2 670
1985	804.80	455.98	276.48	175.71	2 198	3 890
1990	866.25	470.07	284.31	310.95	3 621	6 617
1991	872.63	479.67	291.56	342.75	3 943	7 218
1992	878.97	485.70	293.97	411.24	4 696	8 520
1993	885.89	503.10	293.45	536.10	6 075	10 843
1994	890.55	513.00	291.94	725.14	8 164	14 273
1995	894.67	515.30	289.59	917.65	10 281	17 848
1996	898.45	512.00	283.98	1 099.47	12 263	21 405
1997	899.80	513.33	281.34	1 235.28	13 739	24 095
1998	905.09	508.10	218.56	1 336.38	14 808	26 195
1999	910.17	508.14	211.76	1 450.06	15 976	28 538
2000	912.00	486.89	201.75	1 639.36	17 993	32 951
2001	913.98	488.34	192.30	1 840.10	20 154	37 737
2002	919.05	492.61	185.50	2 051.16	22 380	41 820
2003	926.00	510.90	191.01	2 447.66	26 532	48 782
平均每年递增% Average Annual Increase Rate%						
1953－1957	3.8	3.2	13.8	12.8	8.8	9.0
1958－1962	2.4	1.8	4.3	－1.8	－4.3	－4.2
1963－1965	2.3	3.7	4.2	15.3	12.6	12.4
1966－1970	0.5	3.5	2.5	7.7	7.1	4.6
1971－1975	1.5	4.0	6.0	7.2	5.7	3.3
1976－1980	1.3	3.7	6.0	7.3	6.0	3.1
1981－1985	1.4	2.9	2.6	9.3	7.7	5.7
1986－1990	1.5	0.6	0.6	5.2	3.7	4.4
1991－1995	0.6	1.9	0.4	11.7	10.9	9.8
1996－2000	0.4	－1.1	－7.0	11.3	10.8	12.0
1981－1990	1.5	1.8	1.6	7.3	5.7	5.0
1991－2000	0.5	0.4	－3.4	11.5	10.8	10.9
1953－2003	1.5	2.3	2.9	8.5	6.9	6.1
1979－2003	1.0	1.3	－0.5	9.9	8.7	8.4
1998－2003	0.5	－0.1	－6.3	11.6	11.1	12.0
2003 比 2002	0.8	3.7	3.0	14.8	14.0	12.2

注：1.本表地区生产总值、人均地区生产总值按现价计算，速度按可比价计算。2.社会劳动生产率按现价地区生产总值计算，速度按可比价计算。

Note：a) Gross domestic product, per capita GDP are calculated at current prices, increase rate are based on comparable prices. b) Society labou productivity are calculated at current prices of GDP, increase rate are based on comparable prices.

1-8 续表1 Continued
单位:亿元 (100 million yuan)

年 份 Year	农业总产值 Gross Output Value of Agriculture	工业总产值 Gross Output Value of Industry	轻工业 Light Industry	重工业 Heavy Industry	金融机构人民币存款余额 RMB Deposits of Financial Institutions	#城乡居民储蓄存款余额 Savings Deposits Balance of Rural & Urban Residents
1952	2.73	19.71	16.36	3.35	2.66	0.50
1957	3.23	40.44	29.01	11.43	3.08	1.05
1962	2.78	45.39	29.12	16.27	10.33	0.93
1965	4.82	66.35	39.08	27.27	12.19	1.57
1970	5.20	102.77	54.83	47.94	14.54	1.59
1975	5.39	145.57	74.47	71.10	25.69	2.88
1978	6.72	157.90	81.47	76.43	33.24	4.02
1980	9.25	195.94	106.00	89.94	44.92	7.96
1985	20.44	319.47	164.22	155.25	114.25	29.38
1990	51.72	679.94	354.50	325.44	263.21	126.92
1991	54.55	786.60	392.29	394.31	336.56	163.18
1992	58.50	997.91	465.48	532.43	467.81	202.66
1993	66.32	1 401.84	530.05	871.79	586.12	269.70
1994	88.74	1 754.30	760.80	993.50	800.56	394.50
1995	125.44	1 879.65	752.03	1 127.62	1 079.97	549.97
1996	133.53	2 177.42	1 014.46	1 162.96	1 399.06	724.91
1997	140.47	2 450.21	1 130.04	1 320.17	1 634.95	863.36
1998	156.16	2 562.62	1 157.09	1 405.53	1 860.84	1 020.14
1999	150.11	2 751.37	1 128.47	1 622.90	2 060.02	1 130.19
2000	156.30	3 080.74	1 263.10	1 817.64	2 281.55	1 172.40
2001	169.51	3 366.53	1 153.73	2 212.80	2 562.55	1 284.95
2002	181.07	3 717.72	1 207.88	2 509.84	3 018.26	1 486.38
2003	193.44	4 370.76	1 254.68	3 116.08	4 033.51	1 825.32
平均每年递增% Average Annual Increase Rate%						
1953-1957	3.8	16.6	13.5	29.5	3.0	16.0
1958-1962	-2.6	0.4	-1.3	4.5	27.4	-2.3
1963-1965	18.8	15.5	12.8	20.6	5.7	19.0
1966-1970	1.1	10.3	7.5	14.5	3.6	0.3
1971-1975	1.1	8.5	6.7	10.6	12.1	12.6
1976-1980	3.5	6.0	7.7	4.1	11.8	22.5
1981-1985	9.7	9.7	10.1	9.1	20.5	29.8
1986-1990	8.6	10.6	10.2	11.2	18.2	34.0
1991-1995	7.0	20.7	16.3	24.9	32.6	34.1
1996-2000	6.2	15.2	15.8	14.8	16.1	16.3
1981-1990	9.2	10.2	10.1	10.1	19.6	31.9
1991-2000	6.6	17.9	16.0	19.7	24.1	24.9
1953-2003	5.2	11.5	9.6	14.6	15.4	17.4
1979-2003	8.1	14.3	12.6	15.4	21.2	27.7
1998-2003	6.1	16.0	9.7	20.1	16.2	13.3
2003 比 2002	6.6	24.1	18.5	27.0	33.6	22.8

注:1.农业总产值按现价计算,速度按可比价计算。2.工业总产值1995年以后为现价新规定,以前为原规定,速度按可比价计算,以下各表同。3.金融机构人民币存、贷款余额为当年年末数。

Note:a)Gross output value of agriculture are calculated at current prices,increase rate are based on comparable prices. b)Gross output value of industry are calculated at current prices of new stipulation after 1995, others are former stipulation. Increase rate are based on comparable prices, same to next tables. c)RMB deposits and loans of financial institutions are by the end of the year.

1－8 续表 2　Continued
单位:亿元　　(100 million yuan)

年　份 Year	金融机构人民币贷款余额 RMB Loans of Financial Institutions	全市财政收　入 Total Financial Revenue	全市财政支　出 Total Financial Expenditures	全社会固定资产投资额 Total Investment in Fixed Assets	#地　方 Local	全社会新增固定资产 Total Newly Increased in Fixed Assets
1952	0.46	3.88	1.08	1.03	0.32	
1957	10.91	7.99	1.63	2.40	1.13	
1962	24.96	9.77	2.49	1.86	1.33	
1965	25.25	13.33	3.50	2.91	1.84	
1970	39.04	28.02	6.40	6.17	4.34	
1975	68.59	39.17	10.61	16.25	8.88	
1978	80.14	39.25	14.51	20.30	10.03	
1980	102.66	40.94	14.67	23.92	14.53	17.84
1985	191.04	48.21	26.97	65.90	50.80	42.62
1990	415.91	44.88	40.20	87.69	57.47	65.16
1991	487.43	58.09	47.47	128.95	93.13	74.11
1992	624.82	63.05	46.52	169.88	123.85	102.27
1993	768.57	74.96	51.27	226.56	176.14	140.00
1994	927.05	95.99	69.00	315.97	256.88	261.12
1995	1 113.95	117.34	90.37	393.18	309.75	300.86
1996	1 357.38	137.45	110.19	435.81	325.71	313.12
1997	1 502.91	169.12	140.08	498.66	376.69	320.46
1998	1 629.12	186.55	155.15	575.86	452.11	439.58
1999	1 825.26	206.90	177.62	567.36	405.31	459.54
2000	1 863.60	244.81	209.57	608.80	463.83	434.28
2001	2 159.86	304.52	259.78	705.10	567.40	476.92
2002	2 519.04	375.92	300.07	811.26	677.60	537.98
2003	3 426.02	451.74	350.63	1 046.72	893.73	656.99
平均每年递增% Average Annual Increase Rate%						
1953－1957	88.3	15.5	8.6	20.8	36.6	
1958－1962	18.0	4.1	8.8	24.4	45.7	
1963－1965	0.4	10.9	12.0	26.4	20.7	
1966－1970	9.1	16.0	12.8	6.7	4.1	
1971－1975	11.9	6.9	10.6	22.0	14.0	
1976－1980	8.4	0.9	6.7	6.5	7.7	
1981－1985	13.2	3.3	12.9	20.8	29.6	23.6
1986－1990	16.8	－1.4	8.3	6.7	2.3	13.4
1991－1995	21.8	21.2	17.6	36.8	43.3	35.1
1996－2000	10.8	15.9	18.3	10.6	9.1	9.1
1981－1990	15.1	0.9	10.6	16.8	19.6	17.9
1991－2000	16.2	18.5	18.0	26.3	28.9	25.9
1953－2003	19.1	9.8	12.0	14.2	16.6	
1979－2003	16.2	10.3	13.6	17.2	19.9	
1998－2003	14.7	17.8	16.5	10.6	12.3	12.9
2003 比 2002	35.9	20.2	16.8	29.0	31.9	22.1

注:1994 年以前全市财政收支为原地方预算内财政收支口径;1994 年以后为分税制后的全市财政收支数。
Note:Before 1994,total financial revenue and expenditure intra－budgetary refer to original local financial budgetary revenue and expenditure ;but it has been total financial revenue and expenditure of the city since the reform of tax system was implemented in 1994.

1-8 续表 3　Continued

年　份 Year	房屋建筑竣工面积（万平方米）Floor Space of Buildings Completed (10 000 sq. m)	#住　宅 Residential Buildings	社会货运量（万吨）Freight Traffic (10 000 tons)	港口货物吞吐量（万吨）Freight Handled at Ports (10 000 tons)	邮电业务总量（万元）Total Business of Post and Telecomm－unications Service (10 000 yuan)	社会消费品零售总额（亿元）Total Retail Sales of Consumer Goods (100 million yuan)
1952			1 748	74	894	7.19
1957			2 984	284	935	10.55
1962			3 498	391	1 436	12.31
1965			3 450	549	1 621	12.32
1970			4 837	817	1 660	14.57
1975			6 766	826	2 385	21.18
1978			9 241	1 131	2 710	25.20
1980	395.3	239.0	13 949	1 192	3 163	34.64
1985	598.1	342.1	18 249	1 856	5 290	64.12
1990	363.3	189.5	15 929	2 063	32 735	139.88
1991	361.2	193.8	18 308	2 378	44 527	159.44
1992	406.9	199.4	17 522	2 929	61 063	181.20
1993	467.3	286.5	21 640	3 719	97 062	227.42
1994	636.4	438.6	23 783	4 652	132 464	303.37
1995	736.5	486.9	24 040	5 787	187 195	375.64
1996	725.1	494.7	24 133	6 188	256 978	470.04
1997	655.2	412.0	25 090	6 789	342 848	535.02
1998	790.4	516.5	24 505	6 818	474 067	587.12
1999	873.6	596.2	27 052	7 298	567 242	657.28
2000	968.0	673.3	26 400	9 582	753 669	736.63
2001	1 020.1	682.4	28 608	11 369	702 206	832.70
2002	1 181.2	759.3	31 016	12 906	903 296	941.36
2003	1 255.1	775.3	35 252	16 182	1 157 060	922.27
平均每年递增% Average Annual Increase Rate%						
1953－1957			11.3	30.9	0.9	5.5
1958－1962			3.2	6.6	9.0	0.8
1963－1965			－0.5	12.0	4.1	4.0
1966－1970			7.0	8.3	0.5	3.7
1971－1975			6.9	0.2	7.5	7.8
1976－1980			15.6	7.6	5.8	8.8
1981－1985	12.4	12.2	5.5	9.3	10.8	9.3
1986－1990	－9.6	－13.7	－2.7	2.1	24.9	6.5
1991－1995	12.3	18.1	8.6	22.9	41.7	9.2
1996－2000	2.9	3.4	2.0	10.6	32.1	14.8
1981－1990	4.5	3.1	1.3	5.6	17.7	7.8
1991－2000	10.7	14.5	5.2	16.6	36.8	12.0
1953－2003			6.1	11.1	14.2	7.6
1979－2003			5.5	11.2	25.4	10.9
1998－2003	11.4	11.1	5.8	15.6	28.8	15.0
2003 比 2002	6.3	2.1	13.7	25.4	28.1	13.9

注：2003 年社会消费品零售总额为新口径，原口径为 1074.05 亿元，增长速度 17.1%。增长速度均为可比口径，并已扣除物价因素。

Note: In 2003, retail sales of consumer goods is calculated on new coverage, it is 107405 billion yuan calcullated on original coverage, up by 17.1 percent. The increase rate of retail on sales of consumer goods are calculated at comparable coverage and have deducted price sectors.

1－8 续表 4　Continued

年　份 Year	实际利用外资额（万美元）Foreign Capital Actually Used (USD 10 000)	#客商直投 Foreign Direct Investment	天津口岸进出口总值（亿美元）Total Value of Imports & Exports In Tianjin Port (USD 100 million)	#出　口 Exports	外贸进出口总值（亿美元）Total Value of Imports & Exports in Foreign Trade (USD 100 million)	#出　口 Exports
1952						1.90
1957					2.50	2.48
1962					2.40	2.34
1965					3.54	3.41
1970					3.58	3.19
1975					8.86	7.72
1978					9.88	8.65
1980	271	271			18.27	15.42
1985	7 558	4 409	96.18	20.07	14.86	11.53
1990	33 467	8 315	85.95	42.53	22.10	17.86
1991	48 144	9 388	91.37	46.48	20.20	16.06
1992	83 122	23 138	104.61	54.60	23.76	17.52
1993	93 502	54 120	125.04	66.03	27.77	19.42
1994	177 642	101 499	161.67	86.81	33.12	24.00
1995	211 010	152 064	217.46	127.81	65.46	29.98
1996	298 358	200 587	216.85	122.89	82.97	40.49
1997	342 301	251 135	215.62	131.24	100.23	50.18
1998	305 787	251 803	223.19	134.84	106.16	54.99
1999	274 535	253 203	248.29	139.18	126.05	63.32
2000	282 467	256 000	298.03	165.29	171.57	86.29
2001	329 688	322 000	323.71	178.13	181.86	95.02
2002	386 901	380 591	365.35	190.55	228.27	115.95
2003	170 550	163 325	461.67	259.57	293.71	143.74
平均每年递增% Average Annual Increase Rate%						
1953－1957						5.5
1958－1962					－0.8	－1.2
1963－1965					13.8	13.5
1966－1970					0.2	－1.4
1971－1975					19.9	19.4
1976－1980					15.6	14.8
1981－1985	94.6	74.7			－4.1	－5.7
1986－1990	34.7	13.5	－2.2	16.2	8.3	9.1
1991－1995	44.5	78.8	20.4	24.6	24.3	10.9
1996－2000	6.0	11.0	6.5	5.3	21.3	23.5
1981－1990	61.9	40.8			1.9	1.5
1991－2000	23.8	40.9	13.2	14.5	22.7	17.1
1953－2003						8.9
1979－2003					14.5	11.9
1998－2003	10.4	16.3	13.5	11.0	19.6	19.2
2003 比 2002	60.0	62.9	26.4	28.9	28.7	24.0

注：2003 年实际利用外资额采用商务部口径，速度按可比口径计算；以下相关表同。
Note：since 2003，foreign direct investment refer to new coverage of Ministry of Commerce，its increase rate is calculated on the basis of comparable coverage，same as following next.

1-8续表5 Continued

年 份 Year	单位从业人员劳动报酬总额(亿元) Total Remuneration of Persons Employed in Units (100 million yuan)	#国有经济 State-owned	城镇单位从业人员人均劳动报酬(元) Per Capita Remuneration of Persons Employed in Urban Units(yuan)	#国有经济 State-owned	城市居民人均可支配收入(元) Per Capita Annual Disposable Income of Urban Households (yuan)	城市居民人均消费性支出(元) Per Capita Annual Expenditure for Consumption of Urban Households (yuan)
1952	2.56	2.56		573	200	176
1957	5.05	5.05		749	240	216
1962	7.11	7.11		685	252	238
1965	8.48	7.29	714	745	261	234
1970	8.58	7.17	652	673	281	255
1975	10.66	8.61	618	663	324	295
1978	14.00	11.51	640	690	388	345
1980	19.32	15.77	820	865	527	475
1985	34.14	24.69	1 250	1 223	876	771
1990	69.38	55.50	2 438	2 611	1 639	1 440
1991	79.73	62.34	2 724	2 912	1 845	1 586
1992	91.56	71.97	3 118	3 383	2 238	1 907
1993	116.78	90.32	4 080	4 410	2 769	2 322
1994	154.04	116.07	5 364	5 806	3 982	3 301
1995	184.80	135.22	6 501	6 963	4 930	4 064
1996	212.05	154.34	7 643	8 072	5 968	4 680
1997	223.25	160.47	8 238	8 689	6 609	5 204
1998	225.39	151.80	9 895	10 169	7 111	5 471
1999	234.42	151.93	11 046	11 169	7 650	5 852
2000	253.53	161.86	12 414	12 690	8 141	6 121
2001	277.56	176.26	14 242	14 823	8 959	6 987
2002	304.23	182.27	16 223	16 632	9 338	7 192
2003	350.60	194.80	18 511	18 929	10 313	7 868
平均每年递增% Average Annual Increase Rate%						
1953-1957	12.1	12.1		3.3	1.5	2.0
1958-1962	4.7	4.7		-3.9	-1.3	-0.3
1963-1965	10.0	4.6		6.7	5.0	3.2
1966-1970	0.6	0.1	-1.4	-1.5	1.9	2.1
1971-1975	4.4	3.7	-1.1	-0.3	2.9	3.0
1976-1980	11.2	11.5	4.5	4.1	8.8	8.6
1981-1985	8.4	5.8	5.3	3.7	7.2	6.6
1986-1990	5.2	7.4	4.4	6.3	3.5	3.5
1991-1995	5.2	3.4	5.3	5.3	7.8	6.4
1996-2000	4.4	1.6	11.6	10.5	8.4	6.4
1981-1990	6.8	6.6	4.8	4.4	5.1	5.0
1991-2000	4.9	2.5	8.4	7.9	8.1	6.5
1953-2003	6.7	5.5		3.8	4.7	4.4
1979-2003	7.1	5.4	7.7	7.4	7.3	6.7
1998-2003	7.8	3.3	14.5	13.9	9.0	7.2
2003比2002	14.1	5.8	13.0	12.7	9.4	8.3

注:1.1998年以前有关劳动报酬指标的绝对数为职工工资,计算其平均递增速度时已扣除物价因素。2.计算城市居民人均收支平均递增速度按可比口径,且已扣除物价因素。

Note: a) Before 1998, total remuneration and per capita remuneration refer to wage of staff and workers, average annual increase rate of these indicators have deducted price sectors. b) Increase rate of income and expenditure are calculated at comparable coverage and have deducted price sectors.

1－8 续表 6　Continued

年　份 Year	农民人均纯收入(元) Per Capita Annual Net Income of Rural Households (yuan)	农民人均生活消费支出(元) Per Capita Annual Expenditure for Consumption of Rural Households (yuan)	各类学校在校学生数(万人) Students Enrollment By Level of School (10 000 persons)	国有单位自然科学技术人员数(人) Natural Scientific & Technical Personnel of State-owned Units (person)	医院卫生院床位数(张) Hospital Beds (unit)	卫生技术人员数(人) Medical Technical Personnel (person)	#医　生 Doctors
1952	70		57.14		3 457	8 481	3 326
1957	92		83.92		6 156	15 124	5 522
1962	65		106.37		10 521	23 858	8 627
1965	92		148.10		11 266	26 393	10 585
1970	145		148.17		11 361	23 591	9 046
1975	147		169.71		15 961	33 734	12 326
1978	153	132	162.30	102 022	17 288	40 653	15 776
1980	278	208	139.06	127 803	18 753	50 662	20 474
1985	564	426	121.09	194 837	25 191	60 412	25 555
1990	1 069	733	134.97	271 761	33 382	67 485	32 034
1991	1 169	796	138.01	280 986	35 124	68 887	32 385
1992	1 410	923	140.78	287 709	36 035	69 815	32 320
1993	1 593	1 011	145.27	290 789	36 724	70 920	33 026
1994	1 956	1 274	149.67	241 958	37 157	71 217	33 373
1995	2 531	1 717	155.28	248 739	37 280	71 806	33 693
1996	3 142	2 101	161.40	265 924	38 284	71 014	32 975
1997	3 548	2 110	164.41	260 927	39 467	70 431	32 475
1998	3 890	2 260	164.11	259 374	39 134	68 070	31 482
1999	4 055	2 334	162.53	257 169	38 579	65 901	30 273
2000	4 370	2 393	162.22	249 934	38 842	65 145	30 031
2001	4 825	2 618	160.54	240 361	40 394	63 475	29 215
2002	5 315	2 778	161.69	226 639	38 837	56 705	23 888
2003	5 861	3 015	163.23	232 324	38 074	55 629	22 780
平均每年递增% Average Annual Increase Rate%							
1953－1957	5.6		8.0		12.2	12.3	10.7
1958－1962	－6.7		4.9		11.3	9.5	9.3
1963－1965	12.3		11.7		2.3	3.4	7.1
1966－1970	9.5				0.2	－2.2	－3.1
1971－1975	0.3		2.8		7.0	7.4	6.4
1976－1980	13.6		－3.9		3.3	8.5	10.7
1981－1985	15.2	15.4	－2.7	8.8	6.1	3.6	4.5
1986－1990	13.6	11.5	2.2	6.9	5.8	2.2	4.6
1991－1995	18.8	18.6	2.8	－1.8	2.2	1.2	1.2
1996－2000	11.5	6.7	0.9	0.1	0.8	－1.9	－2.3
1981－1990	14.4	13.4	－0.3	7.8	5.9	2.9	4.6
1991－2000	15.1	12.6	1.9	－0.8	1.5	－0.4	－0.6
1953－2003	9.1		2.1		4.8	3.8	3.8
1979－2003	15.7	13.3		3.3	3.2	1.3	1.5
1998－2003	8.7	6.1	－0.1	－1.9	－0.6	－3.9	－5.7
2003 比 2002	10.3	8.5	1.0	2.5	－2.0	－1.9	－4.6

1－9　国民经济结构和比例指标
MAIN STRUCTURE & PROPORTION INDICATORS ON NATIONAL ECONOMY

单位：%　　　　　　　　　　　　　　　　　　　　　　　　　　　　　　　　（%）

指　　标	Item	1999	2000	2001	2002	2003
人口与就业	**Population and Employment**					
人　口	**Population**					
农非结构	Grouped by Non－agricultural and Agricultural					
非农业	Non－agricultural	58.1	58.4	58.6	58.9	59.4
农　业	Agricultural	41.9	41.6	41.4	41.1	40.6
性别结构	Grouped by Sex					
男	Male	50.5	50.5	50.5	50.5	50.5
女	Female	49.5	49.5	49.5	49.5	49.5
就　业	**Employment**					
社会从业人员产业结构	Grouped by Industry					
第一产业	Primary Industry	15.7	16.7	16.9	16.7	16.3
第二产业	Secondary Industry	45.3	45.6	43.6	41.7	42.9
第三产业	Tertiary Industry	39.0	37.7	39.5	41.6	40.8
宏 观 经 济	**Macro Economy**					
国民经济核算	**National Accounting**					
地区生产总值产业结构	Grouped by Industry					
第一产业	Primary Industry	4.9	4.5	4.3	4.1	3.6
第二产业	Secondary Industry	49.1	50.0	49.2	48.8	50.9
第三产业	Tertiary Industry	46.0	45.5	46.5	47.1	45.5
投　资	**Investment**					
全社会固定资产投资结构	Structure of Total Investment in Fixed Assets					
基本建设	Capital Construction	46.3	46.1	43.9	44.6	47.9
更新改造	Innovation	18.5	18.4	20.1	20.5	20.1
房地产开发	Real Estate	20.6	22.0	22.9	21.7	20.2
其他投资	Others	14.6	13.6	13.1	13.2	11.8
资金来源结构	Structure of Sources of Funds					
国家预算内投资	State Budgetary Appropriation	2.2	3.0	2.3	2.6	1.4
国内贷款	Domestic Loans	25.6	20.0	21.9	22.8	30.2
利用外资	Foreign Investment	14.4	15.9	15.8	8.4	5.9
自筹资金	Self－raised Funds	41.8	44.0	46.5	51.4	46.9
其他投资	Others	16.0	17.1	13.5	14.8	15.6
基建投资比例	Percentage of Investment in Capital Construction					
#能源工业	Energy Industry	34.6	33.7	28.3	24.6	22.4
运输邮电通信业	Transportation, Post and Telecommunications Service	18.9	15.7	21.0	18.6	20.5
全社会固定资产投资相当于地区生产总值比例	Proportion of Total Investment in Fixed Assets to GDP	39.1	37.1	38.3	39.6	42.8

注：本表产业和行业分类为国标 GB/T4754－1994 标准，1－11、1－14 至 1－17 表同。
Note: Sector listed in this table is classified by the standard of GB/T4754－1994, same as following table 1－11, 1－14 to 1－17.

1－9 续表 1　Continued
单位：%　　(%)

指　标	Item	1999	2000	2001	2002	2003
财　政	**Government Finance**					
全市财政收入相当于地区生产总值比例	Proportion of Total Financial Revenue to GDP	14.3	14.9	16.5	18.3	18.5
基建支出相当于财政支出比例	Proportion of Capital Construction Appropriation to Government Expenditures	14.5	15.9	15.9	14.8	15.0
科教文卫事业费相当于财政支出比例	Proportion of Culture, Education, Science & Health Care Funds to Government Expenditures	24.6	24.3	22.6	23.1	20.5
利用外资	**Utilization of Foreign Capital**					
实际利用外资结构	Structure of Foreign Capital Actually Utilized					
对外借款	Foreign Loans	7.8	9.4	2.3	1.6	4.2
客外商直接投资	Foreign Direct Investment	92.2	90.6	97.7	98.4	95.8
客商直接投资相当于签约额比例	Proportion of Foreign Direct Investment to Foreign Investment Contracted	69.9	55.7	69.5	65.5	46.5
能　源	**Energy Consumption**					
能源使用结构	Structure of Energy Consumption					
#第一产业	Primary Industry	2.1	2.1	2.5	2.6	1.9
第二产业	Secondary Industry	56.2	56.7	62.2	65.3	63.3
第三产业	Tertiary Industry	21.0	22.9	22.3	19.4	20.6
产　业	**Industrial**					
农　业	**Agriculture**					
农林牧渔业总产值结构	Structure of Gross Output Value					
农　业(种植业)	Farming (Planting)	61.0	53.4	51.2	47.5	45.6
林　业	Forestry	0.9	0.9	0.9	0.8	0.8
牧　业	Animal Husbandry	26.0	33.1	35.8	38.3	39.9
渔　业	Fishery	12.1	12.6	12.1	13.4	13.7
工　业	**Industry**					
全部工业总产值结构	Structure of Gross Output Value of Industry					
轻工业	Light Industry	41.0	41.0	34.3	32.5	28.7
重工业	Heavy Industry	59.0	59.0	65.7	67.5	71.3
建筑业	**Construction**					
建筑业总产值结构	Structure of Gross Output Value of Construction					
房屋和土木工程建筑业	Building and Civil Engineering	83.2	81.4	80.6	81.9	81.9
建筑安装业	Equipment Installation	15.1	16.6	17.6	13.9	13.8
建筑装饰业	Building Decoration	1.7	2.0	1.8	3.2	3.1
其他建筑业	Others				1.0	1.2

1－9 续表 2　Continued
单位：%　　(%)

指 标	Item	1999	2000	2001	2002	2003
运输业	**Transportation**					
货运量结构	Structure of Freight Traffic					
铁 路(天津地区)	Railway(Tianjin Area)	8.8	11.7	13.0	14.6	16.1
公 路	Highway	74.1	71.1	67.8	63.0	56.9
水运、民航	Waterway and Civil Aviation	14.4	15.8	17.6	20.8	25.4
管道运输	Pipelines	2.7	1.4	1.6	1.6	1.6
国内商业	**Domestic Trade**					
社会消费品零售总额构成	Composition of Retail Sales of Consumer Goods					
吃	Food	41.6	40.9	40.1	39.7	36.9
穿	Clothing	17.1	16.6	16.7	16.9	17.3
用	Used Articles	40.3	41.6	41.7	41.8	44.2
烧	Fuel	1.0	0.9	1.5	1.6	1.6
对外经济贸易	**Foreign Trade**					
进出口贸易总值结构	Structure of Imports and Exports					
出口总值	Exports	50.2	50.3	52.2	50.8	48.9
进口总值	Imports	49.8	49.7	47.8	49.2	51.1
进出口总值相当于地区生产总值比例	Proportion of Total Value of Imports & Exports in Foreign Trade to GDP	72.0	87.1	81.8	92.1	99.3
国际旅游	**International Tourism**					
来津旅游人员结构	Structure of Tourists					
外国人、华侨	Foreigners and Overseas Chinese	81.0	81.8	81.1	81.3	83.7
港澳台同胞	Compatriots form Hongkong,Macao and Taiwan	19.0	18.2	18.9	18.7	16.3
金 融	**Banking**					
金融机构人民币存款结构	Structure of RMB Deposits in Financial Institution					
#企业存款	Deposits of Enterprises	35.7	38.2	37.0	37.0	38.2
城乡储蓄存款	Savings Deposits of Urban and Rural	54.9	51.4	50.1	49.2	45.3
金融机构人民币贷款结构	Structure of RMB Loans in Financial Institution					
#工业贷款	Industrial Loans	23.5	19.8	20.1	17.9	12.5
商业贷款	Commercial Loans	16.0	12.6	11.6	9.6	8.0
中长期贷款	Medium－term & Long－term Loans	22.2	23.1	29.5	33.6	42.9

1－10 国民经济主要指标经济类型变化
MAIN INDICATORS OF NATIONAL ECONOMY BY OWNERSHIP

单位：%　　(%)

指　标	Item	1999	2000	2001	2002	2003
1.社会从业人员数	Employment Personnel					
国有经济	State－owned	34.7	33.7	31.4	28.0	25.2
城镇集体经济	Urban Collective－owned	9.4	8.3	6.6	5.4	4.4
乡村从业人员	Rural Employment Personnel	38.2	39.1	39.5	40.0	41.3
其他经济	Others	17.7	18.9	22.5	26.6	29.1
2.城镇单位从业人员	Urban Employment Personnel Worked in Units					
国有经济	State－owned	63.8	62.0	60.4	58.1	53.2
集体经济	Collective－owned	14.4	12.8	10.4	8.9	7.3
其他经济	Others	21.8	25.2	29.2	33.0	39.5
#“三资”经济	"Foreign－funded" Economy	15.4	17.5	20.1	22.2	23.9
3.全社会固定资产投资额	Total Investment in Fixed Assets					
国有经济	State－owend	58.3	42.0	40.5	39.9	45.3
集体经济	Collective－owned	10.8	10.2	9.3	10.6	9.4
其他经济	Others	30.9	47.8	50.2	49.5	45.3
#“三资”经济	"Foreign－funded" Economy	13.3	15.8	24.2	16.4	10.1
4.限额以上工业总产值	Gross Output Value of Industry Above Designated Size					
国有经济	State－owned	25.3	21.4	18.6	15.6	14.8
集体经济	Collective－owned	24.7	19.2	17.5	16.2	11.0
其他经济	Others	50.0	59.4	63.9	68.2	74.2
#“三资”经济	"Foreign－funded" Economy	43.2	45.9	46.5	48.3	46.8
5.限额以上工业增加值	Value－added of Industry Above Designated Size					
国有经济	State－owned	33.0	24.9	17.4	13.8	16.1
集体经济	Collective－owned	20.6	13.4	12.1	11.9	9.9
其他经济	Others	46.4	61.7	70.5	74.3	74.0
#“三资”经济	"Foreign－funded" Economy	38.3	42.1	44.6	46.2	39.5
6.限额以上工业利税总额	Total Pre－tax Profits of Industry Above Designated Size					
国有经济	State－owned	15.3	6.8	5.2	7.0	13.2
集体经济	Collective－owned	29.4	16.1	14.1	14.7	9.1
其他经济	Others	55.3	77.1	80.7	78.3	77.7
#“三资”经济	"Foreign－funded" Economy	47.7	49.3	47.8	38.7	35.3
7.社会消费品零售总额	Total Retail Sales of Consumer Goods					
国有经济	State－owned	17.7	17.6	17.4	16.6	16.3
集体经济	Collective－owned	14.8	14.0	11.5	9.8	9.1
其他经济	Others	67.5	68.4	71.1	73.6	74.6
#私营经济	Private	8.8	9.6	11.6	13.5	14.5
个体经济	Individual	16.8	14.1	16.4	17.8	19.4

1-11 平均每天社会经济活动
AVERAGE DAILY SOCIAL AND ECONOMIC ACTIVITIES

指 标	Item	单 位	Unit	1999	2000	2001	2002	2003
一、全市每天创造的财富	**Daily Production**							
地区生产总值	Gross Domestic Product	万元	10^4 yuan	39 728	44 914	50 414	56 196	67 059
第一产业	Primary Industry	万元	10^4 yuan	1 945	2 015	2 152	2 301	2 456
第二产业	Secondary Industry	万元	10^4 yuan	19 505	22 470	24 785	27 449	34 118
工 业	Industry	万元	10^4 yuan	17 540	20 473	22 498	24 911	31 130
建筑业	Construction	万元	10^4 yuan	1 965	1 997	2 287	2 539	2 988
第三产业	Tertiary Industry	万元	10^4 yuan	18 277	20 429	23 477	26 445	30 485
#交通运输、仓储和邮电通信业	Transportation, Storage, Post and Telecommunications	万元	10^4 yuan	4 269	4 899	5 588	6 325	6 698
全市财政收入	Total Financial Revenue	万元	10^4 yuan	5 668	6 707	8 342	10 299	12 376
主要工业产品产量	Output of Major Industrial Products							
钢	Steel	吨	ton	8 704	9 774	10 830	13 221	15 505
钢 材	Steel Products	吨	ton	11 110	8 654	12 191	22 086	28 259
水 泥	Cement	吨	ton	6 589	7 337	9 287	10 349	12 310
原 油	Crude Oil	吨	ton	18 814	20 931	26 583	33 313	36 063
原 盐	Salt	吨	ton	6 421	6 616	6 534	6 586	6 041
发电量	Electricity	万千瓦时	10^4 kwh	5 002	5 794	5 957	7 365	8 766
汽 车	Motor Vehicle	辆	unit	353	279	161	259	473
彩色电视机	Color Television	台	set	1 379	1 980	1 409	2 092	3 080
摩托车	Motorcycle	辆	unit	1 789	1 053	1 381	2 178	3 145
自行车	Bicycle	辆	unit	6 693	8 548	8 829	17 373	22 847
微波炉	Microwave Oven	台	set	3 659	4 303	8 768	12 313	26 572
移动电话	Mobile Phone	部	unit	19 627	36 065	41 028	78 100	86 020
布	Cloth	万米	10^4 m	75	80	71	74	69
纱	Yarn	吨	ton	232	241	223	252	205
农用化肥	Chemical Fertilizer	吨	ton	735	467	408	439	449
化学农药	Chemical Pesticide	吨	ton	101	76	19	90	58
硫 酸	Sulfuric Acid	吨	ton	314	306	309	333	300
烧 碱	Caustic Soda	吨	ton	1 825	1 914	1 353	1 744	2 189
合成洗涤剂	Synthetic Detergents	吨	ton	240	197	156	148	139
饮料酒	Alcoholic Beverages	吨	ton	389	432	567	565	677
主要农产品产量	Output of Major Farm Products							
粮 食	Grain	吨	ton	4 790	3 399	3 927	3 776	3 268
棉 花	Cotton	吨	ton	16	48	174	171	259
油 料	Oil bearing Crops	吨	ton	64	91	107	93	84
肉 类	Meat	吨	ton	645	808	997	1 230	1 436
蛋 类	Eggs	吨	ton	645	701	712	670	664
牛 奶	Milk	吨	ton	354	452	659	920	1 184
蔬 菜	Vegetables	吨	ton	13 317	14 537	15 466	16 008	16 515
水产品	Aquatic Products	吨	ton	631	663	725	782	817

1－11 续表　Continued

指　标	Item	单　位	Unit	1999	2000	2001	2002	2003
二、全市每天消费量	**Daily Consumption**							
最终消费	Final Consumption Expenditure	万元	10^4 yuan	19 638	22 047	24 708	27 129	31 087
居民消费	Resident Consumption	万元	10^4 yuan	13 803	15 270	17 014	17 983	19 804
城镇居民	Urban	万元	10^4 yuan	10 566	11 710	13 133	13 864	15 341
农村居民	Rural	万元	10^4 yuan	3 237	3 559	3 881	4 119	4 464
政府消费	Government Consumption Expenditure	万元	10^4 yuan	5 835	6 777	7 694	9 146	11 283
社会消费品零售总额	Total Retail Sales of Consumer Goods	万元	10^4 yuan	18 008	20 182	22 814	25 791	25 268
生活用煤、气、水、电	Coal, Gas, Water & Electricity For Living							
煤	Coal	万吨	10^4 tons	0.33	0.27	0.38	0.22	0.25
液化石油气	Liquid Petroleum Gas	吨	ton	463	322	295	263	293
天然气和煤气	Natural Gas And Coal Gas	万立方米	10^4 cum	55	117	160	105	82.5
水	Water	万吨	10^4 tons	76.8	70.4	89.2	81.9	81.7
电	Electricity	万千瓦时	10^4 kwh	658	677	716	804	869
三、每天其他经济活动	**Other Daily Economic Activities**							
社会货物运输量	Freight Traffic	万吨	10^4 tons	74.1	72.3	78.4	85.0	96.6
客运量	Passenger Traffic	万人次	10^4 persons time	8.9	9.5	9.0	9.5	9.6
港口货物吞吐量	Freight Handled at Ports	万吨	10^4 tons	20.0	26.3	31.1	35.4	44.3
邮电业务总量	Total Business of Post and Telecommunications Service	万元	10^4 yuan	1 554	2 065	1 924	2 475	3 170
铁路客运量	Passenger Traffic By Railway	万人次	10^4 persons time	4.2	4.4	4.0	4.1	3.5
公共汽车客运量	Passenger Traffic By Buses	万人次	10^4 persons time	157.8	146.2	167.0	174.0	172
出版图书	Books Published	万册	10^4 copies	23.7	16.1	17.1	19.0	18.6
出版报纸	Newspapers Published	万份	10^4 copies	154.2	164.1	197.5	221.3	225.7
出版杂志	Magazines Published	万册	10^4 copies	13.4	14.5	12.5	13.2	12.6
邮寄函件	Letters Delivered	万件	10^4 copies	22.2	35.6	46.8	55.2	60.4
外贸出口总值	Total Value of Exports in Foreign Trade	万美元	USD 10^4	1 735	2 364	2 603	3 177	3 938
实际利用外资额	Foreign Capital Actually Used	万美元	USD 10^4	752	774	903	1 060	467
竣工房屋建筑面积	Floor Space of Buildings Completed	万平方米	10^4 sq. m	2.39	2.89	2.67	3.24	3.44
接待来津国际旅游人数	Accommodated International Tourists	人次	person－time	395	437	486	560	472
四、每天人口和婚姻动态	**Daily Population Changes And Marriages**							
出生人口	Births	人	person	201	199	208	206	197
死亡人口	Deaths	人	person	132	167	163	166	167
结婚对数	Marriages	对	couple	158	168	159	148	172
离婚对数	Divorces	对	couple	35	37	27	29	33

注：生活用水为城市数。
Note: Water for Living refer to urban area.

1－12 国民经济主要指标年平均每人水平

PER CAPITA ANNUAL LEVEL OF MAIN INDICATORS ON NATIONAL ECONOMY

指 标	Item	单位 Unit	1999	2000	2001	2002	2003
1.地区生产总值	Gross Domestic Product	元 yuan	15 976	17 993	20 154	22 380	26 532
2.全市财政收入	Total Financial Revenue	元 yuan	2 280	2 687	3 335	4 102	4 897
3.全财政支出	Total Financial Expenditures	元 yuan	1 957	2 300	2 845	3 274	3 801
4.全社会固定资产投资	Total Investment in Fixed Assets	元 yuan	6 251	6 682	7 723	8 852	11 346
5.工业总产值	Gross Output Value of Industry	元 yuan	30 314	33 813	36 874	40 563	47 378
6.主要工业产品产量	Output of Major Industrial Products						
原 油	Crude Oil	吨 ton	0.76	0.84	1.06	1.33	1.43
天然气	Natural Gas	立方米 cu.m	94	100	98	97	92
发电量	Electricity	千瓦时 kwh	2 011	2 321	2 382	2 933	3 468
钢	Steel	吨 ton	0.35	0.39	0.43	0.53	0.61
钢 材	Steel Products	吨 ton	0.45	0.35		0.88	1.12
水 泥	Cement	吨 ton	0.26	0.29	0.37	0.41	0.49
布	Cloth	米 m	30	32	28	30	27
纱	Yarn	公斤 kg	9.3	9.7	8.9	10.0	8.1
7.农业总产值	Gross Output Value of Agriculture	元 yuan	1 654	1 716	1 857	1 976	2 097
8.主要农产品产量	Output of Major Farm Products						
粮 食	Grain	公斤 kg	193	136	157	150	129
棉 花	Cotton	公斤 kg	0.6	1.9	7.0	6.8	10.3
油 料	Oil－Bearing Crops	公斤 kg	2.6	3.6	4.3	3.7	3.3
蔬 菜	Vegetables	公斤 kg	536	582	618	638	653
肉 类	Meat	公斤 kg	26	32	40	49	57
蛋 类	Eggs	公斤 kg	26	28	28	27	26
奶 类	Milk	公斤 kg	14	15	26	37	47
水产品	Aquatic Products	公斤 kg	25.4	26.6	29.0	31.2	32.3
鲜 果	Fresh Fruits	公斤 kg	28.1	31.0	32.1	32.6	34.3
9.社会消费品零售额	Total Retail Sales of Consumer Goods	元 yuan	7 242	8 085	9 121	10 271	9 997
10.城市居民主要商品购买量	Perchase Volume of Major Products of Urban Households						
粮 食	Grain	公斤 kg	95.8	96.2	100.3	74.7	80.8
食用植物油	Edible Vegetable－oil	公斤 kg	8.3	8.0	7.9	7.9	9.3
猪牛羊肉	Pork,Beef and Mutton	公斤 kg	23.7	22.7	21.5	22.0	24.2
鸡 蛋	Eggs	公斤 kg	19.2	19.0	17.5	16.3	18.8
鲜 菜	Fresh Vegetables	公斤 kg	133.7	131.7	128.9	125.0	138.9
鱼	Fish	公斤 kg	10.0	9.7	9.5	9.2	9.5
鲜 奶	Milk	公斤 kg	10.3	13.0	16.2	16.9	23.1
干鲜瓜果	Fresh and Dried Fruits	公斤 kg	78.8	83.8	79.2	68.4	80.4
服 装	Garments	件 piece	7.3	7.4	7.1	6.9	6.3
鞋 类	Shoes	双 pair	2.4	2.6	2.6	2.5	2.4
11.外贸出口总值	Total Value of Exports in Foreign Trade	美元 USD	698	947	1 041	1 265	1 558
12.社会货物运输量	Freight Traffic	吨 ton	29.8	29.0	31.3	33.8	38.2

1-13 按新国民经济行业分地区生产总值构成项目(2003年)
COMPOSITION OF GROSS DOMESTIC PRODUCT GROUPED BY NEW SECTOR,2003

单位:亿元 (100 million yuan)

指标 Item	增加值 Added	劳动者报酬 Compensation of Laborers	生产税净额 Net Taxes On Production	固定资产折旧 Depreciation of Fixed Assets	营业盈余 Operating Surplus
合计					
Total	**2 447.66**	**1 052.94**	**410.51**	**440.20**	**544.01**
第一产业					
Primary Industry	92.20	73.48	1.14	3.30	14.28
第二产业					
Secondary Industry	1 245.29	380.44	269.60	254.06	341.19
工业					
Industry	1 136.24	309.80	253.85	244.03	328.56
建筑业					
Construction	109.05	70.64	15.75	10.03	12.63
第三产业					
Tertiary Industry	1 110.17	599.02	139.77	182.84	188.54
交通运输、仓储和邮政业					
Transport, Storage and Post Services	191.79	111.95	20.64	35.36	23.84
交通运输和仓储业					
Transport and Storage	187.44	108.94	20.28	34.75	23.47
邮政业					
Post Services	4.35	3.01	0.36	0.61	0.37
信息传输、计算机服务和软件业					
Information Transmitting, Computer Services and Software	68.09	16.17	8.76	25.44	17.72
批发和零售业					
Wholesale and Retail Trade	177.78	85.78	62.92	5.68	23.40
住宿和餐饮业					
Accommodation and Catering Services	63.98	57.96	2.83	2.61	0.58
金融业					
Finance	107.02	24.95	11.23	7.49	63.35
房地产业					
Real Estate	125.43	17.74	15.18	63.52	28.99
租赁和商务服务业					
Leasing and Business Services	18.55	13.17	0.82	6.50	-1.94
科学研究、技术服务和地质勘察业					
Scientific Research, Technical Services and Geological Prospecting	45.12	27.10	1.76	7.55	8.71
水利、环境和公共设施管理业					
Management for Water Conservancy, Environment and Public Facilities	15.66	4.41	0.64	6.24	4.37
居民服务和其他服务业					
Resident Services and Other Social Services	68.14	44.52	5.93	5.53	12.16
教育					
Education	91.08	84.85	1.19	4.66	0.38
卫生、社会保障和社会福利业					
Health Care, Social Security and Social Welfare	36.94	30.43	0.08	4.02	2.41
文化、体育和娱乐业					
Culture, Sports and Recreational Services	33.97	24.94	5.44	1.06	2.53
公共管理和社会组织					
Public Management and Social Organizations	66.62	55.05	2.35	7.18	2.04

1－14 地区生产总值
GROSS DOMESTIC PRODUCT
（1978－2003）

单位：亿元 （100 million yuan）

年 份 Year	地区生产总值 Gross Domestic Product	第一产业 Primary Industry	第二产业 Secondary Industry			第三产业 Tertiary Industry
				工 业 Industry	建筑业 Construction	
1978	82.65	5.03	57.53	54.39	3.14	20.09
1979	93.00	6.54	64.76	60.95	3.81	21.70
1980	103.52	6.53	72.43	67.35	5.08	24.56
1981	107.96	5.18	76.77	70.86	5.91	26.01
1982	114.10	7.00	79.59	72.03	7.56	27.51
1983	123.40	7.60	84.11	76.33	7.78	31.69
1984	147.47	11.13	95.97	87.47	8.50	40.37
1985	175.71	12.95	114.23	104.11	10.12	48.53
1986	194.67	16.51	122.49	111.06	11.43	55.67
1987	220.00	19.63	136.96	123.99	12.97	63.41
1988	259.64	26.21	159.58	145.35	14.23	73.85
1989	283.34	26.85	175.88	159.07	16.81	80.61
1990	310.95	27.32	179.51	163.72	15.79	104.12
1991	342.75	29.26	194.41	177.56	16.85	119.08
1992	411.24	30.26	230.61	210.00	20.61	150.37
1993	536.10	35.39	302.48	275.04	27.44	198.23
1994	725.14	46.53	404.08	361.27	42.81	274.53
1995	917.65	60.75	501.22	451.84	49.38	355.68
1996	1 099.47	67.60	584.43	527.07	57.36	447.44
1997	1 235.28	69.43	643.88	580.21	63.67	521.97
1998	1 336.38	74.03	660.00	587.83	72.17	602.35
1999	1 450.06	71.01	711.93	640.21	71.72	667.12
2000	1 639.36	73.54	820.17	747.28	72.89	745.65
2001	1 840.10	78.55	904.64	821.18	83.46	856.91
2002	2 051.16	84.00	1 001.90	909.24	92.66	965.26
2003	2 447.66	89.66	1 245.29	1 136.24	109.05	1 112.71

注：根据国家统计制度的变化，从2000年起金融保险业增加值口径有调整。
Note：According to the change of national statistics institution，the coverage of value－added of banking & insurance has been adjusted since the year of 2000.

1－14 续表 Continued
单位:亿元 (100 million yuan)

年 份 Year	#交通运输仓储邮电业 Transportation, Storage, Post and Telecommunications	#商 业 Commerce	#金融保险业 Banking & Insurance	#房地产业 Real Estate	人均地区生产总值(元) Per Capita GDP (yuan)	社会劳动生产率(元/人) Society Labour Productivity (yuan/person)
1978	4.79	6.95	0.13		1 160	2 300
1979	5.51	7.41	0.14		1 272	2 489
1980	6.36	7.12	0.76		1 392	2 670
1981	6.70	8.52	0.57		1 433	2 672
1982	6.59	7.24	0.74		1 488	2 737
1983	7.58	8.89	1.55		1 583	2 883
1984	11.60	14.61	5.64	0.85	1 868	3 341
1985	11.69	15.64	8.94	1.67	2 198	3 890
1986	13.89	17.40	9.80	1.86	2 406	4 219
1987	14.46	20.36	14.54	1.88	2 682	4 692
1988	16.61	21.55	18.32	3.35	3 117	5 547
1989	21.30	14.26	25.31	3.22	3 353	6 061
1990	30.25	15.85	29.04	5.35	3 621	6 617
1991	27.13	27.65	30.37	5.84	3 943	7 218
1992	35.66	41.05	34.71	6.78	4 696	8 520
1993	47.60	51.21	42.61	9.70	6 075	10 843
1994	66.55	65.41	55.50	12.14	8 164	14 273
1995	86.14	78.27	81.40	16.85	10 281	17 848
1996	98.91	97.97	107.00	26.29	12 263	21 405
1997	113.63	107.40	120.17	34.25	13 739	24 095
1998	133.16	127.29	114.88	43.21	14 808	26 195
1999	155.82	142.54	109.32	47.23	15 976	28 538
2000	178.83	158.56	55.80	69.35	17 993	32 951
2001	203.98	178.25	63.38	85.61	20 154	37 737
2002	230.88	196.38	73.08	97.66	22 380	41 820
2003	244.48	215.89	107.02	125.43	26 532	48 782

1-15 地区生产总值增长速度

INCREASE RATE OF GROSS DOMESTIC PRODUCT

(1978-2003)

单位:%　　　　　　　　　　　　　　　　(%)

年 份 Year	地区生产总值 Gross Domestic Product	第一产业 Primary Industry	第二产业 Secondary Industry	工 业 Industry	建筑业 Construc-tion	第三产业 Tertiary Industry	人均地区生产总值 Per Capita GDP	社 会 劳动生产率 Society Labour Productivity
1978	20.9	15.6	23.3	21.1	67.9	16.0	19.6	17.1
1979	10.0	17.4	10.4	10.4	10.7	7.0	7.2	5.9
1980	10.0	-0.2	11.4	10.6	22.0	8.7	8.1	6.0
1981	4.8	-20.9	7.0	6.6	12.2	4.8	3.4	0.5
1982	4.3	12.9	3.5	2.4	17.5	5.3	2.5	1.1
1983	8.3	9.2	6.0	6.0	6.3	14.8	6.6	5.5
1984	19.3	22.8	16.6	17.5	6.2	25.9	17.7	15.6
1985	10.6	21.1	10.5	10.0	16.5	8.8	9.2	8.1
1986	5.8	8.0	5.5	5.0	11.8	6.0	4.5	3.6
1987	7.6	6.0	8.3	8.2	8.9	6.3	6.1	5.9
1988	5.8	7.7	7.7	8.3	1.2	0.4	4.1	6.0
1989	1.6	11.4	-1.9	-2.2	1.2	9.3	0.2	1.8
1990	5.4	4.6	1.1	2.0	-8.4	16.4	3.8	4.8
1991	6.0	3.4	5.5	5.8	2.1	7.5	4.7	4.9
1992	11.7	0.7	11.5	12.4	1.2	14.6	10.8	9.8
1993	12.1	7.4	12.9	13.6	3.6	11.7	11.2	9.4
1994	14.3	5.3	14.7	14.1	22.7	15.6	13.6	11.2
1995	14.9	6.3	14.1	14.5	9.9	17.9	14.3	13.5
1996	14.3	8.2	14.3	14.6	10.1	15.4	13.6	14.4
1997	12.1	7.7	11.7	11.8	10.1	13.4	12.0	12.3
1998	9.3	6.7	7.4	7.0	12.7	13.0	8.9	9.9
1999	10.0	0.1	11.7	12.6	-0.8	8.9	9.4	10.5
2000	10.8	3.7	11.5	12.2	0.9	10.5	10.3	13.1
2001	12.0	6.3	12.8	12.7	14.3	11.7	11.8	14.3
2002	12.5	6.1	14.3	14.6	12.2	11.2	12.1	11.9
2003	14.8	6.1	18.0	18.6	12.4	11.8	14.0	12.2

1-16 总 产 出
TOTAL OUTPUT
(1999-2003)

单位:亿元 (100 million yuan)

指 标 Item	1999	2000	2001	2002	2003	2003 比 2002 年增长% Increase Rate in 2003 over 2002
总 产 出 **Total Output**	**4 891.00**	**5 312.58**	**5 801.25**	**6 365.42**	**7 547.90**	**16.6**
第一产业 Primary Industry	150.10	156.30	169.51	181.07	193.44	6.4
第二产业 Secondary Industry	3 260.55	3 495.60	3 753.33	4 075.48	4 965.91	19.1
工 业 Industry	3 000.28	3 240.42	3 433.78	3 717.72	4 505.07	18.8
建筑业 Construction	260.27	255.18	319.55	357.76	460.84	22.8
第三产业 Tertiary Industry	1 480.35	1 660.68	1 878.41	2 108.87	2 388.55	12.2
农林牧渔服务业 Services of Farming, Forestry, Animal Husbandry and Fishery	5.41	12.07	13.00	18.20	18.91	3.6
地质勘察业、水利管理业 Geological Prospecting and Water Conservancy	14.21	16.86	18.46	21.56	24.95	7.4
交通运输和仓储业 Transportation and Storage	293.23	323.02	363.47	406.80	427.69	11.7
邮电通信业 Post and Telecommunications	48.39	58.33	64.03	68.74	76.73	12.1
批发和零售贸易、餐饮业 Wholesale, Retail Trades and Catering Services	433.50	486.45	547.77	606.82	660.21	11.7
金融保险业 Banking and Insurance	139.18	121.03	135.42	152.97	192.82	19.6
房地产业 Real Estate	105.15	139.56	169.04	195.93	242.90	19.8
社会服务业 Social Services	189.59	213.83	235.85	265.41	316.55	10.6
卫生、体育、社会福利业 Health Care, Sports and Welfare	46.29	56.89	61.93	73.02	75.08	9.4
教育、文艺广播电影电视业 Education, Culture, Radio and Television	84.51	100.96	125.16	142.24	169.77	7.8
科学研究和综合技术服务业 Scientific Research and Polytechnic Services	39.47	42.51	44.91	48.36	56.69	8.7
国家机关、政党机关和社会团体 Government & Party Agencies and Social Organizations	73.90	80.98	90.36	98.48	114.35	7.7
其他行业 Others	7.52	8.19	9.01	10.34	11.90	6.7

1－17 地区生产总值
GROSS DOMESTIC PRODUCT
(1999－2003)

单位:亿元 (100 million yuan)

指 标 Item	1999	2000	2001	2002	2003	2003 比 2002 年增长% Increase Rate in 2003 over 2002
地区生产总值 Gross Domestic Product	**1 450.06**	**1 639.36**	**1 840.10**	**2 051.16**	**2 447.66**	**14.8**
第一产业 Primary Industry	71.01	73.54	78.55	84.00	89.66	6.1
第二产业 Secondary Industry	711.93	820.17	904.64	1 001.90	1 245.29	18.0
工 业 Industry	640.21	747.28	821.18	909.24	1 136.24	18.6
建筑业 Construction	71.72	72.89	83.46	92.66	109.05	12.4
第三产业 Tertiary Industry	667.12	745.65	856.91	965.26	1 112.71	11.8
农林牧渔服务业 Services of Farming, Forestry, Animal Husbandry and Fishery	0.69	1.68	1.70	2.46	2.54	2.7
地质勘察业、水利管理业 Geological Prospecting and Water Conservancy	7.63	9.17	9.82	11.66	13.60	9.1
交通运输和仓储业 Transportation and Storage	123.47	139.23	159.93	181.76	187.44	11.3
邮电通信业 Post and Telecommunications	32.35	39.60	44.05	49.12	57.04	16.2
批发和零售贸易、餐饮业 Wholesale, Retail Trades and Catering Services	142.54	158.56	178.25	196.38	215.89	10.9
金融保险业 Banking and Insurance	109.32	55.80	63.38	73.08	107.02	25.5
房地产业 Real Estate	47.23	69.35	85.61	97.66	125.43	17.6
社会服务业 Social Services	91.96	104.98	119.64	135.59	166.28	8.1
卫生、体育和社会福利业 Health Care, Sports and Welfare	17.48	29.08	32.46	38.08	39.30	8.2
教育、文艺广播电影电视业 Education, Culture, Radio and Television	41.28	61.90	76.43	85.52	100.03	7.7
科学研究和综合技术服务业 Scientific Research and Polytechnic Services	17.58	25.54	28.11	30.37	31.52	7.2
国家机关、政党机关和社会团体 Government & Party Agencies and Social Organizations	31.77	46.27	52.48	57.98	59.69	7.7
其他行业 Others	3.82	4.49	5.05	5.60	6.93	4.1

1－18 支出法地区生产总值
GROSS DOMESTIC PRODUCT BY EXPENDITURE APPROACH
(1999－2003)

单位:亿元 (100 million yuan)

年 份 Year	1999	2000	2001	2002	2003
地区生产总值					
Gross Domestic Product	**1 450.06**	**1 639.36**	**1 840.10**	**2 051.16**	**2 447.66**
最终消费					
Final Consumption Expenditure	716.80	804.71	901.85	990.21	1 134.69
居民消费					
Household Consumption	503.82	557.34	621.00	656.38	722.86
农村居民					
Rura Households	118.15	129.91	141.64	150.35	162.93
城镇居民					
Urba Households	385.67	427.43	479.36	506.03	559.93
政府消费					
Government Consumption	212.98	247.37	280.85	333.83	411.83
资本形成总额					
Gross Capital Formation	722.70	817.15	934.48	1 055.17	1 320.47
固定资本形成总额					
Gross Fixed Capital Formation	631.92	695.10	805.34	926.65	1 180.54
存货增加					
Changes in Inventories	90.78	122.05	129.14	128.52	139.93
货物和服务净出口					
Net Export of Goods and Services	10.56	17.50	3.77	5.78	－7.5

1－19 分配法地区生产总值
GROSS DOMESTIC PRODUCT BY DISTRIBUTION APPROACH
(1999－2003)

单位:亿元 (100 million yuan)

指 标 Item	1999	2000	2001	2002	2003
地区生产总值					
Gross Domestic Product	**1 450.06**	**1 639.36**	**1 840.10**	**2 051.16**	**2 447.66**
劳动者报酬					
Compensation of Laborers	755.33	765.87	835.08	907.60	1 052.94
固定资产折旧					
Depreciation of Fixed Assets	217.54	269.58	313.01	365.88	440.20
生产税净额					
Net Taxes On Production	241.72	281.14	321.29	341.01	410.51
营业盈余					
Operating Surplus	235.47	322.77	370.72	436.67	544.01

1-20 居民消费水平
HOUSEHOLD CONSUMPTION
(1999-2003)

单位:元/人　(yuan/person)

指　标　Item	1999	2000	2001	2002	2003
全市居民消费水平 All Households	**5 551**	**6 117**	**6 802**	**7 162**	**7 836**
农村居民 Agricultural	3 088	3 414	3 736	3 974	4 321
城镇居民 Non-Agricultural	7 346	8 056	8 979	9 403	10 266
农村居民与城镇居民对比(以农村居民为100) Ratio of Consumption of Agricultural to Non-Agricultural(Agricultural as 100)	**1:2.38**	**1:2.36**	**1:2.40**	**1:2.37**	**1:2.38**

1-21 最终消费
FINAL CONSUMPTION EXPENDITURE
(1999-2003)

单位:亿元　(100 million yuan)

项　目　Item	1999	2000	2001	2002	2003
最终消费 Final Consumption Expenditure	**716.80**	**804.71**	**901.85**	**990.21**	**1 134.69**
一、居民消费 Household Consumption	**503.82**	**557.34**	**621.00**	**656.38**	**722.86**
1.农村居民 Rural Households	118.05	129.91	141.64	150.35	162.93
自给性消费 Self-sufficiency consumption	9.75	9.81	9.98	8.83	4.87
商品性消费 Commodity Consumption	62.35	68.93	74.98	77.68	83.17
文化生活服务性消费 Consumption of Culture and Life Services	18.92	20.19	23.19	28.00	31.56
住房及水电消费 Housing, Water and Power Consumption	27.13	30.98	33.49	35.84	43.33
#住房消费 Housing Consumption	23.38	28.34	29.52	32.15	38.78
2.城镇居民 Urban Households	385.67	427.43	479.36	506.03	559.93
商品性消费 Commodity Consumption	260.86	281.50	295.70	299.57	322.68
文化生活服务性消费 Consumption of Culture and Life Services	86.26	102.28	124.03	140.20	162.30
住房及水电消费 Housing, Water and Power Consumption	38.55	43.65	59.63	66.26	74.95
#住房消费 Housing Consumption	25.35	30.43	41.55	45.49	57.18
二、政府消费 Government Consumption	**212.98**	**247.37**	**280.85**	**333.83**	**411.83**

1－22 主要社会经济效益指标
MAJOR ECONOMIC EFFICIENCY INDICATORS

项　目	Item	2000	2001	2002	2003
社会劳动生产率(元/人)	**Overall Labor Productivity(yuan/person)**	**32 951**	**37 737**	**41 820**	**48 782**
第一产业	Primary Industry	9 143	9 580	10 185	10 839
第二产业	Secondary Industry	36 252	41 612	47 934	58 627
第三产业	Tertiary Industry	39 071	45 527	48 509	53 852
资本形成率(投资率)(%)	**Rate of Capital Formation(%)**	**49.8**	**50.8**	**51.4**	**53.9**
消费率(%)	**Consumption Rate(%)**	**49.1**	**49.0**	**48.3**	**46.4**
总产出中间投入率(%)	**Intermediate Input/Total Output(%)**	**69.1**	**68.3**	**67.8**	**67.6**
第一产业	Primary Industry	52.9	53.7	53.6	53.6
第二产业	Secondary Industry	76.5	75.9	75.4	74.9
第三产业	Tertiary Industry	55.1	54.4	54.2	53.4
增加值率(%)	**GDP/Total Output**	**30.9**	**31.7**	**32.2**	**32.4**
第一产业	Primary Industry	47.1	46.3	46.4	46.4
第二产业	Secondary Industry	23.5	24.1	24.6	25.1
第三产业	Tertiary Industry	44.9	45.6	45.8	46.6

1－23 年末资产负债帐户
YEAR－END BALANCE ACCOUNT

单位:亿元 (100 million yuan)

项　目	Item	2001		2002	
		使　用 Utilization	来　源 Source	使　用 Utilization	来　源 Source
非金融资产	**Non－financial Capital**	**6 400.34**		**6 848.44**	
固定资产	Fixed Assets	4 889.75		5 671.99	
存　货	Inventories	835.83		797.53	
其他非金融资产	Others	674.76		378.92	
金融资产与负债	**Financial Capital and Liabilities**	**9 259.52**	**10 818.92**	**10 981.81**	**12 109.92**
国内金融资产与负债	Domestic Financial Liabilities	9 259.52	9 249.87	10 981.81	10 114.33
#存　款	Deposits	2 899.07	2 943.85	3 356.28	3 356.28
贷　款	Loans	2 461.74	2 461.74	2 864.86	2 846.86
国外金融资产与负债	Foreign Financial Liabilities		1 569.05		1 995.59
资产负债差额	**Balance of Assets and Liabilities**		**4 840.94**		**5 720.33**
资产、负债与差额总计	**Liabilities and Balance of Capital and liabilities**	**15 659.86**	**15 659.86**	**17 830.25**	**17 830.25**

1－24　天津在全国的地位

POSITION OF TIANJIN IN THE WHOLE NATION

指　　标	Item	1997 天　津 Tianjin	1997 占全国比重 As Percentage To Nation (％)	2003 天　津 Tianjin	2003 占全国比重 As Percentage To Nation (％)
一、年末户籍人口(万人)	Registered Population(year－end)(10 000 persons)	899.80	0.7	926.00	0.7
二、社会从业人员(万人)	Total Persons Employed (10 000 persons)	513.33	0.7	510.90	0.7
三、地区生产总值(亿元)	Gross Domestic Product(100 million yuan)	1 235.28	1.7	2 447.66	2.1
第一产业	Primary Industry	69.43	0.5	89.66	0.5
第二产业	Secondary Industry	643.88	1.7	1 245.29	2.0
第三产业	Tertiary Industry	521.97	2.3	1 112.71	2.9
四、财政、金融(亿元)	Governmet Finance and Banking(100 million)				
地方一般预算财政收入	Local General Budgetary Financial Revenue	89.91	2.0	204.53	2.1
一般预算财政支出	General Budgetary Financial Expenditure	122.78	1.8	312.08	1.8
金融机构本币存款余额	Deposits of Financial Institution	1 634.95	2.0	4 033.51	1.9
金融机构本币贷款余额	Loans of Financial Institution	1 502.91	2.0	3 426.02	2.2
五、限额以上工业总产值(亿元)	Gross Output Value of Industry(Above Designated Size)(100 million yuan)	2 838.21	2.5	4 049.61	2.9
轻工业	Light Industry	1 309.11	2.4	1 095.39	2.2
重工业	Heavy Industry	1 529.10	2.7	2 954.22	3.2
六、主要工业产品产量	Output of Major Industrial Products				
钢(万吨)	Steel(10 000 tons)	236.79	2.2	565.95	2.5
生　铁(万吨)	Pig Iron(10 000 tons)	185.33	1.6	342.65	1.7
水　泥(万吨)	Cement(10 000 tons)	209.00	0.4	449.31	0.5
平板玻璃(万重量箱)	Plate Glass(10 000 weight cases)	300.20	1.8	262.77	1.0
发电量(亿千瓦时)	Electricity(100 million kwh)	166.53	1.5	319.95	1.7
原　油(万吨)	Crude Oil(10 000 tons)	645.90	4.0	1 316.30	7.8
原　盐(万吨)	Salt(10 000 tons)	226.31	7.3	220.48	6.8
天然气(亿立方米)	Natural Gas(100 million cu. m)	7.58	3.3	8.49	2.4
汽　车(万辆)	Motor Vehicles(10 000)	16.03	10.1	17.25	3.9
自行车(万辆)	Bicycles(10 000)	336.78	11.2	833.93	18.0
移动电话(万部)	Mobile Phone(10 000 units)	207.90		3 139.72	17.2
化学纤维(万吨)	Chemical Fibers(10 000 tons)	10.79	2.3	29.76	2.5
纱(万吨)	Yarn(10 000 tons)	13.61	2.4	7.47	0.8
布(亿米)	Cloth(100 million m)	4.98	2.0	2.51	0.7
机制纸及纸版(万吨)	Machine－made Papers & Paperboards(10 000 tons)	40.56	1.5	17.76	0.4
彩色电视机(万台)	Color Television Sets(10 000 sets)	59.16	2.2	112.41	1.7
家用电冰箱(万台)	Household Refrigerators(10 000 sets)	0.69	0.1	29.17	1.3

1－24 续表　Continued

指　　标	Item	1997 天　津 Tianjin	1997 占全国比重 As Percentage To Nation (%)	2003 天　津 Tianjin	2003 占全国比重 As Percentage To Nation (%)
空调器(万台)	Air Conditioners(10 000 sets)	17.79	1.8	241.84	4.8
七、农林牧渔业总产值(亿元)	Gross Output Value of Farming, Forestry, Animal Husbandry & Fishery(100 million yuan)	140.47	0.6	193.44	0.7
八、主要农产品产量(万吨)	Output of Major Farm Products (10 000 tons)				
粮　食	Grain	206.16	0.4	119.29	0.3
肉　类	Meat	18.70	0.4	52.41	0.8
蛋　类	Eggs	17.71	0.9	24.25	0.9
水产品	Aquatic Products	18.98	0.5	29.83	0.6
九、全社会固定资产投资(亿元)	Total Investment in Fixed Assets (100 million yuan)	498.66	2.0	1 046.72	1.9
十、运输、邮电、通信	Transportation, Post & Telecommunications Services				
港口货物吞吐量(万吨)	Freight Handled at Ports(10 000 tons)	6 789	7.5	16 182	8.0
社会货物运输量(万吨)	Freight Traffic(10 000 tons)	25 090	2.0	35 252	2.3
邮电业务总量(亿元)	Post & Telecommunications Services (100 million yuan)	34.28	1.9	115.71	1.6
十一、商业、外贸、外经	Commerce, Foreign Trade & Foreign Capital				
社会消费品零售总额(亿元)	Total Retail Sales of Consumer Goods (100 million yuan)	535.02	2.0	922.27	2.0
外贸出口总额(亿美元)	Total Value of Exports in Foreign Trade (USD 100 million)	50.18	2.7	143.74	3.3
实际利用外资额(亿美元)	Foreign Capital Actually Used (USD 100 million)	34.23	5.3	17.06	3.0
十二、教育、科技、卫生、文化	Education, Science & Technology, Health Care, Culture				
学校数(所)	Number of Schools(unit)	4 158	0.6	2 070	0.4
专任教师数(万人)	Full－time Teachers(10 000 persons)	11.19	1.1	11.31	1.0
在校学生数(万人)	Students Enrollment(10 000 persons)	164.41	0.8	163.23	0.7
研究与试验发展经费支出(亿元)	Expenditures of Research and Development(100 million Yuan)			40.43	2.7
国有单位专业技术人员数(万人)	Scientific & Technical Personnel in State－owned Units(10 000 persons)	55.98	2.7	46.50	2.1
医院、卫生院(个)	Number of Hospitals(unit)	483	0.7	485	0.8
医院、卫生院床位(万张)	Number of Hospital Beds(10 000 units)	3.95	1.4	3.81	1.3
医生数(万人)	Number of Doctors(10 000 persons)	3.25	1.6	2.28	1.2
图书出版数(万册)	Number of Books Published(10 000 copies)	8 209	1.1	6 772	1.0
杂志出版数(万册)	Number of Magazines Issued(10 000 copies)	4 867	2.0	4 610	1.6
报纸出版数(亿份)	Number of Newspapers Issued (100 million copies)	5.79	2.0	8.24	2.2

1-25 天津、北京、上海、重庆、广州主要经济指标(2003年)

MAIN ECONOMIC INDICATORS OF TIANJIN, BEIJING, SHANGHAI, CHONGQING & GUANGZHOU, 2003

项 目	Item	天津市 Tianjin	北京市 Beijing	上海市 Shanghai	重庆市 Chongqing	广州市 Guangzhou
土地面积(平方公里)	Land Area(sq.km)	11 919.7	16 807.8	6 340.5	82 403	7 434.40
#城市建成区面积	Developed Area	487.47	654.5		654.95	608.00
户籍人口(万人)	Registered Population(10 000 persons)	926.00	1 148.8	1 341.77	3 130.1	725.19
人口自然增长率(‰)	Natural Growth Rate(‰)	1.10	-0.1	-3.2	2.7	2.24
社会从业人员(万人)	Total Employment Personnel	510.90	703.3	813.05	1 726.36	521.07
第一产业	Primary Industry	83.19	62.7	73.72	892.23	95.88
第二产业	Secondary Industry	219.44	225.8	317.12	298.42	200.17
第三产业	Tertiary Industry	208.27	414.8	422.21	535.71	225.02
城镇单位从业人员(万人)	Persons Employed in the Urban Units(10 000 persons)	191.01	491.2	160.73	557.19	277.46
城镇单位从业人员人均劳动报酬(元)	Per Capita Remuneration of Persons Employed in the Urban Units(yuan)	18 511	24 841.6	25 565	12 440	28 237
地区生产总值(亿元)	Gross Domestic Product(100 million yuan)	2 447.66	3 663.1	6 250.81	2 250.56	3 496.88
第一产业	Primary Industry	89.66	95.6	92.98	336.36	105.63
第二产业	Secondary Industry	1 245.29	1 311.9	3 130.72	977.3	1 508.12
第三产业	Tertiary Industry	1 112.71	2 255.6	3 027.11	936.9	1 883.13
人均地区生产总值(元)	Per Capita Gross Domestic Product(yuan)	26 532	32 061	46 718	8 077	48 372
地区生产总值指数(上年=100)	Indices of Gross Domestic Product (preceding year=100)	114.8	110.7	111.8	111.5	115.2
第一产业	Primary Industry	106.1	103.3	102.3	104.2	100.3
第二产业	Secondary Industry	118.0	111.9	116.1	116.0	121.6
第三产业	Tertiary Industry	111.8	110.3	108.0	109.4	111.2
人均地区生产总值指数(上年=100)	Indices of Per Capita GDP (preceding year=100)	114.0	109.4	111.2	112.1	114.2
全社会固定资产投资总额(亿元)	Total Investment In Fixed Assets (100 million yuan)	1 046.72	2 157.1	2 452.11	1 269.35	1 175.17
地方一般预算内财政收入(亿元)	Local General Budgetary Revenue (100 million yuan)	204.53	592.5	899.29	161.56	274.77
一般预算内财政支出(亿元)	General Budgetary Expenditures (100 million yuan)	312.08	734.8	1 102.64	391.36	370.09
金融机构本外币年末存款余额(亿元)	Deposits of Financial Institutions (year-end)(100 million yuan)	4 362.60	20 243.6	17 318.38	3 512.82	8 676.72
#城乡居民储蓄存款	Savings Deposits of Urban and Rural Residents	1 991.76	5 293.5	6 054.6	1 896.56	3 727.33
金融机构本外币年末贷款余额(亿元)	Loans of Financial Institutions (year-end)(100 million yuan)	3 791.22	11 853.1	13 168.05	2 976.67	6 127.27
保险业务保费收入(亿元)	Premium(100 million yuan)	75.31	278.1	289.93	57.93	117.28
保险业务赔款支出(亿元)	Claim(100 million yuan)	17.36	31.2	61.97	14.53	20.31
城市商品零售价格指数(上年=100)	Retail Price Indices of Urban Commodities (preceding year=100)	97.4	98.2	99.0	99.5	
城市居民消费价格指数(上年=100)	Consumer Price Indices of Urban Households(preceding year=100)	101.0	100.2	100.1	100.6	100.1
工业品出厂价格指数(上年=100)	Ex-factory Price Indices of Industrial Products (preceding year=100)	102.5	101.5	101.4	100.6	99.6
原材料燃料动力购进价格指数(上年=100)	Raw Materials, Fuel and Motive Power Purchasing Price Index(preceding year=100)	108.7	104.7	106.4	104.9	105.7
固定资产投资价格指数(上年=100)	Price Index of Investment in Fixed Assets (preceding year=100)	102.6	102.2	102.4	102.9	
房地产销售价格指数(上年=100)	Price Index of Real Estate Sales (preceding year=100)	104.1	100.3	120.1		
城市居民人均可支配收入(元)	Per Capita Annual Disposable Income of Urban Households(yuan)	10 313	13 883	14 867	8 094	15 003
城市居民人均消费性支出(元)	Per Capita Annual Expenditures for Consumption of Urban Households(yuan)	7 868	11 124	11 040	7 118	11 571

注:上海市单位从业人员及人均劳动报酬均为在岗职工口径。广州市存贷款为中外资金融机构人民币存贷款。
Note: Persons employed in the unit and per capita remuneration in Shanghai refer to working staff and workers. Deposits and loans in Guangzhou refer to RMB deposits and loans of home-funded and foreign-funded finamial institutions.

1-25 续表 Continued

项 目	Item	天津市 Tianjin	北京市 Beijing	上海市 Shanghai	重庆市 Chongqing	广州市 Guangzhou
农民人均纯收入(元)	Per Capita Annual Net Income of Farmers(yuan)	5 861	6 496	6 658	2 215	6 130
农民人均生活费支出(元)	Per Capita Annual Living Expenditures of Farmers(yuan)	3 015	4 655	5 670	1 583	4 116
城市人均住房使用面积(平方米)	Per Capita Using Space of Urban Households(sq. m)	17.5	18.7	19.0	18	17.23
农村人均住房面积(平方米)	Per Capita Dwelling Space of Rural Households(sq. m)	24.44	33.95	59.03	31.45	36.01
农业总产值(亿元)	Gross Output Value of Agriculture (100 million yuan)	193.44	237.9	247.29	488.57	180.67
农业总产值指数(上年=100)	Indices of Gross Output Value of Agriculture (preceding year=100)	106.6	104.2	101.1	104.6	100.65
全部工业总产值(亿元)	Gross Output Value of Industry (100 million yuan)	4 370.76	4 021.4	11 266.62		4 705.91
#限额以上	Above Designated Size	4 049.61	3 810.4		1 588.99	4 017.83
全部工业总产值指数(上年=100)	Indices of Gross Output Value of Industry (preceding year=100)	124.1	119.2	131.4		126.52
#限额以上	Above Designated Size	126.1	120.1		126.7	129.43
港口货物吞吐量(万吨)	Freight Handled at Ports(10 000 tons)	16 182		31 621	3 244	19 200
集装箱吞吐量(万标准箱)	Handled Containers (10 000 TEU)	301.5		1 128.25	48.1	335.07
邮电业务总量(2000年不变价)(亿元)	Post and Telecommunications Services (at 2000 Constant Price)(100 million yuan)	115.71	304.0	278.87	121.29	216.13
社会消费品零售总额(亿元)	Total Retail Sales of Consumer Goods (100 million yuan)	922.27	1 916.7	2 220.64	835.52	1 494.27
外贸进出口总额(亿美元)	Total Value of Imports and Exports In Foreign Trade(USD 100 million)	293.71	189.3	1 123.97	25.95	349.41
#出 口	Exports	143.74	168.5	484.82	15.85	168.89
直接利用外资签订合同数(个)	Number of Foreign Direct Investment Contracted(unit)	941	1 360	4 321	187	870
直接利用外资合同额(亿美元)	Foreign Direct Investment Contracted (USD 100 million)	35.13	32.7	110.64	5.53	35.11
实际利用外资额(亿美元)	Foreign Capital Actually Used (USD 100 million)	17.06	21.5	58.50	5.67	30.64
#客商直投	Foreign Direct Investment	16.33	21.5		3.11	25.81
接待(过夜)旅游人数(万人次)	Accommodated Tourists(10 000 person/time)	17.21	185.1	431.84	23.45	2 369.82
旅游外汇收入(亿美元)	Foreign Exchange Earning from International Tourism (USD 100 million)	3.29	19.0	20.53	1.13	16.22
人均绿地面积(平方米)	Per Capita Public Green Areas in Urban Areas(sq. m)	6.7	11.4	9.16	3.1	9.44
建成区绿化覆盖率(%)	Rate of Green Coverage in Developed Areas(%)	31.0	40.9	35.2	16.6	34.19
高等学校校数(个)	Number of Higher Education Institutions	37	73	57	33	44
高等学校在校学生数(万人)	Number of Students Enrollment of Higher Schools(10 000 persons)	24.52	45.1	37.85	25.53	37.47
研究与发展经费支出(亿元)	Research and Development Expenditures (100 million yuan)	40.43	230.8	128.40	19.64	55.00
研发经费支出相当于GDP比例(%)	Proportion of Research and Development Expenditures to GDP(%)	1.7	6.3	2.06	0.87	1.57
医院、卫生院(个)	Number of Hospitals(unit)	485	459	452	1 682	254
医院、卫生院床位(万张)	Number of Hospital Beds(10 000 units)	3.81	6.7	8.11	6.0	3.77
医 生(万人)	Number of Doctors(10 000 persons)	2.28	4.8	0.74	3.64	2.34

注:上海市农民人均纯收入为可支配收入。
Note: The per capita annual net income of farmers in Shanghai refer to per capita annual disposable income of farmers.

1-26　能源平衡表(标准量)

ENERGY BALANCE (STANDARD EQUIVALENT)

单位:万吨标准煤　　(10 000 tons of SCE)

项　目	Item	2002	2003
一、可供本地区消费的能源量	**Volume of Energy Available for Consumption in This Area**	**3 017.10**	**3 242.98**
1.年初库存量	Stock in The Beginning of The Year	289.10	284.88
2.一次能源生产量	Primary Energy Output	1 844.92	1 983.56
3.回收能	Recovery of Energy		
4.外省(区、市)调入量	Inflow from Other Provinces(Regions,Cities)	3 870.63	4 295.84
5.进口量	Import	261.24	393.61
6.我轮、机在外国加油量	Our Steamship and Plane Oiled Abroad	54.46	54.03
7.本省(区、市)调出量(-)	Outflow to Other Provinces(Regions,Cities)	-2 796.37	-3 261.80
8.出口量(-)	Export	-208.93	-212.47
9.外轮、机在我国加油量(-)	Foreign Steamship and Plane Oiled in China	-15.27	-20.98
10.年末库存量	Stock in Year-end	-282.68	-273.68
二、加工转换投入(-)产出(+)量	**Input(-) or Output(+) of Processing and Transformation**	**8.07**	**-41.34**
1.火力发电	Fuel Power Generation		
2.供　热	Heating		
3.洗选煤	Clean Coal		
4.炼　焦	Coke Making	82.23	53.19
5.炼　油	Oil Refining	-131.95	-61.77
6.制　气	Gas Making	57.79	-32.36
#焦碳再投入量(-)	Input of Coke(-)		-0.40
7.煤制品加工	Processing of Coal Products		
三、损失量	**Loss Volume**	**63.66**	**89.14**
四、终端消费量	**End-user Consumption**	**2 966.56**	**3 084.49**
第一产业	Primary Industry	76.64	58.86
第二产业	Secondary Industry	1 935.92	1 975.56
工　业	Industry	1 913.61	1 957.09
建筑业	Construction	22.31	18.47
第三产业	Tertiary Industry	575.96	650.27
交通运输、仓储及邮电通信业	Transportation,Storage,Post and Telecommunications	261.24	295.32
批发和零售贸易业、餐饮业	Wholesale,Retail Trade and Catering Services	205.02	228.11
其　他	Others	109.70	126.83
生活消费	Living Consumption	378.04	399.80
五、平衡差额	**Balance**	**-5.05**	**28.01**
六、消费量合计	**Total of Consumption**	**3 022.15**	**3 214.97**

主要统计指标解释

生产总值(原国内生产总值)　指按市场价格计算的一个国家(或地区)所有常住单位在一定时期内生产活动的最终成果。

从价值形态看,它是所有常驻单位在一定时期内所生产的全部货物和服务价值超过同期投入的全部非固定资产货物和服务价值的差额,即所有常驻单位的增加值之和;从收入形态看,它是所有常驻单位在一定时期内所创造并分配给常驻单位和非常驻单位的初次分配收入之和;从产品形态看,它是最终使用的货物和服务减去进口货物和服务。在实际核算中,其三种表现形态体现为三种计算方法,即生产法、收入法和支出法。三种方法分别从不同的方面反映生产总值及其构成。根据国务院和国家统计局有关我国 GDP 核算和数据发布制度的规定,天津市国内生产总值自 2004 年起更名为"天津市生产总值"简称"天津市 GDP"。

劳动者报酬　指劳动者因从事生产活动所获得的全部报酬。包括劳动者获得的各种形式的工资、奖金和津贴,既包括货币形式的,也包括实物形式的,还包括劳动者所享受的公费医疗和医药卫生费、上下班交通补贴和单位支付的社会保险费、住房公积金等。对于个体经济来说,其所有者所获得的劳动报酬和经营利润不易区分,这两部分统一作为劳动者报酬处理。

生产税净额　指生产税减生产补贴后的余额。生产税指政府对生产单位生产、销售和从事经营活动以及因从事生产活动使用某些生产要素(如固定资产、土地、劳动力)所征收的各种税、附加费和规费。生产补贴与生产税相反,指政府对生产单位的单方面转移支付,因此视为负生产税,包括政策亏损补贴、价格补贴等。

固定资产折旧　指一定时期内为弥补固定资产损耗按照核定的固定资产折旧率提取的固定资产折旧,或按国民经济核算统一规定的折旧率虚拟计算的固定资产折旧。它反映了固定资产在当期生产中的转移价值。各类企业和企业化管理的事业单位的固定资产折旧是指实际计提的折旧费;不计提折旧的政府机关、非企业化管理的事业单位和居民住房的固定资产折旧是按照统一规定的折旧率和固定资产原值计算的虚拟折旧。原则上,固定资产折旧应按固定资产的重置价值计算,但是目前我国尚不具备对全社会固定资产进行重估价的基础,所以暂时只能采用这种办法。

营业盈余　指常住单位创造的增加值扣除劳动者报酬、生产税净额和固定资产折旧后的余额。它相当于企业的营业利润加上生产补贴,但要扣除从利润中开支的工资和福利等。

最终消费　指常住单位在一定时期内对于货物和服务的全部最终消费支出,也就是常住单位为满足物质、文化和精神生活的需要,从本国经济领土和国外购买的货物和服务的支出。不包括非常住单位在本国经济领土内的消费支出。最终消费分为居民消费和政府消费。

居民消费　指常住住户对货物和服务的全部最终消费支出。它除了常住住户直接以货币形式购买货物和服务的消费之外,还包括以其他方式获得的货物和服务的消费,即单位以实物报酬及实物转移的形式提供给劳动者的货物和服务;住户生产并由住户自己消费的货物和服务,其中的服务仅指住户的自有住房服务和支付报酬的家庭服务;金融机构提供的金融媒介服务;保险公司提供的保险服务。

政府消费　指政府部门为全社会提供公共服务的消费支出和免费或以较低价格向住户提供的货物和服务的净支出。前者等于政府服务的产出价值减去政府单位所获得的经营收入后的价值,政府服务的产出价值等于它的经常性业务支出加上固定资产折旧;后者等于政府部门免费或以较低价格向住户提供的货物和服务的市场价值减去向住户收取的价值。

资本形成总额　指常住单位在一定时期内获得的减去处置的固定资产加存货的净变动额,包括固定资本形成总额和存货增加。

固定资本形成总额　指生产者在一定时期内获得的固定资产减处置的固定资产的价值总额,固定资产是通过生产活动生产出来的,其使用年限在一年以上,单位价值在规定标准以上的资产,不包括自然资产。固定资本形成总额可分为有形固定资本形成总额和无形固定资本形成总额。有形固定资本形成总额包括一定时期内完成的建筑工程、安装工程、设备工器具购置(减处置)价值以及土地改良、新增役、种、奶、毛、娱乐用牲畜和新增经济林木价值。无形固定资本形成总额包括矿藏的勘探、计算机软件等获得减处置。

存货增加 指常住单位在一定时期内存货实物量变动的市场价值，即期末价值减期初价值的差额，再扣除当期由于价格变动而产生的持有收益。存货增加可以是正值，也可以是负值；正值表示存货增加，负值表示存货减少。它包括生产单位购进的原材料、燃料和储备物资等存货，以及生产单位生产的产成品、在制品存货等。

货物和服务净出口 指货物和服务出口减货物和服务进口的差额。出口包括常住单位向非常住单位出售和无偿转让的各种货物和服务的价值；进口包括常住单位从非常住单位购买或无偿得到的各种货物和服务的价值。由于服务活动的提供与使用同时发生，因此服务的进出口业务并不发生出入境现象，一般把常住单位从国外得到的服务作为进口，常住单位向国外提供的服务作为出口。货物的出口和进口都按离岸价格计算。在计算地区货物和服务净出口时，还包括地区间货物和服务的流入流出。

用公式表示：

货物和服务净出口（净流出）= 货物和服务出口（流出）- 进口（流入）

行业划分标准 从2003年年报开始，各专业指标的行业分类标准均采用新修订的《国民经济行业分类》（GB/T 4754－2002）。依据经济活动同质性原则，新标准对GB/T 4754－1994《国民经济行业分类与代码》进行了调整。新行业标准为20个门类，95个大类，396个中类，913个小类。与1994年的行业分类标准比较，门类增加了4个，大类增加了3个，中类增加了28个，小类增加了67个。附：国民经济行业分类新旧结构对照表

国民经济行业分类新旧结构对照表

GB/T 4754－2002				GB/T 4754－1994			
门　类	大类	中类	小类	门　类	大类	中类	小类
A 农、林、牧、渔业	5	18	38	A 农、林、牧、渔业	5	14	16
B 采矿业	6	15	33	B 采掘业	7	18	53
C 制造业	30	169	482	C 制造业	30	172	544
D 电力、燃气及水的生产和供应业	3	7	10	D 电力、煤气及水的生产和供应业	3	7	10
E 建筑业	4	7	11	E 建筑业	3	8	8
F 交通运输、仓储和邮政业	9	24	37	F 地质勘察业、水利管理业	2	8	15
G 信息传输、计算机服务和软件业	3	10	14	G 交通运输、仓储和邮电通信业	9	21	22
H 批发和零售业	2	18	93	H 批发和零售贸易、餐饮业	6	32	67
I 住宿和餐饮业	2	7	7	I 金融、保险业	2	8	11
J 金融业	4	16	16	J 房地产业	3	3	3
K 房地产业	1	4	4	K 社会服务业	9	29	36
L 租赁和商务服务业	2	11	27	L 卫生、体育和社会福利业	3	11	17
M 科学研究、技术服务和地质勘察业	4	19	23	M 教育、文化艺术及广播电影电视业	3	18	25
N 水利、环境和公共设施管理业	3	8	18	N 科学研究和综合技术服务业	2	12	12
O 居民服务和其他服务业	2	12	16	O 国家机关、党政机关和社会团体	4	5	5
P 教育	1	5	13	P 其他行业	1	2	2
Q 卫生、社会保障和社会福利业	3	11	17				
R 文化、体育和娱乐业	5	22	29				
S 公共管理和社会组织	5	12	24				
T 国际组织	1	1	1				
（合计）　20	**95**	**396**	**913**	**（合计）　16**	**92**	**368**	**846**

三次产业 根据2002年新颁布的行业分类标准《国民经济行业分类》（GB/T 4754－2002）规定，2003年国家统计局按照社会生产活动历史发展的顺序，对第三产业的划分进行了重新规定。具体的三次产业划分范围如下：

第一产业：包括农、林、牧、渔业。

第二产业:包括采矿业,制造业,电力、燃气及水的生产和供应业,建筑业。

第三产业:包括除第一、二产业以外的其他行业,具体包括 交通运输、仓储和邮政业,信息传输、计算机服务和软件业,批发和零售业,住宿和餐饮业,金融业,房地产业,租赁和商务服务业,科学研究、技术服务和地质勘查业,水利、环境和公共设施管理业,居民服务和其他服务业,教育,卫生、社会保障和社会福利业,文化、体育和娱乐业,公共管理和社会组织等。

现行价格(或称当年价格) 指报告期的实际价格,如工业品的出厂价格,农副产品的收购价格,商业的零售价格等。它反映当年的实际情况,使国民经济各项指标互相衔接,便于对生产、流通、分配、消费之间进行综合平衡。

可比价格 指计算各种总量指标所采用的扣除了价格变动因素的价格,可进行不同时期总量指标的对比。按可比价格计算总量指标有两种方法:一种是直接用产品产量乘某一年的不变价格计算;另一种是用价格指数进行缩减。

平均增长速度 我国计算平均增长速度有两种方法:一种是习惯上经常使用的"水平法",又称几何平均法,是以间隔期最后一年的水平同基期水平对比来计算平均每年增长(或下降)速度;另一种是"累计法",又称代数平均法或方程法,是以间隔期内各年水平的总和同基期水平对比来计算平均每年增长(或下降)速度。在一般正常情况下,两种方法计算的平均每年增长速度比较接近;但在经济发展不平衡、出现大起大落时,两种方法计算的结果差别较大。

本《年鉴》内所列的平均增长速度,除固定资产投资类指标用"累计法"计算外,其余均用"水平法"计算。从某年到某年平均增长速度的年份,均不包括基期年在内。

企业登记注册类型 以工商行政管理部门对企业登记注册的类型为依据,将企业登记注册类型划分为三大类:第一类是内资企业,包括国有企业、集体企业、股份合作企业、私营企业、股份有限公司、有限责任公司、联营企业和其他内资企业。第二类是港、澳、台商投资企业,包括合资经营企业、合作经营企业、港澳台商独资经营企业、港澳台商投资股份有限公司。第三类是外商投资企业,包括中外合资、中外合作、外资企业和外商投资股份有限公司。由于个体经营不属于企业,因此在《关于划分企业登记注册类型的规定》中,未将个体经营列入。但国家明确规定其仍属于国家统计范围,并在分类中单列。企业登记注册类型不同于经济类型,特别是其中的国有企业和集体企业不同于经济类型中的国有经济和集体经济。

内资企业 包括国有企业、集体企业、股份合作企业、私营企业、股份有限公司、有限责任公司、联营企业和其他内资企业。

国有企业 指企业全部资产归国家所有,并按《中华人民共和国企业法人登记管理条例》规定登记注册的非公司制的经济组织。不包括有限责任公司中的国有独资公司和联营企业中的国有与国有联营企业。

集体企业 指企业资产归集体所有,并按《中华人民共和国企业法人登记管理条例》规定登记注册的经济组织。不包括股份合作企业和联营企业中的集体与集体联营企业。

股份合作企业 指以合作制为基础,由企业职工共同出资入股,吸收一定比例的社会资产投资组建,实行自主经营,自负盈亏,共同劳动,民主管理,按劳分配与按股分红相结合的一种集体经济组织。

私营企业 指由自然人投资设立或由自然人控股,以雇佣劳动为基础的营利性经济组织。包括按照《公司法》、《合伙企业法》、《私营企业暂行条例》规定登记注册的私营有限责任公司、私营股份有限公司、私营合伙企业和私营独资企业。

股份有限公司 指根据《中华人民共和国公司登记管理条例》规定登记注册,其全部注册资本由等额股份构成并通过发行股票筹集资本,股东以其认购的股份对公司承担有限责任,公司以其全部资产对其债务承担责任的经济组织。

有限责任公司 指根据《中华人民共和国公司登记管理条例》规定登记注册,由两个以上,五十个以下的股东共同出资,每个股东以其所认缴的出资额对公司承担有限责任,公司以其全部资产对其债务承担责任的经济组织。有限责任公司包括国有独资公司以及其他有限责任公司。

国有独资公司 指国家授权的投资机构或者国家授权的部门单独投资设立的有限责任公司。

其他有限责任公司 指国有独资公司以外的其他有限责任公司。

联营企业 指两个及两个以上相同或不同所有制性质的企业法人或事业单位法人，按自愿、平等、互利的原则共同投资组成的经济组织。

其他内资企业 指上述内资企业之外的其他内资经济组织。

港澳台商投资企业 包括合资经营企业(港或澳、台资)、合作经营企业(港或澳、台资)、港澳台商独资经营企业和港澳台商投资股份有限公司。

港、澳、台商独资经营企业 指依照《中华人民共和国外资企业法》及有关法律的规定，在内地由港澳台地区投资者全额投资设立的企业。

港、澳、台商投资股份有限公司 指根据国家有关规定，经外经贸部(现为商务部)依法批准设立，其中港、澳、台商的股本占公司注册资本的比例达25%以上的股份有限公司。凡其中港、澳、台商的股本占公司注册资本的比例小于25%的，属于内资企业中的股份有限公司。

外商投资企业 包括中外合资经营企业、中外合作经营企业、外资(独资)企业和外商投资股份有限公司。

个体经营 指除农户外，生产资料归劳动者个人所有，以个体劳动为基础，劳动成果归劳动者个人占有和支配的一种经营单位。包括按照《民法通则》和《城乡个体经营户管理暂行条例》规定登记注册的个体工商户和个人合伙，以及没有领取营业执照，但从事个体经营活动的城镇、农村个体经营单位。

行政机关、事业单位和社会团体填写登记注册类型参照企业登记注册类型，主要按其经费来源和管理方式划分。具体规定如下：

(1)**行政机关**：包括国家机关和政党机关，原则上均列为“国有”。但有特殊规定的，如供销社等，则列为“集体”。

(2)**事业单位**：包括经国家机构编制部门和有关业务主管部门批准成立的各类事业单位，不包括实行企业化管理的事业单位。事业单位的划分办法如下：

① 由国家财政预算拨款或列入财政预算外资金管理以及经费主要来源于国有主管部门或国有上级单位的事业单位，列为“国有”。

②经费主要来源于集体单位的事业单位，列为“集体”。

③ 公民个人(或个人合伙)开办的事业单位，列为“私营”。

④ 上述以外的其他事业单位，如果其经费来源不明确，按管理方式进行归类。

(3)**社会团体**：包括经民政部门批准成立以及未纳入社会团体管理条例范围的工会、妇联等各类社会团体。社会团体的划分办法如下：

① 未纳入民政部社会团体管理条例范围的工会、妇联、共青团、青联、工商联、科协、侨联等社会团体，国家拨款设立的基金会或基金管理组织以及经费主要来源于国有业务主管部门或国有上级单位的社会团体，列为“国有”。

②经费主要来源于集体单位的社会团体，列为“集体”。

③ 公民个人(或个人合伙)开办的社会团体，划为“私营”。

④ 上述以外的其他社会团体，如果其经费来源不明确，改按管理方式进行归类。

经济类型 本《年鉴》中的经济类型分组，从1998年开始是在企业登记注册类型分组基础上的再加工，其中国有经济包括国有企业、国有独资和国有与国有联营企业；集体经济包括集体企业、股份合作企业和集体与集体联营企业。私有经济包括私营企业和个体经营。

建成区面积 指城市行政区内实际已成片开发建设、市政公用设施和公共设施基本具备的区域。对核心城市，它包括集中连片的部分以及分散的若干个已经成片建设起来的市政公用设施和公共设施基本具备的地区；对一城多镇来说，它包括由几个连片开发建设起来的市政公用设施和公共设施基本具备的地区组成。因此建成区范围，一般是指建成区外轮廓线所能包括的地区，也就是这个城市实际建设用地所达到的范围。

Explanatory Notes on Main Statistical Indicators

Gross Domestic Product refers to the final products at market prices produced by all resident units in a country(or a region) during a certain period of time.

The form of value added refers to the total value of all products and services produced by all resident units during a certain period of time minus total value of inputs of non - fixed - assets products and services or the summation of the value added of all resident units; the form of prduct refers to all final goods and services minus improts of goods and services. In the practice of national accounting, it is calculated by three approaches, i. e. product approach, income approach and expenditure approach, respectively, to reflect Gross Product and its composition of different aspects. According to the regulations of GDP national accounting as Tianjin Gross Product Value, for short Tianjin GDP.

Labourer Remuneration refers to the whole payment of various forms earned by the labourers from the productive activities they are engaged in. It includes wages, bonuses and allowances the labourers earned in monetary form and in kind. It also includes the free medical services provided to the labourers and the medicine expenses, traffic subsidies, social insurance fee and housing provident fund paid by the labourer's working units for them. As the individual economy is concerned, since the labourer's remuneration is not easily distinguished from the operating profit, both are treated as labourer's remuneration.

Net Taxes on Production refers to the residual of the taxes on production minus the subsidies on production. The taxes on production refers to the various taxes, extra charges and fees levied on the production units on their production, sale and business activities as well as on some sectors of production, such as fixed assets, land and labour force, used in the production activities they are engaged in. In contrast to the taxes on production, the subsidies on production refer to the unilateral transfer of part of the government's revenue to the production units and are therefore regarded as negative taxes on production. They include subsidies on the loss due to implementation of government policies, price subsidies, etc.

Depreciation of Fixed Assets refers to the depreciation of fixed assets of a given period, drawn in accordance with the stipulated depreciation rate for the purpose of compensating the wear loss of the fixed assets or the depreciation of fixed assets calculated in a fictitious way in accordance with the stipulated unified depreciation rate in the national economic accounting system. It reflects the value of transfer of the fixed assets in the production of the current period. The depreciation of fixed assets in various enterprises and institutions managed as enterprises refers to the depreciation expenses actually drawn. In government agencies and institutions not managed as enterprises which do not draw the depreciation expenses, as well as for the houses of residents, the depreciation of fixed assets is the imputed depreciation, which is calculated in accordance with the stipulated unified depreciation rate. In principle, the depreciation of fixed assets should be calculated on the basis of the re - purchased value of the fixed assets. However, there is no actual condition to re - evaluate all the fixed assets in China. Therefore, this method is temporarily adopted at present.

Operating Surplus refers to the balance of the value added created by the resident units deducting the labourer's remuneration, net taxes on production and the depreciation of fixed assets. It is equivalent to the business profit of the enterprises plus subsidies on production, but the wages and welfare expenses paid from the profits should be deducted.

Final Consumption refers to the total expenditure of resident units on final consumption of goods and services in a certain period, namely the expenditure of the resident units for purchases of goods and services from domestic economic territory and abroad to meet the requirements of material, cultural and spiritual life. It excludes the consumption expenditure of non - resident units on consumption in the economic territory of the country. The final consumption is classified into households consumption and government consumption.

Households Consumption refers to the total expenditure of resident households on the final consumption of goods and services. In addition to the consumption of goods and services bought by the households directly with money, the households consumption also includes expenditure on goods and services obtained by the households on other ways, i.e. the goods and services provided to the households by the units in the form of payment in kind and transfer in kind; the goods and services produced and consumed by the households themselves, in which the services refer only to the owner－occupied housing and domestic services provided by the paid household workers; financial intermediate services provided by financial institutions; insurance services provided by insurance companies.

Government Consumption refers to the expenditure on the consumption of the public services provided by the government to the whole society and the net expenditure on the goods and services provided by the government to the households at free charge or lower prices. The former equals to the output value of the government services minus the value of operating income obtained by the government departments, the output value of the government services equals to its current operating expenditure plus depreciation of fixed assets. The latter equals to the market value of the goods and services provided by the government free of charge or at low prices to the households minus the value received by the government from the households.

Total Capital Formation refers to the fixed assets acquired minus those disposed and the net value of inventory, including the total fixed assets formation and the increase in inventory.

Total Fixed Capital Formation refers to the value of fixed assets acquired minus those disposed of during a given period. Fixed assets are the assets produced through production activities with specified unit value which could be used for over one year, excluding natural assets. Total fixed capital formation can be categorized into total tangible assets formation and total intangible assets formation. The total tangible assets formation include the value of the construction projects, installation projects completed and the equipment, apparatus and instruments purchased as well as the value of land improved, the value of draught animals, breeding stock, animal for milk, wool and for recreational animals purpose and the newly increased forest with economic value during a given period. The total intangible assets formation includes the prospecting of minerals, the acquisition of computer software minus the disposal of them.

Increase in Inventory refers to the market value of the change in inventory of resident units during a given period, i.e. the difference of value between the beginning and the end of the period minus the current gains due to the change in prices. The increase in inventory can be positive or negative. A positive value indicates the increase in inventory while a negative value indicates the decrease in stock. The inventory includes the raw materials, fuel and reserve materials purchased by the production units as well as the inventory of finished products, semi－finished products, etc.

Net Export of Goods and Services refers to the difference of the exports of goods and services minus the imports of goods and services. The imports include the value of various goods and services sold or gratuitously transferred by the resident units to the non－resident units. The imports include the value of various goods and services purchased or gratuitously acquired by the resident units from the non－resident units. Because the provision of services and the use of them happen simultaneously, the import and export of services do not appear to have the phenomena of crossing the border of the country. The acquisition of services by the resident units from abroad is usually treated as import while the acquisition of services by non－resident units in this country is usually treated as export. The export and import of goods are calculated at FOB. The formula for calculating is as follows:

Net export of goods and services = value of export of goods and services － value of import of goods and services

Standard of Industry Categorized From annual report of 2003, the industry category adopts new standard (GB/T 4754－2002). According to the equal content of economic activities, new standard adjusts the category and code of GB/T 4754－1994. The new standard is classified 20 industries, including 95 big type, 396 middle type and 913 small type. Compared to old standard, the new one increases 4 industries, 3 big type, 28 middle type and 67 small type. Attachment: The Comparison of New Standard with Old Standard of National Economy Industry Category

The Comparison of New Standard with Old Standard of National Economy Industry Category

GB/T 4754 - 2002				GB/T 4754 - 1994			
Industry	Large	Middle	Small	Industry	Large	Middle	Small
A Farming, Forestry, Animal Husbandry and Fishery	5	18	38	A Farming, Forestry, Animal Husbandry and Fishery	5	14	16
B Minerals Mining	6	15	33	B Mining and Quarrying	7	18	53
C Manufacturing	30	169	482	C Manufacturing	30	172	544
D Production & Supply of Power, Gas and Water	3	7	10	D Production & Supply of Power, and Water Gas	3	7	10
E Construction	4	7	11	E Construction	3	8	8
F Transport, Storage, Post Services	9	24	37	F Geological Prospecting and Water Conservancy	2	8	15
G Information Transmitting, Computer Services and Software	3	10	14	G Transport, Storage, Post and Telecommunication Services	9	21	22
H Wholesale and Retail Trade	2	18	93	H Wholesale, Retail Trade and Catering Services	6	32	67
I Accommodation and Catering Services	2	7	7	I Finance and Insurance	2	8	11
J Finance	4	16	16	J Real Estate	3	3	3
K Real Estate	1	4	4	K Social Services	9	29	36
L Leasing and Business Services	2	11	27	L Health Care, Sports and Social Welfare	3	11	17
M Scientific Research, Technical Services and Geological Prospecting	4	19	23	M Education, Culture and Arts, Radio, Film and Television	3	18	25
N Management for Water Conservancy, Environment and Public Facilities	3	8	18	N Scientific Research and Polytechnic Services	2	12	12
O Resident Services and Other Social Services	2	12	16	O Government Agencies, Parties Agencies and Social Organizations	4	5	5
P Education	1	5	13	P Others	1	2	2
Q Health Care, Social Security and Social Welfare	3	11	17				
R Culture, Sports and Recreational Services	5	22	29				
S Public Management and Social Organizations	5	12	24				
T International Organizations	1	1	1				
(Total) 20	**95**	**396**	**913**	**(Total) 16**	**92**	**368**	**846**

Three Industries According to the new standard of national economy industry category, i.e. GB/T 4754 - 2002, the classification of tertiary industry is adjusted by National Bureau of Statistics according to the order of social production activity development. Three industries are categorized as following.

Primary Industry include agriculture, forestry, animal husbandry and fishery.

Secondary Industry include minerals mining, manufacturing, production and supply of electricity, gas and water, construction.

Tertiary Industry include all other industries not included in primary or secondary industry, including transport, storage, post services; information transmitting, computer services and software; wholesale and retail trade; accommodation and catering services; finance; real estate; leasing and business services; scientific research, technical services and geological prospecting; management for water conservancy, environment and public facilities; resident services and other social services; education; health care, social security and social welfare; culture, sports and recreational services; public management and social organizations and so on.

Actual Price (current year price) refers to the actual prices during the reference period, i.e. ex-factory prices of industrial products, purchasing prices of farm products, retail prices, etc, reflecting the actually happening in current year, joining various statistical indicators on national economic, general balance among production, circulation, distribution, consumption.

Comparable Prices refer to prices that are used to remove the factors of price change in calculating economic aggregates, so as to facilitate comparison of aggregates over time. Two methods are used for calculating economic aggregates at comparable prices, a) Multiplying the output of products by their constant prices of certain year; b) Deflation of data at current prices by relevant price index.

Average Annual Growth Rate Two methods for calculating average annual growth rate are applied in China, one is often called "level approach", or the method of calculating geometric average, which is derived by comparing the level of the last year of the interval with that of the beginning year; the other is called "accumulative approach" or algebraic average or equation method, which is derived by the summation of the actual figure of each year in the interval divided by the figure in the base year. Usually the results calculated by the two methods are fairly close, but they differed sharply when uneven economic development occurred with striking fluctuations in growth.

The average annual growth rate listed in this statistical yearbook are calculated by "level approach" except for the growth rate of investment in fixed assets. The base years are not listed when the years are listed for average annual growth rates.

Registration Status of Enterprises Enterprises are classified into 3 categories, in the light of the registration status of an enterprise in industrial and commercial administration agencies. Domestic - funded enterprises include state - owned enterprises, collective - owned enterprises, cooperative enterprises, private enterprises, share - holding corporations Ltd., limited liability corporations, joint ownership enterprises and other domestic - funded enterprises. Hongkong, Macao and Taiwan funded enterprises include joint venture enterprises, cooperative enterprises, sole investment enterprises and share - holding corporations Ltd. Foreign funded enterprises include Chinese - foreign joint venture enterprises, Chinese - foreign cooperative enterprises, sole foreign funded enterprises and share - holding corporations Ltd. with foreign investment. Due to individuals don't belong to enterprises, individuals don't be listed according to the "Regulation of Registered Status of Enterprises". But individuals belong to statistical category. Registered status of enterprises is different to ownership, especially, state - owned and collective - owned enterprises are different to state - owned and collective - owned economy.

Domestic - funded Enterprises include state - owned enterprises, collective - owned enterprises, cooperative enterprises, private enterprises, share - holding corporations Ltd., limited liability corporations, joint ownership enterprises and others.

State - owned Enterprises refer to non - corporation economic units where the entire assets are owned by the state and which have registered in accordance with the Regulation of the People's Republic of China on the Management of Registration of Corporate Enterprises. Excluded from this category are sole state - funded corporations in the limited liability corporations. Excluded from this category are enterprises with exclusive investment from state - owned, state - owned cooperative enterprises in the join ownership enterprises.

Collective - owned Enterprises refer to economic units where the assets are owned collectively and which have registered in accordance with the Regulation of the People's Republic of China on the Management of Registration of Corporate Enterprises. Excluded from this category are collective - owned and collective - owned cooperative enterprises in joint ownership enterprises, excluded cooperative enterprises.

Cooperative Enterprises refer to a form of collective economic units (enterprises) where capitals come mainly from employees as their shares, with certain proportion of capital from the outside, where production is organized on the basis of independent operation, independent accounting for profits and losses, joint work, democratic management, and a distribution system that integrates remuneration according to work with divided according to capital share.

Private Enterprises refer to profit - making economic units invested and established by natural persons, or controlled by natural persons using employed labour. Included in this category are private limited liability corporations, private share - holding corporations Ltd., private partnership enterprises and private - funded enterprises registered in accordance with the Corporation Law, Partnership Enterprises Law and Interim Regulations on Private Enterprises.

Share - holding Corporations Ltd. refer to economic units registered in accordance with the Regulation of the People's Republic of China on the Management of Registration of Corporations, with total registered capitals divided into equal shares and raised through issuing stocks. Each investor bears limited liability to the corporation depending on the holding of shares, and the corporation bears liability to its debt to the maximum of its total assets.

Limited Liability Corporations refer to economic units established with investment from 2 - 50 investors and registered in accordance with the Regulation of the People's Republic of China on the Management of Registration of Corporations, each investor bearing limited liability to the corporation depending on its share of investment, and the corporation bearing liability to its debt to the maximum of its total assets. Limited liability corporations include exclusive state - funded limited liability corporations and other limited liability corporations.

Sole State - funded Corporations refer to limited liability corporations established with exclusive investment from investment institutions or departments authorized by the state.

Other Limited Liability Corporations refer to the limited liability corporations other than sole state - funded corporations.

Joint Ownership Enterprises refer to economic units established by two or more corporate enterprises or corporate institutions of the same or different ownership, through joint investment on the basis of equality, voluntary participation and mutual benefits. They include state joint ownership enterprises, collective joint ownership enterprises, joint state - collective enterprises, other joint ownership enterprises.

Other Domestic - funded Enterprises refer to domestic - funded economic units other than those mentioned above.

Enterprises with Investment from Hongkong, Macao and Taiwan include joint venture enterprises with funds from Hongkong, Macao and Taiwan, cooperative enterprises with funds from Hongkong, Macao and Taiwan, enterprises with exclusive investment from Hongkong, Macao and Taiwan, share - holding corporations Ltd. with investment from Hongkong, Macao and Taiwan.

Enterprises with Exclusive Investment from Hongkong, Macao and Taiwan refer to enterprises established in the mainland of China with exclusive investment from investors from Hongkong, Macao and Taiwan in accordance with the Law of the People's Republic of China on Foreign - Funded Enterprises and other relevant laws.

Share - holding Corporations Ltd. with Investment from Hongkong, Macao and Taiwan refer to share - holding corporations Ltd. established with the approval from the Ministry of Foreign Trade and Economic Relations (the Ministry of Commerce) in line with relevant state regulations, where the share of investment from Hongkong, Macao or Taiwan business men exceeds 25% of the total registered capital of the corporation. In case, the share of investment from Hongkong, Macao or Taiwan is less than 25% of the total registered capital, the enterprise is to be classified as domestic - funded share - holding corporation Ltd.

Foreign Funded Enterprises include joint venture enterprises with foreign investment, cooperation enterprises with foreign investment, enterprises with exclusive foreign investment, share - holding corporations Ltd. with foreign investment.

Individual refer to economic units which the production materials are owned by individual, where production is organized on the basis of individual operation, labours results are owned and used by labourer, including economic units where have registered in accordance with Civil Law General Rule and individual industrialists and businessmen or a group of citizens which have registered in urban and rural industrial and commercial administration agencies, urban and rural individual where have no business licenses but undertake individual operation.

Government Agencies, Institutions and Social Organization are classified into following categories by source of funds and way of management taking reference of the registration status of enterprises.

(1)**Government agencies** include state and party agencies, classified in principle as "state - owned". There are exceptions, such as supply and marketing cooperatives which are classified as "collective - owned".

(2)**Institutions** include institutions of various types established with the approval by organization and staffing department of the government, but exclude institutions where enterprise management system is introduced. Institutions are further classified as follows:

(a) Institutions whose main budget is listed in the government budget appropriations or extra - budget funds, or allocated from the budget of their competent government agencies. Such institutions are classified as "state - owned". (b) Institutions whose budget mainly comes from collective units. Such institutions are classified as "collective - owned".

(c) Institutions established by individual(individual partnership), which are classified as "private".

(d) Institutions other than those mentioned above whose source of budget is not clear. Such institutions are classified by way of management.

(3)**Social organizations** include social organizations established with the approval from the Ministry of Civil Affairs, and organizations that are not covered by social organizations management regulations such as trade unions, women's federations etc.. Social organizations are further classified as follows:

(a) Social organizations that are not covered by social organizations management regulations of the Ministry of Civil Affairs, such as trade unions, women's federations, communist youth leagues, youth associations, industrial and commerce associations, scientists associations, overseas Chinese associations, etc., foundations and fund management organization established with funds from state, and social organizations whose funds mainly come from the budget of their competent government agencies. Such institutions are classified as "state - owned".

(b)Social organizations whose budget mainly comes from collective units. Such institutions are classified as "collective - owned".

(c)Social organizations established by individual(individual partnership), which are classified as "private".

(d)Social organizations other than those mentioned above whose source of budget is not clear. Such institutions are classified by way of management.

Type of Ownership refers to enterprises classified as various type of ownership in accordance with registered categories of enterprises after 1998. In which, state - owned economy refer to state - owned enterprises, sole state - funded enterprises, state joint ownership enterprises, collective - owned economy refer to collective - owned enterprises, cooperative enterprises, collective joint ownership enterprises; private economy refer to private enterprises and individual.

Developed Areas refer to the land in administrative areas having been developed concentratedly with municipal public facilities. Forcore city, developed areas include concentrated areas and decentralized areas, having basic perfect municipal public facilities; for the city with several towns, developed areas are composed of several concentrated areas with municipal public facilities. Therefore, the scope of developed areas refers to actual construction land of a city.

第2篇 CHAPTER 2

人口和劳动就业

POPULATION, LABOR AND EMPLOYMENT

2-1 改革开放以来人口主要指标

MAJOR POPULATION STATISTICS SINCE REFORM AND OPENING UP

年　份 Year	常住人口（万人）Permanent Population (10 000 persons)	户籍人口（万人）Registered Population (10 000 persons)	户籍户数（万户）Registered Households (10 000 households)	人口密度（人/平方公里）Population Density (person/sq. km)	人口出生率 Birth Rate (‰)	人口死亡率 Death Rate (‰)	人口自然增长率 Natural Growth Rate (‰)
1978		724.27	171.82	640	15.47	6.26	9.21
1979		739.42	174.77	652	14.57	5.94	8.63
1980		748.91	179.67	660	13.29	6.04	7.25
1981		760.32	188.61	670	17.90	5.99	11.91
1982		774.92	196.63	683	20.05	5.64	14.41
1983		785.28	203.47	692	17.14	5.41	11.73
1984		795.52	209.96	702	15.67	5.43	10.24
1985		804.80	216.86	710	13.94	5.78	8.15
1986		814.97	221.81	718	15.00	5.71	9.29
1987	831.76	828.73	230.71	731	17.07	6.08	10.99
1988	843.44	839.21	241.46	741	15.92	5.65	10.27
1989	856.95	852.35	249.26	752	15.50	6.49	9.01
1990	884.03	866.25	258.31	764	15.62	5.79	9.83
1991	908.89	872.63	262.75	770	11.94	5.78	6.16
1992	920.41	878.97	266.77	776	12.50	6.00	6.50
1993	928.02	885.89	270.77	782	10.71	6.20	4.51
1994	935.28	890.55	273.87	745	10.98	6.19	4.79
1995	941.83	894.67	276.89	749	10.23	6.23	4.00
1996	948.19	898.45	279.62	752	10.09	6.53	3.56
1997	952.59	899.80	284.08	753	9.98	6.95	3.03
1998	956.64	905.09	288.20	757	9.89	6.49	3.40
1999	959.48	910.17	291.32	762	9.68	6.73	2.95
2000	1 001.14	912.00	293.04	763	7.72	6.17	1.55
2001	1 004.06	913.98	295.63	765	7.58	5.94	1.64
2002	1 007.18	919.05	299.67	769	7.49	6.04	1.45
2003	1 011.30	926.00	303.27	775	7.14	6.04	1.10

注：1.人口密度1994年以后按规划局新测定的土地面积计算。2.人口自然变动"三率"从1987年以后为历年人口变动抽样调查或普查数据，以前为公安年报数。

Note: a) After 1994, the population density is calculated with new land areas measured by Tianjin Project Bureau. b) After 1987, the three ratio of population changing are obtained from sample survey, others are obtained from annual reports of Public Security Bureau.

2-2 户籍人口主要构成

COMPOSITION OF REGISTERED POPULATION

(1995－2003)

单位：%　　　　(%)

年　份 Year	按户口性质分 By Registered Character		按性别分 By Sex		
	非农业 Non-agricultural	农　业 Agricultural	男　性 Male	女　性 Female	性别比（女=100）Sex Ratio (Female=100)
1995	56.77	43.23	50.66	49.34	102.67
1996	57.12	42.88	50.62	49.38	102.50
1997	57.27	42.73	50.58	49.42	102.33
1998	57.60	42.40	50.53	49.47	102.14
1999	58.09	41.91	50.51	49.49	102.06
2000	58.39	41.61	50.51	49.49	102.05
2001	58.56	41.44	50.48	49.52	101.92
2002	58.88	41.12	50.45	49.55	101.84
2003	59.37	40.63	50.47	49.53	101.89

2-3 按地区分的户数、人口数及人口密度

HOUSEHOLDS, POPULATION AND POPULATION DENSITY BY REGION

地区	Region	户数(万户) Households (10 000 households) 2002	2003	人口数(万人) Population (10 000 persons) 2002	2003	年平均人口(万人) Average Annual Population (10 000 persons) (2003)	人口密度(人/平方公里) Population Density (person/sq. km) (2003)
全市常住人口	**Total Permanent Population**	**315.65**	**316.95**	**1 007.18**	**1 011.30**	**1 009.24**	**848**
全市户籍人口	**Total Registered Population**	**299.67**	**303.27**	**919.05**	**926.00**	**922.53**	**775**
一、市辖区	**Districts Under City Administration**	**250.72**	**253.73**	**752.21**	**758.78**	**755.50**	**1 019**
#市内六区	Six Urban Districts	131.66	132.72	375.60	380.52	378.06	22 682
滨海区	Coastal Districts	34.41	35.09	98.17	98.85	98.51	438
和平区	Heping District	13.82	13.79	43.95	46.66	45.30	46 657
河东区	Hedong District	23.70	24.10	65.77	66.28	66.03	16 995
河西区	Hexi District	24.96	25.22	71.27	72.05	71.66	19 473
南开区	Nankai District	27.30	27.36	77.96	78.70	78.33	20 179
河北区	Hebei District	21.76	22.07	60.99	61.28	61.14	22 697
红桥区	Hongqiao District	20.11	20.18	55.67	55.55	55.61	26 453
塘沽区	Tanggu District	16.22	16.55	47.21	47.59	47.40	628
#开发区	TEDA	0.54	0.62	1.62	1.85	1.73	
汉沽区	Hangu District	6.06	6.12	16.80	16.80	16.80	380
大港区	Dagang District	12.13	12.42	34.15	34.46	34.31	326
东丽区	Dongli District	10.38	10.79	30.83	31.25	31.04	653
西青区	Xiqing District	10.02	10.18	30.60	30.63	30.61	543
津南区	Jinnan District	12.05	12.24	37.16	37.33	37.24	959
北辰区	Beichen District	10.63	10.79	31.98	31.99	31.98	669
武清区	Wuqing District	22.55	22.72	80.57	80.78	80.68	513
宝坻区	Baodi District	18.13	18.28	64.98	65.08	65.03	431
天津铁厂	Tianjin Iron Works	0.89	0.92	2.33	2.35	2.34	
二、市辖县	**Counties Under City Administration**	**48.95**	**49.54**	**166.84**	**167.22**	**167.03**	**371**
宁河县	Ninghe County	10.74	10.88	35.98	36.15	36.07	253
静海县	Jinghai County	16.38	16.64	50.86	51.10	50.98	345
蓟 县	Jixian County	21.83	22.02	80.00	79.97	79.98	503

注:和平区人数、户数中含全市委培大学生数。
Note: Population and households of Heping District include the students commissioned in the universities.

2-4 按户口性质分的户籍户数
HOUSEHOLDS BY REGISTERED CHARACTER

单位:万户 (10 000 households)

地区	Region	非农业 Non-agricultural Households		农业 Agricultural Households	
		2002	2003	2002	2003
全市总计	**Total**	**189.13**	**191.77**	**110.54**	**111.50**
一、市辖区	**Districts Under City Administration**	**179.37**	**181.41**	**71.35**	**72.32**
#市内六区	Six Urban Districts	130.92	131.98	0.73	0.74
滨海区	Coastal District	27.57	28.08	6.84	7.01
和平区	Heping District	13.82	13.79		
河东区	Hedong District	23.67	24.07	0.03	0.03
河西区	Hexi District	24.79	25.05	0.17	0.17
南开区	Nankai District	26.89	26.94	0.41	0.42
河北区	Hebei District	21.74	22.06	0.01	0.01
红桥区	Hongqiao District	20.01	20.07	0.10	0.11
塘沽区	Tanggu District	14.12	14.36	2.10	2.19
#开发区	TEDA	0.54	0.62		
汉沽区	Hangu District	4.59	4.63	1.47	1.49
大港区	Dagang District	8.86	9.09	3.27	3.33
东丽区	Dongli District	3.87	3.93	6.51	6.86
西青区	Xiqing District	2.57	2.58	7.45	7.60
津南区	Jinnan District	3.30	3.36	8.76	8.88
北辰区	Beichen District	4.21	4.31	6.41	6.48
武清区	Wuqing District	3.02	3.13	19.53	19.59
宝坻区	Baodi District	3.02	3.12	15.11	15.16
天津铁厂	Tianjin Iron Works	0.89	0.92		
二、市辖县	**Counties Under City Administration**	**9.76**	**10.37**	**39.19**	**39.17**
宁河县	Ninghe County	3.08	3.30	7.66	7.58
静海县	Jinghai County	3.41	3.65	12.97	12.99
蓟县	Jixian County	3.27	3.42	18.56	18.60

2－5　按户口性质分的户籍人口数
REGISTERED POPULATION BY REGISTERED CHARACTER

单位:万人　　(10 000 persons)

地　区	Region	非农业 Non－agricultural Population		农　业 Agricultural Population	
		2002	2003	2002	2003
全市总计	**Total**	**541.14**	**549.74**	**377.91**	**376.26**
一、市辖区	**Districts Under City Administration**	**514.53**	**521.70**	**237.70**	**237.08**
#市内六区	Six Urban Districts	373.78	378.70	1.82	1.82
滨海区	Coastal Districts	77.28	78.07	20.88	20.78
和平区	Heping District	43.95	46.66		
河东区	Hedong District	65.70	66.21	0.07	0.07
河西区	Hexi District	70.88	71.66	0.39	0.39
南开区	Nankai District	76.88	77.62	1.08	1.08
河北区	Hebei District	60.96	61.26	0.02	0.02
红桥区	Hongqiao District	55.41	55.29	0.26	0.26
塘沽区	Tanggu District	41.15	41.58	6.07	6.01
#开发区	TEDA	1.62	1.85		
汉沽区	Hangu District	12.32	12.32	4.48	4.48
大港区	Dagang District	23.82	24.17	10.34	10.29
东丽区	Dongli District	11.18	11.38	19.65	19.87
西青区	Xiqing District	7.69	7.75	22.91	22.88
津南区	Jinnan District	9.58	9.84	27.58	27.49
北辰区	Beichen District	12.15	12.27	19.83	19.72
武清区	Wuqing District	10.98	11.52	69.60	69.26
宝坻区	Baodi District	9.54	9.82	55.43	55.26
天津铁厂	Tianjin Iron Works	2.33	2.35		
二、市辖县	**Counties Under City Administration**	**26.61**	**28.04**	**140.21**	**139.18**
宁河县	Ninghe County	7.71	8.30	28.26	27.85
静海县	Jinghai County	8.22	8.65	42.63	42.45
蓟　县	Jixian County	10.68	11.09	69.32	68.88

2－6 按性别分的户籍人口数
REGISTERED POPULATION BY SEX

单位：万人 （10 000 persons）

地区	Region	男性 Male 2002	男性 Male 2003	女性 Female 2002	女性 Female 2003	性别比（女＝100） Sex Ratio(Female＝100) 2002	性别比（女＝100） Sex Ratio(Female＝100) 2003
全市总计	**Total**	**463.71**	**467.33**	**455.35**	**458.67**	**101.84**	**101.89**
一、市辖区	**Districts Under City Administration**	**378.91**	**382.31**	**373.31**	**376.47**	**101.50**	**101.55**
#市内六区	Six Urban Districts	188.26	190.94	187.35	189.58	100.49	100.72
滨海区	Coastal Districts	50.81	51.13	47.35	47.72	107.30	107.15
和平区	Heping District	21.28	22.77	22.67	23.89	93.84	95.30
河东区	Hedong District	33.09	33.37	32.67	32.91	101.28	101.38
河西区	Hexi District	35.42	35.80	35.84	36.25	98.82	98.77
南开区	Nankai District	39.51	39.96	38.45	38.74	102.75	103.14
河北区	Hebei District	30.81	30.96	30.18	30.32	102.11	102.14
红桥区	Hongqiao District	28.14	28.08	27.53	27.47	102.24	102.24
塘沽区	Tanggu District	24.36	24.55	22.85	23.04	106.62	106.57
#开发区	TEDA	0.81	0.93	0.81	0.92	99.91	101.07
汉沽区	Hangu District	8.55	8.54	8.25	8.26	103.53	103.43
大港区	Dagang District	17.90	18.04	16.25	16.42	110.18	109.88
东丽区	Dongli District	15.59	15.75	15.24	15.50	102.28	101.57
西青区	Xiqing District	15.20	15.20	15.40	15.43	98.71	98.54
津南区	Jinnan District	18.60	18.67	18.56	18.66	100.18	100.10
北辰区	Beichen District	16.04	16.04	15.95	15.95	100.56	100.52
武清区	Wuqing District	40.43	40.53	40.14	40.25	100.72	100.69
宝坻区	Baodi District	32.79	32.84	32.18	32.24	101.90	101.87
天津铁厂	Tianjin Iron Works	1.19	1.21	1.14	1.14	105.10	105.24
二、市辖县	**Counties Under City Administration**	**84.80**	**85.02**	**82.04**	**82.20**	**103.36**	**103.42**
宁河县	Ninghe County	18.23	18.32	17.75	17.83	102.70	102.75
静海县	Jinghai County	25.82	25.97	25.04	25.13	103.11	103.36
蓟县	Jixian County	40.75	40.73	39.25	39.24	103.83	103.77

2－7 计划生育情况
FAMILY PLANNING
(1997－2003)

指 标 Item	1997	1998	1999	2000	2001	2002	2003
政策生育率(%) Family Planning Rate(%)	98.27	98.32	98.12	98.51	98.67	98.80	98.73
一孩率(%) One－child Rate(%)	81.22	82.73	78.07	76.55	76.54	70.30	76.36
二孩率(%) Two－child Rate(%)	18.23	16.79	20.99	22.27	22.58	29.19	22.59
多孩率(%) Multi－child Rate(%)	0.55	0.48	0.94	1.19	0.88	0.51	1.05
总和生育率 General Fertility Rate	1.28	1.23	1.24	0.88	1.05	1.02	1.03

资料来源：1.政策生育率为计生委年报数；其余指标为历年人口变动抽样调查数据。2.从1998年起计生委年报的调查期为上年10月1日至当年9月30日。
Data Source: a) Family planning rate is obtained from annual reports of Tianjin Birth Control Committee; other data of this table are obtained from annual sample survey in every year. b) Since 1998, the annual survey is undertaken from Oct.1 of previous year to Sep.30 of this year by Tianjin Birth Control Committee.

2－8 人口婚姻登记情况
MARRIAGE REGISTRATION

指 标 Item	2000	2001	2002	2003
结婚对数合计(对) Total Marriages (couple)	**61 416**	**57 922**	**53 892**	**62 630**
#恢复结婚对数 Remarriage with Former Spouse	695	697	716	513
初婚人数(万人) First Marriages(10 000 persons)	10.7	10.0	9.3	10.9
再婚人数(万人) Remarriages(10 000 persons)	1.6	1.5	1.5	1.6
离婚对数(对) Divorces(couple)	**13 338**	**9 851**	**10 576**	**12 041**
法院判决离婚 Mediated by The Court	4 126	3 791	4 143	3 647
民政协议离婚 Approved by Civil Administration Agencies	9 212	6 060	6 433	8 394
涉外婚姻(人) Chinese－Foreigner Marriage (person)	**342**	**273**	**288**	**343**
#女性 Female	298	235	242	278

资料来源：结婚对数是民政事业统计年报数，离婚对数是民政事业统计年报与法院统计年报数之和。
Data Source: The data of marriage couples are obtained from the annual reports of civil administration agencies, the divorce couples are the sum of data obtained from annual reports of civil administration agencies and courts.

2-9 各种特征年龄组的户籍人口(2003年)
REGISTERED POPULATION BY AGE GROUPS,2003

单位:万人 (10 000 persons)

年龄组	Age Groups	合计 Total	#市内六区 Six Urban Districts	男性 Male	#市内六区 Six Urban Districts	女性 Female	#市内六区 Six Urban Districts
一、按学龄人口分组	**Grouped by School Age**						
0-2 岁	Age 0-2	15.88	3.72	8.48	1.92	7.40	1.80
3-5 岁	Age 3-5	19.77	4.76	10.47	2.44	9.30	2.32
6-14 岁	Age 6-14	89.71	24.11	46.89	12.26	42.82	11.85
15-17 岁	Age 15-17	45.88	16.64	23.62	8.43	22.26	8.21
18-21 岁	Age 18-21	62.90	33.54	32.23	17.27	30.67	16.27
二、按婚育人口分组	**Grouped by Marriage Age and Child-bearing Age**						
进入法定婚龄人口	Reaching Legal Marriage Age	16.06	8.49	8.10	3.92	7.96	4.57
育龄妇女人口	Women at Child-bearing Age						
(15-49 岁)	(Between 15-49)	268.29	111.70			268.29	111.70
三、按劳龄人口分组	**Grouped by Labor Age**						
进入劳龄人口	Reaching Labor Age						
(国内标准)	(Domestic Standard)	15.57	5.55	8.04	2.82	7.53	2.73
(国际标准)	(International Standard)	14.95	5.06	7.69	2.54	7.26	2.52
劳动年龄内人口	Within Labor Age						
(国内标准)	(Domestic Standard)	626.92	266.01	329.03	140.54	297.89	125.47
(国际标准)	(International Standard)	701.73	296.93	353.95	150.65	347.78	146.28
退出劳龄人口	Over Labor Age						
(国内标准)	(Domestic Standard)	8.59	3.55	3.48	1.49	5.11	2.06
(国际标准)	(International Standard)	7.30	3.34	3.54	1.49	3.76	1.85
四、按老年人口分组	**Grouped by Aged Population**						
60 岁及以上人口	Age 60 and over	134.16	66.62	64.74	31.19	69.42	35.43
占总人口比重(%)	Proportion in Total(%)	14.49	17.51	13.86	16.34	15.13	18.68
65 岁及以上人口	Age 65 and over	98.92	50.99	47.52	23.63	51.40	27.36
占总人口比重(%)	Proportion in Total(%)	10.68	13.40	10.17	12.38	11.21	14.43
80 岁及以上人口	Age 80 and over	15.39	8.21	6.89	3.71	8.50	4.50
占总人口比重(%)	Proportion in Total(%)	1.66	2.16	1.48	1.94	1.85	2.37

注:进入法定婚龄人口标准为男22岁、女20岁;进入劳龄人口、劳动年龄内人口、退出劳龄人口的国内标准分别是男16岁、16-59岁、60岁和女16岁、16-54岁、55岁;国际标准男女均为15岁、15-64岁、65岁。

Note:The standard of legal marriage age is 22 for male and 20 for female;the domestic standard of "reaching labor age","within labor age" and "over labor age" are 16,16 to 59,60 for male respectively and 16,16 to 54,55 for female respectively;the international standard of these items are 15,15-64 and 65 respectively for both male and female.

2003 年人口变动情况抽样调查资料说明：

本次抽样调查登记的标准时间为 2003 年 11 月 1 日零时；调查样本设计以地域（层）为原则，采用了分层、三阶段、整群、概率比例的抽样方法，在全市 18 个区县中，抽取了 112 个街（乡、镇）级行政单位的 259 个居委会和 103 个村委会中的 2.7 万户，共调查登记了 8.2 万人，占全市常住人口总数的 0.81%。以下表 2—10 至 2—14 为这次调查机器汇总数据。

Brief introduction for sample survey on population change in 2003:

The reference time of sample survey was zero hour of November 1,2003,the principle of survey district was adopted in the sample survey. The sample survey was conducted with a multi - stage systematic cluster sampling scheme. A total of 0.082 million people were selected as the sample from 0.027 million households in 259 resident's committees & 103 village committees in 112 streets(towns) of 18 districts(counties), its share in the total permanent population was 0.81 percent. From Table 2 - 10 to Table 2 - 14, data were obtained from the computer tabulation.

2-10 人口变动情况抽样调查主要数据(2003 年)

DATA OF SAMPLE SURVEY ON POPULATION CHANGE,2003

指 标 Item	2003
样本总户数(户) **Households (househod)**	**26 554**
# 一人户 One Person	1 611
二人户 Two Persons	5 518
三人户 Three Persons	12 110
四人户 Four Persons	4 561
五人及以上户 Five Persons and Above	2 620
户籍人口中有外出半年以上人口的家庭户 Households in Which Someone Have Gone to Other Places for More Than 6 Months	366
样本总人口(人) **Population (person)**	**81 763**
1.住本调查小区，户口在本乡镇街道 Population Who Reside in the Survey District and Have Their Permanent Household Registration There	70 693
2.住本调查小区半年以上，户口在外乡镇街道 Population Who Have Resided in the Survey District for More Than 6 Months but the places of their Permanent Household Registration are Elsewhere	10 333
3.住本调查小区不满半年，离开户口登记地半年以上 Population Who Have Resided in the Survey District for Less Than 6 Months but have been away from the places of their Permanent Household Registration for More Than 6 Months	488
4.住本调查小区，户口待定 Population Who Reside in the Survey District While the Places of their Permanent Household Have not Yet Settled	249
总负担系数 Total Dependency Ratio	30.89
少儿负担系数 The Juvenile and Children Dependency Ratio	18.14
老年负担系数 The Aged Dependency Ratio	12.75
按周工作时间分 15 岁以上在业人口(人) **Employed Population Aged 15 and Over by Weekly Working Time (person)**	
# 20 - 29 小时 20 - 29 hours	805
30 - 39 小时 30 - 39 hours	1 448
40 - 49 小时 40 - 49 hours	23 131
50 小时以上 Over 50 Hours	11 856

2-11 全市6岁及以上人口分年龄的文化构成(2003年)
COMPOSTION OF EDUCATION BY AGE FOR PEOPLE AGED 6 AND OVER,2003

单位:人 (person)

年龄 Age	6岁及以上人口 Aged 6 and over	#小学 Primary School	#初中 Junior Middle School	#高中 Senior Middle School	#大学专科 Junior College	#大学本科 University	#研究生 Graduate Student
全市合计							
Total	**78 516**	**17 614**	**29 718**	**18 264**	**5 143**	**3 157**	**163**
6-9	2 809	2 664					
10-14	5 273	2 820	2 404	27			
15-19	6 482	286	2 525	3 127	316	200	
20-24	5 769	216	1 902	1 812	953	825	22
25-29	4 975	335	2 196	1 412	592	367	29
30-34	6 413	611	3 104	1 629	626	343	43
35-39	6 884	847	3 547	1 612	466	306	28
40-44	8 117	777	3 135	3 391	472	241	15
45-49	8 794	1 466	4 133	2 330	482	159	9
50-54	6 612	1 837	3 091	857	446	130	9
55-59	4 414	1 512	1 426	788	307	129	1
60-64	3 247	1 116	858	566	183	157	1
65岁及以上							
(≥65)	8 727	3 127	1 397	713	300	300	6
#女性							
Female	**39 565**	**9 164**	**14 110**	**8 995**	**2 412**	**1 409**	**69**
6-9	1 318	1 246					
10-14	2 557	1 327	1 209	13			
15-19	3 159	131	1 192	1 541	178	105	
20-24	2 897	106	920	898	518	433	10
25-29	2 585	185	1 149	715	306	191	18
30-34	3 252	353	1 566	799	327	157	19
35-39	3 505	495	1 742	862	218	131	9
40-44	4 030	486	1 442	1 750	211	71	4
45-49	4 427	918	1 937	1 145	204	64	4
50-54	3 380	1 057	1 482	408	191	54	4
55-59	2 211	840	627	376	117	49	
60-64	1 714	617	410	263	56	60	
65岁及以上							
(≥65)	4 530	1 403	434	225	86	94	1

2－12　全市 15 岁及以上人口分年龄的婚姻状况(2003 年)

MARRIAGE STATUS OF POPULATION AGED 15 AND OVER,2003

单位:人　　　　(person)

年　龄 Age	15 岁及以上人口 Aged 15 and Over	未　婚 Unmarried	初婚有配偶 First Marriages	再婚有配偶 Remarriages	离　婚 Divorces	丧　偶 Widowed
全 市 合 计						
Total	**70 434**	**13 008**	**51 592**	**1 076**	**840**	**3 918**
15－19	6 482	6 419	54			
20－24	5 769	4 441	1 300	9	15	5
25－29	4 975	1 133	3 752	35	55	
30－34	6 413	375	5 805	100	119	14
35－39	6 884	157	6 384	164	151	28
40－44	8 117	128	7 530	178	213	76
45－49	8 794	123	8 219	168	139	145
50－54	6 612	86	6 145	130	72	179
55－59	4 414	57	3 999	78	26	254
60－64	3 247	30	2 781	58	16	362
65 岁及以上						
(≥65)	8 727	59	5 623	156	34	2 855
#女　性						
Female	**35 690**	**5 969**	**25 994**	**555**	**423**	**2 749**
15－19	3 159	3 123	32			
20－24	2 897	2 117	761	5	10	4
25－29	2 585	434	2 099	20	32	
30－34	3 252	123	2 998	60	63	8
35－39	3 505	45	3 280	91	72	17
40－44	4 030	43	3 748	100	105	38
45－49	4 427	39	4 133	82	69	104
50－54	3 380	21	3 115	77	35	132
55－59	2 211	11	1 959	38	16	187
60－64	1 714	2	1 410	22	7	273
65 岁及以上						
(≥65)	4 530	11	2 459	60	14	1 986

2-13 按地区分的家庭户类型(2003年)
TYPE OF HOUSEHOLD BY REGION,2003

单位:户 (household)

地 区	Region	单身户 Single	一对夫妇户 One Couple	二代户 Two Gene-rations	三代及以上户 Three and Over Gene-rations	一代与其他户 One Gene-rations and Other	二代与其他户 Two Gene-rations and Other	三代及以上与其他户 Three and Over Gene-rations and Other
全市总计	**Total**	**1 611**	**4 376**	**15 858**	**3 843**	**175**	**273**	**284**
和平区	Heping District	96	115	458	135	4	13	22
河东区	Hedong District	178	374	1 261	194	14	32	71
河西区	Hexi District	181	386	1 286	232	16	18	12
南开区	Nankai District	131	357	1 471	357	17	32	39
河北区	Hebei District	135	244	959	253	18	22	22
红桥区	Hongqiao District	195	298	1 065	180	11	13	3
塘沽区	Tanggu District	95	306	885	195	18	19	8
汉沽区	Hangu District	52	181	302	54	4	5	3
大港区	Dagang District	44	220	769	61	4	12	22
东丽区	Dongli District	43	218	783	141	11	8	4
西青区	Xiqing District	84	245	903	135	2	8	4
津南区	Jinnan District	45	163	659	161	7	6	4
北辰区	Beichen District	56	183	689	210	6	11	8
武清区	Wuqing District	88	271	1 158	397	12	29	16
宝坻区	Baodi District	33	243	875	321	7	9	4
宁河县	Ninghe County	37	131	514	175	3	4	14
静海县	Jinghai County	32	217	891	209	7	14	8
蓟 县	Jixian County	86	224	930	433	14	18	20

2－14　按地区分有65岁及以上老年人口的家庭户(2003年)

HOUSEHOLDS WITH POPULATION AGED 65 AND OVER BY REGION, 2003

单位:户　　(household)

地　区	Region	合　计 Total	#单身老人户 Single	#一对老夫妇户 One Couple	#一个老人与亲属户 One Aged Population and Relatives	#二个老人与亲属户 Two Aged Population and Relatives
全市总计	**Total**	**6 332**	**820**	**1 233**	**3 136**	**1 124**
和平区	Heping District	300	43	48	139	70
河东区	Hedong District	609	90	141	272	103
河西区	Hexi District	610	96	126	246	141
南开区	Nankai District	727	72	134	363	156
河北区	Hebei District	498	72	87	246	91
红桥区	Hongqiao District	515	127	120	207	60
塘沽区	Tanggu District	371	46	79	182	64
汉沽区	Hangu District	124	31	42	33	18
大港区	Dagang District	166	17	31	96	22
东丽区	Dongli District	202	22	54	105	21
西青区	Xiqing District	246	45	55	120	26
津南区	Jinnan District	173	16	35	89	32
北辰区	Beichen District	269	29	39	137	63
武清区	Wuqing District	395	40	61	229	65
宝坻区	Baodi District	271	10	44	168	48
宁河县	Ninghe County	194	12	31	123	28
静海县	Jinghai County	243	23	41	152	26
蓟　县	Jixian County	419	29	65	229	90

2－15　社会从业人员

TOTAL PERSONS EMPLOYED

（1978－2003）

单位：万人　　　　(10 000 persons)

年　份 Year	劳动力资源总数 Number of Labour Force	社会从业人员合计 Number of Persons Employed	按城乡分组 Grouped by Urban and Rural Areas					
			城　镇 Urban Areas	国有经济 State－owned	集体经济 Collective－owned	其他经济 Other Ownership	个体私营经济 Private and Individual	乡　村 Rural Areas
1978	448.76	366.70	217.50	168.30	49.10		0.10	149.20
1979	466.90	380.54	230.34	178.20	52.04		0.10	150.20
1980	480.80	394.79	243.59	188.08	54.61		0.90	151.20
1981	494.10	413.20	255.00	194.02	59.88		1.10	158.20
1982	503.60	420.52	262.02	198.91	61.61		1.50	158.50
1983	509.50	435.53	270.33	201.27	66.96		2.10	165.20
1984	517.10	447.29	276.39	201.29	71.42	0.98	2.70	170.90
1985	526.10	455.98	281.08	205.26	69.71	1.51	4.60	174.90
1986	532.27	466.90	284.50	209.97	68.47	1.76	4.30	182.40
1987	544.80	470.93	286.63	212.10	66.89	2.54	5.10	184.30
1988	549.97	465.15	286.64	213.99	64.33	3.04	5.28	178.51
1989	555.99	469.79	289.91	217.32	63.45	3.61	5.53	179.88
1990	558.93	470.07	290.01	217.26	62.55	4.50	5.70	180.06
1991	564.15	479.67	300.58	219.34	66.17	6.05	9.02	179.09
1992	569.70	485.70	303.70	212.73	72.39	8.85	9.73	182.00
1993	566.10	503.10	312.70	210.90	75.50	16.30	10.00	190.40
1994	694.30	513.00	318.60	206.50	71.40	24.40	16.30	194.40
1995	701.60	515.30	319.80	202.10	68.40	29.20	20.10	195.50
1996	708.80	512.00	317.10	199.10	62.80	31.00	24.20	194.90
1997	716.26	513.33	318.60	196.16	58.19	35.80	28.45	194.73
1998	728.68	508.10	312.65	183.49	53.00	41.58	34.58	195.45
1999	740.76	508.14	313.89	176.54	47.54	49.80	40.01	194.25
2000	753.27	486.89	296.61	163.84	40.58	55.37	36.82	190.28
2001	761.11	488.34	295.37	153.25	32.13	60.94	49.05	192.97
2002	771.69	492.61	295.71	137.81	26.60	82.54	48.76	196.90
2003	793.86	510.90	299.95	128.52	22.80	93.72	54.91	210.95

年　份 Year	按三次产业分 Grouped by Three Industries					
	绝对数 Number			构　成(％) Composition in Percentage(％)		
	第一产业 Primary Industry	第二产业 Secondary Industry	第三产业 Tertiary Industry	第一产业 Primary Industry	第二产业 Secondary Industry	第三产业 Tertiary Industry
1978						
1979						
1980						
1981						
1982						
1983						
1984						
1985	99.13	228.04	128.73	21.7	50.1	28.2
1986	96.06	231.02	139.86	20.6	49.5	29.9
1987	94.12	232.03	144.78	20.0	49.3	30.7
1988	91.19	229.85	144.11	19.6	49.4	31.1
1989	93.46	231.57	144.76	19.9	49.3	30.8
1990	93.63	232.17	144.27	19.9	49.4	30.7
1991	94.27	237.24	148.16	19.7	49.5	30.8
1992	92.50	238.40	154.80	19.0	49.1	31.9
1993	89.00	245.20	168.90	17.7	48.7	33.6
1994	85.60	246.50	180.90	16.7	48.0	35.3
1995	82.90	247.10	185.30	16.1	47.9	36.0
1996	82.10	241.40	188.50	16.0	47.2	36.8
1997	81.26	235.69	196.38	15.8	45.9	38.3
1998	80.88	233.21	194.01	15.9	45.9	38.2
1999	79.57	230.33	198.24	15.7	45.3	39.0
2000	81.29	222.15	183.45	16.7	45.6	37.7
2001	82.70	212.65	192.99	16.9	43.6	39.5
2002	82.25	205.38	204.98	16.7	41.7	41.6
2003	83.19	219.44	208.27	16.3	42.9	40.8

注：城镇从业人员中包括由于各种原因已经离开本人的生产或工作岗位，但仍与本单位保留劳动关系的职工。

Note：The number of urban employment personnel include those staff and workers who still keep their relation with their units，but have left their working post at there.

2-16 城镇单位从业人员
PERSONS EMPLOYED IN URBAN UNITS
(1978-2003)

单位:万人 (10 000 persons)

年 份 Year	合 计 Total	按三次产业分 Grouped by Three Industries			按经济类型分 Grouped by Ownership		
		第一产业 Primary Industry	第二产业 Secondary Industry	第三产业 Tertiary Industry	国有经济 State-owned	集体经济 Collective-owned	其他经济 Other
总 计 **Total**							
1978	217.40	4.22	131.55	81.63	168.30	49.10	
1979	230.24	3.41	138.63	88.20	178.20	52.04	
1980	242.69	3.34	146.52	92.83	188.08	54.61	
1981	253.90	3.53	153.95	96.42	194.02	59.88	
1982	260.53	3.51	155.71	101.31	198.91	61.62	
1983	268.23	3.62	161.31	103.30	201.27	66.96	
1984	273.69	3.92	163.52	106.25	201.29	71.42	0.98
1985	276.48	3.96	165.69	106.83	205.26	69.71	1.51
1986	280.20	4.51	167.19	108.50	209.97	68.47	1.76
1987	281.53	4.25	172.04	105.24	212.10	66.89	2.54
1988	281.36	4.30	164.82	112.24	213.99	64.33	3.04
1989	284.38	4.22	167.13	113.03	217.32	63.45	3.61
1990	284.31	4.10	167.68	112.53	217.26	62.55	4.50
1991	291.56	4.34	171.57	115.65	219.34	66.17	6.05
1992	293.97	4.10	171.41	118.46	212.73	72.39	8.85
1993	293.45	2.55	171.18	119.72	206.52	70.89	16.04
1994	291.94	2.30	168.72	120.92	201.75	66.21	23.98
1995	289.59	1.90	167.33	120.36	197.01	64.19	28.39
1996	283.98	1.73	163.07	119.18	194.32	59.62	30.04
1997	281.34	1.71	158.68	120.95	191.64	55.28	34.42
1998	218.56	1.43	113.47	103.66	144.18	36.26	38.12
1999	211.76	1.10	110.27	100.39	135.08	30.46	46.22
2000	201.75	1.11	105.63	95.01	125.00	25.82	50.93
2001	192.30	1.09	99.82	91.39	116.24	20.05	56.00
2002	185.50	1.09	92.68	91.73	107.79	16.47	61.24
2003	191.01	0.97	97.60	92.44	101.57	13.95	75.49
#女 性 **Female**							
1978	90.40	1.45	23.06	65.89	60.43	29.97	
1979	95.57	1.04	34.12	60.41	64.82	30.75	
1980	102.05	1.23	38.17	62.65	69.97	32.08	
1981	106.50	0.98	39.91	65.61	72.20	34.30	
1982	109.46	1.00	40.93	67.53	73.82	35.64	
1983	113.23	0.99	41.98	70.26	75.57	37.66	
1984	114.34	1.15	42.16	71.03	75.34	38.53	0.47
1985	115.64	1.18	43.26	71.20	76.26	38.72	0.66
1986	118.29	1.04	44.49	72.76	79.43	38.10	0.76
1987	119.45	1.32	44.46	73.67	81.18	37.12	1.15
1988	119.22	1.37	44.95	72.90	82.27	35.59	1.36
1989	120.48	1.30	71.30	47.88	83.92	34.91	1.65
1990	120.90	1.25	71.76	47.89	84.44	34.39	2.07
1991	124.24	1.44	73.87	48.93	85.78	35.61	2.85
1992	124.05	1.23	73.38	49.44	83.89	35.89	4.27
1993	123.14	0.86	72.00	50.28	81.46	34.00	7.68
1994	123.73	0.81	72.00	50.92	80.64	31.79	11.30
1995	123.60	0.68	72.03	50.89	79.27	30.81	13.52
1996	120.23	0.57	69.84	49.82	77.39	28.59	14.25
1997	118.75	0.55	67.48	50.72	76.61	26.15	15.99
1998	89.89	0.46	46.11	43.32	56.17	15.93	17.79
1999	82.95	0.31	41.33	41.31	51.80	13.22	17.93
2000	77.28	0.33	38.85	38.10	47.26	10.76	19.26
2001	77.40	0.36	40.09	36.95	43.26	8.11	26.03
2002	73.59	0.33	36.00	37.26	39.60	6.52	27.47
2003	76.27	0.28	38.49	37.50	37.73	5.33	33.21

注:1998年以前为职工人数。
Note: Before 1998, the data of this table refer to staff and workers.

2-17 按新国民经济行业分各类从业人员(2003 年)

PERSONS EMPLOYED GROUPED BY NEW SECTOR, 2003

单位:万人 (10 000 persons)

项 目 Item	社会从业人员 Persons Employed	城镇单位从业人员 Persons Employed in Urban Units	在岗职工人数 On - post Staff and Workers	其他从业人员 Other Persons Employed
总 计 Total	**510.90**	**191.01**	**174.89**	**16.12**
农、林、牧、渔业 Farming, Forestry, Animal Husbandry and Fishery	83.19	0.97	0.95	0.02
采矿业 Minerals Mining	7.93	6.97	6.33	0.64
制造业 Manufacturing	178.89	77.14	72.50	4.64
电力、燃气及水的生产和供应业 Production & Supply of Power, Gas and Water	3.94	3.55	3.45	0.10
建筑业 Construction	28.68	9.94	9.11	0.83
交通运输、仓储及邮政业 Transport, Storage, Post Services	28.94	13.47	12.18	1.29
信息传输、计算机服务和软件业 Information Transmitting, Computer Services and Software	1.74	1.54	1.46	0.08
批发和零售业 Wholesale and Retail Trade	67.71	11.87	10.07	1.80
住宿和餐饮业 Accommodation and Catering Services	6.75	3.51	2.79	0.72
金融业 Finance	5.59	5.20	3.59	1.61
房地产业 Real Estate	5.93	1.90	1.65	0.26
租赁和商务服务业 Leasing and Business Services	5.30	4.03	3.64	0.39
科学研究、技术服务和地质勘察业 Scientific Research, Technical Services and Geological Prospecting	5.80	5.27	4.75	0.52
水利、环境和公共设施管理业 Management for Water Conservancy, Environment and Public Facilities	3.64	3.35	3.04	0.31
居民服务和其他服务业 Resident Services and Other Social Services	24.53	3.25	2.89	0.35
教 育 Education	17.64	16.90	16.06	0.84
卫生、社会保障和社会福利业 Health Care, Social Security and Social Welfare	8.04	6.83	6.58	0.25
文化、体育和娱乐业 Culture, Sports and Recreational Services	12.85	2.14	1.96	0.18
公共管理和社会组织 Public Management and Social Organizations	13.81	13.18	11.89	1.29

注:本表行业分类为国标 GB/T4754-2002 标准。
Note: Sector listed in this table is classified by the standard of GB/T4754-2002.

2－18 社会从业人员及构成
NUMBER AND COMPOSITION OF PERSONS EMPLOYMED

项　目	Item	绝对数（万人） Number （10 000 persons）		构　成（%） Composition in Percentage（%）	
		2002	2003	2002	2003
总　计	**Total**	**492.61**	**510.90**	**100.0**	**100.0**
一、按经济类型分	**Grouped by Ownership**				
国有经济	State－owned	137.81	128.52	28.0	25.2
集体经济	Collective－owned	195.31	196.55	39.6	38.5
私营经济	Private	51.07	66.19	10.4	13.0
个体经济	Individual	25.88	25.92	5.3	5.1
港澳台投资经济	Hongkong, Macao and Taiwan Funded	12.34	11.79	2.5	2.3
外商投资经济	Foreign Funded	30.61	35.02	6.2	6.8
其他经济	Other	39.59	46.91	8.0	9.1
二、按国民经济行业分	**Grouped by Sector**				
农、林、牧、渔业	Farming, Forestry, Animal Husbandry and Fishery	82.25	83.19	16.7	16.3
工　业	Industry	178.69	190.76	36.3	37.3
采掘业	Mining and Quarrying	8.83	7.93	1.8	1.5
制造业	Manufacturing	165.84	178.89	33.7	35.0
电力、煤气业及水的生产和供应业	Production and Supply of Electric Power, Gas and Water	4.02	3.94	0.8	0.8
建筑业	Construction	26.69	28.68	5.4	5.6
地质勘察业、水利管理业	Geological Prospecting and Water Conservancy	1.21	3.89	0.2	0.8
交通运输、仓储及邮电通信业	Transportation, Storage, Post and Telecommunications	30.47	29.74	6.2	5.8
批发和零售贸易、餐饮业	Wholesale & Retail Trade and Catering Service	66.42	74.83	13.5	14.7
金融、保险业	Banking and Insurance	4.54	5.59	0.9	1.1
房地产业	Real Estate	4.57	5.93	0.9	1.1
社会服务业	Social Services	30.27	30.52	6.1	6.0
卫生、体育和社会福利业	Health Care, Sports and Social Welfare	8.23	13.40	1.7	2.6
教育、文化艺术及广播电影电视业	Education, Culture & Arts, Radio, Film and Television	22.11	25.13	4.5	4.9
科学研究和综合技术服务业	Scientific Research and Polytechnical Services	5.29	5.80	1.1	1.2
国家机关、政党机关和社会团体	Government Agencies, Party Agencies and Social Organization	12.30	13.44	2.5	2.6
其他行业	Others	19.57		4.0	

注：本表行业分类为国标 GB/T4754－1994 标准，2－19、2－23 表同。
Note: Sector listed in this table is classified by the standard of GB/T4754－1994, same as following table 2－19, 2－23.

2-19 城镇单位从业人员及构成

NUMBER AND COMPOSITION OF PERSONS EMPLOYED IN URBAN UNITS

项目	Item	绝对数（万人）Number (10 000 persons) 2002	2003	构成（%）Composition in Percentage (%) 2002	2003
总计	**Total**	**185.50**	**191.01**	**100.0**	**100.0**
一、按经济类型分	**Grouped by Ownership**				
国有经济	State-owned	107.79	101.57	58.1	53.2
集体经济	Collective-owned	16.47	13.95	8.9	7.3
其他经济	Other	61.24	75.49	33.0	39.5
#“三资”经济	Foreign Funded	41.20	45.61	22.2	23.9
股份制经济	Share Holding	7.76	8.99	4.2	4.7
二、按国民经济行业分	**Grouped by Sector**				
农、林、牧、渔业	Farming, Forestry, Animal Husbandry and Fishery	1.09	0.97	0.6	0.5
工业	Industry	82.82	87.66	44.6	45.9
采掘业	Mining and Quarrying	8.01	6.97	4.3	3.6
制造业	Manufacturing	71.22	77.14	38.4	40.4
电力、煤气业及水的生产和供应业	Production and Supply of Electric Power, Gas and Water	3.59	3.55	1.9	1.9
建筑业	Construction	9.87	9.94	5.3	5.2
地质勘察业、水利管理业	Geological Prospecting and Water Conservancy	1.08	3.59	0.6	1.9
交通运输、仓储及邮电通信业	Transportation, Storage, Post and Telecommunications	13.21	11.22	7.1	5.9
批发和零售贸易、餐饮业	Wholesale & Retail Trade and Catering Services	11.45	15.77	6.2	8.3
金融、保险业	Banking and Insurance	4.12	5.20	2.2	2.7
房地产业	Real Estate	3.53	5.73	1.9	3.0
社会服务业	Social Services	11.63	7.23	6.3	3.8
卫生、体育和社会福利业	Health Care, Sports and Social Welfare	7.00	6.83	3.8	3.6
教育、文化艺术及广播电影电视业	Education, Culture & Arts, Radio, Film and Television	20.14	18.79	10.8	9.8
科学研究和综合技术服务业	Scientific Research and Polytechnical Services	4.56	5.27	2.5	2.7
国家机关、政党机关和社会团体	Government Agencies, Party Agencies and Social Organization	11.97	12.81	6.5	6.7
其他行业	Others	3.03		1.6	
三、按企业、事业、机关分	**Grouped By Enterprise, Institution and Agency**				
企业	Enterprises	140.39	145.41	75.7	76.1
中央	Central	30.13	26.77	16.3	14.0
地方	Local	110.26	118.64	59.4	62.1
#国有	State-owned	39.80	35.97	21.5	18.9
事业	Institutions	33.44	33.25	18.0	17.4
中央	Central	2.73	2.32	1.5	1.2
地方	Local	30.71	30.93	16.5	16.2
机关	Agencies	11.67	12.35	6.3	6.5
中央	Central	0.95	1.09	0.5	0.6
地方	Local	10.72	11.26	5.8	5.9

2-20 城镇单位从业人员变动情况(2003年)
CHANGES OF PERSONS EMPLOYED IN URBAN UNITS, 2003

单位:人 (person)

项目 Item	合计 Total	按经济类型分 Grouped by Ownership			按企事业机关分 Grouped by Enterprise, Institution and Agency		
		国有经济 State-owned	集体经济 Collective-owned	其他经济 Others	企业 Enterprise	事业 Institution	机关 Agency
一、从业人员增加合计 Number of Persons Employed Increased	**246 226**	**85 927**	**16 733**	**143 566**	**211 644**	**24 712**	**9 870**
1.从农村招收人 Recruited from Rural Area	52 738	7 891	3 141	41 706	50 226	1 453	1 059
2.从城镇招收失业人员 Recruited from Urban Area	29 581	9 811	2 036	17 734	25 518	1 785	2 278
3.录用的退伍军人 Employment of Demobilized Soldiers	1 747	1 138	90	519	1 293	226	228
4.录用及使用的大中专技校毕业生 Employment of Graduate	46 704	16 900	1 029	28 775	38 124	6 697	1 883
5.录用的本单位和外单位不在岗人员 Not Fully Employed	38 385	16 043	3 692	18 650	35 673	1 375	1 337
#录用的本单位和外单位下岗人员 Laid-off Personnel	16 476	6 915	1 697	7 864	15 286	596	594
#4050人员 "4050" Personnel	4 935	2 413	614	1 908	4 565	234	136
6.录用的离退休人员 VCSR and RRSW	9 056	4 710	915	3 431	7 316	1 347	393
7.调入人数 Job Changes	68 015	29 434	5 830	32 751	53 494	11 829	2 692
#市外调入 From Outside Tianjin	2 370	1 427	17	926	1 989	342	39
二、从业人员减少合计 Number of Persons Employed Decreased	**244 155**	**115 187**	**26 939**	**102 029**	**215 482**	**23 713**	**4 960**
1.离退休退职人员 Retire and Quit	32 861	20 511	3 700	8 650	24 157	7 445	1 259
2.开除、除名、辞退 Discharge	14 514	4 244	1 106	9 164	12 917	1 339	258
3.终止合同 Contract Expiration	43 363	10 338	4 351	28 674	41 314	1 641	408
4.解除合同 Contract Termination	47 901	15 028	2 800	30 073	47 032	539	330
#协商解除合同 Consultative	20 702	6 980	1 165	12 557	20 575	95	32
5.在岗人员转不在岗 Not On-post from On-post	44 710	27 944	8 635	8 131	41 896	2 693	121
6.调出人数 Job Changes	59 021	35 875	6 182	16 964	46 879	9 680	2 462
#调至市外 To Outside Tianjin	1 309	699	111	499	1 125	164	20
7.死亡 Death	1 785	1 247	165	373	1 287	376	122

2-21 市属各局(总公司)国有经济单位从业人员年末人数
YEAR-END NUMBER OF PERSONS EMPLOYED IN STATE-OWNED UNITS BY BUREAU(CORPORATION)

单位:人 (person)

局(总公司)	Bureau(Corporation)	2002	2003
一、经委系统	**Tianjin Economical Committee System**		
机电工业控股集团公司	Tianjin Machinery & Electric Industry Holding Group Company	18 684	13 803
中环电子信息集团有限公司	Tianjin Zhonghuan Electronics & Information Group	17 844	15 775
冶金集团(控股)有限公司	Tianjin Metallurgical Group (Holding) Corporation	19 183	21 108
渤海化工集团公司	Tianjin Bohai Chemical Industry Group Corporation	37 346	33 512
纺织集团(控股)有限公司	Tianjin Textile Industrial General Corporation	30 473	27 181
一轻集团(控股)有限公司	Tianjin Yiqing Group(Holding Share) Co.,Ltd	8 753	6 183
二轻集团(控股)有限公司	The Second Light Industry Group(Holding) Co.,Ltd	4 620	3 402
医药集团有限公司	Tianjin Pharmaceutical Holdings	5 231	4 495
汽车工业(集团)有限公司	Tianjin Automobile Industry Group Co.,Ltd	7 400	4 409
飞鸽集团有限公司	Tianjin Flying Pigeon Group Co.,Ltd	2 776	2 452
塑料集团	Tianjin Plastics Group	2 420	1 748
天铁冶金集团有限公司	Tianjin Tian Tie Metallurgical Group Co.,Ltd	21 153	19 445
建筑材料集团(控股)有限公司	Tianjin Building Materials Group(Holding) Co.,Ltd	6 876	4 996
二、农委系统	**Tianjin Agricultural Committee System**		
农业局	Tianjin Agriculture Bureau	715	460
畜牧局	Tianjin Animal Husbandry Bureau	383	307
农垦集团总公司	Tianjin State Farms Agribusiness Group Company	5 618	4 972
水产局	Tianjin Aquatic Products Bureau	1 596	1 443
三、建委系统	**Tianjin Construction Committee System**		
建工集团总公司	Tianjin Construction Engineering Group Corporation	12 105	6 844
市政工程局	Tianjin Municipal Engineering Bureau	20 969	19 030
房地产管理局	Tianjin Real Estate Administrative Bureau	9 405	9 047
住宅建设发展集团	Tianjin House Construction Development Group	3 227	2 503
公共交通集团公司	Tianjin Public Traffic Group Corporation	9 624	9 866
自来水集团	Tianjin Tap Water Group	3 435	3 552
燃气集团	Tianjin Gas Group	7 180	6 897
四、交委系统	**Tianjin Transportation Committee System**		
港务局	Tianjin Port Authority	10 863	10 940
交通局	Tianjin Transportation Management Bureau	8 030	7 358
五、商委系统	**Tianjin Commercial Committee System**		
粮食粮油集团有限公司	Tianjin Grain & Oil Group Co.,Ltd	4 345	3 930
一商集团有限公司	Tianjin Yishang Group Co.,Ltd	3 585	3 067
二商集团有限公司	Tianjin Second Commercial Group Co.,Ltd	6 223	5 660

2－22　市属各局(总公司)国有经济单位从业人员年平均人数

AVERAGE NUMBER OF PERSONS EMPLOYED IN STATE－OWNED UNITS BY BUREAU(CORPORATION)

单位:人　　(person)

局(总公司)	Bureau(Corporation)	2002	2003
一、经委系统	**Tianjin Economical Committee System**		
机电工业控股集团公司	Tianjin Machinery & Electric Industry Holding Group Company	20 345	16 188
中环电子信息集团有限公司	Tianjin Zhonghuan Electronics & Information Group	19 392	16 723
冶金集团(控股)有限公司	Tianjin Metallurgical Group(Holding) Corporation	19 268	20 400
渤海化工集团公司	Tianjin Bohai Chemical Industry Group Corporation	39 067	35 240
纺织集团(控股)有限公司	Tianjin Textile Industrial General Corporation	32 430	28 780
一轻集团(控股)有限公司	Tianjin Yiqing Group(Holding Share) Co.,Ltd	9 470	6 912
二轻集团(控股)有限公司	The Second Light Industry Group(Holding) Co.,Ltd	5 682	4 008
医药集团有限公司	Tianjin Pharmaceutical Holdings	5 295	4 450
汽车工业(集团)有限公司	Tianjin Automobile Industry Group Co.,Ltd	9 707	4 950
飞鸽集团有限公司	Tianjin Flying Pigeon Group Co.,Ltd	2 807	2 569
塑料集团	Tianjin Plastics Group	2 610	2 041
天铁冶金集团有限公司	Tianjin Tian Tie Metallurgical Group Co.,Ltd	21 040	19 490
建筑材料集团(控股)有限公司	Tianjin Building Materials Group(Holding)Co.,Ltd	7 524	5 354
二、农委系统	**Tianjin Agricultural Committee System**		
农业局	Tianjin Agriculture Bureau	698	443
畜牧局	Tianjin Animal Husbandry Bureau	404	306
农垦集团总公司	Tianjin State Farms Agribusiness Group Company	5 810	5 418
水产局	Tianjin Aquatic Products Bureau	1 639	1 464
三、建委系统	**Tianjin Construction Committee System**		
建工集团总公司	Tianjin Construction Engineering Group Corporation	12 460	6 955
市政工程局	Tianjin Municipal Engineering Bureau	21 129	19 525
房地产管理局	Tianjin Real Estate Administrative Bureau	9 396	9 107
住宅建设发展集团	Tianjin House Construction Development Group	3 355	2 595
公共交通集团公司	Tianjin Public Traffic Group Corporation	9 640	9 790
自来水集团	Tianjin Tap Water Group	3 716	3 198
燃气集团	Tianjin Gas Group	7 169	6 985
四、交委系统	**Tianjin Transportation Committee System**		
港务局	Tianjin Port Authority	10 839	10 933
交通局	Tianjin Transportation Management Bureau	8 392	7 557
五、商委系统	**Tianjin Commercial Committee System**		
粮食粮油集团有限公司	Tianjin Grain & Oil Group Co.,Ltd	4 377	4 056
一商集团有限公司	Tianjin Yishang Group Co.,Ltd	3 626	3 341
二商集团有限公司	Tianjin Second Commercial Group Co.,Ltd	6 475	5 939

2-23 城乡私营、个体从业人员
PERSONS EMPLOYED OF PRIVATE AND INDIVIDUAL IN URBAN AND RURAL AREAS

单位:万人　(10 000 persons)

项　　目	Item	2002 合　计 Total	2002 私　营 Private	2002 个　体 Individual
总　　计	**Total**	**76.95**	**51.07**	**25.88**
#城　镇	Urban Area	48.76	35.69	13.07
按国民经济行业分	**Grouped by Sector**			
农、林、牧、渔业	Farming, Forestry, Animal Husbandry & Fishery	0.37	0.30	0.07
工　业	Industry	22.85	17.97	4.88
#制造业	Manufacturing	22.82	17.96	4.86
建筑业	Construction	1.76	1.64	0.12
交通运输、仓储及邮电通信业	Transportation, Storage, Post and Telecommunications	2.54	1.33	1.21
批发和零售贸易、餐饮业	Whole & Retail Trade and Catering Services	34.46	17.81	16.65
#餐饮业	Catering Services	3.64	0.66	2.98
社会服务业	Social Services	8.40	5.53	2.87
其他行业	Others	6.57	6.49	0.08

项　　目	Item	2003 合　计 Total	2003 私　营 Private	2003 个　体 Individual
总　　计	**Total**	**92.11**	**66.19**	**25.92**
#城　镇	Urban Area	54.91	42.45	12.46
按国民经济行业分	**Grouped by Sector**			
农、林、牧、渔业	Farming, Forestry, Animal Husbandry & Fishery	0.57	0.44	0.13
工　业	Industry	29.00	23.29	5.71
#制造业	Manufacturing	28.94	23.28	5.66
建筑业	Construction	2.62	2.46	0.16
交通运输、仓储及邮电通信业	Transportation, Storage, Post and Telecommunications	2.84	1.86	0.98
批发和零售贸易、餐饮业	Whole & Retail Trade and Catering Services	37.73	21.88	15.85
#餐饮业	Catering Services	3.65	0.75	2.90
社会服务业	Social Services	9.52	6.58	2.94
其他行业	Others	9.83	9.68	0.15

资料来源:天津市工商局。
Data source: Tianjin Municipal Industry & Commerce Bureau.

2-24 离退休退职人员情况
BASIC STATISTICS ON RETIRED AND QUITED PERSONNEL
(2000-2003)

指标 Item	2000	2001	2002	2003
离退休、退职人数(万人)				
Number of Retired and Quited Personnel (10 000 persons)	**92.8**	**99.2**	**109.9**	**111.2**
劳动部门				
Labour Department	92.3	98.6	109.3	110.6
国有经济				
State-owned	67.7	72.0	76.8	76.6
集体经济				
Collective-owned	15.3	16.8	18.0	18.6
其他经济				
Others	9.3	9.8	14.5	15.4
民政部门				
Civil Administration Department	0.5	0.6	0.6	0.6
离退休退职人员与在职职工之比(以在职职工为100)				
Ratio of Retired and Quited Personnel to On-post Staff and Workers (take on-post staff and workers as 100)	**48.0**	**53.9**	**62.1**	**63.6**

资料来源:天津市劳动和社会保障局、民政局。
Data Source: Tianjin Municipal Labour & Social Insurance Bureau and Tianjin Municipal Civil Administration Bureau.

2-25 城镇登记失业人员情况
BASIC STATISTICS ON REGISTERED UNEMPLOYED PERSONNEL IN URBAN AREA
(2000-2003)

单位:万人 (10 000 persons)

指标 Item	2000	2001	2002	2003
新登记失业人数				
Number of Newly Registered Unemployed Personnel	**9.55**	**9.99**	**11.02**	**7.61**
总计中:女性				
of The Total: Female	5.25	5.49	6.13	3.96
总计中:由就业转失业人数				
of The Total: Unemployment Turned from Employment	6.00	7.45	8.76	5.60
本期失业人员就业人数				
Newly Employed Personnel Turning from Unemployment	**8.25**	**9.09**	**9.51**	**8.48**
期末实有登记失业人数				
Registered Unemployed Personnel Year-end	**10.50**	**11.40**	**12.90**	**12.03**
总计中:女性				
of The Total: Female	5.68	6.27	6.71	6.25
总计中:长期失业者				
of The Total: Permanent Unemployed Personnel	6.71	10.26	10.91	4.81
登记失业率(%)				
Registered Unemployed Rate(%)	**3.20**	**3.60**	**3.91**	**3.80**

资料来源:天津市劳动和社会保障局。
Information Source: Tianjin Municipal Labour & Social Insurance Bureau.

主要统计指标解释

常住人口　指实际经常居住在某地区一定时间(指半年以上)的人口。按人口普查和抽样调查规定,主要包括:1.除离开本地半年以上(不包括在国外工作或学习的人)的全部常住本地的户籍人口;2.户口在外地,但在本地居住半年以上者,或离开户口地半年以上而调查时在本地居住的人口;3.调查时居住在本地,但在任何地方都没有登记常住户口,如手持户口迁移证、出生证、退伍证、劳改劳教释放证等尚未办理常住户口的人,即所谓"口袋户口"的人。

户籍人口　指公民依照《中华人民共和国户口登记条例》,已在其经常居住地的公安户籍管理机关登记了常住户口的人。这类人口不管其是否外出,也不管外出时间长短,只要在某地注册有常住户口,则为该地区的户籍人口。

人口密度　指单位土地面积上的人口数。通常使用常住人口计算人口密度,用于说明人口的拥挤程度。通常以每平方公里的居民人数来表示。计算公式:

人口密度=(常住人口/总土地面积)

人口出生率　指一定时期内出生的人口数与该时期内平均人口数之比,通常以年为单位计算,用千分比来表示,表明某年1000人中活产的人数。计算公式:

人口出生率=(年内出生人数/年平均人口数)×1000‰

人口死亡率　指一定时期内死亡的人口数与该时期内平均人口数之比,通常以年为单位计算,用千分比来表示,表明某年1000人中死亡的人数。计算公式:

人口死亡率=(年内死亡人数/年平均人口数)×1000‰

人口自然增长率　指一定时期内人口自然增长数(出生人数减死亡人数)与该时期内平均人口数之比,通常以年为单位计算,用千分比来表示,计算公式:

人口自然增长率=〔(年内出生人数-年内死亡人数)/年平均人口数〕×1000‰

人口自然增长率=人口出生率-人口死亡率

政策生育率　表明的是平均100个出生人口中符合生育政策规定的存活活产数。计算公式:

政策生育率=(符合政策生育规定的出生人数/本期出生总数)×100%

总和生育率　总和生育率是将特定时点上全体妇女生育率综合起来,以一个数字来表示。实际上,它就是假设一个妇女在整个育龄期都按照某一年的年龄别生育率生育,她所生育孩子的总数,即平均每个妇女在育龄期生育的孩子数。

总负担系数　指14岁及以下少年儿童人口数和65岁及以上老年人口数与15-64岁劳动力年龄人口数的比例。表明的是每百名劳动年龄人口负担多少非劳动年龄人口。计算公式:

总负担系数=〔(14岁及以下人数+65岁及以上人数)/15-64岁人数〕×100%

少儿负担系数　指14岁及以下少年儿童人口数与15-64岁劳动力年龄人口数的比例。表明的是每百名劳动年龄人口负担多少14岁及以下少年儿童人口。计算公式:

少儿负担系数=(14岁及以下人数/15-64岁人数)×100%

老年负担系数　指65岁及以上老年人口数与15-64岁劳动力年龄人口数的比例。表明的是每百名劳动年龄人口负担多少65岁及以上老年人口。计算公式:

老年负担系数=(65岁及以上人数/15-64岁人数)×100%

劳动力资源　指在劳动年龄内,具有劳动能力,在正常情况下,可能或实际参加社会劳动的总人口数。具体的范围是:劳动年龄内(16周岁及以上),有劳动能力、实际参加社会劳动和未参加社会劳动的人员。

社会从业人员　是指在劳动年龄内,有劳动能力,参加社会劳动取得劳动报酬或经营收入的人员。具体指城镇单位从业人员,乡镇企业从业人员,乡村农林牧渔劳动者,私营、个体雇员,私营、个体雇主以及其他从业人员。从空间范围上讲社会从业人员既包括城镇中的从业人员,又包括乡村中的从业人员。

城镇单位从业人员　是指在各级国家机关、政党机关、社会团体、事业单位以及城镇范围内的各类企业中工作,并取得劳动报酬的全部人员。包括在岗职工和其他从业人员,但不包括不在岗职工。

城镇私营和个体从业人员　城镇私营从业人员指在工商管理部门注册登记,其经营地址设在县城关镇(含城关镇)以上的私营企业从业人员;包括私营企业投资者和雇工。城镇个体从业人员指在工商管理部门注册登记,并持有城镇户口或在城镇长期居住,经批准从事个体工商经营的从业人员;包括个体经营者和在个体工商户劳动的家庭帮工和雇工。

在岗职工　是指调查时期(时点)在单位工作并领取工资的职工。具体是指那些与本单位签有劳动合同或在本单位在册,并在本单位从事有报酬的劳动人员,在岗职工还包括单位派出学习、工作及病伤产假(六个月内)且仍在单位支付劳动报酬的人员。

单位其他从业人员 按劳动统计规定不作在岗职工统计，但实际参加各单位生产或工作并取得劳动报酬的人员。包括再就业的离退休人员、民办教师、在各单位工作的港、澳、台、外籍人员、聘用的外单位不在岗人员、聘用的失业人员、聘用和使用的外来人员、聘用的其他人员以及在本单位从事第二职业的外单位人员，但不包括在单位中工作并领取报酬的在校学生。

城镇登记失业人员 指有非农业户口，在一定的劳动年龄（16岁至退休年龄）内，有劳动能力，无业且要求就业，并在当地劳动保障机构进行求职登记的人员。

城镇登记失业率 报告期末城镇登记失业人数占期末从业人员总数与期末实有城镇登记失业人数之和的比重。计算公式：

城镇登记失业率＝〔期末实有城镇登记失业人数/（期末从业人员总数＋期末实有城镇登记失业人数）〕×100%

Explanatory Notes on Main Statistical Indicators

Permanent Resident Population refers to the total number of people alive at a given area within a period (over half a year). According to the regulation of population census and sample survey, permanent resident population include (a) registered population in this area other than those who have left this area over half a year(exclude those going abroad to work or study). (b) population with residence registered in other area, but having actually resided in this area over half a year or having left place of residence registration over half a year and resided in this area during the period of population survey. (c) population with residence registration in this enumeration area not yet settled, i. e. residence card on hand, migration certificate, birth certificate, demobilized soldier card, release certificate, etc.

Registered Population refers to the population with registered in accordance with the regulation of the People's Republic of China on the Management of Registration Residence in public security organs in this area. No matter he is out or not, how long the time is, which is often expressed in.

Population Density refers to the total number of people within unit land area. Usually, population density is calculated using permanent resident population and indicates crowd degree of population. It is often expressed in the number of people per square kilometer. The following formula is used :

Population Density = (permanent resident population)/(Total Area of Land)

Birth Rate refers to the ratio of the number of births to the average population during a certain period of time, usually using a year as unit for calculation, which is often expressed in ‰ and indicates the alive births per 1000 persons. The following formula is used

Birth Rate = (Number of Births)/(Annual Average Number of Population) × 1000‰

Death Rate refers to the ratio of the number of deaths to the average population during a certain period of time, usually using a year as unit for calculation, which is often expressed in ‰ and indicates the deaths per 1000 persons. The following formula is used

Death Rate = (Number of Deaths)/(Annual Average Number of Population) × 1000‰

Natural Growth Rate of Population refers to the ratio of natural increase in population (number of births minus number of deaths) in a certain period of time to the average population of the same period, usually using a year as unit for calculation, which is often expressed in ‰. The following formula is used :

Natural Growth Rate of Population = (Number of Births − Number of Deaths)/(Annual Average Number of Population) × 1000‰

Natural Growth Rate of Population = Birth Rate − Death Rate

Birth Control Rate refers to the number of alive births matching the birth control policy per 100 births. The following formula is used :

Birth Control Rate = (the number of births matching the birth control policy)/(the Total Births of the Same Period) × 1000‰

Total of Birth Rate refers to the total of birth rate of women aged 15 − 49 during a certain period of time, which is expressed in a data. It actually refers to the number of children of average noman aged 15 − 49.

Gross Dependency Coefficient refers to the ratio of children aged 0 − 14 and elderly population aged 65 and over to the working − age population aged 15 − 64. It describes in general the number of non − working - age population that every 100 people at working ages will take care of. The following formula is used:

Gross Dependency Coefficient = [(population aged 0 - 14) + (population aged 65 and over)]/(population aged 15 - 64) × 100%

Children Dependency Coefficient refers to the ratio of children aged 0 - 14 to the working - age population aged 15 - 64. It describes in general the number of children that every 100 people at working ages will take care of. The following formula is used :

Children Dependency Coefficient = (population aged 0 - 14)/(population aged 15 - 64) × 100%

Old Dependency Coefficient refers to the ratio of elderly population aged 65 and over to the working - age population aged 15 - 64. It describes in general the number of elderly population that every 100 people at working ages will take care of. The following formula is used :

Old Dependency Coefficient = (population aged 65 and over) /(population aged 15 - 64) × 100%

Labour Force Resources refer to the number of population at working ages (aged 16 and over) who have capacity for physical labour, have engaged in social labour or not.

Social Employment Personnel refer to the persons aged 16 and over who are engaged in social labour and receive remuneration payment or earn business income, including employment personnel worked in units in urban areas, employment personnel worked in township enterprises, rural labour engaged in farming, forestry, animal husbandry and fishery, employees in private enterprises and individual economy, employers of private enterprises and individual economy and other employment personnel. Social employment personnel not only include those in urban areas, also include those in rural areas.

Persons Employed in Urban Units refer to all the persons working in government agencies of various levels, political and party organizations, social organizations, enterprises and institutions, and receiving remuneration payment. They include on - post staff and workers and other employment personnel in various units, but exclude staff and workers who have left their working units.

Persons Employed in Private Enterprises and Individual Economy in Urban Areas Persons employed in private enterprises refer to the persons employed in the private enterprises which have been registered at the departments of industrial and commercial administration and are situated at a town (i. e. at own where the county government is located) for business operation or at urban areas with the level higher than a county town. The individual economy in urban areas refer to persons who hold the certificates of residence in urban areas or have resided in the urban areas for a long time and have been registered at the departments of industrial and commercial administration and approved to be engaged in individual industrial or commercial business, including self - employed persons as well as helpers and hired labourers who work in the individual households engaged in industrial or commercial business.

On - post Staff and Workers refer to staff and workers who work in and receive wages from their working units during a survey period. They include the persons who have signed working contracts with units or registered in units, also include those receive wages from units but are temporarily absent from work for reasons of study, work or on sick, injury or maternal leave no more than six months.

Other Persons Employed in Various Units refer to the numbers receiving wages or other forms of payment, include re - employed retirees, teachers in schools run by the local people, foreigners and Chinese compatriots from HongKong, Macao, and Taiwan working in various units, employees of other units working temporarily at current posts, unemployment personnel, non - locals, and employees holding the second job of other units, exclude students enrolled in universities and colleges who work at the units and receive wages.

Registered Urban Unemployed Persons refer to the persons who are registered as permanent residents in the urban areas engaged in non - agricultural activities, aged within the range of working age(16 - retired age), capable to labour, unemployed but desirous to be employed and have been registered at the local employment service agencies to apply for a job.

Registered Urban Unemployment Rate refers to the ratio of the number of the registered unemployed persons to the sum of the number of employed persons and the registered unemployed persons. The formula is as follows :

Registered urban unemployment rate = number of urban registered unemployed persons/ (urban employed persons + number of registered urban unemployed persons) × 100%

第3篇 CHAPTER 3

固定资产投资

INVESTMENT IN FIXED ASSETS

3-1 全社会固定资产投资
TOTAL INVESTMENT IN FIXED ASSETS
(1980-2003)

单位:亿元 (100 million yuan)

年份 Year	全社会固定资产投资 Total Investment in Fixed Assets	国有经济 State-owned	集体经济 Collective-owned	#农村 Rural	个体经济 Individuals	#农村 Rural
总计 Total						
1980	23.92	22.13	1.48	0.65	0.31	0.31
1981	27.60	23.72	2.83	1.62	1.05	1.05
1982	35.07	30.04	3.16	1.67	1.87	1.74
1983	41.58	33.47	3.75	2.03	4.36	4.16
1984	48.28	37.90	6.80	3.80	3.58	3.08
1985	65.90	54.16	7.39	3.04	4.35	3.93
1986	71.91	61.03	5.93	2.73	4.95	4.24
1987	76.44	61.32	9.53	6.59	5.59	4.31
1988	82.61	66.11	9.01	6.53	7.49	7.12
1989	83.88	68.39	7.68	5.75	7.81	6.61
1990	87.69	72.18	10.56	9.48	4.95	4.36
1991	128.95	109.69	12.18	10.84	7.08	6.68
1992	169.88	137.81	25.21	23.59	6.86	6.08
1993	226.56	187.83	30.51	27.34	8.22	6.36
1994	315.97	265.32	40.14	36.98	10.51	8.51
1995	393.18	324.20	58.65	46.52	10.33	9.36
1996	435.81	351.59	66.67	57.35	17.55	15.28
1997	498.66	422.84	61.77	52.39	14.05	10.63
1998	575.86	491.87	68.39	56.70	15.60	12.45
1999	567.36	488.45	61.59	49.00	17.32	11.50
2000	608.80	526.20	61.80	56.47	20.80	13.10
2001	705.10	612.50	66.10	61.50	26.50	16.40
2002	811.26	695.75	85.90	74.00	29.61	20.01
2003	1 046.72	919.59	98.04	89.73	29.09	22.86
#地方 Local Investmen						
1980	14.53	12.74	1.48	0.65	0.31	0.31
1981	20.17	16.29	2.83	1.62	1.05	1.05
1982	28.37	23.34	3.16	1.67	1.87	1.74
1983	32.65	24.54	3.75	2.03	4.36	4.16
1984	36.88	26.50	6.80	3.80	3.58	3.08
1985	50.80	39.06	7.39	3.04	4.35	3.93
1986	53.68	42.80	5.93	2.73	4.95	4.24
1987	52.18	37.06	9.53	6.59	5.59	4.31
1988	54.96	38.46	9.01	6.53	7.49	7.12
1989	53.77	38.28	7.68	5.75	7.81	6.61
1990	57.47	41.96	10.56	9.48	4.95	4.36
1991	93.13	73.87	12.18	10.84	7.08	6.68
1992	123.85	91.78	25.21	23.59	6.86	6.08
1993	176.14	137.41	30.51	27.34	8.22	6.36
1994	256.88	206.23	40.14	36.98	10.51	8.51
1995	309.75	240.77	58.65	46.52	10.33	9.36
1996	325.71	241.49	66.67	57.35	17.55	15.28
1997	376.69	300.87	61.77	52.39	14.05	10.63
1998	452.11	368.12	68.39	56.70	15.60	12.45
1999	405.31	326.40	61.59	49.00	17.32	11.50
2000	463.83	381.23	61.80	56.47	20.80	13.10
2001	567.40	474.80	66.10	61.50	26.50	16.40
2002	677.60	562.09	85.90	74.00	29.61	20.01
2003	893.73	766.60	98.04	89.73	29.09	22.86

注:本表国有经济中包括“三资”、股份制、联营、私营经济。以下各表同。
Note: State-owned units of this table included foreign funded economic units, share holding economic units, joint ownership economic units and private economy, Same as following next.

3-2 全社会新增固定资产
TOTAL NEWLY INCREASED IN FIXED ASSETS
(1980-2003)

单位:亿元　　(100 million yuan)

年份 Year	全社会新增固定资产 Total Newly Increased in Fixed Assets	国有经济 State-owned	集体经济 Collective-owned	#农村 Rural	个体经济 Individuals	#农村 Rural
总计 Total						
1980	17.84	16.32	1.21	0.65	0.31	0.31
1981	26.69	23.17	2.47	1.62	1.05	1.05
1982	27.72	23.13	2.72	1.67	1.87	1.74
1983	39.92	32.18	3.38	2.03	4.36	4.16
1984	39.01	29.00	6.43	3.80	3.58	3.08
1985	42.62	32.26	6.01	3.04	4.35	3.93
1986	56.39	46.12	5.32	2.73	4.95	4.24
1987	61.04	46.02	9.43	6.59	5.59	4.31
1988	63.28	47.06	8.73	6.82	7.49	7.12
1989	69.55	50.40	11.34	8.78	7.81	6.61
1990	65.16	49.66	10.55	9.55	4.95	4.36
1991	74.11	54.99	12.03	10.85	7.09	6.68
1992	102.27	73.24	22.17	21.26	6.86	6.08
1993	140.00	105.82	25.96	24.11	8.22	6.36
1994	261.12	216.98	33.63	32.36	10.51	8.51
1995	300.86	247.08	43.45	40.19	10.33	9.36
1996	313.12	246.63	48.94	41.61	17.55	15.28
1997	320.46	259.08	47.33	41.76	14.05	10.63
1998	439.58	379.21	44.77	42.54	15.60	12.45
1999	459.54	383.73	58.49	47.78	17.32	11.50
2000	434.28	372.48	50.48	46.15	11.32	7.14
2001	476.92	385.67	64.75	61.00	26.50	16.40
2002	537.98	427.98	80.39	71.14	29.61	20.01
2003	656.99	534.66	96.66	87.03	25.67	22.86
#地方 Local Investmen						
1980	10.03	8.51	1.21	0.65	0.31	0.31
1981	13.55	10.03	2.47	1.62	1.05	1.05
1982	18.77	14.18	2.72	1.67	1.87	1.74
1983	30.24	22.50	3.38	2.03	4.36	4.16
1984	30.63	20.62	6.43	3.80	3.58	3.08
1985	34.18	23.82	6.01	3.04	4.35	3.93
1986	42.99	32.72	5.32	2.73	4.95	4.24
1987	45.44	30.42	9.43	6.59	5.59	4.31
1988	47.44	31.22	8.73	6.82	7.49	7.12
1989	50.02	30.87	11.34	8.78	7.81	6.61
1990	49.46	33.96	10.55	9.55	4.95	4.36
1991	47.38	28.26	12.03	10.85	7.09	6.68
1992	69.15	40.12	22.17	21.26	6.86	6.08
1993	93.59	59.41	25.96	24.11	8.22	6.36
1994	244.01	199.87	33.63	32.36	10.51	8.51
1995	218.06	164.28	43.45	40.19	10.33	9.36
1996	241.66	175.17	48.94	41.61	17.55	15.28
1997	243.63	182.25	47.33	41.76	14.05	10.63
1998	351.27	290.90	44.77	42.54	15.60	12.45
1999	353.35	277.54	58.49	47.78	17.32	11.50
2000	350.97	289.17	50.48	46.15	11.32	7.14
2001	356.46	263.86	66.10	61.50	26.50	16.40
2002	434.61	324.61	80.39	71.14	29.61	20.01
2003	543.59	421.26	96.66	87.03	25.67	22.86

3-3 全社会固定资产投资和房屋建筑面积
TOTAL INVESTMENT IN FIXED ASSETS AND FLOOR SPACE OF BUILDINGS

指　　标	Item	2001	2002	2003	2003比2002年增长% Increase Rate in 2003 over 2002
一、投资总额(亿元)	**Total Investment (100 million yuan)**	**705.10**	**811.26**	**1 046.72**	**29.0**
1.按经济类型分	**Grouped by Ownership**				
国有经济	State-owned	612.50	695.75	919.59	32.2
集体经济	Collective-owned	66.10	85.90	98.04	14.1
#农　村	Rural	61.50	74.00	89.73	21.3
个体经济	Individuals	26.50	29.61	29.09	-1.8
#农　村	Rural	16.40	20.01	22.86	14.2
2.按隶属关系分	**Grouped by Administrative Relationship**				
中　央	Central Government	137.70	133.66	152.99	14.5
地　方	Local Government	567.40	677.60	893.73	31.9
3.按管理渠道分	**Grouped by Channel of Management**				
基本建设	Capital Construction	309.38	361.85	501.37	38.6
更新改造	Innovation	141.85	166.02	210.89	27.0
房地产开发	Real Estate Development	161.27	175.84	211.39	20.2
其他投资	Others	92.60	107.55	123.07	14.4
4.按三次产业分	**Grouped by Industries**				
第一产业	Primary Industry	1.13	3.77	9.38	148.8
第二产业	Secondary Industry	260.27	312.11	377.64	21.0
第三产业	Tertiary Industry	443.70	495.38	659.70	33.2
二、房屋建筑面积(万平方米)	**Floor Space of Buildings (10 000 sq.m)**				
施工面积	Floor Space Under Construction	3 205.40	3 917.46	4 377.95	11.8
竣工面积	Floor Space Completed	1 614.92	1 835.39	2 072.42	12.9
#住　宅	Residential Buildings	958.73	1 043.38	1 121.96	7.5

3－4 按新国民经济行业分全市固定资产投资建设情况（2003 年）

INVESTMENT IN FIXED ASSETS GROUPED BY NEW SECTOR，2003

行业 Sector	施工项目（个）Number of Projects under Construction (unit)	全部建成投产项目（个）Number of Projects Completed and Put into Use (unit)	固定资产投资总额（万元）Total Investment in Fixed Assets (10 000 yuan)	新增固定资产（万元）Total Newly Increased Fixed Assets (10 000 yuan)
总计 Total	**1 624**	**883**	**9 338 629**	**5 468 620**
农、林、牧、渔业 Farming，Forestry，Animal Husbandry and Fishery	34	9	22 025	18 881
工业 Industry	700	405	3 066 524	1 785 249
采矿业 Minerals Mining	15	11	889 679	703 304
制造业 Manufacturing	570	319	1 762 664	868 667
电力、燃气及水的生产和供应业 Production & Supply of Power，Gas and Water	115	75	414 181	213 278
建筑业 Construction	41	26	99 054	60 706
交通运输、仓储和邮政业 Transport，Storage，Post Services	90	47	963 385	766 013
信息传输、计算机服务和软件业 Information Transmitting，Computer Services and Software	72	15	334 370	192 325
批发和零售业 Wholesale and Retail Trade	68	42	88 962	85 211
住宿和餐饮业 Accommodation and Catering Services	17	9	17 165	6 870
金融业 Finance	2	1	7 702	6 357
房地产业 Real Estate	22	2	2 434 197	1 621 758
租赁和商务服务业 Leasing and Business Services	20	5	45 212	15 111
科学研究、技术服务和地质勘察业 Scientific Research，Technical Services and Geological Prospecting	10	4	14 693	7 522
水利、环境和公共设施管理业 Management for Water Conservancy，Environment and Public Facilities	213	216	1 387 649	501 326
居民服务和其他服务业 Resident Services and Other Social Services	8	5	2 966	2 987
教育 Education	144	89	306 543	231 904
卫生、社会保障和社会福利业 Health Care，Social Security and Social Welfare	46	23	137 726	35 919
文化、体育和娱乐业 Culture，Sports and Recreational Services	37	11	263 314	20 874
公共管理和社会组织 Public Management and Social Organizations	100	64	147 142	109 607

注：本表行业分类为国标 GB/T4754－2002 标准。
Note：Sector listed in this table is classified by the standard of GB/T4754－2002.

3－5 固定资产投资施工项目个数
（不含农村集体及个人投资）
NUMBER OF PROJECTS UNDER CONSTRUCTION IN FIXED ASSETS
（EXCLUDE RURAL COLLECTIVE－OWNED UNITS AND INDIVIDUAL ECONOMY）

单位：个 (unit)

项 目	Item	2001	2002	2003	2003 比 2002 年增长% Increase Rate in 2003 over 2002
总 计	**Total**	**1 381**	**1 630**	**1 624**	**－0.4**
按管理渠道分：	**Grouped by Channel of Management**				
基本建设	Capital Construction	636	744	835	12.2
更新改造	Innovation	600	756	677	－10.4
其他投资	Others	145	130	112	－13.8
按行业分：	**Grouped by Sectors**				
农、林、牧、渔业	Farming, Forestry, Animal Husbandry and Fishery	25	29	34	17.2
工 业	Industry	557	697	700	0.4
采掘业	Mining and Quarrying	8	17	15	－11.8
制造业	Manufacturing	489	631	570	－9.7
电力、煤气及水的生产和供应业	Electric Power, Gas and Water Production and Supply	60	49	115	134.7
建筑业	Construction	54	43	41	－4.7
地质勘察业、水利管理业	Geological Prospecting and Water Conservancy	32	42	58	38.1
交通运输、仓储及邮电通信业	Transportation, Storage, Post and Telecommunications	168	200	161	－19.5
批发和零售贸易、餐饮业	Wholesale & Retail Trade and Catering Services	96	100	78	－22.0
金融、保险业	Banking and Insurance	4	7	2	－71.4
房地产业和社会服务业	Real Estate and Social Services	126	161	209	29.8
房地产业	Real Estate	25	25	22	－12.0
社会服务业	Social Services	101	136	187	37.5
卫生、体育和社会福利业	Health Care, Sports and Social Welfare	37	36	45	25.0
教育、文化艺术及广播电影电视业	Education, Culture and Arts, Radio, Film and Television	116	143	170	18.9
科学研究和综合技术服务业	Scientific Research and Polytechnical Services	30	26	10	－61.5
国家机关、政党机关和社会团体	Government Agencies, Party Agencies and Social Organization	111	117	100	－14.5
其他行业	Others	25	29	16	－44.8

注：本表行业分类为国标 GB/T4754－1994 标准，3－6、3－8 至 12 表同。
Note: Sector listed in this table is classified by the standard of GB/T4754－1994, same as following table 3－6, 3－8 to12.

3－6　固定资产投资建成投产项目个数

（不含农村集体及个人投资）

NUMBER OF PROJECTS IN FIXED ASSETS COMPLETED AND PUT INTO USE

（EXCLUDE RURAL COLLECTIVE－OWNED UNITS AND INDIVIDUAL ECONOMY）

单位：个　　(unit)

项　　目	Item	2001	2002	2003	2003 比2002年增长% Increase Rate in 2003 over 2002
总　　计	**Total**	**726**	**914**	**883**	**－3.4**
按管理渠道分：	**Grouped by Channel of Management**				
基本建设	Capital Construction	319	370	423	14.3
更新改造	Innovation	311	423	381	－9.9
其他投资	Others	96	121	79	－34.7
按行业分：	**Grouped by Sectors**				
农、林、牧、渔业	Farming，Forestry，Animal Husbandry and Fishery	5	10	9	－10.0
工　业	Industry	301	395	405	2.5
采掘业	Mining and Quarrying	4	13	11	－15.4
制造业	Manufacturing	260	358	319	－10.9
电力、煤气及水的生产和供应业	Electric Power，Gas and Water Production and Supply	37	24	75	212.5
建筑业	Construction	29	32	26	－18.8
地质勘察业、水利管理业	Geological Prospecting and Water Conservancy	19	25	38	52.0
交通运输、仓储及邮电通信业	Transportation，Storage，Post and Telecommunications	54	81	62	－23.5
批发和零售贸易、餐饮业	Wholesale & Retail Trade and Catering Services	67	68	49	－27.9
金融、保险业	Banking and Insurance	2	5	1	－80.0
房地产业和社会服务业	Real Estate and Social Services	80	98	102	4.1
房地产业	Real Estate	12	12	2	－83.3
社会服务业	Social Services	68	86	100	16.3
卫生、体育和社会福利业	Health Care，Sports and Social Welfare	22	21	24	14.3
教育、文化艺术及广播电影电视业	Education，Culture and Arts，Radio，Film and Television	58	83	97	16.9
科学研究和综合技术服务业	Scientific Research and Polytechnical Services	20	11	4	－63.6
国家机关、政党机关和社会团体	Government Agencies，Party Agencies and Social Organization	62	73	64	－12.3
其他行业	Others	7	12	2	－83.3

3－7 全市固定资产投资额及新增固定资产
INVESTMENT IN FIXED ASSETS AND NEWLY INCREASED FIXED ASSETS

单位：万元 (10 000 yuan)

项 目	Item	2001	2002	2003	2003 比2002年增长% Increase Rate in 2003 over 2002
固定资产投资额	**Total Investment in Fixed Assets**	**6 226 043**	**7 147 640**	**9 338 629**	**30.7**
一、按三次产业分	**Grouped by Industries**				
第一产业	Primary Industry	11 297	12 534	22 025	75.7
第二产业	Secondary Industry	2 602 670	2 576 375	3 165 578	22.9
第三产业	Tertiary Industry	3 612 076	4 558 731	6 151 026	34.9
二、按隶属关系分	**Grouped by Administrative Relationship**				
中 央	Central Government	1 374 781	1 336 551	1 529 894	14.5
地 方	Local Government	4 851 262	5 811 089	7 808 735	34.4
三、按建设性质分	**Grouped by Type of Construction**				
新 建	New Construction	2 488 985	3 004 038	4 402 321	46.5
改、扩建及其他	Expansion, Reconstruction and Others	2 124 396	2 385 156	2 822 432	18.3
四、按登记注册类型分	**Grouped by Registered Categories**				
1.内资企业	Domestic－funded Enterprises	4 520 890	5 815 366	8 285 372	42.5
国有企业	State－owned Enterprises	2 365 834	2 856 954	4 131 584	44.6
集体企业	Collective－owned Enterprises	149 690	94 491	83 143	－12.0
股份合作企业	Cooperative Enterprises	17 736	67 213	132 661	97.4
私 营	Private Enterprises	565 627	671 317	717 094	6.8
股份有限公司	Share Holding Corporations Ltd.	554 610	633 938	1 144 102	80.5
有限责任公司	Limited Liability Corporations	811 050	1 433 706	1 950 939	36.1
#国有独资	Sole State－funded Corporations	479 003	345 216	559 484	62.1
联营经济	Joint Ownership Enterprises	22 092	36 494	77 114	111.3
#国有与国有联营企业	State Joint Ownership Enterprises	9 944	32 592	53 436	64.0
集体与集体联营企业	Collective Joint Ownership Enterprises	2 168	466	1 542	230.9
其他内资企业	Other Domestic－funded Enterprises	34 251	20 713	48 735	135.3
2.港澳台商投资企业	Enterprises with Investment from Hongkong, Macao and Taiwan	600 775	621 675	302 977	－51.3
3.外商投资企业	Foreign Funded Enterprises	1 104 378	710 599	750 280	5.6
新增固定资产	**Newly Increased Fixed Assets**	**3 894 217**	**4 443 448**	**5 468 620**	**23.1**
第一产业	Primary Industry	7 143	7 825	18 881	141.3
第二产业	Secondary Industry	1 790 688	1 753 871	1 845 955	5.3
第三产业	Tertiary Industry	2 096 386	2 681 752	3 603 784	34.4
固定资产交付使用率(%)	**Rate of Fixed Assets Put into Use(%)**	**62.5**	**62.2**	**58.6**	

注：表中按建设性质分组数据不含房地产开发投资。
Note: The data of this table grouped by type of construction exclude real estate investment.

3-7续表1 Continued
单位:万元 (10 000 yuan)

项目	Item	2001	2002	2003	2003比2002年增长% Increase Rate in 2003 over 2002
基本建设投资额	**Investment in Capital Construction**	**3 093 770**	**3 618 457**	**5 013 698**	**38.6**
一、按三次产业分	**Grouped by Industries**				
第一产业	Primary Industry	9 197	7 224	19 120	164.7
第二产业	Secondary Industry	1 566 693	1 294 637	1 619 907	25.1
第三产业	Tertiary Industry	1 517 880	2 316 596	3 374 671	45.7
二、按隶属关系分	**Grouped by Administrative Relationship**				
中央	Central Government	1 094 895	1 061 744	1 132 170	6.6
地方	Local Government	1 998 875	2 556 713	3 881 528	51.8
三、按建设性质分	**Grouped by Type of Construction**				
新建	New Construction	1 956 428	2 461 510	3 636 963	47.8
改、扩建及其他	Expansion,Reconstruction and Others	1 137 342	1 156 947	1 376 735	19.0
四、按登记注册类型分	**Grouped by Registered Categories**				
1.内资企业	Domestic-funded Enterprises	2 136 744	3 047 113	4 696 129	54.1
国有企业	State-owned Enterprises	1 375 286	1 946 214	2 545 659	30.8
集体企业	Collective-owned Enterprises				
股份合作企业	Cooperative Enterprises	13 427	34 314	84 252	145.5
私营	Private Enterprises	13 612	56 163	32 012	-43.0
股份有限公司	Share Holding Corporations Ltd.	384 859	398 131	828 993	108.2
有限责任公司	Limited Liability Corporations	329 487	584 506	1 138 982	94.9
#国有独资	Sole State-funded Corporations	125 553	158 757	472 679	197.7
联营经济	Joint Ownership Enterprises	20	24 257	57 815	138.3
#国有与国有联营企业	State Joint Ownership Enterprises		23 627	41 240	74.5
集体与集体联营企业	Collective Joint Ownership Enterprises				
其他内资企业	Other Domestic-funded Enterprises	20 053	3 528	8 416	138.5
2.港澳台商投资企业	Enterprises with Investment from Hongkong,Macao and Taiwan	449 101	390 412	166 333	-57.4
3.外商投资企业	Foreign Funded Enterprises	507 925	180 932	151 236	-16.4
新增固定资产	**Newly Increased Fixed Assets**	**2 012 486**	**2 219 138**	**2 840 928**	**28.0**
第一产业	Primary Industry	6 037	2 515	16 871	570.8
第二产业	Secondary Industry	1 064 152	935 352	1 845 955	97.4
第三产业	Tertiary Industry	942 297	1 281 271	978 102	-23.7
固定资产交付使用率(%)	**Rate of Fixed Assets Put into Use(%)**	**65.0**	**61.3**	**56.7**	

3－7 续表 2　Continued
单位:万元　(10 000 yuan)

项　目	Item	2001	2002	2003	2003 比 2002 年增长% Increase Rate in 2003 over 2002
更新改造投资额	**Investment in Innovation**	**1 418 476**	**1 660 172**	**2 108 873**	**27.0**
一、按三次产业分	**Grouped by Industries**				
第一产业	Primary Industry	731	2 920	895	－69.3
第二产业	Secondary Industry	958 087	1 208 090	1 548 097	28.1
第三产业	Tertiary Industry	459 658	449 162	559 881	24.7
二、按隶属关系分	**Grouped by Administrative Relationship**				
中　央	Central Government	252 181	258 840	365 800	41.3
地　方	Local Government	1 166 295	1 401 332	1 743 073	24.4
三、按建设性质分	**Grouped by Type of Construction**				
新　建	New Construction	448 885	509 703	691 084	35.6
改、扩建及其他	Expansion, Reconstruction and Others	969 591	1 150 469	1 417 789	23.2
四、按登记注册类型分	**Grouped by Registered Categories**				
1.内资企业	Domestic－funded Enterprises	794 645	1 009 738	1 543 667	52.9
国有企业	State－owned Enterprises	612 264	580 307	1 104 203	90.3
集体企业	Collective－owned Enterprises				
股份合作企业	Cooperative Enterprises	4 259	9 864	44 341	349.5
私　营	Private Enterprises	2 735		6 474	
股份有限公司	Share Holding Corporations Ltd.	98 006	144 103	143 252	－0.6
有限责任公司	Limited Liability Corporations	57 762	241 147	212 341	－11.9
#国有独资	Sole State－funded Corporations	8 234	142 284	74 291	－47.8
联营经济	Joint Ownership Enterprises	11 294	8 866	14 869	67.7
#国有与国有联营企业	State Joint Ownership Enterprises	7 844	6 060	9 158	51.1
集体与集体联营企业	Collective Joint Ownership Enterprises	500			
其他内资企业	Other Domestic－funded Enterprises	8 325	25 451	18 187	－28.5
2.港澳台商投资企业	Enterprises with Investment from Hongkong, Macao and Taiwan	63 988	148 996	52 947	－64.5
3.外商投资企业	Foreign Funded Enterprises	559 843	501 438	512 259	2.2
新增固定资产	**Newly Increased Fixed Assets**	**793 724**	**1 043 966**	**1 015 290**	**－2.7**
第一产业	Primary Industry	91	2 920		－100.0
第二产业	Secondary Industry	608 034	785 232	725 083	－7.7
第三产业	Tertiary Industry	185 599	255 814	290 207	13.4
固定资产交付使用率(%)	**Rate of Fixed Assets Put into Use(%)**	**56.0**	**62.9**	**48.1**	

3－8　按行业分全市固定资产投资
INVESTMENT IN FIXED ASSETS BY SECTOR

单位:万元　　(10 000 yuan)

项　目	Item	2001	2002	2003	2003比2002年增长% Increase Rate in 2003 over 2002
固定资产投资总额	**Total Investment in Fixed Assets**	**6 226 043**	**7 147 640**	**9 338 629**	**30.7**
农、林、牧、渔业	Farming, Forestry, Animal Husbandry and Fishery	11 297	12 534	22 025	75.7
工　业	Industry	2 501 064	2 478 917	3 066 524	23.7
采掘业	Mining and Quarrying	640 637	608 948	889 679	46.1
制造业	Manufacturing	1 545 896	1 492 031	1 762 664	18.1
电力、煤气及水的生产和供应业	Electric Power, Gas and Water Production and Supply	314 531	377 938	414 181	9.6
建筑业	Construction	101 606	97 458	99 054	1.6
地质勘察业、水利管理业	Geological Prospecting and Water Conservancy	94 426	183 798	199 206	8.4
交通运输、仓储及邮电通信业	Transportation, Storage, Post and Telecommunications	889 282	900 870	1 280 605	42.2
批发和零售贸易、餐饮业	Wholesale & Retail Trade and Catering Services	113 779	116 155	96 214	－17.2
金融、保险业	Banking and Insurance	9 758	12 683	7 702	－39.3
房地产业和社会服务业	Real Estate and Social Services	1 984 333	2 562 503	3 773 454	47.3
房地产业	Real Estate	1 656 197	1 806 799	2 434 197	34.7
社会服务业	Social Services	328 136	755 704	1 339 257	77.2
卫生、体育和社会福利业	Health Care, Sports and Social Welfare	34 429	75 796	213 269	181.4
教育、文化艺术及广播电影电视业	Education, Culture and Arts, Radio, Film and Television	190 308	310 603	379 647	22.2
科学研究和综合技术服务业	Scientific Research and Polytechnical Services	36 249	23 882	14 473	－39.4
国家机关、政党机关和社会团体	Government Agencies, Party Agencies and Social Organization	103 768	169 185	147 142	－13.0
其他行业	Others	155 744	203 256	39 314	－80.7

3－9　按行业分全市新增固定资产
NEWLY INCREASED FIXED ASSETS BY SECTOR

单位:万元　　(10 000 yuan)

项　目	Item	2001	2002	2003	2003比2002年增长% Increase Rate in 2003 over 2002
新增固定资产总额	**Total Newly Increased Fixed Assets**	**3 894 217**	**4 443 448**	**5 468 620**	**23.1**
农、林、牧、渔业	Farming,Forestry,Animal Husbandry and Fishery	7 143	7 825	18 881	141.3
工　业	Industry	1 718 117	1 689 112	1 785 249	5.7
采掘业	Mining and Quarrying	572 702	530 774	703 304	32.5
制造业	Manufacturing	962 401	873 626	868 667	－0.6
电力、煤气及水的生产和供应业	Electric Power,Gas and Water Production and Supply	183 014	284 712	213 278	－25.1
建筑业	Construction	72 571	64 759	60 706	－6.3
地质勘察业、水利管理业	Geological Prospecting and Water Conservancy	59 412	101 110	106 102	4.9
交通运输、仓储及邮电通信业	Transportation,Storage,Post and Telecommunications	448 065	598 582	958 338	60.1
批发和零售贸易、餐饮业	Wholesale & Retail Trade and Catering Services	81 977	120 490	89 741	－25.5
金融、保险业	Banking and Insurance	9 226	8 066	6 357	－21.2
房地产业和社会服务业	Real Estate and Social Services	1 214 456	1 434 616	2 035 649	41.9
房地产业	Real Estate	1 026 398	1 147 575	1 621 758	41.3
社会服务业	Social Services	188 058	287 041	413 891	44.2
卫生、体育和社会福利业	Health Care,Sports and Social Welfare	14 579	21 313	40 899	91.9
教育、文化艺术及广播电影电视业	Education,Culture and Arts,Radio,Film and Television	125 702	208 338	239 724	15.1
科学研究和综合技术服务业	Scientific Research and Polytechnical Services	28 688	13 505	7 302	－45.9
国家机关、政党机关和社会团体	Government Agencies,Party Agencies and Social Organization	88 382	103 146	109 607	6.3
其他行业	Others	25 899	72 586	10 065	－86.1

3－10　能源工业固定资产投资额
INVESTMENT IN FIXED ASSETS OF ENERGY INDUSTRY

单位:万元 (10 000 yuan)

部　门	Department	2001	2002	2003	2003比2002年增长% Increase Rate in 2003 over 2002
总　计	**Total**	**946 094**	**960 015**	**1 313 868**	**36.9**
石油和天然气开采业	Petroleum and Natural Gas Extraction	637 441	583 664	881 913	51.1
电力、蒸气、热水的生产和供应业	Electric Power,Steam and Hot Water Production and Supply	251 723	333 817	379 486	13.7
石油加工及炼焦业	Petroleum Processing and Coking	21 282	16 851	17 774	5.5
煤气生产和供应业	Gas Production and Supply	35 648	25 683	34 695	35.1
能源投资占全市固定资产投资比重(%)	As Percentage of Total Investment in Fixed Assets	15.2	13.4	14.1	
#基本建设	**Capital Construction**	**876 200**	**891 579**	**1 120 916**	**25.7**
石油和天然气开采业	Petroleum and Natural Gas Extraction	633 846	573 247	870 110	51.8
电力、蒸气、热水的生产和供应业	Electric Power,Steam and Hot Water Production and Supply	206 706	298 893	225 082	－24.7
石油加工及炼焦业	Petroleum Processing and Coking		2 085	974	－53.3
煤气生产和供应业	Gas Production and Supply	35 648	17 354	24 750	42.6
能源投资占基本建设投资比重(%)	As Percentage of Total Investment in Fixed Assets	28.3	24.6	22.4	
更新改造	**Innovation**	**69 894**	**61 948**	**189 658**	**206.2**
石油和天然气开采业	Petroleum and Natural Gas Extraction	3 595	9 953	11 803	18.6
电力、蒸气、热水的生产和供应业	Electric Power,Steam and Hot Water Production and Supply	45 017	28 900	151 510	424.3
石油加工及炼焦业	Petroleum Processing and Coking	21 282	14 766	16 400	11.1
煤气生产和供应业	Gas Production and Supply		8 329	9 945	19.4
能源投资占更新改造投资比重(%)	As Percentage of Total Investment in Fixed Assets	4.9	3.7	9.0	

3-11 城市基础设施固定资产投资额
URBAN INFRASTRUCTURE INVESTMENT IN FIXED ASSETS

单位:万元 (10 000 yuan)

部门	Department	2001	2002	2003	2003比2002年增长% Increase Rate in 2003 over 2002
总计	**Total**	**1 434 079**	**1 964 164**	**2 883 449**	**46.8**
交通运输、仓储及邮电通信业	Transportation,Storage,Post and Telecommunications	889 282	900 870	1 280 605	42.2
电力蒸气、热水生产和供应业	Electric Power,Steam and Hot Water Production and Supply	251 723	333 817	313 184	-6.2
煤气生产和供应业	Gas Production and Supply	35 648	25 683	34 695	35.1
自来水的生产和供应业	Tap Water Production and Supply	27 160	18 438	66 302	259.6
公共设施服务业	Public Services	230 266	685 356	1 188 663	73.4
城市基础设施占全市固定资产投资比重(%)	As Percentage of Total Investment in Fixed Assets	23.0	27.5	30.9	
#基本建设	**Capital Construction**	**1 129 680**	**1 643 594**	**2 248 722**	**36.8**
交通运输、仓储及邮电通信业	Transportation,Storage,Post and Telecommunications	649 171	672 281	1 025 849	52.6
电力蒸气、热水生产和供应业	Electric Power,Steam and Hot Water Production and Supply	206 706	298 893	181 638	-39.2
煤气生产和供应业	Gas Production and Supply	35 648	17 354	24 750	42.6
自来水的生产和供应业	Tap Water Production and Supply	14 254	6 739	43 444	544.7
公共设施服务业	Public Services	223 901	648 327	973 041	50.1
城市基础设施占基本建设投资比重(%)	As Percentage of Total Investment in Fixed Assets	36.5	45.4	44.9	
更新改造	**Innovation**	**303 090**	**313 325**	**626 573**	**100.0**
交通运输、仓储及邮电通信业	Transportation,Storage,Post and Telecommunications	238 802	227 368	249 696	9.8
电力蒸气、热水生产和供应业	Electric Power,Steam and Hot Water Production and Supply	45 017	28 900	128 652	345.2
煤气生产和供应业	Gas Production and Supply		8 329	9 945	19.4
自来水的生产和供应业	Tap Water Production and Supply	12 906	11 699	22 858	95.4
公共设施服务业	Public Services	6 365	37 029	215 422	481.8
城市基础设施占更新改造投资比重(%)	As Percentage of Total Investment in Fixed Assets	21.4	18.9	29.7	

3－12 地方固定资产投资额
LOCAL INVESTMENT IN FIXED ASSETS

单位：万元　　　　(10 000 yuan)

项目	Item	2001	2002	2003	2003比2002年增长% Increase Rate in 2003 over 2002
固定资产投资总额	**Total Investment in Fixed Assets**	**4 851 262**	**5 811 089**	**7 808 735**	**34.4**
一、按构成分	**Grouped by Use of Funds**				
建筑工程	Construction	2 776 114	3 407 113	4 362 400	28.0
安装工程	Installation	176 397	235 754	482 435	104.6
设备工器具	Equipment and Instruments	1 044 711	1 125 780	1 234 662	9.7
其他费用	Others	854 040	1 042 442	1 729 238	65.9
二、按建设性质分	**Grouped by Type of Construction**				
新　建	New Construction	1 960 959	2 448 862	3 800 915	55.2
扩　建	Expansion	638 249	928 157	1 197 523	29.0
改　建	Reconstruction	433 141	414 114	405 055	－2.2
其　他	Others	233 956	277 477	323 290	16.5
三、按行业分	**Grouped by Sector**				
农、林、牧、渔业	Farming,Forestry,Animal Husbandry and Fishery	11 297	10 582	21 306	101.3
工　业	Industry	1 543 372	1 574 375	1 958 735	24.4
采掘业	Mining and Quarrying	3 196	25 748	7 766	－69.8
制造业	Manufacturing	1 449 471	1 432 064	1 723 333	20.3
电力、煤气及水生产和供应业	Electric Power,Gas and Water Production and Supply	90 705	116 563	227 636	95.3
建筑业	Construction	82 214	87 484	65 654	－25.0
地质勘察业、水利管理业	Geological Prospecting and Water Conservancy	93 063	181 858	199 206	9.5
交通运输、仓储及邮电通信业	Transportation,Storage,Post and Telecommunications	575 813	562 093	1 032 267	83.6
批发和零售贸易、饮食业	Wholesale & Retail Trade and Catering Services	113 217	104 934	96 214	－8.3
金融、保险业	Banking and Insurance	560	5 864	4 091	－30.2
房地产业和社会服务业	Real Estate and Social Services	1 955 891	2 546 536	3 687 187	44.8
房地产业	Real Estate	1 628 492	1 790 832	2 402 273	34.1
社会服务业	Social Services	327 399	755 704	1 284 914	70.0
卫生、体育和社会福利业	Health Care,Sports and Social Welfare	34 429	75 796	212 292	180.1
教育、文化艺术及广播电影电视业	Education,Culture and Arts,Radio, Film and Television	166 994	275 265	339 306	23.3
科学研究和综合技术服务业	Scientific Research and Polytechnical Services	19 125	16 515	7 021	－57.5
国家机关、政党机关和社会团体	Government Agencies,Party Agencies and Social Organization	99 543	166 531	146 142	－12.2
其他行业	Others	155 744	203 256	39 314	－80.7

注：表中按建设性质分组数据不包括房地产开发投资。
Note:Investment grouped by type of construction excludes real estate development.

3－12 续表 1　Continued

单位：万元　　(10 000 yuan)

项目	Item	2001	2002	2003	2003 比 2002 年增长% Increase Rate in 2003 over 2002
基本建设投资额	**Investment of Capital Construction**	**1 998 875**	**2 556 713**	**3 881 528**	**51.8**
一、按构成分	**Grouped by Use of Funds**				
建筑工程	Construction	1 289 055	1 838 424	2 441 333	32.8
安装工程	Installation	56 539	75 139	154 425	105.5
设备工器具	Equipment and Instruments	377 450	290 644	370 938	27.6
其他费用	Others	275 831	352 506	914 832	159.5
二、按建设性质分	**Grouped by Type of Construction**				
新　建	New Construction	1 526 257	1 946 591	3 158 973	62.3
扩　建	Expansion	308 662	419 798	502 160	19.6
改　建	Reconstruction	91 853	86 939	127 852	47.1
其　他	Others	72 103	103 385	92 543	－10.5
三、按行业分	**Grouped by Sector**				
农、林、牧、渔业	Farming, Forestry, Animal Husbandry and Fishery	9 197	5 272	18 401	249.0
工　业	Industry	600 306	397 053	509 755	28.4
采掘业	Mining and Quarrying		1 383		
制造业	Manufacturing	549 707	316 368	385 133	21.7
电力、煤气及水生产和供应业	Electric Power, Gas and Water Production and Supply	50 599	79 302	124 622	57.1
建筑业	Construction	66 800	49 142	112 026	128.0
地质勘察业、水利管理业	Geological Prospecting and Water Conservancy	90 997	178 718	188 512	5.5
交通运输、仓储及邮电通信业	Transportation, Storage, Post and Telecommunications	509 141	506 608	942 046	86.0
批发和零售贸易、饮食业	Wholesale & Retail Trade and Catering Services	34 825	79 123	66 577	－15.9
金融、保险业	Banking and Insurance	360	3 532	1 520	－57.0
房地产业和社会服务业	Real Estate and Social Services	339 737	750 527	1 134 085	51.1
房地产业	Real Estate	30 135	42 696	271 021	534.8
社会服务业	Social Services	309 602	707 831	863 064	21.9
卫生、体育和社会福利业	Health Care, Sports and Social Welfare	30 512	70 336	204 966	191.4
教育、文化艺术及广播电影电视业	Education, Culture and Arts, Radio, Film and Television	164 160	265 786	332 302	25.0
科学研究和综合技术服务业	Scientific Research and Polytechnical Services	15 345	12 452	4 525	－63.7
国家机关、政党机关和社会团体	Government Agencies, Party Agencies and Social Organization	86 815	159 485	339 225	112.7
其他行业	Others	50 680	78 679	27 588	－64.9

3－12 续表 2　Continued

单位:万元　(10 000 yuan)

项　目	Item	2001	2002	2003	2003 比 2002 年增长% Increase Rate in 2003 over 2002
更新改造投资额	**Investment of Innovation**	**1 166 295**	**1 401 332**	**1 743 073**	**24.4**
一、按构成分	**Grouped by Use of Funds**				
建筑工程	Construction	464 399	478 167	711 681	48.8
安装工程	Installation	57 842	70 831	171 171	141.7
设备工器具	Equipment and Instruments	605 047	787 662	780 655	－0.9
其他费用	Others	39 007	64 672	79 566	23.0
二、按建设性质分	**Grouped by Type of Construction**				
新　建	New Construction	351 030	469 446	562 382	19.8
扩　建	Expansion	317 303	447 689	688 629	53.8
改　建	Reconstruction	338 657	320 228	278 017	－13.2
其　他	Others	159 305	163 969	214 045	30.5
三、按行业分	**Grouped by Sector**				
农、林、牧、渔业	Farming,Forestry,Animal Husbandry and Fishery	731	2 920	895	－69.3
工　业	Industry	892 426	1 113 131	1 381 233	24.1
采掘业	Mining and Quarrying	3 196	10 359	5 832	－43.7
制造业	Manufacturing	849 124	1 071 535	1 275 281	19.0
电力、煤气及水生产和供应业	Electric Power,Gas and Water Production and Supply	40 106	31 237	100 120	220.5
建筑业	Construction	10 741	28 885	23 801	－17.6
地质勘察业、水利管理业	Geological Prospecting and Water Conservancy	2 066	3 140	10 694	240.6
交通运输、仓储及邮电通信业	Transportation,Storage,Post and Telecommunications	65 363	54 264	85 161	56.9
批发和零售贸易、饮食业	Wholesale & Retail Trade and Catering Services	56 787	9 629	17 907	86.0
金融、保险业	Banking and Insurance		2 232	2 571	15.2
房地产业和社会服务业	Real Estate and Social Services	15 517	48 206	187 186	288.3
房地产业	Real Estate		3 285		
社会服务业	Social Services	15 517	44 921	187 186	316.7
卫生、体育和社会福利业	Health Care,Sports and Social Welfare	1 402	4 370	1 915	－56.2
教育、文化艺术及广播电影电视业	Education,Culture and Arts,Radio,Film and Television	2 543	7 125	5 647	－20.7
科学研究和综合技术服务业	Scientific Research and Polytechnical Services	3 780	2 163	2 496	15.4
国家机关、政党机关和社会团体	Government Agencies,Party Agencies and Social Organization	11 306	6 746	13 098	94.2
其他行业	Others	103 633	118 521	10 469	－91.2

3-13 全市固定资产投资资金来源
SOURCE OF FUNDS FOR INVESTMENT IN FIXED ASSETS

单位：万元 (10 000 yuan)

项目	Item	2001	2002	2003	2003比2002年增长% Increase Rate in 2003 over 2002
资金来源合计	**Total Funds**	**6 844 507**	**8 358 164**	**11 114 992**	**33.0**
上年末结余资金	Balance of Funds Brought Forward from The Previous Year	482 898	742 054	826 153	11.3
本年资金来源合计	Subtotal of The Sources of Funds in This Year	6 361 609	7 616 110	10 288 839	35.1
国家预算内资金	State Budgetary Appropriation	144 332	196 866	144 260	-26.7
国内贷款	Domestic Loans	1 394 685	1 736 477	3 111 982	79.2
债　券	Bonds	4 343	23 970	13 671	-43.0
利用外资	Foreign Investment	1 006 563	639 452	604 760	-5.4
#外商直接投资	Foreign Direct Investment	820 296	594 206	430 214	-27.6
自筹资金	Fundraising	2 956 725	3 912 060	4 824 783	23.3
#企、事业单位自有资金	Fundraising of Enterprises and Institutions	2 188 371	2 785 194	3 629 627	30.3
其他资金来源	Others	854 961	1 107 285	1 589 383	43.5
#基本建设	**Capital Construction**	**3 073 041**	**3 816 129**	**5 259 686**	**37.8**
上年末结余资金	Balance of Funds Brought Forward from The Previous Year	86 443	320 509	263 685	-17.7
本年资金来源合计	Subtotal of The Sources of Funds in This Year	2 986 598	3 495 620	4 996 001	42.9
国家预算内资金	State Budgetary Appropriation	128 435	167 212	136 812	-18.2
国内贷款	Domestic Loans	798 617	1 059 957	1 856 884	75.2
债　券	Bonds	3 820	17 847	11 684	-34.5
利用外资	Foreign Investment	630 302	297 693	241 234	-19.0
#外商直接投资	Foreign Direct Investment	478 054	267 317	135 415	-49.3
自筹资金	Fundraising	1 328 487	1 883 301	2 586 594	37.3
#企、事业单位自有资金	Fundraising of Enterprises and Institutions	1 002 766	1 254 729	1 817 248	44.8
其他资金来源	Others	96 937	69 610	162 793	133.9
更新改造	**Innovation**	**1 434 575**	**1 781 205**	**2 108 645**	**18.4**
上年末结余资金	Balance of Funds Brought Forward from The Previous Year	106 352	65 001	144 476	122.3
本年资金来源合计	Subtotal of The Sources of Funds in This Year	1 328 223	1 716 204	1 964 169	14.4
国家预算内资金	State Budgetary Appropriation	15 497	29 604	7 448	-74.8
国内贷款	Domestic Loans	81 935	191 724	339 415	77.0
债　券	Bonds	523	6 113	1 987	-67.5
利用外资	Foreign Investment	347 227	301 220	325 211	8.0
#外商直接投资	Foreign Direct Investment	322 453	301 120	264 336	-12.2
自筹资金	Fundraising	859 987	1 167 599	1 244 309	6.6
#企、事业单位自有资金	Fundraising of Enterprises and Institution	680 632	991 411	1 183 496	19.4
其他资金来源	Others	23 054	19 944	45 799	129.6

3－14 施工和竣工房屋建筑面积
FLOOR SPACE OF BUILDINGS UNDER CONSTRUCTION AND COMPLETED

单位：万平方米 (10 000 sq. m)

项 目	Item	2001	2002	2003	2003 比 2002 年增长％ Increase Rate in 2003 over 2002
一、房屋建筑施工面积	**Floor Space of Buildings under Construction**	**2 596.75**	**3 035.52**	**3 352.20**	**10.4**
基本建设	Capital Construction	521.04	691.55	841.00	21.6
更新改造	Innovation	149.81	142.58	149.19	4.6
其他投资	Others	62.42	65.83	47.58	－27.7
房地产开发	Real Estate Development	1 863.48	2 135.56	2 314.43	8.4
#住　宅	**Residential Buildings**	**1 706.21**	**1 871.64**	**2 045.47**	**9.3**
基本建设	Capital Construction	94.63	96.48	77.14	－20.0
更新改造	Innovation	11.34	18.77	8.18	－56.4
其他投资	Others	9.62	10.26	6.65	－35.2
房地产开发	Real Estate Development	1 590.62	1 746.13	1 953.50	11.9
二、房屋建筑竣工面积	**Floor Space of Buildings Complete**	**1 020.07**	**1 181.22**	**1 255.09**	**6.3**
基本建设	Capital Construction	223.12	281.67	255.47	－9.3
更新改造	Innovation	67.07	99.12	55.54	－44.0
其他投资	Others	39.40	53.99	32.81	－39.2
房地产开发	Real Estate Development	690.48	746.44	911.27	22.1
#住　宅	**Residential Buildings**	**682.37**	**759.29**	**775.29**	**2.1**
基本建设	Capital Construction	47.34	63.01	19.59	－68.9
更新改造	Innovation	5.34	14.32	1.38	－90.4
其他投资	Others	3.06	8.96	3.65	－59.3
房地产开发	Real Estate Development	626.63	673.00	750.67	11.5

注：房屋竣工面积不含农村集体和个人建房数。
Note: Floor space of buildings completed exclude rural collective－owned and individual houses.

3-15 全市房地产开发投资情况
INVESTMENT ON REAL ESTATE DEVELOPMENT

单位:万元 (10 000 yuan)

项目	Item	2001	2002	2003	2003比2002年增长% Increase Rate in 2003 over 2002
本年完成投资额	**Investment Completed in This Year**	**1 612 662**	**1 758 446**	**2 113 876**	**20.2**
一、按隶属关系分	**Grouped by Administrative Relationship**				
中　央	Central Government	27 705	15 967	31 924	99.9
地　方	Local Government	1 584 957	1 742 479	2 081 952	19.5
二、按登记注册类型分组	**Grouped by Registered Categories**				
1.内资企业	Domestic-funded Enterprises	1 488 366	1 647 950	1 943 394	17.9
国有企业	State-owned Enterprises	378 284	330 433	481 722	45.8
集体企业	Collective-owned Enterprises	103 710	55 715	40 807	-26.8
股份合作企业	Cooperative Enterprises	50	23 035	4 068	-82.3
私　营	Private Enterprises	494 125	525 403	618 762	17.8
股份有限公司	Share Holding Corporations Ltd.	71 745	91 704	171 857	87.4
有限责任公司	Limited Liability Corporations	423 801	608 053	599 616	-1.4
#国有独资	Sole State-funded Corporations	1 300	44 175	12 514	-71.7
联营经济	Joint Ownership Enterprises	10 778	3 371	4 430	31.4
#国有联营	State Joint Ownership Enterprises	2 100	2 905	3 038	4.6
集体联营	Collective Joint Ownership Enterprises	1 668	466	1 392	198.7
其他内资企业	Other Domestic-funded Enterprises	5 873	10 236	22 132	116.2
2.港澳台商投资企业	Enterprises with Investment from Hongkong,Macao and Taiwan	87 686	82 267	83 697	1.7
3.外商投资企业	Foreign Funded Enterprises	36 610	28 229	86 785	207.4
三、按构成分	**Grouped by Use of Funds**				
建筑工程	Construction	975 266	1 034 344	1 166 262	12.8
安装工程	Installation	59 768	84 328	156 216	85.2
设备工器具	Equipment and Instruments	37 403	15 320	40 638	165.3
其他费用	Others	540 225	624 454	750 760	20.2
四、按工程用途分	**Grouped by Use of Projects**				
住　宅	Residential Buildings	963 985	1 031 788	1 509 252	46.3
#别墅、高档公寓	Top Grade Apartment	87 147	140 597	176 977	25.9
办公楼	Office Buildings	45 157	75 122	77 808	3.6
商业营业用房	Commerce Buildings	156 497	147 244	242 564	64.7
其　他	Others	447 023	504 292	284 252	-43.6
本年新增固定资产	**Newly Increased Fixed Assets in This Year**	**996 214**	**1 120 878**	**1 553 772**	**38.6**

3－16　全市房地产开发建设及销售情况

CONSTRUCTION AND SALES OF REAL ESTATE DEVELOPMENT

项　目	Item	2001	2002	2003	2003 比2002年增长% Increase Rate in 2003 over 2002
一、施工房屋面积(万平方米)	**Floor Space of Buildings Under Construction(10⁴ sq.m)**	**1 863.48**	**2 135.56**	**2 314.43**	**8.4**
住　宅	Residential Buildings	1 590.62	1 746.13	1 953.5	11.9
办公楼	Office Buildings	80.34	96.29	85.87	－10.8
商业营业用房	Houses for Business Use	163.75	226.72	194.84	－14.1
其　他	Others	28.77	66.42	80.22	20.8
二、竣工房屋面积(万平方米)	**Floor Space of Buildings Completed(10⁴ sq.m)**	**690.48**	**746.44**	**911.27**	**22.1**
住　宅	Residential Buildings	626.63	673.00	750.67	11.5
办公楼	Office Buildings	10.64	8.11	41.49	411.6
商业营业用房	Houses for Business Use	46.06	56.23	89.43	59.0
其　他	Others	7.15	9.10	29.68	226.2
三、商品房销售额(万元)	**Total Sales of Commercial Houses(10⁴ yuan)**	**1 276 363**	**1 402 816**	**1 980 448**	**41.2**
住　宅	Residential Buildings	1 187 443	1 299 236	1 724 256	32.7
办公楼	Office Buildings	23 249	24 965	98 804	295.8
商业营业用房	Houses for Business Use	65 335	76 683	119 637	56.0
其　他	Others	336	1 932	37 751	1 854.0
四、商品房销售面积(万平方米)	**Floor Space of Commercial Houses Sold(10⁴ sq.m)**	**537.48**	**564.00**	**786.50**	**39.5**
住　宅	Residential Buildings	514.59	538.26	720.64	33.9
办公楼	Office Buildings	5.45	6.94	15.72	126.5
商业营业用房	Houses for Business Use	17.31	17.76	28.89	62.7
其　他	Others	0.13	1.04	21.25	1 943.3
五、房屋竣工价值(万元)	**Value of Buildings Completed(10⁴ yuan)**	**705 326**	**724 976**	**1 199 770**	**65.5**
住　宅	Residential Buildings	615 910	662 588	953 018	43.8
办公楼	Office Buildings	15 640	6 837	72 580	961.6
商业营业用房	Houses for Business Use	63 296	45 924	140 920	206.9
其　他	Others	10 480	9 627	33 252	245.4
六、资金来源合计(万元)	**Total Funds (10⁴ yuan)**	**2 236 507**	**2 650 293**	**3 642 129**	**37.4**
上年末结余资金	Balance of Funds Brought Forward from the Previous Year	289 991	356 544	417 992	17.2
本年资金来源合计	Subtotal of The Sources of Funds in This Year	1 946 516	2 293 749	3 224 137	40.6
国家预算内资金	State Budgetary Appropriation				
国内贷款	Domestic Loans	506 094	484 106	911 374	88.3
债　券	Bonds		10		
利用外资	Usage of Foreign Investment	27 094	38 839	38 315	－1.3
#外商直接投资	Foreign Direct Investment	19 049	24 069	30 463	26.6
自筹资金	Fundraising	689 808	819 828	900 460	9.8
#企、事业单位自有资金	Fundraising of Enterprises and Institutions	427 525	499 206	536 460	7.5
其他资金来源	Others	723 520	950 966	1 373 988	44.5

3－17　房地产物业管理基本情况
BASIC STATISTICS ON REAL ESTATE PROPERTY MANAGEMENT

指　　标	Item	2001	2002	2003
一、企业总数(个)	**Number of Enterprises**	**580**	**640**	**673**
所管项目总数	Number of Items Managed	1 302	1 405	1 490
二、管业情况	**Property Managed**			
户　数(户)	Number of Households(household)	446 619	559 037	611 089
管业建筑面积(万平方米)	Floor Space of Buildings(10^4 sq.m)	6 100.00	6 620.00	7 300.00
住　宅	Residential Buildings	5 080.00	5 420.00	5 957.00
办公用房	Office	404.41	470.36	622.50
商业用房	Houses for Business Use	181.00	293.47	244.80
仓储工业用房	Houses for Storage and Industry	281.71	264.80	382.70
其　他	Others	152.88	171.37	93.00
三、人员情况(人)	**Personnel(person)**	**30 018**	**36 101**	**51 768**
自有人员合计	Total Employees	25 154	28 479	40 975
管理人员	Administrative Personnel	4 936	5 589	7 877
维修人员	Maintenance Personnel	4 646	5 129	7 375
保安人员	Security Personnel	6 058	6 907	10 480
保洁人员	Cleaner	5 862	6 589	9 967
其他人员	Others	3 652	4 265	5 276
外聘人员	Personnel Engaged	4 864	7 622	10 793
四、经营情况	**Management**			
年经营收入(万元)	Annual Income(10^4 yuan)	59 910	71 156	100 863
服务费收缴率(%)	Service Charge Paied Rate(%)	72.2	76.6	77.4
从业人员报酬(万元)	Earnings of Employment Personnel (10^4 yuan)	27 486	22 049	31 620

3－18　房地产中介服务业情况
BASIC STATISTICS ON REAL ESTATE AGENCY

项　　目	Item	2001	2002	2003
房屋代理总面积(万平方米)	**Total Floor Space(10^4 sq.m)**	**272.00**	**598.72**	**254.35**
期房代理	Commercial Houses Under Contruction	77.00	173.02	8.78
现房代理	Commercial Houses	179.00	403.70	166.73
旧房代理	Old Houses	16.00	22.00	78.84
房屋代理成交面积(万平方米)	**Transaction Floor Space by Agency(10^4 sq.m)**	**77.40**	**94.45**	**254.35**
期房代理	Commercial Houses Under Contruction	18.40	21.73	8.78
现房代理	Commercial Houses	43.00	50.72	166.73
旧房代理	Old Houses	16.00	22.00	78.84
房屋代理成交合同金额(万元)	**Transaction Value by Agency(10^4 yuan)**	**211 937**	**249 719**	**970 338**
期房代理	Commercial Houses Under Contruction	55 069	61 867	37 971
现房代理	Commercial Houses	128 495	144 354	721 441
旧房代理	Old Houses	28 373	43 498	210 926

3－19 农村集体固定资产投资完成情况
INVESTMENT IN FIXED ASSETS OF RURAL COLLECTIVE UNITS

项目	Item	2001	2002	2003
一、固定资产投资合计(万元)	**Total Investment in Fixed Asstes(10^4 yuan)**	**615 058**	**740 010**	**897 262**
#农、林、牧、渔业	Farming, Forestry, Animal Husbanday, Fishery	62 440	25 211	33 101
工　业	Industry	222 687	374 040	496 264
交通运输业	Transportation	6 052	2 518	12 643
建筑业	Construction	66 261	170 730	77 919
文教卫生社会福利业	Culture, Health Care, Social Welfare	2 041	12 491	3 149
二、新增固定资产(万元)	**Newly Increased Fixed Assets(10^4 yuan)**	**610 149**	**711 358**	**870 309**
三、房屋面积(万平方米)	**Floor Space of Buildings(10^4 sq.m)**			
施工面积	Under Construction	345.0	647.77	734.24
竣工面积	Completed	338.7	420.00	599.84

3－20 城镇和农村个人建房情况
BUILDING CONSTRUCTION BY INDIVIDUAL IN URBAN AND RURAL AREAS

项目	Item	2001	2002	2003
一、城　镇	**Urban**			
建房户数(户)	Number of Households With Building Construction (household)	4 765	2 698	246
竣工房屋面积(平方米)	Floor Space of Buildings Completed (sq.m)	417 564	222 711	33 789
#住　宅	Residential Buildings	387 774	222 711	23 900
竣工房屋价值(万元)	Value of Buildings Completed (10^4 yuan)	45 742	24 878	2 452
#住　宅	Residential Buildings	37 281	24 878	1 722
竣工房屋造价(元/平方米)	Cost of Buildings Completed (yuan/sq.m)	1 095	1 117	726
#住　宅	Residential Buildings	961	1 117	721
二、农　村	**Rural**			
投资总额(万元)	Total Investment(10^4 yuan)	164 086	200 063	228 571
竣工房屋面积(万平方米)	Floor Space of Buildings Completed (10^4 sq.m)	214.4	211.9	214.11
#住　宅	Residential Buildings	166.5	132.7	175.16
竣工住宅价值(万元)	Value of Residential Buildings Completed (10^4 yuan)	85 087	63 217	114 950
竣工住宅造价(元/平方米)	Cost of Residential Buildings Completed (yuan/sq.m)	511	476	656

3-21 重点建设项目一览表(2003年)

BASIC STATISTICS ON KEY PROJECTS,2003

项目名称 Name of project	开工时间 Starting Time	竣工时间 Ending Time	计划总投资(万元) Total Planned Investment (10 000 yuan)	累计完成投资(万元) Investment Accumulated (10 000 yuan)	本年完成投资(万元) Investment in 2003 (10 000 yuan)
合　计 (64项)			**9 858 012**	**4 818 234**	**3 131 779**
一、海河两岸综合开发项目(7项)			**2 428 600**	**512 369**	**512 369**
1.海河两岸基础设施启动工程	2003.02		394 000	143 900	143 900
2.和平广场商贸娱乐区			800 000	65 700	65 700
3.海河水上运动大世界			60 000	16 000	16 000
4.古文化街海河楼商贸区			70 000	51 069	51 069
5.大悲院商贸区(慈航广场)	2003.09		30 000	10 000	10 000
6.运河经济文化商贸区	2003.08		274 600	165 700	165 700
7.南站中心商贸区			800 000	60 000	60 000
二、工业技术改造及高新技术产业化项目(12项)			**613 591**	**589 737**	**492 555**
1.天钢东移改造	2001.01		280 000	349 120	285 818
2.天津钢管公司二套轧机改造	2003.04		97 000	60 301	60 301
3.柔性水泥基复合材料产业化示范工程	2003.03		12 249	724	724
4.天地伟业 UHT 高亮度投影电视光源	2001.07	2003.10	9 180	9 180	1 310
5.中新药业现代中药产业园	2002.10		25 000	19 745	15 745
6.中空纤维膜系列产品产业化示范工程			11 904	9 100	9 100
7.南开戈德自动服务系统升级	2002.04		19 800	22 998	10 988
8.天士力现代中药 GMP 改造	2001.06		53 100	20 075	20 075
9.天津田歌纺织有限公司	2001.05		19 618	19 264	9 264
10.振兴水泥制成系统二期技改	2003.03		19 800	18 653	18 653
11.三和电机公司扩大新型元器件生产	2003.03		17 800	17 804	17 804
12.LG 电子扩大家电生产能力	2003.03		48 140	42 773	42 773
三、能源及交通邮电项目(11项)			**2 564 146**	**1 763 755**	**606 635**
1.城市电网建设及改造工程	1998.09	2003.12	569 000	567 100	28 100
2.盘山电厂配套220千伏输变电工程	2003.01		60 900	30 600	30 600
3.天津大港发电厂	2003.04		149 115	52 588	45 865
4.双港垃圾焚烧发电厂	2003.07		55 819	20 589	20 589
5.津蓟高速公路	1998.12	2003.12	495 840	451 856	120 000
6.丹拉公路支线天津南段	2000.03	2003.12	305 200	263 500	95 000
7.天津港扩建工程	2001.01		269 033	302 643	202 092
8.京沪高速公路天津正线一期工程	2003.12		373 037	5 000	5 000
9.海滨大道	2003.01		220 000	17 096	17 096
10.天津电力公司供用电综合楼	2002.08		39 202	21 500	11 010
11.天津移动 GSM 九期扩容及传输配套工程	2003.04		27 000	31 283	31 283

3-21 续表 Continued

项 目 名 称 Name of project	开工时间 Starting Time	竣工时间 Ending Time	计划总投资（万元） Total Planned Investment (10 000 yuan)	累计完成投资（万元） Investment Accumulated (10 000 yuan)	本年完成投资（万元） Investment in 2003 (10 000 yuan)
四、基础设施和环保项目(6 项)			2 238 177	1 031 818	761 951
1. 天津地铁一号线	2000.10		786 800	314 068	242 333
2. 津滨快速轨道交通工程	2003.03		745 300	363 124	164 992
3. 城市污水处理工程	2003.09		207 577	28 555	28 555
4. 市内道路及排水改造工程	2003.03		394 500	229 370	229 370
5. 卡口道路改造工程	2003.01	2003.08	60 000	54 275	54 275
6. 市区河道改造	2003.03	2003.08	44 000	42 426	42 426
五、农林水利项目(3 项)			424 464	202 764	108 582
1. 引滦入津水质保护工程	2001.09		239 940	148 182	54 000
2. 天津市六条高速公路两侧农林建设工程	2002.10		170 000	48 082	48 082
3. 外环河关贯通与河水循环工程	2003.03		14 524	6 500	6 500
六、社会事业项目(16 项)			744 002	358 725	284 645
1. 天津博物馆	2001.11		33 600	24 326	10 228
2. 人民医院一期工程	2002.04		38 269	3 421	17 894
3. 第三中心医院扩建工程	2001.12		17 156	14 838	4 096
4. 泰达国际心血管医院	2003.03		65 400	54 612	54 612
5. 天津职业技术师范学院"十五"一期扩建工程	2003.02	2003.10	35 000	35 000	14 376
6. 天津职业大学北辰新校区一期工程	2003.05	2003.12	22 000	21 989	21 989
7. 南开中学等五所示范高中校工程	2002.02	2003.12	39 530	39 530	29 825
8. 泰达图书馆	2003.03		38 000	30 340	30 340
9. 奥林匹克中心体育场	2003.08		118 000	9 931	9 931
10. 广播电视宽带综合业务网工程	2002.06		28 850	14 716	14 716
11. 科技大学泰达校区	2003.03		117 000	26 287	26 287
12. 南开大学扩建	2001.01		40 531	23 358	11 133
13. 天津大学扩建	2001.12		77 408	29 445	10 045
14. 眼科医院	2002.11		14 568	8 598	7 016
15. 一中心医院	2002.12		12 998	2 752	2 575
16. 医科大学扩建工程	2003.09		45 692	19 582	19 582
七、商贸项目及其他(9 项)			862 032	421 823	365 042
1. 万达商业广场	2002.08		120 000	78 000	78 000
2. 滨江金耀广场	2003.01	2003.12	110 000	110 000	63 745
3. 市民广场	2003.03		120 000	32 913	32 913
4. 金融服务区	2003.03		75 000	51 244	51 244
5. 北洋舰船游乐港一期工程	2002.08		49 800	68 818	58 292
6. 天津科技广场	2003.02		101 632	2 478	2 478
7. 华信公司信达广场	1992.10		129 600	21 874	21 874
8. 铜锣湾商住区	2003.01		150 000	48 996	48 996
9. 国展中心扩建	2003.01	2003.12	6 000	7 500	7 500

3－22 建设项目主要新增生产能力(2003 年)

MAIN NEWLY INCREASED PRODUCTION CAPACITY OF CONSTRUCTION PROJECTS,2003

生产能力或效益名称	Item	总计 Total	# 基本建设 Capital Construction	# 更新改造 Innovation
天然原油(万吨/年)	Natural Petroleum (10^4 tons/year)	45.0	45.0	
天然气管输(公里)	Natural Gas Pipelines(km)	39.8	39.8	
(亿立方米/年)	(100 million cu. m/year)	11.0	11.0	
热轧钢材(万吨/年)	Steel－Rolling (10^4 tons/year)	25.0		25.0
铜材加工(吨)	Copper Machining(tons)	1 300		1 300
火力发电(万千瓦)	Capacity of Thermal Power Generating Sets(10^4 kw/year)	2.0	2.0	
输电线路长度(公里)	Lenght of Transmit Electricity Line (km)	256.3	169.3	87.0
变电设备能力(万千伏安)	Capacity of Transformer Equipments(10^4 volts)	206	201	5
化学原料药(吨/年)	Medicine of Chemistry Material(tons/year)	1 060		1 060
光纤通讯电缆(芯公里)	Light Fibre Communication Cable(km)	819.14	819.14	
全塑市话电缆(万对公里)	Plastic Local Call Cable(10^4 km)	2.39		2.39
汽车制造(辆/年)	Cars(unit/year)	1 000		1 000
摩托车制造(辆/年)	Motorcycles(unit/year)	180 000		180 000
显像管(万只/年)	Kinescope(10^4 units/year)	350.0		350.0
电子计算机外部设备(台/年)	Peripheral Equipment of Computers(units/year)	50 000		50 000
程控交换机(万线/年)	Telephone Exchanges(10^4 lines/year)	1.71	1.71	
新建高速公路(公里)	Length of New Highways Expressways(km)	168.6	168.6	
改建二级公路(公里)	Length of Reconstructed Second－grade Highways(km)	2.19		2.19
粮食仓库(万公斤)	Grain Storehouses (10^4 tons)	14 500	14 500	
粮食仓库(平方米)	Grain Storehouses (sq. m)	22 000	22 000	
高等院校:学生席位(个)	Universities and Colleges:Students Capacity(unit)	9 000	9 000	
建筑面积(平方米)	Floor Space of Construction(sq. m)	106 582	106 582	
中等学校:学生席位(个)	Secondary Schools:Students Capacity(unit)	23 290	23 290	
建筑面积(平方米)	Floor Space of Construction(sq. m)	356 454	356 454	
小学校:学生席位(个)	Primary School:Students Capacity(unit)	14 590	11 630	360
建筑面积(平方米)	Floor Space of Construction(sq. m)	87 543	77 043	1 200
其他院校:学生席位(个)	Other School:Students Capacity(unit)	400	400	
建筑面积(平方米)	Floor Space of Construction(sq. m)	7 620	7 620	
医院病床(张)	Number of Hospital Beds(bed)	1 860	1 860	
城市自来水管道长度(公里)	Length of Urban Tap Water Pipes(km)	14.93	14.93	
城市道路扩建长度(公里)	Length of Urban Roads Expanded(km)	76.84	60.28	16.56
城市道路扩建面积(万平方米)	Areas of Urban Roads Expanded(10^4 sq. m)	250.07	209.87	40.20
城市排水管道铺设长度(公里)	Length of Urban Drain Pipes Paved(km)	74.77	74.77	
城市污水处理能力(万吨/日)	Capacity of Urban Waste Water Treated(10^4 tons/day)	3.0	3.0	
城市永久性桥梁(座)	Urban Permanent Bridges(unit)	18	18	
城市防洪堤长度(公里)	Length of Urban Flood Water Embankment(km)	16.19	16.19	

主要统计指标解释

固定资产投资额 是以货币表现的建造和购置固定资产的工作量，它是反映固定资产投资规模、速度、比例关系和使用方向的综合指标。

本《年鉴》固定资产投资分为全社会固定资产投资和全市固定资产投资两个口径。全社会固定资产投资的统计范围包括国有经济单位投资、城乡集体所有制单位投资、其他所有制单位投资和城乡个人投资。全市固定资产投资的统计范围包括国有经济单位投资、城镇集体所有制单位投资和其他所有制单位投资，即全社会固定资产投资中扣除农村集体和个人后的投资额。按照管理渠道，全社会固定资产投资总额为基本建设、更新改造、房地产开发投资和其他固定资产四个部分。

基本建设投资 指企业、事业、行政单位以扩大生产能力或工程效益为主要目的的新建、扩建、改建和恢复工程以及设备购置等有关活动。其综合范围为总投资 50 万元以上(含 50 万元)的基本建设项目。基本建设投资额是以货币表现的基本建设工作量，是反映一定时期内基本建设规模和建设进度的综合指标。

更新改造措施投资 指企事业单位利用自有的基本折旧基金、国家更新改造拨款和国内外技术改造贷款等资金，对原有设施进行技术改造和更新，以及相应配套的辅助性生产、生活福利设施等工程(不包括大修理和维护工程)的投资额。其目的是要在技术进步的前提下，通过采取新技术、新工艺、新设备、新材料，努力提高产品质量、增加品种，促进产品升级换代，降低能源和原材料消耗，增强资源综合利用和污染治理等，提高社会综合经济效益和实现以内涵为主的扩大再生产。其综合范围为总投资 50 万元以上(含 50 万元)的更新改造项目。更新改造措施投资额是以货币表现的更新改造措施完成的工作量。

其他固定资产投资 指不划分基本建设和更新改造的固定资产投资，包括国有经济单位按规定不纳入基本建设计划和更新改造措施计划管理，总投资在 50 万元以上(含 50 万元)的固定资产投资。即：用油田维护费和石油开发基金进行的油田维护和开发工程；矿山、森林等采掘、采伐工业用维持简单再生产费用进行的开拓延伸工程；交通部门用养路费对原有公路、桥梁进行的改建工程和商业部门用简易建筑费建造的仓库工程。还包括城镇集体所有制及其它经济类型企业、事业单位建造和购置固定资产投资在 50 万元以上未列入基本建设计划和更新计划的项目的固定资产投资。

房地产开发投资 指房地产开发公司、商品房建设公司及其他房地产开发单位进行土地开发工程、商品房屋建设工程所完成的投资额。是以货币表现的房地产开发工作量。

商品房屋 指有资格的商品房屋开发公司为了出售而统一开发的全部商品房屋，包括商品住宅和其他商品房屋。但不包括开发区内的非商品房屋项目，也不包括开发公司自建自用的房屋和承建的统建住宅。①商品住宅的建设投资包括：a. 开发区内的征地、拆迁等实际费用；b. 商品住宅建筑安装工程费用；c. 开发区红线内的市政配套；d. 为开发区内商品住宅配套的服务网点。②其他商品房屋的建设投资包括：由开发公司统一开发建设的厂房、仓库等其他商品房屋的建筑安装工程费用，以及由此而发生征地、拆迁费用和配套设施建设。

固定资产投资按构成分组：

建筑工程 指各种房屋建筑物的建造工程，又称建筑工程量。这部分投资额必须兴工动料，通过施工才能实现。建筑工程包括各种房屋的建造，设备基础及各种窑炉的砌筑和金属结构工程，为施工而进行的建筑场地布置、地质勘探、平整场地、施工用水、电、气、路和清理绿化等。矿井的开凿、铁路、公路、桥梁、水利及防空、地下建筑等特殊工程。

安装工程 指各种设备、装置的安装工程，又称安装工作量。在安装工程投资额中，不包括被安装设备本身的价值。安装工程包括生产、动力、起重、运输、传动和医疗试验等各种需安装设备的装配与设备相连的工作台、梯子栏杆以及管线敷设、保温、油漆、防腐和单机试运系统联动无负簧试运(不包括投料试运)。

设备、工具、器具购置 指购置和自制达到固定资产标准的设备、工具、器具的价值。但新建单位、扩建单位的新建车间，按照设计和计划要求购置或自制的全部设备、工具、器具，不论是否达到固定资产标准均计入“设备、工具、器具购置”中。

其他费用 指除建筑安装、设备工具器具购置和商品房屋购置以外的构成固定资产投资完成额的各种费用。主要包括牲畜购置费、林木营建费、办公和生活家具、器具购置费、土地青苗补偿费和安置补助费、建设单位管理费、研究试验费、勘察设计费、联合试运转费、引进技术和进口设备项目的其他费用、生产职工培训费、施工机构迁移费、报废工程损失费和供电站费、矿山巷道维修费等。

固定资产投资按建设性质分组： 是反映固定资产投资使用方向，研究各类性质的比重和对比分析投资效果。具体包括：

新建 一般指从无到有"平地起家"新开始建设的企事业和行政单位及新建输电线路、输油管道、铁路、公路等独立工程。有的项目原有基础很小，经扩大建设后，其新增加的固定资产价值（原值）超过原有固定资产价值三倍以上的也应算为新建。

扩建 指为扩大原有产品生产能力或新的产品能力，在厂内或其他地点增建主要生产车间（或主要工程），独立的生产线等。事业单位和行政单位在原单位增建业务用房，也作为扩建。

改建或更新改造 现有企事业单位为了技术进步对现有设施、工艺条件进行技术改造或更新（包括相应配套的辅助性生产、生活设施建设）。有的还充分发挥现有的生产能力，进行填平补齐而增建不直接增加本单位主要产品生产能力的车间等，也属于改建。

新增固定资产 指报告期内交付使用的固定资产价值，包括建成投入生产或交付使用的工程投资和达到固定资产标准的设备、工具器具的投资以及有关的摊入费用和属于增加固定资产价值的其他建设费用。

固定资产交付使用率 指报告期内新增固定资产与同期完成投资额的比率。它反映各个时期固定资产动用速度，衡量建设过程中投资效果的一个综合性指标。

管理物业项目个数 指报告期末物业管理企业已签订《物业管理委托合同》并实施管理的物业项目个数。

管理物业占地面积 指报告期末物业管理企业正在进行管理的物业所占用的全部土地面积。其中：

(1)管理房屋建筑占地： 指报告期末物业管理企业在管的全部房屋所占用的土地面积。包括：住宅、办公楼、商业营业用房等及相配套的公建房屋所占用的土地面积。

(2)管理绿化用地： 指报告期末在管理物业项目内由物业公司管理的公共绿地。

管理房屋面积 指报告期末物业管理企业正在进行管理的《物业项目的物业管理委托合同》上载明的营业面积。

Explanatory Notes on Main Statistical Indicators

Total Investment in Fixed Assets refers to the volume of activities in construction and purchases of fixed assets in monetary terms. It is a comprehensive indicator which shows the size, pace, proportional relations and use orientation of the investment in fixed assets.

Investment in fixed assets statistics is classified into total investment in fixed assets in the whole city and investment in fixed assets in Tianjin. The total investment in fixed assets in the whole city includes, the investment by the state-owned units, urban & rural collective units, other ownership units, as well as investment by individuals. Investment in fixed asset in Tianjin includes, the investment by the state-owned units, urban collective units and other ownership units, i.e. the total investment in fixed assets in the whole city deducted the investment by rural collective units and individuals. According to China's current planning management system, the investment in fixed assets in the whole city is classified into the following four parts investment in capital construction, investment in innovation, investment in real estate development and other investment in fixed assets.

Investment in Capital Construction refers to the new construction projects or extension projects and the related work of the enterprises, institutions or administrative units mainly for the purpose of expanding production capacity or improving project efficiency covering only projects each with a total investment of 500,000 yuan and over. Investment of capital construction shows form of currency. It is a comprehensive indicator which shows the size, pace, proportional relations of the investment in fixed assets.

Investment in Innovation refers to the renewal of fixed assets and technological innovation of the original facilities by the enterprises and institutions using basic depreciation funds, appropriate funds from state, technological innovation loans from domestic and abroad, as well as the corresponding supplementary projects and the related work (excluding major overhaul and maintenance projects). For the purposes of technological advancement, improvement in product quality, enlarging variety of products, promoting new generation of products, reducing production consumption and cost, promoting comprehensive utilization of resources, strengthening treatment of pollution, through application of new technologies and techniques, use of new equipment and new materials, construction of new workshops for improving existing production capacity rather than increasing production capacity is also considered as reconstruction. Covering only projects each with a total investment of 500,000 yuan and over, investment in innovation shows form of currency.

Other Investment in Fixed Assets refers to the construction and purchases of fixed assets not listed in the investment in capital construction, investment in innovation and investment in real estate development. It includes following projects of the state - owned units with the total investment of 500,000 yuan and over. It includes (a) projects of oilfields maintenance and exploitation with the oilfields maintenance funds and petroleum development funds, (b) opening and extending projects with the maintenance funds in coal, ore and other mining enterprises and logging enterprises, (c) project of reconstruction of the original highways and bridges with the highway maintenance funds in the department of communication, (d) projects of construction of warehouses with the funds of simple construction in the commercial department, (e) the investment in fixed assets by urban collective units and other type of economical enterprises, institutions units with the total investment of 500,000 yuan and over.

Investment in Real Estate Development refers to the investment by the real estate development companies, commercial buildings construction companies and other real estate development units of various types of ownership in the construction of house buildings. It is finished work in monetary terms.

Commercial Houses refer to residential buildings and other commercial houses of commercial houses development companies that are qualified for sale, excluding non - commercial houses. (1) Investment commercial houses include (a) making a requisition of land and pull down a houses in development area, (b) funds of residential buildings construction and installation, (c) municipal administration engineering system in red line of development area, (d) residential building complementary service facilities in development area. (2) Investment in construction of other commercial houses include funds of factory buildings, warehouses and other commercial houses.

Investment in Fixed Assets by Structure :

Construction Project refers to the construction of various houses and buildings, it also is called the work volume of construction, including construction of various houses, equipment foundations and industrial kilns and stoves, preparation works for project construction, and clearing up works post project construction, geological examination, land - leveling, water, electricity, gas road - cleaning, planting trees, drilling of mines, pavement of railways and roads, highway, bridge, construction of projects of water conservancy, construction of underground air - raid shelters and construction of other special projects.

Installation Project refers to the installation of various kinds of equipment and instruments (work volume of installation) . The value of equipment installed is excluded in the value of installation projects. Including various kinds of equipment, i.e. production, power - driven, lifting, transport, transmission, medical experiment etc. and working table, stepladder railing, putting up of pipes, keep warm, paint, rot - proofing, try operation (excluding put in material try operation).

Purchase of Equipment and Instruments refers to the total value of equipment, tools, and vessels purchased or self - produced which come up to standards for fixed assets. Equipment, tools and vessels purchased or self- produced for new workshops by newly established or expanded units are categorized as "purchase of equipment and instruments" no matter whether they come up to the standards for fixed assets or not.

Other Expenses refers to investment excluded in above items, which consist of construction and installation, purchase of equipment and instruments, purchase of commercial buildings, including purchase of animals by agricultural and forestry units, planting and operating of various economic forest, purchase of office and home furniture, purchase of instruments and vessels, compensation for the loss of land and young crops, subsidies for moving, administration expenses of construction units, and expenses on research and testing, geological prospecting and designing, joint trial running, and the other purchase introduction of technology and imports of equipment, expenses on training of staff and workers, transportation of construction machines, loss of discarded projects, powers upply station, mine harbor maintenance.

Investment in Fixed Assets by Type of Construction refers to reflect use direction of investment in fixed assets, researching various proportions and analyzing result of investment. It includes:

New Construction refers to newly constructed units. In the case, in which the value of the original fixed assets is quite small, and the value of newly added fixed assets exceeds the original ones by three times, the expansion construction is considered as new construction.

Expansion Construction refers to construction of new major production workshop or independent production line within a factory or in other locations, or construction of a branch factory so as to increase the production capacity of the original products. Newly constructed business houses in institutions and administrative organizations are also classified as expansion.

Reconstruction refers to technical innovation and transformation of the existing equipment and technical conditions undertaken by enterprises and institutions for the purposes of technological advancement, (including accessory facilities for production or for living and welfare purposes). The construction of new workshops for improving existing production capacity rather than increasing production capacity is also considered as reconstruction.

Newly Increased Fixed Assets refers to the newly increased value of fixed assets through investment, including the value of projects completed and put into production, the value of equipment, tools, and vessels considered as fixed assets, as well as the relevant expenses as investmentin fixed assets and other construction expansion of increased the volume in fixed assets.

Rate of Projects of Fixed Assets Completed and Put into Operation refers to the ratio of the newly increased fixed assets to the total investment made in the same period. This is a comprehensive indicator, reflecting the speed of the employment of fixed assets and the investment efficiency.

Number of Property Management Projects refers to the number of property management projects which have been signed "property management entrusting contract" and managed by the end of reference period.

Coverage Areas of Property Management refer to the land areas which are managed by property management enterprises by the end of reference period.

(**a**) **Floor Space** refer to land areas of housing which are managed by property management enterprises by the end of reference period, including the land areas of residential buildings, office buildings, commercial houses and those relative housing.

(**b**) **Green Coverage Areas** refer to the public green areas which are managed by property management enterprises by the end of reference period.

Floor Space of Houses Managed refer to the business areas which are managed according to "property management entrusting contract" by property management enterprises by the end of reference period.

第4篇 CHAPTER 4

价格指数

PRICE INDICES

4-1 改革开放以来城市物价总指数
URBAN GENERAL PRICE INDICES SINCE REFORM AND OPENING UP

(1978-2003)

年份 Year	上年=100 Preceding Year=100		1978=100		1990=100	
	商品零售价格指数 Retail Price Index	居民消费价格指数 Consumer Price Index	商品零售价格指数 Retail Price Index	居民消费价格指数 Consumer Price Index	商品零售价格指数 Retail Price Index	居民消费价格指数 Consumer Price Index
1978	100.0	100.0	100.0	100.0		
1979	101.1	101.0	101.1	101.0		
1980	105.5	105.1	106.7	106.2		
1981	101.5	101.3	108.3	107.5		
1982	100.5	100.5	108.8	108.1		
1983	100.5	100.5	109.3	108.6		
1984	101.8	101.8	111.3	110.6		
1985	113.9	113.1	126.8	125.0		
1986	107.2	106.8	135.9	133.6		
1987	106.9	106.8	145.3	142.6		
1988	117.7	116.9	171.0	166.7		
1989	115.1	114.7	196.8	191.2		
1990	102.7	103.0	202.1	197.0	100.0	100.0
1991	108.0	110.2	218.3	217.1	108.0	110.2
1992	109.4	111.4	238.8	241.8	118.2	122.8
1993	114.3	117.6	273.0	284.4	135.0	144.4
1994	115.6	124.0	315.6	352.6	156.1	179.0
1995	110.6	115.3	349.0	406.6	172.7	206.4
1996	105.1	109.0	366.8	443.2	181.5	225.0
1997	100.7	103.1	369.4	456.9	182.7	232.0
1998	96.6	99.5	356.8	454.6	176.5	230.8
1999	97.5	98.9	347.9	449.6	172.1	228.3
2000	98.6	99.6	343.1	447.8	169.7	227.3
2001	98.6	101.2	338.2	453.2	167.3	230.1
2002	97.4	99.6	329.5	451.4	163.0	229.2
2003	97.4	101.0	320.9	455.9	158.7	231.4

4-2 城市居民消费价格分类指数
(上年=100)

URBAN CONSUMER PRICE INDICES BY CATEGORY

(Preceding Year=100)

项目	Item	2002	2003
居民消费价格总指数	**General Consumer Price Index**	**99.6**	**101.0**
#服务项目价格指数	Services	104.4	107.8
1.食品	Food	99.3	103.3
粮食	Grain	100.0	102.1
淀粉及薯类	Starches and Tubers	100.8	94.6
干豆类及豆制品	Bean and Related Products	97.4	105.5

4－2 续表 Continued

项 目	Item	2002	2003
油脂类	Oil or Fat	98.0	111.5
肉禽及其制品	Meat, Poultry and Related Products	98.8	102.2
蛋 类	Eggs	98.5	102.0
水产品	Aquatic Products	105.9	111.0
菜 类	Vegetables	94.6	121.6
调味品	Flavoring	97.5	104.2
糖	Sugar	102.4	99.6
茶及饮料	Tea and Drink	98.4	99.2
干鲜瓜果	Dried and Fresh Melons and Fruits	99.9	99.8
糕点饼干面包	Pasty, Biscuit and Bread	97.2	100.4
奶及奶制品	Milk and Related Products	93.2	95.7
在外用膳食品	Catering Trade	99.6	100.0
其他食品及食品加工服务	Other Food and Cooking Services	99.7	97.3
2.烟酒及用品	Tobacco, Liquor and Related Goods	100.2	98.8
烟 草	Tobacco	99.4	98.4
酒	Liquor	101.3	99.1
吸烟饮酒用品	Related Goods	100.0	98.9
3.衣 着	Clothing	91.3	88.1
服 装	Garments	91.1	87.6
衣着材料	Clothing Materials	99.2	100.2
鞋袜帽	Shoes, Socks and Hats	89.0	86.0
衣着加工服务	Processing Services	100.0	100.0
4.家庭设备用品及维修服务	Household Appliances, Articles and Repair Services	96.0	96.5
耐用消费品	Durable Consumer Goods	95.4	95.9
室内装饰品	Indoors Decorations	98.2	100.6
床上用品	Bed Articles	99.5	90.7
家庭日用杂品	Daily Use Household Articles	93.4	95.0
家庭服务及加工维修服务	Household Services and Repair Services	100.1	103.0
5.医疗保健和个人用品	Medical, Health Care and Individual Goods	102.1	94.0
医疗保健	Medicine and Medical Services	102.6	92.1
个人用品及服务	Individual Goods and Services	100.4	100.0
6.交通和通讯	Transportation and Telecommunications	97.9	97.0
交 通	Transportations	96.2	99.2
通 信	Telecommunications	99.6	95.3
7.娱乐教育文化用品及服务	Recreational, Educational & Cultural Artcles and Services	102.7	110.7
文娱用耐用消费品及服务	Durable Consumer Goods and Services for Recreational Use	90.1	93.2
教 育	Education	109.4	118.5
文化娱乐用品	Recreation and Culture Articles	104.4	121.4
旅游及外出	Tourism	92.4	83.5
8.居 住	Residence	103.7	101.7
建房及装修材料	Building and Decoration Materials	98.7	98.8
租 房	Rent	109.6	104.6
自有住房	Individual Housing	95.0	99.0
水、电、燃料	Water, Electricity and Fuel	106.6	102.7

4-3 城市商品零售价格分类指数

(上年=100)

URBAN RETAIL PRICE INDICES BY CATEGORY

(Preceding Year=100)

项 目	Item	2001	2002
商品零售价格总指数	**General Retail Price Index**	**98.6**	**97.4**
1.食 品	Food	101.0	98.0
粮 食	Grain	101.4	96.7
油脂类	Oil or Fat	86.2	101.6
肉禽蛋	Meat, Poultry and Eggs	105.5	99.2
水产品	Aquatic Products	98.1	89.6
鲜 菜	Fresh Vegetables	99.9	97.2
干 菜	Dried Vegetables	98.2	96.0
鲜 果	Fresh Fruits	110.3	100.8
干 果	Dried Fruits	100.1	97.9
其他食品	Other Food	101.3	97.9
调味品	Flavoring	101.9	99.0
食 糖	Sugar	115.7	98.9
糖 果	Sweets	100.3	100.4
糕 点	Pastry	99.0	96.6
奶及奶制品	Milk and Related Products	99.0	94.8
罐 头	Tined	103.8	99.4
饮食业	Catering Trade	100.1	100.3
2.饮料烟酒	Beverages, Tobacco and Liquor	98.6	100.1
饮 料	Beverages	99.1	99.3
烟 酒	Tobacco and Liquor	98.5	100.4
3.服装鞋帽	Garments, Shoes and Hats	98.8	96.5
服 装	Garments	97.5	96.1
鞋	Shoes	101.4	97.8
其他衣着	Other Clothing	100.2	95.6
4.纺织品	Textiles	98.2	97.6
棉 布	Cotton Cloth	99.3	99.0
棉花化纤混纺	Mixed Cloth	90.1	100.0
化纤布	Chemical Fiber Cloth	96.9	91.9
呢 绒	Wool Fabric	99.6	91.3
绸 缎	Silk and Satins	97.6	105.2
其他纺织品	Other Textiles	100.5	100.6
5.中西药品	Traditional Chinese and Western Medicines	100.1	98.3
中 药	Traditional Chinese Medicine	101.2	98.0
西 药	Western Medicine	99.2	97.8
医疗用品	Medical Articles	100.0	100.7
6.化妆品	Cosmetics	100.6	98.8
7.书报杂志	Books, Newspapers and Magazines	96.8	114.5
8.文化体育用品	Cultural and Sports Goods	99.0	97.8
文化用品	Culture Articles	99.0	97.3
体育用品	Sports Articles	99.1	100.1
9.日用品	Articles for Daily Use	98.0	96.9
一般日用品	Ordinary Articles for Daily Use	98.0	98.8
家 具	Furniture	99.9	101.0
日用杂品	Sundry Articles	96.4	90.4
10.家用电器	Household Appliances	94.4	91.1
11.首 饰	Jewelry	80.7	109.2
12.燃 料	Fuels	107.6	111.5
13.建筑装璜材料	Building Decoration Materials	100.5	100.9
14.机电产品	Mechanical and Electrical Products	94.5	89.1

4－4 城市商品零售价格分类指数(2003年)

(上年＝100)

URBAN RETAIL PRICE INDICES BY CATEGORY,2003

(Preceding Year＝100)

项　目　　Item	2003	项　目　　Item	2003
商品零售价格总指数		服　装	
General Retail Price Index	**97.4**	Garments	87.8
1.食　品		鞋袜帽	
Food	103.7	Shoes,Socks and Hats	86.1
粮　食		其　他	
Grain	102.1	Others	91.0
淀粉及薯类		4.纺织品	
Starches and Tubers	94.6	Textiles	95.3
干豆类及豆制品		衣着材料	
Bean and Related Product	105.5	Clothing Materials	100.2
油脂类		床上用品	
Oil or Fat	111.5	Bed Articles	90.6
肉禽及其制品		5.家用电器及音像器材	
Meat,Poultry and Related Products	102.0	Household Appliances and Stereo Sets & Camera Facilities	90.9
蛋　类		家庭设备	
Eggs	102.1	Hosehold Facilities	94.3
水产品		文娱用耐用消费品	
Aquatic Products	111.0	Durable Consumer Goods for Recreational Use	84.2
菜　类		音像器材类	
Vegetables	123.7	Stereo Sets & Camera Facilities	94.1
调味品		6.文化办公用品	
Flavoring	104.4	Culture and Office Articles	98.1
糖		7.日用品	
Sugar	99.5	Articles for Daily Use	96.8
干鲜瓜果		日用百货	
Dried and Fresh Melons and Fruits	100.3	General Merchandise for Daily Use	96.4
糕点饼干面包		日用杂品	
Pasty,Biscuit and Bread	100.4	Sundry Articles	99.3
奶及奶制品		洗涤用品	
Milk and Related Products	95.7	Washing Articles	101.1
在外用膳食品		其它日用品	
Catering Trade	100.0	Other Articles for Daily Use	94.2
其它食品		8.体育娱乐用品	
Other Food	97.2	Sport and Recreation Articles	99.2
2.饮料烟酒		体育用品	
Beverages,Tobacco and Liquor	98.8	Sport Article	98.5
茶及饮料		娱乐用品	
Tea and Beverages	99.1	Recreation Articles	99.6
烟　草		9.交通、通信用品	
Tobacco	98.4	Transportation and Telecommunications Articles	90.0
酒		交通运输机械	
Liquor	99.1	Transportation Machine	96.2
3.服装鞋帽		通讯器材类	
Garments,Shoes and Hats	87.4	Telecommunications Facilities	65.3

注:根据国家统计制度的变化,本表为重新调整后的分类指数。
Note: According to the change of national statistics institution,the category of retail price indices has been adjusted.

4-4 续表 Continued

项 目 Item	2003	项 目 Item	2003
10.家 具		教材及参考书	
Furniture	99.2	Teaching Materials and Reference Books	96.9
11.化妆品		书报杂志	
Cosmetics	99.2	Books,Newspapers and Magazines	102.0
12.金银珠宝		电子音像制品	
Gold and Silver Jewelry	115.5	Electronics Music and Picture Goods	99.9
13.中西药品及医疗保健用品		15.燃 料	
Traditional Chinese & Western Medicine and Medical,Health Care Goods	90.1	Fuels	109.9
医疗器具及用品		煤炭及制品类	
Medical Facilities and Goods	103.1	Coal and Related Products	97.1
中药材及中成药		石油及制品类	
Traditional Chinese Medicine Material and Medicine	96.3	Petroleum and Related Products	110.7
西 药		16.建筑材料及五金电料	
Western Medicine	85.2	Construction Materials and Hardware Materials	99.1
保健器具及用品		建筑装璜材料	
Health Care Facilities and Goods	94.7	Construction and Decoration Materials	98.7
14.书报杂志及电子出版物		五金电料类	
Books,Newspapers and Magazines,Electronics Publications	99.5	Hardware Materials	100.0

4-5 居民货币购买力指数

INDICES OF MONETARY PURCHASING POWER OF RESIDENTS

(1991-2003)

年 份 Year	上年=100 Preceding Year=100	1990=100
1991	90.7	90.7
1992	89.8	81.4
1993	85.0	69.3
1994	80.6	55.9
1995	86.7	48.4
1996	91.7	44.4
1997	97.0	43.1
1998	100.5	43.3
1999	101.1	43.8
2000	100.4	44.0
2001	98.8	43.5
2002	100.4	43.6
2003	99.0	43.2

4－6 固定资产投资价格指数

（上年＝100）

PRICE INDICES OF INVESTMENT IN FIXED ASSETS

（Preceding Year＝100）

（1999－2003）

项 目 Item	1999	2000	2001	2002	2003
投资价格总指数 General Price Index of Investment	**99.2**	**99.9**	**99.7**	**99.5**	**102.6**
建筑安装、装饰工程 Building Installation	100.2	100.7	100.1	100.7	104.9
#主要建筑材料费用 Experse of Major Construction Materials	99.6	100.9	99.8	100.3	106.0
设备工器具购置 Purchase of Equipment, Tools and Instruments	96.5	97.8	98.5	94.9	97.8
其他费用 Others	99.8	100.1	100.1	100.2	100.4

4－7 工业品出厂价格指数（上年＝100）

EX－FACTORY PRICE INDICES OF INDUSTRIAL PRODUCTS

（Preceding Year＝100）

（1999－2003）

项 目 Item	1999	2000	2001	2002	2003
工业品出厂价格总指数 General Industrial Producer Price Index	**96.4**	**102.8**	**95.9**	**95.9**	**102.5**
轻工业 Light Industry	96.3	98.8	97.8	97.9	99.6
以农产品为原料 Using Farm Products as Raw Materials	96.5	99.2	97.8	98.4	103.6
以非农产品为原料 Using Non－farm Products as Raw Materials	96.1	98.2	97.9	97.3	98.1
重工业 Heavy Industry	96.4	104.9	94.8	94.5	105.1
采掘业 Mining and Quarrying Industry	118.4	161.1	89.3	100.2	124.7
原料工业 Raw Materials Industry	98.4	116.8	99.7	98.7	113.5
加工工业 Processing Industry	92.9	92.5	93.1	90.7	97.5
生产资料 Production Goods	97.0	105.1	95.0	95.5	103.3
采掘业 Mining and Quarrying Industry	118.0	159.9	89.5	100.3	124.7
原料工业 Raw Materials Industry	98.4	115.6	99.5	98.5	113.0
加工工业 Processing Industry	93.5	92.8	93.3	92.8	98.2
生活资料 Consumer Goods	95.2	98.1	97.6	95.7	100.0
食 品 Food	97.8	99.0	96.6	100.2	103.1
衣 着 Clothing	92.7	99.2	100.1	99.2	101.2
一般日用品 Daily Use Articles·	100.5	99.4	98.5	98.6	99.9
耐用消费品 Durable Consumer Goods	92.3	96.1	97.1	89.7	96.4

4－8　按新行业分工业品出厂价格指数(2003年)

(上年＝100)

EX－FACTORY PRICE INDICES OF INDUSTRIAL PRODUCTS BY NEW SECTOR,2003

(Preceding Year＝100)

行　业　Sector	2003
煤炭开采和洗选业 Coal Mining and Dressing	120.6
石油和天然气开采业 Petroleum and Natural Gas Extraction	126.1
非金属矿采选业 Nonmetal Minerals Mining and Dressing	98.8
农副食品加工业 Agricultural Products and Byproducts Processing	110.7
食品制造业 Food Manufacturing	100.2
饮料制造业 Beverage Manufacturing	99.9
烟草制品业 Tobacco Processing	100.0
纺织业 Textile Industry	107.9
纺织服装、鞋、帽制造业 Textile Garments,Shoes,Caps Manufacturing	100.7
皮革、毛皮、羽毛(绒)及其制品业 Leather, Furs, Down and Related Products	99.4
木材加工及木、竹、藤、棕、草制品业 Timber Processing,Bamboo, Cane,Palm Fiber and Straw Products	99.8
家具制造业 Furniture Manufacturing	99.4
造纸及纸制品业 Papermaking and Paper Products	96.8
印刷业和记录媒介的复制 Printing and Record Medium Reproduction	97.2
文教体育用品制造业 Cultural, Educational and Sports Goods	98.1
石油加工、炼焦及核燃料加工业 Petroleum Processing,Coking and Nuclear Fuel Processing	115.6
化学原料及化学制品制造业 Chemical Raw Materials and Chemical Products	108.4
医药制造业 Medical and Pharmaceutical Products	98.0
化学纤维制造业 Chemical Fiber	114.4
橡胶制品业 Rubber Products	102.5
塑料制品业 Plastic Products	99.7
非金属矿物制品业 Nonmetal Mineral Products	96.6
黑色金属冶炼及压延加工业 Smelting and Pressing of Ferrous Metals	122.6
有色金属冶炼及压延加工业 Smelting and Pressing of Nonferrous Metals	102.8
金属制品业 Metal Products	103.4
通用设备制造业 General Purpose Equipment Manufacturing	99.0
专用设备制造业 Special Purpose Equipment Manufacturing	98.2
交通运输设备制造业 Transport Equipment Manufacturing	93.1
电气机械及器材制造业 Electric Equipment and Machinery	98.3
通信设备、计算机及其他电子设备制造业 Telecommunications Equipment,Computer and Other Electronic Equipment Manufacturing	86.1
仪器仪表及文化、办公用机械制造业 Instruments,Meters,Cultural and Office Machinery	96.1
工艺品及其他制造业 Handiwork and Other Manufacturing	105.1
电力、热力的生产和供应业 Production and Supply of Electric Power and Heat Energy	101.2
煤气生产和供应业 Production and Supply of Gas	105.7
水的生产和供应业 Production and Supply of Tap Water	116.5

注：本表行业分类为国标GB/T4754－2002标准。
Note:Sector listed in this table is classified by the standard of GB/T4754－2002.

4－9　工业主要原材料、燃料及动力购进价格指数

（上年＝100）

MAIN RAW MATERIALS,FUEL AND MOTIVE POWER PURCHASING PRICE INDEX OF INDUSTRY

(Preceding Year＝100)

(1999－2003)

项　目　Item	1999	2000	2001	2002	2003
原材料燃料动力购进价格总指数 Raw Materials Fuel and Motive Power Purchasing Price Index	**96.3**	**104.5**	**98.8**	**95.9**	**108.7**
燃料、动力类 Fuels and Energy	105.5	123.8	98.4	102.0	113.1
黑色金属材料类 Ferrous Metals	94.2	101.8	100.8	98.4	119.6
有色金属材料及电线类 Non ferrous Metals	97.1	108.6	95.3	96.8	107.8
化工原料类 Chemical Raw Materials	94.1	110.7	98.9	94.5	111.3
木材及纸浆类 Wood and Paper Pulps	100.0	100.7	101.1	102.9	100.9
建筑材料及非金属矿类 Construction Materials	100.1	103.6	97.2	98.3	106.9
其他工业原材料及半成品类 Other Industrial Raw Materials and Semi－products	96.3	97.6	97.7	95.1	95.9
农副产品类 Farm and Sideline Products	86.7	98.8	100.5	92.7	122.5
纺织原料类 Textile Raw Materials	95.6	99.5	99.5	89.3	106.2

4－10　房地产价格指数

（上年＝100）

PRICE INDEX OF REAL ESTATE

(Preceding Year＝100)

(1999－2003)

项　目　Item	1999	2000	2001	2002	2003
房屋销售价格指数 Price Index of Real Estate Sales	**100.0**	**100.0**	**101.2**	**101.6**	**104.1**
商品房 Commodity Housing	99.8	99.6	101.9	101.9	104.0
经济适用房 Economic Housing	100.4	101.0	103.9	103.9	106.6
普通住宅 Common Residence	99.7	99.2	101.7	101.1	103.2
豪华住宅 Luxurious Residence	93.8	96.6	98.3	100.9	100.6
公房交易 Transaction of Public Residence	100.5	102.1	100.7	100.0	100.0
私有住房 Private Housing	100.4	99.8	97.0	99.6	105.0
房屋租赁价格指数 Price Index of Real Estate Rent	**99.0**	**100.1**	**110.1**	**106.0**	**100.9**
住　宅 Residence	100.0	100.0	120.9	113.8	107.9
办公用房 Office	99.4	96.0	95.6	95.2	96.1
商业用房 Commercial Housing	100.5	94.6	100.6	102.9	99.9
厂房仓库 Workshop and Storehouse	104.3	112.6	100.1	96.1	90.3
土地交易价格指数 Price Index of Land Transaction	**101.3**	**100.5**	**101.6**	**102.8**	**103.0**

主要统计指标解释

城市商品零售价格指数 是工业、商业、餐饮业和其他零售企业向城市居民、机关团体出售生活消费品和办公用品的价格水平变动趋势和变动程度的相对数。其目的在于掌握零售商品价格的变动趋势，为国家宏观调控和国民经济核算提供参考依据。

商品零售价格的调查范围涉及到各种类型的工业、商业、餐饮业和其他行业的零售商品以及农民对非农业居民出售商品的价格。包括食品、饮料烟酒、服装鞋帽、纺织品、家用电器及音像器材、文化办公用品、日用品、体育娱乐用品、交通通信用品、家具、化妆品、金银珠宝、中西药品及医疗保健用品、书报杂志及电子出版物、燃料、建筑材料及五金电料等16个大类。

城市居民消费价格指数 是反映城市居民购买的消费品及服务价格水平的变动趋势和变动程度的相对数。它是宏观经济分析和决策、价格总水平监测和调控以及国民经济核算的重要指标。其按年度计算的变动率通常被用来作为反映通货膨胀(或紧缩)程度的指标。

城市居民消费价格的调查范围包括城市居民购买并用于日常生活消费的商品和服务项目价格。按用途划分为8个大类，包括食品、烟酒及用品、衣着、家庭设备用品及维修服务费、医疗保健及个人用品、交通和通信、娱乐教育文化用品及服务、居住等。

固定资产投资价格指数 是反映固定资产投资额价格变动趋势和程度的相对数。固定资产投资额是由建筑安装工程投资完成额、设备、工器具购置投资完成额和其他费用投资完成额三部分组成的。编制固定资产投资价格指数首先分别编制上述三部分投资的价格指数，然后采用加权算术平均法求出固定资产投资价格总指数。编制固定资产投资价格指数可以准确地反映固定资产投资中涉及的各类商品和取费项目价格变动趋势和变动幅度，消除按现价计算的固定资产投资指标中的价格变动因素，真实地反映固定资产投资的规模、速度、结构和效益，为国家科学地制定、检查固定资产投资计划并提高宏观调控水平，为完善国民经济核算体系提供科学的、可靠的依据。

工业品出厂价格指数 是反映全部工业产品出厂价格总水平的变动趋势和程度的相对数，包括工业企业售给本企业以外所有单位的各种产品和直接售给居民用于生活消费的产品。通过工业品出厂价格指数能观察出厂价格变动对工业总产值的影响。

工业原材料、燃料及动力购进价格指数 是反映全部工业原材料、燃料、动力购进价格水平的变动趋势和程度的相对数。它是依据我市部分重点企业中主要原材料、燃料、动力购进价格的定期调查资料，按加权算术平均公式计算的。

房地产价格指数 是反映全部房地产价格总水平的变动趋势和程度的相对数。包括土地交易价格指数、房地产销售价格指数、房地产租赁价格指数。

土地交易价格指数 是指房地产开发商或其他建设单位在进行商品房、生产和商业用房及其他生产经营用地开发前为取得土地使用权而实际支付的价格的变动趋势和程度的相对数。

房地产销售价格指数 是指房地产销售价格总水平变动趋势和程度的相对数。

房地产租赁价格指数 是指房地产租赁价格总水平变动趋势和程度的相对数。

Explanatory Notes on Main Statistical Indicators

Urban Retail Price Index reflects the trend and degree of changes in retail prices of living consumer goods and office equipment which are sold to residents and organizations by retail enterprises. It can be used to know about the change tendency of the price of retailed goods, provides reliable data for government decision making and further improving the current national accounting system.

Its survey field covers the retail price of industry, commerce, catering trade and other sectors and prices of goods sold to non - agricultural population by farmers. Now it is classified into 16 categories by food, beverages, tobacco and liquor, garments, shoes and hats, textiles, household appliances, stereo sets & camera facilities, cultural and office goods, articles for daily use, sports and recreational goods, transport and communications goods, furniture, cosmetics, jewelry, traditional Chinese and western medicines, newspapers, magazines and electronics publications, fuels, building decoration materials, hardware materials.

Urban Consumer Price Index reflects the trend and degree of changes in prices of consumer goods and services purchased by urban households. It is a indicator used for government decision making, price monitoring & controlling and improving the current national accounting system. The annual price index is used tp reflect the degree of inflation and deflation.

Its survey field covers the prices of goods and services purchased by urban households and used for living. It is classified into 8 categories by food, tobacco and use articles, clothing, household facilities and articles, repair services, medicine and medical articles, means of transportation and communication, recreation, education and culture articles, residence, services.

Price Index of Investment in Fixed Assets reflects the trend and degree of changes in prices of investment in fixed assets. The investment in fixed assets consists of three components, namely the investment in construction and installation, the investment in purchases of equipment and instrument, and the investment in other items. Price index of investment in fixed assets is calculated as the weighted arithmetic mean of the price indices of the three components of investment in fixed assets. Removing the factor of price change in the aggregates of investment at current prices, this indicator shows the changes in the prices of commodities and fees involved in the investment of fixed assets, and can be used to observe the actual size, growth, structure, and efficiency of investment in fixed assets and provides reliable and scientific data for government planning, management, decision making, and further improving the current national accounting system.

Ex - factory Price Index of Industrial Products reflects the trend and degree of changes in general ex - factory prices of all industrial products, including sales of industrial products by an industrial enterprise to all units outside the enterprise, as well as sales of consumer goods to residents. It can be used to analyze the impact of ex - factory prices on gross industrial output value.

Purchase Price of Industrial Raw Materials, Fuel and Power reflects the trend and degree changes in the general purchase price of all industrial raw materials, fuel and power. It is calculated as the weighted arithmetic mean in order to purchase price of industrial raw materials, fuel and power of part of key enterprises periodical surveys.

Price Indices of Real Estate reflect the trend and degree changes in real estate price, including price index of land transaction, price index of real estate sales, price index of real estate leasing.

Price Index of Land Transaction reflects the trend and degree changes in land transaction price which paid actually by developing enterprises or construction units to get land use rights before development of commodity buildings.

Price Index of Real Estate Sales reflects the trend and degree changes in real estate sales.

Price Index of Real Estate Leasing reflects the trend and degree changes in real estate leasing.

第5篇 CHAPTER 5

人民生活

PEOPLE'S LIFE

5－1 城乡居民物质文化生活水平提高情况

IMPROVEMENT IN URBAN AND RURAL RESIDENTS' MATERIAL AND CULTURAL LIFE

指 标	Item	1999	2000	2001	2002	2003
一、居民收入支出(元)	**Income and Expenditure of Urban and Rural Residents(yuan)**					
单位从业人员年人均劳动报酬	Per Capita Annual Remuneration of Persons Employed in Units	11 046	12 414	14 242	16 223	18 511
城市居民人均可支配收入	Per Capita Annual Disposable Income	7 650	8 141	8 959	9 338	10 313
城市居民人均消费性支出	Per Capita Annual Expenditures for Consumption	5 852	6 121	6 987	7 192	7 868
农民人均年纯收入	Per Capita Annual Net Income of Farmer	4 055	4 370	4 825	5 315	5 861
农民人均年生活消费支出	Per Capita Annual Living Expenditures of Farmer	2 334	2 393	2 618	2 778	3 015
二、居民年平均消费水平(元)	**Average Annual Consumption level of Residents(yuan)**					
全市居民	All Residents	5 551	6 117	6 802	7 162	7 836
农村居民	Rural Residents	3 088	3 414	3 736	3 974	4 321
城镇居民	Urban Residents	7 346	8 056	8 979	9 403	10 266
三、储 蓄(元)	**Savings(yuan)**					
城乡居民人均年末储蓄余额	Per Capita Saving Deposit Balance of Urban and Rural Residents	12 417	12 855	14 059	16 173	19 712
四、住 房(平方米)	**Floor Space of Residential Buildings(sq.m)**					
城市人均住宅使用面积	Per Capita Using Floor Space of Urban Residents	13.1	13.9	15.9	16.7	17.5
农村人均住房面积	Per Capita Living Floor Space of Rural Residents	22.9	23.6	23.9	24.3	24.4
五、交通和通信	**Traffic and Telecommunications**					
城市每万人拥有公共交通车辆(标台)	Number of Public Transportations Vehicles Per 10 000 Persons in City(standard vehicles)	9.8	10.9	8.9	9.3	9.4
城市每万人拥有铺装道路长度(公里)	Length of Paved Roads Per 10 000 Persons In City(km)	7.37	7.41	6.40	6.57	6.55
每人每年函件交寄(件)	Per Capita Annual Letters Delivered(piece)	8.9	14.3	18.7	22.0	23.9
全市每百人拥有电话机(含移动)(部)	Telephones Owned Per 100 Persons (Include Mobile)(sets)	36.2	46.6	56.0	65.4	82.3
六、电、水、燃气、供热	**Electricity,Water,Gas and Heating**					
全市人均生活用电量(千瓦小时)	Per Capita Electric Consumption for Living of All Residents(kwh)	265	271	286	320	344
城市人均生活用水量(吨)	Per Capita Water Consumption for Living of Urban Households(ton)	54	48	53	48.5	47.8
城市用气普及率(%)	Popularization Rate of Urban Households in Gas Use(%)	95.0	96.8	94.8	95.1	97.1
城市住宅集中供热面积(万平方米)	Heating Area of Urbon Residential Buildings(10 000 sq.m)	3 475	4 558	6 591	7 381	8 118

5－1续表 Continued

指 标	Item	1999	2000	2001	2002	2003
七、平均每人消费品零售总额(元)	**Per Capita Value of Retail Sales of Consumer Goods(yuan)**	**7 241**	**8 085**	**9 121**	**10 271**	**11 642**
#食品类	Food	3 012	3 304	3 662	4 077	4 289
衣着类	Clothing	1 238	1 342	1 525	1 738	2 018
用品类	Articles For Use	2 916	3 364	3 800	4 290	5 149
八、文 化	**Culture**					
每百户城市居民家庭拥有(台)	Number of Sets Per 100 Urban Households(set)					
彩色电视机	Color TV Sets	131	132	134	135	135
家用电脑	Micro－Computer	11	16	21	26	35
每百户农村居民家庭拥有(台)	Possession Per 100 Rural Households(set)					
彩色电视机	Color TV Sets	98	98	103	105	110
家用电脑	Micro－Computers		2	3	5	7
平均每人每年有图书(册)	Per Capita Number of Books Per Year(copy)	9.5	6.5	6.8	7.5	7.3
平均每百人每天有报纸(份)	Number of Newspapers Per 100 Persons Per Day(copy)	17.0	18.0	21.6	24.1	24.5
九、教 育	**Education**					
平均每万人口中有各级学校在校学生(人)	Number of Students Enrollment Per 10 000 Population(person)	1 786	1 779	1 759	1 764	1 769
#大学生	University Students	99.4	129	169	215	266
学龄儿童入学率(%)	Enrollment Ratio of School－Age Children(%)	99.9	100.0	100.0	100.0	100.0
十、卫 生	**Public Health**					
每万人拥有医院、卫生院床位(张)	Number of Hospital Beds Per 10 000 Persons(bed)	42.5	42.6	44.2	42.4	41.3
每万人拥有医生(人)	Number of Doctors Per 10 000 Persons (person)	33.3	33.0	32.0	26.0	24.7
十一、赡养人口(人)	**Persons Supported by Others(person)**					
城镇每一就业者赡养人口	Number of Persons Supported by Each Urban Employment	0.38	0.46	0.46	0.46	0.46
农村每一劳动力负担人口	Number of Persons Supported by Each Rural Labourer	0.44	0.49	0.50	0.48	0.48
十二、城市绿化	**City Afforestation**					
建成区绿化覆盖率(%)	Coverage Rate of Afforestation in Developed Area(%)	23.5	25.0	26.0	27.3	31.0
城市人均公共绿地(平方米)	Per Capita Public Green Areas in Urban Areas(sq. m)	4.9	5.4	4.9	5.6	6.7
十三、环境卫生与保护	**Environment Sanitation and Protection**					
年末拥有公共厕所(座)	Public Lavatories(unit)	2 610	2 656	2 740	2 723	2 430
城市环境噪声达标面积(平方公里)	Standardization Areas of City Environment Noise(sq. km)	170	173	375	477	539

注：赡养人口不含劳动者本人。
Note: Supported people exclude laborer himself or herself.

5-2 城镇单位从业人员劳动报酬总额
TOTAL REMUNERATION OF PERSONS EMPLOYED IN URBAN UNITS
(1978-2003)

单位:万元 (10 000 yuan)

年 份 Year	合 计 Total	按三次产业分 Grouped by Three Industries			按经济类型分 Grouped by Ownership		
		第一产业 Primary Industry	第二产业 Secondary Industry	第三产业 Tertiary Industry	国有经济 State-owned	集体经济 Collective-owned	其他经济 Others
1978	140 025.9	2 082.8	84 606.7	53 336.4	115 066.4	24 959.5	
1979	163 378.3	2 260.1	98 785.4	62 332.8	134 797.9	28 580.4	
1980	193 203.8	2 379.0	116 329.2	74 495.6	157 671.3	35 532.5	
1981	199 268.8	2 738.4	119 613.2	76 917.2	160 389.3	38 879.5	
1982	210 261.6	2 690.2	124 680.8	82 890.6	169 746.2	40 515.4	
1983	228 951.3	3 054.6	136 047.4	89 849.3	181 978.2	46 973.1	
1984	289 930.5	4 590.5	176 965.3	108 374.7	224 820.2	64 384.2	726.1
1985	341 395.6	4 580.5	189 914.1	146 901.0	246 890.0	69 379.5	1 842.1
1986	414 996.7	5 374.0	231 191.3	178 431.4	300 832.1	78 743.7	2 603.4
1987	460 891.5	5 732.5	255 239.3	199 919.7	340 298.6	84 153.2	4 140.7
1988	551 631.1	6 830.4	306 011.6	238 789.1	416 602.0	96 152.2	6 306.6
1989	640 232.5	7 505.6	356 973.7	275 753.2	483 663.2	113 059.1	8 595.9
1990	693 799.9	7 922.4	384 745.7	301 131.8	555 045.8	126 263.4	12 490.7
1991	797 340.6	9 044.1	448 747.2	339 549.3	623 445.1	154 187.4	19 708.1
1992	915 613.9	10 256.6	540 256.4	365 100.9	719 664.3	165 127.4	30 822.2
1993	1 167 779.8	7 155.8	691 240.2	469 383.8	903 227.9	192 110.6	72 441.3
1994	1 540 420.1	7 987.2	869 252.5	663 180.4	1 160 716.0	216 900.1	162 804.0
1995	1 848 027.9	8 603.4	1 055 034.7	784 389.8	1 352 214.5	259 963.3	235 850.1
1996	2 120 491.6	9 611.0	1 163 182.5	947 698.1	1 543 422.3	271 357.8	305 711.5
1997	2 232 525.8	10 438.1	1 187 059.3	1 035 028.4	1 604 714.3	264 608.8	363 202.7
1998	2 253 865.6	10 749.2	1 185 574.2	1 057 542.2	1 517 991.3	239 448.3	496 426.0
1999	2 344 186.1	9 713.4	1 215 273.1	1 119 199.6	1 519 302.4	212 537.6	612 346.1
2000	2 535 342.8	10 707.3	1 311 485.3	1 213 150.2	1 618 601.9	198 578.4	718 162.5
2001	2 775 592.7	11 572.1	1 374 770.9	1 389 249.7	1 762 580.1	168 567.3	844 445.3
2002	3 042 326.7	13 831.2	1 457 423.5	1 571 072.0	1 822 701.1	154 713.5	1 064 912.1
2003	3 506 036.0	13 186.3	1 727 566.1	1 765 283.6	1 947 978.7	154 880.0	1 403 177.3

注:1.1998年以前为职工工资总额。2.1985-1991年全市职工工资总额均包括肉价补贴,其他分组不包括。3.1993年以前各项指标中均不包括交通费、洗理费。下同。

Note:a)Before 1998,data of this table refer to total wages of staff and workers. b)In this table,total wages of staff and workers include price subsidy of meat,other group exclude this part from 1985 to 1991. c)Before 1993,each item exclude expenses of transport and washing. Same as following next.

5-3 城镇单位从业人员人均劳动报酬
PER CAPITA REMUNERATION OF PERSONS EMPLOYED IN URBAN UNITS
(1978-2003)

单位:元 (yuan)

年份 Year	合计 Total	按经济类型分 Grouped by Ownership			按主要行业分 Grouped by Main Sectors	
		国有经济 State-owned	集体经济 Collective-owned	其他经济 Others	农林牧渔业 Farming,Forestry Animal Husbandry and Fishery	工业 Industry
1978	640	690	478		492	639
1979	732	781	565		580	738
1980	820	865	667		736	815
1981	805	845	674		789	790
1982	820	865	672		767	792
1983	868	916	721		840	835
1984	1 071	1 132	900		1 157	1 041
1985	1 250	1 223	995	1 272	1 178	1 097
1986	1 498	1 455	1 149	1 479	1 196	1 354
1987	1 651	1 622	1 256	1 630	1 337	1 505
1988	1 975	1 972	1 475	2 212	1 604	1 826
1989	2 262	2 274	1 691	2 479	1 774	2 141
1990	2 438	2 611	1 866	2 946	1 932	2 304
1991	2 724	2 912	2 114	3 455	2 102	2 608
1992	3 118	3 383	2 285	3 553	2 430	3 116
1993	4 080	4 410	2 780	5 869	2 960	4 189
1994	5 364	5 806	3 370	7 100	3 597	5 245
1995	6 501	6 963	4 138	8 640	4 852	6 373
1996	7 643	8 072	4 745	10 522	5 720	7 253
1997	8 238	8 689	5 083	10 599	6 489	7 783
1998	9 895	10 169	6 020	12 818	7 541	9 656
1999	11 046	11 169	6 821	13 601	8 476	10 994
2000	12 414	12 690	7 485	14 317	9 414	12 240
2001	14 242	14 823	8 159	15 263	10 333	13 494
2002	16 223	16 632	9 152	17 449	12 492	15 462
2003	18 511	18 929	10 865	19 424	13 256	17 620

注:1.1998年以前为职工平均工资;2.本表行业分类为国标GB/T4754-1994标准。
Note:a)Before 1998,data of this table refer to average wage of staff and workers; b)Sector listed in this table is classified by the standard of GB/T4754-1994.

5－3 续表 Continued
单位：元 (yuan)

年 份 Year	按主要行业分 Grouped by Main Sectors						
	建筑业 Construction	交通运输仓储及邮电通信业 Transportation, Storage, Post and Telecommunications	批发和零售贸易、餐饮业 Wholesale & Retail Trade and Catering Services	金 融 保险业 Banking, Insurance	卫生、体育和社会福利业 Health Care, Sports and Social Welfare	教育、文艺及广播业 Education, Culture, Arts and Radio	国家、政党机关和社会团体 Government & Party Agencies, Social Organization
1978	603	759	619	678	611	608	687
1979	714	901	726	712	646	655	743
1980	842	978	774	783	776	782	855
1981	865	944	772	810	827	773	842
1982	930	985	759	795	883	848	846
1983	993	1 043	794	805	908	878	949
1984	1 361	1 244	1 017	1 059	962	929	1 037
1985	1 539	1 395	1 104	1 135	1 130	1 153	1 104
1986	1 674	1 642	1 326	1 316	1 337	1 256	1 278
1987	1 831	1 789	1 502	1 541	1 523	1 343	1 442
1988	2 094	2 218	1 842	1 835	1 876	1 697	1 693
1989	2 278	2 566	2 114	2 005	2 098	1 921	1 989
1990	2 412	2 759	2 268	2 197	2 381	2 127	2 193
1991	2 753	3 271	2 555	2 469	2 665	2 276	2 349
1992	3 251	3 931	2 899	3 246	3 368	2 892	2 983
1993	3 890	4 904	3 657	4 489	3 835	3 691	4 039
1994	5 234	6 388	4 764	7 338	5 806	5 406	6 021
1995	6 820	8 423	5 702	8 924	6 748	6 080	6 721
1996	7 918	9 887	6 593	11 540	8 960	7 669	8 750
1997	8 766	11 059	7 120	13 295	9 785	8 598	9 420
1998	10 624	13 041	7 989	13 661	10 639	9 487	10 557
1999	11 041	14 967	8 930	14 803	12 004	10 181	11 336
2000	12 395	16 775	10 099	14 866	14 182	11 991	13 172
2001	13 570	19 987	11 450	18 010	16 430	15 046	16 001
2002	15 190	21 892	13 379	21 593	18 818	16 401	18 209
2003	19 049	25 584	14 897	24 061	20 059	19 662	19 914

5-4 按新国民经济行业分各类从业人员劳动报酬总额(2003年)
TOTAL REMUNERATION OF PERSONS EMPLOYED GROUPED BY NEW SECTOR, 2003

单位:万元 (10 000 yuan)

行业 Sector	城镇单位从业人员 Persons Employed in Urban Units	在岗职工 On-post Staff and Workers	其他从业人员 Other Persons Employed
总计 Total	**3 506 036.0**	**3 254 148.4**	**251 887.6**
农、林、牧、渔业 Farming, Forestry, Animal Husbandry and Fishery	13 186.3	13 003.8	182.5
采矿业 Minerals Mining	158 166.6	149 774.8	8 391.8
制造业 Manufacturing	1 282 526.2	1 167 489.1	115 037.1
电力、燃气及水的生产和供应业 Production & Supply of Power, Gas and Water	90 230.0	89 416.1	813.9
建筑业 Construction	196 643.3	186 560.9	10 082.4
交通运输、仓储及邮政业 Transport, Storage, Post Services	307 989.6	292 658.5	15 331.1
信息传输、计算机服务和软件业 Information Transmitting, Computer Services and Software	50 333.4	48 278.7	2 054.7
批发和零售业 Wholesale and Retail Trade	181 378.0	158 282.5	23 095.5
住宿和餐饮业 Accommodation and Catering Services	42 403.0	34 685.2	7 717.8
金融业 Finance	125 424.8	94 908.6	30 516.2
房地产业 Real Estate	36 341.9	32 749.4	3 592.5
租赁和商务服务业 Leasing and Business Services	52 055.4	47 058.5	4 996.9
科学研究、技术服务和地质勘察业 Scientific Research, Technical Services and Geological Prospecting	122 846.5	115 830.5	7 016.0
水利、环境和公共设施管理业 Management for Water Conservancy, Environment and Public Facilities	56 496.0	54 488.9	2 007.1
居民服务和其他服务业 Resident Services and Other Social Services	41 764.1	38 897.5	2 866.6
教育 Education	316 984.0	309 167.7	7 816.3
卫生、社会保障和社会福利业 Health Care, Social Security and Social Welfare	135 575.6	134 228.6	1 347.0
文化、体育和娱乐业 Culture, Sports and Recreational Services	41 495.3	39 131.5	2 363.8
公共管理和社会组织 Public Management and Social Organizations	254 196.0	247 537.6	6 658.4

注:本表行业分类为国标GB/T4754-2002标准,5-5表同。
Note: Sector listed in this table is classified by the standard of GB/T4754-2002, same as following table 5-4.

5-5 按新国民经济行业分各类从业人员人均劳动报酬(2003年)
PERUCAPITA REMUNERATION OF PERSONS EMPLOYED GROUPED BY NEW SECTOR,2003

单位:元 (yuan)

行 业 Sector	城镇单位从业人员 Persons Employed in Urban Units	在岗职工 On-post Staff and Workers	其他从业人员 Other Persons Employed
总 计			
Total	**18 511**	**18 648**	**16 904**
农、林、牧、渔业			
Farming,Forestry,Animal Husbandry and Fishery	13 256	13 346	8 946
采矿业			
Minerals Mining	22 784	23 605	14 059
制造业			
Manufacturing	16 776	16 179	26 830
电力、燃气及水的生产和供应业			
Production & Supply of Power,Gas and Water	25 789	26 084	11 496
建筑业			
Construction	19 049	19 609	12 466
交通运输、仓储及邮政业			
Transport, Storage, Post Services	23 353	23 748	17 726
信息传输、计算机服务和软件业			
Information Transmitting, Computer Services and Software	33 441	33 784	27 000
批发和零售业			
Wholesale and Retail Trade	15 131	15 605	12 523
住宿和餐饮业			
Accommodation and Catering Services	12 446	12 430	12 523
金融业			
Finance	24 060	26 294	19 032
房地产业			
Real Estate	20 280	21 253	14 307
租赁和商务服务业			
Leasing and Business Services	13 613	13 498	14 801
科学研究、技术服务和地质勘察业			
Scientific Research, Technical Services and Geological Prospecting	23 544	24 548	14 057
水利、环境和公共设施管理业			
Management for Water Conservancy,Environment and Public Facilities	16 270	17 325	6 134
居民服务和其他服务业			
Resident Services and Other Social Services	13 833	14 492	8 554
教 育			
Education	18 794	19 226	9 958
卫生、社会保障和社会福利业			
Health Care, Social Security and Social Welfare	20 059	20 426	7 184
文化、体育和娱乐业			
Culture, Sports and Recreational Services	19 222	19 837	12 702
公共管理和社会组织			
Public Management and Social Organizations	19 875	21 365	5 534

5－6　城镇单位从业人员劳动报酬
REMUNERATION OF PERSONS EMPLOYED IN URBAN UNITS

项　　目	Item	劳动报酬总额(万元) Total Remuneration (10 000 yuan)		人均劳动报酬(元) Per Capita Remuneration(yuan)	
		2002	2003	2002	2003
总　　计	**Total**	**3 042 326.7**	**3 506 036.0**	**16 223**	**18 511**
一、按经济类型分	**Grouped by Ownership**				
国有经济	State－owned	1 822 701.1	1 947 978.7	16 632	18 929
集体经济	Collective－owned	154 713.5	154 880.0	9 152	10 865
其他经济	Other	1 064 912.1	1 403 177.3	17 449	19 424
#"三资"经济	Foreign Funded	722 618.5	864 380.4	18 392	20 037
股份制经济	Share Holding	161 992.7	217 658.4	17 111	24 033
二、按国民经济行业分	**Grouped by Sector**				
农、林、牧、渔业	Farming, Forestry, Animal Husbandry and Fisher	13 831.2	13 186.3	12 492	13 256
工　业	Industry	1 298 104.4	1 530 922.8	15 462	17 620
采掘业	Mining and Quarrying	150 412.0	158 166.6	18 647	22 784
制造业	Manufacturing	1 068 945.4	1 282 526.2	14 781	16 776
电力、煤气业及水的生产和供应业	Production and Supply of Electric Power, Gas and Water	78 747.0	90 230.0	22 093	25 789
建筑业	Construction	159 319.1	196 643.3	15 190	19 049
地质勘察业、水利管理业	Geological Prospecting and Water Conservancy	18 674.8	70 628.3	16 903	19 547
交通运输、仓储及邮电通信业	Transportation, Storage, Post and Telecommunications	292 340.8	279 130.7	21 892	25 584
批发和零售贸易、餐饮业	Wholesale & Retail Trade and Catering Services	157 233.2	214 883.9	13 379	14 897
金融、保险业	Banking and Insurance	89 787.8	125 424.8	21 593	24 061
房地产业	Real Estate	53 016.1	88 487.0	15 295	15 749
社会服务业	Social Services	165 224.7	174 615.7	14 106	18 829
卫生、体育和社会福利业	Health Care, Sports and Social Welfare	131 584.3	140 850.1	18 818	20 059
教育、文化艺术及广播电影电视业	Education, Culture & Arts, Radio, Film and Television	329 259.8	339 021.7	16 401	19 662
科学研究和综合技术服务业	Scientific Research and Polytechnical Services	82 128.3	92 846.5	18 213	16 744
国家机关、政党机关和社会团体	Government Agencies, Party Agencies and Social Organization	216 997.1	239 394.9	18 209	19 914
其他行业	Others	34 825.1		11 862	
三、按企业、事业、机关分	**Grouped By Enterprise, Institution and Agency**				
企　业	Enterprises	2 266 701.2	2 645 941.9	15 899	18 347
中　央	Central	602 795.6	641 462.8	19 797	23 591
地　方	Local	1 663 905.6	2 004 479.1	14 840	17 128
#国　有	State－owned	571 059.4	597 736.3	13 800	16 056
事　业	Institutions	564 507.3	621 725.3	16 928	18 717
中　央	Central	54 483.1	53 980.9	19 778	23 404
地　方	Local	510 024.2	567 744.4	16 671	18 367
机　关	Agencies	211 118.2	238 368.8	18 191	19 915
中　央	Central	24 567.3	27 757.6	26 055	32 476
地　方	Local	186 550.9	210 611.2	17 496	18 949

注：本表行业分类为国标GB/T4754－1994标准，5－7、5－8表同。
Note: Sector listed in this table is classified by the standard of GB/T4754－1994, same as following table 5－7 and 5－8.

5－7 在岗职工劳动报酬
REMUNERATION OF ON－POST STAFF AND WORKERS

行 业 Sector	劳动报酬总额(万元) Total Remuneration (10 000 yuan)		人均劳动报酬(元) Per Capita Remuneration (yuan)	
	2002	2003	2002	2003
总 计 Total	**2 907 250.2**	**3 254 148.4**	**16 258**	**18 648**
农、林、牧、渔业 Farming,Forestry,Animal Husbandry and Fishery	13 776.5	13 003.8	12 505	13 347
工 业 Industry	1 223 075.2	1 406 680.0	15 029	17 169
建筑业 Construction	155 449.2	186 560.9	15 488	19 609
地质勘察业、水利管理业 Geological Prospecting and Water Conservancy	18 574.2	70 355.6	17 023	19 783
交通运输、仓储及邮电通信业 Transportation,Storage,Post and Telecommunications	286 239.9	263 464.7	22 203	26 177
批发和零售贸易、餐饮业 Whole & Retail Trade and Catering Services	140 930.3	192 480.7	13 687	15 275
金融、保险业 Banking and Insurance	83 199.4	94 908.6	22 601	26 295
房地产业 Real Estate	50 160.6	79 897.6	15 589	15 885
社会服务业 Social Services	155 485.2	164 165.1	14 293	19 467
卫生、体育和社会福利业 Health Care,Sports and Social Welfare	130 467.3	132 503.1	19 681	20 426
教育、文化艺术及广播电影电视业 Education,Culture and Arts,Radio,Film and Television	323 856.8	331 748.2	16 693	20 300
科学研究和综合技术服务业 Scientific Research and Polytechnical Services	78 645.4	85 221.5	18 755	17 519
国家机关、政党机关和社会团体 Government Agencies,Party Agencies and Social Organization	213 909.9	233 158.6	19 019	21 436
其他行业 Others	33 480.3		12 091	

5-8 其他从业人员劳动报酬
REMUNERATION OF OTHER PERSONS EMPLOYED

行业 Sector	劳动报酬总额(万元) Total Remuneration (10 000 yuan)		人均劳动报酬(元) Per Capita Remuneration (yuan)	
	2002	2003	2002	2003
总计				
Total	**135 076.5**	**251 887.6**	**15 509**	**16 904**
农、林、牧、渔业				
Farming, Forestry, Animal Husbandry and Fishery	54.7	182.5	9 945	8 946
工业				
Industry	75 029.2	124 242.8	29 192	25 073
建筑业				
Construction	3 869.9	10 082.4	8 575	12 466
地质勘察业、水利管理业				
Geological Prospecting and Water Conservancy	100.6	272.7	7 343	4 793
交通运输、仓储及邮电通信业				
Transportation, Storage, Post and Telecommunications	6 100.9	15 666.0	13 214	18 526
批发和零售贸易、餐饮业				
Whole & Retail Trade and Catering Services	16 302.9	22 403.2	11 197	12 900
金融、保险业				
Banking and Insurance	6 588.4	30 516.2	13 818	19 032
房地产业				
Real Estate	2 855.5	8 589.4	11 491	14 590
社会服务业				
Social Services	9 739.5	10 450.6	11 667	10 153
卫生、体育和社会福利业				
Health Care, Sports and Social Welfare	1 117.0	8 347.0	3 075	7 184
教育、文化艺术及广播电影电视业				
Education, Culture and Arts, Radio, Film and Television	5 403.0	7 273.5	8 006	13 006
科学研究和综合技术服务业				
Scientific Research and Polytechnical Services	3 482.9	7 625.0	11 022	6 536
国家机关、政党机关和社会团体				
Government Agencies, Party Agencies and Social Organization	3 087.2	6 236.3	4 610	5 447
其他行业				
Others	1 344.8		8 058	

5-9 市属各局(总公司)国有经济单位从业人员劳动报酬总额

TOTAL REMUNERATION OF STATE-OWNED PERSONS EMPLOYED IN UNITS BY BUREAU(CORPORATION)

单位:万元 (10 000 yuan)

局(总公司)	Bureau(Corporation)	2002	2003
一、经委系统	**Tianjin Economical Committee System**		
机电工业控股集团公司	Tianjin Machinery & Electric Industry Holding Group Company	20 676.1	18 539.0
中环电子信息集团有限公司	Tianjin Zhonghuan Electronics & Information Group	24 733.7	23 305.4
冶金集团(控股)有限公司	Tianjin Metallurgical Group (Holding) Corporation	27 823.9	33 389.8
渤海化工集团公司	Tianjin Bohai Chemical Industry Group Corporation	56 412.2	61 132.9
纺织集团(控股)有限公司	Tianjin Textile Industrial General Corporation	31 115.3	30 414.4
一轻集团(控股)有限公司	Tianjin Yiqing Group(Holding Share) Co.,Ltd	9 976.8	8 813.9
二轻集团(控股)有限公司	The Second Light Industry Group(Holding) Co.,Ltd	4 671.1	4 155.2
医药集团有限公司	Tianjin Pharmaceutical Holdings	8 698.6	7 714.1
汽车工业(集团)有限公司	Tianjin Automobile Industry Group Co.,Ltd	12 257.9	9 854.7
飞鸽集团有限公司	Tianjin Flying Pigeon Group Co.,Ltd	2 383.3	2 344.6
塑料集团	Tianjin Plastics Group	2 325.4	2 252.1
天铁冶金集团有限公司	Tianjin Tian Tie Metallurgical Group Co.,Ltd	35 809.7	38 736.0
建筑材料集团(控股)有限公司	Tianjin Building Materials Group(Holding)Co.,Ltd	8 037.9	6 199.6
二、农委系统	**Tianjin Agricultural Committee System**		
农业局	Tianjin Agriculture Bureau	823.3	728.2
畜牧局	Tianjin Animal Husbandry Bureau	535.2	543.1
农垦集团总公司	Tianjin State Farms Agribusiness Group Company	6 440.5	7 066.6
水产局	Tianjin Aquatic Products Bureau	3 264.6	3 231.4
三、建委系统	**Tianjin Construction Committee System**		
建工集团总公司	Tianjin Construction Engineering Group Corporation	16 680.7	9 301.4
市政工程局	Tianjin Municipal Engineering Bureau	38 113.3	36 306.5
房地产管理局	Tianjin Real Estate Administrative Bureau	13 744.2	14 476.1
住宅建设发展集团	Tianjin House Construction Development Group	3 932.2	3 554.8
公共交通集团公司	Tianjin Public Traffic Group Corporation	12 736.1	13 018.5
自来水集团	Tianjin Tap Water Group	7 559.2	7 899.3
燃气集团	Tianjin Gas Group	12 634.4	14 713.7
四、交委系统	**Tianjin Transportation Committee System**		
港务局	Tianjin Port Authority	41 947.0	49 167.9
交通局	Tianjin Transportation Management Bureau	7 706.1	8 141.1
五、商委系统	**Tianjin Commercial Committee System**		
粮食粮油集团有限公司	Tianjin Grain & Oil Group Co.,Ltd	5 483.9	6 019.5
一商集团有限公司	Tianjin Yishang Group Co.,Ltd	4 802.3	4 590.7
二商集团有限公司	Tianjin Second Commercial Group Co.,Ltd	7 320.8	7 597.2

5－10 市属各局(总公司)国有经济单位从业人员人均劳动报酬

PER CAPITA REMUNERATION OF STATE－OWNED PERSONS EMPLOYED IN UNITS BY BUREAU(CORPORATION)

单位:元 (yuan)

局(总公司)	Bureau(Corporation)	2002	2003
一、经委系统	**Tianjin Economical Committee System**		
机电工业控股集团公司	Tianjin Machinery & Electric Industry Holding Group Company	10 163	11 452
中环电子信息集团有限公司	Tianjin Zhonghuan Electronics & Information Group	12 755	13 936
冶金集团(控股)有限公司	Tianjin Metallurgical Group (Holding) Corporation	14 440	16 368
渤海化工集团公司	Tianjin Bohai Chemical Industry Group Corporation	14 440	17 348
纺织集团(控股)有限公司	Tianjin Textile Industrial General Corporation	9 595	10 568
一轻集团(控股)有限公司	Tianjin Yiqing Group(Holding Share) Co.,Ltd	10 535	12 752
二轻集团(控股)有限公司	The Second Light Industry Group(Holding) Co.,Ltd	8 221	10 367
医药集团有限公司	Tianjin Pharmaceutical Holdings	16 428	17 335
汽车工业(集团)有限公司	Tianjin Automobile Industry Group Co.,Ltd	12 628	19 908
飞鸽集团有限公司	Tianjin Flying Pigeon Group Co.,Ltd	8 491	9 127
塑料集团	Tianjin Plastics Group	8 910	11 034
天铁冶金集团有限公司	Tianjin Tian Tie Metallurgical Group Co.,Ltd	17 020	19 875
建筑材料集团(控股)有限公司	Tianjin Building Materials Group(Holding)Co.,Ltd	10 683	11 579
二、农委系统	**Tianjin Agricultural Committee System**		
农业局	Tianjin Agriculture Bureau	11 795	16 438
畜牧局	Tianjin Animal Husbandry Bureau	13 248	17 748
农垦集团总公司	Tianjin State Farms Agribusiness Group Company	11 085	13 043
水产局	Tianjin Aquatic Products Bureau	19 918	22 072
三、建委系统	**Tianjin Construction Committee System**		
建工集团总公司	Tianjin Construction Engineering Group Corporation	13 387	13 374
市政工程局	Tianjin Municipal Engineering Bureau	18 038	18 595
房地产管理局	Tianjin Real Estate Administrative Bureau	14 628	15 896
住宅建设发展集团	Tianjin House Construction Development Group	11 720	13 699
公共交通集团公司	Tianjin Public Traffic Group Corporation	13 212	13 298
自来水集团	Tianjin Tap Water Group	20 342	24 701
燃气集团	Tianjin Gas Group	17 624	21 065
四、交委系统	**Tianjin Transportation Committee System**		
港务局	Tianjin Port Authority	38 700	44 972
交通局	Tianjin Transportation Management Bureau	9 183	10 773
五、商委系统	**Tianjin Commercial Committee System**		
粮食粮油集团有限公司	Tianjin Grain & Oil Group Co.,Ltd	12 529	14 841
一商集团有限公司	Tianjin Yishang Group Co.,Ltd	13 244	13 740
二商集团有限公司	Tianjin Second Commercial Group Co.,Ltd	11 306	12 792

5－11 职工劳保福利费发放情况
TOTAL INSURANCE WELFARE OF STAFF AND WORKERS
（2000－2003）

指 标 Item	2000	2001	2002	2003
在职职工保险福利费用总额(万元) Total Insurance Welfare of On－post Staff & Workers (10 000 yuan)	**209 452.1**	**264 423.4**	**221 265.1**	**265 528.4**
国有经济 State－owned	157 276.6	170 572.3	140 320.9	176 980.3
集体经济 Collective－owned	13 668.9	10 314.9	8 231.4	7 738.1
其他经济 Others	38 506.6	83 536.2	72 712.8	80 810.0
非在职职工保险福利费用总额(万元) Total Insurance Welfare of Staff & Workers not On－post(10 000 yuan)	**776 759.8**	**858 471.6**	**997 655.8**	**1 136 250.0**
#国有经济 State－owned	623 245.1	692 157.4	775 335.7	864 488.0
在职职工人均保险福利费(元) Per Capita Insurance Welfare of On－post Staff & Workers (yuan)	**955**	**1 218**	**1 039**	**1 246**
国有经济 State－owned	1 059	1 399	1 079	1 432
集体经济 Collective－owned	395	342	350	373
其他经济 Others	1 063	1 285	1 224	1 175
非在职职工人均保险福利费(元) Per Capita Insurance Welfare of Staff & Workers not On－post (yuan)	**8 415**	**8 705**	**9 127**	**10 270**
#国有经济 State－owned	9 204	9 612	10 094	11 281

注：1.本资料来源于市劳动和社会保障局、民政局。2.非在职职工保险福利费不含民政部门支付。
Note：a) Data are gotten from Tianjin Municipal Labour & Social Insurance Bureau and Tianjin Municipal Civil Administration Bureau. b) Insurance welfare of staff and workers not on the job exclude those paid by civil administration department.

5－12 职工保险福利费构成
COMPOSITION OF INSURANCE WELFARE OF STAFF AND WORKERS
（2000－2003）

单位：万元　　(10 000 yuan)

指 标 Item	2000	2001	2002	2003
在职职工 On－post Staff & Workers	**209 452.1**	**264 423.4**	**221 265.1**	**265 528.4**
集体福利设施、事业补贴费 Collective Welfare Facilities, Insurance Subsidies	30 781.0	42 345.8	40 950.9	46 666.4
文体宣传费 Culture and Sport Expenses	6 398.8	9 229.8	9 088.6	9 300.5
医疗卫生费 Medical, Health Care Expenses	118 777.7	149 881.4	100 772.9	102 014.0
其 他 Others	53 494.6	62 966.4	70 452.7	107 547.5
非在职职工 Staff and Workers not On－post	**776 759.8**	**858 471.6**	**997 655.8**	**1 136 250.0**
离休费 Retirement Pay	33 426.4	40 207.5	46 185.6	51 122.5
退休费 Pension Cost	554 181.9	683 579.8	847 180.6	978 888.5
退职生活费 Resignation Living Fee	5 674.1	4 921.7	7 379.7	7 165.5
医疗卫生费 Medical, Health Care Expenses	130 995.5	93 045.0	60 589.4	64 498.4
其 他 Others	52 481.9	36 717.6	36 320.5	34 575.1

5－13 社会保障事业发展情况
BASIC STATISTICS ON SOCIAL SECURITY

指　标　Item	计量单位　Unit	2002	2003
一、医疗保险参保人员情况			
Medical Insurance			
参加基本医疗保险人数	万人		
Personnnel Participated in Medical Insurance	10 000 persons	208.50	242.92
职工人数	万人		
Staff and Workers	10 000 persons	139.20	165.17
退休人数 Retired Personnel	万人		
Retired Personnel	10 000 persons	69.30	77.75
基本医疗保险基金收入	亿元		
Revenue of Basic Medical Insurance Funds	100 million yuan	17.21	19.53
基本医疗保险基金支出	亿元		
Expenditure of Basic Medical Insurance Funds	100 million yuan	15.07	20.40
基本医疗保险基金累计结余	亿元		
Balance of Basic Medical Insurance Funds	100 million yuan	2.26	1.39
二、失业保险参保人员情况			
Unemployment Insurance			
参加失业保险职工人数	万人		
Personnnel Participated in Unemployment Insurance	10 000 persons	189.55	193.45
领取失业保险金人数	万人		
Drawing Unemployment Insurance Funds	10 000 persons	12.44	9.50
#本年新增	万人		
New Increased in This Year	10 000 persons	7.42	3.40
失业保险基金收入	亿元		
Revenue of Unemployment Insurance Funds	100 million yuan	5.35	5.66
失业保险基金支出	亿元		
Expenditure of Unemployment Insurance Funds	100 million yuan	5.58	4.43
失业保险基金累计结余	亿元		
Balance of Unemployment Insurance Funds	100 million yuan	2.11	3.34
三、基本养老保险参保人员情况			
Pension Insurance			
参加基本养老保险职工人数	万人		
Personnnel Participated in Pension Insurance	10 000 persons	204.61	185.67
基本养老保险实际缴费人数	万人		
Paying Expense for Pension Insurance	10 000 persons	174.82	175.80
基本养老保险基金收入	亿元		
Revenue of Pension Insurance Funds	100 million yuan	74.66	85.33
基本养老保险基金支出	亿元		
Expenditure of Pension Insurance Funds	100 million yuan	67.03	81.78
基本养老保险基金累计结余	亿元		
Balance of Pension Insurance	100 million yuan	18.55	22.10

5－14　城市居民家庭人均收支及增幅
PER CAPITA INCOME & EXPENDITURES AND INCREASE RATE OF URBAN HOUSEHOLDS
（1978－2003）

年　份 Year	人均年可支配收入(元) Per Capita Annual Disposable Income (yuan)	人均年消费性支出(元) Per Capita Annual Expenditures for Consumption (yuan)	人均收入增幅(％) Increase Rate of Per Capita Disposable Income (％)	人均支出增幅(％) Increase Rate of Per Capita Expenditures for Consumption (％)	扣除物价人均收入增幅(％) Increase Rate of Per Capita Disposable Income After Deducting Price Factor (％)	扣除物价人均支出增幅(％) Increase Rate of Per Capita Expenditures for Consumption After Deducting Price Factor (％)
1978	388.32	344.88	9.5	6.8	9.5	6.8
1979	425.40	385.20	9.5	11.7	8.4	10.6
1980	526.92	474.72	23.9	23.2	17.9	17.2
1981	539.52	485.88	2.4	2.4	1.1	1.1
1982	576.72	496.56	6.9	2.2	6.4	1.7
1983	604.31	520.84	4.8	4.9	4.3	4.4
1984	728.17	599.64	20.5	15.1	18.4	13.1
1985	875.52	770.64	20.2	28.5	6.3	13.6
1986	1 069.61	949.08	22.2	23.2	14.4	15.4
1987	1 187.49	1 071.14	11.0	12.9	3.9	5.7
1988	1 329.70	1 278.87	12.0	19.4	－4.2	2.1
1989	1 477.77	1 291.09	11.1	1.0	－3.1	－11.9
1990	1 638.92	1 440.47	10.9	11.6	7.7	8.3
1991	1 844.98	1 585.71	12.6	10.1	2.2	－0.1
1992	2 238.38	1 907.17	21.3	20.3	8.9	8.0
1993	2 769.26	2 322.19	23.7	21.8	5.2	3.6
1994	3 982.13	3 301.37	43.8	42.2	16.0	14.7
1995	4 929.53	4 064.10	23.8	23.1	7.4	6.8
1996	5 967.71	4 679.61	21.1	15.1	11.1	5.6
1997	6 608.56	5 204.29	10.7	11.2	7.4	7.9
1998	7 110.54	5 471.01	7.6	5.1	8.1	5.6
1999	7 649.83	5 851.53	7.6	7.0	8.8	8.1
2000	8 140.55	6 121.07	6.4	4.6	6.8	5.0
2001	8 958.70	6 987.22	10.1	14.2	8.7	12.8
2002	9 337.54	7 191.97	11.6	5.4	12.1	5.8
2003	10 312.91	7 867.53	10.4	9.4	9.4	8.3

5－15　城市居民家庭基本情况
BASIC INDICATORS OF URBAN HOUSEHOLDS

指　标	Item	单位　Unit	2000	2001	2002	2003
调查户数	Number of Households Surveyed	户　household	500	1 500	1 500	1 500
平均每户人口	Average Persons Per Household	人　person	3.08	3.09	3.02	2.99
平均每户就业人口	Average Employees Per Household	人　person	1.63	1.59	1.44	1.41
平均每户就业面	Percentage of Employment Per Household	%	52.9	51.5	47.7	47.2
平均每一就业者负担人口	Persons Supported By Each Employee	人　person	1.89	1.94	2.11	2.12
平均每人年可支配收入	Per Capita Annual Disposable Income	元　yuan	8 140.55	8 958.70	9 337.54	10 312.91
平均每人年消费性支出	Per Capita Annual Expenditures for Consumption	元　yuan	6 121.07	6 987.22	7 191.97	7 867.53

5-16 城市不同收入水平居民家庭基本情况(2003 年)
（按平均每人每月可支配收入分组）

BASIC INDICATORS OF URBAN HOUSEHOLDS WITH DIFFERENT INCOME LEVEL, 2003
(GROUPED BY PER CAPITA DISPOSABLE INCOME PER MONTH)

项目	Item	调查户数（户） Number of Households Surveyed (household)	平均每户人口（人） Average Persons Per Household (person)	平均每户就业人口（人） Average Employees Per Household (person)	平均每一就业者负担人口（人） Persons Supported by Each Employee (person)
全市	**Total**	**1 500**	**2.99**	**1.41**	**2.12**
1. 最低收入户	Lowest Income Households				
（378.47 元以下）	(Below 378.47 yuan)	150	3.25	1.11	2.93
#更低收入户	Even More Lowest Income Households				
（303.47 元以下）	(Below 303.47 yuan)	75	3.33	1.06	3.14
2. 低收入户	Low Income Households				
（378.75 - 487.14 元）	(378.75 - 487.14 yuan)	150	3.20	1.30	2.46
3. 中等偏下收入户	Lower Middle Income Households				
（487.19 - 667.28 元）	(487.19 - 667.28 yuan)	300	3.15	1.47	2.14
4. 中等收入户	Middle Income Households				
（667.97 - 876.00 元）	(667.97 - 876.00 yuan)	300	2.99	1.42	2.11
5. 中等偏上收入户	Upper Middle Income Households				
（876.81 - 1195.67 元）	(876.81 - 1195.67 yuan)	300	2.85	1.42	2.01
6. 高收入户	High Income Households				
（1196.03 - 1487.08 元）	(1196.03 - 1487.08 yuan)	150	2.85	1.55	1.84
7. 最高收入户	Highest Income Households				
（1493.17 元以上）	(Over 1493.17 yuan)	150	2.67	1.53	1.75

项目	Item	平均每人年总收入（元） Per Capita Annual Actual Income (yuan)	平均每人年可支配收入（元） Per Capita Annual Disposable Income (yuan)	平均每人年消费性支出（元） Per Capita Annual Expenditures for Consumption (yuan)	#平均每人年服务性消费支出（元） Per Capita Annual Expenditures for Services (yuan)
全市	**Total**	**10 971.57**	**10 312.91**	**7 867.53**	**2 125.33**
1. 最低收入户	Lowest Income Households				
（378.47 元以下）	(Below 378.47 yuan)	3 642.04	3 483.53	3 963.81	1 116.60
#更低收入户	Even More Lowest Income Households				
（303.47 元以下）	(Below 303.47 yuan)	2 968.41	2 850.15	3 538.92	994.39
2. 低收入户	Low Income Households				
（378.75 - 487.14 元）	(378.75 - 487.14 yuan)	5 488.62	5 238.92	5 102.34	1 502.01
3. 中等偏下收入户	Lower Middle Income Households				
（487.19 - 667.28 元）	(487.19 - 667.28 yuan)	7 298.03	6 850.27	6 027.44	1 609.49
4. 中等收入户	Middle Income Households				
（667.97 - 876.00 元）	(667.97 - 876.00 yuan)	9 794.33	9 204.92	7 351.80	1 941.86
5. 中等偏上收入户	Upper Middle Income Households				
（876.81 - 1195.67 元）	(876.81 - 1195.67 yuan)	12 994.05	12 246.35	9 171.18	2 361.09
6. 高收入户	High Income Households				
（1196.03 - 1487.08 元）	(1196.03 - 1487.08yuan)	17 100.64	15 879.05	11 512.09	3 042.66
7. 最高收入户	Highest Income Households				
（1493.17 元以上）	(Over 1493.17 yuan)	26 527.53	24 930.47	14 574.17	4 198.97

5－17　城市居民家庭平均每人全年消费性支出分类(2003年)

THE CLASSIFICATION OF PER CAPITA ANNUAL EXPENDITURES FOR CONSUMPTION OF URBAN HOUSEHOLDS,2003

单位:元 (yuan)

项目	Item	合计 Total	最低收入 10% Lowest Income (10 percent)	低收入 10% Lower Income (10 percent)	较低收入 20% Low Income (20 percent)
消费性支出	**Total Expenditures for Consumption**	**7 867.53**	**3 963.81**	**5 102.34**	**6 027.44**
一、食　品	Food	2 963.85	1 921.86	2 180.00	2 595.26
(一)粮油类	Grain and Oil	349.63	317.04	322.80	339.37
1.粮　食	Grain	217.41	199.46	201.74	209.48
2.淀粉及薯类	Starches and Tubers	24.71	22.17	22.76	23.43
3.干豆类及豆制品	Beans and Bean Products	28.05	23.02	23.71	25.95
4.油脂类	Oil and Fats	79.46	72.38	74.59	80.52
(二)肉禽蛋水产品类	Meat,Poultry,Egg and Related Products	844.55	584.44	674.16	769.45
1.肉　类	Meat	390.00	289.75	331.33	368.91
2.禽　类	Poultry	89.37	64.97	70.92	80.60
3.蛋　类	Eggs	93.27	80.44	85.46	88.96
4.水产品类	Aquatic Products	271.92	149.28	186.45	231.00
(三)蔬菜类	Vegetables	249.97	189.30	209.91	233.16
(四)调味品	Condiments	56.18	43.95	46.43	53.32
(五)糖烟酒饮料类	Sugar,Tobacco,Liquor and Beverages	307.63	178.60	228.36	268.75
1.糖　类	Sugar	24.24	15.23	17.24	19.36
2.烟草类	Tobacco	112.77	66.19	97.70	104.25
3.酒　类	Liquor	88.80	54.20	60.03	79.58
4.饮　料	Beverages	81.81	42.98	53.39	65.56
(六)鲜瓜果类	Dry and Fresh Melons nad Fruits	241.72	145.40	168.55	212.53
(七)糕点、奶及奶制品	Cake,Milk and Related Produts	223.16	130.14	152.50	185.22
(八)其他食品	Other Food	77.94	41.18	44.15	59.05
(九)饮食服务	Dining	613.07	291.82	333.14	474.42
#在外饮食	Dining Out	612.07	290.13	332.08	473.44
二、衣　着	Clothing	579.70	200.85	308.71	397.38
#服　装	Garments	402.09	129.68	204.33	269.11
衣着材料	Clothing Materials	15.54	5.87	6.15	11.53
鞋　类	Shoes	122.02	49.40	73.47	89.08
衣着加工服务费	Tailoring and Laundering Service Fees	10.05	4.18	3.80	6.54
三、家庭设备、用品及服务	Household Facilities,Articles and Services	467.03	128.99	210.23	268.87
#耐用消费品	Durable Consumer Goods	261.65	47.28	99.43	137.42
室内装饰品	Room Decorations	24.71	1.35	6.19	7.74
家庭服务	Household Services	28.08	5.70	8.94	14.26
四、医疗保健	Medicine and Medical Services	697.76	294.32	331.25	549.06
五、交通与通讯	Transport and Communication Services	721.28	245.76	333.82	460.50
六、娱乐、教育、文化服务	Recreation,Education and Cultural Services	1 083.91	633.82	974.76	809.68
#文化娱乐用品	Cultural and Recreational Articles	318.63	70.31	182.32	193.54
七、居　住	Residence	1 095.61	458.28	662.53	773.89
#燃　料	Fuel	109.27	91.20	102.50	105.93
八、杂项商品与服务	Miscellaneous Commodities and Services	258.39	79.93	101.05	172.79

5－17 续表　Continued
单位:元　(yuan)

项　目	Item	中间收入 20% Middle Income (20 percent)	较高收入 20% High Income (20 percent)	高收入 10% Higher Income (10 percent)	最高收入 10% Highest Income (10 percent)
消费性支出	**Total Expenditures for Consumption**	**7 351.80**	**9 171.18**	**11 512.09**	**14 574.17**
一、食　品	Food	2 997.64	3 426.71	3 678.74	4 214.61
(一)粮油类	Grain and Oil	357.48	367.17	364.83	372.52
1.粮　食	Grain	221.21	232.26	224.04	228.27
2.淀粉及薯类	Starches and Tubers	26.22	24.94	26.79	26.88
3.干豆类及豆制品	Beans and Bean Products	29.02	30.37	30.32	34.50
4.油脂类	Oil and Fats	81.03	79.59	83.68	82.87
(二)肉禽蛋水产品类	Meat,Poultry,Egg and Related Products	861.55	964.38	977.49	1 094.33
1.肉　类	Meat	404.88	437.29	420.37	460.56
2.禽　类	Poultry	92.56	102.05	104.88	109.85
3.蛋　类	Eggs	94.06	98.02	101.51	107.13
4.水产品类	Aquatic Products	270.05	327.01	350.73	416.80
(三)蔬菜类	Vegetables	255.35	275.26	273.14	317.60
(四)调味品	Condiments	56.90	60.75	65.43	67.74
(五)糖烟酒饮料类	Sugar,Tobacco,Liquor and Beverages	313.08	375.71	373.54	417.52
1.糖　类	Sugar	23.22	28.47	32.56	39.04
2.烟草类	Tobacco	113.53	136.34	122.43	143.56
3.酒　类	Liquor	93.04	108.30	111.09	110.57
4.饮　料	Beverages	83.29	102.60	107.46	124.35
(六)鲜瓜果类	Dry and Fresh Melons nad Fruits	233.90	280.04	326.92	356.27
(七)糕点、奶及奶制品	Cake,Milk and Related Produts	232.05	263.61	291.73	326.29
(八)其他食品	Other Food	78.50	96.58	93.61	147.43
(九)饮食服务	Dining	608.84	743.22	862.06	1 114.91
#在外饮食	Dining Out	607.98	742.32	860.78	1 114.51
二、衣　着	Clothing	519.64	741.40	931.02	1 192.54
#服　装	Garments	348.21	519.82	684.94	839.84
衣着材料	Clothing Materials	16.61	22.16	18.33	27.84
鞋　类	Shoes	118.90	144.89	173.37	246.01
衣着加工服务费	Tailoring and Laundering Service Fees	9.24	13.92	16.31	19.50
三、家庭设备、用品及服务	Household Facilities,Articles and Services	362.81	596.32	944.91	1 087.68
#耐用消费品	Durable Consumer Goods	202.58	356.39	562.68	610.42
室内装饰品	Room Decorations	10.14	30.52	71.84	84.55
家庭服务	Household Services	21.39	27.88	66.03	84.79
四、医疗保健	Medicine and Medical Services	686.58	834.15	1 047.07	1 319.12
五、交通与通讯	Transport and Communication Services	619.43	755.92	1 316.60	1 875.99
六、娱乐、教育、文化服务	Recreation,Education and Cultural Services	1 027.86	1 182.59	1 327.02	2 043.48
#文化娱乐用品	Cultural and Recreational Articles	303.04	415.81	438.39	765.62
七、居　住	Residence	924.81	1 326.78	1 907.73	2 147.92
#燃　料	Fuel	104.55	119.94	112.09	131.38
八、杂项商品与服务	Miscellaneous Commodities and Services	213.03	307.30	408.99	692.82

5－18　城市居民家庭平均每人主要消费品全年购买量(2003年)
PER CAPITA ANNUAL PURCHASES OF MAJOR CONSUMER GOODS OF URBAN HOUSEHOLDS,2003

商品名称	Item	单　位	Unit	合　计 Total	最低收入 10% Lowest Income (10 percent)	低收入 10% Lower Income (10 percent)	较低收入 20% Low Income (20 percent)
粮　食	Grain	公斤	kg	80.78	83.51	78.69	79.28
淀粉及薯类	Starches and Tubers	公斤	kg	13.93	14.00	13.33	13.21
油脂类	Oil and Fats	公斤	kg	9.34	9.12	9.04	9.53
#食用植物油	Edible Vegetable Oil	公斤	kg	9.29	9.02	8.97	9.48
肉　类	Meat	公斤	kg	28.88	22.20	24.79	27.60
#猪　肉	Pork	公斤	kg	17.71	14.41	15.12	17.06
牛　肉	Beef	公斤	kg	3.07	2.37	3.33	3.13
羊　肉	Mutton	公斤	kg	3.45	2.54	2.87	3.40
禽　类	Poultry	公斤	kg	6.59	5.19	5.57	6.07
#鸡	Chicken	公斤	kg	3.90	3.33	3.53	3.77
蛋　类	Eggs	公斤	kg	20.28	17.73	18.74	19.30
#鲜　蛋	Fresh Eggs	公斤	kg	18.76	16.57	17.32	17.81
鱼	Fish	公斤	kg	9.48	7.26	7.88	8.81
虾	Shrimp	公斤	kg	4.58	2.63	3.35	3.91
鲜　菜	Fresh Vegetables	公斤	kg	138.88	122.16	126.45	132.42
干　菜	Dry Vegetables	公斤	kg	0.32	0.23	0.23	0.28
酒　类	Liquor	公斤	kg	11.71	9.32	10.84	10.38
#白　酒	Wine	公斤	kg	2.82	2.46	2.21	2.95
啤　酒	Beer	公斤	kg	8.66	6.67	8.45	7.25
碳酸饮料	Beverages	公斤	kg	3.84	2.29	2.79	3.90
茶　叶	Tea	公斤	kg	0.28	0.21	0.26	0.25
鲜　果	Fresh Fruits	公斤	kg	49.05	33.13	37.18	44.43
鲜　瓜	Fresh Melons	公斤	kg	31.38	22.36	27.02	29.04
糕　点	Cake	公斤	kg	6.15	4.40	4.55	5.69
鲜　奶	Milk	公斤	kg	23.10	12.56	16.59	18.53
服　装	Garments	件	piece	6.26	3.04	4.73	5.31
#男士服装	Men's Clothing	件	piece	2.59	1.21	1.96	2.25
女士服装	Women's Clothing	件	piece	3.12	1.62	2.46	2.70
童　装	Children's Clothing	件	piece	0.54	0.21	0.31	0.36
鞋　类	Shoes	双	pair	2.44	1.54	2.00	2.50

5－18 续表 Continued

商品名称	Item	单位	Unit	中间收入 20% Middle Income (20 percent)	较高收入 20% High Income (20 percent)	高收入 10% Higher Income (10 percent)	最高收入 10% Highest Income (10 percent)
粮　食	Grain	公斤	kg	81.22	83.06	80.49	77.88
淀粉及薯类	Starches and Tubers	公斤	kg	14.71	13.79	15.05	13.62
油脂类	Oil and Fats	公斤	kg	9.38	9.25	9.67	9.29
#食用植物油	Edible Vegetable Oil	公斤	kg	9.36	9.18	9.62	9.21
肉　类	Meat	公斤	kg	30.21	32.02	30.52	33.23
#猪　肉	Pork	公斤	kg	18.69	19.50	18.07	19.79
牛　肉	Beef	公斤	kg	3.16	3.07	3.15	3.21
羊　肉	Mutton	公斤	kg	3.77	3.70	3.57	4.00
禽　类	Poultry	公斤	kg	7.05	7.24	7.11	7.71
#鸡	Chicken	公斤	kg	4.34	4.05	3.61	4.29
蛋　类	Eggs	公斤	kg	20.45	21.21	21.94	23.31
#鲜　蛋	Fresh Eggs	公斤	kg	18.93	19.59	20.13	21.69
鱼	Fish	公斤	kg	9.82	10.61	10.26	11.50
虾	Shrimp	公斤	kg	4.80	5.48	5.67	6.29
鲜　菜	Fresh Vegetables	公斤	kg	142.09	146.09	145.33	158.91
干　菜	Dry Vegetables	公斤	kg	0.32	0.35	0.45	0.47
酒　类	Liquor	公斤	kg	13.06	14.43	11.49	10.09
#白　酒	Wine	公斤	kg	3.07	3.27	2.82	2.16
啤　酒	Beer	公斤	kg	9.78	10.87	8.36	7.61
碳酸饮料	Beverages	公斤	kg	3.87	4.37	4.81	4.50
茶　叶	Tea	公斤	kg	0.31	0.32	0.27	0.36
鲜　果	Fresh Fruits	公斤	kg	48.25	54.97	63.07	67.07
鲜　瓜	Fresh Melons	公斤	kg	30.69	32.46	39.11	43.82
糕　点	Cake	公斤	kg	6.44	7.19	7.28	7.05
鲜　奶	Milk	公斤	kg	26.14	25.61	29.51	34.87
服　装	Garments	件	piece	6.16	7.78	7.91	9.31
#男士服装	Men's Clothing	件	piece	2.78	3.03	3.14	3.84
女士服装	Women's Clothing	件	piece	2.79	3.90	4.06	4.79
童　装	Children's Clothing	件	piece	0.60	0.85	0.72	0.69
鞋　类	Shoes	双	pair	2.40	2.66	2.72	3.17

5-19 城市居民家庭平均每百户主要消费品全年购买量
PER 100 URBAN HOUSEHOLDS ANNUAL PURCHASES OF MAJOR CONSUMER GOODS
(1999-2003)

商品名称	Item	1999	2000	2001	2002	2003
摩托车(辆)	Motorcycle(unit)	0.6	0.4	0.2	0.3	0.2
自行车(辆)	Bicycle(unit)	13.8	15.6	13.8	18.9	19.7
电风扇(台)	Electric Fan(unit)	7.4	5.0	4.4	5.3	6.4
洗衣机(台)	Washing Machine(unit)	5.8	3.8	5.6	4.8	6.8
电冰箱(台)	Refrigerator(unit)	5.2	6.0	6.4	5.7	4.9
冰　柜(台)	Freezer(unit)	0.6	0.8	0.6	0.9	0.5
彩色电视机(台)	Color TV Set(unit)	11.8	9.0	9.0	9.9	6.8
影碟机(台)	Video Disc Player(unit)	7.4	2.8	3.6	4.7	4.4
录放像机(台)	Videorecorder(unit)	0.2			0.1	0.2
组合音响(台)	Hi-Fi Stereo Component System(unit)	2.2	0.8	1.2	1.5	1.1
收录机(台)	Recorder(unit)	4.8	3.2	3.6	6.9	6.4
家用电脑(台)	Micro-Computer(unit)	2.4	4.4	5.2	5.7	5.6
照像机(架)	Camera(set)	1.2	0.6	1.6	1.1	1.1
微波炉(台)	Microwave Oven(unit)	8.8	10.2	11.2	6.3	7.0
空调器(台)	Air-conditioner(unit)	8.2	14.0	7.6	6.7	6.7
电炊具(台)	Electric Cooking Appliance(unit)	7.2	9.6	9.4	8.7	9.5
淋浴热水器(台)	Shower (unit)	4.0	7.0	6.8	6.9	6.2
抽油烟机(台)	Smoke Absorber(unit)	5.0	4.2	4.8	5.1	6.2

5-20 城市居民家庭平均每百户耐用消费品年末拥有量
PER 100 URBAN HOUSEHOLDS YEAR-END POSSESSIONS OF MAJOR DURABLE CONSUMER GOODS
(1999-2003)

商品名称	Item	1999	2000	2001	2002	2003
组合家具(套)	Composite Furniture(set)	77.8	76.0	75.0	85.0	91.9
摩托车(辆)	Motorcycle (unit)	10.2	9.4	9.6	8.5	8.9
自行车(辆)	Bicycle (unit)	232.2	230.0	239.0	226.1	228.5
电风扇(台)	Electric Fan(unit)	131.4	127.2	132.6	118.7	119.9
洗衣机(台)	Washing Machine(unit)	97.4	97.6	95.6	96.0	96.3
电冰箱(台)	Refrigerator(unit)	98.8	99.8	102.6	102.1	98.5
冰　柜(台)	Freezer(unit)	20.0	19.4	19.2	18.0	16.7
彩色电视机(台)	Color TV Set(unit)	131.2	132.0	134.0	135.0	134.5
影碟机(台)	Video Disc Player(unit)	23.0	31.2	41.0	45.1	49.6
录放像机(台)	Video-recorder(unit)	39.8	33.8	31.8	30.4	30.3
组合音响(台)	Hi-Fi Stereo Component System(unit)	19.0	19.0	21.4	25.1	26.8
收录机(台)	Recorder(unit)	73.2	64.4	68.4	55.7	56.8
家用电脑(台)	Micro-Computer(unit)	11.2	16.4	21.2	26.3	34.1
照像机(架)	Camera(unit)	64.0	64.6	59.6	60.0	56.3
钢　琴(架)	Piano(unit)	1.6	0.6	0.6	1.5	1.4
微波炉(台)	Microwave Oven(unit)	24.6	30.8	43.0	51.1	61.4
空调器(台)	Air-conditioner(unit)	59.8	65.6	73.8	80.9	90.9
电炊具(台)	Electric Cooking Appliance(unit)	66.0	78.8	95.4	91.9	101.1
淋浴热水器(台)	Shower(unit)	64.6	70.2	78.6	79.0	82.7
抽油烟机(台)	Smoke Absorber(unit)	64.4	70.8	74.8	75.9	82.4

5－21　农村居民家庭基本情况
BASIC INDICATORS OF RURAL HOUSEHOLDS

项　目	Item	单　位　Unit	2001	2002	2003
一、户均常住人口	Average Permanent Residents Per Household	人　person	3.72	3.64	3.60
二、户均整半劳动力	Average Full－time and Part－time Labors Per Household	人　person	2.48	2.46	2.44
整半劳动力占人口比重	Proportion of Full－time and Part－time Labors to Residents	%	66.7	67.6	67.8
三、平均每个劳动力负担人口	Dependents Per Labor	人　person	1.50	1.48	1.48
四、年末户均生产性固定资产原值	Year－end Productive Original Value of Fixed Assets Per Household	元　yuan	6 624	7 228	7 051
五、户均经营耕地面积	Cultivated Land Areas Per Household	公顷　hectare	0.36	0.34	0.31
六、年末人均住房面积	Year－end Living Space Per Capita	平方米　sq.m	23.93	24.33	24.44
七、全年人均纯收入	Annual Net Income Per Capita	元　yuan	4 825	5 315	5 861
八、全年人均生活消费支出	Per Capita Living Expenditures	元　yuan	2 618	2 778	3 015
九、户均乡镇企业人数	Employees in Township and Village Enterprise Per Household	人　person	0.60	0.63	0.60

5－22　农村居民家庭劳动力文化程度
EDUCATION LEVEL OF LABORS IN RURAL HOUSEHOLDS
(1999－2003)

单位：人　(person)

项　目	Item	1999	2000	2001	2002	2003
每百个劳动力中：	In Per 100 Labors：					
不识字或识字很少	Illiterate or Semi－illiterate	2.34	1.77	1.88	1.69	1.65
小　学	Primary School	24.07	27.89	27.35	28.01	25.37
初　中	Junior Middle School	54.75	56.10	56.45	54.94	55.84
高　中	Senior Middle School	13.26	9.78	10.43	10.49	11.13
中　专	Specialized Secondary School	4.32	3.17	2.88	3.65	4.64
大专及以上	Junior College	1.26	1.29	1.01	1.22	1.37

5－23 农村居民人均纯收入
PER CAPITA NET INCOME OF FARMER

单位：元 (yuan)

项　目	Item	2001	2002	2003	2003 比2002年增长% Increase Rat in 2003 over 2002
人均纯收入	**Per Capita Annual Net Income**	**4 825**	**5 315**	**5 861**	**10.3**
1.工资性收入	Rewards of Labours	2 662	2 939	3 248	10.5
#在非企业组织中劳动得到	From Collective Organiza	625	638	676	6.0
在本地企业中劳动得到	From Labour In Enterprises	1 728	1 929	2 143	11.1
#从乡镇集体企业中劳动得到	From Collective Ente	989	980	937	－4.4
2.家庭经营纯收入	Income from Family Busines	1 949	2 140	2 349	9.8
#农　业	Planting	1 016	1 060	1 178	11.1
畜牧业	Animal Husbandry	119	140	166	18.6
工　业	Industry	16	22	26	18.2
建筑业	Construction	137	153	165	7.8
交通运输、仓储和邮政业	Transportation, Post and Telecommunications	169	215	231	7.4
批发和零售业	Wholesale, Retail and Catering Trade	75	95	106	11.6
住宿和餐饮业	Accommodation Catering Service	46	50	55	10.0
社会服务业	Social Service	91	102	109	6.9
文教卫生业	Culture, Education & Health Care	20	26	27	3.8
3.转移性、财产性纯收入	Transfer and Property Income	214	236	264	11.9

5－26 农村居民人均纯收入构成
COMPOSITION OF PER CAPITA NET INCOME OF FARMER

单位：% (%)

项　目	Item	2001	2002	2003
人均纯收入	**Per Capita Annual Net Income**	**100.0**	**100.0**	**100.0**
1.工资性收入	Rewards of Labours	55.2	55.3	55.4
#在非企业组织中劳动得到	From Collective Organiza	13.0	12.0	11.5
在本地企业中劳动得到	From Labour In Enterprises	35.8	36.3	36.6
#从乡镇集体企业中劳动得到	From Collective Ente	20.5	18.4	16.0
2.家庭经营纯收入	Income from Family Busines	40.4	40.3	40.1
#农　业	Planting	21.1	19.9	20.1
畜牧业	Animal Husbandry	2.5	2.6	2.8
工　业	Industry	0.3	0.4	0.4
建筑业	Construction	2.9	2.9	2.8
交通运输、仓储和邮政业	Transportation, Post and Telecommunications	3.5	4.1	3.9
批发和零售业	Wholesale, Retail and Catering Trade	1.6	1.8	1.8
住宿和餐饮业	Accommodation Catering Service	1.0	0.9	0.9
社会服务业	Social Service	1.9	1.9	1.9
文教卫生业	Culture, Education & Health Care	0.4	0.5	0.5
3.转移性、财产性纯收入	Transfer and Property Income	4.4	4.4	4.5

5-25 农村居民人均生活消费支出
PER CAPITA ANNUAL LIVING EXPENDITURES OF FARMER

单位:元 (yuan)

项目	Item	2001	2002	2003	2003比2002年增长% Increase Rate in 2003 over 2002
人均生活消费支出	**Per Capita Annual Living Expenditures**	**2 618**	**2 778**	**3 015**	**8.5**
食品	Food	1 059	1 062	1 156	8.9
衣着	Clothing	241	263	266	1.1
居住	Residence	519	578	694	20.1
家庭设备、用品及服务	Household Facilities,Articles and Services	137	113	105	-7.1
医疗保健	Medicine and Medical Services	171	220	230	4.5
交通通讯	Transportation and Communications	167	195	216	10.8
文教娱乐用品及服务	Culture,Education and Recreation Articles and Services	220	234	246	5.1
其他商品和服务	Other Commodities and Services	104	113	102	-9.7

5-26 农村居民人均生活消费支出构成
COMPOSITION OF PER CAPITA LIVING EXPENDITURES OF FARMER

单位:% (%)

项目	Item	2001	2002	2003
人均生活消费支出	**Per Capita Annual Living Expenditure**	**100.0**	**100.0**	**100.0**
食品	Food	40.5	38.2	38.3
衣着	Clothing	9.2	9.5	8.8
居住	Residence	19.8	20.8	23.0
家庭设备、用品及服务	Household Facilities,Articles and Services	5.2	4.1	3.5
医疗保健	Medicine and Medical Services	6.5	7.9	7.6
交通通讯	Transportation and Communications	6.4	7.0	7.2
文教娱乐用品及服务	Culture,Education and Recreation Articles and Services	8.4	8.4	8.2
其他商品和服务	Other Commodities and Services	4.0	4.1	3.4

5-27 农村居民家庭每百户耐用消费品拥有量
PER 100 RURAL HOUSEHOLDS YEAR-END POSSESSIONS OF DURABLE CONSUMER GOODS
(1999-2003)

商品名称	Item	1999	2000	2001	2002	2003
自行车(辆)	Bicycles(unit)	221	179	200	204	198
电动自行车(辆)	Bicycles(unit)				2	3
摩托车(辆)	Motorcycles(unit)	30	31	40	41	45
生活用汽车(辆)	Cars(unit)		2	2	3	3
电风扇(台)	Electric Fans(set)	159	163	182	180	171
洗衣机(台)	Washing Machines(set)	84	85	90	86	90
电冰箱(台)	Refrigerators(set)	64	65	66	72	75
吸尘器(台)	Vacuum Cleaners(set)	5	5	5	5	6
空调器(台)	Air-Conditioners(set)	9	15	20	26	32
普通电话(部)	Telephone(set)		51	72	80	84
移动电话(部)	Mobile Telephone(set)		11	19	36	54
家用电脑(台)	Micro-Computers(set)		2	3	5	7
微波炉(台)	Oven(Set)			4	7	10
黑白电视机(台)	Black/White TV Sets(set)	33	19	20	17	16
彩色电视机(台)	Color TV Sets(set)	98	98	103	105	110
照相机(架)	Cameras(set)	14	15	19	20	20
影碟机(台)	Video Disc Player(Set)			24	27	31
收录机(台)	Recorders(Set)	50	21	21	19	19
录像机(台)	Video Recorders(Set)	10	8	10	9	7
摄像机(台)	Vidicon(Set)					1

5-28 农村居民人均食品消费量
PER CAPITA ANNUAL CONSUMPTION ON FOOD OF RURAL HOUSEHOLDS
(1999-2003)

单位:千克 (kg)

商品名称	Item	1999	2000	2001	2002	2003
粮　食	Grain	185.0	192.7	207.4	199.0	195.0
蔬菜及其制品	Vegetables and Relative Products	89.3	77.1	117.5	132.4	134.3
食用植物油	Vegetable Oil	7.0	8.1	9.2	10.8	9.3
食用动物油	Animal Oil	1.1	1.2	1.0	0.9	0.7
猪　肉	Pork	9.8	9.5	8.9	8.9	9.4
牛　肉	Beef	0.6	0.7	0.9	0.6	0.7
羊　肉	Mutton	1.3	1.1	1.0	1.1	1.0
家　禽	Poultry	0.6	0.8	0.9	1.1	1.1
肉禽制品	Meat, Poultry and Related Products	1.3	0.9	0.6	0.9	1.2
蛋类及其制品	Eggs and Related Products	11.6	10.8	12.0	14.4	16.6
奶及奶制品	Milk and Related Products			1.0	1.3	1.9
水产品	Aquatic Products	8.8	7.5	7.3	8.7	9.4
干鲜瓜果	Dried and Fresh Melons and Fruits	34.4	37.1	31.8	32.4	32.6
食　糖	Sugar	1.4	0.8	1.2	2.0	1.1
白　酒	Wine	3.2	3.5	3.2	3.3	3.2
啤　酒	Beer	7.8	7.5	8.1	7.3	7.0

主要统计指标解释

城镇单位从业人员劳动报酬 是指各单位在一定时期内直接支付给本单位全部从业人员的劳动报酬总额。包括在岗职工工资总额和本单位其他从业人员劳动报酬两部分。

在岗职工工资总额 指各单位在一定时期内直接支付给本单位在岗职工的全部劳动报酬总额。在岗职工工资总额构成包括:计时工资(含计时标准工资)、计件工资、奖金、计件超额工资、津贴和补贴、加班加点工资、特殊情况下支付的工资等。

其他从业人员劳动报酬 指各单位在一定时期内直接支付给本单位其他从业人员的全部劳动报酬。包括支付给再就业的离退休人员的劳动报酬和民办教师、港澳台和外籍人员的劳动报酬总额。还包括支付给聘用的外单位不在岗人员、聘用的失业人员、聘用和使用的外来人员、聘用的在本单位从事第二职业人员的劳动报酬。

职工保险福利费总额 指各单位在工资以外实际支付给职工个人和用于集体的劳动保险福利费用总额。

城市居民家庭就业人口 指从事社会劳动并取得报酬或经营收入的人口,不论在全民、集体和其他所有制单位工作或从事个体劳动,不论有固定性职业或临时性职业都是就业人口。

城市居民家庭总收入 指城市居民家庭中生活在一起的所有家庭成员在调查期得到的工薪收入、经营净收入、财产性收入、转移性收入的总和,不包括出售财物收入和借贷收入。收入的统计标准以实际发生的数额为准,无论收入是补发还是预发,只要是调查期得到的都应如实计算,不作分摊。

城市居民家庭可支配收入 指城市居民家庭可用于最终消费支出和其他非义务性支出以及储蓄的总和,即居民家庭可以用来自由支配的收入。它是家庭总收入扣除交纳的所得税、个人交纳的社会保障费以及调查户的记帐收入补贴后的收入。计算公式为:

可支配收入 = 家庭总收入 - 交纳所得税 - 个人交纳的社会保障支出 - 记帐补贴

城市居民家庭消费支出 指城市居民家庭用于本家庭日常生活消费需要的全部支出,包括食品、衣着、家庭设备用品及服务、医疗保健、交通和通讯、娱乐教育文化服务、居住、杂项商品和服务等八大类。

城市居民家庭服务性消费支出 指城市居民家庭用于本家庭支付社会提供的各种文化和生活方面的非商品性服务费用。不包括为别人付款的服务费用。

农村居民常住人口 指全年经常在家或在家居住六个月以上,而且经济和生活与本户连成一体的人口。外出从业人员在外居住时间虽然在六个月以上,但收入主要带回家中,经济与本户连成一体,仍视为家庭常住人口;在家居住、生活和本户连成一体的国家职工、退休人员也视为家庭常住人口。但是现役军人、中专及以上(走读生除外)的在校学生、以及常年在外(不包括探亲、看病等)且已有稳定的职业与居住场所的外出从业人员,不应当作为家庭常住人口。

农村居民家庭赡养人口 指农村住户供给其生活的人口。

农村居民纯收入 指农村住户当年从各个来源得到的总收入相应地扣除所发生的费用后的收入总和。纯收入主要用于再生产投入和当年生活消费支出,也可用于储蓄和各种非义务性支出。计算公式为:

农村居民纯收入 = 总收入 - 家庭经营费用支出 - 税费支出—生产性固定资产折旧 - 农村亲友赠送

农村居民工资性收入 指农村住户成员受雇于单位或个人,靠出卖劳动而获得的收入。包括:

(1)在非企业组织中劳动得到的收入:指农村住户成员在不具备企业性质的行政事业单位和各种组织中劳动得到的收入。包括村干部和民办教师的工资(奖金、补贴),乡及以上行政、事业单位工作人员的工资(奖金、补贴)等。

(2)在本地劳动得到的收入:指农村住户成员在所属乡(镇)地域范围内受雇于单位或个人,靠出卖劳动而获得的收入。

(3)常住人口外出从业得到的收入:指农村住户成员到住户所属乡镇地域范围以外从业得到的收入。

农村居民家庭经营收入 指农村住户以家庭为生产经营单位进行生产筹划和管理而获得的收入。家庭经营活动按行业划分为农业、林业、畜牧业、渔业、工业、建筑业、交通运输和邮电业、批发和零售贸易餐饮业、社会服务业、文教卫生业和其他家庭经营。

农村居民财产性收入 指金融资产或有形非生产性资产的所有者向其他机构单位提供资金或将有形非生产性资产供其支配,作为回报而从中获得的收入。包括利息收入、股息收入、租金收入、土地征用补偿收入等。

农村居民转移性收入 指农村住户和住户成员无须付出任何对应物而获得的货物、服务、资金或资产所有权等,不包括无偿提供的用于固定资本形成的资金。一般情况下,指农村住户在二次分配中的所有收入。包括家庭非常住人口寄回或带回、城市亲友赠送、农村亲友赠送等。

农村居民总收入 指调查期内农村住户和住户成员从各种来源渠道得到的收入总和(包括现金收入和实物收入)。按收入的性质划分为工资性收入、家庭经营收入、财产性收入和转移性收入。

农村居民家庭经营费用支出 指农村住户以家庭为基本生产经营单位从事生产经营活动而消费的商品和服务、自产自用产品。所消费的未计算为住户收入的自产自用产品,不计算为费用支出;库存的化肥、农药也不计算为本期费用支出。

农村居民生活消费支出 指农村住户用于物质生活和精神生活方面的支出。包括食品,衣着,居住,家庭设备、用品及服务,医疗保健,交通和通讯,文化教育娱乐用品及服务,其他商品和服务等消费支出。

Explanatory Notes on Main Statistical Indicators

Reward of Employment Personnel Worked in Urban Units refer to total reward payment of employment personnel worked in units during a certain period. It includes total wages of working staff and workers and reward of other employment personnel.

Total Wages of Working Staff and Workers refer to the total reward payment to working staff and workers in their units during a certain period of time. It includes time wage, piece wage, Cash awards, exceed wage, subsidy, working overtime wage and other special wage.

Total Reward Payment to Other Employment Personnel refers to the total reward payment to other persons employed in their units during a certain period of time. It includes reward payment to re - employed retirees, teachers in schools run by the local people, foreigners and Chinese compatriots from HongKong, Macao, and Taiwan working in various units, employees of other units working temporarily at current posts, unemployment personnel, non - locals, and employees holding the second job of other unit.

Total Insurance Welfare Funds of Staff and Workers refer to the total labour insurance welfare funds payment to every staff and worker in various units and collective of the units.

Employment Personnel of Urban Households refers to the persons who are engaged in social labor and receive payment or earn business income, including the staff and workers in the state - owned, the staff and workers in collective - owned, other employed, employed persons individual business, etc. No matter he is permanent or temporary.

Total Income of Urban Households refers to the total income of the sample households, including wage, income from business, income from property, transfer income, excluding proceeds from sales of belongings and credit income. It is calculated on real income, no matter the income is supplied again or beforehand.

Disposable Income of Urban Households refers to the disposable income of the sample households, including those which can be used for final expenditure and other non - obligation expenditure and savings. It refers to the difference of total income minus income tax, expenditure for social security and subsidies of account. The following formula is used

Disposable Income of Urban Households = Total Income - Income Tax - Expenditure for Social Security - Survey Subsidies

Expenditure for Consumption of Urban Households refers to total expenditure of the sample households for consumption in daily life. It is classified into 8 categories food, clothing, household facilities and articles service, medicine and medical service, transportation and communication, recreation, education and culture service, residence, miscellaneous commodities services.

Service Expenditure for Consumption of Urban Households refers to total non - commodity expenditure of the sample households for consumption in culture and life. It excludes service expenditure paid for other persons.

Rural Permanent Resident Population refers to population staying at home permanently or for over

6 months during a year and sharing life economically with the household. Members of the household staying away from the household for over 6 months but keeping a close economic life with the household by sending the majority of income to the household are regarded as resident population of the household. Government staff and workers or retirees living as close members of the household are also considered as resident population. However, servicemen, students of secondary technical schools or schools of higher education and persons with stable jobs and residence outside the household (excluding those visiting relatives or seeking medical service) are not included as resident population of the household.

Dependents of Rural household refer to population provided by rural household.

Net Income of Rural Households refers to the total income of the rural households after the deduction of the expenses for the various cost, which can then be spent for investment in reproduction, expenditure for living consumption, saving, non - productive construction. The formula for calculating is as follows

Net Income of Rural Households = Total Income - Expenses for Productive Operation - Taxes - Depreciation of Fixed Assets for Production - Gifts to Relatives

Income from Wages and Salaries of Rural Households refers to income from labour earned by members of rural households employed by other units or individuals. It includes

(a) Income by members of rural households employed by administration business units and social organizations, including wages (Cash awards and subsidy) of village staff and teachers in schools run by the local people, wages (Cash awards and subsidy) of staff employed by administration business units at township and higher level.

(b) Income earned at local region income from labour earned by members of rural households employed by other units or individuals at local township.

(c) Income of permanent residence outside the household income from labour earned by members of rural households employed by other units or individuals at outside local region.

Income of Productive Operation of Rural Households refers to income obtained from family productive operation. Family productive operation cover farming, forestry, animal husbandry, fishery, industry, construction, transport, post, telecommunication, wholesale and retail trade, catering, social services, culture, education, health care and other household operation.

Property Income of Rural Households refers to the income received as returns by owners of financial assets or tangible non - productive assets by providing capital or tangible non - productive assets to other institutional units. It includes interest income, bonus stock income, rent income, compensatory income of collected land.

Transfer Income of Rural Households refers to the receipt by rural households and their members of goods, services, capitals or rights of assets without giving or repaying accordingly, excluding capitals provided to them for the formation of fixed assets. In general, it refers to all income received by rural household through redistribution. It includes income receipt by non - permanent residents, gifts of urban & rural relatives.

Total Income of Rural Households refers to the sum of income earned from various sources by the rural households and their members during the referance period, and is classified as income from wages and salaries, income from household operations, property income and transfer income.

Expenditure on Rural Household Operations refers to expenditure by rural households on goods and services consumed (including own - produced goods) in household - based production or operations. Consumption of own - produced goods which are not included as household income is not considered as expenditure. Chemical fertilizers and pesticides in stock are not included as expenditure of the current period.

Expenditure on Consumption of Rural Households That Expenditure was use on matter life and energy life by rural households, including food expenditure, clothing expenditure, residence, household facilities, articles and services, medicines and medical services, transportation and communications, cultural, education and recreation articles and services, other commodity and services.

第6篇 CHAPTER 6

农村经济
RURAL ECONOMY

6-1 农村社会经济主要指标

MAJOR INDICATORS OF AGRICULTURAL SOCIETY AND ECONOMY

项　　目	Item	2001	2002	2003	2003比2002年增长% Increase Rate in 2003 over 2002
一、基本情况	**Basic Statistics**				
乡镇政府(个)	Township and Town Governments (unit)	140	140	140	
乡村总户数(万户)	Number of Rural Households(10 000 households)	112.65	112.85	115.27	2.1
乡村总人口(万人)	Rural Population (10 000 persons)	387.24	386.62	391.28	1.2
二、农业现代化	**Agricultural Modernization**				
农机总动力(万千瓦)	Total Power of Agricultural Machinery(10 000 kw)	603.32	612.72	601.66	-1.8
大中型拖拉机(台)	Large and Medium - sized Tractors(set)	9 600	8 900	9 290	4.4
小型拖拉机(万台)	Mini - tractors(10 000 sets)	3.71	3.65	3.58	-1.9
年末实有机电井(眼)	Motor - pumped Well(year - end)	24 972	25 992	25 509	-1.9
有效灌溉面积(万公顷)	Effective Irrigated Areas(10 000 hectares)	35.43	35.44	35.41	-0.1
节水灌溉面积(万公顷)	Water - saving Irrigated Areas(10 000 hectares)	15.20	16.26	17.47	7.4
农村用电量(万千瓦时)	Rural Electricity Consumption(10 000 kwh)	377 823	402 785	423 157	5.1
化肥施用量(折纯)(万吨)	Consumption of Chemical Fertilizers(pureness)(10 000 tons)	17.31	17.59	17.80	1.2
农药使用量(吨)	Consumption of Farm Pesticides(ton)	2 807	2 532	2 547	0.6
三、农作物总播种面积(万公顷)	**Total Sown Areas of Farm Crops (10 000 hectares)**	**54.45**	**52.28**	**50.15**	**-4.1**
#粮　食	Grain	32.85	31.13	25.81	-17.1
蔬　菜	Vegetables	12.95	12.84	13.46	4.8
四、总产量(万吨)	**Yield of Farm Crops(10 000 tons)**				
#粮　食	Grain	143.33	137.82	119.29	-13.4
蔬　菜	Vegetables	564.50	584.31	602.78	3.2
五、水果产量(万吨)	**Yield of Fruits(10 000 tons)**	**91.95**	**79.48**	**84.33**	**6.1**
#果用瓜	Melon - Fruits	62.66	49.61	52.69	6.2
六、年末实有林地面积(万公顷)	**Forest Area(year - end)(10 000 hectares)**	**14.19**	**17.53**	**18.21**	**3.9**
#当年造林面积	Afforested Area in This Year	0.50	0.76	0.69	-9.2

6－1 续表 Continued

项 目	Item	2001	2002	2003	2003 比 2002 年增长% Increase Rate in 2003 over 2002
七、畜牧业生产	**Production of Animal Husbandry**				
生猪出栏(万头)	Number of Slaughtered Pigs(10 000 heads)	306.19	362.36	412.94	14.0
牛出栏(万头)	Number of Slaughtered Cattle(10 000 heads)	21.60	27.93	32.82	17.5
羊出栏(万只)	Number of Slaughtered Sheep and Goats (10 000 heads)	108.61	124.74	142.45	14.2
家禽出栏(万只)	Number of Slaughtered Poultry(10 000 heads)	6 061.78	7 999.92	9 441.88	18.0
八、畜禽产品产量(万吨)	**Output of Animal and Poultry (10 000 tons)**				
肉类总产量	Output of Meat	36.40	44.88	52.41	16.8
#猪 肉	Pork	21.92	26.09	30.56	17.1
牛羊肉	Beef and Mutton	5.97	7.39	8.53	15.4
禽 肉	Poultry	8.07	10.88	12.81	17.7
禽蛋产量	Output of Poultry Eggs	26.00	24.47	24.25	-0.9
奶类产量	Output of Milk	24.05	33.59	43.23	28.7
九、渔业生产	**Production of Fishery**				
水产养殖面积(万公顷)	Cultured Areas of Aquatic Products (10 000 hectares)	3.67	3.82	3.83	0.3
#淡 水	Fresh Water	3.23	3.24	3.33	2.8
水产品产量(万吨)	Output of Aquatic Products(10 000 tons)	26.46	28.56	29.83	4.4
#淡 水	Fresh Water	22.07	23.28	24.74	6.3
十、农林牧渔业总产值(亿元)	**Gross Output Value of Farming, Forestry, Animal Husbandry and Fishery(100 million yuan)**	**169.51**	**181.07**	**193.44**	**6.6**
农 业	Farming	86.73	86.06	88.20	0.02
林 业	Forestry	1.46	1.52	1.61	3.8
牧 业	Animal Husbandry	60.76	69.21	77.22	13.6
渔 业	Fishery	20.56	24.28	26.41	6.7

注:农林牧渔业总产值按当年价格计算,增长速度按可比价格计算(下同)。
Note:Gross output value of farming,forestry,animal husbandry and fishery are calculated at current prices,increase rate are based on comparable prices(same as following next).

6－2　农村基层组织情况
BASIC CONDITION OF RURAL GRASSROOTS UNITS
(1990－2003)

年　份 Year	乡镇政府（个）Township and Town Governments (unit)	#镇政府 Town Governments	村民委员会（个）Villagers' Committees (unit)	乡村总人口（万人）Rural Population (10 000 persons)	乡村总户数（万户）Number of Rural Households (10 000 households)	乡村从业人员（万人）Number of Rural Persons Employed (10 000 persons)
1990	221	35	3 872	393.43	110.35	170.79
1991	221	37	3 870	389.75	109.66	171.00
1992	222	38	3 872	397.37	112.94	172.39
1993	223	43	3 871	411.75	118.80	174.30
1994	226	49	3 877	395.32	112.06	172.03
1995	226	71	3 876	396.26	112.62	169.85
1996	226	78	3 878	394.84	113.19	167.92
1997	225	94	3 877	389.65	112.38	167.39
1998	224	95	3 877	392.92	113.79	166.39
1999	221	103	3 872	388.22	112.48	165.27
2000	218	103	3 850	386.08	112.07	168.07
2001	140	120	3 829	387.24	112.65	169.16
2002	140	120	3 836	386.62	112.85	168.71
2003	140	120	3 836	391.28	115.27	173.32

注：2000 年以前乡村从业人员为乡村劳动力。
Note: Rural employment personnel refer to rural laborer before 2000.

6－3　改革开放以来乡村从业人员分布情况
DISTRIBUTION OF RURAL LABOR FORCE SINCE REFORM AND OPENING UP

单位：万人　　(10 000 persons)

年　份 Year	农林牧渔业 Farming, Forestry, Animal Husbandry and Fishery	工　业 Industry	建筑业 Construction	交通运输邮电仓储业 Transportation, Post, Telecommu－nications and Storage	批发零售贸易餐饮业 Wholesale, Retail Trade and Catering Services
1978	103.37	23.06	0.81		
1979	105.93	24.29	0.91		
1980	105.04	26.15	1.90		
1981	107.42	39.20	2.25		
1982	107.57	38.14	3.84	1.78	1.03
1983	105.06	42.71	5.14	2.47	1.51
1984	95.99	51.11	7.10	3.78	2.32
1985	95.16	52.61	9.25	5.57	3.48
1986	91.55	52.18	9.42	5.62	4.06
1987	89.87	54.06	9.40	5.48	4.34
1988	86.89	54.01	9.20	5.42	4.43
1989	89.23	51.82	8.67	5.35	4.47
1990	89.53	51.75	8.44	5.57	4.73
1991	89.93	51.60	8.44	5.82	4.95
1992	88.43	52.78	8.57	6.94	5.56
1993	86.47	54.43	8.93	7.78	6.12
1994	83.33	53.60	9.23	8.68	6.71
1995	80.90	52.54	9.43	9.28	7.32
1996	80.23	50.82	9.57	9.25	7.64
1997	79.43	49.01	9.72	9.53	8.66
1998	79.07	48.66	9.67	9.46	6.47
1999	78.09	43.65	10.99	10.20	10.42
2000	79.65	42.85	11.03	10.45	10.70
2001	81.02	40.69	11.59	10.40	11.94
2002	80.28	40.65	11.79	10.51	12.45
2003	81.16	45.13	12.87	11.91	14.67

注：2000 年以前乡村从业人员为乡村劳动力。
Note: Rural persons employed refer to rural laborer before 2000.

6-4 改革开放以来农业生产条件情况

CONDITIONS OF AGRICULTURAL PRODUCTION SINCE REFORM AND OPENING UP

年 份 Year	年末实有常用耕地面积(万公顷) Cultivated Area (year-end) (10 000 hectares)	年末实有林地面积(万公顷) Forest Area (year-end) (10 000 hectares)	#当年造林面积 Afforested Area in The Year	水产养殖面积(万公顷) Cultured Area of Aquatic Products (10 000 hectares)	有效灌溉面积(万公顷) Effective Irrigated Area (10 000 hectares)
1978	46.94	2.12	0.07	0.76	37.09
1979	46.84	1.88	0.17	0.61	38.09
1980	46.41	2.68	0.13	0.41	37.93
1981	46.29	2.70	0.09	0.53	37.95
1982	46.10	3.01	0.30	0.61	37.07
1983	45.86	3.18	0.28	1.02	36.52
1984	45.41	3.50	0.35	1.21	36.09
1985	44.70	3.82	0.28	1.73	34.94
1986	44.14	3.69	0.02	2.18	34.06
1987	43.85	3.85	0.19	2.50	34.08
1988	43.33	4.06	0.26	2.68	34.26
1989	43.23	4.36	0.37	2.76	34.22
1990	43.15	4.47	0.73	2.68	32.69
1991	43.16	6.40	0.55	2.65	32.88
1992	42.95	7.12	0.72	2.70	32.75
1993	42.87	7.37	0.77	2.73	32.85
1994	42.74	8.32	0.78	2.90	32.96
1995	42.61	8.70	0.48	3.12	33.24
1996	42.58	9.26	0.62	3.41	33.26
1997	42.52	9.85	0.90	3.81	33.28
1998	42.49	11.14	0.91	3.71	33.29
1999	42.46	12.74	0.94	3.76	34.39
2000	42.43	13.69	0.93	3.64	35.32
2001	42.39	14.19	0.50	3.67	35.43
2002	42.28	17.53	0.76	3.82	35.44
2003	41.85	18.21	0.69	3.83	35.41

年 份 Year	农用机械总动力(万千瓦) Total Power of Agricultural Machinery (10 000 kw)	机耕面积(万公顷) Cultivated Area Using Machinery (10 000 hectares)	机播面积(万公顷) Sown Area Using Machinery (10 000 hectares)	化肥施用量(折纯)(万吨) Consumption of Chemical Fertilizers (Pureness) (10 000 tons)	农村用电量(万千瓦小时) Rural Electricity Consumption (10 000 kwh)
1978	176.84	40.13	14.35	29.03	53 087
1979	189.71	39.75	15.52	32.36	61 067
1980	205.44	39.06	13.20	27.62	67 281
1981	212.66	38.56	10.99	21.17	67 368
1982	218.46	38.03	9.29	21.52	68 783
1983	224.70	33.57	7.55	23.77	82 032
1984	245.06	34.04	8.13	25.56	96 800
1985	248.16	32.02	7.22	27.12	103 093
1986	262.28	35.51	8.73	27.56	112 929
1987	277.61	37.86	8.28	28.04	115 850
1988	298.83	39.52	10.40	34.18	132 128
1989	303.71	39.70	10.90	39.53	154 286
1990	311.27	39.90	13.21	40.99	165 331
1991	303.76	40.17	14.53	42.53	180 834
1992	308.63	40.65	17.13	41.19	218 273
1993	302.22	38.47	15.00	40.13	231 072
1994	335.72	39.93	17.22	41.06	250 611
1995	364.08	38.08	19.50	45.29	325 482
1996	384.22	39.85	22.28	48.82	358 184
1997	417.37	39.66	25.00	49.15	330 249
1998	440.57	40.13	24.99	51.48	337 565
1999	481.54	39.62	24.93	47.24	343 667
2000	593.40	39.62	25.73	16.64	354 946
2001	603.32	37.26	24.11	17.31	377 823
2002	612.72	38.17	23.95	17.59	402 785
2003	601.66	37.05	23.57	17.80	423 157

注：化肥施用量2000年以前为实物量。
Note: Consumption of chemical fertilizers refered to full-scale quantity before 2000.

6-5 改革开放以来农林牧渔业总产值及增长速度情况
GROSS OUTPUT VALUE AND INCREASE RATE OF FARMING, FORESTRY, ANIMAL HUSBANDRY AND FISHERY SINCE REFORM AND OPENING UP

年份 Year	合计 Total	农业 Farming	林业 Forestry	牧业 Animal Husbandry	渔业 Fishery
总产值(亿元) Gross Output Value (100 million yuan)					
1978	6.72	5.40	0.04	1.05	0.22
1979	8.88	7.10	0.04	1.48	0.26
1980	9.25	7.25	0.05	1.63	0.33
1981	8.34	6.11	0.05	1.95	0.23
1982	12.56	10.17	0.11	1.90	0.37
1983	12.68	9.58	0.16	2.47	0.47
1984	16.68	12.17	0.25	3.70	0.56
1985	20.44	13.81	0.27	5.10	1.25
1986	26.93	18.80	0.31	5.67	2.14
1987	32.93	22.47	0.37	7.22	2.87
1988	42.34	29.39	0.72	7.94	4.29
1989	49.08	34.71	0.33	10.09	3.95
1990	51.72	34.71	0.45	11.54	5.02
1991	54.55	36.68	0.34	12.88	4.65
1992	58.50	39.24	0.45	13.44	5.37
1993	66.32	44.28	0.44	15.82	5.78
1994	88.74	57.71	0.60	22.91	7.52
1995	125.44	85.25	0.85	28.76	10.58
1996	133.53	90.17	0.96	30.27	12.13
1997	140.47	89.77	1.00	33.99	15.71
1998	156.16	98.83	1.19	38.09	18.05
1999	150.11	91.58	1.42	38.95	18.16
2000	156.30	83.42	1.37	51.75	19.76
2001	169.51	86.73	1.46	60.76	20.56
2002	181.07	86.06	1.52	69.21	24.28
2003	193.44	88.20	1.61	77.22	26.41
增长速度(比上年)(%) Increase Rate over Preceding Year					
1978	23.0	28.2	-9.8	16.9	-6.8
1979	16.8	16.1	4.9	6.9	-23.8
1980	4.9	4.4	31.9	8.1	-5.7
1981	-10.3	-13.0	-24.9	3.3	-13.1
1982	20.9	26.5	9.1	2.7	16.7
1983	1.3	-3.3	25.0	16.9	18.4
1984	27.7	25.7	73.5	33.9	18.9
1985	12.7	6.5	-15.0	36.1	12.0
1986	11.4	15.9	0.2	-4.3	41.3
1987	9.2	7.6	1.7	4.1	37.0
1988	6.1	-0.5	77.3	15.8	17.3
1989	11.2	15.4	-48.1	5.3	11.5
1990	6.7	6.6	17.4	7.4	5.0
1991	6.7	7.0	-16.3	10.2	-0.2
1992	4.1	4.5	21.5	3.0	3.4
1993	4.3	5.6	-12.3	7.8	-9.6
1994	7.3	4.3	4.1	14.3	8.4
1995	13.0	13.5	-1.0	5.1	33.4
1996	7.5	8.5	10.3	3.5	10.6
1997	7.6	5.1	2.6	10.5	15.7
1998	11.8	8.2	39.7	15.4	21.2
1999	0.4	-6.3	15.1	13.7	3.1
2000	4.2	-4.4	-5.7	19.6	6.1
2001	8.0	4.1	7.2	15.9	3.0
2002	6.0	-8.9	13.7	14.9	36.2
2003	6.6	0.02	3.8	13.6	6.7

6-6 改革开放以来农林牧渔业总产值结构
STRUCTURE OF GROSS OUTPUT VALUE OF FARMING,FORESTRY, ANIMAL HUSBANDRY AND FISHERY SINCE REFORM AND OPENING UP

单位:% (%)

年份 Year	合计 Total	农业 Farming	林业 Forestry	牧业 Animal Husbandry	渔业 Fishery
1978	100.0	80.4	0.6	15.6	3.4
1979	100.0	80.0	0.5	16.7	2.8
1980	100.0	78.4	0.5	17.6	3.5
1981	100.0	73.3	0.6	23.4	2.7
1982	100.0	81.0	0.9	15.1	3.0
1983	100.0	75.6	1.3	19.5	3.6
1984	100.0	73.0	1.5	22.2	3.3
1985	100.0	67.6	1.3	25.0	6.1
1986	100.0	69.8	1.2	21.1	7.9
1987	100.0	68.2	1.1	21.9	8.8
1988	100.0	69.4	1.7	18.8	10.1
1989	100.0	70.7	0.7	20.6	8.0
1990	100.0	67.1	0.9	22.3	9.7
1991	100.0	67.2	0.6	23.6	8.6
1992	100.0	67.1	0.8	23.0	9.1
1993	100.0	66.8	0.7	23.9	8.6
1994	100.0	65.0	0.7	25.8	8.5
1995	100.0	68.0	0.7	22.9	8.4
1996	100.0	67.5	0.7	22.7	9.1
1997	100.0	63.9	0.7	24.2	11.2
1998	100.0	63.3	0.8	24.4	11.5
1999	100.0	61.0	0.9	25.9	12.2
2000	100.0	53.4	0.9	33.1	12.6
2001	100.0	51.2	0.9	35.8	12.1
2002	100.0	47.5	0.8	38.3	13.4
2003	100.0	45.6	0.8	39.9	13.7

6-7 农作物播种面积
SOWN AREAS OF FARM CROPS

(1990-2003)

单位:万公顷 (10 000 hectares)

年份 Year	合计 Total	粮食 Grain	棉花 Cotton	油料 Oil-bearing Crops	蔬菜 Vegetables	其他农作物 other
1990	54.95	45.23	1.04	2.21	5.08	1.39
1991	55.30	45.19	1.74	1.93	5.24	1.20
1992	54.56	44.03	1.67	1.85	5.71	1.30
1993	54.61	44.64	0.57	1.83	6.12	1.45
1994	53.00	41.74	1.33	1.72	7.02	1.19
1995	54.91	43.78	1.00	1.69	7.50	0.94
1996	56.44	45.57	0.38	1.37	8.08	1.04
1997	55.73	43.99	0.28	1.61	8.82	1.03
1998	56.32	44.45	0.35	1.69	8.64	1.19
1999	56.29	43.10	0.60	1.62	9.86	1.11
2000	53.31	34.59	1.51	2.63	12.83	1.75
2001	54.45	32.85	4.50	2.05	12.95	2.10
2002	52.28	31.13	4.48	1.89	12.84	1.94
2003	50.15	25.81	7.06	1.58	13.46	2.24

6-8 改革开放以来主要农产品产量情况
YIELD OF MAJOR FARM CROPS SINCE REFORM AND OPENING UP

单位:万吨 (10 000 tons)

年 份 Year	粮 食 Grain	#小 麦 Wheat	#玉 米 Corn	棉 花 Cotton	油 料 Oil-bearing Crops	蔬 菜 Vegetables
1978	117.10	47.96	31.68	0.23	1.00	122.37
1979	138.69	49.04	42.47	0.11	1.51	127.32
1980	137.76	27.42	57.74	0.16	2.79	111.72
1981	110.00	20.80	55.53	0.23	4.50	111.25
1982	122.51	18.83	68.02	0.45	4.43	129.29
1983	110.87	32.89	47.07	1.14	3.09	128.07
1984	131.30	32.79	56.21	3.29	5.52	147.77
1985	140.52	43.52	55.12	2.38	6.84	151.52
1986	157.60	46.10	64.20	1.33	5.86	193.95
1987	167.67	47.52	69.64	1.28	5.22	202.48
1988	158.30	52.36	52.72	1.01	3.45	215.44
1989	169.80	57.30	63.50	1.10	4.42	260.51
1990	188.75	64.74	74.00	1.53	4.68	268.14
1991	198.50	62.00	79.90	2.55	4.50	282.56
1992	198.74	62.00	76.04	1.63	3.96	310.41
1993	199.82	59.07	80.80	0.76	4.45	354.34
1994	190.33	50.76	77.65	0.93	4.03	407.86
1995	207.46	65.40	80.50	1.12	4.01	434.17
1996	207.00	67.35	75.41	0.51	3.13	452.71
1997	206.16	77.41	65.45	0.39	3.01	486.23
1998	210.12	76.06	75.51	0.63	3.76	505.35
1999	174.85	71.60	56.30	0.57	2.34	486.07
2000	124.05	59.91	40.95	1.75	3.31	530.60
2001	143.33	45.09	75.19	6.36	3.90	564.50
2002	137.82	44.11	71.05	6.24	3.40	584.31
2003	119.29	35.91	64.81	9.47	3.08	602.78

年 份 Year	肉 类 Meats	#猪 肉 Pork	#牛羊肉 Beef and Mutton	禽 蛋 Poultry Eggs	奶 类 Milk	水产品 Aquatic Products
1978	6.51	5.96	0.06	1.64	1.72	4.49
1979	6.63	5.97	0.08	1.94	1.96	3.28
1980	6.46	5.98	0.09	1.27	2.24	3.21
1981	7.14	6.77	0.10	1.91	2.61	2.69
1982	5.90	5.30	0.16	2.63	2.92	3.59
1983	5.50	4.88	0.18	4.49	3.37	4.11
1984	6.54	5.47	0.45	7.19	3.90	4.45
1985	7.12	5.85	0.47	10.62	4.30	4.87
1986	7.57	6.14	0.67	10.65	4.71	6.73
1987	7.14	5.73	0.61	10.88	5.31	8.13
1988	7.76	6.03	0.67	10.83	6.07	9.15
1989	8.23	6.37	0.73	12.18	6.63	10.38
1990	9.13	7.07	0.84	13.01	7.40	10.83
1991	9.89	7.19	1.05	15.01	8.41	10.81
1992	11.31	7.43	1.24	14.95	9.10	11.10
1993	11.47	7.26	1.61	15.08	9.14	11.39
1994	13.69	8.32	2.37	17.48	9.43	12.83
1995	15.86	9.59	3.09	16.94	10.47	15.35
1996	16.94	10.50	3.30	16.65	10.69	16.99
1997	18.70	11.77	3.44	17.71	12.13	18.98
1998	21.74	13.88	3.74	22.68	11.69	21.38
1999	23.53	14.59	4.24	23.56	12.94	23.03
2000	29.49	17.96	4.76	25.60	16.52	24.22
2001	36.40	21.92	5.97	26.00	24.06	26.46
2002	44.88	26.09	7.39	24.47	33.59	28.56
2003	52.41	30.56	8.53	24.25	43.23	29.83

6－9 粮食作物种植结构与产量结构

STRUCTURE OF SOWN AREAS AND YIELD OF GRAIN CROPS

(1983－2003)

单位：%　　　　(%)

年份 Year	粮食作物合计 Grain	小麦 Wheat	水稻 Rice	玉米 Corn	其他粮食 Others
种植结构 Structure of Sown Areas					
1983	100.0	31.0	4.8	35.1	29.1
1984	100.0	33.4	4.9	32.3	29.4
1985	100.0	33.9	6.9	30.5	28.7
1986	100.0	31.6	7.7	32.2	28.5
1987	100.0	30.6	8.9	33.5	27.0
1988	100.0	31.2	10.3	32.5	26.0
1989	100.0	30.4	10.9	33.3	25.4
1990	100.0	31.2	9.5	35.7	23.6
1991	100.0	32.5	12.0	33.7	21.8
1992	100.0	32.5	12.0	34.2	21.3
1993	100.0	31.1	8.7	35.0	25.2
1994	100.0	28.8	9.0	37.1	25.1
1995	100.0	32.4	10.5	36.0	21.1
1996	100.0	32.6	12.7	37.8	16.9
1997	100.0	34.5	14.3	35.9	15.3
1998	100.0	34.6	11.6	37.5	16.3
1999	100.0	33.2	14.2	39.1	13.5
2000	100.0	35.2	10.2	37.9	16.7
2001	100.0	32.5	3.5	42.9	21.1
2002	100.0	30.8	4.8	47.1	17.3
2003	100.0	30.3	2.7	48.4	18.6
产量结构 Structure of Yield					
1983	100.0	29.7	9.1	42.5	18.7
1984	100.0	25.0	10.1	42.8	22.1
1985	100.0	31.0	12.4	39.2	17.4
1986	100.0	29.3	13.6	40.7	16.4
1987	100.0	28.3	14.2	41.5	16.0
1988	100.0	33.1	18.2	33.3	15.4
1989	100.0	33.7	16.3	37.4	12.6
1990	100.0	34.3	14.9	39.2	11.6
1991	100.0	31.2	16.6	40.2	12.0
1992	100.0	31.2	19.8	38.3	10.7
1993	100.0	28.3	15.3	38.8	17.6
1994	100.0	26.7	16.7	40.8	15.8
1995	100.0	31.5	18.7	38.8	11.0
1996	100.0	32.5	22.9	36.4	8.2
1997	100.0	37.5	24.8	31.7	6.0
1998	100.0	36.2	21.5	35.9	6.4
1999	100.0	40.9	23.0	32.2	3.9
2000	100.0	48.3	11.7	33.0	7.0
2001	100.0	31.5	5.2	52.5	10.8
2002	100.0	32.0	8.1	51.6	8.3
2003	100.0	30.1	4.7	54.3	10.9

6-10 农作物种植结构
STRUCTURE OF FARM CROPS SOWN AREAS
(1990-2003)

单位:% (%)

年份 Year	合计 Total	粮食 Grain	棉花 Cotton	油料 Oil-bearing Crops	蔬菜 Vegetables	其他农作物 Others
1990	100.0	82.3	1.9	4.0	9.2	2.6
1991	100.0	81.7	3.1	3.5	9.5	2.2
1992	100.0	80.7	3.1	3.4	10.5	2.3
1993	100.0	81.7	1.0	3.4	11.2	2.7
1994	100.0	78.8	2.5	3.2	13.2	2.3
1995	100.0	79.7	1.8	3.1	13.7	1.7
1996	100.0	80.7	0.7	2.4	14.3	1.9
1997	100.0	78.9	0.5	2.9	15.8	1.9
1998	100.0	78.9	0.6	3.0	15.3	2.2
1999	100.0	76.6	1.1	2.9	17.5	1.9
2000	100.0	64.9	2.8	4.9	24.1	3.3
2001	100.0	60.3	8.3	3.8	23.8	3.8
2002	100.0	59.5	8.6	3.6	24.6	3.7
2003	100.0	51.5	14.1	3.1	26.8	4.5

6-11 各区县农村基层组织建设(2003年)
BASIC CONDITION OF RURAL GRASSROOTS UNITS BY DISTRICT AND COUNTY, 2003

地区 Region	乡镇政府(个) Township and Town Governments (unit)	#镇政府 Town Governments	村民委员会(个) Villagers' Committees (unit)	乡村户数(户) Number of Rural Households (household)	乡村人口(人) Rural Population (person)	乡村从业人员(人) Number of Rural Persons Employed (person)
总计 Total	**140**	**120**	**3 836**	**1 152 701**	**3 912 751**	**1 733 221**
塘沽区 Tanggu District	1	1	34	22 814	68 391	21 465
汉沽区 Hangu District	4	4	58	17 358	53 993	25 071
大港区 Dagang District	3	3	73	32 859	103 807	38 316
东丽区 Dongli District	4	3	109	78 756	227 765	92 989
西青区 Xiqing District	7	7	149	79 541	241 698	110 500
津南区 Jinnan District	8	8	165	91 912	284 477	129 652
北辰区 Beichen District	9	9	126	87 144	272 914	112 704
武清区 Wuqing District	24	19	741	195 886	692 626	365 618
宝坻区 Baodi District	22	19	765	154 211	566 412	254 391
宁河县 Ninghe County	14	11	283	75 788	278 532	109 279
静海县 Jinghai County	18	16	384	129 378	422 973	155 892
蓟县 Jixian County	26	20	949	187 054	699 163	317 344

6－12 农村居民家庭户均生产性固定资产原值
ORIGINAL VALUE OF PRODUCTIVE FIXED ASSETS PER RURAL HOUSEHOLD
(1999－2003)

单位:元 (yuan)

项目	Item	1999	2000	2001	2002	2003
年末户均生产性固定资产原值	**Original Value of Productive Fixed Assets(year－end)**	**6 138**	**6 020**	**6 624**	**7 228**	**7 051**
1.役畜、产品畜	Draught Animals and Commodity Animals	330	294	513	779	729
2.大中型铁木农具	Large and Medium Wood & Iron Farm Tools	78	212	424	335	263
3.农林牧渔业机械	Machinery for Farming,Forestry, Animal Husbandry and Fishery	1 960	1 471	1 484	1 375	1 300
4.工业机械	Industrial Machinery	31	160	148	288	230
5.运输机械	Transport Machinery	1 764	1 708	1 759	1 936	1 893
6.生产用房	Buildings for Production	1 309	1 466	1 610	1 783	1 828
7.其　他	Others	666	709	686	732	808

注:本表数据为农村住户抽样调查数。
Note:The data of this table are collected from sample survey on rural households.

6－13 农村居民家庭每百户生产性固定资产拥有量
NUMBER OF PRODUCTIVE FIXED ASSETS PER 100 RURAL HOUSEHOLDS
(1999－2003)

项目	Item	1999	2000	2001	2002	2003
汽　车(辆)	Motor Vehicles(set)	3.80	5.10	5.17	6.50	5.83
大中型拖拉机(台)	Large and Medium Tractors(set)	2.75	2.00	3.17	1.67	1.83
小型和手扶拖拉机(台)	Mini－tractors(set)	20.00	15.50	23.33	25.67	22.33
机动脱粒机(台)	Motorized Threshing Machines(set)	7.52	2.40	2.27	3.18	2.69
胶轮大车(辆)	Carts with Rubber Tires(set)	13.66	10.50	12.67	9.83	7.17
水　泵(台)	Pumps(set)	13.69	17.90	20.80	20.88	18.67
役　畜(头)	Draught Animals(head)	17.40	18.60	17.25	17.67	17.08
产品畜(头)	Commodity Animals(head)	16.30	11.70	24.00	36.33	35.17

注:本表数据为农村住户抽样调查数。
Note:The data of this table are collected from sample survey on rural households.

6-14 各区县耕地面积(2003年)
AREAS UNDER CULTIVATION BY DISTRICT AND COUNTY,2003

单位:公顷 (hectare)

地区 Region		年末实有耕地 Cultivated Areas (year-end)	水田 Paddy Fields	旱地 Dry Fields	粮食占耕地 Areas for Grain	蔬菜占耕地 Areas for Vegetables
塘沽区	Tanggu District	5 160	604	4 536	3 049	1 067
汉沽区	Hangu District	4 225	373	3 852	462	227
大港区	Dagang District	13 419		13 419	7 323	429
东丽区	Dongli District	13 760	2 177	11 583	2 738	2 096
西青区	Xiqing District	15 948	1 372	14 576	6 732	3 928
津南区	Jinnan District	14 553	476	14 077	5 501	2 283
北辰区	Beiche District	18 473	141	18 332	7 696	3 164
武清区	Wuqing District	90 257	2 256	88 001	42 513	18 745
宝坻区	Baodi District	75 586	3 181	72 405	37 211	14 750
宁河县	Ninghe County	38 668	428	38 240	7 813	4 928
静海县	Jingha County	69 178		69 178	42 000	4 220
蓟县	Jixian County	54 155	408	53 747	27 698	9 511

6-15 各区县农业现代化情况(2003年)
AGRICULTURAL MODERNIZATION BY DISTRICT AND COUNTY,2003

地区 Region		农业机械总动力(万千瓦) Total Power of Agricultural Machinery (10 000 kw)	农村用电量(万千瓦时) Rural Electricity Consumption (10 000 kwh)	有效灌溉面积(万公顷) Effective Irrigated Areas (10 000 hectares)	化肥施用量(折纯)(吨) Consumption of Chemical Fertilizers (Pureness) (ton)	农用薄膜使用量(吨) Consumption of Agricul-tural Membrane (ton)	农药使用量(吨) Consumption of Farm Pesticides (ton)
塘沽区	Tanggu District	25.94	5 843	0.52	951	462	66
汉沽区	Hangu District	13.83	14 860	0.24	1 293	125	160
大港区	Dagang District	25.89	13 086	1.09	1 623	27	52
东丽区	Dongli District	46.44	23 531	1.38	2 357	784	69
西青区	Xiqing District	48.33	50 072	1.55	10 000	1 565	101
津南区	Jinnan District	47.82	32 627	1.38	1 635	410	64
北辰区	Beichen District	46.10	31 654	1.45	6 497	1 487	336
武清区	Wuqing District	95.52	112 185	7.43	45 423	2 209	384
宝坻区	Baodi District	65.06	22 206	6.54	38 705	1 189	323
宁河县	Ninghe County	51.62	25 406	3.59	15 423	1 910	197
静海县	Jinghai County	67.50	87 009	5.55	19 375	1 862	286
蓟县	Jixian County	66.56	27 786	4.22	34 636	855	496

6-16 各区县农林牧渔业总产值和增加值(2003年)
GROSS OUTPUT VALUE AND VALUE-ADDED OF FARMING, FORESTRY, ANIMAL HUSBANDRY AND FISHERY BY DISTRICT AND COUNTY, 2003

单位:万元 (10 000 yuan)

地区 Region	合计 Total	农业 Farming	林业 Forestry	牧业 Animal Husbandry	渔业 Fishery
总产值 Gross Output Value					
塘沽区 Tanggu District	41 385	9 708	320	8 346	23 011
汉沽区 Hangu District	70 324	21 474	74	10 381	38 395
大港区 Dagang District	29 485	7 715	56	16 649	5 065
东丽区 Dongli District	85 748	45 377	1 029	26 273	13 069
西青区 Xiqing District	122 883	59 666	375	30 399	32 443
津南区 Jinnan District	44 943	20 073	292	12 266	12 312
北辰区 Beichen District	109 985	43 136	636	53 285	12 928
武清区 Wuqing District	399 765	210 721	3 366	160 305	25 373
宝坻区 Baodi District	274 537	134 757	846	119 355	19 579
宁河县 Ninghe County	215 796	115 084	798	83 433	16 481
静海县 Jinghai County	214 955	109 526	4 620	85 751	15 058
蓟　县 Jixian County	360 118	140 345	4 249	198 834	16 690
增加值 Value-added					
塘沽区 Tanggu District	16 148	4 489	64	3 040	8 555
汉沽区 Hangu District	29 580	12 045	49	2 421	15 066
大港区 Dagang District	12 960	3 360	27	7 041	2 532
东丽区 Dongli District	34 549	19 737	191	8 519	6 102
西青区 Xiqing District	60 200	29 795	150	13 872	16 383
津南区 Jinnan District	26 858	11 995	175	7 330	7 358
北辰区 Beichen District	53 480	23 112	308	24 554	5 506
武清区 Wuqing District	187 516	114 843	2 169	59 213	11 291
宝坻区 Baodi District	112 622	52 132	514	52 851	7 125
宁河县 Ninghe County	100 187	52 802	239	39 631	7 515
静海县 Jinghai County	109 847	62 905	3 097	37 710	6 135
蓟　县 Jixian County	165 005	75 310	2 807	79 210	7 678

6-17 各区县主要农作物播种面积(2003年)
SOWN AREAS OF MAJOR FARM CROPS BY DISTRICT AND COUNTY,2003

单位:公顷 (hectare)

地区 Region	粮食作物 Grain Crops	#小麦 Wheat	#稻谷 Rice	#玉米 Corn
塘沽区 Tanggu District	997	7		411
汉沽区 Hangu District	584		275	88
大港区 Dagang District	7 044	188	4	3 082
东丽区 Dongli District	2 738		126	895
西青区 Xiqing District	7 732	2 000	1 236	2 019
津南区 Jinnan District	5 687		193	3 104
北辰区 Beichen District	8 828	1 132	107	4 573
武清区 Wuqing District	71 702	30 216	118	36 976
宝坻区 Baodi District	59 181	21 969	3 181	25 441
宁河县 Ninghe County	7 820	85	431	4 176
静海县 Jinghai County	45 499	3 403		27 180
蓟县 Jixian County	47 990	17 397	1 112	27 217

地区 Region	油料作物 Oil-bearing Crops	#花生 Peanuts	棉花 Cotton	蔬菜 Vegetables
塘沽区 Tanggu District			1 512	1 660
汉沽区 Hangu District			811	340
大港区 Dagang District	172	3	273	765
东丽区 Dongli District	160		3 096	4 382
西青区 Xiqing District	36		635	9 407
津南区 Jinnan District			3 014	3 956
北辰区 Beichen District	1 176	398	2 391	7 071
武清区 Wuqing District	5 453	1 246	12 008	42 208
宝坻区 Baodi District	1 335	374	11 564	23 596
宁河县 Ninghe County	758	43	24 430	6 828
静海县 Jinghai County	5 133	317	8 956	7 000
蓟县 Jixian County	1 086	1 073	1 026	19 022

6－18 各区县主要农作物产量(2003 年)

YIELD OF MAJOR FARM CROPS BY DISTRICT AND COUNTY,2003

地 区 Region		粮食作物 Grain Crops	#小 麦 Wheat	#稻 谷 Rice	#玉 米 Corn
产 量(吨)	**Total Yield (ton)**				
塘沽区	Tanggu District	2 316	30		915
汉沽区	Hangu District	2 925		2 072	458
大港区	Dagang District	14 344	92	2	8 881
东丽区	Dongli District	11 069		807	4 218
西青区	Xiqing District	37 549	8 570	7 620	11 438
津南区	Jinnan District	19 164		1 029	10 402
北辰区	Beichen District	35 943	4 543	565	22 540
武清区	Wuqing District	380 248	149 118	874	217 709
宝坻区	Baodi District	292 242	107 513	23 658	137 767
宁河县	Ninghe County	43 591	439	3 624	28 473
静海县	Jinghai County	176 659	8 121		130 439
蓟 县	Jixian County	295 777	109 790	7 763	171 412
单 产	**Unit Yield**				
(公斤/公顷)(kg/hectare)					
塘沽区	Tanggu District	2 323	4 286		2 226
汉沽区	Hangu District	5 009		7 535	5 205
大港区	Dagang District	2 036	489	500	2 882
东丽区	Dongli District	4 043		6 405	4 713
西青区	Xiqing District	4 856	4 285	6 165	5 665
津南区	Jinnan District	3 370		5 332	3 351
北辰区	Beichen District	4 071	4 013	5 280	4 929
武清区	Wuqing District	5 303	4 935	7 407	5 888
宝坻区	Baodi District	4 938	4 894	7 437	5 415
宁河县	Ninghe County	5 574	5 165	8 408	6 818
静海县	Jinghai County	3 883	2 386		4 799
蓟 县	Jixian County	6 163	6 311	6 981	6 298

6-18 续表 Continued

地 区	Region	油料作物 Oil-bearing Crops	#花 生 Peanuts	棉 花 Cotton	蔬 菜 Vegetables
产 量(吨)	**Total Yield (ton)**				
塘沽区	Tanggu District			3 741	60 000
汉沽区	Hangu District			1 141	30 351
大港区	Dagang District	261	2	310	50 777
东丽区	Dongli District	400		11 569	267 682
西青区	Xiqing District	104		2 360	357 919
津南区	Jinnan District			9 003	179 645
北辰区	Beichen District	2 345	1 150	2 576	337 320
武清区	Wuqing District	11 535	3 834	14 522	1 778 034
宝坻区	Baodi District	2 576	869	15 897	888 672
宁河县	Ninghe County	1 685	130	33 835	284 822
静海县	Jinghai County	10 187	1 022	11 637	451 900
蓟 县	Jixian County	3 838	3 832	1 635	1 340 642
单 产	**Unit Yield**				
(公斤/公顷)	**(kg/hectare)**				
塘沽区	Tanggu District			2 474	36 145
汉沽区	Hangu District			1 407	89 268
大港区	Dagang District	1 517	666	1 136	66 375
东丽区	Dongli District	2 500		3 737	61 087
西青区	Xiqing District	2 889		3 717	38 048
津南区	Jinnan District			2 987	45 411
北辰区	Beichen District	1 994	2 889	1 077	47 705
武清区	Wuqing District	2 115	3 077	1 209	42 126
宝坻区	Baodi District	1 930	2 324	1 375	37 662
宁河县	Ninghe County	2 223	3 023	1 385	41 714
静海县	Jinghai County	1 985	3 224	1 299	64 557
蓟 县	Jixian County	3 534	3 571	1 594	70 478

6－19　各区县畜牧业生产情况（2003年）

PRODUCTION OF ANIMAL HUSBANDRY BY DISTRICT AND COUNTY, 2003

地　区　Region	大牲畜存栏（头）Large Animals in Hand (head)	#牛 Cattle and Buffaloes	猪存栏（万头）Pigs in Hand (10 000 heads)	猪出栏（万头）Slaughtered Pigs (10 000 heads)	羊存栏（万只）Sheep & Goats in Hand (10 000 heads)	羊出栏（万只）Slaughtered Sheep and Goats (10 000 heads)	家禽存栏（万只）Poultry in Hand (10 000 heads)	家禽出栏（万只）Slaughtered Poultry (10 000 heads)
塘沽区 Tanggu District	1 400	1 400	4.59	7.47	0.89	1.13	22.38	67.28
汉沽区 Hangu District	1 147	1 123	1.81	4.49	0.36	0.68	25.13	118.14
大港区 Dagang District	4 900	2 800	4.08	4.18	4.77	5.99	109.49	292.90
东丽区 Dongli District	3 918	3 901	5.88	11.92	2.41	4.90	81.78	455.52
西青区 Xiqing District	6 432	6 330	5.85	9.84	2.42	2.51	190.63	976.74
津南区 Jinnan District	4 194	3 780	3.88	6.38	1.81	1.96	361.28	650.74
北辰区 Beichen District	22 912	20 873	5.62	14.84	6.81	12.75	229.34	738.94
武清区 Wuqing District	114 584	104 578	26.36	63.20	24.40	44.33	726.57	2 689.76
宝坻区 Baodi District	83 318	66 175	58.73	106.33	16.69	16.69	352.74	334.27
宁河县 Ninghe County	39 534	36 698	34.77	66.57	7.73	6.01	237.79	621.88
静海县 Jinghai County	42 237	25 229	15.83	32.28	17.45	26.47	414.82	1 611.58
蓟　县 Jixian County	130 623	119 106	83.14	144.35	20.50	23.17	870.96	1 410.81

地　区　Region	肉类总产量（吨）Output of Meat (ton)	#猪　肉 Pork	#牛羊肉 Beef & Mutton	#禽　肉 Meat of Poultry	禽蛋产量（吨）Output of Poultry Eggs (ton)	#鸡　蛋 Eggs	奶类产量（吨）Output of Milk (ton)	#牛　奶 Cow Milk
塘沽区 Tanggu District	7 466	5 236	699	1 350	614	560	1 220	1 220
汉沽区 Hangu District	6 000	3 427	202	1 765	3 443	3 431	2 244	2 244
大港区 Dagang District	8 429	3 350	1 971	3 108	4 700	4 700	180	180
东丽区 Dongli District	20 088	8 740	2 904	8 391	3 587	3 552	6 309	6 309
西青区 Xiqing District	24 706	7 872	848	15 981	3 902	3 322	8 722	8 722
津南区 Jinnan District	13 699	4 139	1 098	8 330	7 633	7 563	2 640	2 640
北辰区 Beichen District	27 386	10 387	6 333	10 630	27 397	26 961	60 175	60 175
武清区 Wuqing District	102 580	41 060	28 813	31 653	50 968	38 891	189 577	189 577
宝坻区 Baodi District	107 919	83 440	14 871	6 059	39 139	37 372	12 094	12 094
宁河县 Ninghe County	58 902	45 881	2 839	9 515	16 219	15 603	53 841	53 841
静海县 Jinghai County	64 697	24 572	11 750	28 355	15 363	14 714	75 279	75 279
蓟　县 Jixian County	154 201	104 186	23 647	23 861	76 894	73 313	2 494	2 494

6－20　林业生产、果园面积及产量
FORESTRY PRODUCTION,ORCHARD AREAS AND OUTPUT
(2001－2003)

项　　目	Item	2001	2002	2003
一、年末实有林地面积(万公顷)	**Forestry Areas(year－end)(10 000 hectares)**	**14.19**	**17.53**	**18.21**
#当年造林面积	Afforested Areas in The Year	0.50	0.76	0.69
二、封山育林面积(万公顷)	**Afforested Areas on Sealed Moutain**	**1.07**	**1.13**	**1.27**
育苗面积(万公顷)	Areas Used for Cultivating Sapling	0.42	0.61	0.79
三、年末实有果园面积(万公顷)	**Areas of Orchards(year－end)(10 000 hectares)**	**4.18**	**4.36**	**4.11**
四、干果产量(吨)	**Output of Dry Fruits(ton)**	**631**	**471**	**666**
#核　桃	Walnuts	360	337	384
栗　子	Chestnut	227	134	239
五、园林水果产量(吨)	**Output of Fruits in Orchards(ton)**	**292 950**	**298 686**	**316 429**
#苹　果	Apples	68 424	67 118	68 069
梨	Pears	27 991	23 220	25 851
桃	Peaches	45 837	45 562	49 071
鲜　枣	Fresh Jujubes	21 698	17 233	15 678
葡　萄	Grapes	114 154	137 992	140 060
柿　子	Persimmons	7 672	1 084	10 036

6－21　各区县渔业生产情况(2003年)
FISHERY PRODUCTION BY DISTRICT AND COUNTY,2003

地　区	Region	水产品总产量(吨) Total Aquatic Products (ton)	海水产品 Seawater Aquatic Products	淡水产品 Freshwater Aquatic Products	水产养殖面积(公顷) Cultured Areas of Aquatic Products (hectare)	海水养殖 Seawater Cultured	淡水养殖 Freshwater Cultured
塘沽区	Tanggu District	22 477	18 767	3 710	3 781	2 179	1 602
汉沽区	Hangu District	23 080	14 404	8 676	1 940	1 059	881
大港区	Dagang District	5 554	1 660	3 894	3 979	1 716	2 263
东丽区	Dongli District	17 965		17 965	2 621		2 621
西青区	Xiqing District	47 268		47 268	4 733		4 733
津南区	Jinnan District	13 200		13 200	2 688		2 688
北辰区	Beichen District	11 978	35	11 943	1 992		1 992
武清区	Wuqing District	42 263		42 263	5 721		5 721
宝坻区	Baodi District	31 077		31 077	3 450		3 450
宁河县	Ninghe County	16 087	135	15 952	2 829	133	2 696
静海县	Jinghai County	21 782		21 782	2 288		2 288
蓟　县	Jixian County	25 600		25 600	1 800		1 800

6－22　农垦集团总公司主要指标

MAJOR INDICATORS STATE FARMS AGRIBUSINESS GROUP CORPORATION

项　目	Item	2001	2002	2003
一、直属企事业单位（个）	**Number of Units**	**39**	**36**	**40**
#农场个数	Farms	15	15	15
工业企业个数	Industrial Enterprises	12	12	12
商业企业个数	Commercial Enterprises	4	3	2
二、土地面积（公顷）	**Land Areas (hectare)**	**11 375**	**10 992**	**9 025**
#耕地面积	Cultivated Areas	4 264	3 965	3 051
三、工农业总产值（万元）	**Gross Output Value of Agriculture and Industry (10 000 yuan)**	**154 370**	**160 151**	**173 676**
#农业总产值	Gross Agricultural Output Value	22 446	25 430	27 154
四、增加值（万元）	**Value－added (10 000 yuan)**	**55 023**	**61 993**	**66 910**
第一产业	Primary Industry	5 528	6 721	7 380
第二产业	Secondary Industry	44 594	47 713	50 767
第三产业	Tertiary Industry	4 901	7 559	8 763
五、种植业生产情况	**Production of Planting**			
农作物播种面积(公顷)	Sown Areas of Farm Crops (hectare)	3 817	3 453	2 513
#粮食作物	Grain	2 049	1 934	1 077
商品蔬菜	Vegetables for Sale	190	63	72
农作物总产量	Total Yield of Farm Crops			
#粮　食（吨）	Grain (ton)	6 210	9 069	5 782
商品菜（吨）	Vegetables for Sale (ton)	8 557	2 115	3 620
六、水果生产情况	**Production of Fruits**			
果园面积（公顷）	Areas of Orchards (hectare)	302	259	184
水果总产量（吨）	Total Yield of Fruits (ton)	2 344	1 193	1 268
七、畜牧水产生产情况	**Production of Animal Husbandry and Fishery**			
奶牛年末存栏（头）	Cows in Hand (year－end) (head)	16 968	19 059	19 979
#成母牛	Female Cows	10 540	10 666	11 966
牛奶总产量（吨）	Output of Milk (ton)	69 035	74 281	79 455

6－22 续表 Continued

项 目	Item	2001	2002	2003
鸡年末存栏（万只）	Cocks and Hens in Hand(year－end)(10 000 heads)	32.21	37.30	22.69
#产蛋鸡	Hens	27.47	35.30	22.29
鸡蛋总产量（吨）	Total Output of Eggs (ton)	4 055	3 369	4 516
肉类总产量（吨）	Total Output of Meat (ton)	866	549	833
养殖水面（公顷）	Cultured Water Areas (hectare)	610	834	516
水产品产量（吨）	Total Aquatic Products (ton)	3 684	5 579	4 077
八、农业机械总动力（万千瓦）	**Total Power of Agricultural Machinery(10 000 kw)**	**1.38**	**1.39**	**1.05**
#大中型拖拉机（台）	Large and Medium－sized Tractors (set)	50	50	38
小型拖拉机（台）	Mini－tractors (set)	12	12	8
汽车拥有量（辆）	Number of Motor Vehicles (set)	355	317	296
#载重汽车（辆）	Trucks (set)	141	87	62
九、用电量（万千瓦小时）	**Electricity Consumption (10 000 kwh)**	**4 438**	**4 635**	**4 328**
十、化肥施用量(折纯)(吨)	**Consumption of Chemical Fertilizers (pureness) (ton)**	**778**	**616**	**758**
十一、主要工业产品产量	**Output of Major Industrial Products**			
葡萄酒（吨）	Wine (ton)	25 246	29 690	27 150
淀 粉（吨）	Starch (ton)	124	60	22
奶 粉（吨）	Milk Powder (ton)	3 009	2 277	2 200
消毒牛奶（吨）	Sterilized Milk (ton)	48 805	52 233	65 157
饲料添加剂（吨）	Added Preparation for Forage (ton)	317	404	151
十二、固定资产投资总额(万元)	**Total Investment in Fixed Assets (10 000 yuan)**	**6 304**	**13 302**	**16 744**
新增固定资产	Newly Increased Fixed Assets	3 404	12 702	7 697
十三、外贸出口总值（万元）	**Total Value of Exports (10 000 yuan)**	**12 785**	**13 708**	**14 010**
十四、利润总额（万元）	**Total Profits (10 000 yuan)**	**5 377**	**6 712**	**7 808**
十五、年末职工人数（人）	**Number of Staff and Workers(year－end) (person)**	**10 695**	**9 349**	**7 958**
十六、工资总额（万元）	**Total Wages (10 000 yuan)**	**9 448**	**9 857**	**10 392**
职工年平均工资（元）	Annual Average Wage (yuan)	8 092	9 706	11 829
十七、年末固定资产原值(万元)	**Original Value of Fixed Assets(year－end) (10 000 yuan)**	**103 367**	**107 317**	**111 067**
年末固定资产净值（万元）	Net Value of Fixed Assets(year－end)(10 000 yuan)	50 724	74 772	76 113

6－23　乡镇企业主要经济指标(2003年)

BASIC STATISTICS ON TOWNSHIP ENTERPRISES(GROUPED BY OWNERSHIP),2003

指　标	Item	总　计	集体企业 Collect－iveowned Enterp－rises	私营企业 Private Enterp－rises	个体企业 Individua Enterp－rises
一、企业个数(个)	**Number of Enterprises(unit)**	**136 003**	**7 563**	**23 377**	**105 063**
工　业	Industry	38 384	2 952	12 285	23 147
建筑业	Construction	2 124	65	706	1 353
交运仓储业	Transportation,Storage	33 071	1 365	1 734	29 972
批发零售业	Wholesale and Retail Trade	41 570	1 199	7 181	33 190
住宿餐饮业	Accommodation and Catering Services	11 560	213	715	10 632
社会服务业	Social Services	8 845	1 728	691	6 426
其　他	Others	449	41	65	343
二、年末人数(人)	**Number of Staff and Workers(year－end)(person)**	**1 392 803**	**445 941**	**494 469**	**452 393**
工　业	Industry	979 128	373 873	407 322	197 933
建筑业	Construction	76 843	23 396	25 749	27 698
交运仓储业	Transportation,Storage	97 063	11 388	10 874	74 801
批发零售业	Wholesale and Retail Trade	137 559	11 749	35 893	89 917
住宿餐饮业	Accommodation and Catering Services	53 589	5 417	6 516	41 656
社会服务业	Social Services	33 223	8 047	6 373	18 803
其　他	Others	15 398	12 071	1 742	1 585
三、营业收入(万元)	**Business Income(10 000 yuan)**	**23 733 735**	**8 496 141**	**8 581 668**	**6 655 926**
工　业	Industry	17 582 838	7 643 995	6 525 882	3 412 961
建筑业	Construction	527 327	188 889	178 998	159 440
交运仓储业	Transportation,Storage	1 458 474	131 378	279 258	1 047 838
批发零售业	Wholesale and Retail Trade	2 997 641	319 450	1 396 162	1 282 029
住宿餐饮业	Accommodation and Catering Services	649 199	49 317	86 789	513 093
社会服务业	Social Services	366 086	59 045	88 110	218 931
其　他	Others	152 170	104 067	26 469	21 634
四、利润总额(万元)	**Total Profits(10 000 yuan)**	**2 092 485**	**630 982**	**735 111**	**726 392**
工　业	Industry	1 460 347	553 033	573 087	334 227
建筑业	Construction	47 414	14 073	20 141	13 200
交运仓储业	Transportation,Storage	182 365	16 958	17 706	147 701
批发零售业	Wholesale and Retail Trade	258 816	26 749	98 752	133 315
住宿餐饮业	Accommodation and Catering Services	80 318	5 382	9 746	65 190
社会服务业	Social Services	49 836	6 735	14 148	28 953
其　他	Others	13 389	8 052	1 531	3 806
五、总产值(万元)	**Gross Output Value**	**23 967 278**	**8 936 703**	**8 500 503**	**6 530 072**
工　业	Industry	1 915 112	8 193 379	7 076 327	3 881 416
建筑业	Construction	586 319	188 455	216 599	181 265
交运仓储业	Transportation,Storage	1 414 419	129 083	273 739	1 011 597
批发零售业	Wholesale and Retail Trade	1 689 289	214 824	744 131	730 334
住宿餐饮业	Accommodation and Catering Services	625 679	59 061	79 911	486 707
社会服务业	Social Services	355 858	53 918	84 446	217 494
其　他	Others	144 592	97 983	25 350	21 259

6-23 续表 Continued

指标	Item	总计	集体企业 Collect-iveowned Enterp-rises	私营企业 Private Enterp-rises	个体企业 Individua Enterp-rises
六、增加值(万元)	**Added Value (10 000 yuan)**	**5 464 152**	**1 735 682**	**1 841 786**	**1 886 684**
工　业	Industry	3 728 996	1 517 283	1 429 867	781 846
建筑业	Construction	160 730	48 654	59 147	52 929
交运仓储业	Transportation, Storage	520 794	52 127	49 705	418 962
批发零售业	Wholesale and Retail Trade	663 987	60 357	235 092	368 538
住宿餐饮业	Accommodation and Catering Services	231 340	17 334	26 990	187 016
社会服务业	Social Services	125 169	20 252	36 786	68 131
其　他	Others	33 136	19 675	4 199	9 262
七、实交税金(万元)	**Taxes Paid (10 000 yuan)**	**550 558**	**258 333**	**183 878**	**108 347**
工　业	Industry	437 426	243 374	138 270	55 782
建筑业	Construction	12 919	4 037	4 748	4 134
交运仓储业	Transportation, Storage	22 759	1 701	4 301	16 757
批发零售业	Wholesale and Retail Trade	56 141	4 776	31 339	20 026
住宿餐饮业	Accommodation and Catering Services	9 250	995	965	7 290
社会服务业	Social Services	8 282	256	3 936	4 090
其　他	Others	3 781	3 194	319	268
八、固定资产原值(万元)	**Original Value of Fixed Assets(10 000 yuan)**	**6 735 779**	**2 959 420**	**2 321 292**	**1 455 067**
工　业	Industry	4 898 824	2 733 885	1 582 144	582 795
建筑业	Construction	70 135	17 915	34 418	17 802
交运仓储业	Transportation, Storage	478 693	74 467	84 176	320 050
批发零售业	Wholesale and Retail Trade	792 861	63 271	438 866	290 724
住宿餐饮业	Accommodation and Catering Services	260 862	18 421	62 243	180 198
社会服务业	Social Services	192 865	21 493	114 834	56 538
其　他	Others	41 539	29 968	4 611	6 960
九、资产总计(万元)	**Total Capital(10 000 yuan)**	**13 435 511**	**6 190 103**	**5 162 256**	**2 083 152**
工　业	Industry	10 558 014	5 644 385	3 905 063	1 008 566
建筑业	Construction	559 677	98 390	419 731	41 556
交运仓储业	Transportation, Storage	545 196	73 824	107 490	363 882
批发零售业	Wholesale and Retail Trade	1 084 338	190 810	523 697	369 831
住宿餐饮业	Accommodation and Catering Services	283 510	21 085	61 010	201 415
社会服务业	Social Services	254 692	35 429	131 358	87 905
其　他	Others	150 084	126 180	13 907	9 997
十、所有者权益(万元)	**Ownership Rights and Interests(10 000 yuan)**	**7 455 586**	**2 696 922**	**3 020 911**	**1 737 753**
工　业	Industry	5 139 590	2 346 434	2 050 575	742 581
建筑业	Construction	270 275	46 757	186 884	36 634
交运仓储业	Transportation, Storage	482 629	60 976	94 943	326 710
批发零售业	Wholesale and Retail Trade	938 332	115 967	472 991	349 374
住宿餐饮业	Accommodation and Catering Services	265 238	18 591	57 152	189 495
社会服务业	Social Services	272 844	40 670	149 094	83 080
其　他	Others	86 678	67 527	9 272	9 879
十一、出口交货值(万元)	**Delivery Value of Exports(10 000 yuan)**	**2 653 371**	**2 074 455**	**538 054**	**40 862**

注：出口交货值为集体工业和销售收入100万元以上的私营企业。
Note: Delivery value of exports refer to all collective-owned enterprises and private enterprises with annual business revenue of over 1 million yuan.

6－24 各区县乡镇企业主要经济指标(2003年)

MAJOR INDICATORS OF TOWNSHIP ENTERPRISES BY DISTRICT AND COUNTY, 2003

地区 Region	企业数(个) Number of Enterprises (unit)	年末人数(人) Staff and Workers (year－end) (person)	总产值(万元) Gross Output Value (10 000 yuan)	增加值(万元) Added Value (10 000 yuan)	营业收入(万元) Business Income (10 000 yuan)	利税总额(万元) Total Pre－tax Profits (10 000 yuan)
全市总计 Total	**136 003**	**1 392 803**	**23 967 278**	**5 464 152**	**23 733 735**	**2 816 939**
塘沽区 Tanggu District	3 885	26 836	392 899	131 650	464 458	67 118
汉沽区 Hangu District	2 826	18 180	311 061	80 849	300 759	36 868
大港区 Dagang District	4 964	56 781	1 135 080	222 055	1 048 389	91 853
东丽区 Dongli District	4 377	70 271	1 973 585	417 038	2 106 478	206 808
西青区 Xiqing District	18 474	151 796	2 802 924	794 348	2 848 470	409 227
津南区 Jinnan District	11 465	159 667	1 863 003	448 818	1 717 643	164 080
北辰区 Beichen District	11 640	154 926	4 133 261	1 028 518	4 772 862	597 461
武清区 Wuqing District	14 145	160 122	2 346 962	474 201	1 905 089	308 282
宝坻区 Baodi District	17 812	170 745	2 145 021	467 014	2 128 011	265 007
宁河县 Ninghe County	16 190	100 747	2 229 228	418 635	2 055 268	192 651
静海县 Jinghai County	5 035	142 070	2 789 873	525 700	2 793 318	285 875
蓟县 Jixian County	25 190	180 662	1 844 381	455 326	1 592 990	191 709

地区 Region	实交税金(万元) Taxes Paid (10 000 yuan)	固定资产原值(万元) Original Value of Fixed Assets (10 000 yuan)	资产总计(万元) Total Capital (10 000 yuan)	所有者权益(万元) Ownership Rights and Interests (10 000 yuan)	固定资产原值利税率 Ratio of Pre－tax Profits to Original Value of Fixed Assets (%)	营业收入利税率 Ratio of Pre-tax Profits to Business Income (%)
全市总计 Total	**550 558**	**6 735 779**	**13 435 511**	**7 455 586**	**41.8**	**11.9**
塘沽区 Tanggu District	19 908	140 542	267 034	142 907	47.8	14.5
汉沽区 Hangu District	2 982	48 664	106 250	32 669	75.8	12.3
大港区 Dagang District	30 336	261 611	519 813	308 380	35.1	8.8
东丽区 Dongli District	55 438	870 849	1 243 856	958 527	23.7	9.8
西青区 Xiqing District	80 661	995 341	1 702 093	1 011 242	41.1	14.4
津南区 Jinnan District	39 301	633 434	2 608 853	1 174 350	25.9	9.6
北辰区 Beichen District	150 668	1 618 321	3 245 141	1 731 845	36.9	12.5
武清区 Wuqing District	45 079	628 770	1 177 529	699 706	49.0	16.2
宝坻区 Baodi District	22 164	308 198	519 620	196 714	86.0	12.5
宁河县 Ninghe County	16 296	348 852	509 726	325 059	55.2	9.4
静海县 Jinghai County	36 717	524 382	986 495	513 244	54.5	10.2
蓟县 Jixian County	51 008	356 815	549 101	360 943	53.7	12.0

6－25 用水情况
WATER CONSUMPTION
(2000－2003)

单位:万立方米 (10 000 cu. m)

地区 Region		2000 小计 Total	2000 地表水 Surface Water	2000 地下水 Underground Water	2001 小计 Total	2001 地表水 Surface Water	2001 地下水 Underground Water
全市总计	**Total**	**226 345**	**144 164**	**82 181**	**188 141**	**111 848**	**76 293**
市内六区	Six Urban Districts	79 705	70 486	9 219	64 959	56 322	8 637
塘沽区	Tanggu District	2 931	100	2 831	2 499	989	1 510
汉沽区	Hangu District	8 114	900	7 214	2 874	850	2 024
大港区	Dagang District	5 863		5 863	2 280		2 280
东丽区	Dongli District	2 759	1 187	1 572	2 325	745	1 580
西青区	Xiqing District	14 398	12 209	2 189	14 471	11 109	3 362
津南区	Jinnan District	4 472	1 447	3 025	5 411	3 000	2 411
北辰区	Beichen District	2 969	1 514	1 455	2 798	1 200	1 598
武清区	Wuqing District	28 001	17 261	10 740	27 511	16 124	11 387
宝坻区	Baodi District	42 828	34 243	8 585	33 127	19 049	14 078
宁河县	Ninghe County	13 209	3 200	10 009	9 229		9 229
静海县	Jinghai County	5 899	380	5 519	6 670	1 700	4 970
蓟县	Jixian County	15 197	1 237	13 960	13 987	760	13 227

地区 Region		2002 小计 Total	2002 地表水 Surface Water	2002 地下水 Underground Water	2003 小计 Total	2003 地表水 Surface Water	2003 地下水 Underground Water
全市总计	**Total**	**199 610**	**117 421**	**82 189**	**205 118**	**133 713**	**71 405**
市内六区	Six Urban Districts	57 978	56 984	994	60 492	59 713	779
塘沽区	Tanggu District	1 878		1 878	1 771		1 771
汉沽区	Hangu District	5 177		5 177	4 673	520	4 153
大港区	Dagang District	5 268		5 268	3 930	150	3 780
东丽区	Dongli District	2 560	565	1 995	2 576	565	2 011
西青区	Xiqing District	15 432	11 800	3 632	15 211	11 650	3 561
津南区	Jinnan District	4 027	860	3 167	6 381	3 375	3 006
北辰区	Beichen District	3 624	1 220	2 404	3 745	1 450	2 295
武清区	Wuqing District	28 203	16 759	11 444	29 052	17 552	11 500
宝坻区	Baodi District	38 074	24 213	13 861	40 026	31 480	8 546
宁河县	Ninghe County	12 451	1 800	10 651	15 851	6 815	9 036
静海县	Jinghai County	8 908	2 900	6 008	5 822		5 822
蓟县	Jixian County	16 030	320	15 710	15 588	443	15 145

资料来源:天津市水利局,以下两表同。
Information Source: Tianjin Municipal Water Conservancy Bureau, same as following next two tables.

6－26 大型水库基本情况(2003 年)
LARGE RESERVOIRS OF TIANJIN,2003

项目	Item	于桥水库 Yuqiao Reservoir	团泊洼水库 Tuanbowa Reservoir	北大港水库 Beidagang Reservoir
建设地点	Construction Site	蓟县 Jixian	静海县 Jinghai	大港区 Dagang
所属河系	Location River	蓟运河 Jiyun River	独流碱河 Duliujian River	大青河 Daqing River
总库容(万立方米)	Total Capacity of Reservoir(10 000 cu. m)	155 900	18 000	50 000
设计灌溉面积(万公顷)	Designed Irrigated Areas(10 000 hectares)	4.20	3.00	1.38
有效灌溉面积(万公顷)	Effective Irrigated Areas(10 000 hectares)	3.00	2.60	0.66

6－27 中型水库基本情况(2003 年)
MEDIUM RESERVOIRS OF TIANJIN,2003

水库名称 Name of Reservoir	座落地点 Site	所在河系 Location River	总库容(万立方米) Total Capacity of Reservoir (10 000 cu. m)	灌溉面积(万公顷) Irrigated Areas (10 000 hectares)		年设计灌溉用水(万立方米) Annual Irrigated Water (10 000 cu. m)
				设计 Designed Areas	有效 Effective Areas	
七里海水库 Qilihai Reservoir	宁河县 Ninghe	潮白新河 Chaobaixin River	2 400	1.00	0.40	1 800
新地河水库 Xindihe Reservoir	东丽区 Dongli	金钟河 Jinzhong River	2 200	0.27	0.27	1 000
鸭淀水库 Yadian Reservoir	西青区 Xiqing	津港运河 Jingang Canal	3 150	0.47	0.47	1 997
黄港一库 Huanggang Ⅰ Reservoir	塘沽区 Tanggu	黑猪河 Heizhu River	1 295	0.09	0.06	800
黄港二库 Huanggang Ⅱ Reservoir	塘沽区 Tanggu	黑猪河 Heizhu River	4 615	0.21	0.18	400
北塘水库 Beitang Reservoir	塘沽区 Tanggu	永定新河 Yongdingxin River	1 580			
营城水库 Yingcheng Reservoir	汉沽区 Hangu	蓟运河 Jixian Canal	3 000	0.04	0.04	400
钱圈水库 Qianquan Reservoir	大港区 Dagang	马厂减河 Machangjian River	2 650	0.20	0.10	
沙井子水库 Shajingzi Reservoir	大港区 Dagang	青县、静海县、黄骅县 Qingxian,Jinghai & Huanghua County	2 000	0.07	0.07	300
上马台水库 Shangmatai Reservoir	武清区 Wuqing	北运河 North Canal	2 680	0.86	0.86	1 900
津南水库 Jinnan Reservoir	津南区 Jinnan	海河 Haihe River	2 966	0.15	0.15	600
尔王庄水库 Erwangzhuang Reservoir	宝坻区 Baodi	潮白新河 Chaobaixin River	4 530			

主要统计指标解释

农村总人口 指乡村户数中的常住人口。包括常住人口中外出的民工、合同工及户口在家的在外学生。但不包括户口在家领取工资的国家正式职工。

乡村从业人员 指乡村人口中16岁以上实际参加生产经营活动并取得实物或货币收入的人员，即包括劳动年龄内经常参加劳动的人员，也包括超过劳动年龄但经常参加劳动的人员，但不包括户口在家的在外学生、现役军人和丧失能力的人，也不包括待业人员和家务劳动者。从业人员年龄为16岁以上。从业人员按从事主业时间最长（时间相同按收入算），分为农业从业人员、工业从业人员、建筑业从业人员、交运仓储及邮电通讯业从业人员、批发零售及餐饮业从业人员、其它从业人员。

农林牧渔业总产值 指以货币表现的农林牧渔业全部产品总量。它用价值量形式综合说明了一定时期（通常指一年）农林牧渔业生产的总成果和总规模，是观察农林牧渔业生产水平和发展速度；研究农林牧渔业内部比例关系和农林牧渔业在国民经济中的产业布局的一个重要指标，同时，也是计算农林牧渔业劳动生产率和农林牧渔业增加值的基础资料。

农林牧渔业中间消耗 指在农业生产过程中所投入和消耗的各种物质产品和劳务价值总和。分为中间物质消耗和中间劳务消耗。

农林牧渔业增加值 指各种经济类型的农业生产单位和农户从事农业生产经营活动所提供的社会最终产品的货币表现。其计算方法有两种，一是生产法：农牧渔业增加值＝农林牧渔业总产值－农林牧渔业中间消耗；二是分配法：农林牧渔业增加值＝固定资产折旧＋劳动者报酬＋生产税净额（生产税－生产补贴）＋营业盈余。

农业机械总动力 指主要用于农、林、牧、渔业的各种动力机械的动力总和。包括耕作机械、收获机械、农产品加工机械、运输机械、植保机械、牧业机械、林业机械、渔业机械和其它农业机械的动力。

农村用电量 指在本年度内，农村生产上和生活上的全年用电总度数（全年累计数）。但不包括农村中的全民所有制工业、交通、基建单位的用电量，也不包括县办工业和城镇生活用电量。

有效灌溉面积 指灌溉工程或设备已基本配套，有一定水源，土地比较平整，在一般年景可以进行正常灌溉的耕地面积。在一般情况下，有效灌溉面积应等于灌溉工程或设备已经配套，能够进行灌溉的水田和水浇地面积之和。

造林面积 指报告期内在荒地、荒山、沙丘等一切可造林的土地上，采用人工播种、植苗、飞机播种等方法种植成片的乔木林和灌木林，经过检查验收符合技术规程要求，并按《中华人民共和国森林法实施细则》规定，成活率达85%以上的造林面积。包括四旁植树如一侧在四行以上，连续面积0.066公顷以上的面积，造林面积不包括补植面积和治沙及沿河种草面积。

当年出栏头数 指农林牧渔企业生产单位饲养的，供屠宰并已出栏的全部牲畜头数。包括交售给国家，集市上出售的部分。

肉类总产量 指当年出栏并已屠宰的猪、牛、羊、马、骡、驴、家禽、兔等肉产量。即屠宰后除去头、蹄、下水后带骨肉的重量，也叫胴体重。

水产品产量 指本年度内捕捞的水产品（包括人工养殖并捕捞的水产品和捕捞天然生长的水产品）产量。不论自食或出售的，都应计算在内。用作继续扩大再生产的水产品（如鱼苗、鱼种、鱼饵及转塘鱼、存塘鱼等）不作水产品产量统计。在淡水生长的各种水生植物，如莲藕、菱角等，因属农作物范畴，均不包括在水产品产量之内。

Explanatory Notes on Main Statistical Indicators

Total Population of Rural refer to the permanent residents in rural, including those work in other places, contract workers, students having left place of residence registration in other places of which permanent population, excluding the staff and worker of receiving wages from state－owned units and having resided in this enumeration area.

Employment Personnel in Rural Areas refers to the total number of people aged over 16 who are engaged in production and business activities that generate incomes in cash or in kind. It includes all the working laborers, no matter whether they are within the working age or not. But students studying outside with their registered residence at home, active army, people who lost their ability to work, unemployed people and those engaged in housework are not included. The age of employment personnel are 16 and over. Employment personnel in rural areas are divided into agricultural personnel, industrial personnel, construction personnel, personnel engaged in transportation, storage, post and telecommunications, personnel engaged in wholesale, retail and catering business, other employment personnel according to the working time of main working.

Gross Output Value of Farming, Forestry, Animal Husbandry and Fishery refers to the total volume of products of farming, forestry, animal husbandry and fishery in value terms, which reflects the total scale and total result of agricultural production during a given period of time, which observe development level and speed of farming, forestry, animal husbandry and fishery, study proportional relations of farming, forestry, animal husbandry and fishery and proportional relations in national economic, which is also calculated labor productivity of farming, forestry, animal husbandry and fishery and value - added of farming, forestry, animal husbandry and fishery.

Intermediate Consumption of Farming, Forestry, Animal Husbandry and Fishery refers to total value input and consumption in the process of agriculture production and various physical products. It is classified into intermediate material consumption and intermediate service consumption.

Value - added of Farming, Forestry, Animal Husbandry and Fishery refers to the final results of various agricultural production and trade units in money terms. It is calculated with two approaches. First, production approach, value - added of farming, forestry, animal husbandry and fishery = gross output value of farming, forestry, animal husbandry and fishery - intermediate input of farming, forestry, animal husbandry and fishery. Second, distribution approach, value - a dded of farming, forestry, animal husbandry and fishery = depreciation of fixed assets + laborers remuneration + net taxes on production (taxes on production subsidies production) + operating surplus.

Total Power of Farm Machinery refers to total mechanical power of machinery used in farming, forestry, animal husbandry, and fishery, including cultivating, harvesting, farming products process, transport, plant protection, stock breeding, forestry and fishery and other power of farm machinery.

Rural Electricity Consumption refers to the value of consumption electricity of rural in a year on production and life, but excluding value of consumption electricity by state - owned industry, transport, basic construction units and county - run industry, urban household consumption of electricity.

Irrigated Area refers to areas that are effectively irrigated, i.e. level land which has water source and complete sets of irrigation facilities to lift and move adequate water for irrigation purpose under normal conditions. In general, irrigated area equal sum area of paddy fields and irrigated land for irrigated engineering or complete sets.

Afforested Area refers to the area of forest land where tree and bush by artificially seed, young plant, plane seed on the waste land, barren mountain, dune. during the reference period. Live rate of forest area coverage above 85% in accordance with the Regulation of the People's Republic of China on the Management of Forest Law, including the area of forest land inside farm land and the area of tree planted by the side of farm houses and along the roads, continuing area coverage above 0.066 hectare, excluding the area of sand and planted grass lands along the river.

Number of Livestock Slaughtered refers to the total number of animals for butchering by farming, forestry, animal husbandry and fishery, including parts of selling to country and markets.

Output of Meal refers to output of having butchered of pork, beef, mutton, horse, mule, donkey, fowls, rabbit in the current year, namely the heaviness minus head, hoof, offal.

Total Output of Aquatic Products Amount of fishing (including artificially cultured, naturally grown) ,in respective consumption by peasants themselves or sold. It excludes aquatic (i.e. fish fry, fish grows, fish bait and transferred fish from piscina, leave fish) for continuing expanded reproduction aquatic. Various fresh water plants (i.e. lotus roots, water chestnut) are not included.

第7篇 CHAPTER 7

工　业

INDUSTRY

7-1 工业总产值及增长速度

GROSS OUTPUT VALUE AND INCREASE RATE OF INDUSTRY

(1978-2003)

年 份 Year	全部工业总产值 Total	按轻重分 Grouped by Light & Heavy Industry		按经济类型分 Grouped by Ownership		
		轻工业 Light Industry	重工业 Heavy Industry	国有经济 State-owned	集体经济 Collective-owned	其他经济 Others
绝对数(亿元) Gross Output Value (100 million yuan)						
1978	157.90	81.47	76.43	127.49	30.41	
1979	175.52	89.73	85.79	141.43	34.07	0.02
1980	195.94	106.00	89.94	156.11	39.44	0.39
1981	205.87	121.92	83.95	161.96	42.84	1.07
1982	218.41	123.87	94.54	170.49	46.46	1.46
1983	235.33	127.83	107.50	182.47	50.90	1.96
1984	259.10	138.36	120.74	195.34	60.50	3.26
1985	319.47	164.22	155.25	230.34	83.89	5.24
1986	344.73	174.84	169.89	243.52	92.77	8.44
1987	405.49	205.51	199.98	273.06	119.98	12.45
1988	521.10	267.48	253.62	320.06	179.73	21.31
1989	635.22	318.41	316.81	386.40	221.93	26.89
1990	679.94	354.50	325.44	404.28	243.44	36.73
1991	786.60	392.29	394.31	436.43	295.72	54.45
1992	997.91	465.48	532.43	492.15	402.42	103.34
1993	1 401.84	530.05	871.79	628.76	573.51	199.57
1994	1 754.30	760.80	993.50	648.10	675.59	430.61
1995	1 879.65	752.03	1 127.62	582.51	704.36	592.78
1996	2 177.42	1 014.46	1 162.96	587.86	798.77	790.79
1997	2 450.21	1 130.04	1 320.17	636.94	963.77	849.50
1998	2 562.62	1 157.09	1 405.53	572.64	731.59	1 258.39
1999	2 751.37	1 128.47	1 622.90	572.33	704.71	1 474.33
2000	3 080.74	1 263.10	1 817.64	558.50	815.26	1 706.98
2001	3 366.53	1 153.73	2 212.80	546.00	643.48	2 177.05
2002	3 717.72	1 207.88	2 509.84	519.19	660.91	2 537.62
2003	4 370.76	1 254.68	3 116.08	599.97	542.67	3 228.12
比上年增长% Increase Rate over Preceding year						
1978	14.3	14.6	13.9	15.6	7.4	
1979	9.6	10.7	8.5	9.7	10.8	
1980	11.4	18.9	3.4	9.6	14.9	1 950
1981	6.5	15.1	-3.9	6.0	11.0	170
1982	6.4	4.1	9.7	5.1	10.5	32.7
1983	8.5	7.2	10.3	7.8	10.3	34.0
1984	11.3	11.8	10.6	8.2	20.1	69.2
1985	15.9	12.8	20.1	10.8	30.4	50.9
1986	6.5	7.3	5.6	4.4	9.2	58.9
1987	11.8	7.1	18.1	6.6	23.0	40.1
1988	18.4	19.7	16.9	8.0	38.0	57.9
1989	9.0	12.3	5.0	-1.0	23.5	37.1
1990	7.8	5.3	11.2	-0.1	16.0	38.6
1991	12.2	7.1	17.8	2.4	24.5	42.2
1992	24.2	22.5	26.3	7.3	37.2	90.0
1993	25.1	8.9	40.5	-1.6	37.5	95.7
1994	19.1	33.8	8.2	-6.6	29.0	99.1
1995	23.5	11.2	34.8	-3.3	-22.6	110
1996	24.7	31.8	19.5	4.9	45.8	18.7
1997	12.9	13.6	12.2	7.8	-8.8	48.2
1998	8.5	9.9	7.2	-2.1	-1.3	19.9
1999	13.0	5.9	19.4	-0.2	3.2	22.2
2000	17.5	19.7	16.0	13.9	6.1	20.8
2001	14.0	-6.6	28.4	2.0	-17.7	33.0
2002	19.6	13.3	23.7	16.8	9.58	22.7
2003	24.1	18.5	27.0	12.2	8.3	28.7

注:工业总产值绝对数按当年价格计算,增长速度按可比价格计算(下同)。
Note:Gross output value of industry are at current prices,increase rate are based on comparable prices (same as following next).

7-2 按新国民经济行业分工业企业单位数(2003年)
(限额以上工业)

NUMBER OF INDUSTRIAL ENTERPRISES GROUPED BY NEW SECTOR,2003(ABOVE DESIGNATED SIZE)

单位:个 (unit)

项目	Item	全部 Total	#地方 Local
总计	**Total**	**5 341**	**5 250**
煤炭开采和洗选业	Coal Mining and Dressing	2	2
石油和天然气开采业	Petroleum and Natural Gas Extraction	4	
有色金属矿采选业	Nonferrous Metals Mining and Dressing	1	1
非金属矿采选业	Nonmetal Minerals Mining and Dressing	19	18
农副食品加工业	Agricultural Products and Byproducts Processing	186	186
食品制造业	Food Manufacturing	133	133
饮料制造业	Beverage Manufacturing	65	65
烟草制品业	Tobacco Products	1	
纺织业	Textile Industry	327	327
纺织服装鞋帽制造业	Textile Garments,Shoes,Caps Manufacturing	286	286
皮革毛皮羽毛(绒)及其制品业	Leather, Furs, Down and Related Products	81	81
木材加工及木、竹、藤、棕、草制品业	Timber Processing,Bamboo, Cane, Palm Fiber and Straw Products	66	64
家具制造业	Furniture Manufacturing	68	68
造纸及纸制品业	Papermaking and Paper Products	169	168
印刷业和记录媒介的复制	Printing and Record Medium Reproduction	97	92
文教体育用品制造业	Cultural, Educational and Sports Goods	69	67
石油加工炼焦及核燃料加工业	Petroleum Processing, Coking and Nuclear Fuel Processing	34	32
化学原料及化学制品制造业	Raw Chemical Materials and Chemical Products	502	492
医药制造业	Medical and Pharmaceutical Products	101	100
化学纤维制造业	Chemical Fiber	18	18
橡胶制品业	Rubber Products	111	111
塑料制品业	Plastic Products	210	208
非金属矿物制品业	Nonmetal Mineral Products	210	208
黑色金属冶炼及压延加工业	Smelting and Pressing of Ferrous Metals	139	138
有色金属冶炼及压延加工业	Smelting and Pressing of Nonferrous Metals	87	86
金属制品业	Metal Products	440	436
通用设备制造业	General Purpose Equipment Manufacturing	390	384
专用设备制造业	Special Purpose Equipment Manufacturing	244	235
交通运输设备制造业	Transport Equipment Manufacturing	377	357
电气机械及器材制造业	Electric Equipment and Machinery	305	303
通信设备计算机及其他电子设备制造业	Telecommunications Equipment,Computer and Other Electronic Equipment Manufacturing	262	257
仪器仪表及文化办公用机械制造业	Instruments, Meters, Cultural and Office Machinery	133	131
工艺品及其他制造业	Craftwork and Other Manufacturing	128	128
废弃资源和废旧材料回收加工业	Waste Resources and Materials Recovering and Processing	4	4
电力热力的生产和供应业	Production and Supply of Electric & Heat Energy	45	37
燃气生产和供应业	Production and Supply of Gas	11	11
水的生产和供应业	Production and Supply of Water	16	16

注:本表行业分类为国标GB/T4754-2002标准,7-5、7-14、7-24表同。
Note:Sector listed in this table is classified by the standard of GB/T4754-2002,same as following table 7-5,7-14 and 7-24.

7－3　工业企业单位数
（限额及以上工业）
NUMBER OF INDUSTRIAL ENTERPRISES(ABOVE DESIGNATED SIZE)

单位：个　　　　(unit)

项　　目	Item	2002	2003
全 市 总 计	**Total**	**5 346**	**5 341**
#国有及国有控股企业	State－owned and State－holding Enterprises	1 636	1 625
按登记注册类型分组：	**Grouped by Status of Registration**		
一、内资企业	Domestic－funded Enterprises	4 019	3 996
国有企业	State－owned Enterprises	1 202	1 111
集体企业	Collective－owned Enterprises	1 444	1 220
股份合作企业	Cooperative Enterprises	246	172
私营企业	Private Enterprises	594	753
股份有限公司	Share－holding Corporations Ltd.	90	83
有限责任公司	Limited Liability Corporations	347	589
#国有独资	Sole State－funded Corporations	48	56
联营经济	Joint Ownership Enterprises	90	61
#国有与国有联营企业	State Joint Ownership Enterprises	10	12
集体与集体联营企业	Collective Joint Ownership Enterprises	12	14
其他内资企业	Other Domestic－funded Enterprises	6	7
二、港澳台商投资企业	Enterprises with Investment from Hongkong, Macao and Taiwan	409	389
三、外商投资企业	Foreign Funded Enterprises	918	956
按经济类型分组：	**Grouped by Ownership**		
国有经济	State－owned	1 260	1 179
集体经济	Collective－owned	1 702	1 406
私有经济	Private and Individual	594	753
港澳台商投资经济	Hongkong, Macao and Taiwan Funded	409	389
外商投资经济	Foreign Funded	918	956
其　他	Others	463	658
按隶属关系分组：	**Grouped by Administrative Relationship**		
中央工业	Central Industry	85	91
地方工业	Local Industry	5 261	5 250
#市管工业	City Industry	2 318	2 292
#工业系统	Industry System	1 140	1 271
县管工业	County Industry	85	77
区管工业	District Industry	553	597
街管工业	Neighbour Industry	26	14
乡镇管工业	Town and Country Industry	1 205	1 330
按轻重分组：	**Grouped by Light & Heavy Industry**		
轻工业	Light Industry	2 672	2 378
重工业	Heavy Industry	2 674	2 963

注：本表行业分类为国标 GB/T4754—1994 标准，7－4、7－6、7－7 表同。
Note: Sector listed in this table is classifed by the standard of GB/T4754－1994. Same as following table 7－4, 7－6 and 7－7.

7-3 续表　Continued

单位:个　(unit)

项　目	Item	2002	2003
按规模分组:	**Grouped by Size of Enterprises**		
大　型	Large-sized	356	46
中　型	Medium-sized	470	435
小　型	Small-sized	4 520	4 860
按行业分组:	**Grouped by Sector**		
#石油天然气开采业	Petroleum and Natural Gas Extraction	4	4
非金属矿采选业	Nonmetal Minerals Mining and Dressing	24	19
食品加工业	Food Processing	191	182
食品制造业	Food Manufacturing	149	126
饮料制造业	Beverage Manufacturing	69	65
烟草加工业	Tobacco Processing	1	1
纺织业	Textile Industry	316	327
服装及其它纤维制品制造业	Garments and Other Fiber Products	297	286
皮革毛皮羽绒及其制品业	Leather, Furs, Down and Related Products	78	81
木材加工及竹、藤、棕、草制品业	Timber Processing, Bamboo, Cane, Palm Fiber and Straw Products	71	66
家具制造业	Furniture Manufacturing	57	68
造纸及纸制品业	Papermaking and Paper Products	165	169
印刷业记录媒介的复制	Printing and Record Medium Reproduction	94	79
文教体育用品制造业	Cultural, Educational and Sports Goods	69	87
石油加工及炼焦业	Petroleum Processing and Coking	30	34
化学原料及化学制品制造业	Raw Chemical Materials and Chemical Products	504	513
医药制造业	Medical and Pharmaceutical Products	92	91
化学纤维制造业	Chemical Fiber	19	18
橡胶制品业	Rubber Products	119	111
塑料制品业	Plastic Products	207	210
非金属矿物制品业	Nonmetal Mineral Products	218	210
黑色金属冶炼及压延加工业	Smelting and Pressing of Ferrous Metals	133	139
有色金属冶炼及压延加工业	Smelting and Pressing of Nonferrous Metals	88	87
金属制品业	Metal Products	508	472
普通机械制造业	Ordinary Machinery Manufacturing	358	377
专用设备制造业	Equipment Manufacturing for Special Purpose	227	233
交通运输设备制造业	Transport Equipment Manufacturing	355	374
电气机械及器材制造业	Electric Equipment and Machinery	311	305
电子及通信设备制造业	Electronic and Telecommunications Equipment	257	264
仪器仪表及文化办公用机械制造业	Instruments, Meters, Cultural and Office Machinery	123	131
其他制造业	Other Manufacturing	139	136
电力蒸汽热水的生产和供应业	Production and Supply of Electric Power, Steam and Hot Water	44	45
煤气生产和供应业	Production and Supply of Gas	13	11
自来水的生产和供应业	Production and Supply of Tap Water	13	16

7－4 地方工业企业单位数
（限额及以上工业）
NUMBER OF LOCAL INDUSTRIAL ENTERPRISES(ABOVE DESIGNATED SIZE)

单位：个 (unit)

项 目	Item	2002	2003
全市总计	**Total**	**5 261**	**5 250**
按登记注册类型分组：	**Grouped by Status of Registration**		
一、内资企业	Domestic－funded Enterprises	3 949	3 917
国有企业	State－owned Enterprises	1 152	1 057
集体企业	Collective－owned Enterprises	1 442	1 219
股份合作企业	Cooperative Enterprises	246	171
私营企业	Private Enterprises	594	753
股份有限公司	Share－holding Corporations Ltd.	85	77
有限责任公司	Limited Liability Corporations	336	572
#国有独资	Sole State－funded Corporations	46	54
联营经济	Joint Ownership Enterprises	89	61
#国有与国有联营企业	State Joint Ownership Enterprises	10	12
集体与集体联营企业	Collective Joint Ownership Enterprises	12	14
其他内资企业	Other Domestic－funded Enterprises	5	7
二、港澳台商投资企业	Enterprises with Investment from Hongkong,Macao and Taiwan	405	385
三、外商投资企业	Foreign Funded Enterprises	907	948
按经济类型分组：	**Grouped by Ownership**		
国有经济	State－owned	1 208	1 123
集体经济	Collective－owned	1 700	1 404
私有经济	Private and Individual	594	753
港澳台商投资经济	Hongkong,Macao and Taiwan Funded	405	385
外商投资经济	Foreign Funded	907	948
其 他	Others	447	637
按隶属关系分组：	**Grouped by Administrative Relationship**		
#市管工业	City Industry	2 318	2 292
#工业系统	Industry System	1 140	1 271
县管工业	County Industry	85	77
区管工业	District Industry	553	597
街管工业	Neighbour Industry	26	14
乡镇管工业	Town and Country Industry	1 205	1 330
按轻重分组：	**Grouped by Light & Heavy Industry**		
轻工业	Light Industry	2 655	2 363
重工业	Heavy Industry	2 606	2 887

7－4 续表　Continued

单位:个　(unit)

项　目	Item	2002	2003
按规模分组:	**Grouped by Size of Enterprises**		
大　型	Large－sized	327	38
中　型	Medium－sized	455	412
小　型	Small－sized	4 479	4 800
按行业分组:	**Grouped by Sector**		
#非金属矿采选业	Nonmetal Minerals Mining and Dressing	23	18
食品加工业	Food Processing	191	182
食品制造业	Food Manufacturing	149	126
饮料制造业	Beverage Manufacturing	69	65
纺织业	Textile Industry	316	327
服装及其它纤维制品制造业	Garments and Other Fiber Products	297	286
皮革、毛皮、羽绒及其制品业	Leather,Furs,Down and Related Products	78	81
木材加工及竹、藤、棕、草制品业	Timber Processing,Bamboo, Cane, Palm Fiber and Straw Products	69	64
家具制造业	Furniture Manufacturing	57	68
造纸及纸制品业	Papermaking and Paper Products	164	168
印刷业、记录媒介的复制	Printing and Record Medium Reproduction	90	74
文教体育用品制造业	Cultural,Educationaland Sports Goods	69	85
石油加工及炼焦业	Petroleum Processing and Coking	28	32
化学原料及化学制品制造业	Chemical Raw Materials and Chemical Products	498	503
医药制造业	Medical and Pharmaceutical Products	91	90
化学纤维制造业	Chemical Fiber	19	18
橡胶制品业	Rubber Products	119	111
塑料制品业	Plastic Products	206	208
非金属矿物制品业	Nonmetal Mineral Products	217	208
黑色金属冶炼及压延加工业	Smelting and Pressing of Ferrous Metals	133	138
有色金属冶炼及压延加工业	Smelting and Pressing of Nonferrous Metal	87	86
金属制品业	Metal Products	503	468
普通机械制造业	Ordinary Machinery Manufacturing	356	372
专用设备制造业	Equipment Manufacturing for Special Purpose	218	224
交通运输设备制造业	Transport Equipment Manufacturing	334	354
电气机械及器材制造业	Electric Equipment and Machinery	301	302
电子及通信设备制造业	Electronic and Telecommunications Equipment	254	259
仪器仪表及文化、办公用机械制造业	Instruments,Meters,Cultural and Office Machinery	122	129
其他制造业	Other Manufacturing	139	136
电力、蒸汽、热水的生产和供应业	Production and Supply of Electric Power, Steam and Hot Water	35	37
煤气生产和供应业	Production and Supply of Gas	13	11
自来水的生产和供应业	Production and Supply of Tap Water	13	16

7－5 按新国民经济行业分工业总产值(2003年)
(限额以上工业)

GROSS INDUSTRIAL OUTPUT VALUE GROUPED BY NEW SECTOR(ABOVE DESIGNATED SIZE),2003

单位:亿元 (100 million yuan)

项 目	Item	全 部 Total	#地 方 Local
总 计	**Total**	**4 049.61**	**3 442.36**
煤炭开采和洗选业	Coal Mining and Dressing	2.04	2.04
石油和天然气开采业	Petroleum and Natural Gas Extraction	229.50	
有色金属矿采选业	Nonferrous Metals Mining and Dressing	19.75	19.75
非金属矿采选业	Nonmetal Minerals Mining and Dressing	6.32	6.18
农副食品加工业	Agricultural Products and Byproducts Processing	107.92	107.92
食品制造业	Food Manufacturing	59.00	59.00
饮料制造业	Beverage Manufacturing	50.08	50.08
烟草制品业	Tobacco Products	8.67	
纺织业	Textile Industry	76.09	76.09
纺织服装鞋帽制造业	Textile Garments,Shoes,Caps Manufacturing	78.07	78.07
皮革毛皮羽毛(绒)及其制品业	Leather, Furs, Down and Related Products	30.04	30.04
木材加工及木、竹、藤、棕、草制品业	Timber Processing,Bamboo, Cane, Palm Fiber and Straw Products	14.14	13.87
家具制造业	Furniture Manufacturing	37.05	37.05
造纸及纸制品业	Papermaking and Paper Products	37.81	37.62
印刷业和记录媒介的复制	Printing and Record Medium Reproduction	19.99	19.68
文教体育用品制造业	Cultural, Educational and Sports Goods	27.70	27.31
石油加工炼焦及核燃料加工业	Petroleum Processing, Coking and Nuclear Fuel Processing	201.59	40.81
化学原料及化学制品制造业	Raw Chemical Materials and Chemical Products	314.01	240.53
医药制造业	Medical and Pharmaceutical Products	107.06	104.64
化学纤维制造业	Chemical Fiber	9.27	9.27
橡胶制品业	Rubber Products	50.89	50.89
塑料制品业	Plastic Products	72.03	71.88
非金属矿物制品业	Nonmetal Mineral Products	64.34	63.41
黑色金属冶炼及压延加工业	Smelting and Pressing of Ferrous Metals	430.14	430.14
有色金属冶炼及压延加工业	Smelting and Pressing of Nonferrous Metals	54.03	52.32
金属制品业	Metal Products	161.59	159.88
通用设备制造业	General Purpose Equipment Manufacturing	130.14	130.00
专用设备制造业	Special Purpose Equipment Manufacturing	68.58	62.51
交通运输设备制造业	Transport Equipment Manufacturing	314.60	300.11
电气机械及器材制造业	Electric Equipment and Machinery	195.94	190.31
通信设备计算机及其他电子设备制造业	Telecommunications Equipment,Computer and Other Electronic Equipment Manufacturing	886.17	869.54
仪器仪表及文化办公用机械制造业	Instruments, Meters, Cultural and Office Machinery	39.95	39.08
工艺品及其他制造业	Craftwork and Other Manufacturing	28.60	28.60
废弃资源和废旧材料回收加工业	Waste Resources and Materials Recovering and Processing	1.81	1.81
电力热力的生产和供应业	Production and Supply of Electric & Heat Energy	99.62	16.85
燃气生产和供应业	Production and Supply of Gas	8.01	8.01
水的生产和供应业	Production and Supply of Water	7.07	7.07

7－6　工业总产值
（限额及以上工业）
GROSS OUTPUT VALUE OF INDUSTRY(ABOVE DESIGNATED SIZE)

单位：亿元　　(100 million yuan)

项　　目	Item	2002	2003	2003 比2002年增长% Increase Rate in 2003 over 2002
全市总计	**Total**	**3 323.12**	**4 049.61**	**26.1**
#国有及国有控股企业	State－owned and State－holding Enterprises	1 078.27	1 456.51	28.6
按登记注册类型分组：	**Grouped by Status of Registration**			
一、内资企业	Domestic－funded Enterprises			
国有企业	State－owned Enterprises	336.65	419.09	10.6
集体企业	Collective－owned Enterprises	381.12	384.05	7.8
股份合作企业	Cooperative Enterprises	151.18	57.38	－63.0
私营企业	Private Enterprises	134.10	232.51	41.2
股份有限公司	Share－holding Corporations Ltd.	365.70	514.08	21.7
有限责任公司	Limited Liability Corporations	322.81	525.47	29.7
#国有独资	Sole State－funded Corporations	179.93	177.21	14.2
联营经济	Joint Ownership Enterprises	29.20	17.95	－9.1
#国有与国有联营企业	State Joint Ownership Enterprises	2.61	3.67	24.0
集体与集体联营企业	Collective Joint Ownership Enterprises	4.91	2.72	－46.0
其他内资企业	Other Domestic－funded Enterprises	1.07	3.02	119.6
二、港澳台商投资企业	Enterprises with Investment from Hongkong,Macao and Taiwan	236.45	262.07	21.0
三、外商投资企业	Foreign Funded Enterprises	1 364.84	1 633.98	31.3
按经济类型分组：	**Grouped by Ownership**			
国有经济	State－owned	519.19	599.97	12.2
集体经济	Collective－owned	537.21	444.15	－19.3
私有经济	Private and Individual	134.10	232.51	41.2
港澳台商投资经济	Hongkong,Macao and Taiwan Funded	236.45	262.07	21.0
外商投资经济	Foreign Funded	1 364.84	1 633.98	31.3
其　他	Others	531.33	876.92	30.7

注：规模分组增长速度按新标准可比口径计算，7－7表同。
Note：Increase rate grouped by size of enterprise is calculated on the basis of comparable coverage according to new standard，same as following table 7－7.

7-6续表1　Continued

单位:亿元　(100 million yuan)

项　目	Item	2002	2003	2003比2002年增长% Increase Rate in 2003 over 2002
按隶属关系分组:	**Grouped by Administrative Relationship**			
中央工业	Central Industry	464.41	607.25	14.8
地方工业	Local Industry	2 858.72	3 442.36	27.0
#市管工业	City Industry	1 900.37	2 277.65	29.2
#工业系统	Industry System	952.37	1 351.91	43.1
县管工业	County Industry	29.85	36.56	41.1
区管工业	District Industry	120.12	178.87	26.7
街管工业	Neighbour Industry	1.59	1.55	-4.9
乡镇管工业	Town and Country Industry	396.66	531.34	25.4
按轻重分组:	**Grouped by Light & Heavy Industry**			
轻工业	Light Industry	1 012.41	1 095.39	20.8
重工业	Heavy Industry	2 310.71	2 954.22	28.7
按规模分组:	**Grouped by Size of Enterprises**			
大　型	Large-sized	1 901.87	1 576.77	20.1
中　型	Medium-sized	283.23	1 238.04	45.9
小　型	Small-sized	1 138.02	1 234.81	17.2
按行业分组:	**Grouped by Sector**			
#石油天然气开采业	Petroleum and Natural Gas Extraction	163.56	229.50	7.9
非金属矿采选业	Nonmetal Minerals Mining and Dressing	8.95	6.32	-28.5
食品加工业	Food Processing	87.66	107.43	22.6
食品制造业	Food Manufacturing	57.20	56.83	-0.8
饮料制造业	Beverage Manufacturing	48.83	50.08	8.3
烟草加工业	Tobacco Processing	8.01	8.67	-0.1
纺织业	Textile Industry	71.34	76.09	5.7
服装及其它纤维制品制造业	Garments and Other Fiber Products	77.03	78.07	14.4
皮革毛皮羽绒及其制品业	Leather, Furs, Down and Related Products	26.77	30.04	10.5
木材加工及竹藤棕草制品业	Timber Processing, Bamboo, Cane, Palm Fiber and Straw Product	12.74	14.14	20.5

7－6续表2　Continued

单位:亿元　(100 million yuan)

项　目	Item	2002	2003	2003比2002年增长% Increase Rate in 2003 over 2002
家具制造业	Furniture Manufacturing	30.84	37.05	14.6
造纸及纸制品业	Papermaking and Paper Products	32.98	37.81	6.1
印刷业、记录媒介的复制	Printing and Record Medium Reproduction	27.82	17.95	－33.6
文教体育用品制造业	Cultural, Educational and Sports Goods	26.09	29.73	7.9
石油加工及炼焦业	Petroleum Processing and Coking	149.32	201.59	23.9
化学原料及化学制品制造业	Chemical Raw Materials and Chemical Products	263.30	316.67	13.5
医药制造业	Medical and Pharmaceutical Products	83.22	103.62	24.1
化学纤维制造业	Chemical Fiber	7.03	9.27	15.5
橡胶制品业	Rubber Products	43.13	50.89	15.3
塑料制品业	Plastic Products	59.56	72.03	14.9
非金属矿物制品业	Nonmetal Mineral Products	50.67	64.34	32.5
黑色金属冶炼及压延加工业	Smelting and Pressing of Ferrous Metals	284.37	430.14	42.9
有色金属冶炼及压延加工业	Smelting and Pressing of Nonferrous Metals	53.50	54.03	18.1
金属制品业	Metal Products	134.14	166.03	26.2
普通机械制造业	Ordinary Machinery Manufacturing	102.00	127.68	27.5
专用设备制造业	Equipment Manufacturing For Special Purpose	56.28	69.38	28.2
交通运输设备制造业	Transport Equipment Manufacturing	187.72	314.46	54.7
电气机械及器材制造业	Electric Equipment and Machinery	166.64	196.36	46.9
电子及通信设备制造业	Electronic and Telecommunications Equipment	829.36	886.52	22.5
仪器仪表及文化、办公用机械制造业	Instruments, Meters, Cultural and Office Machinery	28.09	39.29	54.1
其他制造业	Other Manufacturing	31.05	30.99	9.6
电力蒸汽热水的生产和供应业	Production and Supply of Electric Power, Steam and Hot Water	83.46	99.62	18.0
煤气生产和供应业	Production and Supply of Gas	14.83	8.01	－4.0
自来水的生产和供应业	Production and Supply of Tap Water	6.57	7.07	3.7

7-7 地方工业总产值
（限额及以上工业）
GROSS OUTPUT VALUE OF LOCAL INDUSTRY (ABOVE DESIGNATED SIZE)

单位：亿元 (100 million yuan)

项 目	Item	2002	2003	2003比2002年增长% Increase Rate in 2003 over 2002
全市总计	**Total**	**2 858.72**	**3 442.36**	**27.0**
按登记注册类型分组：	**Grouped by Status of Registration**			
一、内资企业	Domestic - funded Enterprises			
国有企业	State - owned Enterprises	212.54	278.42	13.6
集体企业	Collective - owned Enterprises	381.11	383.98	7.8
股份合作企业	Cooperative Enterprises	151.18	57.12	-63.1
私营企业	Private Eenterprises	134.10	232.51	41.2
股份有限公司	Share - holding Corporations Ltd.	83.97	154.29	25.1
有限责任公司	Limited Liability Corporations	280.25	444.46	31.4
#国有独资	Sole State - funded Corporations	175.52	146.09	-18.8
联营经济	Joint Ownership Enterprises	29.14	17.95	-9.1
#国有与国有联营企业	State Joint Ownership Enterprises	2.61	3.67	24.0
集体与集体联营企业	Collective Joint Ownership Enterprises	4.91	2.72	-46.0
其他内资企业	Other Domestic - funded Enterprises	1.05	3.02	119.6
二、港澳台商投资企业	Enterprises with Investment from Hongkong, Macao and Taiwan	236.09	261.63	21.1
三、外商投资企业	Foreign Funded Enterprises	1 349.29	1 608.98	30.9
按经济类型分组：	**Grouped by Ownership**			
国有经济	State - owned	390.67	428.18	14.5
集体经济	Collective - owned	537.20	443.81	-19.4
私有经济	Private and Individual	134.10	232.51	41.2
港澳台商投资经济	Hongkong, Macao and Taiwan Funded	236.09	261.63	21.1
外商投资经济	Foreign Funded	1 349.29	1 608.98	30.9
其 他	Others	211.37	467.24	34.0

7－7 续表 1　Continued

单位:亿元 (100 million yuan)

项　目	Item	2002	2003	2003 比 2002 年增长% Increase Rate in 2003 over 2002
按隶属关系分组:	**Grouped by Administrative Relationship**			
#市管工业	City Industry	1 900.37	2 277.65	29.0
#工业系统	Industry System	952.37	1 351.91	43.1
县管工业	County Industry	29.85	36.56	32.8
区管工业	District Industry	120.12	178.87	25.6
街管工业	Neighbour Industry	1.59	1.55	－4.9
乡镇管工业	Town and Country Industry	396.66	531.34	25.2
按轻重分组:	**Grouped by Light & Heavy Industry**			
轻工业	Light Industry	999.43	1 080.8	20.9
重工业	Heavy Industry	1 859.29	2 361.56	30.2
按规模分组:	**Grouped by Size of Enterprises**			
大　型	Large－sized	1 493.76	1 205.82	21.1
中　型	Medium－sized	235.94	1 030.71	47.9
小　型	Small－sized	1 129.02	1 205.83	17.1
按行业分组:	**Grouped by Sector**			
#非金属矿采选业	Nonmetal Minerals Mining and Dressing	8.86	6.18	－29.4
食品加工业	Food Processing	87.66	107.43	22.6
食品制造业	Food Manufacturing	57.20	56.83	－0.8
饮料制造业	Beverage Manufacturing	48.83	50.08	8.3
纺织业	Textile Industry	71.34	76.09	5.7
服装及其它纤维制品制造业	Garments and Other Fiber Products	77.03	78.07	14.4
皮革毛皮羽绒及其制品业	Leather，Furs，Down and Related Products	26.77	30.04	10.5

7-7 续表 2 Continued
单位:亿元 (100 million yuan)

项 目	Item	2002	2003	2003 比 2002 年增长% Increase Rate in 2003 over 2002
木材加工及竹、藤、棕、草制品业	Timber Processing, Bamboo, Cane, Palm Fiber and Straw Product	12.58	13.87	19.9
家具制造业	Furniture Manufacturing	30.84	37.05	14.6
造纸及纸制品业	Papermaking and Paper Products	32.81	37.62	6.1
印刷业、记录媒介的复制	Printing and Record Medium Reproduction	27.54	17.64	34.1
文教体育用品制造业	Cultural, Educational and Sports Goods	26.09	29.34	7.8
石油加工及炼焦业	Petroleum Processing and Coking	26.90	40.81	27.0
化学原料及化学制品制造业	Chemical Raw Materials and Chemical Products	205.07	243.19	15.0
医药制造业	Medical and Pharmaceutical Products	80.93	101.20	24.3
化学纤维制造业	Chemical Fiber	7.03	9.27	15.5
橡胶制品业	Rubber Products	43.13	50.89	15.3
塑料制品业	Plastic Products	59.49	71.88	14.8
非金属矿物制品业	Nonmetal Mineral Products	50.64	63.41	32.4
黑色金属冶炼及压延加工业	Smelting and Pressing of Ferrous Metals	284.37	430.14	42.9
有色金属冶炼及压延加工业	Smelting and Pressing of Nonferrous Metals	52.27	52.32	17.5
金属制品业	Metal Products	132.07	164.33	26.6
普通机械制造业	Ordinary Machinery Manufacturing	101.96	127.63	27.5
专用设备制造业	Equipment Manufacturing for Special Purpose	51.79	63.31	28.0
交通运输设备制造业	Transport Equipment Manufacturing	175.17	299.97	56.4
电气机械及器材制造业	Electric Equipment and Machinery	158.16	190.64	46.2
电子及通信设备制造业	Electronic and Telecommunications Equipment	819.91	869.88	22.2
仪器仪表及文化办公用机械制造业	Instruments, Meters, Cultural and Office Machinery	28.08	38.43	56.4
其他制造业	Other Manufacturing	31.05	30.99	9.6
电力蒸汽热水的生产和供应业	Production and Supply of Electric Power, Steam and Hot Water	12.67	16.85	17.5
煤气生产和供应业	Production and Supply of Gas	14.83	8.01	-4.0
自来水的生产和供应业	Production and Supply of Tap Water	6.57	7.07	3.7

7-8 主要工业产品产量
OUTPUT OF MAJOR INDUSTRIAL PRODUCTS
(1978-2003)

年份 Year	布（万米） Cloth (10 000 m)	纱（万吨） Yarn (10 000 tons)	机制纸及纸板（万吨） Machine-made Paper and Paperboards (10 000 tons)	合成洗涤剂（万吨） Synthetic Detergent (10 000 tons)	饮料酒（万吨） Alcoholic Beverages (10 000 tons)	家用电冰箱（万台） Household Refrige-rators (10 000 units)	电视机（万台） Television Sets (10 000 units)	#彩色电视机 Color Television Sets
1978	33 727	8.30	9.26	2.38	2.88	0.50	2.54	
1979	36 067	9.20	21.46	2.70	3.66	0.55	8.11	
1980	39 215	9.96	22.75	2.95	4.49	0.40	15.28	0.60
1981	42 427	10.73	21.25	3.19	5.86	0.14	36.70	2.01
1982	45 831	11.50	22.82	3.53	5.76	0.23	36.11	5.00
1983	46 803	11.95		3.70	6.75	0.51	43.62	8.28
1984	44 865	11.67		4.12	7.46	2.01	61.59	15.72
1985	44 043	11.95	24.60	5.04	8.40	6.89	90.22	34.02
1986	43 798	12.22	26.45	5.39	9.79	9.79	89.85	33.54
1987	43 885	12.57	27.92	5.56	10.60	14.53	100.02	55.46
1988	43 410	12.67	27.10	5.88	10.96	33.32	135.25	62.07
1989	41 729	11.30	28.31	7.36	9.47	40.41	137.85	57.32
1990	49 194	11.69	26.75	8.54	9.28	23.34	143.93	62.46
1991	46 790	11.23	27.18	9.34	10.75	6.71	140.27	72.63
1992	43 031	10.86	33.32	10.56	10.88	9.27	140.99	68.29
1993	39 259	11.59	36.84	10.00	11.40	2.71	134.88	73.30
1994	41 437	13.19	31.01	9.68	11.09	3.95	124.00	80.37
1995	49 803	12.35	41.42	11.95	12.34	3.70	160.82	109.54
1996	39 662	10.51	45.89	12.07	10.72	0.29	157.34	117.80
1997	49 845	13.61	40.56	10.28	13.73	0.69	84.36	59.16
1998	33 326	8.37	33.64	9.65	15.25	2.29	82.94	47.87
1999	27 308	8.45	25.50	8.75	14.21	9.93	84.67	50.34
2000	29 217	8.80	25.18	7.19	15.75	8.42	94.27	72.28
2001	25 861	8.13	20.63	5.68	20.71	3.85	66.24	51.42
2002	27 082	9.18	27.98	5.41	20.64	19.14	87.06	76.35
2003	25 114	7.47	17.76	5.09	24.72	29.17	121.09	112.41

7－8 续表 Continued

年 份 Year	原 油 （万吨） Crude Oil （10 000 tons）	发电量 （亿千瓦小时） Electricity （100 million kwh）	钢 （万吨） Steel （10 000 tons）	水 泥 （万吨） Cement （10 000 tons）	硫 酸 （万吨） Sulfuric Acid （10 000 tons）	烧 碱 （万吨） Caustic Soda （10 000 tons）	农用化肥 （万吨） Chemical Fertilizer （10 000 tons）	化学农药 （万吨） Chemical Pesticide （10 000 tons）
1978	316.90	51.68	101.75	47.34	10.52	17.02	4.67	7.31
1979	307.30	52.56	109.53	56.52	11.86	19.26	5.39	7.50
1980	307.41	63.20	124.94	62.55	12.38	19.93	6.22	7.82
1981	303.84	72.96	125.15	75.71	12.41	19.19	4.78	7.32
1982	302.24	75.01	124.56	81.80	13.53	21.21	5.85	6.91
1983	310.41	77.34	133.86	82.68	13.22	21.27	7.05	3.65
1984	320.81	79.57	132.49	90.52	12.00	21.97	7.66	2.69
1985	374.63	80.65	111.93	105.11	11.72	23.36	5.56	2.31
1986	413.33	78.38	150.32	112.41	10.33	23.97	4.09	2.14
1987	453.01	81.09	162.96	120.19	11.30	24.73	6.56	1.67
1988	462.79	91.07	156.44	129.37	8.32	25.18	7.61	1.75
1989	470.43	96.60	151.57	127.84	8.09	24.90	7.79	1.75
1990	469.50	94.85	166.74	122.14	7.70	25.23	7.21	1.97
1991	474.90	90.27	175.43	137.24	8.31	27.25	7.85	2.12
1992	491.76	98.62	183.45	144.58	8.15	27.99	7.84	2.01
1993	517.00	126.65	221.98	152.39	7.36	28.27	10.61	2.37
1994	589.00	122.47	188.55	177.00	7.79	29.28	15.75	2.81
1995	620.82	133.65	171.57	200.62	5.58	32.57	9.74	1.69
1996	646.60	146.04	200.99	207.88	8.11	50.75	11.31	2.95
1997	645.90	166.53	236.79	209.00	11.33	44.15	10.91	3.27
1998	691.28	172.51	255.27	250.00	10.36	39.90	10.26	3.38
1999	686.72	182.56	317.69	240.51	11.47	47.04	26.82	3.68
2000	763.99	211.49	356.76	267.81	11.17	49.28	17.04	2.79
2001	970.29	217.43	395.30	338.99	11.27	49.39	14.91	0.71
2002	1 215.94	268.83	482.58	377.75	12.15	63.65	16.03	3.30
2003	1 316.30	319.95	565.95	449.31	10.96	79.89	16.40	2.10

7－9 主要工业产品产量

OUTPUT OF MAJOR INDUSTRIAL PRODUCTS

产品名称	Item	单位	Unit	2002	2003
原　油	Crude Oil	万吨	10 000 tons	1 215.94	1 316.30
原油加工量	Crude Oil Processed	万吨	10 000 tons	644.58	710.19
发电量	Electricity	亿千瓦小时	100 million kwh	268.83	319.95
供热量	Heating Supply	万百万千焦	10 billion kilo－joule	1 931.08	2 458.00
天然气	Natural Gas	亿立方米	100 million cu. m	8.88	8.49
液化气	Liquefied Petroleum Gas	万吨	10 000 tons	50.36	55.12
原　盐	Salt	万吨	10 000 tons	240.40	220.48
食用植物油	Edible Vegetable Oil	万吨	10 000 tons	19.99	17.35
饮料酒	Alcoholic Beverages	万吨	10 000 tons	20.64	24.72
#啤　酒	Beer	万吨	10 000 tons	14.51	17.33
方便主食品	Staple Foods	万吨	10 000 tons	10.85	14.47
软饮料	Soft Drinking	万吨	10 000 tons	71.47	89.97
卷　烟	Cigarettes	万箱	10 000 cases	22.00	22.00
家　具	Furniture	万件	10 000 pcs	382.08	439.51
地　毯	Carpet	万元	10 000 yuan	124 919	122 559
化学纤维	Chemical Fiber	万吨	10 000 tons	22.41	29.76
纱(混合)	Yarn	万吨	10 000 tons	9.18	7.47
布(混合)	Cloth	万米	10 000 m	27 082	25 114
丝织品	Silk Knitwear	万米	10 000 m	4 242.00	1 693.00
毛　线	Knitting Wool	吨	ton	7 333	8 693
呢　绒	Woolen Piece Goods	万米	10 000 m	719	689
服　装	Garments	万件	10 000 pieces	20 151	22 211
人造板	Artificial Board	万立方米	10 000 cu. m	17.66	9.95
机制纸及纸板	Machine－made Paper and Paperboard	万吨	10 000 tons	27.98	17.76
电子琴	Electronic Organ	万架	10 000 units	109.74	110.71
硫　酸	Sulfuric Acid	吨	10 000 tons	12.15	10.96
纯　碱	Soda Ash	万吨	10 000 tons	79.46	82.01
烧　碱	Caustic Soda	万吨	10 000 tons	63.65	79.89
电　石	Calcium Carbide	万吨	10 000 tons	1.90	0.96
合成氨	Synthetic Ammonia	万吨	10 000 tons	14.48	23.15
农用化肥	Chemical Fertilizer	万吨	10 000 tons	16.03	16.40
化学农药	Chemical Pesticide	吨	ton	32 990	21 026
乙　烯	Ethene	万吨	10 000 tons	21.28	23.00

7－9 续表　Continued

产品名称	Item	单　位	Unit	2002	2003
油　漆	Paint	吨	ton	119 452	130 412
染　料	Dyestuff	吨	ton	92 773	91 732
轮胎外胎	Tires	万条	10 000 units	538.55	603.76
农用塑料薄膜	Plastic Film for Farm Use	吨	ton	13 824	14 690
合成洗涤剂	Synthetic Detergents	万吨	10 000 tons	5.41	5.09
化学原料药	Chemical Raw Medicine	吨	ton	11 325	8 513
中成药	Traditional Chinese Patent Medicine	万吨	10 000 tons	0.58	0.62
水　泥	Cement	万吨	10 000 tons	377.75	449.31
平板玻璃	Plate Glass	万重量箱	10 000 weight cases	329.58	262.77
生　铁	Pig Iron	万吨	10 000 tons	247.71	342.65
钢	Steel	万吨	10 000 tons	482.58	565.95
钢　材	Steel Products	万吨	10 000 tons	806.13	1 031.47
黄　金	Gold	千克	kg	9 264	19 479
焦　炭	Coke	万吨	10 000 tons	282.38	307.65
电焊条	Welding Rod	万吨	10 000 tons	76.67	89.24
内燃机	Internal Combustion Engine	万千瓦	10 000 kw	563.42	973.91
金属切削机床	Metal－cutting Machine	台	unit	174	1 208
升降移动机械	Lift	台	unit	4 059	5 150
汽　车	Motor Vehicle	辆	unit	94 397	172 473
#轿　车	Car	辆	unit	92 067	172 473
摩托车	Motorcycle	万辆	10 000 units	79.49	114.79
自行车	Bicycle	万辆	10 000 units	634.11	833.93
家用电冰箱	Household Refrigerator	万台	10 000 units	19.14	29.17
房间空气调节器	Air Conditioner	万台	10 000 units	121.62	241.84
微波炉	Microwave Oven	万台	10 000 units	449.42	969.87
移动电话	Mobile Phone	万部	10 000 units	2 850.66	3 139.72
微型计算机	Micro－computer	万部	10 000 units	0.92	0.42
半导体集成电路	Semiconductor Integrated Circuit	亿块	100 million pcs	3.22	3.69
电视机	Television Sets	万台	10 000 units	87.06	121.09
#彩色电视机	Color Television Sets	万台	10 000 units	76.35	112.41
录像机	Videocorder	万台	10 000 units	334.12	279.06
吸尘器	Vacuum Cleaners	万台	10 000 units	155.60	302.83

7－10 主要产品销售量和产销率
SALES VOLUME AND SALES RATIO OF MAJOR INDUSTRIAL PRODUCTS

产品名称	Item	单 位	Unit	2002 销售量 Sales Volume	2002 产销率(%) Sales Ratio(%)	2003 销售量 Sales Volume	2003 产销率(%) Sales Ratio(%)
生 铁	Pig Iron	万吨	10 000 tons	26.73	10.79	80.81	23.58
钢 材	Steel Products	万吨	10 000 tons	769.48	95.45	1 044.71	101.28
无缝钢管	Seamless Steel Pipe	万吨	10 000 tons	85.70	99.71	92.68	101.10
硫 酸	Sulfuric Acid	万吨	10 000 tons	10.61	87.34	10.10	92.17
烧 碱	Caustic Soda	万吨	10 000 tons	55.69	87.48	69.63	87.15
纯 碱	Soda Ash	万吨	10 000 tons	75.38	94.85	78.99	96.31
轮胎外胎	Tires	万条	10 000 units	533.09	98.98	603.26	99.91
水 泥	Cement	万吨	10 000 tons	360.82	95.52	455.19	101.30
平板玻璃	Plate Glass	万重量箱	10 000 weight cases	333.38	101.51	274.49	104.46
焦 碳	Coke	万吨	10 000 tons	183.31	64.91	207.23	67.35
原 油	Crude Oil	万吨	10 000 tons	1 192.75	98.09	1 294.29	98.32
汽 车	Motor Vehicle	万辆	10 000 units	10.18	107.84	16.78	97.26
电视机	Television Sets	万台	10 000 units	88.04	98.75	119.36	98.57
#彩色电视机	Color Television Sets	万台	10 000 units	76.26	99.87	111.21	98.93
家用电冰箱(柜)	Household Refrigerator	万台	10 000 units	15.09	78.85	29.61	99.88
吸尘器	Vacuum Cleaners	万台	10 000 units	160.29	103.01	302.69	99.95
房间空气调节器	Air Conditioner	万台	10 000 units	123.30	101.40	241.65	99.56
微波炉	Microwave Ovens	万台	10 000 units	466.98	103.90	970.25	100.03
移动电话机	Mobile Phone	万部	10 000 units	2 858.79	100.28	3 151.65	100.37
纱(混合)	Yarn	万吨	10 000 tons	5.78	62.92	4.53	60.62
布(混合)	Cloth	万米	10 000 m	27 845.28	102.81	25 589.74	101.89
毛 线	Knitting Wool	吨	ton	6 661.80	90.83	8 489.85	97.66
呢 绒	Woolen Piece Goods	万米	10 000 m	732.60	101.89	700.65	101.72
合成洗涤剂	Synthetic Detergents	万吨	10 000 tons	5.32	98.31	5.07	99.66
录像机	Videocorder	万部	10 000 units	332.90	99.63	276.11	98.94
照相机	Cameras	万台	10 000 units	148.78	100.22	78.33	91.15
服 装	Garments	万件	10 000 pieces	19 165.06	95.10	22 181.45	99.85
自行车	Bicycle	万辆	10 000 units	612.64	96.61	736.00	97.96
微型计算机	Micro－computer	万部	10 000 units	0.91	98.88	0.39	92.27
人造板	Artificial Board	万立方米	10 000 cu.m	16.32	92.40	10.01	100.64
摩托车	Motorcycles	万辆	10 000 units	76.12	95.75	117.85	102.66

7-11 工业企业主要财务指标
MAIN FINANCIAL INDICATORS OF INDUSTRIAL ENTERPRISES
(1978-2003)

单位:亿元 (100 million yuan)

年份 Year	固定资产原值 Original Value of Fixed Assets	固定资产净值平均余额 Annual Average Balance of Net Value of Fixed Assets	流动资产平均余额 Annual Average Balance of Circulating Funds	产品销售收入 Sales Revenue	利税总额 Total Pre-tax Profits	从业人员年平均人数(万人) Annual Average Persons Employed (10 000 persons)
全市 **Total**						
1978	88.75	54.45	46.51	141.56	37.06	121.31
1979	97.39	60.93	45.30	160.28	41.29	121.85
1980	106.71	67.55	46.14	173.94	43.94	127.30
1981	117.75	74.77	49.03	186.44	47.33	134.76
1982	124.22	77.87	52.36	195.79	46.38	141.96
1983	132.50	82.64	54.94	209.79	47.95	138.01
1984	156.68	101.72	61.42	230.99	51.54	144.21
1985	183.01	119.09	66.91	280.08	65.40	149.18
1986	203.55	132.18	80.72	306.38	65.04	152.08
1987	229.71	150.86	89.12	347.11	67.82	157.81
1988	264.70	174.58	100.56	423.08	69.63	157.21
1989	310.87	195.30	123.71	454.76	59.75	157.35
1990	329.93	217.17	148.83	465.55	48.36	159.31
1991	379.97	252.86	173.89	538.50	52.61	155.64
1992	458.50	276.80	207.99	646.92	59.40	160.30
1993	611.67	312.14	559.47	1 040.49	83.94	178.08
1994	852.75	429.40	756.09	1 101.71	109.86	177.93
1995	1 273.46	628.11	888.92	1 376.70	133.51	173.58
1996	1 338.28	892.14	1 044.83	1 498.67	139.73	165.56
1997	1 590.96	1 092.54	1 232.07	1 668.15	139.96	158.52
1998	1 899.35	1 289.83	1 386.17	1 943.89	148.69	142.99
1999	2 157.03	1 446.46	1 490.98	2 182.17	175.66	128.75
2000	2 488.60	1 561.39	1 488.27	2 656.98	274.27	120.19
2001	2 763.94	1 657.85	1 772.75	2 983.26	326.55	122.15
2002	2 940.21	1 729.50	1 874.76	3 437.46	325.07	120.95
2003	3 036.78	1 793.13	1 991.12	4 202.02	401.35	115.28
#国有经济 **State-owned**						
1978	79.47	47.87	38.24		32.09	81.13
1979	86.83	53.37	36.23		35.75	80.59
1980	94.64	58.87	37.05	146.58	38.17	83.51
1981	103.83	64.62	39.18	156.59	41.40	87.03
1982	108.52	66.51	41.08	162.09	39.73	91.57
1983	115.06	70.25	43.72	173.37	40.69	88.03
1984	136.56	87.68	49.26	190.86	41.31	90.51
1985	159.35	102.07	51.58	225.75	54.51	94.27
1986	174.96	111.83	61.81	244.76	53.19	94.90
1987	196.15	126.57	69.58	275.53	55.63	97.35
1988	223.16	144.22	76.64	331.61	56.03	97.73
1989	258.69	160.37	93.85	352.99	46.77	97.94
1990	273.52	176.86	112.41	356.60	37.35	97.07
1991	314.71	207.30	129.89	407.79	39.01	96.74
1992	376.34	245.69	255.46	459.59	37.32	96.08
1993	467.63	292.18	345.77	663.86	37.91	117.79
1994	612.46	363.96	444.30	584.78	44.50	93.50
1995	942.91	644.15	474.69	625.98	44.91	90.70
1996	910.56	647.65	518.45	594.08	37.06	83.05
1997	1 031.89	732.58	577.59	625.22	39.26	78.99
1998	1 130.86	773.73	601.69	587.69	29.63	69.34
1999	1 261.91	817.29	631.78	594.55	26.88	56.84
2000	1 193.87	836.48	648.06	667.84	18.70	48.12
2001	1 151.07	699.45	615.11	649.26	17.08	42.99
2002	1 087.90	693.21	605.08	629.86	22.63	36.42
2003	1 066.98	704.47	576.42	817.42	52.83	30.71

注:1.本表数据范围1997年及以前为街乡及以上工业,1998年开始为限额以上工业。2.固定资产净值平均余额1991年及以前为固定资产净值。3.流动资产平均余额1991年及以前为定额流动资金平均余额。4.从业人员年平均人数1998年以前为职工平均人数。

Note:a)Before 1998, figures of this table refer to industrial enterprises at township and higher level, since 1998, figures refer to enterprises above designated size. b)Before 1992, annual average balance of net value of fixed assets refer to net value of fixed assets . c)Before 1992, annual average balance of circulating funds refer to average balance of quota circulating funds . d)Before 1998, annual average employment personnel refer to staff and workers.

7－12 分地区工业企业主要财务指标(2003年)

MAIN FINANCIAL INDICATORS OF INDUSTRIAL ENTERPRISES BY REGION,2003

单位:亿元 (100 million yuan)

地区 Region		企业单位数(个) Number of Enter-prises (unit)	资产总计 Total Assets	固定资产原价 Original Value of Fixed Assets	固定资产净值年平均余额 Annual Average Balance of Net Value of Fixed Assets	流动资产年平均余额 Annual Average Balance of Circulating Funds
全市总计	**Total**	**5 341**	**4 626.67**	**3 036.78**	**1 793.13**	**1 991.12**
和平区	Heping District	100	119.34	68.83	44.48	40.99
河东区	Hedong District	237	366.76	156.07	97.82	174.51
河西区	Hexi District	290	281.29	140.28	84.28	119.73
南开区	Nankai District	498	282.70	103.64	69.00	142.66
河北区	Hebei District	259	324.58	233.93	164.53	107.62
红桥区	Hongqiao District	137	47.26	19.63	12.07	24.29
塘沽区	Tanggu District	404	930.91	758.48	364.63	438.26
汉沽区	Hangu District	84	51.43	35.65	21.71	22.95
大港区	Dagang District	154	442.79	565.85	309.50	136.05
东丽区	Dongli District	385	314.49	180.96	111.33	125.45
西青区	Xiqing District	476	517.78	283.73	173.40	254.49
津南区	Jinnan District	356	105.41	48.35	30.24	54.03
北辰区	Beichen District	540	372.87	146.18	88.39	157.96
武清区	Wuqing District	363	170.70	111.81	73.66	76.82
宝坻区	Baodi District	337	37.45	21.05	14.48	18.20
宁河县	Ninghe County	161	43.79	19.54	13.79	21.60
静海县	Jinghai County	276	101.32	40.87	32.43	50.37
蓟　县	Jixian County	284	115.77	101.93	87.38	25.14

地区 Region		产品销售收入 Sales Revenue	销售税金及附加 Sales Tax and Extra Charge	利税总额 Total Pre-tax Profit	利润总额 Total Profit	工业总产值 Gross Industrial Output Value	工业增加值 Value Added of Industry
全市总计	**Total**	**4 202.02**	**39.29**	**401.35**	**237.62**	**4 049.61**	**1 074.78**
和平区	Heping District	55.36	0.24	1.83	0.14	23.30	8.61
河东区	Hedong District	283.12	0.80	22.74	13.82	191.02	43.84
河西区	Hexi District	155.55	2.42	10.52	3.33	152.25	38.75
南开区	Nankai District	164.56	0.52	13.25	7.23	142.68	39.61
河北区	Hebei District	153.47	0.63	7.55	0.22	97.23	33.05
红桥区	Hongqiao District	27.36	0.27	1.16	0.01	24.74	5.33
塘沽区	Tanggu District	1 000.82	12.04	116.38	82.81	1 002.62	314.96
汉沽区	Hangu District	47.01	0.33	4.18	1.14	46.79	18.68
大港区	Dagang District	415.67	9.03	37.37	10.65	406.48	109.04
东丽区	Dongli District	239.34	4.01	24.56	12.10	241.00	61.56
西青区	Xiqing District	641.34	4.52	49.33	30.54	638.20	127.61
津南区	Jinnan District	115.20	0.36	7.88	4.43	118.04	45.41
北辰区	Beichen District	328.35	1.63	38.85	25.01	344.30	66.84
武清区	Wuqing District	173.01	0.23	22.78	17.43	196.78	42.44
宝坻区	Baodi District	63.02	0.03	5.63	3.96	66.88	12.26
宁河县	Ninghe County	54.59	0.35	4.20	2.95	58.25	8.28
静海县	Jinghai County	179.81	0.51	14.09	10.81	184.40	62.67
蓟　县	Jixian County	104.44	1.38	19.04	11.04	114.65	35.81

7－13　工业企业主要

MAIN FINANCIAL INDICATORS OF

项　目	Item	企业单位数（个）Number of Enter－prises (unit)	从业人员年平均人数（人）Annual Average Persons Employed (person)	工业总产值（万元）Gross Industrial Output Value (10 000 yuan)
全市总计	**Total**	**5 341**	**1 152 757**	**40 496 103**
#国有及国有控股企业	State－owned and State－holding Enterprises	1 625	452 090	14 565 133
按登记注册类型分组:	**Grouped by Status of Registration**			
一、内资企业	Domestic－funded Enterprises	3 996	807 485	21 535 552
国有企业	State－owned Enterprises	1 111	211 900	4 190 888
集体企业	Collective－owned Enterprise	1 220	184 610	3 840 546
股份合作企业	Cooperative Enterprises	172	24 003	573 780
私营企业	Private Enterprises	753	98 063	2 325 143
股份有限公司	Share－holding Corporations Ltd.	83	68 002	5 140 814
有限责任公司	Limited Liability Corporations	589	208 372	5 254 707
#国有独资	Sole State－funded Corporations	56	93 145	1 772 105
联营经济	Joint Ownership Enterprises	61	12 022	179 458
#国有与国有联营企业	State Joint Ownership Enterprises	12	2 019	36 686
集体与集体联营企业	Collective Joint Ownership Enterprises	14	1 655	27 203
其他内资企业	Other Domestic－funded Enterprises	7	513	30 216
二、港澳台商投资企业	Enterprises with Investment from Hongkong, Macao and Taiwan	389	84 912	2 620 712
三、外商投资企业	Foreign Funded Enterprises	956	260 360	16 339 839
按经济类型分组:	**Grouped by Ownership**			
国有经济	State－owned	1 179	307 064	5 999 679
集体经济	Collective－owned	1 406	210 268	4 441 529
私有经济	Private and Individual	753	98 063	2 325 143
港澳台商投资经济	Hongkong, Macao and Taiwan Funded	389	84 912	2 620 712
外商投资经济	Foreign Funded	956	260 360	16 339 839
其　他	Others	658	192 090	8 769 201
按隶属关系分组:	**Grouped by Administrative Relationship**			
中央工业	Central Industry	91	110 902	6 072 491
地方工业	Local Industry	5 250	1 041 855	34 423 612
#市管工业	City Industry	2 292	557 971	22 776 516
#工业系统	Industry System	1 271	362 859	13 519 139
县管工业	County Industry	77	21 171	365 605
区管工业	District Industry	597	70 120	1 788 651
街管工业	Neighbour Industry	14	1 607	15 473
乡镇管工业	Town and Country Industry	1 330	250 348	5 313 354
按轻重分组:	**Grouped by Light & Heavy Industry**			
轻工业	Light Industry	2 378	479 555	10 953 875
重工业	Heavy Industry	2 963	673 202	29 542 228
按规模分组:	**Grouped by Size of Enterprises**			
大　型	Large－sized	46	246 303	15 767 697
中　型	Medium－sized	435	342 082	12 380 350
小　型	Small－sized	4 860	564 372	12 348 056

财务指标(2003年)

INDUSTRIAL ENTERPRISES, 2003

工业增加值(万元) Value Added of Industry (10 000 yuan)	实收资本(万元) Total Capital Hold (10 000 yuan)	资产总计(万元) Total Assets (10 000 yuan)	流动资产年平均余额(万元) Annual Average Balance of Circulating Funds (10 000 yuan)	固定资产原价合计(万元) Original Value of Fixed Assets (10 000 yuan)	固定资产净值年平均余额(万元) Annual Average Balance of Net Value of Fixed Assets (10 000 yuan)	产品销售收入(万元) Sales Revenue (10 000 yuan)	利税总额(万元) Total Pre-tax Profits (10 000 yuan)	#利润总额 Total Profits
10 747 773	**12 834 149**	**46 266 686**	**19 911 227**	**30 367 761**	**17 931 300**	**42 020 153**	**4 013 533**	**2 376 194**
4 702 041	6 759 560	27 152 693	9 566 298	20 701 645	12 224 606	16 678 612	2 087 728	1 071 291
6 500 220	6 744 807	30 685 047	11 491 294	21 857 222	12 935 575	22 880 049	2 596 999	1 451 917
1 146 591	2 261 276	11 226 917	4 036 944	7 458 714	5 071 846	6 091 775	387 038	108 219
933 172	436 436	2 157 696	1 185 307	898 797	558 546	3 441 287	300 676	193 785
130 137	57 063	345 438	189 063	132 368	81 701	503 960	60 705	41 888
490 557	280 980	1 240 320	568 877	446 861	268 787	2 228 601	206 649	151 635
2 029 596	1 016 960	6 416 018	2 229 535	7 079 535	3 131 177	5 117 372	1 105 434	703 761
1 702 391	2 642 507	9 096 170	3 190 276	5 731 307	3 760 874	5 290 222	516 008	239 029
579 585	1 705 155	5 095 014	1 714 514	3 187 018	1 954 117	2 048 386	139 699	21 151
44 494	45 761	190 260	85 236	106 343	60 608	176 866	17 894	11 589
5 718	11 187	36 483	12 775	24 086	18 691	34 004	1 562	-536
4 335	2 979	14 236	8 189	5 690	3 106	27 045	2 120	1 603
23 283	3 825	12 227	6 055	3 296	2 036	29 965	2 596	2 012
682 244	1 177 860	2 899 231	1 438 707	1 573 594	919 515	2 534 860	242 136	169 452
3 565 309	4 911 482	12 682 408	6 981 227	6 936 946	4 076 210	16 605 244	1 174 398	754 825
1 731 894	3 977 617	16 358 415	5 764 234	10 669 818	7 044 653	8 174 165	528 299	128 833
1 067 644	496 478	2 517 370	1 382 559	1 036 855	643 353	3 972 291	363 500	237 276
490 557	280 980	1 240 320	568 877	446 861	268 787	2 228 601	206 649	151 635
682 244	1 177 860	2 899 231	1 438 707	1 573 594	919 515	2 534 860	242 136	169 452
3 565 309	4 911 482	12 682 408	6 981 227	6 936 946	4 076 210	16 605 244	1 174 398	754 825
3 210 127	1 989 732	10 568 942	3 775 624	9 703 687	4 978 782	8 504 991	1 498 551	934 173
2 680 088	1 903 549	9 078 525	2 031 312	11 838 726	6 616 370	6 738 111	1 315 141	718 303
8 067 685	10 930 600	37 188 160	17 879 916	18 529 035	11 314 930	35 282 042	2 698 393	1 657 891
5 087 962	8 420 779	28 558 197	13 736 561	14 509 876	8 784 802	24 095 895	1 628 541	887 254
2 878 453	5 415 565	18 902 446	8 702 477	9 435 869	5 908 212	14 635 396	1 174 099	613 759
87 724	178 255	570 262	225 258	328 178	240 547	408 616	23 148	3 234
430 605	990 099	2 539 735	1 147 408	1 289 882	869 353	2 076 335	168 931	125 233
1 802	3 214	13 399	4 753	6 911	1 268	16 123	941	244
1 154 593	867 397	3 314 988	1 614 083	1 449 773	825 347	4 886 761	540 631	391 754
2 678 013	3 971 227	13 731 268	6 079 526	6 474 277	4 051 160	11 023 396	1 081 154	638 747
8 069 760	8 862 922	32 535 418	13 831 702	23 893 483	13 880 140	30 996 757	2 932 380	1 737 448
3 696 022	4 265 494	17 651 617	7 390 967	13 280 159	7 821 056	18 068 272	1 248 933	579 206
3 929 674	4 164 114	14 021 496	5 711 232	10 188 684	5 682 032	12 354 114	1 718 173	1 162 650
3 122 077	4 404 540	14 593 573	6 809 029	6 898 918	4 428 212	11 597 767	1 046 427	634 338

7-14 地方工业企业

MAIN FINANCIAL INDICATORS OF

项 目	Item	企业单位数（个）Number of Enter-prises (unit)	从业人员年平均人数（人）Annual Average Persons Employed (person)	工业总产值（万元）Gross Industrial Output Value (10 000 yuan)
全市总计	**Total**	**5 250**	**1 041 855**	**34 423 612**
按登记注册类型分组：	**Grouped by Status of Registration**			
一、内资企业	Domestic-funded Enterprises	3 917	699 643	15 717 454
国有企业	State-owned Enterprises	1 057	161 671	2 784 186
集体企业	Collective-owned Enterprise	1 219	184 548	3 839 766
股份合作企业	Cooperative Enterprises	171	23 987	571 166
私营企业	Private Enterprises	753	98 063	2 325 143
股份有限公司	Share-holding Corporations Ltd.	77	47 426	1 542 881
有限责任公司	Limited Liability Corporations	572	171 413	4 444 638
#国有独资	Sole State-funded Corporations	54	60 027	1 460 895
联营经济	Joint Ownership Enterprises	61	12 022	179 458
#国有与国有联营企业	State Joint Ownership Enterprises	12	2 019	36 686
集体与集体联营企业	Collective Joint Ownership Enterprises	14	1 655	27 203
其他内资企业	Other Domestic-funded Enterprises	7	513	30 216
二、港澳台商投资企业	Enterprises with Investment from Hongkong, Macao and Taiwan	385	84 162	2 616 316
三、外商投资企业	Foreign Funded Enterprises	948	258 050	16 089 842
按经济类型分组：	**Grouped by Ownership**			
国有经济	State-owned	1 123	223 717	4 281 767
集体经济	Collective-owned	1 404	210 190	4 438 135
私有经济	Private and Individual	753	98 063	2 325 143
港澳台商投资经济	Hongkong, Macao and Taiwan Funded	385	84 162	2 616 316
外商投资经济	Foreign Funded	948	258 050	16 089 842
其 他	Others	637	167 673	4 672 409
按隶属关系分组：	**Grouped by Administrative Relationship**			
#市管工业	City Industry	2 292	557 971	22 776 516
#工业系统	Industry System	1 271	362 859	13 519 139
县管工业	County Industry	77	21 171	365 605
区管工业	District Industry	597	70 120	1 788 651
街管工业	Neighbour Industry	14	1 607	15 473
乡镇管工业	Town and Country Industry	1 330	250 348	5 313 354
按轻重分组：	**Grouped by Light & Heavy Industry**			
轻工业	Light Industry	2 363	476 544	10 807 997
重工业	Heavy Industry	2 887	565 311	23 615 615
按规模分组：	**Grouped by Size of Enterprises**			
大 型	Large	38	162 944	12 058 201
中 型	Medium-sized	412	321 880	10 307 092
小 型	Small-sized	4 800	557 031	12 058 319

主要财务指标(2003 年)
LOCAL INDUSTRIAL ENTERPRISES,2003

工业增加值(万元) Value Added of Industry (10 000 yuan)	实收资本(万元) Total Capital Hold (10 000 yuan)	资产总计(万元) Total Assets (10 000 yuan)	流动资产年平均余额(万元) Annual Average Balance of Circulating Funds (10 000 yuan)	固定资产原价合计(万元) Original Value of Fixed Assets (10 000 yuan)	固定资产净值年平均余额(万元) Annual Average Balance of Net Value of Fixed Assets (10 000 yuan)	产品销售收入(万元) Sales Revenue (10 000 yuan)	利税总额(万元) Total Pre-tax Profits (10 000 yuan)	#利润总额 Total Profits
8 067 685	**10 930 600**	**37 188 160**	**17 879 916**	**18 529 035**	**11 314 930**	**35 282 042**	**2 698 393**	**1 657 891**
3 892 742	4 973 996	21 819 934	9 577 355	10 104 072	6 375 133	16 386 682	1 326 216	761 702
631 724	1 565 715	7 632 360	3 221 428	3 736 312	2 431 842	3 938 395	197 965	68 898
933 035	436 386	2 157 388	1 185 047	898 715	558 508	3 440 523	300 638	193 789
129 873	56 912	343 387	187 678	132 148	81 565	501 347	60 441	41 633
490 557	280 980	1 240 320	568 877	446 861	268 787	2 228 601	206 649	151 635
374 739	706 618	3 173 797	1 688 803	1 069 673	611 381	1 697 258	159 138	97 864
1 265 038	1 877 800	7 070 196	2 634 231	3 710 724	2 360 406	4 373 728	380 896	194 283
449 364	1 174 365	4 266 646	1 288 388	2 598 024	1 631 658	1 632 163	142 686	51 662
44 494	45 761	190 260	85 236	106 343	60 608	176 866	17 894	11 589
5 718	11 187	36 483	12 775	24 086	18 691	34 004	1 562	-536
4 335	2 979	14 236	8 189	5 690	3 106	27 045	2 120	1 603
23 283	3 825	12 227	6 055	3 296	2 036	29 965	2 596	2 012
682 819	1 149 651	2 865 272	1 418 589	1 565 423	918 482	2 530 574	244 069	171 633
3 492 125	4 806 953	12 502 955	6 883 972	6 859 540	4 021 316	16 364 786	1 128 108	724 557
1 086 806	2 751 267	11 935 489	4 522 591	6 358 422	4 082 191	5 604 562	342 213	120 023
1 067 243	496 277	2 515 011	1 380 914	1 036 553	643 178	3 968 914	363 199	237 025
490 557	280 980	1 240 320	568 877	446 861	268 787	2 228 601	206 649	151 635
682 819	1 149 651	2 865 272	1 418 589	1 565 423	918 482	2 530 574	244 069	171 633
3 492 125	4 806 953	12 502 955	6 883 972	6 859 540	4 021 316	16 364 786	1 128 108	724 557
1 248 136	1 445 473	6 129 115	3 104 974	2 262 237	1 380 977	4 584 604	414 156	253 019
5 087 962	8 420 779	28 558 197	13 736 561	14 509 876	8 784 802	24 095 895	1 628 541	887 254
2 878 453	5 415 565	18 902 446	8 702 477	9 435 869	5 908 212	14 635 396	1 174 099	613 759
87 724	178 255	570 262	225 258	328 178	240 547	408 616	23 148	3 234
430 605	990 099	2 539 735	1 147 408	1 289 882	869 353	2 076 335	168 931	125 233
1 802	3 214	13 399	4 753	6 911	1 268	16 123	941	244
1 154 593	867 397	3 314 988	1 614 083	1 449 773	825 347	4 886 761	540 631	391 754
2 603 208	3 923 143	13 561 825	5 964 109	6 392 357	4 002 134	10 874 543	1 031 604	633 968
5 464 477	7 007 457	23 626 335	11 915 807	12 136 678	7 312 796	24 407 499	1 666 789	1 023 924
2 581 831	3 106 681	11 810 001	5 959 946	6 330 030	3 607 340	13 532 539	869 206	501 090
2 516 604	3 602 666	11 396 255	5 259 330	5 917 379	3 729 908	10 459 796	847 895	556 991
2 969 250	4 221 254	13 981 905	6 660 640	6 281 627	3 977 682	11 289 708	981 292	599 811

7－15　分行业工业企业

MAIN FINANCIAL INDICATORS OF INDUSTRIAL

行　业	Sector	企　业单位数（个）Number of Enter－prises (unit)	从业人员年平均人数（人）Annual Average Persons Employed (person)	工业总产　值（万元）Gross Industrial Output Value (10 000 yuan)
总　计	**Total**	**5 341**	**1 152 757**	**40 496 103**
#煤炭开采和洗选业	Coal Mining and Dressing	2	75	20 438
石油和天然气开采业	Petroleum and Natural Gas Extraction	4	54 547	2 294 966
有色金属矿采选业	Nonferrous Metals Mining and Dressing	1	2 990	197 463
非金属矿采选业	Nonmetal Minerals Mining and Dressing	19	13 013	63 193
农副食品加工业	Agricultural Products and Byproducts Processing	186	26 621	1 079 249
食品制造业	Food Manufacturing	133	21 889	589 969
饮料制造业	Beverage Manufacturing	65	14 519	500 768
烟草制品业	Tobacco Products	1	1 157	86 672
纺织业	Textile Industry	327	72 714	760 930
纺织服装鞋帽制造业	Textile Garments,Shoes,Caps Manufacturing	286	81 944	780 667
皮革毛皮羽毛(绒)及其制品业	Leather, Furs, Down and Related Products	81	18 381	300 433
木材加工及木、竹、藤、棕、草制品业	Timber Processing,Bamboo, Cane, Palm Fiber and Straw Products	66	7 401	141 433
家具制造业	Furniture Manufacturing	68	17 082	370 531
造纸及纸制品业	Papermaking and Paper Products	169	19 225	378 059
印刷业和记录媒介的复制	Printing and Record Medium Reproduction	97	8 820	199 865
文教体育用品制造业	Cultural, Educational and Sports Goods	69	14 958	276 986
石油加工炼焦及核燃料加工业	Petroleum Processing, Coking and Nuclear Fuel Processing	34	10 577	2 015 948
化学原料及化学制品制造业	Raw Chemical Materials and Chemical Products	502	83 834	3 140 063
医药制造业	Medical and Pharmaceutical Products	101	39 010	1 070 625
化学纤维制造业	Chemical Fiber	18	3 873	92 700
橡胶制品业	Rubber Products	111	23 798	508 881
塑料制品业	Plastic Products	210	31 817	720 303
非金属矿物制品业	Nonmetal Mineral Products	210	27 389	643 390
黑色金属冶炼及压延加工业	Smelting and Pressing of Ferrous Metals	139	75 329	4 301 360
有色金属冶炼及压延加工业	Smelting and Pressing of Nonferrous Metals	87	11 870	540 326
金属制品业	Metal Products	440	60 050	1 615 874
通用设备制造业	General Purpose Equipment Manufacturing	390	58 793	1 301 373
专用设备制造业	Special Purpose Equipment Manufacturing	244	35 035	685 772
交通运输设备制造业	Transport Equipment Manufacturing	377	87 112	3 146 022
电气机械及器材制造业	Electric Equipment and Machinery	305	47 253	1 959 410
通信设备计算机及其他电子设备制造业	Telecommunications Equipment,Computer and Other Electronic Equipment Manufacturing	262	98 641	8 861 705
仪器仪表及文化办公用机械制造业	Instruments, Meters, Cultural and Office Machinery	133	22 932	399 486
工艺品及其他制造业	Craftwork and Other Manufacturing	128	26 120	286 072
废弃资源和废旧材料回收加工业	Waste Resources and Materials Recovering and Processing	4	456	18 109
电力热力的生产和供应业	Production and Supply of Electric & Heat Energy	45	22 320	996 240
燃气生产和供应业	Production and Supply of Gas	11	7 162	80 146
水的生产和供应业	Production and Supply of Water	16	4 050	70 676

主要财务指标（2003 年）

ENTERPRISES BY INDUSTRIAL SECTOR,2003

工业增加值（万元）Value Added of Industry (10 000 yuan)	实收资本（万元）Total Capital Hold (10 000 yuan)	资产总计（万元）Total Assets (10 000 yuan)	流动资产年平均余额（万元）Annual Average Balance of Circulating Funds (10 000 yuan)	固定资产原价合计（万元）Original Value of Fixed Assets (10 000 yuan)	固定资产净值年平均余额（万元）Annuale Average Balance of Net Value of Fixed Assets (10 000 yuan)	产品销售收入（万元）Sales Revenue (10 000 yuan)	利税总额（万元）Total Pre-tax Profits (10 000 yuan)	#利润总额 Total Profits
10 747 773	**12 834 149**	**46 266 686**	**19 911 227**	**30 367 761**	**17 931 300**	**42 020 153**	**4 013 533**	**2 376 194**
2 835	5 202	67 467	56 242	7 790	9 105	24 923	45	-1 957
1 576 400	734 857	3 597 094	710 606	6 013 433	2 543 183	2 350 560	903 859	630 541
29 637	28 000	112 944	48 371	50 028	29 067	218 039	7 475	6 177
33 817	51 278	256 908	117 014	143 929	94 613	59 550	9 057	304
176 179	203 242	665 932	352 205	353 937	207 958	1 180 755	60 950	41 987
166 476	195 123	610 033	300 800	431 767	241 845	482 063	46 251	22 803
157 893	239 237	657 790	274 222	357 143	221 496	475 336	98 255	44 702
57 883	29 958	112 469	77 152	59 606	38 312	84 269	42 582	367
162 334	466 452	2 013 347	717 326	968 037	611 839	791 033	44 113	26 301
187 659	121 891	461 072	256 541	194 019	125 899	698 565	57 862	35 097
41 090	47 174	210 058	91 884	99 301	56 851	279 856	17 046	12 742
29 418	60 979	170 131	128 197	82 288	49 480	139 909	9 907	7 084
93 990	142 387	426 720	170 105	146 878	103 600	378 762	38 089	30 364
66 793	131 395	637 809	202 512	419 413	236 858	364 442	26 104	14 031
73 859	97 911	635 061	318 459	143 426	87 570	136 722	21 240	15 312
83 381	98 761	217 041	112 811	141 692	70 634	241 932	18 045	14 296
325 679	203 343	849 958	353 138	893 107	501 123	1 919 890	92 490	-22 753
823 384	1 122 306	3 779 737	1 305 269	3 030 435	2 086 890	3 094 368	324 218	188 807
434 606	633 252	2 351 784	1 072 422	745 444	466 976	1 499 898	210 288	118 076
33 567	16 258	93 475	26 621	64 612	51 757	84 213	5 518	1 695
116 593	149 780	537 297	260 584	264 353	153 754	481 561	44 037	24 640
229 363	250 198	880 595	370 213	491 715	335 527	695 837	81 690	55 370
154 929	358 830	1 109 488	494 376	590 474	402 914	600 882	42 920	18 483
967 145	1 215 146	4 556 940	2 057 340	2 298 184	1 485 109	4 965 393	340 778	223 443
100 420	91 827	398 133	203 021	162 590	119 813	534 785	31 491	23 761
375 604	299 619	1 449 783	784 694	519 728	317 845	1 670 685	110 319	73 151
430 320	540 582	1 642 203	794 898	765 223	469 763	1 322 130	135 437	87 924
198 120	269 012	983 895	579 487	430 082	251 338	670 441	68 332	42 198
730 845	1 348 121	3 330 389	1 695 785	1 649 848	933 858	3 067 604	377 715	214 176
352 642	681 129	2 187 072	1 066 198	1 024 611	650 702	1 933 933	159 701	100 222
1 717 540	1 640 473	5 920 120	3 665 145	2 998 258	1 609 874	8 752 701	304 277	210 979
89 479	180 754	625 303	325 936	244 020	168 862	454 178	21 686	10 582
68 764	51 686	198 260	115 916	78 927	51 612	231 794	25 614	20 738
6 110	7 689	24 813	23 792	2 201	1 558	20 345	187	145
594 116	727 471	3 551 114	601 605	3 795 930	2 703 792	1 769 135	205 922	71 612
31 851	143 683	373 727	104 487	320 043	170 501	251 229	24 533	12 980
27 187	249 239	570 860	76 483	385 431	269 997	92 565	5 547	-182

7-16 分行业国有大中型工业

MAIN FINANCIAL INDICATORS OF LARGE AND MEDIUM-SIZED

行 业	Sector	企业单位数（个）Number of Enter-prises (unit)	从业人员年平均人数（人）Annual Average Persons Employed (persons)	工业总产值（万元）Gross Industrial Output Value (10 000 yuan)
总 计	**Total**	**96**	**207 668**	**5 302 751**
#石油和天然气开采业	Petroleum and Natural Gas Extraction	2	40 691	311 845
非金属矿采选业	Nonmetal Minerals Mining and Dressing	2	11 339	43 137
农副食品加工业	Farm and Sideline Foods Processing	4	2 558	54 355
食品制造业	Food Manufacturing	1	581	8 643
饮料制造业	Beverage Manufacturing	3	1 841	60 645
烟草制品业	Tobacco Products	1	1 157	86 672
纺织业	Textile Industry	4	12 591	66 323
纺织服装鞋帽制造业	Textile Garments,Shoes and Cap Products	1	582	3 929
造纸及纸制品业	Papermaking and Paper Products	1	514	9 074
印刷业和记录媒介的复制	Printing and Record Medium Reproduction	2	1 038	8 954
化学原料及化学制品制造业	Raw Chemical Materials and Chemical Products	10	27 880	1 284 230
医药制造业	Medical and Pharmaceutical Products	5	7 144	245 590
橡胶制品业	Rubber Products	1	615	6 414
塑料制品业	Plastic Products	2	1 684	24 703
非金属矿物制品业	Nonmetal Mineral Products	2	2 329	26 012
黑色金属冶炼及压延加工业	Smelting and Pressing of Ferrous Metals	7	40 784	2 017 283
有色金属冶炼及压延加工业	Smelting and Pressing of Nonferrous Metals	1	460	22 510
金属制品业	Metal Products	5	3 149	59 664
通用设备制造业	Ordinary Machinery Manufacturing	5	4 051	91 013
专用设备制造业	Equipment Manufacturing for Special Purpose	4	2 873	28 030
交通运输设备制造业	Transport Equipment Manufacturing	9	13 029	179 682
电气机械及器材制造业	Electric Equipment and Machinery	1	1 695	11 066
通信设备计算机及其他电子设备制造业	Computer ,Telecommunications and else Electronic Equipment	5	3 220	88 244
仪器仪表及文化办公用机械制造业	Instruments, Meters, Cultural and Office Machinery	1	722	8 671
电力热力的生产和供应业	Production and Supply of Electric & Hot Power	11	16 833	428 882
燃气生产和供应业	Production and Supply of Gas	4	6 340	70 666
水的生产和供应业	Production and Supply of Water	2	1 968	56 514

企业主要财务指标(2003 年)

STATE - OWNED ENTERPRISES BY INDUSTRIAL SECTOR,2003

工业增加值(万元) Value Added of Industry (10 000 yuan)	实收资本(万元) Total Capital Hold (10 000 yuan)	资产总计(万元) Total Assets (10 000 yuan)	流动资产年平均余额(万元) Annual Average Balance of Circulating Funds (10 000 yuan)	固定资产原价合计(万元) Original Value of Fixed Assets (10 000 yuan)	固定资产净值年平均余额(万元) Annual Average Balance of Net Value of Fixed Assets (10 000 yuan)	产品销售收入(万元) Sales Revenue (10 000 yuan)	利税总额(万元) Total Pre - tax Profits (10 000 yuan)	#利润总额 Total Profits
1 523 601	**3 160 555**	**11 782 860**	**3 959 905**	**8 654 397**	**5 716 998**	**7 641 359**	**559 674**	**190 301**
127 764	531 355	995 541	436 933	751 087	431 854	546 526	1 208	- 31 190
27 870	39 506	219 060	110 396	109 566	68 898	43 766	6 782	- 589
6 239	17 642	55 358	25 137	39 565	25 694	72 007	143	83
2 342	4 322	9 722	4 160	4 218	2 388	8 394	448	127
16 689	19 869	70 576	26 299	44 310	31 101	58 528	7 916	- 115
57 883	29 958	112 469	77 152	59 606	38 312	84 269	42 582	367
21 563	51 272	140 998	52 008	116 343	70 046	84 130	- 1 415	- 3 022
315	1 832	6 074	2 276	3 032	1 660	6 239	217	- 2
786	3 921	9 036	5 066	5 958	2 340	9 830	455	15
4 963	3 242	16 098	5 811	14 969	9 660	8 955	1 276	465
314 523	454 587	1 982 918	489 557	2 124 836	1 521 799	1 303 270	117 887	45 678
82 809	95 375	844 815	323 758	121 831	76 140	388 512	51 343	37 499
3 525	1 100	12 002	6 317	3 746	2 095	6 076	431	
3 047	30 657	91 726	18 234	49 577	38 029	25 730	- 1 072	- 1 540
7 253	6 209	56 938	20 158	33 800	23 736	25 463	3 392	1 152
411 067	976 535	3 306 624	1 378 310	1 940 031	1 236 148	3 111 908	228 351	136 748
1 163	2 500	9 540	1 923	6 808	6 407	21 422	315	96
10 695	36 547	142 146	65 053	61 983	45 448	64 626	2 346	866
19 988	15 521	212 079	71 535	59 221	35 259	88 830	3 961	66
5 789	20 928	55 076	26 992	41 440	23 435	32 880	1 091	9
52 192	87 516	358 779	165 253	240 948	131 308	180 038	10 483	3 624
4 944	8 126	26 621	13 679	17 102	6 988	11 317	1 249	451
23 563	91 133	205 272	86 906	88 031	45 042	82 972	10 714	8 357
1 083	6 230	26 328	14 941	11 433	7 308	10 999	641	419
263 600	374 945	2 127 964	421 176	2 149 369	1 480 974	1 163 919	60 701	- 4 033
28 983	104 170	276 390	75 211	242 208	137 925	145 713	10 835	1 088
22 968	145 561	412 716	35 667	313 385	217 007	55 046	- 2 604	- 6 319

7-17 工业企业主要经济效益指标
MAIN INDICATORS ON ECONOMIC BENEFIT OF INDUSTRIAL ENTERPRISES
(1978-2003)

年 份 Year	产销率 (%) Sales Ratio (%)	资 金 利税率 (%) Ratio of Pre-tax Profits to Total Assets (%)	总资产 贡献率 (%) Ratio of Total Assets to Industrial Output Value (%)	成本费用 利润率 (%) Ratio of Profits to Industrial Cost (%)	万元产值 耗能源 (吨标准煤) Energy Consumption per 10 000 yuan Output Value (tons of SCE)	工 业 增加值率 (%) Ratio of Value Added to Gross Industrial Output Value (%)	全员劳动 生产率 (元/人) Overall Labor Productivity (yuan/person)
全 市 合 计 **Total**							
1978	93.74	37.7			4.83		
1979	97.81	38.4			4.27		
1980	94.82	39.1			4.18		
1981	97.74	38.2			3.90		
1982	97.39	36.8			3.80		
1983	97.70	35.7			3.71		
1984	98.31	31.6			3.56		
1985	98.17	35.2			3.47		
1986	99.11	30.6			3.38		
1987	98.44	28.3			3.40		
1988	98.13	25.3			3.18		
1989	92.14	18.7			3.12		
1990	88.76	10.7			2.03		
1991	93.13	9.6			1.85	22.5	8 574
1992	92.69	9.2			1.70	22.7	9 864
1993	97.62	9.6	9.11	3.50	1.60	20.8	11 814
1994	85.15	9.3			1.86	20.9	15 214
1995	86.35	8.8	9.60	4.47	1.70	21.9	20 084
1996	91.61	7.2	8.25	4.99	1.29	21.3	20 993
1997	96.43	6.0	7.10	3.74	0.88	20.4	23 073
1998	97.87	5.56	6.61	2.92	0.91	20.1	29 055
1999	98.59	5.98	6.47	3.60	0.77	20.7	35 730
2000	98.39	8.99	8.86	6.48	0.68	24.2	52 425
2001	96.71	9.52	9.32	6.59	0.66	24.8	59 605
2002	99.08	9.02	8.66	5.77	0.64	25.4	69 728
2003	98.88	10.61	9.89	6.03	0.56	26.5	93 235
#国有经济 **State-owned**							
1978							
1979	98.84	39.09					
1980	95.26	40.26					
1981	98.09	38.65					
1982							
1983	97.87	35.71					
1984	98.74	32.36					
1985	98.18	35.48					
1986	99.97	30.63					
1987	100.09	28.36					
1988	100.26	25.37					
1989	94.44	18.40					
1990	92.14	10.65					
1991	97.56	7.33				22.9	10 126
1992	98.23	7.87				23.2	11 371
1993	100.81	6.69	6.95	0.66		20.3	10 813
1994	97.85	6.26				23.0	15 910
1995	107.46	5.6	6.51	0.54		27.3	20 536
1996	98.21	3.3	5.00	0.34		27.3	18 365
1997	95.84	3.2	4.66			25.0	19 587
1998	99.21	2.15	4.08			25.8	21 340
1999	100.98	1.86	3.17			28.4	26 743
2000	99.96	1.26	1.26			28.0	32 545
2001	98.97	1.30	2.39			23.2	29 470
2002	100.54	1.74	2.43			22.5	32 058
2003	100.16	4.12	4.15	1.59		28.9	56 402

7－18　工业企业主要经济效益指标(2003年)

MAIN INDICATORS ON ECONOMIC BENEFIT OF INDUSTRIAL ENTERPRISES，2003

项　目	Item	单　位	Unit	全　市 Total	#地　方 Local
全　市	**Total**				
总资产贡献率	Ratio of Total Assets to Industrial Output Value	%		9.89	8.36
增加值率	Ratio of Value Added to Gross Industrial Output Value	%		26.5	23.44
全员劳动生产率	Overall Labor Productivity	元/人	yuan/person	93 235	77 436
流动资产周转次数	Number of Times of Turnover of Circulating Funds	次	times	2.11	1.97
亏损企业个数	Number of Loss－suffering Enterprises	个	unit	1 385	1 352
亏损企业亏损额	Total Loss of Loss－suffering Enterprises	亿元	100 million yuan	52.40	40.73
国有及国有控股经济	**State－owned and State－holding**				
总资产贡献率	Ratio of Total Assets to Industrial Output Value	%		9.01	5.60
增加值率	Ratio of Value Added to Gross Industrial Output Value	%		32.28	23.96
全员劳动生产率	Overall Labor Productivity	元/人	yuan/person	104 007	60 980
流动资产周转次数	Number of Times of Turnover of Circulating Funds	次	times	1.74	1.33
亏损企业个数	Number of Loss－suffering Enterprises	个	unit	792	762
亏损企业亏损额	Total Loss of Loss－suffering Enterprises	亿元	100 million yuan	28.26	16.60
国有经济	**State－owned**				
总资产贡献率	Ratio of Total Assets to Industrial Output Value	%		4.15	3.63
增加值率	Ratio of Value Added to Gross Industrial Output Value	%		28.87	25.38
全员劳动生产率	Overall Labor Productivity	元/人	yuan/person	56 402	48 580
流动资产周转次数	Number of Times of Turnover of Circulating Funds	次	times	1.42	1.24
亏损企业个数	Number of Loss－suffering Enterprises	个	unit	655	633
亏损企业亏损额	Total Loss of Loss－suffering Enterprises	亿元	100 million yuan	15.61	10.88
集体经济	**Collective－owned**				
总资产贡献率	Ratio of Total Assets to Industrial Output Value	%		13.54	13.55
增加值率	Ratio of Value Added to Gross Industrial Output Value	%		24.04	24.05
全员劳动生产率	Overall Labor Productivity	元/人	yuan/person	50 775	50 775
流动资产周转次数	Number of Times of Turnover of Circulating Funds	次	times	2.87	2.87
亏损企业个数	Number of Loss－suffering Enterprises	个	unit	162	161
亏损企业亏损额	Total Loss of Loss－suffering Enterprises	亿元	100 million yuan	1.64	1.64
“三资”经济	**Foreign，Hongkong，Macao and Taiwan Funded**				
总资产贡献率	Ratio of Total Assets to Industrial Output Value	%		10.04	9.89
增加值率	Ratio of Value Added to Gross Industrial Output Value	%		22.40	22.32
全员劳动生产率	Overall Labor Productivity	元/人	yuan/person	123 020	121 999
流动资产周转次数	Number of Times of Turnover of Circulating Funds	次	times	2.27	2.28
亏损企业个数	Number of Loss－suffering Enterprises	个	unit	383	378
亏损企业亏损额	Total Loss of Loss－suffering Enterprises	亿元	100 million yuan	23.68	23.44
股份制经济	**Share－holding**				
总资产贡献率	Ratio of Total Assets to Industrial Output Value	%		17.62	9.48
增加值率	Ratio of Value Added to Gross Industrial Output Value	%		36.56	26.30
全员劳动生产率	Overall Labor Productivity	元/人	yuan/person	172 047	74 957
流动资产周转次数	Number of Times of Turnover of Circulating Funds	次	times	2.26	1.46
亏损企业个数	Number of Loss－suffering Enterprises	个	unit	132	127
亏损企业亏损额	Total Loss of Loss－suffering Enterprises	亿元	100 million yuan	11.30	4.59

7－19　国有及国有控股大中型工业企业主要经济指标及占全市比重
MAIN ECONOMIC INDICATORS OF LARGE & MEDIUM－SIZED STATE－OWNED AND STATE－HOLDING ENTERPRISES AND AS PERCENTAGE OF WHOLE INDUSTRY

单位:亿元　　(100 million yuan)

指　标	Item	全市工业 Total	国有及国有控股大中型 Large & Medium－sized State－owned and State－holding 绝对数 Absolute Number	占全市% As Percentage of Whole Industry (%)
2002				
企业单位数(个)	Number of Enterprises(unit)	5 346	459	8.6
从业人员年平均人数(万人)	Annual Average Employment Personnel (10 000 persons)	120.95	39.49	32.7
工业总产值	Gross Industrial Output Value	3 323.12	973.05	29.3
工业增加值	Value Added of Industry	843.38	298.45	35.4
资产总计	Total Assets	4 383.04	2 310.50	52.7
#流动资产年平均余额	Annual Average Balance of Circulating Funds	1 874.76	790.43	42.2
固定资产净值年平均余额	Annual Average Balance of Net Value of Fixed Assets	1 729.50	1 086.37	62.8
所有者权益	Creditor's Equity	1 836.65	938.47	51.1
#实收资本	Paid－up Capital	1 289.40	618.61	48.0
产品销售收入	Sales Revenue	3 437.46	1 122.99	32.7
#产品销售成本	Cost of Sales	2 846.70	917.96	32.3
产品销售税金及附加	Sales Tax and Extra Charges	31.46	24.42	77.6
利税总额	Total Pre－tax Profits	325.07	128.55	39.6
总资产贡献率(%)	Ratio of Total Assets to Industrial Output Value(%)	8.66	7.07	
全员劳动生产率(元/人)	Overall Labor Productivity(yuan/person)	69 728	75 579	
亏损企业个数(个)	Number of Loss－suffering Enterprises(unit)	1 399	227	16.2
亏损企业亏损额	Total Loss of Loss－suffering Enterprises	60.40	33.05	54.7
2003				
企业单位数(个)	Number of Enterprises(unit)	5 341	187	3.5
从业人员年平均人数(万人)	Annual Average Employment Personnel (10 000 persons)	115.28	30.93	26.8
工业总产值	Gross Industrial Output Value	4 049.61	1 230.79	30.4
工业增加值	Value Added of Industry	1 074.78	411.31	38.3
资产总计	Total Assets	4 626.67	2 053.17	44.4
#流动资产年平均余额	Annual Average Balance of Circulating Funds	1 991.12	690.31	34.7
固定资产净值年平均余额	Annual Average Balance of Net Value of Fixed Assets	1 793.13	1 008.31	56.2
所有者权益	Creditors Equity	1 908.36	872.06	45.7
#实收资本	Paid－up Capital	1 283.41	517.26	40.3
产品销售收入	Sales Revenue	4 202.02	1 485.30	35.3
#产品销售成本	Cost of Sales	3 546.84	1 212.82	34.2
产品销售税金及附加	Sales Tax and Extra Charges	39.29	30.11	76.6
利税总额	Total Pre－tax Profits	401.35	197.03	49.1
总资产贡献率(%)	Ratio of Total Assets to Industrial Output Value(%)	9.89	11.13	
全员劳动生产率(元/人)	Overall Labor Productivity(yuan/person)	93 235	133 002	
亏损企业个数(个)	Number of Loss－suffering Enterprises(unit)	1 385	57	4.1
亏损企业亏损额	Total Loss of Loss－suffering Enterprises	52.40	16.92	32.3

7-20 大中型工业企业主要经济指标及占全市比重
MAIN ECONOMIC INDICATORS OF LARGE & MEDIUM-SIZED INDUSTRIAL ENTERPRISES AND AS PERCENTAGE OF WHOLE INDUSTRY

单位:亿元 (100 million yuan)

指标	Item	大中型 Large & Medium-sized		#国有大中型 State-owned	
		绝对数 Absolute Number	占全市% As Percentage of Whole Industry	绝对数 Absolute Number	占全市% As Percentage of Whole Industry(%)
2002					
企业单位数(个)	Number of Enterprises(unit)	826	15.5	326	6.1
从业人员年平均人数(万人)	Annual Average Employment Personnel (10 000 persons)	56.46	46.7	29.73	24.6
工业总产值	Gross Industrial Output Value	2 185.10	65.8	479.70	14.4
工业增加值	Value Added of Industry	609.46	72.3	106.21	12.6
资产总计	Total Assets	3 323.50	75.8	1 515.05	34.6
#流动资产年平均余额	Annual Average Balance of Circulating Funds	1 319.23	70.4	530.51	28.3
固定资产净值年平均余额	Annual Average Balance of Net Value of Fixed Assets	1 432.18	82.8	637.86	36.9
所有者权益	Creditor's Equity	1 432.99	78.0	553.57	30.1
#实收资本	Paid-up Capital	979.28	76.0	419.32	32.5
产品销售收入	Sales Revenue	2 311.47	67.2	591.63	17.2
#产品销售成本	Cost of Sales	1 904.82	66.9	528.05	18.6
产品销售税金及附加	Sales Tax and Extra Charges	27.85	88.5	6.46	20.5
利税总额	Total Pre-tax Profits	217.61	66.9	23.41	7.2
总资产贡献率(%)	Ratio of Total Assets to Industrial Output Value(%)	7.87		2.75	
全员劳动生产率(元/人)	Overall Labor Productivity(yuan/person)	107 946		35 702	
亏损企业个数(个)	Number of Loss-suffering Enterprises(unit)	366	26.2	187	13.4
亏损企业亏损额	Total Loss of Loss-suffering Enterprises	47.19	78.1	20.63	34.2
2003					
企业单位数(个)	Number of Enterprises(unit)	481	9.0	96	1.8
从业人员年平均人数(万人)	Annual Average Employment Personnel (10 000 persons)	58.84	51.0	20.77	18.0
工业总产值	Gross Industrial Output Value	2 814.80	69.5	530.28	13.1
工业增加值	Value Added of Industry	762.57	71.0	152.36	14.2
资产总计	Total Assets	3 167.31	68.5	1 178.29	25.5
#流动资产年平均余额	Annual Average Balance of Circulating Funds	1 310.22	65.8	395.99	19.9
固定资产净值年平均余额	Annual Average Balance of Net Value of Fixed Assets	1 350.31	75.3	571.70	31.9
所有者权益	Creditor's Equity	1 379.59	72.3	425.61	22.3
#实收资本	Paid-up Capital	842.96	65.7	316.06	24.6
产品销售收入	Sales Revenue	3 042.24	72.4	764.14	18.2
#产品销售成本	Cost of Sales	2 567.46	72.4	677.03	19.1
产品销售税金及附加	Sales Tax and Extra Charges	34.22	87.1	7.61	19.4
利税总额	Total Pre-tax Profits	296.71	73.9	55.97	13.9
总资产贡献率(%)	Ratio of Total Assets to Industrial Output Value(%)	10.72		5.85	
全员劳动生产率(元/人)	Overall Labor Productivity(yuan/person)	129 604		73 367	
亏损企业个数(个)	Number of Loss-suffering Enterprises(unit)	99	7.1	36	2.6
亏损企业亏损额	Total Loss of Loss-suffering Enterprises	27.01	51.5	7.84	15.0

7-21 工业系统分主管部门工业企业主要财务指标(2003年)

MAIN FINANCIAL INDICATORS OF INDUSTRIAL ENTERPRISES BY ADMINISTRATIVE DEPARTMENT,2003

单位:万元 (10 000 yuan)

主管系统 Administrative Department	企业单位数(个) Number of Enterprises (unit)	资产总计 Total Assets	固定资产原价 Original Value of Fixed Assets	固定资产净值年平均余额 Annual Average Balance of Net Value of Fixed Assets	流动资产年平均余额 Annual Average Balance of Circu-lating Funds	产品销售收入 Sales Revenue
冶金集团(控股)有限公司 Tianjin Metallurgical Group(Holding) Corporation	84	1 436 611	526 539	341 517	830 469	1 302 332
渤海化工集团公司 Tianjin Bohai Chemical Industry Group Corporation	209	1 957 961	1 333 788	796 415	763 944	1 167 816
机电工业控股集团公司 Tianjin Machinery & Electric Industry Holding Group Company	262	1 764 349	675 476	401 247	778 044	952 554
中环电子信息集团有限公司 Tianjin Zhonghuan Electronics & Information Group	370	2 634 320	1 333 450	820 634	1 415 997	4 004 975
纺织集团(控股)有限公司 Tianjin Textile Industrial General Corporation	358	1 261 159	757 462	502 839	458 341	383 640
一轻集团(控股)有限公司 Tianjin Yiqing Group(Holding Share) Co.,Ltd	265	992 292	487 997	307 946	468 949	502 984
二轻集团(控股)有限公司 The Second Light Industry Group(Holding) Co.,Ltd	261	918 655	480 110	316 521	424 411	781 655
医药集团有限公司 Tianjin Pharmaceutical Holdings	45	844 507	317 349	194 381	442 617	718 597
建筑材料集团(控股)有限公司 Tianjin Building Materials Group(Holding)Co.,Ltd	47	550 801	355 337	259 006	202 339	152 879
汽车工业(集团)有限公司 Tianjin Automobile Industry Group Co.,Ltd	48	1 836 790	983 542	557 871	1 000 608	1 625 873
飞鸽集团有限公司 Tianjin Flying Pigeon Group Co.,Ltd	87	142 871	50 849	31 140	76 210	41 302
钢管有限责任公司 Tianjin Pipe Corporation Ltd	9	1 219 277	925 125	604 216	302 112	570 085
有色金属集团有限公司 Tianjin Non-ferrous Metals Group Co.,Ltd	41	148 312	44 078	31 486	75 843	131 833
天铁冶金集团有限公司 Tianjin Tian Tie Metallurgical Group Co.,Ltd	10	1 215 041	663 825	418 115	568 703	1 488 091
摩托集团 Tianjin Motors Group Inc	2	239 461	152 839	95 770	102 726	336 420
塑料集团 Tianjin Plastics Group	54	157 260	83 319	57 220	45 375	55 207

7－21 续表 Continued
单位:万元 (10 000 yuan)

主管系统 Administrative Department	销售税金及附加 Sales Tax and Extra Charges	利税总额 Total Pre－tax Profits	利润总额 Total Profits	工业总产值 Gross Indus－trial Output Value	工业总产值比上年增长% Increase Rate of Gross Industrial Output Value Preceding Year	工业增加值 Value Added of Industry
冶金集团(控股)有限公司 Tianjin Metallurgical Group(Holding) Corporation	2 366	77 792	52 600	1 182 029	91.5	146 364
渤海化工集团公司 Tianjin Bohai Chemical Industry Group Corporation	7 725	81 007	21 371	1 164 181	16.2	294 806
机电工业控股集团公司 Tianjin Machinery & Electric Industry Holding Group Company	2 421	45 952	11 436	868 749	30.2	193 478
中环电子信息集团有限公司 Tianjin Zhonghuan Electronics & Information Group	1 532	267 019	191 593	4 019 956	39.4	632 303
纺织集团(控股)有限公司 Tianjin Textile Industrial General Corporation	327	8 592	－380	360 094	19.9	87 685
一轻集团(控股)有限公司 Tianjin Yiqing Group(Holding Share) Co.,Ltd	6 580	61 317	27 165	487 996	13.6	142 977
二轻集团(控股)有限公司 The Second Light Industry Group(Holding) Co.,Ltd	223	33 989	8 899	800 376	53.2	89 938
医药集团有限公司 Tianjin Pharmaceutical Holdings	2 108	82 124	37 995	400 236	23.1	160 351
建筑材料集团(控股)有限公司 Tianjin Building Materials Group(Holding)Co.,Ltd	879	7 638	－2 172	162 263	12.3	32 949
汽车工业(集团)有限公司 Tianjin Automobile Industry Group Co.,Ltd	39 259	202 835	105 359	1 656 752	91.0	387 809
飞鸽集团有限公司 Tianjin Flying Pigeon Group Co.,Ltd	41	119	－869	45 057	20.2	7 909
钢管有限责任公司 Tianjin Pipe Corporation Ltd	3 035	61 514	28 149	550 667	41.1	153 192
有色金属集团有限公司 Tianjin Non－ferrous Metals Group Co.,Ltd	59	－6 570	－8 334	132 166	36.9	4 924
天铁冶金集团有限公司 Tianjin Tian Tie Metallurgical Group Co.,Ltd	3 192	100 655	58 778	1 010 006	38.0	221 927
摩托集团 Tianjin Motors Group Inc	19 428	31 589	2 052	318 322	4.4	50 918
塑料集团 Tianjin Plastics Group	133	－564	－2 140	56 207	9.1	8 807

7-22 高新技术产业主要经济指标
MAIN INDICATORS OF HIGH & NEW TECHNOLOGY INDUSTRY

单位:亿元 (100 million yuan)

项 目 Item	产 值 Output Value		销售收入 Sales Revenue		利税总额 Total Pre - tax Profits	
	2002	2003	2002	2003	2002	2003
全 市 总 计 **Total**	**1 097.40**	**1 235.87**	**1 080.16**	**1 243.14**	**86.77**	**82.24**
一、按规模分 **Grouped by Size of Enterprises**						
大型企业 Large - sized	892.46	675.94	887.99	709.01	68.49	34.05
中型企业 Medium - sized	79.95	389.58	76.52	373.72	3.92	36.21
小型企业 Small - sized	124.99	170.35	115.65	160.41	14.36	11.98
二、按经济类型分 **Grouped by Ownership**						
国有经济 State - owned	45.04	45.95	48.79	57.46	6.60	7.91
集体经济 Collective - owned	42.42	56.17	41.03	48.52	4.75	4.58
私营经济 Private	8.62	11.09	8.63	12.25	1.32	1.58
外商投资经济 Foreign Funded	912.09	1 014.68	874.94	995.03	60.84	59.51
港澳台商投资经济 Hongkong, Macao and Taiwan Funded	26.22	31.50	24.43	29.45	2.38	2.92
其他经济 Others	63.01	76.48	82.34	100.43	10.88	5.74
三、按技术领域分 **Grouped by Fields**						
1.电子信息 Electronics and Information	888.56	954.06	848.01	931.84	54.63	40.49
2.航空航天 Aviation and Spaceflight	0.39	0.49	0.34	0.42	0.18	0.22
3.光机电一体化 Photoeletric Mechanical Electron Incorporated	80.51	106.01	79.81	106.90	8.46	12.63
4.生物技术和医药 Biology Technology and Pharmaceutical	88.98	110.45	115.43	147.45	19.23	23.33
5.新材料 New Materials	18.06	44.55	17.47	37.96	2.86	4.71
6.新能源和节能材料 New Energy and Energy Saving Materials	18.49	19.15	17.09	17.52	1.12	0.89
7.环境保护 Environmental Protection	2.41	1.16	2.01	1.05	0.29	-0.03
8.地球、空间及海洋工程 Earth, Space and Ocean Engineering						
9.核应用技术 Nucleus Utilization Technology						

7-23 电子信息产品制造业主要经济指标(2003年)
MAIN INDICATORS OF ELECTRONIC AND INFORMATION PRODUCTS MANUFACTURING,2003

单位:亿元 (100 million yuan)

项目 Item	产值 Output Value	销售收入 Sales Revenue	利税总额 Total Pre-tax Profits
全市总计 Total	**1 010.89**	**988.52**	**43.05**
一、按规模分 Grouped by Size of Enterprises			
大型企业 Large-sized	520.16	507.73	1.95
中型企业 Medium-sized	424.26	416.68	35.88
小型企业 Small-sized	66.47	64.11	5.22
二、按经济类型分 Grouped by Ownership			
国有经济 State-owned	11.44	10.71	0.19
集体经济 Collective-owned	2.78	28.50	0.13
私营经济 Private and Individual			
外商及港澳台商投资经济 Foreign,Hongkong,Macao and Taiwan Funded	967.01	948.40	39.05
其他经济 Others	29.66	0.91	3.68
三、按行业分 Grouped by Sector			
1.雷达业 Radar	0.23	0.02	
2.通信设备业 Telecommunications Equipment	518.84	503.33	7.55
3.广播电视设备业 Equipment of Radio and Television	1.88	1.34	0.22
4.电子计算机业 Electronic Computer	96.68	105.65	6.17
5.家电业 Home Appliances	163.43	156.15	13.18
6.电子测量仪器业 Instruments of Electronic Survey	3.62	3.49	0.69
7.电子工业专用设备业 Industrial Electronic Equipment for Special Use	2.60	2.50	0.13
8.电子元件业 Electronic Element	173.93	133.45	3.50
9.电子器件业 Electronic Implements	23.55	58.42	9.14
10.电子信息机电产品业 Machinery & Electric Products	24.71	23.34	2.05
11.电子信息专用材料业 Electronic and Information Materials for Special Use	1.42	0.83	0.42

7-24 工业行业主要能
THE FINAL CONSUMPTION OF MAIN

行 业	Sector	煤 炭（万吨）Coal (10 000 tons)	焦 炭（万吨）Coke (10 000 tons)	原 油（万吨）Crude Oil (10 000 tons)	汽 油（万吨）Gasoline (10 000 tons)
总 计	**Total**	**767.99**	**140.57**	**33.22**	**14.06**
煤炭开采和洗选业	Coal Mining and Dressing				
石油和天然气开采业	Petroleum and Natural Gas Extraction	17.08			1.94
有色金属矿采选业	Nonferrous Metals Mining and Dressing			20.98	
非金属矿采选业	Nonmetal Minerals Mining and Dressing	4.39			0.17
农副食品加工业	Agricultural Products and Byproducts Processing	15.06			0.42
食品制造业	Food Manufacturing	13.57			0.32
饮料制造业	Beverage Manufacturing	38.98			0.20
烟草制品业	Tobacco Products	3.13			0.05
纺织业	Textile Industry	41.74			0.39
纺织服装鞋帽制造业	Textile Garments,Shoes,Caps Manufacturing	8.26			0.66
皮革毛皮羽毛(绒)及其制品业	Leather, Furs, Down and Related Products	3.20			0.14
木材加工及木、竹、藤、棕、草制品业	Timber Processing,Bamboo, Cane, Palm Fiber and Straw Products	4.82			0.08
家具制造业	Furniture Manufacturing	3.09	0.14		0.13
造纸及纸制品业	Papermaking and Paper Products	27.37	0.34		0.44
印刷业和记录媒介的复制	Printing and Record Medium Reproduction	1.93			0.10
文教体育用品制造业	Cultural, Educational and Sports Goods	1.37			0.13
石油加工炼焦及核燃料加工业	Petroleum Processing, Coking and Nuclear Fuel Processing	1.71	0.01		0.08
化学原料及化学制品制造业	Raw Chemical Materials and Chemical Products	140.88	2.51		1.31
医药制造业	Medical and Pharmaceutical Products	23.31	0.05	0.05	0.21
化学纤维制造业	Chemical Fiber	4.7	0.05	0.70	0.04
橡胶制品业	Rubber Products	23.62		0.01	0.55
塑料制品业	Plastic Products	4.89			0.28
非金属矿物制品业	Nonmetal Mineral Products	94.77	0.30		0.34
黑色金属冶炼及压延加工业	Smelting and Pressing of Ferrous Metals	99.71	130.15	0.07	0.60
有色金属冶炼及压延加工业	Smelting and Pressing of Nonferrous Metals	7.13	0.41		0.21
金属制品业	Metal Products	24.19	1.58	10.47	0.81
通用设备制造业	General Purpose Equipment Manufacturing	79.63	3.83	0.17	0.72
专用设备制造业	Special Purpose Equipment Manufacturing	6.66	0.59	0.65	0.28
交通运输设备制造业	Transport Equipment Manufacturing	26.58	0.25	0.06	1.11
电气机械及器材制造业	Electric Equipment and Machinery	12.27	0.36	0.02	
通信设备计算机及其他电子设备制造业	Telecommunications Equipment,Computer and Other Electronic Equipment Manufacturing	8.35			0.26
仪器仪表及文化办公用机械制造业	Instruments, Meters, Cultural and Office Machinery	4.16		0.04	1.62
工艺品及其他制造业	Craftwork and Other Manufacturing	5.91			
废弃资源和废旧材料回收加工业	Waste Resources and Materials Recovering and Processing	0.01			
电力热力的生产和供应业	Production and Supply of Electric & Heat Energy	10.73			0.35
燃气生产和供应业	Production and Supply of Gas	4.28			0.08
水的生产和供应业	Production and Supply of Water	0.51			0.04

源终端消费量(2003 年)

ENERGY BY INDUSTRIAL SECTOR,2003

柴 油 (万吨) Diesel Oil (10 000 tons)	燃料油 (万吨) Fuel Oil (10 000 tons)	天然气 (亿立方米) Natural Gas (100 million cu.m)	热 力 (万百万千焦) Heat (10 000 million kilo-joule)	电 力 (亿千瓦时) Electricity (100 million kwh)	其他石油制品 (万吨) Other Petroleum Product (10 000 tons)
29.30	**52.57**	**2.48**	**4 272.18**	**211.01**	**142.06**
14.48	2.47	0.93		11.31	
0.38			194.95	1.43	
0.52			18.13	1.83	
0.35		0.01	95.52	2.88	
0.39			17.35	1.88	
0.02			2.75	0.16	
0.22		0.02	109.20	6.67	
0.22			1.09	1.06	
0.07			0.11	0.51	
0.27		0.03		0.57	
0.11				0.65	
0.37			18.31	34.11	
0.09			4.84	0.39	
0.04			4.41	0.49	
0.36	7.12		325.33	4.29	79.52
1.56	21.39	0.19	3 124.21	47.21	60.08
0.23		0.03	72.26	2.71	0.02
			0.03	0.63	
0.11	0.95		44.58	2.73	0.06
0.27		0.04	15.87	12.03	
1.94	8.24	0.03	1.32	7.37	
2.54	12.21	0.58	83.43	27.51	
0.13			1.01	1.45	
0.76	0.19		0.94	4.54	0.02
0.34		0.01	17.83	3.78	0.23
0.18			6.81	1.47	0.18
0.93		0.01	11.40	5.34	0.84
0.27			5.67		1.09
0.86		0.22	34.16	9.30	
1.16		0.01	3.89	1.02	
0.05			3.99	0.43	
0.05		0.06	52.01	13.15	0.02
0.03		0.31		0.62	
			0.78	1.49	

主要统计指标解释

工业总产值 是以货币表现的工业企业在报告期内生产的工业产品总量。它是反映一定时间内工业生产总规模和总水平的重要指标。工业总产值采用“工厂法”计算。1995 年全国第三次工业普查对工业总产值的范围和计算方法作出新规定。工业总产值包括本年生产成品价值，对外加工费收入，自制半成品、在产品期末期初差额价值。新规定与原规定的变化：一是对工业产值中凡自备原材料，不论其加工繁简程度如何，一律按全价计算产值。凡来料加工，一律按加工费计算总产值；二是自制半成品、在产品期末期初差额价值的计算改变了生产周期六个月以上的原则，而以当期会计是否将其计入成本核算作为是否计入产值的依据；三是现价产值按不含增值税的价格计算。1995 年以后各年工业总产值均是按新规定计算的。

限额以上工业企业 包括全部国有（含国有联营、国有独资公司）和年销售收入在 500 万元及以上的非国有工业企业。

工业行业类别 根据新颁布的行业分类标准《国民经济行业分类》(GB/T 4754－2002) “工业”包括“采矿业”、“制造业”和“电力、燃气及水的生产和供应业”三个门类。

轻工业 一般指提供生活消费品和制作手工工具的工业。

重工业 一般指生产生产资料为国民经济各部门提供物质技术基础的工业。

大、中、小型企业 根据 2003 年国家统计局制定的《统计上大中小型企业划分办法(暂行)》，以从业人员数、销售额和资产总额三项指标为依据，将工业企业划分为大、中、小型，而不再按照企业产品的年生产能力和生产用固定资产原值划分。划分标准如下：

指标名称	单 位	大 型	中 型	小 型
从业人员数	人	2 000 及以上	300－2 000 以下	300 以下
销售额	万元	30 000 及以上	3 000－30 000 以下	3 000 以下
资产总额	万元	40 000 及以上	4 000－40 000 以下	4 000 以下

实收资本(股本) 指投资人作为资本投入到企业中的各种资产的价值。企业实收资本按照投资主体一般分为六种：

①**国家资本：** 是指有权代表国家投资的政府部门或机构以国有资产投入企业形成的资本。不论企业的资本是哪个政府部门或机构投入的，只要是以国家资本形式投资的，均作为国家资本计算。

②**集体资本：** 是指由本企业劳动群众集体所有和集体企业联合经济组织范围内的劳动群众集体所有的资产投入形成的资本金，以及企业在实行新制度以前国家减免税款形成的资本金。

③**法人资本：** 是指其他法人单位投入本企业的资本。

④**个人资本：** 是指社会个人或者本企业内部职工以个人合法财产投入企业形成的资本。

⑤**港澳台资本：** 是指我国香港、澳门和台湾地区的投资者投入企业的资本。

⑥**外商资本：** 是指外国投资者投入企业的资本。

产品销售收入 指企业销售产品的销售收入和提供劳务等主要经营业务取得的收入总额。现行的会计制度要求企业采用“权责发生制”原则计算产品销售收入，即以销售实现为依据。

产品销售成本 指企业销售产品和提供劳务等主要经营业务的实际成本。该指标不包括期间费用，即不包括管理费用、销售费用和财务费用。企业应当按照权责发生制原则确认当期费用，即对应属于本期的各项费用，不论其是否实际支付，均应确认为本期的费用；对于不属于本期的费用，即使款项已经在本期付出，也不应确认为本期费用。

产品销售费用 指企业在销售产品、自制半成品和提供劳务等主要经营业务过程中所发生的各项费用以及专设销售机构的各项费用。包括运输费、装卸费、包装费、保险费、展览费、广告费、租赁费（不包括融资租赁费），以及为销售本企业产品而专设的销售机构的职工工资、福利费、业务费、折旧费等其他费用。

产品销售税金及附加 指企业销售产品和提供劳务等主要经营业务应负担的城市维护建设税、消费税、资源税和教育费附加。

产品销售利润 指企业销售产品和提供劳务等主要经营业务收入扣除其成本、费用、税金后的利润。该指标计算公式为：

产品销售利润＝产品销售收入－产品销售成本－产品销售费用－产品销售税金

营业利润 指企业生产经营活动所取得的利润，包括主营业务利润和其他业务利润。其计算公式为：

营业利润 = 产品销售利润 + 其他业务利润 - 管理费用 - 财务费用

利润总额 指企业在一定时期的最终经营成果。企业在生产经营过程中，通过销售过程将产品卖给购买方，实现收入，收入扣除当初的投入成本以及其他一系列费用，再加减非经营性质的收支及投资收益，即为企业的利润总额或亏损总额。亏损以"－"号表示，计算公式为：

利润总额 = 营业利润 + 投资收益 + 补贴收入 + 营业外收入 - 营业外支出 + 以前年度损益调整

利税总额 指利润总额、产品销售税金及附加和本期应交增值税之和。

能源消费量 指能源使用单位在报告期内实际消费的一次能源或二次能源的数量。

能源折标准煤 各种能源由于原始计量单位不同，热值也不一样，因此必须折算成同一标准计量单位，才能汇总、对比和分析。本资料采用的标准计量单位是"吨标准煤"。

Explanatory Notes on Main Statistical Indicators

Gross Industrial Output Value is the total volume of industrial products sold or available for sale in value terms which reflect the total achievements and overall scale of industrial production during a given period. The gross industrial output value is calculated with "factory method" . Data of the gross industrial output value were adjusted in accordance with the 1995 industrial census. It includes the value of the finished products, the value of industrial services rendered to other units, and the changes in the value of the semi - finished products and products in process between the beginning and closing of the period. The changes between the new regulation and the old regulation the first, calculating output value as whole price for ready source materials by themselves, calculating output value as cost for processed with imported materials; the second, the changes producing circulation above six months for the value of the semi - finished products and products in process between the beginning and closing of the period, calculating output value in accordance with financial accounting in current period; the third, output value of current price excluded value added tax. It is not comparable with the data before 1995.

Industrial Enterprises above Designated Size refer to all state - owned(including sole state - funded enterprises, state - owned joint ownership enterprises), and other non - state - owned industrial enterprises with annual sales of over 5 million yuan.

Industrial Sector Classification State draws up the new industrial classification of China Industrial Classification by Sector of the National Economy (GB/T4754 - 2002) in 2003. Industry is classified into three categories, minerals mining, manufacturing, production & supply of power, gas & water.

Light Industry refers to the industry that produces consumer goods and hand tools.

Heavy Industry refers to the industry which produces capital goods, and provides various sectors of the national economy with necessary material and technical basis.

Large, Medium, Small - sized Enterprises Industrial enterprises are classified into large, medium, small - sized enterprises according to employment personnel, sales revenue and total assets in accordance with the regulation of Classification (temporary) of Large, Medium, Small - sized Enterprises on Statistics, are not classified according to production capacity and original value of fixed assets. The standard of classification as following

Indicator	Unit	Large - sized	Medium - sized	Small - sized
Employment personnel	person	2 000 and over	300 - 2 000 below	below 300
Sales Revenue	10 000 yuan	30 000 and over	30 00 - 30 000 below	below 3 000
Total assets	10 000 yuan	40 000 and over	4 000 - 40 000 below	below 4 000

Capital Obtained refers to the sum of capital received by the enterprise from investors. It can be classified into 6 kinds according to investors.

(a) **State capital** refers to capital which is formed through state - owned investment into the enerprises by government agencies or institutions that could represent the state in the investment.

(**b**)**Collective capital** refers to capital which is formed through state－owned investment into the enterprises by collective institutions or units that could represent the state in the investment, also include the capital which is formed through decrease tax before the enterprise implement new regulation.

(**c**)**Corporate capital** refers to capital which is formed through investment by other corporate units.

(**d**) **Individual capital** refers to capital which is formed through investment by individuals outside the enterprise or employees of the enterprise using their personal legal properties.

(**e**) **Capital from Hongkong, Macao and Taiwan** refers to capital which is formed through investment by investors from Hongkong,Macao and Taiwan of China using their assets of various forms.

(**f**)**Foreign capital** refers to capital which is formed through investment by foreign investors.

Sales Revenue of Products refers to the revenue from the sales of products by industrial enterprises and the revenue from services provided, etc. According to the requirement of current accountancy regulation,enterprise calculate sales revenue of products using the principle of power occurrence system,i. e. it is calculated on the basis of sales.

Sales Cost of Products refers to the actual cost of products of industrial enterprises and industrial services provided, etc. It excludes period cost,i. e. management cost,sales cost and finance cost. Enterprise should calculate sales cost according to the principle of power occurrence system,i. e. cost of current period should be calculated no matter it has be paid or not; cost of non－current period should not be calculated even it has been paid at current period.

Sales Expenses of Products refers to the expenses of selling products, semi－processed goods of industrial enterprises and industrial services provided, expenses of sales department, which is included the expenses on transportation, load and unload, package, insurance, exhibition,advertisement and wage of staff and workers of sales department, welfare, business and depreciation.

Tax and Extra Charges on Sales of Products refer to the tax on city maintenance and construction, consumption tax,resources tax and extra charges for education, which should be borne by the enterprises in selling products and providing industrial services during the reference period.

Sales Profit of Products refers to the profit gained by the enterprises by deducting cost, charges and taxes from the business income of the enterprises obtained in selling products and providing industrial services. The following formula is used

Sales Profit of Products = Sales Revenue － Sales Cost of Products － Sales Expensesof Products － Sales Tax of Products

Business Profits refers to the profits on producing and operating by the enterprises, including main operating profits and other profits. The following formula is used

Business Profits = Sales Profits + Other Profits － overhead costs － financial expenses

Total Profits refer to the final achievements of production and operation of the enterprises, represented by the total profits or losses (loss is expressed by the negative figure) , i.e. sales revenue deduce devotion cost, expenses, expenditure of activities other than operation, add income of activities other than operation and investment earnings. The following formula is used

Total Profits = Profits from Operation + Investment Earnings + Income from Subsidies + Income of Activities other than Operation － Expenditure of Activities other than Operation + Adjustment of Profits and Losses of Previous Years

Total Value of Profit and Tax (Pre－tax) refers to the sum of the total net profits, products sales tax & surcharges and the value added tax payable of industrial enterprises, namely pre－tax profits.

Total Energy Consumption refers to the total consumption of one－time energy and second－time energy of units.

Energy Conversed to Ton－standard－coal Various energies are conversed into the standard coal equivalent, because the unit of original calculation is not same,heat value is not same.

第8篇 CHAPTER 8

建筑业

CONSTRUCTION

8-1 改革开放以来建筑企业基本情况

BASIC STATISTICS ON CONSTRUCTION ENTERPRISES SINCE REFORM AND OPENING UP

年 份 Year	企业个数（个） Number of Enterprises	从业人员平均人数（万人） Annual Average Employed Personnel (10 000 persons)	建筑业总产值（万元） Gross Output Value of Construction (10 000 yuan)	房屋建筑施工面积（万平方米） Floor Space of Building Under Construction (10 000 sq.m)	房屋建筑竣工面积（万平方米） Floor Space of Building Completed (10 000 sq.m)	#住 宅 Residential Buildings
1978	45	16.71	87 817			
1979	47	20.20	122 110	650.56	290.46	
1980	77	21.40	116 448	693.43	332.80	
1981	70	19.60	101 540	703.36	336.20	
1982	72	20.20	125 518	782.66	421.20	
1983	77	18.40	143 691	818.17	397.40	
1984	84	20.90	203 376	921.23	464.40	
1985	88	21.76	261 710	1 040.02	505.50	
1986	88	22.23	275 938	902.13	483.00	
1987	85	21.85	295 390	917.42	451.90	
1988	83	20.20	310 770	865.15	409.80	
1989	81	19.70	323 534	774.30	399.10	
1990	82	18.71	317 009	675.46	333.60	
1991	83	18.95	361 739	582.73	295.41	
1992	96	18.76	484 293	721.50	344.70	158.50
1993	237	25.87	826 585	1 210.94	505.02	270.70
1994	482	36.28	1 305 160	1 359.96	600.15	376.97
1995	693	31.53	1 656 748	1 604.10	640.25	328.40
1996	461	29.06	1 735 679	1 579.53	567.98	285.82
1997	477	29.26	1 909 999	1 752.13	727.61	398.82
1998	500	29.34	2 111 208	2 059.23	868.00	527.98
1999	491	28.71	2 227 406	2 087.01	901.88	637.85
2000	456	27.44	2 380 991	2 253.99	1 056.40	658.85
2001	420	25.96	2 886 808	2 140.04	924.92	562.40
2002	925	34.56	4 061 628	2 817.84	1 332.10	726.87
2003	900	35.55	5 208 402	3 395.94	1 465.75	797.72

注：1.本表1993年以前不含乡镇企业数据。2.从2002年起建筑业统计范围由原资质四级及以上企业改为具有建筑业资质等级的所有独立核算企业，但不包括劳务分包企业。3.2002年以前的建筑业总产值为企业自行完成的施工产值。4.以下各相关表同。

Note: a) Before 1993, figures in this table exclude township enterprises. b) In 2002, the statistical coverage of construction includes all the construction enterprises with qualification criteria and independent accounting system, but excludes engineering sub-contractors, the original coverage includes the construction enterprises with qualification criteria at or above Class 4. c) Before 2002, gross output value of construction refer to output value under construction. d) Same as following next.

8－2 建筑企业主要经济效益指标和工程质量
MAIN INDICATORS OF ECONOMIC EFFICIENCY AND ENGINEERING QUALITY OF CONSTRUCTION ENTERPRISES
(1980－2003)

年　份 Year	全员劳动生产率 (元/人) Overall Labor Productivity (yuan/person)	平均每一从业人员竣工面积 (平方米) Per Capita Floor Space of Building Completed (sq. m)	产值利润率 (%) Ratio of Profit to Gross Output Value (%)	产值利税率 (%) Ratio of Pre－tax Profit to Gross Output Value (%)	按面积计算竣工率 (%) Percentage of Building Completed in terms of Floor Space (%)
1980	5 638	16.1	7.0	7.5	48.0
1981	4 988	18.0	9.0	9.5	52.1
1982	5 999	20.1	9.3	10.0	53.8
1983	7 030	19.4	10.2	13.1	48.6
1984	8 896	22.2	8.3	8.8	50.4
1985	10 633	20.5	7.0	7.8	48.6
1986	11 538	20.2	4.6	5.1	53.5
1987	12 460	19.1	4.5	4.9	49.3
1988	13 487	17.8	2.7	4.7	47.4
1989	15 041	18.6	0.6	4.3	51.5
1990	15 874	16.7	－0.3	2.7	49.4
1991	17 952	14.7	0.8	3.4	50.7
1992	23 578	16.8	1.0	3.5	38.2
1993	33 126	18.6	2.9	5.5	38.7
1994	36 762	16.0	0.5	3.2	42.3
1995	52 545	19.6	0.6	3.4	37.2
1996	59 724	19.5	1.0	3.6	36.0
1997	65 274	24.9	1.1	3.7	41.5
1998	71 958	29.6	1.4	3.9	42.2
1999	77 583	31.4	1.0	3.6	43.2
2000	86 771	38.5	1.1	4.0	46.9
2001	111 194	35.6	1.3	4.2	43.2
2002	117 536	38.5	1.8	4.7	47.3
2003	146 499	41.2	1.9	4.8	43.2

8-3 建筑企业基本情况(2003年)
(按行业和资质等级分)
BASIC STATISTICS ON CONSTRUCTION ENTERPRISES,2003
(GROUPED BY SECTOR AND QUALIFICATION GRADE)

指标 Item	企业个数(个) Number of Enterprises	从业人员平均人数(万人) Average Employed Personnel (10 000 persons)	建筑业总产值(万元) Gross Output Value of Construction (10 000 yuan)	竣工产值(万元) Gross Output Value Completed (10 000 yuan)	房屋建筑施工面积(万平方米) Floor Space of Building Under Construction (10 000 sq.m)	房屋建筑竣工面积(万平方米) Floor Space of Building Completed (10 000 sq.m)	#住宅 Residential Buildings
一、按行业分							
Grouped by Sector							
房屋工程建筑业							
Building Engineering	172	16.53	1 814 471	1 365 553	2 783.12	1 306.02	729.99
土木工程建筑业							
Civil Engineering	159	11.17	2 452 731	1 616 718	377.37	105.83	43.36
建筑安装业							
Building Installation	254	5.68	716 208	511 602	210.21	49.84	24.37
建筑装饰业							
Building Decoration	233	1.57	162 491	123 583			
其他建筑业							
Others	82	0.60	62 501	41 160	25.24	4.06	
二、按资质等级分							
Grouped by Quali-fication Grade							
施工总承包							
General Contractor	239	27.32	4 021 856	2 848 022	3 058.74	1 436.73	793.02
特级							
Super Grade	3	5.52	970 179	638 784	246.94	110.17	34.43
一级							
First Grade	43	11.20	2 075 197	1 398 315	1 601.28	625.23	319.81
二级							
Second Grade	77	6.94	690 239	576 299	906.12	512.91	333.13
三级							
Third Grade	116	3.66	286 241	234 624	304.40	188.42	105.65
专业承包							
Specialized Contractor	661	8.23	1 186 546	810 594	337.20	29.02	4.70
一级							
First Grade	38	1.74	478 268	248 988	49.02	6.88	
二级							
Second Grade	99	2.23	294 439	214 335	108.23	1.41	0.74
三级							
Third Grade	524	4.26	413 839	347 271	179.95	20.73	3.96

注:本表行业分类为国标GB/T4754-2002标准。
Note: Sector listed in this table is classified by the standard of GB/T4754-2002.

8-4 建筑企业基本情况
（按经济类型分）
BASIC STATISTICS ON CONSTRUCTION ENTERPRISES
（GROUPED BY OWNERSHIP）

指　标 Item	全市总计 Total		# 国有经济 State - owned		# 地　方 Local	
	2002	2003	2002	2003	2002	2003
企业个数（个） Number of Enterprises(unit)	925	900	160	154	112	106
全部从业人员平均人数（万人） Average Employed Personnel (10 000 persons)	34.56	35.55	11.71	11.56	6.97	6.54
从业人员劳动报酬（万元）(10 000 yuan) Earnings of Employed Personnel	329 865	416 189	130 721	157 498	51 119	62 432
建筑业总产值（万元） Gross Output Value of Construction (10 000 yuan)	4 061 628	5 208 402	1 581 077	1 976 613	732 365	871 595
竣工产值（万元）(10 000 yuan) Gross Output Value Completed	2 690 174	3 658 616	1 047 316	1 323 523	560 597	608 177
房屋建筑施工面积（万平方米） Floor Space of Buildings Under Construction (10 000 sq. m)	2 817.84	3 395.94	1 087.10	1 252.58	637.19	675.56
房屋建筑竣工面积（万平方米） Floor Space of Buildings Completed (10 000 sq. m)	1 332.10	1 465.75	473.48	503.19	316.04	304.91
# 住　宅 Residential Buildings	726.87	797.72	294.45	294.32	227.77	225.30

指　标 Item	# 集体经济 Collective - owned		# 私有经济 Private		# 港澳台投资经济 Hongkong, Macao and Taiwan Funded		# 外商投资经济 Foreign Funded	
	2002	2003	2002	2003	2002	2003	2002	2003
企业个数（个） Number of Enterprises(unit)	221	195	224	240	16	15	9	8
全部从业人员平均人数（万人） Average Employed Personnel (10 000 persons)	6.32	6.75	1.60	2.11	0.22	0.29	0.09	0.07
从业人员劳动报酬（万元）(10 000 yuan) Earnings of Employed Personnel	53 495	62 506	12 672	17 296	3 091	3 838	1 834	934
建筑业总产值（万元） Gross Output Value of Construction (10 000 yuan)	512 354	566 917	103 519	224 968	37 165	41 028	22 192	20 382
竣工产值（万元）(10 000 yuan) Gross Output Value Completed	424 220	473 172	71 893	163 242	17 187	20 448	8 278	22 004
房屋建筑施工面积（万平方米） Floor Space of Buildings Under Construction (10 000 sq. m)	477.70	497.47	128.37	238.08	2.66	5.80	22.81	23.24
房屋建筑竣工面积（万平方米） Floor Space of Buildings Completed (10 000 sq. m)	312.74	292.45	79.88	33.84	0.42		3.1	20.13
# 住　宅 Residential Buildings	187.73	192.51	16.35	6.25				

8-5 建筑企业主要财务指标(2003年)

MAIN FINANCIAL INDICATORS OF CONSTRUCTION ENTERPRISES,2003

单位:万元 (10 000 yuan)

指标	Item	全市总计 Total	#国有经济 State-owned	#地方 Local
1.资本金	**Capital**			
资本金合计	Total Capital	1 392 672	646 332	356 922
2.年末资产负债	**Assets and Liabilities at Year-end**			
流动资产合计	Total Circulating Funds	4 135 163	1 833 325	1 001 521
固定资产合计	Total Fixed Assets	1 208 952	432 264	199 835
固定资产原价	Original Value of Fixed Assets	1 752 793	711 698	257 937
#生产经营用	Used in Production and Management	1 460 655	578 474	177 969
累计折旧	Accumulative Depreciation	635 802	307 195	70 932
资产总计	Total Assets	5 769 987	2 525 115	1 371 296
3.损益及分配	**Profit,Loss and Distribution**			
工程结算收入	Revenue of Project Settle Accounts	5 172 545	1 946 775	871 573
工程结算成本	Costs of Project Settle Accounts	4 627 196	1 758 967	800 399
工程结算税金及附加	Taxes and Extra Charges of Project Settle Accounts	142 031	51 440	19 458
工程结算利润	Profits of Project Settle Accounts	403 318	136 368	51 716
其他业务收入	Other Revenue from Business	166 328	90 734	59 951
其他业务利润	Other Profits from Business	10 821	3 566	2 577
管理费用	Management Expenses	298 074	127 632	50 297
#税金	Taxes	10 987	5 182	1 580
利润总额	Total Profits	98 544	14 161	3 326
应交所得税	Income Taxes Payable	25 232	4 827	2 027
应付利润	Profits Payable	31 839	3 904	2 414
利税总额	Total Pre-tax Profits	251 562	70 783	24 364
4.工资、福利费	**Wage and Welfare Expenses**			
应付工资总额	Total Wage Payable	367 117	137 656	54 416
应付福利费总额	Total Welfare Expenses Payable	49 072	19 842	8 016

8－5 续表 Continued

单位:万元 (10 000 yuan)

指标	Item	#集体经济 Collective－owned	#私有经济 Private	#港澳台投资经济 Hongkong,Macao & Taiwan Funded	#外商投资经济 Foreign Funded
1.资本金	**Capital**				
资本金合计	Total Capital	161 821	110 024	18 231	7 359
2.年末资产负债	**Assets and Liabilities at Year－end**				
流动资产合计	Total Circulating Funds	471 577	170 974	52 818	14 365
固定资产合计	Total Fixed Assets	100 264	51 910	12 673	726
固定资产原价	Original Value of Fixed Assets	123 862	56 570	14 491	1 191
#生产经营用	Used in Production & Management	94 445	46 489	14 018	1 002
累计折旧	Accumulative Depreciation	34 265	10 910	2 857	603
资产总计	Total Assets	602 233	232 537	66 719	16 125
3.损益及分配	**Profit,Loss and Distribution**				
工程结算收入	Revenue of Project Settle Accounts	546 302	215 153	37 862	20 621
工程结算成本	Costs of Project Settle Accounts	470 718	183 892	30 737	18 808
工程结算税金及附加	Taxes and Extra Charges of Project Settle Accounts	20 598	6 397	1 611	484
工程结算利润	Profits of Project Settle Accounts	54 986	24 864	5 514	1 329
其他业务收入	Other Revenue from Business	7 492	5 332	30 659	21
其他业务利润	Other Profits from Business	2 721	583	454	20
管理费用	Management Expenses	32 224	14 429	9 828	1 184
#税　金	Taxes	1 014	361	32	18
利润总额	Total Profits	19 399	7 405	－4 200	153
应交所得税	Income Taxes Payable	5 641	1 734	22	73
应付利润	Profits Payable	8 536	2 711	37	154
利税总额	Total Pre－tax Profits	41 011	14 163	－2 557	655
4.工资、福利费	**Wage and Welfare Expenses**				
应付工资总额	Total Wage Payable	57 330	15 863	3 137	900
应付福利费总额	Total Welfare Expenses Payable	5 176	1 433	701	34

8－6 建筑企业年末自有机械设备总功率和净值

TOTAL POWER AND NET VALUE OF MACHINERY AND EQUIPMENT OWNED BY CONSTRUCTION ENTERPRISES (YEAR－END)

(1980－2003)

年份 Year	年末自有机械设备总功率（万千瓦） Total Power of Machinery and Equipment Owned (year－end) (10 000 kw)	# 国有经济 State－owned	# 地方 Local	年末自有机械设备净值（万元） Net Value of Machinery and Equipment Owned (year－end) (10 000 yuan)	# 国有经济 State－owned	# 地方 Local
1980	64.2	60.8	35.4	46 513	45 147	20 790
1981	68.4	65.6	34.9	45 824	44 466	20 459
1982	68.6	64.8	40.2	45 035	43 619	25 128
1983	71.7	68.2	43.6	45 036	44 004	25 740
1984	77.3	71.9	26.1	43 919	42 718	24 178
1985	93.6	88.7	47.6	55 340	54 071	28 085
1986	91.1	87.1	47.7	59 434	58 449	29 073
1987	93.9	90.1	46.5	64 381	63 306	29 882
1988	90.9	86.6	46.6	78 774	77 552	30 761
1989	94.6	90.1	43.7	80 086	78 496	27 416
1990	91.7	86.7	41.4	79 168	77 633	28 493
1991	89.74	85.46	42.95	76 234	74 526	27 722
1992	94.60	89.90	42.60	76 234	74 252	29 646
1993	98.92	89.57	41.20	116 608	108 817	55 009
1994	116.58	103.91	37.47	172 348	153 207	47 757
1995	138.36	110.17	43.77	179 888	164 162	60 526
1996	137.98	109.22	40.47	384 677	178 790	47 006
1997	151.18	119.22	43.87	207 571	173 245	54 521
1998	173.03	111.19	39.28	206 033	163 854	49 153
1999	185.54	146.77	38.00	214 052	174 687	67 470
2000	157.27	102.26	36.14	217 748	122 519	45 433
2001	168.83	87.31	32.16	231 546	126 407	51 157
2002	221.56	85.37	33.03	529 838	166 556	83 098
2003	227.81	86.32	34.65	582 022	208 634	79 305

8-7 建筑企业技术装备率和动力装备率
VALUE AND POWER OF MACHINES PER LABORER OF CONSTRUCTION ENTERPRISES
(1980-2003)

年份 Year	全部职工技术装备率(元/人) Value of Machines per Laborer (yuan/person)	#国有经济 State-owned	#地方 Local	全部职工动力装备率(千瓦/人) Power of Machines Per Laborer (kw/person)	#国有经济 State-owned	#地方 Local
1980	2 178	2 309	1 583	3.0	3.1	2.4
1981	2 344	2 506	1 672	3.5	3.7	2.6
1982	2 325	2 466	1 940	3.4	3.5	3.0
1983	2 465	2 652	2 209	3.9	4.1	3.7
1984	2 102	2 200	2 035	3.7	3.7	2.2
1985	2 533	2 669	2 242	4.3	4.4	3.8
1986	2 674	2 819	2 256	4.1	4.2	3.7
1987	2 952	3 097	2 374	4.3	4.4	3.7
1988	3 900	4 118	2 571	4.5	4.6	3.9
1989	4 065	4 270	2 573	4.8	4.9	4.1
1990	4 231	4 480	2 893	4.9	5.0	4.2
1991	4 023	4 259	2 697	4.7	4.9	4.1
1992	4 063	4 279	2 878	5.00	5.20	4.10
1993	4 507	5 490	4 461	3.80	4.50	3.30
1994	5 114	5 075	2 350	3.46	3.44	1.84
1995	6 281	6 622	4 299	4.83	4.44	3.11
1996	13 237	7 677	3 647	4.75	4.69	3.14
1997	7 094	7 680	4 300	5.17	5.28	3.46
1998	7 022	7 908	4 134	5.90	5.37	3.30
1999	8 774	11 542	10 233	7.61	9.70	5.76
2000	10 714	9 483	9 008	7.74	7.92	7.17
2001	12 881	14 697	11 768	9.39	10.15	7.40
2002	19 423	18 366	16 571	8.12	9.41	6.59
2003	24 203	27 824	24 187	9.47	11.51	10.57

8－8　建筑企业机械设备情况及经济效益指标
MACHINERY EQUIPMENT AND ECONOMIC EFFICIENCY INDICATORS OF CONSTRUCTION ENTERPRISES

指　　标　　Item	全　市 Total	#国有经济 State－owned	#地　方 Local
2002			
建筑业机械设备情况			
Machinery and Equipment of Construction Enterprises			
自有机械设备总台数(台)			
Number of Machinery and Equipment Owned(set)	107 138	37 699	18 643
自有机械设备总功率(万千瓦)			
Power of Machinery and Equipment Owned(10 000 kw)	221.56	85.37	33.03
#施工机械功率			
Power of Construction Machines	174.80	66.19	25.01
自有机械设备净值(万元)			
Net Value of Machinery and Equipment Owned(10 000 yuan)	529 838	166 556	83 098
技术装备率(元/人)			
Value of Machines Per Laborer(yuan/person)	19 423	18 366	16 571
动力装备率(千瓦/人)			
Power of Machines Per Laborer(kw/person)	8.12	9.41	6.59
建筑业经济效益指标			
Economic Efficiency Indicators of Construction Enterprises			
全员劳动生产率(元/人)			
Overall Labor Productivity(yuan/person)	117 536	135 007	105 075
房屋竣工率(%)			
Percentage of Buildings Completed(%)	47.3	43.6	49.6
平均每一从业人员竣工面积(平方米/人)			
Per Capita Floor Space of Buildings Completed (sq. m/person)	38.5	40.4	45.3
每百元产值实现利税(元)			
Ratio of Pre－tax Profit to Gross Output Value(yuan)	4.7	3.5	3.2
百元产值占用流动资产(元)			
Ratio of Circulating Funds to Gross Output Value(yuan)	84.0	98.2	118.3
全员资金占有率(元/人)			
Per Capita Owned Capital(yuan/person)	129 828	167 207	153 628
2003			
建筑业机械设备情况			
Machinery and Equipment of Construction Enterprises			
自有机械设备总台数(台)			
Number of Machinery and Equipment Owned(set)	105 861	35 567	18 058
自有机械设备总功率(万千瓦)			
Power of Machinery and Equipment Owned(10 000 kw)	227.81	86.32	34.65
#施工机械功率			
Power of Construction Machines	164.07	62.63	24.29
自有机械设备净值(万元)			
Net Value of Machinery and Equipment Owned (10 000 yuan)	582 022	208 634	79 305
技术装备率(元/人)			
Value of Machines Per Laborer(yuan/person)	24 203	27 824	24 187
动力装备率(千瓦/人)			
Power of Machines Per Laborer(kw/person)	9.47	11.51	10.57
建筑业经济效益指标			
Economic Efficiency Indicators of Construction Enterprises			
全员劳动生产率(元/人)			
Overall Labor Productivity(yuan/person)	146 499	171 031	133 302
房屋竣工率(%)			
Percentage of Buildings Completed(%)	43.2	40.2	45.1
平均每一从业人员竣工面积(平方米/人)			
Per Capita Floor Space of Buildings Completed(sq. m/person)	41.2	43.5	46.6
每百元产值实现利税(元)			
Ratio of Pre－tax Profit to Gross Output Value(yuan)	4.8	3.6	2.8
百元产值占用流动资产(元)			
Ratio of Circulating Funds to Gross Output Value(yuan)	79.4	92.7	114.9
全员资金占有率(元/人)			
Per Capita Owned Capital(yuan/person)	150 316	196 036	173 736

主要统计指标解释

建筑业总产值 是以货币表现的建筑安装企业在一定时期内生产的建筑业产品的总和。建筑业总产值包括三部分内容：

(1)建筑工程产值 指列入建筑工程预算内的各种工程价值，主要包括：各种用途的房屋、构筑物的建筑工程和暖气、卫生、通风、照明、煤气等设备安装价值；设备基础、支柱、操作台、梯子、烟囱、凉水塔的砌筑工程；各种锅炉炉体砌筑和金属结构安装工程；施工现场布置、场地平整、施工临时用水、电、道路的铺筑与架设；矿井的开凿、井巷掘进延伸、露天矿的剥离、石油、天然气钻井工程；铁路、公路、港口、桥梁的建筑工程；水利工程；防空、地下建筑等特殊工程。和对建筑物内部或外部进行装饰、装修的价值。

(2)设备安装工程产值 指设备安装工程价值，主要包括生产、动力、起重、运输、传动、医疗、实验、电讯、光纤、电话、计算机和电子设备等各种需要安装设备的装配与安装，与设备相联接的工作台、梯子、栏杆等装设工程；附属于被安装设备的管线敷设工程；被安装设备的绝缘、防腐保温、油漆等工作；为测定安装工作质量，对单个设备、系统设备进行单机试车和系统联动无负荷试运转工作，但产值中不包括被安装设备的价值。

(3)其他产值 建筑业总产值中除建筑工程、安装工程以外的产值。包括房屋、构筑物修理产值、非标准设备制造产值、总包企业向分包企业收取的管理费以及不能明确划分的施工活动所完成的产值。

①房屋、构筑物修理产值 指房屋和构筑物修理所完成的产值，但不包括被修理房屋、构筑物本身产值和生产设备的修理产值。

②非标准设备制造产值 指加工制造没有定型的非标准生产设备的加工费和原材料价值。

Explanatory Notes on Main Statistical Indicators

Gross Output Value of Construction refers to total of construction products, expressed in money terms, completed by construction and installation enterprises during a given period of time. It includes three parts :

(a) **Output Value of Construction Projects** is the value of projects covered by the project budgets, including the value of various buildings and structures, the value of the installation projects of central heating, public health, ventilation, lighting, gas, etc., the building of the base of equipment, pillar, operation desk, ladder, funnel, water tower, the building boiler room and installation of metals construction, arrange construction site, level the land, temporary expenses of water, electrical, pave the way, cutting mine, well drilling construction of oil, gas, the building engineering of railways, highways, port and bridges, water engineering, output value of building decoration, air defense,underground.

(b) **Output Value of Installation Projects** is the value of the installation of equipment, (excluding the value of the equipment to be installed) , mainly including production, power, lifting, transportation, medical treatment, experimentation, telecommunications, fiber optics, telephone, computer, electronic equipment, working desk, ladder, banisters, insulation,heat preservation, paint, etc.

(c) **Other Output Value** refers to output value outside of output value of construction projects and installation projects. It includes output value of repair of buildings and structures, output value of manufactured non - standard equipment, management fee of chief contractor received from subcontractor, other output value of construction.

a. Output value of repair of buildings and structures refer to the value created through the repairs of buildings or structures, but does not include the value of buildings or structures being repaired and the value of the repair of production equipment.

b. Output value of manufactured non - standard equipment refer to the value of non - standard production equipment (including raw materials and manufacturing cost)made for the construction projects.

第9篇 CHAPTER 9

交通运输和邮电通信

TRANSPORTATION, POST AND TELECOMMUNICATIONS

9-1 社会客、货运输量和周转量

PASSENGER & FREIGHT TRAFFIC AND THE TURNOVER VOLUME OF PASSENGER & FREIGHT TRAFFIC

(1985-2003)

年 份 Year	客运量(万人) Passenger Traffic (10 000 persons)	#铁 路 Railways	#公 路 Highways	#水 运 Waterways	旅客周转量(百万人公里) Turnover Volume of Passenger Traffic (million passenger-km)	#铁 路 Railways	#公 路 Highways	#水 运 Waterways
1985	2 984	2 192	788			5 234	456	
1986	2 873	2 088	779			5 558	467	
1987	2 838	2 111	718			5 960	448	
1988	2 601	1 976	616			6 745	424	
1989	2 550	2 047	496			6 214	329	
1990	2 175	1 722	447			5 409	307	
1991	2 922	1 718	1 196			4 974	941	
1992	2 662	1 731	897			6 242	819	
1993	3 225	1 812	1 380	4	8 825	6 584	1 463	92
1994	3 373	1 863	1 463	6	8 299	5 778	1 639	49
1995	3 308	1 802	1 464	5	7 927	5 437	1 680	41
1996	3 125	1 580	1 496	5	7 599	4 917	1 772	43
1997	3 136	1 449	1 640	5	7 921	5 050	2 017	41
1998	3 207	1 511	1 651	4	7 950	5 280	1 914	33
1999	3 259	1 546	1 671	3	8 277	5 780	1 782	25
2000	3 474	1 594	1 820	2	8 845	6 022	1 864	26
2001	3 302	1 456	1 780	6	9 197	5 996	2 205	34
2002	3 457	1 498	1 870	5	9 255	5 782	2 272	33
2003	3 507	1 281	2 109	2	9 274	5 526	2 158	23

年 份 Year	货运量(万吨) Freight Traffic (10 000 tons)	#铁 路 Railways	#公 路 Highways	#水 运 Waterways	货物周转量(亿吨公里) Turnover Volume of Freight Traffic (100 million ton-km)	#铁 路 Railways	#公 路 Highways	#水 运 Waterways
1985	18 249	2 595	14 500	818	765	190	34	540
1986	18 525	2 351	14 935	882	881	204	34	641
1987	18 400	2 544	14 618	896	930	222	35	671
1988	16 693	2 529	12 829	975	1 022	230	44	746
1989	15 543	2 723	11 426	1 014	1 035	235	42	756
1990	15 929	2 228	12 329	1 046	1 139	234	52	852
1991	18 308	2 290	14 537	1 163	1 216	204	37	973
1992	17 522	2 392	13 562	1 248	1 321	217	37	1 067
1993	21 640	2 618	17 244	1 347	1 341	264	46	1 030
1994	23 783	2 634	19 270	1 421	1 325	225	46	1 053
1995	24 040	2 722	19 323	1 517	1 412	230	41	1 139
1996	24 133	2 668	19 491	1 489	1 052	224	41	784
1997	25 090	2 548	20 515	1 390	1 031	219	44	765
1998	24 505	2 467	18 584	2 867	3 710	198	60	3 449
1999	27 052	2 380	20 049	3 884	4 759	200	60	4 497
2000	26 400	3 079	18 764	4 165	4 674	275	63	4 334
2001	28 608	3 727	19 382	5 037	5 166	230	65	4 870
2002	31 016	4 519	19 554	6 452	6 484	228	66	6 188
2003	35 252	5 662	20 072	8 944	8 169	259	68	7 840

注：铁路数据为天津地区辖区数，下同。
Note: The data of railways cover the regions under Tianjin administration, same as following next.

9－2　社会客、货运输量和周转量

PASSENGER & FREIGHT TRAFFIC AND THE TURNOVER VOLUME OF PASSENGER & FREIGHT TRAFFIC

指　标	Item	2001	2002	2003	2003 比 2002 年 增长% Increase Rate in 2003 over 2002
客运量(万人)	**Passenger Traffic (10 000 persons)**	**3 302**	**3 457**	**3 507**	**1.4**
铁　路	Railways	1 456	1 498	1 281	－14.5
公　路	Highways	1 780	1 870	2 109	12.8
水　运	Waterways	6	5	2	－60.0
民　航	Civil Aviation	60	84	115	36.9
旅客周转量	**Turnover Volume of Passenger Traffic**				
(百万人公里)	**(million passenger－km)**	**9 197**	**9 255**	**9 274**	**0.2**
铁　路	Railways	5 996	5 782	5 526	－4.4
公　路	Highways	2 205	2 272	2 158	－5.0
水　运	Waterways	34	33	23	－30.3
民　航	Civil Aviation	962	1 168	1 567	34.2
货运量(万吨)	**Freight Traffic (10 000 tons)**	**28 608**	**31 016**	**35 252**	**13.7**
铁　路	Railways	3 727	4 519	5 662	25.3
公　路	Highways	19 382	19 554	20 072	2.6
水　运	Waterways	5 037	6 452	8 944	38.6
民　航	Civil Aviation	1	1	1	
管道输油气量	Traffic of Petroleum & Gas Pipelines	461	490	573	16.9
货物周转量	**Turnover Volume of Freight Traffic**				
(亿吨公里)	**(100 million ton－km)**	**5 166**	**6 484**	**8 169**	**26.0**
铁　路	Railways	230	228	259	13.6
公　路	Highways	65	66	68	3.0
水　运	Waterways	4 870	6 188	7 840	26.7
民　航	Civil Aviation	0.2	0.2	0.2	
管道输油气量	Traffic of Petroleum & Gas Pipelines	1.2	1.9	1.9	

9－3 运输线路长度
LENGTH OF TRANSPORT ROUTES

单位:公里 (km)

指标	Item	2001	2002	2003	2003比2002年增长% Increase Rate in 2003 over 2002
一、铁路	**Railways**				
延展里程	Extention Length	4 372	4 435	4 455	0.5
营业里程	Length of Railways in Operation	1 424	1 501	1 454	-3.1
二、公路	**Highways**				
通车里程	Length of Highways Having Transport Service	9 647	9 696	10 168	4.9
等级公路	Expressway and Class I to IV Highway	9 067	9 126	9 901	8.5
#高速公路	Expressway	304	331	517	56.2
等外公路	Highway Below Class IV	580	570	267	-53.2
三、内河航道	**Navigable Inland Waterways**				
航道里程	Length of Navigable Inland Waterways	443	443	412	-7.0
四、民航	**Civil Aviation**				
民用航空航线里程	Length of Civil Aviation	17 712	19 922	18 519	-7.0
五、管道	**Pipelines**				
输油气管道里程	Length of Petroleum & Gas Pipelines	462	462	495	7.1

注:内河航道里程为内河清淤里程。民用航空航线里程为国航天津分公司在天津机场起落飞机的里程。
Note: Length of navigable inland waterways refer to length of cleaning up the silt inland waterways. Length of civil aviation refer to the length of China International Aviation Corporation Tianjin Company flights at Tianjin airport.

9－4 民用车辆拥有量(2003年)
NUMBER OF CIVIL MOTOR VEHICLES OWNED, 2003

单位:辆 (unit)

指标	Item	合计 Total	#个人 Private－owned	#当年新注册 Registered in 2003
总计	**Total**	**1 005 482**	**749 318**	**95 666**
一、民用汽车	Civil Motor Vehicles	537 797	309 622	77 851
1.载客汽车	Passenger Vehicles	382 438	248 136	65 914
大型	Large－sized	13 809	1 193	2 262
中型	Medium－sized	29 675	12 412	2 281
小型	Small－sized	227 836	141 279	56 487
微型	Minisize	111 118	93 252	4 884
#轿车	Cars	199 769	127 238	47 434
2.载货汽车	Trucks	140 938	59 730	9 778
重型	Heavy Trucks	23 373	6 185	929
中型	Medium－sized Trucks	22 835	7 428	1 157
轻型	Light Trucks	77 909	33 255	7 271
微型	Minisize Trucks	16 821	12 862	421
#普通载货	Ordinary Trucks	110 240	47 531	5 894
3.其他汽车	Other Civil Motor Vehicles	14 421	1 756	2 159
二、摩托车	Motorcycles	363 865	344 862	15 793
三、农用运输车	Vehicles for Agriculture	37 795	37 157	633
四、拖拉机	Tractor	53 415	53 415	
五、挂车	Trailer	11 111	4 038	1 277
六、其他类型车	Other Vehicles	1 499	224	112

9－5　港口客、货吞吐量

VOLUME OF PASSENGER & FREIGHT HANDLED IN PORTS

(1978－2003)

年　份 Year	港口旅客吞吐量 (万人次) Volume of Passenger Handled in Ports (10 000 person－times)	港口货物吞吐量 (万吨) Volume of Freight Handled in Ports (10 000 tons)	出　港 Out－port	比　重(%) Proportion (%)	进　港 In－port	比　重(%) Proportion (%)	集装箱吞吐量 (万国际标准箱) Handled Containers (10 000 TEU)
1978	6.2	1 131	280	24.8	851	75.2	0.7
1979	7.7	1 270	302	23.8	968	76.2	0.8
1980	6.0	1 192	393	33.0	799	67.0	1.6
1981	18.1	1 175	460	39.2	715	60.8	2.6
1982	19.7	1 287	496	38.5	791	61.5	4.2
1983	24.9	1 506	430	28.6	1 076	71.4	6.1
1984	26.5	1 611	449	27.9	1 162	72.1	8.5
1985	33.8	1 856	360	19.4	1 496	80.6	14.9
1986	40.7	1 818	695	38.2	1 123	61.8	16.8
1987	47.0	1 725	670	38.8	1 055	61.2	16.3
1988	42.8	2 109	1 052	49.9	1 057	50.1	21.4
1989	34.7	2 437	1 341	55.0	1 096	45.0	26.6
1990	37.0	2 063	1 195	57.9	868	42.1	28.7
1991	47.7	2 378	1 488	62.6	890	37.4	33.9
1992	61.2	2 929	1 915	65.4	1 014	34.6	39.4
1993	57.6	3 719	2 527	68.0	1 192	32.0	48.2
1994	51.9	4 652	3 507	75.4	1 145	24.6	63.1
1995	50.4	5 787	4 551	78.6	1 236	21.4	70.2
1996	58.7	6 188	4 839	78.2	1 349	21.8	82.3
1997	52.7	6 789	5 198	76.6	1 591	23.4	93.6
1998	45.3	6 818	5 124	75.2	1 694	24.8	101.8
1999	48.7	7 298	5 280	72.4	2 018	27.6	130.2
2000	40.2	9 582	6 936	72.4	2 646	27.6	170.8
2001	37.1	11 369	8 086	71.1	3 283	28.9	201.1
2002	33.0	12 906	8 802	68.2	4 104	31.8	240.8
2003	22.7	16 182	10 912	67.4	5 270	32.6	301.5

注：货物吞吐量是全港数据，即包括货主码头数据。
Note：Volume of freight handled in ports refer to the figure of ports，including those of docks.

9－6 港口设施

PORTS FACILITIES

指　标	Item	2001	2002	2003	2003比2002年增长% Increase Rate in 2003 over 2002
码头长度(米)	Length of Quay Line(m)	13 934	14 464	14 443	－0.1
港口泊位(个)	Number of Berths(unit)	107	108	108	
港务局	Tianjin Port Authority	75	76	76	
货主码头	Docks	32	32	32	
#万吨级泊位	10,000 Ton Class	53	55	54	－1.8
#港务局	Tianjin Port Authority	51	53	52	－1.9
铁路专用线长度(米)	Length of Railways(m)	69 971	65 464	75 650	15.6
仓库总面积(平方米)	Areas of Store Houses(sq.m)	206 886	197 509	200 445	1.5
堆场总面积(平方米)	Areas of Goods Pile(sq.m)	2 658 032	3 185 411	3 295 601	3.5
集装箱堆场堆存能力(TEU)	Capacity of Piling Containers(TEU)	56 764	66 677	98 129	47.2
装卸机械台数(台)	Number of Loading & Unloading Machines(unit)	1 040	1 084	1 102	1.7

注：本表除港口泊位含货主码头数据外，其余设施均为港务局数据。
Note: Number of berths include docks, other ports facilities refer to those owned by Tianjin Port Authority.

9－7 港口分货类吞吐量

VOLUME OF FREIGHT HANDLED IN PORTS BY CATEGORY

单位：万吨　　(10 000 tons)

指　标	Item	合计 Total		出港量 Out－port		进港量 In－port	
		2002	2003	2002	2003	2002	2003
港口货物吞吐量	**Volume of Freight Handled in Ports**	**12 906**	**16 182**	**8 802**	**10 912**	**4 104**	**5 270**
国　外	Abroad	7 006	8 758	4 144	5 140	2 862	3 618
国　内	Domestic	5 900	7 424	4 658	5 772	1 242	1 652
分品种货物吞吐量	**Volume of Freight Handled by Category**						
煤炭及制品	Coal and Related Products	5 638	6 754	5 637	6 726	1	28
石油、天然气及制品	Petroleum, Natural Gas and Related Products	1 004	1 480	473	771	531	709
金属矿石	Metal Ores	1 212	1 743	13	24	1 199	1 719
钢　铁	Steel and Iron	793	1 141	579	883	214	258
矿建材料	Mineral Building Materials	606	822	66	90	540	732
水　泥	Cement	4	4	4	4		
木　材	Timber	35	35	19	22	16	13
非金属矿石	Nonmetal Ores	182	206	165	190	17	16
化学肥料及农药	Chemical Fertilizers and Pesticides	160	81	9	6	151	75
盐	Salt	36	32	36	32		
粮　食	Grain	142	222	56	97	86	125
机械、电器、设备	Machine, Electric Machine, Equipment	628	834	333	425	295	409
化工原料及制品	Chemical Materials and Related Products	522	635	364	420	158	215
有色金属	Nonferrous Metals	101	111	72	80	29	31
轻工、医药产品	Light Industry, Medical and Pharmaceutical Products	614	658	473	499	141	159
农林牧渔产品	Agricultural Products	314	368	177	191	137	177
其　他	Others	915	1 056	326	452	589	604
集装箱吞吐量(万国际标准箱)	**Handled Containers (10 000 TEU)**	**241**	**302**	**115**	**154**	**126**	**147**

9-8 铁路、公路、民航运输主要技术经济指标
MAIN TECHNICAL AND ECONOMIC INDICATORS OF RAILWAY,HIGHWAY AND CIVIL AVIATION TRANSPORT

指 标	Item	2001	2002	2003
一、铁 路	**Railways**			
货运机车日产量(万吨公里)	Average Daily Ton-kilometers of Freight Locomotives (10 000 ton-km)	144.6	143.5	147.1
货车周转时间(天)	Turning Around Time of Freight Cars(day)	1.5	1.4	1.4
货物列车旅行速度(公里/小时)	Running Speed of Freight Trains(km/hr)	36.2	35.1	35.9
旅客列车旅行速度(公里/小时)	Travelling Speed of Passenger Train(km/hr)	71.2	71.1	70.8
货物列车运行正点率(%)	Punctuality Rate of Freight Trains in Running(%)	91.0	91.7	91.2
旅客列车运行正点率(%)	Punctuality Rate of Passenger Trains in Running(%)	99.1	99.2	99.4
运输全员劳动生产率 (千换算吨公里/人)	Labour Productivity (1 000 comparable ton-km. person)	1 959	1 907	2 033
二、公 路	**Highways**			
载货汽车里程利用率(%)	Utilization Rate of Length of Trucks in Operation(%)	52.7	52.1	59.6
载客汽车里程利用率(%)	Utilization Rate of Length of Passenger Vehicles in Operation(%)	99.6	99.6	70.4
载货汽车每百吨公里耗汽油(升)	Gasoline Consumption of Trucks(L/100 ton-km)	7.4	7.0	7.9
载客汽车每百吨公里耗汽油(升)	Gasoline Consumption of Passenger Vehicles(L/100 ton-km)	21.3	21.1	15.1
载货汽车每百吨公里耗柴油(升)	Diesel Oil Consumption of Trucks(L/100 ton-km)	3.5	3.6	4.2
载客汽车每百吨公里耗柴油(升)	Diesel Oil Consumption of Passenger Vehicles(L/100 ton-km)	22.1	21.0	21.4
载货汽车实载率(%)	Utilization Rate of Capacity of Freight Trucks(%)	60.9	62.7	70.5
载客汽车实载率(%)	Utilization Rate of Capcity of Passenger Vehicles	34.9	38.4	79.2
三、民 航	**Civil Aviation**			
飞行小时(小时)	Flying Time(hour)	18 248	23 117	28 901
平均每可用机飞行小时(小时)	Flying Time Per Avaliable Aircraft(hour)	3 402	3 450	2 627
正班飞行距离(万公里)	Distance under Normal Conditions(10 000 km)	1 069.4	1 310.8	1 793.1
平均每可用机日生产飞行小时(小时)	Average Daily Flying Time Per Avaliable Aircraft (hour)	9.1	9.3	7.2
正班平均载运率(%)	Average Utilization Rate of Capacity under Normal Conditions(%)	59.8	61.1	66.0

注:1.本表铁路数据为铁路分局数据,公路数据为交通局数据,民航数据为国航数据。2.2003年公路、民航数据的统计口径有较大调整。

Note: a) In this table, the data of railway is provided by Tianjin Railway Bureau, highway is provided by Tianjin Communication Bureau, civil aviation is provided by China International Aviation Corporation . b) In 2003, the statistical coverage of highway and civil aviation have been adjusted.

9－9　邮电业基本情况

BASIC STATISTICS ON POST AND TELECOMMUNICATIONS

(1978－2003)

年　份 Year	邮电业务总量 (万元) Business Value of Post and Telecommunications (10 000 yuan)	邮电局所数 (处) Number of Post and Telecommunications Offices(unit)	局用电话交换机容量 (门) Capacity of Office Telephone Exchanges (line)	电话机(含移动) (万部) Telephone (Include Mobile) (10 000)	平均每百人拥有电话机数(含移动)(部/百人) Popularization Rate of Telephone (Include Mobile) (unit/100 persons)
1978	2 710	217	59 390	8.36	1.2
1979	2 901	220	60 710	9.43	1.3
1980	3 163	223	64 195	9.98	1.3
1981	3 441	230	66 660	11.65	1.5
1982	3 641	240	62 460	11.38	1.5
1983	3 890	249	68 460	12.37	1.6
1984	4 478	253	81 790	13.37	1.7
1985	5 290	268	100 770	15.06	1.9
1986	6 155	272	112 910	17.74	2.2
1987	7 244	274	130 880	20.36	2.5
1988	11 092	273	195 850	23.32	2.8
1989	12 538	278	231 520	26.74	3.1
1990	32 735	281	230 586	31.78	3.7
1991	44 527	280	271 356	34.28	3.9
1992	61 063	273	359 932	42.27	4.8
1993	97 062	277	532 118	63.91	7.2
1994	132 464	297	1 137 748	96.03	10.8
1995	187 195	300	1 522 493	135.61	15.2
1996	256 978	314	1 694 092	174.65	19.4
1997	342 848	328	1 945 020	207.82	23.1
1998	474 067	399	2 447 630	259.58	28.7
1999	567 242	470	2 761 633	329.30	36.2
2000	753 669	563	3 182 465	431.28	46.6
2001	702 206	543	3 645 600	511.57	56.0
2002	903 296	597	3 865 700	601.45	65.4
2003	1 157 060	619	4 024 500	761.91	82.3

注：邮电业务总量1990年以前为1980年不变价，1990年至2000年为1990年不变价，2001年开始为2000年不变价(下同)。

Note: The business value of post and telecommunications is calculated at 1980 constant prices before 1990, it is calculated at 1990 constant prices in 1990－2000, it has been calculated at 2000 constant prices since 2001(same as following next).

9－10 通信网络和设备能力情况

TELECOMMUNICATIONS NET AND FACILITY CAPABILITIES

指　　标　　Item	2001	2002	2003	2003 比 2002 年增长% Increase Rate in 2003 over 2002
一、通信网络情况				
Telecommunications Net				
邮电局所数(处)				
Number of Post & Telecommunications Office	543	597	619	3.7
邮路总长度(公里)				
Length of Postal Routes(km)	19 636	21 689	19 986	-7.9
长途电话业务电路(路)				
Number of Long－distance Telephones(line)	45 695	46 829	55 176	17.8
数据通信网长途电路(路)				
Digital Long－distance Communication(line)	12 366	14 556	12 795	-12.1
二、通信设备能力情况				
Facility Capabilities of Telecommunications				
邮政汽车(辆)				
Automobile for Post Bussiness(unit)	706	729	744	2.1
长途电话交换机容量(路端)				
Capacity of Long－Distance Telephone Exchanges(circuit)	81 000	90 000	265 427	194.9
局用电话交换机容量(万门)				
Capacity of Office Telephone Exchanges(10 000 lines)	364.6	386.6	402.5	4.1
移动电话交换机容量(万门)				
Capacity of Mobile Telephone Exchanges(10 000 subscribers)	287	357	515	44.3
无线寻呼系统容量(万户)				
Capacity of Pagering Service (10 000 subscribers)	154	155	155	
电话机(含移动)(万部)				
Telephone(Include Mobile)(10 000 subscribers)	511.6	601.5	761.9	26.7
三、长途电信线路				
Long－distance Telecommunications lines				
长途光缆线路长度(公里)				
Length of Optical Cable Line(km)	995.5	1 724.4	2 386.6	38.4
数字微波线路长度(公里)				
Length of Digital Microwave Line(km)	1 808.4	1 712.3	1 482	-13.4

注:根据专业制度规定,2003 年数据通信网长途电路数据的统计口径有较大调整。
Note:According to relative regulation,the statistical coverage of long－distance telecommunications lines is adjusted in 2003.

9-11 邮电业务量

POST AND TELECOMMUNICATIONS SERVICES

指 标	Item	2001	2002	2003	2003 比2002年 增长% Increase Rate in 2003 over 2002
一、邮电业务总量	**Business Value of Post and**				
(万元)	**Telecommunications(10 000 yuan)**	**702 206**	**903 296**	**1 157 060**	**28.1**
二、主要业务情况	**Main Business**				
函 件(万件)	Letters(10 000 pcs)	17 066.18	20 132.48	22 033.93	9.4
特快专递(万件)	Pieces of Express Mail Services(10 000 pcs)	254.34	287.67	321.50	11.8
订销报刊期发数	Number of Newspapers and Magazines				
(万份)	Subscibed (10 000 pcs)	222.39	407.90	314.07	-23.0
邮政储蓄收储余额	Balance of Deposit of Postal Services				
(亿元)	(100 million yuan)	90.43	100.70	117.47	16.7
集邮业务(万枚)	Philately(10 000 pcs)	7 446.22	6 690.45	6 793.54	1.5
长途电话(万次)	Long Distance Calls(10 000 times)	33 855.42	34 586.74	48 978.07	41.6
国内长途电话	Domestic	33 149.75	33 589.12	48 367.01	44.0
国际电话及港澳台电话	International and Hongkong, Macao & Taiwan	705.67	997.62	611.06	-38.7
无线寻呼年末用户	Number of Subscribers of Pagering Services				
(万户)	(10 000 subscribers)	52.2	26.2	9.84	-62.4
移动电话年末用户	Number of Mobile Telephone Subscribers				
(万户)	(10 000 subscribers)	214.48	306.40	383.31	25.1
本地电话年末用户	Number of Local Telephone Subscribers				
(万户)	(10 000 subscribers)	275.00	295.05	354.54	20.2
住宅电话年末用户	Number of Residential Telephone Subscribers				
(万户)	at Year-end(10 000 subscribers)	219.10	232.75	238.36	2.4
公用电话(万部)	Number of Public Telephone Sets(10 000 sets)	6.90	20.21	22.69	12.3
数字数据用户(户)	Digital and Data Users(subscriber)	7 677	7 781	7 690	-1.2
国际互联网络用户	Number of Subscriber of Internet				
(户)	Services (subscriber)	685 502	1 249 791	2 045 731	63.7

9－12 分地区邮电局所数

NUMBER OF POST AND TELECOMMUNICATIONS OFFICES BY REGION

单位:处　　(unit)

地　区	Region	2001	2002	2003
全　市	**Total**	**543**	**597**	**619**
一、市辖区	**Districts Under City Administration**	**431**	**500**	**483**
#市内六区	Six Urban Districts	189	231	199
滨海三区	Three Coastal Districts	99	100	107
和平区	Heping District	32	35	34
河东区	Hedong District	35	49	40
河西区	Hexi District	32	46	36
南开区	Nankai District	40	46	43
河北区	Hebei District	31	34	30
红桥区	Hongqiao District	19	21	16
塘沽区	Tanggu District	43	41	50
汉沽区	Hangu District	16	17	19
大港区	Dagang District	40	42	38
东丽区	Dongli District	15	22	18
西青区	Xiqing District	22	24	22
津南区	Jinnan District	15	19	22
北辰区	Beichen District	17	22	20
武清区	Wuqing District	37	41	54
宝坻区	Baodi District	37	41	41
二、市辖县	**Counties Under City Administration**	**112**	**97**	**136**
宁河县	Ninghe County	32	26	42
静海县	Jinghai County	46	32	51
蓟　县	Jixian County	34	39	43
每一局所服务面积	**Average Service Areas Per Office**			
(平方公里)	**(sq.km)**	**21.95**	**19.93**	**19.26**
每一局所服务人口	**Population Serviced Per Office**			
(万人)	**(10 000 persons)**	**1.68**	**1.54**	**1.50**

主要统计指标解释

货运量　指在一定时期内，以重量单位（吨）计算的由各种运输工具实际完成运送过程的货物数量。

货物周转量　指在一定时期内，由各种运输工具实际完成运送过程的以综合货物运量和运送距离的乘积之和。

客运量　指在一定时期内，各运输部门实际运送的旅客人数，计算单位为人。

旅客周转量　指在一定时期内，实际运送的旅客人数与其相应的旅客运输距离乘积之和。

港口货物吞吐量　又称港口吞吐量，指经由水路运进、出港区范围，并经过装卸的货物数量。按货物流向分为进港吞吐量和出港吞吐量；按货物的贸易性质分为内贸和外贸吞吐量；按货物的类别分，可根据现行的交通行业标准《运输货物分类和代码》分类。

邮电业务总量（又称通信业务总量）　指以货币形式表现的通信企业为社会提供各类通信服务的总和。是用于观察通信业务发展变化总趋势的综合性总量指标。根据专业性质分为邮政业务总量和电信业务总量。电信业务总量又可细分为本地网通信业务总量、长途通信业务总量、移动通信业务总量、数据通信业务总量、电报业务总量等。按通信范围可分为：国内通信业务总量、国际及港澳台通信业务总量。

Explanatory Notes on Main Statistical Indicators

Freight Traffic refers to the volume (tons) of freight transported with various traffic facilities.

Turnover Volume of Freight Traffic refers to the sum of the volume of transported cargo multiplying by the transport distance.

Passengers Traffic refers to the sum of the passengers transported in some time.

Turnover Volume of Passengers Traffic refers to the sum of the volume of transported passengers multiplied by the transport distance.

Ports Cargo Handled Capacity refers to the volume of cargo passing in and out the harbor area and having been loaded and unloaded. The volume of freight handled may be classified as in - port & out - port. It can also be classified as national trade and international trade by the attribute of trade or be classified by the classification of cargo according to the standard of traffic in use "The Classification and Code of Transported Cargo".

Business Volume of Post and Telecommunications (also called business volume of communications) refers to the total value of the information delivered and other posts and telecommunications services provided by the post and telecommunications departments for the customers. It is a comprehensive gross index to observe the trend of development and change of telecommunications services. It can be classified as post services and telecommunications services by major. Telecommunications services can also be classified as local communications service volume, communications service volume of long distance, mobile communications service volume, digital mobile communications service volume, telegraph service volume etc. It is classified as national communications service volume, Hongkong, Macao, Taiwan and international communications service volume by region.

第10篇 CHAPTER 10

批发零售贸易餐饮业

WHOLESALE, RETAIL TRADE AND CATERING SERVICES

10-1 改革开放以来社会消费品零售总额
TOTAL RETAIL SALES OF CONSUMER GOODS SINCE REFORM AND OPENING UP

单位：万元 (10 000 yuan)

年份 Year	社会消费品零售总额 Total Retail Sales of Consumer Goods	按经济类型分 Grouped by Ownership		
		国有 State-owned	集体 Collective-owned	其他 Others
1978	252 049	205 093	77 766	
1979	290 837	234 828	84 706	
1980	346 414	261 306	108 376	
1981-1985	2 387 235	1 648 044	783 599	
1981	380 427	274 209	127 149	
1982	397 624	291 871	126 895	
1983	446 277	314 208	143 543	
1984	521 738	365 178	168 653	
1985	641 169	402 578	217 359	
1986-1990	5 724 290	2 827 606	1 923 724	
1986	813 933	438 003	290 192	
1987	955 671	503 113	327 064	
1988	1 212 831	605 854	423 263	
1989	1 343 010	625 616	451 054	
1990	1 398 845	655 020	432 151	
1991-1995	12 470 655	3 749 330	2 369 270	
1991	1 594 432	748 758	454 722	
1992	1 811 969	612 502	423 681	775 786
1993	2 274 197	704 178	457 575	1 112 444
1994	3 033 695	788 098	480 306	1 765 291
1995	3 756 362	895 794	552 986	2 307 582
1996-2000	29 860 922	6 044 730	4 876 577	18 939 615
1996	4 700 449	1 156 852	998 016	2 545 581
1997	5 350 162	1 270 153	925 880	3 154 129
1998	5 871 198	1 157 102	948 726	3 765 370
1999	6 572 816	1 166 364	971 562	4 434 890
2000	7 366 297	1 294 259	1 032 393	5 039 645
2001	8 326 969	1 450 623	960 377	5 915 969
2002	9 413 642	1 562 192	922 553	6 928 897
2003(原口径)	10 740 504	1 748 882	981 688	8 009 934

注：1.1992年以前的经济类型和行业分组数为社会商品零售额。2.根据国家统计局规定，从2003年起社会消费品零售总额不包括"制造业"、"农业生产者"的零售额。本表2003年数据为原口径，新口径见10-3表。

Note: a)Before 1992, the figures grouped by ownership and sector refer to total retail sales of commodities. b)According to the institution of National Bureau of Statistics of China, total retail sales of consumer goods exclude those of manufacturing and agricultural producers. the figure in this table refer to original coverage, the figure calculated by new coverage is listed in table 10-3.

10－1 续表 1　Continued
单位:万元　(10 000 yuan)

年份 Year	按行业分 Grouped by Sector			
	批发零售贸易业 Wholesale and Retail Trade	餐饮业 Catering Trade	制造业 Manufacturing	其他行业 Others
1978	255 941	12 021	11 260	3 637
1979	287 271	13 868	14 523	3 904
1980	322 555	15 566	24 080	7 747
1981－1985	2 144 085	107 938	214 081	53 672
1981	345 396	16 406	32 812	8 393
1982	359 353	17 180	36 327	10 097
1983	401 918	18 332	40 934	10 080
1984	470 288	25 143	47 214	11 042
1985	567 130	30 877	56 794	14 060
1986－1990	5 040 424	323 508	417 356	86 700
1986	720 674	41 973	64 308	18 577
1987	844 202	49 616	73 747	23 607
1988	1 077 290	62 589	92 650	19 893
1989	1 171 777	79 188	105 855	15 681
1990	1 226 481	90 142	80 796	8 942
1991－1995	8 998 662	853 651	535 286	2 180 534
1991	1 377 565	113 262	69 741	131 342
1992	1 422 957	125 997	74 653	188 362
1993	1 738 624	145 885	94 755	294 933
1994	2 087 661	210 081	113 927	622 026
1995	2 371 855	258 426	182 210	943 871
1996－2000	16 182 475	2 864 063	1 250 000	9 564 384
1996	2 671 350	364 726	187 451	1 476 922
1997	2 952 633	461 368	213 828	1 722 333
1998	3 260 718	573 401	266 505	1 770 574
1999	3 505 923	674 279	271 828	2 120 786
2000	3 791 851	790 289	310 388	2 473 769
2001	4 417 948	910 487	340 395	2 658 139
2002	5 146 671	1 025 749	396 490	2 844 732
2003(原口径)	5 863 677	1 099 120	440 867	3 336 840

10－1 续表 2　Continued
单位:万元　(10 000 yuan)

年份 Year	按类别分 Grouped by Sort			
	吃 Food	穿 Clothing	用 Used Articles	烧 Fuel
1978	121 373	50 620	71 045	9 011
1979	134 289	60 715	86 718	9 115
1980	151 791	76 209	108 894	9 520
1981－1985	999 626	444 598	882 614	60 397
1981	162 955	82 161	125 225	10 086
1982	172 521	76 785	137 668	10 650
1983	189 395	86 021	159 640	11 221
1984	223 179	86 396	199 238	12 925
1985	251 576	113 235	260 843	15 515
1986－1990	2 227 297	1 022 321	2 380 713	93 959
1986	317 896	150 212	329 515	16 310
1987	372 388	170 854	396 448	15 981
1988	443 703	225 913	521 879	21 336
1989	534 771	234 834	554 567	18 838
1990	558 539	240 508	578 304	21 494
1991－1995	5 263 703	2 109 623	4 843 225	254 104
1991	662 047	276 846	626 243	29 296
1992	748 510	305 706	711 774	45 979
1993	869 432	400 857	946 526	57 382
1994	1 292 145	499 044	1 187 194	55 312
1995	1 691 569	627 170	1 371 488	66 135
1996－2000	12 433 054	4 934 713	12 108 211	384 944
1996	2 057 810	763 542	1 799 534	79 563
1997	2 258 422	865 522	2 137 253	88 965
1998	2 373 175	959 281	2 459 573	79 169
1999	2 733 574	1 123 695	2 646 514	69 033
2000	3 010 073	1 222 673	3 065 337	68 214
2001	3 343 257	1 392 390	3 469 838	121 484
2002	3 736 466	1 593 133	3 932 004	152 039
2003(原口径)	3 956 971	1 861 831	4 750 103	171 599

10－2 改革开放以来社会消费品零售总额增长速度

INCREASE RATE OF TOTAL RETAIL SALES OF CONSUMER GOODS SINCE REFORM AND OPENING UP

单位：%　　(%)

年份 Year	社会消费品零售总额增长速度 Increase Rate of Total Retail Sales of Consumer Goods	吃 Food	穿 Clothing	用 Used Articles	烧 Fuel	社会消费品零售总额扣除物价增长速度 Increase Rate After Deducting Price Factor
1978	6.7	8.1	8.3	4.7	-3.9	6.7
1979	15.4	10.6	19.9	22.1	1.2	14.1
1980	19.1	13.0	25.5	25.6	4.4	12.9
1981-1985	13.1	10.6	8.2	19.1	10.3	9.3
1981	9.8	7.4	7.8	15.0	5.9	8.2
1982	4.5	5.9	-6.5	9.9	5.6	4.0
1983	12.2	9.8	12.0	16.0	5.4	11.6
1984	16.9	17.8	0.4	24.8	15.2	14.8
1985	22.9	12.7	31.1	30.9	20.0	7.9
1986-1990	16.9	17.3	16.3	17.3	6.7	6.5
1986	26.9	26.4	32.7	26.3	5.1	18.4
1987	17.4	17.1	13.7	20.3	-2.0	9.8
1988	26.9	19.2	32.2	31.6	33.5	7.8
1989	10.7	20.5	3.9	6.3	-11.7	-3.8
1990	4.2	4.4	2.4	4.3	14.1	1.5
1991-1995	21.8	24.8	21.1	18.9	25.2	9.2
1991	14.0	18.5	15.1	8.3	36.3	5.6
1992	13.6	13.1	10.4	13.7	56.9	3.8
1993	25.5	16.2	31.1	33.0	24.8	9.8
1994	33.4	48.6	24.5	25.4	-3.6	15.4
1995	23.8	30.9	25.7	15.5	19.6	11.9
1996-2000	14.4	12.2	14.3	17.5	0.6	14.9
1996	25.1	21.7	21.7	31.2	20.3	19.0
1997	13.8	9.7	13.4	18.8	11.8	13.0
1998	10.2	4.3	10.8	15.9	-11.0	14.1
1999	12.0	15.2	17.1	7.6	-12.8	14.8
2000	12.1	10.1	8.8	15.8	-1.2	13.7
2001	13.0	11.1	13.9	13.2	78.1	14.6
2002	13.1	11.8	14.4	13.3	25.2	16.1
2003(原口径)	14.1	5.9	16.9	20.8	12.9	17.1

10－3 社会消费品零售总额
TOTAL RETAIL SALES OF CONSUMER GOODS

指 标	Item	2002	2003	2003 比2002年增长% Increase Rate in 2003 over 2002
社会消费品零售总额	**Total Retail Sales of Consumer Goods**	**8 317 506**	**9 222 673**	**10.9**
一、按销售地区分	**Grouped by Region**			
市	City	7 768 277	8 591 908	10.6
县	County	294 484	352 577	19.7
县以下	Under County Level	254 745	278 188	9.2
二、按行业分	**Grouped by Sector**			
批发零售贸易业	Wholesale and Retail Trade	6 460 596	7 271 020	12.5
餐饮业	Catering Trade	1 025 749	1 099 120	7.2
其他行业	Others	831 161	852 533	2.6

注：本表数据已调整为新口径。
Note：The data of this table have been adjusted to the new coverage of statistics.

10－4 按新国民经济行业分批发零售贸易业商品销售总额（2003年）
TOTAL SALES OF WHOLESALE AND RETAIL TRADE BY NEW SECTOR，2003

单位：万元 (10 000 yuan)

项 目	Item	商品销售总额 Total Sales	#批发 Wholesale
总计	**Total**	**24 700 204**	**17 429 183**
批发业	**Wholesale Trade**	**18 904 583**	**17 009 307**
农畜产品批发	Farm & Livestock Products	169 760	168 765
食品、饮料及烟草制品批发	Food，Beverage and Tobacco	1 526 998	897 084
纺织、服装及日用品批发	Textile，Garments and Daily Articles	991 141	775 282
文化、体育用品及器材批发	Cultural and Sports Goods & Equipment	220 786	214 746
医药及医疗器械批发	Medicine and Medical Appliance	951 436	715 760
矿产品、建材及化工产品批发	Mineral Products，Building Material and Chemical Products	10 934 784	10 788 866
机械设备、五金交电及电子产品批发	Machinery Equipment，Hardware，Transport，Electric and Electronic Products	3 180 340	2 954 271
其他批发	Others	929 339	494 533
零售业	**Retail Trade**	**5 795 621**	**419 876**
综合零售	Comprehensive Retail	2 573 689	291 447
食品、饮料及烟草制品专门零售	Special Retail of Food，Beverage and Tobacco	1 029 561	11 643
纺织、服装及日用品专门零售	Special Retail of Textile，Garments and Daily Articles	220 878	39 818
文化、体育用品及器材专门零售	Special Retail of Cultural and Sports Goods & Equipment	70 176	2 041
医药及医疗器械专门零售	Special Retail of Medicine and Medical Appliance	11 704	4 539
汽车、摩托车、燃料及零配件专门零售	Special Retail of Motor Vehicles，Motorcycles，Parts and fuel	160 065	36 981
家用电器及电子产品专门零售	Special Retail of Household Appliances and Electronic Products	227 212	13 445
五金、家具及室内装修材料专门零售	Special Retail of Hardware，Furniture and Decoration Materials for Indoors	245 358	6 284
无店铺及其他零售	Have no Stores and Other Retail	1 256 977	13 677

注：本表行业分类为国标GB/T4754－2002标准。10－5、10－8表同。
Note：Sector listed in this table is classified by the standard of GB/T4754－2002. same as following table 10－5 and 10－8.

10－5 按新国民经济行业分批发零售贸易业商品购销存总额（2003 年）
TOTAL PURCHASES,SALES AND INVENTORY OF WHOLESALE AND RETAIL TRADE ABOVE DESIGNATED SIZE BY NEW SECTOR,2003
（限额以上批发零售贸易业）

单位：万元 (10 000 yuan)

项 目 Item	商品购进总额 Total Goods Purchases	#生产者 Prod－ucers	#进 口 Imports	商品销售总额 Total Sales	#批 发 Whole－sale	年末库存总额 Inventory (year－end)
总 计 Total	**18 581 946**	**11 514 152**	**928 121**	**19 150 523**	**16 788 626**	**1 079 329**
批发业 Wholesale Trade	**16 612 517**	**10 633 932**	**927 339**	**16 972 169**	**16 397 447**	**910 592**
农畜产品批发 Farm & Livestock Products	144 939	75 803	7 157	169 760	168 765	102 446
食品、饮料及烟草制品批发 Food,Beverage and Tobacco	555 823	254 841	53 239	619 923	609 877	51 188
纺织、服装及日用品批发 Textile,Garments and Daily Articles	672 582	429 005	77 065	693 550	681 056	44 433
文化、体育用品及器材批发 Cultural and Sports Goods & Equipment	198 337	151 070	5 904	220 786	214 746	18 163
医药及医疗器械批发 Medicine and Medical Appliance	1 040 227	457 912	55 654	951 436	715 760	91 285
矿产品、建材及化工产品批发 Mineral Products,Building Material and Chemical Products	10 679 926	7 740 071	197 803	10 934 784	10 788 866	286 154
机械设备、五金交电及电子产品批发 Machinery Equipment,Hardware ,Transport,Electric and Electronic Products	3 043 795	1 435 850	497 104	3 080 820	2 922 760	271 401
其他批发 Others	276 890	89 380	33 412	301 111	295 617	45 523
零售业 Retail Trade	**1 969 429**	**880 221**	**782**	**2 178 354**	**391 179**	**168 736**
综合零售 Comprehensive Retail	1 278 282	523 167		1 488 509	282 838	88 744
食品、饮料及烟草制品专门零售 Special Retail of Food,Beverage and Tobacco	42 509	14 520	780	56 517	3 924	7 935
纺织、服装及日用品专门零售 Special Retail of Textile,Garments and Daily Articles	111 371	79 161		94 997	38 819	12 656
文化、体育用品及器材专门零售 Special Retail of Cultural and Sports Goods & Equipment	65 784	16 800	3	70 176	2 041	15 388
医药及医疗器械专门零售 Special Retail of Medicine and Medical Appliance	10 748	2 425		11 704	4 539	9 968
汽车、摩托车、燃料及零配件专门零售 Special Retail of Motor Vehicles,Motorcycles,Parts and fuel	148 576	37 492		160 065	36 981	5 513
家用电器及电子产品专门零售 Special Retail of Household Appliances and Electronic Products	247 468	152 769		227 212	13 445	18 288
五金、家具及室内装修材料专门零售 Special Retail of Hardware,Furniture and Decoration Materials for Indoors	56 705	48 587		59 069	4 806	8 704
无店铺及其他零售 Have no Stores and Other Retail	7 985	5 302		10 105	3 785	1 539

注：限额标准见本篇末附表（下同）。
Note:Standard of designated size can be gotten from added table on the end of this chapter(same to next).

10－6 限额以上批发零售贸易业商品购进总额
TOTAL PURCHASES OF WHOLESALE AND RETAIL TRADE ABOVE DESIGNATED SIZE

单位：万元 (10 000 yuan)

项目 Item	商品购进总额 Total Goods Purchases		#从生产者购进 From Producers		#进口 Imports	
	2002	2003	2002	2003	2002	2003
总计 Total	**13 566 808**	**18 581 946**	**9 210 555**	**11 514 152**	**572 698**	**928 121**
在总计中：国有及国有控股企业 In the Total: State－owned and State－holding Enterprises	9 890 088	13 691 114	7 398 882	9 688 700	340 646	542 180
一、按登记注册类型分 Grouped by Registered Type						
内资企业 Domestic－funded Enterprises	12 575 185	17 019 881	8 926 121	11 208 338	397 004	597 421
#国有企业 State－owned Enterprises	6 707 835	8 927 254	5 117 187	6 750 766	245 659	301 576
集体企业 Collective－owned Enterprises	741 739	947 187	303 701	388 018	3 660	11 728
股份合作企业 Cooperative Enterprises	86 317	77 861	35 046	42 605		
私营 Private Economy	651 415	1 351 041	373 466	560 928	9 606	41 753
股份有限公司 Share－holding Corporations Ltd.	1 130 189	1 540 329	755 016	414 937	12 736	45 151
有限责任公司 Limited Liability Corporations	2 671 834	3 154 758	1 836 392	2 066 343	125 343	197 213
#国有独资 Sole State－funded Corporations	827 615	424 495	759 357	262 851	44 174	102 943
联营经济 Joint Ownership Enterprises	578 015	1 019 482	505 314	984 740		
#国有与国有联营企业 State Joint Ownership Enterprises	510 458	985 964	466 000	956 614		
港澳台商投资企业 Enterprises with Investment from Hongkong, Macao and Taiwan	151 858	353 437	22 002	93 277	61 087	160 403
外商投资企业 Foreign Funded Enterprises	839 765	1 208 628	262 432	212 537	114 607	170 297
二、按经济类型分 Grouped by Ownership						
国有经济 State－owned	8 045 908	10 337 713	6 342 544	7 970 231	289 833	404 518
集体经济 Collective－owned	841 503	1 025 048	338 747	430 624	3 660	11 728
私有经济 Private and Individual	651 415	1 351 041	373 466	560 928	9 606	41 753
港澳台商投资经济 Hongkong, Macao and Taiwan Funded	151 858	353 437	22 002	93 277	61 087	160 403
外商投资经济 Foreign Funded	839 765	1 208 628	262 432	212 537	114 607	170 297
其他 Others	3 036 359	4 306 080	1 871 364	2 246 555	93 905	139 422
三、按国民经济行业分 Grouped by Sector						
食品饮料烟草和家庭用品批发业 Wholesale of Food, Beverage, Tobacco and Family Articles Goods	**2 337 844**	**3 023 372**	**1 246 475**	**1 501 067**	**138 880**	**199 769**
食品、饮料、烟草批发业 Food, Beverage and Tobacco	612 061	715 867	271 551	290 540	33 502	68 632
棉、麻、土畜产品批发业 Cotton, Flax, Local Animal Products	63 227	46 459	20 503	27 545	4 009	4 626
纺织品、服装和鞋帽批发业 Textile, Garments Shoes and Hats	344 379	544 573	275 784	396 255	28 194	64 440

注：本表行业分类为国标 GB/T4754－1994 标准，10－7 表同。
Note: Setcor listed in this table is classified by the standard of GB/T4754－1994, same as following table 10－7.

10－6 续表　Continued

单位：万元　　　　(10 000 yuan)

项　目 Item	商品购进总额 TotalGoods Purchases		#从生产者购进 From Producers		#进　口 Imports	
	2002	2003	2002	2003	2002	2003
日用百货批发业 Daily Used Goods	301 755	264 252	188 778	184 077	17 609	6 056
日用杂品批发业 Grocery						
五金、交电、化工批发业 Hardware, Electrical Appliance and Chemical Products	374 923	422 718	132 009	144 703	23 610	2 356
药品及医疗器械批发业 Medicine and Medical Appliance	641 499	1 029 503	357 851	457 947	31 957	53 661
能源、材料和机械电子设备批发业 Wholesale of Energy, Materials, Machinery and Electronic Equipment	**8 873 716**	**12 345 210**	**6 842 958**	**8 699 226**	**352 314**	**653 752**
能源批发业 Energy	3 965 353	5 270 817	3 490 677	3 843 790		
化工材料批发业 Chemical Materials	510 086	591 818	291 891	105 194	59 522	144 564
木材批发业 Timber	23 876	84 548	11 317	33 340		442
建筑材料批发业 Building Materials	49 596	87 999	31 403	19 722	3 935	
矿产品批发业 Mineral Products						
金属材料批发业 Metal Materials	2 683 126	4 142 944	2 011 288	3 551 830	40 655	55 826
机械、电子设备批发业 Machinery and Electronic Equipments	497 345	830 168	296 051	344 001	101 895	173 838
汽车、摩托车及零配件批发业 Motor Vehicles, Motorcycles and Related Spares and Fittings	1 070 107	1 223 743	684 700	761 748	144 129	275 743
再生物资回收批发业 Recovery of Reclaimed Materials	74 228	113 174	25 631	39 602	2 178	3 339
其他批发业 Others	**509 227**	**587 390**	**187 731**	**247 152**	**77 008**	**57 718**
工艺美术品批发业 Handicrafts	19 785	17 427	13 625	11 218		
图书报刊批发业 Books, Newspapers and Magazines	59 835	61 244	42 321	42 496		
农业生产资料批发业 Agricultural Production Materials	176 893	257 272	81 857	98 035	28 039	3 029
其他类未包括的批发业 Others	252 714	251 448	49 928	95 402	48 969	54 689
零售业 Retail Trade	**1 846 021**	**2 625 975**	**933 391**	**1 066 707**	**4 496**	**16 883**
食品、饮料和烟草零售业 Food, Beverage and Tobacco	109 756	68 946	17 054	15 755		
日用百货零售业 Daily Used Goods	1 044 986	1 241 547	477 359	511 864	240	3
纺织品、服装和鞋帽零售业 Textile, Garments, Shoes and Hats	87 491	180 870	54 632	115 718		
日用杂品零售业 Grocery	2 824	1 888	1 551	731		780
五金、交电、化工零售业 Handware, Electrical Appliance and Chemical Products	181 468	380 758	141 572	180 088	4 233	2 406
药品及医疗器械零售业 Medicine and Medical Appliance	6 523	17 419	965	1 916	23	
图书报刊零售业 Books, Newspapers and Magazines	53 533	50 047	16 211	11 446		
其他零售业 Others	359 440	684 499	224 047	229 190		13 695

10－7 限额以上批发零售贸易业商品销售和库存总额

TOTAL SALES AND INVENTORY OF WHOLESALE AND RETAIL TRADE ABOVE DESIGNATED SIZE

单位：万元 (10 000 yuan)

项目 Item	商品销售总额 Total Sales		#批发 Wholesale		年末库存总额 Inventory(year－end)	
	2002	2003	2002	2003	2002	2003
总计 Total	**14 383 322**	**19 150 523**	**12 155 554**	**16 788 626**	**1 058 678**	**1 079 329**
在总计中：国有及国有控股企业 of the Total：State－owned and State－holding Enterprises	10 576 213	14 217 501	9 545 673	13 051 566	708 637	718 059
一、按登记注册类型分 Grouped by Registered Type						
#内资企业 Domestic－funded Enterprises	13 343 573	17 508 877	11 493 273	15 504 633	939 306	931 587
国有企业 State－owned Enterprises	7 096 275	9 338 951	6 673 094	8 932 172	404 998	379 007
集体企业 Collective－owned Enterprises	781 603	968 972	541 562	828 719	92 847	77 523
股份合作企业 Cooperative Enterprises	93 057	90 154	72 193	56 886	11 626	9 103
私营 Private Economy	662 286	1 306 433	439 465	907 289	49 012	81 163
股份有限公司 Share－holding Corporations Ltd	1 231 387	1 433 552	783 620	1 055 798	84 297	109 020
有限责任公司 Limited Liability Corporations	2 857 907	3 331 104	2 374 450	2 708 582	256 309	215 689
#国有独资 Sole State－funded Corporations	916 017	471 534	903 379	458 182	127 194	62 311
联营企业 Joint Ownership Enterprises	597 735	1 037 768	585 567	1 013 246	37 849	59 987
#国有与国有联营企业 State Joint Ownership Enterprises	526 545	1 002 771	520 223	978 830	33 343	58 269
港澳台商投资企业 Enterprises with Investment from Hongkong，Macao and Taiwan	175 576	337 285	60 499	258 962	22 060	50 901
外商投资企业 Foreign Funded Enterprises	864 173	1 304 361	601 782	1 025 031	97 312	96 841
二、按经济类型分 Grouped by Ownership						
国有经济 State－owned	8 538 838	10 813 256	8 096 697	10 369 184	565 535	499 587
集体经济 Collective－owned	888 413	1 059 126	622 155	885 604	104 472	86 625
私有经济 Private and Individual	662 286	1 306 433	439 465	907 289	49 012	81 163
港澳台商投资经济 Hongkong，Macao and Taiwan	175 576	337 285	60 499	258 962	22 060	50 901
外商投资经济 Foreign Funded	864 173	1 304 361	601 782	1 025 031	97 312	96 841
其他 Others	3 254 037	4 330 062	2 334 956	3 342 556	220 287	264 211
三、按国民经济行业分 Grouped by Sector						
食品饮料烟草和家庭用品批发业 Wholesale of Food，Beverage，Tobacco and Family Articles Goods	**2 626 452**	**3 052 288**	**2 374 266**	**2 796 331**	**385 270**	**355 662**
食品、饮料、烟草批发业 Food，Beverage and Tobacco	712 846	788 232	704 153	779 131	190 326	171 941
棉、麻、土畜产品批发业 Cotton，Flax，Local Animal Product	73 591	66 756	72 185	66 637	9 599	10 130
纺织品、服装和鞋帽批发业 Textile，Garments Shoes and Hats	397 019	544 794	393 900	544 687	58 756	37 401

10－7 续表 Continued
单位:万元 (10 000 yuan)

项目 Item	商品销售总额 Total Sales		#批发 Wholesale		年末库存总额 Inventory(year－end)	
	2002	2003	2002	2003	2002	2003
日用百货批发业 Daily Used Goods	331 523	286 357	310 772	270 862	25 075	16 514
日用杂品批发业 Grocery						
五金、交电、化工批发业 Hardware,Electrical Appliance and Chemical Products	399 170	427 128	380 347	419 831	31 346	29 896
药品及医疗器械批发业 Medicine and Medical Appliance	712 304	939 021	512 908	715 184	70 168	89 779
能源、材料和机械电子设备批发业 Wholesale of Energy,Materials, Machinery and Electronic Equipments	**9 139 478**	**12 685 454**	**8 841 200**	**12 461 747**	**432 960**	**466 574**
能源批发业 Energy	4 182 545	5 548 711	4 132 202	5 474 958	42 236	36 443
化工材料批发业 Chemical Materials	507 504	594 498	495 811	589 285	28 254	19 075
木材批发业 Timber	24 490	83 833	24 490	83 833	283	1 261
建筑材料批发业 Building Materials	53 902	87 123	35 951	85 887	6 005	7 213
矿产品批发业 Mineral Products						
金属材料批发业 Metal Materials	2 737 151	4 153 122	2 681 922	4 143 269	134 464	225 572
机械、电子设备批发业 Machinery and Electronic Equipments	570 984	919 589	549 850	885 821	68 286	82 835
汽车、摩托车及零配件批发业 Motor Vehicles,Motorcycles and Related Spares and Fittings	986 709	1 179 903	845 579	1 080 544	146 746	85 847
再生物资回收批发业 Recovery of Reclaimed Materials	76 194	118 674	75 396	118 152	6 686	8 328
其他批发业 Others	**530 404**	**644 065**	**480 779**	**633 427**	**44 401**	**52 706**
工艺美术品批发业 Handicrafts	38 871	38 970	38 871	38 970	3 502	412
图书报刊批发业 Books,Newspapers and Magazines	56 882	66 721	40 696	63 329	9 104	9 549
农业生产资料批发业 Agricultural Production Materials	179 745	264 032	178 842	262 415	18 115	21 862
其他类未包括的批发业 Others	254 906	274 342	222 370	268 713	13 680	20 883
零售业 Retail Trade	**2 086 989**	**2 768 716**	**459 309**	**897 121**	**196 047**	**204 386**
食品、饮料和烟草零售业 Food,Beverage and Tobacco	118 737	90 709	24 878	27 254	16 360	15 771
日用百货零售业 Daily Used Goods	1 215 315	1 450 541	248 914	301 428	98 081	93 306
纺织品、服装和鞋帽零售业 Textile,Garments,Shoes and Hats	108 965	168 754	13 717	38 013	8 801	12 380
日用杂品零售业 Grocery	3 495	2 492	1 651	979	1 134	950
五金、交电、化工零售业 Handware,Electrical Appliance and Chemical Products	180 309	298 217	37 538	121 709	27 699	22 079
药品及医疗器械零售业 Medicine and Medical Appliance	7 976	18 560	3 096	5 191	2 350	10 529
图书报刊零售业 Books,Newspapers and Magazines	51 719	50 223	1 061	1 083	10 097	9 317
其他零售业 Others	400 475	689 221	128 454	401 465	31 526	40 054

10－8　限额以上国有及国有控股批发零售贸易业主要指标(2003 年)

MAIN INDICATORS OF STATE－OWNED & STATE－HOLDING WHOLESALE AND RETAIL TRADE ABOVE DESIGNATED SIZE,2003

项　目 Item	机　构 (个) Organization (unit)	商品购进 总　额 Total Purchases (万元) (10 000 yuan)	商品销售 总　额 Total Sales (万元) (10 000 yuan)
总　计 **Total**	**347**	**13 691 114**	**14 217 501**
批发业 **Wholesale Trade**	**245**	**12 823 542**	**13 164 269**
农畜产品批发 Farm & Livestock Products	16	104 033	129 564
食品、饮料及烟草制品批发 Food,Beverage and Tobacco	34	402 177	458 363
纺织、服装及日用品批发 Textile,Garments and Daily Articles	26	599 144	616 759
文化、体育用品及器材批发 Cultural and Sports Goods & Equipment	11	133 580	146 990
医药及医疗器械批发 Medicine and Medical Appliance	18	917 634	797 098
矿产品、建材及化工产品批发 Mineral Products,Building Material and Chemical Products	80	8 703 765	9 008 805
机械设备、五金交电及、电子产品批发 Machinery Equipment,Hardware,Transport ,Electri and Electronic Products	49	1 830 971	1 853 885
其他批发 Others	11	132 238	152 805
零售业 **Retail Trade**	**102**	**867 572**	**1 053 232**
综合零售 Comprehensive Retail	26	682 634	849 156
食品、饮料及烟草制品专门零售 Special Retail of Food,Beverage and Tobacco	19	10 845	14 954
纺织、服装及日用品专门零售 Special Retail of Textile,Garments and Daily Articles	5	28 184	31 871
文化、体育用品及器材专门零售 Special Retail of Cultural and Sports Goods & Equipment	30	62 081	66 349
医药及医疗器械专门零售 Special Retail of Medicine and Medical Appliance	2	5 218	5 840
汽车、摩托车、燃料及零配件专门零售 Special Retail of Motor Vehicles,Motorcycles, Parts and fuel	9	74 835	80 268
家用电器及电子产品专门零售 Special Retail of Household Appliances and Electronic Products			
五金、家具及室内装修材料专门零售 Special Retail of Hardware,Furniture and Decoration Materials for Indoors	5	765	1 264
无店铺及其他零售 Have no Stores and Other Retail	6	3 011	3 531

10-9 限额以上批发零售贸易业主要商品销售数量(2003年)

SALES OF MAIN COMMODITIES IN WHOLESALE AND RETAIL TRADE ABOVE DESIGNATED SIZE,2003

品名		Item		销售合计 Total Sales	批发 Wholesale	零售 Retail
粮食	(吨)	Grain	(ton)	477 204	435 804	41 400
食用植物油	(吨)	Edible Vegetable Oil	(ton)	264 809	232 637	32 172
食糖	(吨)	Sugar	(ton)	63 146	56 823	6 323
卷烟	(万支)	Tobacco	(10000)	1 762 614	1 624 666	137 948
酒	(吨)	Liquor	(ton)	17 017	9 598	7 419
棉花	(吨)	Cotton	(ton)	63 834	63 834	
布	(百米)	Cloth	(100 meters)	786 135	775 348	10 787
各种服装	(百件)	Garment	(100 pieces)	1 777 184	1 399 224	377 960
鞋	(百双)	Shoes	(100 pairs)	94 420	41 869	52 551
照相机	(架)	Cameras	(set)	49 454	1 758	47 696
电视机	(台)	Television Sets	(set)	520 065	226 832	293 233
组合音响	(台)	Stereo System	(set)	33 357	2 814	30 543
摄像机	(台)	Video Camera	(set)	13 486	718	12 768
录像机	(台)	Video Recorders	(set)	339	25	314
影碟机	(台)	VCD Players	(set)	202 112	5 742	196 370
家用电冰箱	(台)	Refrigerators	(set)	486 956	311 011	175 945
家用洗衣机	(台)	Washing Machines	(set)	230 014	48 377	181 637
房间空调器	(台)	Air-conditioners	(set)	627 588	395 909	231 679
电暖器	(台)	Electric Warmers	(set)	65 258	936	64 322
淋浴器	(台)	Shower	(set)	129 875	1 474	128 401
家用电风扇	(台)	Electric Fans	(set)	215 055	127 324	87 731
微波炉	(台)	Microwave Ovens	(set)	364 251	183 646	180 605
自行车	(辆)	Bicycles	(set)	526 563	447 807	78 756
微型计算机	(台)	Micro computers	(set)	185 121	131 353	53 768
普通电话机	(部)	Telephone Sets	(set)	986 096	26 800	959 296
移动电话机	(部)	Mobile Telephone Sets	(set)	2 012 472	1 351 808	660 664
化学肥料	(吨)	Chemical Fertilizers	(ton)	522 742	522 742	
化学农药	(吨)	Chemical Pesticide	(ton)	7 699	7 699	
农用薄膜	(吨)	Agricultural Film	(ton)	1 596	1 596	
煤炭	(吨)	Coal	(ton)	5 214 570	4 977 169	237 401
木材	(立方米)	Timber	(cu.m)	37 765	37 765	
汽油	(吨)	Gasoline	(ton)	6 037 184	5 847 372	189 812
煤油	(吨)	Kerosene	(ton)	788 778	788 775	3
柴油	(吨)	Diesel Oil	(ton)	9 825 101	9 757 615	67 486
硫酸	(吨)	Sulphuric Acid	(ton)	158 200	158 200	
纯碱	(吨)	Soda	(ton)	6 679	6 674	5
烧碱	(吨)	Ashcaustic Soda	(ton)	15 859	15 855	4
橡胶	(吨)	Rubber	(ton)	1 156 228	1 156 228	
钢材	(吨)	Steel Products	(ton)	11 856 881	11 830 716	26 165
铜	(吨)	Copper	(ton)	11 693	11 693	
铝	(吨)	Aluminum	(ton)	19 609	19 609	
铜材	(吨)	Copper Products	(ton)	34 458	34 458	
铝材	(吨)	Aluminum Products	(ton)	14 098	14 098	
水泥	(吨)	Cement	(ton)	387 894	387 894	
汽车	(辆)	Motor Vehicles	(set)	187 047	163 100	23 947
#轿车	(辆)	Motor Vehicles	(set)	165 903	148 435	17 468
摩托车	(辆)	Motorcycles	(set)	5 853	49	5 804
拖拉机	(台)	Tractors	(set)	1 000	1 000	

10－10 限额以上批发零售贸易业财务状况(2003年)

FINANCIAL STATUS OF WHOLESALE AND RETAIL TRADE ABOVE DESIGNATED SIZE,2003

单位:万元 (10 000 yuan)

指　标	Item	合　计 Total	#国有经济 State－owned	#集体经济 Collective－owned
一、资产负债	Total Assets and Liabilities			
资产合计	Total Assets	7 029 858.0	3 634 572.1	409 577.4
#流动资产年末合计	Total Circulating Assets(year－end)	5 300 147.7	2 822 615.1	325 517.0
#存　货	Inventory	1 048 146.9	542 837.1	82 239.0
固定资产合计	Total Fixed Assets	1 044 249.2	547 686.4	52 195.8
固定资产原值	Original Value of Fixed Assets	1 168 481.5	637 635.5	57 616.4
#生产经营用	For Production	711 611.3	374 158.2	31 564.6
累计折旧	Accumulative Depreciation	281 849.8	160 863.7	18 683.2
#本年折旧	Occured in 2003	48 986.7	20 453.3	3 505.2
负债合计	Total Liabilities	5 531 830.8	3 077 107.6	304 353.8
流动负债合计	Total Circulating Liabilities	4 831 793.0	2 580 623.7	284 069.3
长期负债合计	Total Long－term Liabilities	520 369.4	345 508.2	11 432.4
所有者权益合计	Ownership Interest	1 498 027.2	557 464.5	105 223.6
#实收资本	Proceeds of Capital	1 575 780.2	788 020.0	62 897.0
#国家资本	State－owned	514 030.8	314 907.1	4 272.5
集体资本	Collective－owned	57 418.8	2 412.1	35 746.6
港澳台商资本	Hongkong,Macao and Taiwan	40 964.0	62.3	
外商资本	Foreign	77 689.6		
二、损益及分配	Profit,Loss and Distribution			
商品销售收入	Sales Revenue	16 053 329.6	9 034 208.2	984 763.4
商品销售收入净额	Net Value of Sales Revenue	16 034 423.2	9 027 556.8	981 752.6
商品销售成本	Sales Cost	15 229 857.0	8 665 084.3	936 642.8
经营费用	Operating Expense	467 585.8	182 513.9	24 035.2
商品销售税金及附加	Sales Tax and Extra Charges	11 650.5	6 008.2	916.4
商品销售利润	Sales Profits	325 329.9	173 950.4	20 158.2
代购代销收入	Revenue from Agency Activity	11 699.3	10 785.2	－42.0
主营业务利润	Profits of Major Business	337 029.2	184 735.6	20 116.2
其他业务利润	Profits of Other Business	85 293.3	21 438.8	4 122.9
管理费用	Overhead Expenses	258 528.3	110 754.1	15 765.8
财务费用	Financial Expenses	77 058.3	44 921.7	2 616.5
营业利润	Operating Profits	131 148.5	49 573.6	5 743.5
利润总额	Total Profits	151 995.2	71 445.9	6 950.1

10－11 限额以上批发贸易业财务状况(2003 年)
FINANCIAL STATUS OF WHOLESALE ABOVE DESIGNATED SIZE,2003

单位:万元 (10 000 yuan)

指标	Item	合计 Total	#国有经济 State－owned	#集体经济 Collective－owned
一、资产负债	**Total Assets and Liabilities**			
资产合计	Total Assets	5 523 550.8	3 340 786.4	328 432.1
#流动资产年末合计	Total Circulating Assets(year－end)	4 498 223.3	2 626 120.5	276 640.1
#存货	Inventory	898 570.8	515 731.6	71 246.8
固定资产合计	Total Fixed Assets	595 896.9	463 818.3	28 022.0
固定资产原值	Original Value of Fixed Assets	692 212.9	527 699.0	39 667.7
#生产经营用	For Production	412 047.4	318 960.0	20 332.0
累计折旧	Accumulative Depreciation	177 396.2	132 451.3	14 079.0
#本年折旧	Occured in 2003	28 110.8	16 604.9	3 112.2
负债合计	Total Liabilities	4 501 094.7	2 841 687.9	250 737.3
流动负债合计	Total Circulating Liabilities	3 927 945.5	2 378 254.6	241 298.1
长期负债合计	Total Long－term Liabilities	426 601.3	339 457.7	6 278.4
所有者权益合计	Ownership Interest	1 022 456.1	499 098.5	77 694.8
#实收资本	Proceeds of Capital	1 161 554.6	742 533.5	45 194.1
#国家资本	State－owned	346 404.0	284 949.0	3 551.4
集体资本	Collective－owned	37 397.1	2 412.1	27 799.1
港澳台商资本	Hongkong,Macao and Taiwan	29 941.8	62.3	
外商资本	Foreign	38 930.1		
二、损益及分配	**Profit,Loss and Distribution**			
商品销售收入	Sales Revenue	14 179 055.0	8 742 290.3	896 896.8
商品销售收入净额	Net Value of Sales Revenue	14 161 894.6	8 736 644.0	893 936.3
商品销售成本	Sales Cost	13 562 160.9	8 410 367.9	857 250.7
经营费用	Operating Expense	320 270.1	166 410.2	19 119.3
商品销售税金及附加	Sales Tax and Extra Charges	7 796.4	5 167.3	519.7
商品销售利润	Sales Profits	271 667.2	154 698.6	17 046.6
代购代销收入	Revenue from Agency Activity	11 575.3	10 785.2	－42.0
主营业务利润	Profits of Major Business	283 242.5	165 483.8	17 004.6
其他业务利润	Profits of Other Business	32 614.2	17 604.3	2 564.5
管理费用	Overhead Expenses	170 154.9	92 177.9	11 161.3
财务费用	Financial Expenses	64 468.7	40 691.2	2 107.5
营业利润	Operating Profits	119 656.6	48 858.7	6 055.0
利润总额	Total Profits	135 852.7	70 814.3	6 447.2

10－12　限额以上零售贸易业财务状况(2003年)

FINANCIAL STATUS OF RETAIL TRADE ABOVE DESIGNATED SIZE,2003

单位:万元　　　　(10 000 yuan)

指　　标	Item	合　计 Total	#国有经济 State－owned	#集体经济 Collective－owned
一、资产负债	**Total Assets and Liabilities**			
资产合计	Total Assets	1 506 307.2	285 539.1	81 145.3
#流动资产年末合计	Total Circulating Assets(year－end)	801 924.4	29 007.1	48 876.9
#存　货	Inventory	149 576.1	4 441.0	10 992.2
固定资产合计	Total Fixed Assets	448 352.3	16 313.1	24 173.8
固定资产原值	Original Value of Fixed Assets	476 268.6	19 812.8	17 948.7
#生产经营用	For Production	299 563.9	16 786.7	11 232.6
累计折旧	Accumulative Depreciation	104 453.6	3 519.7	4 604.2
#本年折旧	Occured in 2003	20 875.9	249.8	393.0
负债合计	Total Liabilities	1 030 736.1	42 601.3	53 616.5
流动负债合计	Total Circulating Liabilities	903 847.5	41 497.6	42 771.2
长期负债合计	Total Long－term Liabilities	93 768.1	967.8	5 154.0
所有者权益合计	Ownership Interest	475 571.1	5 461.7	27 528.8
#实收资本	Proceeds of Capital	414 225.6	9 729.6	17 702.9
#国家资本	State－owned	167 626.8	7 994.1	721.1
集体资本	Collective－owned	20 021.7	486.6	7 947.5
港澳台商资本	Hongkong,Macao and Taiwan	11 022.2		
外商资本	Foreign	38 759.5		
二、损益及分配	**Profit,Loss and Distribution**			
商品销售收入	Sales Revenue	1 874 274.6	45 372.1	87 866.6
商品销售收入净额	Net Value of Sales Revenue	1 872 528.6	45 372.0	87 816.3
商品销售成本	Sales Cost	1 667 696.1	41 555.3	79 392.1
经营费用	Operating Expense	147 315.7	2 719.2	4 915.9
商品销售税金及附加	Sales Tax and Extra Charges	3 854.1	75.6	396.7
商品销售利润	Sales Profits	53 662.7	1 021.9	3 111.6
代购代销收入	Revenue from Agency Activity	124.0		
主营业务利润	Profits of Major Business	53 786.7	1 021.9	3 111.6
其他业务利润	Profits of Other Business	52 679.1	1 049.2	1 558.4
管理费用	Overhead Expenses	88 373.4	2 487.9	4 604.5
财务费用	Financial Expenses	12 589.6	946.2	509.0
营业利润	Operating Profits	11 491.9	－1 064.3	－311.5
利润总额	Total Profits	16 142.5	－1 817.6	502.9

10－13　限额以上餐饮业财务状况(2003 年)

FINANCIAL STATUS OF CATERING SERVICE ABOVE DESIGNATED SIZE,2003

单位:万元　　　　(10 000 yuan)

指　标	Item	合　计 Total	#国有经济 State－owned	#集体经济 Collective－owned
一、资产负债	**Total Assets and Liabilities**			
资产合计	Total Assets	202 294.9	55 308.7	8 445.5
#流动资产年末合计	Total Circulating Assets(year－end)	59 725.5	11 541.1	1 496.6
#存　货	Inventory	6 798.4	607.6	237.7
固定资产合计	Total Fixed Assets	82 299.3	30 897.7	5 486.0
固定资产原值	Original Value of Fixed Assets	88 041.3	23 775.0	6 195.2
#生产经营用	For Production	44 906.5	6 762.2	5 587.8
累计折旧	Accumulative Depreciation	21 759.1	3 940.2	932.3
#本年折旧	Occured in 2003	4 179.6	359.0	151.4
负债合计	Total Liabilities	141 049.4	41 027.7	6 581.7
流动负债合计	Total Circulating Liabilities	109 308.9	22 552.7	5 326.7
长期负债合计	Total Long－term Liabilities	29 692.1	18 475.0	1 220.8
所有者权益合计	Ownership Interest	61 245.5	14 281.0	1 863.8
#实收资本	Proceeds of Capital	62 501.4	12 006.6	1 749.1
#国家资本	State－owned	12 810.4	10 410.5	
集体资本	Collective－owned	1 957.9		1 633.3
港澳台商资本	Hongkong,Macao and Taiwan	2 355.5	225.0	
外商资本	Foreign	20 170.7		
二、损益及分配	**Profit,Loss and Distribution**			
营业收入	Operating Revenue	179 936.8	17 362.6	4 059.4
营业成本	Operating Cost	90 484.6	9 860.5	2 462.1
营业费用	Business Expenses	59 685.5	4 641.0	877.0
营业税金及附加	Business Tax and Extra Charges	7 912.3	555.5	185.0
经营利润	Operating Profits	21 854.4	2 305.6	535.3
管理费用	Overhead Expenses	15 530.7	2 002.1	504.0
财务费用	Financial Expenses	2 468.7	312.2	86.3
营业利润	Operating Profits	3 855.0	－8.7	－55.0
利润总额	Total Profits	3 781.1	－331.0	－88.6

10－14　限额以上零售贸易业业态情况(2003年)
BUSINESS MODE OF RETAIL TRADE ABOVE DESIGNATED SIZE,2003

单位:万元　　(10 000 yuan)

指标	Item	百货商店 Department Store	超级市场 Supermarket	专业(专卖)店 Monopolization Shop	其他 Others
企业数(个)	Number of Units	55	26	76	85
商品销售收入(营业收入)	Sales Revenue(Business Revenue)	881 978.0	450 343.9	423 179.4	118 773.3
商品销售收入净额	Net Value of Sales Revenue	881 765.1	450 286.8	421 874.8	118 601.9
商品销售成本(营业成本)	Sales Cost(Business Cost)	811 337.1	398 470.1	354 476.7	103 412.2
经营费用(营业费用)	Operating Expense(Business Cost)	32 075.9	72 297.0	33 664.4	9 278.4
商品销售税金及附加	Sales Tax and Extra Charges	1 946.4	637.1	811.6	459.0
商品销售利润	Sales Profits	36 405.7	－21 117.4	32 922.1	5 452.3
代购代销收入	Revenue from Agency Activity			4.0	120.0
主营业务利润	Main Business Profits	36 405.7	－21 117.4	32 926.1	5 572.3
其他业务利润	Other Business Profits	17 137.1	28 647.5	5 488.5	1 406.0
管理费用	Overhead Expenses	51 041.0	12 759.0	18 811.2	5 762.2
#税　金	Tax	1 354.3	675.6	288.5	114.4
财务费用	Financial Expenses	7 772.4	3 890.1	405.1	522.0
营业利润	Operating Profits	－4 722.2	－5 907.7	21 460.5	661.3
利润总额	Total Profits	－2 854.7	－3 957.3	22 493.7	460.8

10－15　限额以上连锁店(公司)基本情况(2003年)
BASIC STATISTICS FOR CHAIN ENTERPRISES ABOVE DESIGNATED SIZE,2003

指标	Item	连锁总店数(个) Number of Chain Headquaretrs (unit)	连锁门店数(个) Number of Subbranches (unit)	营业面积(平方平米) Area for Business (sq.m)	从业人人员(人) Persons Employed (person)	销售总额(万元) Total Sale Revenue (10^4 yuan)
总　计	**Total**	**34**	**629**	**24 850**	**450 927**	**930 456**
一、零售业	**Retail Trade**	**20**	**424**	**16 164**	**373 418**	**865 106**
#国有及国有控股	State－owned and State－controlling Enterprises	6	41	2 451	10 754	254 020
外商及港澳台商投资	Foreign Funded, Hongkong,Macao and Taiwan	5	99	4 379	78 615	151 909
按零售业态分	Grouped by Business					
超级市场	Supermarket	9	321	11 542	283 407	431 957
二、餐饮业	**Catering Services**	**14**	**205**	**8 686**	**77 509**	**65 350**
#外商及港澳台商投资	Foreign Funded, Hongkong,Macao and Taiwan	7	143	7 359	52 929	56 127
按餐饮活动分	Grouped by Business					
正　餐	Dinner	6	20	1 291	14 500	9 494
快　餐	Fast Food	7	160	7 105	55 664	54 606
其　他	Others	1	25	290	7 345	1 251

附表:批发零售贸易餐饮业统计限额标准
ADDED TABLE: DESIGNATED SIZE OF WHOLESALE,RETAIL AND CATERING TRADE

行业类别 Type of Sector	统计指标名称 Indicator	计量单位 Unit	限额标准 Designated Size
批发业 Wholesale	年末从业人员 Employment Personnel(year－end)	人 person	20及以上 20 and over
	年销售额 Annual Sales	万元 10 000 yuan	2 000及以上 2 000 and over
零售业 Retail	年末从业人员 Employment Personnel(year－end)	人 person	60及以上 60 and over
	年销售额 Annual Sales	万元 10 000 yuan	500及以上 500 and over
餐饮业 Catering Service	年末从业人员 Employment Personnel(year－end)	人 person	40及以上 40 and over
	年营业额 Annual Operating Revenue	万元 10 000 yuan	200及以上 200 and over

主要统计指标解释

批发和零售贸易业 根据新颁布的行业分类标准《国民经济行业分类》(GB/T4754 - 2002),将原批发零售贸易、餐饮业门类中的餐饮业调出,且不含原“金属和非金属废料和碎屑的加工处理”部分。

社会消费品零售总额 各种经济类型的批发零售贸易业、餐饮业和其他行业对城乡居民和社会集团的消费品零售额总和。

商品购进总额 指从本企业以外的单位和个人购进(包括从国外直接进口)作为转卖或加工后转卖的商品金额。包括从工农业生产者购进额,从批发零售贸易业购进额,进口额和其他购进组成。这个指标反映批发零售贸易企业从国内外市场上购进商品的总量。

商品销售总额 指对本企业以外的单位和个人出售(包括对国(境)外直接出口)的商品(包括售给本单位消费用的商品)金额。本指标由对生产经营单位批发额、对批发零售贸易业批发额、出口额、对居民和社会集团商品零售额项目组成。这个指标反映批发零售贸易企业在国内市场上销售商品以及出口商品总量。

商品销售收入(营业收入) 指批发零售贸易企业商品销售收入、接受其他单位委托代销商品的收入和餐饮企业的营业收入。1994 年实行增值税为价外税,因此商品销售收入不含增值税。与 1994 年前数字不可比。

商品销售收入净额 指批发零售贸易企业商品销售收入,减去商品销售折扣与折让后的净额。

商品销售税金及附加 批发零售贸易企业销售商品应负担的税金和餐饮企业应由各项经营业务负担的税金及附加。包括营业税、城市维护建设税、出口关税和教育费附加等。

Explanatory Notes on Main Statistical Indicators

Wholesale and Retail Trade refers to original wholesale, retail trade and catering deducting catering according to the new classification of "national economic classification and code" (GB T4754 - 2002),excluding original "metal and non - metal waste materials processing".

Total Retail Sales of Consumer Goods refers to the sum of retail sales of consumer goods to urban and rural residents and social groups by the establishments in wholesale, retail, catering and other industries of various ownerships.

Total Purchases of Commodities refers to the total value of purchases of commodities by the establishments from other establishments or individuals (including direct import from abroad) for the purpose of reselling, either with or without further processing of the commodities purchased. The total purchases include agricultural and industrial products purchased from producers, commodities purchased from wholesale and retail trades,commodities directly imported from abroad,commodities purchased from other units. This indicator issued to show the total value of purchases of commodities by wholesale and retail establishments from domestic and overseas markets.

Total Sales of Commodities refers to selling of commodities by the establishments to other establishments and individuals (including direct export) . The total sales include commodities sold to establishments in industry, wholesale and retail trades for their production and operation, commodities for direct export to other countries, commodities sold to urban and rural residents and social groups for their consumption. This indicator is used to show the total value of sales of commodities at domestic markets and export.

Sales Revenue (Business income) refers to the sales revenue of wholesale and retail trades, incomes of selling goods on a commission and catering trade. Value added tax is not included. It is not comparable with the data before 1994.

Net Sales Revenue Sales revenue in wholesale and retail trades minus discount of sales.

Tax and Extra Charges on Sales of Commodity refers to tax of sold goods supported by wholesale and retail enterprises,tax and extra charges supported by catering enterprises,including business tax,tax on city maintenance,export tax and extra charges for education.

第11篇 CHAPTER 11

对外经济贸易和旅游

FOREIGN ECONOMY TRADE AND TOURISM

11－1 对外贸易进出口商品总值
TOTAL VALUE OF IMPORTS AND EXPORTS
(1981－2003)

年份 Year	绝对数(万美元) Absolute Value(USD 10 000)			增长速度(%)(比上年) Increase Rate(%)(Over Preceding Year)		
	进出口总值 Imports & Exports	出口总值 Exports	进口总值 Imports	进出口总值 Imports & Exports	出口总值 Exports	进口总值 Imports
1981	168 330	153 670	14 660	－7.9	－0.4	－48.5
1982	153 729	142 411	11 318	－8.7	－7.3	－22.8
1983	157 817	142 734	15 083	2.7	0.2	33.3
1984	146 749	123 365	23 384	－7.0	－13.6	55.0
1985	148 603	115 274	33 329	1.3	－6.6	43.9
1986	166 405	125 494	40 911	12.0	8.9	21.6
1987	201 281	151 712	49 569	21.0	20.9	21.2
1988	227 846	168 268	59 578	13.2	10.9	20.2
1989	221 421	168 604	52 817	－2.8	0.2	－11.3
1990	220 979	178 555	42 424	－0.2	5.9	－19.7
1991	202 013	160 636	41 377	－8.6	－10.0	－2.5
1992	237 577	175 234	62 343	17.6	9.1	50.7
1993	277 666	194 234	83 432	16.9	10.8	33.8
1994	331 232	239 978	91 254	19.3	23.6	9.4
1995	654 556	299 841	354 715	97.6	24.9	288.7
1996	829 743	404 913	424 830	26.8	35.0	19.8
1997	1 002 286	501 818	500 468	20.8	23.9	17.8
1998	1 061 595	549 856	511 739	5.9	9.6	2.3
1999	1 260 465	633 199	627 265	18.7	15.2	22.6
2000	1 715 741	862 906	852 835	36.1	36.3	36.0
2001	1 818 636	950 177	868 459	6.0	10.1	1.8
2002	2 282 658	1 159 490	1 123 168	25.5	22.0	29.3
2003	2 937 141	1 437 396	1 499 745	28.7	24.0	33.5

注：自1998年始，用海关数据。
Note: Since 1998, the data of this table are gotten from Tianjin Custom.

11－2 天津口岸进出口贸易总值
TOTAL VALUE OF IMPORTS AND EXPORTS IN TIANJIN PORT
(1981－2003)

年份 Year	按美元计算(亿美元) Calculated by USD(USD 100 million)			按人民币计算(亿元) Calculated by RMB(100 million yuan)		
	进出口总值 Imports & Exports	出口总值 Exports	进口总值 Imports	进出口总值 Imports & Exports	出口总值 Exports	进口总值 Imports
1981	57.84	22.74	35.10	96.62	37.99	58.63
1982	58.36	25.80	32.56	108.21	47.84	60.37
1983	60.55	22.92	37.63	119.42	45.19	74.23
1984	69.35	21.77	47.58	154.21	48.06	106.15
1985	96.18	20.07	76.11	283.30	59.13	224.17
1986	96.82	26.37	70.45	338.13	92.11	246.02
1987	89.98	32.85	57.13	334.91	122.27	212.64
1988	102.77	38.78	63.99	388.00	146.00	242.00
1989	106.30	39.70	66.60	399.69	149.27	250.42
1990	85.95	42.53	43.42	410.84	203.29	207.55
1991	91.37	46.48	44.89	486.98	239.59	247.39
1992	104.61	54.60	50.01	572.23	298.68	273.55
1993	125.04	66.03	59.01	726.48	383.63	342.85
1994	161.67	86.81	74.86	1 397.96	750.65	647.31
1995	217.46	127.81	89.65	1 821.23	1 070.41	750.82
1996	216.85	122.89	93.96	1 804.19	1 022.44	781.75
1997	215.62	131.24	84.38	1 787.55	1 088.02	699.53
1998	223.19	134.84	88.35	1 852.48	1 119.17	733.31
1999	248.29	139.18	109.11	2 055.34	1 152.13	903.21
2000	298.03	165.29	132.74	2 479.60	1 375.20	1 104.40
2001	323.71	178.13	145.58	2 679.30	1 474.40	1 204.90
2002	365.35	190.55	174.80	3 025.46	1 577.94	1 447.52
2003	461.67	259.57	202.10	3 831.86	2 154.43	1 677.43

11-3 改革开放以来利用外资情况

UTILIZATION OF FOREIGN CAPITAL SINCE REFORM AND OPENING UP

年份 Year	绝对数(万美元) Absolute Value(USD 10 000)		增长速度(%)(比上年) Increase Rate(%)(Over Preceding Year)	
	直接利用外资 Foreign Direct Investment	借用国外资金 Foreign Loans	直接利用外资 Foreign Direct Investment	借用国外资金 Foreign Loans
合同额 Foreign Investment Contracted				
1978				
1979	279			
1980	511		83.2	
1981	204		-60.1	
1982	150		-26.5	
1983	555		270.0	
1984	6 290		1 033.3	
1985	5 452	6 037	-13.3	
1986	6 583	19 969	20.7	230.8
1987	1 417	7 620	-78.5	-61.8
1988	8 931	16 904	530.3	121.8
1989	8 452	15 743	-5.4	-6.9
1990	16 367	2 000	93.6	-87.3
1991	19 656	4 100	20.1	87.0
1992	121 927	12 100	520.3	195.1
1993	225 567	9 154	85.0	-24.3
1994	350 234	52 000	55.3	468.1
1995	385 053	35 600	9.9	-31.5
1996	392 431	120 400	1.9	238.2
1997	385 066	202 100	-1.9	67.9
1998	363 729	132 989	-5.5	-34.2
1999	362 034	102 545	-0.5	-22.9
2000	460 000		27.1	
2001	463 000		0.7	
2002	581 220		25.5	
2003	351 297		74.3	
实际利用外资 Foreign Capital Actually Used				
1978				
1979				
1980	271			
1981	40		-85.2	
1982	578		1 345.0	
1983	40	251	-93.1	
1984	1 190	933	2 875.0	271.7
1985	4 409	2 098	270.5	124.9
1986	4 287	11 229	-2.8	435.2
1987	5 491	18 547	28.1	65.2
1988	2 395	42 878	-56.4	131.2
1989	8 134	35 178	239.6	-18.0
1990	8 315	25 122	2.7	-28.6
1991	9 388	38 711	12.9	54.1
1992	23 138	59 922	146.5	54.8
1993	54 120	39 112	133.9	-34.7
1994	101 499	75 985	87.5	94.3
1995	152 064	58 924	49.8	-22.5
1996	200 587	97 771	31.9	65.9
1997	251 135	91 166	25.2	-6.8
1998	251 803	53 984	0.3	-40.8
1999	253 203	21 332	0.6	-60.5
2000	256 000	26 467	1.1	24.1
2001	322 000	7 688	25.8	-71.0
2002	380 591	6 310	18.2	-17.9
2003	163 325	7 225	62.9	14.5

注:2003 年直接利用外资额采用商务部新口径,速度为可比口径;11-8、11-9、11-11 表同。

Note: Since 2003, foreign direct investment refer to new coverage of Ministry of Commerce, its increase rate is calculated on the basis of comparable coverage; same as following table 11-8, 11-9 and 11-11.

11－4　对外贸易进出口商品总值
TOTAL VALUE OF IMPORTS AND EXPORTS IN FOREIGN TRADE

单位:万美元　　(USD 10 000)

项　目	Item	2002 进出口总值 Imports & Exports	2002 出口总值 Exports	2002 进口总值 Imports
合　计	**Total**	**2 282 658**	**1 159 490**	**1 123 168**
1.按口岸分	**By Port**			
本口岸	Local Port	1 748 008	777 009	970 999
外口岸	Outside Port	534 650	382 481	152 169
2.按经营单位分	**By Managing Unit**			
#国有企业	State－owned Enterprises	370 468	216 726	153 742
中外合资企业	Joint Venture Enterprises	692 828	326 500	366 328
中外合作企业	Cooperative Operation Enterprises	24 577	12 520	12 057
外商独资企业	Foreign－funded Sole Enterprises	1 120 936	571 949	548 987
3.按贸易性质分	**By Trade Kind**			
#一般贸易	General Trade	699 947	357 928	342 019
进料加工	Processing Using Import Material	1 179 937	704 233	475 705
外商投资企业进口设备	Equipments of Foreign－funded Enterprises Import	65 103		65 103
来料加工	Processing Using Provided Material	128 074	74 734	53 339
易货贸易	Dicker Trade			
捐　赠	Donation	1 035	1 020	15
保税区仓储进出境货物	Goods Passed in and out TPFTZ	9 024	2 303	6 722
保税区仓储转口货物	Goods Transited in TPFTZ	190 114	13 738	176 376
4.按商品类别分	**By Category of Commodities**			
#食品及活动物	Food and Live Animals	34 972	26 784	8 188
饮料及烟类	Beverages and Tobacco	815	589	226
非食用原料(燃料油除外)	Non－edible Raw Materials(exclude Fuel Oil)	69 488	16 708	52 780
矿物燃料、润滑油及有关原料	Mineral Fuels, Lubricants and Related Materials	84 819	74 314	10 505
动植物油、脂及蜡	Animal and Vegetable Oils, Fats and Wax	17 982	29	17 953
化学成品及有关产品	Chemicals and Related Products	199 206	56 079	143 127
按原料分类的制成品	Related Products By Raw Materials	242 442	118 131	124 311
机械及运输设备	Machinery and Transport Equipment	1 363 291	672 270	691 021
杂项制品	Miscellaneous Products	261 524	191 947	69 577

11－4 续表　Continued

单位:万美元　(USD 10 000)

项　目	Item	2003 进出口总值 Imports & Exports	2003 出口总值 Exports	2003 进口总值 Imports
合　计	**Total**	**2 937 141**	**1 437 396**	**1 499 745**
1.按口岸分	**By Port**			
本口岸	Local Port	2 229 718	998 036	1 231 682
外口岸	Outside Port	707 423	439 360	268 063
2.按经营单位分	**By Managing Unit**			
#国有企业	State－owned Enterprises	474 646	247 461	227 185
中外合资企业	Joint Venture Enterprises	953 581	441 308	512 273
中外合作企业	Cooperative Operation Enterprises	42 322	19 931	22 391
外商独资企业	Foreign－funded Sole Enterprises	1 334 350	681 440	652 910
3.按贸易性质分	**By Trade Kind**			
#一般贸易	General Trade	1 048 412	483 629	564 783
进料加工	Processing Using Import Material	1 319 739	831 298	488 441
外商投资企业进口设备	Equipments of Foreign－funded Enterprises Import	65 188		65 188
来料加工	Processing Using Provided Material	142 912	83 442	59 470
易货贸易	Dicker Trade	1 051	9	1 042
捐　赠	Donation	928	272	656
保税区仓储进出境货物	Goods Passed in and out TPFTZ	11 465	2 791	8 674
保税区仓储转口货物	Goods Transited in TPFTZ	334 677	26 645	308 032
4.按商品类别分	**By Category of Commodities**			
#食品及活动物	Food and Live Animals	41 857	31 478	10 379
饮料及烟类	Beverages and Tobacco	947	771	176
非食用原料(燃料油除外)	Non－edible Raw Materials(exclude Fuel Oil)	92 606	24 710	67 896
矿物燃料、润滑油及有关原料	Mineral Fuels, Lubricants and Related Materials	118 781	105 996	12 785
动植物油、脂及蜡	Animal and Vegetable Oils, Fats and Wax	41 910	289	41 621
化学成品及有关产品	Chemicals and Related Products	230 441	73 794	156 647
按原料分类的制成品	Related Products By Raw Materials	311 011	146 442	164 569
机械及运输设备	Machinery and Transport Equipment	1 776 684	835 454	941 230
杂项制品	Miscellaneous Products	81 058	57 593	23 465

11－5 对外贸易分国别、地区进出口总值

TOTAL VALUE OF IMPORTS AND EXPORTS IN FOREIGN TRADE BY COUNTRY AND REGION

单位:万美元 (USD 10 000)

国 别、地 区 Country, Region	2002			2003		
	进出口总值 Imports & Exports	出口总值 Exports	进口总值 Imports	进出口总值 Imports & Exports	出口总值 Exports	进口总值 Imports
合 计 Total	**2 282 658**	**1 159 490**	**1 123 168**	**2 937 141**	**1 437 396**	**1 499 745**
亚 洲 Asia	**1 364 773**	**544 522**	**820 250**	**1 743 282**	**675 827**	**1 067 455**
#中国香港 Hongkong, China	124 917	69 797	55 120	132 477	88 876	43 601
中国澳门 Macao, China	435	434	1	153	150	3
朝 鲜 Democratic People's Republic of Korea	362	192	170	560	443	117
韩 国 Republic of Korea	392 170	114 570	277 600	540 206	151 600	388 606
日 本 Japan	450 832	166 714	284 118	571 910	181 582	390 328
菲律宾 Philippines	17 385	6 844	10 541	19 506	8 673	10 833
缅 甸 Burma	3 753	3 723	30	2 072	2 019	53
泰 国 Thailand	24 050	14 364	9 685	28 554	17 586	10 968
马来西亚 Malaysia	52 997	25 487	27 510	69 282	22 827	46 455
新加坡 Singapore	77 930	36 859	41 071	120 116	63 170	56 946
巴基斯坦 Pakistan	4 008	3 811	197	4 638	4 398	240
伊 朗 Iran	3 666	3 500	166	4 075	3 679	396
叙利亚 Syria	871	871		998	6	992
中国台湾 Taiwan, China	107 685	16 512	91 174	107 450	19 943	87 507
黎巴嫩 Lebanon	589	435	154	544	347	197
约 旦 Jordan	790	784	6	759	747	12
也 门 Yeman	690	662	28	1 069	1 030	39
沙 特 Saudi Arabia	6 539	5 176	1 363	5 170	3 941	1 229
科威特 Koweit	557	321	236	601	331	270
巴 林 Bahrein	48	46	2	219	83	136
非 洲 Africa	**20 204**	**18 301**	**1 903**	**26 317**	**23 161**	**3 156**
#埃 及 Egypt	2 609	2 139	470	2 806	2 451	355
苏 丹 Sudan	611	586	25	1 333	1 273	60
利比亚 Libya	112	112		21	21	
肯尼亚 Kenya	510	393	117	643	571	72
坦桑尼亚 Tanzania	372	360	12	554	523	31
欧 洲 Europe	**312 604**	**174 973**	**137 631**	**468 999**	**245 966**	**223 033**
#波 兰 Poland	2 043	1 361	682	3 540	2 200	1 340

11－5 续表 Continued
单位:万美元 (USD 10 000)

国别、地区	Country, Region	2002 进出口总值 Imports & Exports	2002 出口总值 Exports	2002 进口总值 Imports	2003 进出口总值 Imports & Exports	2003 出口总值 Exports	2003 进口总值 Imports
匈牙利	Hungary	3 161	3 091	70	4 026	3 603	423
捷　克	Czech	2 291	1 734	557	2 797	2 187	610
保加利亚	Bulgaria	193	183	10	784	319	465
阿尔巴尼亚	Albania	93	93		286	286	
罗马尼亚	Roumania	2 470	959	1 511	1 409	1 294	115
德　国	Germany	110 136	50 855	59 282	189 748	79 275	110 473
南斯拉夫	Yugoslavia	464	440	24	69	67	2
法　国	France	35 329	14 601	20 728	37 139	16 159	20 980
意大利	Italy	18 616	9 436	9 180	22 966	10 865	12 101
荷　兰	Netherlands	29 223	26 720	2 503	39 308	36 102	3 206
比利时	Belgium	7 686	5 223	2 463	11 571	7 543	4 028
英　国	United Kingdom	32 012	18 625	13 387	43 102	26 440	16 662
爱尔兰	Ireland	1 899	1 069	829	2 250	1 430	820
丹　麦	Danmark	7 847	2 563	5 284	11 557	3 542	8 015
芬　兰	Finland	12 095	9 905	2 189	27 313	22 868	4 445
瑞　典	Sweden	5 931	1 953	3 978	10 953	2 755	8 198
挪　威	Norway	2 164	1 014	1 150	5 594	1 333	4 261
瑞　士	Switzerland	5 808	1 848	3 960	6 425	1 902	4 523
奥地利	Austria	1 310	240	1 070	3 429	218	3 211
西班牙	Spain	9 653	7 507	2 146	10 581	7 358	3 223
拉丁美洲及北美洲	**Latin and North America**	**561 771**	**406 334**	**155 437**	**668 615**	**471 723**	**196 892**
#墨西哥	Mexico	14 051	9 624	4 427	15 595	10 326	5 269
古　巴	Cuba	274	273	1	636	634	2
智　利	Chile	3 319	2 652	667	4 042	3 078	964
加拿大	Canada	20 284	14 545	5 739	25 616	18 232	7 384
美　国	United States	493 480	364 583	128 897	570 457	417 583	152 874
大洋洲及太平洋地区	**Oceania and Pacific Region**	**23 307**	**15 359**	**7 947**	**29 929**	**20 718**	**9 211**
#澳大利亚	Australia	20 412	14 026	6 386	25 490	18 986	6 504
新西兰	New Zealand	2 707	1 146	1 561	4 167	1 460	2 707

11－6　天津口岸进出口商品检验情况
TEST OF IMPORTS AND EXPORTS COMMODITIES IN TIANJIN PORT
(1999－2003)

项　目	Item	1999	2000	2001	2002	2003
一、进口商品检验	**Imports Test**					
批　数(批)	Batches(batch)	14 583	21 895	57 285	76 426	105 340
金　额(万美元)	Value(USD 10 000)	119 835	279 811	539 748	651 968	1 035 630
#经检验发现不合格商品	Substandard					
批　数(批)	Batches(batch)		252	292	505	602
金　额(万美元)	Value(USD 10 000)	1 528	6 562	13 620	20 431	24 721
二、出口商品检验	**Exports Test**					
批　数(批)	Batches(batch)	31 648	62 694	125 642	147 379	171 394
金　额(万美元)	Value(USD 10 000)	153 709	414 287	636 064	774 081	1 030 159
#经检验发现不合格商品	Substandard					
批　数(批)	Batches(batch)	85	53	129	140	163
金　额(万美元)	Value(USD 10 000)	584	246	192	288	355

11－7　境外投资企业地区分布(截止2003年底)
DISTRIBUTION OF OVERSEAS ENTERPRISES (BY THE END OF 2003)

地　区　Region	境外企业数(个) Number of Enterprises (unit)	投资总额 Value of Investment		#中方投资额 Investment by Chinese Partner	
		金　额(万美元) Value(USD 10 000)	构　成(%) Proportion(%)	金　额(万美元) Value(USD 10 000)	构　成(%) Proportion(%)
合　计　Total	**373**	**30 925.99**	**100.0**	**17 291.50**	**100.0**
亚　洲 Asia	163	10 502.51	34.0	5 907.85	34.2
欧　洲 Europe	72	3 361.59	10.9	2 903.92	16.8
北美洲 North America	71	3 341.14	10.8	2 366.04	13.7
南美洲 South America	18	1 628.00	5.3	1 267.50	7.3
大洋洲 Oceania	14	1 906.26	6.1	1 574.41	9.1
非　洲 Africa	35	10 186.49	32.9	3 271.78	18.9

11－8 直接利用外资签约情况

UTILIZATION OF FOREIGN DIRECT INVESTMENT

项 目	Item	至2003年底累计 Accumulative Total (by the end of 2003)	2001	2002	2003	2003比2002年增长% Increased Rate in 2003 over 2002
一、合同数(个)	**Number of Contracts(unit)**	**15 990**	**618**	**816**	**941**	**15.3**
合资企业	Joint Venture Enterprises	5 948	156	198	218	10.7
合作企业	Cooperative Operation Enterprises	558	16	30	23	－23.3
独资企业	Foreign－funded Sole Enterprises	9 484	446	588	700	18.9
二、合同投资总额（万美元）	**Total Investment Contracted(USD 10 000)**	**5 649 688**	**490 640**	**640 604**	**591 200**	**－7.7**
合资企业	Joint Venture Enterprises	2 420 777	126 938	140 356	156 229	9.0
合作企业	Cooperative Operation Enterprises	554 045	9 481	38 513	20 385	－47.1
独资企业	Foreign－funded Sole Enterprises	2 674 866	354 221	461 735	414 586	－9.6
三、合同外资金额（万美元）	**Foreign Investment Contracted(USD 10 000)**	**4 530 145**	**463 000**	**581 220**	**351 297**	**74.3**
合资企业	Joint Venture Enterprises	1 536 776	100 889	100 809	62 060	44.6
合作企业	Cooperative Operation Enterprises	469 187	8 161	29 272	14 471	－23.4
独资企业	Foreign－funded Sole Enterprises	2 524 182	353 950	451 139	274 766	96.6

11－9 实际利用外资情况

FOREIGN CAPITAL ACTUALLY USED

单位：万美元 (USD 10 000)

项 目	Item	至2003年底累计 Accumulative Total (by the end of 2003)	2001	2002	2003	2003比2002年增长% Increased Rate in 2003over 2002
总 计	**Total**	**3 180 891**	**329 688**	**386 901**	**170 550**	**60.0**
1.借用国外资金	**Foreign Loans**	**720 833**	**7 688**	**6 310**	**7 225**	**14.5**
外国政府贷款	Foreign Government Loans	71 172	116	861		
国际金融组织贷款	Loans from International Financial Organizations	70 051	1 481	2 423		
出口信贷	Export Loans	88 722	5 094	1 751	247	－89.8
外国银行商业贷款	Commercial Loans from Foreign Banks	445 152	997	1 275	6 978	298.5
对外发行债券、股票	External Bonds，Stocks	45 736				
2.直接利用外资	**Foreign Direct Investment**	**2 454 003**	**322 000**	**380 591**	**163 325**	**62.9**
合资企业	Joint Venture Enterprises	1 041 112	144 560	80 088	49 201	133.2
合作企业	Cooperative Operation Enterprises	170 817	20 304	45 521	2 967	－75.3
独资企业	Foreign－funded Sole Enterprises	1 242 074	157 136	254 982	111 157	65.5
3.其他投资	**Other Foreign Investment**	**6 055**				

11－10 借用国外资金情况
BORROWING FOREIGN CAPITAL

单位:万美元 (USD 10 000)

项 目 Item	上年结转资金 Capital Carried From Last Year		当年新增借款 New Increased Loans		偿还本金 Repaid Principal	
	2002	2003	2002	2003	2002	2003
国外贷款合计 Total Loans	**158 985**	**114 006**	**6 310**	**7 225**	**51 707**	**15 820**
1.按债务期限分 By Period of Debt						
中长期 Long－term & Medium－term	157 608	112 531	5 041	247	50 532	13 556
短 期 Short－term	1 377	1 475	1 269	6 978	1 175	2 264
2.按借款方式分 By Mode of Borrowing						
外国政府贷款 Government Loans	51 515	45 710	861		5 328	2 716
国际金融组织贷款 Loans from International Financial Organization	39 815	24 090	2 423		18 148	3 670
出口信贷 Export Loans	36 476	24 409	1 751	247	15 334	4 293
外国银行商业贷款 Commercial Loans of Foreign Banks	31 179	19 797	1 275	6 978	12 897	5 141

项 目 Item	外汇汇率差额 Margin of Foreign Exchange Rate		期末借款余额 Loaned Balance Year－end		偿还利息 Repaid Interest	
	2002	2003	2002	2003	2002	2003
国外贷款合计 Total Loans	**418**	**1 840**	**114 006**	**107 251**	**4 535**	**2 700**
1.按债务期限分 By Period of Debt						
中长期 Long－term & Medium－term	414	1 831	112 531	101 053	4 534	2 687
短 期 Short－term	4	9	1 475	6 198	1	13
2.按借款方式分 By Mode of Borrowing						
外国政府贷款 Government Loans	－1 338	50	45 710	43 044	1 524	915
国际金融组织贷款 Loans from International Financial Organization		2	24 090	20 422	457	200
出口信贷 Export Loans	1 516	1 672	24 409	22 035	2 019	1 249
外国银行商业贷款 Commercial Loans of Foreign Banks	240	5 141	19 797	21 750	535	336

11－11　外商及港澳台商投资企业投资情况(2003年)

INVESTMENT OF FOREIGN－FUNDED AND HONGKONG ,MACAO AND TAIWAN FUNDED ENTERPRISES,2003

项　目	Item	直接利用外资合同数(个) Contractual Projects of Foreign Direct Investment (unit)		直接利用外资合同投资总额(万美元) Total Volume of Foreign Direct Investment Contracted (USD 10 000)	
		2003	至2003年底累计 Accumulative Total (by the end of 2003)	2003	至2003年底累计 Accumulative Total (by the end of 2003)
总　计	**Total**	**941**	**15 990**	**591 200**	**5 649 689**
一、按投资方式分	**By Mode of Investment**				
合资企业	Joint Venture Enterprises	218	5 948	156 229	2 420 778
合作企业	Cooperative Operation Enterprises	23	558	20 385	554 045
独资企业	Foreign－funded Sole Enterprises	700	9 484	414 586	2 674 866
二、按行业分	**By Sector**				
农　业	Agriculture	7	104	3 975	19 808
制造业	Manufacturing	594	8 962	379 600	3 263 040
建筑业	Construction	2	309	109	75 727
交通运输及仓储业	Transportation and Storage	12	148	12 703	198 547
批发零售贸易及餐饮业	Wholesale,Retail Trade and Catering	191	4 403	67 265	717 236
房地产业	Real Estate	32	587	2 465	1 006 643
社会服务业	Social Services	75	1 013	1 789	65 503
其他行业	Others	28	464	123 294	303 186
三、按国别(地区)分	**By Country(Region)**				
#中国香港	Hongkong,China	142	5 280	142 047	2 084 550
中国台湾	Taiwan,China	58	1 597	27 851	220 490
韩　国	Republic of Korea	240	1 801	48 470	507 635
日　本	Japan	120	1 498	106 953	479 529
美　国	United States	144	2 574	83 277	910 418
新加坡	Singapore	30	477	12 012	179 721
英　国	United Kingdom	11	146	4 244	1 153 621
德　国	Germany	16	185	16 290	90 078
法　国	France	6	118	3 467	46 907
意大利	Italy	3	65	1 744	21 884
英属维尔京群岛	Virgin Islands of United Kingdom	40	244	36 931	399 151

11－11 续表 Continued

项　　目	Item	#直接利用外资合同额（万美元）Foreign Capital of Foreign Direct Investment Contracted (USD 10 000)		实际直接利用外资（万美元）Foreign Capital Actually Used (USD 10 000)	
		2003	至2003年底累计 Accumulative Total (by the end of 2003)	2003	至2003年底累计 Accumulative Total (by the end of 2003)
总　　计	**Total**	**351 297**	**4 530 145**	**163 325**	**2 454 003**
一、按投资方式分	**By Mode of Investment**				
合资企业	Joint Venture Enterprises	62 060	1 536 776	49 201	1 041 112
合作企业	Cooperative Operation Enterprises	14 471	59 887	2 967	170 817
独资企业	Foreign－funded Sole Enterprises	274 766	2 524 182	111 157	1 242 074
二、按行业分	**By Sector**				
农　业	Agriculture	3 015	13 577	21	4 707
制造业	Manufacturing	215 409	2 615 080	108 554	1 514 441
建筑业	Construction	56	63 218	6 141	39 546
交通运输及仓储业	Transportation and Storage	6 820	165 220	6 174	101 382
批发零售贸易及餐饮业	Wholesale, Retail Trade and Catering	44 296	593 535	23 135	423 103
房地产业	Real Estate	34 624	840 335	6 366	155 528
社会服务业	Social Services	37 947	90 752	11 989	61 423
其他行业	Others	9 130	148 428	945	153 873
三、按国别(地区)分	**By Country(Region)**				
#中国香港	Hongkong, China	95 543	1 664 845	32 595	886 648
中国台湾	Taiwan, China	14 589	166 101	3 253	84 569
韩　国	Republic of Korea	29 917	286 028	20 731	173 757
日　本	Japan	55 252	334 880	24 403	255 674
美　国	United States	53 435	783 426	35 185	355 852
新加坡	Singapore	6 185	80 405	6 362	73 468
英　国	United Kingdom	2 860	44 969	3 744	37 084
德　国	Germany	10 782	64 073	7 030	46 263
法　国	France	3 359	32 967	2 305	18 535
意大利	Italy	1 664	12 804	1 459	7 566
英属维尔京群岛	Virgin Islands of United Kingdom	21 551	288 187	9 015	155 174

11－12　外商及港澳台商投资企业生产经营情况(2003年)

PRODUCTION AND OPERATION OF FOREIGN－FUNDED AND HONGKONG,MACAO AND TAIWAN FUNDED ENTERPRISES,2003

单位:万元　(10 000 yuan)

项　目　Item	企业个数(个) Number of Enterprises (unit)	全部从业人员数(人) Number of Persons Employed (person)	全部从业人员劳动报酬 Total Remuneration of Persons Employed	销售(营业)收入 Sales (Business) Revenue	利润总额 Total Profits
合　计　Total	**4 517**	**444 891**	**891 583**	**22 330 729**	**976 016**
一、按投资方式分　By Mode of Investment					
港澳台合资 Hongkong,Macao and Taiwan Joint Venture	813	67 714	104 220	2 274 429	103 169
港澳台合作 Hongkong,Macao and Taiwan Cooperative Operation	73	3 269	6 088	181 500	13 537
港澳台独资 Hongkong,Macao and Taiwan Funded	826	52 502	98 562	1 676 731	97 068
中外合资 Joint Venture	961	142 495	276 716	9 305 178	491 064
中外合作 Cooperative Operation	106	11 080	18 032	352 963	37 576
外商独资 Foreign－funded Sole	1 738	167 831	387 965	8 539 928	233 602
二、按国民经济行业分　By Sector					
农、林、牧、渔业 Farming,Forestry,Animal Husbandry and Fishery	17	1 034	1 725	44 321	－266
采矿业 Minerals Mining	7	88	176	25 434	－1 956
制造业 Manufacturing	2 986	388 434	756 078	19 156 642	898 780
#食品制造业 Food Manufacturing	121	12 529	21 459	444 943	22 055
饮料制造业 Beverage Manufacturing	64	7 467	14 839	326 786	23 359
纺织业 Textile Industry	115	11 790	14 532	234 099	2 315
纺织服装、鞋、帽制造业 Textile Industry	245	33 892	32 855	283 344	3 885
家具制造业 Furniture Manufacturing	54	6 102	7 955	140 057	9 454
化学原料及化学制品制造业 Chemical Raw Materials and Chemical Products	178	10 172	30 689	701 774	64 957
医药制造业 Medical and Pharmaceutical Products	66	9 849	33 092	394 642	25 799
塑料制品业 Plastic Products	179	21 741	30 763	492 538	53 934
非金属矿物制品业 Nonmetal Mineral Products	108	7 146	12 169	258 526	－974
黑色金属冶炼及压延加工业 Smelting and Pressing of Ferrous Metals	20	3 345	4 246	182 348	1 369
通用设备制造业 General Purpose Equipment Manufacturing	137	17 675	51 192	835 101	92 183
专用设备制造业 Special Purposes Equipment Manufacturing	175	11 865	21 805	340 568	32 867
交通运输设备制造业 Transport Equipment Manufacturing	160	32 669	53 886	1 643 538	108 930

11－12 续表 1　Continued

单位：万元　(10 000 yuan)

项　目　Item	企业个数（个）Number of Enterprises (unit)	全部从业人员数（人）Number of Persons Employed (person)	全部从业人员劳动报酬 Total Remuneration of Persons Employed	销售（营业）收入 Sales (Business) Revenue	利润总额 Total Profits
电气机械及器材制造业 Electric Equipment and Machinery	94	15 229	27 573	972 969	53 987
通信设备、计算机及其他电子设备制造业 Telecommunications Equipment, Computer and Other Electronic Equipment Manufacturing	319	87 460	245 655	8 734 526	241 435
电力、燃气及水的生产和供应业 Production & Supply of Power, Gas and Water	10	2 360	8 810	201 808	16 564
建筑业 Construction	123	2 815	6 040	77 166	－5 539
交通运输、仓储及邮政业 Transport, Storage, Post Services	183	9 991	37 889	386 933	62 097
信息传输、计算机服务和软件业 Information Transmitting, Computer Services and Software	40	1 003	5 254	25 503	3 972
批发和零售业 Wholesale and Retail Trade	679	11 780	27 381	1 909 682	10 797
住宿和餐饮业 Accommodation and Catering Services	81	12 849	14 461	142 385	3 341
金融业 Finance	14	277	4 069	52 468	10 507
房地产业 Real Estate	169	4 461	9 627	230 327	－22 070
租赁和商务服务业 Leasing and Business Services	81	1 243	6 329	24 306	1 561
科学研究、技术服务和地质勘察业 Scientific Research, Technical Services and Geological Prospecting	56	954	4 741	22 978	409
水利、环境和公共设施管理业 Management for Water Conservancy, Environment and Public Facilities	4	72	64	1 494	－26
居民服务和社会服务业 Resident Services and Other Social Services	50	6 729	7 957	22 642	－632
卫生、社会保障和社会福利业 Health Care, Social Security and Social Welfare	1	22	76	580	－4
文化、体育和娱乐业 Culture, Sports and Recreational Services	16	779	907	6 059	－1 520
三、按坐落地点分组 By Site of Location					
和平区 Heping District	421	13 670	30 188	1 030 591	11 786
河东区 Hedong District	206	14 632	28 045	481 991	2 475
河西区 Hexi District	562	45 839	92 456	1 726 505	34 898
南开区 Nankai District	468	34 154	63 774	1 139 515	52 198
河北区 Hebei District	162	10 303	17 675	234 071	－307
红桥区 Hongqiao District	54	3 449	4 533	82 531	7 642
塘沽区 Tanggu District	908	104 096	330 661	9 053 611	334 568
汉沽区 Hangu District	23	1 611	2 497	71 684	8 460
大港区 Dagang District	55	7 585	13 321	259 231	4 092
东丽区 Dongli District	387	41 070	61 894	1 087 775	55 324
西青区 Xiqing District	315	47 636	78 435	3 674 140	219 575
津南区 Jinnan District	219	27 550	37 801	463 378	26 774
北辰区 Beichen District	275	22 232	43 849	1 427 854	63 620
武清区 Wuqing District	197	38 875	54 541	1 072 412	117 037
宝坻区 Baodi District	79	12 414	10 752	94 690	1 166
宁河县 Ninghe County	47	3 887	3 552	69 887	5 361
静海县 Jinghai County	104	11 364	11 635	186 853	13 974
蓟　县 Jixian County	35	4 524	5 974	174 009	17 374

11－12 续表 2　Continued

单位:万元　(10 000 yuan)

项　目	Item	企业个数(个) Number of Enterprises (unit)	全部从业人员数(人) Number of Persons Employed (person)	全部从业人员劳动报酬 Total Remuneration of Persons Employed	销售(营业)收入 Sales (Business) Revenue	利润总额 Total Profits
四、按国别(地区)分组	**by Country(Region)**					
亚　洲	**Asia**	**3 197**	**318 001**	**532 585**	**13 755 605**	**676 227**
#孟加拉国	Bengal	7	505	453	12 943	－455
中国香港	Hongkong,China	1 315	86 404	150 632	2 969 219	146 295
印度尼西亚	Indonesia	5	50	126	3 531	－406
日　本	Japan	615	79 612	143 344	3 765 588	181 016
老　挝	Laos	1	215	273	7 398	473
中国澳门	Macao,China	27	1 484	1 703	21 812	1 252
马来西亚	Malaysia	30	4 815	7 935	48 231	－11 201
新加坡	Singapore	146	11 456	19 959	307 612	19 920
韩　国	Republic of Korea	612	93 361	142 926	5 308 685	269 513
泰　国	Thailand	16	1 374	3 372	115 435	2 390
中国台湾	Taiwan,China	370	35 597	56 535	1 141 628	66 228
亚洲其他国家(地区)	Others	6	232	343	4 795	－310
非　洲	**Africa**	**15**	**846**	**1 791**	**45 495**	**2 576**
欧　洲	**Europe**	**333**	**27 641**	**79 825**	**1 757 065**	**89 441**
#比利时	Belgium	9	488	917	15 566	1 038
丹　麦	Danmark	10	1 097	7 882	135 299	15 026
英　国	United Kingdom	65	7 528	17 282	286 555	13 389
德　国	Germany	69	4 165	13 438	566 644	35 884
法　国	France	50	4 873	16 405	349 570	45 213
意大利	Italy	23	2 144	4 572	84 319	－6 787
荷　兰	Netherlands	25	1 657	5 345	126 532	－1 622
西班牙	Spain	13	1 577	2 270	30 064	－1 592
芬　兰	Finland	8	214	1 448	51 599	－2 015
匈牙利	Hungary	7	219	80	1 137	152
挪　威	Norway	2	135	530	3 575	958
罗马尼亚	Roumania	4	124	142	3 276	－52
瑞　典	Sweden	13	752	1 193	5 764	－944
瑞　士	Switzerland	17	2 150	7 283	90 674	－9 268
俄罗斯	Russia	3	64	78	691	－21
捷克共和国	Czech Rep.	2	12	12	14	－22
拉丁美洲	**Latin**	**95**	**14 492**	**18 244**	**239 345**	**25 619**
#巴　西	Brazil	26	3 348	4 440	27 737	530
凯曼群岛	Cayman	9	1 928	1 663	50 648	－423
巴拿马	Panama	7	97	215	1 253	－14
英属维尔京群岛	Virgin Islands of the United kingdom	36	8 594	11 067	153 014	27 831
北美洲	**North America**	**806**	**78 400**	**252 008**	**6 317 240**	**189 763**
#加拿大	Canada	76	4 341	5 612	113 322	1 373
美　国	United States	725	72 312	243 280	6 007 357	185 851
大洋洲	**Oceania**	**71**	**5 511**	**7 131**	**215 979**	**－7 610**
#澳大利亚	Australia	53	4 104	5 376	195 032	－7 644

11－13 新批准外商及港澳台商投资企业名单(合同

NEW APPROVED FOREIGN－FUNDED AND HONGKONG,MACAO AND TAIWAN FUNDED

企业名称 Name of Enterprise	投资方式 Investment Manner	投资国别(地区) Investment Country (Region)
联台国际事业(天津)有限公司	外资企业	中国台湾
LIEAN－TAI International Enterprise Co.,Ltd.(Tianjin)	Foreign－funded Enterprise	Taiwan,China
天津优奈米国际科技有限公司	外资企业	中国香港
Tianjin U－NaNo International Technology Co.,Ltd.	Foreign－funded Enterprise	Hongkong,China
天津家荣房地产发展有限公司	中外合资	日　本
Tianjin Jiarong Real Estate Development Co.,Ltd.	Joint Venture Enterprise	Japan
赛威传动(中国)投资有限公司	外资企业	德　国
Sew－Eurodrive(China) Holding Co.,Ltd.	Foreign－funded Enterprise	Germany
天津恒信港务实业发展有限公司	外资企业	中国香港
Tinjin Hengxin Port Operating & Entity Development Co.,Ltd.	Foreign－funded Enterprise	Hongkong,China
天津术鼎医药品有限公司	外资企业	中国澳门
Tianjin Shuding Pharmaceutical Production Co.,Ltd.	Foreign－funded Enterprise	Macao,China
天津福利德投资咨询有限公司	外资企业	英属维尔京
Tianjin Fulide I&C Co.,Ltd.	Foreign－funded Enterprise	Virgin Islands
诚保利亚泰(天津)房地产开发有限公司	外资企业	美　国
Singpoli Pacifica (Tianjin) Real Estate Development Co.,Ltd.	Foreign－funded Enterprise	United States
沃芬(天津)实业发展有限公司	外资企业	美　国
Walfen (Tianjin) Enterprise Development Co.,Ltd.	Foreign－funded Enterprise	United States
天津港保税区嘉士德国际烟草有限公司	外资企业	中国香港
Tianjin Portfree Trade Zone Jiashide International Tobacco Co.,Ltd.	Foreign－funded Enterprise	Hongkong,China
天津天任车料有限公司	外资企业	中国香港
Tianjin Tianren Auto Part Co.,Ltd.	Foreign－funded Enterprise	Hongkong,China
天津杨柳青文化公园开发有限公司	外资企业	中国香港
Tianjin Yangliuqing Cultural Park Develotment Co.,Ltd.	Foreign－funded Enterprise	Hongkong,China
天津科能实业发展有限公司	外资企业	中国香港
Tianjin Keneng Industry Development Co.,Ltd.	Foreign－funded Enterprise	Hongkong,China
联业(天津)置业有限公司	外资企业	中国香港
Unilink (Tian Jin) Real Estate Co.,Ltd.	Foreign－funded Enterprise	Hongkong,China
天津术鼎保健品有限公司	外资企业	中国澳门
Tianjin Shuding Health Care Article Co.,Ltd.	Foreign－funded Enterprise	Macao,China
天津术鼎生物技术有限公司	外资企业	中国澳门
Tianjin Shuding Living Creature Technique Co.,Ltd.	Foreign－funded Enterprise	Macao,China
北亚渤迪(天津)物流有限公司	外资企业	马来西亚
North Asia Bodi(Tianjin) Logistics Co.,Ltd.	Foreign－funded Enterprise	Malaysia
豪圣电机(天津)有限公司	外资企业	韩　国
Hyo Seong Electric (Tianjin) Co.,Ltd.	Foreign－funded Enterprise	Korea
天津东方普勒国际贸易有限公司	外资企业	德　国
Tianjin East－Kepler International Trade Co.,Ltd.	Foreign－funded Enterprise	Germany
天津孚宝乙烯仓储有限公司	中外合资	荷　兰
Vopak Ethylene Terminal Tianjin Co.,Ltd.	Joint Venture Enterprise	Netherlands

投资总额在 2500 万美元以上)(2003 年)
ENTERPRISES WITH CONTRACTED INVESTMENT OF OVER 25 MILLION USD, 2003

经营范围 Businesse Field	合同投资总额(万美元) Value of Investment Contracted (USD 10 000)	合同外资额(万美元) Foreign Capital Contracted (USD 10 000)
资源再生及综合利用技术，农副产品、果蔬饮料的开发生产，生物工程技术开发等 Resources Rebirth and Comprehensive Usage, Development and Production of Farm and Sideline Products, etc	12 500	4 500
生产、销售和开发电子及通信设备、半导体、集成电路和新型电子元器件等 Production, Sales and Development of Electric and Communication Equipment, Semi - conductor, etc	12 000	12 000
房地产开发、管理、转让、出租，建设和经营商业，服务业，金融设施和公用事业 Real Estate Development, Management, Rent, etc	7 324	1 901
在机电工业和相关领域进行投资；新产品及高新技术的研究、开发、转让 Investment in the field of Machine Electricity Industry	4 300	4 300
港口设施的建设、开发、经营，代办保税仓储，国际贸易，简单加工 Construction, Development and Management of Port Facilities, International Trade	2 999	2 999
开发、生产、加工和销售小容量注射剂、颗粒剂、外用散剂和硬胶囊剂医药产品 Development, Production, Processing and Sales of Medical Products	2 999	1 200
国际贸易及相关的简单加工，代办保税仓储，商品展示展览 International Trade, Processing, Agent for Storage, Exhibition	2 999	2 999
房地产及物流设施的建设、开发、经营；会展及物流项目的策划及咨询服务；物流分拨配送 Construction, Development of Real Estate and Logistics Facilities, Consulting Services, Logistics	2 999	2 000
城市基础设施建设、开发；高科技产品的研发、销售；国际贸易；房地产开发；健身俱乐部；旅游咨询服务 Construction and Development of Urban Infrastruction, Development and Sales of Hi - tech Products, etc	2 999	2 999
卷烟及原材料、附属材料的国际贸易；保税仓储及相关的委托加工 International Trade, Free Trade Storage and Relative Processing	2 998	2 998
有色金属复合材料、新型合金材料生产、加工、制造；自行车零部件、整车、运动器材生产制造、销售 Production, Processing of Metal Alloy Material, etc	2 998	1 500
开发和经营杨柳青文化公园 Development and Management of Yangliuqing Culture Park	2 998	2 998
对工业项目、基础设施、商业设施的开发、经营、管理，房地产经营，投资咨询，高科技产品的研制、开发 Development, Management of Industrial Projects, Infrastructure, Commerce Facilities, etc	2 998	2 998
国际贸易，简单加工，代办保税仓储，物流运转，商品的展示展销；基础设施和房地产项目的开发、建设和经营 International Trade, Agent for Storage, Exhibition, Real Estate Development, etc	2 998	2 998
生产、加工、销售功能饮料及饮品、茶饮料、软饮料 Production, Processing and Sales of Beverage	2 998	1 200
生物医药的研制、开发、技术转让 Research, Development, Technique Transmit of Living Creature Medicine	2 998	1 200
物流分拨；国际贸易；集装箱维修及简单加工；代办保税仓储服务 Logistics, International Trade, Agent for Free Trade Storage, Maintainment of Containers, etc	2 998	1 250
汽车马达及相关产品的生产、制造、销售，国际贸易，代办保税仓储 Production, Manufacturing, Sales of Auto Motor and Relative Products, International Trade, etc	2 998	2 998
国际贸易及相关的简单加工，国际物流及保税仓储 International Trade, Processing, International Logistics, Free Trade Storage	2 998	1 200
乙烯产品的储存及相关服务；技术咨询服务 Storage of Ethylene, Technique Consulting Services	2 998	1 000

11－13 续表 1　Continued

企　业　名　称 Name of Enterprise	投资方式 Investment Manner	投资国别（地区） Investment Country (Region)
天津北奥生物医药有限公司 Bioch Med－Pharma Co.,Ltd.	外资企业 Foreign－funded Enterprise	加拿大 Canada
天津华益食品有限公司 Manna Food Stuff Co.,Ltd. TianJin	外资企业 Foreign－funded Enterprise	加拿大 Canada
天津澳林文化传媒有限公司 Tianjin Only Cultrual Communication Co.,Ltd.	外资企业 Foreign－funded Enterprise	美　国 United States
新能基(天津)发展有限公司 Newsynergy Wa－do(Tianjin) Development Co.,Ltd.	外资企业 Foreign－funded Enterprise	美　国 United States
天津沣佳柔性电路有限公司 Tianjin Fengjia Gentle Electric Circuit Co.,Ltd.	外资企业 Foreign－funded Enterprise	中国香港 Hongkong,China
天津天通实业发展有限公司 Tianjin Tiantong Industrial Development Co.,Ltd.	外资企业 Foreign－funded Enterprise	中国香港 Hongkong,China
天津台荣投资咨询有限公司 Tairung Investment (Tianjin) Co.,Ltd.	外资企业 Foreign－funded Enterprise	中国台湾 Taiwan,China
天津宝润光电科技有限公司 Baorun Optical Elecrical Science and Technology Co.,Ltd.	外资企业 Foreign－funded Enterprise	中国台湾 Taiwan,China
天津达祥精密工业有限公司 Tianjin Daxiang Precision Industry Co.,Ltd.	外资企业 Foreign－funded Enterprise	英属维尔京 Virgin Islands
天津德来房地产开发有限公司 Tianjin Delai Real Estate Development Co.,Ltd.	外资企业 Foreign－funded Enterprise	萨摩亚 Samoa
天津鑫聚銮发展有限公司 Tianjin Xin Juluan Development Co.,Ltd.	中外合作 Cooperative Operation Enterprise	中国香港 Hongkong,China
天津倡億实业有限公司 Tianjin Billon Champ Industry Co.,Ltd.	中外合作 Cooperative Operation Enterprise	中国香港 Hongkong,China
天津昌京物流有限公司 Tianjin Champking Logistics Co.,Ltd.	外资企业 Foreign－funded Enterprise	中国香港 Hongkong,China
天津唐财建设开发有限公司 Tang Cai (Tianjin) Development & Construction Co.,Ltd.	外资企业 Foreign－funded Enterprise	中国香港 Hongkong,China
天津中迈投资(集团)有限公司 Tianjin Zhongmai Investment(Group) Co.,Ltd.	中外合资 Joint Venture Enterprise	新加坡 Singapore
天津天威制药有限公司 Tianjin Tianwei Natural Pharmacy Co.,Ltd.	中外合资 Joint Venture Enterprise	美　国 United States
银河富乐顿度假中心(天津)有限公司 Galaxy Fullerton Town Resort Center (Tianjin) Co.,Ltd.	中外合资 Joint Venture Enterprise	美　国 United States
天津中天元药业有限公司 Tianjin Zhongtianyuan Natural Pharmacy Co.,Ltd.	中外合资 Joint Venture Enterprise	美　国 United States
天津易航科技发展有限公司 Aegis High－Tech Development Co.,Ltd.	外资企业 Foreign－funded Enterprise	美　国 United States
天津特爱特科技开发有限公司 Tianjin Tit Science and Technology Development Co.,Ltd.	外资企业 Foreign－funded Enterprise	美　国 United States
艾尔工业气体(天津)有限公司 Air Industrial Products (TianJin) Co.,Ltd.	外资企业 Foreign－funded Enterprise	美　国 United States

经营范围 Businesse Field	合同投资总额（万美元） Value of Investment Contracted (USD 10 000)	合同外资额（万美元） Agreement Foreign Capital (USD 10 000)
生物医药研发及咨询服务；国际贸易及简单加工 Development,Consulting of Living Creature Medicine,International Trade,Processing	2 998	2 998
粮食、蔬菜、食品加工及相关配套产品的生产、销售 Production and Sales of Grain,Vegetable,Foods and Relative Products	2 998	1 200
文化交流咨询、管理咨询、广告传媒、艺术培训、音乐制作、形象设计、娱乐咨询 Cultural Exchange,Management Consulting,Advertisement Media,Art Training,etc	2 998	2 998
房地产开发建设咨询服务；高新技术及产品开发咨询服务；国际经济科技、环保信息咨询服务 Consulting Services on Real Estate Development,Hi - tech Products,etc	2 998	2 000
生产、加工、销售、研究开发柔性电路及相关产品 Production,Processing,Sales of Gentle Electric Circuit and Relative Products	2 990	1 300
国际贸易及简单加工；物流分拨配送；高科技产品及环保产品的开发等 International Trade ,Processing,Logistics,Development of Hi - tech and Environment Protection Products	2 990	1 280
国际贸易，基础设施投资，代办保税仓储，物流分拨配送，高科技产品开发 International Trade,Investment on Infrastructure,Agent for Free Trade Storage,Logistics,etc	2 990	1 250
超精硅薄膜液晶显示屏制造、生产及销售 Manufacturing,Production and Sales of Monitor	2 990	2 990
汽车用铸锻毛坯件及涡轮增压器、发动机零部件的制造、加工、装配与销售 Manufacturing,Processing,Installation and Sales of Auto Parts	2 990	1 200
房地产开发及销售；国际贸易；畜产品贸易；绿化、园林建设、养护；基础设施建设；物流分拨配送等 Real Estate Development,International Trade,Park Development,etc	2 990	1 250
包括仿古建筑在内的旅游设施开发的咨询和旅游服务相关的咨询业务 Consulting on Tourism Facility Development,Tourism Services	2 988	2 988
农副产品加工、绿菌肥、汽车关键零配件的开发、钢材压延、服装生产和销售；标准厂房的开发建设 Processing of Farm and Sideline Products,Development of Auto Parts,etc	2 980	2 520
国际贸易，简单加工，代办保税仓储，物流配送，高科技开发 International Trade,Processing,Agent for Free Trade Storage,Logistics,etc	2 980	2 980
房地产开发、销售、出租；高新科技的开发、转让 Development,Sales,Rent of Real Estate,Development and Transmit of Hi - tech	2 980	1 200
生产、加工、销售有色金属及制品 Production,Processing and Sales of Nonferrous Metal and Relative Products	2 980	1 400
中药材、中药提取物、中成药、新型心脑血管药的开发、研究及相关的技术转让和咨询服务 Development,Research,Technique Transmit and Consulting Services of Medicine	2 980	1 175
开发、建设、经营度假住宅区及国际老年公寓 Development,Construction and Management of Holiday Residential Zone,International Old - age Apartment	2 980	1 800
中西药片剂、硬胶囊剂、口服液、糊剂和化学原料药的研制、生产及销售 Research,Production and Sales of Medicine	2 980	375
在天津市范围内从事基础设施项目的投资，并提供相关的服务 Investment on Infrastructure	2 980	2 980
水及空气净化装置和成套设备、环保科技产品、生物工程设备的研发生产销售 Research,Production and Sales of Decontamination Facility,Environment Protection Products,etc	2 980	1 680
液化空气制造、提纯、销售 Manufacturing,Decontamination and Sales of Liquefaction Air	2 980	2 980

11－13 续表 2　Continued

企　业　名　称 Name of Enterprise	投资方式 Investment Manner	投资国别（地区） Investment Country (Region)
天津捷通不锈钢管材有限公司 Tianjin Jietong Stainless Steel Pipe Co.,Ltd.	外资企业 Foreign－funded Enterprise	美　国 United States
天津顺驰地产发展有限公司 Tianjin Sunco Real Estate Development Co.,Ltd.	外资企业 Foreign－funded Enterprise	英属维尔京 Virgin Islands
天津空港国际汽车园发展有限公司 Tianjin Airprort International Automobil Area Development Limited Company Co.,Ltd.	中外合资 Joint Venture Enterprise	美　国 United States
天津德新软件技术开发有限公司 Tianjin Fawer Denso Air－Conditioner Co.,Ltd.	外资企业 Foreign－funded Enterprise	英属维尔京 Virgin Islands
天津剑纳沃特印刷机械有限公司 Tianjin Janawater Printing Machinery Co.,Ltd.	外资企业 Foreign－funded Enterprise	英属维尔京 Virgin Islands
天津摩斯特制衣有限公司 Tianjin Most Garment Co.,Ltd.	中外合作 Cooperative Operation Enterprise	美　国 United States
裕田(天津)科技园开发有限公司 Grandland (Tianjin) Technology Park Co.,Ltd.	外资企业 Foreign－funded Enterprise	美　国 United States
天津泰利桦科技发展有限公司 Tianjin Tailihua Technology Development Co.,Ltd.	中外合作 Cooperative Operation Enterprise	澳大利亚 Australia
爱三(天津)汽车部件有限公司 Aisan (Tianjin) Auto Parts Co.,Ltd.	外资企业 Foreign－funded Enterprise	日　本 Japan
太平置业(天津)有限公司 Pgc (Tianjin) Co.,Ltd.	外资企业 Foreign－funded Enterprise	美　国 United States
天津康源生物工程有限公司 Tianjin Kang Yuan Biology Engineering Co.,Ltd.	外资企业 Foreign－funded Enterprise	中国香港 Hongkong,China
天津瑞克思包装材料有限公司 Tianjin RIX Package Materials Co.,Ltd.	外资企业 Foreign－funded Enterprise	中国香港 Hongkong,China
天津博瑞尔包装机械有限公司 Tianjin Borel Package Machinery Co.,Ltd.	外资企业 Foreign－funded Enterprise	英属维尔京 Virgin Islands
天津凯斯特型材有限公司 Tianjin Kaisi Special Profiles Co.,Ltd.	外资企业 Foreign－funded Enterprise	德　国 Germany
天津空港保华公共保税仓有限公司 Tianjin Airport Baohua Bond Warehouse Co.,Ltd.	中外合资 Joint Venture Enterprise	中国香港 Hongkong,China
天津益林特建材有限公司 Tianjin Yilinte Construction Materials Co.,Ltd.	外资企业 Foreign－funded Enterprise	中国香港 Hongkong,China
矽谷华孚(天津)科技发展有限公司 Top Trend & Hwafu (Tianjin) Science & Development Co.,Ltd.	外资企业 Foreign－funded Enterprise	中国香港 Hongkong,China
天津聚洋生物技术开发有限公司 Tianjin Ju Yang Bio－tech Development Co.,Ltd.	中外合资 Joint Venture Enterprise	日　本 Japan
天津尼普罗注塑有限公司 Tianjin Nipro Plastics Co.,Ltd.	外资企业 Foreign－funded Enterprise	马来西亚 Malaysia
天津劝业家乐福超市有限公司 Tianjin Quanye Carrefour Hypermarket Co.,Ltd.	中外合资 Joint Venture Enterprise	荷　兰 Netherlands
格恩(天津)公路机械有限公司 GEEN(Tianjin) Highway Machinery Co.,Ltd.	外资企业 Foreign－funded Enterprise	加拿大 Canada

经营范围 Businesse Field	合同投资总额（万美元） Value of Investment Contracted (USD 10 000)	合同外资额（万美元） Agreement Foreign Capital (USD 10 000)
生产、加工、销售不锈钢复合管材 Production, Processing and Sales of Stainless Steel Tube Materials	2 980	2 580
房地产开发与商品房销售；物业管理；建筑材料、装饰材料的生产与销售；房产经营 Real Estate Development, Commercial Houses Sales, Property Management, etc	2 972	1 812
中外品牌汽车展示、展销；中外品牌汽车 3S、4S 店经营；中外汽车仓储、分拨、配送；汽车零部件展示及交易 Exhibition, Storage, Logistics of Automobile, etc	2 960	483
计算机软件、硬件和相关产品的开发、生产及销售 Development, Production and Sales of Computer Software, Hardware and Relative Products	2 950	2 950
印刷机械，包装机械的制造、销售及印刷材料、包装材料的生产、销售；印刷、包装制品及辅助配件的生产 Manufacturing of Printing Machinery, Package Machinery and Relative Products, etc	2 900	2 000
生产、销售服装、服饰系列及服饰展示 Production and Sales of Garment, Dress Series, Dress Exhibition	2 900	2 900
区内房地产开发、建设及经营；电子、生物产品的开发、生产及销售；相关的物流仓储服务 Real Estate Development, Development, Production and Sales of Electronic & Living Creature Products, etc	2 900	2 900
环保产品，高科技产品的研发及技术服务；农业技术改造；房地产开发经营；物流分拨配送及物流咨询服务 Research, Technology Services of Environment Protection Products, Hi－tech Products, etc	2 900	2 000
汽车产业用车辆、船舶、摩托车用零部件、内燃机及其零部件和通用机械及其零部件的制造、销售和维修 Manufacturing, Sales and Maintainment of Vehicle, Ships, Parts, Machinery, etc	2 827	1 540
区内房地产和物流设施的开发、建设及经营；电子、生物产品的开发、生产、销售；相关的物流服务 Development, Construction and Management of Real Estate, Logistics Facility, etc	2 788	2 788
养殖、种植、生物提取、深加工防癌美容长寿饮品、用品；微生物肥料；抗口蹄疫饲料的生产及销售等 Farming, Processing of Anti－cancer Hairdressing Longevity Products, Microorganism Fertilizer, etc	2 750	1 100
新型食品包装材料的开发、生产和销售 Development, Production and Sales of New Food Package Materials	2 740	1 200
新型包装机械、包装材料的生产、加工、销售 Production, Processing and Sales of New Package Machinery, Package Materials	2 700	1 080
新型门窗材料的生产和销售。 Production and Sales of New Doors and Windows Materials	2 600	1 250
仓储，加工贸易，物流分拨，简单加工，自有房屋租赁 Storage, Processing Trade, Logistics, Housing Rent	2 500	780
生产、销售新型建筑材料 Production and Sales of New Construction Materials	2 500	2 500
电子产品、网络设备、纺织设备、针纺织品、服装、箱包、五金制品及相关原料的生产和销售；仓储、物流 Production and Sales of Electronic Products, Network Equipment, Textile Equipment, etc	2 500	2 500
开发、生产、销售无公害农产品及系列产品；生产、销售生物饲料 Development, Production and Sales of Harmfulness Agricultural Products, etc	2 500	1 020
加工、生产和销售精密注塑件 Processing, Production and Sales of Precise Plastics	2 500	2 500
食品、生活用品及相关商品零售及相关配套服务；配套餐饮服务及相关服务设施的经营等 Retail and Relative Services of Food, Living Articles and Relative Goods, etc	2 500	650
生产、销售公路维护机械 Production and Sales of Highway Maintainment Machinery	2 500	1 250

11-14 接待其他国家和地区旅游人数和居住天数
NUMBER OF INTERNATIONAL TOURISTS AND DWELLING DAYS
(1999-2003)

单位:人次、天 (person-times)(day)

项目	Item	1999	2000	2001	2002	2003
一、接待人数(含不过夜)	**Total Tourists(include not stay for night**	**320 777**	**356 203**	**421 422**	**506 038**	**489 017**
接待人数(过夜)	Accommodated Tourists(stay for night)	144 321	159 662	177 330	204 559	172 104
1.外国人	Foreigners	112 503	130 553	143 735	166 205	144 087
#日　本	Japan	32 862	42 530	47 418	52 748	45 268
菲律宾	Philippines	669	662	566	553	438
新加坡	Singapore	4 674	5 024	4 449	5 251	4 198
泰　国	Thailand	611	496	530	622	425
印　尼	Indonesia	574	907	689	562	510
美　国	United States	11 838	12 392	12 279	16 197	10 705
加拿大	Canada	2 010	1 745	2 031	2 055	1 651
英　国	United Kingdom	3 499	2 958	3 050	3 199	2 754
法　国	France	2 387	2 130	2 389	2 079	2 030
德　国	Germany	3 134	2 728	2 896	3 381	3 409
意大利	Italy	2 019	1 032	1 155	1 330	1 277
俄罗斯	Russia	3 699	7 312	6 654	4 352	3 337
澳大利亚	Australia	2 506	2 557	2 394	2 828	1 875
2.港澳台同胞	Hongkong,Macao & Taiwan Compatriot	27 408	29 109	33 595	38 354	28 017
二、平均每人居住天数	**Per Capita Staying Days in Tianjin**	**7.2**	**7.8**	**8.4**	**8.9**	**9.6**

11-15 接待其他国家和地区旅游外汇收入
FOREIGN EXCHANGE EARNING FROM INTERNATIONAL TOURISTS
(1999-2003)

单位:万美元 (USD 10 000)

项目	Item	1999	2000	2001	2002	2003
合　计	**Total**	**20 903**	**23 176**	**28 017**	**34 238**	**32 947**
长途交通	Long-distance Transportation Expense	8 638	9 862	12 385	12 905	12 403
飞　机	Civil Aviation	7 321	8 513	10 039	10 460	10 047
火　车	Railway	331	89	446	1 391	1 326
汽　车	Motor Vehicles	884	996	1 394	443	447
海　运	Sea Transportation	102	264	507	611	583
游　览	Tour	1 151	776	1 388	2 004	1 916
住　宿	Accommodation	3 570	2 520	3 424	4 496	4 333
餐　饮	Catering Service	1 578	1 712	2 202	2 479	2 394
娱　乐	Entertainment	1 173	936	1 362	2 528	2 427
购　物	Shopping	2 404	4 117	4 747	5 451	5 266
邮电通讯	Posts and Tele-communications	537	825	781	1 231	1 177
市内交通	Local Transportation Expense	720	339	581	1 151	1 117
其　他	Others	1 132	2 089	1 147	1 993	1 913

11－16 天津市星级饭店一览表(2003年)
LIST OF STAR－LEVEL HOTELS,2003

宾馆名称 Name of Hotel	星 级 Star Level	客房数 Number of Guest Room	床位数 Number of Beds	地 址 Address
喜来登大酒店	五 星			河西区紫金山路
SHERATON TIANJIN HOTEL	★★★★★	300	366	Zijinshan Road,Hexi Dist.
凯悦饭店	四 星			和平区解放北路219号
HYATT TIANJIN	★★★★	428	632	No.219 North Jiefang Road,Heping Dist.
水晶宫饭店	四 星			河西区友谊路28号
THE CRYSTAL PALACE HOTEL	★★★★	346	618	No.28 Youyi Road,Hexi Dist.
利顺德大饭店	四 星			和平区台儿庄路33号
ASTOR HOTEL	★★★★	208	431	No.33 Taĭerzhuang Road,Heping Dist.
津利华大酒店	四 星			河西区友谊路32号
GENEVA HOTEL	★★★★	261	460	No.32 Youyi Road,Hexi Dist.
泰达国际酒店	四 星			开发区第二大街
TEDA INTERNATIONAL HOTEL	★★★★	164	287	Second Avenue of TEDA
天津假日饭店	四 星			河北区中山路288号
HOLIDAY INN TIAN JIN	★★★★	256	345	No.288 Zhongshan Road,Hebei Dist.
美都大酒店	四 星			河西区围堤道117号
MEIDU HOTEL	★★★★	158	243	No.117 Weidi Road,Hexi Dist.
泰达中心酒店	四 星			开发区第三大街16号
TEDA CENTRAL HOTEL	★★★★	187	276	No.16 Third Avenue of TEDA
天宇大酒店	四 星			和平区卫津路143号
TIAN JIN TIAN YU HOTEL	★★★★	136	242	No.143 Weijin Road,Heping Dist.
君悦大酒店	四 星			和平区贵州路16号
JUNYUE HOTEL	★★★★	188	225	NO.16 Guizhou Road,Heping Dist.
天鹅湖温泉度假村	四 星			武清开发区福源道北
SAWN LAKE SPRING VACATION VILLAGE	★★★★	298	508	North of Fuyuan Road,Wuqing Development Area
天津利顺德大厦	四 星			和平区台儿庄路33号
ASTOR PLAZA	★★★★	83	120	No.33 Taĭerzhuang Road,Heping Dist.
友谊宾馆	三 星			和平区南京路94号
TIANJIN FRIENDSHIP HOTEL	★★★	185	598	No.94 Nanjing Road,Heping Dist.
凯撒皇宫大酒店	三 星			河西区气象台路4号
CAESAR PALACE HOTEL	★★★	72	100	No.4 Qixiangtai Road,Hexi Dist.
天津市皇宫饭店	三 星			和平区解放北路177号
TIANJIN IMPERIAC HOTEL	★★★	70	120	No.177 North Jiefang Road,Heping Dist.
华富宫大饭店	三 星			和平区南市旅馆街
GHA FU PALACE GRAND HOTEL	★★★	429	1 000	Nanshi Hotel Mall,Heping Dist.
东亚大酒店	三 星			和平区汉阳道41号
EAST ASIA HOTEL CO.LTD	★★★	109	222	No.41 Hanyang Road,Heping Dist.
龙凤酒店	三 星			河东区光华路甲1号
LONG FENG HOTEL	★★★	150	320	No.1 Guanghua road,Hedong Dist.
天津宾馆	三 星			河西区宾水道1号
TIAN JIN GRAND HOTEL	★★★	643	1 300	No.1 Binshui Road,Hexi Dist.
先达大酒店	三 星			河西区环湖中路
SINTA HOTEL	★★★	140	364	Middle Hunhu Road,Hexi Dist.
金禧国际大酒店	三 星			南开区南开三马路
CAIRNHILL INTERNATIONAL HOTEL	★★★	320	473	Sanmalu ,Nankai Dist.

11－16 续表 1　Continued

宾馆名称 Name of Hotel	星级 Star Level	客房数 Number of Guest Room	床位数 Number of Beds	地址 Address
双鹿大厦	三　星			南开区南开三马路
SHUANG LU HOTEL	★★★	109	175	Sanmalu ,Nankai Dist.
凯德大酒店	三　星			河北区自由道 15 号
KIND HOTEL	★★★	148	278	No.15 Ziyou Road,Hebei Dist.
北方宾馆	三　星			塘沽区东沽闸北路 1 号
TIAN JIN VIEW HOTEL	★★★	173	600	No.1 Zhabei Road of Donggu,Tanggu Dist.
胜利宾馆	三　星			塘沽区津塘公路 11 号
VICTORY HOTEL TIAN JIN CHINA	★★★	278	538	No.11 Jintang Highway,Tanggu Dist.
金帆大厦	三　星			天津开发区第一大街 49
GOLDEN SAIL HOTEL	★★★	80	112	NO.49 First Avenue of TEDA
夏日酒店	三　星			塘沽区滨海游乐城内
SUMMRE HOTEL	★★★	76	140	Binhai Entertainment City,Tanggu Dist.
天大天财酒店	三　星			华苑新技术产业园区榕苑路 1 号
TIANCAI HOTEL	★★★	150	289	No.1 Rongyuan Road,Hi－tech Industry Park,Huayuan
升云大酒店	三　星			大港区上古林东环海鲜街 88 号
SHENGYUN HOTEL	★★★	45	85	No.88 Haixian Street,Shanggulin,Dagang Dist.
正达酒店	三　星			河北区万柳村大街 6 号
ZHENGDA HOTEL	★★★	84	140	No.6 Wanliucun Street, Hebei Dist.
贵达酒店	三　星			宁河县苗庄镇
GUIDA HOTEL	★★★	80	190	Miaozhuang Town,Ninghe County
津海大酒店	三　星			静海县大邱庄镇
JIN HAI RESTAURANT	★★★	130	224	Daqiuzhuang Village,Jinghai County
尧舜大酒店	三　星			静海县大邱庄镇尧舜街
TIAN JIN YAO SHUN HOTEL	★★★	65	110	Raoshun Street,Daqiuzhuang Village,Jinghai County
天华宾馆	三　星			大港区津港公路南
TIANHUA HOTEL	★★★	99	433	South of Jingang Highway,Dagang Dist.
天波大酒店	三　星			河东区六经路 11 号
TIAN BO HOTEL	★★★	170	300	No.11 Liujing Road,Hedong Dist.
建设大厦	三　星			蓟县西昌北路
JIAN SHE BUILDING TIANJIN	★★★	53	104	North Xichang Road,Ji County
水上会宾园饭店	三　星			南开区水上公园路
HUI BIN YUAN HOTEL	★★★	185	180	Water Park Road,Nankai Dist.
体育宾馆	三　星			南开区宾水道延长线
SPORTS HOTEL	★★★	152	201	Continuation of Binshui Road,Nankai Dist.
红楼大酒店	三　星			南开区津淄公路 28 号
RED BUILDING HOTEL	★★★	85	174	NO.28 Jinzi Road,Nankai Dist.
温泉宾馆	三　星			河西区小围堤道
HOT SPRING HOTEL TIAN JIN	★★★	259	500	Xiaoweidi Road,Hexi Dist.
渤海度假村	三　星			塘沽区新北公路 21 号
BO HAI HOLIDAY RESORT TIAN JIN	★★★	345	820	No.21 Xinbei Road,Tanggu Dist.
天津远洋宾馆	三　星			河北区远洋广场 5 号
OCEAN HOTEL TIAN JIN	★★★	163	330	No.5 Ocean Square,Hebei Dist.
渔阳宾馆	三　星			蓟县城内迎宾路 12 号
YUYANG HOTEL	★★★	68	132	No.12 Yingbin Road of County,JiXian

11－16 续表 2　Continued

宾馆名称 Name of Hotel	星　级 Star Level	客房数 Number of Guest Room	床位数 Number of Beds	地　　址 Address
大港油田宾馆	三　星			大港油田三号院团结西路
DAGANG OIL FIELD HOTEL	★★★	164	275	No.3 yard, Tuanjie West Road, Dagang Oil Field
东丽湖度假村	三　星			东丽区东丽湖北侧
DONGLI LAKE HOLIDAY VILLAGE	★★★	111	212	North of Dongli Lake, Dongli Dist.
宝坻宾馆	三　星			宝坻区城关镇广川路 23 号
BAODI HOTEL	★★★	205	461	NO.23 Guangchuan Road,Chengguan Village,Baodi County
雍阳宾馆	三　星			武清区杨村镇
YONG YANG HOTEL	★★★	137	274	Yangcun Town,Wuqing Dist.
枫林宾馆	三　星			南开区宾水西道 2 号
FENG LIN HOTEL	★★★	84	131	No.2 West Binshui Road,Nankai Dist.
鸿发大厦	三　星			开发区洞庭路 41 号
HONGFA BUILDING	★★★	128	245	No.41 Dongting Road, TEDA
富蓝特大酒店	三　星			和平区新华路 231 号
TIAN JIN FRIEND HOTEL	★★★	58	114	No.231 Xinhua Road,Heping Dist.
憩园山庄	三　星			蓟县官庄镇
QIYUAN HOTEL	★★★	101	258	Guanzhuang Town, Jixian County
建行蓟县休养所	三　星			蓟县兴华大街 20 号
CHINA CONSTRUCTION BANK				No.20 Xinghua Street, Jixian County
JIXIAN SANATORIUM	★★★	40	90	
鸿发花园	二　星			塘沽中心北路 22 号
HONG FA HOTEL	★★	63	117	No.22 North Center Road,Tanggu Dist.
职工之家	二　星			河东区津塘路 79 号
TJFTU HOTEL	★★	152	250	No.79 Jintang Highway,Hedong Dist.
第一饭店	二　星			和平区解放北路 158 号
TIAN JIN FIRST HOTEL	★★	101	156	No.158 North Jiefang Road,Heping Dist.
贾苑大酒店	二　星			静海县东方红路 50 号
GU YUAN HOTEL	★★	120	343	No.50 Dongfanghong Road,Jinghai County
胜利宾馆度假村	二　星			蓟县逯庄子乡东大屯北
TIANJIN MUNICIPAL ENGINEERING				North of Dongdatun,Luzhuangzi Country,Jixian County
BUREAU JIXIAN WORKERS SANATORIUM	★★	90	223	
沃特文化娱乐总汇	二　星			和平区湖北路
TIAN JIN WATER HOTEL	★★	70	140	Hubei Road,Heping Dist.
富利华大酒店	二　星			河东区七纬路 104 号
FU LI HUA HOTEL	★★	61	126	No.104 Qiwei Road,Hedong Dist.
天馨宾馆	二　星			河东区六纬路 112 号
TIAN XIN HOTEL	★★	102	204	No.112 Liuwei Road,Hedong Dist.
中冀宾馆	二　星			河西区围堤道 1 号路
ZHONG JI HOTEL	★★	128	256	No.1 Weidi Road,Hexi Dist.
国际科技咨询大厦	二　星			河西区友谊路 25 号
INTER TECH HOTEL	★★	119	230	No.25 Youxi Road,Hexi Dist.
金竹宾馆	二　星			河西区尖山路 2 号
TIAN JIN GLODEN BAMBOO HOTEL	★★	86	111	No.2 Jianshan Road,Hexi Dist.
华城宾馆	二　星			南开区红旗路南路 253 号
HUA CHENG HOTEL TIAN JIN	★★	121	285	No.253 Hongqi South Road,Nankai Dist.

11－16 续表 3 Continued

宾馆名称 Name of Hotel	星 级 Star Level	客房数 Number of Guest Room	床位数 Number of Beds	地 址 Address
新港国际海员俱乐部 XIN GANG INTERNATAONAL SEAMAN'S CLUB	二 星 ★★	94	178	塘沽区新港二号路 No. 2 Road of Xingang, Tanggu Dist.
赣津宾馆 GANJIN HOTEL	二 星 ★★	88	176	河东区新开路江西大厦 Jiangxi Building, Jinkai Road, Hedong Dist.
内蒙古金马宾馆 INNER MONGOLIA JINMA HOTEL	二 星 ★★	122	200	河东区华兴街 9 号 No. 9 Huaxing Street, Hedong Dist.
康衢大酒店 COUNTRY HOTEL	二 星 ★★	140	270	南开区复康路 208 号 No. 208 Fukang Road, Nankai Dist.
麓林宾馆 LULIN HOTEL	二 星 ★★	141	228	西青区大任庄路 7 号 No. 7 Darenzhuang Road, Xiqing Dist.
杨柳青高尔夫俱乐部宾馆 YANGLIUQING GOLF CLUB HOTEL	二 星 ★★	23	40	西青区杨柳青镇一经路立交桥北 North of Yijinglu Crossroads, Yangliuqing Town, Xiqing Dist.
天津邮电蓟县疗养院 SANATORIUM OF TIANJIN POST & TELECOMMUNICATIONS	二 星 ★★	128	256	蓟县兴华大街 53 号 No. 53 Xinghua Street, Jixian County
世纪宾馆 CENTURY HOTEL	二 星 ★★	68	128	蓟县县城文昌街 42 号 No. 42 Wenchang Street, Jixian County
星尔特大酒店 XINGERTE GRAND HOTEL	二 星 ★★	119	238	河东区六纬路 91 号 No. 91 Liuwei Road, Hedong Dist
超杰大饭店 CHAOJIE HOTEL	二 星 ★★	75	150	河西区友谊路 58 号 No. 58 Youyi Road, Hexi Dist
凯特饭店 KAITE HOTEL	二 星 ★★	63	121	河西区佟楼三合里 121 号 No. 121 Sanheli Tonglou, Hexi Dist
新业国际饭店 XINYE INTERNATIONAL HOTEL	二 星 ★★	46	92	塘沽区新港路 97 号 No. 97 XIngang Road, Tanggu Dist.
宝坻长城宾馆 THE GREAT WALL HOTEL	二 星 ★★	69	152	宝坻区石华街 Shihua Street, Baodi County
新纪元大酒店 NEW CENTURY HOTEL	二 星 ★★	60	121	河西区埔口道 28 号 No. 28 Pukou Road, Hexi Dist.
碧缘宾馆 BI YUAN HOTEL	一 星 ★	85	194	河东区程林庄道 63 号 No. 63 Chenglinzhuang Road, Hedong Dist.
静海宾馆 JINGHAI HOTEL	一 星 ★	148	413	静海县城静文路 20 号 No. 20 Jingwen Road, Jinghai County
物流货运中心宾馆 OLIVE HOTEL	一 星 ★	155	298	河北区金钟河大街与外环线交口 Joint of Jinzhonghe Street and Outer Circle, Hebei Dist.
东丽宾馆 DONGLI HOTEL	一 星 ★	101	241	东丽区跃进路 30 号 No. 30 Yuejin Road, Dongli Dist.
龙脉宾馆 LONGMAI HOTEL	一 星 ★	23	60	河西区尖山路 2－1 号 No. 2－1 Jianshan Road, Hexi Dist.
学府宾馆 XUEFU HOTEL	一 星 ★	80	150	河西区水上公园北路 16 号 No. 16 Water Park North Road, Hexi Dist.

11－17 天津与国外结成友好城市一览表
LIST OF FOREIGN SISTER CITIES WITH TIANJIN

友好城市 Sister City	国 别 Country of Origin	缔结时间 Time of Conclusion	友好城市 Sister City	国 别 Country of Origin	缔结时间 Time of Conclusion
神户市	日 本	1973 年 6 月 24 日	阿比让市	科特迪瓦	1992 年 9 月 26 日
Kobe	Japan	June 24,1973	La Ville D'abidjan	Cote Divoire	Sept. 26,1992
费 城	美 国	1980 年 2 月 10 日	乌兰巴托市	蒙 古	1992 年 9 月 27 日
Philadephia	U.S.A	Feb. 10,1980	Ulan Bator	Mongolia	Sept. 27,1992
墨尔本市	澳大利亚	1980 年 5 月 5 日	哈尔科夫市	乌克兰	1993 年 6 月 14 日
Melbourne	Australia	May 5,1980	Kharkov	Ukraine	June 14,1993
四日市	日 本	1980 年 10 月 28 日	延雪坪市	瑞 典	1993 年 9 月 23 日
Yokkaichi	Japan	Oct. 28,1980	Jon Koping	Sweden	Sept. 23,1993
萨拉耶沃市	波黑共和国	1980 年 5 月 28 日	仁川市	韩 国	1993 年 12 月 7 日
Sarajevo	Bosnia Herzegovina	May 28,1980	Inchon	Republic of Korea	Dec. 7,1993
北加莱海峡大区	法 国	1984 年 10 月 10 日	萨尔州	德 国	1994 年 9 月 27 日
Region Nord Pas de Clais	France	Oct. 10,1984	State of Saarland	Germany	Sept. 27,1994
伦巴第大区	意大利	1985 年 5 月 9 日	罗兹市	波 兰	1994 年 10 月 11 日
Lombardia Region	Italy	May 9,1985	Lodz	Poland	Oct. 11,1994
格罗宁根市	荷 兰	1985 年 9 月 12 日	里约热内卢市	巴 西	1995 年 4 月 18 日
Groningen	Holand	Sept. 12,1985	Rio de Janeiro	Brazil	Apr. 18,1995
千叶市	日 本	1989 年 5 月 7 日	橘 郡	美 国	1997 年 8 月 1 日
Chiba	Japan	May 7,1989	Orange County	U.S.A	Aug. 1,1997
普罗夫迪夫大区	保加利亚	1989 年 10 月 15 日	亚马逊洲	巴 西	1997 年 10 月 21 日
Plovdiv	Bulgaria	Oct. 15,1989	State of Amazon	Brazil	Oct. 21,1997
伊兹密尔市	土耳其	1991 年 9 月 25 日	海防市	越 南	1999 年 1 月 8 日
Izmir	Turkey	Sept. 25,1991	Haiphong City	Vietnam	Jan. 8,1999

11－18 对外承包工程和劳务合作
CONTRACTED FOREIGN PROJECTS AND LABOR COOPERATION

项 目	Item	1999	2000	2001	2002	2003
签订合同份数(个)	Number of Contracts(unit)	386	574	811	501	1 107
#对外承包工程	Contracted Foreign Projects	71	83	15	89	633
劳务合作	Labor Cooperation	274	447	496	405	461
签订合同金额(万美元)	Contracted Value(USD 10 000)	21 170	22 711	30 829	28 532	40 419
#对外承包工程	Contracted Foreign Projects	10 051	14 619	10 712	17 373	31 227
劳务合作	Labor Cooperation	10 427	7 650	9 458	10 736	8 746
实际营业额(万美元)	Fulfilling Value(USD 10 000)	19 802	22 823	30 499	26 834	40 515
#对外承包工程	Contracted Foreign Projects	10 151	12 123	6 084	16 443	28 863
劳务合作	Labor Cooperation	9 277	10 261	9 691	10 139	11 161
年末在外劳动人数(人)	Number of Outside Laborers Year－end(person)	11 282	11 943	15 069	11 876	11 320
#对外承包工程	Contracted Foreign Projects	544	663	789	415	768
劳务合作	Labor Cooperation	10 736	11 278	14 265	11 421	10 544

11－19　按国别(地区)分对外承包工程和劳务合作(2003 年)

CONTRACTED FOREIGN PROJECTS AND LABOR COOPERATION BY COUNTRY (REGION),2003

国　家、地　区	Country,　Region	对外承包工程 Contracted Foreign Projects		劳务合作 Labor Cooperation	
		合同个数(个) Number of Projects	合同金额(万美元) Contracted Value(USD 10 000)	合同个数(个) Number of Projects	合同金额(万美元) Contracted Value(USD 10 000)
合　　计	**Total**	**633**	**31 227**	**461**	**8 746**
亚　洲	**Asia**	**23**	**10 877**	**149**	**5 095**
阿拉伯联合酋长国	United Arab Emirates	1	327		
阿　曼	Oman	1	5 911		
韩　国	Republic of Korea	3	22	31	1 313
伊　朗	Iran	4			
新加坡	Singapore			63	343
中国香港	Hongkong,China	3	43		913
柬埔寨	Cambodia			22	197
日　本	Japan	3	14	14	887
印度尼西亚	Indonesia	6			
越　南	Vietnam	1	2 989	3	10
中国台湾	Taiwan,China			14	1 295
马来西亚	Malaysia			1	72
约　旦	Jordan			1	65
沙特阿拉伯	Saudi Arabia	1	1 571		
非　洲	**Africa**	**18**	**2 384**	**17**	**388**
厄立特里亚	Eritrea	1	79		
南　非	South Africa			1	3
莱索托	Lesotho			6	173
赞比亚	Zambia			1	9
尼日利亚	Nigeria	6	2 114		
多　哥	Togo			1	7
突尼斯	Tunis	2			
苏　丹	Sudan	8	140		
加　纳	Ghana	1	51		
马达加斯加	Madagascar			8	196
欧　洲	**Europe**	**1**	**2**	**3**	**42**
俄罗斯联邦	Russia			2	29
英　国	United Kingdom			1	13
德　国	Germany	1	2		
拉丁美洲	**Latin America**	**9**	**788**	**6**	**87**
巴拿马	Panama			3	71
墨西哥	Mexico	5	480	3	16
委内瑞拉	Venezuela	4	308		
北美洲	**North America**	**2**	**11**	**17**	**2 773**
美　国	United States	2	11	17	2 773
大洋洲	**Oceania**			**1**	**216**
密克罗尼西亚联邦	Micronesia FS			1	216
其他国家	**Others**	**1**	**2**		
国　内	**Domestic**	**579**	**17 163**	**268**	**145**

主要统计指标解释

利用外资 包括三部分，一是对外借款；二是客商直接投资；三是客商其他投资。外资包括现金、实物、工业产权或专有技术等。凡是本年内实际投资（不论是执行本年签订的协议或是执行过去几年签订的协议）均应计算在内。

对外借款 指由我国政府、部门、企业或其他经济组织从境外借入的资金或在境外发行的外币债券。按借款类别不同划分为：外国政府贷款、国际金融组织贷款、外国银行商业贷款、出口信贷和其他：包括对外发行债券、股票等。本年鉴公布的我市的对外借款统计数据中，不含外国及港、澳、台在津投资企业的对外借款。

客商直接投资 指国外及港澳台地区的法人和自然人按照我国有关政策、法规在中国大陆地区以现金、实物、无形资产等各种方式投资于非上市公司中的全部投资及在单个外国投资者所占股权比例不低于10%的上市公司中的投资。

客商其他投资 凡是国外及港澳台地区的法人和自然人按照我国有关政策、法规在中国大陆地区以现金、实物、无形资产等各种方式进行的投资中不属于客商直接投资的部分，均列入本类。

客商直接投资协议（合同）外资额 是根据外商投资企业合同（章程）规定，外方投资者应缴付的注册资本。包括外方从企业获得的利润对企业的再投资以及批准的企业投资总额内的外方股东贷款（2002年以前还包括以企业名义从境内外借入的其他外资）。

实际利用外资 包括对外借款、客商直接投资和客商其他投资三部分实际到位的外资。对外借款按实际提取或拨交的使用数、客商直接投资按外方实际到位资金统计（以会计师事务所出具的验资报告为准）、外商其他投资按到位数计算。

口岸进出口总值 指天津口岸实际进出的货物总金额。包括天津经营单位和其他省市经营单位经天津口岸实现的进出口货物总额。按海关监管的贸易方式分为：一般贸易实际进出口货物，来料加工装配进出口货物，国家间、联合国及国际组织无偿援助物资和赠送品，华侨、港澳台同胞和外籍华人捐赠品，租赁期满归承租人所有的租赁货物，进料加工进出口货物，边境地方贸易及边境地区小额贸易进出口货物（边民互市贸易除外），中外合资企业、中外合作经营企业、外商独资经营企业进出口货物和公用物品，到、离岸价格在规定限额以上的进出口货样和广告品（无商业价值、无使用价值和免费提供出口的除外），从保税仓库提取在中国境内销售的进口货物，以及其他进出口货物。进出口总额用以观察一个国家在对外贸易方面的总规模。我国规定出口货物按离岸价格统计，进口货物按到岸价格统计。

外贸进出口总额 指所有天津进出口经营单位经天津口岸和其他省市口岸进出口货物的总金额。自1999年1月开始使用海关统计数据。

Explanatory Notes on Main Statistical Indicators

Utilization of Foreign Capital includes foreign loans, foreign direct investment, other foreign investment. Foreign capital includes cash, foods, industrial property right, special technique, etc. It includes actual investment in current year or signed in previous years.

Foreign Borrowing refer to funds borrowed from abroad by the Chinese government, departments, enterprises and other economic units, foreign currency bond issued abroad. Grouped by the category of borrowing, it includes (a) loans of foreign governments, (b) loans of international financial institutions, (c) commercial loans of foreign banks, (d) export credit of foreign banks, (e) bonds, shares issued abroad, etc. The data in this yearbook excludes foreign borrowing of foreign funded and Hongkong, Macao and Taiwan funded enterprises.

Foreign Direct Investment refers to the investment inside China by foreign funded and Hongkong, Macao and Taiwan funded enterprises, economic organizations or individuals, following the relevant policies and laws of China and using cash, practicalities technology, for the investment of corporations that are not listed in stock market, share ownership of single foreign investor is not lower than 10%.

Other Investment by Foreign Enterprises refers to the investment other than foreign direct investment inside China by foreign funded and Hongkong, Macao and Taiwan funded enterprises, economic organizations or individuals, following the relevant policies and laws of China and using cash, practicalities technology.

Foreign Direct Investment Contracted refer to the total registered capital that according to the contract, foreign investor should provide. It includes re－investment of foreign investor using the profits obtained from enterprise, loans of foreigns shareholder among the total investment (also includes other investment of enterprise borrowed from China and abroad before 2002).

Foreign Capital Actually Used refers to the actual investment of foreign borrowing, foreign direct investment and other investment by foreign enterprises. It includes actual withdraw of foreign borrowing, actual capital of foreign direct investment (in accordance with the capital report of Accountant Services), actual capital of other investment by foreign enterprises.

Total Imports and Exports at Customs refer to the value of commodities imported into and exported from Tianjin Custom. It includes the value of commodities imported into and exported from Tianjin Custom of Tianjin business units and business units of other provinces(municipalities). Imports and exports trade are the base on customs supervision, being divided into the actual imports and exports from common trade, imported and exported goods under the processing and assembling trades and materials, supplies and gifts as aid given gratis between governments and by the United Nations and other international organizations, and contributions donated by overseas Chinese, compatriots in HongKong and Macao and Chinese with foreign citizenship, leasing commodities owned by tenant at the expiration of leasing period, imported and exported commodities processed with imported materials, commodities trading in border areas (excluding mutual exchange goods), the imported and exported commodities and articles for public use of the Sino－foreign joint ventures, cooperative enterprises and ventures exclusively with foreign own investment. Also included are import and export of samples and advertising goods for whose CIF or FOB value are beyond the permitted ceiling (excluding goods of no trading or use value and free commodities for export), imported goods sold in China from bonded warehouses and other imported or exported goods. The indicator of the total imports and exports at customs can be used to observe the total size of external trade in a country. In accordance with the stipulation of the Chinese government, imports are calculated at CIF, while exports are calculated at FOB.

Foreign Trade Imports & Exports include imports and exports of business units of Tianjin at Tianjin customs and other customs. The data of customs statistics has been used since January, 1999.

第12篇 CHAPTER 12

财政和金融

GOVERNMENT FINANCE AND BANKING

12－1　全市财政收支
TOTAL FINANCIAL REVENUE AND EXPENDITURE
（1994－2003）

年　份 Year	全市财政收入 Total Financial Revenue	一般预算收入 General Budgetary Financial Revenue	基金收入 Fund Revenue	全市财政支出 Total Financial Expenditure	一般预算支出 General Budgetary Financial Expenditure	基金支出 Fund Expenditure
绝对数(亿元)						
Value						
(100 million yuan)						
1994	95.99	95.99		69.00	69.00	
1995	117.34	117.34		90.37	90.37	
1996	137.45	137.45		110.19	110.19	
1997	169.12	151.42	17.70	140.08	122.78	17.30
1998	186.55	170.07	16.47	155.15	137.93	17.22
1999	206.89	187.14	19.75	177.62	157.41	20.21
2000	244.81	222.70	22.11	209.57	187.05	22.52
2001	304.52	279.41	25.12	259.78	234.67	25.11
2002	375.92	339.81	36.11	300.07	265.21	34.86
2003	451.74	410.95	40.79	350.63	312.08	38.56
比上年增长%						
Increase Rate over						
Preceding Year						
1995	22.2	22.2		31.0	31.0	
1996	15.8	15.8		21.9	21.9	
1997	13.5	10.2		13.8	11.4	
1998	10.3	12.3	－6.9	8.0	6.9	16.8
1999	10.9	10.0	19.9	14.5	14.1	17.3
2000	18.3	19.0	11.9	16.4	17.1	11.2
2001	24.4	25.5	13.6	25.7	27.3	11.8
2002	18.4	14.7	43.8	15.5	13.0	39.6
2003	20.2	21.0	12.9	16.8	17.8	10.0

资料来源：天津市财政局
Information source：Tianjin Municipal Finance Bureau.
注：1.本表收支均未含以港养港收支。2.增长速度均按可比口径计算。3.12－2至12－5表同。
Note：a) Revenue and expenditure in this table exclude expenses charged and used for operation of Tianjin Port. b) Increase rate is calculated on the basis of comparable coverage. c) Same as following table 12－2 to 12－5.

12-2 地方一般预算财政收入
LOCAL GENERAL BUDGETARY FINANCIAL REVENUE
(1994-2003)

年 份 Year	地方一般预算收入 Local General Budgetary Finan-cial Revenue	#增值税(25%) Value-added Tax(25%)	#营业税 Operating Tax	#企业所得税 Income Tax of Enterprises	#个人所得税 Individual Income Tax
绝对数(亿元) Value (100 million yuan)					
1994	46.83	14.26	15.17	11.21	2.41
1995	58.94	16.66	19.86	12.67	3.77
1996	76.02	17.25	24.67	19.06	5.30
1997	89.91	17.30	27.60	21.48	6.49
1998	101.40	18.99	30.71	20.34	7.91
1999	112.81	20.83	33.88	24.02	8.86
2000	133.61	26.12	38.16	29.25	11.34
2001	163.64	34.87	42.99	39.38	16.58
2002	171.83	38.73	51.65	26.24	13.20
2003	204.53	45.19	64.32	23.80	12.53
比上年增长% Increase Rate over Preceding year					
1995	16.0	28.8	42.6	13.0	56.5
1996	29.0	3.6	24.2	50.4	40.4
1997	18.3	0.3	11.9	12.7	22.5
1998	12.8	9.8	11.3	-5.3	21.9
1999	11.3	9.7	10.3	18.1	12.1
2000	18.4	25.4	12.6	21.8	27.9
2001	22.5	33.5	12.7	34.6	46.2
2002	16.9	11.1	20.1	9.6	23.1
2003	24.8	16.7	24.5	13.6	18.7

注:2002年开始中央与地方实施所得税收入分享改革,所得税中央与地方分享比例2002年为5:5,2003年为6:4。下同。
Note:Since 2002,the distribution of income tax is reformed, central government and local government go shares for income tax at equal share of 50% each in 2002,central government shares 60% and local government shares 40% in 2003.Same as following table next.

12-3 一般预算财政支出
GENERAL BUDGETARY FINANCIAL EXPENDITURE
(1994-2003)

年 份 Year	一般预算支出 General Budgetary Financial Expenditure	#基本建设 Capital Construction	#支援农业 Supporting Agriculture	#教育事业费 Operating Expense of Education	#城市维护费 City Maintenance	#科技三项费用 Science and Technology Promotion
绝对数(亿元) Value (100 million yuan)						
1994	69.00	9.69	2.29	11.41	6.88	0.94
1995	90.37	17.95	2.81	13.41	7.82	0.99
1996	110.19	23.20	3.11	16.62	10.33	1.16
1997	122.78	22.69	3.72	19.07	12.30	1.43
1998	137.93	24.16	4.00	21.74	15.13	1.58
1999	157.41	22.87	4.38	25.33	14.89	2.32
2000	187.05	29.71	4.65	30.87	15.90	3.69
2001	234.67	37.43	5.74	36.26	16.09	6.06
2002	265.21	39.36	7.05	41.57	20.44	6.68
2003	312.08	52.43	8.04	47.58	27.61	7.80
比上年增长% Increase Rate over Preceding year						
1994	39.6	38.7	14.5	44.1	39.5	6.1
1995	31.0	85.3	22.7	17.5	13.7	10.3
1996	21.9	29.3	10.6	23.9	32.1	17.4
1997	11.4	-2.2	19.6	14.7	19.1	22.8
1998	6.9	6.5	7.6	14.0	23.0	10.4
1999	14.1	-5.4	9.5	16.5	-1.6	47.0
2000	17.1	29.9	6.2	21.9	6.7	59.2
2001	27.3	26.0	23.4	17.4	1.2	64.0
2002	13.0	5.2	22.9	14.7	27.0	10.2
2003	17.8	33.2	14.3	14.4	35.1	16.8

12-4 财政收支
FINANCIAL REVENUE AND EXPENDITURE

单位:万元 (10 000 yuan)

项目	Item	2002	2003	2003 比2002年增长% Increase Rate in 2003 over 2002
财政收入合计	**Total Revenue**	**3 759 184**	**4 517 368**	**20.2**
#一般预算收入	General Budgetary Financial Revenue	3 398 056	4 109 493	21.0
一、地方财政收入	**Local Financial Revenue**	**2 079 451**	**2 453 170**	**22.6**
1.一般预算收入	**General Budgetary Financial Revenue**	**1 718 323**	**2 045 295**	**24.8**
#税收收入	Revenue from Taxs	1 548 131	1 775 553	20.9
#增值税(25%)	Value-added Tax(25%)	387 315	451 925	16.7
营业税	Operating Tax	516 467	643 231	24.5
个人所得税	Individual Income Tax	132 035	125 347	18.7
企业所得税	Income Tax of Enterprises	262 430	238 022	13.6
国有企业计划亏损补贴类	Planning Subsidies to Loss-suffering State-owned Enterprises	-30 000	-30 000	
罚没收入	Penalty and Confiscatory Income	62 545	59 786	-4.4
行政性收费收入	Income from Administrative Fees	73 124	147 274	101.4
专项收入类	Special Project Income	49 095	60 031	22.3
基金预算收入	**Budgetary Fund Revenue**	**361 128**	**407 875**	**12.9**
2.市级财政收入	**Financial Revenue at City Level**	**1 079 411**	**1 255 540**	**19.5**
一般预算收入	General Budgetary Financial Revenue	786 750	1 001 900	32.2
基金收入	Budgetary Fund Revenue	292 661	253 640	-13.3
区县级财政收入	**Financial Revenue at District & County Level**	**1 000 040**	**1 197 630**	**26.1**
一般预算收入	General Budgetary Financial Revenue	931 573	1 043 395	18.4
基金收入	Budgetary Fund Revenue	68 467	154 235	125.3
二、上划中央收入小计	**Revenue Transferred to Central Government**	**1 679 733**	**2 064 198**	**17.4**
财政支出合计	**Total Expenditures**	**3 000 699**	**3 506 322**	**16.8**
1.一般预算支出合计	**General Budgetary Financial Expenditure**	**2 652 103**	**3 120 771**	**17.8**
#基本建设支出	Capital Construction	393 565	524 274	33.2
企业挖潜改造资金	Innovation Funds of Enterprises	307 820	293 732	-4.6
科技三项费用	Science and Technology Promotion	66 774	78 023	16.8
支援农村生产支出	Supporting Agricultural Production	70 476	80 363	14.3
工交流通等部门事业费	Operating Expenses of Industrial, Transportation and Commercial Departments	11 830	16 492	39.4
城市维护建设费	Expenditure for City Maintenance	204 363	276 061	35.1
文体广播事业费	Operating Expenses of Culture, Sports and Broadcasting	63 087	71 864	14.3
教育事业费	Operating Expenses of Education	415 730	475 804	14.4
科学事业费	Operating Expenses of Science	15 593	19 403	24.4
卫生经费	Funds of Health Care	117 052	153 135	30.8
社会保障和优抚救济支出	Social Security and Pensions, Relief	286 165	334 399	16.8
政策性补贴支出	Expenditure for Price Subsidies	23 969	31 147	30.0
基金预算支出	**Budgetary Fund Expenditures**	**348 596**	**385 551**	**10.0**
2.市级财政支出	**Financial Expenditures at City Level**	**1 534 221**	**1 752 792**	**14.2**
一般预算支出	General Budgetary Financial Expenditure	1 236 551	1 496 701	21.0
基金支出	Fund Expenditures	297 670	256 091	-14.0
区县级财政支出	**Financial Expenditures at District & County Level**	**1 466 478**	**1 753 530**	**19.6**
一般预算支出	General Budgetary Financial Expenditure	1 415 552	1 624 070	14.7
基金支出	Fund Expenditures	50 926	129 460	154.2

12－5 区县级一般预算财政收支(2003年)

GENERAL BUDGETARY FINANCIAL REVENUE & EXPENDITURE AT DISTRICT & COUNTY LEVEL,2003

单位:万元 (10 000 yuan)

地区	Region	一般预算财政收入 General Budgetary Financial Revenue	增值税 Value－added Tax	营业税 Operating Tax	个人所得税 Individual Income Tax
总计	**Total**	**1 043 395**	**239 671**	**289 635**	**47 405**
和平区	Heping District	59 815	4 295	26 327	3 045
河东区	Hedong District	43 822	4 581	15 924	1 656
河西区	Hexi District	68 999	6 267	22 977	3 040
南开区	Nankai District	58 051	7 111	16 663	2 276
河北区	Hebei District	32 359	4 334	10 428	1 211
红桥区	Hongqiao District	19 273	2 627	5 969	817
塘沽区	Tanggu District	49 763	5 846	18 195	1 978
汉沽区	Hangu District	10 683	2 511	1 648	194
大港区	Dagang District	28 261	3 752	6 788	800
东丽区	Dongli District	39 504	9 869	9 106	1 934
西青区	Xiqing District	60 064	11 038	16 793	1 730
津南区	Jinnan District	24 766	5 613	7 202	1 120
北辰区	Beichen District	44 699	11 771	11 455	1 665
武清区	Wuqing District	43 995	9 036	12 264	2 532
宝坻区	Baodi District	18 068	2 473	3 980	540
宁河县	Ninghe County	14 767	1 897	3 748	392
静海县	Jinghai County	17 554	3 205	4 325	538
蓟　县	Jixian County	16 805	2 156	3 049	594
开发区	TEDA	313 829	124 303	68 196	15 780
保税区	TPFTZ	40 858	6 720	15 255	3 243
新技术产业园区	THIP	37 460	10 266	9 343	2 320

地区	Region	城市维护建设税 Tax on Urban Maintenance and Construction	农业各税 Agricultural and Related Taxes	企业所得税 Income Tax of Enterprises	其他各项收入 Others
总计	**Total**	**53 261**	**98 750**	**131 898**	**182 775**
和平区	Heping District	2 812	5 710	4 431	13 195
河东区	Hedong District	2 348	8 009	2 074	9 230
河西区	Hexi District	2 360	18 240	3 797	12 318
南开区	Nankai District	2 368	13 869	3 746	12 018
河北区	Hebei District	1 605	4 815	2 548	7 418
红桥区	Hongqiao District	1 012	3 499	1 110	4 239
塘沽区	Tanggu District	5 725	3 159	2 255	12 605
汉沽区	Hangu District	1 431	412	549	3 938
大港区	Dagang District	2 583	1 210	1 632	11 496
东丽区	Dongli District	4 031	3 624	3 854	7 086
西青区	Xiqing District	3 700	10 579	5 805	10 419
津南区	Jinnan District	1 333	2 543	2 820	4 135
北辰区	Beichen District	2 813	4 934	5 271	6 790
武清区	Wuqing District	3 499	5 366	4 330	6 968
宝坻区	Baodi District	1 476	2 541	687	6 371
宁河县	Ninghe County	1 065	865	837	5 963
静海县	Jinghai County	1 322	2 439	1 051	4 674
蓟　县	Jixian County	2 553	716	606	7 131
开发区	TEDA	5 306	3 612	68 836	27 796
保税区	TPFTZ	1 171	949	8 584	4 936
新技术产业园区	THIP	2 748	1 659	7 075	4 049

12－5 续表 Continued
单位:万元 (10 000 yuan)

地区	Region	一般预算财政支出 Financial Expenditure at District and County Level	#基本建设支出 Capital Construction	#支援农村生产支出 Supporting Agricultural Production	#教育事业费 Operating Expenses of Education
总计	**Total**	**1 624 070**	**382 194**	**33 865**	**315 662**
和平区	Heping District	78 409	12 913		20 171
河东区	Hedong District	60 803	300		19 660
河西区	Hexi District	70 595	5 129		22 549
南开区	Nankai District	60 574	399		20 907
河北区	Hebei District	56 052	1 065		18 550
红桥区	Hongqiao District	47 505	75		16 821
塘沽区	Tanggu District	82 836		1 711	22 980
汉沽区	Hangu District	24 459	330	721	6 515
大港区	Dagang District	48 664	3 487	1 617	11 089
东丽区	Dongli District	57 729	9 342	4 754	15 282
西青区	Xiqing District	96 576	46 384	1 559	12 933
津南区	Jinnan District	52 165	7 279	1 836	11 827
北辰区	Beichen District	73 219	17 416	1 950	18 137
武清区	Wuqing District	95 038	1 149	7 266	26 039
宝坻区	Baodi District	46 584	750	3 427	18 869
宁河县	Ninghe County	30 933		1 428	10 203
静海县	Jinghai County	42 785	700	5 639	14 514
蓟县	Jixian County	36 429	320	1 957	16 142
开发区	TEDA	428 833	183 392		8 474
保税区	TPFTZ	104 812	77 245		2 000
新技术产业园区	THIP	29 070	14 519		2 000

地区	Region	#医疗卫生支出 Funds of Health Care	#社会保障补助支出 Subsidies for Social Security	#公检法司支出 Public Security Agency,Procuratorial Agency & Court of Justice
总计	**Total**	**70 978**	**7 010**	**81 412**
和平区	Heping District	4 989	112	6 554
河东区	Hedong District	4 387	220	5 510
河西区	Hexi District	5 251	415	5 511
南开区	Nankai District	4 848	164	6 070
河北区	Hebei District	5 494	222	5 075
红桥区	Hongqiao District	4 293	346	4 583
塘沽区	Tanggu District	3 277	3 756	7 962
汉沽区	Hangu District	2 176	189	2 120
大港区	Dagang District	2 367	224	3 715
东丽区	Dongli District	4 768	116	3 057
西青区	Xiqing District	2 982	19	3 262
津南区	Jinnan District	4 627	57	2 140
北辰区	Beichen District	4 130	33	2 514
武清区	Wuqing District	4 755	55	4 680
宝坻区	Baodi District	2 501	228	1 464
宁河县	Ninghe County	780	110	1 590
静海县	Jinghai County	2 748	10	4 318
蓟县	Jixian County	1 952	112	4 991
开发区	TEDA	4 329	362	5 681
保税区	TPFTZ	282	200	560
新技术产业园区	THIP	42	60	55

12－6 天津市国家税务局各项税收情况
TAX REVENUE OF TIANJIN NATIONAL TAX BUREAU
(1999－2003)

单位:万元 (10 000 yuan)

项目	Item	1999	2000	2001	2002	2003
总计	**Total**	**1 819 120**	**2 576 539**	**2 913 569**	**3 412 625**	**4 064 420**
一、税收合计	**Total Tax**	**1 816 151**	**2 570 504**	**2 895 242**	**3 876 635**	**4 693 511**
#增值税	Value－added Tax	1 461 335	2 005 818	2 057 409	2 952 659	3 595 089
消费税	Consumption Tax	143 795	142 186	147 029	200 445	289 421
营业税	Operating Tax	52 001	53 496	44 771	33 876	28 396
企业所得税	Income Tax of Enterprises	23 569	78 624	107 394	72 838	134 168
#国有企业	State－owned Enterprises	11 068	22 789	23 030	23 975	22 144
集体企业	Collective－owned Enterprises	3 904	3 505	1 340	4 558	4 933
股份合作企业	Cooperative Enterprises				87	711
联营企业	Joint Ownership Enterprises	323	338	745	613	322
有限责任公司	Limited Liability Corporations				5 204	22 057
股份有限公司	Share－holding Corporations Ltd.	8 162	51 833	82 261	38 156	82 605
私营企业	Private Enterprises				245	1 396
外商投资企业和外国企业所得税	Income Tax of Foreign and Foreign－founded Enterprises	126 823	248 107	463 259	531 775	553 412
个人所得税	Individual Income Tax	6 827	38 390	71 130	80 752	86 507
城市维护建设税	Tax on Urban Maintenance and Construction	1 138	2 704	2 167	2 104	3 223
房产税	Tax on Real Estates			502	526	574
印花税	Stamp Tax	653	1 179	1 403	1 473	2 562
城镇土地使用税	Tax on the Use of Town Land			153	153	129
车船使用税	Tax on the Use of Vehicle and Ship			25	34	30
二、出口退税合计	**Tax Returned from Export Enterprises**				**－495 912**	**－679 190**
三、其他收入合计	**Others**	**2 969**	**6 035**	**18 327**	**31 902**	**50 099**
#教育费附加收入	Revenue from Extra－Charges for Education	487	1 159	929	902	1 381

12－7　各类金融机构和人员
FINANCIAL INSTITUTIONS AND PERSONNEL

项　目	Item	机　构（个）Institutions (unit) 2001	2002	2003
各类金融机构	**Financial Institutions**	**2 761**	**2 850**	**2 837**
一、银行类机构	**Banking Institutions**	**1 703**	**1 653**	**1 594**
中央银行	Central Banks	2	2	2
政策性银行	Policy Banks	10	10	10
商业银行	Commercial Banks	1 677	1 627	1 567
国有独资商业银行	State－owned Sole Commercial Banks	1 426	1 361	1 279
股份制商业银行	Share－holding Commercial Banks	92	104	108
天津城市商业银行	Tianjin City Commercial Banks	159	160	180
外资银行	Foreign Funded Banks	14	14	15
二、非银行类机构	**Non－banking Institutions**	**1 058**	**1 197**	**1 243**
保险公司	Insurance Companies	105	311	369
信托投资公司	Trust Investment Companies	3	3	2
证券经营公司	Securities Business Companies	93	85	78
农村信用社	Rural Credit Cooperatives	566	507	503
财务公司	Financial Affairs Companies	1	1	1
邮局储蓄所	Savings Deposit Offices of Postal Offices	286	286	286
金融资产管理	Finance Assets Supervision Corporation	4	4	4

项　目	Item	人　员（人）Personnel (person) 2001	2002	2003
各类金融机构	**Financial Institutions**	**43 724**	**41 765**	**46 436**
一、银行类机构	**Banking Institutions**	**32 613**	**29 293**	**32 777**
中央银行	Central Banks	733	678	575
政策性银行	Policy Banks	284	288	292
商业银行	Commercial Banks	31 338	28 059	31 630
国有独资商业银行	State－owned Sole Commercial Banks	25 402	22 658	25 563
股份制商业银行	Share－holding Commercial Banks	1 924	1 934	2 362
天津城市商业银行	Tianjin City Commercial Banks	4 012	4 032	3 705
外资银行	Foreign Funded Banks	258	268	280
二、非银行类机构	**Non－banking Institutions**	**11 111**	**12 472**	**13 659**
保险公司	Insurance Companies	2 790	3 246	5 000
信托投资公司	Trust Investment Companies	404	376	277
证券经营公司	Securities Business Companies	2 190	3 000	3 000
农村信用社	Rural Credit Cooperatives	4 711	4 701	4 701
财务公司	Financial Affairs Companies	17	16	16
邮局储蓄所	Savings Deposit Offices of Postal Offices	800	800	435
金融资产管理	Finance Assets Supervision Corporation	199	333	230

12－8　改革开放以来金融机构各项存贷款余额
DEPOSITS AND LOANS OF FINANCIAL INSTITUTIONS SINCE REFORM AND OPENING UP

单位:亿元　　　　(100 million yuan)

年份 Year	存款合计 Total Deposits	企业存款 Deposits of Enterprises	财政性存款 Treasury Deposits	储蓄存款 Savings Deposits	农业存款 Agricultural Deposits	信托及其他类存款 Trusted Deposits and Others	贷款合计 Total Loans	#工业贷款 Industrial Loans
1978	33.24	15.80	11.02	4.02	2.40		80.14	34.27
1979	44.59	19.34	12.63	5.77	3.10		88.74	38.71
1980	44.92	23.83	8.99	7.96	3.55	0.59	102.66	38.60
1981	53.25	25.08	10.23	9.70	4.70	3.54	107.73	37.09
1982	68.05	32.97	11.73	12.50	6.18	4.67	112.61	36.89
1983	75.83	35.62	11.58	16.67	7.85	4.11	125.38	39.01
1984	95.52	45.76	10.98	22.19	6.87	9.72	138.99	46.76
1985	114.25	58.48	13.82	29.38	4.52	8.05	191.04	65.99
1986	129.14	63.22	11.32	40.52	5.61	8.48	224.49	77.91
1987	156.48	70.41	12.65	54.95	6.77	11.70	260.12	83.64
1988	176.44	72.77	14.35	62.72	9.45	17.16	296.18	92.32
1989	203.44	70.24	16.20	89.71	8.51	18.79	341.60	110.60
1990	263.21	86.66	19.15	126.92	9.42	21.07	415.91	136.49
1991	336.56	106.84	24.73	163.18	13.15	28.67	487.43	158.14
1992	467.81	157.39	23.50	202.66	18.51	65.75	624.82	182.23
1993	586.12	193.71	23.78	269.70	21.75	77.19	768.57	223.91
1994	800.56	301.12	24.26	394.50	18.26	62.43	927.05	248.74
1995	1 079.97	385.21	37.59	549.97	22.87	84.33	1 113.95	289.50
1996	1 399.06	527.68	28.54	724.91	25.82	98.64	1 357.38	340.91
1997	1 634.95	638.88	26.22	863.36	28.76	77.73	1 502.91	379.86
1998	1 860.84	655.38	12.53	1 020.14	34.28	138.50	1 629.12	407.52
1999	2 060.02	736.03	45.78	1 130.19	37.94	110.08	1 825.26	429.22
2000	2 281.55	871.31	53.97	1 172.40	44.10	139.76	1 863.60	369.25
2001	2 562.55	946.89	63.82	1 284.95	56.32	210.56	2 159.86	433.16
2002	3 018.26	1 115.35	102.30	1 486.38	73.86	240.37	2 519.04	450.32
2003	4 033.51	1 542.75	136.89	1 825.32	164.72	363.83	3 426.02	429.13

年份 Year	#商业贷款 Commercial Loans	#建筑业贷款 Construction Loans	#私营及个体贷款 Loans to Private and Individuals	#乡镇企业贷款 Loans to Township Enterprises	#农业贷款 Agricultural Loans	#中长期贷款 Medium－term & Long－term Loans	#信托类贷款及其他 Credit Loans and Others
1978	45.16	0.01			0.42	0.28	
1979	49.14				0.46	0.43	0.01
1980	60.07	0.23		0.33	0.44	2.82	0.17
1981	63.57	0.25		0.60	0.49	5.64	0.17
1982	65.14	0.26		0.81	0.54	8.70	0.27
1983	72.38	0.38		1.15	0.64	10.70	1.12
1984	64.07	2.66	0.02	3.00	1.37	14.21	6.90
1985	76.72	5.46	0.01	3.50	11.61	19.63	8.11
1986	90.76	6.39	0.01	5.68	7.86	26.59	9.29
1987	102.27	7.00	0.02	7.52	11.58	32.35	15.74
1988	118.21	7.37	0.06	8.90	14.97	35.47	18.89
1989	138.68	7.54	0.06	9.24	19.59	37.55	18.33
1990	162.49	8.23	0.09	10.75	27.29	50.00	20.57
1991	173.04	8.86	0.11	12.20	36.26	73.88	24.95
1992	196.20	9.75	0.14	13.50	49.78	105.67	67.56
1993	223.91	10.76	0.80	16.18	65.83	143.93	83.25
1994	219.58	13.06	1.44	67.29	16.58	210.87	71.98
1995	242.71	16.18	3.47	85.70	22.46	262.01	85.70
1996	278.76	31.82	11.48	106.12	29.66	305.50	116.22
1997	297.74	36.28	8.63	125.32	41.46	298.81	67.61
1998	295.91	37.38	10.11	147.17	50.65	302.69	94.42
1999	292.08	36.00	10.15	163.59	51.33	405.04	113.77
2000	235.64	44.85	15.64	163.14	42.65	431.27	113.89
2001	249.95	60.84	38.96	174.28	47.55	637.76	137.91
2002	240.68	77.45	34.76	192.22	74.99	846.93	179.49
2003	275.22	95.23	31.50	239.98	132.30	1 468.35	283.53

注:1.从1993年起存款合计中含"中央财政存款"。2.中长期贷款1994年以前为固定资产贷款,1998年起中长期贷款中含中期流动资金贷款。3.农业存款1996年以前为农村存款。4.12－9表同。

Note:a) Since 1993, Total deposits includes central treasury deposits. b) Before 1994, medium－term & long－term loans refers to fixed assets loans, it has included medium－term circulating capital loans since 1998. c) Agricultural deposits refers to rural deposits before 1996. d) Same as following table 12－9.

12－9 改革开放以来银行机构各项存贷款余额

DEPOSITS AND LOANS OF BANKING INSTITUTIONS SINCE REFORM AND OPENING UP

单位：亿元 (100 million yuan)

年份 Year	存款合计 Total Deposits	企业存款 Deposits of Enterprises	财政性存款 Treasury Deposits	储蓄存款 Savings Deposits	农业存款 Agricultural Deposits	信托及其他类存款 Trusted Deposits and Others	贷款合计 Total Loans	#工业贷款 Industrial Loans
1978	32.85	15.80	11.02	3.64	2.40		80.14	34.27
1979	40.30	19.34	12.63	5.23	3.10		88.74	38.71
1980	44.05	23.83	8.99	7.10	3.55	0.59	102.66	38.60
1981	51.93	25.08	10.23	8.39	4.70	3.54	107.73	37.09
1982	66.12	32.97	11.73	10.57	6.18	4.67	112.61	36.89
1983	72.70	35.62	11.58	13.54	7.85	4.11	125.38	39.01
1984	91.38	45.76	10.98	18.06	6.87	9.72	138.99	46.76
1985	111.14	58.48	13.82	23.77	7.03	8.05	181.00	65.99
1986	122.55	63.31	11.08	32.48	9.58	6.10	217.77	77.88
1987	143.36	69.84	12.38	43.81	10.61	6.71	247.39	83.26
1988	157.55	70.71	14.82	49.83	12.83	9.35	277.08	91.29
1989	180.08	68.11	16.20	72.30	11.80	11.68	320.59	109.07
1990	236.31	83.78	19.15	101.88	18.58	12.92	387.72	134.42
1991	297.65	103.33	24.73	130.31	22.86	16.43	449.95	155.69
1992	376.19	141.99	23.50	160.47	24.27	25.96	539.53	178.32
1993	461.52	158.42	23.77	215.28	28.74	35.29	655.99	218.90
1994	596.96	250.75	24.26	317.46	2.31	2.18	788.51	243.47
1995	812.45	321.99	37.59	445.14	2.89	4.83	898.43	283.26
1996	1 071.75	443.35	28.54	593.35	2.59	3.93	1 147.90	332.65
1997	1 415.43	630.45	26.22	741.43	2.70	14.62	1 334.79	379.27
1998	1 605.63	648.00	12.53	880.82	2.78	61.50	1 427.53	406.79
1999	1 801.79	728.74	45.69	975.06	2.89	49.41	1 606.22	428.54
2000	2 000.58	861.62	53.88	1 011.47	2.54	71.07	1 635.99	368.86
2001	2 255.95	934.36	63.67	1 117.34	3.76	136.83	1 918.86	432.23
2002	2 672.47	1 090.57	102.16	1 308.25	3.69	167.80	2 233.48	448.66
2003	3 482.63	1 466.20	136.63	1 593.74	4.33	281.73	2 973.90	427.43

年份 Year	#商业贷款 Commercial Loans	#建筑业贷款 Construction Loans	#私营及个体贷款 Loans to Private and Individuals	#乡镇企业贷款 Loans to Township Enterprises	#农业贷款 Agricultural Loans	#中长期贷款 Medium－term & Long－term Loans	#信托类贷款及其他 Credit Loans and Others
1978	45.16	0.01			0.42	0.28	
1979	49.14				0.46	0.43	0.01
1980	60.07	0.23		0.33	0.44	2.82	0.17
1981	63.57	0.25		0.60	0.49	5.64	0.17
1982	65.14	0.26		0.81	0.54	8.70	0.27
1983	72.38	0.38		1.15	0.64	10.70	1.12
1984	64.07	2.66	0.02	3.00	1.37	14.21	6.90
1985	76.72	5.46	0.01	3.50	1.58	19.63	7.08
1986	90.72	6.39	0.01	5.68	2.08	26.59	6.46
1987	101.82	7.00	0.01	7.52	2.98	32.35	7.39
1988	117.16	7.37	0.03	8.90	4.11	35.47	6.98
1989	137.44	7.54	0.04	9.24	5.70	37.55	14.00
1990	160.99	8.23	0.04	10.75	7.86	50.00	15.43
1991	171.22	8.86	0.03	12.20	9.74	73.88	18.34
1992	190.01	9.75	0.03	13.50	11.16	105.67	31.09
1993	210.73	10.76	0.05	16.18	14.20	143.93	41.23
1994	214.48	13.06	0.14	21.00	12.31	203.97	18.82
1995	237.52	16.18	0.10	25.42	16.37	257.00	21.28
1996	271.66	31.82	0.29	35.78	22.66	303.03	37.28
1997	297.74	36.28	8.63	41.29	30.43	297.02	12.53
1998	295.91	37.38	10.11	51.22	35.08	301.56	19.02
1999	292.08	35.99	10.15	57.22	31.64	404.36	34.23
2000	235.64	44.85	15.64	47.34	21.57	430.05	36.89
2001	249.93	60.81	38.96	49.35	19.92	634.26	66.47
2002	240.66	77.45	34.76	53.41	20.35	841.14	109.68
2003	275.20	95.23	31.50	59.10	16.52	1 460.80	167.50

注：自2001年起，银行机构没有信托类存款。“信托类贷款及其他”含“票据融资”及““各项垫款”项目。
Note: Since 2001, banking institutions have no trusted deposits. Trusted deposits and others include bill financing and other money advanced for to be paid back later.

12－10　现金收入和支出
CASH INCOME AND EXPENDITURES

单位:亿元　　(100 million yuan)

项　目	Item	2001	2002	2003	2003 比2002年 增长% Increase Rate in 2003 over 2002
一、现金收入总计	**Total Cash Income**	**4 782.14**	**5 081.47**	**6 561.94**	**29.1**
商品销售收入	Income from Commodity Sales	784.51	881.88	1 122.42	27.3
服务事业收入	Income from Service Trade	237.90	243.45	281.56	15.7
税款收入	Income from Taxes	21.29	26.37	30.66	16.3
城乡个体经营收入	Income from Urban and Rural Individual Business	251.48	251.21	295.27	17.5
储蓄存款收入	Income from Savings Deposits	2 957.21	3 207.78	4 233.60	32.0
其他金融机构收入	Income from Other Financial Institutions	92.25	81.15	104.87	29.2
居民归还贷款收入	Income from Repayment of Loans by Residents	27.89	40.83	91.78	124.8
汇兑收入	Income from Remittances	53.69	51.04	36.07	－29.3
有价证券收入	Income from Securities	50.01	18.13	28.04	54.7
其他收入	Other Income	305.90	279.64	337.67	20.8
二、现金支出总计	**Total Cash Expenditures**	**4 793.23**	**5 126.79**	**6 651.99**	**29.8**
工资性支出	Wages	448.82	435.08	582.02	33.8
#国家职工工资奖金	Wages and Bonuses to the Staff and Workers From Government	199.28	209.06	269.13	28.7
国家对个人其他支出	Other Payments to Individuals From Government	119.07	100.23	128.81	28.5
其他单位工资性支出	Wages from Other Units	119.06	113.82	171.73	50.9
农副产品采购支出	Purchases of Agricultural and Sideline Products	76.12	98.06	112.90	15.1
工矿及其他产品采购支出	Expenditure for Purchases of Industrial and Mineral Products	56.20	70.01	88.07	25.8
行政企事业管理费支出	Government and Enterprises Overhead	256.28	290.95	351.52	20.8
城乡个体经营支出	Expenditure for Individual Business	374.89	447.24	569.39	27.3
储蓄存款支出	Expenditure for Savings Deposits	3 055.65	3 275.96	4 303.18	31.4
其他金融机构支出	Expenditure for Other Financial Institutions	83.07	87.93	96.22	9.4
居民提取贷款支出	Expenditure for Loans by Residents	23.23	46.37	119.38	157.5
汇兑支出	Expenditure for Remittances	25.86	26.27	16.36	－37.7
有价证券支出	Expenditure for Securities	28.23	19.11	22.90	19.8
其他支出	Others	364.89	329.81	390.05	18.3
三、货币投放(＋)或回笼(－)	**Currency Issuance and Cash Withdrawal**	**11.09**	**45.32**	**90.05**	**98.7**

12-11 金融机构人民币信贷收支情况

RMB CREDIT INCOME & EXPENDITURES OF FINANCIAL INSTITUTIONS

单位:亿元 (100 million yuan)

项目	Item	2001	2002	2003	2003比2002年增长% Increase Rate in 2003 over 2002
一、各项存款总计	**Total Deposits**	**2 562.56**	**3 018.21**	**4 033.51**	**33.6**
1.企业存款	Deposits of Enterprises	939.31	1 115.35	1 542.75	38.3
2.财政性存款	Treasury Deposits	71.16	102.30	136.89	35.0
3.储蓄存款	Savings Deposits	1 284.99	1 486.38	1 825.32	22.8
#定期储蓄	Fixed Deposits	976.74	1 096.34	1 294.04	18.0
4.农业存款	Agricultural Deposits	56.40	73.86	164.72	123.0
5.信托类存款	Trusted Deposits	72.87	72.40	81.92	29.9
6.其他类存款	Other Deposits	137.83	167.92	281.91	67.9
二、各项贷款总计	**Total Loans**	**2 181.33**	**2 520.89**	**3 426.02**	**35.9**
1.短期贷款	Short-term Loans	1 364.17	1 492.59	1 674.14	12.2
#工业贷款	Industrial Loans	460.10	450.32	429.13	-4.7
商业贷款	Commercial Loans	223.82	240.68	275.22	14.4
建筑业贷款	Construction Loans	62.43	77.45	95.23	23.0
私营及个体贷款	Loans to Private and Individuals	32.66	34.76	31.50	-9.4
乡镇企业贷款	Loans to Township Enterprises	174.28	192.22	239.98	24.9
农业贷款	Agricultural Loans	47.72	74.99	132.30	76.4
三资企业贷款	Loans to Hongkong, Macao, Taiwan and Foreign Funded Enterprise	130.06	114.21	83.41	-27.0
其他短期贷款	Other Short-term Loans	233.10	307.96	387.37	25.8
2.中期流动资金贷款	Medium-term Circulating Capital Loans	89.57	123.72	158.43	28.1
3.中长期贷款	Medium-term and Long-term Loans	568.51	725.09	1 309.92	80.7
#技术改造贷款	Loans to Technical Innovation	25.04	22.80	26.71	17.2
基本建设贷款	Loans to Capital Construction	331.61	412.25	806.36	95.6
4.信托类贷款	Credit Loans	71.07	69.66	87.90	26.2
5.票据融资	Bill Financing	78.01	93.88	187.55	99.8
6.各项垫款	Money Advanced for sb. to be Paid Back Later	10.00	15.95	8.08	-49.3

注:2002年数据已调整为2003年同口径,12-12、12-13表同。
Note: The data of this table in 2002 have been adjusted to the same coverage of statistics in 2003, same as following table 12-12, 12-13.

12-12 银行机构人民币信贷收支情况

RMB CREDIT INCOME & EXPENDITURES OF BANKING INSTITUTIONS

单位：亿元 (100 million yuan)

项目	Item	2001	2002	2003	2003比2002年增长% Increase Rate in 2003 over 2002
一、各项存款总计	**Total Deposits**	**2 255.97**	**2 672.47**	**3 482.63**	**30.3**
1.企业存款	Deposits of Enterprises	926.77	1 090.57	1 466.20	34.4
2.财政性存款	Treasury Deposits	71.00	102.16	136.63	33.7
3.储蓄存款	Savings Deposits	1 117.37	1 308.25	1 593.74	21.8
#定期储蓄	Fixed Deposits	845.55	1 014.68	1 132.10	16.7
4.农业存款	Agricultural Deposits	3.83	3.69	4.33	17.3
5.其他类存款	Other Deposits	137.00	167.80	281.73	67.9
二、各项贷款总计	**Total Loans**	**1 931.51**	**2 235.31**	**2 973.90**	**33.0**
1.短期贷款	Short - term Loans	1 198.13	1 282.62	1 345.60	4.9
#工业贷款	Industrial Loans	459.17	448.66	427.43	-4.7
商业贷款	Commercial Loans	223.80	240.66	275.20	14.4
建筑业贷款	Construction Loans	62.40	77.45	95.23	23.0
私营及个体贷款	Loans to Private and Individuals	32.66	34.76	31.50	-9.4
乡镇企业贷款	Loans toTownship Enterprises	49.35	53.41	59.10	10.7
农业贷款	Agricultural Loans	20.09	20.35	16.52	-18.8
三资企业贷款	Loans to Hongkong, Macao, Taiwan and Foreign Funded Enterprises	130.06	114.21	83.41	-27.0
其他短期贷款	Other Short - term Loans	220.60	293.12	357.21	21.9
2.中期流动资金贷款	Medium - term Circulating Capital Loans	89.57	123.72	158.43	28.1
3.中长期贷款	Medium - term and Long - term Loans	564.70	719.29	1 302.37	81.1
#技术改造贷款	Loans to Technical Innovation	25.04	22.80	26.71	17.2
基本建设贷款	Loans to Capital Construction	331.61	412.25	806.36	95.6
4.票据融资	Bill Financing	69.11	93.73	159.42	70.1
5.各项垫款	Money Advanced for sb. to be Paid Back Later	10.00	15.95	8.08	-49.3

12－13　金融机构本外币信贷收支情况

RMB & FOREIGN CURRENCY CREDIT INCOME AND EXPENDITURES OF FINANCIAL INSTITUTIONS

单位：亿元　　(100 million yuan)

项　目	Item	2002	2003	2003比2002年增长% Increase Rate in 2003 over 2002
一、各项存款总计	**Total Deposits**	**3 358.83**	**4 362.60**	**29.9**
1.企业存款	Deposits of Enterprises	1 261.89	1 678.00	33.0
#定期储蓄	Fixed Deposits	275.35	416.15	51.1
2.储蓄存款	Savings Deposits	1 659.49	1 991.76	20.0
#定期储蓄	Fixed Deposits	1 250.60	1 438.17	15.0
3.信托类存款	Trusted Deposits	72.68	82.00	12.8
4.其他存款	Other Deposits	364.77	610.84	67.5
二、各项贷款总计	**Total Loans**	**2 870.91**	**3 791.22**	**32.1**
1.短期贷款	Short－term Loans	1 611.39	1 812.48	12.5
2.中长期贷款	Medium－term and Long－term Loans	960.09	1 573.93	63.9
3.信托类贷款	Credit Loans	94.96	112.66	18.6
4.其他贷款	Other Loans	69.87	75.59	8.2
5.票据融资	Bill Financing	112.84	203.09	80.0
6.各项垫款	Money Advanced for sb. to be Paid Back Later	21.76	13.47	－38.1

注：本表金融机构含外资金融机构。
Note：Financial institutions in this table include foreign funded institutions.

12－14　保险业务主要指标

MAIN INDICATORS OF INSURANCE BUSINESS

(1990－2003)

年份 Year	保险金额(亿元) Amount Insured (100 million yuan)	保费(万元) Premium (10 000 yuan)	#人身险 Life Insurance	#财产险 Property Insurance	赔款及给付(万元) Claim and Payment (10 000 yuan)	#人身险 Life Insurance	#财产险 Property Insurance
1990	918.00	34 327	4 384	17 896	9 827	334	5 237
1991	1 009.18	39 474	5 832	20 222	14 715	894	8 651
1992	1 136.06	49 624	10 185	23 639	22 843	1 637	12 963
1993	1 514.16	67 412	14 492	32 496	34 689	4 866	17 885
1994	2 434.06	100 561	24 628	47 147	47 434	6 642	27 405
1995	2 274.74	123 655	31 588	61 338	52 985	6 545	30 973
1996	2 488.21	171 768	63 373	74 399	62 613	10 186	33 257
1997	3 306.04	243 377	125 327	112 401	83 528	18 334	61 900
1998	3 949.15	271 654	161 097	110 557	70 075	14 206	55 869
1999	4 848.10	291 382	175 804	115 578	69 163	14 703	54 460
2000	3 696.19	314 663	191 786	122 877	71 950	7 714	64 236
2001	5 176.91	417 049	276 050	140 999	119 062	56 364	62 698
2002	5 632.35	649 698	505 966	143 732	114 818	46 513	68 305
2003	6 497.87	753 098	597 450	155 648	173 608	72 493	101 115

12－15 保险业务情况
BASIC INDICATORS OF INSURANCE BUSINESS

项　　目	Item	2002	2003	2003比2002年增长% Increase Rate in 2003 over 2002
保险金额（亿元）	**Amount Insured (100 million yuan)**	**5 632.35**	**6 497.87**	**15.4**
财产保险	Property Insurance	5 081.88	5 656.82	11.3
财产险	Property Insurance	1 907.06	2 156.00	13.1
机动车险	Motor Vehicle Insurance	581.64	891.74	53.3
货运险	Freight Transport Insurance	598.75	721.32	20.5
责任险	Liability Insurance	1 285.16	755.51	-41.2
保证险	Guarantee Insurance	8.00	22.61	182.6
其他财产险	Others	701.27	1 109.64	58.2
人寿保险	Life Insurance	550.47	841.05	52.8
保　费（万元）	**Premium (10 000 yuan)**	**649 698**	**753 098**	**15.9**
财产保险	Property Insurance	143 732	155 648	8.3
财产险	Property Insurance	24 195	26 375	9.0
机动车险	Motor Vehicle Insurance	79 168	77 757	-1.8
货运险	Freight Insurance	12 741	11 770	-7.6
责任险	Liability Insurance	9 457	9 360	-1.0
保证险	Guarantee Insurance	1 733	3 477	100.6
其他财产险	Others	16 438	26 909	63.7
人寿保险	Life Insurance	505 966	597 450	18.1
赔款及给付额（万元）	**Claim and Payment (10 000 yuan)**	**114 818**	**173 608**	**51.2**
财产保险	Property Insurance	68 305	101 115	48.0
财产险	Property Insurance	4 983	5 763	15.7
机动车险	Motor Vehicle Insurance	47 512	56 545	19.0
货运险	Freight Transport Insurance	5 167	5 042	-2.4
责任险	Liability Insurance	4 707	5 747	22.1
保证险	Guarantee Insurance	280	678	142.1
其他财产险	Others	5 656	27 340	383.4
人寿保险	Life Insurance	46 513	72 493	55.9
保险密度（元）	**Insurance Density (yuan)**	**649.13**	**752.43**	**15.9**
财产保险	Property Insurance	143.61	155.51	8.3
人寿保险	Life Insurance	505.52	596.92	18.1
保险深度（%）	**Insurance Depth (%)**	**2.72**	**3.15**	**15.6**
财产保险	Property Insurance	0.60	0.65	8.3
人寿保险	Life Insurance	2.12	2.50	18.1
赔付率（%）	**Claim and Payment Rate (%)**	**17.67**	**23.05**	**30.4**
财产保险	Property Insurance	47.52	64.96	36.7
人寿保险	Life Insurance	9.19	12.13	32.0

12－16 外资银行、保险公司在津分行、代表处一览(2003 年)

BRANCHES OR OFFICES OF FOREIGN FUNDED BANKS AND INSURANCE COMPANIES IN TIANJIN,2003

名 称 Name	行长、首席代表 Director	办公地址 Address
英国渣打银行天津分行	张文耀	天津津汇广场 2008
Standard Chartered Bank Tianjin Branch	Cheung Man Yiu	Rm. 2008 Exchange Office Tower of Tianjin
法国巴黎银行天津分行	宋宝成	天津国际大厦 16 层
BNP PARIBAS Tianjin Branch	Victor Song	16 Floor International Building of Tianjin
香港上海汇丰银行有限公司天津分行	管致中	天津远洋广场 1 层
The Hongkong and Shanghai Banking Corporation Limited,Tianjin Branch	Koon Chi Chung	1 Floor Ocean Shipping Plaza of Tianjin
法国里昂信贷银行天津分行	张家麟	天津国际大厦 710
Credit Lyonnais of France,Tianjin Branch	Charles Chang	Rm. 710 International Building of Tianjin
法国兴业银行天津分行	汪雁龄	天津河川大厦 22 层
Societe Generale of France,Tianjin Branch	Denny Wong	22 Floor Innotec Tower of Tianjin
新加坡华侨银行天津分行	陈殿升	天津国际大厦 511
Overseas－Chinese Banking Co., Ltd. of Singapore,Tianjin Branch	Tan Tian Seng	Rm. 511 International Building of Tianjin
摩根大通银行天津分行	佟静星	天津国际大厦 14 层
J.P.Morgan Chase Bank,Tianjin Branch	Charles Tong	14 Floor International Building of Tianjin
韩国外换银行天津分行	李炳锡	天津利顺德饭店 1 层
Korea Exchange Bank,Tianjin Branch	Lee BYung Seok	1 Floor Astor Hotel of Tianjin
韩国朝兴银行股份有限公司天津分行	金容吉	天津国际大厦 1901
Chohung Branch Tianjin Branch	Yong Kil Kim	Rm. 1901 International Building of Tianjin
三井住友银行天津分行	西山敏朗	天津国际大厦 1210
Sumitomo Mitsui Banking Corporation, Tianjin Branch	Toshiro nishiyama	Rm. 1210 International Building of Tianjin
日本日联银行股份有限公司天津分行	森川幸好	天津国际大厦 811
UFJ Bank Limited. Tianjin Branch	Morikawa Yukiyoshi	Rm. 811 International Building of Tianjin
韩国新韩银行天津分行	洪万基	天津国际大厦 507
Korea Shinhan Bank,Tianjin Branch	Hong Man Ki	Rm. 507 International Building of Tianjin
韩国中小企业银行天津分行	李钟赞	天津国际大厦 911
Industrial Bank of Korea,Tianjin Branch	Jong－Chang,Lee	Rm.911 International Building of Tianjin

12－16 续表　Continued

名　　称 Name	行长、首席代表 Director	办公地址 Address
日本东京三菱银行天津分行	平山亮	天津国际大厦 21 层
The Bank of Tokyo－Mitsubishi，Ltd. Japan， Tianjin Branch	Ryo Hirayama	21 Floor International Building of Tianjin
花旗银行天津分行	沈筑非	天津津汇广场 1801
Citibank. N. A. Tianjin Branch	Fred Shen	Rm. 1801 Exchange Office Tower of Tianjin
星展银行(香港)有限公司天津代表处	李　虹	天津津汇广场 1902
DBS Bank (Hongkong) Limited，Tianjin Office Representative	Lillian H li	Rm. 1902 Exchange Tower of Tianjin
日本瑞穗实业银行股份有限公司天津代表处	孙国贤	天津国际大厦 2202
The Fuji Bank of Japan，Tianjin Office	Guo Xian Sun	Rm. 2202 International Building of Tianjin
荷兰银行天津代表处处	许　燕	天津国际大厦 912
ABN AMRO Bank N. V. ，Tianjin Rep. Office	Jennifer Xu	Rm. 912 International Building of Tianjin
香港东亚银行天津代表处	魏玉琨	天津国际大厦 907
The Bank of East Asia Limited of Hongkong， Tianjin Office	Yu Kun Wei	Rm. 907 International Building of Tianjin
日本三井住友海上火灾保险公司天津代表处	小泽龙雄	天津国际大厦 1703
Mitsui Sumitomo Insurance Co. ，Ltd. Tianjin Representative Office	Tatsuo Ozawa	Rm. 1703 International Building of Tianjin
日本东京海上火灾保险公司天津代表处	滨田幸司	天津国际大厦 2309
The Tokio Marine and Fire Insurace Co. ，Ltd. Tianjin Representative Office	Koji Hamada	Rm. 2309 International Building of Tianjin
爱和谊保险公司天津代表处	村中弘幸	天津国际大厦 1609
Aioi Insurance Co. ，Ltd. Tianjin Representative Office	Hiroyuki Muranaka	Rm. 1609 International Building of Tianjin
裕利安宜信用保险股份公司天津代表处	王　洁	天津津汇广场 905
Euler Hermes Kreditversicherungs－AG Tianjin Representative Office	John Wang	Rm. 905 Exchange Office Tower of Tianjin

12－17　金融机构法定存款利率表
NOMINAL INTEREST RATES ON DEPOSITS OF FINANCIAL INSTITUTIONS
(1996－2003)

单位:年利率%　　(annual interest rate %)

项　　目	Item	1996年5月1日 May 1,1996	1996年8月23日 Aug. 23,1996	1997年10月23日 Oct. 23,1997	1998年3月25日 Mar. 25,1998
个人人民币储蓄存款	**RMB Household Deposits**				
一、活　期	Current Deposits	2.97	1.98	1.71	1.71
二、定　期	Fixed Deposits				
三个月	3 Months	4.86	3.33	2.88	2.88
半　年	6 Months	7.20	5.40	4.14	4.14
一　年	1 Year	9.18	7.47	5.67	5.22
二　年	2 Years	9.90	7.92	5.94	5.58
三　年	3 Years	10.80	8.28	6.21	6.21
五　年	5 Years	12.06	9.00	6.66	6.66
八年及以上	8 Years and Over	17.10	17.10		
三、存本取息、零存整取、整存零取	Three Convenients & Flexible Ways of Savings Deposits				
一　年	1 Year	7.20	5.40	4.14	4.14
三　年	3 Years	9.18	7.47	5.67	5.22
五　年	5 Years	10.80	8.28	6.21	6.21
四、定活两便	Current or Fixed Deposits				
不满三个月	Less than 3 Months	2.97	1.98	1.71	
三个月	3 Months	2.916	1.998	1.728	
半　年	6 Months	4.32	3.24	2.484	
一年及一年以上	1 Year and Over	5.508	4.482	3.402	
企业单位存款	**Enterprises Deposits**				
一、活　期	Current Deposits	2.97	1.98	1.71	1.71
二、定　期	Fixed Deposits				
三个月	3 Months	4.86	3.33	2.88	2.88
半　年	6 Months	7.20	5.40	4.14	4.14
一　年	1 Year	9.18	7.47	5.67	5.22
二　年	2 Years	9.90	7.92	5.94	5.58
三　年	3 Years	10.80	8.28	6.21	6.21
五　年	5 Years	12.06	9.00	6.66	6.66

项　　目	Item	1998年7月1日 Jul. 1,1998	1998年12月7日 Dec. 7,1998	1999年6月10日 June 10,1999	2002年2月21日 Feb.21,2002
个人人民币储蓄存款	**RMB Household Deposits**				
一、活　期	Current Deposits	1.44	1.44	0.99	0.72
二、定　期	Fixed Deposits				
三个月	3 Months	2.79	2.79	1.98	1.71
半　年	6 Months	3.96	3.33	2.16	1.89
一　年	1 Year	4.77	3.78	2.25	1.98
二　年	2 Years	4.86	3.96	2.43	2.25
三　年	3 Years	4.95	4.14	2.70	2.52
五　年	5 Years	5.22	4.50	2.88	2.79
三、存本取息、零存整取、整存零取	Three Convenients & Flexible Ways of Savings Deposits				
一　年	1 Year	3.96	3.33	1.98	1.71
三　年	3 Years	4.77	3.78	2.16	1.89
五　年	5 Years	4.95	4.14	2.25	1.98
企业单位存款	**Enterprises Deposits**				
一、活　期	Current Deposits	1.44	1.44	0.99	0.72
二、定　期	Fixed Deposits				
三个月	3 Months	2.79	2.79	1.98	1.71
半　年	6 Months	3.96	3.33	2.16	1.89
一　年	1 Year	4.77	3.78	2.25	1.98
二　年	2 Years	4.86	3.96	2.43	2.25
三　年	3 Years	4.95	4.14	2.70	2.52
五　年	5 Years	5.22	4.50	2.88	2.79

12－18　金融机构法定贷款利率表
NOMINAL INTEREST RATES ON LOANS OF FINANCIAL INSTITUTIONS
(1996－2003)

单位:年利率%　　(annual interest rate %)

项　目	Item	1996年5月1日 May 1,1996	1996年8月23日 Aug. 23,1996	1997年10月23日 Oct. 23,1997	1998年3月25日 Mar. 25,1998
流动资金贷款	**Loans for Circulating Funds**				
1.一般流动资金	General Circulating Funds				
半　年	6 Months	9.72	9.18	7.65	7.02
一　年	1 Year	10.98	10.08	8.64	7.92
2.个体工商户贷款	Loans to Individuals Engaged in Industrial and Business	在10.98%基础上上浮10% 10% Floating Over 10.98%	在10.08%基础上上浮10% 10% Floating Over 10.08%	同前 Ditto	同前 Ditto
固定资产贷款	**Loans for Fixed Assets**				
1.技术改造贷款	Loans to Technical Innovation				
2.基本建设贷款	Loans to Capital Construction				
一年以内	Less than 1 Year	11.52	10.08		
一年以上至三年	1－3 Years	13.14	10.98	9.36	9.00
三年以上至五年	3－5 Years	14.94	11.70	9.90	9.72
五年以上至十年	5－10 Years	15.12	12.42	10.53	10.35

项　目	Item	1998年7月1日 Jul. 1,1998	1998年12月7日 Dec. 7,1998	1999年6月10日 June 10,1999	2002年2月21日 Feb. 21,2002
短期贷款	**Short－term Loans**				
1.一般流动资金	General Circulating Funds				
半年以内	Less than 6 Months	6.57	6.12	5.58	5.04
一年(6个月至一年)	1 Year(6 months to 1 year)	6.93	6.39	5.85	5.31
2.个体工商户贷款	Loans to Individuals Engaged in Industrial and Business	同前 Ditto	同前 Ditto		
长期贷款	**Long－term Loans**				
1.技术改造贷款	Loans to Technical Innovation				
2.基本建设贷款	Loans to Capital Construction				
一年以内	Less than 1 Year				
一年以上至三年	1－3 Years	7.11	6.66	5.94	5.49
三年以上至五年	3－5 Years	7.65	7.20	6.03	5.58
五年以上至十年	5－10 Years	8.01	7.56	6.21	5.76
住房贷款	**Housing Loans**				
1.个人住房公积金贷款	Accumulation Fund Loans				
五年以内	Less than 5 Years			4.14	3.60
五年以上	More than 5 Years			4.59	4.05
2.商业银行自营性住房贷款	Self－supported by Commercial Banks				
五年以内	Less than 5 Years			5.31	4.77
五年以上	More than 5 Years			5.58	4.77

主要统计指标解释

财政收入 指国家可直接支配的财力，主要包括税收收入和其他收入两大类。1994 年我国统一实行分税制财政体制，按税种分为上划中央收入和地方财政收入。上划中央收入包括：增值税的 75% 和消费税的 100%等；地方财政收入包括：增值税的 25%、营业税（不含银行总行、铁道、保险总公司的营业税）、地方企业交纳的企业所得税、外商投资企业和外国企业所得税、个人所得税、土地使用税、固定资产投资方向调节税、城市维护建设税（不含银行总行、铁道、保险总公司集中交纳的部分）、资源税（不包括海洋石油资源税）、房产税、车船使用税、印花税、屠宰税、农牧业税、耕地占用税、契税、遗产和赠与税、土地增值税、国有土地有偿使用收入以及基金收入等。地方财政收入加上划中央收入为全市财政收入。需要指出的是，1994 年以后地方财政收入与以前实行的总额分成财政体制下的地方财政收入在内容和范围上有一定差别，从 2002 年 1 月 1 日起我国所得税收入分配方式又有重大改革，2002 年所得税收入中央分享 50%，地方分享 50%。因此，历年数据不完全可比。

一般预算财政收入 是通过一定的形式和程序，由各级财政部门组织并纳入预算管理的各项收入，也就是会计制度改革以前所称的"预算收入"。

基金预算收入 是按规定收取，转入或通过当年财政安排，由财政管理并具有指定用途的政府性基金预算收入等。

一般预算财政支出 是各级财政部门对集中的一般预算收入有计划地分配和使用而安排的支出。

基金预算支出 是各级财政部门用基金预算收入安排的支出。

保险密度 为按常住人口计算的人均保费收入。

保险深度 指保费收入相当于国内生产总值的比例。

存款 指企业、机关、团体或居民根据资金必须收回的原则，把货币资金存入金融机构保管并取得一定利息的一种信用活动形式。根据存款对象的不同可划分为企业存款、财政性存款、城乡储蓄存款、农村存款、信托及其他存款等，它是银行信贷资金的主要来源。

贷款 指金融机构根据资金必须归还的原则，按一定利率，为企业、个人等提供资金的一种信用活动形式。我国银行贷款分为工业贷款、农业贷款、商业贷款、建筑业贷款、私营和个体贷款、乡镇企业贷款、中长期贷款、信托及其他贷款等。

保险金额 指保险人承担赔偿或者给付保险金责任的最高限额。

保费 指投保人为取得保险人在约定范围内所承担赔偿责任而支付给保险人的费用。

赔款 指保险人根据保险合同的规定，向被保险人支付的赔偿保险责任损失的金额。

给付 包括死伤医疗给付和满期给付。死伤医疗给付是指保险人根据人寿保险及长期健康保险合同的规定，因被保险人在保险期内发生保险责任范围内的保险事故支付给被保险人（或受益人）的金额。满期给付是指被保险人生存期满，保险人按人寿保险合同规定支付给被保险人的满期保险金额。

Explanatory Notes on Main Statistical Indicators

Government Revenue refers to the revenue of the government directly disposable finance, including various tax revenue and other revenue. In accordance with the classification of the structure of the government finance in 1994 on the basis of the classification of channels for collection of tax revenue, the revenue of the central government and the revenue of the local governments have different coverage. Revenue of the central government includes 75% of the value added tax and 100% of the value consumption tax, etc, The revenue of the local governments includes 25% of the value added tax, business tax, (excluding business taxes of head offices of bank, profits of railways, head office of insurance company) , income tax of the local enterprises subordinated to the local government, income tax of foreign, Hongkong, Macao and Taiwan funded enterprises, personal income tax, tax on the use of urban land, tax on the adjustment of the investment in fixed assets, tax on town maintenance and construction, tax on resources (excluding tax on ocean petroleum resources), tax on real estates, tax on the use of vehicles and ships, stamp tax, slaughter tax, tax on agriculture and animal husbandry, tax on the occupancy of cultivated land, contract tax, inheritance tax, gift tax, land value added tax, income of non - gratuitous use on the state - owned land and income of funds. Total of government revenue included the revenue of the central government and the revenue of the local governments. Now the content and coverage of the local financial revenue is difference from that before 1994, please pay attention to distinguish when you use. From January 1,2002 , distribution of income tax changed, central government share in 50% and local government share in 50% , the figures in 2002 are not comparable with the previous years.

General Budgetary Financial Revenue refers to financial revenue with budgetary management through certain form and procedure by financial departments at each level, also called "budgetary revenue" before reformation of accounting system.

Fund Budgetary Revenue refers to government fund budgetary revenue with financial management and assigned uses gathered by rules or through financial arrangement.

General Budgetary Financial Expenditure refers to expenditure distributed and used from general budgetary financial revenue by financial departments at each level.

Fund Budgetary Expenditure refers to expenditure arranged from fund budgetary revenue by financial departments at each level.

Insurance Density refers to per capita premiums which is based on permanent resident population.

Insurance Depth refers to the proportion of premiums to gross domestic product.

Deposit is a form of credit by which enterprises, institutions, organizations or households can put money into banks and other credit institutions for safekeeping and interest earning under the principle of free withdrawal. According to different depositors, deposits are divided into enterprise deposits, treasury deposits, urban and rural savings deposits, rural deposits, entrust and other deposits. Deposits are major sources of credit funds of banks.

Loan is a from of credit by which banks and other credit institutions provide funds at certain interest rate to enterprises and individuals in the light of the principle of unconditional repayment. Loans from Chinese banks include industry loans, agriculture loans, commerce loans, construction loans, loans to private and individuals, township enterprises loans, medium & long term loans, entrust and other loans.

Amount Insured refers to the maximum that the insurant will get for the claim of the case insured.

Premium is the fee paid by the insurant to the insurer to obtain the obligation of compensation from the insurance within the agreed terms.

Settled Claim is the compensation paid by the insurer to insurant in accordance with the insurance contract.

Payment includes payment for death, injury or medical treatment and mature payment. Payment for death, injury or medical treatment refers to the money paid to insurant (or the beneficiary) in accordance with the life or health insurance contract when the insurant encounters accidents within the insured period covered in the contract. Mature payment refers to the mature payment to the insurant in accordance with the life insurance contract at the end of the insured period.

第13篇 CHAPTER 13

城市建设和环境保护

URBAN CONSTRUCTION
AND ENVIRONMENT PROTECTION

13－1 市政公用设施水平
LEVEL OF MUNICIPAL PUBLIC FACILITIES

指标	Item	单位	Unit	2001	2002	2003
城市人口密度	Population Density of Urban Districts	人/平方公里	person/sq.km	1 388	831	841
人均城市建设维护基金	Per Capita Fund on Urban Construction and Maintenance	元/人	yuan/person	1 149	1 305	2 219
人均住房使用面积	Per Capita Using Space of Residential Buildings	平方米	sq.m	15.9	16.7	17.5
人均日生活用水量	Per Capita Daily Consumption of Tap Water for Residential Use	公斤	kg	144.9	132.9	131.0
用水普及率	Percentage of Population with Access to Tap Water	%	%	100	100	100
每万人拥有公共交通车辆	Number of Public Transportation Vehicles per 10 000 Persons	标台	unit	8.9	9.3	9.4
用气普及率	Percentage of Population with Access to Gas	%	%	94.8	95.1	97.1
人均拥有道路面积	Per Capita Area of Paved Roads	平方米	sq.m	8.5	8.5	8.8
排水管道密度	Density of Drainpipes	公里/平方公里	km/sq.km	18.3	19.4	18.7
污水处理率	Percentage of Sewage Disposed	%	%	61.2	43.2	43.9
人均公共绿地面积	Per Capita Public Green Areas	平方米	sq.m	4.9	5.6	6.7
建成区绿化覆盖率	Coverage Rate of Afforestation in Developed Area	%	%	26.0	27.3	31.0
垃圾粪便无害化处理率	Innocuous Disposal Rate of Garbage,Excrement and Urine	%	%	55.9	54.9	60.6

13－2 城市自来水
URBAN TAP WATER

指标	Item	单位	Unit	2001	2002	2003
综合生产能力	Production Capacity	万吨/日	10^4 tons/day	359.0	362.8	343.1
供水管道	Length of Water Supply Pipelines	公里	km	5 810	6 691	6 822
供水总量	Total Annual Volume of Water Supply	万吨	10^4 tons	69 592	68 114	64 537
售水总量	Total Annual Volume of Water Sold	万吨	10^4 tons	61 040	60 118	54 758
#生活用水	For Residential Use	万吨	10^4 tons	32 569	29 881	29 829
生产用水	For Productive Use	万吨	10^4 tons	28 471	30 236	24 889
市内最高一日供水	Urban Maximum Volume of Water Supply of One Day	万吨/日	10^4 tons/day	206.1	202.3	194.0
用水人口	Number of Residents With Access to Tap Water	万人	10^4 persons	608.6	616.2	623.9

13－3 城市房屋建筑面积
FLOOR SPACE OF BUILDINGS IN CITY
(1978－2003)

单位:万平方米 (10 000 sq.m)

年 份 Year	年末实有房屋建筑面积 Total Floor Space of Buildings (year－end)	#住 宅 Residential Buildings	本年新建房屋建筑面积 Total Floor Space of Newly Constructed Buildings	#住 宅 Residential Buildings	住宅使用面积 Total Using Space of Residential Buildings	人均住宅使用面积(平方米/人) Per Capita Using Space of Residential Buildings (sq.m)
1978	4 005.67	1 766.00	193.79	85.80	1 358.00	4.32
1979	4 262.60	1 892.05	266.55	136.00	1 455.00	4.39
1980	4 509.04	2 049.04	265.57	176.14	1 576.00	4.64
1981	5 103.90	2 474.33	405.00	256.00	1 903.00	5.51
1982	5 475.00	2 732.00	435.00	313.00	2 102.00	5.94
1983	6 246.00	3 185.00	521.00	323.00	2 450.00	6.31
1984	6 660.00	3 463.00	447.00	302.00	2 664.00	6.76
1985	8 914.00	4 166.90	579.00	323.00	2 849.00	7.10
1986	9 541.00	4 524.00	660.00	369.00	3 659.00	8.69
1987	9 881.00	4 699.00	424.00	213.30	3 792.00	8.86
1988	10 437.30	5 085.00	528.60	322.00	4 086.00	9.32
1989	10 875.60	5 368.60	485.90	309.30	4 301.00	9.63
1990	11 189.80	5 553.00	363.20	203.10	4 439.00	9.79
1991	11 476.00	5 722.56	344.50	194.50	4 566.00	9.99
1992	11 768.44	5 872.00	395.70	214.70	4 662.00	10.19
1993	12 056.10	6 021.00	492.00	302.20	4 764.00	10.32
1994	12 509.50	6 349.10	614.60	448.40	5 003.00	10.77
1995	13 085.27	6 404.40	688.30	487.70	5 326.00	11.39
1996	13 608.00	6 803.60	657.20	483.40	5 598.00	11.88
1997	14 019.00	7 096.00	599.90	401.00	5 790.00	12.27
1998	14 434.00	7 412.00	728.23	512.09	5 987.00	12.58
1999	15 042.00	7 831.00	796.28	580.88	6 309.00	13.10
2000	15 789.00	8 404.00	874.86	626.58	6 709.00	13.88
2001	17 550.26	11 201.80	961.82	676.66	8 462.00	15.91
2002	18 695.40	11 897.01	1 071.58	711.19	8 969.00	16.71
2003	19 324.10	12 575.38	1 190.45	739.29	9 507.00	17.46

13－4 城市房屋建筑面积
(按产权管理分)
FLOOR SPACE OF BUILDINGS IN CITY (BY PROPERTY RIGHT MANAGEMENT)

单位:万平方米 (10 000 sq.m)

项 目	Item	年末实有房屋建筑面积 Total Floor Space of Buildings (year－end)			#住宅建筑面积 Residential Buildings		
		2001	2002	2003	2001	2002	2003
总 计	**Total**	**17 550.26**	**18 695.40**	**19 324.10**	**11 201.80**	**11 897.01**	**12 575.38**
#房管部门直管产	Under House Management Department	2 968.83	3 146.89	3 052.42	1 952.52	1 871.58	1 780.52
私 产	Private Property	6 842.84	7 505.64	8 564.05	6 598.80	7 199.62	8 093.38
#物业管理房	Under Products Management	6 100.00	6 620.00	7 300.00	5 080.00	5 420.00	5 957.00

13－5 城市燃气设备能力
GAS EQUIPMENT CAPACITY IN CITY

项目	Item	2001	2002	2003	2003 比2002年增长% Increase Rate in 2003 over 2002
液化石油气	**Liquefied Petroleum Gas**				
储气能力(吨)	Storage Capacity(ton)	19 856	21 237	14 881	－29.9
天然气	**Natural Gas**				
储气能力(万立方米)	Storage Capacity(10 000 cu. m)	101.2	126.0	126.0	
管道长度(公里)	Length of Pipelines(km)	4 911	5 026	5 380	7.0
煤制气	**Coal Gas**				
储气能力(万立方米)	Storage Capacity(10 000 cu. m)	50.0	50.0	60.0	20.0
管道长度(公里)	Length of Pipelines(km)	1 348	1 384	1 423	2.8

13－6 城市燃气销售量和用气户数
GAS SOLD AND GAS USERS IN CITY

项目	Item	销售量(吨、万立方米) Volume of Gas Sold (ton, 10 000 cu. m)			用气户数(户) Gas Users (household)		
		2001	2002	2003	2001	2002	2003
液化石油气	**Liquefied Petroleum Gas**	**137 364**	**115 210**	**79 736**	**547 398**	**457 560**	**419 502**
工业用	For Industrial Use	98 214	76 422	36 942	27 188	8 838	11 880
民　用	For Residential Use	39 150	38 788	42 794	520 210	448 722	407 622
天然气	**Natural Gas**	**32 567**	**35 457**	**41 567**	**1 200 230**	**1 286 335**	**1 361 443**
#工业用	For Industrial Use	12 156	12 229	15 630	79	100	148
福利用	For Welfare Use	6 750	8 673	11 190	5 445	5 921	6 678
民　用	For Residentail Use	13 617	13 917	14 180	1 194 706	1 280 314	1 354 617
煤制气	**Coal Gas**	**13 667**	**21 272**	**24 172**	**264 634**	**313 958**	**334 505**
#工业用	For Industrial Use	4 807	12 062	14 820	15	12	12
福利用	For Welfare Use	442	1 112	1 413	587	946	1 135
民　用	For Residentail Use	8 414	7 986	7 938	264 032	313 000	333 358

注：工业用液化石油气数据含福利、商业和其他用。
Note: Volume of liquefied petroleum gas sold for industrial use include those of welfare, commerce and other use.

13－7 城市市政设施情况
MUNICIPAL FACILITIES IN CITY

指标	Item	单位	Unit	2001	2002	2003	2003比2002年增长% Increase Rate in 2003 over 2002
年末实有道路	**Road(year－end)**						
铺装道路长度	Length of Paved Roads	公里	km	3 893	4 051	4 084	0.8
铺装道路面积	Area of Paved Roads	万平方米	10^4 sq.m	5 164	5 213	5 489	5.3
#人行道面积	Area of Footway	万平方米	10^4 sq.m	891	922	969	5.1
年末实有桥梁	**Bridges(year－end)**						
桥梁座数	Number of Bridges	座	unit	469	486	490	0.8
#立交桥	Flyover	座	unit	41	47	51	8.5
年末实有路灯盏数	**Number of Road Lamps(year－end)**	**盏**	**unit**	**109 741**	**139 194**	**178 826**	**28.5**
排泄污水能力	**Capacity of Sewage Drainage**						
污水年排放量	Annual Volume of Sewage Drainage	万吨	10^4 tons	57 051	52 263	53 730	2.8
排水管道长度	Length of Drainpipes	公里	km	7 756	8 828	9 124	3.4
污水处理厂	Sewage Treatment Works	座	set	3	3	3	
污水处理厂能力	Disposal Capacity of Sewage Treatment Works	万吨/日	10^4 tons/day	76.8	76.8	76.8	

注:铺装道路含市区公路。
Note:Paved roads include highway of urban areas.

13－8 城市公共交通
PUBLIC TRAFFIC IN CITY

指标	Item	单位	Unit	2001	2002	2003	2003比2002年增长% Increase Rate in 2003 over 2002
公共汽车	**Public Transportation Vehicles**						
营运车辆	Operation Vehicles	辆	unit	5 836	5 821	6 066	4.2
线路条数	Number of Routes	条	route	330	335	347	3.6
线路长度	Length of Routes	公里	km	7 602	7 936	8 206	3.4
乘客人数	Passengers	万人次	10^4 person－time	60 238	62 713	62 048	－1.1
日均乘客人数	Average Daily Passengers	万人次	10^4 person－time	167	174	172	－1.1
营运出租汽车	**Operating Taxis**	**辆**	**unit**	**31 939**	**31 939**	**31 939**	

13－9 城市园林绿化情况

PARKS,GARDENS AND GREEN AREAS IN CITY

指标	Item	2001	2002	2003	2003比2002年增长% Increase Rate in 2003 over 2002
公园(含动物园)(个)	Parks (Including Zoo)(unit)	187	195	196	0.5
花圃(个)	Gardens(unit)	27	24	23	－4.2
园林绿地总面积(公顷)	Total Area of Parks,Gardens and Green Areas(hectare)	8 872.4	10 113.8	13 238.8	30.9
#公共绿地	Public Green Area	2 993.1	3 466.6	4 161.3	20.0
#公园面积	Area of Parks	1 204.3	2 005.3	2 829.4	41.1
花圃面积	Area of Gardens	71.6	61.3	71.4	16.5
专用绿地	Special－purpose Green Area	2 041.2	2 025.0	2 338.4	15.5
年末实有树木(万株)	Trees(year－end)(10 000 trees)	2 147.9	2 349.9	2 386.9	1.6
#行道树	Roadside Trees	191.8	191.2	171.6	－10.3
全年植树(万株)	Trees Planted(10 000 trees)	113.3	133.6	213.0	59.4

13－10 公园分布

DISTRIBUTION OF PARKS

地区	Region	公园个数(个) Number of Parks (unit)			公园面积(公顷) Area of Parks (hectare)		
		2001	2002	2003	2001	2002	2003
合计	**Total**	**187**	**195**	**196**	**1 204.3**	**2 005.3**	**2 829.4**
和平区	Heping District	14	14	14	30.2	31.3	30.9
河东区	Hedong District	16	16	16	52.8	52.8	52.8
河西区	Hexi District	26	27	28	117.7	118.8	136.9
南开区	Nankai District	16	16	16	257.9	257.9	262.2
河北区	Hebei District	25	24	20	77.4	78.7	75.6
红桥区	Hongqiao District	25	25	25	51.2	51.2	51.2
塘沽区	Tanggu District	7	8	9	109.6	195.6	368.6
开发区	TEDA District	12	15	16	87.7	113.3	147.3
汉沽区	Hangu District	6	6	6	36.1	69.6	58.1
大港区	Dagang District	5	7	6	52.6	693.7	757.5
东丽区	Dongli District	6	7	10	14.2	17.4	398.5
西青区	Xiqing District	6	6	4	132.7	132.7	208.5
津南区	Jinnan District	7	8	9	33.8	41.9	124.4
北辰区	Beichen District	4	4	5	6.8	6.8	11.5
武清区	Wuqing District	10	10	10	115.9	115.9	117.7
宝坻区	Baodi District	2	2	2	27.7	27.7	27.7

13－11 城市集中供热
HEATING IN CITY

项 目 Item		单 位 Unit		2001	2002	2003	2003 比2002年增长% Increase Rate in 2003 over 2002
供热能力	Heating Capacity						
蒸 汽	Steam	吨/小时	ton/hour	2 391	3 121	3 234	3.6
热 水	Hot Water	兆瓦/小时	10^6 w/hour	6 904	9 122	9 390	2.9
供热总量	Volume Supplied						
蒸 汽	Steam	万吉焦/年	10^{13} joule/year	1 270	1 404	1 486	5.8
热 水	Hot Water	万吉焦/年	10^{13} joule/year	4 170	5 660	6 191	9.4
管道长度	Length of Pipelines	公里	km	4 550	5 852	7 387	26.2
供热面积	Heating Area	万平方米	10^4 sq.m	8 167	9 527	10 787	13.2
#住 宅	Residential Buildings	万平方米	10^4 sq.m	6 591	7 381	8 118	10.0

13－12 城市环境卫生事业发展情况
DEVELOPMENT OF URBAN ENVIRONMENT SANITATION

指 标 Item		单 位 Unit		2001	2002	2003	2003 比2002年增长% Increase Rate in 2003 over 2002
清运垃圾粪便工作量	**Volume of Garbage, Excrement and Urine Disposal**						
清扫街道面积	Area Cleaned	万平方米	10^4 sq.m	5 418	5 910	6 408	8.4
清运垃圾	Volume of Garbage Disposal	万吨	10^4 ton	219	163	172	5.5
清运粪便	Volume of Excrement and Urine Disposal	万吨	10^4 ton	25	26	25.2	-3.1
垃圾无害化处理量	Volume of Garbage Innocuous Disposal	万吨	10^4 ton	122	89	104.1	17.0
环境卫生设施	**Environmental Sanitation Facilities**						
公共厕所	Lavatories	座	unit	2 740	2 723	2 430	-10.8
垃圾无害化处理厂	Garbage Innocuous Disposal Plant	座	unit	1	1	3	200.0
无害化处理厂能力	Capacity of Innocuous Disposal Plant	吨/日	ton/day	2 700	2 700	3 800	40.7
环卫职工人数	**Number of Environment Sanitation Staff & Workers**	**人**	**person**	**11 156**	**18 186**	**16 857**	**-7.3**

13－13 工业废水、废气、废渣、粉尘排放及处理情况

EMISSION AND TREATMENT OF INDUSTRIAL WASTE WATER，WASTE GAS，WASTE RESIDUE AND DUST

指　标　Item	2000	2001	2002	2003
一、工业废水				
Industrial Waste Water				
工业废水排放量(万吨)				
Volume of Waste Water Discharged(10 000 tons)	17 604	21 250	21 959	21 605
工业废水达标率(%)				
Rate of Reaching the Standard of Industrial Waste Water (%)	98	100	100	100
二、工业废气				
Industrial Waste Gas				
工业废气排放总量(亿标立方米)				
Total Volume of Industrial Waste Gas Emission (100 million cu. m)	1 749	2 858	3 678	4 360
生产工艺过程中废气排放量				
Volume of Waste Gas from the Process of Production	408	978	956	893
燃料燃烧过程中废气排放量				
Volume of Waste Gas from the Burning Process of Fuel	1 341	1 880	2 722	3 467
废气中二氧化硫(万吨)				
Sulphur Dioxide in Waste Gas(10 000 tons)	16	20	20	26
三、工业废渣				
Industrial Waste Residue				
工业废渣产生量(万吨)				
Amount of Industrial Waste Residue Produced(10 000 tons)	470	575	643	644
#已处理量				
Volume of Treatment	25	22	26	57
已综合利用量				
Volume of Comprehensive Utilization	457	642	643	619
工业废渣处理率(%)				
Disposal Rate of Industrial Waste Residue(%)	8	4	4	8
工业废渣综合利用率(%)				
Rate of Comprehensive Using Industrial Waste Residue(%)	88	95	96	96
四、工业粉尘				
Industrial Dust				
工业粉尘产生量(万吨)				
Amount of Industrial Dust Producted(10 000 tons)	26	20	24	21
工业粉尘排放量				
Volume of Industrial Dust Emission	3	2	3	2
工业粉尘去除量				
Volume of Industrial Dust Removed	23	18	21	19
工业粉尘去除率(%)				
Rate of Industrial Dust Removed(%)	88	90	89	90

13－14　城市环境噪声情况
NOISE OF URBAN ENVIRONMENT

指　标　Item	2000	2001	2002	2003
城市交通噪声等效声级(分贝) Equivalent Sound Level of City Traffic Noise(decibel)	69	69	68	68
城市环境噪声达标面积(平方公里) Standardization Areas of City Environment Noise(sq. km)	173	375	477	539

注:城市环境噪声达标面积2000年以前为建成区数据,2001年以后为全市数据。
Note:Figures on standardization areas of city environment noise refer to developed areas before 2000,after 2001,they refer to the total areas of city.

13－15　环境保护系统人员构成
COMPOSITION OF ENVIRONMENT PROTECTION PERSONNEL

指　标	Item	2000	2001	2002	2003
年末实有人数(人)	**Persons(year－end)(person)**	**1 423**	**1 672**	**1 679**	**1 703**
科技人员	Science and Technology Personnel	730	848	737	724
#科研人员	Scientific Research Personnel	178	188	175	176
监测人员	Monitoring Personnel	361	454	391	402
行政干部	Administrative Personnel	426	448	418	438
科技业务人员占全部人员比重(%)	**Percentage of Science and Technology Personnel in Total(%)**	**51**	**51**	**44**	**43**

13－16　环境管理"三同时"制度执行情况
IMPLEMENTATION OF "THREE MEANTIME" SYSTEM OF ENVIRONMENTAL MANAGEMENT

指　标	Item	2000	2001	2002	2003
当年建成投产项目数(个)	Projects Putting into Use (unit)	78	185	4 464	1 439
应执行"三同时"项目数(个)	Number of Project Executing "Three Meantime"(unit)	78	185	4 464	1 439
实际执行"三同时"项目(个)	Number of Actual Executing Project (unit)	78	185	4 464	1 439
项目实际投资额(亿元)	Actual Investment of Project (100 million yuan)	24	29	82	93
#环保工程实际投资额	Actual Investment of Protecting Environment	1	1	2	3
"三同时"执行率(%)	Rate of Executing "Three Meantime"(%)	100	100	100	100
"三同时"合格率(%)	Qualified Rate of Executing "Three Meantime"(%)	100	100	100	100

注:"三同时"指同时设计、同时施工、同时使用。
Note:"Three Meantime" refers to design,construction,and use at the same time.

13－17　排污费征收、企事业单位污染治理情况

COLLECTION OF DISCHARGE FEE AND TREATMENT OF POLLUTION IN ENTERPRISES AND INSTITUTIONS

指　标　Item	单　位　unit	2000	2001	2002	2003
一、排污费收支情况					
Revenue And Expenditure of Discharge Fee					
排污费交纳单位	个				
Unit of Paying Discharge Fee	unit	12 983	12 599	1 252	6 766
排污费征收额	万元				
Collection of Discharge Fee	10 000 yuan	6 744	8 153	11 157	14 219
排污费支出额	万元				
Expenditure of Discharge Fee	10 000 yuan	7 841	7 202	9 120	13 011
二、企事业单位污染治理情况					
Treating Pollution of Enterprises					
1.资金合计	万元				
Total Expense	10 000 yuan	76 993	26 254	99 227	87 152
治理废水	万元				
Treating Waste Water	10 000 yuan	22 793	12 251	23 152	28 612
治理废气	万元				
Treating Waste Gas	10 000 yuan	5 329	12 138	44 391	45 627
治理废渣	万元				
Treating Waste Residue	10 000 yuan	1 130	322	18 487	6 587
治理噪声	万元				
Treating Noise	10 000 yuan	46 595	134	1 128	719
其　他	万元				
Others	10 000 yuan	1 146	1 409	12 069	5 608
2.当年安排治理项目	个				
Numer of Project of Treated This Year	unit	433	447	445	319
3.当年竣工项目	个				
Numer of Project Completed This Year	unit	304	419	295	182
治理废水	个				
Treating Waste Water	unit	110	64	79	58
治理废气	个				
Treating Waste Gas	unit	163	303	150	79
治理废渣	个				
Treating Waste Residue	unit	9	6	9	10
治理噪声	个				
Treating Noise	unit	13	16	19	3
其　他	个				
Others	unit	9	30	38	32

主要统计指标解释

城市园林绿地面积 指报告期末用作园林和绿化的各种绿地面积。包括公共绿地、居住区绿地、单位附属绿地、防护绿地、生产绿地、道路绿地和风景林地面积。

建成区绿化覆盖率 指报告期末建成区内绿化覆盖面积与建成区面积之比。用百分数表示。计算公式：

建成区绿化覆盖率＝（建成区内绿化覆盖面积/建成区面积）×100％

公共绿地 指向公众开放的市级、区级、居住区级各类公园、街旁游园，包括其范围内的水域。其中居住区级公园应不小于1万平方米，街旁游园的宽度不小于8米，面积不小于400平方米。

人均公共绿地面积 指报告期末区域内城市人口平均每人拥有的公共绿地面积。计算公式：人均公共绿地面积＝区域内公共绿地面积/区域内城市人口数

城市人口平均每人居住面积 指按城市人口（市辖区的非农业人口）计算的平均居住面积。其中的居住面积是指全部住宅中，专供日常生活起居使用的卧室、起居室的房间面积，不包括客厅、厨房、厕所等附属面积。居住面积按居住用房的内墙线计算。

噪声等效声级（简称LEQ） 指在规定的时间内，某一连续稳态声的A〔计权〕声压，具有与时变的噪声相同的均方A〔计权〕声压，则这一连续稳态声的声级，就是此时变噪声的等效声级。噪声等效声级（分贝）数值越小越好。

Explanatory Notes on Main Statistical Indicators

Area of Urban Gardens and Green Areas refers to the total area used for gardens and green by the report period, including public green land, residential zone green land, units green land, protection green land, production green land, roadside green land and suburban scenic spots.

The Rate of Green Coverage of the Developed Zones is the ratio of gardens and green areas to the developed zones areas, which is often expressed in %. The following formula is used

The Rate of Green Coverage of the Developed Zones = (gardens and green areas) / (the developed zones areas) × 100%

Public Green Area refers to green area of various parks and roadside gardens opened to the public, including waters within the above region. Of which, residential zone gardens should not less than 10,000 square meters, roadside gardens should not less than 8 meters wide and 400 square meters.

Per Capita Public Green Area refers to public green owned by each urban population. The following formula is used

Per Capita Public Green Area = public green area/number of urban population

Per Capita Living Space of Urban Population The population in urban refer to the non－agriculture population in urban, Net living space include bedroom, area of living room, exclude drawing room, kitchen, toilet, etc. It is calculated in order to the interior wall line of house.

Level of Equivalent Noise (LEQ) In the specified time interval, it refer to the A sound pressure of a continuous steady state sound, with the same mean square A sound pressure as the time variant noise. This sound level of a continuous steady state sound is the equivalent sound level of the time variant noise. The smaller of the value of noise equivalent sound level (dB), the better.

第14篇 CHAPTER 14

教 育
EDUCATION

14－1 各类学校在校学生数和专任教师数
STUDENTS ENROLLMENT AND TEACHERS BY TYPE OF SCHOOL

(1978－2003)

年 份 Year	学校数(所) Number of Schools (unit)			在校学生数(万人) Students Enrollment (10 000 persons)			专任教师数(人) Full－time Teachers (person)		
	高等学校 Institutions of Higher Education	中等学校 Secondary Schools	小 学 Primary Schools	高等学校 Institutions of Higher Education	中等学校 Secondary Schools	小 学 Primary Schools	高等学校 Institutions of Higher Education	中等学校 Secondary Schools	小 学 Primary Schools
1978	22	1 191	3 357	2	81	79	6 327	45 632	40 550
1979	26	1 228	3 371	3	70	80	7 696	45 581	40 330
1980	28	1 217	3 399	3	57	79	8 312	46 447	40 720
1981	27	1 173	3 381	4	48	76	8 290	45 515	41 858
1982	27	1 075	3 405	3	45	73	9 117	43 352	42 265
1983	28	1 067	3 382	3	42	72	9 820	42 157	41 121
1984	28	1 028	3 334	4	41	74	10 012	40 528	39 863
1985	28	1 085	3 302	5	43	73	10 527	42 634	39 871
1986	28	1 089	3 274	5	45	73	11 108	44 499	40 948
1987	28	1 073	3 261	5	46	73	11 474	47 353	42 872
1988	28	1 053	3 277	5	44	76	11 143	48 252	44 309
1989	28	1 041	3 275	5	43	81	11 124	46 446	43 241
1990	28	1 013	3 259	5	44	86	11 121	47 056	47 110
1991	27	1 003	3 232	5	46	87	10 704	46 460	47 762
1992	26	981	3 238	5	48	87	10 391	46 935	49 030
1993	26	975	3 243	6	50	89	10 160	46 688	50 448
1994	26	991	3 219	7	53	90	10 170	46 591	51 616
1995	25	1 059	3 216	7	60	88	10 490	47 196	51 401
1996	20	1 098	3 185	7	66	88	9 811	48 771	51 202
1997	20	1 108	3 030	7	69	88	9 589	51 309	51 048
1998	20	1 091	2 841	8	74	83	9 496	51 643	49 420
1999	21	1 041	2 642	9	76	77	9 647	53 012	48 293
2000	21	1 006	2 323	12	79	72	10 137	53 844	46 697
2001	33	1 012	1 307	15	79	67	12 552	52 732	45 651
2002	37	978	1 208	20	79	63	14 175	53 386	44 922
2003	37	897	1 136	25	80	59	15 553	53 706	43 829

14－2 各类学校数、学生数和教职工数

SCHOOLS, STUDENTS AND TEACHERS BY TYPE OF SCHOOL

学校类别	Item	学校数(所) Number of Schools (unit)		毕业生数(人) Graduates (person)		招生数(人) New Students Enrollment (person)	
		2002	2003	2002	2003	2002	2003
合　计	**Total**	**2 223**	**2 070**	**395 307**	**416 641**	**406 589**	**430 252**
高等学校	Institutions of Higher Education	37	37	27 295	40 221	69 453	86 115
中等专业学校	Specialized Secondary Schools	73	51	26 397	23 071	20 743	23 844
技工学校	Secondary Technical Schools	87	79	15 266	13 023	15 090	16 796
农业、职业中学	Rural, Vocational Secondary Schools	123	103	23 538	24 065	20 089	20 231
普通中学	Regular Secondary Schools	695	664	169 510	184 239	188 259	198 303
高　中	Senior Secondary Schools	224	222	41 486	44 968	58 855	69 875
初　中	Junior Secondary Schools	471	442	128 024	139 271	129 404	128 428
小　学	Primary Schools	1 208	1 136	133 301	132 022	92 955	84 963

学校类别	Item	在校学生数(人) Students Enrollment (person)		教职工数(人) Teachers, Staff and Workers(person)		#专任教师 Full－time Teachers	
		2002	2003	2002	2003	2002	2003
合　计	**Total**	**1 616 906**	**1 632 339**	**162 846**	**161 505**	**112 483**	**113 088**
高等学校	Institutions of Higher Education	196 892	245 213	32 019	33 371	14 175	15 553
中等专业学校	Specialized Secondary Schools	74 690	73 254	8 309	6 814	4 381	3 600
技工学校	Secondary Technical Schools	47 309	51 977	6 088	6 051	3 923	4 047
农业、职业中学	Rural, Vocational Secondary Schools	65 583	61 415	7 400	7 559	4 470	4 637
普通中学	Regular Secondary Schools	605 190	615 034	54 793	55 107	40 612	41 422
高　中	Senior Secondary Schools	157 902	182 529			10 805	12 024
初　中	Junior Secondary Schools	447 288	432 505			29 807	29 398
小　学	Primary Schools	627 242	585 446	54 237	52 603	44 922	43 829

14－3 各级学校平均每万人口拥有学生数
NUMBER OF STUDENT ENROLLMENT PER 10 000 POPULATION

单位：人 (person)

项 目	Item	平均每万人口中有在校学生 Students Enrollment Per 10 000 Population 2000	2001	2002	2003
合 计	**Total**	**1 779**	**1 759**	**1 764**	**1 769**
高等学校	Institutions of Higher Education	129	169	215	266
中等学校	Secondary Schools	863	861	865	842
中等专业学校	Specialized Secondary Schools	98	89	81	79
技工学校	Secondary Technical Schools	58	47	52	56
农业、职业中学	Rural，Vocational Schools	82	76	72	67
普通中学	Regular Secondary Schools	626	649	660	667
高 中	Senior Secondary Schools	136	155	172	198
初 中	Junior Secondary Schools	490	494	488	469
小 学	Primary Schools	786	729	684	635

14－4 各级学校平均每一教师负担学生数
STUDENT－TEACHER RATIO BY LEVEL OF SCHOOL

单位：人 (person)

项 目	Item	平均每一教师负担学生数 Students－ Teacher Ratio 2000	2001	2002	2003
合 计	**Total**	**15**	**14**	**15**	**14**
高等学校	Institutions of Higher Education	12	13	14	16
中等学校	Secondary Schools	15	15	16	15
中等专业学校	Specialized Secondary Schools	16	17	17	20
技工学校	Secondary Technical Schools	12	12	12	13
农业、职业中学	Rural，Vocational Schools	16	16	15	13
普通中学	Regular Secondary Schools	15	15	15	15
高 中	Senior Secondary Schools	14	14	15	15
初 中	Junior Secondary Schools	15	15	15	15
小 学	Primary Schools	16	15	14	13

14－5 各级学校学生升学率
PERCENTAGE OF GRADUATE STUDENTS IN ALL SCHOOLS BY LEVEL

单位：% (%)

指 标 Item	2000	2001	2002	2003
初中毕业生升学率 Percentage of Graduates in Junior Secondary Schools Entering Senior Secondary Schools	89.40	91.00	92.02	93.10
初中入学率 Percentage of Graduates in Primary Schools Entering Junior Secondary Schools	96.13	98.79	99.21	98.97
学龄儿童入学率 Percentage of School－age Children Enrolled	99.99	99.99	100.00	99.97

14－6　研究生在学、毕业、招生及指导教师人数
ENROLLED,GRADUATED AND RECRUITED
STUDENTS FOR MASTER & DOCTOR DEGREE AND THEIR TEACHERS

单位：人　　　　(person)

指　标　Item	2000	2001	2002	2003
总　计　Total				
在校生数　Students Enrollment	10 392	12 185	15 922	20 657
毕业生数　Graduates	2 059	2 100	2 790	3 252
招生人数　New Students Enrollment	4 563	5 354	6 574	8 506
指导教师　Teachers	2 538	2 885	3 056	3 273
攻读博士学位 Postgraduate for Doctor Degree				
在校生数　Students Enrollment	2 168	2 788	3 500	4 304
毕业生数　Graduates	444	484	642	585
招生人数　New Students Enrollment	902	1 173	1 387	1 680
攻读硕士学位 Postgraduate for Master Degree				
在校生数　Students Enrollment	8 224	9 397	12 422	16 353
毕业生数　Graduates	1 615	1 616	2 148	2 667
招生人数　New Students Enrollment	3 661	4 181	5 187	6 826

14－7　分学科研究生人数
NUMBER OF GRADUATE STUDENTS BY SUBJECT

单位：人　　　　(person)

学　科　Item	博士生 Doctor		硕士生 Master	
	2002	2003	2002	2003
总　计　Total	**3 500**	**4 304**	**12 422**	**16 353**
哲　学　Philosophy	56	73	142	175
经济学　Economics	1 123	1 358	3 053	4 188
法　学　Law	110	143	420	703
教育学　Education	15	18	558	846
文　学　Literature	112	132	702	1 002
历史学　History	198	213	200	251
理　学　Science	428	545	1 246	1 583
工　学　Engineering	1 191	1 478	5 209	6 425
医　学　Medicine	244	320	875	1 160
农　学　Agriculture	23	24	17	20

14－8 高等学校基本情况
BASIC STATISTICS ON INSTITUTIONS OF HIGHER EDUCATION

项 目 Item		学校数(所) Number of Schools (unit)		在校学生数(人) Students Enrollment (person)		毕业生数(人) Graduates (person)	
		2002	2003	2002	2003	2002	2003
总 计	**Total**	**37**	**37**	**196 892**	**245 213**	**27 295**	**40 221**
综合大学	Comprehensive Universities	1	1	11 906	12 432	2 386	2 834
理工院校	Science and Engineering	6	6	69 679	76 550	11 914	15 417
农林院校	Agriculture and Forestry	1	1	4 516	6 568	270	693
医药院校	Medicine	3	3	10 634	12 673	1 233	2 094
师范院校	Teacher Training	2	2	20 385	23 648	3 906	4 721
语文院校	Linguistics and Literary	1	1	4 982	6 175	474	1 140
财经院校	Economics and Finance	2	2	24 060	28 754	2 968	5 486
体育院校	Physical Culture	1	1	3 988	5 200	644	896
艺术院校	Art Institutes	2	2	3 491	4 412	364	500
职业大学	Vocational Colleges	18	18	43 251	68 801	3 136	6 440

项 目 Item		招生数(人) New Students Enrollment (person)		教职工数(人) Teachers,Staff and Workers (person)		#专任教师 Full－time	
		2002	2003	2002	2003	2002	2003
总 计	**Total**	**69 453**	**86 115**	**32 019**	**33 371**	**14 175**	**15 553**
综合大学	Comprehensive Universities	3 162	3 390	4 029	4 033	1 472	1 455
理工院校	Science and Engineering	19 466	22 942	11 333	11 819	4 566	5 022
农林院校	Agriculture and Forestry	1 836	2 769	714	743	338	354
医药院校	Medicine	3 366	4 229	2 340	2 365	826	1 038
师范院校	Teacher Training	6 125	7 513	2 994	3 007	1 480	1 561
语文院校	Linguistics and Literary	1 419	2 102	573	622	307	339
财经院校	Economics and Finance	6 791	8 757	2 489	2 656	1 332	1 420
体育院校	Physical Culture	1 396	2 170	436	590	184	305
艺术院校	Art Institutes	1 307	1 455	666	719	339	357
职业大学	Vocational Colleges	24 585	30 788	6 445	6 817	3 331	3 702

14－9 普通高等学校分科学生数

NUMBER OF STUDENTS ENROLLMENT IN INSTITUTIONS OF HIGHER EDUCATION BY SUBJECT

单位：人 (person)

学 科 Item	毕业生数 Graduates 合 计 Total 2002	2003	本 科 Regular College Course 2002	2003	专 科 Specialized Subject 2002	2003
总 计 Total	**27 295**	**40 221**	**17 722**	**22 756**	**9 573**	**17 465**
哲 学 Philosophy	30	35	30	35		
经济学 Economics	5 831	9 959	3 735	5 213	2 096	4 746
法 学 Law	942	1 559	591	721	351	838
教育学 Education	2 034	2 643	974	1 257	1 060	1 386
文 学 Literature	3 096	4 805	2 075	2 863	1 021	1 942
历史学 History	180	155	99	126	81	29
理 学 Science	1 851	2 225	1 476	1 639	375	586
工 学 Engineering	11 927	16 384	7 641	9 557	4 286	6 827
农 学 Agriculture	154	362	154	270		92
医 学 Medicine	1 250	2 094	947	1 075	303	1 019
总计中：师范 In total：Teacher Training	3 472	3 415	2 148	2 765	1 324	650

学 科 Item	招生数 New Students Enrollment 合 计 Total 2002	2003	本 科 Regular College Course 2002	2003	专 科 Specialized Subject 2002	2003
总 计 Total	**69 453**	**86 115**	**36 274**	**44 427**	**33 179**	**41 688**
哲 学 Philosophy	58	66	58	66		
经济学 Economics	18 758	24 172	9 089	10 680	9 669	13 492
法 学 Law	3 021	3 102	1 347	1 534	1 674	1 568
教育学 Education	3 854	4 308	1 916	2 118	1 938	2 190
文 学 Literature	9 889	12 490	5 540	7 274	4 349	5 216
历史学 History	119	177	119	125		52
理 学 Science	5 556	6 089	3 435	3 984	2 121	2 105
工 学 Engineering	24 012	30 691	12 438	15 710	11 574	14 981
农 学 Agriculture	730	980	490	728	240	252
医 学 Medicine	3 456	4 040	1 842	2 208	1 614	1 832
总计中：师范 In total：Teacher Training	3 497	3 056	2 790	2 341	707	715

学 科 Item	在校学生数 Students Enrollment 合 计 Total 2002	2003	本 科 Regular College Course 2002	2003	专 科 Specialized Subject 2002	2003
总 计 Total	**196 892**	**245 213**	**123 775**	**145 159**	**73 117**	**100 054**
哲 学 Philosophy	202	229	202	229		
经济学 Economics	48 831	65 180	28 972	34 877	19 859	30 303
法 学 Law	7 835	9 535	4 057	5 023	3 778	4 512
教育学 Education	10 921	12 525	7 077	7 948	3 844	4 577
文 学 Literature	26 357	34 272	16 519	21 048	9 838	13 224
历史学 History	578	598	548	546	30	52
理 学 Science	14 148	17 819	10 345	12 531	3 803	5 288
工 学 Engineering	74 996	89 869	47 273	52 923	27 723	36 946
农 学 Agriculture	2 095	2 664	1 554	1 990	541	674
医 学 Medicine	10 929	12 522	7 228	8 044	3 701	4 478
总计中：师范 In total：Teacher Training	13 883	13 162	12 304	11 778	1 579	1 384

14－10 高等学校分科专任教师数(按职称分)

NUMBER OF FULL－TIME TEACHERS IN INSTITUTIONS OF HIGHER EDUCATION BY SUBJECT

单位:人 (person)

学科	Item	合计 Total		正高级 Senior Title		副高级 Asso. Senior Title	
		2002	2003	2002	2003	2002	2003
总计	**Total**	**14 175**	**15 553**	**1 832**	**2 171**	**4 997**	**5 388**
哲学	Philosophy	338	414	49	63	140	174
经济学	Economics	2 269	2 150	347	311	753	711
法学	Law	443	453	48	49	139	148
教育学	Education	986	1 171	67	89	340	400
文学	Literature	3 044	3 198	268	284	908	955
历史学	History	191	187	50	56	79	79
理学	Science	1 968	2 135	365	444	757	804
工学	Engineering	4 489	4 847	587	671	1 709	1 749
农学	Agriculture	111	146	17	19	45	60
医学	Medicine	336	852	34	185	127	308

学科	Item	中级 Middle Title		初级 Junior Title		无职称 No Title	
		2002	2003	2002	2003	2002	2003
总计	**Total**	**4 248**	**4 625**	**2 326**	**2 727**	**772**	**642**
哲学	Philosophy	104	136	35	39	10	2
经济学	Economics	688	648	386	397	95	83
法学	Law	149	140	89	96	18	20
教育学	Education	333	394	182	227	64	61
文学	Literature	974	1 016	667	712	227	231
历史学	History	56	47	6	4		1
理学	Science	546	548	228	301	72	38
工学	Engineering	1 250	1 399	680	848	263	180
农学	Agriculture	31	49	13	15	5	3
医学	Medicine	117	248	40	88	18	23

14－11　中等专业学校分科学生数及专业课教师数

NUMBER OF STUDENTS AND SPECIAL COURSE TEACHERS IN SPECIALIZED SECONDARY SCHOOLS BY SUBJECT

单位:人　　(person)

学　科	Item	在校学生数 Students Enrollment 2002	在校学生数 Students Enrollment 2003	毕业生数 Graduates 2002	毕业生数 Graduates 2003
总　计	**Total**	**74 690**	**73 254**	**26 397**	**23 071**
农林类	Agriculture, Forestry	2 015	1 670	669	546
资源与环境类	Resource and Environment	1 235	1 070	270	383
能源类	Power	374	338	211	144
土木水利工程类	Construction and Water Conservancy Engineering	5 974	5 799	2 220	1 688
加工制造类	Processing and Manufacturing	10 979	11 818	5 280	4 008
交通运输类	Transport	1 676	1 833	415	1 068
信息技术类	Information Technology	22 770	22 902	5 494	6 530
医药卫生类	Medicine, Health	3 217	3 043	1 363	704
商贸与旅游类	Trade and Tour	11 747	13 908	2 732	2 812
财经类	Finance and Economics	3 842	2 394	2 743	1 980
文化艺术与体育类	Arts and Physical Culture	3 795	2 660	1 094	1 166
社会公共事业类	Society Commonality Business	5 166	3 611	2 292	1 158
其　他	Others	1 900	2 208	1 614	884

学　科	Item	招生数 New students Enrollment 2002	招生数 New students Enrollment 2003	专业课教师数 Special Course Teachers 2002	专业课教师数 Special Course Teachers 2003
总　计	**Total**	**20 743**	**23 844**	**2 391**	**1 810**
农林类	Agriculture, Forestry	501	461	80	62
资源与环境类	Resource and Environment	415	244	48	42
能源类	Power	88	104	25	20
土木水利工程类	Construction and Water Conservancy Engineering	1 841	1 904	145	175
加工制造类	Processing and Manufacturing	2 985	4 828	217	279
交通运输类	Transport	687	545	84	65
信息技术类	Information Technology	6 292	7 117	349	321
医药卫生类	Medicine, Health	725	1 017	218	80
商贸与旅游类	Trade and Tour	4 079	4 510	232	124
财经类	Finance and Economics	392	629	238	213
文化艺术与体育类	Arts and Physical Culture	909	730	527	240
社会公共事业类	Society Commonality Business	1 343	869	137	102
其　他	Others	486	886	91	87

14－12　普通中学分课程专任教师学历情况(2003年)

EDUCATIONAL BACKGROUND OF FULL－TIME TEACHERS IN REGULAR SECONDARY SCHOOLS BY COURSE,2003

单位:人　(person)

项　目	Item	合　计 Total	#政　治 Politics	#语　文 Chinese	#数　学 Math	#物　理 Physics
总　计	**Total**	**41 422**	**2 936**	**6 713**	**6 931**	**3 675**
初　中	**Junior Middle School**	**29 398**	**2 164**	**4 936**	**5 183**	**2 387**
大学本科毕业及以上	University and The Level Above	9 704	748	1 868	1 679	700
大学专科毕业	Junior College	16 429	1 235	2 767	3 037	1 475
中专毕业	Specialized Secondary School	3 214	180	299	462	212
高中毕业及以下	Senior Middle School and The Level below	51	1	2	5	
高　中	**Senior Middle School**	**12 024**	**772**	**1 777**	**1 748**	**1 288**
大学本科毕业及以上	University and The Level Above	9 891	656	1 510	1 474	1 047
大学专科毕业	Junior College	2 056	112	265	269	238
中专毕业	Specialized Secondary School	75	3	2	5	3
高中毕业及以下	Senior Middle School and The Level below	2	1			

项　目	Item	#化　学 Chemical	#生　物 Biology	#外　语 Foreign Language	#历史地理 History & Geography
总　计	**Total**	**2 854**	**1 594**	**6 434**	**3 139**
初　中	**Junior Middle School**	**1 633**	**964**	**4 687**	**1 910**
大学本科毕业及以上	University and The Level Above	480	371	1 540	679
大学专科毕业	Junior College	985	427	2 704	907
中专毕业	Specialized Secondary School	168	164	438	318
高中毕业及以下	Senior Middle School and The Level below		2	5	6
高　中	**Senior Middle School**	**1 221**	**630**	**1 747**	**1 229**
大学本科毕业及以上	University and The Level Above	1 004	554	1 414	1 067
大学专科毕业	Junior College	212	75	328	160
中专毕业	Specialized Secondary School	5	1	5	2
高中毕业及以下	Senior Middle School and The Level below				

14－13　天津市重点中学一览表(2003年)

LIST OF KEY MIDDLE SCHOOLS,2003

学校名称 Name of School	班　级(个) Classes (unit)		在校学生数(人) Students Enrollment (person)		教职工数(人) Teachers,Staff and Workers (person)	
	合　计 Total	#高　中 Senior Middle Schools	合　计 Total	#高　中 Senior Middle Schools	合　计 Total	#高　中 Senior Middle Schools
南开中学 Nankai Middle School	26	26	1 249	1 249	259	111
一　　中 No.1 Middle School	26	26	1 125	1 125	368	123
耀华中学 Yaohua Middle School	48	44	2 154	1 972	249	129
新华中学 Xinhua Middle School	27	27	1 174	1 174	255	104
实验中学 Shiyan Middle School	21	21	1 002	1 002	247	89
二十中学 No.20 Middle School	24	24	1 010	1 010	200	90
南开二中 No.2 Nankai Middle School	37	37	1 682	1 682	384	163
二十一中 No.21 Middle School	40	24	1 942	1 076	269	112
五十五中 No.55 Middle School	36	24	1 736	1 076	223	77
七　　中 No.7 Middle School	30	30	1 313	1 313	229	88
四十五中 No.45 Middle School	18	18	884	884	255	89
津华中学 Jinhua Middle School	18	18	884	884	200	57
海河中学 Haihe Middle School	32	32	1 124	1 124	288	85
四十二中 No.42 Middle School	25	25	1 085	1 085	315	98
四　　中 No.4 Middle School	24	24	1 097	1 097	283	86
三十一中 No.31 Middle School	20	20	844	844	240	68
一0九中 No.109 Middle School	18	18	856	856	195	66
天大附中 Tianda Middle School	21	14	829	538	96	34
南大附中 Nanda Middle School	25	12	1 121	575	106	34
四十三中 No.43 Middle School	33	33	1 439	1 439	264	120
二十五中 No.25 Middle School	20	20	947	947	291	64
天津中学 Tianjin Middle School	20	20	928	928	166	57
二　　中 No.2 Middle School	34	34	1 455	1 455	277	96
十　四　中 No.14 Middle School	24	24	887	887	218	71
五十七中 No.57 Middle School	22	22	939	939	241	91
外语学校 Foreign Language School	19	13	803	549	236	68
红光中学 Hongguang Middle School	31	12	781	395	188	39
铁　一　中 No.1 Railway Middle School	38	15	2 054	660	152	61
三　　中 No.3 Middle School	26	26	1 212	1 212	274	63
五　　中 No.5 Middle School	25	25	1 213	1 213	345	116
民族中学 Nationality Middle School	22	22	1 036	1 036	347	107
五十一中 No.51 Middle School	20	17	857	801	247	85

14－13 续表 Continued

学校名称 Name of School	班 级(个) Classes(unit)		在校学生数(人) Students Enrollment (person)		教职工数(人) Teachers,Staff and Workers(person)	
	合 计 Total	#高 中 Senior Middle Schools	合 计 Total	#高 中 Senior Middle Schools	合 计 Total	#高 中 Senior Middle Schools
英才中学 Yingcai Middle School	8	8	369	369		
塘沽一中 Tanggu No.1 Middle School	26	26	1 225	1 225	342	261
塘沽二中 Tanggu No.2 Middle School	47	30	2 419	1 348	312	94
渤海石油一 Bohai No.1 Middle School	26	14	903	424	118	48
汉沽一中 Hangu No.1 Middle School	44	38	2 172	1 837	197	132
大港一中 Dagang No.1 Middle School	19	19	829	829	98	61
油田实验中学 Oilfield Shiyan Middle School	21	21	834	834	115	86
一00中学 No.100 Middle School	24	24	1 509	1 509	158	105
杨柳青一中 Yangliuqing No.1 Middle School	30	30	1 421	1 421	162	113
咸水沽一中 Xianshuigu No.1 Middle School	22	22	1 028	1 028	203	114
四十七中 No.47 Middle School	26	26	1 096	1 096	206	137
芦台一中 Lutai No.1 Middle School	44	40	2 027	1 855	226	136
杨村一中 Yangcun No.1 Middle School	43	43	1 792	1 792	238	144
静海一中 Jinghai No.1 Middle School	43	43	2 407	2 407	248	163
宝坻一中 Baodi No.1 Middle School	23	23	1 507	1 507	147	84
蓟县一中 Jixian No.1 Middle School	33	33	1 755	1 755	179	111

14－14 按部门分普通中小学生基本情况

BASIC STATISTICS ON SECONDARY SCHOOLS AND PRIMARY SCHOOLS BY DEPARTMENT

单位:人 (person)

项 目 Item	教育部门 Education Department		其他部门 Other Departments		民 办 Private Units	
	2002	2003	2002	2003	2002	2003
普通中学 Middle Schools						
在校学生数 Students Enrollment	553 223	559 076	24 936	25 010	27 031	30 948
毕业生数 Graduates	155 358	168 129	7 555	7 496	6 597	8 614
招生数 New Students Enrollment	172 203	180 406	7 280	7 024	8 776	10 873
小 学 Primary Schools						
在校学生数 Students Enrollment	598 952	557 260	25 298	24 412	2 992	3 774
毕业生数 Graduates	127 356	126 312	5 556	5 117	389	593
招生数 New Students Enrollment	88 224	80 158	4 264	4 368	467	437

注:本表不含民办公助和公办民助学校。
Note:This table exclude private units supported by state and state－owned units supported by private units.

14－15　普通中小学分布情况(2003 年)
DISTRIBUTION OF REGULAR SECONDARY SCHOOLS AND PRIMARY SCHOOLS,2003

地　区　Region	学校数(所) Number of Schools(Unit)		在校学生数(人) Students Enrollment(person)		专任教师数(人) Full－time Teachers(person)	
	普通中学 Regular Middle Schools	小　学 Primary Schools	普通中学 Regular Middle Schools	小　学 Primary Schools	普通中学 Regular Middle Schools	小　学 Primary Schools
全　市　Total	**664**	**1 136**	**615 034**	**585 446**	**41 422**	**43 829**
一、市辖区　Districts Under City Administration	**525**	**837**	**459 288**	**448 352**	**31 780**	**35 298**
和平区　Heping District	33	39	36 943	29 143	2 300	2 295
河东区　Hedong District	34	33	30 425	25 009	2 011	2 202
河西区　Hexi District	53	60	43 046	32 386	2 446	2 263
南开区　Nankai District	43	43	35 296	29 421	2 592	2 587
河北区　Hebei District	41	46	37 401	27 804	2 159	2 077
红桥区　Hongqiao District	36	37	32 104	21 215	2 160	2 193
塘沽区　Tanggu District	41	62	29 263	34 200	2 221	2 671
汉沽区　Hangu District	15	26	10 408	11 692	881	1 082
大港区　Dagang District	39	32	27 567	23 624	2 536	1 958
东丽区　Dongli District	28	43	17 146	25 190	1 313	1 974
西青区　Xiqing District	17	41	15 992	20 206	1 223	2 023
津南区　Jinnan District	20	45	19 446	28 502	1 009	1 621
北辰区　Beichen District	20	46	15 292	19 741	1 205	1 766
武清区　Wuqing District	52	144	51 033	55 955	3 690	4 082
宝坻区　Baodi District	51	135	56 425	62 682	3 877	4 316
天津铁厂　Tianjin Iron Works	2	5	1 501	1 582	157	188
二、市辖县　Counties Under City Administration	**139**	**299**	**155 746**	**137 094**	**9 642**	**8 531**
宁河县　Ninghe County	29	65	36 042	26 695	2 112	1 910
静海县　Jinghai County	47	99	38 392	43 228	2 590	2 867
蓟　县　Jixian County	63	135	81 312	67 171	4 940	3 754

注:专任教师数中不包括民办教师数。
Note:Number of full－time teachers exclude civilian teachers.

14－16 普通中学、职业中学及小学校舍情况(2003年)
STATISTICS FOR SCHOOLHOUSES OF REGULAR SECONDARY SCHOOLS, VOCATIONAL SECONDARY SCHOOLS AND PRIMARY SCHOOLS, 2003

单位:平方米 (sq. m)

地 区 Region		占地面积 Areas	校舍建筑面积 Floor Space of Schoolhouses			学生人均建筑面积 Average Floor Space of Students		
			普通中学 Regular Secondary Schools	职业中学 Vocational Secondary Schools	小 学 Primary Schools	普通中学 Regular Secondary Schools	职业中学 Vocational Secondary Schools	小 学 Primary Schools
全 市	**Total**	**33 480 625**	**4 873 623**	**890 204**	**3 446 301**	**7.92**	**14.49**	**5.89**
一、市辖区	**Districts Under City Administration**	**24 944 921**	**4 003 100**	**780 251**	**2 676 422**	**8.72**	**20.38**	**5.97**
和平区	Heping District	376 877	171 746	32 864	123 472	5.40	5.52	4.43
河东区	Hedong District	1 021 293	278 111	76 107	146 510	9.14	14.83	5.86
河西区	Hexi District	1 235 498	277 130	104 741	182 568	7.70	9.77	5.64
南开区	Nankai District	1 169 123	275 306	129 211	158 664	8.59	14.99	5.39
河北区	Hebei District	1 069 338	300 095	69 881	149 775	8.02	13.18	5.39
红桥区	Hongqiao District	776 715	216 117	80 534	138 810	6.84	18.92	6.54
直属校	Directly Under City	480 745	306 086	8 688	23 808	19.25	17.34	19.05
塘沽区	Tanggu District	1 854 887	397 249	64 158	299 468	13.58	12.97	8.76
汉沽区	Hangu District	518 099	76 163		55 600	7.32		4.76
大港区	Dagang District	3 092 741	364 182	81 909	178 822	13.21	64.70	7.57
东丽区	Dongli District	1 464 557	182 638	20 347	195 466	10.65	13.68	7.76
西青区	Xiqing District	1 241 180	155 908	18 560	160 880	9.75	59.87	7.96
津南区	Jinnan District	1 021 905	137 508	11 232	135 170	7.07	14.36	4.74
北辰区	Beichen District	1 337 732	190 284	24 494	158 965	12.44	11.88	8.05
武清区	Wuqing District	4 598 790	382 171	32 837	319 045	7.49	10.61	5.70
宝坻区	Baodi District	3 616 168	274 071	24 688	237 240	4.86	23.16	3.78
天津铁厂	Tianjin Iron Works	69 273	18 335		12 159	12.22		7.69
二、市辖县	**Counties Under City Administration**	**8 535 704**	**870 523**	**109 953**	**769 879**	**5.59**	**24.65**	**5.62**
宁河县	Ninghe County	1 635 568	178 077	19 572	158 935	4.94	29.21	5.95
静海县	Jinghai County	2 733 000	215 846	28 142	264 749	5.62	27.62	6.12
蓟 县	Jixian County	4 167 136	476 600	62 239	346 195	5.86	17.12	5.15

注:占地面积包括中等师范学校、幼儿园教师进修学校、特殊教育学校及其他。
Note: Areas of schools include middle teacher training, kindergarten teacher training, special education and other schools.

14－17 其他教育基本情况
BASIC STATISTICS ON OTHER EDUCATION

单位:所、人 (unit)(person)

指标	Item	2000	2001	2002	2003
成人教育	**Adult Education**				
成人高等学校	**Adult Higher Education Schools**				
学校数	Number of Schools	35	26	22	22
在校学生数	Students Enrollment	71 345	83 262	104 270	115 770
成人中等学校	**Secondary Schools for Adults**				
学校数	Number of Schools	96	85	74	29
在校学生数	Students Enrollment	42 511	32 292	20 505	7 619
特殊教育	**Specific Education**				
盲聋哑学校	**Blind and Deaf－Mute Schools**				
学校数	Number of Schools	9	9	7	8
在校学生数	Students Enrollment	684	680	651	751
初中	Junior Middle Schools	231	232	247	249
小学	Primary Schools	453	448	404	502
教职工人数	Teachers,Staff and Workers	335	331	408	402
#专任教师数	Full－time Teachers	226	229	257	254
弱智学校	**Schools for Low Intelligence Student**				
学校数	Number of Schools	15	15	14	13
在校学生数	Students Enrollment	1 033	979	945	2 416
初中	Junior Middle Schools		336	348	451
小学	Primary Schools	1 033	643	597	1 965
教职工人数	Teachers,Staff and Workers	323	305	304	304
#专任教师数	Full－time teachers	235	214	220	200
工读学校	**Schools for Mistaken Students**				
学校数	Number of Schools	3	3	3	3
在校学生数	Students Enrollment	247	190	152	82
教职工人数	Teachers,Staff and Workers	122	121	117	113
#专任教师数	Full－time Eeachers	62	38	35	28

14－18 托幼园所基本情况
BASIC STATISTICS ON KINDERGARTENS AND NURSERIES

指标	Item	2000	2001	2002	2003
托幼园所数(所)	Number of Nurseries and Kindergartens (unit)	2 996	2 566	2 286	2 152
#幼儿园	Kindergartens	806	2 068	1 166	1 778
入托园儿童数(人)	Children Enrollment(person)	216 618	204 427	203 627	199 551
三岁及以上儿童	Children over Three Age	209 607	197 390	195 695	192 552
三岁及以下儿童	Children under Three Age	7 011	7 037	7 932	6 999
教职工数(人)	Teachers,Staff and Workers(person)	17 673	12 439	16 356	15 309
#教养员	Teachers and Health Workers	10 866	7 035	10 436	10 046

主要统计指标解释

学校(机构)　是指按国家规定的设置标准和审批程序批准设立的，招收适龄人口实施各级各类教育活动的教育机构。

普通高等学校　是按国家规定的设置标准和审批程序批准举办的，通过全国普通高等教育统一招生考试，招收高中毕业生为主要培养对象，实施高等学历教育的全日制大学、独立设置的学院和高等专科学校、高等职业学校和其他机构。大学、独立设置的学院主要实施本科及本科层次以上的教育。高等专科学校、高等职业学校实施专科层次教育。

成人高等学校：　是按国家规定的设置标准和审批程序批准举办的，通过全国成人高等教育统一招生考试，招收高中毕业或同等学历的人员为主要培养对象，利用函授、业余、脱产的多种形式对其实施高等学历教育的学校。包括：职工高等学校、农民高等学校、管理干部学院、教育学院、独立函授学院、广播电视大学、其他机构。

中等职业学校　是指按国家规定的设置标准和审批程序批准成立的实施中等职业教育的学校(机构)。调整后的中等职业学校是指将普通中等专业学校(中等技术学校、中等师范学校)、成人中等专业学校、职业高中学校等各种实施中等职业教育的办学类型，通过合并、共建、联办、划转等形式调整为统一的办学类型，即中等职业学校。

职业中学(职业高中、职业初中)　职业中学是指经县或县以上教育行政部门批准设立，招收小学或初中毕业生实施中等职业技术教育的教学机构。职业中学按学校性质类别可分为：独立设置的职业中学(包括：职业初中、职业高中、职业初高中合设学校)；附设有普通中学班的职业中学。

普通中等学校(普通高中、普通初中)　普通中等学校通常称普通中学，分为普通高级中学和普通初级中学两个阶段。普通初级中学是指独立设置的招收小学毕业的适龄人口进行初级中等基础教育的机构；普通高级中学是指独立设置的招收初中毕业的适龄人口进行高级中等基础教育的机构；完全中学是指普通初、高中合设的教育机构；一贯制学校是指在一所学校连续实施中小学教育的机构。其中包括实施九年义务教育的九年一贯制学校和实施高中教育的十二年一贯制学校。(说明：一贯制学校的办学条件如能划分为小学、初中、高中，则分开填报；如不能划分清楚，可按就高不就低的方法填入初中、高中报表中，不能重复填写。)

初等教育(普通小学)　普通小学是指由县或县以上教育行政部门批准，招收学龄儿童实施初等教育的教学机构。

学前教育(幼儿园)　幼儿园是指招收三周岁以上(含三周岁)学龄前幼儿，对其进行保育和教育的单位，包括全市各幼儿教学点；幼儿园以游戏为基本活动形式，寓教于乐、寓教于动。

工读学校　是指由教育和公安部门联合举办的，对有轻微违法行为的中学生进行挽救教育的教学机构。

特殊教育学校　是指某地独立设置的招收盲聋哑和智残儿童，以及其他特殊需要的儿童、青少年进行普通或职业初、中等教育的教学机构。

毕业生数　是指上学年，具有学籍的学生学完教学计划规定的全部课程，考试及格，取得毕业证书，实际毕业的学生数。

招生数　是指通过国家统一招生考试，按照国家招生计划实际招收入学的新生数。(高等教育包括春秋两季招收的学生。)

在校生数　是指本学年初，具有学籍的注册学生总数。

教职工数　是指在学校(机构)工作并由学校(机构)支付劳动报酬的教职工，人员包括在编人员，即根据原人事管理制度，人事关系和档案均在学校的人员；聘任制人员，即人事制度改革后，高校(机构)招聘录用的长期、全时工作人员。聘任制人员的人事关系在学校但档案不在学校。教职工数包括校本部教职工、科研机构人员、校办企业职工、其他附设机构人员。

专任教师　是指具有教师资格，专门从事教学工作的人员。

Explanatory Notes on Main Statistical Indicators

School (Institution) refer to educational establishments at different levels set up according to the government evaluation and approval procedures, enrolling school - age population.

Regular Institutions of Higher Learning refer to educational establishments set up according to the government evaluation and approval procedures, enrolling graduates from senior secondary schools and providing higher education courses and training for senior professionals. They include full - time universities, colleges, high professional schools, high professional vocational schools and others. Universities and colleges are mainly providing undergraduate courses; those high professional schools and high professional vocational schools are mainly providing professional trainings.

Institutions of Higher Learning for Adults refer to educational establishments, set up in line with relevant rules approved by the government, enrolling staff and workers with senior secondary school or equivalent education, and providing higher education courses in many forms of correspondence, spare time, or full time for adults. Professionals thus trained receive a qualification equivalent to graduates studying regular courses at regular universities, colleges and professional colleges. Institutions of higher learning for adults include schools of high education for staff and workers, schools of high education for peasants, colleges for management cadres, pedagogical colleges, independent correspondence colleges, Radio and TV universities and other educational establishments.

Secondary Professional Schools refer to educational establishments, set up in line with relevant rules approved by the government, implementing secondary professional education. Secondary professional schools are original specialized secondary schools (secondary technical schools, secondary teacher training schools), specialized secondary schools for adults, vocational secondary schools, which are named secondary professional schools after they are merged, constructed together and adjusted to be a kind of education type.

Vocational Secondary Schools (vocational senior secondary schools, vocational junior secondary schools) refer to educational establishments approved by county or above education administrative department, enrolling graduates from primary schools and junior secondary schools and providing vocational secondary education courses. They include vocational secondary schools (including vocational senior secondary schools, vocational junior secondary schools, vocational junior & senior secondary schools), vocational secondary schools with regular secondary school classes.

Regular Secondary Schools (regular senior secondary schools, regular junior secondary schools) are divided into regular senior secondary schools and regular junior secondary schools. Regular junior secondary schools refer to educational establishments enrolling graduates from primary schools and providing junior secondary education courses. Regular senior secondary schools refer to educational establishments enrolling graduates from junior secondary schools and providing senior secondary education courses. Whole seconary schools refer to educational establishments including senior secondary school and junior secondary school. Successive schools refer to educational establishments providing successive primary and secondary education courses, include nine – year successive schools and twelve – year successive schools. (Note: If successive schools can be divided into primary school, junior secondary school and senior secondary school, should fill in respectively, otherwise, should fill in junior secondary school or senior secondary school and have no repetition.

Primary Education (Regular Primary Schools) refer to educational establishments approved by county or above education administrative department, enrolling school – age children and providing primary education courses.

Baby Education (Kindergartens) Kindergartens refer to educational units enrolling children aged 3 – 6, include all baby education units. Kindergartens take games as basic activities.

Schools for Juvenile Delinquents refer to educational establishments founded by education deparment and public security department, enrolling students of secondary schools with slight illegal behavior.

Special Education Schools refer to educational establishments, enrolling blind, deaf, dumb children, weak – minded children and providing regular or vocational primary and seconary education courses.

Graduates refer to the number of students who have student status, learn over all education courses, pass the examination and receive diploma.

New Students Enrollment refer to number of new students who have passed enrollment examination (Higher Learning include students enrolled in spring and autumn).

Students Enrollment refer to number of students with student status at the beginning of the school year.

Number of Teachers, Officers and Workers refer to work at schools (institutions) and receive wages from schools (institutions). They include personnel whose personal connections and files put in schools, engaged personnel, i.e. full – time personnel engaged by higher learning (institutions). The personal connections of engaged personnel are put in schools but files are not put in schools. Number of teachers, officers and workers include staff, personnel of science rearch institutions, staff and workers of enterprises founded by schools and personnel of other subordinated institutions.

Full – time Teachers refer to personnel who have qualifications of teacher and undertake educational working.

第15篇 CHAPTER 15

科学技术

SCIENCE & TECHNOLOGY

15－1　专业技术人员
SPECIAL TECHNICAL PERSONNEL

单位：人　　　　(person)

项　目 Item	全　市 Total			平均每万人口有科技人员 Scientific and Technological Personnel Per 10 000 Persons (2003)	平均每万名从业人员有科技人员 Scientific and Technological Personnel Per 10 000 Employees (2003)
	2001	2002	2003		
合　计 Total	**509 624**	**482 778**	**465 039**	**460**	**2 435**
一、自然科学专业技术人员 Natural Science	**240 361**	**226 639**	**232 324**	**230**	**1 216**
#工程技术人员 Engineering	143 753	128 997	134 556	133	705
农业技术人员 Agriculture	3 238	3 030	3 197	3	17
科学研究人员 Scientific Research	2 462	2 852	3 671	4	19
卫生技术人员 Health Care	64 096	60 737	60 517	60	317
教学人员 Teaching	26 812	31 023	30 383	30	159
二、社会科学专业技术人员 Social Science	**269 263**	**256 139**	**232 715**	**230**	**1 218**
#科学研究人员 Scientific Research	1 482	916	1 040	1	6
教学人员 Teaching	108 451	98 066	97 685	97	511
经济人员 Economy	61 943	50 485	48 594	48	254
财会人员 Accountant	45 837	39 594	39 977	40	209
统计人员 Statistician	7 027	4 978	4 776	5	25
翻译人员 Translator	1 185	912	823	1	4
图书、档案、资料人员 Librarian and Archivist	6 521	5 860	5 828	6	31
编辑、记者、播音员 Editor, Reporter and Broadcasting	2 558	2 651	2 760	3	15
体育教练人员 Coach	546	551	548	1	3
工艺美术人员 Arts and Craft	553	418	437		2
文艺人员 Literature and Art	2 640	2 010	2 170	2	11

注：专业技术人员统计范围为国有经济单位。
Note: Special technical personnel refer to state－owned units.

15－2　专业技术人员构成(2003 年)
COMPOSITION OF SPECIAL TECHNICAL PERSONNEL,2003

单位:人　　　　(person)

项　目 Item	按性别分 By Sex	按受教育程度分 By Education Status		按职称分 By Title	
	#女专业技术人员数 Female	#受过高等专业教育人数 Having Higher Special Education Background	#受过中等专业教育人数 Having Special Secondary School Background	#高级职称人数 Senior Professional Certification	#中级职称人数 Medium Professional Certification
合　计 **Total**	**221 290**	**280 894**	**138 064**	**52 419**	**148 667**
一、自然科学专业技术人员 **Natural Science**	**97 365**	**141 454**	**76 804**	**30 085**	**68 276**
#工程技术人员 Engineering	36 161	83 330	42 432	16 071	37 222
农业技术人员 Agriculture	978	1 608	1 208	367	896
科学研究人员 Scientific Research	1 445	3 556	76	1 482	1 321
卫生技术人员 Health Care	41 953	27 838	28 471	5 029	16 817
教学人员 Teaching	16 828	25 122	4 617	7 136	12 020
二、社会科学专业技术人员 **Social Science**	**123 925**	**139 440**	**61 260**	**22 334**	**80 391**
#科学研究人员 Scientific Research	459	964	36	381	421
教学人员 Teaching	61 599	65 906	27 678	12 232	45 437
经济人员 Economy	16 686	23 639	12 408	1 876	8 647
财会人员 Accountant	25 727	20 292	13 122	783	6 670
统计人员 Statistician	3 468	2 069	1 378	179	977
翻译人员 Translator	417	796	21	227	291
图书、档案、资料人员 Librarian and Archivist	4 257	4 129	917	701	2 555
编辑、记者、播音员 Editor,Reporter and Broadcasting	1 200	2 493	116	859	975
体育教练人员 Coach	148	470	50	148	188
工艺美术人员 Arts and Craft	128	241	127	60	148
文艺人员 Literature and Art	765	632	1 077	674	1 019

15-3 国民经济各行业专业技术人员
SPECIAL TECHNICAL PERSONNEL BY SECTORS OF NATIONAL ECONOMY

单位:人 (person)

项目	Item	自然科学专业技术人员 Special Technical Personnel of Natural Science 2001	2002	2003
总计	**Total**	**247 014**	**226 639**	**232 324**
农、林、牧、渔业	Farming, Forestry, Animal Husbandry and Fishery	6 010	5 822	6 104
工业	Industry	77 756	56 308	54 824
地质普查和勘探业	Geological Survey and Prospecting	1 158	1 495	3 721
建筑业	Construction	25 687	23 333	18 392
交通运输、邮电通讯业	Transportation, Post and Telecommunications	17 361	22 961	32 046
商业、公共饮食业、物资供销和仓储业	Commerce, Public Catering Trade, Material Supply and Storage	5 044	2 062	1 661
房地产管理、公共事业、居民服务和咨询服务业	Real Estate Management, Public Services, Residential Services and Consultancy Services	5 910	5 533	6 854
卫生、体育和社会福利业	Health Care, Sports and Social Welfare	51 813	50 235	50 820
教育、文化艺术及广播电视业	Education, Culture and Arts, Radio and Television	33 611	38 806	37 979
科学研究和综合技术服务业	Scientific Research and Polytechnical Services	14 942	13 640	15 083
金融、保险业	Banking and Insurance	1 045	1 786	1 081
国家政党机关和社会团体	Government Agencies, Party Agencies & Social Organizations	4 726	434	56
其他	Others	1 951	4 224	3 703

项目	Item	社会科学专业技术人员 Special Technical Personnel of Social Science 2001	2002	2003
总计	**Total**	**279 637**	**256 139**	**232 715**
农、林、牧、渔业	Farming, Forestry, Animal Husbandry and Fishery	2 508	2 699	2 480
工业	Industry	61 036	46 349	39 096
地质普查和勘探业	Geological Survey and Prospecting	477	473	881
建筑业	Construction	11 578	11 672	8 915
交通运输、邮电通讯业	Transportation, Post and Telecommunications	11 970	17 779	13 039
商业、公共饮食业、物资供销和仓储业	Commerce, Public Catering Trade, Material Supply and Storage	27 441	15 893	14 262
房地产管理、公共事业、居民服务和咨询服务业	Real Estate Management, Public Services, Residential Services and Consultancy Services	6 844	6 868	6 795
卫生、体育和社会福利业	Health Care, Sports and Social Welfare	5 778	7 230	6 197
教育、文化艺术及广播电视业	Education, Cultureand Arts, Radio and Television	118 079	111 694	108 348
科学研究和综合技术服务业	Scientific Research and Polytechnical Services	3 264	2 813	2 862
金融、保险业	Banking and Insurance	22 501	24 784	23 914
国家政党机关和社会团体	Government Agencies, Party Agencies & Social Organizations	5 408	919	164
其他	Others	2 753	6 966	5 762

注:本表行业分类为国标 GB/T4754-1994 标准,15-3、15-4、15-5 表同。
Note: Sector listed in this table is classified by the standard of GB/T4754-1994, same as following table 15-3, 15-4 and 15-5.

15－4 自然科学专业技术人员构成(2003年)

COMPOSITION OF SPECIAL TECHNICAL PERSONNEL OF NATURAL SCIENCE, 2003

单位:人 (person)

行业	Sector	合计 Total	#工程技术人员 Engineering	#农业技术人员 Agriculture
总计	**Total**	**232 324**	**134 556**	**3 197**
农、林、牧、渔业	Farming, Forestry, Animal Husbandry and Fishery	6 104	3 189	2 671
工业	Industry	54 824	48 794	90
地质普查和勘探业	Geological Survey and Prospecting	3 721	3 593	
建筑业	Construction	18 392	17 356	
交通运输、邮电通讯业	Transportation, Post and Telecommunications	32 046	29 005	
商业、公共饮食业、物资供销和仓储业	Commerce, Public Catering Trade, Material Supply and Storage	1 661	1 234	
房地产管理、公共事业、居民服务和咨询服务业	Real Estate Management, Public Services, Residential Services and Consultancy Services	6 854	6 446	98
卫生、体育和社会福利业	Health Care, Sports and Social Welfare	50 820	1 111	
教育、文化艺术及广播电视业	Education, Culture and Arts, Radio and Television	37 979	6 534	41
科学研究和综合技术服务业	Scientific Research and Polytechnical Services	15 083	12 946	77
金融、保险业	Banking and Insurance	1 081	1 031	
国家政党机关和社会团体	Government Agencies, Party Agencies & Social Organizations	56	44	7
其他	Others	3 703	3 273	213

行业	Sector	#科学研究人员 Science Research	#卫生技术人员 Health Care	#教学人员 Teaching
总计	**Total**	**3 671**	**60 517**	**30 383**
农、林、牧、渔业	Farming, Forestry, Animal Husbandry and Fishery	125	110	9
工业	Industry	6	4 968	966
地质普查和勘探业	Geological Survey and Prospecting		93	35
建筑业	Construction	5	984	47
交通运输、邮电通讯业	Transportation, Post and Telecommunications		2 663	378
商业、公共饮食业、物资供销和仓储业	Commerce, Public Catering Trade, Material Supply and Storage		422	5
房地产管理、公共事业、居民服务和咨询服务业	Real Estate Management, Public Services, Residential Services and Consultancy Services	5	272	33
卫生、体育和社会福利业	Health Care, Sports and Social Welfare	260	49 280	169
教育、文化艺术及广播电视业	Education, Culture and Arts, Radio and Television	1 552	1 207	28 645
科学研究和综合技术服务业	Scientific Research and Polytechnical Services	1 691	345	24
金融、保险业	Banking and Insurance	22	28	
国家政党机关和社会团体	Government Agencies, Party Agencies & Social Organizations		5	
其他	Others	5	140	72

15－5 社会科学专业技术人员构成(2003年)
COMPOSITION OF SPECIAL TECHNICAL PERSONNEL OF SOCIAL SCIENCE,2003

单位:人 (person)

行 业	Sector	合 计 Total	科学研究人员 Science Research	教学人员 Teaching
总 计	**Total**	**232 715**	**1 040**	**97 685**
农、林、牧、渔业	Farming,Forestry,Animal Husbandry and Fishery	2 480		156
工 业	Industry	39 096		4 223
地质普查和勘探业	Geological Survey and Prospecting	881		135
建筑业	Construction	8 915		238
交通运输、邮电通讯业	Transportation,Post and Telecommunications	13 039		1 206
商业、公共饮食业、物资供销和仓储业	Commerce,Public Catering Trade,Material Supply and Storage	14 262		39
房地产管理、公共事业、居民服务和咨询服务业	Real Estate Management,Public Services,Residential Services & Consultancy Services	6 795		260
卫生、体育和社会福利业	Health Care,Sports and Social Welfare	6 197	26	357
教育、文化艺术及广播电视业	Education,Culture and Arts,Radio and Television	108 348	855	90 630
科学研究和综合技术服务业	Scientific Research and Polytechnical Services	2 862	158	75
金融、保险业	Banking and Insurance	23 914		45
国家政党机关和社会团体	Government Agencies,Party Agencies & Social Organizations	164		4
其 他	Others	5 762	1	317

行 业	Sector	财会人员 Accountant	统计人员 Statistician	编辑、记者、播音员 Editor, Reporter and Broadcasting
总 计	**Total**	**39 977**	**4 776**	**2 760**
农、林、牧、渔业	Farming,Forestry,Animal Husbandry and Fishery	1 086	93	11
工 业	Industry	8 810	2 439	70
地质普查和勘探业	Geological Survey and Prospecting	312	25	4
建筑业	Construction	3 260	310	11
交通运输、邮电通讯业	Transportation,Post and Telecommunications	2 831	380	17
商业、公共饮食业、物资供销和仓储业	Commerce,Public Catering Trade,Material Supply and Storage	3 663	388	6
房地产管理、公共事业、居民服务和咨询服务业	Real Estate Management,Public Services Residential Services and Consultancy Services	2 230	353	11
卫生、体育和社会福利业	Health Care,Sports and Social Welfare	2 994	221	27
教育、文化艺术及广播电视业	Education,Culture and Arts,Radio and Television	3 586	114	2 432
科学研究和综合技术服务业	Scientific Research and Polytechnical Services	863	80	83
金融、保险业	Banking and Insurance	8 594	49	
国家政党机关和社会团体	Government Agencies,Party Agencies & Social Organizations	30	7	3
其 他	Others	1 718	317	85

15－5 续表　Continued
单位：人　(person)

行　业	Sector	翻译人员 Translator	经济人员 Economy	体育教练人员 Coach
总　计	**Total**	**823**	**48 594**	**548**
农、林、牧、渔业	Farming, Forestry, Animal Husbandry and Fishery	3	465	
工　业	Industry	293	12 575	
地质普查和勘探业	Geological Survey and Prospecting	7	143	
建筑业	Construction	48	2 841	
交通运输、邮电通讯业	Transportation, Post and Telecommunications	51	5 085	
商业、公共饮食业、物资供销和仓储业	Commerce, Public Catering Trade, Material Supply and Storage	42	8 086	
房地产管理、公共事业、居民服务和咨询服务业	Real Estate Management, Public Services, Resi－dential Services and Consultancy Services	83	1 893	6
卫生、体育和社会福利业	Health Care, Sports and Social Welfare	26	407	514
教育、文化艺术及广播电视业	Education, Culture and Arts, Radio and Television	96	490	28
科学研究和综合技术服务业	Scientific Research and Polytechnical Services	91	337	
金融、保险业	Banking and Insurance	11	14 157	
国家政党机关和社会团体	Government Agencies, Party Agencies & Social Organizations	16	73	
其　他	Others	56	2 042	

行　业	Sector	图书、档案、资料人员 Librarian and Archivist	工艺美术人员 Arts & Craft	其　他 Others
总　计	**Total**	**5 828**	**437**	**30 247**
农、林、牧、渔业	Farming, Forestry, Animal Husbandry and Fishery	53		613
工　业	Industry	954	126	9 606
地质普查和勘探业	Geological Survey and Prospecting	34		221
建筑业	Construction	97	15	2 095
交通运输、邮电通讯业	Transportation, Post and Telecommunications	142		3 327
商业、公共饮食业、物资供销和仓储业	Commerce, Public Catering Trade, Material Supply and Storage	98	46	1 894
房地产管理、公共事业、居民服务和咨询服务业	Real Estate Management, Public Services, Resi－dential Services and Consultancy Services	144	41	1 774
卫生、体育和社会福利业	Health Care, Sports and Social Welfare	248	7	1 370
教育、文化艺术及广播电视业	Education, Culture and Arts, Radio and Television	3 553	170	6 394
科学研究和综合技术服务业	Scientific Research and Polytechnical Services	315	14	846
金融、保险业	Banking and Insurance	44		1 014
国家政党机关和社会团体	Government Agencies, Party Agencies & Social Organizations	3	5	23
其　他	Others	143	13	1 070

15－6 独立科学研究和技术开发机构情况
BASIC INDICATORS OF INDEPENDENT INSTITUTIONS OF SCIENTIFIC RESEARCH AND TECHNOLOGICAL DEVELOPMENT

指 标	Indicator	自然科学研究与技术开发机构 Institutions of Natural Scien－tific Research and Technical Development		社会、人文科研与开发机构 Institutions of Social Science and Humanities of Research and Development		科学技术情报和文献机构 Institutions of Scientific and Technological Information and Documents	
		2002	2003	2002	2003	2002	2003
机构数(个)	**Number of Institutions (unit)**	**132**	**131**	**3**	**3**	**11**	**11**
科技活动人员(人)	**Number of Persons Engaged in Scientific and Technological Activities (person)**	**11 387**	**10 876**	**278**	**289**	**604**	**597**
高级职称	Senior Professional Certification	3 488	3 504	153	135	218	231
中级职称	Medium Professional Certification	3 638	3 435	91	90	253	233
初级职称	Junior Professional Certification	2 613	2 735	33	48	85	112
其 他	Others	1 648	1 202	1	16	48	21
经费支出总额(万元)	**Total Expenditures of Operating Expenses (10 000 yuan)**	**143 005**	**163 400**	**2 517**	**2 395**	**5 721**	**5 592**

15－7 独立自然科学研究机构课题开展和投入
PROJECTS AND INPUT OF INDEPENDENT INSTITUTIONS OF NATURAL SCIENCE RESEARCH

项 目	Item	课题数(项) Number of Projects (item)		投入人力(人年) Labor Force Input (person－year)		投入经费(万元) Funds Input (10 000 yuan)	
		2002	2003	2002	2003	2002	2003
合 计	**Total**	**1 471**	**1 520**	**4 312**	**4 746**	**36 029**	**43 896**
按课题类型分	Grouped by Type of Projects						
基础研究	Basic Research	20	22	48	60	302	395
应用研究	Application Research	150	196	520	702	4 034	4 298
试验发展	Experiment Development	456	467	1 710	1 864	15 194	19 661
研究与试验发展成果应用	Achievements Application of Research and Experiment Development	471	453	1 075	1 077	9 428	12 571
科技服务	Services of Science and Technology	332	337	881	948	6 575	6 087
生产性活动	Activities of Production	42	45	78	95	496	884

15－8 三项专利申请受理量和批准量
THREE TYPES OF PATENT APPLICATIONS EXAMINED AND CERTIFIED

单位：项 (item)

项　目 Item	申请量 Number of Applications Examined			批准量 Number of Applications Certified		
	2001	2002	2003	2001	2002	2003
合　计 Total	**3 081**	**5 357**	**6 812**	**1 829**	**1 827**	**2 505**
一、按种类分 Grouped by Type						
发　明 Creation and Inventions	784	2 067	3 328	96	102	241
实用新型 Utility Models	1 707	2 361	2 713	1 214	1 165	1 547
外观设计 Designs	590	929	771	519	560	717
二、按对象分 Grouped by Applicator						
工矿企业 Industrial and Mineral Enterprises	881	1 875	2 791	505	513	675
大专院校 Universities and Colleges	162	363	436	49	77	175
科研单位 Scientific Research Institutions	102	117	193	61	68	97
机关团体 Agencies and Organizations	23	24	34	24	15	22
个　人 Individuals	1 913	2 978	3 358	1 190	1 154	1 536

15－9 重大科技研究成果和获奖成果
MAJOR ACHIEVEMENTS IN SCIENTIFIC AND TECHNOLOGICAL RESEARCH AND PRIZES AWARDED

单位：项 (item)

项　目 Item	2000	2001	2002	2003
重大科学技术研究成果数 Number of Major Achievements in Scientific and Technological Research	1 263	1 200	1 020	1 203
获天津市科技进步奖 Number of Tianjin Scientific and Technological Progress Prizes Awarded	296	239	248	246
一等奖 First Class Awards	9	7	14	13
二等奖 Second Class Awards	72	41	67	64
三等奖 Third Class Awards	215	191	167	169
获国家科技奖 Number of National Scientific and Technological Prizes Awarded	13	9	13	14

15－10 天津市获国家科学技术奖科技成果一览(2003 年)

LIST OF NATIONAL SCIENTIFIC AND TECHNOLOGICAL PRIZES AWARDED IN TIANJIN,2003

获奖项目和等级 Project and Grade Awarded	完成单位和个人 Name of Unit and Individual
自然科学二等奖(3 项) **Second Class National Awards for Natural Science(three itmes)**	
1.分子磁性的基础研究 Basic Research on Numerator Magnetism	廖代正、王耕霖、姜宗慧、阎世平、程鹏 Liao Daizheng Wang Genglin Jiang Zonghui Yan SHiping Cheng Peng
2.中国主要植物染色体研究 Study on Chromosome of Major Plant in China	陈瑞阳、宋文芹、李秀兰、李懋学、林盛华 Chen Ruiyang Song Wenqin Li Xiulan Li Maoxue Lin Shenghua
3.复杂非线性系统的动力学理论与应用 Dynamics Theories and Application of Complicacy Non－line System	陈予恕、陆启韶、褚福磊、徐健学、吴志强 Chen Yushu Lu Qishao Chu Fulei Xu Jianxue Wu Zhiqiang
科技进步一等奖(1 项) **First Class National Awards for Progress(one itmes)**	
1.秦岭特长铁路隧道修建技术 Technology of Constructing Qinling Railways Tunnel	铁路第一勘察设计院、中国铁路工程总公司等 The First Survey and Design Institute Ministry of Railways, China Railways Engineering General Corporation
科技进步二等奖(10 项) **Second Class National Awards for Progress(ten itmes)**	
1.中低焓地热工程建设技术 Technology of Constructing Subterranean Heat Engineering	天津大学、中国地质大学(北京)天津市地热管理处、天津地热勘察开发设计院等 Tianjin University,China University of Geosciences,Tianjin Subterranean Heat Office, Tianjin Subterranean Heat Office,Tianjin Subterranean Heat Survey & Design Institute
2.通里攻下法在腹部外科疾病中的应用与基础研究 Application and Basic Research of the Method in Belly Surgery Disease	天津市中西医结合急腹症研究所、南开大学、天津医科大学基础医学、天津医科大学总医院 Tianjin Chinese & Western Medicine Belly Disease Research Institute, Nankai University,Basic Medical Science Dept. of Tianjin Medical Science University, The General Hospital of Tianjin Medical Science University
3.新型干法水泥生产关键技术与装备开发及工程化应用 Key Technology,Equipment Development & Application of New Drying Method for Cement Produces	天津水泥工业设计研究院 Tianjin Cement Industry Design Institute
4.煤层气勘探技术研究与试验 Study and Experiment on the Suvey Technology of Coal & Gas	中国石油勘探开发科学研究院廊坊分院 大港油田集团钻采工艺研究院 Petrochina Exploration & Development Science Research Institute(Lang Fang), Dagang Oilfield Group Exploration & Development Institute
5.数字高清晰度电视系统关键技术与设备 Key Technology and Equipment of High and Clear Digit－Television System	上海交通大学、浙江大学、天津大学等 Shanghai Jiao Tong University, Zhejiang University, Tianjin University
6.资源环境、区域经济空间信息共享应用网络 Application Network of Information Share on Resource Environment and District Economy	中国科学院遥感应用研究所、国家信息中心等 Institute of Remote Sensing Application Chinese Academy of Sciences, State Information Center
7.钢筋混凝土多层及高层异型柱框架结构成套技术 A Technique of Multi－layer Reinforced Concrete Pillar Frame Construction	河北工业大学、天津市轻工业设计院等 Hebei Industry University,Tianjin Light Industry Design Institute
8.公路工程灾害预防与治理综合技术研究及工程应用 Study and Application on Disaster Prevention Bureau,and Comprehensive Treatment of Highways	山东省交通厅公路局、北京科技大学等 Shandong Transportation Department Highways University of Science and Technology Beijing
9.镧系元素时间分辨荧光分析技术及仪器的配套研究 Analysis Technology and Relative Appliance of Chemical Element Time Distinguishes Fluorescence	解放军第二军医大学、解放军总医院等 Second Military Medical University,General Hospital of PLA
10.海洋平台结构检测维修、安全评定与实时监测系统 Test Maintainment,Safety Approval and Monitors System of Sea Platform	哈尔滨工业大学、中海石油(中国)有限公司天津分公司等 Harbin Industry University, China Offshore Oil(China) Ltd. Tianjin Corporation

15-11 高等学校科研课题开展与投入(2003年)
(理、工、农、医类)

PROJECTS OF DEVELOPMENT AND INPUT OF SCIENTIFIC RESEARCH IN UNIVERSITIES AND COLLEGES,2003
(SCIENCE, ENGINEERING, AGRICULTURE AND MEDICINE)

项目	Item	课题数(项) Number of Projects (item)	投入人力(人年) Labor Force Input (person)	#科学家和工程师 Scientist and Engineer	投入经费(万元) Funds Input (10 000 yuan)
总计	**Total**	**4 645**	**4 730**	**4 544**	**61 589**
按课题活动类型分	**Grouped by Type of Projects**				
基础研究	Basic Research	1 015	1 131	1 099	6 938
应用研究	Application Research	2 622	2 442	2 358	26 381
试验发展	Experiment Development	550	567	526	21 535
R&D成果应用	R&D Achievement Used	79	119	105	1 574
科技服务	Service of Science and Technology	379	471	456	5 161
按(课题)项目类别分	**Grouped by Project**				
国家"973"项目	State "973" Project	32	45	42	1 557
国家科技攻关项目	State S&T Strategical Project	30	42	40	693
国家"863"项目	State "863" Project	75	84	79	3 236
国家自然科学基金项目	State Natural Scientific Fund Project	450	448	430	3 968
主管部门科技项目	S&T Project from Administrative Department	664	702	678	3 317
国家部委其他科技项目	S&T Project from Ministry	288	370	358	5 323
省、市、自治区科技项目	S&T Project from Province, Municipality, Autonomous Region	1 002	1 167	1 130	8 718
企事业单位委托科技项目	S&T Project from Enterprise, Institution	1 503	1 356	1 288	33 135
国际合作项目	International Cooperate Project	39	42	39	531
自选项目	Self-choosing Project	560	473	459	1 102
其他项目	Other Project	2	1	1	9

15-12 高等学校研究发展机构科技专著和论文
(理、工、农、医类)

S&T WORKS AND PAPERS OF RESEARCH & DEVELOPMENT INSTITUTIONS IN UNIVERSITIES AND COLLEGES
(SCIENCE, ENGINEERING, AGRICULTURE AND MEDICINE)

项目	Item	单位	Unit	2000	2001	2002	2003
科技专著	**Scientific and Technological Work**	**部**	**copy**	**183**	**157**	**143**	**135**
		万字	**10 000 words**	**5 123**	**4 085**	**4 209**	**4 056**
#自然科学	Natural Science	部	copy	46	42	25	26
		万字	10 000 words	1 028	940	503	910
工程科学	Engineering	部	copy	103	74	68	65
		万字	10 000 words	2 761	1 846	2 116	1 957
医学科学	Medicine	部	copy	32	39	48	43
		万字	10 000 words	1 311	1 269	1 571	1 186
农业科学	Agriculture	部	copy	2	2	2	1
		万字	10 000 words	22	30	19	3
科学论文	**Scientific Papers**	**篇**	**piece**	**7 608**	**8 280**	**8 624**	**9 540**
#国外发表	Published Abroad	篇	piece	1 054	1 105	1 201	1 312

15－13　新技术产业园区基本情况
BASIC STATISTICS ON TIANJIN HIGH－TECH INDUSTRY PARK

项　目	Item	2000	2001	2002	2003
年末企业单位数(个)	Number of Enterprises Year－end(unit)	4 080	4 350	4 500	4 700
从业人员数　(人)	Number of Employment Personnel(person)	121 235	130 645	142 012	128 605
#大专以上学历	College Record and Above	40 349	42 734	49 565	43 270
中级以上职称	With Middle－grade Title and Above	23 050	23 087	20 866	16 655
研究与开发人员(人)	Research and Development Personnel(person)	17 284	16 766	25 877	23 637
技工贸总产值(亿元)	Gross Output Value of Technology,Industry and Trade (100 million yuan)	274.61	322.72	416.6	561.96
技工贸总收入(亿元)	Total Income from Technology,Industry and Trade (100 million yuan)	296.99	383.28	498.4	668.94
#技术收入	Income from Technology	13.88	17.72	20.9	12.79
利润总额　(亿元)	Profit (100 million yuan)	16.31	17.68	23.7	25.73
出口创汇总额(亿美元)	Exports (USD 100 million)	9.13	7.98	12.9	13.63
交纳税金总额(亿元)	Taxes (100 million yuan)	14.73	19.70	20.4	28.84

15－14　计量仪器检定情况
STATISTICS FOR MEASURING IMPLEMENTS TEST

单位:台、件　　(set)(piece)

类　别	Sort	2000	2001	2002	2003
总　计	**Total**	**1 305 309**	**1 316 548**	**1 309 119**	**1 325 488**
长　度	Length	31 777	35 144	34 040	30 525
温　度	Temperature	22 219	28 750	50 037	41 102
力　学	Mechanics	494 279	510 462	431 922	447 634
#衡　器	Weighing Apparatus	143 228	85 789	83 406	87 179
电　磁	Electromagnetism	86 041	87 549	102 870	105 670
光　学	Optics	272	315	260	254
声　学	Acoustics	294	247	219	385
化　学	Chemistry	2 444	2 897	2 751	3 018
电离辐射	Ionization Radiation	219	226	267	460
无线电	Radio	547 615	543 683	587 952	598 194
时间频率	Time Frequency	1 571	1 250	1 708	1 341
其　他	Others	118 578	106 025	97 093	96 905

15－15　技术监督机构人员、行政执法及科技成果情况
PERSONNEL, EXECUTING LAW OF ADMINISTRATION AND ACHIEVEMENT OF SCIENCE AND TECHNOLOGY OF PRODUCT QUALITY AND TECHNIQUE SUPERVISION AGENCIES

项　目	Item	2002年 全　市 Total(2002)	#市级单位 City Level	2003年 全　市 Total(2003)	#市级单位 City Level
一、机构人员情况	**Agencies and Personnel**				
机构数(个)	Number of Agencies(unit)	82	13	82	14
职工人数(人)	Number of Employees(person)	2 045	806	2 061	810
行政机构人员	Administrative Agencies	685	144	662	111
事业机构人员	Institutions	1 360	662	1 399	699
#执法人员(人)	Staff of Executing Law(person)	1 123	295	1 184	314
二、行政案件情况	**Administrative Cases**				
现场处罚案件(件)	Penalized Cases(piece)	1 465	148	1 948	73
立案受理案件(件)	Registerd Cases(piece)	2 418	227	2 328	231
立案处罚案件(件)	Punished Cases(piece)	2 411	220	2 320	223
罚没金额(万元)	Total Value of Punishment(10 000 yuan)	2 011	441	2 509	587
三、科技项目情况	**Items of Science and Technology**				
项目总数(项)	Number of Items(item)	18	11	26	23
#市　级	City Level	11	11		
经费金额(万元)	Outlay(10 000 yuan)	35	30	67	65
#市　级	City Level	30	30		
四、科技成果情况	**Achievement of Science and Technology**				
成果鉴定(项)	Authorized(item)	15	14	20	20
五、科技成果获奖情况	**Prizes Awarded of Science and Technology Achievement**				
获奖项目数(项)	Number of Prizes Awarded(item)	12	8	11	6
#省部级三等奖	Third Class Provincial and Ministerial Awards	3	2	1	
地方级二等奖	Second Class Municipal Awards	3	2	6	4
地方级三等奖	Third Class Municipal Awards	4	3	4	2

15－16　产品质量监督检验情况(2003年)

ESULTS OF SAMPLING CHECK ON THE QUALITY OF PRODUCTS UNDER STATE SUPERVISION，2003

项目	Item	监督检查企业(个) Number of Enterprises Supervised & Checked (unit)	查出不合格产品企业(个) Number of Enterprises with Products Unqualified (unit)	不合格产品企业所占比例(%) Proportion of Enterprises with Products Unqualified (%)	检验批次(批次) Batch－times Checked (batch/times)
合　计	**Total**	**3 990**	**733**	**18.4**	**5 107**
一、农用产品	Agricultural Products	193	35	18.1	210
#农用化肥	Chemical Fertilizers	32	2	6.3	47
饲　料	Forages	92	13	14.1	94
二、加工食品和饮料	Food and Beverage	1 219	233	19.1	1 393
#小麦粉、大米	Rice，Wheat Powder	312	9	2.9	321
肉制品	Meat and Related Products	88	24	27.3	102
调味品	Condiment	135	31	23.0	176
白　酒	White Liquor	25	3	12.0	46
黄酒、果酒	Yellow Liquor & Wine	10	3	30.0	14
食用植物油	Edible Vegetable Oil	34			34
糕点、糖果	Cake，Candy	212	48	22.6	222
非酒精液体饮料	Non－alcoholic Beverage	178	43	24.2	192
冷冻饮品	Frozed Beverage	19	12	63.2	21
方便主食品	Quick Foods	42	11	26.2	47
乳制品	Dairy Products	13	3	23.1	24
三、家用电器	Household Electric Appliances	2			2
四、轻工产品	Light Industry Products	384	56	14.6	437
#纸制品	Paper Products	41	5	12.2	49
合成洗涤剂	Synthetic Detergent	7			7
化妆品	Cosmetic	1	1	100.0	1
橡胶、塑料制品	Rubber Products，Plastic Products	50	8	16.0	52
五、纺织、鞋类产品	Textile and Shoes	60	7	11.7	77
#棉纺织	Cotton Textiles	7			11
鞋	Shoes	16	2	12.5	18
六、化工产品	Chemical Products	238	59	24.8	279
#涂料、油漆	Paint	75	13	17.3	80
染　料	Dyestuff	13			16
化学试剂	Chemical Reagent	17	9	53.0	33
七、建材产品	Building Raw Materials	299	37	12.4	475
#砖、瓦	Brick，Tiles	35			35
装饰材料	Decoration Materials	105	16	15.2	111
八、机电产品	Mechanical and Electrical Product	854	142	16.6	992
#阀类、泵	Valves，Pumps	53	21	39.6	55
电线、电缆	Electric Wire，Cable	135	22	16.3	189
电工仪器仪表	Electrician Instrument	6			6
安全防范设备	Security & Protect Appliance	60	7	11.7	60
电动机、柴油机	Motor Machinery & Diesel Engine	193	27	14.0	216
自行车	Bicycle	240	33	13.8	258
九、冶金产品、金属制品	Metallurgical and Metal Products	238	98	41.2	259
#型　材	Profiled Bar	20	10	50.0	28
十、能源产品	Energy Sources Products	492	62	12.6	951
十一、医疗器械	Medical Treatment Instrument				
十二、其　他	Others	11	4	36.4	32

资料来源：天津市质量技术监督局，下表同。
Information Source：Tianjin Municipal Quality & Technology Supervision Bureau，same to next.

15－16 续表　Continued

项　目	Item	合格批次（批次）Batch－times with Qualified Quality (batch/times)	批次合格率（%）Rate of Batch－times Qualified	上年批次合格率（%）Rate of Batch－times Qualified in Previous Year	批次合格率比上年增减百分点 Percentage Batch－times Qualified over Previous Year
合　计	**Total**	**4 332**	**84.8**	**84.9**	**－0.1**
一、农用产品	Agricultural Products	174	82.9	94.5	－11.6
#农用化肥	Chemical Fertilizers	45	95.7	98.3	－2.6
饲　料	Forages	80	85.1	91.8	－6.7
二、加工食品和饮料	Food and Beverage	1 141	81.9	77.3	4.6
#小麦粉、大米	Rice, Wheat Powder	312	97.2	87.6	9.6
肉制品	Meat and Related Products	78	76.5	78.9	－2.4
调味品	Condiment	142	80.7	74.4	6.3
白　酒	White Liquor	43	93.5	74.9	18.6
黄酒、果酒	Yellow Liquor & Wine	11	78.6	100.0	－21.4
食用植物油	Edible Vegetable Oil	34	100.0	98.1	1.9
糕点、糖果	Cake, Candy	173	77.9	76.2	1.7
非酒精液体饮料	Non－alcoholic Beverage	149	77.6	69.6	8.0
冷冻饮品	Frozed Beverage	9	42.9	45.0	－2.1
方便主食品	Quick Foods	36	76.6	95.5	－18.9
乳制品	Dairy Products	19	79.2	83.0	－3.8
三、家用电器	Household Electric Appliances	2	100.0	63.5	36.5
四、轻工产品	Light Industry Products	379	86.7	88.3	－1.6
#纸制品	Paper Products	44	89.8	95.0	－5.2
合成洗涤剂	Synthetic Detergent	7	100.0	85.7	14.3
橡胶、塑料制品	Rubber Products, Plastic Products	44	84.6	84.6	
五、纺织、鞋类产品	Textile and Shoes	70	90.9	94.6	－3.7
#棉纺织	Cotton Textiles	11	100.0	95.7	4.3
鞋	Shoes	16	88.9	100.0	－11.1
六、化工产品	Chemical Products	216	77.4	85.2	－7.8
#涂料、油漆	Paint	67	83.8	88.5	－4.7
染　料	Dyestuff	16	100.0	83.3	16.7
化学试剂	Chemical Reagent	20	60.6	79.6	－19.0
七、建材产品	Building Raw Materials	438	92.2	89.6	2.6
#砖、瓦	Brick, Tiles	35	100.0	79.7	20.3
装饰材料	Decoration Materials	95	85.6	73.3	12.3
八、机电产品	Mechanical and Electrical Product	843	85.0	87.6	－2.6
#阀类、泵	Valves, Pumps	34	61.8	96.3	－34.5
电线、电缆	Electric Wire, Cable	166	87.8	87.9	－0.1
电工仪器仪表	Electrician Instrument	6	100.0	62.5	37.5
安全防范设备	Security & Protect Appliance	53	88.3	96.2	－7.9
电动机、柴油机	Motor Machinery & Diesel Engine	187	86.6	100.0	－13.4
自行车	Bicycle	225	87.2	88.4	－1.2
九、冶金产品、金属制品	Metallurgical and Metal Products	159	61.4	89.3	－27.9
#型　材	Profiled Bar	18	64.3	79.5	－15.2
十、能源产品	Energy Sources Products	882	92.9	89.4	3.5
十一、医疗器械	Medical Treatment Instrument			100.0	
十二、其　他	Others	28	87.5	81.8	5.7

15－17　商品质量监督检验情况(2003 年)

RESULTS OF SAMPLING CHECK ON THE QUALITY OF COMMODITIES UNDER STATE SUPERVISION,2003

项　　目	Item	检查商业企业数(个) Number of Trade Enterprises Checked (unit)	检查商品批次(批次) Batch－times Checked (batch/times)	合格批次(批次) Batch－times with Qualified Quality (batch/times)
合　　计	**Total**	**4 299**	**11 415**	**9 323**
一、农用产品	Agricultural Products	200	611	539
#农用化肥	Chemical Fertilizers	15	53	41
化学农药	Chemical Pesticide	141	504	462
二、加工食品和饮料	Food and Beverage	1 961	5 512	4 455
#小麦粉、大米	Rice,Wheat Powder	132	256	213
肉制品	Meat and Related Products	158	422	355
调味品	Condiment	215	431	330
保健食品	Health Care Foods	13	13	8
白　酒	White Liquor	463	2 023	1 680
啤　酒	Beer	38	84	62
黄酒、果酒	Yellow Liquor & Wine	111	378	340
食用植物油	Edible Vegetable Oil	37	68	65
糕点、糖果	Cake,Candy	244	524	447
非酒精液体饮料	Non－alcoholic Beverage	25	65	55
冷冻饮品	Freezed Beverage	71	98	69
方便主食品	Quick Foods	102	293	238
乳制品	Dairy Products	41	89	62
三、家用电器	Household Electric Appliances	237	871	785
#计算机	Computer	19	31	26
电话机	Telephone sets	17	45	40
四、轻工产品	Light Industry Products	533	1 847	1 588
#家　具	Furniture	6	16	8
眼　镜(架、片)	Glasses	44	116	102
灯泡、灯管	Electric Bulbs,Fluorescence Tube	49	114	97
日用五金	Daily－use Metals	13	15	5
合成洗涤剂	Synthetic Detergent	19	41	40
化妆品	Cosmetic	69	320	271
橡胶、塑料制品	Rubber Products,Plastic Products	17	19	11
五、纺织、鞋类产品	Textile and Shoes	251	642	525
#服　装	Garments	94	394	334
棉纺织	Cotton Textiles	18	21	11
六、化工产品	Chemical Products	149	209	130
#涂料、油漆	Paint	31	46	20
七、建材产品	Building Raw Materials	273	423	294
#水　泥	Cement	22	23	14
油毡、油纸	Asphalt Felts,Oilpaper	2	2	
人造板	Artificial Board	115	134	86
八、机电产品	Mechanical and Electrical Products	262	580	420
#轴　承	Bearing	14	36	33
电线、电缆	Electric Wire,Cable	72	173	108
电动工具	Electric Tools	31	53	48
低压电器及元件	Low－voltage Electric Elements	44	110	95
九、冶金产品、金属制品	Metallurgical and Metal Products	116	194	170
十、能源产品	Energy Sources Products	101	144	117
#汽油、柴油	Gasoline,Diesel Oil	58	71	60
十一、医疗器械	Medical Treatment Instrument	62	112	83
十二、其　他	Others	154	270	217

15－17 续表 Continued

项 目	Item	批次合格率(％) Rate of Batch－times Qualified	查出伪劣商品批次(批次) Batch－times of Commodities with Low Quality (batch/times)	查出不合格商品价值(万元) Value of Commodities Unqualified (10 000 yuan)	#伪劣商品 Commodities with Low Quality
合 计	**Total**	**81.7**	**1 055**	**930.83**	**490.41**
一、农用产品	Agricultural Products	88.2	20	36.16	13.41
#农用化肥	Chemical Fertilizers	77.4	1	14.00	5.00
化学农药	Chemical Pesticide	91.7	5	14.57	4.82
二、加工食品和饮料	Food and Beverage	80.8	641	178.67	92.36
#小麦粉、大米	Rice, Wheat Powder	83.2	9	23.11	5.61
肉制品	Meat and Related Products	84.1	15	4.12	2.10
调味品	Condiment	76.6	81	12.65	10.51
保健食品	Health Care Foods	61.5	3	0.70	0.20
白 酒	White Liquor	83.0	318	31.31	26.38
啤 酒	Beer	73.8	3	6.47	2.60
黄酒、果酒	Yellow Liquor & Wine	90.0	35	7.66	6.51
食用植物油	Edible Vegetable Oil	95.6	1	1.71	1.70
糕点、糖果	Cake, Candy	85.3	41	8.65	4.60
非酒精液体饮料	Non－alcoholic Beverage	84.6	1	2.80	0.12
冷冻饮品	Freezed Beverage	70.4	21	1.28	1.05
方便主食品	Quick Foods	81.2	9	1.17	0.21
乳制品	Dairy Products	69.7	12	12.95	1.62
三、家用电器	Household Electric Appliances	90.1	20	80.08	13.10
#计算器	Computer	38.2	5	6.00	6.00
电话机	Telephone sets	129.0	1	3.71	0.01
四、轻工产品	Light Industry Products	86.0	118	71.55	29.55
家 具	Furniture	50.0	8	3.55	3.55
眼 镜(架、片)	Glasses	87.9	13	7.00	6.80
灯泡、灯管	Electric Bulbs, Fluorescence Tube	85.1	12	2.42	1.91
日用五金	Daily－use Metals	33.3	7	2.92	0.40
合成洗涤剂	Synthetic Detergent	97.6			
化妆品	Cosmetic	84.7	12	12.74	6.74
橡胶、塑料制品	Rubber Products, Plastic Products	57.9	3	8.26	1.26
五、纺织、鞋类产品	Textile and Shoes	81.8	39	36.16	8.13
#服 装	Garments	84.8	13	23.69	3.50
棉纺织	Cotton Textiles	52.4	10	0.63	0.63
六、化工产品	Chemical Products	62.2	24	81.39	5.61
#涂料、油漆	Paint	43.5	11	8.00	3.72
七、建材产品	Building Raw Materials	69.5	62	210.55	176.11
#水 泥	Cement	60.9	2	6.90	2.20
油毡、油纸	Asphalt Felts, Oilpaper		2	2.40	2.40
人造板	Artificial Board	64.2	25	3.85	3.00
八、机电产品	Mechanical and Electrical Products	72.4	53	166.46	119.31
#轴 承	Bearing	91.7	3	0.22	0.22
电线、电缆	Electric Wire, Cable	62.4	19	118.29	107.71
电动工具	Electric Tools	90.6	5	1.85	1.85
低压电器及元件	Low－voltage Electric Elements	86.4	8	3.61	2.76
九、冶金产品、金属制品	Metallurgical and Metal Products	87.6	19	23.03	15.75
十、能源产品	Energy Sources Products	81.3	25	8.90	7.90
#汽油、柴油	Gasoline, Diesel Oil	84.5	10	8.40	7.50
十一、医疗器械	Medical Treatment Instrument	74.1	10	21.70	1.70
十二、其 他	Others	80.0	24	16.18	7.48

15－18 天津市科学技术协会和所属学会科技活动(2003 年)

SCIENTIFIC AND TECHNOLOGICAL ACTIVITIES OF TIANJIN SCIENCE AND TECHNOLOGY ASSOCIATIONS AND AFFILIATED LEARNED SOCIETIES,2003

项　目	Item	合　计 Total	市及区、县科协 Science Association of City,District and County	市级学会 Institution of City Level
一、机构与人员	**Institutions and Personnel**			
机　构(个)	Institutions(unit)	481	19	462
人　员(人)	Personnel(person)	122 636	204	122 432
二、学术交流情况	**Academic Activities of Exchange**			
1.学术会议(次)	1.Academic Meetings(time)	778	537	241
国　内	Domestic	777	537	240
国　际	International	1		1
参加人数(人次)	Number of Participants(person－times)	36 072	4 887	31 185
国　内	Domestic	35 952	4 887	31 065
国　际	International	120		120
交流论文(篇)	Number of Papers Presented(pieces)	4 703	64	4 639
国　内	Domestic	4 598	64	4 534
国　际	International	105		105
2.科技交流(个)	2.Exchange of Science and Technological(unit)	88	16	72
接　待	Received	51	10	41
外　派	Sent Abroad	37	6	31
交流人数(人次)	Number of Exchange(person－times)	360	138	222
接　待	Received	179	71	108
外　派	Sent Abroad	181	67	114
三、科学普及	**Activities for Popular Science**			
科普讲座(次)	Lectures of Popular Science(time)	1 326	897	429
参加人数(人次)	Number of Participants(person－times)	191 890	128 150	63 740
科普展览(次)	Exhibitions of Popular Science(time)	519	410	109
参加人数(人次)	Number of Participants(person－times)	439 504	241 866	197 638
四、科技培训	**Science and Technological Training**			
培训班数(个(期))	Number of Training Classes(unit(period))	1 775	1 541	234
培训人数(人次)	Number of Persons in Training Classes (person－times)	120 262	98 929	21 333
五、科技咨询服务(项)	**Service of Consultative Activities(item)**			
无偿咨询项目	Gratis Consultative Projects	1 246	554	692
完成技术合同数	Number of Consultative Contracts Completed	1 229	1 017	212
六、青少年科技活动	**Scientific and Technological Activities of Teenager**			
科技夏(冬)令营(次)	Scientific and Technological Summer (Winter) Camp(time)	64	57	7
参加人数(人次)	Number of Participants(person－times)	31 295	30 797	498
青少年科技竞赛(次)	Number of Teenagers Participating in Science and Technology Competition(time)	363	337	26
七、科技出版物	**Science and Technology Publication**			
出版科技期刊(种)	Science and Technology Magazine(kind)	38	3	35
年发行总数(册)	Number of Issue(volume)	1 823 830	1 401 000	422 830
年发表学术论文(篇)	Number of Papers Presented(piece)	2 570	3	2 567

15－19　大中型工业企业科技活动基本情况(2003年)
(按企业类型和经济类型分)
S&T ACTIVITIES IN LARGE AND MEDIUM－SIZED ENTERPRISES, 2003
(GROUPED BY TYPE AND OWNERSHIP)

项　目　Item	合　计 Total	按企业类型分 Grouped by Type of Enterprises	
		大　型 Large	中　型 Medium
1.有科技活动企业数(个)			
Number of Enterprises with Scientific and Technological Activities	146	26	120
2.从事科技活动人员(人)			
Employees Engaged in Scientific and Technological Activities (person)	21 294	12 137	9 157
#科学家和工程师			
Scientists and Engineers	13 509	8 037	5 472
研究与试验发展人员			
Personnel of R&D	11 472	6 209	5 263
3.科技活动经费筹集(万元)			
Funding for Scientific and Technological Activities (10 000 yuan)	394 295.3	272 033.7	122 261.6
4.科技活动经费支出(万元)			
Expenditures of Scientific and Technological Activities (10 000 yuan)	377 445.9	263 272.4	114 173.5
#研究与试验发展经费支出			
Expenditures of R&D	153 220.6	120 727.8	32 492.8
#新产品开发经费支出			
Expenditures of New Product Development	132 167.7	94 487.0	37 680.7
5.科技活动项目数(项)			
Number of Scientific and Technological Activities	2 433	1 016	1 417
#研究与试验发展项目数			
Number of R&D	1 322	585	737
6.科技机构数(个)			
Number of Scientific and Technological Institutions (unit)	99	36	63
科技机构人员数(人)			
Persons in Scientific and Technological Institutions (person)	10 330	7 322	3 008
科技机构经费支出(万元)			
Expenditures of Scientific and Technological Institutions (10 000 yuan)	184 138.3	160 234.8	23 903.5
#研究与试验发展经费支出(万元)			
Expenditures of R&D (10 000 yuan)	49 019.4	35 065.0	13 954.4
7.新产品产值(万元)			
Output Value of New Products (10 000 yuan)	7 972 812.7	6 056 874.1	1 915 938.6
新产品销售收入(万元)			
Sales Revenue of New Products (10 000 yuan)	7 909 689.2	6 086 745.8	1 822 943.4
新产品销售利润(万元)			
Sales Profits of New Products (10 000 yuan)	299 104.8	237 698.1	61 406.7
8.专利申请数(件)			
Number of Patent Applications (piece)	2 423	2 301	122
拥有发明专利数(件)			
Number of Patent Granted (piece)	438	388	50
9.技术改造经费支出(万元)			
Expenditures of Technical Innovation (10 000 yuan)	294 294.1	245 934.5	48 359.6
10.技术引进经费支出(万元)			
Expenditures of Technical Introduction (10 000 yuan)	135 850.2	74 646.1	61 204.1

15－19 续表 Continued

项 目 Item	按经济类型分 Grouped by Ownership 国有经济 State－owned	集体经济 Collective－owned	“三资”经济 Hongkong，Macao，Taiwan and Foreign Funded	其他经济 Others
1.有科技活动企业数(个) Number of Enterprises with Scientific and Technological Activities	40	1	35	70
2.从事科技活动人员(人) Employees Engaged in Scientific and Technological Activities (person)	5 885	11	5 272	10 126
#科学家和工程师 Scientists and Engineers	3 822	5	2 649	7 033
研究与发展人员 Personnel of R&D	2 310	10	3 170	5 982
3.企业科技活动经费筹集（万元） Funding for Scientific and Technological Activities (10 000 yuan)	70 122.3	54.0	175 875.4	148 243.6
4.企业科技活动经费支出（万元） Expenditures of Scientific and Technological Activities (10 000 yuan)	64 577.7	54.0	179 888.1	132 926.1
#研究与试验发展经费支出 Expenditures of R&D	18 039.8	54.0	78 691.9	56 434.9
#新产品开发经费支出 Expenditures of New Product Development	17 377.2	54.0	42 037.8	72 698.7
5.企业科技活动项目数（项） Number of Scientific and Technological Activities	721	4	277	1 431
#研究与试验发展项目数 Number of R&D	285	2	172	863
6.科技机构数(个) Scientific and Technological Institutions(unit)	26		10	63
科技机构人员数(人) Persons in Scientific and Technological Institutions (person)	2 949		2 714	4 667
科技机构经费支出（万元） Expenditures of Scientific and Technological Institutions (10 000 yuan)	31 796.2		84 115.7	68 226.4
#研究与试验发展经费支出 Expenditures of R&D (10 000 yuan)	5 222.0		4 687.1	39 110.3
7.新产品产值(万元) Output Value of New Products (10 000 yuan)	463 416.6	222.0	6 422 287.0	1 086 887.1
新产品销售收入(万元) Sales Revenue of New Products (10 000 yuan)	381 714.4	222.0	6 435 880.3	1 091 872.5
新产品销售利润(万元) Sales Profits of New Products(10 000 yuan)	－17 042.3	52.3	196 396.0	119 698.8
8.专利申请数(件) Number of Patent Applications(piece)	52		2 089	282
拥有发明专利数(件) Number of Patent Granted(piece)	31		345	62
9.技术改造经费支出(万元) Expenditures of Technical Innovation (10 000 yuan)	106 652.6		45 540.3	142 101.2
10.技术引进经费支出(万元) Expenditures of Technical Introduction (10 000 yuan)	13 924.8		109 979.2	11 946.2

15－20　大中型工业企业科技活动基本情况(2003年)
（按新国民经济行业分）
S&T ACTIVITIES IN LARGE AND MEDIUM－SIZED ENTERPRISES,2003
(GROUPED BY NEW SECTOR)

项　目	Item	有科技活动企业数(个) Number of Enterprises with Scientific Technological Activities	从事科技活动人员(人) Employees Engaged in Scientific and Technological Activities (person)	#科学家和工程师 Scientists and Engineers	研究与试验发展人员(人) Personnel of R&D
总　计	**Total**	**146**	**21 294**	**13 509**	**11 472**
#石油和天然气开采业	Petroleum and Natural Gas Extraction	4	2 619	2 319	2 064
非金属矿采选业	Nonmetal Minerals Mining and Dressing	2	159	102	159
农副食品加工业	Agricultural Products and Byproducts Processing				
食品制造业	Food Manufacturing	3	67	54	59
饮料制造业	Beverage Manufacturing	3	63	36	58
烟草制品业	Tobacco Processing	1	56	34	34
纺织业	Textile Industry	3	300	150	182
纺织服装、鞋、帽制造业	Textile Garments,Shoes,Caps Manufacturing	1	16	8	
皮革、毛皮、羽毛(绒)及其制品业	Leather, Furs, Down and Related Products	1	33		
木材加工及木、竹、藤、棕、草制品业	Timber Processing,Bamboo, Cane,Palm Fiber and Straw Products				
家具制造业	Furniture Manufacturing	1	54	38	42
造纸及纸制品业	Papermaking and Paper Products				
印刷业和记录媒介的复制	Printing and Record Medium Reproduction	1	155	120	132
文教体育用品制造业	Cultural, Educational and Sports Goods	1	10	10	
石油加工、炼焦及核燃料加工业	Petroleum Processing,Coking and Nuclear Fuel Processing	2	530	507	127
化学原料及化学制品制造业	Chemical Raw Materials and Chemical Products	17	1 979	1 167	1 351
医药制造业	Medical and Pharmaceutical Products	13	1 494	1 017	832
化学纤维制造业	Chemical Fiber	1	11	5	10
橡胶制品业	Rubber Products	2	54	40	52
塑料制品业	Plastic Products	1	69	29	47
非金属矿物制品业	Nonmetal Mineral Products	5	374	53	6
黑色金属冶炼及压延加工业	Smelting and Pressing of Ferrous Metals	5	2 352	1 600	323
有色金属冶炼及压延加工业	Smelting and Pressing of Nonferrous Metals	1	26	26	
金属制品业	Metal Products	5	193	128	58
通用设备制造业	General Purpose Equipment Manufacturing	11	1 450	977	1 288
专用设备制造业	Special Purpose Equipment Manufacturing	8	771	438	356
交通运输设备制造业	Transport Equipment Manufacturing	18	1 897	1 160	1 195
电气机械及器材制造业	Electric Equipment and Machinery	12	1 993	1 107	1 035
通信设备、计算机及其他电子设备制造业	Telecommunications Equipment,Computer and Other Electronic Equipment Manufacturing	15	3 168	1 375	1 741
仪器仪表及文化、办公用机械制造业	Instruments,Meters,Cultural and Office Machinery	1	27	14	11
电力、热力的生产和供应业	Production and Supply of Electric Power and Heat Energy	5	1 213	866	149
煤气生产和供应业	Production and Supply of Gas	2	16	16	16
水的生产和供应业	Production and Supply of Tap Water	1	145	113	145

注:本表行业分类为国标GB/T4754－2002标准。
Note: Sector listed in this table is classified by the standard of GB/T4754－2002.

15－20 续表 1　Continued

项　目	Item	企业科技活动经费筹集总额（万元）Funding for Scientific and Technological Activities of Enterprises (10 000 yuan)	企业科技活动经费支出总额（万元）Expenditures of Scientific and Technological Activities of Enterprises (10 000 yuan)	#研究与试验发展经费支出 Expenditures of R&D	#新产品开发经费支出 Expenditures of New Product Development
总　计	**Total**	**394 295.3**	**377 445.9**	**153 220.6**	**132 167.7**
#石油和天然气开采业	Petroleum and Natural Gas Extraction	31 337.7	26 109.7	13 453.5	13 424.7
非金属矿采选业	Nonmetal Minerals Mining and Dressing	2 180.0	1 940.0	1 887.0	1 445.3
农副食品加工业	Agricultural Products and Byproducts Processing				
食品制造业	Food Manufacturing	252.0	219.0	122.0	122.0
饮料制造业	Beverage Manufacturing	546.3	559.3	236.3	293.3
烟草制品业	Tobacco Processing	52.7	1 092.0	288.0	
纺织业	Textile Industry	2 935.6	2 256.8	1 818.2	1 849.2
纺织服装、鞋、帽制造业	Textile Garments, Shoes, Caps Manufacturing	25.7	23.7		23.7
皮革、毛皮、羽毛(绒)及其制品业	Leather, Furs, Down and Related Products	59.7	59.7		7.1
木材加工及木、竹、藤、棕、草制品业	Timber Processing, Bamboo, Cane, Palm Fiber and Straw Products				
家具制造业	Furniture Manufacturing	198.1	198.1	133.1	158.7
造纸及纸制品业	Papermaking and Paper Products				
印刷业和记录媒介的复制	Printing and Record Medium Reproduction	2 016.0	2 016.0	1 409.8	2 014.0
文教体育用品制造业	Cultural, Educational and Sports Goods	24.0	24.0		24.0
石油加工、炼焦及核燃料加工业	Petroleum Processing, Coking and Nuclear Fuel Processing	238.0	1 933.4	170.0	170.0
化学原料及化学制品制造业	Chemical Raw Materials and Chemical Products	37 765.6	30 436.6	19 944.2	12 972.2
医药制造业	Medical and Pharmaceutical Products	41 496.9	35 846.8	11 844.4	10 908.8
化学纤维制造业	Chemical Fiber	54.0	54.0	54.0	54.0
橡胶制品业	Rubber Products	1 219.0	959.0	649.2	653.0
塑料制品业	Plastic Products	680.0	680.0	680.0	680.0
非金属矿物制品业	Nonmetal Mineral Products	3 332.5	3 327.7	52.0	1 684.4
黑色金属冶炼及压延加工业	Smelting and Pressing of Ferrous Metals	57 344.7	57 159.7	5 843.7	25 497.5
有色金属冶炼及压延加工业	Smelting and Pressing of Nonferrous Metals	138.5	138.5		85.0
金属制品业	Metal Products	463.3	465.3	96.8	363.1
通用设备制造业	General Purpose Equipment Manufacturing	14 614.4	14 183.8	13 162.5	13 653.4
专用设备制造业	Special Purpose Equipment Manufacturing	4 803.0	4 724.0	3 104.8	3 620.3
交通运输设备制造业	Transport Equipment Manufacturing	7 589.7	9 028.9	4 025.7	7 814.7
电气机械及器材制造业	Electric Equipment and Machinery	45 389.4	45 327.8	8 319.5	17 218.2
通信设备、计算机及其他电子设备制造业	Telecommunications Equipment, Computer and Other Electronic Equipment Manufacturing	127 145.6	125 375.0	63 071.2	14 974.7
仪器仪表及文化、办公用机械制造业	Instruments, Meters, Cultural and Office Machinery	33.8	33.8	22.3	22.3
电力、热力的生产和供应业	Production and Supply of Electric Power and Heat Energy	7 440.5	9 004.2	1 052.4	810.1
煤气生产和供应业	Production and Supply of Gas	2 862.0	2 396.0	156.0	
水的生产和供应业	Production and Supply of Tap Water	2 056.6	1 873.0	1 624.0	1 624.0

15－20 续表 2　Continued

项　目	Item	企业科技活动项目数（项） Number of Scientific and Technological Activities	#研究与试验发展项目数 Number of R&D	新产品产值（万元） Output Value of New Products (10 000 yuan)	新产品销售收入（万元） Sales Revenue of New Products (10 000 yuan)	新产品销售利润（万元） Sales Profits of New Products (10 000 yuan)
总　计	**Total**	**2 433**	**1 322**	**7 972 812.7**	**7 909 689.2**	**299 104.8**
#石油和天然气开采业	Petroleum and Natural Gas Extraction	240	211	17 450.8	17 380.8	3 288.1
非金属矿采选业	Nonmetal Minerals Mining and Dressing	24	24	3 579.7	3 695.4	416.8
农副食品加工业	Agricultural Products and Byproducts Processing			76 421.5	76 421.5	60.0
食品制造业	Food Manufacturing	17	6	70 023.1	70 062.7	221.0
饮料制造业	Beverage Manufacturing	17	8	59 888.1	44 347.7	2 196.1
烟草制品业	Tobacco Processing	12	12	67 227.8	35 983.5	
纺织业	Textile Industry	84	27	33 772.8	31 939.1	4 195.5
纺织服装、鞋、帽制造业	Textile Garments, Shoes, Caps Manufacturing	64		238.4	238.4	14.3
皮革、毛皮、羽毛(绒)及其制品业	Leather, Furs, Down and Related Products	1		399.4	414.7	37.7
木材加工及木、竹、藤、棕、草制品业	Timber Processing, Bamboo, Cane, Palm Fiber and Straw Products			4 027.8	4 027.8	
家具制造业	Furniture Manufacturing	8	1	23 434.3	23 079.7	365.3
造纸及纸制品业	Papermaking and Paper Products					
印刷业和记录媒介的复制	rinting and Record Medium Reproduction	15	9	31 619.7	28 214.7	2 462.0
文教体育用品制造业	Cultural, Educational and Sports Goods	4		200.0	200.0	
石油加工、炼焦及核燃料加工业	Petroleum Processing, Coking and Nuclear Fuel Processing	9	8	30 384.6	30 384.6	2 317.0
化学原料及化学制品制造业	Chemical Raw Materials and Chemical Products	239	138	201 772.4	160 510.9	7 221.9
医药制造业	Medical and Pharmaceutical Products	261	146	120 790.7	121 888.8	30 240.1
化学纤维制造业	Chemical Fiber	4	2	222.0	222.0	52.3
橡胶制品业	Rubber Products	7	6	88 034.7	84 711.2	7 378.4
塑料制品业	Plastic Products	6	6	40 904.4	39 999.2	3 777.1
非金属矿物制品业	Nonmetal Mineral Products	7	2	48 329.3	47 963.8	7 778.3
黑色金属冶炼及压延加工业	Smelting and Pressing of Ferrous Metals	152	17	434 670.0	436 217.0	45 505.8
有色金属冶炼及压延加工业	Smelting and Pressing of Nonferrous Metals	38		11 348.2	10 853.2	－138.5
金属制品业	Metal Products	26	10	76 311.2	75 615.0	917.6
通用设备制造业	General Purpose Equipment Manufacturing	177	132	147 649.8	181 639.5	13 051.7
专用设备制造业	Special Purpose Equipment Manufacturing	41	34	57 330.5	51 709.8	11 006.6
交通运输设备制造业	Transport Equipment Manufacturing	295	93	762 024.4	807 890.9	73 425.5
电气机械及器材制造业	Electric Equipment and Machinery	258	207	662 428.8	651 665.4	15 602.8
通信设备、计算机及其他电子设备制造业	Telecommunications Equipment, Computer and Other Electronic Equipment Manufacturing	294	190	4 826 720.5	4 797 813.1	118 637.7
仪器仪表及文化、办公用机械制造业	Instruments, Meters, Cultural and Office Machinery	4	4	75 563.0	74 554.0	4 536.5
电力、热力的生产和供应业	Production and Supply of Electric Power and Heat Energy	125	25	44.8	44.8	－48 112.0
煤气生产和供应业	Production and Supply of Gas	2	2			
水的生产和供应业	Production and Supply of Tap Water	2	2			－7 350.8

15－20 续表 3　Continued

项　　目	Item	科　技机构数（个）Number of Scientific and Technological Research Institutions	科技机构人员数（人）Personnel of Scientific and Technological Research Institutions	科技机构经费支出（万元）Expenditures of Scientific and Technological Research Institutions	#研究与试验发展经费支出 Expenditures of R&D
总　计	**Total**	**99**	**10 330**	**184 138.3**	**49 019.4**
#石油和天然气开采业	Petroleum and Natural Gas Extraction	13	1 576	14 085.3	11 753.0
非金属矿采选业	Nonmetal Minerals Mining and Dressing	1	109	832.0	660.3
农副食品加工业	Agricultural Products and Byproducts Processing				
食品制造业	Food Manufacturing	3	37	57.0	31.0
饮料制造业	Beverage Manufacturing	1	35	26.0	20.0
烟草制品业	Tobacco Processing				
纺织业	Textile Industry	1	105	1 220.8	1 220.8
纺织服装、鞋、帽制造业	Textile Garments,Shoes,Caps Manufacturing				
皮革、毛皮、羽毛(绒)及其制品业	Leather, Furs, Down and Related Products				
木材加工及木、竹、藤、棕、草制品业	Timber Processing,Bamboo, Cane,Palm Fiber and Straw Products				
家具制造业	Furniture Manufacturing				
造纸及纸制品业	Papermaking and Paper Products				
印刷业和记录媒介的复制	Printing and Record Medium Reproduction	1	155	2 014.0	1 409.8
文教体育用品制造业	Cultural, Educational and Sports Goods				
石油加工、炼焦及核燃料加工业	Petroleum Processing,Coking and Nuclear Fuel Processing	1	32	20.0	20.0
化学原料及化学制品制造业	Chemical Raw Materials and Chemical Products	14	839	5 751.0	4 391.5
医药制造业	Medical and Pharmaceutical Products	14	578	12 499.2	9 774.4
化学纤维制造业	Chemical Fiber				
橡胶制品业	Rubber Products	1	3	1.4	1.4
塑料制品业	Plastic Products	1	20	479.8	479.8
非金属矿物制品业	Nonmetal Mineral Products				
黑色金属冶炼及压延加工业	Smelting and Pressing of Ferrous Metals	4	2 161	48 795.9	5 693.7
有色金属冶炼及压延加工业	Smelting and Pressing of Nonferrous Metals				
金属制品业	Metal Products	3	132	350.5	48.8
通用设备制造业	General Purpose Equipment Manufacturing	6	482	2 964.4	2 344.7
专用设备制造业	Special Purpose Equipment Manufacturing	5	226	2 320.0	1 564.1
交通运输设备制造业	Transport Equipment Manufacturing	11	654	6 019.2	2 669.7
电气机械及器材制造业	Electric Equipment and Machinery	6	921	21 725.4	3 962.5
通信设备、计算机及其他电子设备制造业	Telecommunications Equipment,Computer and Other Electronic Equipment Manufacturing	12	2 132	63 923.5	2 867.9
仪器仪表及文化、办公用机械制造业	Instruments,Meters,Cultural and Office Machinery				
电力、热力的生产和供应业	Production and Supply of Electric Power and Heat Energy	1	133	1 052.9	106.0
煤气生产和供应业	Production and Supply of Gas				
水的生产和供应业	Production and Supply of Tap Water				

15－20 续表 4　Continued

项　目	Item	专利申请数（件）Number of Patent Applications (piece)	拥有发明专利数（件）Number of Invent Patent Owned (piece)	技术改造经费支出（万元）Expenditures of Technical Transformation (10 000 yuan)	技术引进经费支出（万元）Expenditures of Technical Introduction (10 000 yuan)
总　计	**Total**	**2 423**	**438**	**294 294.1**	**135 850.2**
#石油和天然气开采业	Petroleum and Natural Gas Extraction	52	8	497.3	101.0
非金属矿采选业	Nonmetal Minerals Mining and Dressing		6	723.0	
农副食品加工业	Agricultural Products and Byproducts Processing			20.0	
食品制造业	Food Manufacturing	5	2	413.0	
饮料制造业	Beverage Manufacturing	2		2 243.0	56.0
烟草制品业	Tobacco Processing	3	3		
纺织业	Textile Industry	3		7 179.6	5 136.0
纺织服装、鞋、帽制造业	Textile Garments, Shoes, Caps Manufacturing				
皮革、毛皮、羽毛(绒)及其制品业	Leather, Furs, Down and Related Products				
木材加工及木、竹、藤、棕、草制品业	Timber Processing, Bamboo, Cane, Palm Fiber and Straw Products				
家具制造业	Furniture Manufacturing				
造纸及纸制品业	Papermaking and Paper Products			1 184.0	1 184.0
印刷业和记录媒介的复制	Printing and Record Medium Reproduction	11	2	5 089.0	
文教体育用品制造业	Cultural, Educational and Sports Goods				
石油加工、炼焦及核燃料加工业	Petroleum Processing, Coking and Nuclear Fuel Processing			8 390.0	730.0
化学原料及化学制品制造业	Chemical Raw Materials and Chemical Products	53	24	72 289.0	6 550.7
医药制造业	Medical and Pharmaceutical Products	100	4	16 791.9	2 457.7
化学纤维制造业	Chemical Fiber				
橡胶制品业	Rubber Products			42.2	
塑料制品业	Plastic Products	9		1 597.0	
非金属矿物制品业	Nonmetal Mineral Products			2 493.2	
黑色金属冶炼及压延加工业	Smelting and Pressing of Ferrous Metals	15	10	97 113.0	9 011.1
有色金属冶炼及压延加工业	Smelting and Pressing of Nonferrous Metals				
金属制品业	Metal Products	1		86.7	
通用设备制造业	General Purpose Equipment Manufacturing	16		4 631.5	3 022.8
专用设备制造业	Special Purpose Equipment Manufacturing	9	10	1 077.7	509.7
交通运输设备制造业	Transport Equipment Manufacturing	7	4	29 225.9	14 391.2
电气机械及器材制造业	Electric Equipment and Machinery	1 773	16	13 021.4	14 396.4
通信设备、计算机及其他电子设备制造业	Telecommunications Equipment, Computer and Other Electronic Equipment Manufacturing	361	343	10 414.0	78 206.2
仪器仪表及文化、办公用机械制造业	Instruments, Meters, Cultural and Office Machinery				
电力、热力的生产和供应业	Production and Supply of Electric Power and Heat Energy		3	15 901.8	97.4
煤气生产和供应业	Production and Supply of Gas			412.3	
水的生产和供应业	Production and Supply of Tap Water	3	3	3 457.6	

主要统计指标解释

科技活动　指在自然科学、农业科学、医药科学、工程与技术科学、人文与社会科学领域(简称科学技术领域)中与科技知识的产生、发展、传播和应用密切相关的有组织的活动。为核算科技投入的需要,科技活动可分为科学研究与试验发展(R&D)、科学研究与试验发展成果应用及相关的科技服务三类活动。

科学研究与试验发展　指在科学技术领域,为增加知识总量、以及运用这些知识去创造新的应用进行的系统的创造性的活动,包括基础研究、应用研究、试验发展三类活动。在工业企业开展的科学研究与试验发展(R&D)活动中,较为普遍的和大量的活动属于试验发展活动。

基础研究　指为了获得关于现象和可观察事实的基本原理的新知识(揭示客观事物的本质、运动规律,获得新发现、新学说)而进行的实验性或理论性研究,它不以任何专门或特定的应用或使用为目的。其成果以科学论文和科学著作为主要形式。

应用研究　指为获得新知识而进行的创造性研究,主要针对某一特定的目的或目标。应用研究是为了确定基础研究成果可能的用途,或是为达到预定的目标探索应采取的新方法(原理性)或新途径。其成果形式以科学论文、专著、原理性模型或发明专利为主。

试验发展　指利用从基础研究、应用研究和实际经验所获得的现有知识,为产生新的产品、材料和装置,建立新的工艺、系统和服务,以及对已生产和建立的上述各项作实质性的改进而进行的系统性工作。其成果形式主要是专利、专有技术、新产品原型或样机样件等。

研究与试验发展成果应用　指为使试验发展阶段产生的新产品、材料和装置,建立的新工艺、系统和服务以及作实质性改进后的上述各项能够投入生产或实际应用,解决所存在的技术问题而进行的系统性的工作。这类活动的成果形式大多是可供生产和实际操作的带有技术和工艺参数的图纸、技术标准和操作规范。

科技服务　与科学研究与试验发展有关并有助于科学技术知识的产生、传播和应用的活动,包括为扩大科技成果的使用范围而进行的示范性推广工作;为用户提供科技信息和文献服务的系统性工作;为用户提供可行性报告、技术方案、建议及进行技术论证等技术咨询工作;自然、生物现象的日常观测、监测,资源的考察和勘探;有关社会、人文、经济现象的通用资料的收集,如统计、市场调查等,以及这些资料的常规分析与整理;为社会和公众提供的测试、标准化、计量、计算、质量控制和专利服务,不包括工商企业为进行正常生产而开展的上述活动。

Explanatory Notes on Main Statistical Indicators

Science and Technology Activity refer to organizational activity aimed at developing, spreading and applying the scientific technology about natural science, agriculture science, medicine science, engineering and technology science, human and social science. In order to calculate the input of science and technology, science and technology activities are divided into R&D, Achievements Applying on Researches & Experiments Developing and Science and Technique Services.

Research and Experimental Development(R&D) refers to systematic and creative endeavor aimed at expanding the overall volume of knowledge and applying the knowledge in inventing new uses. It includes basic studies, application research and experimental development. For industrial enterprises, their R&D mainly belongs to experimental development activities.

Basic Research refers to empirical or theoretical research aiming at obtaining new knowledge on the fundamental principles of phenomena of observable facts to reveal the nature and law of movement of objects and to acquire new discoveries or new theories. Basic research takes no specific or designated application as the aim of the research. Results of basic research are mainly released or disseminated in the form of scientific papers or monographs.

Applied Research refers to creative research aiming at obtaining new knowledge on a specific objective or target. Purpose of the applied research is to identify the possible use of results from basic research, or to explore new (fundamental) methods or new approaches. Results of applied research are expressed in the form of scientific papers, monographs, fundamental models or invention patents.

Experiments and Development refer to systematic activities aiming at using the knowledge from basic and applied researches or from practical experience to develop new products, materials and equipment, to establish new production process, system and service, or to make substantial improvement on the existing products, process and services. Results of experiment and development activities are embodied in patents, exclusive technology, monotype of new products or equipment.

Achievements Applying on Researches & Experiments Developing It is meant that a lot of work is systematically taken to find solutions applicable both/either to technological problems in products, materials and devices put into production and in skills, systems and services into practical use. This kind of achievements include blueprint, technical standard and operating rules with technology and technological parameter for the purpose of production and practical operation.

Science and Technique Services A forward movement in research of the science and development of experiment is a help in creation, spread and application of scientific and technological knowledge, including seven principal matters: (a) extending application, on scope, of an achievement in science and technique by setting an example related there to in popularization, (b) furnishing users with the systematic information on sciences and value - lasting documents as a study, (c) making technique - inquiring business available to users for requirement of technologies either by way of a suggestion or of a scheme, either analysis or feasibility report, (d) people observing day by day and/or listening and reporting on or testing, by apparatus, things appearing in or changes brought about by the nature and living beings, (e) inspecting and/or searching for resources, (f) collecting, analyzing routinely and sorting out the general - purpose information on societies, humanities and economics, e.g. statistics and on - the - spot investigationon markets, (g) providing a test, standardization, measure, calculation, quality control and patent - related services to the society and the public, not to industrial enterprises and/or firms engaged in the above items - developing dealings made available to their normal production and/or operation.

第16篇 CHAPTER 16

卫生、社会保障和社会福利

PUBLIC HEALTH，SOCIAL SECURITY AND SOCIAL WELFARE

16－1　卫生机构、床位及技术人员数
NUMBER OF HEALTH CARE INSTITUTIONS,BEDS AND MEDICAL TECHNICAL PERSONNEL

（1980－2003）

年　份 Year	卫生事业机构（个） Number of Health Care Institutions (unit)	#医院、卫生院 Hospitals	卫生机构床位数（张） Beds (unit)	#医院、卫生院 Hospitals	卫生技术人员数（人） Medical Technical Personnel (persons)	#医　生 Doctors	#护理人员 Nurses
1980	3 535	332	20 911	18 753	50 662	20 474	15 839
1981	3 610	332	21 987	20 301	54 535	22 941	16 555
1982	3 548	337	23 332	21 503	56 152	23 765	16 929
1983	3 582	344	24 351	22 658	58 645	25 033	17 745
1984	3 592	353	25 611	23 906	59 405	25 517	17 762
1985	3 550	285	27 402	25 191	60 412	25 555	18 520
1986	3 631	282	29 218	27 247	62 897	26 750	19 463
1987	3 465	282	30 786	28 371	63 067	27 222	19 303
1988	3 363	285	33 245	30 640	63 924	29 968	19 372
1989	3 420	291	34 122	32 224	65 766	31 619	20 264
1990	3 392	293	35 581	33 382	67 485	32 034	21 228
1991	3 397	300	37 504	35 124	68 887	32 385	22 086
1992	3 287	301	38 137	36 035	69 815	32 320	22 804
1993	3 182	304	39 023	36 724	70 920	33 026	22 884
1994	3 182	419	38 986	37 157	71 217	33 373	22 936
1995	3 182	416	39 092	37 280	71 806	33 693	23 177
1996	4 171	476	39 612	38 284	71 014	32 975	23 156
1997	3 571	483	40 758	39 467	70 431	32 475	23 045
1998	3 190	482	40 471	39 134	68 070	31 482	22 209
1999	2 969	487	39 779	38 579	65 901	30 273	21 977
2000	2 983	488	40 039	38 842	65 145	30 031	21 667
2001	2 665	495	41 637	40 394	63 475	29 215	21 298
2002	2 636	486	40 090	38 837	56 705	23 888	19 257
2003	2 671	485	40 194	38 074	55 629	22 780	19 173

16－2　卫生事业机构
HEALTH CARE INSTITUTIONS

单位：个　　　　(unit)

名　称	Item	2000	2001	2002	2003
总　计	**Total**	**2 983**	**2 665**	**2 636**	**2 671**
医院、卫生院	Hospitals	488	495	486	485
疗养院、所	Sanatoriums	3	2	3	3
门诊部、所	Clinics	2 348	2 044	2 040	2 051
专科防治所、站	Specialized Prevention Stations	20	20	17	17
卫生防疫站	Sanitation and Antiepidemic Stations	25	24	25	25
妇幼保健站、所	Maternity and Child Care Centers	18	13	21	22
药品检验所、站	Medicines and Chemical Reagent labs	10	9		3
医学科学研究机构	Research Institutes of Medical Science	15	15	9	8
高等医学教育机构	Education Institutions of High Medicine	3	3	3	3
其他卫生事业机构	Other Health Care Institutions	53	40	32	54
平均每个医院负担人口（人）	Average Burden Population of Each Hospital (person)	18 686	18 464	18 858	19 021

16-3 全市卫生技术人员数(2003年)
NUMBER OF MEDICAL TECHNICAL PERSONNEL,2003

单位:人 (person)

项目	Item	总计 Total	#医生 Doctor	#护士 Nurse	#药剂人员 Pharmacist	#检验人员 Laboratory Technicians
总计	**Total**	**55 629**	**22 780**	**19 173**	**4 547**	**3 232**
一、医院	Hospitals	44 628	16 851	17 399	3 753	2 389
#综合医院	Comprehensive Hospitals	29 002	11 120	11 396	2 429	1 647
专科医院	Special Hospitals	9 471	2 972	4 088	591	476
#口腔医院	Stomatitis Hospitals	632	301	176	21	4
眼科医院	Eye Hospitals	266	100	108	20	9
耳鼻喉科医院	E.N.T. Hospitals	27	9	10	1	1
肿瘤医院	Tumour Hospitals	934	303	416	50	31
胸科医院	Chest Hospitals	673	223	323	4	24
血液病医院	Blood Disease Hospitals	501	123	145	22	51
妇产科医院	Gynecology Hospitals	1 097	319	542	68	80
儿童医院	Children Hospitals	987	318	484	79	46
精神病医院	Mental Disease Hospitals	1 203	263	563	67	36
传染病医院	Infectious Disease Hospitals	426	103	186	47	36
皮肤病医院	Skin Disease Hospitals	44	16	12	8	3
结核病医院	Tuberculosis Hospitals	372	100	135	31	29
骨科医院	Orthopaedics Hospitals	994	324	448	75	43
二、社区卫生服务中心	Community Health Care Centers	68	48	19	1	
三、卫生院	Hospitals in Township	4 713	2 719	672	481	243
四、门诊部	Clinics	1 276	740	147	142	41
五、急救中心(站)	First-aid Centers	53	33	15	1	
六、采供血机构	Blood Collection and Supplying Institutions	122	23	32	5	42
七、妇幼保健院(所、站)	Maternity and Child Care Centers	1 604	766	502	87	114
八、专科疾病防治院(所、站)	Special Disease Prevention Stations	546	215	176	37	51
九、疾病预防控制中心(防疫站)	Disease Prevention and Control Centers	1 681	1 026	60	12	299
十、卫生监督所	Sanitation Supervision Institutions	164	107	4	1	18
十一、其他卫生机构	Other Health Care Institutions	774	252	147	27	35

16－4　卫生机构的床位数

NUMBER OF BEDS IN HEALTH CARE INSTITUTIONS

单位：张　　(unit)

名　称	Item	2000	2001	2002	2003
总　计	**Total**	**40 039**	**41 637**	**40 090**	**40 194**
医院、卫生院	Hospitals	38 842	40 394	38 837	38 074
疗养院、所	Sanatoriums	459	513	633	633
门诊部、所	Clinics	185	145	59	114
专科防治所、站	Specialized Prevention Stations	310	340	380	499
其他卫生机构	Other Health Care Institutions	158	245	291	874
平均每千人口有医院床位	Hospital Beds per 1000 Population	4.26	4.42	4.24	4.13

16－5　按管理部门和性质分的卫生机构基本情况(2003 年)

BASIC STATUS OF PUBLIC HEALTH BY DEPARTMENT AND CHARACTER,2003

部　门	Department	卫生机构（个）Health Care Institutions (unit)	卫生机构床位（张）Number of Institutions Beds (unit)	卫生技术人员(人) Medical Technical Personnel(person)	
				合　计 Total	医　生 Doctors
总　计	**Total**	**731**	**40 194**	**55 629**	**22 780**
政府办	Run by Government	497	30 205	45 376	18 299
企业办	Run by Enterprises	93	7 932	7 734	3 102
集体办	Run by Collective Units	61	1 242	1 013	564
联营、私营	Run by Joint Ownership Enterprises and Private	57	564	849	456
其　他	Others	23	251	657	359

部　门	Department	卫生技术人员(人) Medical Technical Personnel(person)			
		护理人员 Nurse Personnel	药剂人员 Pharmacist	检验人员 Laboratory Technicians	其他人员 Others
总　计	**Total**	**19 173**	**4 547**	**3 232**	**5 897**
政府办	Run by Government	15 935	3 644	2 752	4 746
企业办	Run by Enterprises	2 866	610	387	769
集体办	Run by Collective Units	135	111	35	168
联营、私营	Run by Joint Ownership Enterprises and Private	159	122	39	73
其　他	Others	78	60	19	141

16-6 医疗机构运营情况(2003年)

OPERATION OF MEDICAL INSTITUTIONS, 2003

指标	Item	医院 Hospitals at and above County Level	卫生院 Hospitals in Township	门诊部 Clinics
机构数(个)	Number of Institutions(unit)	267	212	102
总诊疗人次数(万人次)	Patients Treated(10^4 person-times)	2 226	529	93
#门诊人次数	Out-patients	1 910	509	93
健康检查人数(人)	Health Check(person)	768 601	42 452	400
入院人数(人)	In-patients(person)	451 139	68 450	10
出院人数(人)	Leaving Hospital(person)	450 050	68 399	10

16-7 医疗机构诊疗和病床使用情况

DIAGNOSIS, TREATMENT AND BEDS USED OF MEDICAL INSTITUTIONS

项目 Item	2000	2001	2002	2003
诊疗情况(万人次)				
Diagnosis and Treatment(10^4 person-times)				
诊疗人数				
Patients Treated	1 849	1 916	2 277	2 226
#门诊				
Out-patients	1 577	1 622	1 930	1 910
入院人数				
In-patients	42	44	46	45
平均每月诊疗人数(万人次)				
Number of Patients Treated Per Month(10^4 person-times)				
门诊诊疗人数				
Number of Out-patients	131	135	161	159
入院诊疗人数				
In-patients	4	4	4	4
病床使用情况				
Sickbeds Used				
病人治愈率(%)				
Recovering Rate(%)	50	47	40	37
病床周转次数(次)				
Turnover Beds(times)	13	14	13	13
病床使用率(%)				
Utilization Rate (%)	56	56	60	62
病床工作日(日)				
Working Days of Beds(day)	205	204	217	227
出院者平均 住院日数(日)				
Average Hospitalization Period(day)	14	14	16	16

16－8　适龄儿童疫苗率

STATUS OF VACCINE INOCULATION CHILDREN ON AGE

（1980－2003）

单位：%　　　　（%）

年　份 Year	麻　疹 Measles	脊髓灰质炎 Poliomyeliti	百白破 Pertussis	卡介苗 Bcg Vaccine
1980	93.60	96.60	95.40	93.60
1981	93.10	97.50	91.00	93.30
1982	95.80	98.00	93.70	94.80
1983	91.70	97.40	96.60	94.50
1984	94.60	96.30	95.10	95.20
1985	96.40	97.30	95.40	96.40
1986	96.90	97.50	97.10	96.40
1987	97.90	97.90	97.00	85.00
1988	96.70	95.60	97.40	96.90
1989	97.08	97.81	96.98	96.98
1990	98.04	98.31	97.63	98.05
1991	98.50	99.40	98.69	98.90
1992	98.49	99.12	98.86	97.30
1993	96.03	99.50	98.51	97.80
1994	98.81	99.48	98.78	94.60
1995	98.33	99.19	97.55	99.03
1996	99.17	99.05	99.34	99.35
1997	95.81	96.61	99.38	99.11
1998	99.27	99.59	99.58	98.61
1999	99.44	99.10	99.30	98.69
2000	99.58	99.57	99.48	99.41
2001	99.30	99.78	99.70	98.36
2002	98.64	97.40	98.07	99.91
2003	99.48	98.56	98.15	97.41

16－9　全市居民前十位死亡原因、死亡专率

CAUSE OF DEATH AND DEATH RATE OF 10 MAJOR DISEASES

序位及死因	Position and Cause of Death	死亡专率 Death Rate (1/100 000)		占全部死亡人数的% Proportion（%）	
		2002	2003	2002	2003
1.心脏病	Heart Trouble	146.71	151.23	23.96	24.62
2.脑血管病	Cerebrovascular Disease	142.90	143.61	23.34	23.38
3.恶性肿瘤	Malignant Tumour	124.46	123.88	20.33	20.17
4.呼吸系病	Respiratory Disease	86.87	80.90	14.19	13.17
5.损伤和中毒	Trauma and Toxicosis	27.75	30.52	4.53	4.97
6.消化系病	Digestive Disease	17.13	18.69	2.80	3.04
7.内分泌、营养和代谢及免疫疾病	Internal System, Nutrition, Metabolive and Immunity Disease	17.87	17.87	2.92	2.91
8.泌尿、生殖系统病	Urinary Disease	11.31	13.04	1.85	2.12
9.神经系病	Neuropathy	7.84	7.88	1.28	1.28
10.先天畸形、变性和染色体异常	Inborn Abnormaliy, Chromosome Abnormality	2.53	2.69	0.41	0.44

16－10　优抚对象及优抚事业单位情况
MARTYRS & DISABLED VETERANS AND ADMINISTRATION AGENCIES FOR MARTYRS

指　标	Item	2000	2001	2002	2003
优抚人数(人)	**Martyrs and Disabled Veterans(person)**	**262 990**	**248 622**	**244 876**	**242 465**
烈　属	Members of Revolutionary Martyr's Family	9 524	9 043	8 754	8 646
牺牲病故军人家属	Families of Soldiers Sacrificed or Died of Illness	2 882	2 159	1 668	1 620
现役军人家属	Servicemen's Families	123 540	110 591	107 227	96 793
革命伤残人员	Revolutionary Disabled	7 541	7 233	7 103	7 106
在乡复员军人	Demobilized Soldiers in Hometown	8 881	8 301	8 659	7 927
在乡退伍军人	Veterans in Hometown	110 619	111 292	111 465	120 371
在乡退伍老红军战士	Demobilized Old Red Army Men in Hometown	3	3	3	2
优抚事业单位	**Administration Agencies for Martyrs**				
1.单位数(个)	Number of Units(unit)	9	9	9	9
复退军人疗养院	Convalescent Homes for Disabled Veterans	1	1	1	1
复退军人精神病院	Psychopathy Homes for Disabled Veterans	1	1	1	1
光荣院	Homes for Disabled Veterans	7	7	7	7
2.床位数(张)	Number of Beds(unit)	924	1 006	1 078	1 078
复退军人疗养院	Convalescent Homes for Disabled Veterans	50	100	100	100
复退军人精神病院	Psychopath Homes for Disabled Veterans	130	130	120	120
光荣院	Homes for Disabled Veterans	744	776	858	858
3.收养人员数(人)	Adopted Persons(person)	544	605	674	793
复退军人疗养院	Convalescent Home for Disabled Veterans		30	50	71
复退军人精神病院	Psychopath Homes for Disabled Veterans	98	98	98	108
光荣院	Homes for Disabled Veterans	446	477	526	614
4.职工人数(人)	Staff and Workers(person)	397	392	406	397
#医护人员	Doctors and Nurses	124	106	120	136

16－11 社会福利事业、企业单位和工作人员数
NUMBER OF SOCIAL WELFARE INSTITUTIONS, ENTERPRISES, PERSONS ENGAGED

指标	Item	机构(个) Institutions or Enterprises(unit)			工作人员(人) Persons Engaged (person)		
		2001	2002	2003	2001	2002	2003
福利事业单位	Social Welfare Institutions	274	283	281	3 246	3 507	3 688
民政部门办	Run by Civil Administration Organs	23	24	24	1 346	1 395	1 559
社会集体办	Run by Collectivie Units	265	259	257	2 854	2 112	2 129
福利企业单位	Social Welfare Enterprises	1 019	894	843	48 460	41 081	36 873
民政部门办	Run by Civil Administration Organs	39	92	36	5 498	6 003	4 182
社会集体办	Run by Collectivie Units	980	802	807	42 962	35 078	32 691
烈士纪念建筑物管理单位	Martyr Memorial Building Management Units	10	10	10	161	162	166
社会救助单位	Collecting and Repatriation Units	7	7	7	168	155	151
殡葬管理单位	Funeral and Interment Units	7	7	7	353	201	220

16－12 收养性社会福利事业单位基本情况(2003年)
BASIC STATISTICS ON SOCIAL WELFARE INSTITUTIONS, 2003

指标	Item	单位数(个) Institutions (unit)	床位数(张) Number of Beds (unit)	职工人数(人) Staff and Workers (person)	年末在院收养人员(人) Adopted Personnel at the Year－end (person)	#女性 Female
总计	**Total**	**271**	**15 693**	**3 092**	**9 931**	**5 173**
民政部门办	**Run by Civil Administration Organs**	**9**	**2 087**	**801**	**1 916**	**817**
社会福利院	Social Welfare Homes	6	820	362	700	231
儿童福利院	Welfare Homes for Children	2	693	153	642	291
#SOS儿童村	SOS Children's Village	1	200	26	149	61
精神病人福利院	Psychopath Welfare Homes	1	574	286	574	295
社会办敬老院	**Homes for Old People**	**262**	**13 606**	**2 291**	**8 015**	**4 356**
城镇办敬老院	Run by Urban	149	10 147	1 815	6 249	3 843
农村办敬老院	Run by Rural	113	3 459	476	1 766	513

16-13 社会福利企业情况
BASIC STATISTICS ON SOCIAL WELFARE ENTERPRISES

指 标	Item	2000	2001	2002	2003
一、民政部门办福利企业	**Welfare Enterprise Run by Civil Administration Organs**				
工 业	**Industry**				
单位数(个)	Number of Units(unit)	91	96	92	106
国有经济	Stated-owned	33	39	37	36
集体经济	Collective-owned	58	57	55	70
职工人数(人)	Staff and Workers(person)	6 980	7 006	6 003	5 873
#盲聋哑残人数	Blind,Deaf,Mute,Disabled	2 562	2 464	2 352	2 340
销售收入(万元)	Sales Revenue(10 000 yuan)	54 608	53 326	46 577	59 398
国有经济	Stated-owned	36 365	32 394	33 717	35 158
集体经济	Collective-owned	18 243	18 468	12 860	24 240
盈利金额(万元)	Profit(10 000 yuan)	2 488	2 300	2 685	3 557
亏损金额(万元)	Losses(10 000 yuan)	593	1 088	1 377	1 772
商业服务业	**Commerce and Service**				
单位数(个)	Number of Units(unit)	44	75	15	13
职工人数(人)	Staff and Workers(person)	603	3 158	286	211
#盲聋哑残人数	Blind,Deaf,Mute,Disabled	211	818	96	61
销售收入(万元)	Sales Revenue(10000 yuan)	5 220	10 059	1 150	1 452
盈利金额(万元)	Profit(10000 yuan)	277	798	25	82
亏损金额(万元)	Losses(10000 yuan)	111	103	174	252
二、社会办福利企业	**Welfare Enterprise Run by Society**				
单位数(个)	Number of Units(unit)	1 092	980	802	763
职工人数(人)	Staff and Workers(person)	44 823	42 962	35 078	31 680
#盲聋哑残人数	Blind,Deaf,Mute,Disabled	20 058	18 021	16 204	14 668
销售收入(万元)	Sales Revenue(10000 yuan)	376 357	380 799	389 057	495 872

16-14 抚恤、社会救济事业费
PENSIONS AND RELIEF FUNDS

单位:万元 (10 000 yuan)

指 标	Item	2000	2001	2002	2003
抚恤事业费	Pensions	8 415	11 097	8 159	8 472
社会救济费	Relief Funds	8 544	15 355	29 772	33 499
#农村社会救济费	Rural Relief Funds	447	579	689	1 036
城镇低保救济费	Urban Relief Funds	3 211	8 143	20 153	22 187
精简退职老职工救济费	Relief for Old Staff and Workers Reduced and Discharged	731	689	712	487
自然灾害救济费	Relief for Natural Disaster	1 298	1 417	804	1 745

注:2001以年前抚恤事业费中含优抚事业单位经费和烈士陵园经费。
Note: Before 2001,Pensions include outlay of administration agencies for martyrs and martyr cemetery .

16-15 享受补助、救济人员情况
PERSONS RECEIVING SUBSIDIES AND RELIEF FUNDS

单位:人 (person)

指　标 Item	2000	2001	2002	2003
社会救济总人数 Number of Persons Receiving Relief Funds	14 806	12 976	332 470	273 627
城乡居民最低生活保障人数 Number of Persons Receiving Lowest Cost-of-living in Urban & Rural Areas	3 941	3 014	323 953	267 448
#农业人口 Agricultural Population	2 176	3 014	22 560	26 140
集体供养孤老残幼 Orphan, Elder, Disabled Persons Fended by Collective Units	3 766	3 230	2 083	1 980
精减退职老职工救济人数 Number of Laid-off, Retired, Elderly Staff and Workers Receiving Relief Funds	7 099	6 732	6 434	6 179
#享受40%救济 Persons Receiving 40% of Relief Funds	3 307	3 102	2 934	2 862
#享受定期定量救济 Persons Receiving Periodical and Fixed Relief Funds	3 792	3 630	3 500	3 317
临时救济人次数(人次) Number of Poor Persons Receiving Temporary Almsgiving(person-times)	61 913	80 473	85 972	118 987
#农业人口 Agricultural Population	32 186	44 644	29 385	42 410

注:2001年以前的城乡居民最低生活保障人数为定期定量救济人数。
Note: Before 2001, persons receiving lowest cost-of-living in urban & rural areas refer to persons receiving periodical and fixed relief funds.

16-16 集体优待供给补助金额
COLLECTIVE SUPPLY SUBSIDIES

单位:万元 (10 000 yuan)

指　标 Item	2000	2001	2002	2003
优待烈军属总金额 Subsidies for Relutionary Martyr's Family	2 339	2 254	2 179	1 906
社会散居孤老残幼供给金额 Funds for Scattered Orphans, Elder, Disabled Persons	675	555	610	564
供给敬老院金额 Supply to Homes for Old People	454	615	742	502

16-17 城镇社区服务情况
BASIC STATISTICS ON URBAN COMMUNITY SERVICE

指　标	Item	2000	2001	2002	2003
城镇社区服务设施数(个)	Number of Urban Welfare Facilities(unit)	1 922	1 955	2 425	1 913
便民利民服务网点(个)	Urban Service Points for Civilian(unit)	7 933	8 067	8 923	8 373
城镇社区服务中心	Urban Community Service Center				
单位数(个)	Number of Units(unit)	89	93	98	105
年末职工人数(人)	Number of Staff and Workers Year-end (person)	619	745	794	792
活动人次(人次数)	Number of Persons Coming to Center(person-times)	545 341	610 535	554 855	594 781

主要统计指标解释

卫生技术人员 指卫生事业机构支付工资的全部固定职工和合同制职工中现任职务为卫生技术工作的人员。包括中医师、西医师、中西医结合高级医师、护师、中药师、西药师、检验师、其他技师、中医士、西医士、护士、助产士、中药剂士、西药剂士、检验士、其他技士、其他中医、护理员、中药剂员、西药剂员、检验员和其他初级卫生技术人员。不包括从事管理工作的卫生技术人员。

医生 指经卫生部门审查合格，从事医疗工作的专业人员。分为中医医生和西医医生。包括卫生技术人员中的中医师、西医师、中西医结合高级医师、中医士、西医士和其他中医。

Explanatory Notes on Main Statistical Indicators

Medical Technical Personnel refer to all medical staff and workers employed by medical institutions, including doctors of Chinese and Western medicine, senior doctors who integrate traditional Chinese therapeutics with Western therapeutics in practice, senior nurses, pharmacists of Chinese and Western medicine, laboratory specialists, other specialists, paramedics of Chinese and Western medicine, nurses, midwives, druggists in Chinese and Western medicine, laboratory technicians, other technicians, other practitioners of Chinese medicine, nursing attendants, pharmacological workers of Chinese and Western medicine, laboratory workers, and other primary medical personnel, excluding management personnel.

Doctors refer to qualified professional medical workers approved to practice by public health departments. They are classified into doctors of Chinese medicine, doctors of Western medicine, senior doctors who integrate traditional Chinese therapeutics with Western therapeutics in practice, paramedics of Chinese medicine and Western medicine, and other specialists of Chinese medicine.

第17篇 CHAPTER 17

文化、体育

CULTURE, SPORTS

17－1　文化事业机构和人员情况
BASIC STATISTICS OF CULTURAL INSTITUTIONS AND PERSONNEL
（1978－2003）

年　份 Year	电影事业 Film	艺术事业 Art	公共图书馆 Public Library	文物事业 Culturd Relic	群众文化事业 Mass Culture
机构数(个) **Institutions(unit)**					
1978	1 702	39	19	7	18
1979	2 232	37	17	7	18
1980	1 755	39	19	7	19
1981	1 781	41	19	7	19
1982	1 809	40	23	7	19
1983	1 625	40	23	7	19
1984	1 590	37	26	10	19
1985	1 158	41	26	13	19
1986	1 033	39	27	13	19
1987	929	36	29	15	19
1988	949	39	30	15	19
1989	722	39	30	15	19
1990	668	39	30	16	19
1991	669	38	31	20	19
1992	659	37	31	20	20
1993	662	36	31	20	19
1994	661	51	31	21	19
1995	662	49	31	21	19
1996	662	47	31	21	19
1997	255	48	31	24	19
1998	255	48	31	23	19
1999	238	47	31	23	19
2000	236	49	31	23	19
2001	236	49	31	23	19
2002	236	49	31	24	19
2003	236	49	31	26	19
人员数(人) **Personnel(person)**					
1978	6 571	3 000	446	405	650
1979	7 922	3 490	576	474	723
1980	7 012	3 309	545	399	804
1981	7 247	3 834	594	409	834
1982	6 492	3 811	681	431	758
1983	6 731	3 338	721	415	752
1984	6 706	3 209	756	437	789
1985	5 689	3 195	837	437	849
1986	5 442	3 032	896	506	926
1987	5 047	2 779	993	569	955
1988	5 308	2 794	1 010	567	950
1989	4 755	2 773	1 056	560	928
1990	4 521	2 729	1 182	562	955
1991	4 200	2 772	1 081	562	943
1992	4 107	2 717	1 146	562	955
1993	4 193	2 835	1 118	625	1 282
1994	4 003	2 851	1 087	549	873
1995	4 003	3 552	1 084	549	847
1996	4 003	2 817	1 156	609	868
1997	1 507	2 565	1 025	612	828
1998	1 930	2 532	1 122	801	837
1999	1 930	2 616	1 129	731	807
2000	1 930	2 468	1 111	887	798
2001	1 930	2 562	1 014	887	752
2002	1 930	2 483	974	918	755
2003	1 930	2 322	1 095	862	750

17－2 图书出版
BOOKS PUBLICATION

项　目 Item	种　类(种) Number of Publications (kind)			总印数(万册) Total Copies (10 000 volumes)		
	2001	2002	2003	2001	2002	2003
总　计 Total	**3 400**	**3 711**	**3 798**	**6 236**	**6 917**	**6 772**
#本　版 Local Publications	3 248	3 560	3 615	4 985	5 646	5 440
书　籍 Books	2 364	2 785	2 918	2 115	4 370	4 364
课　本 Textbook	921	818	815	3 980	2 414	2 332
图　片 Picture	115	108	65	141	133	76

17－3 报纸出版
NEWSPAPERS PUBLICATION

项　目 Item	种　类(种) Number of Publications (kind)			总印数(万份) Total Copies (10 000 volumes)		
	2001	2002	2003	2001	2002	2003
总　计 Total	**25**	**43**	**45**	**72 080**	**80 782**	**82 387**
综合报 Comprehensive Newspapers	11	15	20	60 722	70 822	76 327
专业报 Professional Newspapers	14	28	25	11 358	9 960	6 060
省、直辖市级报纸合计 Newspapers at Provincial or Municipal Level	24	24	24	71 711	79 833	80 746
综合报 Comprehensive Newspapers	11	11	14	60 517	70 129	74 923
专业报 Professional Newspapers	13	13	10	11 194	9 704	5 823
区(市)级报纸合计 Newspapers at District (City) Level	2	19	21	369	949	1 641
综合报 Comprehensive Newspapers	1	4	6	205	693	1 404
专业报 Professional Newspapers	1	15	15	164	256	237

17－4 杂志出版
MAGAZINES PUBLICATION

项　目 Item	种　类(种) Number of Publications (kind)			总印数(万册) Total Copies (10 000 volumes)		
	2001	2002	2003	2001	2002	2003
总　计 Total	**237**	**239**	**245**	**4 572**	**4 469**	**4 610**
综　合 Comprehensive	34	3	9	633	18	338
哲学、社会科学 Philosophy and Social Sciences	25	41	41	766	760	803
自然科学、技术 Natural Sciences and Technology	137	141	146	1 322	1 107	1 063
文化、教育 Culture and Education	28	39	33	1 024	1 821	1 569
文学、艺术 Literature and Art	10	14	14	672	736	802
#少年儿童读物 Juvenile and Children's Book	3	3	4	326	326	462
画　刊 Pictorial	3	1	2	155	27	34

17－5　书籍和课本分类出版情况

PUBLICATION OF BOOKS AND TEXTBOOKS BY CATEGORY

类　别　Item	种　类(种) Number of Publication (kind)			总印数(万册) Total Copies (10 000 volumes)		
	2001	2002	2003	2001	2002	2003
总　计 Total	**3 285**	**3 603**	**3 733**	**6 093**	**6 784**	**6 696**
马列主义、毛泽东思想 Marxism－Leninism, Mao Zedong Thought	6	7	6	6	3	11
哲　学 Philosophy	14	29	39	9	20	29
社会科学总论 General Social Sciences	27	19	14	12	6	6
政治、法律 Politics and Law	57	62	52	15	21	18
军　事 Military Affairs	2	8	1		2	1
经　济 Economics	202	218	255	110	104	125
文化、科学、教育、体育 Culture, Science, Education and Sports	1 046	1 403	1 579	4 692	5 377	5 349
语言、文字 Languages	246	272	286	155	182	166
文　学 Literature	360	303	277	224	198	205
艺　术 Art	549	521	611	453	435	506
历史、地理 History and Geography	54	42	42	25	17	21
自然科学总论 General Natural Sciences	81	53	29	41	42	13
数理科学、化学 Mathematics and Chemistry	100	95	87	79	95	39
天文学、地球科学 Astronomy and Geology			2			1
生物科学 Biology	12	6	5	7	4	1
医药、卫生 Medicine and Health Care	256	204	194	117	77	75
农业科学 Agricultural Science	4	30	15	1	11	3
工业技术 Industrial Technology	239	294	222	138	182	116
交通运输 Transportation	8	13	4	1	4	2
航天、航空 Aeronautics and Aerospace	1	1				
环境科学 Environmental Science	2	3	5			1
综合性图书 Comprehensive Books	19	20	8	8	4	10

17－6　广播电台和电视台情况
STATISTICS OF BROADCASTING AND TELEVISION STATIONS
(1978－2003)

单位：套、时：分、%　　(set)(hour：minute)(%)

年　份 Year	广播电台 Broadcasting Stations				电视台 Television Stations			
	节目套数 Number of Programs	平均每日播音时间 Broad－casting Hours Per Day	平均每日自办节目 Self－produced Programs Per Day	广播覆盖率 Listener Rating	节目套数 Number of Programs	平均每周播出时间 Program Hours Per Week	平均每周自办节目 Self－produced Programs Per Week	电视覆盖率 Viewer Rating
1978	4	45:35	44:05	90	1	41:00	18:40	50
1979	4	48:20	46:50	95	1	40:00	18:40	50
1980	4	51:55	49:40	95	1	25:00	19:20	50
1981	4	51:55	49:40	95	1	24:45	24:38	50
1982	4	53:00	49:15	95	1	21:48	12:22	50
1983	4	53:05	42:00	95	1	38:18	11:04	50
1984	4	53:20	30:30	95	1	36:33	16:06	70
1985	4	53:20	43:07	95	2	72:00	45:50	70
1986	5	60:10	47:55	95	3	116:59	115:04	89
1987	5	65:35	56:25	95	3	76:42	72:02	89
1988	5	65:35	56:55	95	3	76:42	72:02	89
1989	5	68:50	59:00	95	3	110:30	107:00	89
1990	5	68:50	58:50	95	3	162:26	103:46	89
1991	5	68:50	59:30	95	4	133:50	130:20	89
1992	5	70:16	68:16	95	4	135:12	131:42	89
1993	5	77:30	75:00	100	10	352:48	255:22	95
1994	5	89:58	84:48	100	11	293:18	276:43	95
1995	6	87:10	84:48	100	11	373:46	360:28	95
1996	6	96:22	93:52	100	11	428:54	416:03	95
1997	6	94:42	91:42	100	11	427:57	416:23	95
1998	6	103:02	99:02	100	11	500:16	477:46	95
1999	6	105:00	100:20	100	11	546:22	525:27	99
2000	6	110:42	105:12	100	11	560:29	533:38	99
2001	6	116:30	112:25	100	15	1 192:30	1 168:30	99
2002	7	130:07	123:25	100	15	1 278:42	1 177:57	99
2003	7	148:32	139:11	100	16	1 509:51	1 353:44	99

17－7　广播和电视节目制作情况（2003年）
PRODUCTION OF BROADCASTING AND TELEVISION,2003

单位：小时　　　　(hour)

项　目	Item	自制节目时间 Self－produced Programs	#新　闻 News	#专　题 Special Topic	#教　育 Educa－tion	#文　艺 Entertain－ment	#服务性 Service
一、广　播	**Broadcasting**						
天津人民广播电台	Tianjin People Broadcasting Station	41 190	7 288	12 471		15 306	851
二、电　视	**Television Stations**						
平均每周播出时间合计	Program Hours Per Week	7 155	2 115	2 327	139	1 531	531
天津电视台	Tianjin Television Station	4 287	1 441	1 848	117	524	357
塘沽区电视台	Tanggu District Television Station	446	65	87	20	183	47
汉沽区电视台	Hangu District Television Station	55	41	4	2	5	
大港区电视台	Dagang District Television Station	141	60	35			6
武清区电视台	Wuqing District Television Station	279	57	64		69	49
宝坻区电视台	Baodi District Television Station	409	113	70		104	
宁河县电视台	Ninghe County Television Station	594	109	42		248	55
静海县电视台	Jinghai County Television Station	220	121	73		6	17
蓟县电视台	Jixian County Television Station	724	108	104		392	

17－8　广播和电视节目播出自办节目情况（2003年）
SELF－PRODUCED PROGRAMS OF BROADCASTING AND TELEVISION,2003

单位：小时：分　　　　(hour:minute)

项　目	Item	平均播出时间 Program Hours	#新　闻 News	#专　题 Special Topic	#教　育 Educa－tion	#文　艺 Entertain－ment	#服务性 Service
一、广　播	**Broadcasting**						
平均每日播音时间	Program Hours Per Day	139:11	23:53	34:20	2:00	62:06	2:25
二、电　视	**Television Stations**						
平均每周播出时间合计	Program Hours Per Week	1 353:44	78:49	509:55	5:06	596:49	140:11
天津电视台	Tianjin Television Station	859:53	50:55	481:47		238:19	88:52
塘沽区电视台	Tanggu District Television Station	123:10	7:00	2:07	2:35	108:34	1:30
汉沽区电视台	Hangu District Television Station	36:35	1:30	3:37	2:31	28:05	
大港区电视台	Dagang District Television Station	63:27	3:50	3:00		55:20	0:07
武清区电视台	Wuqing District Television Station	59:19	3:40	11:20		31:45	3:54
宝坻区电视台	Baodi District Television Station	7:50	2:10	1:20		2:00	
宁河县电视台	Ninghe County Television Station	39:24	4:36	2:39		27:24	1:09
静海县电视台	Jinghai County Television Station	78:01	3:30	2:20		26:50	44:39
蓟县电视台	Jixian County Television Station	86:05	1:38	1:45		78:32	

17－9　天津电视台节目播出情况(2003年)

PROPAGANDA OF TELEVISION PROGRAMS OF TIANJIN TELEVISION STATION,2003

指标 Item		节目套数(套) Programs (set)	平均每周播出时间合计(时:分) Program Hours Per Week (hour:minute)	#自办节目 Self－produced Programs	#新闻 News	专题 Special Topic	文艺 Entertain－ment
合计	**Total**	**7**	**863:33**	**859:53**	**50:55**	**481:47**	**238:19**
天津电视台	Channel	1	127:33	127:33	9:55	64:42	35:43
天津电视台1	Channel 1	1	119:05	119:05	0:00	68:44	40:12
天津电视台2	Channel 2	1	129:42	129:42	2:46	29:42	69:44
天津电视台3	Channel 3	1	128:16	128:16	13:46	61:48	40:20
天津电视台4	Channel,4	1	130:34	130:34	8:03	119:21	0:00
天津电视台5	Channel 5	1	88:10	88:10	0:09	65:09	18:26
天津电视台6	Channel 6	1	140:13	136:33	16:16	72:21	33:54

17－10　电影放映单位基本情况

FILM PROJECTING UNITS

(1978－2003)

单位:个　　(unit)

年份 Year	电影院 Cinema	影剧院 Theater	开放礼堂俱乐部 Opening Auditorium	电影放映队 Projecting Team	对内俱乐部 Internal Club	电影放映单位拥有座席数 Seats
1978	33	12	36	827	775	104 100
1979	35	13	42	1 165	957	104 110
1980	30	24	38	1 209	433	104 050
1981	32	41	34	1 237	416	104 061
1982	33	25	22	1 289	419	105 174
1983	34	29	41	1 200	299	107 693
1984	32	33	40	1 152	311	105 462
1985	35	36	37	809	218	113 847
1986	35	36	40	697	204	118 200
1987	34	37	41	602	194	114 913
1988	34	49	46	612	187	124 879
1989	33	48	46	424	151	130 977
1990	55	26	46	372	148	132 162
1991	54	27	46	372	150	115 379
1992	54	28	44	366	147	116 574
1993	54	28	45	366	149	130 432
1994	54	28	45	366	149	130 432
1995	54	28	45	366	149	130 432
1996	54	28	45	366	149	130 432
1997	23	27	23	134	39	67 783
1998	23	19	19	103	36	67 783
1999	19	22	17	118	35	56 044
2000	19	22	17	139	35	48 592
2001	19	22	17	139	35	47 189
2002	16	13	14	139	15	44 282
2003	12	11	8	139	15	31 718

17－11 电影放映情况
FILM PROJECTING

项 目 Item		单位数（个） Units (unit)		放映场次（场次） Projecting Performances (times)		观众人次（万人次） Audience (10 000 person－times)	
		2002	2003	2002	2003	2002	2003
35m/m 电影放映单位	**Projecting Units of 35m/m Film**	**58**	**31**	**55 290**	**41 970**	**180**	**103**
专业电影院	Speciality Cinema	16	12	27 450	20 949	90	46
影剧院	Theater	13	11	23 535	18 533	50	37
礼 堂	Auditoriums	14	8	4 135	2 382	23	10
对内俱乐部	Internal Clubs	15	15	170	106	17	10

17－12 艺术事业基本情况
BASIC STATISTICS ON ART

指 标	Item	2000	2001	2002	2003
艺术表演团体	**Art Performance Troupes**				
机构数(个)	Institutions(unit)	16	15	15	15
话剧团、儿童剧团	Drama and Children Troupes	2	2	2	2
歌舞剧团	Song and Dance Troupes	1	1	1	1
文工团、文宣队	Culturaland Performance Troupe	2	1	1	1
戏曲剧团	Local Opera Troupes	7	7	7	7
#京 剧	Local Beijing Opera Troupes	2	3	2	2
曲剧团、杂技团、木偶团	Recitation and Ballad Troupes, Acrobatic and Circus Troupes, Puppet Show Troup	3	3	3	3
乐团、合唱团	Philharmonic Troupes and Chorus	1	1	1	1
工作人员数(人)	Employment(person)	1 754	1 800	1 781	1 769
艺术表演场所	**Art Performance Places**				
机构数(个)	Institutions(unit)	32	32	32	32
剧场、音乐厅	Theatre and Concert Hall	31	31	31	31
书场、曲艺厅	Storytelling Places, Rectation and Balled Places	1	1	1	1
座席数(个)	Seats(unit)		19 315	17 858	15 792
工作人员数(人)	Employment(person)	672	707	650	537

17－13　艺术表演活动情况
ART PERFORMANCE

单位:场、万人次　　(times)(10 000 person－times)

指　标	Item	2000	2001	2002	2003
艺术表演团体	**Art Performance Troupes**				
演出场次	Number of Performances	2 000	2 000	2 242	2 191
#到农村演出	Shows In Rural Areas	1 000	800	452	433
观众人次	Number of Spectators	241	287	272	260
艺术表演场所	**Art Performance Places**				
演出场次	Number of Performances	47 000	41 000	39 000	30 336
观众人次	Number of Spectator	172	221	113	73

17－14　公共图书馆情况
PUBLIC LIBRARIES
(1978－2003)

年　份 Year	工作人员 (人) Employment (person)	藏　书 (万册) Collections (10 000 volumes)	借阅人次 (万人次) Person－times of Borrowing (10 000 person－times)	借阅册次 (万册次) Number of Books Borrowed (10 000 volume－times)	建筑面积 (平方米) Floor Space of Buildings (sq. m)	阅览室座席 (个) Seating Capacity of Reading room (unit)
1978	446	519	113	208	17 154	983
1979	576	568	213	488	19 935	1 583
1980	545	553	214	472	20 184	1 944
1981	594	677	249	502	23 409	2 249
1982	681	644	238	644	25 522	2 795
1983	721	664	295	683	27 138	3 390
1984	756	678	277	849	38 568	5 168
1985	837	584	291	581	38 813	4 793
1986	896	625	251	495	42 000	4 850
1987	993	646	301	523	45 100	5 293
1988	1 010	648	268	490	45 290	4 990
1989	1 056	666	269	514	45 290	4 819
1990	1 182	665	245	468	46 251	4 996
1991	1 081	645	201	273	47 000	4 800
1992	1 146	650	303	200	72 800	5 900
1993	1 118	652	203	216	78 000	5 500
1994	1 087	667	280	145	80 500	4 900
1995	1 084	677	265	237	76 900	4 800
1996	1 156	659	148	190	76 421	4 876
1997	1 025	717	206	271	87 000	6 000
1998	1 122	735	201	369	79 489	6 620
1999	1 129	762	352	337	85 965	6 660
2000	1 111	786	198	533	100 000	7 000
2001	1 014	804	331	483	100 000	8 000
2002	974	822	232	413	103 000	8 000
2003	1 095	840	187	339	100 444	7 467

17－15　档案事业基本情况
BASIC STATISTICS ON ARCHIVES

项　目	Item	2000	2001	2002	2003
机构数(个)	**Number of Institutions(unit)**	**543**	**494**	**508**	**497**
#档案馆	Archives	31	31	32	32
机关事业单位档案室	Archives in Government and Institutions	193	182	176	186
大型工业企业档案馆	Archives in Large Industrial Enterprises	319	281	300	279
专职工作人员(人)	**Full－time Personnel(person)**	**1 117**	**1 044**	**1 046**	**999**
#档案馆	Archives	378	372	388	410
机关事业单位档案室	Archives in Government and Institutions	247	220	220	218
大型工业企业档案馆	Archives in Large Industrial Enterprises	492	452	438	371
兼职工作人员(人)	**Part－time Personnel(person)**	**3 369**	**2 900**	**2 690**	**2 466**
#机关事业单位档案室	Archives in Government and Institutions	1 165	1 074	1 037	1 003
大型工业企业档案馆	Archives in Large Industrial Enterprises	2 204	1 826	1 653	1 463

17－16　档案馆档案资料馆藏与开发利用情况
COLLECTION，DEVELOPMENT AND UTILIZATION OF MATERIALS IN ARCHIVES

项　目	Item	2000	2001	2002	2003
馆藏档案	**Collection of Archives**				
全　宗(个)	Full－Records(unit)	2 412	2 491	2 607	2 713
案　卷(万卷)	Files(10 000 volumes)	350	361	386	393
录音、录像、影片(盘)	Sounds and Movies Files(cassette)	6 400	5 300	5 500	20 300
照　片(张)	Photo Files(picture)	206 500	224 200	263 200	253 600
保存资料	**Collection of Materials**				
资料数量(万册)	Materials(10 000 volumes)	31	31	29	26
利用档案资料	**Utilization**				
利用人次(万人次)	Users(10 000 person－times)	3	4	4	3
利用档案(万卷次)	Access to Files(10 000 volume－times)	10	11	20	11
利用资料(册次)	Materials(volume－times)	15 600	12 300	10 500	6 700
利用档案资料(万页)	Copy Materials(10 000 pages)	4	20	8	8
编研档案资料	**Editing Materials**				
公开出版(种)	Public Publication(kind)	5	5	3	2
(万字)	(10 000 words)	269	115	270	11
内部参考(种)	Internal Reference(kind)	59	50	87	55
(万字)	(10 000 words)	256	389	1 764	278

17－17 机关事业单位档案资料保存与开发利用情况
KEEPING,DEVELOPMENT AND UTILIZATION OF MATERIALS IN ARCHIVES

项　　目	Item	2000	2001	2002	2003
保存档案	**Keeping Archives**				
全　宗(个)	Full－Records(unit)	287	233	254	263
案　卷(万卷)	Files(10 000 volumes)	101	82	91	125
底　图(万张)	Chart(10 000 pictures)	197	120	131	83
微缩胶片(万张)	Compressed Film(10 000 pictures)		15	9	
保存资料	**Keeping Materials**				
保存数量(万册)	Number of Materials(10 000 volumes)	13	11	5	5
借阅利用档案资料	**Lending**				
利用人次(万人次)	Users(10 000 person－times)	5	5	5	5
利用档案资料数量(万卷册数)	Access to Files(10 000 volumes)	11	12	11	12
编研档案资料	**Editing Materials and Archives**				
公开出版(种)	Public Publication(kind)	26	35	24	28
(万字)	(10 000 words)	629	446	302	1 247
内部参考(种)	Internal Reference(kind)	158	101	119	139
(万字)	(10 000 words)	5 054	1 044	1 165	1 335

17－18 大型工业企业档案资料保存与开发利用情况
KEEPING,DEVELOPMENT AND UTILIZATION OF ARCHIVES MATERIALS IN LARGE－SIZED INDUSTRIAL ENTERPRISES

项　　目	Item	2000	2001	2002	2003
保存档案	**Keeping Archives**				
全　宗(个)	Full－Records(unit)	454	449	477	444
案　卷(万卷)	Files(10 000 volumes)	211	192	193	167
底　图(万张)	Chart(10 000 pictures)	374	338	345	333
缩微胶片(万张)	Compressed Film(10 000 pictures)			1	8
保存资料	**Keeping Materials**				
保存数量(万册)	Number of Materials(10 000 volumes)	15	18	15	13
借阅利用档案资料	**Lending**				
利用人次(万人次)	Users(10 000 person－times)	9	10	9	8
利用档案资料数量(万卷册数)	Access to Files(10 000 volumes)	24	26	20	19
编研档案资料	**Editing Materials and Archives**				
公开出版(种)	Public Publication(kind)	21	21	4	
(万字)	(10 000 words)	101	63	4	
内部参考(种)	Internal Reference(kind)	287	322	262	266
(万字)	(10 000 words)	2 423	24 314	898	725

17－19　博物馆和文物保护单位基本情况

BASIC STATISTICS ON MUSEUMS AND CULTURAL RELIC PROTECTION UNITS

指　标	Item	单　位	Unit	2000	2001	2002	2003
博物馆	**Museums**						
单位数	Number of Units	个	unit	14	14	15	17
工作人员数	Employment	人	person	686	672	689	629
文物藏品	Number of Collection	万件	10^4 pieces	55	50	54	55
举办陈列	Number of Displays	个	unit	49	46	26	11
举办展览	Number of Exhibitions	个	unit	54	62	53	46
参观人次	Numbers of Visitors	万人次	10^4 person－times	103	76	97	58
文物保护单位	**Cultural Relic Protection Units**						
单位数	Number of Units	个	unit	8	8	8	8
工作人员数	Employment	人	person	102	116	127	131
藏　品	Number of Collection	件	piece	2 368	2 270	3 073	2 975

17－20　群众文化事业基本情况

BASIC STATISTICS ON MASS ART

指　标	Item	单　位	Unit	2000	2001	2002	2003
单位数	Number of Units	个	unit	19	19	19	19
群众艺术馆	Mass Art Centers	个	unit	1	1	1	1
文化馆	Cultural Centers	个	unit	18	18	18	18
工作人员数	Employment	人	person	798	752	755	750
文化活动情况	Cultural Activity						
举办展览	Number of Exhibitions	次	time	619	194	238	144
组织文艺活动次数	Art Performances	次	time	3 069	1 196	1 422	1 097
举办训练班	Training Courses						
班　次	Number of Classes	班	class	3 062	490	431	595
结业人数	Number of Persons Completing Course	人	person	76 000	21 000	9 000	10 000
放映录像	Projecting Kinescope						
场　次	Scene	场	scene	15 461	13 835	5 900	4 170
观众人次	Audience	万人次	10^4 person－times	172	52	6	24

17－21　天津市举办运动竞赛情况(县及县以上)
SPORTS MEETINGS HELD IN TIANJIN(COUNTY－RUN AND OVER)
(1997－2003)

单位:次、万人　(times)(10 000 persons)

年份 Year	举办运动会次数 Sports Meetings	参加运动会人数 Athletes Attending Sports Meetings	体委系统 Physical Culture and Sports Commissions		其他系统 Other Departments	
			运动会次数 Times	参加人数 Person－times	运动会次数 Times	参加人数 Person－times
1997	354	20	149	11	205	9
1998	206	12	103	8	103	4
1999	186	12	107	8	79	4
2000	200	10	101	6	99	4
2001	566	19	105	6	118	7
2002	348	21	87	8	261	13
2003	367	25	82	12	285	13

17－22　体委系统体育工作者
PERSONNEL IN SPORTS COMMISSIONS SYSTEM

单位:人　(person)

指标 Item	2000	2001	2002	2003
体育工作者人数 Personnel of Sports	3 520	3 587	3 602	4 100
专职教练员 Full－time Coaches	508	506	504	512
国家级教练员 National Coaches	6	6	6	6
每十万人口中体育工作者 Number of Physical Personnel in Per 100 000 Persons	39	39	39	41

17－23　等级裁判员和运动员发展人数
NUMBER OF ATHLETES AND REFEREES IN GRADES
(1997－2003)

单位:人　(person)

项目 Item	合计 Total		#一级 First Grade		#二级 Second Grade		#三级 Third Grade	
	总人数 Total	#女性 Female	总人数 Total	#女性 Female	总人数 Total	#女性 Female	总人数 Total	#女性 Female
裁判员 Referees								
1997	366	135	84	34	163	60	93	32
1998	823	246	323	95	331	107	140	34
1999	535	156	111	38	318	91	97	24
2000	396	114	30	21	319	84	47	9
2001	592	187	57	21	336	94	182	68
2002	395	130	71	23	324	107		
2003	404	136	68	22	336	114		
运动员 Athletes								
1997	2 094	1 050	56	32	818	382	619	251
1998	1 474	580	66	36	859	344	519	177
1999	1 547	556	151	47	1 001	369	367	130
2000	1 464	577	48	20	1 078	422	338	135
2001	1 216	485	51	26	963	377	181	82
2002	1 112	572	64	28	1 048	544		
2003	1 283	538	72	36	1 211	502		

主要统计指标解释

电视人口覆盖率 指用普通的电视接收机，室外天线在离地面4米高处能在晚上正常收看电视节目的人数与全市总人口数之比。

广播人口覆盖率 指用普通的收音机在中午能正常收听广播节目的人数与全市总人口数之比。

文化事业机构 指从事专业文化工作和为专业文化工作服务的单独核算、独立建制的单位，不包括文化主管部门直属单位举办的其他行业和各部门的业余文化组织。

艺术表演团体 指从事戏曲、音乐、舞蹈、杂技等专业艺术表演有独立帐户、实行单独核算的团体。

电影放映单位 指具有放映机器设备，固定或不固定的放映场所与专职或兼职的放映技术人员，经文化部门登记批准，经常为一定的观众对象映出电影的机构。包括经批准对外开放进行营业、并与电影发行放映管理机构分帐的专用放映单位或军委系统租片在内。

体育场 指有米跑道(中心含足球场)，有固定车道，跑道6条以上，并有固定看台的田径场。

体育馆 指有固定看台可供篮球、排球、羽毛球、乒乓球、体操等项目训练比赛活动用的室内场地。

等级运动员人数 指经考核正式批准授予等级运动员称号的人数。分为国际级运动健将、运动健将、一、二、三级运动员和少年级运动员。

等级裁判员人数 指经考核正式批准授予等级裁判员称号的人数。分为国际裁判、国家级裁判、一、二、三级裁判。

Explanatory Notes on Main Statistical Indicators

Viewer Rate refers to the ratio of the number of watching TV to the total population using normal television sets with outdoor antenna four meters apart from ground in the evening.

Listener Rate refers to the ratio of the number of listening radio to the total population using normal radiogram at noon.

Cultural Institutions refer to units which have their own organizational system and independent accounting system and specialize in or serve cutural development. They exclude other establishments run by these cultural institutions and amateur cultural groups established by various departments.

Art Troupe refers to the troupe which is engaged in drama, opera, music, dance, acrobatics or other art performance, opens independent accounts with banks and has self - supporting accounting system.

Film Projection Units refer to these units with film projection equipment, full or part - time projectionists, permanent or non - permanent places, approved by related administrative departments to show films regularly for certain groups of audience, including those film projection units which have been approved to give commercial shows and run business with independent accounting system as well as those film - renting units of the military system.

Stadiums refer to stadiums for track and field events with six tracks around soccer fields, permanent track marks and permanent bleachers.

Gymnasiums refer to indoor sports grounds with permanent seats in which basketball, volleyball, badminton, table tennis and gymnastics competitions can be held.

Number of Athletes in Grades refers to the number of athletes who have been given titles through examination. The titles of athletes include international masters of sports, masters of sports, first - grade, second - grade and third - grade sportsmen and young athletes.

Number of Referees in Grades refers to the number of referees who have been given titles after examination. They are classified as international referees, national referees and referees of the first, second and third grades.

第18篇 CHAPTER 18

公共管理和社会组织

PUBLIC MANAGEMENT AND SOCIAL ORGANIZATIONS

18-1 检察机关立案侦察经济案件情况(2003 年)
ECONOMIC CASES UNDER INVESTIGATION BY PROCURATORIAL OFFICES, 2003

项 目 Item	侦查经济案件 Economic Cases Investigated	#贪 污 Corrup-tion	#挪用公款 Misappropriate Public Funds	#贿赂案 Bribery	#受 贿 Accepting Bribe
立 案(件) Cases Registered(case)	**466**	**250**	**121**	**90**	**76**
#5 万元至 10 万元 50000-100000 Yuan	169	122	4	43	42
10 万元至 50 万元 100000-500000 Yuan	161	78	66	16	12
50 万元至 100 万元 500000-1000000 Yuan	38	11		6	4
100 万元以上 Over 1000000 Yuan	43	11	26	3	3
犯罪嫌疑人(人) Criminal in Cases Registered(person)	**477**	**257**	**125**	**90**	**76**
机关工作人员 Civil Servant	47	21	10	16	15
国有公司企业工作人员 Personnel of State-owned Enterprises	268	152	72	40	37
国有事业单位工作人员 Personnel of State-owned Institutions	67	36	16	15	15
委派到非国有单位从事公务人员 Functionary Appointed to Non-state Units	8	6	1	1	1
其他依法从事公务人员 Other Personnel Line of Duty	30	19	7	4	4
其 他 Others	56	22	19	14	4
结 案 Cases Settled					
件 数(件) Number of Cases(case)	376	178	96	91	82
人 数(人) Number of Persons(person)	383	183	98	91	82
#1.移送起诉 Hand over to Suit					
件 数(件) Number of Cases(case)	340	164	85	80	73
人 数(人) Number of Persons(person)	346	168	87	80	73
2.撤销案件 Cases Withdrawed					
件 数(件) Number of Cases(case)	26	8	9	9	7
人 数(人) Number of Persons(person)	27	9	9	9	7
侦结认定金额(万元) Value Approved by Procuratorial Organs in Cases Settled(10 000 yuan)	**12 660.67**	**3 890.66**	**6 281.34**	**1 753.7**	**1 335.7**
挽回经济损失(万元) Retrieve Pecuniary Losses(10 000 yuan)	**3 951.68**	**1 088.64**	**1 998.94**	**833.13**	**810.73**

18－2 法院收案和结案情况（2003 年）
CASES ACCEPTED & SETTLED BY COURTS, 2003

单位：件 (case)

项目	Item	收案 Cases Accepted	结案 Cases Settled	#调解 Mediation	#判决 Judgement
合同纠纷案件	**Contracts Disputes**	**54 598**	**54 018**	**10 624**	**25 511**
#买卖合同纠纷	Purchases and Sales Contracts	8 916	8 768	2 259	3 982
房地产合同纠纷	Real Estate Contracts	1 697	1 572	147	1 087
借款合同纠纷	Debts Contracts	9 486	9 365	2 293	5 060
建设工程公司纠纷	Construction Projest Contracts	1 198	1 203	280	577
运输合同纠纷	Transportation Contracts	580	568	167	258
婚姻家庭案件	**Marriages and Family Affair**	**14 019**	**13 998**	**6 145**	**4 898**
#离婚	Divorce	11 314	11 306	5 281	3 647
抚育	Foster	835	839	295	364
赡养	Support	704	703	189	327
继承纠纷案件	**Inheritance Disputes**	**287**	**286**	**89**	**129**
#继承	Inheritance	160	156	46	73
遗嘱	Will	23	23	8	9
继承权	Inheritance Right	24	27	10	12
遗赠	Bequest	2	3		2
抚养	Bring－up	3	3	2	
其他	Others	75	73	23	32

18－3 法院行政案件收案和结案情况（2003 年）
ADMINISTRATIVE CASES ACCEPTED AND SETTLED BY COURTS, 2003

单位：件 (case)

项目	Item	收案 Cases Accepted	结案 Cases Settled	#维持 Affirmation of Original Judgement	#撤消 Cancel Settled	#变更 Modifi－cation	#撤诉 Withdraw	未结 Cases Unsettled
合计	**Total**	**862**	**839**	**187**	**52**	**2**	**277**	**90**
公安	Publice Security	96	92	34	4		31	8
资源	Resources	49	40	5	13		4	9
城建	City Construction	357	368	87	16	1	170	28
工商	Industry and Commerce	19	18	1			5	3
技术监督	Technology Supervision	4	4	3			1	
计划生育	Family Planning	20	20	1	2		1	
卫生	Health Care	7	6				4	1
物价	Price	2	1	1				1
环保	Environment Protection	41	41	11				
交通	Transportation	29	25	8	2		8	4
税务	Tax	4	4		1		1	
海关（含商检）	Customs(including inspection and quarantine)	1	1	1				
劳动和社会保障局	Labour and Social Security	44	46	22	6	1	10	3
烟草专卖	Tobacco	3	3		1		2	
司法行政	Judicature	37	41	5	2		12	5
民政	Civil Affairs	2	2	2				
教育	Education	6	12		2		4	
乡政府	Township Government	3	3				2	
其他	Others	138	112	6	3		22	28

18－4　调解工作基本情况
BASIC STATISTICS ON MEDIATION

项　目　Item	单　位　Unit	2000	2001	2002	2003
司法助理员 Judicial Assistants	人 person	495	261	426	585
人民调解委员会 People's Mediation Committees	个 unit	6 855	6 500	6 095	6 136
调解民间纠纷 Civil Disputes	件 case	33 609	29 179	28 277	25 377
调解成功 Success	件 case	32 500	28 216	27 343	24 583
防止民事案件转化为刑事案件	件 case	126	138	94	57
Prevent Intensification of Civil Disputes	人 person	378	330	238	243
防止非正常死亡案件	件 case	52	67	48	27
Avoid Injuries and Deaths	人 person	71	42	80	34

18－5　律师工作基本情况
BASIC STATISTICS ON LAWYERS

项　目　Item	单　位　Unit	2000	2001	2002	2003
律师事务所 Law Offices	所 unit	172	179	199	210
职业律师 Lawyers	人 person	1 882	2 081	2 177	1 729
# 专职律师 Full－time Lawyers	人 person	903	1 313	1 398	1 618
兼职律师 Part－time Lawyers	人 person	349	263	304	111
聘请常年法律顾问的单位 Units with Permanent Legal A advisers isers	家 unit	6 650	3 330	3 093	6 026
民事代理 Civil Case	件 case	10 052	8 930	9 782	10 632
经济代理 Economic Case	件 case	6 791	6 071	6 486	6 084
刑事辩护 Criminal Defense	件 case	4 922	4 907	4 130	3 619
行政诉讼代理 Agent of Administrative Action	件 case	213	287	528	372
非诉讼事务 Off－court Case	件 case	7 672	8 785	8 135	17 621
解答法律咨询 Legal Advisory Services	人次 person－times	34 929	26 535	60 741	23 774
代写法律文书 Legal Document Written on Behalf of Clients	件 case	10 414	11 740	10 427	7 966

18－6　部分基层法律服务所主要业务情况(2003 年)
STATISTICS FOR MAJOR BASIC LAW OFFICES, 2003

地　区　Region	担任常年法律顾问(家) Acted as Permanent Legal Advisers (unit)	代理诉讼事务(件) Agent For Lawsuit Case (case)	代理非诉讼事务(件) Agent For Non－litigation Action (case)	代写法律文书(份) Legal Documents Written on Behalf of Clients (case)	协办公证(件) Deal Notarization Jointly (case)	解答法律咨询(人次) Legal Advisory Services (person－times)
总　计　Total	**515**	**2 258**	**915**	**4 324**	**179**	**15 942**
和平区 Heping District	2	52	11	28		121
河东区 Hedong District	8	85	11	120		1 300
河西区 Hexi District	8	34	6	54		303
南开区 Nankai District	31	321	149	451		1 687
河北区 Hebei District	8	173	38	219		1 242
红桥区 Hongqiao District	28	244	8	57	5	306
塘沽区 Tanggu District	4	24	2	21		288
汉沽区 Hangu District	10	87	11	179		321
大港区 Dagang District	33	35	28	77		712
东丽区 Dongli District	4	80	3	352		614
西青区 Xiqing District	20	332	164	767	18	1 446
津南区 Jinnan District	44	142	78	150	69	1 250
北辰区 Beichen District	113	156	137	456	11	666
武清区 Wuqing District	2	163	8	310	20	238
宝坻区 Baodi District	12	128	47	498	12	1 272
宁河县 Ninghe County	58	20	26	95		620
静海县 Jinghai County	38	40	54	174	44	1 036
蓟　县 Jixian County	92	142	134	316		2 520

18－7　公证工作
NOTARIZATION

项　目	Item	单　位	Unit	2000	2001	2002	2003
公证机构	Notary Offices	个	unit	20	20	20	21
公证员	Notarial Personnel	人	person	278	259	253	262
办理公证	Notarized Documents	件	case	175 486	188 641	159 238	182 581
国内公证	Domestic Affairs	件	case	107 198	113 945	87 392	125 682
#经济公证	Economic Affairs	件	case	69 949	66 128	56 818	57 594
涉外公证	Foreign Affairs	件	case	67 803	74 237	71 246	56 899

18－8 主要年份国内公证文书分类情况
DOMESTIC NOTARIAL DOCUMENTS BY TYPE IN MAIN YESRS

单位：件 (case)

项 目	Item	1990	1995	2000	2003
民事公证数总计	**Civil Legal Relations Notarized Total**	**15 224**	**35 055**	**37 249**	**68 088**
#收 养	Child Adoption	691	398	172	84
解除收养	Adoption Renouncements	11	44	3	3
继 承 权	Rights of Inheritance	2 275	2 378	3 526	6 376
遗 嘱	Testaments	818	804	1 606	842
亲属关系	Kinship Confirmation	102	252	429	250
房屋买卖	Purchases and Sales of House	29	660	2 926	5 216
房屋租赁	House Leases	55	198	12	362
委 托 书	Certificate of Entrustment	256	874	1 463	6 067
赠 予 书	Presentation Documents	2 342	3 334	2 453	1 180
声 明 书	Declarations	475	642	2 390	2 481
经济公证数总计	**Business Notarized Total**	**11 420**	**47 261**	**69 949**	**57 594**
#购 销	Purchases and Sales of Contracts	315	485	38	582
联 营	Joint Business Contracts	77	42	3	3
贷 款	Loans Contracts	3 548	16 572	44 570	36 305
招标投标	Bidding	169	227	385	793
劳务合同	Labour Contracts	1 863	1 660	426	2
建筑工程承包	Construction Project Contracts	362	521	178	446
农林牧副渔业承包	Farming,Forestry,Animal Husbandry,Sideline	1 152	492	783	652
财产租赁	Property Leases	189	2 831	620	3 067
法人资格	Legal Person Identification	244	782	153	46
法人委托书	Legal Person Certificate of Entrustment	317	303	401	3 039

18－9 主要年份涉外公证文书分类情况
FOREIGN－RELATED NOTARIAL DOCUMENTS BY TYPE IN MAIN YESRS

单位：件 (case)

类 别	Types	1990	1995	2000	2003
总 计	**Total**	**9 736**	**29 495**	**67 803**	**56 899**
#出 生	Births	1 165	4 254	11 308	6 842
学 历	Schooling	1 759	5 632	11 919	6 955
经 历	Personal Histories	769	1 845	2 517	1 182
生存、居住	Survial and Residence	4		89	41
死 亡	Deaths	19		120	78
收 养	Children Adoption				84
亲属关系	Kinship	1 293	2 011	5 313	4 899
婚姻状况	Marriages	1 092	3 056	5 067	3 534
继承权	Rights of Inheritance	2		3	6 376
遗 嘱	Testaments	5			842
委托书	Trust Deeds	97		244	351
声明书	Declarations	9		450	697
受、未受刑事处分	Criminal Reeords & Undcriminal Records		3 444	9 131	6 438
文本相符	Confirmation of Copies and Photo－Offset Copies to Originals	276	581	7 445	9 455
其 他	Others	1 468	2 241	3 411	4 433

18－10 基层工会组织情况
STATISTICS ON GRASSROOTS UNIONS

项 目	Item	2000	2001	2002	2003
机构数(个)	**Institutions(unit)**	**15 029**	**22 361**	**13 947**	**12 440**
#国有企业	State－owned Enterprises		2 449	2 538	2 278
集体企业	Collective－owned Enterprises		2 011	1 850	1 862
私营企业	Private Enterprises		5 875	1 780	1 726
港澳台商投资企业	Enterprises with Investment from Homgkong, Macao and Taiwan		433	212	162
外商投资企业	Foreign Funded Enterprises		1 984	1 527	1 215
事 业	Institutions		2 574	2 615	2 979
机 关	Agencies		797	744	902
#建立职工代表大会制度的单位	Unit of Founding Employee Congress System	6 497	6 759	6 659	5 415
#建立平等协商集体合同制度单位	Unit of Founding Equal & Consultabe Collective Contract System		8 370	4 504	5 570
职工人数(人)	**Staff and Workers (person)**	**1 933 400**	**2 516 984**	**2 759 122**	**1 984 048**
#国有企业	State－owned Enterprises		950 947	1 045 361	805 061
集体企业	Collective－owned Enterprises		237 947	288 713	251 563
私营企业	Private Enterprises		129 202	108 924	125 662
港澳台商投资企业	Enterprises with Investment from Homgkong, Macao and Taiwan		29 937	33 680	16 026
外商投资企业	Foreign Funded Enterprises		213 584	178 955	119 011
事 业	Institutions		288 747	548 533	321 334
机 关	Agencies		75 676	84 984	85 860
#女职工	Female	971 802		894 837	798 939
#工会专职干部	Full－time Personnel	1 112	1 212	959	970

注:2003年职工人数不包括离退休及不在岗职工。
Note: In 2003, staff and workers exclude VCSR, RRSW and those who are not on the job.

18－11 妇联组织情况
STATISTICS FOR WOMAN FEDERATION ORGANIZATIONS

项 目	Item	2000	2001	2002	2003
妇联组织机构(个)	**Woman Organizations(unit)**	**319**	**268**	**290**	**253**
区妇联	District Woman Organizations	14	15	15	15
县妇联	County Woman Organizations	4	3	3	3
乡妇联	Township Woman Organizations	215	153	177	140
街妇联	Street Woman Organizations	86	97	95	95
妇联干部总数(人)	**Cadres in Woman Organizations(person)**	**570**	**570**	**570**	**484**
市妇联	Municipal Woman Organizations	74	74	74	66
区妇联	District Woman Organizations	101	101	101	119
县妇联	County Woman Organizations	55	55	55	22
乡镇、街道妇联	Township and Street Woman Organizations	340	340	340	277

18－12 妇联工作情况
WOMAN FEDERATION WORKS

项　目　Item	单　位　Unit		2000	2001	2002	2003
双学双比活动						
Double Study And Double Compare Activity						
实用技术培训情况						
Training of Practical Technology						
接受技术培训的妇女数						
Women Received Technology Training	人	person	263 807	208 172	163 239	152 426
女农民技术员						
Female Peasant Technician	人	person	8 443	3 823	8 035	3 010
获绿色证书人数						
Persons Obtaining Green Certificate	人	person	9 007	5 608	10 200	4 166
扶贫情况						
Poverty Helping						
"三八"绿色基地个数						
Number of "3.8" Green Base	个	unit	70	151	92	88
脱贫户数						
Number of Female of Escaping from Poverty	人	person	5 562	2 623	3 952	3 086
巾帼建功活动						
Activity of Women Making Contribution						
岗位建功成材						
Making Professional Contribution						
评选巾帼文明示范岗数						
Number of Civilization Post Chosen	个	unit	134	313	188	132
表彰标兵数						
Number of Prised Pacesetter	人	person	164	2 172	2 343	2 325
下岗女工再就业情况						
Reemployment of Laid－off Female Workers						
培训下岗女工人数						
Laid－off Trained	人	person	22 062	17 773	17 826	19 431
介绍下岗女工就业人数						
Laid－off Introduced to Employ	人	person	19 395	21 902	17 781	5 835
三八红旗手						
"3.8" Advanced Individual	人	person	713	2 480	1 969	554
三八红旗集体						
"3.8" Advanced Collectivity	个	unit	165	640	414	140
五好文明家庭						
"Five Good" Families	户	household	1 638	142 649	38 329	41 256
家庭教育场所						
Families Educational Places						
家长学校						
Householder School	个	unit	3 243	1 730	1 577	2 034
广播电视父母学校						
Broadcasting Parents School	个	unit	99	257	513	162
实施春蕾计划						
Actualizing Spring Bud Project						
资助女童入学或返校数						
Supporting Female Child Entering School	人	person	826	1 372	1 213	1 278
社会捐资总额						
Total of Social Donation	万元	10 000 yuan	63	50	99	80

18－13　受理消费者投诉情况(2003 年)

BASIC STATISTICS ON ACCEPTED CASES OF CONSUMER INSTITUTION,2003

项目	Item	总计 Total	质量 Quality	安全 Safety	价格 Price
一、受理投诉件数总计(件)	**Total Number of Accepted Cases(item)**	**4 083**	**3 217**	**72**	**172**
1.家用电子电器类	Household Electric Appliance	1 015	894	4	12
电视机	Television Set	160	135	1	
家庭影院	Household Cinema	21	19		
空调器类产品	Air－conditioner	112	86		1
洗衣机类产品	Washing Machines	23	18		1
电冰箱(冰柜)	Refrigerators(Freezers)	58	53	1	
厨房电器及相关产品	Kitchen Electric Appliances and Relative Product	48	45	1	
照摄像产品	Camera and DV	4	3		
通讯类产品	Telecommunications Product	483	457	1	8
#移动电话	Mobile Phone	392	368	1	2
计算机类产品	Computer Series	54	38		2
#计算机	Computer	35	29		2
其　他	Others	52	40		
2.家用机械类	Household Machinery	283	241	4	3
汽　车	Car	55	40	1	1
摩托车	Motorcycle	69	65		1
热水器	Water Heater	53	47	2	
其　他	Others	106	89	1	1
3.百货类	Daily Using Commodities	1 825	1 456	37	98
#化妆用品	Cosmetic	33	23	8	1
保健用品	Health Care Goods	19	15	2	
家俱类产品	Furniture	169	152		2
服装鞋帽	Garments,Shoes & hat	858	711		65
文化体育用品	Cultural and Sports Goods	34	29	1	
食　品	Foodstuff	408	304	17	10
保健食品	Health Care Foodstuff	19	13	2	1
药　品	Medicine	41	14	4	15
医疗辅助用品	Medical Treatment Articles	14	11	1	
4.房屋及装修建材	House and Decoration Materials	267	191	5	11
#房　屋	House	72	50		4
装修建材	Decoration Materials	156	115	5	7
5.农用生产资料类	Agricultural Production Materials	87	78	5	
#种子苗木、化肥	Seed,Young Plant,Chemical Fertilizer	42	41		
6.服务类	Service	536	319	14	46
#美　容	Hairdressing	59	39	3	4
邮　电	Posts and Telecommunications	41	14		14
洗衣业	Laundry	115	96	2	0
旅　游	Tourism	13	6	1	2
房屋装修与物业管理	Building Decoration and Property Management	59	43	0	1
7.其他商品类	Other Commodities	70	38	3	2
二、解决件数总计(件)	**Total Cases Solved(item)**	**3 968**			
三、为消费者挽回损失(万元)	**Exempting Expense for Consumers(10 000 yuan)**	**1 098.76**			

注:本资料为天津市消费者协会系统的统计数据,不含各监测站的统计资料。
Note: The data of this table are provided by Tianjin Municipal Consumer Institution,exclude those data calculated by each monitor station.

18－13 续表 Continued

项 目	Item	计 量 Measure	广 告 Adverti－sement	假 冒 Counter－feit	其 他 Other
一、受理投诉件数总计(件)	**Total Number of Accepted Cases(item)**	**98**	**20**	**9**	**495**
1.家用电子电器类	Household Electric Appliance		8	2	95
电视机	Television Set		2		22
家庭影院	Household Cinema		1		1
空调器类产品	Air－conditioner		1		24
洗衣机类产品	Washing Machines				4
电冰箱(冰柜)	Refrigerators(Freezers)				4
厨房电器及相关产品	Kitchen Electric Appliances and Relative Product				2
照摄像产品	Camera and DV		1		
通讯类产品	Telecommunications Product		1	2	14
#移动电话	Mobile Phone			2	19
计算机类产品	Computer Series		2		12
#计算机	Computer		1		3
其 他	Others				12
2.家用机械类	Household Machinery	2	2		31
汽 车	Car	1	1		11
摩托车	Motorcycle				3
热水器	Water Heater				4
其 他	Others	1	1		13
3.百货类	Daily Using Commodities	78	3	5	148
#化妆用品	Cosmetic				1
保健用品	Health Care Goods		1		1
家俱类产品	Furniture				15
服装鞋帽	Garments,Shoes & hat	11		2	69
文化体育用品	Cultural and Sports Goods	1			3
食 品	Foodstuff	47	1	1	28
保健食品	Health Care Foodstuff				3
药 品	Medicine	1			7
医疗辅助用品	Medical Treatment Articles				2
4.房屋及装修建材	House and Decoration Materials	5	1		54
#房 屋	House	1			17
装修建材	Decoration Materials		1		28
5.农用生产资料类	Agricultural Production Materials	2			2
#种子苗木、化肥	Seed,Young Plant,Chemical Fertilizer	1			
6.服务类	Service	7	5	1	144
#美 容	Hairdressing	2			11
邮 电	Posts and Telecommunications	2	1		10
洗衣业	Laundry				17
旅 游	Tourism				4
房屋装修与物业管理	Building Decoration and Property Management				15
7.其他商品类	Other Commodities	4	1	1	21
二、解决件数总计(件)	**Total Cases Solved(item)**				
三、为消费者挽回损失(万元)	**Exempting Expense for Consumers(10 000 yuan)**				

第19篇 CHAPTER 19

滨海新区

NEW COASTAL AREA

19-1 滨海新区
MAIN STATISTICS ON
(1994 -

项　目	Item	1994	1995
户籍人口(万人)	Registered Population(10 000 persons)	99.82	100.24
#非农业人口	Non-agricultural Population	69.57	70.28
从业人员期末人数(万人)	Number of Persons Employed Year-end(10 000 persons)	50.03	55.81
从业人员劳动报酬(亿元)	Total Remuneration of Persons Employed(100 million yuan)		46.25
从业人员人均劳动报酬(元)	Per Capita Remuneration of Persons Employed(yuan)		8 287
地区生产总值(亿元)	Gross Domestic Product(100 million yuan)	168.66	241.64
第一产业	Primary Industry	3.36	4.74
第二产业	Secondary Industry	114.55	166.90
第三产业	Tertiary Industry	50.75	70.00
地区生产总值增长速度(%)	Increase Rate of Gross Domestic Product over Preceding Year(%)	27.6	27.3
地区生产总值占全市比重(%)	Percentage of the City's GDP(%)	23.3	26.3
农业总产值(亿元)	Gross Output Value of Agriculture(100 million yuan)	6.92	9.01
工业总产值(亿元)	Gross Output Value of Industry(100 million yuan)	346.27	510.34
全社会固定资产投资(亿元)	Total Investment In Fixed Assets (100 million yuan)	108.03	152.40
#基础设施	Infrastructure	15.50	20.62
市重点项目	Key Projects	38.98	29.30
全社会固定资产投资占全市比重(%)	Percentage of the City's Total Investment In Fixed Assets(%)	34.2	38.8
区级地方一般预算财政收入(亿元)	General Budgetary Financial Revenue at District Level(100 million yuan)	7.82	12.77
区级地方一般预算财政支出(亿元)	General Budgetary Financial Expenditures at District Level(100 million yuan)	13.03	23.17
社会消费品零售总额(亿元)	Total Retail Sales of Consumer Goods(100 million yuan)	25.92	33.85
外贸出口总额(亿美元)	Exports(USD 100 million)	5.90	10.10
外贸出口总额占全市比重(%)	Percentage of the City's Exports(%)	24.6	33.7
直接利用外资合同数(个)	Number of Foreign Investment Enterprises Newly Signed	987	761
直接利用外资合同金额(亿美元)	Contract Foreign Capital of Foreign Investment Enterprises Newly Signed(USD 100 million)	16.04	18.41
直接利用外资合同金额占全市比重(%)	Percentage of the City's Contract Foreign Capital(%)	45.8	47.8
实际直接利用外资(亿美元)	Actual Direct Utilization of Foreign Capital(USD 100 million)		
内联协议合同数(个)	Number of Projects Signed Contracts(unit)	193	102
外地在津投资协议额(亿元)	Total Domestic Investment Signed in Tianjin(100 million)	3.67	4.12
外地在津投资实际到位额(亿元)	Total Domestic Investment Actually Used in Tianjin(100 million)		3.66

注:2003年直接利用外资采用商务部新口径,速度为可比口径,19-4、19-7、19-8、19-10、19-11、19-12表同。
Note:In 2003,Direct Utilization of Foreign Capital is calculated on new coverage of the Ministry of Commerce,the growth rate is calculated on the basis of comparable coverage,same as following table 19-4,19-7,19-8,19-10,19-11 and 19-12.

主要经济指标
NEW COASTAL AREA
2003）

1996	1997	1998	1999	2000	2001	2002	2003	2003 比2002年 增长% Increase Rate in 2003 over 2002
100.79	101.08	102.70	103.86	104.59	105.35	106.38	107.05	0.6
72.31	73.15	74.94	76.86	78.03	78.99	80.27	81.05	1.0
58.31	59.81	55.31	56.53	55.31	56.16	55.25	58.93	6.7
55.54	62.17	66.30	70.68	77.77	85.53	99.58	116.68	17.2
9525	10 707	11 754	11 825	14 011	15 281	18 086	20 468	13.2
320.29	382.06	416.96	464.35	562.40	667.14	820.52	999.75	20.4
4.84	4.92	5.39	4.86	5.24	5.73	6.16	7.39	17.1
224.78	262.72	264.04	299.07	382.08	452.25	567.65	693.18	20.8
90.67	114.42	147.53	160.42	175.08	209.16	246.71	299.18	19.6
28.3	20.0	13.8	14.7	18.3	17.8	20.1	20.4	
29.1	30.9	31.2	32.0	34.3	36.5	40.0	40.9	
9.86	9.96	11.52	10.71	11.44	12.80	14.02	15.81	11.5
701.44	864.05	895.50	986.00	1 244.43	1 463.38	1 700.04	2 133.21	30.3
157.05	155.83	178.76	173.50	184.34	243.45	280.89	464.08	65.2
26.29	32.82	42.54	52.18	58.04	68.20	85.62	122.57	43.2
26.80	30.89	38.76	48.11	52.35	82.24	73.20	105.64	44.3
36.0	31.2	31.1	30.6	35.0	34.5	34.6	44.3	
20.43	24.32	24.59	28.26	39.13	45.86	44.66	44.34	-0.7
45.29	29.61	28.23	30.87	41.40	51.90	62.66	68.96	10.1
46.90	57.21	64.12	69.69	104.48	118.61	134.22	156.11	16.3
17.46	24.33	28.09	30.01	44.62	54.31	72.01	89.38	24.1
43.1	48.5	49.3	47.4	51.7	57.2	62.1	62.2	
606	623	658	346	292	276	343	458	33.5
18.67	21.12	18.47	19.25	33.09	32.03	15.47	24.52	58.5
47.6	54.8	50.8	53.2	71.9	69.2	76.8	69.8	
				14.23	24.49	8.23	12.15	47.6
123	156	63	48	284	133	138	503	264.5
6.24	11.32	13.33	10.98	14.78	15.53	21.58	36.12	67.4
5.21	6.51	6.55	6.04	7.99	10.65	14.59	25.41	74.2

19－2　滨海新区生产总值
GROSS DOMESTIC PRODUCT OF NEW COASTAL AREA

项　　目	Item	1993	2000	2001	2002	2003
绝对数(亿元)	**Value(100 million yuan)**					
地区生产总值	Gross Domestic Product	112.36	562.40	667.14	820.52	999.75
第一产业	Primary Industry	2.43	5.24	5.73	6.16	7.39
第二产业	Secondary Industry	74.09	382.08	452.25	567.65	693.18
第三产业	Tertiary Industry	35.84	175.08	209.16	246.71	299.18
环比增长速度(%)	**Increase Rate Over Preceding Year(%)**					
地区生产总值	Gross Domestic Product		18.3	17.8	20.1	20.4
第一产业	Primary Industry		4.7	8.9	7.1	17.1
第二产业	Secondary Industry		22.5	18.6	21.8	20.8
第三产业	Tertiary Industry		6.9	16.2	16.6	19.6
三次产业构成(%)	**Composition of Three Industries as Percentage(%)**					
地区生产总值	Gross Domestic Product	100.0	100.0	100.0	100.0	100.0
第一产业	Primary Industry	2.2	0.9	0.9	0.7	0.7
第二产业	Secondary Industry	65.9	67.9	67.8	69.2	69.3
第三产业	Tertiary Industry	31.9	31.1	31.4	30.1	30.0
占全市比重(%)	**Percentage of The City's GDP(%)**					
地区生产总值	Gross Domestic Product	21.0	34.3	36.5	40.0	40.9
第一产业	Primary Industry	6.9	7.1	7.3	7.3	8.2
第二产业	Secondary Industry	24.5	47.1	50.7	56.7	55.7
第三产业	Tertiary Industry	18.1	23.2	24.4	25.6	26.9

19－3　滨海新区基础设施投资完成情况
INFRASTRUCTURE INVESTMENT OF NEW COASTAL AREA

单位:万元　　　　(10 000 yuan)

项　　目	Item	2000	2001	2002	2003	2003 比2002年增长% Increase Rate in 2003 over 2002
合　　计	**Total**	**580 376**	**681 998**	**856 168**	**1 225 676**	**43.2**
铁路和轨道交通	Railway and Track Transportation	32 200	19 855	182 427	247 176	35.5
道路桥梁	Road and Bridge	137 258	239 145	219 427	230 354	5.0
港　口	Port	130 625	153 271	164 214	146 713	-10.7
排　水	Drainage	9 458	14 923	13 339	25 622	92.1
供　水	Water Supply	2 329	6 207	10 243	2 333	-77.2
供电供热	Power and Heat Supply	38 500	33 077	31 134	25 255	-18.9
通　讯	Communication	19 283	22 354	14 493	1 500	-89.7
绿化和环境工程	Afforest and Environment Engineering	21 218	84 364	73 585	110 983	50.8
其　他	Others	189 505	108 802	147 306	435 740	195.8

19－4　滨海新区直接利用外资情况(2003 年)

DIRECT UTILIZATION OF FOREIGN CAPITAL OF NEW COASTAL AREA(2003)

项　目	Item	直接利用外资合同数(个) Number of Contracts (unit)	直接利用外资合同金　额(万美元) Foreign Invest－ment Contracted (USD 10 000)	实际直接利用外资金　额(万美元) Actual Direct Utilization of Foreign Capital (USD 10 000)
合　计	**Total**	**458**	**245 212**	**121 486**
按投资方式分	**By Mode of Investment**			
合资企业	Joint Venture Enterprises	99	32 011	35 711
合作企业	Cooperative Operation Enterprises	5	1 286	12 296
独资企业	Foreign－funded Sole Enterprises	354	211 916	73 479
按行业分	**By Sector**			
农　业	Agriculture	1	1 000	
采矿业	Minerals Mining			10 167
制造业	Manufacturing	203	4 090	2 229
建筑业	Construction	2	135 734	63 098
交通运输及仓储业	Transportation and Storage	1	121	5 112
批发零售及餐饮业	Wholesale,Retail Trade and Catering	169	43 258	24 087
房地产业	Real Estate	38	10 299	5 605
社会服务业	Social Services	33	43 709	10 507
其他行业	Others	11	7 001	680
按国别、地区分	**By Country(Region)**			
#中国香港	Hongkong,China	82	60 747	31 264
中国台湾	Taiwan,China	27	4 139	4 241
韩　国	Republic of Korea	75	22 288	11 640
日　本	Japan	55	40 488	17 147
美　国	United States	75	35 567	21 058
新加坡	Singapore	16	3 097	2 726
英　国	United Kingdom	8	1 680	1 846
德　国	Germany	11	10 347	6 108
法　国	France	3	2 128	1 447
意大利	Italy	2	1 331	195
英属维尔京群岛	Virgin Islands of United Kingdom	29	13 636	7 895

19－5　滨海新区城市市政设施

MUNICIPAL INFRASTRUCTURE OF NEW COASTAL AREA

项　目	Item	2000	2001	2002	2003	2003 比 2002 年 增长% Increase Rate in 2003 over 2002
铺装道路长度(公里)	Length of Paved Roads(km)	1 058.91	1 085.47	1 096.82	1 135.56	3.5
铺装道路面积(万平方米)	Area of Paved Roads(10^4 sq.m)	1 167.69	1 143.11	1 191.60	1 333.49	11.9
桥梁座数(座)	Number of Bridges(unit)	123	153	154	153	－0.6
#立交桥(座)	Flyover(unit)	17	19	20	23	15.0
排水水泵站(座)	Pumping Station(unit)	112	113	116	136	17.2
排水管道长度(公里)	Length of Drainpipes(km)	1 461.02	1 496.19	1 549.55	1 684.14	8.7

19－6 滨海新区区级地方一般预算财政收支情况

LOCAL GENERAL BUDGETARY FINANCIAL REVENUE AND EXPENDITURE OF NEW COASTAL AREA

项目	Item	1993	2000	2001	2002	2003
绝对数(万元)	**Value(10 000 yuan)**					
财政收入	**Financial Revenue**	**79 313**	**391 293**	**458 638**	**446 621**	**443 394**
增值税	Value－added Tax		78 104	122 191	133 484	143 132
营业税	Operation Tax		74 685	88 274	109 823	110 082
企业收入	Enterprises Income	6 417	148 574	156 859	111 553	81 856
个人所得税	Private Income Tax		29 781	42 092	23 139	21 995
城市维护建设税	City Maintenance and Construction Tax	4 446	12 445	12 285	14 032	16 216
农业五税	Five Taxes of Agriculture		2 068	3 158	4 976	9 342
其他各项收入	Others	68 450	45 636	33 779	49 614	60 771
财政支出	**Financial Expenditure**	**74 529**	**413 972**	**518 953**	**626 560**	**689 604**
基本建设支出	Capital Construction	24 623	159 503	168 429	212 065	264 454
农林水利气象支出	Administration of Hydraulic and Meteoro－logical Branch on Farming & Forestry	859	2 590	2 417	2 827	4 049
教育支出	Administration of Education	11 431	35 294	36 000	41 742	51 058
社会保障补助支出	Subsidies of Social Welfare		2 792	3 268	4 379	4 731
行政管理费	Administration Cost	6 020	12 062	16 008	21 277	45 746
公检法司支出	Public Security, Judicial Agencies and Justice System	1 962	9 795	12 346	14 569	20 038
其他各项支出	Others	29 634	191 936	280 485	329 701	299 528
占全市同级比重(%)	**Percentage of the City's Total(%)**					
财政收入	**Financial Revenue**	**28.3**	**51.7**	**48.6**	**47.9**	**44.6**
增值税	Value－added Tax		51.6	56.6	54.8	61.6
营业税	Operation Tax		38.6	37.7	37.4	39.5
企业收入	Enterprises Income		70.0	59.1	66.0	63.3
个人所得税	Private Income Tax		42.7	43.0	40.9	47.9
城市维护建设税	City Maintenance and Construction Tax		75.6	70.9	65.7	33.6
农业五税	Five Taxes of Agriculture		21.0	21.9	20.2	9.9
其他各项收入	Others		43.8	34.8	40.5	36.8
财政支出	**Financial Expenditure**	**32.3**	**45.3**	**44.1**	**44.3**	**45.6**
基本建设支出	Capital Construction	84.5	79.6	73.9	74.0	69.4
农林水利气象支出	Administration of Hydraulic and Meteoro－logical Branch on Farming & Forestry	20.4	25.9	20.9	20.8	16.3
教育支出	Administration of Education	19.1	17.3	15.0	15.1	18.6
社会保障补助支出	Subsidies of Social Welfare		61.9	56.5	46.6	69.8
行政管理费	Administration Cost	28.3	19.9	20.5	22.2	39.2
公检法司支出	Public Security, Judicial Agencies and Justice System	19.0	20.4	20.5	21.5	28.4
其他各项支出	Others	27.9	49.5	50.7	49.6	46.9

19－7 建区以来经济技术开发区国民经济主要指标
MAIN STATISTICS ON ECONOMIC－TECHNOLOGICAL DEVELOPMENT AREA SINCE ITS ESTABLISHMENT

年份 Year	地区生产总值（万元）Gross Domestic Product (10 000 yuan)	工业总产值（万元）Gross Output Value of Industry (10 000 yuan)	#外商及港澳台投资企业 Foreign Funded Enterprises	工业产品销售收入（万元）Sales Revenue of Industrial Product (10 000 yuan)	#外商及港澳台投资企业 Foreign Funded Enterprises
1985					
1986	935	3 872	3 872	1 994	1 994
1987	8 765	18 873	17 373	10 814	9 805
1988	19 282	36 500	33 500	33 945	31 561
1989	18 437	46 518	41 630	46 937	41 424
1990	25 011	78 060	68 859	73 767	60 546
1991	67 129	187 019	163 370	157 434	139 924
1992	128 274	320 762	294 137	288 577	264 635
1993	254 591	702 517	675 260	653 382	624 162
1994	487 678	1 490 806	1 469 665	1 377 942	1 349 440
1995	801 102	2 664 551	2 621 361	2 526 011	2 483 428
1996	1 310 135	3 701 106	3 646 558	3 617 960	3 563 872
1997	1 536 270	4 702 422	4 590 240	4 630 014	4 519 091
1998	1 801 056	5 402 180	5 203 573	5 337 354	5 141 130
1999	2 084 516	6 085 483	5 863 637	6 018 543	5 802 137
2000	2 564 432	7 318 248	7 089 316	7 274 338	7 049 651
2001	3 120 259	8 651 050	8 394 351	8 633 748	8 378 463
2002	3 800 899	10 312 373	10 016 307	10 291 748	9 996 025
2003	4 452 278	12 513 994	12 158 648	12 494 722	12 143 923

年份 Year	直接利用外资合同数（个）Number of Foreign Funded Enterprises Newly Signed (unit)	直接利用外资项目合同投资总额（万美元）Contract Investment of Foreign Funded Enterprises Newly Signed (USD 10 000)	出口总额（万美元）Exports (USD 10 000)	从业人员（人）Persons Employed (person)	#外商及港澳台投资企业 Foreign Funded Enterprises
1985	15	3 192		823	137
1986	27	4 342	202	1 504	667
1987	34	2 280	1 616	6 397	3 000
1988	48	8 482	3 780	8 635	4 493
1989	40	10 569	4 604	8 014	5 801
1990	54	12 237	6 370	14 462	8 115
1991	121	18 565	11 348	21 419	12 010
1992	462	70 261	16 022	37 914	21 071
1993	909	123 536	29 235	55 189	34 553
1994	487	152 278	54 426	84 218	61 152
1995	361	181 129	90 103	112 874	79 682
1996	187	191 604	145 020	140 150	99 853
1997	172	149 576	200 415	157 934	113 473
1998	194	148 207	208 135	171 604	121 093
1999	106	142 884	255 380	180 466	127 156
2000	99	277 902	326 691	191 058	134 496
2001	94	248 779	403 531	195 012	137 702
2002	109	260 675	570 563	205 884	146 808
2003	167	233 952	688 617	231 957	159 666

19－8 经济技术开发区国民经济主要指标
MAIN STATISTICS ON ECONOMIC－TECHNOLOGICAL DEVELOPMENT AREA

项 目	Item	2002	2003	2003 比2002年增长% Increase Rate in 2003 over 2002
1.地区生产总值(万元)	Gross Domestic Product (10 000 yuan)	3 800 899	4 452 278	25.1
第二产业	Secondary Industry	2 998 874	3 548 992	28.3
#工 业	Industry	2 967 824	3 511 682	28.4
第三产业	Tertiary Industry	802 025	903 286	11.5
#交通、仓储及邮电通信业	Transportation, Storage, Post and Telecommunications	63 092	78 159	28.9
批发和零售贸易、餐饮业	Wholesale, Retail Tade and Catering Business	319 013	339 349	8.7
金融、保险业	Banking and Insurance	116 235	136 895	13.3
房地产业	Real Estate	83 356	110 268	26.3
2.工业产品销售收入(万元)	Sales Revenue of Industrial Products (10 000 yuan)	10 291 748	12 494 722	21.4
#外商及港澳台投资企业	Foreign Funded Enterprises	9 996 025	12 143 923	21.5
3.工业总产值(万元)	Gross Output Value of Industry (10 000 yuan)	10 312 373	12 513 994	30.2
#外商及港澳台投资企业	Foreign Funded Enterprises	10 016 037	12 158 648	30.3
4.出口总额(万美元)	Exports (USD 10 000)	570 563	688 617	20.7
5.直接利用外资合同数(个)	Number of Foreign Funded Enterprises Newly Signed(unit)	111	167	50.5
6.直接利用外资合同额(万美元)	Foreign Capital Contracted (USD 10 000)	89 324	127 751	43.0
7.实际直接利用外资金额(万美元)	Actual Direct Utilization of Foreign Capital(USD 10 000)	41 000	63 251	54.3
8.从业人员(人)	Persons Employed (person)	205 884	231 957	12.7
外商及港澳台投资企业	Foreign Funded Enterprises	146 808	159 666	8.8
内资企业	Domestic Funded Enterprises	59 076	72 291	22.4
按产业分组	Grouped by Industry			
第二产业	Secondary Industry	151 050	172 169	14.0
第三产业	Tertiary Industry	54 834	59 788	9.0
9.从业人员人均劳动报酬(元)	Per Capita Remuneration of Persons Employed (yuan)	16 836	19 020	13.0

19－9　经济技术开发区城市建设情况

（截止 2003 年底）

URBAN CONSTRUCTION OF THE ECONOMIC－TECHNOLOGICAL DEVELOPMENT AREA

(By the End of 2003)

项　目	Item	单　位	Unit	数　量 Amount
累计房屋开工面积	Total Floor Space Under Construction	万平方米	10 000 sq. m	1 056.67
#2003 年	in 2003			217.26
累计房屋竣工面积	Total Floor Space Completed	万平方米	10 000 sq. m	660.38
#2003 年	in 2003			67.90
已开发土地面积	Developed Area	平方公里	sq. km	37
桥　梁	Bridge	座	unit	9
路　灯	Street Lamp	盏	unit	8 950
绿化面积	Area of Green Land	万平方米	10 000 sq. m	586.1
公交客运车辆	Number of Public Passenger Vehicles	辆	unit	567
出租车辆	Number of Taxis	辆	unit	847
客运总量	Passenger Traffic	万人次	10 000 person－times	763

19－10　经济技术开发区外商及港澳台投资企业批准情况(1985－2003 年)

MAIN STATISTICS ON FOREIGN FUNDED ENTERPRISES APPROVED OF ECONOMIC－TECHNOLOGICAL DEVELOPMENT AREA, 1985－2003

年　份 Year	直接利用外资合同数(个) Number of Foreign Funded Enterprises Approved(unit)	直接利用外资项目合同投资总额(万美元) Contract Investment (USD 10 000)	#直接利用外资合同金　额(万美元) Contract Foreign Capital (USD 10 000)
1985－2003 年累计 Total of 1985－2003	**3 685**	**2 240 450**	**1 837 015**
1985	14	3 192	1 436
1986	27	4 342	1 693
1987	34	2 280	844
1988	48	8 482	4 835
1989	40	10 569	6 764
1990	54	12 237	10 034
1991	121	18 565	12 653
1992	462	70 261	50 685
1993	909	123 536	75 853
1994	487	152 278	119 908
1995	361	181 129	158 959
1996	187	191 604	158 846
1997	172	149 576	130 815
1998	194	148 207	122 845
1999	106	142 884	127 987
2000	99	277 902	264 034
2001	94	248 779	220 008
2002	109	260 675	241 065
2003	167	233 952	127 751

注：表中数字以核发批准证书为准。

Note: The figures of this table are calculated according to the certificate of agreement.

19－11　经济技术开发区外商及港澳台投资企业按投资方式及国别(地区)分类

(截止2003年底)

TEDA'S FOREIGN FUNDED ENTERPRISES BY INVESTING WAY AND COUNTRY(REGION)

(By the End of 2003)

国别(地区) Country (Region)		企业个数(个) Number of Enterprises(unit)	直接利用外资项目合同投资总额(万美元) Contract Investment (USD 10 000)	#直接利用外资合同金额(万美元) Contract Foreign Investment(USD 10 000)
合　计	**Total**	**1 993**	**1 668 970**	**700 192**
按投资方式分	**Grouped by Investing Way**			
合资企业	Joint Ventures	849	695 460	259 211
合作企业	Cooperative Enterprises	57	74 770	25 207
独资企业	Sole－foreign Enterprises	1 087	898 740	415 774
按国别、地区分	**Grouped by Country, Region**			
美　国	United State	354	448 270	126 179
中国香港	Hongkong, China	650	313 102	129 669
韩　国	Republic of Korea	124	107 675	51 208
英属维尔京群岛	Virgin Islands of United Kingdom	67	121 399	59 653
日　本	Japan	229	174 210	78 201
英　国	United Kingdom	39	42 999	16 764
新加坡	Singapore	82	35 207	15 180
中国台湾	Taiwan, China	141	27 315	12 972
开曼群岛	Qaman Islands	19	160 425	94 928
丹　麦	Denmark	4	28 428	12 520
德　国	Germany	27	23 311	14 296
荷　兰	Netherlands	13	28 781	15 474
瑞　士	Swiss	12	35 044	17 691
加拿大	Canada	49	35 458	17 704
中国澳门	Macao, China	22	16 969	6 648
法　国	France	22	18 638	6 882
西萨摩亚	Samoa Western	8	13 544	4 318
泰　国	Thailand	10	2 138	849
澳大利亚	Australia	25	6 393	2 324
马来西亚	Malaysia	9	3 587	2 450
芬　兰	Finland	5	1 198	715
比利时	Belgium	5	430	157
印度尼西亚	Indonesia	4	393	241
巴哈马	Bahamas	1	600	300
以色列	Israel	1	556	186

注：表中数字以核发营业执照的企业为准，19－12表同。

Note: The figures of this table refer to enterprises which have gotten business license, same as following table 19－12.

19－11 续表　Continued

国　别　(地　区)　Country (Region)		企业个数(个) Number of Enterprises(unit)	直接利用外资项目合同投资总额(万美元) Contract Investment (USD 10 000)	#直接利用外资合同金　额(万美元) Contract Foreign Investment (USD 10 000)
新西兰	New Zealand	8	3 479	1 543
意大利	Italy	3	185	93
毛里求斯	Mauritius	6	11 092	6 807
菲律宾	Philippines	2	364	159
匈牙利	Hungary	7	331	266
罗马尼亚	Romania	1	50	50
巴拿马	Panama	5	252	113
捷　克	Czech	2	104	68
波　兰	Poland	1	150	105
瑞　典	Sweden	2	1 344	587
蒙　古	Mongolia	1	200	120
西班牙	Spain	4	97	45
俄罗斯	Russia	3	112	54
挪　威	Norway	2	80	65
塞浦路斯	Cyprus	3	39	27
乌拉圭	Uruguay	1	68	24
约　旦	Jordan	1	42	10
奥地利	Austria	1	20	20
巴基斯坦	Pakistan	1	34	10
拉脱维亚	Latvia	1	30	30
秘　鲁	Peru	1	30	21
乌兹别克斯坦	Uzbekstan	1	28	10
塞拉利昂	Sierra Leone	1	20	14
柬埔寨	Cambodia	2	45	34
百慕大群岛	Bermuda	4	1 759	955
墨西哥	Mexico	1	14	10
巴巴多斯	Barbados	1	1 200	600
卢森堡	Luxembourg	1	900	315
哥斯达黎加	Costa Rica	1	200	180
基里巴斯	Kiribas	1	100	75
美属萨摩亚	American Samoa	1	500	250
也　门	Yemen	1	28	20

19－12　经济技术开发区外商及港澳台投资企业按行业分类

（截止 2003 年底）

TEDA'S FOREIGN FUNDED ENTERPRISES BY SECTOR

(By the End of 2003)

行　业	Sector	企业个数（个）Number of Enterprises (unit)	直接利用外资项目合同投资总额（万美元）Contract Investment (USD 10 000)	#直接利用外资合同金额（万美元）Contract Foreign Investment (USD 10 000)
合　计	**Total**	**1 993**	**1 668 970**	**700 192**
#通信设备、计算机及其他电子设备制造业	Telecommunication Equipment, Computer and Other Electronic Equipment	181	623 963	222 904
化工原料及化学品制造业	Raw Chemical Material and Chemical Product	110	95 481	40 245
房地产业	Real Estate	125	82 121	31 619
交通运输设备制造业	Transportation Equipment	65	74 707	36 865
农副食品加工业	Agriculture and Sideline Food Processing	87	61 296	33 345
医药制造业	Medical and Pharmaceutical Products	30	54 717	25 418
商务服务业	Commercial Services	116	52 016	40 547
电气机械及器材制造业	Electric Equipment and Machinery	72	51 076	27 829
公共设施服务业	Public Facilities Services	16	50 074	20 491
非金属矿物制品业	Nonmetal Mineral Products	72	47 977	12 142
食品制造业	Food Products	48	47 574	20 719
饮料制造业	Beverage Products	34	35 352	15 470
专用设备制造业	Equipment for Special Purposes	96	34 065	15 396
房屋和土木工程建筑业	Buildings and Civil Engineering Construction	17	32 254	7 135
通用设备制造业	General Equipment	58	30 152	17 380
金属制品业	Metal Products	68	29 305	15 140
塑料制品业	Plastic Products	65	28 864	11 692
纺织业	Textile	36	19 513	6 459
家具制造业	Furniture Products	27	16 974	7 319
仓储业	Storage	25	16 955	5 824
橡胶制品业	Rubber Products	21	16 145	7 242
科技交流和推广服务业	Scientific and Technological Exchange and Promotion Services	39	14 846	8 570
娱乐业	Entertainment	14	14 633	7 476
造纸及纸制品业	Paper Marking and Paper Products	19	12 605	4 811
电力、热力的生产和供应业	Generation, Supply of Power and Heat	2	11 654	6 461
黑色金属冶炼及压延加工业	Smelting and Pressing of Ferrous Metals	7	11 142	3 743
文教体育用品制造业	Cultural, Educational and Sports Goods	31	10 232	3 663
仪器仪表及文化办公用机械制造业	Instruments, Meters, Cultural and Office Machinery	48	9 387	3 896
石油和天然气开采业	Petroleum and Natural Gas Extraction	1	8 940	1 050
纺织服装、鞋、帽制造业	Garments, Shoes and Hats	103	8 131	4 568

19－12 续表　Continued

行　　业	Sector	企业个数(个) Number of Enterprises (unit)	直接利用外资项目合同投资总额(万美元) Contract Investment (USD 10 000)	#直接利用外资合同金额(万美元) Contract Foreign Investment (USD 10 000)
皮革、毛皮、羽毛(绒)及其制品业	Leather, Fur, Down and Related Products	27	7 438	4 038
印刷业和记录媒介的复制	Printing and Record Medium Reproduction	25	6 573	3 563
装卸搬运和其他运输服务业	Loading, Transportation and Other Transportation Services	18	5 222	2 539
有色金属冶炼及压延加工业	Smelting and Pressing of Non－ferrous Metals	5	5 097	1 702
软件业	Software	53	5 089	3 533
计算机服务业	Computer Services	24	4 435	2 677
石油加工、炼焦及核燃料加工业	Petroleum Processing and Coking and Nuclear Fuel Processing	9	4 370	2 323
建筑装饰业	Building Decoration	50	3 945	2 018
水的生产和供应业	Production and Supply of Water	1	3 928	1 803
工艺品及其他制造业	Handicraft and Related Products	42	3 701	2 209
木材加工及木竹藤棕草制品业	Timber Processing and Timber, Bamboo, Cane, Palm Fiber and Straw Products	19	2 619	2 036
煤炭开采和洗选业	Coal Extraction and Washing	4	2 395	1 349
研究与试验发展	R&D	4	1 943	403
批发业	Wholesale	9	1 556	772
燃气生产和供应业	Gas Production and Supply	1	1 449	562
文化艺术业	Culture and Arts	1	1 399	289
道路运输业	Road Transportation	5	1 271	573
水上运输业	Water Transportation	4	968	364
餐饮业	Catering	15	939	680
专业技术服务业	Professional Technology Services	17	764	431
农　业	Agriculture	4	316	89
零售业	Retail	4	234	108
住宿业	Hotels	1	200	98
地质勘查业	Geophysical Exploration	1	189	109
铁路运输业	Railroad Transportation	1	169	101
建筑安装业	Equipment Installation	4	139	67
居民服务业	Resident Services	5	138	82
有色金属矿采选业	Non－ferrous Minerals Mining and Processing	1	77	60
其他矿采选业	Other Minerals Mining and Processing	1	70	70
体　育	Sports	1	70	60
城市公共交通业	Urban Public Transportation	2	68	35
水利管理业	Water Conservancy	1	28	7
渔　业	Fishery	1	20	20

19－13　天津港保税区主要经济指标

MAIN STATISTICS ON TIANJIN PORT FREE TRADE ZONE

项　目　Item	2000	2001	2002	2003	2003 比 2002 年增长% Increase Rate in 2003 over 2002
一、地区生产总值(万元) Gross Domestic Product(10 000 yuan)	346 214	443 851	615 109	830 186	38.2
第二产业 Secondary Industry	13 010	21 304	45 954	86 997	58.6
第三产业 Tertiary Industry	333 204	422 547	569 155	743 189	36.1
二、工业总产值(万元) Gross Output Value of Industry(10 000 yuan)	112 921	169 446	225 396	418 136	92.1
三、进出区货物总值(亿美元) Total Value of Goods from and to The Zone (USD 100 million)	47.00	50.01	65.00	92.31	42.0
四、企业进出口额(万美元) Foreign Trade of The Enterprises(USD 10 000)	99 284	121 482	212 003	361 912	70.7
#进　口 Import	76 873	92 580	173 978	311 927	79.3
五、通关进出口额(万美元) Foreign Trade Through The Customs(USD 10 000)	133 186	149 590	234 537	382 657	63.2
#进　口 Import	76 902	92 574	174 152	312 180	79.3
六、各项税收总额(万元) Various Taxes(10 000 yuan)	429 554	519 613	831 390	1 207 810	45.3
#工商税及所得税 Industrial, Commercial and Income Tax	39 038	98 485	108 499	132 561	22.2
海关关税 Tariffs	239 685	253 234	389 133	547 814	40.8
海关代征税 Tax Levied by The Customs as An Agent	150 831	167 894	333 758	527 435	58.0
七、企业销售(营业)收入(亿元) Sales Revenue of Enterprises(100 million yuan)	118.80	132.90	181.03	300.51	66.0
八、固定资产投资总额(万元) Investment in Fixed Assets(10 000 yuan)	34 703	55 034	155 020	312 017	101.3
#基础设施投资 Infrastructure Investment	17 536	17 623	39 764	144 962	264.6
九、竣工房屋面积(平方米) Floor Space of Buildings Completed(sq. m)	77 602	36 000	308 000	262 310	－14.8

注：从 2002 年起固定资产投资总额按注册口径统计。
Note: Since 2002, investment in fixed assets is calculated according to registered units of TPFTZ.

19－14　滨海三区概况(2003年)

GENERAL SITUATION OF THREE DISTRICTS OF SEASIDE REGION,2003

指标名称	Item	塘沽区 Tanggu District	汉沽区 Hangu District	大港区 Dagang District
户籍户数(户)	Registered Households(household)	159 321	61 176	124 249
户籍人口(人)	Registered Population(person)	457 456	167 979	344 607
单位从业人员(万人)	Persons Employed in Unit(10 000 persons)		3.33	9.02
乡村从业人员(万人)	Rural Persons Employed(10 000 persons)	2.28	2.51	3.80
地区生产总值(万元)	Gross Domestic Product(10 000 yuan)	2 145 297	295 254	1 535 824
第一产业	Primary Industry	19 359	29 580	13 233
第二产业	Secondary Industry	1 345 324	164 644	1 261 900
第三产业	Tertiary Industry	780 614	101 030	260 691
地区生产总值增速(%)	Increase Rate of Gross Domestic Product(%)	17.51	10.3	15.1
区级地方一般预算财政收入(万元)	Local General Budgetary Financial Revenue at District Level (10 000 yuan)	49 763	10 683	32 497
*固定资产投资(万元)	Investment in Fixed Assets(10 000 yuan)	1 390 863	140 354	366 525
城市人均可支配收入(元)	Per Capita Annual Disposable Income of Urban Households(yuan)	12 588		12 680
城市人均消费性支出(元)	Per Capita Annual Expenditure for Consumption of Urban Households (yuan)	10 028		8 677
年末实有耕地面积(万公顷)	Cultivated Land (year－end)(10 000 hectares)	0.52	0.42	1.34
农林牧渔业总产值(万元)	Gross Output Value of Farming,Forestry,Animal Husbandry and Fishery(10 000 yuan)	57 167	70 324	29 485
农林牧渔业总产值增速(%)	Inrease Rate of Gross Output Value of Farming,Forestry, Animal Husbandry and Fishery(%)	4.3	8.0	16.0
乡镇企业单位数(个)	Number of Township Enterprises(unit)	90	126	4 964
#工　业	Industry	62	126	809
乡镇企业人数(万人)	Personnel of Township Enterprises(10 000 persons)	0.73	1.11	5.68
#工　业	Industry	0.22	1.11	3.20
限额以上工业企业	Industrial Enterprises above Designated Size			
单位数(个)	Number of Unit(unit)	164	61	294
总产值(万元)	Gross Output Value(10 000 yuan)	2 437 947	476 251	4 095 628
利税总额(万元)	Total Pre－tax Profits(10 000 yuan)	727 378	41 076	373 942
固定资产原值(万元)	Original Value of Fixed Assets(10 000 yuan)	4 039 940	363 702	5 853 940
社会消费品零售总额(万元)	Total Retail Sales of Consumer Goods(10 000 yuan)	639 536	146 650	301 484
私营工商企业	Private Industrial and Commercial Enterprise			
户　数(户)	Number of Enterprises (unit)	2 406	621	1 583
注册资本(万元)	Registered Capital(10 000 yuan)	378 651	34 305	82 216
营业收入(万元)	Operating Revenue(10 000 yuan)	218 406	80 872	100 038
个体工商业	Individual Industrial and Commercial Enterprise			
户　数(户)	Number of Enterprises(unit)	10 937	4 030	6 226
资　金(万元)	Fund(10 000 yuan)	61 579	5 423	46 989
营业额(万元)	Income(10 000 yuan)	220 903	61 195	109 660
外贸出口交货值(万元)	Delivery Value of Exports in Foreign Trade(10 000 yuan)	413 512	59 625	243 171
小学校数(所)	Number of Primary Schools(unit)	60	26	32
普通中学校数(所)	Number of Regular Secondary Schools(unit)	37	16	39
卫生机构数(个)	Health Care Institutions(unit)	171	16	26
#医院、卫生院	Hospital and Health Center	20	12	24

注:本表为全区数,但塘沽区数据不含开发区和保税区,* 不含农村集体和个人投资。
Note:The data of this table refer to sum of units located at this district,excluding TEDA and PFTA of Tanggu district,the data with " * " exclude rural collective & individual investment.

第20篇 CHAPTER 20

企业改革与市场发展

REFORM OF ENTERPRISE AND
DEVELOPMENT OF MARKET

20－1　企业集团主要指标(2003 年)

MAIN INDICATORS OF ENTERPRISE GROUPS,2003

项　目	Item	企业数(个) Number of Enterprises	从业人员(人) Employment Personnel (person)	从业人员劳动报酬总额(亿元) Total Reward of Employment Personnel (100 million yuan)
总　计	**Total**	**177**	**491 085**	**88.14**
一、按审批部门分	**By Examining Department**			
国务院	The State Council	1	53 839	10.40
国务院主管部门	Governing Departments of the State Council	2	50 363	10.60
省级政府	Provincial Government	129	349 931	60.54
其　他	Others	45	36 952	6.60
二、按国民经济行业分	**By Main Business Sector**			
农、林、牧、渔业	Agriculture	1	355	0.02
工　业	Industry	85	316 955	59.11
#制造业	Manufacturing	82	271 769	48.65
建筑业	Construction	8	51 241	9.18
交通运输、仓储和邮政业	Transportation,Storage and Post	8	22 224	4.57
批发和零售业	Wholesale and Retail Trade	31	68 705	9.70
住宿和餐饮业	Accommodation and Catering Services	3	3 354	0.55
房地产业	Real Estate Industry	35	21 122	3.04
其　他	Others	6	7 129	1.97
三、按登记注册类型分	**By Registered Type**			
国有企业	State－owned Enterprises	5	7 636	1.43
国有独资公司	Sole State－funded Corporation	55	321 686	60.53
其他有限责任公司	Other Limited Liability Corporations	100	139 768	22.09
股份有限公司	Share－holding Corporations Ltd.	13	17 016	3.56
其　他	Others	4	4 979	0.53
四、按控股情况分	**By Controlling Shares**			
国有绝对控股	State－owned Absolute Holding	69	382 260	73.89
国有相对控股	State－owned Relative Holding	6	6 603	1.04
集体绝对控股	Collective－owned Absolute Holding	38	35 364	3.53
集体相对控股	Collective－owned Relative Holding	2	926	0.26
其　他	Others	62	65 932	9.42
五、按企业规模分	**By Size of Enterprises**			
大　型	Large－sized	20	206 401	39.63
中　型	Medium－sized	48	132 155	23.84
小　型	Small－sized	50	59 427	6.74
其　他	Others	59	93 102	17.93

注:1.本表范围为资产总计亿元以上企业集团。2.本表行业分类为国标 GB/T4754－2002 标准。3.20－2 至 20－6 表同。
Note:a)The data of this table refer to those enterprise groups with total assets of over 100 million yuan. b)Sector listed in this table is classified by the standard of GB/T4754－2002. c)Same as following table 20－2 to 20－6.

20－1 续表 1　Continued

单位：亿元　(100 million yuan)

项　目	Item	资　产 总　计 Total Assets	固定资产 净　值 Net Value of Fixed Assets	流动资产年 平均余额 Annual Average Balance of Circulating Funds
总　计	**Total**	**3 404.37**	**755.90**	**1 619.13**
一、按审批部门分	**By Examining Department**			
国务院	The State Council	239.25	90.66	96.47
国务院主管部门	Governing Departments of the State Council	122.47	43.78	72.09
省级政府	Provincial Government	2 268.17	473.31	1 095.44
其　他	Others	774.48	148.15	355.13
二、按国民经济行业分	**By Main Business Sector**			
农、林、牧、渔业	Agriculture	1.64	0.27	0.48
工　业	Industry	1 675.38	518.28	718.96
#制造业	Manufacturing	1 502.57	448.56	655.38
建筑业	Construction	205.11	38.59	134.32
交通运输、仓储和邮政业	Transportation, Storage and Post	104.15	38.48	22.27
批发和零售业	Wholesale and Retail Trade	507.24	89.15	283.15
住宿和餐饮业	Accommodation and Catering Services	12.08	3.63	4.08
房地产业	Real Estate Industry	359.00	20.23	207.60
其　他	Others	539.77	47.27	248.27
三、按登记注册类型分	**By Registered Type**			
国有企业	State－owned Enterprises	166.34	18.03	111.95
国有独资公司	Sole State－funded Corporation	2 248.85	518.36	1 026.07
其他有限责任公司	Other Limited Liability Corporations	810.74	163.33	394.16
股份有限公司	Share－holding Corporations Ltd.	140.81	40.77	64.04
其　他	Others	37.63	15.41	22.91
四、按控股情况分	**By Controlling Shares**			
国有绝对控股	State－owned Absolute Holding	2 668.72	623.84	1 259.28
国有相对控股	State－owned Relative Holding	99.07	15.60	49.99
集体绝对控股	Collective－owned Absolute Holding	156.07	25.85	58.06
集体相对控股	Collective－owned Relative Holding	4.36	0.98	0.95
其　他	Others	476.16	89.63	250.85
五、按企业规模分	**By Size of Enterprises**			
大　型	Large－sized	1 017.30	322.01	437.44
中　型	Medium－sized	974.91	230.64	511.87
小　型	Small－sized	207.66	44.28	102.32
其　他	Others	1 204.50	158.97	567.50

20－1续表2　Continued

单位：亿元　(100 million yuan)

项　目	Item	主营业务收入 Revenue of Main Business	利税总额 Total Pre－tax Profits	#利润总额 Total Profits
总　计	**Total**	**1 969.01**	**109.83**	**50.33**
一、按审批部门分	**By Examining Department**			
国务院	The State Council	135.43	7.95	1.81
国务院主管部门	Governing Departments of the State Council	105.97	1.78	－2.69
省级政府	Provincial Government	1 495.66	73.37	33.71
其　他	Others	231.95	26.73	17.50
二、按国民经济行业分	**By Main Business Sector**			
农、林、牧、渔业	Agriculture	0.49		
工　业	Industry	1 065.06	84.45	39.48
#制造业	Manufacturing	993.59	84.44	43.89
建筑业	Construction	194.90	6.37	1.70
交通运输、仓储和邮政业	Transportation, Storage and Post	36.08	－0.09	－1.18
批发和零售业	Wholesale and Retail Trade	527.01	4.45	1.41
住宿和餐饮业	Accommodation and Catering Services	4.66	0.17	－0.05
房地产业	Real Estate Industry	99.63	12.69	8.23
其　他	Others	41.18	1.79	0.74
三、按登记注册类型分	**By Registered Type**			
国有企业	State－owned Enterprises	202.32	2.00	1.39
国有独资公司	Sole State－funded Corporation	1 127.35	60.73	22.47
其他有限责任公司	Other Limited Liability Corporations	565.08	48.08	29.36
股份有限公司	Share－holding Corporations Ltd.	55.02	－2.20	－3.70
其　他	Others	19.24	1.22	0.81
四、按控股情况分	**By Controlling Shares**			
国有绝对控股	State－owned Absolute Holding	1 572.28	77.01	31.25
国有相对控股	State－owned Relative Holding	13.82	1.26	0.53
集体绝对控股	Collective－owned Absolute Holding	102.45	8.66	5.71
集体相对控股	Collective－owned Relative Holding	1.68	0.10	0.04
其　他	Others	278.78	22.80	12.80
五、按企业规模分	**By Size of Enterprises**			
大　型	Large－sized	686.82	37.25	13.56
中　型	Medium－sized	734.75	24.40	9.15
小　型	Small－sized	135.18	11.62	6.85
其　他	Others	412.26	36.56	20.77

20－2 重点企业建立现代企业制度情况(2003年)
ESTABLISHING MODERN CORPORATE SYSTEM OF KEY ENTERPRISES,2003

项 目	Item	企业数(个) Number of Enterprises	从业人员(人) Employment Personnel (person)	资本金合计(亿元) Total Capital (100 million yuan)
总 计	**Total**	**170**	**313 344**	**547.20**
一、按国民经济行业分	**By Main Business Sector**			
农、林、牧、渔业	Agriculture	1	601	0.96
工 业	Industry	107	243 451	424.00
#制造业	Manufacturing	96	174 879	310.12
建筑业	Construction	17	28 082	18.58
交通运输、仓储和邮政业	Transportation,Storage and Post	4	21 037	55.85
批发和零售业	Wholesale and Retail Trade	30	16 688	21.02
住宿和餐饮业	Accommodation and Catering Services	2	703	0.95
房地产业	Real Estate Industry	6	1 493	19.33
其 他	Others	3	1 289	6.51
二、按登记注册类型分	**By Registered Type**			
国有企业	State－owned Enterprises	23	34 878	85.50
国有独资公司	Sole State－funded Corporation	47	146 164	196.94
其他有限责任公司	Other Limited Liability Corporations	52	67 543	128.45
股份有限公司	Share－holding Corporations Ltd.	31	51 953	81.62
中外合资企业	Joint Ventures Enterprises with Foreign	12	9 738	48.27
港澳台合资企业	Joint Ventures Enterprises with Hongkong,Macao & Taiwan	4	2 667	6.34
其 他	Others	1	401	0.08
三、按控股情况分	**By Controlling Shares**			
国有绝对控股	State－owned Absolute Holding	128	275 319	457.30
国有相对控股	State－owned Relative Holding	18	13 820	53.21
集体绝对控股	Collective－owned Absolute Holding	6	7 410	5.37
集体相对控股	Collective－owned Relative Holding	1	892	0.53
其 他	Others	17	15 903	30.79
四、按企业规模分	**By Size of Enterprises**			
大 型	Large－sized	45	210 030	313.08
中 型	Medium－sized	101	96 811	191.27
小 型	Small－sized	17	4 455	10.22
其 他	Others	7	2 048	32.63

20－2 续表1　Continued

单位:亿元　(100 million yuan)

项　目	Item	资　产 总　计 Total Assets	固定资产 净　值 Net Value of Fixed Assets	流动资产年 平均余额 Annual Average Balance of Circulating Funds
总　计	**Total**	**2 234.43**	**849.64**	**928.62**
一、按国民经济行业分	**By Main Business Sector**			
农、林、牧、渔业	Agriculture	3.21	1.77	1.08
工　业	Industry	1 528.12	671.74	604.22
#制造业	Manufacturing	1 143.45	437.53	508.32
建筑业	Construction	131.89	23.17	90.87
交通运输、仓储和邮政业	Transportation, Storage and Post	252.92	118.36	53.34
批发和零售业	Wholesale and Retail Trade	164.02	27.81	94.15
住宿和餐饮业	Accommodation and Catering Services	1.31	0.47	0.23
房地产业	Real Estate Industry	106.22	3.73	77.08
其　他	Others	46.74	2.59	7.65
二、按登记注册类型分	**By Registered Type**			
国有企业	State－owned Enterprises	211.36	69.73	66.02
国有独资公司	Sole State－funded Corporation	800.48	286.06	361.94
其他有限责任公司	Other Limited Liability Corporations	559.75	232.34	212.91
股份有限公司	Share－holding Corporations Ltd.	551.73	216.48	226.11
中外合资企业	Joint Ventures Enterprises with Foreign	93.96	42.14	48.37
港澳台合资企业	Joint Ventures Enterprises with Hongkong, Macao & Taiwan	16.53	2.77	12.82
其　他	Others	0.62	0.12	0.45
三、按控股情况分	**By Controlling Shares**			
国有绝对控股	State－owned Absolute Holding	1 902.65	776.85	757.99
国有相对控股	State－owned Relative Holding	191.01	28.39	87.08
集体绝对控股	Collective－owned Absolute Holding	23.39	4.23	14.93
集体相对控股	Collective－owned Relative Holding	7.79	1.16	5.68
其　他	Others	109.59	39.01	62.94
四、按企业规模分	**By Size of Enterprises**			
大　型	Large－sized	1 429.70	641.13	555.54
中　型	Medium－sized	619.08	183.73	261.49
小　型	Small－sized	47.56	7.99	28.04
其　他	Others	138.09	16.79	83.55

20－2 续表 2　Continued
单位:亿元　(100 million yuan)

项　目	Item	主营业务收入 Revenue of Main Business	利税总额 Total Pre－tax Profits	#利润总额 Total Profits
总　计	**Total**	**1 486.63**	**115.10**	**50.90**
一、按国民经济行业分	**By Main Business Sector**			
农、林、牧、渔业	Agriculture	1.36		
工　业	Industry	1 046.38	100.16	41.68
#制造业	Manufacturing	876.50	73.75	29.68
建筑业	Construction	124.53	3.79	1.12
交通运输、仓储和邮政业	Transportation, Storage and Post	103.69	7.43	6.38
批发和零售业	Wholesale and Retail Trade	186.94	0.95	－0.04
住宿和餐饮业	Accommodation and Catering Services	0.37	－0.06	－0.07
房地产业	Real Estate Industry	16.75	1.91	1.11
其　他	Others	6.61	0.92	0.72
二、按登记注册类型分	**By Registered Type**			
国有企业	State－owned Enterprises	75.90	8.12	2.10
国有独资公司	Sole State－funded Corporation	501.57	30.75	10.20
其他有限责任公司	Other Limited Liability Corporations	406.73	21.03	8.79
股份有限公司	Share－holding Corporations Ltd.	368.38	46.25	25.88
中外合资企业	Joint Ventures Enterprises with Foreign	102.80	8.32	3.45
港澳台合资企业	Joint Ventures Enterprises with Hongkong, Macao & Taiwan	30.89	0.52	0.40
其　他	Others	0.36	0.11	0.08
三、按控股情况分	**By Controlling Shares**			
国有绝对控股	State－owned Absolute Holding	1 239.44	97.46	41.09
国有相对控股	State－owned Relative Holding	71.26	7.61	5.30
集体绝对控股	Collective－owned Absolute Holding	33.42	0.89	0.37
集体相对控股	Collective－owned Relative Holding	4.17	0.26	0.25
其　他	Others	138.34	8.88	3.89
四、按企业规模分	**By Size of Enterprises**			
大　型	Large－sized	1 080.37	84.18	37.91
中　型	Medium－sized	346.02	26.67	10.14
小　型	Small－sized	37.20	－2.14	－2.39
其　他	Others	23.04	6.39	5.24

20－3 企业家信心指数(2003 年)

CONFIDENCE INDEX OF ENTREPRENEUR,2003

指 标	Item	一季度 First Quarter	二季度 Second Quarter	三季度 Third Quarter	四季度 Fourth Quarter
总体状况	**Overall Confidence Index**	**132.71**	**126.68**	**124.54**	**124.32**
一、按行业门类分	**Grouped By Sector**				
1.工 业	Industry	134.38	134.21	124.14	122.82
采矿业	Minerals Mining	181.79	156.71	180.55	197.99
制造业	Manufacturing	130.72	132.18	120.77	118.71
电力、煤气及水的生产和供应业	Production & Supply of Electric Power,Gas & Water	166.76	168.72	119.17	124.67
2.建筑业	Construction	149.88	155.41	134.20	133.93
#房屋和土木工程建筑业	House & Civil Engineering	154.90	158.34	138.05	134.70
建筑安装业	Construction Installation	100.00	125.00	100.00	150.00
3.交通运输、仓储和邮政业	Transportation,Storage,Post Services	118.30	105.32	111.28	115.67
#铁路运输业	Railway Transport	100.00	100.00	100.00	100.00
公路运输业	Highway Transport	104.76	95.24	78.57	78.57
水上运输业	Waterway Transport	173.75	136.39	175.00	175.00
航空运输业	Civil Aviation Transport	100.00	100.00	100.00	100.00
邮政业	Post Services	100.00	100.00	100.00	100.00
4.批发和零售业	Wholesale,Retail	130.10	125.63	121.56	109.37
批发业	Wholesale Trade	123.40	123.18	122.61	110.75
零售业	Retail Trade	128.53	115.32	100.29	103.18
5.房地产业	Real Estate Trade	150.97	165.85	160.69	165.44
6.社会服务业	Social Services	142.31	100.00	121.62	137.50
租赁业	Leasing	133.33	66.67	133.33	133.33
商务服务业	Business Services	146.15	114.29	105.26	138.89
居民服务业	Resident Services	128.57	85.71	133.33	133.33
其他服务业	Other Social Services	150.00	100.00	140.00	125.00
7.信息传输和计算机服务及软件	Information Transmitting,Computer Services and Software	105.98	86.93	107.74	109.83
信息传输业	Information Transmitting	118.32	100.00	118.32	117.25

20－3 续表 Continued

指　　标	Item	一季度 First Quarter	二季度 Second Quarter	三季度 Third Quarter	四季度 Fourth Quarter
计算机服务业	Computer Services	85.71	85.71	71.43	100.00
软件业	Software	114.29	84.62	123.08	115.38
8.住宿和餐饮业	Accommodation and Catering Services	102.81	22.55	132.31	134.48
住宿业	Accommodation	98.87	12.69	130.61	132.89
餐饮业	Catering Services	118.18	60.00	140.00	145.45
二、按企业登记注册类型分	**Grouped By Status of Registration**				
国有企业	State－owned Enterprises	124.06	113.97	123.50	115.16
集体企业	Collective－owned Enterprises	99.55	79.54	100.31	107.16
股份合作企业	Cooperative Enterprises	104.82	84.82	104.38	95.29
联营企业	Joint Ownership Enterprises	100.00	87.50	87.50	112.50
有限责任公司	Limited Liability Corporations	131.95	130.77	140.36	138.33
股份有限公司	Share－holding Corporations Ltd.	150.59	118.39	152.00	154.55
私营企业	Private Enterprises	118.75	141.18	123.53	118.75
外商及港澳台商投资企业	Enterprises with Investment from Foreign, Hongkong, Macao and Taiwan	147.23	137.29	131.72	130.21
三、按企业规模分	**Grouped By Size of Enterprises**				
大型及特大型	Large and Super－sized	166.89	163.78	145.76	135.11
#特大型	Super－sized	186.64	172.47	129.78	129.80
大　型	Large－sized	154.96	158.54	155.38	138.29
中小型	Medium and Small－sized	112.43	98.48	118.20	119.43
#中　型	Medium－sized	124.89	111.67	129.10	127.62
小　型	Small－sized	102.10	87.50	109.33	112.59
附:国家重点联系企业	Attachment:State Key Enterprises	123.79	177.11	177.11	177.11
国家试点企业集团成员	State Experimental Enterprises Groups	90.97	118.84	110.16	96.34
乡镇企业	Township Enterprises	127.27	118.18	140.00	120.00
上市公司	Corporations Listed in the Stock Market	132.34	127.34	136.41	136.48

20－4　企业景气指数(2003年)

CLIMATE INDEX OF ENTERPRISES,2003

指　　标	Item	一季度 First Quarter	二季度 Second Quarter	三季度 Third Quarter	四季度 Fourth Quarter
总体状况	**Overall Climate Index**	**126.93**	**107.01**	**122.62**	**124.44**
一、按行业门类分	**Grouped By Sector**				
1.工　业	Industry	136.21	117.60	126.42	124.20
采矿业	Minerals Mining	182.56	164.96	181.32	181.32
制造业	Manufacturing	135.16	113.79	122.98	120.17
电力、煤气及水的生产和供应业	Production & Supply of Electric Power,Gas & Water	124.46	132.47	124.52	132.89
2.建筑业	Construction	84.98	146.80	112.71	150.93
#房屋和土木工程建筑业	House & Civil Engineering	83.47	148.96	114.20	153.61
建筑安装业	Construction Installation	100.00	125.00	100.00	125.00
3.交通运输、仓储和邮政业	Transportation,Storage,Post Services	119.54	82.38	114.30	113.24
#铁路运输业	Railway Transport	100.00	100.00	200.00	100.00
公路运输业	Highway Transport	118.47	81.53	71.43	92.86
水上运输业	Waterway Transport	138.14	125.28	157.97	162.50
航空运输业	Civil Aviation Transport	100.00	100.00	200.00	100.00
邮政业	Post Services	100.00	100.00	100.00	111.55
4.批发和零售业	Wholesale,Retail	127.18	93.65	118.17	126.27
批发业	Wholesale Trade	126.46	93.15	120.40	124.24
零售业	Retail Trade	108.11	91.85	100.00	119.02
5.房地产业	Real Estate Trade	132.62	131.38	136.97	141.82
6.社会服务业	Social Services	103.85	70.00	113.51	112.50
租赁业	Leasing	66.67	33.33	133.33	100.00
商务服务业	Business Services	115.38	100.00	126.32	116.67
居民服务业	Resident Services	85.71	42.86	88.89	100.00
其他服务业	Other Social Services	100.00	50.00	80.00	100.00
7.信息传输和计算机服务及软件	Information Transmitting,Computer Services and Software	126.46	84.43	113.63	107.51
信息传输业	Information Transmitting	198.94	117.25	182.27	117.25

20－4 续表　Continued

指　　标	Item	一季度 First Quarter	二季度 Second Quarter	三季度 Third Quarter	四季度 Fourth Quarter
计算机服务业	Computer Services	71.43	71.43	100.00	100.00
软件业	Software	128.57	76.92	92.31	107.69
8.住宿和餐饮业	Accommodation and Catering Services	101.02	17.56	122.97	122.35
住宿业	Accommodation	92.49	10.53	120.44	118.61
餐饮业	Catering Services	136.36	50.00	130.00	136.36
二、按企业登记注册类型分	**Grouped By Status of Registration**				
国有企业	State－owned Enterprises	114.85	86.83	121.83	121.71
集体企业	Collective－owned Enterprises	89.09	72.50	92.77	96.65
股份合作企业	Cooperative Enterprises	89.64	94.82	86.20	95.29
联营企业	Joint Ownership Enterprises	128.57	112.50	112.50	112.50
有限责任公司	Limited Liability Corporations	137.35	119.69	134.62	139.26
股份有限公司	Share－holding Corporations Ltd.	146.30	129.32	161.56	158.60
私营企业	Private Enterprises	106.25	88.24	123.53	112.50
外商及港澳台商投资企业	Enterprises with Investment from Foreign, Hongkong, Macao and Taiwan	142.72	112.27	125.12	125.34
三、按企业规模分	**Grouped By Size of Enterprises**				
大型及特大型	Large and Super－sized	160.06	125.25	147.07	149.75
#特大型	Super－sized	184.33	111.46	133.48	133.48
大　型	Large－sized	145.38	133.55	155.25	159.50
中小型	Medium and Small－sized	109.56	88.64	112.50	112.98
#中　型	Medium－sized	117.72	97.08	124.59	121.01
小　型	Small－sized	102.80	81.60	102.67	106.29
附:国家重点联系企业	Attachment:State Key Enterprises	160.45	177.11	171.98	160.45
国家试点企业集团成员	State Experimental Enterprises Groups	114.80	125.28	143.12	137.71
乡镇企业	Township Enterprises	127.27	136.36	120.00	130.00
上市公司	Corporations Listed in the Stock Market	118.51	138.63	165.09	156.63

20－5　工业行业企业家信心指数(2003年)

CONFIDENCE INDEX OF INDUSTRIAL ENTREPRENEUR,2003

指　　标	Item	一季度 First Quarter	二季度 Second Quarter	三季度 Third Quarter	四季度 Fourth Quarter
工业行业整体状况	**Overall Industrial Confidence Index**	**134.38**	**134.21**	**124.14**	**122.82**
一、按企业登记注册类型分	**Grouped By Status of Registration**				
国有企业	State－owned Enterprises	115.06	126.44	103.47	101.68
集体企业	Collective－owned Enterprises	86.67	100.00	82.76	96.43
有限责任公司	Limited Liability Corporations	123.93	133.13	139.28	133.05
股份有限公司	Share－holding Corporations Ltd.	156.56	118.60	161.14	163.87
私营企业	Private Enterprises	140.00	160.00	100.00	120.00
外商及港澳台商投资企业	Enterprises with Investment from Foreign,Hongkong,Macao and Taiwan	150.27	146.02	131.16	127.71
二、按行业门类分	**Grouped By Sector**				
采矿业	Minerals Mining	181.79	156.71	180.55	197.99
#石油和天然气开采业	#Petroleum and Natural Gas Extraction	200.00	170.69	200.00	200.00
制造业	Manufacturing	130.72	132.18	120.77	118.71
#饮料制造业	#Beverage Manufacturing	163.20	146.79	183.40	188.02
纺织业	Textile Industry	112.10	127.53	104.30	106.21
纺织服装鞋帽制造业	Textile Garments,Shoes,Caps Manufacturing	118.75	105.56	94.44	117.65
造纸及纸制品业	Papermaking and Paper Products	121.62	121.62	113.73	100.00
化学原料及化学制品制造业	Chemical Raw Materials and Products	98.98	106.84	112.38	101.41
医药制造业	Medical and Pharmaceutical Products	138.04	144.40	139.08	141.48
化学纤维制造业	Chemical Fiber	100.00	100.00	150.00	100.00
塑料制品业	Plastic Products	118.12	132.56	133.58	124.49
黑色金属冶炼及压延加工业	Smelting and Pressing of Ferrous Metals	114.95	144.23	153.66	139.68
交通运输设备制造业	Transport Equipment Manufacturing	98.01	115.29	112.14	103.71
电气机械及器材制造业	Electric Equipment and Machinery	151.40	152.66	156.76	151.40
通信设备、计算机及其他电子设备制造业	Telecommunications Equipment,Computer and Other Electronic Equipment Manufacturing	157.24	153.97	105.60	114.49
电力、煤气及水的生产供应业	Production & Supply of Electric Power,Gas & Water	166.76	168.72	119.17	124.67
三、按企业规模分	**Grouped By Size of Enterprises**				
大型及特大型	Large and Super－sized	164.97	162.48	134.94	134.67
中小型	Medium and Small－sized	110.81	113.10	116.24	113.91
#中　型	Medium－sized	121.67	123.77	126.98	122.58
小　型	Small－sized	98.04	100.93	103.70	103.77
附:国家重点企业	Attachment:State Key Enterprises	109.78	172.67	172.67	172.67
国家试点企业集团成员	State Experimental Enterprises Groups	90.97	118.84	110.16	96.34
乡镇企业	Township Enterprises	137.50	137.50	142.86	100.00
上市公司	Corporations Listed in the Stock Market	119.98	119.98	122.22	127.49

20－6　工业企业景气指数(2003年)

CLIMATE INDEX OF INDUSTRIAL ENTERPRISES, 2003

指　标	Item	一季度 First Quarter	二季度 Second Quarter	三季度 Third Quarter	四季度 Fourth Quarter
工业行业整体状况	**Overall Industrial Climate Index**	**136.21**	**117.60**	**126.42**	**124.20**
一、按企业登记注册类型分	**Grouped By Status of Registration**				
国有企业	State－owned Enterprises	110.44	96.83	103.94	107.43
集体企业	Collective－owned Enterprises	86.67	96.67	93.10	89.29
有限责任公司	Limited Liability Corporations	144.76	128.62	151.29	138.60
股份有限公司	Share－holding Corporations Ltd.	158.39	143.98	174.53	169.27
私营企业	Private Enterprises	120.00	140.00	140.00	100.00
外商及港澳台商投资企业	Enterprises with Investment from Foreign, Hongkong, Macao and Taiwan	148.58	122.15	126.80	128.50
二、按行业门类分	**Grouped By Sector**				
采矿业	Mining and Quarrying	182.56	164.96	181.32	181.32
制造业	Manufacturing	135.16	113.79	122.98	120.17
电力、煤气及水的生产供应业	Production & Supply of Electric Power, Gas and Water	124.46	132.47	124.52	132.89
三、按企业规模分	**Grouped By Size of Enterprises**				
大型及特大型	Large and Super－sized	165.69	124.21	137.43	137.87
中小型	Medium and Small－sized	113.51	112.66	118.38	113.91
#中　型	Medium－sized	116.67	113.11	126.19	119.35
小　型	Small－sized	109.80	112.15	109.26	107.55
四、不同观察指标景气指数	**Climate Index on Different Indicators**				
生产成本	Cost	60.69	78.12	67.67	74.55
生产总量	Gross Output	127.86	109.15	134.84	128.60
产品订货情况	Order for Product	125.54	101.19	109.67	119.06
产品销售量	Total Volume of Sales	120.85	99.25	136.45	133.94
产品销售价格	Price of Sales	105.32	71.95	89.09	94.97
产成品库存	Inventory of Product	125.75	121.34	115.95	120.29
税后利润	Profits after Tax	121.28	97.53	92.27	105.10
劳动力需求	Labour Demand	101.72	83.29	103.72	111.82
固定资产投资情况	Investment in Fixed Assets	105.19	116.88	116.66	113.41
科技开发情况	Science and Technology Development	122.54	124.56	111.26	109.84
附：国家重点企业	Attachment: State Key Enterprises	152.67	172.67	166.61	152.67
国家试点企业集团成员	State Experimental Enterprises Groups	114.80	125.28	143.12	137.71
乡镇企业	Township Enterprises	137.50	162.50	128.57	114.29
上市公司	Corporations Listed in the Stock Market	103.81	138.39	169.43	140.59

20－7　内联引资情况(2003年)

DOMESTIC UNION AND ABSORBED CAPITAL,2003

单位	Unit	新签协议合同数(项) Number of Newly Signed Contracts (unit)	协议合同金额(万元) Total Amount of Capital in Projects Signed (10 000 yuan)	实际利用内资金额(万元) Total Amount of Domestic Capital Actually Used (10 000 yuan)	外地投资 From Other Regions	国家部门投资 From Departments of State
总　计	**Total**	**1 404**	**1 722 189**	**1 122 103**	**890 990**	**231 113**
一、各区县	**Districts and Counties**	**478**	**1 137 223**	**603 411**	**547 255**	**56 156**
和平区	Heping District	11	185 000	92 099	92 099	
河东区	Hedong District	13	66 660	28 180	28 180	
河西区	Hexi District	7	70 600	32 650	32 650	
河北区	Hebei District	8	66 600	32 400	25 700	6 700
红桥区	Hongqiao District	6	67 000	35 000	20 000	15 000
南开区	Nankai District	6	65 510	24 690	24 690	
塘沽区	Tanggu District	68	134 532	82 862	56 434	26 428
汉沽区	Hangu District	3	30 420	10 900	10 900	
大港区	Dagang District	19	56 705	22 365	20 265	2 100
东丽区	Dongli District	60	64 031	42 176	42 176	
西青区	Xiqing District	11	43 563	38 863	38 863	
津南区	Jinnan District	20	54 030	21 210	21 210	
北辰区	Beichen District	44	50 846	35 101	35 101	
武清区	Wuqing District	58	29 236	19 121	19 121	
宝坻区	Baodi District	14	39 560	18 390	18 390	
宁河县	Ninghe County	13	23 600	6 650	6 650	
静海县	Jinghai County	10	60 755	39 229	37 829	1 400
蓟　县	Jixian County	107	28 575	21 525	16 997	4 528
二、"三区"	**"Three Districts"**	**447**	**168 769**	**167 230**	**167 230**	
天津经济技术开发区	TEDA	154	45 107	43 568	43 568	
天津港保税区	TPFTZ	257	56 151	56 151	56 151	
天津新技术产业园区	THIP	36	67 511	67 511	67 511	
三、市属各局	**Bureau Under City Administration**	**354**	**239 005**	**174 545**	**65 491**	**109 054**
机电工业控股集团公司	Tianjin Machinery & Electric Industry Holding Group Company	4	2 596	2 393	1 393	1 000
中环电子信息集团有限公司	Tianjin Zhonghuan Electronics & Information Group	8	2 700	2 700	900	1 800
一轻集团(控股)有限公司	Tianjin Yiqing Group(Holding Share) Co.,Ltd	4	1 596	1 578	1 578	
二轻集团(控股)有限公司	The Second Light Industry Group(Holding) Co.,Ltd	7	4 200	4 200	4 200	
纺织集团(控股)有限公司	Tianjin Textile Industrial General Corporation	16	5 510	5 005	4 405	600
医药集团有限公司	Tianjin Pharmaceutical Holdings	1	10 000			
天铁冶金集团有限公司	Tianjin Tian Tie Metallurgical Group Co.,Ltd	1	3 000	3 000	3 000	
飞鸽集团有限公司	Tianjin Flying Pigeon Group Co.,Ltd	240	118	118	118	
钢管有限责任公司	Tianjin Pipe Corporation Ltd	2	38 300	38 300	3 300	35 000
渤海化工集团公司	Tianjin Bohai Chemical Industry Group Corporation	1	7 000	7 000		7 000

20－7 续表 Continued

单位	Unit	新签协议合同数（项）Number of Newly Signed Contracts (unit)	协议合同金额（万元）Total Amount of Capital in Projects Signed (10 000 yuan)	实际利用内资金额（万元）Total Amount of Domestic Capital Actually Used (10 000 yuan)	外地投资 From Other Regions	国家部门投资 From Departments of State
港务局	Tianjin Port Authority	6	10 510	10 510	510	10 000
交通局	Tianjin Transportation Management Bureau	6	5 900	5 900	5 000	900
建工集团	Tianjin Construction Engineering Group	5	5 480	5 480	5 480	
建材集团总公司	Tianjin Building Materials Group General Corporation	7	26 400	26 400	26 400	
市供销合作总社	Tianjin Supply and Marketing General Cooperation	8	1 800	1 927	1 927	
物资集团公司	Tianjin Material Group Corporation	6	1 100	1 100	1 100	
水利局	Tianjin Water Conservancy Bureau	15	30 900	32 477		32 477
其　他	Others	17	81 898	26 457	6 180	20 277
四、驻津单位	**Units Stayed in Tianjin**	**125**	**177 192**	**176 917**	**111 014**	**65 903**
安徽驻津办	Anhui Office Residence in Tianjin	8	4 380	4 380	4 380	
福建驻津办	Fujian Office Residence in Tianjin	8	27 500	27 500	27 500	
黑龙江驻津办	Heilongjiang Office Residence in Tianjin	4	15 700	15 700	15 700	
江西驻津办	Jiangxi Office Residence in Tianjin	6	2 080	2 080		
河北驻津办	Hebei Office Residence in Tianjin	11	14 889	14 889	14 889	
山西驻津办	Shanxi Office Residence in Tianjin	28	6 575	6 575	6 575	
辽宁驻津办	Liaoning Office Residence in Tianjin	2	254	254	254	
内蒙古驻津办	Inner Mongolia Office Residence	2	66	66	66	
新疆驻津办	Xinjiang Office Residence in Tianjin	1	300	300	300	
温州驻津办	Wenzhou Office Residence in Tianjin	11	39 120	39 120	39 120	
中储发展股份有限公司	Zhongchu Development Stock Co., Ltd.	5	8 766	8 766		8 766
中国精密机械进出口天津分公司	Tianjin Filiale of China Precision Machine Import and Export Corporation	4	8 620	8 620		8 620
中国汽车技术研究中心	China Automotive Technology and Research Center	6	8 913	8 638		8 638
国家物资储备局天津办事处	National Materials Storage Bureau Tianjin Office	1	8 000	8 000		8 000
中国电子物资华北公司	North China Corporation of National Electronic Material Corporation	3	1 500	1 500		1 500
天津工程机械研究院	Tianjin Engineering Machinery Research Institute	12	4 777	4 777	150	4 627
中国石油物资天津分公司	Tianjin Corporation of National Petroleum Goods & Materials Branch Company	2	2 000	2 000		2 000
中国钢铁炉料华北公司	China Metallurgical Raw Materials Huabei Company	1	4 000	4 000		4 000
中国地质物资天津公司	China Geological Materials Tianjin Corporation	1	280	280		280
电子科技集团第18研究所	Tianjin Institute of Power Sources	1	6 650	6 650		6 650
天津石化公司	Tianjin Petroleum and Chemical Corporation	4	9 322	9 322		9 322
交通物资华北公司	North China Corporation of Transportation Material	2	500	500		500
中国农业机械华北公司	North China Corporation of National Agricultural Machinery Corporation	2	3 000	3 000		3 000

20－8 人才和劳务市场情况
STATISTICS ON TALENT AND LABOUR FORCE MARKET
(1993－2003)

年 份 Year	劳务市场 Labour Force Market			人才市场 Talent Market		
	进场单位数(个) Number of Units Entering	进场人次(人次) Number of Persons Entering (person time)	达成意向人次(人次) Number of Persons Reached Initial Intent (person time)	进场单位数(个) Number of Units Entering	进场人次(人次) Number of Persons Entering (person time)	达成意向人次(人次) Number of Persons Reached Initial Intent (person time)
1993		296 000	98 300		83 896	34 897
1994	8 561	716 300	224 100	2 886	180 088	45 028
1995	13 737	1 366 000	308 400	4 002	235 433	70 677
1996	13 961	1 498 000	359 000	6 327	292 128	85 202
1997	15 769	1 615 400	337 300		298 873	97 436
1998	20 152	2 471 700	497 000	11 122	500 813	151 637
1999	27 226	2 766 800	502 700	12 285	422 600	122 600
2000	28 724	2 750 000	512 300	12 979	311 000	110 500
2001	28 855	2 698 500	505 600	15 455	348 852	111 739
2002	30 941	2 931 000	536 100	19 903	526 108	164 244
2003	32 939	2 490 000	455 000	19 142	432 600	157 200

20－9 城市房产市场交易情况
EXCHANGE STATUS OF CITY REAL ESTATE MARKET

指 标	Item	2001	2002	2003
房产买卖	**Housing Buying & Selling**			
成交面积(万平方米)	Areas Exchanged(10 000 sq. m)	861.90	875.00	1 526.44
#住 宅	Residential Buildings	829.10	843.20	1 431.32
办公用房	Office Buildings	5.00	4.20	8.98
商业用房	Commercial Buildings	27.80	27.60	86.14
交易金额(亿元)	Amount of Housing Exchanged(100 million yuan)	188.56	198.70	357.06
#住 宅	Residential Buildings	180.09	187.16	320.13
办公用房	Office Buildings	1.02	1.45	5.65
商业用房	Commercial Buildings	7.45	10.09	31.28
房产租赁	**Housing Leased**			
出租面积(万平方米)	Areas(10 000 sq. m)	117.00	162.00	373.80
#住 宅	Residential Buildings	33.00	24.50	27.80
办公用房	Office Buildings	16.00	33.00	37.80
商业用房	Commercial Buildings	68.00	104.50	182.80
租金收入(亿元)	Income(100million yuan)	5.27	6.64	15.66
#住 宅	Residential Buildings	0.51	0.43	0.58
办公用房	Office Buildings	0.72	1.26	1.88
商业用房	Commercial Buildings	4.04	4.95	11.70

20－10　技术市场基本情况
BASIC STATISTICS ON TECHNICAL MARKET

项　目	Item	签订合同数(项) Number of Contracts Signed (item)			合同金额(万元) Value of Contracts Signed (10 000 yuan)		
		2001	2002	2003	2001	2002	2003
合　计	**Total**	**7 335**	**6 889**	**7 278**	**306 009**	**363 262**	**420 008**
一、按技术合同类别分	**Grouped by the Type of Technical Contract**						
技术开发合同	Technology Development Contracts	1 699	1 642	2 349	187 013	164 723	278 607
技术转让合同	Technology Transfer Contracts	613	508	398	37 424	132 474	50 416
技术咨询合同	Technology Inquiry Contracts	1 386	1 387	1 462	14 229	13 996	17 579
技术服务合同	Technology Services Contracts	3 637	3 352	3 069	67 343	52 069	73 406
二、按合同卖方类别分	**Grouped by the Type of Sellers**						
#科技机构	Technical Institution	1 694	1 753	1 673	85 638	84 231	98 857
高等院校	University	672	675	1 225	18 083	20 671	40 449
工业企业	Industrial Enterprises	944	1 097	1 043	118 777	90 895	167 206
技术贸易机构	Technology Trade Organization	2 764	2 753	2 325	39 226	35 407	41 937
个人及个人合伙	Private	236	63	81	1 984	741	1 381
三、按合同买方类别分	**Grouped by the Type of Buyers**						
#工业企业	Industrial Enterprises	5 164	5 403	5 187	137 644	242 327	215 121
科研机构	Technology Research Institution	383	387	409	8 687	11 513	10 877
各级管理部门	Various Management Sections	311	323	901	121 241	68 463	170 783
技术贸易机构	Technology Trade Organization	266	61	25	5 477	5 455	508
个人及个人合伙	Private	25	17	4	471	198	267
四、按社会经济目标分	**Grouped by the Social and Economic Activitie**						
#农业、林业与渔业的发展	Development of Farming,Forestry and Fishery	111	49	73	52 214	14 208	42 163
促进工业的发展	Promoting the Development of Industry	4 156	3 874	3 895	91 834	122 572	175 961
能源生产储存和分配	Production,Store and Distribution of Energy	393	319	362	14 395	12 320	16 934
交通、通讯事业的发展	Development of Transportation and Telecommunications	405	475	629	16 401	62 291	56 961
教育、卫生事业发展	Development of Education & Health Care	267	242	423	21 835	23 192	31 381
社会发展和社会经济服务	Social Development and Social Economic Services	745	592	808	27 495	21 477	34 529
环境保护	Environmental Protecting	449	529	406	12 713	13 416	14 104
五、按技术流向分类	**Grouped by the Buyer's Region**						
天　津	Tianjin	5 030	4 405	4 488	209 293	278 812	301 466
外　地	Others	2 305	2 484	2 790	96 716	84 450	118 542

20－11　天津市主要亿元商

COMMODITY EXCHANGE MARKETS WITH TRANSACTION

市场名称	Name of Market	交易场所面积（平方米）Area of the Transaction Place (sq. m)	交易额（万元）Transactio Value (10 000 yuan)
大胡同集团百货批发商场	Dahutong Small Goods Wholesale Market	78 300	643 981
天津储宝钢材现货交易市场	Chubao Steel Spot Exchange Market	8 518	404 647
天津滨海国际汽车城	Tianjin Binhai International Motor City	2 800	241 942
北方日用工业品中心批发市场	North(Tianjin)Daily－use Industrial Products Wholesale Market	80 000	221 217
红旗农贸批发市场	Hongqi Wholesale Market	180 000	188 665
环渤海建筑材料中心批发市场	Huanbohai Wholesale Market of Building Materials	175 000	156 671
天津不锈钢材市场	Tianjin Stainless Steel Market	7 000	136 679
中国(天津)粮油批发交易市场	China(Tianjin) Grain & Oil Wholesale Market	1 000	133 250
何庄子蔬菜批发市场	Hezhuangzi Vegetables Wholesale Market	100 000	128 784
天津石化交易中心市场	Tianjin Petroleum Chemical Products Exchange Market	1 786	122 794
天津登发装饰基地	Tianjin Dengfa Decoration Base	180 000	108 000
天津钢铁炉料交易市场	Tianjin Steel & Iron Materials Exchange Market	450	104 676
天津市冷冻食品批发市场	Tianjin Freezing Food Wholesale Market	1 200	95 189
天昊集团铁东路摩托市场	Tianhao Group Tiedong Motorcycle Market	10 000	91 110
金钟蔬菜批发市场	Jinzhong Vegetable Wholesale Market	6 600	72 522
天津轻纺商城	Tianjin Light and Textile Goods Market	16 000	69 983
静海县津海商城	Jinghai County Jinhai Market	40 000	64 702
兴业鞋帽批发市场	Xingye Shoes and Hats Market	7 650	62 480
体北食品批发市场	Tibei Foodstuff Wholesale Market	18 000	62 340
津南区葛沽集贸综合市场	Jinnan Gegu Comprehensive Trade Market	51 294	61 501
兴耀消费批发市场	Xingyao Comprehensive Wholesale Market	2 660	60 634
天津市兆鑫食品批销市场	Zhaoxin Eatable Wholesale & Sale Co. ,Ltd.	2 240	58 709
天津百货大楼家具城	Tianjin Department Store Furniture Center	15 000	58 573
天津市珠江装饰家具城	Tianjin Zhujiang Decoration & Furniture Center	30 000	57 075
河北区幸福道农贸市场	Xingfu Road Farm Products Market	3 000	56 850
旧机动车交易中心	Second Hand Motor Vehicle Exchange Market	2 000	46 600
信托贸易公司南开车辆商场	Trust Trade Corporation Nankai Vehicle Market	10 000	37 487
天津市温州城	Tianjin Wenzhou Market	7 000	35 640
零号路农贸市场	Linghao Road Farm Products Market	3 314	34 822
天津果品中心批发市场	Tianjin Fruit Center Wholesale Market	3 150	34 015
河北区宜白路农贸批发市场	Hebei Yibai Road Farm Products Wholesale Market	20 000	33 129
天津华北建材陶瓷批发市场	Huabei Building Material,Ceramic Wholesale Market	11 800	32 517
东丽商贸城	Dongli Trade Market	30 000	31 492
红桥区彰武路市场	Zhangwu Road Farm Products Market	1 782	31 297
蓟县城关市场	Chengguan Town Jixian County Bazaar Market	60 000	28 441
蝶桥旧机动车交易市场	Dieqiao Second Hand Motor Vehicle Exchange Market	150 000	21 099
天津市王顶堤集团汽车产品交易中心	Tianjin Wangdingdi Group Motor Vehicle Exchange Center	20 000	18 120
武清泉州路市场	Wuqing Quanzhou Road Market	20 000	16 650
南开区烈士路市场	Nankai District Lieshi Road Market	7 660	13 130
河北区乌江路摊群市场	Hebei Wujiang Road Market	2 080	12 790
塘沽区新村市场	Tanggu Xincun Market	2 700	10 974
蓟县邦钧农贸市场	Jixian Bangjun Farm Products Market	50 000	10 267
南马路五金城	Nanma Road Hardware Market	39 675	3 996

品交易市场情况(2003 年)
VALUE OF OVER 100 MILLION IN TIANJIN,2003

市场类别	Market Type	交易地址	Transaction Place
服装、小百货、鞋帽	Garments,Daily Consumer Goods,Shoes & Hats	红桥区南运河南路 9 号	No.9 Nanyunhénanlu Road,Hongqiao District
金属材料	Metal Materials	北辰区顺义道	Shunyi Road,Beichen District
机动车	Motor Vehicle	天津保税区天保大道 86 号	No.86 Tianbao Street TPFTZ
灯具、花卉及其它	Lamp,Flower and Other Products	河东区张贵庄路 160 号	No.160 Zhuangguizhuang Road,Hedong District
蔬菜、水果、水产品	Vegetables,Fruits and Aquatic Products	南开区王顶堤复康路立交桥北侧	North of Wangdingdi Crossbridge,Nankai District
建筑及装潢材料	Building and Decoration Materials	河西区解放南路 473 号	No.473 Jiefangnan Road,Hexi District
不锈钢材	Stainless Steel	南开区黄河道 481 号	No.481 Huanghe Road,Nankai District
粮　油	Grain and Oil	河西区台儿庄路 39 号	No.39 Taierzhuang Road,Hexi District
蔬　菜	Vegetables	津南区双港镇何庄子南	South of Hezhuangzi,Shuanggang Town ,Jinnan District
化工材料及制品	Chemical Materials and Related Products	河西区珠江道 58 号	No.58 Zhujiang Road,Hexi District
建筑及装潢材料	Building and Decoration Materials	大沽路与解放南路交口	Cross of Dagu Road and Jiefangnan Road
金属材料	Metal Materials	河西区马场道 103 号	No.103 Machang Road,Hexi District
食　品	Food	南开区天拖南保山道 18 号	No.18 Baoshan Road, Tiantuonan, Nankai District
摩托车	Motorcycle	北辰区铁东路普济河道立交桥北－1 公里	North of Pujihe Crossbridge,Tiedong Road,Beichen District
蔬　菜	Vegetables	东丽区大毕庄赵沽里	Zhaoguli Dabizhuang,Dongli District
纺织品	Textiles	和平区张自忠路 227 号	No.227 Zhangzizhong Road, Heping District
工业品综合	Industrial Products	静海县东方红路 15 号	NO.15 Dofanghong Road,Jinghai County
鞋	Shoes	南开区西湖道 78 号	No.78 Xihu Road,Nankai District
食品、饮料、烟酒	Food,Beverages,Tobacco and Liquor	河西区体北道一号	No.1 Tibei Road,Hexi District
食品、饮料、烟酒	Food,Beverages,Tobacco and Liquor	津南区葛沽镇葛沽二村	Gegu Second Village,Gegu Town ,Jinnan District
农产品综合	Farm Products	河北区建昌道与外环交口处	Gross of Jianchang Road and Waihuan Hebei District
食　品	Food	东丽区张贵庄街跃进路	Yuejin Road Zhangguizhuang Street,Dongli District
家　具	Furniture	和平区和平路 172 号	No.172 Heping Road,Heping District
装饰、家具	Decoration, Furniture	河东区十一经路 87 号	No.87 Shiyijing Road,Hedong District
农产品综合	Farm Products	河北区幸福道 1 号路	No.1 Road,Xingfu Street,Hebei District
机动车	Motor Vehicle	河北区真理道 54 号	No.54 Zhenli Road,Hebei District
机动车	Motor Vehicle	南开区南马路 52 号	No.52 Nanmalu, Nankai District
服装、鞋帽、针纺织	Garments,Shoes and Hats,Textiles	东丽区大毕庄常青村	Changqing Village,Dabizhuang,Dongli District
农产品综合	Farm Products	红桥区南运河南路 9 号	No.9 Nanyunhénanlu Road,Hongqiao District
干鲜果品	Dry and Fresh Fruits	河西区珠江道 55 号增 1 号	Added No.1,No.55 Zhujiang Road,Hexi District
农产品综合	Farm Products	河北区仓联庄宜白路	Yibai Road Canglianzhuang,Hebei District
建筑及装潢材料	Building and Decoration Materials	塘沽区津塘公路 7－189 号	No.7－189 Jintang Highway,Tanggu District
农产品综合	Farm Products	东丽区先锋路一号	No.1 Xianfeng Road,Dongli District
农产品综合	Farm Products	红桥区红桥三号路咸阳北	North of Hongqiao Third Road,Hongqiao District
农产品综合	Farm Products	蓟县城关市场科	Market Dept.Chengguan, Jixian County
机动车	Motor Vehicle	河东区卫国道万东马路交口	Cross of Wandong Road and Weiguo Road,Hedong District
机动车	Motor Vehicle	天津市西青区西营门王顶堤村	Wangdingdi Village,Xiyingmen,Xiqing District
农产品综合	Farm Products	武清区泉州路南 23 号	No.23 Quanzhou Road, Wuqing District
农产品综合	Farm Products	南开区烈士路长虹公园	Changhong Park,Lieshi Road,Nankai District
农产品综合	Farm Products	河北区乌江路 1 号	No.1 Wujiang Road, Hebei Distrcict
农产品综合	Farm Products	塘沽区新村街烟台西道	Yantaixi Road,Xincun Street,Tanggu District
农产品综合	Farm Products	蓟县京哈公路	Jingha Highroad,Jixian Country
五金	Hardware	天津市南开区南马路	Nanma Road Nankai District

主要统计指标解释

企业家信心指数 是根据企业家对企业外部市场经济环境与宏观政策的认识、看法、判断与预期而编制的指数，用以综合反映企业家对宏观经济环境的感受与信心。分行业企业家信心指数为各行业企业家对本行业企业外部市场经济环境与宏观政策的认识、看法、判断与预期。其表现形式为纯正数，以 100 作为景气指数的临界值，其数值范围在 0—200 之间。

企业景气指数 是根据企业家对本企业综合生产经营情况的判断和预期而编制的指数，用以综合反映企业的生产经营状况。分行业企业景气指数用以反映各行业企业的生产经营状况。其表现形式为纯正数，以 100 作为景气指数的临界值，其数值范围在 0—200 之间。

劳务人才市场交易情况 劳务人才市场是指劳动力供求双方实现劳务交换和劳动力流动的场所。主要反映进场单位数、进场人次、达成意向人次等情况。

技术市场 从狭义看，是指在一定时间、地点进行技术转让和技术商品交易的场所。目前统计反映的是企业购买技术开发、技术转让、技术咨询、技术服务项目的合同数和成交额。

房地产交易市场 主要反映房地产的开发、生产、交换、消费活动等情况。如国有土地使用权出让的地块数、面积、收入；房产买卖的成交面积和成交金额；房屋租赁的出租面积和出租金额，以及向个人出售住宅的面积和收回资金数等。

Explanatory Notes on Main Statistical Indicators

Entrepreneur Confidence Index is an index made according to the entrepreneur´s understanding, view, judgment and forecast of the market economic environment out of the enterprise and macroscopic policy. It reflects the entrepreneur′s feeling and confidence in macroeconomic environment comprehensively. The enterprise confidence index by sectors is a reflection of the entrepreneur's understanding, view, judgment and forecast of the market economic environment out of his own sector. It is expressed by a pure positive number between 0 and 200 with 100 as the boundary value of climate index.

Climate Index of Enterprise is an index made according to the entrepreneur's judgment and forecast of the comprehensive production and management. The climate index by sectors reflects the production and management of each sector comprehensively. It is expressed by a pure positive number between 0 and 200 with 100 as the boundary value.

Employees Supply and Demand Dealings Market It is often known as an office to which employees made an application for having been either supplied or demanded daily. The principal datum there of are including numbers of the market entrance - making sectors or enterprises, of employees suppliers and demanders registered together with their agreements to have been reached between them.

Technique Market It can be regarded narrowly as technical - dealings office where technique transfer is made or technology - related good straded at certain time. As shown in statistical datum presently, turnovers are resulting either from purchase or from transfer of techniques, together with numbers related to the inquiry or services involved in technologies.

Real Estate Dealings Market It means working at the real estate - related development, production, exchange and consumption, all, those are shown in such datum either as incomes arising there from, or square meters of houses purchased or sold and turnovers there from, or square meters for houses offered for renting and amounts received accordingly, or square ones for houses sold to individual and corresponding funds. or as total numbers for each piece of and square meters of the state - owned land, which the ownerthere of (the lessor) agrees to let another (lessee) have right to use.

第21篇 CHAPTER 21

排行榜

SENIORITY BY MAIN STATISTICAL INDICATORS

21-1 企业集团年末资产前50名(2003年)
TOP 50 ENTERPRISE GROUPS BY ASSETS (YEAR-END),2003

名 次 Position	企业集团名称 Name of Enterprise Groups	名 次 Position	企业集团名称 Name of Enterprise Groups
1	天津泰达投资控股有限公司	26	天津市宁发集团
2	天津渤海化工集团	27	天津顺驰投资集团
3	天津市物资集团	28	天津农垦集团
4	天津钢管有限责任公司	29	天津一商集团
5	天津医药集团	30	天津实发集团
6	天津天铁冶金集团	31	天津北方国际集团
7	天津金耀集团	32	天津滨江集团
8	天津经济建设投资集团	33	天津纺织集团
9	大港油田集团	34	天津劝业华联集团
10	天津市隆庆集团	35	天津摩托集团
11	天津城建集团	36	天津万隆集团
12	天津环球磁卡集团	37	天津二商集团
13	天津建筑材料集团	38	天津荣程联合钢铁集团
14	天津天钢集团	39	天津中迈投资集团
15	天津市建工集团	40	天津机电国际贸易集团
16	天津南开允公集团	41	天津市天海集团
17	天津市自来水集团	42	天津天大天财股份有限公司
18	天津家世界连锁商业集团	43	天津钢线钢缆集团
19	天津市粮油集团	44	天津市铁路集团
20	天津市房地产开发经营集团	45	天津市房地产信托集团
21	天津港集团	46	天津立达集团
22	天津住宅建设发展集团	47	天津市塑料集团
23	天津市燃气集团	48	天津华泰集团
24	中铁十八局集团	49	天津市飞鸽集团
25	天津天士力集团	50	天津三源电力集团

21－2 企业集团主营业务收入前50名(2003年)

TOP 50 ENTERPRISE GROUPS BY MAIN BUSINESS REVENUE,2003

名 次 Position	企业集团名称 Name of Enterprise Groups	名 次 Position	企业集团名称 Name of Enterprise Groups
1	天津市物资集团	26	天津顺驰投资集团
2	天津天铁冶金集团	27	天津市宁发集团
3	天津渤海化工集团	28	天津农垦集团
4	天津医药集团	29	天津纺织集团
5	天津市隆庆集团	30	天津大桥焊材集团
6	天津钢管有限责任公司	31	天津中迈投资集团
7	天津一商集团	32	天津市金桥焊材集团
8	天津天钢集团	33	天津建筑材料集团
9	中铁十八局集团	34	天津住宅建设发展集团
10	天津市建工集团	35	天津外总集团
11	天津家世界连锁商业集团	36	天津港集团
12	天津城建集团	37	天津市自来水集团
13	大港油田集团	38	天津星河工贸集团
14	天津北方国际集团	39	天津天狮集团
15	天津荣程联合钢铁集团	40	天津二商集团
16	天津金耀集团	41	天津市万达轮胎集团
17	天津摩托集团	42	天津市天海集团
18	天津劝业华联集团	43	天津三源电力集团
19	天津泰达投资控股有限公司	44	天津有色金属集团
20	天津滨江集团	45	天津市房地产开发经营集团
21	天津实发集团	46	天津贻成集团
22	天津天士力集团	47	天津天昊集团
23	天津机电国际贸易集团	48	天津天马企业集团
24	天津市粮油集团	49	天津华泰集团
25	天津市燃气集团	50	天津金元宝商厦集团

21－3　企业集团利税前50名(2003年)

TOP 50 ENTERPRISE GROUPS BY TOTAL PRE－TAX PROFIT,2003

名　次 Position	企业集团名称 Name of Enterprise Groups	名　次 Position	企业集团名称 Name of Enterprise Groups
1	天津天铁冶金集团	26	天津三源电力集团
2	天津医药集团	27	天津建筑材料集团
3	天津泰达投资控股有限公司	28	天津市燃气集团
4	天津渤海化工集团	29	天津天女化工集团
5	天津天钢集团	30	天津市万达轮胎集团
6	天津钢管有限责任公司	31	天津市王顶堤工贸集团
7	天津荣程联合钢铁集团	32	天津天昊集团
8	天津港集团	33	天津市房地产开发经营集团
9	天津金耀集团	34	天津东海投资集团
10	天津天士力集团	35	天津天马企业集团
11	天津实发集团	36	天津纺织集团
12	天津市隆庆集团	37	天津宝成机械集团
13	天津摩托集团	38	天津中迈投资集团
14	天津天狮集团	39	天津市房地产信托集团
15	天津经济建设投资集团	40	天津泰丰工业园投资集团
16	天津农垦集团	41	天津万隆集团
17	天津顺驰投资集团	42	天津住宅建设发展集团
18	天津市宁发集团	43	天津郁美净集团
19	中铁十八局集团	44	天津一商集团
20	天津贻成集团	45	天津井田科工贸集团
21	天津市建工集团	46	天津劝业华联集团
22	天津城建集团	47	天津市铁路集团
23	天津市金桥焊材集团	48	天津蓝天集团
24	天津市物资集团	49	天津市鸿发投资集团
25	天津家世界连锁商业集团	50	天津市高达投资集团

21－4　产品销售收入百强工业企业(2003年)

TOP 100 INDUSTRIAL ENTERPRISES ON PRODUCTION SALES REVENUE,2003

名　次 Position	企业名称 Name of Enterprises	名　次 Position	企业名称 Name of Enterprises
1	摩托罗拉(中国)电子有限公司	51	天津华能杨柳青热电有限责任公司
2	天津天铁冶金集团有限公司	52	康地万达(天津)有限公司
3	中海石油(中国)有限公司天津分公司	53	三星高新电机(天津)有限公司
4	中国石油化工股份有限公司天津分公司	54	中美天津史克制药有限公司
5	天津市电力公司	55	天津市景田实业有限公司
6	天津三星通信技术有限公司	56	天津市荣程钢铁集团有限公司
7	中国石化集团天津石油化工公司	57	天津市飞龙制管厂
8	中国石油天然气股份有限公司大港油田公司	58	天津渤海化工有限责任公司天津碱厂
9	天津三星电子显示器有限公司	59	天津卷烟厂
10	乐金电子(天津)电器有限公司	60	天津市大桥集团有限公司
11	天津一汽丰田汽车有限公司	61	天津新港船厂
12	天津汽车夏利股份有限公司	62	西迪斯(天津)电子有限公司
13	天津市亚益成工贸有限责任公司	63	天津松下电子部品有限公司
14	天津天钢集团有限公司	64	天津三星光电子有限公司
15	中国石油天然气股份有限公司大港石化分公司	65	天津可口可乐饮料有限公司
16	大港油田集团有限公司	66	普利司通(天津)轮胎有限公司
17	天津钢管有限责任公司	67	天津大通铜业有限公司
18	天津三星视界有限公司	68	天津矢崎汽车配件有限公司
19	天津三星电子有限公司	69	天津市第二煤气厂
20	天津金耀集团有限公司	70	中法合营王朝葡萄酿酒有限公司
21	新大洲本田摩托有限公司	71	日新(天津)塑胶有限公司
22	天津通广三星电子有限公司	72	天津市兆博实业有限公司
23	奥的斯电梯有限公司	73	天津津住汽车线束有限公司
24	天津大沽化工有限责任公司	74	天津市万达轮胎集团有限公司
25	天津中新药业集团股份有限公司	75	天津市大邱庄薄板有限公司
26	天津三星电机有限公司	76	美克国际家私(天津)制造有限公司
27	中金黄金股份有限公司	77	SEW 传动设备(天津)有限公司
28	天津太平(集团)有限公司	78	鹏思特(天津)实业有限公司
29	北海粮油工业(天津)有限公司	79	天津爱普生有限公司
30	天津乐金大沽化学有限公司	80	天津市大桥大寺电焊条有限公司
31	天津国华盘山发电有限责任公司	81	天津市华北电缆厂
32	天津渤海化工有限责任公司天津化工厂	82	大宇微波炉(天津)有限公司
33	天津大唐盘山发电有限责任公司	83	天津市染料厂分厂
34	天津顶益国际食品有限公司	84	美孚石油(天津)有限公司
35	中国海洋石油渤海公司	85	PPG 涂料(天津)有限公司
36	天津三洋通信设备有限公司	86	天津燃气集团有限公司
37	天津市金桥焊材集团有限公司	87	天津市九州钢管有限公司
38	天津三美电机有限公司	88	天津市江天型钢有限公司
39	天津丰田汽车发动机有限公司	89	诺和诺德(中国)制药有限公司
40	中盛粮油工业(天津)有限公司	90	天津市静海供电有限公司
41	现代电子(天津)多媒体有限公司	91	正大集团(天津)实业有限公司
42	天津市友发钢管有限公司	92	天津市天宇有色金属集团公司
43	天津胜达轧钢有限公司	93	天津市静海县舜丰钢业有限公司
44	天津中集北洋集装箱有限公司	94	施耐德电气低压(天津)有限公司
45	天津富士通天电子有限公司	95	天津华燊能源发展有限公司
46	天津市轧三制钢有限公司	96	中国华北电力集团公司天津大港发电厂
47	天津天士力集团有限公司	97	天津合全钢铁有限公司
48	天津市利达钢管厂	98	壳牌(天津)石油化工有限公司
49	天津阿尔卑斯电子有限公司	99	天津市大邱庄尧舜轧钢总厂
50	天津雅马哈电子乐器有限公司	100	富川新兴电机(天津)有限公司

21－5　实现利税百强工业企业(2003年)

TOP 100 INDUSTRIAL ENTERPRISES ON TOTAL PRE－TAX PROFITS,2003

名　次 Position	企业名称 Name of Enterprises	名　次 Position	企业名称 Name of Enterprises
1	中海石油(中国)有限公司天津分公司	51	天津华燊能源发展有限公司
2	中国石油天然气股份有限公司大港油田公司	52	天津市金桥焊材集团有限公司
3	天津一汽丰田汽车有限公司	53	天津华能大港发电有限责任公司
4	天津天铁冶金集团有限公司	54	天津市亚益成工贸有限责任公司
5	中国石化集团天津石油化工公司	55	天津渤海化工有限责任公司天津化工厂
6	天津三星视界有限公司	56	天津士名机械装备有限责任公司
7	天津国华盘山发电有限责任公司	57	天津可口可乐饮料有限公司
8	天津天钢集团有限公司	58	天津电装电子有限公司
9	天津汽车夏利股份有限公司	59	美克国际家私(天津)制造有限公司
10	天津钢管有限责任公司	60	中盛粮油工业(天津)有限公司
11	天津市电力公司	61	天津有容蒂康通讯发展有限公司
12	天津三星电子有限公司	62	天津有容蒂康通讯技术有限公司
13	天津大唐盘山发电有限责任公司	63	天津市中环半导体公司
14	天津金耀集团有限公司	64	天津市友发钢管有限公司
15	天津三星通信技术有限公司	65	天津市景田实业有限公司
16	天津卷烟厂	66	天津先进信息产品有限公司
17	天津通广三星电子有限公司	67	天津市染料厂分厂
18	天津天士力集团有限公司	68	西门子电气传动有限公司
19	乐金电子(天津)电器有限公司	69	天津胜达轧钢有限公司
20	天津三星电子显示器有限公司	70	天马缝纫机制造有限公司
21	中法合营王朝葡萄酿酒有限公司	71	天津市长城化工厂
22	新大洲本田摩托有限公司	72	天津南辰钢铁有限公司
23	奥的斯电梯有限公司	73	中金黄金股份有限公司
24	中美天津史克制药有限公司	74	天津丰津汽车传动部件有限公司
25	施耐德电气低压(天津)有限公司	75	天津市新伟祥工业有限公司
26	中国石油天然气股份有限公司大港石化分公司	76	中国海洋石油渤海公司
27	天津丰田汽车发动机有限公司	77	天津雅马哈电子乐器有限公司
28	美孚石油(天津)有限公司	78	天津天宫葡萄酿酒有限公司
29	天津天狮生物发展有限公司	79	天津市万达轮胎集团有限公司
30	天津中新药业集团股份有限公司	80	丹佛斯天津有限公司
31	PPG 涂料(天津)有限公司	81	天津正大饲料科技有限公司
32	天津大沽化工有限责任公司	82	天津三电汽车空调有限公司
33	日新(天津)塑胶有限公司	83	天津力生制药股份有限公司
34	诺维信(中国)生物技术有限公司	84	天津汽车齿轮有限公司
35	SEW 传动设备(天津)有限公司	85	天津市天宇有色金属集团公司
36	天津市第二煤气厂	86	北方气体产品天津有限公司
37	天津乐金大沽化学有限公司	87	天津市华北电缆厂
38	天津顶益国际食品有限公司	88	亚光耐普罗精密注塑天津有限公司
39	天津津住汽车线束有限公司	89	天津中集北洋集装箱有限公司
40	天津三星电机有限公司	90	飞马天津缝纫机有限公司
41	天津泰达股份有限公司	91	天津东洋油墨有限公司
42	中国石油化工股份有限公司天津分公司	92	天津振兴水泥有限公司
43	卡夫天美食品(天津)有限公司	93	诺和诺德(中国)制药有限公司
44	天津三洋通信设备有限公司	94	天津南侨油脂有限公司
45	摩托罗拉(中国)电子有限公司	95	威娜化妆品(中国)有限公司
46	天津市荣程钢铁集团有限公司	96	天津渤海化工有限责任公司天津碱厂
47	壳牌(天津)石油化工有限公司	97	劲量(中国)有限公司
48	麦格昆磁天津有限公司	98	天津水泥股份有限公司
49	天津环球磁卡股份有限公司	99	世讯工业(天津)有限公司
50	普利司通(天津)轮胎有限公司	100	天津市北方实业发展有限公司

21－6　房地产开发企业投资额、销售额五十强(2003年)

TOP 50 REAL ESTATE ENTERPRISES ORDERED BY INVESTMENT AND SALES,2003

投资额名次 Position of Investment	企业名称 Name of Enterprise	销售额名次 Position of Sales	企业名称 Name of Enterprise
1	天津顺驰发展有限公司	1	天津市房地产发展(集团)股份有限公司
2	天津经济技术开发区建设集团有限公司	2	天津顺驰建设有限公司
3	天津市房地产发展(集团)股份有限公司	3	天津市万顺置业有限公司
4	天津市古文化街海河楼开发经营有限公司	4	天津顺驰发展有限公司
5	天津开发区翔达房地产开发有限公司	5	天津开发区永泰房地产开发有限公司
6	天津万科房地产有限公司	6	天津市塘沽区金达房地产开发有限责任公司
7	天津顺驰建设有限公司	7	天津顺驰滨海置地有限公司
8	天津塘沽贻成实业有限公司	8	天津塘沽贻成实业有限公司
9	天津阳光壹佰房地产开发有限公司	9	天津浩地集团有限公司
10	天津顺驰投资集团有限公司	10	天津开发区翔达房地产开发有限公司
11	天津万隆集团有限公司	11	天津奥林匹克花园置业投资有限公司
12	天津滨江金耀广场有限公司	12	天津华厦建设发展股份有限公司
13	天津经济技术开发区房地产开发公司	13	天津市隆杰置业有限公司
14	天津市凯立城市建设开发公司	14	天津开发区亚资置业有限公司
15	天津开发区永泰房地产开发有限公司	15	天津新技术产业园区武清开发区总公司
16	天津乐康置业有限公司	16	天津津基安居发展有限公司
17	天津市建德房地产开发有限公司	17	天津市商业房地产建设开发总公司
18	天津万兆投资发展集团有限公司	18	天津万隆集团有限公司
19	天津市巨川置业发展有限公司	19	天津市恒泰房地产开发有限公司
20	天津开发区晟达房地产开发有限公司	20	天津远洋房地产开发公司
21	天津市河东房地产开发总公司	21	天津市大通建设发展集团有限公司
22	天津市大通建设发展集团有限公司	22	天津顺驰投资集团有限公司
23	天津顺驰滨海置地有限公司	23	天津乐康置业有限公司
24	天津市仁爱房地产开发有限公司	24	天津市骏达房地产综合开发公司
25	天津市市政建设开发有限责任公司	25	天津市美震房地产开发有限公司
26	天津广顺房地产开发有限责任公司	26	天津众成置业有限公司
27	天津华厦建设发展股份有限公司	27	天津市北辰区建设开发公司
28	天津市恒泰房地产开发有限公司	28	天津津港亚太房地产开发有限公司
29	天津开发区鸿发房地产开发有限公司	29	天津市蓟县建设开发公司
30	天津奥林匹克花园置业投资有限公司	30	天津万科房地产有限公司
31	天津开发区福林发展有限公司	31	天津松江置业发展有限公司
32	天津市万顺置业有限公司	32	天津经济技术开发区房地产开发公司
33	天津市塘沽区金达房地产开发有限责任公司	33	天津市凯兴房地产开发公司
34	天津市春港房地产开发有限公司	34	天津市通利房地产开发公司
35	天津市海达房地产开发实业总公司	35	天津市建德房地产开发有限公司
36	天津海泰科技发展股份有限公司	36	天津市鼎基房地产开发有限公司
37	天津六建滨海置业发展有限公司	37	天津市巨川置业发展有限公司
38	天津开发区亚资置业有限公司	38	天津市金谊房地产开发建设公司
39	天津万春房地产开发有限公司	39	天津市华利得房地产有限公司
40	天津市盛星房地产开发有限公司	40	天津开发区福林发展有限公司
41	天津市华利得房地产有限公司	41	天津津投金厦房地产发展股份有限公司
42	天津市商业房地产建设开发总公司	42	天津市天祥房地产开发公司
43	天津市骏达房地产综合开发公司	43	天津市房地产信托集团公司
44	天津市凯兴房地产开发公司	44	天津开发区同圆房地产开发有限公司
45	天津市蓟县建设开发公司	45	天津腾远房地产开发有限公司
46	天津市赛达房地产开发有限公司	46	天津市鑫森置业有限公司
47	天津开发区鼎盛房地产开发有限公司	47	天津龙都置业投资集团有限公司
48	天津众成置业有限公司	48	天津市君利房地产开发有限公司
49	天津市农垦集团房地产开发建设有限公司	49	天津飞林房地产开发有限公司
50	天津市大港区城市建设综合开发公司	50	天津市仁爱房地产开发有限公司

21－7　全市建筑企业建筑业总产值、利税总额五十强(2003年)

TOP 50 CONSTRUCTION ENTERPRISES BY GROSS OUTPUT VALUE OF CONSTRUCTION AND TOTAL PRE－TAX PROFITS,2003

总产值名次 By Output Value	单位名称 Name of Enterprise	利税总额名次 By Total Pre－tax Profits	单位名称 Name of Enterprise
1	中铁十八局集团有限公司	1	中铁十八局集团有限公司
2	海洋石油工程股份有限公司	2	海洋石油工程股份有限公司
3	天津城建集团有限公司	3	中港第一航务工程局第一工程公司
4	中港第一航务工程局第一工程公司	4	天津城建集团有限公司
5	天津市建工工程总承包有限公司	5	天津电力建设公司
6	中国建筑第六工程局	6	天津二十冶金建设有限公司
7	天津第一市政公路工程有限公司	7	中国建筑第六工程局
8	天津五市政公路工程有限公司	8	天津五市政公路工程有限公司
9	天津二十冶金建设有限公司	9	天津市建工工程总承包有限公司
10	天津三建建筑工程有限公司	10	天津航道局
11	天津六建建筑工程有限公司	11	天津第一市政公路工程有限公司
12	天津二建建筑工程有限公司	12	天津三建建筑工程有限公司
13	天津航道局	13	中港第一航务工程局第四工程公司
14	天津一建建筑工程有限公司	14	天津市管道工程集团有限公司
15	天津电力建设公司	15	路桥集团第一公路工程局天津工程处
16	中港第一航务工程局第四工程公司	16	中国石化集团第四建设公司
17	中国石化集团第四建设公司	17	天津六建建筑工程有限公司
18	天津四建建筑工程有限公司	18	中国建筑第六工程局第二建筑工程公司
19	路桥集团第一公路工程局天津工程处	19	天津渔阳建工集团有限公司
20	中国建筑第六工程局土木工程公司	20	天津送变电工程公司
21	中国建筑第六工程局第一建筑工程公司	21	中国建筑第六工程局土木工程公司
22	中国建筑第六工程局第四建筑工程公司	22	天津一建建筑工程有限公司
23	中国建筑第六工程局第二建筑工程公司	23	中国建筑第六工程局第四建筑工程公司
24	中国水利水电基础工程局	24	天津市青龙建筑安装工程公司
25	天津送变电工程公司	25	天津二建建筑工程有限公司
26	天津振津工程集团有限公司	26	中国建筑第六工程局第三建筑工程公司
27	天津市公路工程总公司	27	天津市水利工程有限公司
28	天津市水利工程有限公司	28	天津四建建筑工程有限公司
29	中国建筑第六工程局第三建筑工程公司	29	中国水利水电基础工程局
30	天津电信建设工程有限公司	30	北京铁路建设集团有限公司天津分公司
31	天津五建建筑工程有限公司	31	天津市地方铁路工程公司
32	天津市管道工程集团有限公司	32	天津市华水自来水建设有限公司
33	天津市津南建筑安装工程总公司	33	中国建筑第六工程局第五建筑工程公司
34	天津市地方铁路工程公司	34	西门子楼宇科技(天津)有限公司
35	中国建筑第六工程局第五建筑工程公司	35	天津振津工程集团有限公司
36	天津住一建筑工程总承包有限公司	36	天津开发区建源建筑工程有限责任公司
37	北京铁路建设集团有限公司天津分公司	37	天津市建城地基基础工程有限公司
38	天津市华水自来水建设有限公司	38	天津和平建工集团有限公司
39	天津渔阳建工集团有限公司	39	天津市华方实业有限公司
40	天津市龙祥建材建设工程有限公司	40	中国建筑第六工程局第一建筑工程公司
41	天津市机电设备安装公司	41	天津市龙祥建材建设工程有限公司
42	天津第四市政建筑工程有限公司	42	天津市津南建筑安装工程总公司
43	天津市建城地基基础工程有限公司	43	天津住一建筑工程总承包有限公司
44	天津市青龙建筑安装工程公司	44	天津市正元建筑基础工程有限公司
45	天津和平建工集团有限公司	45	天津市津水建筑工程公司
46	天津市市政道桥建筑工程公司	46	天津市第三房屋建筑工程公司
47	天津大港油田集团工程建设有限公司	47	天津二建机施钢结构工程有限公司
48	天津市万力特建筑钢品有限公司	48	天津市源禹水利工程有限公司
49	天津大港油田集团路桥工程有限责任公司	49	武清区建筑工程总公司
50	天津市第三房屋建筑工程公司	50	天津市武清建筑建材集团有限公司

21－8 物流百强企业(2003年)
TOP 100 GOODS FLOW ENTERPRISES,2003

名 次 Position	企业名称 Name of Enterprises	名 次 Position	企业名称 Name of Enterprises
1	天津天士力制药股份有限公司	51	环发(天津)国际货运代理有限公司
2	天津市轧一制钢有限公司	52	天津中远物流有限公司
3	天津碱厂	53	中国汽车运输天津分公司
4	天津奥的斯电梯	54	金阳国际货运公司
5	天津蓝天集团	55	克运船务(天津)代理有限公司
6	乐金电子(天津)电器有限公司	56	招商局国际货运公司天津分公司
7	天津一汽夏利股份有限公司	57	美极物流运输(中国)有限公司天津分公司
8	天津大无缝物流发展有限公司	58	天津宝运国际物流有限公司
9	天津纺织工业供销公司	59	天津天保国际物流有限公司
10	天津北海实业有限公司	60	天津天保冈谷国际物流有限公司
11	天津港(集团)股份有限公司储运分公司	61	天津远华海运有限公司
12	天津港货运公司	62	天津天惠公司
13	天津开发区陆海矿业贸易有限公司	63	三星一津运(天津)国际货运有限公司
14	天津港贸易公司	64	天津华航国际物流有限公司
15	中国船舶燃料供应天津分公司	65	力生(天津)国际贸易有限公司
16	天津港商业保税库有限公司	66	铁宇公司国际运输(天津)有限公司
17	天津外轮代理公司	67	天津港保税区新世纪国际物流有限公司
18	天津港散货物流有限责任公司	68	天津华日国际物流基地有限公司
19	天津港物资供应有限责任公司	69	亚洲物流(天津)有限公司
20	天津港集装箱货运有限公司	70	天津振华国际货运有限公司
21	天津市津交货运有限公司	71	天昌船务工程有限公司
22	天津市起重打包运输场	72	天津开发区华锡贸易储运有限公司
23	天津市和平汽车运输场	73	华韩(天津)货箱有限公司
24	天津市河西运输场	74	天津鑫达物流发展有限公司
25	天津市联运公司	75	天津津丰集装箱储运有限公司
26	天津市塘沽国际集装箱运输场	76	天津滨海储运贸易有限公司
27	天津物流货运中心	77	天津宏保物流有限公司
28	天津市汽车运输六场	78	胜狮货柜有限公司
29	天津市中邮物流有限责任公司	79	金狮储运有限公司
30	天津港强物流有限公司	80	渤海石油运输公司
31	天津市航铁物流服务有限公司	81	塘沽货箱储运联营公司
32	天津天虹货运代理有限公司	82	天津市物资集团
33	金鹰国际货代有限公司天津分公司	83	天津市津沽粮食工业有限公司
34	北京康捷空货运代理有限公司天津分公司	84	天津远东集团有限公司
35	金龙红旗运输有限公司	85	天津市月坛商厦食品配送有限公司
36	和新物流有限公司	86	天津港保税区瀚通国际贸易有限公司
37	讯达物流有限公司	87	天津市浩通物产有限公司
38	德利得物流有限公司	88	天津石油集团运输公司
39	天津市安达集团有限公司	89	天津市全程物流有限公司
40	东环物流有限公司	90	天津市达润五金机械有限公司
41	捷运物流有限公司	91	天津市石化管件有限公司
42	上海佳吉快运有限公司天津分公司	92	天津市油脂公司新港油脂库
43	中国外运天津有限公司	93	兴达运输配货中心
44	天津松昌国际货运有限责任公司	94	环渤海建筑材料中心批发市场
45	中外运集装箱运输有限公司天津分公司	95	汉沽国家粮食储备库
46	天津大田集团有限公司	96	奥森汽车运输有限公司
47	天津中远国际货运有限公司	97	天津南方物流有限公司
48	天津中通国际货运代理有限责任公司	98	当城无公害农产品市场
49	五矿国际货运天津公司	99	振东物流中心
50	大通国际运输有限公司天津分公司	100	东大旅馆物流中心

21－9　销售总额百强批发贸易企业(2003年)

TOP 100 WHOLESALE TRADE ENTERPRISES BY TOTAL SALES,2003

名　次 Position	单位名称 Name of Enterprise	名　次 Position	单位名称 Name of Enterprise
1	中国石化销售华北公司	51	天津食品进出口股份有限公司
2	天津宝钢北方贸易有限公司	52	丰田通商(天津)有限公司
3	天津石油化工股份有限公司天津石油分公司	53	天津市森博商贸有限公司
4	天津汽车工业销售有限公司	54	永立建机(天津)国际贸易有限公司
5	石油天然气股份有限公司华北销售大港分公司	55	天津市纺织工业供销公司
6	中国铁路物资天津公司	56	天津中北进出口股份有限公司
7	天津港保税区瀚通国际贸易有限公司	57	天津市京津工贸开发公司
8	天津天铁冶金集团商贸有限公司	58	天津东洋油墨印刷物资有限公司
9	天津市基建物资总公司	59	天津市南开金属经营公司
10	中国烟草总公司天津市公司	60	中油大港公司天津开发区销售公司
11	天津市浩通物产有限公司	61	天津市金昌物资贸易公司
12	天津太平(集团)有限公司	62	天津百货商务贸易总公司
13	天津中新药业集团股份有限公司	63	天津五金矿产进出口集团公司
14	上海上汽大众汽车销售有限公司天津销售服务	64	天津国信电讯科技有限公司
15	天津市盈通物资有限公司	65	天津市联琪钢铁贸易公司
16	天津市丽兴贸易公司	66	天津万泰进出口贸易有限公司
17	中国医药(集团)天津公司	67	中国有色金属工业华北供销公司
18	中国农业机械华北集团有限公司	68	天津外总集团有限公司
19	天津市咸通生产资料有限责任公司	69	北方国际集团天津丝绸进出口股份有限公司
20	天津市金属材料总公司	70	渤海石油物资供应公司
21	中化天津进出口公司	71	天津休波顿钢铁有限公司
22	松下电器机电(天津)有限公司	72	天津中化沧狮商贸有限公司
23	中国钢铁炉料华北公司	73	天津市经济技术开发区机电设备总公司
24	天津住友商事有限公司	74	天津汽车工业进出口公司
25	天津机械进出口集团有限公司	75	天津裕华经济贸易总公司
26	天津大桥集团电焊条供销有限公司	76	天津市畜产进出口集团有限公司
27	天津市燃料油公司	77	天津广茂物流有限公司
28	天津天士力医药有限公司	78	天津顺达胜天工贸发展有限公司
29	天津市化轻贸易有限公司	79	天津市油脂(集团)有限公司
30	北星(天津)汽车有限公司	80	天津市长芦实业开发公司
31	天津纺织集团进出口股份有限公司	81	天津土产进出口集团有限公司
32	中化物产股份有限公司天津分公司	82	天津市宏桥汇鑫商贸中心
33	北方国际集团天津纺织品进出有限公司	83	天津威麟国际贸易有限公司
34	天津钢管进出口有限责任公司	84	天津汽车工业物资有限公司
35	中国交通物资华北公司	85	北方国际集团天津医药保健品进出口有限公司
36	天津服装进出口股份有限公司	86	天津港保税区安邦国际贸易有限公司
37	天津市正泰实业总公司	87	天津开发区国信集团有限公司
38	天津市时合钢铁有限公司	88	天津开发区英之杰汽车贸易有限公司
39	天津市化工轻工材料总公司	89	天津市新华书店教材发行部
40	天津利和进出口集团有限公司	90	天津市永兆物资有限公司
41	中谷集团(天津)植物油工贸有限公司	91	蓟县物资供销总公司
42	天津市浩物机电汽车贸易有限公司	92	天津港保税区祥通国际工贸公司
43	中国邮电器材华北公司	93	天津市贸顺汽车销售有限公司
44	天津中煤进出口有限公司	94	天津市物资实业发展中心
45	天津晟达石化有限公司	95	天津市机电设备总公司
46	北方国际集团天津文教体育用品进出口公司	96	欧姆龙贸易(天津)有限公司
47	上海大众汽车有限公司天津分公司	97	天津市通泰实业发展有限公司
48	天津市电话器材公司	98	天津市润飞贸易有限公司
49	天津港保税区捷丰国际贸易有限公司	99	天津港保税区捷拓国际贸易有限公司
50	天津滨江集团有限公司	100	天津市安正电力物资有限公司

21－10　销售总额百强零售贸易企业(2003年)

TOP 100 RETAIL TRADE ENTERPRISES BY TOTAL SALES,2003

名　次 Position	单位名称 Name of Enterprise	名　次 Position	单位名称 Name of Enterprise
1	天津克瑞思(集团)有限公司家乐分公司	51	天津津泰石油有限公司
2	天津百货大楼集团有限公司	52	天津市亨得利钟表眼镜有限公司
3	天津国美电器有限公司	53	天津市大港商厦有限责任公司
4	天津滨江商厦有限公司	54	天津中新药业滨海有限公司
5	天津市劝业场(集团)股份有限公司	55	天津市北川工贸有限公司
6	天津华联商厦股份有限公司	56	天津新世界百货有限公司
7	一商发展有限公司	57	天津南希极玖超级市场有限公司
8	天津滨江购物中心	58	天津市健龙商贸有限公司
9	天津金元宝商厦集团有限公司	59	天津市蓟县金城电器有限公司
10	天津东方集团有限公司	60	天津市西青区百顺商贸有限公司
11	绫致时装(天津)有限公司	61	天津市静海县百货有限公司
12	家福(天津)国际贸易有限公司	62	天津市五和超市
13	天津市津工超市有限公司	63	天津市宝路捷汽车销售服务有限公司
14	天津家居装饰建材中心	64	天津物美万家利实业发展有限公司
15	天津劝业家乐福超市有限公司	65	蓟县综合商场
16	天津伊势丹有限公司	66	天津眼科医院验光配镜中心
17	天津壳牌机动车加油服务有限公司	67	天津百货大楼凯莱塞商厦有限公司
18	天津华润超级市场有限公司	68	天津市汉沽百货大楼有限公司
19	天津塘沽乐购生活购物有限公司	69	天津市文物公司
20	大荣贸易国际有限公司	70	天津市武清区第二百货公司
21	天津长信国脉通信科技股份有限公司	71	蓟县新华书店
22	天津市月坛商厦有限公司	72	华钜百货有限公司
23	天津市大中电器有限公司	73	天津市武清商业大厦
24	天津市新安瑞泰购物广场有限公司	74	天津鑫茂钜业商贸有限公司
25	天津市大港滨城商贸有限责任公司	75	天津市陶陶鞋业服饰有限公司
26	天津滨江服饰商厦	76	天津开发区津港石油联合服务供应公司
27	天津凯通汽车服务发展有限公司	77	天津市宝坻区新华书店
28	天津市四联汽车贸易有限公司	78	天津市新华书店和平区店
29	天津市成功汽车销售服务有限公司	79	天津市东丽区军粮城供销合作社
30	天津市大唐通信有限公司	80	武清区新华书店
31	天津汽车工业交通出租车销售有限公司	81	天津市新华书店河西区店
32	天津滨江金耀广场有限公司	82	天津市津南区小站供销社
33	天津国际商场有限公司	83	天津市运达加油站
34	天津劝业华联集团天津商场	84	天津市武清区庆丰国美电器有限公司
35	天津市新中国现代文化用品有限责任公司	85	天津市龙门大厦有限公司龙马购物广场
36	金元宝商厦集团大五金超级市场有限责任公司	86	天津市天正化工有限公司
37	天津凯旋门百货有限公司	87	上海颐盛商贸有限公司天津分公司
38	天津市大港区迎宾超市	88	天津市渔阳商厦
39	天津天杭汽车工业贸易联营公司	89	天津市河东区大桥道食品店
40	天津市好利来食品有限公司	90	天津市煤业建筑器材宁河公司
41	天津好又多百货商贸有限公司	91	加德士(天津)油品有限公司
42	天津市金角汽车销售有限公司	92	天津市新华书店南开区店
43	天津市路顺汽车经销中心	93	天津市鸿达汽车联销公司
44	天津大港油田炼达超市有限公司	94	天津市桂顺斋糕点有限公司
45	天津日报社报刊发行部	95	天津市汉沽宏叶通信发展有限责任公司
46	天津市东丽区供销社东丽商场	96	天津宝华金店
47	天津市米兰商业有限公司	97	天津市塘沽区新华书店
48	天津市武清区海隆商贸有限公司	98	天津开发区滨海大药房有限公司
49	天津市新华职业教育书店	99	静海县新华书店
50	天津市宁河县家乐超市有限责任公司	100	天津市南开区宏业肉食品南丰路专卖店

21-11　营业收入五十强餐饮业企业(2003年)

TOP 50 CATERING TRADE ENTERPRISES BY BUSINESS REVENUE,2003

名　次 Position	单位名称 Name of Enterprise	名　次 Position	单位名称 Name of Enterprise
1	天津肯德基有限公司	26	宝德福酒店
2	天津麦当劳食品有限公司	27	天津市月坛酒店有限公司
3	天津市渔夫码头美食有限责任公司	28	天津耳朵眼炸糕公司
4	天津市桂发祥十八街麻花总店	29	天津市食为天粮油便民连锁公司
5	天津市瀚金佰餐饮有限公司	30	家必得(天津)比萨饼有限公司
6	渤海石油配餐公司	31	天津市环美大酒楼
7	天府饮食文化有限公司	32	天津市小肥羊餐饮有限责任公司
8	天津市桂发祥麻花饮食集团有限公司	33	天津有乐和食食品有限公司
9	天津家世界集团有限公司家和巨无霸海鲜城	34	天津市鹏天阁酒楼有限公司
10	天津市翠享邨餐饮有限公司	35	天津烤鸭店
11	中华砘品(森泰酒楼)	36	天津市河东区向阳屯大酒楼
12	天津市鸿起顺餐饮有限公司	37	天津市渤海利达配餐服务有限公司
13	天津市狗不理大酒店	38	宴宾楼饭庄
14	天津市峰光大酒楼有限公司	39	天津百世威餐饮发展有限公司
15	天津市天北餐饮有限公司	40	天津东海渔村演歌台有限公司
16	天津德克士食品开发有限公司	41	天津市苏闽菜馆有限公司
17	天津渤海湾餐饮广场有限公司	42	天津市成安饮食有限公司
18	天津大圆碗食品有限公司	43	天津市登瀛楼饭庄有限公司
19	天津市康乐饮料有限公司	44	天津市红桥区饮食公司红旗饭庄
20	天津狗不理包子饮食(集团)公司	45	天津市新业国际酒店有限公司
21	天津市粤唯鲜娱乐苑集团有限公司	46	天津狗不理集团物流有限责任公司
22	天津市集贤大酒家有限公司	47	天津狗不理集团公司速冻食品销售中心
23	天津市美膳酒楼	48	天津市琪琪商贸有限公司
24	天津市金太阳餐饮有限公司	49	万顺阿鲍鱼餐饮有限公司
25	天津市起士林大饭店	50	天津市南开区翠亨邨餐饮有限公司

21－12　外商及港澳台商投资企业利润总额百强企业(2003年)

TOP 100 FOREIGN－FUNDED AND HONGKONG,MACAO AND TAIWAN FUNDED ENTERPRISES BY PROFITS,2003

名　次 Position	企业名称 Name of Enterprise	名　次 Position	企业名称 Name of Enterprise
1	天津丰田汽车有限公司	51	飞马(天津)缝纫机有限公司
2	天津三星视界有限公司	52	北方气体产品(天津)有限公司
3	天津三星电子有限公司	53	掌中万维(中国)信息科技有限公司
4	天津通广三星电子有限公司	54	劲量(中国)有限公司
5	天津三星电子显示器有限公司	55	天津华维斯特实业有限公司
6	天津三星通信技术有限公司	56	天津三美电机有限公司
7	施耐德电气低压(天津)有限公司	57	海赛(天津)特种材料有限公司
8	中国天津奥的斯电梯有限公司	58	天津天利航空机电有限公司
9	天津天狮生物发展有限公司	59	天津富士通天电子有限公司
10	中法合营王朝葡萄酿酒有限公司	60	天津泰丰工业园投资(集团)有限公司
11	天津丰田汽车发动机有限公司	61	赫比(天津)电子有限公司
12	美孚石油(天津)有限公司	62	天津可口可乐饮料有限公司
13	天津东方海陆集装箱码头有限公司	63	永立建机(天津)国际贸易有限公司
14	乐金电子(天津)电器有限公司	64	天津三洋通信设备有限公司
15	SEW 传动设备(天津)有限公司	65	世讯工业(天津)有限公司
16	中美天津史克制药有限公司	66	天津新世界康居有限公司
17	绫致时装(天津)有限公司	67	天津关西涂料化工有限公司
18	PPG 涂料(天津)有限公司	68	德芬工业减速机(天津)有限公司
19	日新(天津)塑胶有限公司	69	天津南侨油脂有限公司
20	天津三星电机有限公司	70	万新精密制品(天津)有限公司
21	天津乐金大沽化学有限公司	72	天津通用水务有限公司
22	天津津住汽车线束有限公司	73	天津东洋油墨有限公司
23	天津津政交通发展有限公司	74	天津爱普生有限公司
24	麦格昆磁(天津)有限公司	75	天津泰达国际仓储运输有限公司
25	天津华 SEN 能源发展有限公司	76	天津汇宇实业有限公司
26	卡夫天美食品(天津)有限公司	77	亚光耐普罗精密注塑天津有限公司
27	仙妮蕾德(天津)企业有限公司	78	天津勤美达工业有限公司
28	壳牌润滑油有限公司	79	松下电器机电(天津)有限公司
29	天津顶益国际食品有限公司	80	天津电装空调有限公司
30	天津肯德基有限公司	81	天津日石润滑油脂有限公司
31	美克国际家私(天津)制造有限公司	82	天津富川电机有限公司
32	天津港集装箱码头有限公司	83	天津新晟工艺美容用品有限公司
33	诺维信(中国)生物技术有限公司	84	天津津信塑料制品有限公司
34	天津天永高速公路有限公司	85	欣阳塑胶工业(天津)有限公司
35	天津丰津汽车传动部件有限公司	86	天津太平(集团)有限公司
36	天津先进信息产品有限公司	87	天津华住金属制品有限公司
37	天津电装电子有限公司	88	富港电子(天津)有限公司
38	天津天马缝纫机制造有限公司	89	美和工业发展有限公司
39	普利司通(天津)轮胎有限公司	90	天津杰普智能卡有限公司
40	中盛粮油工业(天津)有限公司	91	天津斯坦雷电气有限公司
41	天津有容蒂康通讯技术有限公司	92	威娜化妆品(中国)有限公司
42	摩托罗拉(中国)电子有限公司	92	韩国外换银行天津分行
43	天津雅马哈电子乐器有限公司	93	天津顶正印刷包材有限公司
44	天津正大饲料科技有限公司	94	桑莱特(天津)节能材料有限公司
45	西门子电气传动有限公司	95	天津津美饮料有限公司
46	丹佛斯(天津)有限公司	96	光宝电子有限公司
47	天津天昂高速公路有限公司	97	通用半导体(中国)有限公司
48	天津中集北洋集装箱有限公司	98	东海橡塑(天津)有限公司
49	天津新伟祥工业有限公司	99	弗兰德机电传动(天津)有限公司
50	天津三电汽车空调有限公司	100	奥的斯电梯(中国)投资有限公司

21-13 外商及港澳台商投资企业出口创汇百强企业(2003年)

TOP 100 FOREIGN-FUNDED AND HONGKONG,MACAO AND TAIWAN FUNDED ENTERPRISES BY EXPORTS,2003

名 次 Position	企业名称 Name of Enterprise	名 次 Position	企业名称 Name of Enterprise
1	摩托罗拉(中国)电子有限公司	51	科莱恩颜料(天津)有限公司
2	天津三星电子显示器有限公司	52	天津爱津服装有限公司
3	乐金电子(天津)电器有限公司	53	天津蓝天三洋电源有限公司
4	天津三星电子有限公司	54	中国天津奥的斯电梯有限公司
5	天津三星通信技术有限公司	55	日新(天津)塑胶有限公司
6	天津三星电机有限公司	56	劲量(中国)有限公司
7	天津通广三星电子有限公司	57	诺曼地橡胶有限公司
8	天津三美电机有限公司	58	飞马(天津)缝纫机有限公司
9	天津中集北洋集装箱有限公司	59	天津新伟祥工业有限公司
10	天津富士通天电子有限公司	60	九维机电(天津)有限公司
11	现代电子(天津)多媒体有限公司	61	天津津住汽车线束有限公司
12	新大洲本田摩托有限公司	62	天津天石休闲用品有限公司
13	天津雅马哈电子乐器有限公司	63	天津磁化电子有限公司
14	三星高新电机(天津)有限公司	64	天津新晟工艺美容用品有限公司
15	天津三洋通信设备有限公司	65	天津新韩精机有限公司
16	美克国际家私(天津)制造有限公司	66	天津三星康宁有限公司
17	大宇微波炉(天津)有限公司	67	天津泽希矿产加工有限公司
18	天津爱普生有限公司	68	迪恩电子(天津)有限公司
19	天津矢崎汽车配件有限公司	69	天津三王丰展轮胎有限公司
20	天津松下电子部品有限公司	70	天津长威科技有限公司
21	天津三星光电子有限公司	71	荣汉电子(天津)有限公司
22	天津三星视界有限公司	72	博克奥电子(天津)有限公司
23	天津阿尔卑斯电子有限公司	73	亚光耐普罗精密注塑天津有限公司
24	天津太平货柜有限公司	74	天津大星电子有限公司
25	西迪斯(天津)电子有限公司	75	天津斯坦雷电气有限公司
26	大真空有限公司	76	光宝电子有限公司
27	天津富川电机有限公司	77	天津高丽亚那工艺品有限公司
28	天津富士光机有限公司	78	天津美式家具有限公司
29	天津丽通炭素制品有限公司	79	天津联盛化纤棉有限公司
30	天津三和电机有限公司	80	天津统一工业有限公司
31	天津星湖实业有限公司	81	天津天狮生物发展有限公司
32	通用半导体(中国)有限公司	82	天津华住金属制品有限公司
33	天津富士达自行车有限公司	83	盖泽工业(天津)有限公司
34	大宇空调(天津)有限公司	84	天津三星毛纺织有限公司
35	英保达资讯(天津)有限公司	85	丹佛斯(天津)有限公司
36	鹏思特(天津)实业有限公司	86	天津三德木业有限公司
37	万新精密制品(天津)有限公司	87	天津鑫山家具有限公司
38	天津成湖实业有限公司	88	天津新午星机电有限公司
39	罗姆华科电子(天津)有限公司	89	天津柯雅美术材料有限公司
40	功学社	90	东海橡塑(天津)有限公司
41	诺维信(中国)生物技术有限公司	91	科莱恩(天津)有限公司
42	天津韩飞鞋业有限公司	92	新宝企业(天津)有限公司
43	麦格昆磁(天津)有限公司	93	天禧(天津)餐具有限公司
44	现代电子(天津)有限公司	94	天津哈娜好医材有限公司
45	天津科林自行车有限公司	95	天津华宇房地产建设有限公司
46	天津欣御金属家具有限公司	96	天星科龙皮革制品有限公司
47	天津汇宇实业有限公司	97	普利司通(天津)轮胎有限公司
48	天津关西涂料化工有限公司	98	天津福助工业有限公司
49	雅士佳(天津)汽车零件有限公司	99	天津普林电路有限公司
50	天津国际联合轮胎橡胶有限公司	100	天津南华制鞋有限公司

21－14　外商及港澳台商投资企业实缴税金总额百强企业(2003 年)

TOP 100 FOREIGN－FUNDED AND HONGKONG,MACAO AND TAIWAN FUNDED ENTERPRISES BY PAID－UP TAXES,2003

名　次 Position	企业名称 Name of Enterprise	名　次 Position	企业名称 Name of Enterprise
1	摩托罗拉(中国)电子有限公司	51	天津统一工业有限公司
2	天津丰田汽车有限公司	52	天津松下电子部品有限公司
3	天津三星视界有限公司	53	加德士润滑油有限公司
4	天津通广三星电子有限公司	54	天津雅马哈电子乐器有限公司
5	新大洲本田摩托有限公司	55	北星(天津)汽车有限公司
6	乐金电子(天津)电器有限公司	56	天津泰达津联电力有限公司
7	中法合营王朝葡萄酿酒有限公司	57	天津天狮生物发展有限公司
8	天津三星通信技术有限公司	58	天津港集装箱码头有限公司
9	中美天津史克制药有限公司	59	天津有容蒂康通讯技术有限公司
10	天津乐金大沽化学有限公司	60	麦格昆磁(天津)有限公司
11	天津顶益国际食品有限公司	61	威娜化妆品(中国)有限公司
12	天津三星电子有限公司	62	天津南侨油脂有限公司
13	绫致时装(天津)有限公司	63	汉高(天津)国际贸易有限公司
14	天津三洋通信设备有限公司	64	美克国际家私(天津)制造有限公司
15	天津丰田汽车发动机有限公司	65	金普斯(天津)新技术有限公司
16	永立建机(天津)国际贸易有限公司	66	美卓戴纳源克
17	仙妮蕾德(天津)企业有限公司	67	天津国际联合轮胎橡胶有限公司
18	美孚石油(天津)有限公司	68	北方气体产品(天津)有限公司
19	PPG 涂料(天津)有限公司	69	天津华丰汽车装饰有限公司
20	丰田通商(天津)有限公司	70	诺维信(中国)生物技术有限公司
21	北海粮油工业(天津)有限公司	72	天津南辰钢铁有限公司
22	普利司通(天津)轮胎有限公司	73	天津丰田合成有限公司
23	天津三星电子显示器有限公司	74	天津矢崎汽车配件有限公司
24	天津宝洁工业有限公司	75	天津天马缝纫机制造有限公司
25	施耐德电气低压(天津)有限公司	76	天津天永高速公路有限公司
26	天津津住汽车线束有限公司	77	天津关西涂料化工有限公司
27	天津三星电机有限公司	78	松下电器机电(天津)有限公司
28	卡夫天美食品(天津)有限公司	79	天津先进信息产品有限公司
29	日新(天津)塑胶有限公司	80	一汽华利(天津)汽车有限公司
30	天津可口可乐饮料有限公司	81	天津泰丰工业园投资(集团)有限公司
31	中盛粮油工业(天津)有限公司	82	俊安(天津)实业有限公司
32	西门子电气传动有限公司	83	霍尼韦尔(天津)有限公司
33	壳牌润滑油有限公司	84	天津太平货柜有限公司
34	天津东洋油墨有限公司	85	天津伊势丹有限公司
35	SEW 传动设备(天津)有限公司	86	天津瑞升金属工业有限公司
36	诺和诺德(中国)制药有限公司	87	天津华住金属制品有限公司
37	天津华润啤酒有限公司	88	天津三星光电子有限公司
38	天津罗升企业有限公司	89	天津华人酒饮有限公司
39	中国大冢制药有限公司	90	琳得科(天津)实业有限公司
40	天津肯德基有限公司	91	天津太平(集团)有限公司
41	天津电装电子有限公司	92	天津富川电机有限公司
42	天津电装空调有限公司	92	天津乐达利印刷制品有限公司
43	顺驰地产有限公司	93	天津津美饮料有限公司
44	天津顶津食品有限公司	94	天津日板浮法玻璃有限公司
45	现代电子(天津)有限公司	95	西迪斯(天津)电子有限公司
46	博福－益普生(天津)制药有限公司	96	天津顶园国际食品有限公司
47	欧姆龙贸易(天津)有限公司	97	液化空气(天津)有限公司
48	天津雀巢有限公司	98	天津高乐高食品有限公司
49	天津日石润滑油脂有限公司	99	富裕注塑制模(天津)有限公司
50	亚光耐普罗精密注塑天津有限公司	100	三星(天津)国际贸易有限公司

21－15　乡村工业销售收入百强企业(2003 年)
TOP 100 TOWNSHIP AND VILLAGE INDUSTRIAL ENTERPRISES BY SALES REVENUE,2003

名　次 Position	企业名称 Name of Enterprise	名　次 Position	企业名称 Name of Enterprise
1	乐金电子天津电器有限公司	51	天津市金轮自行车集团有限公司
2	天津市友发钢管有限公司	52	天津市环球企业集团公司
3	天津胜达轧钢有限公司	53	飞马天津缝纫机有限公司
4	天津市利达钢管厂	54	天津市塑力电缆厂
5	天津市荣程钢铁集团有限公司	55	天津市智宇有限公司
6	天津天士力制药股份有限公司	56	天津市钢锉厂
7	天津市景田实业有限公司	57	天津明春实业有限公司
8	天津市飞龙制管厂	58	天津三千科技集团有限公司
9	天津市万达轮胎集团有限公司	59	天津市昌升带钢有限公司
10	天津市兆博实业有限公司	60	天津汇宇实业有限公司
11	天津市大邱庄薄板有限公司	61	天津市富强工贸集团公司
12	天津市大桥大寺电焊条有限公司	62	大宝冷冻厂
13	天津市华北电缆厂	63	天津市新宇彩板有限公司
14	天津市染料厂分厂	64	天津通汇集团
15	日新天津塑胶有限公司	65	天津市北方实业发展有限公司
16	天津市九州钢管有限公司	66	天津三电汽车空调有限公司
17	天津市天宇有色金属集团公司	67	天津市蓟县燕南福利股份合作公司
18	天津市静海县舜丰钢业有限公司	68	天津春泰工贸有限公司
19	天津市瑞丰带钢有限公司	69	天津市大站集团公司
20	天津合全钢铁有限公司	70	天津成湖实业有限公司
21	天津市大邱庄尧舜轧钢总厂	71	天津市电装空调有限公司
22	天津南辰钢铁有限公司	72	天津北方渔网集团有限责任公司
23	天津市红联橡胶制品厂	73	天津市中津药业股份有限公司
24	天津市长城化工厂	74	天津腾达集团有限公司
25	天津双街钢管集团有限公司	75	天津市北方制药厂
26	天津富士达自行车有限公司	76	天津市先达汽车工贸公司
27	一汽华利(天津)汽车有限公司	77	天津新午星机电有限公司
28	天津市光辉集团有限公司	78	天津东塔服装集团
29	天津市宝成集团有限公司	79	天津市祥云电缆厂
30	天津士名机械装备有限责任公司	80	天津金美达针织集团有限公司
31	天津市振龙铝业有限公司	81	天津市恒兴汽车冲压件厂
32	天津营城滨海集团有限公司	82	天津丰田钢材加工有限公司
33	万新精密制品(天津)有限公司	83	天津市江天型钢有限公司
34	博克莱(天津)有限公司	84	天津市永明油脂制造厂
35	天津市星湖实业有限公司	85	天津三德木业有限公司
36	天津市永益钢材制品厂	86	天津市金锚进出口有限公司
37	天津田歌纺织有限公司	87	天津力港摩托车有限公司
38	天津荣亨集团股份有限公司	88	天津市鼎盛带钢有限公司
39	新宝企业(天津)有限公司	89	天津海河乳业有限公司
40	天津市北辰区中捷彩涂板材有限公司	90	大港区天成化工厂
41	天津有容蒂康通讯发展有限公司	91	天津华润啤酒有限公司
42	天津市天丰钢铁有限公司	92	科莱恩(天津)有限公司
43	天津市顺豪工贸有限公司	93	天津市永兴集团永隆线缆有限公司
44	天津市北辰区津海植物油厂	94	天津市奥海石油化工综合加工厂
45	天津嘉文实业有限公司	95	天津市顺意钢管有限公司
46	天津市新伟祥工业有限公司	96	天津市大邱庄铝加工厂
47	天津科林自行车有限公司	97	天津市桦成木业有限公司
48	天津通达集团有限公司	98	天津市飞鸽自行车有限公司
49	天津丰津汽车传动部件有限公司	99	天津市神州通钢管有限公司
50	天津市铁中煤化工有限公司	100	天津市宝坻区肆强肉食品公司

21－16 乡村工业实现利税百强企业(2003 年)

TOP 100 TOWNSHIP AND VILLAGE INDUSTRIAL ENTERPRISES BY TOTAL PRE－TAXS PROFITS, 2003

名 次 Position	企业名称 Name of Enterprise	名 次 Position	企业名称 Name of Enterprise
1	天津天士力制药股份有限公司	51	天津春泰工贸有限公司
2	乐金电子天津电器有限公司	52	天津市铁中煤化工有限公司
3	日新天津塑胶有限公司	53	天津市奥海石油化工综合加工厂
4	天津市荣程钢铁集团有限公司	54	天津市华明纸箱厂
5	天津士名机械装备有限责任公司	55	天津春发香精香料有限公司
6	天津丰津汽车传动部件有限公司	56	天津通达集团有限公司
7	天津有容蒂康通讯发展有限公司	57	天津市宝成集团有限公司
8	天津市友发钢管有限公司	58	天津市永益钢材制品厂
9	天津市景田实业有限公司	59	天津市金轮自行车集团有限公司
10	天津市染料厂分厂	60	天津天重车轴制造有限公司
11	天津胜达轧钢有限公司	61	天津星光橡塑有限公司
12	天津宝洁工业有限公司	62	天津摩天电子有限公司
13	天津市长城化工厂	63	天津市振龙铝业有限公司
14	天津南辰钢铁有限公司	64	天津市江天型钢有限公司
15	北方气体产品天津有限公司	65	成真化妆用具(天津)有限公司
16	天津市新伟祥工业有限公司	66	天津市祥云电缆厂
17	天津市万达轮胎集团有限公司	67	天津市胜利化工厂
18	天津三电汽车空调有限公司	68	天津天海同步器有限公司
19	天津市天宇有色金属集团公司	69	天津长荣印刷包装设备有限公司
20	天津市华北电缆厂	70	天津乐达利印刷制品有限公司
21	飞马天津缝纫机有限公司	71	天津市先达汽车工贸公司
22	天津汇宇实业有限公司	72	天津市中津药业股份有限公司
23	天津市北方实业发展有限公司	73	天津市永明油脂制造厂
24	天津市兆博实业有限公司	74	加利(天津)电子有限公司
25	大宝冷冻厂	75	天津市华源工业公司
26	天津市大邱庄薄板有限公司	76	天津市津宝乐器有限公司
27	天津市大桥大寺电焊条有限公司	77	天津金美达针织集团有限公司
28	天津市光辉集团有限公司	78	博克莱(天津)有限公司
29	天津荣亨集团股份有限公司	79	天津市鼎盛带钢有限公司
30	天津市津信塑料制品有限公司	80	天津中川电化有限公司
31	天津市九州钢管有限公司	81	天津市东海液化集团有限公司
32	天津市静海县舜丰钢业有限公司	82	天津市华云自动化工程有限公司
33	天津市瑞丰带钢有限公司	83	天津市北方制药厂
34	天津市北辰区津海植物油厂	84	泰信电机天津有限公司
35	万新精密制品(天津)有限公司	85	天津惠利集团有限公司
36	天津合全钢铁有限公司	86	天津雍阳减水剂厂
37	天津市大邱庄尧舜轧钢总厂	87	天津丰田钢材加工有限公司
38	奥科亚国际瓶盖系统天津有限公司	88	天津市蓟县燕南福利股份合作公司
39	天津双街钢管集团有限公司	89	天津三千科技集团有限公司
40	弗兰德机电传动天津有限公司	90	天津东塔服装集团
41	天津市红联橡胶制品厂	91	天津通汇集团
42	天津嘉文实业有限公司	92	天津市凯通高频焊管厂
43	天津市环球企业集团公司	93	天津市天丰钢铁有限公司
44	桑莱特天津节能材料有限公司	94	天津市顺豪工贸有限公司
45	天津市塑力电缆厂	95	天津市桦成木业有限公司
46	天津腾达集团有限公司	96	博科林(天津)包装技术有限公司
47	盖泽工业天津有限公司	97	天津市天锻压力机有限公司
48	天津三德木业有限公司	98	大港鹏翎胶管股份有限公司
49	天津明春实业有限公司	99	天津市朋业铜材厂
50	天津市顺达汽车零部件厂	100	天津市环球镀锌钢管总厂

21-17　乡村工业出口创汇百强企业(2003年)

TOP 100 TOWNSHIP AND VILLAGE INDUSTRIAL ENTERPRISES BY EXPORTS,2003

名　次 Position	企业名称 Name of Enterprise	名　次 Position	企业名称 Name of Enterprise
1	乐金电子天津电器有限公司	51	天津卡斯特木业有限公司
2	天津市星湖实业有限公司	52	天津天成制药有限公司
3	天津春泰工贸有限公司	53	天津市飞鸽自行车有限公司
4	天津成湖实业有限公司	54	天津胜利集团有限公司
5	天津腾达集团有限公司	55	长城服装集团有限公司
6	万新精密制品(天津)有限公司	56	天津通汇集团
7	天津市环球企业集团公司	57	天津市京津农药厂
8	天津田歌纺织有限公司	58	天津北方渔网集团有限责任公司
9	天津东塔服装集团	59	天津耐迪电子有限公司
10	天津市金轮自行车集团有限公司	60	天津凯兴股份有限公司
11	天津汇宇实业有限公司	61	天津市华强纸制品有限公司
12	天津欣御金属家具有限公司	62	天津市金锚家居用品有限公司
13	天津三德木业有限公司	63	天津迪拜工业品有限公司
14	天津市桦成木业有限公司	64	天津市永久电焊条厂
15	天津双街钢管集团有限公司	65	天津英昌乐器有限公司
16	天津科林自行车有限公司	66	天津欧格运动自行车车料有限公司
17	天津联盛化纤棉公司	67	天津市富强工贸集团公司
18	日新天津塑胶有限公司	68	大风纺织工业有限公司
19	天津市染料厂分厂	69	天津市梦得舒羊绒制品有限公司
20	天津嘉文实业有限公司	70	天津三千科技集团有限公司
21	天津市新伟祥工业有限公司	71	天津协进旅游制品有限公司
22	博克莱(天津)有限公司	72	天津市宝坻区东方木制品厂
23	飞马天津缝纫机有限公司	73	天津市庆洋土特产有限公司
24	天津市银龙预应力钢丝有限公司	74	天津中安药业有限公司
25	天津通达集团有限公司	75	成真化妆用具(天津)有限公司
26	九维天津机电有限公司	76	天津永进缝制品有限公司
27	天津市中津药业股份有限公司	77	天津市三华建筑材料有限公司
28	天津腾发纺织品工贸有限公司	78	大港区天成化工厂
29	天津明春实业有限公司	79	天津百里富工业有限公司
30	韩非鞋业有限公司	80	天津鑫海地毯有限公司
31	天津金美达针织集团有限公司	81	天津北方制衣总厂一分厂
32	天津市长城化工厂	82	天津市华瑞木业有限公司
33	天津惠利集团有限公司	83	天津市振宇集团有限公司
34	天津意劳士炊具有限公司	84	天津市蓟县燕南福利股份合作公司
35	天津市津津制药厂	85	天津鸿美食品有限公司
36	盖泽工业天津有限公司	86	天津三环化学有限公司
37	天津市金锚进出口有限公司	87	成珉机电天津有限公司
38	天津市三王丰展轮胎有限公司	88	天津市江兴实业总公司
39	科莱恩(天津)有限公司	89	天津市凯业体育用品有限公司
40	天津市天星新马皮革制品有限公司	90	天津市冀东服装厂
41	天禧(天津)餐具有限公司	91	宏光车料(天津)有限公司
42	迦拿(天津)五金工业有限公司	92	天津丰津汽车传动部件有限公司
43	天津环宇集团公司	93	天津市凯威化工有限公司
44	天津市华悦制衣有限公司	94	天津市澳蒙制衣有限公司
45	天津市华源工业公司	95	天津民昌工艺品有限公司
46	天津市天利粮油食品有限公司	96	天津市渤海阀门厂
47	天津新午星机电有限公司	97	天津市三尚行食品有限公司
48	天津市静海县前尚集团	98	天津韩昌工艺有限公司
49	新宝企业(天津)有限公司	99	天津广联纤维工业有限公司
50	天津市现代化工有限公司	100	天津市天宇有色金属集团公司

第22篇 CHAPTER 22

区县基本情况

BASIC STATISTICS ON DISTRICTS AND COUNTIES

22－1　和平区基本情况
BASIC STATISTICS OF HEPING DISTRICT

指标名称	Item	2001	2002	2003
＊户籍户数(万户)	Registered Households(10 000 househols)	13.81	13.78	13.73
＊户籍人口(万人)	Registered Population (10 000 persons)	42.00	41.59	41.26
男	Male	20.24	20.05	19.89
女	Female	21.76	21.54	21.37
＊人口出生率(‰)	Birth Rate of Population(‰)	3.44	3.53	2.44
＊人口自然增长率(‰)	Natural Growth Rate of Population(‰)	－2.97	－2.60	－2.62
城镇单位从业人员(万人)	Persons Employed in Urban Units(10^4 persons)	3.07	2.69	2.74
#在岗职工	On－post Staff and Workers	2.80	2.41	2.38
地区生产总值(万元)	Gross Domestic Product(10 000 yuan)	367 200	440 153	550 606
第二产业	Secondary Industry	21 800	10 879	11 913
#工　业	Industry	18 312	7 610	8 060
第三产业	Tertiary Industry	345 400	429 274	538 693
地区生产总值增速(%)	Increase Rate of Gross Domestic Product (%)	18.2	20.2	25.1
一般预算内区级财政收入(万元)	General Intra－budgetary Financial Revenue at District Level (10 000 yuan)	47 290	42 824	59 200
一般预算内区级财政支出(万元)	General Intra－budgetary Financial Expenditure at District Level (10 000 yuan)	61 698	68 468	52 500
#教育经费支出	Operating Expenses for Education	16 610	18 338	19 163
＊固定资产投资(万元)	Investment in Fixed Assets (10 000 yuan)	581 097	634 737	869 255
限额以上工业企业	Industrial Enterprises above Designated Size			
单位数(个)	Number of Units(unit)	35	31	24
从业人员(万人)	Persons Employed(10 000 persons)	0.18	0.17	0.19
总产值(万元)	Gross Output Value(10 000 yuan)	18 936	18 962	17 583
产品销售收入(万元)	Sales Revenue(10 000 yuan)	22 279	22 593	21 850

注:1.“＊”为全区数据,其余为区属数。2.固定资产投资不含农村集体和个人投资。3.22－2至22－6表同。
Note:a) The data with "＊" of this table refer to the whole district,others refer to that of units under the leadership of this district. b)The investment in fixed assets exclude rural collective and individual. c)Same as following table 22－2to22－6.

22－1 续表　Continued

指标名称	Item	2001	2002	2003
利税总额(万元)	Total Pre－tax Profits(10 000 yuan)	691	311	1 378
固定资产原值(万元)	Original Value of Fixed Assets(10 000 yuan)	10 555	11 160	3 506
流动资产合计(万元)	Total Circulating Funds(10 000 yuan)	16 494	21 911	22 794
社会消费品零售总额(万元)	Retail Sales of Consumer Goods(10 000 yuan)	565 003	615 271	740 776
集市贸易市场数(个)	Number of Free Markets(unit)	31	40	31
集市贸易成交额(万元)	Transaction Value of Free Markets (10 000 yuan)	150 040	94 498	116 166
* 私营工商企业	Private Industrial and Commercial Enterprises			
户　数(户)	Number of Enterprises(unit)	2 815	3 923	4 873
雇工人数(人)	Employees(person)	15 735	21 758	27 347
注册资本(万元)	Registered Capital(10 000 yuan)	195 134	276 614	376 411
总产值(万元)	Gross Output Value(10 000 yuan)	4 400	830	11 275
营业收入(万元)	Business Revenue(10 000 yuan)	264 724	726 612	1 210 421
* 个体工商业	Individual Industrial and Commercial Enterprises			
户　数(户)	Number of Enterprises(unit)	13 861	12 911	5 962
从业人员(人)	Persons Employed(person)	14 957	13 809	6 810
资　金(万元)	Fund(10 000 yuan)	18 118	17 851	15 369
营业额(万元)	Turnover(10 000 yuan)	476 225	330 973	247 541
直接利用外资协议额(万美元)	Foreign Direct Investment Contracted(USD 10 000)	1 303	1 516	4 148
外贸出口交货值(万元)	Delivery Value of Exports (10 000 yuan)	4 370	5 344	8 327
* 小学校数(所)	Number of Primary Schools(unit)	54	47	32
* 小学在校学生数(人)	Students Enrollment of Primary Schools(person)	32 321	30 075	28 480
* 普通中学校数(所)	Number of Regular Secondary Schools(unit)	41	36	25
* 普通中学在校学生(人)	Students Enrollment of Regular Secondary Schools(person)	34 933	36 667	33 705
幼儿园数(所)	Number of Kindergartens(unit)	60	50	11
卫生机构数(个)	Health Care Institutions(unit)	27	31	25
# 医院、卫生院	Hospital and Health Center	10	14	11
卫生机构床位数(张)	Beds (unit)	713	693	663
# 医院、卫生院	Hospital and Health Center	713	673	643
* 人均公共绿地面积(平方米)	Per Capita Public Green Areas (sq. m)	2.48	2.48	2.18

22－2　河东区基本情况
BASIC STATISTICS OF HEDONG DISTRICT

指标名称	Item	2001	2002	2003
*户籍户数(万户)	Registered Households(10 000 househols)	23.12	23.70	24.10
*户籍人口(万人)	Registered Population (10 000 persons)	65.13	65.77	66.28
男	Male	32.79	33.09	33.37
女	Female	32.34	32.67	32.91
*人口出生率(‰)	Birth Rate of Population(‰)	3.86	4.06	2.99
*人口自然增长率(‰)	Natural Growth Rate of Population(‰)	－3.15	－2.06	－2.78
城镇单位从业人员(万人)	Persons Employed in Urban Units(10^4 persons)	2.50	2.24	2.42
#在岗职工	On－post Staff and Workers	2.20	1.84	1.86
地区生产总值(万元)	Gross Domestic Product(10 000 yuan)	268 600	325 180	398 037
第二产业	Secondary Industry	58 000	72 663	79 232
#工　业	Industry	47 026	58 057	62 977
第三产业	Tertiary Industry	210 600	252 517	318 805
地区生产总值增速(%)	Increase Rate of Gross Domestic Product (%)	19.3	21.1	21.7
一般预算内区级财政收入(万元)	General Intra－budgetary Financial Revenue at District Level (10 000 yuan)	25 426	25 192	43 822
一般预算内区级财政支出(万元)	General Intra－budgetary Financial Expenditure at District Level (10 000 yuan)	42 998	51 089	60 803
#教育经费支出	Operating Expenses for Education	16 165	17 334	19 660
*固定资产投资(万元)	Investment in Fixed Assets (10 000 yuan)	317 810	323 983	487 357
限额以上工业企业	Industrial Enterprises above Designated Size			
单位数(个)	Number of Units(unit)	19	16	26
从业人员(万人)	Persons Employed(10 000 persons)	2.33	0.14	0.29
总产值(万元)	Gross Output Value(10 000 yuan)	28 550	25 087	56 442
产品销售收入(万元)	Sales Revenue(10 000 yuan)	30 090	28 005	58 092

22－2 续表 Continued

指标名称	Item	2001	2002	2003
利税总额(万元)	Total Pre－tax Profits(10 000 yuan)	205	1 765	5 486
固定资产原值(万元)	Original Value of Fixed Assets(10 000 yuan)	15 313	15 788	13 379
流动资产合计(万元)	Total Circulating Funds(10 000 yuan)	16 323	17 206	35 320
社会消费品零售总额(万元)	Retail Sales of Consumer Goods(10 000 yuan)	301 585	355 910	429 948
集市贸易市场数(个)	Number of Free Markets(unit)	60	32	34
集市贸易成交额(万元)	Transaction Value of Free Markets (10 000 yuan)	179 863	141 560	155 697
* 私营工商企业	Private Industrial and Commercial Enterprises			
户　数(户)	Number of Enterprises(unit)	2 100	2 303	2 945
雇工人数(人)	Employees(person)	15 522	17 418	21 004
注册资本(万元)	Registered Capital(10 000 yuan)	139 533	174 666	289 600
总产值(万元)	Gross Output Value(10 000 yuan)	87 770	105 800	112 595
营业收入(万元)	Business Revenue(10 000 yuan)	117 270	154 078	219 355
* 个体工商业	Individual Industrial and Commercial Enterprises			
户　数(户)	Number of Enterprises(unit)	18 422	13 458	13 986
从业人员(人)	Persons Employed(person)	20 736	15 766	16 340
资　金(万元)	Fund(10 000 yuan)	26 372	21 384	22 323
营业额(万元)	Turnover(10 000 yuan)	135 745	172 520	217 495
直接利用外资协议额(万美元)	Foreign Direct Investment Contracted(USD 10 000)	1 567	1 360	2 650
外贸出口交货值(万元)	Delivery Value of Exports (10 000 yuan)	5 065	5 173	7 698
* 小学校数(所)	Number of Primary Schools(unit)	48	38	33
* 小学在校学生数(人)	Students Enrollment of Primary Schools(person)	30 906	27 328	25 009
* 普通中学校数(所)	Number of Regular Secondary Schools(unit)	43	39	34
* 普通中学在校学生(人)	Students Enrollment of Regular Secondary Schools(person)	30 774	30 448	30 425
幼儿园数(所)	Number of Kindergartens(unit)	52	67	62
卫生机构数(个)	Health Care Institutions(unit)	19	19	19
# 医院、卫生院	Hospital and Health Center	16	16	16
卫生机构床位数(张)	Beds (unit)	1 185	1 273	1 274
# 医院、卫生院	Hospital and Health Center	1 008	1 008	1 008
* 人均公共绿地面积(平方米)	Per Capita Public Green Areas (sq. m)	4.38	5.08	6.00

22－3　河西区基本情况

BASIC STATISTICS OF HEXI DISTRICT

指标名称	Item	2001	2002	2003
＊户籍户数(万户)	Registered Households(10 000 households)	24.53	24.96	25.22
＊户籍人口(万人)	Registered Population (10 000 persons)	70.49	71.27	72.05
男	Male	35.10	35.42	35.80
女	Female	35.39	35.84	36.25
＊人口出生率(‰)	Birth Rate of Population(‰)	3.95	4.19	3.03
＊人口自然增长率(‰)	Natural Growth Rate of Population(‰)	－2.70	－1.39	－1.64
城镇单位从业人员(万人)	Persons Employed in Urban Units(10^4 persons)	3.29	2.89	2.91
#在岗职工	On－post Staff and Workers	2.80	2.55	2.32
地区生产总值(万元)	Gross Domestic Product(10 000 yuan)	300 847	361 100	447 720
第二产业	Secondary Industry	38 045	31 933	45 838
#工　业	Industry	35 854	30 008	41 091
第三产业	Tertiary Industry	262 802	329 167	401 882
地区生产总值增速(%)	Increase Rate of Gross Domestic Product (%)	18.16	20.27	24.19
一般预算内区级财政收入(万元)	General Intra－budgetary Financial Revenue at District Level (10 000 yuan)	29 042	29 438	68 999
一般预算内区级财政支出(万元)	General Intra－budgetary Financial Expenditure at District Level (10 000 yuan)	48 638	57 191	70 595
#教育经费支出	Operating Expenses for Education	18 118	20 314	22 549
＊固定资产投资(万元)	Investment in Fixed Assets (10 000 yuan)	464 836	660 662	577 230
限额以上工业企业	Industrial Enterprises above Designated Size			
单位数(个)	Number of Units(unit)	60	69	56
从业人员(万人)	Persons Employed(10 000 persons)	0.51	0.66	0.35
总产值(万元)	Gross Output Value(10 000 yuan)	79 434	44 610	43 738
产品销售收入(万元)	Sales Revenue(10 000 yuan)	57 651	43 649	43 353

22－3 续表 Continued

指标名称	Item	2001	2002	2003
利税总额(万元)	Total Pre－tax Profits(10 000 yuan)	2 065	2 852	2 065
固定资产原值(万元)	Original Value of Fixed Assets(10 000 yuan)	50 678	57 193	49 187
流动资产合计(万元)	Total Circulating Funds(10 000 yuan)	37 458	42 938	37 217
社会消费品零售总额(万元)	Retail Sales of Consumer Goods(10 000 yuan)	588 940	709 276	822 777
集市贸易市场数(个)	Number of Free Markets(unit)	40	38	41
集市贸易成交额(万元)	Transaction Value of Free Markets (10 000 yuan)	310 000	337 876	380 384
* 私营工商企业	Private Industrial and Commercial Enterprises			
户　数(户)	Number of Enterprises(unit)	3 272	4 026	4 870
雇工人数(人)	Employees(person)	25 162	35 471	39 188
注册资本(万元)	Registered Capital(10 000 yuan)	232 027	242 800	372 287
总产值(万元)	Gross Output Value(10 000 yuan)	14 480	15 600	79 800
营业收入(万元)	Business Revenue(10 000 yuan)	82 080	91 857	161 760
* 个体工商业	Individual Industrial and Commercial Enterprises			
户　数(户)	Number of Enterprises(unit)	10 822	14 004	12 830
从业人员(人)	Persons Employed(person)	11 061	14 600	13 697
资　金(万元)	Fund(10 000 yuan)	21 140	24 000	31 529
营业额(万元)	Turnover(10 000 yuan)	144 632	182 400	189 080
直接利用外资协议额(万美元)	Foreign Direct Investment Contracted(USD 10 000)	1 218	1 396	1 324
外贸出口交货值(万元)	Delivery Value of Exports (10 000 yuan)	12 323	12 745	14 344
* 小学校数(所)	Number of Primary Schools(unit)	68	60	58
* 小学在校学生数(人)	Students Enrollment of Primary Schools(person)	37 102	34 365	32 386
* 普通中学校数(所)	Number of Regular Secondary Schools(unit)	54	53	53
* 普通中学在校学生(人)	Students Enrollment of Regular Secondary Schools(person)	42 396	43 050	43 046
幼儿园数(所)	Number of Kindergartens(unit)	43	44	43
卫生机构数(个)	Health Care Institutions(unit)	27	22	24
# 医院、卫生院	Hospital and Health Center	16	16	18
卫生机构床位数(张)	Beds(unit)	1 311	1 311	782
# 医院、卫生院	Hospital and Health Center	1 201	1 201	782
* 人均公共绿地面积(平方米)	Per Capita Public Green Areas(sq. m)	5.66	5.90	5.48

22－4　南开区基本情况
BASIC STATISTICS OF NANKAI DISTRICT

指标名称	Item	2001	2002	2003
*户籍户数(万户)	Registered Households(10 000 households)	26.75	27.03	27.36
*户籍人口(万人)	Registered Population (10 000 persons)	77.20	77.96	78.70
男	Male	39.09	39.51	39.96
女	Female	38.11	38.45	38.74
*人口出生率(‰)	Birth Rate of Population(‰)	3.65	3.79	3.20
*人口自然增长率(‰)	Natural Growth Rate of Population(‰)	－2.49	－2.17	－1.89
城镇单位从业人员(万人)	Persons Employed in Urban Units(10^4 persons)	3.25	2.92	3.95
#在岗职工	On－post Staff and Workers	2.79	2.41	2.79
地区生产总值(万元)	Gross Domestic Product(10 000 yuan)	277 385	338 116	418 469
第二产业	Secondary Industry	29 860	63 782	69 462
#工　业	Industry	28 003	59 110	65 186
第三产业	Tertiary Industry	247 525	274 334	349 007
地区生产总值增速(％)	Increase Rate of Gross Domestic Product (％)	22.2	21.6	23.0
一般预算内区级财政收入(万元)	General Intra－budgetary Financial Revenue at District Level (10 000 yuan)	25 735	25 918	58 051
一般预算内区级财政支出(万元)	General Intra－budgetary Financial Expenditure at District Level (10 000 yuan)	49 897	56 149	60 574
#教育经费支出	Operating Expenses for Education	16 919	19 014	20 907
*固定资产投资 (万元)	Investment in Fixed Assets (10 000 yuan)	773 345	845 473	737 131
限额以上工业企业	Industrial Enterprises above Designated Size			
单位数(个)	Number of Units(unit)	92	97	105
从业人员(万人)	Persons Employed(10 000 persons)	0.72	0.56	0.71
总产值(万元)	Gross Output Value(10 000 yuan)	47 181	48 024	71 350
产品销售收入(万元)	Sales Revenue(10 000 yuan)	48 240	52 296	76 004

22－4 续表　Continued

指标名称	Item	2001	2002	2003
利税总额(万元)	Total Pre－tax Profits(10 000 yuan)	3 016	2 857	4 731
固定资产原值(万元)	Original Value of Fixed Assets(10 000 yuan)	34 158	35 384	37 902
流动资产合计(万元)	Total Circulating Funds(10 000 yuan)	41 528	49 289	62 088
社会消费品零售总额(万元)	Retail Sales of Consumer Goods(10 000 yuan)	545 243	638 944	767 637
集市贸易市场数(个)	Number of Free Markets(unit)			
集市贸易成交额(万元)	Transaction Value of Free Markets (10 000 yuan)			
* 私营工商企业	Private Industrial and Commercial Enterprises			
户　数(户)	Number of Enterprises(unit)	2 147	2 954	5 815
雇工人数(人)	Employees(person)	16 037	20 472	47 751
注册资本(万元)	Registered Capital(10 000 yuan)	80 748	138 328	473 114
总产值(万元)	Gross Output Value(10 000 yuan)	22 136	27 861	378 817
营业收入(万元)	Business Revenue(10 000 yuan)	63 464	77 882	395 311
* 个体工商业	Individual Industrial and Commercial Enterprises			
户　数(户)	Number of Enterprises(unit)	6 591	6 615	8 377
从业人员(人)	Persons Employed(person)	7 706	7 655	13 770
资　金(万元)	Fund(10 000 yuan)	16 179	18 819	22 951
营业额(万元)	Turnover(10 000 yuan)	43 178	48 408	351 949
直接利用外资协议额(万美元)	Foreign Direct Investment Contracted(USD 10 000)	1 523	3 500	2 435
外贸出口交货值(万元)	Delivery Value of Exports (10 000 yuan)	23 702	17 846	17 639
* 小学校数(所)	Number of Primary Schools(unit)	57	53	43
* 小学在校学生数(人)	Students Enrollment of Primary Schools(person)	35 340	31 691	29 421
* 普通中学校数(所)	Number of Regular Secondary Schools(unit)	54	52	43
* 普通中学在校学生(人)	Students Enrollment of Regular Secondary Schools(person)	35 936	36 135	35 296
幼儿园数(所)	Number of Kindergartens(unit)	50	53	48
卫生机构数(个)	Health Care Institutions(unit)	26	25	25
# 医院、卫生院	Hospital and Health Center	17	17	17
卫生机构床位数(张)	Beds(unit)	1 423	1 423	1 423
# 医院、卫生院	Hospital and Health Center	969	969	969
* 人均公共绿地面积(平方米)	Per Capita Public Green Areas(sq. m)	6.00	6.24	7.50

22－5　河北区基本情况
BASIC STATISTICS OF HEBEI DISTRICT

指标名称	Item	2001	2002	2003
* 户籍户数(万户)	Registered Households(10 000 househols)	21.48	21.76	22.07
* 户籍人口(万人)	Registered Population (10 000 persons)	61.00	60.99	61.28
男	Male	30.82	30.81	30.97
女	Female	30.18	30.18	30.32
* 人口出生率(‰)	Birth Rate of Population(‰)	3.35	3.54	2.96
* 人口自然增长率(‰)	Natural Growth Rate of Population(‰)	－3.81	－2.89	－2.53
城镇单位从业人员(万人)	Persons Employed in Urban Units(10^4 persons)	2.8	2.6	2.5
# 在岗职工	On－post Staff and Workers	2.5	2.2	2.1
地区生产总值(万元)	Gross Domestic Product(10 000 yuan)	253 962	298 751	359 674
第二产业	Secondary Industry	50 741	55 251	66 914
# 工　业	Industry	45 897	49 266	58 095
第三产业	Tertiary Industry	203 221	243 500	292 760
地区生产总值增速(%)	Increase Rate of Gross Domestic Product (%)	16.5	18.4	20.8
一般预算内区级财政收入(万元)	General Intra－budgetary Financial Revenue at District Level (10 000 yuan)	24 728	24 640	32 359
一般预算内区级财政支出(万元)	General Intra－budgetary Financial Expenditure at District Level (10 000 yuan)	43 423	54 233	56 052
# 教育经费支出	Operating Expenses for Education	14 807	17 212	18 550
* 固定资产投资 (万元)	Investment in Fixed Assets (10 000 yuan)	354 102	494 069	392 794
限额以上工业企业	Industrial Enterprises above Designated Size			
单位数(个)	Number of Units(unit)	40	39	28
从业人员(万人)	Persons Employed(10 000 persons)	0.27	0.27	0.21
总产值(万元)	Gross Output Value(10 000 yuan)	27 289	27 406	25 844
产品销售收入(万元)	Sales Revenue(10 000 yuan)	26 481	27 591	25 736

22－5 续表 Continued

指标名称	Item	2001	2002	2003
利税总额(万元)	Total Pre－tax Profits(10 000 yuan)	2 553	3 823	3 132
固定资产原值(万元)	Original Value of Fixed Assets(10 000 yuan)	8 930	8 882	6 945
流动资产合计(万元)	Total Circulating Funds(10 000 yuan)	16 608	21 122	19 938
社会消费品零售总额(万元)	Retail Sales of Consumer Goods(10 000 yuan)	466 380	553 882	662 322
集市贸易市场数(个)	Number of Free Markets(unit)	44	44	52
集市贸易成交额(万元)	Transaction Value of Free Markets (10 000 yuan)	311 681	418 244	
* 私营工商企业	Private Industrial and Commercial Enterprises			
户　数(户)	Number of Enterprises(unit)	1 629	2 133	2 700
雇工人数(人)	Employees(person)	13 131	17 930	24 412
注册资本(万元)	Registered Capital(10 000 yuan)	107 704	169 532	235 753
总产值(万元)	Gross Output Value(10 000 yuan)	74 952	86 891	90 589
营业收入(万元)	Business Revenue(10 000 yuan)	209 577	240 537	262 114
* 个体工商业	Individual Industrial and Commercial Enterprises			
户　数(户)	Number of Enterprises(unit)	7 900	8 851	10 000
从业人员(人)	Persons Employed(person)	9 693	11 236	13 035
资　金(万元)	Fund(10 000 yuan)	18 066	23 012	25 676
营业额(万元)	Turnover(10 000 yuan)	90 038	114 627	126 598
直接利用外资协议额(万美元)	Foreign Direct Investment Contracted(USD 10 000)	1 617	1 650	3 519
外贸出口交货值(万元)	Delivery Value of Exports (10 000 yuan)	10 097	8 698	10 286
* 小学校数(所)	Number of Primary Schools(unit)	60	57	46
* 小学在校学生数(人)	Students Enrollment of Primary Schools(person)	32 175	29 844	27 804
* 普通中学校数(所)	Number of Regular Secondary Schools(unit)	47	46	41
* 普通中学在校学生(人)	Students Enrollment of Regular Secondary Schools(person)	38 907	38 938	37 401
幼儿园数(所)	Number of Kindergartens(unit)	64	60	55
卫生机构数(个)	Health Care Institutions(unit)	21	21	22
# 医院、卫生院	Hospital and Health Center	17	17	18
卫生机构床位数(张)	Beds(unit)	1 841	1 717	1 537
# 医院、卫生院	Hospital and Health Center	1 841	1 717	1 537
* 人均公共绿地面积(平方米)	Per Capita Public Green Areas(sq. m)	5.76	8.75	6.44

22－6　红桥区基本情况
BASIC STATISTICS OF HONGQIAO DISTRICT

指标名称	Item	2001	2002	2003
* 户籍户数(万户)	Registered Households(10 000 househols)	19.85	20.11	20.18
* 户籍人口(万人)	Registered Population (10 000 persons)	55.79	55.67	55.55
男	Male	28.23	28.14	28.08
女	Female	27.56	27.53	27.47
* 人口出生率(‰)	Birth Rate of Population(‰)	4.11	4.19	3.91
* 人口自然增长率(‰)	Natural Growth Rate of Population(‰)	－3.65	－2.17	－2.48
城镇单位从业人员(万人)	Persons Employed in Urban Units(10^4 persons)	3.14	2.60	2.55
#在岗职工	On－post Staff and Workers	2.70	2.25	2.04
地区生产总值(万元)	Gross Domestic Product(10 000 yuan)	259 587	302 000	371 469
第二产业	Secondary Industry	35 401	35 862	38 515
#工　业	Industry	23 143	22 047	22 604
第三产业	Tertiary Industry	224 186	266 138	332 954
地区生产总值增速(%)	Increase Rate of Gross Domestic Product (%)	20.3	17.5	22.9
一般预算内区级财政收入(万元)	General Intra－budgetary Financial Revenue at District Level (10 000 yuan)	17 913	17 156	19 273
一般预算内区级财政支出(万元)	General Intra－budgetary Financial Expenditure at District Level (10 000 yuan)	36 414	42 804	47 505
#教育经费支出	Operating Expenses for Education	15 353	15 126	16 821
* 固定资产投资(万元)	Investment in Fixed Assets (10 000 yuan)	85 681	192 106	431 352
限额以上工业企业	Industrial Enterprises above Designated Size			
单位数(个)	Number of Units(unit)	16	18	16
从业人员(万人)	Persons Employed(10 000 persons)	0.20	0.20	0.17
总产值(万元)	Gross Output Value(10 000 yuan)	26 564	33 395	42 942
产品销售收入(万元)	Sales Revenue(10 000 yuan)	15 935	27 743	37 868

22－6 续表 Continued

指标名称	Item	2001	2002	2003
利税总额(万元)	Total Pre－tax Profits(10 000 yuan)	1 056	762	1 168
固定资产原值(万元)	Original Value of Fixed Assets(10 000 yuan)	8 795	8 207	7 976
流动资产合计(万元)	Total Circulating Funds(10 000 yuan)	11 337	13 975	15 309
社会消费品零售总额(万元)	Retail Sales of Consumer Goods(10 000 yuan)	316 346	369 200	442 802
集市贸易市场数(个)	Number of Free Markets(unit)	41	37	38
集市贸易成交额(万元)	Transaction Value of Free Markets (10 000 yuan)	544 873	655 048	762 641
* 私营工商企业	Private Industrial and Commercial Enterprises			
户　数(户)	Number of Enterprises(unit)	1 585	1 451	1 493
雇工人数(人)	Employees(person)	12 812	12 199	13 155
注册资本(万元)	Registered Capital(10 000 yuan)	121 694	149 105	140 659
总产值(万元)	Gross Output Value(10 000 yuan)	31 697	34 938	32 304
营业收入(万元)	Business Revenue(10 000 yuan)	67 079	100 196	96 346
* 个体工商业	Individual Industrial and Commercial Enterprises			
户　数(户)	Number of Enterprises(unit)	13 634	13 862	15 007
从业人员(人)	Persons Employed(person)	14 758	14 268	15 402
资　金(万元)	Fund(10 000 yuan)	24 900	32 201	35 620
营业额(万元)	Turnover(10 000 yuan)	165 359	190 331	198 285
直接利用外资协议额(万美元)	Foreign Direct Investment Contracted(USD 10 000)	501	650	2 390
外贸出口交货值(万元)	Delivery Value of Exports (10 000 yuan)	11 322	5 793	6 953
* 小学校数(所)	Number of Primary Schools(unit)	46	43	37
* 小学在校学生数(人)	Students Enrollment of Primary Schools(person)	27 800	23 924	21 215
* 普通中学校数(所)	Number of Regular Secondary Schools(unit)	41	41	36
* 普通中学在校学生(人)	Students Enrollment of Regular Secondary Schools(person)	32 551	32 460	32 104
幼儿园数(所)	Number of Kindergartens(unit)	41	38	20
卫生机构数(个)	Health Care Institutions(unit)	185	121	112
# 医院、卫生院	Hospital and Health Center	15	15	15
卫生机构床位数(张)	Beds(unit)	1 202	1 392	1 283
# 医院、卫生院	Hospital and Health Center	1 061	1 141	1 074
* 人均公共绿地面积(平方米)	Per Capita Public Green Areas(sq. m)	4.59	2.30	2.88

22－7 塘沽区基本情况

BASIC STATISTICS OF TANGGU DISTRICT

指标名称	Item	2001	2002	2003
*户籍户数(万户)	Registered Households (10 000 househols)	15.92	16.22	16.54
#农业户	Agricultural Households	2.19	2.10	2.18
*户籍人口(万人)	Registered Population (10 000 persons)	46.84	47.21	47.59
1.农业人口	Agricultural Population	6.38	6.07	6.01
非农业人口	Non－agricultural Population	40.46	41.15	41.58
2.男	Male	24.20	24.36	24.55
女	Female	22.63	22.85	23.04
*人口出生率(‰)	Birth Rate of Population (‰)	6.30	6.57	5.27
*人口自然增长率(‰)	Natural Growth Rate of Population (‰)	－0.66	－1.63	1.27
城镇单位从业人员(万人)	Persons Employed in Urban Units (10^4 persons)	3.09	3.57	3.56
#在岗职工	On－post Staff and Workers	2.95	3.44	3.29
*乡村从业人员(万人)	Rural Persons Employed(10 000 persons)	2.39	2.35	2.15
#农林牧渔业劳动者人数	Farming,Forestry,Animal Husbandry and Fishery	0.84	0.82	0.65
地区生产总值(万元)	Gross Domestic Product (10 000 yuan)	312 589	412 846	531 941
第一产业	Primary Industry	13 063	13 913	16 148
第二产业	Secondary Industry	75 362	85 795	120 801
#工　业	Industry	55 422	63 224	92 588
第三产业	Tertiary Industry	224 164	313 138	394 992
地区生产总值增速(%)	Increase Rate of Gross Domestic Product (%)	18.0	31.1	25.6
一般预算内区级财政收入(万元)	General Intra－budgetary Financial Revenue at District Level (10 000 yuan)	50 592	47 430	49 763
一般预算内区级财政支出(万元)	General Intra－budgetary Financial Expenditure at District Level (10 000 yuan)	58 117	73 468	82 836
#教育经费支出	Operating Expenses for Education	17 809	20 156	22 980
*固定资产投资(万元)	Investment in Fixed Assets(10 000 yuan)	858 687	919 592	1 390 863
年末实有耕地面积(万公顷)	Cultivated Land (year－end) (10 000 hectare)	0.52	0.52	0.52
农业机械总动力(万千瓦)	Total Power of Agricultural Machinery (10 000 kw)	22.44	27.49	25.94
化肥折纯量(吨)	Consumption of Chemical Fertilizers (Pureness) (ton)	1 581	1 253	951
农村用电量(万千瓦小时)	Rural Electricity Consumption (10 000 kwh)	5 042	5 104	5 843
农林牧渔业总产值(万元)	Gross Output Value of Farming,Forestry,Animal Husbandry and Fishery (10 000 yuan)	30 626	36 472	41 385
农林牧渔业总产值增速(%)	Increase Rate of Gross Output Value of Farming,Forestry,Animal Husbandry and Fishery(%)	24.6	19.1	13.5
粮食产量(万吨)	Total Yield of Grain (10 000 tons)	0.59	0.51	0.23
水产品产量(吨)	Total Yield of Aquatic Products (ton)	18 845	19 472	22 477
蔬菜总产量(吨)	Total Yield of Vegetable (ton)	61 278	60 400	60 000
*农民人均年纯收入(元)	Per Capita Annual Net Income of Rural Households(yuan)	5 399	5 950	6 555
*农民人均生活消费支出(元)	Per Capita Annual Expenditure for Consumption of Rural Households (yuan)	3 451	3 653	4 259

注:1."*"为全区数据,其余为区属数。2.固定资产投资不含农村集体和个人投资。3.乡镇企业为乡村两级数。4.22－8至22－15表同。
Note:a)The data with "*" of this table reler to the whole district,others reler to units under the leadership ofthis district. b)The investment in fixed assets exclude rural collective and individual. c)Township enterprises include that of village and town level. d)Same as following table 22－8to22－15.

22－7 续表　Continued

指标名称	Item	2001	2002	2003
乡镇企业单位数(个)	Number of Township Enterprises(unit)	150	134	90
#工　业	Industry	75	61	62
乡镇企业人数(万人)	Employment of Township Enterprises(10 000 persons)	1.39	1.62	0.73
#工　业	Industry	0.49	0.64	0.22
乡镇企业主营业务收入(万元)	Major Business Revenue of Township Enterprises(10 000 yuan)	161 577	151 590	74 025
#工　业	Industry	41 648	40 046	21 790
限额以上工业企业	Industrial Enterprises above Designated Size			
单位数(个)	Number of Units(unit)	95	124	113
从业人员(万人)	Persons Employed(10 000 persons)	0.61	0.89	0.72
总产值(万元)	Gross Output Value(10 000 yuan)	215 074	269 676	294 187
产品销售收入(万元)	Sales Revenue(10 000 yuan)	206 857	265 670	303 710
利税总额(万元)	Total Pre－tax Profits(10 000 yuan)	25 076	36 797	52 137
固定资产原值(万元)	Original Value of Fixed Assets(10 000 yuan)	203 255	242 562	198 405
流动资产合计(万元)	Total Circulating Funds(10 000 yuan)	107 708	158 548	175 227
社会消费品零售总额(万元)	Total Retail Sales of Consumer Goods(10 000 yuan)	396 301	503 934	601 105
集市贸易市场数(个)	Number of Free Markets	59	64	65
集市贸易成交额(万元)	Transaction Value of Free Markets(10 000 yuan)	310 471	408 372	462 018
*私营工商企业	Private Industrial and Commercial Enterprises			
户　数(户)	Number of Enterprises(unit)	1 624	2 184	2 406
雇工人数(人)	Employees(person)	14 151	18 905	18 528
注册资本(万元)	Registered Capital(10 000 yuan)	182 441	224 404	378 651
总产值(万元)	Gross Output Value(10 000 yuan)	48 882	59 143	76 803
营业收入(万元)	Business Revenue(10 000 yuan)	130 982	186 987	218 406
*个体工商业	Individual Industrial and Commercial Enterprises			
户　数(户)	Number of Enterprises (unit)	7 304	8 432	10 937
从业人员(人)	Persons Employed(person)	8 963	10 253	13 285
资　金(万元)	Fund(10 000 yuan)	49 052	54 865	61 579
营业额(万元)	Turnover(10 000 yuan)	160 219	189 800	220 903
直接利用外资协议额(万美元)	Foreign Direct Investment Contracted(USD 10 000)	8 412	11 119	7 089
外贸出口交货值(万元)	Delivery Value of Exports Trade(10 000 yuan)	56 699	85 127	153 956
*小学校数(所)	Number of Primary Schools(unit)	64	61	60
*小学在校学生数(人)	Students Enrollment of Primary Schools(person)	34 307	34 847	31 975
*普通中学校数(所)	Number of Regular Secondary Schools(unit)	40	42	37
*普通中学在校学生数(人)	Students Enrollment of Regular Secondary Schools(person)	25 997	28 407	26 621
幼儿园数(所)	Number of Kindergartens(unit)	46	47	88
卫生机构数(个)	Health Care Institutions(unit)	210	172	171
#医院、卫生院	Hospital and Health Center	20	20	20
卫生机构床位数(张)	Beds(unit)	2 409	2 410	2 410
#医院、卫生院	Hospital and Health Center	2 371	2 371	2 167

22－8 汉沽区基本情况

BASIC STATISTICS OF HANGU DISTRICT

指标名称	Item	2001	2002	2003
*户籍户数(万户)	Registered Households(10 000 househols)	6.00	6.06	6.12
#农业户	Agricultural Households	1.46	1.47	1.48
*户籍人口(万人)	Registered Population (10 000 persons)	16.79	16.80	16.80
1.农业人口	Agricultural Population	4.49	4.48	4.47
非农业人口	Non－agricultural Population	12.30	12.32	12.32
2.男	Male	8.55	8.55	8.54
女	Female	8.24	8.25	8.26
*人口出生率(‰)	Birth Rate of Population (‰)	6.40	8.2	8.7
*人口自然增长率(‰)	Natural Growth Rate of Population (‰)	1.70	2.7	2.1
城镇单位从业人员(万人)	Persons Employed in Urban Units (10^4 persons)	1.38	1.28	1.27
#在岗职工	On－post Staff and Workers	1.36	1.27	1.23
*乡村从业人员(万人)	Rural Persons Employed(10 000 persons)	2.4	2.37	2.51
#农林牧渔业劳动者人数	Farming,Forestry,Animal Husbandry and Fishery		1.36	1.54
地区生产总值(万元)	Gross Domestic Product (10 000 yuan)	164 372	188 450	222 117
第一产业	Primary Industry	26 048	27 636	29 580
第二产业	Secondary Industry	70 000	81 266	99 325
#工　业	Industry	62 689	73 486	87 670
第三产业	Tertiary Industry	68 324	79 548	93 212
地区生产总值增速(%)	Increase Rate of Gross Domestic Product (%)	16.1	16.2	15.3
一般预算内区级财政收入(万元)	General Intra－budgetary Financial Revenue at District Level (10 000 yuan)	10 323	9 638	10 683
一般预算内区级财政支出(万元)	General Intra－budgetary Financial Expenditure at District Level (10 000 yuan)	16 966	20 490	24 459
#教育经费支出	Operating Expenses for Education	5 042	5 993	6 515
*固定资产投资(万元)	Investment in Fixed Assets(10 000 yuan)	32 238	41 268	110 337
年末实有耕地面积(万公顷)	Cultivated Land (year－end) (10 000 hectare)	0.43	0.42	0.42
农业机械总动力(万千瓦)	Total Power of Agricultural Machinery (10 000 kw)	16.27	15.03	13.83
化肥折纯量(吨)	Consumption of Chemical Fertilizers (Pureness) (ton)	1 784	1 539	1 293
农村用电量(万千瓦小时)	Rural Electricity Consumption (10 000 kwh)	18 669	16 785	14 860
农林牧渔业总产值(万元)	Gross Output Value of Farming,Forestry,Animal Husbandry and Fishery (10 000 yuan)	61 315	65 101	70 324
农林牧渔业总产值增速(%)	Increase Rate of Gross Output Value of Farming, Forestry,Animal Husbandry and Fishery(%)	15.1	6.2	8.0
粮食产量(万吨)	Total Yield of Grain (10 000 tons)	0.56	0.50	0.29
水产品产量(吨)	Total Yield of Aquatic Products (ton)	26 777	26 375	23 080
蔬菜总产量(吨)	Total Yield of Vegetable (ton)	31 220	26 997	30 351
*农民人均年纯收入(元)	Per Capita Annual Net Income of Rural Households(yuan)	5 161	5 678	6 247
*农民人均生活消费支出(元)	Per Capita Annual Expenditure for Consumption of Rural Households (yuan)	2 773	3 165	3 433

22－8续表 Continued

指标名称	Item	2001	2002	2003
乡镇企业单位数(个)	Number of Township Enterprises(unit)	125	116	126
#工 业	Industry	125	116	126
乡镇企业人数(万人)	Employment of Township Enterprises(10 000 persons)	1.21	1.12	1.11
#工 业	Industry	1.21	1.12	1.11
乡镇企业主营业务收入(万元)	Major Business Revenue of Township Enterprises(10 000 yuan)	156 400	187 680	225 238
#工 业	Industry	156 400	187 680	225 238
限额以上工业企业	Industrial Enterprises above Designated Size			
单位数(个)	Number of Units(unit)	57	51	55
从业人员(万人)	Persons Employed(10 000 persons)	1.35	1.37	1.33
总产值(万元)	Gross Output Value(10 000 yuan)	177 859	214 638	283 242
产品销售收入(万元)	Sales Revenue(10 000 yuan)	169 132	207 060	271 491
利税总额(万元)	Total Pre－tax Profits(10 000 yuan)	14 428	15 776	23 156
固定资产原值(万元)	Original Value of Fixed Assets(10 000 yuan)	66 345	45 901	42 468
流动资产合计(万元)	Total Circulating Funds(10 000 yuan)	83 250	84 731	91 594
社会消费品零售总额(万元)	Total Retail Sales of Consumer Goods(10 000 yuan)	96 957	115 890	142 781
集市贸易市场数(个)	Number of Free Markets	12	10	10
集市贸易成交额(万元)	Transaction Value of Free Markets(10 000 yuan)	35 390	41 785	49 298
*私营工商企业	Private Industrial and Commercial Enterprises			
户 数(户)	Number of Enterprises (unit)	500	547	621
雇工人数(人)	Employees(person)	5 847	6 097	7 264
注册资本(万元)	Registered Capital(10 000 yuan)	20 849	24 909	34 305
总产值(万元)	Gross Output Value(10 000 yuan)	14 065	32 440	42 484
营业收入(万元)	Business Revenue(10 000 yuan)	25 343	23 881	38 388
*个体工商业	Individual Industrial and Commercial Enterprises			
户 数(户)	Number of Enterprises (unit)	5 929	3 967	4 030
从业人员(人)	Persons Employed(person)	6 818	4 466	4 726
资 金(万元)	Fund(10 000 yuan)	7 464	5 185	5 423
营业额(万元)	Turnover(10 000 yuan)	24 359	59 171	61 195
直接利用外资协议额(万美元)	Foreign Direct Investment Contracted(USD 10 000)	616	765	2 164
外贸出口交货值(万元)	Delivery Value of Exports Trade(10 000 yuan)	25 103	47 873	53 724
*小学校数(所)	Number of Primary Schools(unit)	29	28	26
*小学在校学生数(人)	Students Enrollment of Primary Schools(person)	12 914	12 314	11 692
*普通中学校数(所)	Number of Regular Secondary Schools(unit)	18	16	15
*普通中学在校学生数(人)	Students Enrollment of Regular Secondary Schools(person)	10 009	10 278	10 408
幼儿园数(所)	Number of Kindergartens(unit)	27	24	24
卫生机构数(个)	Health Care Institutions(unit)	20	16	16
#医院、卫生院	Hospital and Health Center	8	12	8
卫生机构床位数(张)	Beds(unit)	1 002	1 012	992
#医院、卫生院	Hospital and Health Center	952	992	972

22－9 大港区基本情况
BASIC STATISTICS OF DAGANG DISTRICT

指标名称	Item	2001	2002	2003
* 户籍户数(万户)	Registered Households(10 000 househols)	11.91	12.13	12.42
# 农业户	Agricultural Households	3.28	3.27	3.33
* 户籍人口(万人)	Registered Population(10 000 persons)	33.51	34.15	34.46
1.农业人口	Agricultural Population	10.25	10.34	10.29
非农业人口	Non－agricultural Population	23.26	23.82	24.17
2.男	Male	17.64	17.90	18.04
女	Female	15.86	16.25	16.42
* 人口出生率(‰)	Birth Rate of Population(‰)	11.92	13.08	9.11
* 人口自然增长率(‰)	Natural Growth Rate of Population(‰)	8.56	9.31	4.94
城镇单位从业人员(万人)	Persons Employed in Urban Units(10^4 persons)	1.46	1.57	1.75
# 在岗职工	On－post Staff and Workers	1.44	1.55	1.70
* 乡村从业人员(万人)	Rural Persons Employed(10 000 persons)	3.57	3.6	3.80
# 农林牧渔业劳动者人数	Farming, Forestry, Animal Husbandry and Fishery	1.60	1.5	1.60
地区生产总值(万元)	Gross Domestic Product (10 000 yuan)	356 635	425 557	532 421
第一产业	Primary Industry	9 207	10 465	12 960
第二产业	Secondary Industry	214 380	247 550	311 723
# 工　业	Industry	167 646	190 720	242 419
第三产业	Tertiary Industry	133 048	167 542	207 738
地区生产总值增速(％)	Increase Rate of Gross Domestic Product(％)	18.3	20.8	22.0
一般预算内区级财政收入(万元)	General Intra－budgetary Financial Revenue at District Level(10 000 yuan)	33 117	32 495	28 261
一般预算内区级财政支出(万元)	General Intra－budgetary Financial Expenditure at District Level(10 000 yuan)	42 775	45 791	48 664
# 教育经费支出	Operating Expenses for Education	8 094	10 403	11 089
* 固定资产投资(万元)	Investment in Fixed Assets(10 000 yuan)	453 158	406 102	466 476
年末实有耕地面积(万公顷)	Cultivated Land(year－end)(10 000 hectare)	1.35	1.35	1.34
农业机械总动力(万千瓦)	Total Power of Agricultural Machinery(10 000 kw)	28	27.61	25.89
化肥折纯量(吨)	Consumption of Chemical Fertilizers(Pureness)(ton)	1 751	1 612	1 623
农村用电量(万千瓦小时)	Rural Electricity Consumption(10 000 kwh)	12 287	12 697	13 086
农林牧渔业总产值(万元)	Gross Output Value of Farming, Forestry, Animal Husbandry and Fishery(10 000 yuan)	22 442	25 015	29 485
农林牧渔业总产值增速(％)	Increase Rate of Gross Output Value of Farming, Forestry, Animal Husbandry and Fishery(％)	41.8	0.7	16.0
粮食产量(万吨)	Total Yield of Grain(10 000 tons)	1.86	0.45	1.43
水产品产量(吨)	Total Yield of Aquatic Products(ton)	6 329	5 355	5 554
蔬菜总产量(吨)	Total Yield of Vegetable(ton)	50 050	50 033	50 777
* 农民人均年纯收入(元)	Per Capita Annual Net Income of Rural Households(yuan)	5 162	5 679	6 253
* 农民人均生活消费支出(元)	Per Capita Annual Expenditure for Consumption of Rural Households (yuan)	2 394	4 037	4 845

22－9 续表　Continued

指标名称	Item	2001	2002	2003
乡镇企业单位数(个)	Number of Township Enterprises(unit)	234	228	214
#工　业	Industry	234	228	214
乡镇企业人数(万人)	Employment of Township Enterprises(10 000 persons)	1.70	1.76	1.67
#工　业	Industry	1.70	1.76	1.67
乡镇企业主营业务收入(万元)	Major Business Revenue of Township Enterprises(10 000 yuan)	215 564	275 677	350 508
#工　业	Industry	215 564	275 677	350 508
限额以上工业企业	Industrial Enterprises above Designated Size			
单位数(个)	Number of Units(unit)	522	424	287
从业人员(万人)	Persons Employed(10 000 persons)	3.04	3.69	2.58
总产值(万元)	Gross Output Value(10 000 yuan)	543 878	884 256	671 153
产品销售收入(万元)	Sales Revenue(10 000 yuan)	509 069	760 089	668 153
利税总额(万元)	Total Pre－tax Profits(10 000 yuan)	58 797	18 492	30 372
固定资产原值(万元)	Original Value of Fixed Assets(10 000 yuan)	197 062	307 345	261 976
流动资产合计(万元)	Total Circulating Funds(10 000 yuan)	198 152	335 947	342 414
社会消费品零售总额(万元)	Total Retail Sales of Consumer Goods(10 000 yuan)	216 625	253 022	265 492
集市贸易市场数(个)	Number of Free Markets	33	36	36
集市贸易成交额(万元)	Transaction Value of Free Markets(10 000 yuan)	36 000	28 800	31 800
*私营工商企业	Private Industrial and Commercial Enterprises			
户　数(户)	Number of Enterprises (unit)	1 117	1 231	1 583
雇工人数(人)	Employees(person)	10 070	14 330	18 098
注册资本(万元)	Registered Capital(10 000 yuan)	61 428	82 216	82 216
总产值(万元)	Gross Output Value(10 000 yuan)	34 804	43 167	55 128
营业收入(万元)	Business Revenue(10 000 yuan)	54 116	72 517	100 038
*个体工商业	Individual Industrial and Commercial Enterprises			
户　数(户)	Number of Enterprises (unit)	5 254	5 924	6 226
从业人员(人)	Persons Employed(person)	11 408	12 781	14 191
资　金(万元)	Fund(10 000 yuan)	33 728	46 989	46 989
营业额(万元)	Turnover(10 000 yuan)	71 294	86 031	109 660
直接利用外资协议额(万美元)	Foreign Direct Investment Contracted(USD 10 000)	7 217	13 905	3 409
外贸出口交货值(万元)	Delivery Value of Exports Trade(10 000 yuan)	210 000	186 135	243 171
*小学校数(所)	Number of Primary Schools(unit)	39	32	32
*小学在校学生数(人)	Students Enrollment of Primary Schools(person)	23 872	23 262	23 624
*普通中学校数(所)	Number of Regular Secondary Schools(unit)	40	41	39
*普通中学在校学生数(人)	Students Enrollment of Regular Secondary Schools(person)	23 891	26 254	27 567
幼儿园数(所)	Number of Kindergartens(unit)	82	55	84
卫生机构数(个)	Health Care Institutions(unit)	13	12	12
#医院、卫生院	Hospital and Health Center	10	10	10
卫生机构床位数(张)	Beds(unit)	437	490	442
#医院、卫生院	Hospital and Health Center	302	302	382

22－10　东丽区基本情况
BASIC STATISTICS OF DONGLI DISTRICT

指标名称	Item	2001	2002	2003
*户籍户数(万户)	Registered Households(10 000 househols)	10.26	10.38	10.79
#农业户	Agricultural Households	6.47	6.51	6.86
*户籍人口(万人)	Registered Population(10 000 persons)	30.59	30.83	31.25
1.农业人口	Agricultural Population	19.64	19.65	19.87
非农业人口	Non－agricultural Population	10.95	11.18	11.37
2.男	Male	15.45	15.59	15.75
女	Female	15.14	15.24	15.50
*人口出生率(‰)	Birth Rate of Population(‰)	8.33	8.03	5.44
*人口自然增长率(‰)	Natural Growth Rate of Population(‰)	2.62	2.55	0.51
城镇单位从业人员(万人)	Persons Employed in Urban Units (10^4 persons)	3.94	4.37	3.88
#在岗职工	On－post Staff and Workers	3.88	4.37	3.59
*乡村从业人员(万人)	Rural Persons Employed(10 000 persons)	8.17	8.13	9.29
#农林牧渔业劳动者人数	Farming, Forestry, Animal Husbandry and Fishery	1.84	1.87	2.08
地区生产总值(万元)	Gross Domestic Product(10 000 yuan)	736 047	850 000	1 011 590
第一产业	Primary Industry	25 937	32 532	34 548
第二产业	Secondary Industry	319 000	367 655	462 392
#工　业	Industry	272 693	312 146	387 784
第三产业	Tertiary Industry	391 110	449 813	514 650
地区生产总值增速(%)	Increase Rate of Gross Domestic Product(%)	11.5	17.7	17.6
一般预算内区级财政收入(万元)	General Intra－budgetary Financial Revenue at District Level(10 000 yuan)	37 917	38 226	39 504
一般预算内区级财政支出(万元)	General Intra－budgetary Financial Expenditure at District Level (10 000 yuan)	40 053	49 816	57 729
#教育经费支出	Operating Expenses for Education	9 860	13 329	15 282
*固定资产投资(万元)	Investment in Fixed Assets(10 000 yuan)	188 018	288 383	735 363
年末实有耕地面积(万公顷)	Cultivated Land (year－end) (10 000 hectare)	1.39	1.39	1.38
农业机械总动力(万千瓦)	Total Power of Agricultural Machinery (10 000 kw)	48.28	46.60	46.4
化肥折纯量(吨)	Consumption of Chemical Fertilizers (Pureness) (ton)	2 686	2 464	2 357
农村用电量(万千瓦小时)	Rural Electricity Consumption (10 000 kwh)	22 862	22 608	23 531
农林牧渔业总产值(万元)	Gross Output Value of Farming, Forestry, Animal Husbandry and Fishery (10 000 yuan)	66 115	83 877	85 748
农林牧渔业总产值增速(%)	Increase Rate of Gross Output Value of Farming, Forestry, Animal Husbandry and Fishery(%)	－6.7	26.9	2.2
粮食产量(万吨)	Total Yield of Grain (10 000 tons)	3.71	3.44	1.11
水产品产量(吨)	Total Yield of Aquatic Products (ton)	16 411	18 415	17 965
蔬菜总产量(吨)	Total Yield of Vegetable (ton)	250 972	220 187	267 682
*农民人均年纯收入(元)	Per Capita Annual Net Income of Rural Households(yuan)	5 851	6 451	7 161
*农民人均生活消费支出(元)	Per Capita Annual Expenditure for Consumption of Rural Households (yuan)	4 284	4 151	4 854

22－10 续表　Continued

指标名称	Item	2001	2002	2003
乡镇企业单位数(个)	Number of Township Enterprises(unit)	1 003	1 911	1 945
#工　业	Industry	618	1 500	1 482
乡镇企业人数(万人)	Employment of Township Enterprises(10 000 persons)	5.31	8.4	8.3
#工　业	Industry	4.17	6.2	6.1
乡镇企业主营业务收入(万元)	Major Business Revenue of Township Enterprises(10 000 yuan)	1 272 132	908 376	1 178 327
#工　业	Industry	679 248	803 500	849 037
限额以上工业企业	Industrial Enterprises above Designated Size			
单位数(个)	Number of Units(unit)	157	169	167
从业人员(万人)	Persons Employed(10 000 persons)	2.25	3.02	3.48
总产值(万元)	Gross Output Value(10 000 yuan)	462 059	616 662	666 257
产品销售收入(万元)	Sales Revenue(10 000 yuan)	385 429	623 400	619 845
利税总额(万元)	Total Pre－tax Profits(10 000 yuan)	45 517	72 086	75 175
固定资产原值(万元)	Original Value of Fixed Assets(10 000 yuan)	145 561	268 790	2 888 351
流动资产合计(万元)	Total Circulating Funds(10 000 yuan)	195 221	326 235	343 873
社会消费品零售总额(万元)	Total Retail Sales of Consumer Goods(10 000 yuan)	430 843	509 200	604 931
集市贸易市场数(个)	Number of Free Markets	34	34	34
集市贸易成交额(万元)	Transaction Value of Free Markets(10 000 yuan)	341 421	341 421	467 442
*私营工商企业	Private Industrial and Commercial Enterprises			
户　数(户)	Number of Enterprises (unit)	2 494	2 527	3 133
雇工人数(人)	Employees(person)	22 500	23 251	27 306
注册资本(万元)	Registered Capital(10 000 yuan)	231 600	233 522	335 816
总产值(万元)	Gross Output Value(10 000 yuan)	331 100	410 800	510 037
营业收入(万元)	Business Revenue(10 000 yuan)	302 600	343 035	425 880
*个体工商业	Individual Industrial and Commercial Enterprises			
户　数(户)	Number of Enterprises (unit)	4 441	4 852	5 963
从业人员(人)	Persons Employed(person)	7 800	8 172	10 273
资　金(万元)	Fund(10 000 yuan)	14 100	14 988	19 459
营业额(万元)	Turnover(10 000 yuan)	242 600	64 201	79 601
直接利用外资协议额(万美元)	Foreign Direct Investment Contracted(USD 10 000)	16 507	5 845	13 169
外贸出口交货值(万元)	Delivery Value of Exports Trade(10 000 yuan)	260 544	306 947	388 622
*小学校数(所)	Number of Primary Schools(unit)	49	46	43
*小学在校学生数(人)	Students Enrollment of Primary Schools(person)	19 458	20 997	25 190
*普通中学校数(所)	Number of Regular Secondary Schools(unit)	27	28	28
*普通中学在校学生数(人)	Students Enrollment of Regular Secondary Schools(person)	18 819	16 916	17 146
幼儿园数(所)	Number of Kindergartens(unit)	45	59	55
卫生机构数(个)	Health Care Institutions(unit)	15	18	18
#医院、卫生院	Hospital and Health Center	4	4	11
卫生机构床位数(张)	Beds(unit)	700	700	722
#医院、卫生院	Hospital and Health Center	700	700	700

22－11　西青区基本情况
BASIC STATISTICS OF XIQING DISTRICT

指标名称	Item	2001	2002	2003
*户籍户数(万户)	Registered Households(10 000 households)	9.84	10.02	10.18
#农业户	Agricultural Households	7.30	7.45	7.60
*户籍人口(万人)	Registered Population(10 000 persons)	30.61	30.60	30.63
1.农业人口	Agricultural Population	22.86	22.91	22.88
非农业人口	Non－agricultural Population	7.75	7.69	7.75
2.男	Male	15.22	15.20	15.20
女	Female	15.39	15.40	15.43
*人口出生率(‰)	Birth Rate of Population(‰)	10.91	10.9	8.99
*人口自然增长率(‰)	Natural Growth Rate of Population(‰)	4.62	5.8	3.73
城镇单位从业人员(万人)	Persons Employed in Urban Units (10^4 persons)	2.47	3.78	3.61
#在岗职工	On－post Staff and Workers	2.38	3.37	3.14
*乡村从业人员(万人)	Rural Persons Employed(10 000 persons)	10.92	10.60	11.05
#农林牧渔业劳动者人数	Farming,Forestry,Animal Husbandry and Fishery	3.71	3.80	3.96
地区生产总值(万元)	Gross Domestic Product(10 000 yuan)	828 322	1 000 033	1 233 215
第一产业	Primary Industry	48 200	53 300	60 200
第二产业	Secondary Industry	442 900	550 900	711 000
#工　业	Industry	431 400	539 900	700 000
第三产业	Tertiary Industry	337 222	395 833	462 015
地区生产总值增速(%)	Increase Rate of Gross Domestic Product(%)	15.1	24.3	20.9
一般预算内区级财政收入(万元)	General Intra－budgetary Financial Revenue at District Level(10 000 yuan)	53 708	50 864	60 064
一般预算内区级财政支出(万元)	General Intra－budgetary Financial Expenditure at District Level(10 000 yuan)	60 044	68 011	96 576
#教育经费支出	Operating Expenses for Education	9 403	11 509	12 933
*固定资产投资(万元)	Investment in Fixed Assets(10 000 yuan)	420 631	432 597	357 143
年末实有耕地面积(万公顷)	Cultivated Land(year－end)(10 000 hectare)	1.62	1.61	1.59
农业机械总动力(万千瓦)	Total Power of Agricultural Machinery(10 000 kw)	47.99	50.31	48.33
化肥折纯量(吨)	Consumption of Chemical Fertilizers(Pureness)(ton)	11 926	7 921	10 000
农村用电量(万千瓦小时)	Rural Electricity Consumption(10 000 kwh)	53 712	49 297	50 072
农林牧渔业总产值(万元)	Gross Output Value of Farming,Forestry,Animal Husbandry and Fishery(10 000 yuan)	104 167	114 624	122 883
农林牧渔业总产值增速(%)	Increase Rate of Gross Output Value of Farming, Forestry,Animal Husbandry and Fishery(%)	17.7	10.0	8.7
粮食产量(万吨)	Total Yield of Grain(10 000 tons)	4.20	4.35	3.75
水产品产量(吨)	Total Yield of Aquatic Products(ton)	39 392	44 310	47 268
蔬菜总产量(吨)	Total Yield of Vegetable(ton)	385 442	369 077	357 919
*农民人均年纯收入(元)	Per Capita Annual Net Income of Rural Households(yuan)	6 010	6 615	7 288
*农民人均生活消费支出(元)	Per Capita Annual Expenditure for Consumption of Rural Households (yuan)	3 287	3 366	3 439

22－11 续表 Continued

指标名称	Item	2001	2002	2003
乡镇企业单位数(个)	Number of Township Enterprises(unit)	663	644	707
#工　业	Industry	536	465	443
乡镇企业人数(万人)	Employment of Township Enterprises(10 000 persons)	6.48	6.53	6.31
#工　业	Industry	5.59	5.81	5.40
乡镇企业主营业务收入(万元)	Major Business Revenue of Township Enterprises(10 000 yuan)	1 295 178	1 346 296	1 425 310
#工　业	Industry	1 126 570	1 180 912	1 227 165
限额以上工业企业	Industrial Enterprises above Designated Size			
单位数(个)	Number of Units(unit)	401	233	347
从业人员(万人)	Persons Employed(10 000 persons)	6.41	5.37	7.45
总产值(万元)	Gross Output Value(10 000 yuan)	1 711 601	1 369 923	2 149 836
产品销售收入(万元)	Sales Revenue(10 000 yuan)	1 575 981	1 241 973	2 076 071
利税总额(万元)	Total Pre－tax Profits(10 000 yuan)	193 964	133 888	441 244
固定资产原值(万元)	Original Value of Fixed Assets(10 000 yuan)	475 400	524 470	903 166
流动资产合计(万元)	Total Circulating Funds(10 000 yuan)	634 930	516 302	940 473
社会消费品零售总额(万元)	Total Retail Sales of Consumer Goods(10 000 yuan)	50 034	151 891	20.72
集市贸易市场数(个)	Number of Free Markets	50	31	36
集市贸易成交额(万元)	Transaction Value of Free Markets(10 000 yuan)	209 924	22 810	143 195
* 私营工商企业	Private Industrial and Commercial Enterprises			
户　数(户)	Number of Enterprises (unit)	1 531	1 942	2 630
雇工人数(人)	Employees(person)	14 138	20 722	22 651
注册资本(万元)	Registered Capital(10 000 yuan)	109 387	162 150	298 919
总产值(万元)	Gross Output Value(10 000 yuan)	54 697	42 722	51 603
营业收入(万元)	Business Revenue(10 000 yuan)	26 401	21 226	32 287
* 个体工商业	Individual Industrial and Commercial Enterprises			
户　数(户)	Number of Enterprises (unit)	3 831	5 167	4 539
从业人员(人)	Persons Employed(person)	8 826	9 352	8 878
资　金(万元)	Fund(10 000 yuan)	16 065	17 045	19 198
营业额(万元)	Turnover(10 000 yuan)	36 377	36 087	46 563
直接利用外资协议额(万美元)	Foreign Direct Investment Contracted(USD 10 000)	14 575	21 300	15 528
外贸出口交货值(万元)	Delivery Value of Exports Trade (10 000 yuan)	257 340	307 838	435 365
* 小学校数(所)	Number of Primary Schools(unit)	42	42	41
* 小学在校学生数(人)	Students Enrollment of Primary Schools(person)	21 992	20 995	20 206
* 普通中学校数(所)	Number of Regular Secondary Schools(unit)	19	19	17
* 普通中学在校学生数(人)	Students Enrollment of Regular Secondary Schools(person)	17 485	16 817	14 006
幼儿园数(所)	Number of Kindergartens(unit)	84	62	70
卫生机构数(个)	Health Care Institutions(unit)	15	16	18
#医院、卫生院	Hospital and Health Center	11	11	11
卫生机构床位数(张)	Beds(unit)	700	700	700
#医院、卫生院	Hospital and Health Center	700	700	700

22－12　津南区基本情况

BASIC STATISTICS OF JINNAN DISTRICT

指标名称	Item	2001	2002	2003
* 户籍户数(万户)	Registered Households(10 000 househols)	11.90	12.05	12.24
# 农业户	Agricultural Households	8.69	8.76	8.88
* 户籍人口(万人)	Registered Population(10 000 persons)	37.01	37.16	37.32
1.农业人口	Agricultural Population	27.66	27.58	27.49
非农业人口	Non－agricultural Population	9.35	9.58	9.83
2.男	Male	18.54	18.60	18.67
女	Female	18.47	18.56	18.65
* 人口出生率(‰)	Birth Rate of Population(‰)	9.42	11.57	7.44
* 人口自然增长率(‰)	Natural Growth Rate of Population(‰)	5.11	6.67	2.68
城镇单位从业人员(万人)	Persons Employed in Urban Units (10^4 persons)	2.42	3.23	3.53
# 在岗职工	On－post Staff and Workers	2.37	3.18	3.4
* 乡村从业人员(万人)	Rural Persons Employed(10 000 persons)	13.72	13.62	13.03
# 农林牧渔业劳动者人数	Farming, Forestry, Animal Husbandry and Fishery	3.70	3.40	3.31
地区生产总值(万元)	Gross Domestic Product(10 000 yuan)	622 052	698 895	852 443
第一产业	Primary Industry	22 695	24 798	26 858
第二产业	Secondary Industry	333 790	370 767	454 822
# 工　业	Industry	292 209	320 660	396 338
第三产业	Tertiary Industry	256 657	303 330	370 763
地区生产总值增速(%)	Increase Rate of Gross Domestic Product(%)	15.1	20.1	19.7
一般预算内区级财政收入(万元)	General Intra－budgetary Financial Revenue at District Level(10 000 yuan)	27 685	30 666	24 766
一般预算内区级财政支出(万元)	General Intra－budgetary Financial Expenditure at District Level(10 000 yuan)	29 113	38 577	52 165
# 教育经费支出	Operating Expenses for Education	8 928	10 565	11 827
* 固定资产投资(万元)	Investment in Fixed Assets(10 000 yuan)	87 922	94 897	133 607
年末实有耕地面积(万公顷)	Cultivated Land(year－end)(10 000 hectare)	1.46	1.46	1.46
农业机械总动力(万千瓦)	Total Power of Agricultural Machinery(10 000 kw)	47.78	47.82	47.82
化肥折纯量(吨)	Consumption of Chemical Fertilizers(Pureness)(ton)	1 734	1 597	1 635
农村用电量(万千瓦小时)	Rural Electricity Consumption(10 000 kwh)	27 066	30 586	32 627
农林牧渔业总产值(万元)	Gross Output Value of Farming, Forestry, Animal Husbandry and Fishery(10 000 yuan)	42 444	43 717	44 943
农林牧渔业总产值增速(%)	Increase Rate of Gross Output Value of Farming, Forestry, Animal Husbandry and Fishery(%)	7.4	9.5	2.8
粮食产量(万吨)	Total Yield of Grain(10 000 tons)	3.97	2.73	1.92
水产品产量(吨)	Total Yield of Aquatic Products(ton)	10 982	11 273	13 200
蔬菜总产量(吨)	Total Yield of Vegetable (ton)	170 123	176 927	179 645
* 农民人均年纯收入(元)	Per Capita Annual Net Income of Rural Households(yuan)	5 327	5 866	6 467
* 农民人均生活消费支出(元)	Per Capita Annual Expenditure for Consumption of Rural Households(yuan)	3 664	3 457	3 820

22－12 续表　Continued

指标名称	Item	2001	2002	2003
乡镇企业单位数(个)	Number of Township Enterprises(unit)	11 218	11 178	11 465
#工　业	Industry	2 067	2 018	2 886
乡镇企业人数(万人)	Employment of Township Enterprises(10 000 persons)	13.16	13.92	15.97
#工　业	Industry	8.23	9.78	9.37
乡镇企业主营业务收入(万元)	Major Business Revenue of Township Enterprises(10 000 yuan)	1 297 174	1 434 673	1 717 643
#工　业	Industry	826 909	964 408	1 107 191
限额以上工业企业	Industrial Enterprises above Designated Size			
单位数(个)	Number of Units(unit)	212	227	228
从业人员(万人)	Persons Employed(10 000 persons)	4.00	5.29	6.22
总产值(万元)	Gross Output Value(10 000 yuan)	597 416	690 478	1 129 875
产品销售收入(万元)	Sales Revenue(10 000 yuan)	567 386	661 987	1 075 900
利税总额(万元)	Total Pre－tax Profits(10 000 yuan)	47 579	58 637	85 932
固定资产原值(万元)	Original Value of Fixed Assets(10 000 yuan)	183 902	214 842	374 603
流动资产合计(万元)	Total Circulating Funds(10 000 yuan)	259 161	298 333	463 306
社会消费品零售总额(万元)	Total Retail Sales of Consumer Goods(10 000 yuan)	224 987	263 327	314 843
集市贸易市场数(个)	Number of Free Markets	9	7	7
集市贸易成交额(万元)	Transaction Value of Free Markets(10 000 yuan)	200 993	217 146	217 120
*私营工商企业	Private Industrial and Commercial Enterprises			
户　数(户)	Number of Enterprises (unit)	1 993	2 118	2 484
雇工人数(人)	Employees(person)	24 460	49 950	32 905
注册资本(万元)	Registered Capital(10 000 yuan)	135 591	183 058	280 552
总产值(万元)	Gross Output Value(10 000 yuan)	299 909	313 500	358 192
营业收入(万元)	Business Revenue(10 000 yuan)	295 281	348 200	374 426
*个体工商业	Individual Industrial and Commercial Enterprises			
户　数(户)	Number of Enterprises (unit)	7 731	8 010	7 655
从业人员(人)	Persons Employed(person)	13 229	15 420	13 658
资　金(万元)	Fund(10 000 yuan)	15 966	16 992	17 678
营业额(万元)	Turnover(10 000 yuan)	684 630	673 300	631 109
直接利用外资协议额(万美元)	Foreign Direct Investment Contracted(USD 10 000)	8 250	10 889	27 035
外贸出口交货值(万元)	Delivery Value of Exports Trade(10 000 yuan)	131 149	295 505	296 373
*小学校数(所)	Number of Primary Schools(unit)	44	45	44
*小学在校学生数(人)	Students Enrollment of Primary Schools(person)	30 265	29 870	28 922
*普通中学校数(所)	Number of Regular Secondary Schools(unit)	22	21	26
*普通中学在校学生数(人)	Students Enrollment of Regular Secondary Schools(person)	18 942	19 331	19 965
幼儿园数(所)	Number of Kindergartens(unit)	77	48	103
卫生机构数(个)	Health Care Institutions(unit)	20	19	16
#医院、卫生院	Hospital and Health Center	3	3	12
卫生机构床位数(张)	Beds(unit)	507	533	553
#医院、卫生院	Hospital and Health Center	468	470	529

22－13　北辰区基本情况
BASIC STATISTICS OF BEICHEN DISTRICT

指标名称	Item	2001	2002	2003
*户籍户数(万户)	Registered Households(10 000 households)	10.48	10.63	10.79
#农业户	Agricultural Households	6.39	6.41	6.48
*户籍人口(万人)	Registered Population(10 000 persons)	31.70	31.98	31.99
1.农业人口	Agricultural Population	19.91	19.83	19.72
非农业人口	Non－agricultural Population	11.79	12.15	12.27
2.男	Male	15.90	16.04	16.04
女	Female	15.80	15.95	15.95
*人口出生率(‰)	Birth Rate of Population(‰)	9.15	8.78	7.14
*人口自然增长率(‰)	Natural Growth Rate of Population(‰)	1.57	4.51	1.07
城镇单位从业人员(万人)	Persons Employed in Urban Units (10^4 persons)	2.81	2.62	3.05
#在岗职工	On－post Staff and Workers	2.64	2.47	2.79
*乡村从业人员(万人)	Rural Persons Employed(10 000 persons)	8.05	8.09	9.53
#农林牧渔业劳动者人数	Farming,Forestry,Animal Husbandry and Fishery	2.99	3.04	3.23
地区生产总值(万元)	Gross Domestic Product(10 000 yuan)	837 642	984 474	1 172 331
第一产业	Primary Industry	47 688	50 668	53 480
第二产业	Secondary Industry	514 324	603 662	728 834
#工　业	Industry	509 097	598 883	716 102
第三产业	Tertiary Industry	275 630	330 144	390 017
地区生产总值增速(%)	Increase Rate of Gross Domestic Product(%)	19.5	20.7	15.9
一般预算内区级财政收入(万元)	General Intra－budgetary Financial Revenue at District Level(10 000 yuan)	43 641	46 636	44 699
一般预算内区级财政支出(万元)	General Intra－budgetary Financial Expenditure at District Level(10 000 yuan)	47 679	59 965	73 219
#教育经费支出	Operating Expenses for Education	12 258	17 780	18 137
*固定资产投资(万元)	Investment in Fixed Assets(10 000 yuan)	190 803	203 141	301 400
年末实有耕地面积(万公顷)	Cultivated Land(year－end)(10 000 hectare)	1.85	1.85	1.85
农业机械总动力(万千瓦)	Total Power of Agricultural Machinery(10 000 kw)	48.30	47.67	46.1
化肥折纯量(吨)	Consumption of Chemical Fertilizers(Pureness)(ton)	6 246	6 972	6 497
农村用电量(万千瓦小时)	Rural Electricity Consumption(10 000 kwh)	25 133	26 404	31 654
农林牧渔业总产值(万元)	Gross Output Value of Farming,Forestry,Animal Husbandry and Fishery(10 000 yuan)	97 504	103 441	109 985
农林牧渔业总产值增速(%)	Increase Rate of Gross Output Value of Farming, Forestry,Animal Husbandry and Fishery(%)	10.6	6.1	6.3
粮食产量(万吨)	Total Yield of Grain(10 000 tons)	4.36	4.62	3.59
水产品产量(吨)	Total Yield of Aquatic Products (ton)	11 796	12 529	11 978
蔬菜总产量(吨)	Total Yield of Vegetable (ton)	401 192	375 345	337 320
*农民人均年纯收入(元)	Per Capita Annual Net Income of Rural Households(yuan)	6 005	6 606	7 268
*农民人均生活消费支出(元)	Per Capita Annual Expenditure for Consumption of Rural Households(yuan)	3 545	3 686	3 731

22－13 续表 Continued

指标名称	Item	2001	2002	2003
乡镇企业单位数(个)	Number of Township Enterprises(unit)	2 964	3 299	1 370
#工 业	Industry	658	623	581
乡镇企业人数(万人)	Employment of Township Enterprises(10 000 persons)	7.84	8.08	7.13
#工 业	Industry	5.83	6.08	6.25
乡镇企业主营业务收入(万元)	Major Business Revenue of Township Enterprises(10 000 yuan)	2 175 577	2 441 498	2 577 068
#工 业	Industry	1 719 668	1 951 498	2 223 592
限额以上工业企业	Industrial Enterprises above Designated Size			
单位数(个)	Number of Units(unit)	431	456	475
从业人员(万人)	Persons Employed(10 000 persons)	5.52	6.16	6.75
总产值(万元)	Gross Output Value(10 000 yuan)	2 030 936	2 298 507	2 723 578
产品销售收入(万元)	Sales Revenue(10 000 yuan)	1 916 386	2 269 201	2 713 396
利税总额(万元)	Total Pre－tax Profits(10 000 yuan)	256 313	297 022	353 969
固定资产原值(万元)	Original Value of Fixed Assets(10 000 yuan)	579 401	702 103	854 065
流动资产合计(万元)	Total Circulating Funds(10 000 yuan)	908 162	1 090 936	1 336 326
社会消费品零售总额(万元)	Total Retail Sales of Consumer Goods(10 000 yuan)	238 307	284 100	329 457
集市贸易市场数(个)	Number of Free Markets	33	27	
集市贸易成交额(万元)	Transaction Value of Free Markets(10 000 yuan)	87 731	85 620	
*私营工商企业	Private Industrial and Commercial Enterprises			
户 数(户)	Number of Enterprises (unit)	2 353	2 778	3 703
雇工人数(人)	Employees(person)	19 488	22 633	38 510
注册资本(万元)	Registered Capital(10 000 yuan)	241 124	323 880	523 278
总产值(万元)	Gross Output Value(10 000 yuan)	145 403	171 612	225 607
营业收入(万元)	Business Revenue(10 000 yuan)	247 165	296 958	434 063
*个体工商业	Individual Industrial and Commercial Enterprises			
户 数(户)	Number of Enterprises (unit)	7 065	5 366	6 416
从业人员(人)	Persons Employed(person)	10 970	8 052	10 026
资 金(万元)	Fund(10 000 yuan)	20 776	18 452	23 318
营业额(万元)	Turnover(10 000 yuan)	278 160	369 738	413 556
直接利用外资协议额(万美元)	Foreign Direct Investment Contracted(USD 10 000)	12 600	20 263	8 131
外贸出口交货值(万元)	Delivery Value of Exports Trade(10 000 yuan)	453 108	548 461	703 573
*小学校数(所)	Number of Primary Schools(unit)	46	46	46
*小学在校学生数(人)	Students Enrollment of Primary Schools(person)	22 560	21 086	19 741
*普通中学校数(所)	Number of Regular Secondary Schools(unit)	20	20	20
*普通中学在校学生数(人)	Students Enrollment of Regular Secondary Schools(person)	15 182	15 284	15 292
幼儿园数(所)	Number of Kindergartens(unit)	92	98	105
卫生机构数(个)	Health Care Institutions(unit)	19	19	19
#医院、卫生院	Hospital and Health Center	15	15	15
卫生机构床位数(张)	Beds(unit)	607	607	547
#医院、卫生院	Hospital and Health Center	607	607	547

22－14 武清区基本情况
BASIC STATISTICS OF WUQING DISTRICT

指标名称	Item	2001	2002	2003
*户籍户数(万户)	Registered Households(10 000 households)	22.42	22.55	22.72
#农业户	Agricultural Households	19.53	19.53	19.59
*户籍人口(万人)	Registered Population(10 000 persons)	80.17	80.57	80.78
1.农业人口	Agricultural Population	69.74	69.60	69.26
非农业人口	Non－agricultural Population	10.43	10.98	11.52
2.男	Male	39.79	40.43	40.53
女	Female	39.92	40.14	40.25
*人口出生率(‰)	Birth Rate of Population(‰)	10.1	9.6	8.3
*人口自然增长率(‰)	Natural Growth Rate of Population(‰)	3.6	3.2	2.1
城镇单位从业人员(万人)	Persons Employed in Urban Units (10^4 persons)	3.44	2.82	6.20
#在岗职工	On－post Staff and Workers	2.95	2.79	6.14
*乡村从业人员(万人)	Rural Persons Employed(10 000 persons)	36.32	36.33	36.56
#农林牧渔业劳动者人数	Farming,Forestry,Animal Husbandry and Fishery	20.18	20.58	20.43
地区生产总值(万元)	Gross Domestic Product(10 000 yuan)	916 984	1 007 269	1 181 796
第一产业	Primary Industry	164 463	173 785	187 516
第二产业	Secondary Industry	437 363	473 807	564 094
#工　业	Industry	422 209	462 847	551 800
第三产业	Tertiary Industry	315 158	359 677	430 186
地区生产总值增速(%)	Increase Rate of Gross Domestic Product(%)	14.0	14.0	15.0
一般预算内区级财政收入(万元)	General Intra－budgetary Financial Revenue at District Level(10 000 yuan)	46 925	51 152	43 995
一般预算内区级财政支出(万元)	General Intra－budgetary Financial Expenditure at District Level(10 000 yuan)	53 562	76 098	95 038
#教育经费支出	Operating Expenses for Education	19 507	21 477	26 039
*固定资产投资(万元)	Investment in Fixed Assets(10 000 yuan)	124 793	207 047	217 192
年末实有耕地面积(万公顷)	Cultivated Land(year－end)(10 000 hectare)	9.13	9.07	9.03
农业机械总动力(万千瓦)	Total Power of Agricultural Machinery(10 000 kw)	99.55	99.4	95.52
化肥折纯量(吨)	Consumption of Chemical Fertilizers(Pureness)(ton)	42 317	44 920	45 423
农村用电量(万千瓦小时)	Rural Electricity Consumption(10 000 kwh)	82 659	93 205	112 185
农林牧渔业总产值(万元)	Gross Output Value of Farming,Forestry,Animal Husbandry and Fishery(10 000 yuan)	368 302	383 048	399 765
农林牧渔业总产值增速(%)	Increase Rate of Gross Output Value of Farming,Forestry,Animal Husbandry and Fishery(%)	10.0	4.0	4.4
粮食产量(万吨)	Total Yield of Grain(10 000 tons)	44.2	35.97	38.02
水产品产量(吨)	Total Yield of Aquatic Products(ton)	35 113	36 766	42 263
蔬菜总产量(吨)	Total Yield of Vegetable(ton)	1 793 040	1 764 796	1 778 034
*农民人均年纯收入(元)	Per Capita Annual Net Income of Rural Households(yuan)	4 754	5 230	5 758
*农民人均生活消费支出(元)	Per Capita Annual Expenditure for Consumption of Rural Households(yuan)	2 627	2 474	2 533

22－14 续表 Continued

指标名称	Item	2001	2002	2003
乡镇企业单位数(个)	Number of Township Enterprises(unit)	420	405	375
#工　业	Industry	377	375	357
乡镇企业人数(万人)	Employment of Township Enterprises(10 000 persons)	5.89	5.56	4.33
#工　业	Industry	5.75	5.45	4.29
乡镇企业主营业务收入(万元)	Major Business Revenue of Township Enterprises(10 000 yuan)	635 974	599 465	564 781
#工　业	Industry	627 507	591 456	563 042
限额以上工业企业	Industrial Enterprises above Designated Size			
单位数(个)	Number of Units(unit)	389	369	428
从业人员(万人)	Persons Employed(10 000 persons)	6.11	7.74	8.09
总产值(万元)	Gross Output Value(10 000 yuan)	1 270 354	1 215 773	1 523 851
产品销售收入(万元)	Sales Revenue(10 000 yuan)	1 012 620	1 056 268	1 407 262
利税总额(万元)	Total Pre－tax Profits(10 000 yuan)	126 764	121 092	154 435
固定资产原值(万元)	Original Value of Fixed Assets(10 000 yuan)	594 768	556 563	795 785
流动资产合计(万元)	Total Circulating Funds(10 000 yuan)	513 472	539 760	749 724
社会消费品零售总额(万元)	Total Retail Sales of Consumer Goods(10 000 yuan)	262 300	309 151	364 702
集市贸易市场数(个)	Number of Free Markets	27	32	29
集市贸易成交额(万元)	Transaction Value of Free Markets(10 000 yuan)	164 872	159 845	149 015
*私营工商企业	Private Industrial and Commercial Enterprises			
户　数(户)	Number of Enterprises (unit)	1 977	2 354	2 823
雇工人数(人)	Employees(person)	13 062	15 319	20 300
注册资本(万元)	Registered Capital(10 000 yuan)	141 428	183 249	305 700
总产值(万元)	Gross Output Value(10 000 yuan)	163 772	173 708	217 700
营业收入(万元)	Business Revenue(10 000 yuan)	214 231	257 908	289 369
*个体工商业	Individual Industrial and Commercial Enterprises			
户　数(户)	Number of Enterprises (unit)	17 519	19 251	22 040
从业人员(人)	Persons Employed(person)	27 513	29 664	29 900
资　金(万元)	Fund(10 000 yuan)	25 637	29 058	44 200
营业额(万元)	Turnover(10 000 yuan)	389 591	438 998	464 656
直接利用外资协议额(万美元)	Foreign Direct Investment Contracted(USD 10 000)	10 600	10 838	4 915
外贸出口交货值(万元)	Delivery Value of Exports Trade(10 000 yuan)	460 000	510 000	570 000
*小学校数(所)	Number of Primary Schools(unit)	211	162	202
*小学在校学生数(人)	Students Enrollment of Primary Schools(person)	65 136	60 329	55 469
*普通中学校数(所)	Number of Regular Secondary Schools(unit)	52	51	52
*普通中学在校学生数(人)	Students Enrollment of Regular Secondary Schools(person)	49 731	51 367	50 736
幼儿园数(所)	Number of Kindergartens(unit)	394	300	273
卫生机构数(个)	Health Care Institutions(unit)	44	43	42
#医院、卫生院	Hospital and Health Center	36	36	36
卫生机构床位数(张)	Beds(unit)	1 161	1 161	1 170
#医院、卫生院	Hospital and Health Center	1 051	1 051	1 051

22－15　宝坻区基本情况

BASIC STATISTICS OF BAODI DISTRICT

指标名称	Item	2001	2002	2003
*户籍户数(万户)	Registered Households(10 000 househols)	18.03	18.13	18.28
#农业户	Agricultural Households	15.10	15.11	15.16
*户籍人口(万人)	Registered Population(10 000 persons)	64.94	64.98	65.08
1.农业人口	Agricultural Population	55.63	55.43	55.27
非农业人口	Non－agricultural Population	9.30	9.54	9.82
2.男	Male	32.79	32.79	32.84
女	Female	32.15	32.18	32.24
*人口出生率(‰)	Birth Rate of Population(‰)	7.1	7.38	8.11
*人口自然增长率(‰)	Natural Growth Rate of Population(‰)	0.9	1.89	2.67
城镇单位从业人员(万人)	Persons Employed in Urban Units(10^4 persons)	3.2	2.64	3.11
#在岗职工	On－post Staff and Workers	3.2	2.63	3.11
*乡村从业人员(万人)	Rural Persons Employed(10 000 persons)	25.43	25.43	25.44
#农林牧渔业劳动者人数	Farming,Forestry,Animal Husbandry and Fishery	13.81	13.56	13.71
地区生产总值(万元)	Gross Domestic Product(10 000 yuan)	792 834	875 010	1 024 271
第一产业	Primary Industry	101 913	104 300	112 622
第二产业	Secondary Industry	400 110	443 800	533 248
#工　业	Industry	349 720	381 228	490 290
第三产业	Tertiary Industry	292 811	326 910	378 401
地区生产总值增速(%)	Increase Rate of Gross Domestic Product (%)	14.6	14.0	15.2
一般预算内区级财政收入(万元)	General Intra－budgetary Financial Revenue at District Level(10 000 yuan)	18 651	19 316	18 068
一般预算内区级财政支出(万元)	General Intra－budgetary Financial Expenditure at District Level(10 000 yuan)	34 807	39 318	46 584
#教育经费支出	Operating Expenses for Education	12 851	16 434	18 869
*固定资产投资(万元)	Investment in Fixed Assets(10 000 yuan)	31 942	69 149	105 044
年末实有耕地面积(万公顷)	Cultivated Land(year－end)(10 000 hectare)	7.72	7.72	7.56
农业机械总动力(万千瓦)	Total Power of Agricultural Machinery(10 000 kw)	58.84	63.46	65.06
化肥折纯量(吨)	Consumption of Chemical Fertilizers(Pureness)(ton)	32 684	37 596	38 705
农村用电量(万千瓦小时)	Rural Electricity Consumption(10 000 kwh)	35 481	43 812	44 807
农林牧渔业总产值(万元)	Gross Output Value of Farming,Forestry,Animal Husbandry and Fishery(10 000 yuan)	233 861	261 786	274 537
农林牧渔业总产值增速(%)	Increase Rate of Gross Output Value of Farming, Forestry,Animal Husbandry and Fishery(%)	29.3	11.9	4.9
粮食产量(万吨)	Total Yield of Grain(10 000 tons)	31.56	31.22	29.22
水产品产量(吨)	Total Yield of Aquatic Products(ton)	26 790	29 198	31 077
蔬菜总产量(吨)	Total Yield of Vegetable(ton)	720 561	922 145	888 672
*农民人均年纯收入(元)	Per Capita Annual Net Income of Rural Households(yuan)	4 464	4 915	5 416
*农民人均生活消费支出(元)	Per Capita Annual Expenditure for Consumption of Rural Households (yuan)	2 182	2 274	2 347

22－15 续表　Continued

指标名称	Item	2001	2002	2003
乡镇企业单位数(个)	Number of Township Enterprises(unit)	267	295	319
#工　业	Industry	252	289	313
乡镇企业人数(万人)	Employment of Township Enterprises(10 000 persons)	3.77	6.12	6.45
#工　业	Industry	3.45	5.85	6.14
乡镇企业主营业务收入(万元)	Major Business Revenue of Township Enterprises(10 000 yuan)	288 385	522 463	600 739
#工　业	Industry	272 862	510 294	586 044
限额以上工业企业	Industrial Enterprises above Designated Size			
单位数(个)	Number of Units(unit)	307	341	343
从业人员(万人)	Persons Employed(10 000 persons)	5.34	6.60	6.8
总产值(万元)	Gross Output Value(10 000 yuan)	471 264	618 859	663 668
产品销售收入(万元)	Sales Revenue(10 000 yuan)	465 643	608 309	589 743
利税总额(万元)	Total Pre－tax Profits(10 000 yuan)	45 701	52 418	67 629
固定资产原值(万元)	Original Value of Fixed Assets(10 000 yuan)	167 203	203 146	210 013
流动资产合计(万元)	Total Circulating Funds(10 000 yuan)	162 458	197 419	193 462
社会消费品零售总额(万元)	Total Retail Sales of Consumer Goods(10 000 yuan)	226 915	266 100	315 982
集市贸易市场数(个)	Number of Free Markets	32	32	32
集市贸易成交额(万元)	Transaction Value of Free Markets(10 000 yuan)	112 577	126 000	110 488
*私营工商企业	Private Industrial and Commercial Enterprises			
户　数(户)	Number of Enterprises (unit)	579	865	1 153
雇工人数(人)	Employees(person)	23 894	50 400	59 900
注册资本(万元)	Registered Capital(10 000 yuan)	39 559	73 149	146 337
总产值(万元)	Gross Output Value(10 000 yuan)	203 441	279 612	466 499
营业收入(万元)	Business Revenue(10 000 yuan)	20 545	33 849	80 516
*个体工商业	Individual Industrial and Commercial Enterprises			
户　数(户)	Number of Enterprises (unit)	11 029	13 287	11 522
从业人员(人)	Persons Employed(person)		54 322	58 700
资　金(万元)	Fund(10 000 yuan)	26 414	41 195	34 294
营业额(万元)	Turnover(10 000 yuan)	152 768	173 649	208 995
直接利用外资协议额(万美元)	Foreign Direct Investment Contracted(USD 10 000)	4 800	7 100	14 189
外贸出口交货值(万元)	Delivery Value of Exports Trade(10 000 yuan)	220 037	241 600	281 000
*小学校数(所)	Number of Primary Schools(unit)	141	141	211
*小学在校学生数(人)	Students Enrollment of Primary Schools(person)	69 861	71 921	62 477
*普通中学校数(所)	Number of Regular Secondary Schools(unit)	51	51	51
*普通中学在校学生数(人)	Students Enrollment of Regular Secondary Schools(person)	54 895	50 854	54 459
幼儿园数(所)	Number of Kindergartens(unit)	247	51	51
卫生机构数(个)	Health Care Institutions(unit)	47	47	46
#医院、卫生院	Hospital and Health Center	41	41	41
卫生机构床位数(张)	Beds(unit)	955	995	995
#医院、卫生院	Hospital and Health Center	955.00	995	995

22－16　宁河县基本情况
BASIC STATISTICS OF NINGHE COUNTY

指标名称	Item	2001	2002	2003
*户籍户数(万户)	Registered Households(10 000 households)	10.62	10.74	10.88
#农业户	Agricultural Households	7.64	7.66	7.58
*户籍人口(万人)	Registered Population(10 000 persons)	35.74	35.98	36.15
1.农业人口	Agricultural Population	28.26	28.26	27.85
非农业人口	Non－agricultural Population	7.48	7.71	8.30
2.男	Male	18.11	18.23	18.32
女	Female	17.64	17.75	17.83
*人口出生率(‰)	Birth Rate of Population(‰)	8.29	8.07	7.77
*人口自然增长率(‰)	Natural Growth Rate of Population(‰)	3.49	3.53	3.28
城镇单位从业人员(万人)	Persons Employed in Urban Units(10^4 persons)	2.71	2.40	2.29
#在岗职工	On－post Staff and Workers	2.36	2.29	2.20
*乡村从业人员(万人)	Rural Persons Employed(10 000 persons)	11.29	11.21	10.93
#农林牧渔业劳动者人数	Farming,Forestry,Animal Husbandry and Fishery	6.47	6.36	6.46
地区生产总值(万元)	Gross Domestic Product(10 000 yuan)	584 639	672 340	806 079
第一产业	Primary Industry	87 249	92 103	100 187
第二产业	Secondary Industry	276 586	320 184	382 831
#工　业	Industry	220 900	236 100	340 220
第三产业	Tertiary Industry	220 804	260 053	323 061
地区生产总值增速(%)	Increase Rate of Gross Domestic Product(%)	16.2	16.9	17.5
一般预算内县级财政收入(万元)	General Intra－budgetary Financial Revenue at County Level (10 000 yuan)	20 716	18 132	14 767
一般预算内县级财政支出(万元)	General Intra－budgetary Financial Expenditure at County Level(10 000 yuan)	27 335	28 043	30 933
#教育经费支出	Operating Expenses for Education	7 936	8 920	10 203
*固定资产投资(万元)	Investment in Fixed Assets(10 000 yuan)	24 463	41 954	90 092
年末实有耕地面积(万公顷)	Cultivated Land(year－end)(10 000 hectare)	3.95	3.95	3.87
农业机械总动力(万千瓦)	Total Power of Agricultural Machinery(10 000 kw)	51.21	51.3	51.6
化肥折纯量(吨)	Consumption of Chemical Fertilizers(Pureness)(ton)	15 086	15 240	15 423
农村用电量(万千瓦小时)	Rural Electricity Consumption(10 000 kwh)	14 250	20 967	25 406
农林牧渔业总产值(万元)	Gross Output Value of Farming,Forestry,Animal Husbandry and Fishery(10 000 yuan)	173 417	188 427	215 796
农林牧渔业总产值增速(%)	Increase Rate of Gross Output Value of Farming, Forestry,Animal Husbandry and Fishery(%)	2.8	8.7	15.4
粮食产量(万吨)	Total Yield of Grain(10 000 tons)	5.75	6.3	4.4
水产品产量(吨)	Total Yield of Aquatic Products(ton)	15 528	15 529	16 087
蔬菜总产量(吨)	Total Yield of Vegetable(ton)	338 625	272 643	284 822
*农民人均年纯收入(元)	Per Capita Annual Net Income of Rural Households(yuan)	4 649	5 102	5 628
*农民人均生活消费支出(元)	Per Capita Annual Expenditure for Consumption of Rural Households(yuan)	2 025	2 023	2 211

注:1."*"为全县数据,其余为县属数。2.固定资产投资不含农村集体和个人投资。3.乡镇企业为乡村两级数。4.22－17和22－18表同。
Note:a)The data with "*" of this table reler to the whole county,others reler to units under the leadership of this county. b)The investment in fixed assets exclude rural collective and individual. c)Township enterprises include that of village and town level. d)Same as following table 22－17 and 22－18.

22－16 续表　Continued

指标名称	Item	2001	2002	2003
乡镇企业单位数(个)	Number of Township Enterprises(unit)	178	161	136
#工　业	Industry	167	145	118
乡镇企业人数(万人)	Employment of Township Enterprises(10 000 persons)	1.54	1.44	1.35
#工　业	Industry	1.50	1.37	1.24
乡镇企业主营业务收入(万元)	Major Business Revenue of Township Enterprises(10 000 yuan)	295 957	278 509	248 062
#工　业	Industry	283 987	266 523	238 088
限额以上工业企业	Industrial Enterprises above Designated Size			
单位数(个)	Number of Units(unit)	154	156	156
从业人员(万人)	Persons Employed(10 000 persons)	1.87	2.08	2.15
总产值(万元)	Gross Output Value(10 000 yuan)	463 115	485 785	551 507
产品销售收入(万元)	Sales Revenue(10 000 yuan)	415 183	464 166	547 382
利税总额(万元)	Total Pre－tax Profits(10 000 yuan)	33 239	34 328	42 851
固定资产原值(万元)	Original Value of Fixed Assets(10 000 yuan)	167 856	191 690	196 789
流动资产合计(万元)	Total Circulating Funds(10 000 yuan)	145 403	149 569	233 865
社会消费品零售总额(万元)	Total Retail Sales of Consumer Goods(10 000 yuan)	178 000	256 151	255 300
集市贸易市场数(个)	Number of Free Markets	36	36	36
集市贸易成交额(万元)	Transaction Value of Free Markets(10 000 yuan)	65 400	76 800	110 000
* 私营工商企业	Private Industrial and Commercial Enterprises			
户　数(户)	Number of Enterprises (unit)	879	1 043	1 301
雇工人数(人)	Employees(person)	11 317	16 023	16 909
注册资本(万元)	Registered Capital(10 000 yuan)	86 062	114 799	225 830
总产值(万元)	Gross Output Value(10 000 yuan)	120 063	110 427	126 982
营业收入(万元)	Business Revenue(10 000 yuan)	9 129	9 379	10 766
* 个体工商业	Individual Industrial and Commercial Enterprises			
户　数(户)	Number of Enterprises (unit)	10 082	10 008	10 060
从业人员(人)	Persons Employed(person)	12 157	12 053	12 413
资　金(万元)	Fund(10 000 yuan)	8 285	9 423	11 660
营业额(万元)	Turnover(10 000 yuan)	83 250	87 620	114 384
直接利用外资协议额(万美元)	Foreign Direct Investment Contracted(USD 10 000)	3 200	5 200	3 284
外贸出口交货值(万元)	Delivery Value of Exports Trade(10 000 yuan)	185 000	266 800	320 000
* 小学校数(所)	Number of Primary Schools(unit)	68	65	65
* 小学在校学生数(人)	Students Enrollment of Primary Schools(person)	35 760	31 139	26 695
* 普通中学校数(所)	Number of Regular Secondary Schools(unit)	28	28	29
* 普通中学在校学生数(人)	Students Enrollment of Regular Secondary Schools(person)	29 784	34 030	34 030
幼儿园数(所)	Number of Kindergartens(unit)	96	79	140
卫生机构数(个)	Health Care Institutions(unit)	71	71	70
#医院、卫生院	Hospital and Health Center	8	8	8
卫生机构床位数(张)	Beds(unit)	569	569	569
#医院、卫生院	Hospital and Health Center	569	569	569

22－17 静海县基本情况
BASIC STATISTICS OF JINGHAI COUNTY

指标名称	Item	2001	2002	2003
* 户籍户数(万户)	Registered Households(10 000 househols)	16.11	16.38	16.64
# 农业户	Agricultural Households	12.92	12.97	12.99
* 户籍人口(万人)	Registered Population(10 000 persons)	50.53	50.86	51.09
1.农业人口	Agricultural Population	42.65	42.63	42.45
非农业人口	Non－agricultural Population	7.88	8.22	8.64
2.男	Male	25.63	25.82	25.97
女	Female	24.90	25.04	25.12
* 人口出生率(‰)	Birth Rate of Population(‰)	9.99	10.5	8.94
* 人口自然增长率(‰)	Natural Growth Rate of Population(‰)	3.49	5.45	2.94
城镇单位从业人员(万人)	Persons Employed in Urban Units(10^4 persons)	3.26	3.00	2.64
# 在岗职工	On－post Staff and Workers	3.21	2.96	2.59
* 乡村从业人员(万人)	Rural Persons Employed(10 000 persons)	15.55	15.61	15.59
# 农林牧渔业劳动者人数	Farming,Forestry,Animal Husbandry and Fishery	7.48	7.55	7.57
地区生产总值(万元)	Gross Domestic Product(10 000 yuan)	678 770	781 084	925 447
第一产业	Primary Industry	93 626	100 568	109 847
第二产业	Secondary Industry	397 770	459 934	546 677
# 工　业	Industry	388 353	446 543	527 234
第三产业	Tertiary Industry	187 374	220 582	268 923
地区生产总值增速(%)	Increase Rate of Gross Domestic Product(%)	14.2	17.8	15.6
一般预算县级财政收入(万元)	General Intra－budgetary Financial Revenue at County Level(10 000 yuan)	19 766	21 004	17 554
一般预算内县级财政支出(万元)	General Intra－budgetary Financial Expenditure at County Level(10 000 yuan)	28 976	35 365	42 785
# 教育经费支出	Operating Expenses for Education	10 946	13 143	14 514
* 固定资产投资(万元)	Investment in Fixed Assets(10 000 yuan)	38 909	60 462	116 324
年末实有耕地面积(万公顷)	Cultivated Land(year－end)(10 000 hectare)	6.92	6.92	6.92
农业机械总动力(万千瓦)	Total Power of Agricultural Machinery(10 000 kw)	67.10	67.30	67.5
化肥折纯量(吨)	Consumption of Chemical Fertilizers(Pureness)(ton)	21 860	19 700	19 376
农村用电量(万千瓦小时)	Rural Electricity Consumption(10 000 kwh)	65 568	74 074	87 009
农林牧渔业总产值(万元)	Gross Output Value of Farming,Forestry,Animal Husbandry and Fishery(10 000 yuan)	186 165	206 536	214 955
农林牧渔业总产值增速(%)	Increase Rate of Gross Output Value of Farming,Forestry,Animal Husbandry and Fishery(%)	12.6	10.9	21.2
粮食产量(万吨)	Total Yield of Grain(10 000 tons)	17.62	10.73	17.67
水产品产量(吨)	Total Yield of Aquatic Products(ton)	20 325	20 022	21 782
蔬菜总产量(吨)	Total Yield of Vegetable(ton)	377 327	395 191	451 900
* 农民人均年纯收入(元)	Per Capita Annual Net Income of Rural Households(yuan)	4 350	4 873	5 417
* 农民人均生活消费支出(元)	Per Capita Annual Expenditure for Consumption of Rural Households(yuan)	2 833	2 599	2 844

22－17 续表 Continued

指标名称	Item	2001	2002	2003
乡镇企业单位数(个)	Number of Township Enterprises(unit)	735	604	144
#工 业	Industry	676	541	144
乡镇企业人数(万人)	Employment of Township Enterprises(10 000 persons)	6.53	6.75	1.67
#工 业	Industry	6.07	6.23	1.67
乡镇企业主营业务收入(万元)	Major Business Revenue of Township Enterprises(10 000 yuan)	1 438 265	1 585 870	567 903
#工 业	Industry	1 412 597	1 555 853	567 903
限额以上工业企业	Industrial Enterprises above Designated Size			
单位数(个)	Number of Units(unit)	276	258	247
从业人员(万人)	Persons Employed(10 000 persons)	4.85	5.67	5.00
总产值(万元)	Gross Output Value(10 000 yuan)	1 474 533	1 620 508	1 828 819
产品销售收入(万元)	Sales Revenue(10 000 yuan)	1 438 754	1 596 900	1 828 893
利税总额(万元)	Total Pre－tax Profits(10 000 yuan)	122 624	132 031	141 419
固定资产原值(万元)	Original Value of Fixed Assets(10 000 yuan)	412 924	619 000	556 502
流动资产合计(万元)	Total Circulating Funds(10 000 yuan)	415 770	554 045	599 221
社会消费品零售总额(万元)	Total Retail Sales of Consumer Goods(10 000 yuan)	201 029	235 561	279 400
集市贸易市场数(个)	Number of Free Markets	33	33	32
集市贸易成交额(万元)	Transaction Value of Free Markets(10 000 yuan)	157 679	190 915	220 775
* 私营工商企业	Private Industrial and Commercial Enterprises			
户 数(户)	Number of Enterprises (unit)	948	1 290	2 002
雇工人数(人)	Employees(person)	11 609	13 603	19 203
注册资本(万元)	Registered Capital(10 000 yuan)	104 675	157 454	329 579
总产值(万元)	Gross Output Value(10 000 yuan)	21 947	22 584	24 584
营业收入(万元)	Business Revenue(10 000 yuan)	17 645	16 764	21 412
* 个体工商业	Individual Industrial and Commercial Enterprises			
户 数(户)	Number of Enterprises (unit)	11 770	11 836	11 434
从业人员(人)	Persons Employed(person)	22 087	22 704	24 316
资 金(万元)	Fund(10 000 yuan)	21 810	25 989	28 556
营业额(万元)	Turnover(10 000 yuan)	68 813	68 610	81 602
直接利用外资协议额(万美元)	Foreign Direct Investment Contracted(USD 10 000)	3 421	4 469	4 105
外贸出口交货值(万元)	Delivery Value of Exports Trade(10 000 yuan)	157 662	197 797	190 000
* 小学校数(所)	Number of Primary Schools(unit)	98	100	99
* 小学在校学生数(人)	Students Enrollment of Primary Schools(person)	44 638	43 880	43 228
* 普通中学校数(所)	Number of Regular Secondary Schools(unit)	44	46	47
* 普通中学在校学生数(人)	Students Enrollment of Regular Secondary Schools(person)	34 805	37 378	38 392
幼儿园数(所)	Number of Kindergartens(unit)	281	115	264
卫生机构数(个)	Health Care Institutions(unit)	117	117	108
#医院、卫生院	Hospital and Health Center	7	7	7
卫生机构床位数(张)	Beds(unit)	990	1 075	996
#医院、卫生院	Hospital and Health Center	644	685	700

22－18 蓟县基本情况
BASIC STATISTICS OF JIXIAN COUNTY

指标名称	Item	2001	2002	2003
*户籍户数(万户)	Registered Households(10 000 househols)	21.66	21.83	22.02
#农业户	Agricultural Households	18.53	18.56	18.60
*户籍人口(万人)	Registered Population(10 000 persons)	79.71	80.00	79.97
1.农业人口	Agricultural Population	69.46	69.32	68.88
非农业人口	Non－agricultural Population	10.25	10.68	11.09
2.男	Male	38.87	40.75	40.73
女	Female	39.08	39.25	39.24
*人口出生率(‰)	Birth Rate of Population(‰)	6.46	6.68	6.04
*人口自然增长率(‰)	Natural Growth Rate of Population(‰)	1.60	1.78	1.07
城镇单位从业人员(万人)	Persons Employed in Urban Units(10^4 persons)	4.71	4.82	4.75
#在岗职工	On－post Staff and Workers	4.24	4.34	4.18
*乡村从业人员(万人)	Rural Persons Employed(10 000 persons)	31.56	31.65	31.73
#农林牧渔业劳动者人数	Farming,Forestry,Animal Husbandry and Fishery	17.01	16.43	16.51
地区生产总值(万元)	Gross Domestic Product(10 000 yuan)	754 528	867 013	1 024 657
第一产业	Primary Industry	129 266	145 163	165 005
第二产业	Secondary Industry	313 988	366 653	435 759
#工　业	Industry	264 951	307 398	368 591
第三产业	Tertiary Industry	311 274	355 197	423 893
地区生产总值增速(%)	Increase Rate of Gross Domestic Product(%)	16.2	18.6	16.4
一般预算内县级财政收入(万元)	General Intra－budgetary Financial Revenue at County Level (10 000 yuan)	20 220	20 563	16 805
一般预算内县级财政支出(万元)	General Intra－budgetary Financial Expenditure at County Level(10 000 yuan)	31 752	37 605	36 429
#教育经费支出	Operating Expenses for Education	14 510	15 472	16 142
*固定资产投资(万元)	Investment in Fixed Assets(10 000 yuan)	181 538	157 456	150 649
年末实有耕地面积(万公顷)	Cultivated Land(year－end)(10 000 hectare)	5.44	5.42	5.42
农业机械总动力(万千瓦)	Total Power of Agricultural Machinery(10 000 kw)	66.36	64.90	66.56
化肥折纯量(吨)	Consumption of Chemical Fertilizers(Pureness)(ton)	32 643	34 518	34 636
农村用电量(万千瓦小时)	Rural Electricity Consumption(10 000 kwh)	26 251	27 364	27 786
农林牧渔业总产值(万元)	Gross Output Value of Farming,Forestry,Animal Husbandry and Fishery(10 000 yuan)	286 586	313 729	360 118
农林牧渔业总产值增速(%)	Increase Rate of Gross Output Value of Farming, Forestry,Animal Husbandry and Fishery(%)	17.1	9.5	14.8
粮食产量(万吨)	Total Yield of Grain(10 000 tons)	32.53	31.80	29.58
水产品产量(吨)	Total Yield of Aquatic Products(ton)	20 487	21 259	25 600
蔬菜总产量(吨)	Total Yield of Vegetable(ton)	1 056 750	1 171 781	1 340 642
*农民人均年纯收入(元)	Per Capita Annual Net Income of Rural Households(yuan)	4 452	4 908	5 420
*农民人均生活消费支出(元)	Per Capita Annual Expenditure for Consumption of Rural Households(yuan)	1 907	1 967	2 568

22－18 续表 Continued

指标名称	Item	2001	2002	2003
乡镇企业单位数(个)	Number of Township Enterprises(unit)	675	523	494
#工　业	Industry	554	472	438
乡镇企业人数(万人)	Employment of Township Enterprises(10 000 persons)	6.04	5.94	6.17
#工　业	Industry	4.79	5.23	5.47
乡镇企业主营业务收入(万元)	Major Business Revenue of Township Enterprises(10 000 yuan)	491 019	549 580	663 935
#工　业	Industry	455 618	513 576	623 640
限额以上工业企业	Industrial Enterprises above Designated Size			
单位数(个)	Number of Units(unit)	261	285	302
从业人员(万人)	Persons Employed(10 000 persons)	4.43	5.41	6.35
总产值(万元)	Gross Output Value(10 000 yuan)	570 437	684 317	866 890
产品销售收入(万元)	Sales Revenue(10 000 yuan)	473 321	583 627	764 649
利税总额(万元)	Total Pre－tax Profits(10 000 yuan)	48 510	56 067	78 890
固定资产原值(万元)	Original Value of Fixed Assets(10 000 yuan)	187 461	217 339	279 987
流动资产合计(万元)	Total Circulating Funds(10 000 yuan)	153 463	189 847	205 020
社会消费品零售总额(万元)	Total Retail Sales of Consumer Goods(10 000 yuan)	251 196	295 124	293 271
集市贸易市场数(个)	Number of Free Markets	32	32	32
集市贸易成交额(万元)	Transaction Value of Free Markets(10 000 yuan)	123 000	138 920	144 007
*私营工商企业	Private Industrial and Commercial Enterprises			
户　数(户)	Number of Enterprises (unit)	524	546	569
雇工人数(人)	Employees(person)	5 077	4 836	7 315
注册资本(万元)	Registered Capital(10 000 yuan)	20 806	25 708	52 164
总产值(万元)	Gross Output Value(10 000 yuan)	13 708	22 422	74 001
营业收入(万元)	Business Revenue(10 000 yuan)	7 767	13 318	24 420
*个体工商业	Individual Industrial and Commercial Enterprises			
户　数(户)	Number of Enterprises (unit)	23 328	12 922	13 386
从业人员(人)	Persons Employed(person)	27 104	20 655	22 405
资　金(万元)	Fund(10 000 yuan)	28 361	25 993	26 441
营业额(万元)	Turnover(10 000 yuan)	118 172	103 724	80 085
直接利用外资协议额(万美元)	Foreign Direct Investment Contracted(USD 10 000)	1 609	3 001	12 600
外贸出口交货值(万元)	Delivery Value of Exports Trade(10 000 yuan)	210 000	260 000	315 000
*小学校数(所)	Number of Primary Schools(unit)	137	137	397
*小学在校学生数(人)	Students Enrollment of Primary Schools(person)	85 981	77 795	82 094
*普通中学校数(所)	Number of Regular Secondary Schools(unit)	63	63	66
*普通中学在校学生数(人)	Students Enrollment of Regular Secondary Schools(person)	74 553	79 037	80 145
幼儿园数(所)	Number of Kindergartens(unit)	247	117	275
卫生机构数(个)	Health Care Institutions(unit)	135	401	338
#医院、卫生院	Hospital and Health Center	43	37	36
卫生机构床位数(张)	Beds(unit)	1 483	1 438	1 410
#医院、卫生院	Hospital and Health Center	1 483	1 438	1 410

企业采风

BRIEF INTRODUCTION OF ENTERPRISES

1 天津钢管有限责任公司
TIANJIN PIPE CORPORATION LTD.

2 天津海关
TIANJIN CUSTOM

3 中国工商银行天津市分行
INDUSTRIAL & COMMERCIAL BANK OF CHINA
TIANJIN MUNICIPAL BRANCH

4 中国石化集团天津石油化工公司
SINOPEC TIANJIN PETROCHEMICAL CORPORATION

5 中国石化股份天津分公司
CHINA PETROLEUMICAL CO,LTD. TIANJIN CORPORATION

6 中国石油大港石化公司
CHINA PETROLEUM DAGANG PETROLEUM
& COMMERCIAL CORPORATION

7 天津鑫茂科技投资集团
TIANJIN XINMAO SCIENCE AND TECHNOLOGY
INVESTMENT GROUP

8 天津城市建设学院
TIANJIN INSTITUTE OF URBAN CONSTRUCTION

9 天津工业大学
TIANJIN POLYTECHNIC UNIVERSITY

10 天津图书大厦
TIANJIN BOOK BUILDING

11 天津市建筑设计院
TIANJIN CONSTRUCTION DESIGN INSTITUTE

12 天津市勘察院
TIANJIN INSTITUTE OF GEOTECHNICAL
INVESTTIGATION & SURVEYING

13 天津市建设投资集团
TIANJIN CONSTRUCTION INVESTMENT CORPORATION

14 天士力集团
TASLY GROUP

15 天津金耀集团有限公司
TIANJIN JINYAO GROUP CO., LTD.

16 天津市中央药业有限公司
TIANJIN ZHONGYANG PHARMACEUTICAL
CORPORATION LIMITED

17 天津药物研究院
TIANJIN MEDICINE RESERCH INSTITUTE

18 中法合营王朝葡萄酿酒有限公司
SINO－FRENCH JOINT－VENTURE DYNASTY
WINERY CORPORATION LTD.

19 天津农垦集团总公司
TIANJIN STATE FARMS AGRIBUSINESS
GROUP CORPORATION

20 天津丰田汽车发动机有限公司
TIANJIN TOYOTA MOTOR ENGINE CO., LTD.

21 中国农业机械华北集团有限公司
CHINA AGRICULTURAL MACHINERY NORTH
CHINA GROUP CO.,LTD.

22 天津泰达建设集团有限公司
TEDA CONSTRUCTION GROUP CO.,LTD.

23 天津市安居建设发展总公司
TIANJIN ANJU CONSTRUCTION
DEVELOPMENT CORPORATION

24－25 龙都集团
LONGDU GROUP

26 天津市东达房地产开发公司
DONGDA REAL ESTATE DEVELOPMENT COMPANY

27 河北区建设开发公司
HEBEI CONSTRUCTION DEVELOPMENT CORPORATION

28 天津市河东房地产开发总公司
TIANJIN HEDONG REAL ESTATE GENERAL COMPANY

29 天津第一市政公路工程有限公司
TIANJIN NO.1 MUNICIPAL HIGHWAY ENGINEERING CO., LTD.

30 天津第二市政公路工程有限公司
TIANJIN NO.2 MUNICIPAL HIGHWAY ENGINEERING CO., LTD.

31 天津第三市政公路工程有限公司
TIANJIN NO.3 MUNICIPAL HIGHWAY ENGINEERING CO., LTD.

32 天津第四市政建筑工程有限公司
TIANJIN NO.4 MUNICIPAL HIGHWAY ENGINEERING CO., LTD.

33 天津第五市政公路工程有限公司
TIANJIN NO.5 MUNICIPAL HIGHWAY ENGINEERING Co., LTD.

34 华明集团
HUAMING GROUP

35 津英纺纱有限公司
JINYING SPINNING CO.,LTD.

36－37 刘房子经济发展总公司
LIUFANGZI ECONOMY DEVELOPMENT
GENERAL COMPANY

38 天津送变电工程公司
TIANJIN POWER TRANSMISSION ENGINEERING
CORPORATION

39 天津大港发电厂
TIANJIN DAGANG POWER PLANT

40 天津兴业置业集团
TIANJIN XINGYE PROPERTY GROUP

中国统计出版社最新资料书简目

中国统计年鉴—2004
中国统计摘要—2004
2004 中国发展报告
中国城市统计年鉴—2003
中国农村统计年鉴—2004
中国劳动统计年鉴—2004
中国人口统计年鉴—2004
中国工业经济统计年鉴—2004
中国市场统计年鉴—2004
2003 中国城市发展报告
中国建筑业统计年鉴—2003
中国价格及城镇居民家庭收支调查统计年鉴—2004
国际统计年鉴—2004
中国对外经济贸易统计年鉴—2003
中国基本单位统计年鉴—2003
中国民政统计年鉴—2004
中国高技术产业统计年鉴—2004
中国房地产行业名录
北京统计年鉴—2004
天津统计年鉴—2004
河北经济年鉴—2004
山西统计年鉴—2004
内蒙古统计年鉴—2004
辽宁统计年鉴—2004
吉林统计年鉴—2004
黑龙江统计年鉴—2004
上海统计年鉴—2004
江苏统计年鉴—2004
浙江统计年鉴—2004
安徽统计年鉴—2004
福建统计年鉴—2004
江西统计年鉴—2004
山东统计年鉴—2004
河南统计年鉴—2004
湖北统计年鉴—2004
湖南统计年鉴—2004
广东统计年鉴—2004
广西统计年鉴—2004
海南统计年鉴—2004
重庆统计年鉴—2004
四川统计年鉴—2004
贵州统计年鉴—2004
云南统计年鉴—2004
西藏统计年鉴—2004
陕西统计年鉴—2004
甘肃年鉴—2004
青海统计年鉴—2004
宁夏统计年鉴—2004
新疆统计年鉴—2004
新疆生产建设兵团统计年鉴—2004
石家庄统计年鉴—2004
唐山统计年鉴—2004
邯郸统计年鉴—2004
呼和浩特经济统计年鉴—2004
鄂尔多斯市统计年鉴—2004
包头统计年鉴—2004
赤峰统计年鉴—2004
沈阳年鉴—2004
大连统计年鉴—2004
鞍山统计年鉴—2004
长春统计年鉴—2004
吉林市社会经济统计年鉴—2004
四平统计年鉴—2004
延吉统计年鉴—2004
哈尔滨统计年鉴—2004
齐齐哈尔经济统计年鉴—2004
牡丹江统计年鉴—2004
大庆统计年鉴—2004
黑龙江垦区统计年鉴—2004
上海浦东新区统计年鉴—2004
南京统计年鉴—2004
苏州统计年鉴—2004
无锡统计年鉴—2004
常州统计年鉴—2004
徐州统计年鉴—2004
南通统计年鉴—2004
盐城统计年鉴—2004
镇江统计年鉴—2004
杭州统计年鉴—2004
宁波统计年鉴—2004
绍兴统计年鉴—2004
台州统计年鉴—2004
舟山统计年鉴—2004
温州统计年鉴—2004
金华统计年鉴—2004
嘉兴统计年鉴—2004
丽水统计年鉴—2004
福州年鉴—2004
厦门经济特区年鉴—2004
福州经济技术开发区年鉴—2004
南昌经济社会统计年鉴—2004
九江经济统计年鉴—2004
济南统计年鉴—2004
青岛统计年鉴—2004
潍坊统计年鉴—2004
郑州统计年鉴—2004
洛阳统计年鉴—2004
三门峡统计年鉴—2004
平顶山统计年鉴—2004
南阳经济统计年鉴—2004
武汉统计年鉴—2004
宜昌统计年鉴—2004
十堰统计年鉴—2004
荆州统计年鉴—2004
广州统计年鉴—2004
东莞统计年鉴—2004
惠州统计年鉴—2004
深圳统计年鉴—2004
南宁统计年鉴—2004
桂林经济社会统计年鉴—2004
柳州经济统计年鉴—2004
来宾统计年鉴—2004
河池地区经济社会统计年鉴—2004
海口统计年鉴—2004
成都统计年鉴—2004
贵阳统计年鉴—2004
昆明统计年鉴—2004
西安统计年鉴—2004
兰州年鉴—2004
西宁统计年鉴—2004
银川统计年鉴—2004
乌鲁木齐统计年鉴—2004
巴音郭楞统计年鉴—2004
吐鲁番统计年鉴—2004

(京)新登字 041 号

图书在版编目(CIP)数据

天津统计年鉴. 2004/天津市统计局编.
—北京: 中国统计出版社,2004.6
ISBN 7—5037—4322—0

Ⅰ.天…
Ⅱ.天…
Ⅲ.统计资料—天津市—2004—年鉴
Ⅳ.C832.21—54

中国版本图书馆 CIP 数据核字(2004)第 031569 号

天津统计年鉴—2004

作　　者/天津市统计局
责任编辑/蔡启新
E—mail/yearbook@stats.gov.cn
责任校对/李立新　戴　华
封面设计/天津市河图广告传播有限公司
出版发行/中国统计出版社
通信地址/北京市西城区三里河月坛南街 75 号　中国统计出版社
邮　　编/100826
电　　话/(010)63262295
印　　刷/国家海洋信息中心印刷厂
经　　销/新华书店
开　　本/890×1240 毫米　1/16
字　　数/113 万字
印　　张/37 印张
印　　数/1—5000 册
版　　别/2004 年 7 月第 1 版
版　　次/2004 年 7 月第 1 次印刷
书　　号/ISBN 7—5037—4322—0/F·1787
定　　价/280.00 元(含光盘)

本书附同版本 CD—ROM 一张,光盘内容以书面文字为准。

天津海关

TIANJIN CUSTOM

提高监管服务水平

打造一流服务型海关

天津是我国重要的外贸口岸，在天津口岸担负进出口监管任务的天津海关认真贯彻“依法行政、为国把关，服务经济、促进发展”的海关工作方针，以争一流为目标，努力打造服务型海关，不断促进地方经济发展。2003年共监管进出口货物8178万吨，货物总值461.7亿美元，征收税款290.24亿元，同比分别增长29.4%、26.4%和31.2%，有力保证了口岸对外贸易的健康快速发展。

——以高效便捷的服务促进外贸发展。2003年，天津海关以实施关衔制度为契机，采取有力措施，克服“非典”影响，通关效率不断提高。拓宽了便捷通关适用范围，使占天津市进出口51%的货物享受到了便捷通关措施，解决了通关“瓶颈”问题；建立了节假日通关和疑难单据快速督办等应急机制，年内“通关110”热线接听电话万余次，及时解决疑难问题3000余件；在全国率先实行了保税区“分批出区，集中报关”的现代物流便捷通关措施，取得了良好的经济效益和社会效益。

——以改革创新不断提高服务层次。2003年，天津海关以科技应用为保障，深化通关作业改革，促进了监管水平和服务水平的不断提高。改变了加工贸易监管的低效运作方式，初步确立了具有天津特色的“电子账册＋联网核查”的新型加工贸易监管模式。截至年底已成功联通36家大型加工贸易企业，占天津市加工贸易进出口总值的64%。完成了关区“三网合一”的光纤网络建设，自行开发了63个应用程序，有效提升了通关监管作业的信息化水平。

——以监管效能的提高创造良好口岸环境。2003年，天津海关积极推行并初步形成了领导有力、层级分明、全员参与、全程覆盖、反应灵敏的风险管理机制，为确保税款应收尽收、监管严密有效和加大打私力度打下坚实基础。坚持标本兼治、齐抓共管的综合治税思路，深入开展了打击归类、价格和加工贸易伪瞒报行为的专项治理；依托箱号识别、视像监控等高科技设备和千兆光纤网络，全面建成了卡口通道式物流监控体系，做到了对口岸的全封闭、全方位、全过程的不间断监控；组织了“流火”缉私战役，相继查办了一批案值大、偷逃税额高的大要案，有效维护了天津口岸良好的外贸进出口秩序。多年来，该关采取积极有效措施，严厉打击天津口岸文物走私活动，为保护国家文物做出了巨大的贡献，受到了海关总署、国家文物总局、天津市政府的表彰和奖励。2003年12月22日，该关举行了隆重的走私文物移交仪式，将1995—2001年间查扣的8691件文物移交给天津市文物局，中央电视台对此作了全程现场直播。海关总署署长牟新生参加了仪式，对该关的文物监管工作给予了充分肯定。

Tianjin Custom is authorized to supervise import & export at Tianjin Port, seriously implements the working policy of “handle affairs by law, guard the port for the country, serve for economy and promote the development”, promotes the development of Tianjin economy continuously. In 2003, the volume of import & export at Tianjin Port reached 81.78 million tons with the total value of 46.17 billion US$, tax totaled 29.024 billion yuan, up by 29.4%, 26.4% and 31.2% respectively, ensured the rapid and sound development of foreign trade.

The effective and convenient services of Tianjin Custom have promoted the development of foreign trade. In 2003, Tianjin Custom devoted every effort to eliminate the negative effect brought by the SARS epidemic, the efficiency of entry-exit custom is improved continuously. The field of quick entry-exit custom is widened. AT present, 51% of import & export goods enjoy the measure of quick entry-exit custom. The emergency mechanism for holiday entry-exit custom and solving difficulty is established. Hotline telephone received totaled over 10,000 times and solved over 3,000 questions in this year. Tianjin Custom is the first one to implement the measure of “goods leave group by group and pay customs duties together” for TPFTZ and has earned good economic and social benefit.

Tianjin Custom improves the service level through reform and innovation. It deepens the reform of entry-exit custom depending on science and technology. The new supervision mode, i.e. “e-account book + network check” for processing trade, is established preliminarily. By the end of 2003, it has successfully connected 36 large-sized processing enterprises with network, accounting for 64% of total import & export of processing trade. It has completed the establishment of fiber optic network, developed 63 application procedure, improved the information level of supervision for entry-exit custom.

It has created a good port environment through the improvement of supervision efficiency. In 2003, Tianjin Custom established risk management mechanism preliminarily. It developed the management for illegal activities, established logistics supervision system and supervised port without break, investigated and dealt with some evading taxes cases, effectively maintained the rule of Tianjin Port.

中国工商银行 天津市分行

INDUSTRIAL AND COMMERCIAL BANK OF CHINA TIANJIN MUNICIPAL BRANCH

“您身边的银行，可信赖的银行”

工商银行天津市分行办公大楼

中国工商银行天津市分行以其雄厚的资金实力、遍及城乡的营业网点、彰显实力的电子化优势、高素质的人才后备力量，构筑起津门金融界的脊梁。

截止2002年末，全行本外币各项存款余额828.1亿元，各项贷款余额656.4亿元，位居天津市同业之首。遍布城乡的400多家营业网点，全部实现上机联网，更让百姓切身体会到“您身边的银行，可信赖的银行”的方便快捷。

近两年，工商银行网上银行、电话银行业务发展迅速，推出了以“金融e通道”为品牌的一批全新网上银行业务品种。2002年，依托全新的综合业务处理系统，全行结算业务实现了全国通存通兑。如今，客户持工商银行储蓄存折或牡丹卡便可在全国3万多家营业网点办理存、取款、转帐、个人汇款等业务及ATM（自动柜员机）自动取款，为您的工作和生活带来无限方便。

目前，工商银行天津市分行经营资产业务、负债业务、中间业务和国际业务四大种类，近百个业务品种，为企业及个人客户提供全方位的金融服务。

营业大厅

Industrial and Commercial Bank of China Tianjin Municipal Branch becomes the pillar of Tianjin Banking, depending on its abundant funds, wide-spread business offices, e-bank, high quality personnel.

By the end of 2002, the balance of deposit of Industrial and Commercial Bank of China Tianjin Municipal Branch was 82.81 billion yuan, the balance of loans was 65.64 billion yuan, ranking the first position amongall banks in Tianjin. There are over 400 business offices linked with network in urban and rural areas. People can enjoy its convenient services and faithfulness.

In recent two years, it quickens to develop e-bank and telephone-bank business, including a series of new network varieties. In 2002, customers can transact business using bankbook or Mudan card in over 30,000 offices of Industrial and Commercial Bank of China. It is convenient for customers no matter which places they locate in China.

At present, Tianjin Municipal Branch engages in four varieties of business, including capital business, debt business, medium business and international business, and about 100 kinds of business. All these business can provide overall services for enterprises and residents.

地址：天津市河西区围堤道123号 Add: No. 123 Weidi Road, Hexi District, Tianjin

邮政编码 Postal Code: 300074 电话 Tel: 95588

中国石化股份公司天津分公司

China Petrochemical Co., Ltd. Tianjin Corporation

董事长：常振勇

装置区外景

中国石化股份公司天津分公司是中国石油化工股份公司的分支机构，是生产管理和成本控制中心。天津分公司位于天津滨海新区的大港区，地处渤海之滨，扼京、冀、鲁之咽喉，环境优美，交通便利，

油罐

拥有自己的天津港库区和专用油码头。天津分公司以炼油、化工、化纤为主业，主要生产装置引进日本、美国、德国的先进技术，拥有炼油装置14套，化工装置2套，化纤装置7套。原油加工能力500万吨/年，对二甲苯生产能力8万吨，聚酯生产能力10万吨/年，合成纤维生产能力6.8万吨/年，生产油、化、纤三大类产品30余种。

截止到2003年底，天津分公司总资产36.57亿元，销售收入超百亿元。在分公司科技人员的不断努力下，不断有炼油和化纤的新品和专利问世。中国石化股份公司天津分公司将继续以优质的产品、先进的技术、严细的管理和良好的服务为中国石化事业的发展和全球经济的繁荣做出应有的贡献。

China Petrochemical Co., Ltd. Tianjin Corporation is a center of production management and cost control, which is subordinated to China Petrochemical Co., Ltd.. It is situated in Dagang District of the new coastal area, lying near to Bohai with beautiful environment and convenient traffic. The corporation owns its Tianjin Port warehouse and oil dock. Its production fields mainly cover petroleum coking, chemical industry and chemical fibers. The major production equipment are imported from Japan, United States and Germany, including 14 sets of petroleum coking equipment,

油码头外景

2 sets of chemical industry equipment and 7 sets of chemical fibers. It can produce more than 30 kinds products with Production capacity of 5 million tons crude oil, 80,000 tons C6H4(CH3) , 2,100,000 tons polyester and 68,000 tons synthetic fibre.

By the end of 2003, the corporation owned 3.657 billion yuan of total capital and sales revenue reached more than 10

10万吨涤纶短丝装置

billion yuan. With the hard work of technical personnel, the corporation emerges new products and patents continuously. It will continue to contribute itself for the development of petrochemical industry, depending on its good quality products, advanced technique, rigorous management and good services.

地址：天津市大港区
Add: Dagang District, Tianjin
邮政编码 Postal Code: 300271
电话 Tel: (022) 63804610
传真 Fax: (022) 63803000

新厂门全景

中国石油大港石化公司

PETROCHINA DAGANG PETROCHEMICAL CORPORATION

中油集团副总经理段文德来我公司进行视察调研

中国石油大港石化公司，是中国石油天然气股份有限公司直属的地区分公司，位于天津滨海新区，地处国家重点石油化工基地，海陆交通便利，基础设施完善，具有得天独厚的区域优势和资源优势。目前该公司已发展成为拥有固定资产净值14.7亿元，原油配套加工能力250万吨/年，可生产七大系列五十多种产品的现代炼化企业，被誉为渤海之滨的一颗璀璨明珠。

大港石化公司始建于1965年，在近四十年的发展历程中，大港石化公司走过了一条由小到大、由弱到强的持续发展之路。特别是1996年以来，该公司抓住机遇、创新管理、与时俱进、乘势而上，使企业从规模到效益实现了快速发展。该公司始终坚持“效益领先”的发展思路，不断进行技术改造和创新，使生产装备和工艺技术达到了国内同行业先进水平。1996年该公司通过ISO 9002质量体系认证，2000年QHSE体系正式运行，奠定了企业管理制度化、标准化、规范化的基础。该公司生产的“滨海”牌系列产品，多次荣获国家和行业优质产品称号，行销国内20多个省市和东南亚地区，深受国内外用户赞誉。

随着经济全球化步伐的加快，炼化行业的生存和发展环境正在发生新的、历史性的变化；该公司放眼未来，未雨绸缪，以可持续发展为着力点，大力实施低成本战略，努力提高参与大市场竞争的实力。

中国石油大港石化公司愿与国内外同行真诚合作，共创美好明天！

培养高素质员工队伍

Petrochina Dagang Petrochemical Corporation is subordinated to China Petroleum & Gas Co., Ltd.. It is situated at new coastal area and located at national key petrochemical base. It has good geographical location, abundant resources, convenient traffic and complete infrastructure. By now, it has been a modern enterprise which owns 1.47 billion yuan of net value of fixed assets and can produce more than 50 kinds of 7 series products with annual processing capacity of 2.5 billion tons.

The corporation was established in 1965. During the past 40 years, it has developed continuously. Especially since 1996, it seizes opportunity and quickens to develop. It always takes “benefit the first” as its development idea and carries out technological innovation so that its production equipment and technological level have reached domestic advanced level. In 1996, it passed ISO 9002 quality system certification, QHSE system began to operate in 2000. All these lay a foundation to form regular management institution. “Binhai” brand series products have been named “good quality product” and sold to more than 20 provinces (municipalities) and Southeast Asia.

Along with the pace of global economic development, the development environment of petrochemical industry is changing. The corporation will work hard for sustained development and hope to improve competitive power through implementing low cost strategy.

We sincerely hope to cooperate and develop with all the friends.

石化公司厂区夜景

地址：天津市大港油田花园路东口
Add: The East Joint of Huayuan Road, Dagang Oil Field, Tianjin
邮编 Postal Code: 300280
电话 Tel: (022) 25921144 25924140
传真 Fax: (022) 25979268

天津鑫茂科技投资集团

Tianjin Xinmao Science And Technology Investment Group

天津鑫茂科技投资集团是以投资建设高新技术产业园、创新工业物业管理、以培育科技产业孵化基地、实现发展科技产业为主的私营企业集团。

鑫茂集团拥有控股和参股子公司33家，经营范围涉及工业房地产开发、产业园物业管理、高新技术产业投资、进出口贸易、商业零售、培训咨询、餐饮娱乐酒店业等多个领域。2003年名列天津市百强私营企业，并荣获天津市优秀企业称号。董事长杜克荣为全国军队模范转业干部、全国民营科技园专业委员会副主任、全国民营企业文化建设委员会委员、全国民营企业报刊研究会副会长、天津市工商业联合会副会长、天津市企业联合会副会长、天津市人大代表、天津市南开区政协常委，2003年荣获天津市优秀企业家称号和国家科技部中国民营科技创新奖，2004年因其创业业绩突出而被纳入天津市档案馆“杰出人才档案”。

董事长兼总裁：杜克荣

鑫茂科技投资集团自1992年创业以来，始终践行“实现自我，奉献社会”的企业理念，形成了“永不满足、勇于创新、主动变革、与入园企业共创卓越、共享辉煌”的核心价值观。秉承“与人争路，不如自己开路”的经营理念，随时根据市场需求变化，调整资本结构和产业结构，通过整合已有资源，不断加大对科技园、科技企业、零售服务业的投入；构筑了“主业突出、三位一体、优势互补”的发展平台，提高了集团的整体运营能力。其中，集团倾情开发建设的南开鑫茂民营科技园和华苑民营科技园厂房总建筑面积25.6万平米，引进中外科技企业240余家，以其“民投、民建、民管、民享”的鑫茂特色。2002年被国家科技部评为“全国十佳民营科技园”，2003年又荣获国家科技部“中国民营科技促进奖”。

Tianjin Xinmao Science and Technology Investment Group is a private group, mainly engages in construction and property management of hi-tech park, developing of incubation base of science and technology industry.

The group is a holding company or a stock-holder of 33 companies. Its business fields cover real estate, property management, domestic & international trade, catering and hotel, retail trade, high and new technology and training consulting. In 2003, it was awarded one of “top 100 private enterprises in Tianjin” and “Tianjin excellent enterprises”. Mr. Du kerong, chairman of the board, is a national model cadre transferred to civilian work from army, vice director of National Private Science and Technology Park Committee, member of National Private Enterprise Culture Construction Committee, vice president of National Enterprise Newspaper Research Committee, vice president of Tianjin Industry & Commerce League, vice president of Tianjin Enterprise League, delegate of Tianjin People's Congress, a standing member of Nankai District Political Consultative Committee. He was awarded “Tianjin excellent enterpriser” and “private science and technology innovation awards of the Ministry of Science and Technology” in 2003. He was listed in Tianjin Archives as outstanding talented person.

Since its establishment in 1992, the group always takes “develop itself, contribute for society” as its motto, carries forward the core worth view of “no satisfactory, actively proceeding reform, with a pioneering spirit, developing with the enterprises of park”, takes “scramble for road with the person, not equal to open a new road” as management motto. Following the change of requirement, the group adjusts capital structure and industry structure, increases investment in science and technology park, hi-tech enterprises and retail services. It has established development platform and improved the whole strength of group. Nankai Xinmao Private Science and Technology Park and Huayuan Private Science and Technology Park, occupy construction area of 0.256 million square meters, locate more than 240 Chinese and foreign science and technology enterprises, was awarded “10 national excellent private science and technology park” in 2002 and “private science and technology promotion awards” by the Ministry of Science and Technology in 2003.

天津城市建设学院

李瑞环

党委书记：杜金岭

院长、博士生导师：杜东菊

天津城市建设学院是一所以城市领域为主要服务对象的高等院校，前身是天津大学建筑分校，始建于1978年，1987年发展为独立办学的高等工科院校。1996年首批通过国家教委本科教学合格评估，1998年成为硕士学位授予权单位。学院与改革开放同龄同步，沐浴时代春风，事业发展日新月异。

学院目前占地321亩（规划用地1300亩），建筑面积24.16万平方米。设有建筑系、土木工程系、热能工程系、材料科学与工程系、管理工程系、市政与环境工程系、计算机科学与工程系、艺术系8个系，3个高职校区，1个成人教育学院；5个硕士学位点，23个本科专业，15个高职（专科）专业。学科专业涵盖工、理、管、文、农五大学科门类，在校学生万余名，教职工1千余人。近五年来学院投资上亿元，新建单元式学生公寓、商住型教师住宅、先进的远程教育中心、多功能食堂、多媒体阶梯教室、高标准学术报告厅、数字化电子图书阅览室、现代化塑胶运动场。校园布局新颖和谐，楼堂错落有致，满目绿树草坪，兼有碧水池塘，山石雕塑亭阁，环境品位高雅，文化底蕴厚重，是致力于城市科学研究的理想院校，是培养高素质城市人才的美好摇篮。

“十五”期间，学院以创建城市大学为目标，到2005年办学规模达12000人，将拥有本科专业25个，硕士学位授予学科点9个，取得博士学位授予权，学科专业涵盖工、理、经、管、文、林、法、艺八个门类，办学实力进入国内同类院校前列。功崇唯志，业广唯勤。建园人紧紧把握城市发展脉搏，解放思想，大胆创新，努力把学院建设成为一所多学科交融、特色鲜明的高水平的城市大学。

Tianjin Institute of Urban Construction is a institution of higher education, mainly serves for urban areas, the former Tianjin University at Construction which founded in 1978, it became a independent engineering institution of higher education in 1987. It is one of the first schools which passed the evaluation of undergraduate course by Commission of Education in 1996, it was authorized to confer master degree in 1998. Following the reform and opening to the outside world, the institute develops with continuous changes and improvements.

The institute occupies an land area of 321 mu(planning area of 1,300 mu), the construction area is 241,600 square meters. It has 8 departments, namely construction department, civil engineering department, heat energy engineering department, material science and engineering department, management engineering department, municipal and environment engineering department, computer and engineering department, art department, 3 higher vocational schools and 1 adult education institute. There are 5 units can confer master degree, 23 undergraduate subjects and 15 higher vocational subjects. These subjects cover engineering, science, management, literature and agriculture. There are over 10,000 enrolled undergraduate students and over 1,000 teachers and staff. In recent five years, the institute invests over 0.2 billion yuan to construct student apartment, teacher residential building, advanced remote education center, multi-function dining room, multi-media classroom, scholarship report hall, e-library, stadium. You can enjoy the sight of teaching building, green trees and lawn, clear waters and loft. It is a ideal institute for you to carry out urban science reach, the cradle of cultivate high quality talents.

The institute takes establishing urban university as its objective, the enrolled students will reach 12,000 in 2005, the institute will have 25 subjects covering engineering, science, economy, management, literature, forestry, law and art, 9 units can confer master degree and can be authorized to confer doctor degree. The education strength can list the leading position among domestic same kind of institutes. We will work hard with a pioneering spirit, try to make the institute be a multi-subject urban university with special features and high level.

地址：天津市西青区津静路26号　邮政编码 Postal Code: 300384　电话 Tel: (022)23792015　传真 Fax: (022)23792528
Add: No.26, Jin-jing Highway, Xiqing District, Tianjin　http: //www.tjuci.edu.cn　E-mail: office@tjuci.edu.cn

天津工業大學

TIANJIN POLYTECHNIC UNIVERSITY

地址：天津市河东区程林庄路63号
Add: No.63 Chenglinzhuang Road, Hedong District, Tianjin
电话 Tel: (022) 24528000
邮政编码 Postal Code: 300160
http://www.tjpu.edu.cn
E-mail: xzb@tjpu.edu.cn

天／津／工／业／大／学

天津工业大学历史悠久，其最早的系建于1912年，现已发展成一所以工为主，工理结合，工、理、文、管、经、法协调发展的多科性教学研究型大学，是具有学士、硕士、博士学位授予权的中国北方重要高等学府。学校目前拥有1个博士后流动站、1个一级学科博士点、6个二级学科博士点、3个自主设置博士点、26个硕士点（其中3个硕士点还具有高校教师在职攻读硕士学位授予权）和5个工程硕士领域、34个本科专业；拥有1个国家级重点学科，3个省部级重点学科，5个天津市重点建设学科；学校设有14个院系、多个研究所、室，现有全日制在校生12000余人。学校占地近九百多亩，建筑面积三十多万平方米，现正在规划建设占地四千余亩的新校区。

该校特色学科在国际国内处于领先水平，教学、科研、管理诸方面都跻身于全国普通高校前列，并正以坚实的步伐向着“立足天津、面向全国，在国内有较大影响，在国际有一定知名度”的办学目标大步迈进。

洋湖

语音室

Tianjin Polytechnic University has a long history, its earliest department founded in 1912. Now it has become a multi-disciplinary university dominated by engineering and integrating engineering, sciences, liberal arts, management, economics and law. It can grant degree for scholar, master and doctor. At present, there are 1 doctoral working station, 1 doctoral degree program of the first-level branch of learning, 6 doctoral degree program of the second-level branch of learning, 3 doctoral degree program offered by itself, 26 master degree programs (including 3 programs which can grant master degree for the teachers of universities) , 5 engineering master degree programs and 34 scholar degree subjects. It has 1 state-level key subject, 3 ministry-level key subjects and 5 Tianjin key subjects. It has 14 institutes, many research institutes, 12,000 enrolled undergraduate students. The university occupies an area of 900 mu and the construction area reaches 0.3 million square meters. Now it plans to construct the new campus of 4,000 mous .

Its distinguishing subjects reach national and international advanced level, which teaching, science research, management have listed the leading position among national general colleges and universities. The university will develop along the target "having a foothold in Tianjin, facing to China, being a famous university" .

天津市建筑设计院
Tianjin Construction Design Institute

Tianjin Construction Design Institute, founded 50 years before, has become the biggest comprehensive construction design institute in Tianjin and one of "top 100 national investigation and design enterprises" which is equipped with strong strength and abundant talented persons. In recent ten years, there are 165 projects made by the institute be awarded good design prizes by State, the Ministry of Construction and Tianjin Municipal. Of which, Tianjin No.2 Nankai Middle School was awarded state-grade excellent design gold prize in 2002, Zhou Enlai and Deng Yingchao Memorial was awarded silver prize, Huayuan Bihuali zone was awarded bronze prize. Among the project collecting of six comprehensive development and rebuilding projects along Haihe River, Tianjin Construction Design Institute won three prizes, namely Dabeiyuan Culture Trade Center, CBD South Railway Station and Heping Trade Center of Haihe Square were awarded excellent plans. "Tianjin Steel Structure Residential Building Design Rules" compiled by the institute passed the appraisal of state-grade experts, is the first rule of steel structure residential building design and has reached the leading level in China.

It has 2 state-grade engineering design experts, 18 chief senior engineers, 296 senior engineers, 65 first-class registered architects, 80 first-class registered construction teachers, 27 registered supervisors. In 1996, it passed ISO 9001 International Quality System Certification and transferred to ISO 9001:2000 Quality Management System on March, 2000.

天津市建筑设计院至今走过了50多年历程，已经发展成为技术实力雄厚、人才济济的天津市最大的综合性建筑设计院，是中国勘察设计综合实力百强企业。近十年来，天津建院共有165项工程分别获得国家、建设部、天津市优秀设计奖。其中：天津市第二南开中学获2002年度国家级优秀设计金质奖；周恩来、邓颖超纪念馆获银质奖；华苑居住区碧华里小区获铜质奖。在天津海河两岸综合开发工程六个节点设计方案国际征集中，天津建院就有三项获奖：大悲院文化商贸区获优胜方案；中心商务区南站地区获优胜方案；海河广场和和平商贸区获优秀方案。由天津建院主编的《天津市钢结构住宅设计规程》的科研成果通过了国家级专家鉴定，它是国内第一部钢结构住宅设计规程，达到国内领先水平。

天津市建筑设计院拥有国家工程设计大师2人，正高级建筑（工程）师18人，高级规划师、建筑（工程）师296人，国家一级注册建筑师65人，一级注册结构工程师80人、注册监理工程师27人。1996年获得ISO 9001国际质量体系认证。2000年3月实现2000版ISO 9001标准质量管理体系转换。

地址: 天津市河西区气象台路95号
Add: No. 95 Qixiangtai Street, Hexi District, Tianjin
电话 Tel: (022) 23543000 23345260
邮政编码 Postal Code: 300074

天津市勘察院

Tianjin Institute of Geotechnical Investigation & Surveying

院长：李文春

天津市勘察院成立于1979年，是以岩土工程勘察、工程测量、建筑与岩土工程设计和桩基施工、工程测试为主的专业化综合性生产科研单位，拥有工程勘察国家级综合甲级资质、岩土工程国家一级承包资质、桩基测试国家甲级资质、工程测量国家甲级资质、建筑设计国家乙级资质、工程监理国家乙级资质和深基坑支护设计专项资质，是全国大型综合勘察单位之一，被评为全国勘察设计综合实力百强单位，并通过ISO 9001：2000国际质量认证。

我院目前有职工300名，其中49人具有高级技术职称，56人具有中级技术职称，同时我院还拥有1名国家勘察大师，2名国务院特贴专家，3名市级特贴专家，技术实力雄厚。

本院拥有国内一流的专业生产及施工设备，以及高素质的人才队伍。本院以团结、拼搏、求实、创新为企业精神，坚持职工为本、科技兴院的方针，以先进的技术、优质的服务为宗旨，为顾客提供高质量、高水平的勘测、设计、施工和科研成果。

地址：天津市南开区红旗南路428号
Add: No. 428 Hongqinan Road,
Nankai District, Tianjin
电话 Tel: (022) 23679610, 23679557
传真 Fax: (022) 23679610
邮政编码 Postal Code: 300191
http://www.tigis.com.cn
E-mail: tjgis@tigis.com.cn

Tianjin Institute of Geotechnical Investigation & Surveying founded in 1979, is a comprehensive production and scientific research unit, mainly undertakes investigation & surveying on rock soil engineering, measure, construction and design of engineering. It is a large-sized investigation & surveying unit in China, which is the first grade national unit in terms of capital and quality, first grade unit in rock soil engineering, first grade unit in foundation test, first grade unit in engineering measure, second grade unit in construction design, second grade unit in engineering supervision, special qualification in design for deep pit support. It is awarded "top 100 national institute of investigation & surveying in terms of comprehensive strength" and has passed ISO 9001:2000 International Quality Standard Certification. It has 300 staff and workers, of which, 49 persons have senior professional certification, 56 persons have medium professional certification, 1 national investigation master, two experts enjoy the special subsidy of the State Council, 3 experts enjoy the special subsidy of the Tianjin Municipal. Its technical strength is strong.

It is equipped with top-grade production and construction equipment, high quality talented person's troops. It takes "solidify, working diligently with pioneering spirit" as enterprise spirit, takes "care for staff and workers, technology makes the institute strong" as principle, takes "advanced technology and high quality services" as aim. It can provide high quality investigation, design, construction and scientific research results for customers.

天津市建设投资公司
TIANJIN CONSTRUCTION INVESTMENT CORPORATION

改造后的谦德庄新景

河北区小树林地块拆迁后现状

拆迁后的老城厢地块现状

老城厢地块围挡现状

天津市建设投资公司成立于1993年。为落实天津市委、市政府提出的“三、五、八、十”奋斗目标，建设投资公司承担了危陋平房难点大片的改造重任；通过多种融资手段，投资50亿元先后启动了谦德庄、春华里、西广开、南门西、芥园道等大面积危陋平房改造，占地总面积约210公顷，有力的组织和推动了全市危改。

2003年，围绕海河综合开发改造，为适应规模资本运作，建设投资公司与曾为天津市安居工程建设做出突出贡献的安居建设发展总公司整合，形成新公司架构。按照市政府提出的市场化经营思路和建委总体部署，利用百亿授信额度对旧城区和平广场、老城厢、小伙巷等30余片危旧房屋进行了拆迁改造，并将地块挂牌上市，为海河综合开发改造提供了良好的前提条件。

面向未来，建设投资公司将继续发扬世纪危改精神，遵循为民造福宗旨，围绕天津经济总体发展目标和海河经济发展规划，以创新发展的经营思路和良好的资信能力，竭诚与海内外投资者积极合作，为加速天津发展做出更大的贡献。

Tianjin Construction Investment Corporation founded in 1993. In order to implement the struggle target of “Four objectives”, the corporation undertook reconstruction of dilapidated houses. Through kinds of ways to raise funds, it invested 5 billion yuan to carry out the reconstruction of Qiandezhuang, Chunhuali, Xiguangkai, Nanmenxi and Jieyuandao with the total land area of 210 hectares. All these projects pushed the reconstruction of dilapidated houses of Tianjin.

In 2003, the corporation united Anju Construction Development Corporation and established a new corporation. Around comprehensive development and rebuilding project along Haihe River, the corporation undertook the reconstruction of old and dilapidated houses, including old downtown Heping Square, Laochengxiang, Xiaohuoxiang and so on. These projects had provided good prerequisite for comprehensive development and rebuilding project along Haihe River.

Facing to future, the corporation will continue to carry forward Weigai spirit and bring benefit to people. According to objectives for the development of Tianjin economy and the development plan of Haihe economy, it will sincerely cooperate with investors from home and abroad and contribute a lot for the development of Tianjin with a pioneering spirit and good credit.

地址：天津市和平区常德道23号
Add: No.23 Changde Road, Heping District, Tianjin
电话 Tel: (022) 23040616
传真 Fax: (022) 23040619
邮政编码 Postal Code: 300050

天津药物研究院

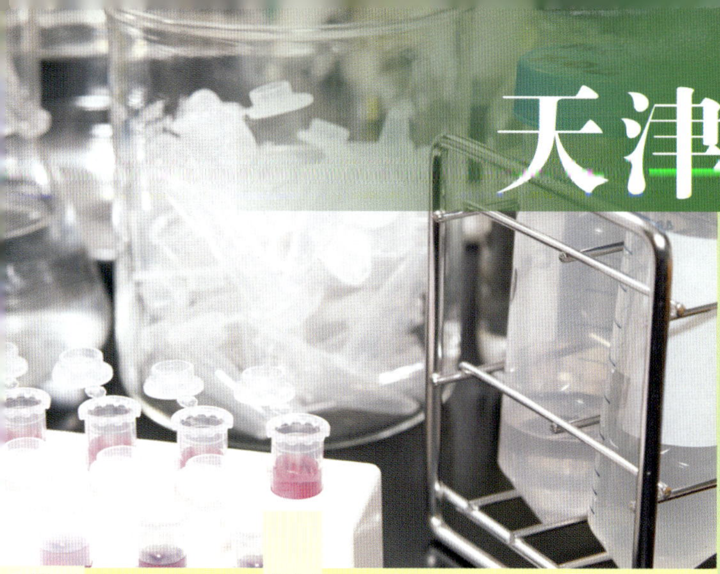

Tianjin Medicine Research Institute

Tianjin Medicine Research Institute is a large-sized comprehensive medicine research organization, is subordinated to former State Medicine Management Bureau. It mainly undertakes research working of new medicine, natural medicine and relative products. It owns strong scientific research ability and has made in over 500 scientific research achievements, of which, 200 projects have won scientific research achievement awards of state, ministry and Tianjin. In 2001, it acquired 22 new medicine certifications and a total of 60 million yuan contracts on the transfer of technology. Tianjin Medicine Research Institute Pharmaceutical Co., Ltd. is a hi-tech enterprise with scientific research, production and selling together, is formerly Tianjin Medicine Research Institute Experiment Pharmaceutical Factory, undertakes conversion of research achievement and has become the pillar of the institute. The corporation is the specified manufacturer of spirit medicine and is listed as "Tianjin 10 Billion Project" unit. It has been awarded excellent hi-tech enterprise for several times and passed GMP Certification.

The corporation has sales department, production department, quality department, material management department, financing department, human resource department. About two third employees have medium or high class titles, one third employees have pharmacist qualifications. Sales department has formed sales network covering the whole country and some foreign countries. Production department has four workshops with new special equipment, namely raw material medicine, injection, solid medicine and traditional Chinese medicine. The corporation can produce 0.6-0.8 billion grains of solid medicine, 30 million units of injection, 0.2 million tons of raw material medicine per year. Quality department is equipped with complete quality control system and over 10 technical personnel.

The corporation has developed over 10 kinds of medicine, produced and sold raw material medicine, injection, medicine grain, capsule and so on, including pain relieving, inflammation eliminating, lowing blood sugar, spirit illness treatment, top blood pressure treatment, heart blood vessel illness treatment series medicine.

In recent years, the corporation relies on scientific research achievement of Tianjin Medicine Research Institute and develops with a rapid speed. Following the aim of "scientific innovation, serve healthy", it will continue to produce hi-tech products and improve the life quality of patients.

天津药物研究院为大型、综合性医药科研机构，原直属于前国家医药管理局，主要承担国家创新药物、仿制药物、天然药物及其制剂的研究工作，具有很强的科研开发能力。四十多年来，共取得500多项科研成果，其中200余项曾获国家、部委、市级科研成果奖。2001年又取得新药证书22个，技术转让合同金额6000多万元。

天津药物研究院药业有限责任公司为天津药物研究院主办的集科、工、贸为一体的高新技术企业，公司的前身是药物研究院试验药厂，承担院科研成果的中试、放大，为适应研究院的发展需要，目前以实施本院重大科研成果产业化为主，已成为院科研的支柱。公司目前是国家精神药品的定点生产单位，并被列为“天津百亿工程”项目的承担单位，多次被评为优秀高新技术企业，已通过GMP认证。

公司设有营销部、生产部、质量部、物资管理部、财务部、人事行政部等部门，现有在册员工三分之二具有中级以上技术职称，三分之一具有执业药师资格。营销部已形成了覆盖全国及部分国外市场的营销网络。生产部下设原料药、针剂、固体制剂和中药四个车间，均采用最新型的制药专用设备。年生产能力为：固体制剂6–8亿片/粒，针剂3000万支，原料药20吨。质量部具备完善的质量控制体系，并拥有十余名技术骨干。

公司生产和销售原料药、针剂、片剂、胶囊剂和口服液，包括：镇痛、抗炎、戒毒、降血糖、抗精神病、抗高血压、改善心脑血管病等方面的系列产品，历年来共开发生产二十余个品种。

公司依托于天津药物研究院的科研力量和成果，近几年得到了迅猛的发展，本着科技创新，服务健康的宗旨，今后将继续以不断提供高科技含量的产品作为发展方向，以期为商业伙伴、医生和患者提供更优质的产品，为提高患者的生命质量而努力。

地址: 天津市南开区鞍山道308号
Add: No.308 Anshanxi Street, Nankai District, Tianjin
邮政编码 Postal Code: 300193
电话 Tel: (022) 23006946
传真 Fax: (022) 27377355

天津农垦集团总公司

Tianjin State Farms Agribusiness Group Corporation

天津农垦集团总公司为具有企业法人资格的国有独资性质的经济实体。下辖4个分公司、27个全资子公司、4个控股子公司、并参股3家公司，拥有资产22亿元，土地16.5万亩（含耕5.9万亩），职工1.26万人。2002年集团总公司实现国内生产总值6.2亿元，实现利润总额1.75亿元。集团总公司所属企业的经营范围涉及农、工、商、房地产、社会服务等各业；所生产的王朝牌葡萄酒享誉海内外，海河及帕玛拉特品牌的奶制品、红港牌草坪草卷等也属国内知名产品。

2000年5月天津农垦集团被批准列入市政府重点支持的大型企业集团，享受市政府规定的投资审批权、股票上市、兼并重组、所得税返还、土地出让、技术改造、生产要素指标、进出口配额等扶持政策，使天津农垦集团总公司获得了更大的发展空间。

领导视察王朝酒销售情况

Tianjin State Farms Agribusiness Group Corporation is a state-owned corporate group. It has 4 subsidiary companies, 27 subsidiaries under its control, and is a holding company of 4 comparies and a stock holder of 3 companies. It owns a property of 2.2 billion yuan, 165 thousand mou of earth (A plowland of 59 thousand mou). There are 12.6 thousand employees in this corporation. In 2002, it realized a GDP of 0.62 billion yuan and a profit of 175,000 thousand yuan. Its management covers agriculture, industry, business, real estate and social service. The Dynasty Wine it produces enjoys a good reputation and the Haihe and Pamalat Milk it produces and known throughout China.

天津农垦奶牛养殖场

In May 2000, it was approved as an important company by Tianjin Government. It also enjoys the privilege to approve, put its stock into market, annexation and recombination, repayment of income tax, remising earth, technique reform, support of production element and quota of imports and exports. As a result, Tianjin State Farms Agribusiness Group Corporation gains a greater development space.

地址：天津市南开区士英路20号
Add: No. 20 Shiying Road, Nankai District, Tianjin
邮政编码 Postal Code: 300381
电话 Tel: (022) 23943341, 23943355

天津丰田汽车发动机有限公司

TTME TIANJIN TOYOTA MOTOR ENGINE CO., LTD.

总经理：三重野英治

副总经理：栾广辰

天津丰田汽车发动机有限公司（TIANJIN TOYOTA MOTOR ENGINE CO., LTD. 简称 TTME）是经国务院 1996 年 5 月批准，由天津汽车工业（集团）有限公司和日本丰田汽车公司共同出资兴建的合资企业，注册资本 2.48 亿美元，中日双方各占 50% 的出资比率。经国家商务部批准，2003 年 12 月天津汽车工业（集团）有限公司将所占有的 50% 全部转让给中国第一汽车集团公司。

公司占地面积 21 万平方米，建筑面积 8.6 万平方米。主要产品是从日本丰田汽车公司引进的具有先进水平的 A 系列、K3/SZ 系列、ZZ 系列发动机及汽车铸件。为国内特锐、威姿、威乐、威驰、花冠等多种车型配套。

公司于 2000 年 2 月，通过 ISO 9002：1994 标准的认证，并于 2002 年 6 月进行了换版认证（即 ISO 9001：2000）；同时公司为保护地球生态环境，注重并致力于环境管理，于 2002 年 9 月通过 ISO 14001：1996 环境管理体系国内及 UKAS 国际认证。

公司以先进的丰田生产方式，不断地生产高品质、高性能、环保型的发动机来更好地服务于广大客户。

Tianjin Toyota Motor Engine Co., Ltd. (TTME) is a joint-venture enterprise invested by Tianjin Auto Industrial(Group) Co., Ltd. and Japan Toyota Auto Corporation. Approved by the State Council, it was founded in May, 1996. It registered capital is USD 0.248 billion at equal share of 50% each. Approved by the Ministry of Commerce, Tianjin Motor Industrial(Group) Co., Ltd. made over its total registered capital to China No.1 Auto Group in December, 2003.

The corporation occupies an area of 210,000 square meters, the construction area reaches 86,000 square meters. Its major products include A series, K3/SZ series and ZZ series engine and auto casting parts which are equipped with international advanced technology imported from Japan Toyota Auto Corporation. The products are used for TERIOS, Vizi, VELA, Vios, COROLLA and other domestic cars.

The corporation passed ISO 9002:1994 Quality Standard System Certification in February, 2000 and ISO 9001:2000 Quality Standard System Certification in June, 2002. Meanwhile, it pays attention to environmental management and passed ISO 14001:1996 Environmental Management System Certification in September, 2002.

The corporation takes Toyota management pattern and produces engines with high quality, good performance and pollution-free for all customers.

地址：天津市西青区杨柳青西青道266号
Add: No. 266 Xiqing Road, Yangliuqing, Xiqing District, Tianjin
邮政编码 Postal Code: 300380　电话 Tel: (022) 27911049　传真 Fax: (022) 27390960

TOYOTA

天津汽车

天津泰达建设集团有限公司

TEDA Construction Group Co., Ltd.

风荷新园

云琅大厦

泰达园

天津泰达建设集团有限公司（简称泰达建设）是以房地产开发为主业的大型企业，并具有物业管理、基础设施建设、建筑规划设计、装修装饰、金融投资等综合能力。集团拥有两家建设部一级资质的房地产开发公司，旗下的建设分公司、滨海分公司和全资子公司开发区房地产开发公司是集团房地产开发的三家主要企业，拥有“天江格调空间”、“泰达园”、“风荷园”、“翠亨村”、“云琅新居”等一批知名房地产品牌；公司长期在天津开发区从事标准工业厂房和基础设施的开发建设，是开发区最主要的标准工业厂房开发商，为完善开发区的投资环境创造了条件；公司控股的天孚物业管理公司为国家一级资质的物业管理企业，物业管理规模居天津市首位。

泰达建设前身是开发区建设开发公司，1984年与天津开发区同时成立，为开发区的建设做出了突出贡献。1988年公司进入房地产开发领域，1995正式改组为集团公司，1999年实施资产重组，将原建设集团、开发区房地产开发公司和职工住房合作社等重组为新的建设集团，是天津开发区第一家国有独资授权经营公司，2002年公司成为天津泰达投资控股公司的房地产开发支柱企业。

泰达建设规模和实力在天津市房地产开发企业中名列前茅，总资产已达到51亿元。公司参与发起了全国百家开发企业承诺销售“放心房”活动，在2001年和2003年被连续评为“天津市房地产开发企业二十强”之首，2002年公司进入“全国房地产领先企业”行列。公司多次获得“天津市优秀企业”、“开发区百强企业”等荣誉称号。公司自1994年至今连续获得“重合同守信誉单位”荣誉称号，2003年获得国家级“守合同重信用单位”称号，2003年全国第五届住交会被评为“2003年度中国房地产品牌企业五十强”，2004年被评为“天津市房地产开发AAA级信誉企业”。

TEDA Construction Group Co., Ltd. (TEDA Construction in brief) is a large-sized enterprise, mainly undertakes real estate development, has the comprehensive ability to undertake property management, infrastructure construction, building design, repair and decoration, banking investment. The group has two first class real estate enterprises in terms of capital and quality approved by the Ministry of Construction. Its major real estate enterprises, namely Construction Corporation, Binhai Corporation and TEDA Real Estate Development Corporation, have developed some famous projects, including TEDA Garden, Fenghe Garden, Cuihengcun, Yunlang Building. The corporation develops and constructs the standard workshop and infrastructure at TEDA all the year round. Its holding company, Tianfu Property Management Corporation is a first class property management enterprise in terms of capital and quality, occupies the first position on the scope of property management in Tianjin.

Its former, TEDA Construction Development Corporation founded in 1984 and had contributed a lot for the construction of TEDA. Since 1988, it began to relate to real estate development, became a group corporation in 1995. In 1999, the new construction group established as the first sole state-owned enterprise, which was merged from original Construction Group, TEDA Real Estate Development Corporation and Staff and Workers Housing Cooperation Agency, became he pillar enterprise of TEDA Investment Holdings.

天江格调空间

TEDA Construction Group Co., Ltd. lists the leading position on the scope and strength among real estate enterprises in Tianjin, its total capital reaches 5.1 billion yuan. It takes part in the activity of selling satisfied houses with 100 national real estate development enterprises. It was awarded “top 20 real estate development enterprises in Tianjin” and occupied the first position in 2001 and 2003. It listed “top real estate development enterprises” in China in 2002. It was awarded “Tianjin excellent enterprises” and “top 100 TEDA enterprises” for several times. From 1994 to now, the corporation was awarded “honor construction and abide by its words” for the successive years. In 2003, it was awarded state-grade enterprise of “honor construction and abide by its words”, “top 50 real estate development enterprises in China” in the fifth House Fair. In 2004, it was awarded “AAA credit enterprise of real estate development in Tianjin”.

地址：天津开发区第一大街
Add: No. 65 the First Street, TEDA
联系电话 Tel: (022)2532
传真 Fax: (022)2532
邮政编码 Postal Code: 30

安居建设发展总公司

Anju Construction Development General Corporation

天津市安居建设发展总公司成立于1995年4月，为国有独资企业，注册资本金9200万人民币，从1997年以来历年被评为天津市房地产建设开发20强企业。

总公司自1995年以来先后组织实施了总建筑面积185万平方米的华苑居住区和总建筑面积270万平方米的丽苑居住区的规划设计竞赛和市政基础设施大配套建设，并实施了瑞景居住区的地块开发、组织规划设计与前期准备及招商工作。总公司还自行开发建设了总建筑面积19.4万平方米的国家重大科技产业工程项目华苑碧华里小区和总建筑面积21.8万平方米的国家建设部"住宅产业化"和"建筑节能试点"项目华苑绮华里小区。

其中碧华里于九九年六月被国家科技部和建设授予"国家小康住宅示范小区"称号，并获得规划设计、工程质量、环境质量和科技进步等四项优秀奖。绮华里小区作为建设部节能试点示范小区，于2001年4月全国首家通过建设部专家组验收，综合节能技术处于全国领先水平。碧华里、绮华里还在联合国人居中心北京信息办和《中国建设报》举办的首届"东方园林杯"全国优秀住宅社区环境评选中分别荣获特别金奖和金奖。几个小区还先后获得全国城市物业管理优秀住宅小区称号。2001年11月，在中国房地产业协会和《中国房地产报》主办的中国（天津）房地产成功经营模式典范推介活动中，华苑碧华里、绮华里被推介为部、省级试点示范小区开发模式。

新开发的瑞景居住区占地面积212.23公顷，规划建筑面积168.93万平方米，其规划宗旨为创造健康人居环境，整合各种生活元素。居住区中心为10.7公顷的体育文化公园（包括绿地及30米宽的环行水面）。地铁一号线刘园—双林，预计于2005年建成通车，形成交通线路快速便捷，内外网络天地互连的局面。目前以健康理念为主题的天津奥林匹克花园项目，做为瑞景新苑一期工程已于2002年3月开工，至2003年8月已有12万平方米商品房入住。

地址: 天津市河西区宁波道15号
Add: No. 15 Ningbo Road, Hexi District, Tianjin
邮政编码 Postal Code: 300202
电话 Tel: (022) 23259996

Tianjin Anju Construction Development General Corporation founded on April, 1995, is a sole state-funded corporation with the registered capital of 92 million yuan. Since the year of 1997, it was awarded "top 20 real estate enterprises in Tianjin" for consecutive years.

Since the foundation of the corporation, it has organized the design competition and construction of civil infrastructure for Huayuan zone of 1.85 million square meters and Liyuan zone of 2.7 million square meters. It also developed and designed Ruijing zone, developed and constructed Huayuan Bihuali zone of 0.194 million square meters and Qihuali zone of 0.218 million square meters. Bihuali zone was awarded "national comfortable model zone" by the Ministry of Science and Technology and the Ministry of Construction on June, 1999, was also awarded four excellent prizes for design, quality, environmental quality and science & technology achievement. Bing the energy-saving model zone, Qihuali zone was the first to pass the check of energy-saving organized by the Ministry of Construction and its comprehensive energy-saving technology reached national leading level. Bihuali and Qihuali were awarded special gold prize and gold prize of "The East Garden Cup" and " property management advanced zone" ,was recommended as development model zone during the period of China (Tianjin) Real Estate Model Recommending Activity on November, 2001. Ruijing zone, which is newly developed by the corporation, occupies an area of 212.23 hectares and designed construction area reaches 1.6893 million square meters including sport culture park of 10.7 hectares. Being phase 1 engineering of Ruijingxinyuan, Olympic Garden began to construct on March, 2002. By the end of August, 2003, there are 0.12 million square meter of residential housing put into use.

龙都集团

天津龙都置业投资集团有限公司

龙都集团总经理：王洪泉

龙都馨园鸟瞰图

天津龙都置业投资集团有限公司是天津市大型国有企业，是天津市房地产行业二十强企业之一。龙都集团以天津龙都置业投资集团有限公司为核心，由天津龙都房地产开发有限公司、天津市开发区龙都物业管理有限公司、天津龙都置业网络有限公司、天津市兆丰房地产开发有限公司、天津市津房置换河西连锁有限公司等五个紧密层企业和天津龙都装饰有限公司、天津龙都广告文化发展有限公司等十余个半紧密层企业组成。龙都集团实行以资产为纽带的母子公司体制，通过投资及生产经营协作等多种形式，与众多企业、事业单位共同组成经济联合体。

龙都集团经营范围：房地产投资；房地产开发；房地产经营；房地服务；房地产咨询服务；物业管理；商品房销售；商品房销售代理；住房贷款担保室内外装修；建筑材料高新技术开发、装饰；建筑材料、装饰材料、五金、交电批发；房地产信息；广告；餐饮娱乐等方面业务。

龙都集团发展战略和目标：按照现代化企业制度和市场经济的要求，以房地产市场为导向，通过改革、重组、改造和加强管理，建立新型高效、与国际接轨的现代企业管理体制和运行机制。充分发挥龙都置业投资集团有限公司核心企业的主导作用。通过资产运营，不断优化资源配置，形成群体优势，使龙都集团逐步发展成为集房地产投资、房地产开发、房地产经营、住房贷款担保、物业管理、建筑材料高新技术开发等综合功能，多种产业经营一体化的跨行业、跨地区、跨所有制，具有管理密集、资金密集的大型企业集团。逐步发展成为天津市房地产业的龙头企业，在国内市场竞争中占有明显优势，形成规模效应，创出全国知名品牌。

公司自创业以来，本着“诚信、服务、交朋友”的宗旨，以城市新区成片综合开发及旧城市改造为主要任务，先后完成了龙海公寓、龙都花园、西南楼同惠里、西楼后街、信昌厚大楼、奉化道同业里、体院北十区、五号路育红新里、西南楼白云里、小海地凤致里等十余片危旧房开发改造项目，累计竣工面积三百万平方米，总投资额达三十亿元。

三味舒屋

集团公司部分奖项

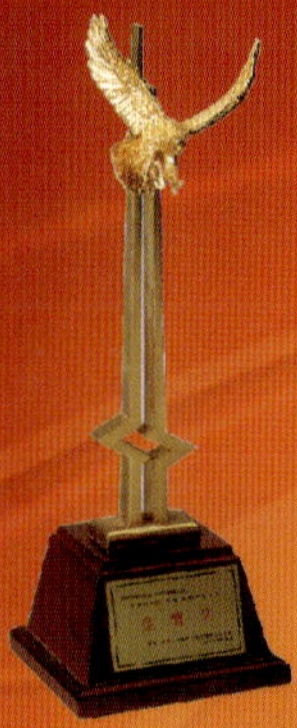

联系电话：(022) 28236868（十六线）　传真：(022) 28309900　http://www.longdu.cn

天津市东达房地产开发公司

Tianjin Dongda Real Estate Development Company

总经理：牛世清

天津市东达房地产开发公司是组建于1992年的全民企业，经过近7年的奋斗，目前已经发展到已开发和即将开发118万平方米的住宅、具有上千万元固定资产、运作着上亿元资金的房地产公司。

东达房地产开发公司在“投入危陋平房改造，造福于民”的思想指导下，1994年率先开发改造大直沽危陋平房难点大片。在5年的城市危房改造建设进程中，共拆除危陋平房近30万平方米。投资7000万元开了两条路（大直沽中路和八纬路），为挖掘保护大直沽文化遗存和600年古树，投资3000万元拆迁安置了高台近400户居民，为建设历史陈列馆创造了条件。

东达房地产开发公司在开发改造大直沽中提出了“六个负责”的原则，把“对历史负责，挖掘保护历史文化遗产；对未来负责，建造楼板全现浇，质量可靠，抗震性能强的住宅；对现实负责，提供优质、优价、优服务的优秀物业群；对整体环境负责，清除污染源，充分利用海河资源，营造自然人居环境空间；对子女负责，加大教育、文化、体育的配套投入，解除居民后顾之忧，创造良好的教育和心理成长环境；对政府负责，加速危改平房改造，促进区域经济发展建设新城区”作为企业发展和建设的宗旨。

我们相信，在不久的将来，“直沽旅游商城”将充分显示东达房地产开发公司对社会、对津门父老的奉献。

神州花园俯视图

大直沽历史陈列馆

神州花园

地址：天津市河东区大直沽五号路八纬路口

Add: The Joint of No. 5 Road and Bawei Road, Hedong District, Tianjin

电话 Tel: (022) 24145678

邮政编码 Postal Code: 300170

Dongda Real Estate Development Company is a state-owned enterprise which was setup in 1992. As a result of development of seven years, it has achieved and developed a total residential buildings area of 1,180,000 square meters. It has fixed assets of over 10 million yuan and operation funds of over 100 million yuan.

Under the guideline of “Reform old and dangerous residential building, bring benefit to people”, the company is the first to develop Dazhigu area. During the construction of urban dangerous residential building, the company has demolished 300,000 square meters of old and dangerous residential buildings. It invested 70 million yuan two roads (Dazhiguzhong Road and Bawei Road). In order to protect Dazhigu cultural ruins and six hundreds years old tree, it invested 30 million yuan to arrange for 400 households and provided condition to construct History Exhibition Hall.

During the development and reconstruction of Dazhigu, the company advances the principle of “Six responsibilities”, concerns history to protect historic cultural heritage; concerns future to construct high quality residential buildings; concerns reality to provide excellent products management; concerns the whole environment to clear away the source of pollution, use the resources of HaiHe River and build natural living environment; concerns childrens to enlarge the investment of education, culture, sports and build good education & mentality environment; concerns government to quicken the reform of old and dangerous houses, accelerate the construction of new urban region.

We believe Zhigu Tour Market District will show the contribution of the company for the society and people in the coming future.

天津市河东房地产开发总公司

Tianjin Hedong Real Estate General Company

嘉华国际城坐落于华昌大街商圈中轴——天津站后广场中心地段，西临内环新开路，北临华龙道，南临华昌大街、东临新泰路。项目所处地域属天津市市级规划的物流主动脉，周边交通网络密集，四通八达。尽善尽美的大区成熟营造出了天津商业不可否认的消费主卖场。

嘉华国际城总投资约30亿元，总占地面积42.8万平米，总建筑面积达64.2万多平米，计划五年内完成。

其一期商业区——嘉华国际商业中心已于2003年4月开始建设，2004年5月投入使用。该中心坐落在新开路与华昌大街交口，占地约18000平米，建筑面积8.5万平米，主体为五层框架结构建筑，具有购物餐饮、娱乐休闲、康体健身、家居装饰与金融等“一站式”全方位的服务功能，是海河东岸不可复制的多功能大型购物休闲中心。

嘉华国际商业中心投资赢利三大途径

自行经营：投资者买商铺作为自己的经营场地，占据新商业轴心最旺地段，节省不断飙升的租金成本，所营商品自然货如轮转！

出租赢利：商铺租金逐年上升，投资购铺后租给第三者经营，可获取高额租金回报。

低入高出：善于把握最佳赚钱时机的“买卖人”一致认同：先人一步的投资观念是获取巨大差额利润的不二法门！

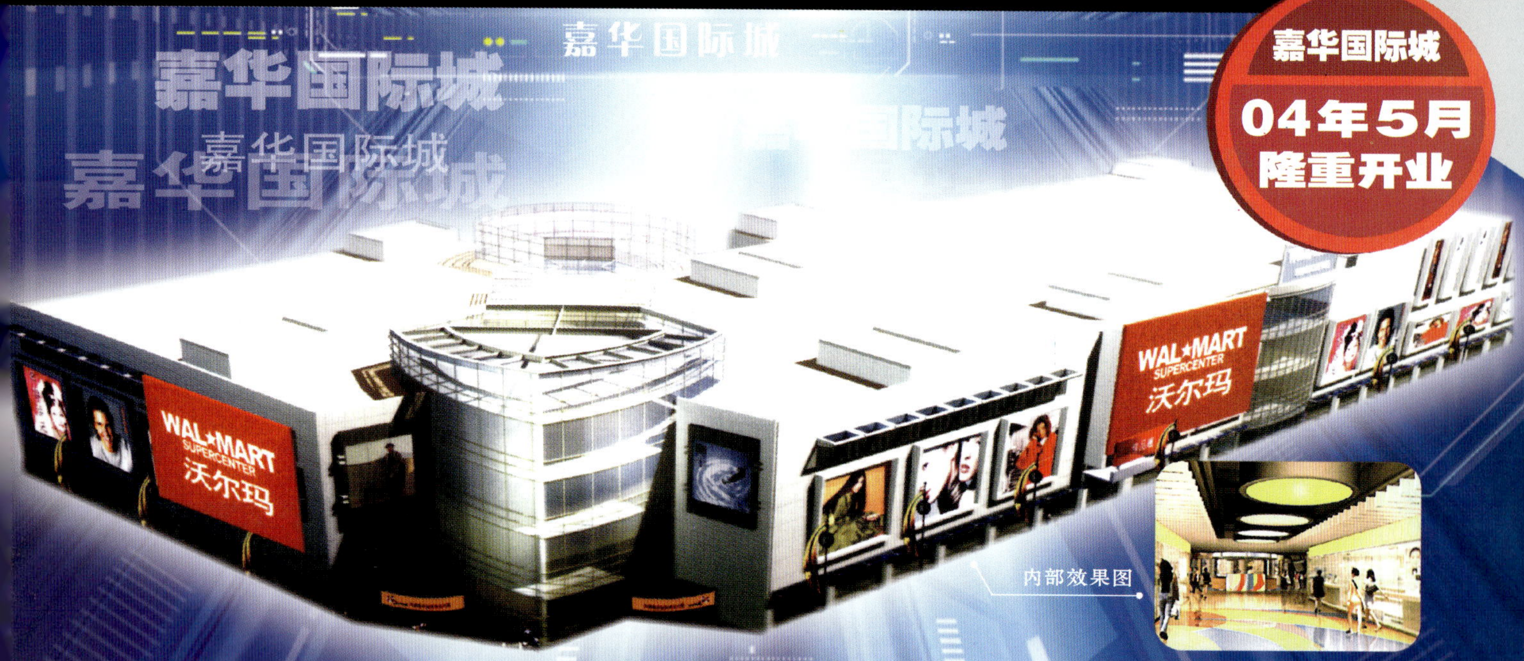

内部效果图

Jiahua International City is situated at the center of Huachang Trade Street and the square behind of Tianjin Railway Station, with Xinkai Road on the west, Hualong Road on the north, Huachang Street on the south and Xintai Road on the east. The project locates at the main line of the planned Tianjin logistics passage. It has traffic accessible to all directions. Good consumer environment has made it become the major consumer place in Tianjin.

The total investment of Jiahua International City total 3 billion yuan, it occupies land area of 0.428 million square meters and the construction area reaches 0.642 million square meters. The project will be completed in five years.

Jiahua Shopping Mall, the phase I trade city, began to construct on April, 2003 and plan to put into use on May, 2004. It is situated at the junction of Xinkai road and Huachang street, occupies land area of 0.018 million square meters and the construction area reaches 0.085 million square meters. The main construction is a five-story building, is a multi-function large-sized shopping center covering catering, entertainment, keeping fit, decoration and financing.

地址：天津市河东区程林庄路与红星路交口嘉华小区

Add: Jiahua zone, the joint of chenglinzhuang Road and Hongxing Road, Hedong District, Tianjin

电话 Tel: (022) 24493568 24015180

天津第二市政公路工程有限公司
Tianjin No. 2 Municipal Highway Engineering Co., Ltd.

总经理：王清泉

天津第二市政公路工程有限公司是天津城建集团有限公司的母体支柱企业之一，公司现有职工2850人，有职称的工程技术人员和经济管理人员682人，其中高、中级240人，有资质的项目经理155人。拥有大中型机械设备1236台，其中有原装进口沥青砼搅拌站、沥青砼摊铺设备及其他进口大型机械设备40余部。公司技术力量雄厚，设备先进，能承揽各类市政工程和各等公路工程、桥梁、隧道工程的设施工及建筑工程等。

近年来，公司承建的主要工程有：获全国优质工程金奖的引滦入津输水工程，获全国优质工程银奖的天津市外环线工程，获建设部优质工程的大邱庄住宅楼工程，获交通部优质工程的京津塘高速公路工程，获建设部优质工程和全国用户满意工程的天津宾水西道立交桥工程，获鲁班奖的上海共和新路立交桥（北段）工程及获鲁班奖和全国用户满意工程奖的天津（卫国道）顺驰立交桥工程，天津市金纬路跨铁路立交桥荣获全国市政金杯奖等。承建的大型工程还有天津四十万吨污水处理厂，上海—南京、石家庄—安阳、北京—福州、北京—沈阳高速公路工程，天津万家码头千米大桥工程，珠海赛车场工程，重庆大班油库设备安装工程，以及蒙古、呼和浩特、海口、福州、苏州、天津等排水、道路、顶管工程。公司具有综合施工能力，可承担各等级公路、桥梁、软土地基处理，大型土方，自来水厂，污水处理厂，地上、地下大型结构，给排水管道、泵站、热力、电力、电讯、机电设备安装，房地产开发，建筑工程设计，沥青砼和水泥制品的加工等工程项目。公司还具有交通工程专用施工设备和专业测试仪器等。

公司曾荣获“中国五百家最大建筑施工企业”、“天津建筑业骨干企业”、“全国优秀施工企业”、“全国市政工程优秀施工企业”、“全国工程建设管理先进单位”、“全国用户满意施工企业”、“天津市信用等级AAA企业”称号，并获“全国五一劳动奖状”和“安康杯”先进单位、精神文明建设先进单位等荣誉。公司作为“重合同、守信誉”企业，坚持“质量第一、信誉至上、造价合理”的经营宗旨，将继续不断开拓，与各届合作，为国内、国外用户提供更多、更好、更全面的服务。

Tianjin No.2 Municipal Highway Engineering Co., Ltd. is one of pillar enterprises of Tianjin City Construction Group Co., Ltd. Now the corporation has 2,850 employees, including 682 technicians and managing persons, of which, 240 are medium & high-class qualified employees, 55 are project managers with intelligence. It has 1,236 sets of large and medium-sized mechanical equipment, including over 40 sets imported equipment. It has a abundant technique staff and advanced equipment, can undertakes kinds of municipal engineering and construction of highway, bridge and tunnel. In recent years, it has constructed many projects, such as Leading Luanhe river into Tianjin project which was awarded gold prize of national high quality project, Tianjin Outer circulating roads which was awarded silver prize of national high quality project, Daqiuzhuang residential building which was awarded high quality project by the Ministry of Construction, Jing-Jin-Tang Expressway which was awarded high quality project by the Ministry of Communication, Binshuixidao Flyover which was awarded high quality project by the Ministry of Construction and customer satisfactory project, Shanghai Gonghexinlu Flyover(north part) which was awarded Luban prize, Shunchi Flyover which was awarded Luban prize and customer satisfactory project, Jinweilu Flyover which was awarded Gold Cup Prize of national municipal projects. It also constructed Tianjin Sewage Disposal Factory of 0.4 million tons, Shanghai-Nanjing expressway, Shijiazhuang-Anyang Expressway, Beijing-Fuzhou Expressway, Beijing-Shenyang Expressway, Tianjin Wanjiamatou Bridge, Zhuhai Race car field, Chongqing Daban Oil depot equipment installation, draining, road engineering of Menggu, Huhehaote, Haikou, Fuzhou, Suzhou, Tianjin. The corporation owns comprehensive construction ability, can undertake highway, bridge, soft foundation engineering, construction of tap water factory, sewage disposal factory, supply & drain water pipe, pump station, equipment installation, real estate development, project design and so on. It is equipped with special facility of communication engineering and special test instrument.

The corporation was awarded "top 500 national construction enterprises", "Tianjin key construction enterprise", "national advanced municipal construction enterp-rise", "national engineering management advanced unit", "national customer satisfactory enterprise", "Tianjin AAA credit enterprise", "Labor Day Prize", "Ankang Cup advanced unit" and so on. Following the principle of "credibility, efficiency, low cost and high quality", we will cooperate with friends and provide better service for our clients.

京蓟高速公路

津滨快速轨道

地址: 天津市南开区宜宾道13号

Add: No. 13 Yibin Street, Nankai District, Tianjin

邮政编码 Postal Code: 300113

电话 Tel: (022) 27615665

传真 Fax: (022) 27616538

Tianjin No.3 Municipal Highway Engineering Co., Ltd.

天津第三市政公路工程有限公司

天津第三市政公路工程有限公司始建于1970年，1998年按照现代企业制度依法改为有限公司，系交通部颁发的市政公用工程施工总承包和桥梁工程专业承包一级资质企业，主要承担大型市政桥涵、道路工程、地下铁路、污水处理厂、泵站、给排水管道和民用建筑安装及市政公用工程施工。

公司拥有12个分公司，各类工程技术和经营管理人员570人，其中具有中高级职称的158人，成套大中型先进设备683台。30多年来，公司在桥梁、地铁、污水处理厂等施工领域形成了特有的工艺技术、管理经验和综合优势，具有精、快、新的施工特点，有多项科技成果获得国家和天津市科技进步奖、质量金奖等。以八里台立交桥为代表的5项工程荣获国家优质工程银质奖，无锡芦村污水处理厂等2项工程获中国市政工程金杯奖，京沈高速公路宝坻大桥等2项工程获国家鲁班奖。

1998年通过ISO 9000质量管理体系认证，1999年获全国精神文明建设先进单位，2001年获全国“五一”劳动奖状先进集体，2004年顺利通过质量、环境和职业健康安全体系认证。

Tianjin No.3 Municipal Highway Engineering Co., Ltd. founded in 1970 and established a corporation Ltd. in accordance with modem corporate system in 1998. It is a first class enterprise approved by the Ministry of Communications in terms of contracting for public engineering and bridge engineering, mainly engages in diversified business activities in fields of large-scale bridge & culvert, kinds of highway, subway, sewage treatment works, pump station, supply & drainage pipelines, installation for civil building and municipal public engineering.

It has 12 subsidiaries with advanced equipment of 683 sets. There are 570 technique and management personnel, of which, 158 have medium & senior professional certification. During the past three decades, the corporation has formed own technique, management experience and comprehensive superiority with the specialties of precision, quick and new in fields of bridge, subway, sewage treatment construction. Its some scientific and technological achievements are awarded national and municipal awards for progress and golden prizes for quality. We have won 5 silver prizes of national excellent projects including Balitai Crossroad, 2 national golden cup prizes for municipal projects including Wuxi Lucun Sewage Treatment Works, 2 Luban prizes including JingShen Expressway Baodi Bridge.

In 1998, it passed the certification of ISO 9000 Quality Man-agement System. In 1999, it was granted national excellent unit in spirit civilization. In 2001, it was granted May Day Labor Prize. In 2004, it passed Quality, Environment and Occupation Health Safety System Certification.

地址: 天津市河西区紫金山路3号

Add: No. 3 Zijinshan Road, Hexi District, Tianjin

邮政编码 Postal Code: 300074

电话 Tel: (022) 23359888

传真 Fax: (022) 23352313

天津第四市政建筑工程有限公司

Tianjin No. 4 Municipal Construction Co., Ltd.

党委书记、董事长：孙洪年

副董事长、总经理：韩明华

天津第四市政建筑工程有限公司是国家建筑总承包工程一级、市政工程二级企业。主要经营建筑安装、高级装饰、基础施工、钢结构安装、市政工程、公路配套工程和房地产开发等项目。公司2003年通过了质量、职业健康安全和环境管理体系认证。靠科学的管理建设了一大批颇有影响的工程，曾获得鲁班奖一项、国家质量奖银质奖两项、全国十大公路工程奖一项、全国用户满意工程一项、全国市政金杯示范工程三项、市优工程、示范工程奖十三项。03年承建的津蓟、丹拉高速公路收费站和服务区工程受到市委书记张立昌同志的高度赞扬。

津蓟高速公路起始站

公司连续十四年被评为“重合同守信誉”单位，连续五年被评为市级“文明单位”；并被评为全国“优秀市政施工企业”。

Tianjin No.4 Municipal Construction Co., Ltd is a first class engineering contracting enterprise and second class civil-planning enterprise. It mainly engages in installation, luxurious decoration, basic construction, steel structure installation, civil projects, highway engineering and real estate development.

In 2003, the corporation passed quality, safety and environmental management system certification. Depending on scientific management, it has constructed many influential projects. One project we built is awarded "Luban awards", two projects are awarded silver prizes in terms of quality by State, one project is ranked one of ten national perfect highway projects, one project is awarded as a satisfactory project for customer, 3 projects are named national model municipal projects, 13 projects are named city-level perfect projects or model projects. Charge station and service site of Jinji expressway and Danla expressway built by the corporation in 2003, won the approval of Zhang Lichang, secretary of municipal Party committee.

It has been granted as an enterprise that has excellent credit standing and does well in carrying out contracts for 14 consecutive years. It has awarded city-level civilized unit for 5 consecutive years. It also was named "national advanced municipal construction enterprise".

地址：天津市河西区紫金山路4号
Add: No. 4 Zijinshan Road, Hexi District, Tianjin
邮政编码 Postal Code: 300074
电话/传真 Tel/Fax: (022) 23542985

天津第五市政公路工程有限公司
Tianjin No. 5 Municipal Highway Engineering Co., Ltd.

董事长：刘宪生

天津第五市政公路工程有限公司（以下称公司）具有国家公路工程施工总承包一级、市政公用工程施工总承包一级、桥梁工程专业承包一级、公路路面工程专业承包一级、公路路基工程专业承包一级、公路交通工程专业承包交通安全设施等企业资质，主要承担各等级公路、桥梁、隧道、地铁和各类型市政公用工程的施工。

公司注册资本1.082亿元，总资产6.44亿元，其中固定资产2.08亿元。公司拥有各类专业技术人员600余人，具有高中级职称专业人员230余人，国家一级项目经理36人，公司年施工能力超过10亿元。

公司承建的京津塘高速公路、沪宁高速公路和津晋汉港立交先后荣获国家建筑最高奖“鲁班奖”和“中国土木工程（詹天佑）大奖”；唐津高速公路跨东南环铁路特大桥获得“国家银质奖章”；天津津围公路改造工程获得“2002年度交通部公路工程优质工程三等奖”；武汉军山长江大桥钢箱梁沥青砼桥面的铺筑工程被交通部评为“优质工程”。

公司拥有雄厚的施工能力。先后引进了360多台套德国、美国、瑞典、瑞士、澳大利亚等具有国际先进水平的大型机械设备。

公司在经营管理方面取得了一系列令人瞩目的成就。1998年和2002年分别通过了ISO 9000质量管理体系认证及职业安全健康管理体系认证；近年来先后多次被评为全国和天津市“优秀企业”，2000年又荣获“全国质量效益型先进企业”称号；2003年被评为“天津市2002年百强企业”；董事长、总经理先后被评为“天津市优秀企业家”；公司连续数年被天津市人民政府授予“守合同，重信用”称号，并被中国建设银行评为AAA级信用企业。

地址：天津市河东区十经路11号
Add: No. 11 Shijing Road, Hedong District, Tianjin
邮政编码 Postal Code: 300171
电话 Tel: (022) 24251800
传真 Fax: (022) 24251686
http://www.tjwsz.com

总经理：吴秉军

Tianjin No.5 Municipal Highway Engineering Co., Ltd. mainly undertakes construction of highway, bridge, tunnel, subway and municipal public engineering projects, which is the first class contractor in national highway engineering, municipal public engineering, bridge engineering, highway roadbed engineering, highway traffic engineering.

Its registered capital is 0.1082 billion yuan, the total assets is 0.644 billion yuan, including 0.208 billion yuan of fixed assets. The corporation has more than 600 special technique personnel, over 230 have medium & senior professional certification, 36 are Grade I national project managers. Its annual value of output reaches 1 billion yuan.

Jing-Jin-Tang expressway, Hu-Ning expressway and Jin-Jin-Han flyover was awarded “Luban awards” and “Zhan Tianyou awards”. Railway bridge of Tang-Jin expressway was awarded “national silver awards”. Reconstruction of Jin-Wei highway project was awarded “the third-grade awards of highway projects” by the Ministry of Communications in 2002. Surfacing engineering of Wuhan Junshan Changjiang bridge was awarded “good quality project” by the Ministry of Communications.

The corporation owns strong construction power. It has imported over 360 sets international advanced equipment from Germany, United States, Sweden, Switzerland and Australia.

It passed ISO 9000 quality system certification and vocational safety & healthy management certification in 1998 and 2002 respectively. In recent years, it has been named “perfect enterprise” by State and Tianjin Municipal. In 2000, it was awarded “national quality & benefit advanced enterprise”. In 2003, it was named “Top 100 enterprises in Tianjin”. The chairman of the board and general manager are awarded “Tianjin perfect enterprisers”. It was named “put stress on prestige and faithfulness to contracts” by Tianjin Municipal Government, “AAA grade credit enterprise” by China Construction Bank.

Huaming Group

华明集团

总经理：刘乃兰

德国高宝KBA 105对开五色胶印机

台湾产2.5米7层瓦楞纸板生产线

The general manager, Liu Nailan who is the committee member of National Political Consultative Committee and the stanging committee member of Tianjin Municipal Women's Federation creates great progress through working hard and developing of 20 years. She wins honour of national labour model, national May Day labour merit, "Ruzinu" award of Civil Affair Ministry and Tianjin top grade model worker award.

Under the leadership of the general manager, Liu Nailan, the enterprise is enlarged continuously. It occupies 138,500 square meters' land with a total construction area of 55,360 square meters, its capital is over 200 million yuan, its output value increases up to 300 million yuan. It involves six industries of packing, cold drink and snacks, printing, commerce and trade, service, communication. It includes Paper Case Factory, Kangle Food Factory, Printing Factory, Technology Internal Box Factory and cooperative enterprises, such as: Kaitong Automobile Development Co., Ltd., that is first one to sell and repair Guangzhou Honda automobile; Yourong Dikang Communication Co., Ltd. that is rich in production strength and largely market prospect; Yutian Wooden-paper Factory products packing raw material. It is a comprehensive state class township enterprise group which its business concentrates in primary industry, secondary industry, tertiary industry, it is a across-region, across-industries enterprise. It is awarded Tianjin "the Ninth Five" advanced unit, State first class awards of profit-tax township enter prise and one of top 100 paper manufacturers.

In new century and new developing, Huaming Group will continue to strive and bring forth new spirit to serve the old and new users according to creditable quality, lowest price and high quality service.

集全国政协委员、天津市妇联常委等众多职务于一身的刘乃兰总经理，经过20年的努力拼搏、勇于开拓，创造了华明集团的骄人业绩。先后荣获全国劳动模范、全国五一劳动奖章、国家民政部最高荣誉"孺子牛"奖、天津市特等劳动模范等荣誉称号。

在刘乃兰总经理的带领下，企业不断发展壮大，现已发展成为占地面积138500平方米，建筑面积55360平方米，资产总值超2亿元，年产值突破3亿元，集包装、冷食、印刷、商贸、服务、通讯六大行业包括纸箱厂、康乐食品厂、印刷厂、工艺内盒厂以及合资企业：天津首家经销、维修广州本田汽车的公司——凯通汽车服务发展有限公司；具有雄厚生产技术实力和广阔市场前景的公司——有容蒂康通讯技术有限公司；生产包装原料的企业——玉田板纸厂等十余个企业，集一、二、三产业兼有的跨地区、跨行业、跨所有制的综合国家级乡镇企业集团。连续多年被评为天津市"九五"立功先进单位，全国最高利税乡镇企业等荣誉称号，成为全国纸制品行业百强之一。

新世纪、新发展，华明集团将继续秉承拼搏、创新的华明精神，以可靠的质量、低廉的价格、优质的服务，竭诚为各界新老客户服务。

地址：天津市东丽区外环线三号桥东

Add: The East of No. 3 Bridge, Outer Circle, Dongli District, Tianjin

邮政编码 Postal Code: 300300

电话 Tel: (022) 84780805

E-mail: hmzx@163.com

津英纺纱有限公司
Jinying Spinning Co., Ltd.

理想成为世界顶级缝纫制造商

天津津英纺纱有限公司于1988年成立，1990年开业，尔后不断拓展运营规模，现公司投资总额累计已达4300余万美元，中外方各占50%。本公司原料以进口为主，主要生产高档纯涤短纤缝纫线、包芯线、长丝绣花装饰线及绳编类产品，产品70%以上出口。10余年来，公司一直在盈利中运营，在国际市场激烈竞争中不断地创新和发展，是具备一定规模，较强竞争力和世界一流技术和装备的合资经营企业。

李鹏等有关首脑要员，我市主要领导及国家有关部委领导人，均先后莅临公司参观视察。公司开业运营近十四年来，连年荣获国家及市政府授予的“最佳”、“双优”外商投资企业、“天津市工业百强企业”、“天津市优秀企业”、“全国纺织工业思想政治工作优秀企业”、“天津市模范职工之家”等荣誉称号，并于1991年跨入“中国规模最大500家外商投资工业企业”行列。2000年6月，天津市政府又对1990—1999年度连续10年荣获天津市先进外商投资企业称号的津英纺纱等8家企业，颁发奖牌，登报表彰。

十余年来，中外双方均能在友好协商、互惠互利的基础上，共谋企业发展。将来双方仍将致力于创新发展，不断调整产品结构、开发新品种、提高经济效益和社会效益，给投资者以合理回报。

Jinying Spinning Co., Ltd. was established in 1988 and started from operation in 1990, then further developed. The total investment is USD 43 million, at equal share of 50% each the Sino-British. The company is export-oriented with major raw material is imported. The business scope of the company is to produce SSP synthetic yarn thread, PPC, filament and braid, and to maintain over 70% export. During the last ten years, the company has been running with profit and developing in the keen competitive market.

For the past years, the company received a lot of visitors from central and municipal government, including Premier Li Peng and many senior officials and guests from other countries. Jinying Spinning Co., Ltd. has received a lot of awards every year, such as “Double Excellent”, “Double Good” enterprises with foreign investment, “100 leading Industrial Enterprises in Tianjin” and “the excellent enterprise of Tianjin”, “the Ideological and Political excellent enterprise of Chinese Textile Industry”, “the Exemplary Family of employee in Tianjin”. In 1991, the company also listed in “the Largest 500 industrial Enterprises with Foreign Investment in China”. In June 2000, Jinying Spinning Co., Ltd. and other seven companies received special award of achievement for consecutive 10 years by Tianjin government.

During the last ten years, both sides were in friendly negotiation and on the mutual reciprocity & benefit to developed Jinying Spinning. In the future, we will be devoted to innovating and developing, pushing forward new product development, to create the best economic and social benefit and to give investor the good result.

地址: 天津市西青区李七庄津涞公路南
Add: Jinlai Road, Liqizhuang, xiqing District, Tianjin
邮政编码 Postal Code: 300381
电话 Tel: (022) 83912847, 83912940
传真 Fax: (022) 83913935
E-mail: tjjysc@public 1.tpt.tj.cn

FM66227

Vision

To be the world's outstanding manufacturer of grey sewing thread

刘房子经济发展总公司

Liufangzi Economy Development General Company

总经理：田东平

公司承建的住宅小区

刘房子为我市西北部一颗璀璨的明珠，被市政府评为市级明星小康村。地理位置优越，与津霸公路、中环线、外环线、子牙河形成环围。远期规划前景宏大，在9平方公里的辖区内，780余户近2700人正以饱满的热情迎接二十一世纪的挑战。

改革开放十几年的发展，村经济已初具规模。现有村办集体企业十几家，三资企业数家；农业生产逐步走上科学、规模、效益型，现已形成的津霸公路刘房子村商业一条街，为第三产业的发展起到了促进作用。工业产值在村经济的比重日渐上升，已初步形成农、工、商合理发展，相互促进，比翼齐飞良性循环之势。

几年来教育事业得到长足发展。同时加大了社会福利、社会保障的投入。村容、村貌焕然一新，治安良好，民风纯朴，已实现精神文明与物质文明的共同发展。

刘房子领导正用战略眼光审视自己，以高度责任感率领全体人民共同努力、继往开来。

我们将敞开胸怀，与各方有识之士积极合作、共创未来

高级别墅

村民住宅小区

教育从娃娃抓起

与天津商学院联建的教学楼

天津海洋开关厂车间一角

建设峻工后的高级别墅一角

Liufangzi, as a shining star in Northwest Tianjin, is a municipal level well-off star town with good geographic location, connected with Jin-ba Expressway, Middle Ring Road, Extra-Ring Road and Ziya River, having a good developing potential. In its 9 square kilometers area, there are more than 780 families, nearly 2,700 people, who are heartedly welcoming the challenge of the 21st century.

After more than 10 years, development since the reform and opening to outside, the town's economy becomes scaled. There are over 10 township collective enterprises and several joint ventures in the town. Its agricultural production is becoming scientific efficient and on scale, a commercial street is setup in the town near Jin-Ba Expressway, which plays an important role in the development of its tertiary industry. Its development of agriculture, industry and service industry become coordinated with each other.

Its education has also gotten improved rapidly. Its input in social welfare and social protection system is also enlarged. The town`s environment and outlook are changed freshly which is socially securitied and civilized. The town is also realized co-development of spirital and material civilization.

The leaders of the town are inspecting themselves strategically, and leading its people to work hard together and success the past and looking forward the future. We are heartedly looking forward to actively cooperating with friends in different walks to achieve an excellent future.

地址: 天津市北辰区津霸公路
Add: Jinba Expressway, Beichen District, Tianjin
邮政编码 Postal Code: 300400
电话 Tel: (022)26654384

天津送变电工程公司

TIANJIN POWER TRANSMISSION ENGINEERING CORPORATION

党委书记：周顺起

经理：张嘉利

天津送变电工程公司成立于1953年，是具有国家一级资质的电力工程总承包施工企业（同时具有工民建、市政管网、电讯通讯等施工资质和能力）。其电缆对接及终端技术居全国领先地位，是瑞士布鲁克公司在东南亚的总代理。该公司隶属于天津市电力公司，注册资金9257万元，年施工能力为架设110千伏—500千伏输电线路200公里，敷设330千伏及以下电缆100公里，安装35千伏以上主变容器100万伏安，工民建200000平方米。2002年通过了ISO 9001：2000国际标准体系认证，2001年获国家外经贸委批准的境外承包工程经营权。

公司历年来承建的数千项目工程合格率100%，优良品率在85%以上。先后被天津市人民政府授予"市级先进企业"、市"八五"、"九五"立功先进集体，连续十四年荣获"守合同，重信用"单位称号。并具备"AAA"信用等级。

Tianjin Power Transmission Engineering Corporation founded in 1953, is a first grade power engineering construction enterprise in terms of capital and quality (also including industry & civil construction, municipal pipe works, communication engineering). The cable joint and relative technology reaches national leading level. It is awarded general agent of Switzerland Cable Corporation in Southeast Asia. The corporation is subordinated to Tianjin Municipal Power Corporation with the registered capital of 92.57 million yuan. It can lay 200 kilometers of power transmission line from 110KV to 500KV, 100 kilometers cable of 330KV & under, construct 0.2 million square meters of industry & civil buildings per year. In 2002, it passed ISO 9001:2000 International Standard System Certification. In 2001, it enjoyed autonomous right on undertaking foreign projects.

Thousands of projects constructed by the corporation are up to standard, of which, 85 percent of all the projects are high quality projects. The corporation was awarded "municipal-level advanced enterprise", "eighth-five and ninth-five advanced unit", "honor construction and abide by its words" unit for the successive 14 years. It also obtains "AAA" grade credit.

地址：天津市河东区卫国道122号　邮政编码 Postal Code: 300161　电话/传真 Tel/Fax: (022) 24565026
Add: No. 122 Weiguo Road, Hedong District, Tianjin

厂长：李瑞欣

Tianjin Dagang Power Plant is situated in the south part of Tianjin, closes to Bohai Sea, 52 kilometers north to downtown of Tianjin, 7 kilometers east to Bohai Sea, Duliujian River on the south, covering an land area of 52.86 hectares.

It is equipped with 4 generator sets of 328.5tw imported from Italy and the total machine capacity reaches 1314tw. Tianjin Dagang Power Plant began to build in 1974, the Phase I project, two fuel generator sets generated electricity in October,1978 and April, 1979 respectively; the Phase II project, two burning coal generator sets began to build in April, 1988 and put into operation in October, 1991 and May, 1992 respectively.

Tianjin Dagang Power Plant is a thermal power plant with advanced equipment, high automation and strong control ability. During the past two decades, it always maintains the principle of "safety the first, pay attention to prevention", the safety and economic efficiency are improved continuously through deep treatment on equipment and environment.

Because it lays stress on management, Tianjin Dagang Power Plant has been awarded standardization unit in terms of safety production, non-seep thermal Power Plant, two-star grade enterprise, double civilization unit, top-grade thermal Power Plant successively. At present, we are working hard and trying to make the plant become a international top-grade thermal Power Plant.

发电厂厂景

天津大港发电厂
Tianjin Dagang Power Plant

天津大港发电厂地处天津市南部的渤海之滨，坐落在大港区境内，北距天津市中心 52 公里，东距渤海 7 公里，南傍独流减河，占地 52.86 公顷。

大港发电厂现有 4 台 328.5 兆瓦发电机组，总装机容量 1314 兆瓦，成套设备由意大利引进。电厂于 1974 年动工兴建，一期工程两台燃油机组分别于 1978 年 10 月、1979 年 4 月并网发电（2002 年 2 月退出备用进行燃油锅炉改燃煤锅炉的技术改造，预计 2004 年改造完成，投产发电）；二期工程两台燃煤机组 1988 年 4 月开工，分别于 1991 年 10 月、1992 年 5 月投产。

大港发电厂是一座设备先进、自动化程度高、调峰能力较强的火力发电厂。建厂二十多年来，大港电厂始终坚持“安全第一，预防为主”的方针，通过对设备、环境进行全方位的深层次治理，使安全生产水平和经济效益不断提高。

抓管理、创一流，使大港发电厂先后成为电力系统安全文明生产“达标”企业、华北电力系统“无渗漏火电厂”、“二星级企业”、国家电力公司“双文明单位”、国家电力公司“一流火力发电厂”。目前，大港发电厂全体干部职工正以崭新的姿态，饱满的工作热情，艰苦奋斗的工作作风，向国际一流火力发电厂迈进。

地址：天津市大港区古林街　　电话 Tel: (022) 25903333
Add: Gulin Street, Dagang District, Tianjin　　邮政编码 Postal Code: 300272

天津兴业置业集团

TIANJIN XINGYE PROPERTY GROUP

兴科大厦

天津兴业置业集团组建于一九九三年十月，是以高科技、贸易、运输、三产业、房地产业、批发、零售、代购、代销，以及仓储、租赁、商品贸易为一体的大型综合性群体。

集团公司地处南开区中心，座落于鞍山西道、灵隐道，占地面积22万多平方米，交通便利，地理位置优越，拥有资产5.3亿元，利税3000万元。

集团下属企业天津市业兴电子有限公司、必兴商贸有限公司、兴业劳务服务有限公司、兴运机械施工有限公司、兴业房地产开发有限公司、兴业贸易商行，以及兴业鞋帽批发市场、兴业天宝旧物市场、农贸副食烟酒批发市场等。

为了加快发展步伐，集团正在进行产权制度改革，改革后的集团公司将以崭新的面貌展示于社会，诚信于社会，欢迎国内外商界朋友进行合作，共同发展。

董事长兼总经理刘长海向社会各界同仁致意。

Tianjin Xingye Property Group founded in October, 1993, is a large-sized comprehensive group, covering the fields of hi-tech, trade, transport, tertiary industry, real estate, wholesale, retail trade, agent for purchasing and sales, storage, rent and commodity trade.

The group locates at the center of Nankai District with convenient traffic and advantageous geographic location, occupying an area of 220,000 square meters. Its assets reaches 0.53 billion yuan and pre-tax profits total 30 million yuan.

Its subordinated enterprises include Tianjin Yexing Electronics Co., Ltd., Bixing Trade Co., Ltd., Xingye Labor Service Co., Ltd., Xingyun Machinery Construction Co., Ltd., Xingye Real Estate Development Co., Ltd., Xingye Trade Corporation, Xingye Shoes & Caps Wholesale Market, Xingye Tianbao Old Goods Market, Farm Products, Tobacco and Liquor Wholesale Market and so on.

In order to quicken the pace of development, the group is carrying out the reform of property rights. After the reform, the group will face to society with new feature. We hope to cooperate with friends at home and abroad and develop together.

The president, general manager, Mr. Liu Changhai gives his best wishes to social friends of all circles.

地址：天津市南开区鞍山西道445号

Add: No. 445 Anshanxi Road, Nankai District, Tianjin

电话 Tel: (022) 27384817

2004天津统计年鉴
TIANJIN STATISTICAL YEARBOOK

电子版

使用说明

《天津统计年鉴2004（电子版）》是新型的阅读工具，它使用简捷，界面美观，便于携带，全部文档均采用HTM格式。文字及图形资料装于一张光盘中，借助于计算机，可以方便快速地进行查询，并可将所需的资料打印出来。随着科学技术的发展，电子版资料必将越来越流行，为广大用户所喜爱。

[硬件配置] 586及以上微机，VGA显示器，带鼠标

[软件环境] 中文Windows 9x/2000/XP系统，Internet Explorer 5.0及以上，分辨率为800*600

[使用方法] 将光盘插入CD-ROM中，系统自动启动年鉴程序或者执行光驱中\2004nj\index.htm文件

User's Guide

Tianjin Statistical Yearbook 2004 (electric version) is a new type reading tool. It is equipped with beautiful interface and HTM files. You have the aid of computer to use the CD and it is convenient for you to search & read materials and print. Electric edition will be more popular along with the development of science and technology.

[Hardware Requirement]

PC 586 or higher with VGA and mouse

[Software Requirement]

Windows 9x/2000/XP, Internet Explorer 5.0 or higher, resolution 800*600

[Usage Method]

Insert CD into CD-ROM, then Yearbook program will start or to run \2004nj\index.htm